TREASURY OF WORLD MASTERPIECES

ROBERT LOUIS STEVENSON

TREASURY OF WORLD MASTERPIECES

ROBERT LOUIS STEVENSON

TREASURE ISLAND

KIDNAPPED

WEIR OF HERMISTON

THE MASTER OF BALLANTRAE

THE BLACK ARROW

THE STRANGE CASE OF
DR JEKYLL AND MR HYDE

OCTOPUS BOOKS LIMITED

Treasure Island appeared as a serial for a boys' newspaper in 1881
Kidnapped was first published in 1886
Weir of Hermiston was first published in 1896
The Master of Ballantrae was first published in 1889
The Black Arrow was first published in 1888
The Strange Case of Dr Jekyll and Mr Hyde was first published in 1886

This edition first published in Great Britain in 1984 by
Octopus Books Limited
59 Grosvenor Street
London W1

Illustrated by Duncan Smith

ISBN 0 7064 2134 5

Printed in the United States of America
by Kingsport Press

CONTENTS

Introduction 9

Treasure Island 13

Kidnapped 137

Weir of Hermiston 273

The Master of Ballantrae 349

The Black Arrow 495

The Strange Case of Dr Jekyll and Mr Hyde . 643

INTRODUCTION

ROBERT LOUIS STEVENSON, the son of a well-to-do Presbyterian engineer, was born in 1850 in the city of Edinburgh. An only child with a delicate disposition, his life was fraught with illness. However, despite the fact that he was forever ailing the power of his imagination was unflagging.

Stevenson studied engineering at Edinburgh University and was expected to follow in his father's footsteps. He was discontented with this chosen subject, however, and later transferred to law – again unhappily, for his heart lay in writing. By this stage he had already begun to write numerous pieces several of which were published by the time he became a qualified advocate. Articles by him were to be seen in the *Cornhill Magazine* and the *Portfolio* and his contributions, initialled 'RLS' were rapidly becoming popular. But just as his circle of friends was expanding and other well-renowned talents of the time (e.g. W. E. Henley and Edmund Gosse) were seen to be acquainted with him, Stevenson's relationship with his father deteriorated. The young Stevenson was opposed to the strictness of his father's Calvinistic faith and at the age of twenty-three he became an agnostic, a decision that was to cause a rift with his parents which took many years to heal.

In 1873, on leaving university, Stevenson went abroad, and his travels were to provide the basis for many of his early works. *An Inland Voyage* (1878) described his wanderings through France on foot and by canoe, and *Travels With A Donkey in the Cevennes* (1879) has for its inspiration the author's experiences in Languedoc. It was near here that Stevenson was to meet someone who would prove to be a major influence on his life. In 1876 at Brez-sur-Loing, near Fontainebleau he fell in love with an American, Fanny Osbourne, a lady ten years his senior, who was married with three children. Mrs Osbourne's husband had deserted her and Stevenson's affection for her was mutual. She consequently left France for California to initiate divorce proceedings. Stevenson later journeyed to America to join her having won the wholehearted approval of his parents, and an income from his father, and soon they were happily married. They returned to Scotland with Fanny's son, Lloyd, who became his loyal and trusted companion. The years that followed were marked by constant travel for the Stevensons with visits to and from different climates. They ventured to Switzerland, the South of France and also Bournemouth. It was during this period that several collections of Stevenson's poems and essays were published. *Virginibus Puerisque*, a collection of essays for boys and girls appeared in 1881; *Familiar Studies of Men and Books* and *New Arabian Nights* in 1882, and in 1885 *A Child's Garden of Verses* (poems about children).

In 1883 *Treasure Island*, probably the most famous story of a hunt for buried treasure ever written, became Stevenson's most popular success. Originally called *The Sea Cook or Treasure Island* the novel was conceived while the Stevenson family were staying at Braemar in Scotland. One rainswept afternoon Lloyd Osbourne, then twelve, began to map out an imaginary desert island, and Stevenson decided to write a story fashioned around this. 'It was to be a story for boys; no need of psychology or fine writing, and I had a boy at hand to be a touchstone. . . . On a chill September morning, by the cheek of a brisk fire, and the rain drumming on the window, I began *The Sea Cook*, for that was the original title!' *Treasure Island* did in fact begin life as a serial in 1881 but its reception was lukewarm. As a book, however, it was an immediate success.

A compelling story of blood-thirsty pirates, the novel still lives on as the exciting adventure surrounding the discovery of Billy Bones' map of Skeleton Island with hidden treasure, the fight across a tropical island, the terror of the 'black spot' and one-legged Long John Silver with his parrot calling 'pieces of eight'. Another novel which appeared at the time in serial form (and was later published as a novel in 1888) was *The Black Arrow*. This tremendously popular tale for young readers tells of Richard Shelton, who fighting for the Yorkists in the icy winter weather, meets not only 'crookback' Richard III, but the outlaw band of archers who send their dreaded black arrows to rescue his love Joanna.

In 1896 came two more masterpieces. *Kidnapped*, set in the Western Highlands of Scotland, is the classic adventure tale of the troubled days following the Jacobite Rebellion, and Alan Breck Stewart, fearless and romantic, is one of Stevenson's most engaging heroes. Henry James believed *Kidnapped* to be one of Stevenson's finest novels and of it Stevenson wrote: 'In one of my books, and in one only, the characters took the bit in their teeth, all at once they became detached from the flat paper, they turned their backs on me and walked off bodily . . . it was they who spoke, it was they who made the remainder of the story.'

The Strange Case of Dr Jekyll and Mr Hyde (1886) was another of Stevenson's books which commanded both an extensive and an adult audience, especially in America. Based on a dream, it was written while Stevenson was living at Bournemouth and suffering from severe ill-health. Although physically ill his mind was alert and, having dreamt one night a considerable section of his novel, he was to write several drafts before he was entirely satisfied. Astonishingly the book was ready for sale ten weeks from its inception and a perceptive critic in *The Times* drew much attention to its content. Subsequently reports suggested that the novel was widely referred to in pulpits throughout the country. *The Strange Case of Dr Jekyll and Mr Hyde* is both a thriller and an allegory, a tale rich in symbolic meaning concerning the duality of human nature and the way in which evil and good uneasily dwell together. The novel tells the bizarre story of the doctor who, by means of a drug he has discovered, is able to create for himself a separate personality that is evil in instinct and repulsive in appearance. *The Strange Case of Dr Jekyll and Mr Hyde* is immensely credible, a tale which drives home a truth, set within the parameters of a first-rate thriller. Such was its success that 40,000 copies were sold in the first six months.

In 1887 Stevenson's father died and the writer, still in poor health returned to America with his mother, wife and stepson. They finally settled in Samoa where Stevenson's interest in the South Seas was evident in *The Beach of Falesa*

(1892), A *Footnote to History* (1892) and *In the South Seas* (1896). Here, from 1887 until 1894 his literary output was prolific and in 1889 he wrote *The Master of Ballantrae* which tells of the lifelong feud between Master Ballantrae and his younger brother Henry. This novel in particular underlines Stevenson's preoccupation with destiny and the belief that in life there are those born to lose. In *The Master of Ballantrae* the loser is the young brother whose persecution by the Master changes him into a wretch craving for revenge.

Stevenson wrote about *The Master of Ballantrae* to Burlingame, the editor of Scribner's, who was to publish the novel in serial form. He described his work as 'a tragedy. Five parts of it are sound human tragedy, the last one or two, I regret to say, not so soundly designed; I almost hesitate to write them; they shame, perhaps degrade, the beginning, they are very picturesque but they are fantastic.' More significantly, however, he commented that the book contained 'more human work than anything of mine but *Kidnapped*'.

Catriona (the sequel to *Kidnapped*) appeared in 1893, and a number of novels were written in collaboration with Lloyd Osbourne, *The Wrong Box* in 1889, *The Wrecker* in 1892 and *The Ebb-Tide* in 1894. *Weir of Hermiston* (1896), thought to be Stevenson's greatest novel, was never finished. At the age of forty-four and after many years of illness he died in 1894 at a time when critics believed he was at his peak. A vibrant story about the austere Scottish judge and his son, *Weir of Hermiston* displays the fruition of Stevenson's narrative abilities. A rivetting tension races through the story and his characters, handled with precision, rise from the page. Another novel written at the same time, *St Ives*, was later completed by Quiller-Couch.

The short stories and collections which emanated from Stevenson's pen during this period included: *The Silverado Squatters* (1883); *Prince Otto* (1885); *The Merry Men* (1887); *Memories and Portraits* (1887); *Across the Plains* (1892); *Island Nights' Entertainment* (1893) and a further collection of poems, *Underwoods* (1887). Although he was often dogged by illness Stevenson loved to dabble in the world of adventure, swashbuckling deeds and escapades and undoubtedly wrote his best when dealing with Scotland, the country, the people and the tongue that he knew and loved.

Robert Louis Stevenson's legacy to us of novels, South Seas stories and adventures is considerable. For children and adults alike his books are rich in colourful characters and settings and will live in the imagination forever.

TREASURE ISLAND

PART ONE

CHAPTER ONE

The Old Sea Dog at the 'Admiral Benbow'

SQUIRE TRELAWNEY, DR. LIVESEY, and the rest of these gentlemen having asked me to write down the whole particulars about Treasure Island, from the beginning to the end, keeping nothing back but the bearings of the island, and that only because there is still treasure not yet lifted, I take up my pen in the year of grace 17—, and go back to the time when my father kept the 'Admiral Benbow' inn, and the brown old seaman, with the sabre cut, first took up his lodging under our roof.

I remember him as if it were yesterday, as he came plodding to the inn door, his sea-chest following behind him in a hand-barrow; a tall, strong, heavy, nut-brown man; his tarry pigtail falling over the shoulders of his soiled blue coat; his hands ragged and scarred, with black, broken nails; and the sabre cut across one cheek, a dirty, livid white. I remember him looking round the cove and whistling to himself as he did so, and then breaking out in that old sea-song that he sang so often afterwards:

> 'Fifteen men on the dead man's chest –
> Yo-ho-ho, and a bottle of rum!'

in the high old tottering voice that seemed to have been tuned and broken at the capstan bars. Then he rapped on the door with a bit of stick like a handspike that he carried, and when my father appeared, called roughly for a glass of rum. This, when it was brought to him, he drank slowly, like a connoisseur, lingering on the taste, and still looking about him at the cliffs and up at our signboard.

'This is a handy cove,' says he, at length; 'and a pleasant sittyated grog-shop. Much company, mate?'

My father told him no, very little company, the more was the pity.

'Well, then,' said he, 'this is the berth for me. Here you, matey,' he cried to the man who trundled the barrow; 'bring up alongside and help up my chest. I'll stay here a bit,' he continued. 'I'm a plain man; rum and bacon and eggs is what I want, and that head up there for to watch ships off. What you mought call me? You mought call me captain. Oh, I see what you're at – there'; and he threw down three or four gold pieces on the threshold. 'You can tell me when I've worked through that,' says he, looking as fierce as a commander.

And, indeed, bad as his clothes were, and coarsely as he spoke, he had none of the appearance of a man who sailed before the mast; but seemed like a mate or skipper, accustomed to be obeyed or to strike. The man who came with the barrow told us the mail had set him down the morning before at the 'Royal George'; that he had inquired what inns there were along the coast, and hearing ours well spoken of, I suppose, and described as lonely, had chosen it from the others for his place of residence. And that was all we could learn of our guest.

He was a very silent man by custom. All day he hung round the cove, or upon the cliffs, with a brass telescope; all evening he sat in a corner of the parlour next the fire, and drank rum and water very strong. Mostly he would not speak when spoken to; only look up sudden and fierce, and blow through his nose like a fog-horn; and we and the people who came about our house soon learned to let him be. Every day, when he came back from his stroll, he would ask if any seafaring men had gone by along the road. At first we thought it was the want of company of his own kind that made him ask this question; but at last we began to see he was desirous to avoid them. When a seaman put up at the 'Admiral Benbow' (as now and then some did, making by the coast road for Bristol), he would look in at him through the curtained door before he entered the parlour; and he was always sure to be as silent as a mouse when any such was present. For me, at least, there was no secret about the matter; for I was, in a way, a sharer in his alarms. He had taken me aside one day, and promised me a silver fourpenny on the first of every month if I would only keep my 'weather-eye open for a seafaring man with one leg,' and let him know the moment he appeared. Often enough, when the first of the month came round, and I applied for my wage, he would only blow through his nose at me, and stare me down; but before the week was out he was sure to think better of it, bring me my fourpenny piece, and repeat his orders to look out for 'the seafaring man with one leg.'

How that personage haunted my dreams, I need scarcely tell you. On stormy nights, when the wind shook the four corners of the house, and the surf roared along the cove and up the cliffs, I would see him in a thousand forms, and with a thousand diabolical expressions. Now the leg would be cut off at the knee, now at the hip; now he was a monstrous kind of a creature who had never had but the one leg, and that in the middle of his body. To see him leap and run and pursue me over hedge and ditch was the worst of nightmares. And altogether I paid pretty dear for my monthly fourpenny piece, in the shape of these abominable fancies.

But though I was so terrified by the idea of the seafaring man with one leg, I was far less afraid of the captain himself than anybody else who knew him. There were nights when he took a deal more rum and water than his head would carry; and then he would sometimes sit and sing his wicked, old, wild sea-songs, minding nobody; but sometimes he would call for glasses round, and force all the trembling company to listen to his stories or bear a chorus to his singing. Often I have heard the house shaking with 'Yo-ho-ho, and a bottle of rum'; all the neighbours joining in for dear life, with the fear of death upon them, and each singing louder than the other, to avoid remark. For in these fits he was the most overriding companion ever known; he would slap his hand on the table for silence all round; he would fly up in a passion of anger at a question, or sometimes because none was put, and so he judged the company was not following his story. Nor would he allow any one to leave the inn till he had drunk himself sleepy and reeled off to bed.

His stories were what frightened people worst of all. Dreadful stories they were; about hanging, and walking the plank, and storms at sea, and the Dry Tortugas, and wild deeds and places on the Spanish Main. By his own account he must have lived his life among some of the wickedest men that God ever allowed upon the sea; and the language in which he told these stories shocked our plain country people almost as much as the crimes that he described. My father was always saying the inn would be ruined, for people would soon cease coming there to be tyrannized over and put down, and sent shivering to their beds; but I really believed his presence did us good. People were frightened at the time, but on looking back they rather liked it; it was a fine excitement in a quiet country life; and there was even a party of the younger men who pretended to admire him, calling him a 'true sea dog,' and a 'real old salt,' and such-like names, and saying there was the sort of man that made England terrible at sea.

In one way, indeed, he bade fair to ruin us; for he kept on staying week after week, and at last month after month, so that all the money had been long exhausted, and still my father never plucked up the heart to insist on having more. If ever he mentioned it, the captain blew through his nose so loudly, that you might say he roared, and stared my poor father out of the room. I have seen him wringing his hands after such a rebuff, and I am sure the annoyance and the terror he lived in must have greatly hastened his early and unhappy death.

All the time he lived with us the captain made no change whatever in his dress but to buy some stockings from a hawker. One of the cocks of his hat having fallen down, he let it hang from that day forth, though it was a great annoyance when it blew. I remember the appearance of his coat, which he patched himself upstairs in his room, and which, before the end, was nothing but patches. He never wrote or received a letter, and he never spoke with any but the neighbours, and with these, for the most part, only when drunk on rum. The great sea-chest none of us had ever seen open.

He was only once crossed, and that was towards the end, when my poor father was far gone in a decline that took him off. Dr Livesey came late one afternoon to see the patient, took a bit of dinner from my mother, and went into the parlour to smoke a pipe until his horse should come down from the hamlet, for we had no stabling at the old 'Benbow.' I followed him in, and I remember observing the contrast the neat, bright doctor, with his powder as white as snow, and his bright, black eyes and pleasant manners, made with the coltish country folk, and above all, with that filthy, heavy, bleared scarecrow of a pirate of ours, sitting far gone in rum, with his arms on the table. Suddenly he – the captain, that is – began to pipe up his eternal song:

> 'Fifteen men on the dead man's chest –
> Yo-ho-ho, and a bottle of rum!
> Drink and the devil had done for the rest –
> Yo-ho-ho, and a bottle of rum!'

At first I had supposed 'the dead man's chest' to be that identical big box of his upstairs in the front room, and the thought had been mingled in my nightmares with that of the one-legged seafaring man. But by this time we had all long ceased to pay any particular notice to the song; it was new, that night, to nobody but Dr Livesey, and on him I observed it did not produce an agreeable effect, for he looked up for a moment quite angrily before he went on with his talk to old Taylor, the gardener, on a new cure for the rheumatics. In the meantime, the captain gradually brightened up at his own music, and at last flapped his hand upon the table before him in a way we all knew to mean – silence. The voices stopped at once, all but Dr Livesey's; he went on as before, speaking clear and kind, and drawing briskly at his pipe between every word or two. The captain glared at him for a while, flapped his hand again, glared still harder, and at last broke out with a villainous, low oath: 'Silence, there, between decks!'

'Were you addressing me, sir?' says the doctor; and when the ruffian had told him, with another oath, that this was so, 'I have only one thing to say to you, sir,' replies the doctor, 'that if you keep on drinking rum, the world will soon be quit of a very dirty scoundrel!'

The old fellow's fury was awful. He sprang to his feet, drew and opened a sailor's clasp-knife, and, balancing it open on the palm of his hand, threatened to pin the doctor to the wall.

The doctor never so much as moved. He spoke to him, as before, over his shoulder, and in the same tone of voice; rather high, so that all the room might hear, but perfectly calm and steady:

'If you do not put that knife this instant in your pocket, I promise, upon my honour, you shall hang at next assizes.'

Then followed a battle of looks between them; but the captain soon knuckled under, put up his weapon, and resumed his seat, grumbling like a beaten dog.

'And now, sir,' continued the doctor, 'since I now know there's such a fellow in my district, you may count I'll have an eye upon you day and night. I'm not a doctor only; I'm a magistrate; and if I catch a breath of complaint against you, if it's only for a piece of incivility like to-night's, I'll take effectual means to have you hunted down and routed out of this. Let that suffice.'

Soon after Dr Livesey's horse came to the door, and he rode away; but the captain held his peace that evening, and for many evenings to come.

CHAPTER TWO

Black Dog Appears and Disappears

IT WAS NOT VERY LONG after this that there occurred the first of the mysterious events that rid us at last of the captain, though not, as you will see, of his affairs. It was a bitter cold winter, with long, hard frosts and heavy gales; and it was plain from the first that my poor father was little likely to see the spring. He sank daily, and my mother and I had all the inn upon our hands; and were kept busy enough, without paying much regard to our unpleasant guest.

It was one January morning, very early – a pinching, frosty morning – the cove all grey with hoar-frost, the ripple lapping softly on the stones, the sun still low and only touching the hill-tops and shining far to seaward. The captain had risen earlier than usual, and set out down the beach, his cutlass swinging under the broad skirts of the old blue coat, his brass telescope under his arm, his hat tilted back upon his head. I remember his breath hanging like smoke in his wake as he strode off, and the last sound I heard of him, as he turned the big rock, was a loud snort of indignation, as though his mind was still running upon Dr Livesey.

Well, mother was upstairs with father; and I was laying the breakfast table against the captain's return, when the parlour door opened, and a man stepped in on whom I had never set my eyes before. He was a pale, tallowy creature, wanting two fingers of the left hand; and, though he wore a cutlass, he did not look much like a fighter. I had always kept my eye open for seafaring men, with one leg or two, and I remember this one puzzled me. He was not sailorly, and yet he had a smack of the sea about him too.

I asked him what was for his service, and he said he would take rum; but as I was going out of the room to fetch it he sat down upon a table and motioned to me to draw near. I paused where I was with my napkin in my hand.

'Come here, sonny,' says he. 'Come nearer here.'

I took a step nearer.

'Is this here table for my mate Bill?' he asked, with a kind of a leer.

I told him I did not know his mate Bill; and this was for a person who stayed in our house, whom we called the captain.

'Well,' said he, 'my mate Bill would be called the captain, as like as not. He has a cut on one cheek, and a mighty pleasant way with him, particularly in drink, has my mate Bill. We'll put it, for argument like, that your captain has a cut on one cheek – and we'll put it, if you like, that that cheek's the right one. Ah, well! I told you. Now, is my mate Bill in this here house?'

I told him he was out walking.

'Which way, sonny? Which way is he gone?'

And when I had pointed out the rock and told him how the captain was likely to return, and how soon, and answered a few other questions, 'Ah,' said he, 'this'll be as good as drink to my mate Bill.'

The expression of his face as he said these words was not at all pleasant, and I had my own reasons for thinking that the stranger was mistaken, even supposing he meant what he said. But it was no affair of mine, I thought; and besides, it was difficult to know what to do. The stranger kept hanging about just outside the inn door, peering round the corner like a cat waiting for a mouse. Once I stepped out myself into the road, but he immediately called me back, and, as I did not obey quick enough for his fancy, a most horrible change came over his tallowy face and he ordered me in, with an oath that made me jump. As soon as I was back again he returned to his former manner, half fawning, half sneering, patted me on the shoulder, told me I was a good boy, and he had taken quite a fancy to me. 'I have a son of my own,' said he, 'as like you as two blocks, and he's all the pride of my 'art. But the great thing for boys is discipline, sonny – discipline. Now, if you had sailed along of Bill, you wouldn't have stood there to be spoke to twice – not you. That was never Bill's way, nor the way of sich as sailed with him. And here, sure enough, is my mate Bill, with a spyglass under his arm, bless his old 'art to be sure. You and me'll just go back into the parlour, sonny, and get behind the door, and we'll give Bill a little surprise – bless his 'art, I say again.'

So saying, the stranger backed along with me into the parlour, and put me

behind him in the corner, so that we were both hidden by the open door. I was
very uneasy and alarmed, as you may fancy, and it rather added to my fears to
observe that the stranger was certainly frightened himself. He cleared the hilt of
his cutlass and loosened the blade sheath; and all the time we were waiting there
he kept swallowing as if he felt what we used to call a lump in the throat.

At last in strode the captain, slammed the door behind him, without looking
to the right or left, and marched straight across the room to where his breakfast
awaited him.

'Bill,' said the stranger, in a voice that I thought he had tried to make bold
and big.

The captain spun round on his heel and fronted us; all the brown had gone
out of his face, and even his nose was blue; he had the look of a man who sees a
ghost, or the evil one, or something worse, if anything can be; and, upon my
word, I felt sorry to see him, all in a moment, turn so old and sick.

'Come, Bill, you know me; you know an old shipmate, Bill, surely,' said the
stranger.

The captain made a sort of gasp.

'Black Dog!' said he.

'And who else?' returned the other, getting more at his ease. 'Black Dog as
ever was, come for to see his old shipmate, Billy, at the "Admiral Benbow" inn.
Ah, Bill, Bill, we have seen a sight of times, us two, since I lost them two
talons,' holding up his mutilated hand.

'Now look here,' said the captain; 'you've run me down; here I am; well, then,
speak up: what is it?'

'That's you, Bill,' returned Black Dog, 'you're in the right of it, Billy. I'll have
a glass of rum from this dear child here, as I've took such a liking to; and we'll sit
down, if you please, and talk square, like old shipmates.'

When I returned with the rum, they were already seated on either side of the
captain's breakfast table – Black Dog next to the door, and sitting sideways, so as
to have one eye on his old shipmate, and one, as I thought, on his retreat.

He bade me go, and leave the door wide open. 'None of your keyholes for me,
sonny,' he said; and I left them together, and retired into the bar.

For a long time, though I certainly did my best to listen, I could hear nothing
but a low gabbling; but at last the voices began to grow higher, and I picked up a
word or two, mostly oaths, from the captain.

'No, no, no, no; and an end of it!' he cried once. And again: 'If it comes to
swinging, swing all, say I.'

Then all of a sudden there was a trememdous explosion of oaths and other
noises – the chair went over in a lump, a clash of steel followed, and then a cry
of pain, and the next instant I saw Black Dog in full flight, and the captain hotly
pursuing, both with drawn cutlasses, and the former streaming blood from the
left shoulder. Just at the door, the captain aimed at the fugitive one last
tremendous cut, which would certainly have split him to the chine had it not
been intercepted by our big signboard of Admiral Benbow. You may see the
notch on the lower side of the frame to this day.

That blow was the last of the battle. Once out upon the road, Black Dog, in
spite of his wound, showed a wonderful clean pair of heels, and disappeared over
the edge of the hill in half a minute. The captain, for his part, stood staring at

the signboard like a bewildered man. Then he passed his hand over his eyes several times, and at last turned back into the house.

'Jim,' says he, 'rum'; and as he spoke, he reeled a little, and caught himself with one hand against the wall.

'Are you hurt?' cried I.

'Rum,' he repeated. 'I must get away from here. Rum! rum!'

I ran to fetch it; but I was quite unsteadied by all that had fallen out, and I broke one glass and fouled the tap, and while I was still getting in my own way, I heard a loud fall in the parlour, and, running in, beheld the captain lying full length upon the floor. At the same instant my mother, alarmed by the cries and fighting, came running downstairs to help me. Between us we raised his head. He was breathing very loud and hard; but his eyes were closed, and his face a horrible colour.

'Dear, deary me!' cried my mother, 'what a disgrace upon the house! And your poor father sick!'

In the meantime, we had no idea what to do to help the captain, nor any other thought but that he had got his death-hurt in the scuffle with the stranger. I got the rum, to be sure, and tried to put it down his throat; but his teeth were tightly shut, and his jaws as strong as iron. It was a happy relief for us when the door opened and Dr Livesey came in, on his visit to my father.

'Oh, doctor,' we cried, 'what shall we do? Where is he wounded?'

'Wounded? A fiddle-stick's end!' said the doctor. 'No more wounded than you or I. The man has had a stroke, as I warned him. Now, Mrs Hawkins, just you run upstairs to your husband, and tell him, if possible, nothing about it. For my part, I must do my best to save this fellow's trebly worthless life; and Jim here will get me a basin.'

When I got back with the basin, the doctor had already ripped up the captain's sleeve, and exposed his great sinewy arm. It was tattooed in several places: 'Here's luck,' 'A fair wind,' and 'Billy Bones his fancy,' were very neatly and clearly executed on the forearm; and up near the shoulder there was a sketch of a gallows and a man hanging from it – done, as I thought, with great spirit.

'Prophetic,' said the doctor, touching this picture with his finger. 'And now, Master Billy Bones, if that be your name, we'll have a look at the colour of your blood. Jim,' he said, 'are you afraid of blood?'

'No, sir,' said I.

'Well, then,' said he, 'you hold the basin'; and with that he took his lancet and opened a vein.

A great deal of blood was taken before the captain opened his eyes and looked mistily about him. First he recognized the doctor with an unmistakable frown; then his glance fell upon me, and he looked relieved. But suddenly his colour changed, and he tried to raise himself, crying:

'Where's Black Dog?'

'There's no Black Dog here,' said the doctor, 'except what you have on your own back. You have been drinking rum; you have had a stroke, precisely as I told you; and I have just, very much against my own will, dragged you head foremost out of the grave. Now, Mr Bones——'

'That's not my name,' he interrupted.

'Much I care,' returned the doctor. 'It's the name of a buccaneer of my acquaintance; and I call you by it for the sake of shortness, and what I have to say to you is this: one glass of rum won't kill you, but if you take one you'll take another and another, and I stake my wig if you don't break off short, you'll die – do you understand that? – die, and go to your own place, like the man in the Bible. Come, now, make an effort. I'll help you to your bed for once.'

Between us, with much trouble, we managed to hoist him upstairs, and laid him on his bed, where his head fell back on the pillow, as if he were almost fainting.

'Now, mind you,' said the doctor, 'I clear my conscience – the name of rum for you is death.'

And with that he went off to see my father, taking me with him by the arm.

'This is nothing,' he said, as soon as he had closed the door. 'I have drawn blood enough to keep him quiet a while; he should lie for a week where he is – that is the best thing for him and you; but another stroke would settle him.'

CHAPTER THREE

The Black Spot

ABOUT NOON I STOPPED AT the captain's door with some cooling drinks and medicines. He was lying very much as we had left him, only a little higher, and he seemed both weak and excited.

'Jim,' he said, 'You're the only one here that's worth anything; and you know I've been always good to you. Never a month but I've given you a silver fourpenny for yourself. And now you see, mate, I'm pretty low, and deserted by all; and Jim, you'll bring me one noggin of rum, now, won't you, matey?'

'The doctor——' I began.

But he broke in cursing the doctor, in a feeble voice, but heartily. 'Doctors is all swabs,' he said; 'and that doctor there, why, what do he know about seafaring men? I been in places hot as pitch, and mates dropping round with Yellow Jack, and the blessed land a-heaving like the sea with earthquakes – what do the doctor know of lands like that? – and I lived on rum, I tell you. It's been meat and drink, and man and wife, to me; and if I'm not to have my rum now I'm a poor old hulk on a lee-shore, my blood'll be on you, Jim, and that doctor swab'; and he ran on again for a while with curses. 'Look, Jim, how my fingers fidget,' he continued, in the pleading tone. 'I can't keep 'em still, not I. I haven't had a drop this blessed day. That doctor's a fool, I tell you. If I don't have a drain o' rum, Jim, I'll have the horrors; I seen some on 'em already. I seen old Flint in the corner there, behind you; as plain as print, I seen him; and if I get the horrors, I'm a man that has lived rough, and I'll raise Cain. Your doctor hisself said one glass wouldn't hurt me. I'll give you a golden guinea for a noggin, Jim.'

He was growing more and more excited, and this alarmed me for my father, who was very low that day, and needed quiet; besides, I was reassured by the doctor's words, now quoted to me, and rather offended by the offer of a bribe.

'I want none of your money,' said I, 'but what you owe my father. I'll get you one glass, and no more.'

When I brought it to him, he seized it greedily, and drank it out.

'Ay, ay,' said he, 'that's some better, sure enough. And now, matey, did that doctor say how long I was to lie here in this old berth?'

'A week at least,' said I.

'Thunder!' he cried. 'A week! I can't do that: they'd have the black spot on me by then. The lubbers is going about to get the wind of me this blessed moment; lubbers as couldn't keep what they got, and want to nail what is another's. Is that seamanly behaviour, now, I want to know? But I'm a saving soul. I never wasted good money of mine, nor lost it neither; and I'll trick 'em again. I'm not afraid on 'em. I'll shake out another reef, matey, and daddle 'em again.'

As he was thus speaking, he had risen from bed with great difficulty, holding to my shoulder with a grip that almost made me cry out, and moving his legs like so much dead weight. His words, spirited as they were in meaning, contrasted sadly with the weakness of the voice in which they were uttered. He paused when he had got into a sitting position on the edge.

'That doctor's done me,' he murmured. 'My ears is singing. Lay me back.'

Before I could do much to help him he had fallen back again to his former place, where he lay for a while silent.

'Jim,' he said, at length, 'you saw that seafaring man to-day?'

'Black Dog?' I asked.

'Ah! Black Dog,' says he. 'He's a bad 'un; but there's worse that put him on. Now, if I can't get away nohow, and they tip me the black spot, mind you, it's my old sea-chest they're after; you get on a horse – you can, can't you? Well, then, you get on a horse, and go to – well, yes, I will! – to that eternal doctor swab, and tell him to pipe all hands – magistrates and sich – and he'll lay 'em aboard at the "Admiral Benbow" – all old Flint's crew, man and boy, all on 'em that's left. I was first mate, I was, old Flint's first mate, and I'm the on'y one as knows the place. He gave it me to Savannah, when he lay a-dying, like as if I was to now, you see. But you won't peach unless they get the black spot on me, or unless you see that Black Dog again, or a seafaring man with one leg, Jim – him above all.'

'But what is the black spot, captain?' I asked.

'That's a summons, mate. I'll tell you if they get that. But you keep your weather-eye open, Jim, and I'll share with you equals, upon my honour.'

He wandered a little longer, his voice growing weaker; but soon after I had given him his medicine, which he took like a child, with the remark: 'If ever a seaman wanted drugs, it's me,' he fell at last into a heavy, swoon-like sleep, in which I left him. What I should have done had all gone well I do not know. Probably I should have told the whole story to the doctor; for I was in mortal fear lest the captain should repent of his confessions and make an end of me. But as things fell out, my poor father died quite suddenly that evening, which put all other matters on one side. Our natural distress, the visits of the neighbours, the arranging of the funeral, and all the work of the inn to be carried on in the meanwhile, kept me so busy that I had scarcely time to think of the captain, far less to be afraid of him.

He got downstairs next morning, to be sure, and had his meals as usual, though he ate little, and had more, I am afraid, than his usual supply of rum, for he helped himself out of the bar, scowling and blowing through his nose, and no one dared to cross him. On the night before the funeral he was as drunk as ever; and it was shocking, in that house of mourning, to hear him singing away at his ugly old sea-song; but, weak as he was, we were all in the fear of death for him, and the doctor was suddenly taken up with a case many miles away, and was never near the house after my father's death. I have said the captain was weak; and indeed he seemed rather to grow weaker than regain his strength. He clambered up and down stairs, and went from the parlour to the bar and back again, and sometimes put his nose out of doors to smell the sea, holding on to the walls as he went for support, and breathing hard and fast like a man on a steep mountain. He never particularly addressed me, and it is my belief he had as good as forgotten his confidences; but his temper was more flighty, and, allowing for his bodily weakness, more violent than ever. He had an alarming way now when he was drunk of drawing his cutlass and laying it bare before him on the table. But, with all that, he minded people less, and seemed shut up in his own thoughts and rather wandering. Once, for instance, to our extreme wonder, he piped up to a different air, a kind of country love-song, that he must have learned in his youth before he had begun to follow the sea.

So things passed, until the day after the funeral, and about three o'clock of a bitter, foggy, frosty afternoon, I was standing at the door for a moment, full of sad thoughts about my father, when I saw someone drawing slowly near along the road. He was plainly blind, for he tapped before him with a stick, and wore a great green shade over his eyes and nose; and he was hunched, as if with age or weakness, and wore a huge old tattered sea-cloak with a hood, that made him appear positively deformed. I never saw in my life a more dreadful-looking figure. He stopped a little from the inn, and, raising his voice in an odd sing-song, addressed the air in front of him:

'Will any kind friend inform a poor blind man, who has lost the precious sight of his eyes in the gracious defence of his country, England, and God bless King George! – where or in what part of this country he may now be?'

'You are at the "Admiral Benbow." Black Hill Cove, my good man,' said I.

'I hear a voice,' said he – 'a young voice. Will you give me your hand, my kind young friend, and lead me in?'

I held out my hand, and the horrible, soft-spoken, eyeless creature gripped it in a moment like a vice. I was so much startled that I struggled to withdraw; but the blind man pulled me close up to him with a single action of his arm.

'Now, boy,' he said, 'take me in to the captain.'

'Sir,' said I, 'upon my word I dare not.'

'Oh,' he sneered, that's it! Take me in straight, or I'll break your arm.'

And he gave it, as he spoke, a wrench that made me cry out.

'Sir,' I said, 'it is for yourself I mean. The captain is not what he used to be. He sits with a drawn cutlass. Another gentleman——'

'Come, now, march,' interrupted he; and I never heard a voice so cruel, and cold, and ugly as that blind man's. It cowed me more than the pain, and I began to obey him at once, walking straight in at the door and towards the parlour where our sick old buccaneer was sitting, dazed with rum. The blind man clung close to me, holding me in one iron fist, and leaning almost more of his weight on me than I could carry. 'Lead me straight up to him, and when I'm in view, cry out: "Here's a friend for you, Bill." If you don't, I'll do this'; and with that he gave me a twitch that I thought would have made me faint. Between this and that, I was so utterly terrified of the blind beggar that I forgot my terror of the captain, and as I opened the parlour door, cried out the words he had ordered in a trembling voice.

The poor captain raised his eyes, and at one look the rum went out of him, and left him staring sober. The expression of his face was not so much of terror as of mortal sickness. He made a movement to rise, but I do not believe he had enough force left in his body.

'Now, Bill, sit where you are,' said the beggar. 'If I can't see, I can hear a finger stirring. Business is business. Hold out your left hand. Boy, take his left hand by the wrist, and bring it near to my right.'

We both obeyed him to the letter, and I saw him pass something from the hollow of the hand that held his stick into the palm of the captain's, which closed upon it instantly.

'And now that's done,' said the blind man; and at the words he suddenly left hold of me, and, with incredible accuracy and nimbleness, skipped out of the parlour and into the road, where, as I still stood motionless, I could hear his stick go tap-tap-tapping into the distance.

It was some time before either I or the captain seemed to gather our sense; but at length, and about at the same moment, I released his wrist, which I was still holding, and he drew his hand and looked sharply into the palm.

'Ten o'clock!' he cried. 'Six hours. We'll do them yet'; and he sprang to his feet.

Even as he did so, he reeled, put his hand to his throat, stood swaying for a moment, and then, with a peculiar sound, fell from his whole height face foremost to the floor.

I ran to him at once, calling to my mother. But haste was all in vain. The captain had been struck dead by thundering apoplexy. It is a curious thing to understand, for I had certainly never liked the man, though of late I had begun to pity him, but as soon as I saw that he was dead, I burst into a flood of tears. It was the second death I had known, and the sorrow of the first was still fresh in my heart.

CHAPTER FOUR

The Sea-Chest

I LOST NO TIME, OF COURSE, in telling my mother all that I knew, and perhaps should have told her long before, and we saw ourselves at once in a difficult and dangerous position. Some of the man's money – if he had any – was certainly due to us; but it was not likely that our captain's shipmates, above all the two specimens seen by me, Black Dog and the blind beggar, would be inclined to give up their booty in payment of the dead man's debts. The captain's order to mount at once and ride for Dr Livesey would have left my mother alone and unprotected, which was not to be thought of. Indeed, it seemed impossible for either of us to remain much longer in the house: the fall of coals in the kitchen grate, the very ticking of the clock, filled us with alarms. The neighbourhood, to our ears, seemed haunted by approaching footsteps; and what between the dead body of the captain on the parlour floor, and the thought of that detestable blind beggar hovering near at hand, and ready to return, there were moments when, as the saying goes, I jumped in my skin for terror. Something must speedily be resolved upon; and it occurred to us at last to go forth together and seek help in the neighbouring hamlet. No sooner said than done. Bareheaded as we were, we ran out at once in the gathering evening and the frosty fog.

The hamlet lay not many hundred yards away though out of view, on the other side of the next cove; and what greatly encouraged me, it was in an opposite direction from that whence the blind man had made his appearance, and whither he had presumably returned. We were not many minutes on the road, though we sometimes stopped to lay hold of each other and hearken. But there was no unusual sound – nothing but the low wash of the ripple and the croaking of the crows in the wood.

It was already candle-light when we reached the hamlet, and I shall never forget how much I was cheered to see the yellow shine in doors and windows; but that, as it proved, was the best of the help we were likely to get in that quarter. For – you would have thought men would have been ashamed of themselves – no soul would consent to return with us to the 'Admiral Benbow.' The more we told of our troubles, the more – man, woman, and child – they clung to the shelter of their houses. The name of Captain Flint, though it was strange to me, was well enough known to some there, and carried a great weight of terror. Some of the men who had been to field-work on the far side of the 'Admiral Benbow' remembered, besides, to have seen several strangers on the road, and, taking them to be smugglers, to have bolted away; and one at least had seen a little lugger in what we called Kitt's Hole. For that matter, any one who was a comrade of the captain's was enough to frighten them to death. And the short and the long of the matter was, that while we could get several who were willing enough to ride to Dr Livesey's, which lay in another direction, not one would help us to defend the inn.

They say cowardice is infectious; but then argument is, on the other hand, a great emboldener; and so when each had said his say, my mother made them a speech. She would not, she declared, lose money that belonged to her fatherless boy; 'if none of the rest of you dare,' she said, 'Jim and I dare. Back we will go, the way we came, and small thanks to you big, hulking, chicken-hearted men. We'll have that chest open, if we die for it. And I'll thank you for that bag, Mrs Crossley, to bring back our lawful money in.

Of course, I said I would go with my mother; and of course they all cried out at our foolhardiness; but even then not a man would go along with us. All they would do was to give me a loaded pistol, lest we were attacked; and to promise to have horses ready saddled, in case we were pursued on our return; while one lad was to ride forward to the doctor's in search of armed assistance.

My heart was beating finely when we two set forth in the cold night upon this dangerous venture. A full moon was beginning to rise and peered redly through the upper edges of the fog, and this increased our haste, for it was plain, before we came forth again, that all would be as bright as day, and our departure exposed to the eyes of any watchers. We slipped along the hedges, noiseless and swift, nor did we see or hear anything to increase our terrors, till, to our huge relief, the door of the 'Admiral Benbow' had closed behind us.

I slipped the bolt at once, and we stood and panted for a moment in the dark, alone in the house with the dead captain's body. Then my mother got a candle in the bar, and, holding each other's hands, we advanced into the parlour. He lay as we had left him, on his back, with his eyes open, and one arm stretched out.

'Draw down the blind, Jim,' whispered my mother; 'they might come and watch outside. And now,' said she, when I had done so, 'we have to get the key off *that*; and who's to touch it, I should like to know!' and she gave a kind of sob as she said the words.

I went down on my knees at once. On the floor close to his hand there was a little round of paper, blackened on the one side. I could not doubt that this was the *black spot*; and taking it up, I found written on the other side, in a very good, clear hand, this short message: 'You have till ten to-night.'

'He had till ten, mother,' said I; and just as I said it, our old clock began striking. This sudden noise startled us shockingly; but the news was good, for it was only six.

'Now, Jim,' she said, 'that key.'

I felt in his pockets, one after another. A few small coins, a thimble, and some thread and a big needle, a piece of pigtail tobacco bitten away at the end, his gully with the crooked handle, a pocket compass, and a tinder-box, were all that they contained, and I began to despair.

'Perhaps it's round his neck,' suggested my mother.

Overcoming a strong repugnance, I tore open his shirt at the neck, and there, sure enough, hanging to a bit of tarry string, which I cut with his own gully, we found the key. At this triumph we were filled with hope, and hurried upstairs, without delay, to the little room where he had slept so long, and where his box had stood since the day of his arrival.

It was like any other seaman's chest on the outside, the initial 'B.' burned on the top of it with a hot iron, and the corners somewhat smashed and broken as by long, rough usage.

'Give me the key,' said my mother; and though the lock was very stiff, she had turned it and thrown back the lid in a twinkling.

A strong smell of tobacco and tar rose from the interior, but nothing was to be seen on the top except a suit of very good clothes, carefully brushed and folded. They had never been worn, my mother said. Under that, the miscellany began – a quadrant, a tin cannikin, several sticks of tobacco, two brace of very handsome pistols, a piece of bar silver, an old Spanish watch and some other trinkets of little value and mostly of foreign make, a pair of compasses mounted with brass, and five or six curious West Indian shells. It has often set me thinking since that he should have carried about these shells with him in his wandering, guilty, and hunted life.

In the meantime we had found nothing of any value but the silver and the trinkets, and neither of these were in our way. Underneath there was an old boat-cloak, whitened with sea salt on many a harbour bar. My mother pulled it up with impatience, and there lay before us, the last things in the chest, a bundle tied up in oil-cloth, and looking like papers, and a canvas bag, that gave forth, at a touch, the jingle of gold.

'I'll show these rogues that I'm an honest woman,' said my mother. I'll have my dues, and not a farthing over. Hold Mrs Crossley's bag.' And she began to count over the amount of the captain's score from the sailor's bag into the one that I was holding.

It was a long, difficult business, for the coins were of all countries and sizes – doubloons, and louis-d'ors, and guineas, and pieces of eight, and I know not what besides, all shaken together at random. The guineas, too, were about the scarcest, and it was with these only that my mother knew how to make her count.

When we were about half-way through, I suddenly put my hand upon her arm; for I had heard in the silent, frosty air, a sound that brought my heart into my mouth – the tap-tapping of the blind man's stick upon the frozen road. It drew nearer and nearer, while we sat holding our breath. Then it struck sharp on the inn door, and then we could hear the handle being turned, and the bolt rattling as the wretched being tried to enter; and then there was a long time of silence both within and without. At last the tapping recommenced, and, to our indescribable joy and gratitude, died slowly away again until it ceased to be heard.

'Mother,' said I, 'take the whole and let's be going'; for I was sure the bolted door must have seemed suspicious, and would bring the whole hornets' nest about our ears; though how thankful I was that I had bolted it, none could tell who had never met that terrible blind man.

But my mother, frightened as she was, would not consent to take a fraction more than was due to her, and was obstinately unwilling to be content with less. It was not yet seven, she said, by a long way; she knew her rights and she would have them; and she was still arguing with me, when a little low whistle sounded a good way off upon the hill. That was enough, and more than enough, for both of us.

'I'll take what I have,' she said, jumping to her feet.

'And I'll take this to square the count,' said I, picking up the oilskin packet.

Next moment we were both groping downstairs, leaving the candle by the empty chest; and the next we had opened the door and were in full retreat. We had not started a moment too soon. The fog was rapidly dispersing; already the moon shone quite clear on the high ground on either side; and it was only in the exact bottom of the dell and round the tavern door that a thin veil still hung unbroken to conceal the first steps of our escape. Far less than half-way to the hamlet, very little beyond the bottom of the hill, we must come forth into the moonlight. Nor was this all; for the sound of several footsteps running came already to our ears, and as we looked back in their direction, a light tossing to and fro and still rapidly advancing, showed that one of the newcomers carried a lantern.

'My dear,' said my mother suddenly, 'take the money and run on. I am going to faint.'

This was certainly the end for both of us, I thought. How I cursed the cowardice of the neighbours; how I blamed my poor mother for her honesty and her greed, for her past foolhardiness and present weakness!

We were just at the little bridge, by good fortune; and I helped her, tottering as she was, to the edge of the bank, where, sure enough, she gave a sigh and fell on my shoulder. I do not know how I found the strength to do it at all, and I am afraid it was roughly done; but I managed to drag her down the bank and a little way under the arch. Farther I could not move her, for the bridge was too low to let me do more than crawl below it. So there we had to stay – my mother almost entirely exposed, and both of us within earshot of the inn.

CHAPTER FIVE

The Last of the Blind Man

MY CURIOSITY, IN A SENSE, was stronger than my fear; for I could not remain where I was, but crept back to the bank again, whence, sheltering my head behind a bush of broom, I might command the road before our door. I was scarcely in position ere my enemies began to arrive, seven or eight of them, running hard, their feet beating out of time along the road, and the man with the lantern some paces in front. Three men ran together, hand in hand; and I made out, even through the mist, that the middle man of this trio was the blind beggar. The next moment his voice showed me that I was right.

'Down with the door!' he cried.

'Ay, ay, sir!' answered two or three; and a rush was made upon the 'Admiral Benbow,' the lantern-bearer following; and then I could see them pause, and hear speeches passed in a lower key, as if they were surprised to find the door open. But the pause was brief, for the blind man again issued his commands. His voice sounded louder and higher, as if he were afire with eagerness and rage.

'In, in, in!' he shouted, and cursed them for their delay.

Four or five of them obeyed at once, two remaining on the road with the formidable beggar. There was a pause, then a cry of surprise, and then a voice shouting from the house:

'Bill's dead!'

But the blind man swore at them again for their delay.

'Search him, some of you shirking lubbers, and the rest of you aloft and get the chest,' he cried.

I could hear their feet rattling up our old stairs, so that the house must have shook with it. Promptly afterwards, fresh sounds of astonishment arose; the window of the captain's room was thrown open with a slam and a jingle of broken glass, and a man leaned out into the moonlight, head and shoulders, and addressed the blind beggar on the road below him.

'Pew,' he cried, 'they've been before us. Someone's turned the chest out alow and aloft.'

'Is it there?' roared Pew.

'The money's there.'

The blind man cursed the money.

'Flint's fist, I mean,' he cried.

'We don't see it here nohow,' returned the man.

'Here, you below there, is it on Bill?' cried the blind man again.

At that, another fellow, probably he who had remained below to search the captain's body, came to the door of the inn. 'Bill's been overhauled a'ready,' said he, 'nothin' left.'

'It's these people of the inn – it's that boy. I wish I had put his eyes out!' cried the blind man, Pew. 'They were here no time ago – they had the door bolted when I tried it. Scatter, lads, and find 'em.'

'Sure enough, they left their glim here,' said the fellow from the window.

'Scatter and find 'em! Rout the house out!' reiterated Pew, striking with his stick upon the road.

Then there followed a great to-do through all our old inn, heavy feet pounding to and fro, furniture thrown over, doors kicked in, until the very rocks re-echoed, and the men came out again, one after another, on the road, and declared that we were nowhere to be found. And just then the same whistle that had alarmed my mother and myself over the dead captain's money was once more clearly audible through the night, but this time twice repeated. I had thought it to be the blind man's trumpet, so to speak, summoning his crew to the assault; but I now found that it was a signal from the hillside towards the hamlet, and, from its effect upon the buccaneers, a signal to warn them of approaching danger.

'There's Dirk again,' said one. 'Twice! We'll have to budge, mates.'

'Budge, you skulk!' cried Pew. 'Dirk was a fool and a coward from the first – you wouldn't mind him. They must be close by; they can't be far; you have your hands on it. Scatter and look for them, dogs! Oh, shiver my soul,' he cried, 'if I had eyes!'

This appeal seemed to produce some effect, for two of the fellows began to look here and there among the lumber, but half-heartedly, I thought, and with half an eye to their own danger all the time, while the rest stood irresolute on the road.

'You have your hands on thousands, you fools, and you hang a leg! You'd be as rich as kings if you could find it, and you know it's here, and you stand there malingering. There wasn't one of you dared face Bill, and I did – a blind man! And I'm to lose my chance for you! I'm to be a poor, crawling beggar, sponging for rum, when I might be rolling in a coach! If you had the pluck of a weevil in a biscuit you would catch them still.'

'Hang it, Pew, we've got the doubloons!' grumbled one.

'They might have hid the blessed thing,' said another. 'Take the Georges, Pew, and don't stand here squalling.'

Squalling was the word for it, Pew's anger rose so high at these objections; till at last, his passion completely taking the upper hand, he struck at them right and left in his blindness, and his stick sounded heavily on more than one.

These, in their turn, cursed back at the blind miscreant, threatening him in horrid terms, and tried in vain to catch the stick and wrest it from his grasp.

This quarrel was the saving for us; for while it was still raging, another sound came from the top of the hill on the side of the hamlet – the tramp of horses galloping. Almost at the same time, a pistol shot, flash and report, came from the hedge-side. And that was plainly the last signal of danger; for the buccaneers turned at once and ran, separating in every direction, one seaward along the cove, one slant across the hill, and so on, so that in half a minute not a sign of them remained but Pew. Him they had deserted, whether in sheer panic or out of revenge for his ill words and blows, I know not; but there he remained behind, tapping up and down the road in a frenzy, and groping and calling for his comrades. Finally he took the wrong turn, and ran a few steps past me, towards the hamlet, crying:

'Johnny, Black Dog, Dirk,' and other names, 'you won't leave old Pew, mates – not old Pew!'

Just then the noise of horses topped the rise, and four or five riders came in sight in the moonlight, and swept at full gallop down the slope.

At this Pew saw his error, turned with a scream, and ran straight for the ditch, into which he rolled. But he was on his feet again in a second, and made another dash, now utterly bewildered, right under the nearest of the coming horses.

The rider tried to save him, but in vain. Down went Pew with a cry that rang high into the night; and the four hoofs trampled and spurned him and passed by. He fell on his side, then gently collapsed upon his face, and moved no more.

I leaped to my feet and hailed the riders. They were pulling up at any rate, horrified at the accident; and I soon saw what they were. One, tailing out behind the rest, was a lad that had gone from the hamlet to Dr Livesey's; the rest were revenue officers, whom he had met by the way, and with whom he had had the intelligence to return at once. Some news of the lugger in Kitt's Hole had found its way to Supervisor Dance, and set him forth that night in our direction, and to that circumstance my mother and I owed our preservation from death.

Pew was dead, stone dead. As for my mother, when we had carried her up to the hamlet, a little cold water and salts and that soon brought her back again, and she was none the worse for her terror, though she still continued to deplore the balance of the money. In the meantime, the supervisor rode on, as fast as he could, to Kitt's Hole; but his men had to dismount and grope down the dingle, leading, and sometimes supporting, their horses, and in continual fear of ambushes; so it was no great matter for surprise that when they got down to the Hole the lugger was already under way, though still close in. He hailed her. A voice replied, telling him to keep out of the moonlight, or he would get some lead in him, and at the same time a bullet whistled close by his arm. Soon after, the lugger doubled the point and disappeared. Mr Dance stood there, as he said, 'like a fish out of water,' and all he could do was to dispatch a man to B—— to warn the cutter. 'And that,' said he, 'is just about as good as nothing. They've got off clean, and there's an end. Only,' he added, 'I'm glad I trod on Master Pew's corns'; for by this time he had heard my story.

I went back with him to the 'Admiral Benbow,' and you cannot imagine a house in such a state of smash; the very clock had been thrown down by these fellows in their furious hunt after my mother and myself; and though nothing had actually been taken away except the captain's money-bag and a little silver from the till, I could see at once that we were ruined. Mr Dance could make nothing of the scene.

'They got the money, you say? Well then, Hawkins, what in fortune were they after? More money, I suppose?'

'No, sir; not money, I think,' replied I. 'In fact, sir, I believe I have the thing in my breast-pocket; and, to tell you the truth, I should like to get it put in safety.'

'To be sure, boy; quite right,' said he. 'I'll take it, if you like.'

'I thought, perhaps, Dr Livesey——' I began

'Perfectly right,' he interrupted very cheerily, 'perfectly right – a gentleman and a magistrate. And, now I come to think of it, I might as well ride round there myself and report to him or squire. Master Pew's dead, when all's done; not that I regret it, but he's dead, you see, and people will make it out against an officer of His Majesty's revenue, if make it out they can. Now, I'll tell you, Hawkins: if you like, I'll take you along.'

I thanked him heartily for the offer, and we walked back to the hamlet where the horses were. By the time I had told mother of my purpose they were all in the saddle.

'Dogger,' said Mr Dance, 'you have a good horse; take up this lad behind you.'

As soon as I was mounted, holding on to Dogger's belt, the supervisor gave the word, and the party struck out at a bouncing trot on the road to Dr Livesey's house.

CHAPTER SIX

The Captain's Papers

WE RODE HARD ALL THE way, till we drew up before Dr Livesey's door. The house was all dark to the front.

Mr Dance told me to jump down and knock, and Dogger gave me a stirrup to descend by. The door was opened almost at once by the maid.

'Is Dr Livesey in?' I asked.

No, she said; he had come home in the afternoon, but had gone up to the Hall to dine and pass the evening with the squire.

'So there we go, boys,' said Mr Dance.

This time, as the distance was short, I did not mount, but ran with Dogger's stirrup-leather to the lodge gates, and up the long, leafless, moonlit avenue to where the white line of the Hall buildings looked on either hand on great old gardens. Here Mr Dance dismounted, and, taking me along with him, was admitted at a word into the house.

The servant led us down a matted passage, and showed us at the end into a great library, all lined with bookcases and busts upon the top of them, where the squire and Dr Livesey sat, pipe in hand, on either side of a bright fire.

I had never seen the squire so near at hand. He was a tall man, over six feet high, and broad in proportion, and he had a bluff, rough-and-ready face, all roughened and reddened and lined in his long travels. His eyebrows were very black, and moved readily, and this gave him a look of some temper, not bad, you would say, but quick and high.

'Come in, Mr Dance,' says he, very stately and condescending.

'Good evening, Dance,' says the doctor, with a nod. 'And good evening to you, friend Jim. What good wind brings you here?'

The supervisor stood up straight and stiff, and told his story like a lesson; and you should have seen how the two gentlemen leaned forward and looked at each other, and forgot to smoke in their surprise and interest. When they heard how my mother went back to the inn, Dr Livesey fairly slapped his thigh, and the squire cried 'Bravo!' and broke his long pipe against the grate. Long before it was done, Mr Trelawney (that, you will remember, was the squire's name) had got up from his seat, and was striding about the room, and the doctor, as if to hear the better, had taken off his powdered wig, and sat there, looking very strange indeed with his own close-cropped, black poll.

At last Mr Dance finished the story.

'Mr Dance,' said the squire, 'you are a very noble fellow. And as for riding down that black, atrocious miscreant, I regard it as an act of virtue, sir, like stamping on a cockroach. This lad Hawkins is a trump, I perceive. Hawkins, will you ring that bell? Mr Dance must have some ale.'

'And so, Jim,' said the doctor, 'you have the thing that they were after, have you?'

'Here it is, sir,' said I, and gave him the oilskin packet.

The doctor looked it all over, as if his fingers were itching to open it; but instead of doing that, he put it quietly in the pocket of his coat.

'Squire,' said he, 'when Dance has had his ale he must, of course, be off on His Majesty's service; but I mean to keep Jim Hawkins here to sleep at my house, and, with your permission, I propose we should have up the cold pie, and let him sup.'

'As you will, Livesey,' said the squire; 'Hawkins has earned better than cold pie.'

So a big pigeon pie was brought in and put on a side table, and I made a hearty supper, for I was as hungry as a hawk, while Mr Dance was further complimented, and at last dismissed.

'And now, squire,' said the doctor.

'And now, Livesey,' said the squire, in the same breath.

'One at a time, one at a time,' laughed Dr Livesey. 'You have heard of this Flint, I suppose?'

'Heard of him!' cried the squire. 'Heard of him, you say! He was the bloodthirstiest buccaneer that sailed. Blackbeard was a child to Flint. The Spaniards were so prodigiously afraid of him, that, I tell you, sir, I was sometimes proud he was an Englishman. I've seen his topsails with these eyes, off Trinidad, and the cowardly son of a rumpuncheon that I sailed with put back – put back, sir, into Port of Spain.'

'Well, I've heard of him myself, in England,' said the doctor. 'But the point is, had he money?'

'Money!' cried the squire. 'Have you heard the story?' What were these villains after but money? What do they care for but money? For what would they risk their rascal carcasses but money?'

'That we shall soon know,' replied the doctor. 'But you are so confoundedly hot-headed and exclamatory that I cannot get a word in. What I want to know is this: Supposing that I have here in my pocket some clue to where Flint buried his treasure, will that treasure amount to much?'

'Amount, sir!' cried the squire. 'It will amount to this; if we have the clue you talk about, I fit out a ship in Bristol dock, and take you and Hawkins here along, and I'll have that treasure if I search a year.'

'Very well,' said the doctor. 'Now, then, if Jim is agreeable, we'll open the packet'; and he laid it before him on the table.

The bundle was sewn together, and the doctor had to get out his instrument case and cut the stitches with his medical scissors. It contained two things – a book and a sealed paper.

'First of all we'll try the book,' observed the doctor.

The squire and I were both peering over his shoulder as he opened it, for Dr Livesey had kindly motioned me to come round from the side table, where I had been eating, to enjoy the sport of the search. On the first page there were only some scraps of writing, such as a man with a pen in his hand might make for idleness or practice. One was the same as the tattoo mark: 'Billy Bones his fancy'; then there was 'Mr W. Bones, mate.' 'No more rum.' 'Off Palm Key he

got itt'; and some other snatches, mostly single words and unintelligible. I could
not help wondering who it was that had 'got itt,' and what 'itt' was that he got.
A knife in his back as like as not.

'Not much instruction there,' said Dr Livesey, as he passed on.

The next ten or twelve pages were filled with a curious series of entries. There
was a date at one end of the line and at the other a sum of money, as in common
account books; but instead of explanatory writing, only a varying number of
crosses between the two. On the 12th of June 1745, for instance, a sum of
seventy pounds had plainly become due to someone, and there was nothing but
six crosses to explain the cause. In a few cases, to be sure, the name of a place
would be added, as 'Offe Caraccas'; or a mere entry of latitude and longitude, as
'62° 17' 20", 19° 2' 40".'

The record lasted over nearly twenty years, the amount of the separate entries
growing larger as time went on, and at the end a grand total had been made out
after five or six wrong additions, and these words appended: 'Bones, his pile.'

'I can't make head or tail of this,' said Dr Livesey.

'The thing is as clear as noonday,' cried the squire. 'This is the black-hearted
hound's account book. These crosses stand for the names of ships or towns that
they sank or plundered. The sums are the scoundrel's share, and where he feared
an ambiguity, you see he added something clearer. "Offe Caraccas," now; you
see, here was some unhappy vessel boarded off that coast. God help the poor
souls that manned her – coral long ago.'

'Right!' said the doctor. 'See what it is to be a traveller. Right! And the
amounts increase, you see, as he rose in rank.'

There was little else in the volume but a few bearings of places noted in the
blank leaves towards the end, and a table for reducing French, English, and
Spanish moneys to a common value.

'Thrifty man!' cried the doctor. 'He wasn't the one to be cheated.'

'And now,' said the squire, 'for the other.'

The paper had been sealed in several places with a thimble, by the way of seal;
the very thimble, perhaps, that I had found in the captain's pocket. The doctor
opened the seals with great care, and there fell out the map of an island, with
latitude and longitude, soundings, names of hills, and bays and inlets, and every
particular that would be needed to bring a ship to a safe anchorage upon its
shores. It was about nine miles long and five across, shaped, you might say, like a
fat dragon standing up, and had two fine landlocked harbours, and a hill in the
centre part marked 'The Spy-glass.' There were several additions of a later date;
but, above all, three crosses of red ink – two on the north part of the island, one
in the south-west, and, beside this last, in the same red ink, and in a small neat
hand, very different from the captain's tottery characters, these words: 'Bulk of
treasure here.'

Over on the back the same hand had written this further information:

Tall tree, Spy-glass Shoulder, bearing a point to the N. of N.N.E.
Skeleton Island E.S.E. and by E.
Ten feet.
The bar silver is in the north cache; you can find it by the trend of the
east hummock, ten fathoms south of the black crag with the face on it.

The arms are easy found, in the sand hill, N. point of north inlet cape, bearing E. and a quarter N.   J. F.

That was all; but brief as it was, and, to me, incomprehensible, it filled the squire and Dr Livesey with delight.

'Livesey,' said the squire, 'you will give up this wretched practice at once. To-morrow I start for Bristol. In three weeks' time – three weeks! – two weeks – ten days – we'll have the best ship, sir, and the choicest crew in England. Hawkins shall come as cabin-boy. You'll make a famous cabin-boy, Hawkins. You, Livesey, are ship's doctor; I am admiral. We'll take Redruth, Joyce, and Hunter. We'll have favourable winds, a quick passage, and not the least difficulty in finding the spot, and money to eat – to roll in – to play duck and drake with ever after.'

'Trelawney,' said the doctor, 'I'll go with you; and, I'll go bail for it, so will Jim, and be a credit to the undertaking. There's only one man I'm afraid of.'

'And who's that?' cried the squire. 'Name the dog, sir!'

'You,' replied the doctor; 'for you cannot hold your tongue. We are not the only men who know of this paper. These fellows who attacked the inn to-night – bold, desperate blades, for sure – and the rest who stayed aboard that lugger, and more, I dare say, not far off, are, one and all, through thick and thin, bound that they'll get that money. We must none of us go alone till we get to sea. Jim and I shall stick together in the meanwhile; you'll take Joyce and Hunter when you ride to Bristol, and, from first to last, not one of us must breathe a word of what we've found.'

'Livesey,' returned the squire, 'you are always in the right of it. I'll be as silent as the grave.'

PART TWO

CHAPTER ONE

I Go To Bristol

IT WAS LONGER THAN THE squire imagined ere we were ready for the sea, and none of our first plans – not even Dr Livesey's, of keeping me beside him – could be carried out as we intended. The doctor had to go to London for a physician to take charge of his practice; the squire was hard at work at Bristol; and I lived on at the Hall under the charge of old Redruth, the gamekeeper, almost a prisoner, but full of sea-dreams and the most charming anticipations of strange islands and adventures. I brooded by the hour together over the map, all the details of which I well remembered. Sitting by the fire in the housekeeper's room, I approached that island, in my fancy, from every possible direction; I explored every acre of its surface; I climbed a thousand times to that tall hill they call the Spy-glass, and from the top enjoyed the most wonderful and changing prospects. Sometimes the isle was thick with savages, with whom we fought; sometimes full of dangerous animals that hunted us; but in all my fancies nothing occurred to me so strange and tragic as our actual adventures.

So the weeks passed on – till one fine day there came a letter addressed to Dr Livesey, with this addition: 'To be opened, in the case of his absence, by Tom Redruth, or young Hawkins.' Obeying this order we found, or rather I found – for the gamekeeper was a poor hand at reading anything but print – the following important news:

> *Old Anchor Inn, Bristol, March 1, 17—.*
> DEAR LIVESEY,—As I do not know whether you are at the Hall or still in London, I send this in double to both places.
> The ship is bought and fitted. She lies at anchor, ready for sea. You never imagined a sweeter schooner – a child might sail her – two hundred tons; name, *Hispaniola*.
> I got her through my old friend, Blandly, who has proved himself throughout the most surprising trump. The admirable fellow literally slaved in my interest, and, I may say, did every one in Bristol, as soon as they got wind of the port we sailed for – treasure, I mean.

'Redruth,' said I, interrupting the letter, 'Dr Livesey will not like that. The squire has been talking, after all.'

'Well, who's a better right?' growled the gamekeeper. 'A pretty rum go if squire ain't to talk for Dr Livesey, I should think.'

At that I gave up all attempt at commentary, and read straight on:

> Blandly himself found the *Hispaniola*, and by the most admirable

management got her for the merest trifle. There is a class of men in Bristol
monstrously prejudiced against Blandly. They go the length of declaring
that this honest creature would do anything for money, that the *Hispaniola*
belonged to him, and that he sold it me absurdly high – the most
transparent calumnies. None of them dare, however, to deny the merits of
the ship.

So far there was not a hitch. The workpeople, to be sure – riggers and
what not – were most annoyingly slow; but time cured that. It was the crew
that troubled me.

I wished a round score of men – in case of natives, buccaneers, or the
odious French – and I had the worry of the deuce itself to find so much as
half a dozen, till the most remarkable stroke of fortune brought me the very
man that I required.

I was standing on the dock, when, by the merest accident, I fell in talk
with him. I found he was an old sailor, kept a public-house, knew all the
seafaring men in Bristol, had lost his health ashore, and wanted a good
berth as cook to get to sea again. He had hobbled down there that morning,
he said, to get a smell of the salt.

I was monstrously touched – so would you have been – and, out of pure
pity, I engaged him on the spot to be ship's cook. Long John Silver, he is
called, and has lost a leg; but that I regarded as a recommendation, since he
lost it in his country's service under the immortal Hawke. He has no
pension, Livesey. Imagine the abominable age we live in!

Well, sir, I thought I had only found a cook, but it was a crew I had
discovered. Between Silver and myself we got together in a few days a
company of the toughest old salts imaginable – not pretty to look at, but
fellows, by their faces, of the most indomitable spirit. I declare we could
fight a frigate.

Long John even got rid of two out of the six or seven I had already
engaged. He showed me in a moment that they were just the sort of fresh-
water swabs we had to fear in an adventure of importance.

I am in the most magnificent health and spirits, eating like a bull,
sleeping like a tree, yet I shall not enjoy a moment till I hear my old
tarpaulins tramping round the capstan. Seaward ho! Hang the treasure! It's
the glory of the sea that has turned my head. So now, Livesey, come post;
do not lose an hour, if you respect me.

Let young Hawkins go at once to see his mother, with Redruth for a
guard; and then both come full speed to Bristol.

JOHN TRELAWNEY.

Postscript. I did not tell you that Blandly, who, by the way, is to send a
consort after us if we don't turn up by the end of August, had found an
admirable fellow for sailing master – a stiff man, which I regret, but in all
other respects, a treasure. Long John Silver unearthed a very competent
man for a mate, a man named Arrow. I have a boatswain who pipes,
Livesey; so things shall go man-o'-war fashion on board the good ship
Hispaniola.

I forgot to tell you that Silver is a man of substance; I know of my own knowledge that he has a banker's account, which has never been overdrawn. He leaves his wife to manage the inn; and as she is a woman of colour, a pair of old bachelors like you and I may be excused for guessing that it is the wife, quite as much as the health, that sends him back to roving.   J.T.

PPS. Hawkins may stay one night with his mother.   J.T.

You can fancy the excitement into which that letter put me. I was half beside myself with glee; and if ever I despised a man, it was old Tom Redruth, who could do nothing but grumble and lament. Any of the under-gamekeepers would gladly have changed places with him; but such was not the squire's pleasure, and the squire's pleasure was like law among them all. Nobody but old Redruth would have dared so much as even to grumble.

The next morning he and I set out on foot for the 'Admiral Benbow,' and there I found my mother in good health and spirits. The captain, who had so long been a cause of so much discomfort, was gone where the wicked cease from troubling. The squire had had everything repaired, and the public rooms and the sign repainted, and had added some furniture – above all, a beautiful armchair for mother in the bar. He had found her a boy as an apprentice also, so that she should not want help while I was gone.

It was on seeing that boy that I understood, for the first time, my situation. I had thought up to that moment of the adventures before me, not at all of the home that I was leaving; and now at sight of this clumsy stranger, who was to stay here in my place beside my mother, I had my first attack of tears. I am afraid I led that boy a dog's life; for as he was new to the work, I had a hundred opportunities of setting him right and putting him down, and I was not slow to profit by them.

The night passed, and the next day, after dinner, Redruth and I were afoot again, and on the road. I said good-bye to mother and the cove where I had lived since I was born, and the dear old 'Admiral Benbow' – since he was repainted, no longer quite so dear. One of my last thoughts was of the captain, who had so often strode along the beach with his cocked hat, his sabre-cut cheek, and his old brass telescope. Next moment we had turned the corner and my home was out of sight.

The mail picked us up about dusk at the 'Royal George' on the heath. I was wedged in between Redruth and a stout old gentleman, and in spite of the swift motion and the cold night air, I must have dozed a great deal from the very first, and then slept like a log, up hill and down dale through stage after stage; for when I was awakened at last, it was by a punch in the ribs, and I opened my eyes, to find that we were standing still before a large building in a city street, and that the day had already broken a long time.

'Where are we?' I asked.

'Bristol,' said Tom. 'Get down.'

Mr Trelawney had taken up his residence at an inn far down the docks, to superintend the work upon the schooner. Thither we had now to walk, and our way, to my great delight, lay along the quays and beside the great multitude of ships of all sizes and rigs and nations. In one, sailors were singing at their work; in another, there were men aloft, high over my head, hanging to threads that seemed no thicker than a spider's. Though I have lived by the shore all my life, I seemed never to have been near the sea till then. The smell of tar and salt was something new. I saw the most wonderful figureheads, that had all been far over the ocean. I saw, besides, many old sailors, with rings in their ears, and whiskers curled in ringlets, and tarry pigtails, and their swaggering, clumsy sea-walk; and if I had seen as many kings or archbishops I could not have been more delighted.

And I was going to sea myself; to sea in a schooner, with a piping boatswain, and pig-tailed singing seamen; to sea, bound for an unknown island, and to seek for buried treasures!

While I was still in this delightful dream, we came suddenly in front of a large inn, and met Squire Trelawney, all dressed out like a sea-officer, in stout blue cloth, coming out of the door with a smile on his face, and a capital imitation of a sailor's walk.

'Here you are,' he cried, 'and the doctor came last night from London. Bravo! the ship's company complete!'

'Oh, sir,' cried I, 'when do we sail?'

Sail!' says he. 'We sail to-morrow!'

CHAPTER TWO

At the Sign of the 'Spy-Glass'

WHEN I HAD DONE BREAKFASTING the squire gave me a note addressed to John Silver, at the sign of the 'Spy-glass,' and told me I should easily find the place by following the line of the docks, and keeping a bright look-out for a little tavern with a large brass telescope for sign. I set off, overjoyed at this opportunity to see some more of the ships and seamen, and picked my way among a great crowd of people and carts and bales, for the dock was now at its busiest, until I found the tavern in question.

It was a bright enough little place of entertainment. The sign was newly painted; the windows had neat red curtains; the floor was cleanly sanded. There was a street on either side, and an open door on both, which made the large, low room pretty clear to see in, in spite of clouds of tobacco smoke.

The customers were mostly seafaring men; and they talked so loudly that I hung at the door, almost afraid to enter.

As I was waiting, a man came out of a side-room, and, at a glance, I was sure he must be Long John. His left leg was cut off close by the hip, and under the left shoulder he carried a crutch, which he managed with wonderful dexterity, hopping about upon it like a bird. He was very tall and strong, with a face as big as a ham – plain and pale, but intelligent and smiling. Indeed, he seemed in the most cheerful spirits, whistling as he moved about among the tables, with a merry word or a slap on the shoulder for the more favoured of his guests.

Now, to tell you the truth, from the very first mention of Long John in Squire

Trelawney's letter, I had taken a fear in my mind that he might prove to be the very one-legged sailor whom I had watched for so long at the old 'Benbow.' But one look at the man before me was enough. I had seen the captain, and Black Dog, and the blind man Pew, and I thought I knew what a buccaneer was like – a very different creature, according to me, from this clean and pleasant-tempered landlord.

I plucked up courage at once, crossed the threshold, and walked right up to the man where he stood, propped on his crutch, talking to a customer.

'Mr Silver, sir?' I asked, holding out the note.

'Yes, my lad,' said he; 'such is my name, to be sure. And who may you be?' And then as he saw the squire's letter, he seemed to me to give something almost like a start.

'Oh!' said he, quite loud, and offering his hand, 'I see. You are our new cabin-boy; pleased I am to see you.'

And he took my hand in his large firm grasp.

Just then one of the customers at the far side rose suddenly and made for the door. It was close by him, and he was out in the street in a moment. But his hurry had attracted my notice, and I recognized him at a glance. It was the tallow-faced man, wanting two fingers, who had come first to the 'Admiral Benbow.'

'Oh,' I cried, 'stop him! it's Black Dog!'

'I don't care two coppers who he is,' cried Silver. 'But he hasn't paid his score. Harry, run and catch him.'

One of the others who was nearest the door leaped up, and started in pursuit.

'If he were Admiral Hawke he shall pay his score,' cried Silver; and then, relinquishing my hand – 'Who did you say he was?' he asked: 'Black what?'

'Dog, sir,' said I. 'Has Mr Trelawney not told you of the buccaneers? He was one of them.'

'So?' cried Silver. 'In my house! Ben, run and help Harry. One of those swabs, was he? Was that you drinking with him, Morgan? Step up here.'

The man whom he called Morgan – an old, grey-haired, mahogany-faced sailor – came forward pretty sheepishly, rolling his quid.

'Now, Morgan,' said Long John, very sternly; 'you never clapped your eyes on that Black – Black Dog before, did you, now?'

'Not I, sir,' said Morgan, with a salute.

'You didn't know his name, did you?'

'No, sir.'

'By the powers, Tom Morgan, it's as good for you!' exclaimed the landlord. 'If you had been mixed up with the life of that, you would never have put another foot in my house, you may lay to that. And what was he saying to you?'

'I don't rightly know, sir,' answered Morgan.

'Do you call that a head on your shoulders, or a blessed dead-eye?' cried Long John. 'Don't rightly know, don't you! Perhaps you don't happen to rightly know who you was speaking to, perhaps? Come, now, what was he jawing – v'yages, cap'ns, ships? Pipe up! What was it?'

'We was a-talkin' of keel-hauling,' answered Morgan.

'Keel-hauling, was you? and a mighty suitable thing, too, and you may lay to that. Get back to your place for a lubber, Tom.'

And then, as Morgan rolled back his seat, Silver added to me in a confidential whisper, that was very flattering, as I thought:

'He's quite an honest man, Tom Morgan, on'y stupid. And now,' he ran on again aloud, 'let's see – Black Dog? No, I don't know the name, not I. Yet I kind of think I've – yes, I've seen the swab. He used to come here with a blind beggar, he used.'

'That he did, you may be sure,' said I. 'I knew that blind man, too. His name was Pew.'

'It was!' cried Silver, now quite excited. 'Pew! That were his name for certain. Ah, he looked a shark, he did! If we run down this Black Dog, now, there'll be news for Cap'n Trelawney! Ben's a good runner; few seamen run better than Ben. He should run him down, hand over hand, by the powers. He talked o' keel-hauling, did he? I'll keel-haul him!'

All the time he was jerking out these phrases he was stumping up and down the tavern on his crutch, slapping tables with his hand, and giving such a show of excitement as would have convinced an Old Bailey judge or a Bow Street runner. My suspicions had been thoroughly reawakened on finding Black Dog at the 'Spy-glass,' and I watched the cook narrowly. But he was too deep, and too ready, and too clever for me, and by the time the two men had come back out of breath, and confessed that they had lost the track in a crowd, and been scolded like thieves, I would have gone bail for the innocence of Long John Silver.

'See here, now, Hawkins,' said he, 'here's a blessed hard thing on a man like me, now, ain't it? There's Cap'n Trelawney – what's he to think? Here I have this confounded son of a Dutchman sitting in my own house, drinking of my own rum! Here you comes and tells me of it plain; and here I let him give us all the slip before my blessed deadlights! Now, Hawkins, you do me justice with the cap'n. You're a lad, you are, but you're as smart as paint. I see that when you first came in. Now, here it is: What could I do, with this old timber I hobble on? When I was an A.B. master mariner I'd have come up alongside of him, hand over hand, and broached him to in a brace of old shakes, I would; but now——'

And then, all of a sudden, he stopped, and his jaw dropped as though he had remembered something.

'The score!' he burst out. 'Three goes o' rum! Why, shiver my timbers, if I hadn't forgotten my score!'

And, falling on a bench, he laughed until the tears ran down his cheeks. I could not help joining; and we laughed together, peal after peal, until the tavern rang again.

'Why, what a precious old sea-calf I am!' he said, at last, wiping his cheeks. 'You and me should get on well, Hawkins, for I'll take my davy I should be rated ship's boy. But, come now, stand by to go about. This won't do. Dooty is dooty, messmates. I'll put on my old cocked hat, and step along of you to Cap'n Trelawney, and report this here affair. For, mind you, it's serious, young Hawkins; and neither you nor me's come out of it with what I should make so bold as to call credit. Nor you neither, says you; not smart – none of the pair of us smart. But dash my buttons! that was a good 'un about my score.'

And he began to laugh again, and that so heartily, that though I did not see the joke as he did, I was again obliged to join him in his mirth.

On our little walk along the quays, he made himself the most interesting companion, telling me about the different ships that we passed by, their rig, tonnage, and nationality, explaining the work that was going forward – how one was discharging, another taking in cargo, and a third making ready for sea; and every now and then telling me some little anecdote of ships or seamen, or repeating a nautical phrase till I had learned it perfectly. I began to see that here was one of the best possible shipmates.

When we got to the inn, the squire and Dr Livesey were seated together, finishing a quart of ale with a toast in it, before they should go aboard the schooner on a visit of inspection.

Long John told the story from first to last, with a great deal of spirit and the most perfect truth. 'That was how it were, now, weren't it, Hawkins?' he would say, now and again, and I could always bear him entirely out.

The two gentlemen regretted that Black Dog had got away; but we all agreed there was nothing to be done, and after he had been complimented, Long John took up his crutch and departed.

'All hands aboard by four this afternoon,' shouted the squire after him.

'Ay, ay, sir,' cried the cook, in the passage.

'Well, squire,' said Dr Livesey, 'I don't put much faith in your discoveries, as a general thing; but I will say this, John Silver suits me.'

'The man's a perfect trump,' declared the squire.

'And now,' added the doctor, 'Jim may come on board with us, may he not?'

'To be sure he may,' says squire. 'Take your hat, Hawkins, and we'll see the ship.'

CHAPTER THREE

Powder and Arms

THE HISPANIOLA LAY SOME way out, and we went under the figureheads and round the sterns of many other ships, and their cables sometimes grated underneath our keel, and sometimes swung above us. At last, however, we got alongside, and were met and saluted as we stepped aboard by the mate, Mr Arrow, a brown old sailor, with earrings in his ears and a squint. He and the squire were very thick and friendly, but I soon observed that things were not the same between Mr Trelawney and the captain.

This last was a sharp-looking man, who seemed angry with everything aboard, and was soon to tell us why, for we had hardly got down into the cabin when a sailor followed us.

'Captain Smollett, sir, axing to speak with you,' said he.

'I am always at the captain's orders. Show him in,' said the squire.

The captain, who was close behind his messenger, entered at once, and shut the door behind him.

'Well, Captain Smollett, what have you to say? All well, I hope; all shipshape and seaworthy?'

'Well, sir,' said the captain, 'better speak plain, I believe, even at the risk of offence. I don't like this cruise; I don't like the men; and I don't like my officer. That's short and sweet.'

'Perhaps, sir, you don't like the ship?' inquired the squire, very angry, as I could see.

'I can't speak as to that, sir, not having seen her tried,' said the captain. 'She seems a clever craft; more I can't say.'

'Possibly, sir, you may not like your employer, either?' says the squire.

But here Dr Livesey cut in.

'Stay a bit,' said he, 'stay a bit. No use of such questions as that but to produce ill feeling. The captain has said too much or he has said too little, and I'm bound to say that I require an explanation of his words. You don't, you say, like the cruise. Now, why?'

'I was engaged, sir, on what we called sealed orders, to sail this ship for that gentleman where he should bid me,' said the captain. 'So far so good. But now I find that every man before the mast knows more than I do. I don't call that fair, do you?'

'No,' said Dr Livesey, 'I don't.'

'Next,' said the captain, 'I learn we are going after treasure – hear it from my own hands, mind you. Now, treasure is ticklish work; I don't like treasure voyages on any account; and I don't like them, above all, when they are secret, and when (begging your pardon, Mr Trelawney) the secret has been told to the parrot.'

'Silver's parrot?' asked the squire.

'It's a way of speaking,' said the captain. 'Blabbed, I mean. It's my belief neither of you gentlemen know what you are about; but I'll tell you my way of it – life or death, and a close run.'

'That is all clear, and, I dare say, true enough,' replied Dr Livesey. 'We take the risk; but we are not so ignorant as you believe us. Next, you say you don't like the crew. Are they not good seamen?'

'I don't like them, sir,' returned Captain Smollett. 'And I think I should have had the choosing of my own hands, if you go to that.'

'Perhaps you should,' replied the doctor. 'My friend should, perhaps, have taken you along with him; but the slight, if there be one, was unintentional. And you don't like Mr Arrow?'

'I don't, sir. I believe he's a good seaman; but he's too free with the crew to be a good officer. A mate should keep himself to himself – shouldn't drink with the men before the mast!'

'Do you mean he drinks?' cried the squire.

'No, sir,' replied the captain; 'only that he's too familiar.'

'Well, now, and the short and long of it, captain?' asked the doctor. 'Tell us what you want.'

'Well, gentlemen, are you determined to go on this cruise?'

'Like iron,' answered the squire.

'Very good,' said the captain. 'Then, as you've heard me very patiently, saying things that I could not prove, hear me a few words more. They are putting the powder and the arms in the fore-hold. Now, you have a good place under the cabin; why not put them there? – first point. Then you are bringing four of your own people with you, and they tell me some of them are to be berthed forward.

Why not give them the berths here beside the cabin? – second point.'

'Any more?' asked Mr Trelawney.

'One more,' said the captain. 'There's been too much blabbing already.'

'Far too much,' agreed the doctor.

'I'll tell you what I've heard myself,' continued Captain Smollett: 'that you have a map of an island; that there's crosses on the map to show where treasure is; and that the island lies——' And then he named the latitude and longitude exactly.

'I never told that,' cried the squire, 'to a soul!'

The hands know it, sir,' returned the captain.

'Livesey, that must have been you or Hawkins,' cried the squire.

'It doesn't much matter who it was,' replied the doctor. And I could see that neither he nor the captain paid much regard to Mr Trelawney's protestations. Neither did I, to be sure, he was so loose a talker; yet in this case I believe he was really right, and that nobody had told the situation of the island.

'Well, gentlemen,' continued the captain, 'I don't know who has this map; but I make a point, it shall be kept secret even from me and Mr Arrow. Otherwise I would ask you to let me resign.'

'I see,' said the doctor. 'You wish us to keep this matter dark, and to make a garrison of the stern part of the ship, manned with my friend's own people, and provided with all the arms and powder on board. In other words, you fear a mutiny.'

'Sir,' said Captain Smollett, 'with no intention to take offence, I deny your right to put words into my mouth. No captain, sir, would be justified in going to sea at all if he had ground enough to say that. As for Mr Arrow, I believe him thoroughly honest; some of the men are the same: all may be for what I know. But I am responsible for the ship's safety and the life of every man Jack aboard of her. I see things going, as I think, not quite right. And I ask you to take certain precautions, or let me resign my berth. And that's all.'

'Captain Smollett,' began the doctor, with a smile, 'did you ever hear the fable of the mountain and the mouse? You'll excuse me, I dare say, but you remind me of that fable. When you came in here I'll stake my wig that you meant more than this.'

'Doctor,' said the captain, 'you are smart. When I came in here I meant to get discharged. I had no thought that Mr Trelawney would hear a word.'

'No more I would,' cried the squire. 'Had Livesey not been here I should have seen you to the deuce. As it is, I have heard you. I will do as you desire; but I think the worse of you.'

'That's as you please, sir,' said the captain. 'You'll find I do my duty.'

And with that he took his leave.

'Trelawney,' said the doctor, 'contrary to all my notions, I believe you have managed to get two honest men on board with you – that man and John Silver.'

'Silver, if you like,' cried the squire; 'but as for that intolerable humbug, I declare I think his conduct unmanly, unsailorly, and downright un-English.'

'Well,' says the doctor, 'we shall see.'

When we came on deck, the men had begun already to take out the arms and powder, yo-ho-ing at their work, while the captain and Mr Arrow stood by superintending.

The new arrangement was quite to my liking. The whole schooner had been overhauled; six berths had been made astern, out of what had been the after-part of the main hold; and this set of cabins was only joined to the galley and forecastle by a sparred passage on the port side. It had originally meant that the captain, Mr Arrow, Hunter, Joyce, the doctor, and the squire, were to occupy these six berths. Now, Redruth and I were to get two of them, and Mr Arrow and the captain were to sleep on deck in the companion, which had been enlarged on each side till you might almost have called it a round-house. Very low it was still, of course; but there was room to swing two hammocks, and even the mate seemed pleased with the arrangement. Even he, perhaps, had been doubtful as to the crew, but that is only guess; for, as you shall hear, we had not long the benefit of his opinion.

We were all hard at work, changing the powder and the berths, when the last man or two, and Long John along with them, came off in a shore-boat.

The cook came up the side like a monkey for cleverness, and, as soon as he saw what was doing, 'So ho, mates!' says he, 'what's this?'

'We're a-changing of the powder, Jack,' answers one.

'Why, by the powers,' cried Long John, 'if we do, we'll miss the morning tide!'

'My orders!' said the captain shortly. 'You may go below, my man. Hands will want supper.'

'Ay, ay, sir,' answered the cook; and, touching his forelock, he disappeared at once in the direction of his galley.

'That's a good man, captain,' said the doctor.

'Very likely, sir,' replied Captain Smollett. 'Easy with that, men – easy,' he ran on, to the fellows who were shifting the powder; and then suddenly observing me examining the swivel we carried amidships, a long brass nine – 'Here, you ship's boy,' he cried out, 'out o' that! Off with you to the cook and get some work.'

And then as I was hurrying off I heard him say, quite loudly, to the doctor: 'I'll have no favourites on my ship.'

I assure you I was quite of the squire's way of thinking, and hated the captain deeply.

CHAPTER FOUR

The Voyage

ALL THAT NIGHT WE WERE in a great bustle getting things stowed in their place, and boatfuls of the squire's friends, Mr. Blandly and the like, coming off to wish him a good voyage and a safe return. We never had a night at the 'Admiral Benbow' when I had half the work; and I was dog-tired when, a little before dawn, the boatswain sounded his pipe, and the crew began to man the capstan-bars. I might have been twice as weary, yet I would not have left the deck; all was so new and interesting to me – the brief commands, the shrill note of the whistle, the men bustling to their places in the glimmer of the ship's lanterns.

'Now, Barbecue, tip us a stave,' cried one voice.

'The old one,' cried another.

'Ay, ay, mates,' said Long John, who was standing by, with his crutch under his arm, and at once broke out in the air and words I knew so well:

'Fifteen men on the dead man's chest—'

And then the whole crew bore chorus:

'Yo-ho-ho, and a bottle of rum!'

And at the third 'ho!' drove the bars before them with a will.

Even at that exciting moment it carried me back to the old 'Admiral Benbow' in a second; and I seemed to hear the voice of the captain piping in the chorus. But soon the anchor was short up; soon it was hanging dripping at the bows; soon the sails began to draw, and the land and shipping to flit by on either side; and before I could lie down to snatch an hour of slumber the *Hispaniola* had begun her voyage to the Isle of Treasure.

I am not going to relate that voyage in detail. It was fairly prosperous. The ship proved to be a good ship, the crew were capable seamen, and the captain thoroughly understood his business. But before we came the length of Treasure Island, two or three things had happened which required to be known.

Mr Arrow, first of all, turned out even worse than the captain had feared. He had no command among the men, and people did what they pleased with him. But that was by no means the worst of it; for after a day or two at sea he began to appear on deck with hazy eye, red cheeks, stuttering tongue, and other marks of drunkenness. Time after time he was ordered below in disgrace. Sometimes he fell and cut himself; sometimes he lay all day long in his little bunk at one side of the companion; sometimes for a day or two he would be almost sober and attend to his work at least passably.

In the meantime, we could never make out where he got the drink. That was the ship's mystery. Watch him as we pleased, we could do nothing to solve it; and when we asked him to his face, he would only laugh, if he were drunk, and if he were sober, deny solemnly that he ever tasted anything but water.

He was not only useless as an officer, and a bad influence amongst the men, but it was plain that at this rate he must soon kill himself outright; so nobody was much surprised nor very sorry when one dark night, with a head sea, he disappeared entirely and was seen no more.

'Overboard!' said the captain. 'Well, gentlemen, that saves the trouble of putting him in irons.'

But there we were, without a mate; and it was necessary, of course, to advance one of the men. The boatswain, Job Anderson, was the likeliest man aboard, and, though he kept his old title, he served in a way as mate. Mr Trelawney had followed the sea, and his knowledge made him very useful, for he often took watch himself in easy weather. And the coxswain, Israel Hands, was a careful, wily, old, experienced seaman, who could be trusted at a pinch with almost anything.

He was a great confidant of Long John Silver, and so the mention of his name leads me on to speak of our ship's cook, Barbecue, as the men called him.

Aboard ship he carried his crutch by a lanyard round his neck, to have both hands as free as possible. It was something to see him wedge the foot of the crutch against a bulkhead, and, propped against it, yielding to every movement of the ship, get on with his cooking like someone safe ashore. Still more strange was it to see him in the heaviest of weather cross the deck. He had a line or two rigged up to help him across the widest spaces – Long John's earrings, they were called; and he would hand himself from one place to another, now using the crutch, now trailing it alongside by the lanyard, as quickly as another man could walk. Yet some of the men who had sailed with him before expressed their pity to see him so reduced.

'He's no common man, Barbecue,' said the coxswain to me. 'He had good schooling in his young days, and can speak like a book when so minded; and brave – a lion's nothing alongside of Long John! I seen him grapple four, and knock their heads together – him unarmed.'

All the crew respected and even obeyed him. He had a way of talking to each, and doing everybody some particular service. To me he was unweariedly kind; and always glad to see me in the galley, which he kept as clean as a new pin; the dishes hanging up burnished, and his parrot in a cage in one corner.

'Come away, Hawkins,' he would say; 'come and have a yarn with John. Nobody more welcome than yourself, my son. Sit you down, and hear the news. Here's Cap'n Flint – I calls my parrot Cap'n Flint, after the famous buccaneer – here's Cap'n Flint predicting success to our v'yage. Wasn't you, Cap'n?'

And the parrot would say, with great rapidity: 'Pieces of eight! pieces of eight! pieces of eight!' till you wondered that it was not out of breath, or till John threw his handkerchief over the cage.

'Now, that bird,' he would say, 'is, may be, two hundred years old, Hawkins – they lives for ever mostly; and if anybody's seen more wickedness, it must be the devil himself. She's sailed with England, the great Cap'n England, the pirate. She's been at Madagascar, and at Malabar, and Surinam, and Providence, and Portobello. She was at the fishing up of the wrecked Plate ships. It's there she learned "Pieces of eight," and little wonder; three hundred and fifty thousand of 'em, Hawkins! She was at the boarding of the *Viceroy of the Indies* out of Goa, she was; and to look at her you would think she was a baby. But you smelt powder – didn't you, Cap'n?'

'Stand by to go about,' the parrot would scream.

'Ah, she's a handsome craft, she is,' the cook would say, and give her sugar from his pocket, and then the bird would peck at the bars and swear straight on, passing belief for wickedness. 'There,' John would add, 'you can't touch pitch and not be mucked, lad. Here's this poor old innocent bird o' mine swearing blue fire, and none the wiser, you may lay to that. She would swear the same, in a manner of speaking, before chaplain.' And John would touch his forelock with a solemn way he had, that made me think he was the best of men.

In the meantime, squire and Captain Smollett were still on pretty distant terms with one another. The squire made no bones about the matter; he despised the captain. The captain, on his part, never spoke but when he was spoken to, and then sharp and short and dry, and not a word wasted. He owned, when driven into a corner, that he seemed to have been wrong about the crew, that some of them were as brisk as he wanted to see, and all had behaved fairly well. As for the ship, he had taken a downright fancy to her. 'She'll lie a point nearer the wind than a man has a right to expect of his own married wife, sir. But,' he would add, 'all I say is we're not home again, and I don't like the cruise.'

The squire, at this, would turn away and march up and down the deck, chin in air.

'A trifle more of that man,' he would say, 'and I should explode.'

We had some heavy weather, which only proved the qualities of the *Hispaniola*. Every man on board seemed well content, and they must have been hard to please if they had been otherwise; for it is my belief there was never a ship's company so spoiled since Noah put to sea. Double grog was going on the least excuse; there was duff on odd days, as, for instance, if the squire heard it was any man's birthday; and always a barrel of apples standing broached in the waist, for any one to help himself that had a fancy.

'Never knew good come of it, yet,' the captain said to Dr Livesey. 'Spoil foc's'le hands, make devils. That's my belief.'

But good did come of the apple barrel, as you shall hear; for if it had not been for that, we should have had no note of warning, and might all have perished by the hand of treachery.

This was how it came about.

We had run up the trades to get the wind of the island we were after – I am not allowed to be more plain – and now we were running down for it with a bright look-out day and night. It was about the last day of our outward voyage, by the largest computation; some time that night, or, at latest, before noon of the morrow, we should sight the Treasure Island. We were heading S.S.W., and had a steady breeze abeam and a quiet sea. The *Hispaniola* rolled steadily, dipping her bowsprit now and then with a whiff of spray. All was drawing alow and aloft; every one was in the bravest spirits; because we were now so near an end of the first part of our adventure.

Now, just after sundown, when all my work was over, and I was on my way to my berth, it occurred to me that I should like an apple. I ran on deck. The watch was all forward looking out for the island. The man at the helm was watching the luff of the sail, and whistling away gently to himself; and that was the only sound excepting the swish of the sea against the bows and around the sides of the ship.

In I got bodily into the apple barrel, and found there was scarce an apple left; but sitting down there in the dark, what with the sound of the waters and the rocking movement of the ship, I had either fallen asleep, or was on the point of doing so, when a heavy man sat down with rather a clash close by. The barrel shook as he leaned his shoulder against it, and I was about to jump up when the man began to speak. It was Silver's voice, and, before I had heard a dozen words, I would not have shown myself for all the world, but lay there, trembling and listening, in the extreme of fear and curiosity; for from these dozen words I understood that the lives of all the honest men aboard depended upon me alone.

CHAPTER FIVE

What I Heard in the Apple Barrel

'NO, NOT I,' SAID SILVER. 'Flint was cap'n; I was quartermaster, along of my timber leg. The same broadside I lost my leg, old Pew lost his deadlights. It was a master surgeon, him that ampytated me – out of college and all – Latin by the bucket, and what not; but he was hanged like a dog, and sun-dried like the rest, at Corso Castle. That was Roberts's men, that was, and comed of changing names to their ships – *Royal Fortune* and so on. Now, what a ship was christened, so let her stay, I says. So it was with the *Cassandra*, as brought us all safe home from Malabar, after England took the *Viceroy of the Indies*; so it was with the old *Walrus*, Flint's old ship, as I've seen a-muck with the red blood and fit to sink with gold.'

'Ah!' cried another voice, that of the youngest hand on board, and evidently full of admiration, 'he was the flower of the flock, was Flint!'

'Davis was a man, too, by all accounts,' said Silver. 'I never sailed along of him; first with England, then with Flint, that's my story; and now here on my own account, in a manner of speaking. I laid by nine hundred safe, from England, and two thousand after Flint. That ain't bad for a man before the mast – all safe in bank. 'Tain't earning now, it's saving does it, you may lay to that. Where's all England's men now? I dunno. Where's Flint's? Why, most on 'em aboard here, and glad to get the duff – been begging before that, some on 'em. Old Pew, as had lost his sight, and might have thought shame, spends twelve hundred pounds in a year, like a lord in Parliament. Where is he now? Well, he's dead now and under hatches; but for two year before that, shiver my timbers! the man was starving. He begged, and he stole, and he cut throats, and starved at that, by the powers!'

'Well, it ain't much use, after all,' said the young seaman.

"Tain't much use for fools, you may lay to it – that, nor nothing,' cried Silver. 'But now, you look here: you're young, you are, but you're as smart as paint. I see that when I set my eyes on you, and I'll talk to you like a man.'

You may imagine how I felt when I heard this abominable old rogue addressing another in the very same words of flattery as he had used to myself. I think, if I had been able, that I would have killed him through the barrel. Meantime, he ran on, little supposing he was overheard.

'Here it is about gentlemen of fortune. They lives rough, and they risk swinging, but they eat and drink like fighting-cocks, and when a cruise is done, why it's hundreds of pounds instead of hundreds of farthings in their pockets. Now, the most goes for rum and a good fling, and to sea again in their shirts. But that's not the course I lay. I puts it all away, some here, some there, and none too much anywhere, by reason of suspicion. I'm fifty, mark you; once back from this cruise, I set up gentleman in earnest. Time enough, too, says you. Ah, but I've lived easy in the meantime; never denied myself o' nothing heart desires, and slep' soft and ate dainty all my days, but when at sea. And how did I begin? Before the mast, like you!'

'Well,' said the other, 'but all the other money's gone now, ain't it? You daren't show face in Bristol after this.'

'Why, where might you suppose it was?' asked Silver, derisively.

'At Bristol, in banks and places,' answered his companion.

'It were,' said the cook; 'it were when we weighed anchor. But my old missus has it all by now. And the "Spy-glass" is sold, lease and goodwill and rigging; and the old girl's off to meet me. I would tell you where, for I trust you; but it 'ud make jealousy among the mates.'

'And can you trust your missus?' asked the other.

'Gentlemen of fortune,' returned the cook, 'usually trust little among themselves, and right they are, you may lay to it. But I have a way with me, I have. When a mate brings a slip on his cable – one as knows me, I mean – it won't be in the same world with old John. There was some that was feared of Pew, and some that was feared of Flint; and Flint his own self was feared of me. Feared he was, and proud. They was the roughest crew afloat, was Flint's; the devil himself would have been feared to go to sea with them. Well, now, I tell you, I'm not a boasting man, and you seen yourself how easy I keep company; but when I was quartermaster, *lambs* wasn't the word for Flint's old buccaneers. Ah, you may be sure of yourself in old John's ship.'

'Well, I tell you now,' replied the lad, 'I didn't half a quarter like the job till I had this talk with you, John; but there's my hand on it now.'

'And a brave lad you were, and smart, too,' answered Silver, shaking hands so heartily that all the barrel shook, 'and a finer figurehead for a gentleman of fortune I never clapped my eyes on.'

By this time I had begun to understand the meaning of their terms. By a 'gentleman of fortune' they plainly meant neither more nor less than a common pirate, and the little scene that I had overheard was the last act in the corruption of one of the honest hands – perhaps of the last one left aboard. But on this point I was soon to be relieved, for Silver giving a little whistle, a third man strolled up and sat down by the party.

'Dick's square,' said Silver.

'Oh, I know'd Dick was square,' returned the voice of the coxswain, Israel Hands. 'He's no fool, is Dick.' And he turned his quid and spat. 'But look here,' he went on, 'here's what I want to know, Barbecue: how long are we a-going to stand off and on like a blessed bum-boat? I've had a'most enough o' Cap'n Smollett; he's hazed me long enough, by thunder! I want to go into that cabin, I do. I want their pickles and wines, and that.'

'Israel,' said Silver, 'your head ain't much account, nor ever was. But you're able to hear, I reckon; leastways, your ears is big enough. Now, here's what I say: you'll berth forward, and you'll live hard, and you'll speak soft, and you'll keep sober, till I give the word; and you may lay to that, my son.'

'Well, I don't say no, do I?' growled the coxswain. 'What I say is, when? That's what I say.'

'When! by the powers!' cried Silver. 'Well, now, if you want to know, I'll tell

you when. The last moment I can manage; and that's when. Here's a first-rate
seaman, Cap'n Smollett, sails the blessed ship for us. Here's this squire and
doctor with a map and such – I don't know where it is, do I? No more do you,
says you. Well, then, I mean this squire and doctor shall find the stuff, and help
us to get it aboard, by the powers. Then we'll see. If I was sure of you all, sons of
double Dutchmen, I'd have Cap'n Smollett navigate us half-way back again
before I struck.'

'Why, we're all seamen aboard here, I should think,' said the lad Dick.

'We're all foc's'le hands, you mean,' snapped Silver. 'We can steer a course,
but who's to set one? That's what all you gentlemen split on, first and last. If I
had my way, I'd have Cap'n Smollett work us back into the trades at least; then
we'd have no blessed miscalculations and a spoonful of water a day. But I know
the sort you are. I'll finish with 'em at the island, as soon's the blunt's on board,
and a pity it is. But you're never happy till you're drunk. Split my sides, I've a
sick heart to sail with the likes of you!'

'Easy all, Long John,' cried Israel. 'Who's acrossin' of you?'

'Why, how many tall ships, think ye, now, have I seen laid aboard? and how
many brisk lads drying in the sun at Execution Dock?' cried Silver, 'and all for
this same hurry and hurry and hurry. You hear me? I seen a thing or two at sea, I
have. If you would on'y lay your course, and a p'int to windward, you would ride
in carriages, you would. But not you! I know you. You'll have your mouthful of
rum to-morrow, and go hang.'

'Everybody know'd you was a kind of a chapling, John; but there's others as
could hand and steer as well as you,' said Israel. 'They liked a bit o'fun, they did.
They wasn't so high and dry, nohow, but took their fling, like jolly companions
every one.'

'So?' says Silver. 'Well, and where are they now? Pew was that sort, and he
died a beggar-man. Flint was, and he died of rum at Savannah. Ah, they was a
sweet crew, they was! on'y, where are they?'

'But,' asked Dick, 'when we do lay 'em athwart, what are we to do with 'em,
anyhow?'

'There's the man for me!' cried the cook, admiringly. 'That's what I call
business. Well, what would you think? Put 'em ashore like maroons? That would
have been England's way. Or cut 'em down like that much pork? That would
have been Flint's or Billy Bones's.'

'Billy was the man for that,' said Israel. '"Dead men don't bite," says he.
Well, he's dead now hisself; he knows the long and short on it now; and if ever a
rough hand come to port, it was Billy.'

'Right you are,' said Silver, 'rough and ready. But mark you here: I'm an easy
man – I'm quite the gentleman, says you; but this time it's serious. Dooty is
dooty, mates. I give my vote – death. When I'm in Parlyment, and riding in my
coach, I don't want none of these sea-lawyers in the cabin a-coming home,
unlooked for, like the devil at prayers. Wait is what I say; but when the time
comes, why let her rip!'

'John,' cries the coxswain, 'you're a man!'

'You'll say so, Israel, when you see,' said Silver. 'Only one thing I claim – I
claim Trelawney. I'll wring his calf's head off his body with these hands. Dick!'
he added, breaking off, 'you just jump up, like a sweet lad, and get me an apple,

to wet my pipe like.'

You may fancy the terror I was in! I should have leaped out and run for it, if I had found the strength; but my limbs and heart alike misgave me. I heard Dick begin to rise, and then someone seemingly stopped him, and the voice of Hands exclaimed:

'Oh, stow that! Don't you get sucking of that bilge, John. Let's have a go of the rum.'

'Dick,' said Silver, 'I trust you. I've a gauge on the keg, mind. There's the key; you fill a pannikin and bring it up.'

Terrified as I was, I could not help thinking to myself that this must have been how Mr Arrow got the strong waters that destroyed him.

Dick was gone but a little while, and during his absence Israel spoke straight on in the cook's ear. It was but a word or two that I could catch, and yet I gathered some important news; for, besides other scraps that tended to the same purpose, this whole clause was audible: 'Not another man of them'll jine.' Hence there were still faithful men on board.

When Dick returned, one after another of the trio took the pannikin and drank – one 'To luck'; another with a 'Here's to old Flint'; and Silver himself saying, in a kind of song: 'Here's to ourselves, and hold your luff, plenty of prizes and plenty of duff.'

Just then a sort of brightness fell upon me in the barrel, and, looking up, I found the moon had risen, and was silvering the mizzentop and shining white on the luff of the foresail; and almost at the same time the voice of the look-out shouted: 'Land ho!'

CHAPTER SIX

Council of War

THERE WAS A GREAT RUSH of feet across the deck. I could hear people tumbling up from the cabin and the foc's'le; and, slipping in an instant outside my barrel, I dived behind the foresail, and made a double towards the stern, and came out upon the open deck in time to join Hunter and Dr Livesey in the rush for the weather bow.

There all hands were already congregated. A belt of fog had lifted almost simultaneously with the appearance of the moon. Away to the south-west of us we saw two low hills, about a couple of miles apart, and rising behind one of them a third and higher hill, whose peak was still buried in the fog. All three seemed sharp and conical in figure.

So much I saw, almost in a dream, for I had not yet recovered from my horrid fear of a minute or two before. And then I heard the voice of Captain Smollett issuing orders. The *Hispaniola* was laid a couple of points nearer the wind, and now sailed a course that would just clear the island on the east.

'And now, men,' said the captain, when all was sheeted home, 'has any one of you ever seen that land ahead?'

'I have, sir,' said Silver. 'I've watered there with a trader I was cook in.'

'The anchorage is on the south, behind an islet, I fancy?' asked the captain.

'Yes, sir; Skeleton Island they calls it. It were a main place for pirates once, and a hand we had on board knowed all their names for it. That hill to the nor'ard they calls the Fore-mast Hill; there are three hills in a row running south'ard – fore, main, and mizzen, sir. But the main – that's the big 'un with the cloud on it – they usually calls the Spy-glass, by reason of a look-out they kept when they was in the anchorage cleaning; for it's there they cleaned their ships, sir, asking your pardon.'

'I have a chart here,' says Captain Smollett. 'See if that's the place.'

Long John's eyes burned in his head as he took the chart; but by the fresh look of the paper, I knew he was doomed to disappointment. This was not the map we found in Billy Bones's chest, but an accurate copy, complete in all things – names and heights and soundings – with the single exception of the red crosses and the written notes. Sharp as must have been his annoyance, Silver had the strength of mind to hide it.

'Yes, sir,' said he, 'this is the spot to be sure; and very prettily drawed out. Who might have done that, I wonder? The pirates were too ignorant, I reckon. Ay, here it is: "Capt. Kidd's Anchorage" – just the name my shipmate called it. There's a strong current runs along the south, and then away nor'ard up to the west coast. Right you was, sir,' says he, 'to haul your wind and keep the weather of the island. Leastways, if such was your intention as to enter and careen, and there ain't no better place for that in these waters.'

'Thank you, my man,' says Captain Smollett. 'I'll ask you, later on, to give us a help. You may go.'

I was surprised at the coolness with which John avowed his knowledge of the island; and I own I was half frightened when I saw him drawing nearer to myself. He did not know, to be sure, that I had overheard his council from the apple barrel, and yet I had, by this time, taken such a horror of his cruelty, duplicity, and power, that I could scarce conceal a shudder when he laid his hand upon my arm.

'Ah,' says he, 'this is a sweet spot, this island – a sweet spot for a lad to get ashore on. You'll bathe, and you'll climb trees, and you'll hunt goats, you will; and you'll get aloft on them hills like a goat yourself. Why, it makes me young again. I was going to forget my timber leg, I was. It's a pleasant thing to be young, and have ten toes, and you may lay to that. When you want to go a bit of exploring, you must ask old John, and he'll put up a snack for you to take along.'

And clapping me in the friendliest way upon the shoulder, he hobbled off forward and went below.

Captain Smollett, the squire, and Dr Livesey, were talking together on the quarter-deck, and anxious as I was to tell them my story, I durst not interrupt them openly. While I was still casting about in my thoughts to find some probable excuse, Dr Livesey called me to his side. He had left his pipe below, and being a slave to tobacco, had meant that I should fetch it; but as soon as I was near enough to speak and not to be overheard, I broke out immediately: 'Doctor, let me speak. Get the captain and squire down to the cabin, and then make some pretence to send for me. I have terrible news.'

The doctor changed countenance a little, but next moment he was master of himself.

'Thank you, Jim,' said he, quite loudly, 'that was all I wanted to know,' as if he had asked me a question.

And with that he turned on his heel and rejoined the other two. They spoke together for a little, and though none of them started, or raised his voice, or so much as whistled, it was plain enough that Dr Livesey had communicated my request; for the next thing that I heard was the captain giving an order to Job Anderson, and all hands were piped on deck.

'My lads,' said Captain Smollett, 'I've a word to say to you. This land that we have sighted is the place we have been sailing to. Mr Trelawney, being a very open-handed gentleman, as we all know, has just asked me a word or two, and as I was able to tell him that every man on board had done his duty, alow and aloft, as I never ask to see it done better, he and I and the doctor are going below to the cabin to drink *your* health and luck, and you'll have grog served out for you to drink *our* health and luck. I'll tell you what I think of this: I think it handsome. And if you think as I do, you'll give a good sea cheer for the gentleman that does it.'

The cheer followed – that was a matter of course; but it rang out so full and hearty, that I confess I could hardly believe these same men were plotting for our blood.

'One more cheer for Cap'n Smollett,' cried Long John, when the first had subsided.

And this also was given with a will.

On the top of that the three gentlemen went below, and not long after, word was sent forward that Jim Hawkins was wanted in the cabin.

I found them all three seated round the table, a bottle of Spanish wine and some raisins before them, and the doctor smoking away, with his wig on his lap, and that, I knew, was a sign that he was agitated. The stern window was open, for it was a warm night, and you could see the moon shining behind on the ship's wake.

'Now, Hawkins,' said the squire, 'you have something to say. Speak up.'

I did as I was bid, and, as short as I could make it, told the whole details of Silver's conversation. Nobody interrupted me till I was done, nor did any one of the three of them make so much as a movement, but they kept their eyes upon my face from first to last.

'Jim,' said Dr Livesey, 'take a seat.'

And they made me sit down at table beside them, poured me out a glass of wine, filled my hands with raisins, and all three, one after the other, and each with a bow, drank my good health, and their service to me, for my luck and courage.

'Now, captain,' said the squire, 'you were right, and I was wrong. I own myself an ass, and I await your orders.'

'No more an ass than I, sir,' returned the captain. 'I never heard of a crew that meant to mutiny but what showed signs before, for any man that had an eye in his head to see the mischief and take steps according. But this crew,' he added, 'beats me.'

'Captain,' said the doctor, 'with your permission, that's Silver. A very remarkable man.'

'He'd look remarkably well from a yard-arm, sir,' returned the captain. 'But this is talk; this don't lead to anything. I see three or four points, and with Mr Trelawney's permission, I'll name them.'

'You, sir, are the captain. It is for you to speak,' says Mr Trelawney, grandly.

'First point,' began Mr Smollett. 'We must go on, because we can't turn back. If I gave the word to go about, they would rise at once. Second point, we have time before us – at least, until this treasure's found. Third point, there are faithful hands. Now, sir, it's got to come to blows sooner or later; and what I propose is, to take time by the forelock, as the saying is, and come to blows some fine day when they least expect it. We can count, I take it, on your own home servants, Mr Trelawney?'

'As upon myself,' declared the squire.

'Three,' reckoned the captain, 'ourselves make seven, counting Hawkins, here. Now, about the honest hands?'

'Most likely Trelawney's own men,' said the doctor; 'those he had picked up for himself, before he lit on Silver.'

'Nay,' replied the squire, 'Hands was one of mine.'

'I did think I could have trusted Hands,' added the captain.

'And to think that they're all Englishmen!' broke out the squire. 'Sir, I could find it in my heart to blow the ship up.'

'Well, gentlemen,' said the captain, 'the best that I can say is not much. We must lay to, if you please, and keep a bright look-out. It's trying on a man, I know. It would be pleasanter to come to blows. But there's no help for it till we know our men. Lay to, and whistle for a wind, that's my view.'

'Jim here,' said the doctor, 'can help us more than any one. The men are not shy with him, and Jim is a noticing lad.'

'Hawkins, I put prodigious faith in you,' added the squire.

I began to feel pretty desperate at this, for I felt altogether helpless; and yet, by an odd train of circumstances, it was indeed through me that safety came. In the meantime, talk as we pleased, there were only seven out of the twenty-six on whom we knew we could rely; and out of these seven one was a boy, so that the grown men on our side were six to their nineteen.

PART THREE

CHAPTER ONE

How I Began My Shore Adventure

THE APPEARANCE OF THE ISLAND when I came on deck next morning was altogether changed. Although the breeze had now utterly failed, we had made a
great deal of way during the night, and were now lying becalmed about half a
mile to the south-east of the low eastern coast. Grey-coloured woods covered a
large part of the surface. This even tint was indeed broken up by many tall trees
of the pine family, out-topping the others – some singly, some in clumps; but
the general colouring was uniform and sad. The hills ran up clear above the
vegetation in spires of naked rock. All were strangely shaped, and the Spy-glass,
which was by three or four hundred feet the tallest on the island, was likewise
the strangest in configuration, running up sheer from almost every side, and
then suddenly cut off at the top like a pedestal to put a statue on.

The *Hispaniola* was rolling scuppers under in the ocean swell. The booms were
tearing at the blocks, the rudder was banging to and fro, and the whole ship
creaking, groaning, and jumping like a manufactory. I had to cling tight to the
backstay, and the world turned giddily before my eyes; for though I was a good
sailor when there was way on, this standing still and being rolled about like a
bottle was a thing I never learned to stand without a qualm or so, above all in
the morning, on an empty stomach.

Perhaps it was this – perhaps it was the look of the island with its grey,
melancholy woods, and wild stone spires, and the surf that we could both see
and hear foaming and thundering on the steep beach – at least, although the sun
shone bright and hot, and the shore birds were fishing and crying all around us,
and you would have thought any one would have been glad to get to land after
being so long at sea, my heart sank, as the saying is, into my boots; and from that
first look onward, I hated the very thought of Treasure Island.

We had a dreary morning's work before us, for there was no sign of any wind,
and the boats had to be got out and manned, and the ship warped three or four
miles round the corner of the island, and up the narrow passage to the haven
behind Skeleton Island. I volunteered for one of the boats, where I had, of
course, no business. The heat was sweltering, and the men grumbled fiercely
over their work. Anderson was in command of my boat, and instead of keeping
the crew in order, he grumbled as loud as the worst.

'Well,' he said, with an oath, 'it's not for ever.'

I thought this was a very bad sign; for up to that day, the men had gone briskly
and willingly about their business; but the very sight of the island had relaxed
the cords of discipline.

All the way in, Long John stood by the steersman and conned the ship. He
knew the passage like the palm of his hand; and though the man in the chains

got everywhere more water than was down in the chart, John never hesitated once.

'There's a strong scour with the ebb,' he said, 'and this here passage has been dug out, in a manner of speaking, with a spade.'

We brought up just where the anchor was in the chart, about a third of a mile from either shore, the mainland on one side and Skeleton Island on the other. The bottom was clean sand. The plunge of our anchor sent up clouds of birds wheeling and crying over the woods; but in less than a minute they were down again, and all was once more silent.

The place was entirely land-locked, buried in woods, the trees coming right down to high-water mark, the shores mostly flat, and the hill-tops standing round at a distance in a sort of amphitheatre, one here, one there. Two little rivers, or, rather, two swamps, emptied out into this pond, as you might call it; and the foliage round that part of the shore had a kind of poisonous brightness. From the ship, we could see nothing of the house or stockade, for they were quite buried among trees; and if it had not been for the chart on the companion, we might have been the first that had ever anchored there since the island arose out of the seas.

There was not a breath of air moving, nor a sound but that of the surf booming half a mile away along the beaches and against the rocks outside. A peculiar stagnant smell hung over the anchorage – a smell of sodden leaves and rotting tree trunks. I observed the doctor sniffing and sniffing, like someone tasting a bad egg.

'I don't know about treasure,' he said, 'but I'll stake my wig there's fever here.'

If the conduct of the men had been alarming in the boat, it became truly threatening when they had come aboard. They lay about the deck growling together in talk. The slightest order was received with a black look, and grudgingly and carelessly obeyed. Even the honest hands must have caught the infection, for there was not one man aboard to mend another. Mutiny, it was plain, hung over us like a thunder-cloud.

And it was not only we of the cabin party who perceived the danger. Long John was hard at work going from group to group, spending himself in good advice, and as for example no man could have shown a better. He fairly outstripped himself in willingness and civility; he was all smiles to every one. If an order were given, John would be on his crutch in an instant, with the cheeriest 'Ay, ay, sir!' in the world; and when there was nothing else to do, he kept up one song after another, as if to conceal the discontent of the rest.

Of all the gloomy features of that gloomy afternoon, this obvious anxiety on the part of Long John appeared the worst.

We held a council in the cabin.

'Sir,' said the captain, 'if I risk another order, the whole ship'll come about our ears by the run. You see, sir, here it is. I get rough answer, do I not? Well, if I speak back, pikes will be going in two shakes; if I don't, Silver will see there's something under that, and the game's up. Now, we've only one man to rely on.'

'And who is that?' asked the squire.

'Silver, sir,' returned the captain; 'he's as anxious as you and I to smother things up. This is a tiff; he'd soon talk 'em out of it if he had the chance, and what I propose to do is to give him the chance. Let's allow the men an afternoon ashore. If they all go, why, we'll fight the ship. If they none of them go, well, then, we hold the cabin, and God defend the right. If some go, you mark my words, sir, Silver'll bring 'em aboard again as mild as lambs.'

It was so decided; loaded pistols were served out to all the sure men; Hunter, Joyce, and Redruth were taken into our confidence, and received the news with less surprise and a better spirit than we had looked for, and then the captain went on deck and addressed the crew.

'My lads,' said he, 'we've had a hot day, and are all tired and out of sorts. A turn ashore'll hurt nobody – the boats are still in the water; you can take the gigs, and as many as please can go ashore for the afternoon. I'll fire a gun half an hour before sundown.'

I believe the silly fellows must have thought they would break their shins over treasure as soon as they were landed; for they all came out of their sulks in a moment, and gave a cheer that started the echo in a far-away hill, and sent the birds once more flying and squalling round the anchorage.

The captain was too bright to be in the way. He whipped out of sight in a moment, leaving Silver to arrange the party, and I fancy it was as well he did so. Had he been on deck, he could no longer so much as have pretended not to understand the situation. It was as plain as day. Silver was the captain, and a mighty rebellious crew he had of it. The honest hands – and I was soon to see it proved that there were such on board – must have been very stupid fellows. Or, rather, I suppose the truth was this, that all hands were disaffected by the example of the ringleaders – only some more, some less; and a few, being good fellows in the main, could neither be led nor driven any further. It is one thing to be idle and skulk, and quite another to take a ship and murder a number of innocent men.

At last, however, the party was made up. Six fellows were to stay on board, and the remaining thirteen, including Silver, began to embark.

Then it was that there came into my head the first of the mad notions that contributed so much to save our lives. If six men were left by Silver, it was plain our party could not take and fight the ship; and since only six were left, it was equally plain that the cabin party had no present need of my assistance. It occurred to me at once to go ashore. In a jiffy I had slipped over the side, and curled up in the foresheets of the nearest boat, and almost at the same moment she shoved off.

No one took notice of me, only the bow oar saying: 'Is that you, Jim? Keep your head down.' But Silver, from the other boat, looked sharply over and called out to know if that were me; and from that moment I began to regret what I had done.

The crews raced for the beach; but the boat I was in, having some start, and being at once the lighter and the better manned, shot far ahead of her consort, and the bow had struck among the shore-side trees, and I had caught a branch and swung myself out, and plunged into the nearest thicket, while Silver and the rest were still a hundred yards behind.

'Jim, Jim!' I heard him shouting.

But you may suppose I paid no heed; jumping, ducking, and breaking through, I ran straight before my nose, till I could run no longer.

CHAPTER TWO

The First Blow

I WAS SO PLEASED AT HAVING given the slip to Long John, that I began to enjoy myself and look round me with some interest on the strange land that I was in.

I had crossed a marshy tract full of willows, bulrushes, and odd, outlandish, swampy trees; and I had now come out upon the skirts of an open piece of undulating, sandy country, about a mile long, dotted with a few pines, and a great number of contorted trees, not unlike the oak in growth, but pale in the foliage, like willows. On the far side of the open stood one of the hills, with two quaint, craggy peaks, shining vividly in the sun.

I now felt for the first time the joy of exploration. The isle was uninhabited; my shipmates I had left behind, and nothing lived in front of me but dumb brutes and fowls. I turned hither and thither among the trees. Here and there were flowering plants, unknown to me; here and there I saw snakes, and one raised his head from a ledge of rock and hissed at me with a noise not unlike the spinning of a top. Little did I suppose that he was a deadly enemy, and that the noise was the famous rattle.

Then I came to a long thicket of these oak-like trees – live, or evergreen, oaks, I heard afterwards they should be called – which grew low along the sand like brambles, the boughs curiously twisted, the foliage compact, like thatch. The thicket stretched down from the top of one of the sandy knolls, spreading and growing taller as it went, until it reached the margin of the broad, reedy fen, through which the nearest of the little rivers soaked its way into the anchorage. The marsh was steaming in the strong sun, and the outline of the Spy-glass trembled through the haze.

All at once there began to go a sort of bustle among the bulrushes; a wild duck flew up with a quack, another followed, and soon over the whole surface of the marsh a great cloud of birds hung screaming and circling in the air. I judged at once that some of my shipmates must be drawing near along the borders of the fen. Nor was I deceived; for soon I heard the very distant and low tones of a human voice, which, as I continued to give ear, grew steadily louder and nearer.

This put me in a great fear, and I crawled under cover of the nearest live oak, and squatted there, hearkening, as silent as a mouse.

Another voice answered; and then the first voice, which I now recognized to be Silver's, once more took up the story, and ran on for a long while in a stream, only now and again interrupted by the other. By the sound they must have been talking earnestly, and almost fiercely; but no distinct word came to my hearing.

At last the speakers seemed to have paused, and perhaps to have sat down; for not only did they cease to draw any nearer, but the birds themselves began to grow more quiet, and to settle again to their places in the swamp.

And now I began to feel that I was neglecting my business; that since I had been so foolhardy as to come ashore with these desperadoes, the least I could do was to overhear them at their councils; and that my plain and obvious duty was to draw as close as I could manage, under the favourable ambush of the crouching trees.

I could tell the direction of the speakers pretty exactly, not only by the sound of their voices, but by the behaviour of the few birds that still hung in alarm above the heads of the intruders.

Crawling on all-fours, I made steadily but slowly towards them; till at last, raising my head to an aperture among the leaves, I could see clear down into a little green dell beside the marsh, and closely set about with trees, where Long John Silver and another of the crew stood face to face in conversation.

The sun beat full upon them. Silver had thrown his hat beside him on the ground, and his great smooth, blond face, all shining with heat, was lifted to the other man's in a kind of appeal.

'Mate,' he was saying, 'it's because I thinks gold dust of you – gold dust, and you may lay to that! If I hadn't took to you like pitch, do you think I'd have been here a-warning of you? All's up – you can't make nor mend; it's to save your neck that I'm a-speaking, and if one of the wild 'uns knew it, where 'ud I be, Tom – now, tell me, where 'ud I be?'

'Silver,' said the other man – and I observed he was not only red in the face, but spoke as hoarse as a crow, and his voice shook, too, like a taut rope – 'Silver,' says he, 'you're old, and you're honest, or has the name for it; and you've money, too, which lots of poor sailors hasn't; and you're brave, or I'm mistook. And will you tell me you'll let yourself be led away with that kind of a mess of swabs? not you!' As sure as God sees me, I'd sooner lose my hand. If I turn agin my dooty——'

And then all of a sudden he was interrupted by a noise. I had found one of the honest hands – well, here, at the same moment, came news of another. Far away out in the marsh there arose, all of a sudden, a sound like the cry of anger, then another on the back of it; and then one horrid, long-drawn scream. The rocks of the Spy-glass re-echoed it a score of times; the whole troop of marsh-birds rose again, darkening heaven, with a simultaneous whirr; and long after that death-yell was still ringing in my brain, silence had re-established its empire, and only the rustle of the re-descending birds and the boom of the distant surges disturbed the languor of the afternoon.

Tom had leaped at the sound, like a horse at the spur; but Silver had not winked an eye. He stood where he was, resting lightly on his crutch, watching his companion like a snake about to spring.

'John!' said the sailor, stretching out his hand.

'Hands off!' cried Silver, leaping back a yard, as it seemed to me, with the speed and security of a trained gymnast.

'Hands off, if you like, John Silver,' said the other. 'It's a black conscience that can make you feared of me. But, in heaven's name, tell me what was that?'

'That?' returned Silver, smiling away, but warier than ever, his eye a mere pin-point in his big face, but gleaming like a crumb of glass. 'That? O, I reckon that'll be Alan.'

And at this poor Tom flashed out like a hero.

'Alan!' he cried. 'Then rest his soul for a true seaman! And as for you, John Silver, long you've been a mate of mine, but you're mate of mine no more. If I die like a dog, I'll die in my dooty. You've killed Alan, have you? Kill me, too, if you can. But I defies you.'

And with that, this brave fellow turned his back directly on the cook, and set off walking for the beach. But he was not destined to go far. With a cry, John seized the branch of a tree, whipped the crutch out of his armpit, and sent that uncouth missile hurtling through the air. It struck poor Tom, point foremost, and with stunning violence, right between the shoulders in the middle of his back. His hands flew up, he gave a sort of gasp, and fell.

Whether he were injured much or little, none could ever tell. Like enough, to judge from the sound, his back was broken on the spot. But he had no time given him to recover. Silver, agile as a monkey, even without leg or crutch, was on the top of him next moment, and had twice buried his knife up to the hilt in that defenceless body. From my place of ambush, I could hear him pant aloud as he struck the blows.

I do not know what it rightly is to faint, but I do know that for the next little while the whole world swam away from before me in a whirling mist; Silver and the birds and the tall Spy-glass hill-top going round and round and topsy-turvy before my eyes, and all manner of bells ringing and distant voices shouting in my ear.

When I came again to myself, the monster had pulled himself together, his crutch under his arm, his hat upon his head. Just before him Tom lay motionless upon the sward; but the murderer minded him not a whit, cleansing his blood-stained knife the while upon a wisp of grass. Everything else was unchanged, the sun still shining mercilessly on the steaming marsh and the tall pinnacle of the mountain, and I could scarce persuade myself that murder had been actually done, and a human life cruelly cut short a moment since, before my eyes.

But now John put his hand into his pocket, brought out a whistle, and blew upon it several modulated blasts, that rang far across the heated air. I could not tell, of course, the meaning of the signal; but it instantly awoke my fears. More men would be coming. I might be discovered. They had already slain two of the honest people; after Tom and Alan, might not I come next?

Instantly I began to extricate myself and crawl back again, with what speed and silence I could manage, to the more open portion of the wood. As I did so, I could hear hails coming and going between the old buccaneer and his comrades, and this sound of danger lent me wings. As soon as I was clear of the thicket, I ran as I never ran before, scarce minding the direction of my flight, so long as it led me from the murderers; and as I ran, fear grew and grew upon me, until it turned into a kind of frenzy.

Indeed, could any one be more entirely lost than I? When the gun fired, how should I dare to go down to the boats among those fiends, still smoking from their crime? Would not the first of them who saw me wring my neck like a snipe's? Would not my absence itself be an evidence to them of my alarm, and therefore of my fatal knowledge? It was all over, I thought. Good-bye to the Hispaniola; good-bye to the squire, the doctor, and the captain! There was nothing left for me but death by starvation, or death by the hands of the mutineers.

All this while, as I say, I was still running, and, without taking any notice, I had drawn near to the foot of the little hill with the two peaks, and had got into a part of the island where the live oaks grew more widely apart, and seemed more like forest trees in their bearing and dimensions. Mingled with these were a few scattered pines, some fifty, some nearer seventy, feet high. The air, too, smelt more freshly than down beside the marsh.

And here a fresh alarm brought me to a standstill with a thumping heart.

CHAPTER THREE

The Man of the Island

FROM THE SIDE OF THE HILL, which was here steep and stony, a spout of gravel was dislodged and fell rattling and bounding through the trees. My eyes turned instinctively in that direction, and I saw a figure leap with great rapidity behind the trunk of a pine. What it was, whether bear or monkey, I could in no wise tell. It seemed dark and shaggy; more I knew not. But the terror of this new apparition brought me to a stand.

I was now, if seemed, cut off upon both sides; behind me the murderers, before me this lurking nondescript. And immediately I began to prefer the dangers that I knew to those I knew not. Silver himself appeared less terrible in contrast with this creature of the woods, and I turned on my heel, and, looking sharply behind me over my shoulder, began to retrace my steps in the direction of the boats.

Instantly the figure reappeared, and, making a wide circuit, began to head me off. I was tired, at any rate; but had I been as fresh as when I rose, I could see it was in vain for me to contend in speed with such an adversary. From trunk to trunk the creature flitted like a deer, running manlike on two legs, but unlike any man that I had ever seen, stooping almost double as it ran. Yet man it was, I could no longer be in doubt about that.

I began to recall what I had heard of cannibals. I was within an ace of calling for help. But the mere fact that he was a man, however wild, had somewhat reassured me, and my fear of Silver began to revive in proportion. I stood still, therefore, and cast about for some method of escape; and as I was so thinking, the recollection of my pistol flashed into my mind. As soon as I remembered I was not defenceless, courage glowed again in my heart; and I set my face resolutely for this man of the island, and walked briskly towards him.

He was concealed by this time, behind another tree trunk; but he must have been watching me closely, for as soon as I began to move in his direction he reappeared and took a step to meet me. Then he hesitated, drew back, came forward again, and at last, to my wonder and confusion, threw himself on his knees, and held out his clasped hands in supplication.

At that I once more stopped.

'Who are you?' I asked.

'Ben Gunn,' he answered, and his voice sounded hoarse and awkward, like a rusty lock. 'I'm poor Ben Gunn, I am; and I haven't spoke with a Christian these three years.'

I could now see that he was a white man like myself, and that his features were even pleasing. His skin, wherever it was exposed, was burnt by the sun; even his lips were black; and his fair eyes looked quite startling in so dark a face. Of all the beggar-men that I had seen or fancied, he was the chief for raggedness. He was clothed with tatters of old ship's canvas and old sea cloth; and this extraordinary patchwork was all held together by a system of the most various and incongruous fastenings, brass buttons, bits of stick, and loops of tarry gaskin. About his waist he wore an old brass-buckled leather belt, which was the one thing solid in his whole accoutrement.

'Three years!' I cried. 'Were you shipwrecked?'

'Nay, mate,' said he – 'marooned.'

I had heard the word, and I knew it stood for a horrible kind of punishment common enough among the buccaneers, in which the offender is put ashore with a little powder and shot, and left behind on some desolate and distant island.

'Marooned three years agone,' he continued, 'and lived on goats since then, and berries, and oysters. Wherever a man is, says I, a man can do for himself. But, mate, my heart is sore for Christian diet. You mightn't happen to have a piece of cheese about you, now? No? Well, many's the long night I've dreamed of cheese – toasted, mostly – and woke up again, and here I were.'

'If ever I can get aboard again,' said I, 'you shall have cheese by the stone.'

All this time he had been feeling the stuff of my jacket, smoothing my hands, looking at my boots, and generally, in the intervals of his speech, showing a childish pleasure in the presence of a fellow creature. But at my last words he perked up into a kind of startled shyness.

'If ever you can get aboard again, says you?' he repeated. 'Why, now, who's to hinder you?'

'Not you, I know,' was my reply.

'And right you was,' he cried. 'Now you – what do you call yourself, mate?'

'Jim,' I told him.

'Jim, Jim,' says he, quite pleased apparently. 'Well, now, Jim, I've lived that rough as you'd be ashamed to hear of. Now, for instance, you wouldn't think I had had a pious mother – to look at me? he asked.

'Why, no, not in particular,' I answered.

'Ah, well,' said he, 'but I had – remarkable pious. And I was a civil, pious boy, and could rattle off my catechism that fast, as you couldn't tell one word from another. And here's what it come to, Jim, and it begun with chuck-farthen on the blessed grave-stones! That's what it begun with, but it went further'n that; and so my mother told me, and predicked the whole, she did, the pious woman! But it were Providence that put me here. I've thought it all out in this here lonely island, and I'm back on piety. You don't catch me tasting rum so much; but just a thimbleful for luck, of course, the first chance I have. I'm bound I'll be good, and I see the way to. And, Jim' – looking all round him, and lowering his voice to a whisper – 'I'm rich.'

I now felt sure that the poor fellow had gone crazy in his solitude, and I suppose I must have shown the feeling in my face; for he repeated the statement hotly:

'Rich! rich! I says. And I'll tell you what: I'll make a man of you, Jim. Ah, Jim, you'll bless your stars, you will, you was the first that found me!'

And at this there came suddenly a lowering shadow over his face, and he tightened his grasp upon my hand, and raised a forefinger threateningly before my eyes.

'Now, Jim, you tell me true; that ain't Flint's ship?' he asked.

At this I had a happy inspiration. I began to believe that I had found an ally, and I answered him at once.

'It's not Flint's ship, and Flint is dead; but I'll tell you true, as you ask me – there are some of Flint's hands aboard; worse luck for the rest of us.'

'Not a man – with one – leg?' he gasped.

'Silver?' I asked.

'Ah, Silver!' says he; 'that were his name.'

'He's the cook; and the ringleader, too.'

He was still holding me by the wrist, and at that he gave it quite a wring.

'If you was sent by Long John,' he said, 'I'm as good as pork, and I know it. But where was you, do you suppose?'

I had made up my mind in a moment, and by way of answer told him the whole story of our voyage, and the predicament in which we found ourselves. He heard me with the keenest interest, and when I had done he patted me on the head.

'You're a good lad, Jim,' he said, 'and you're all in a clove-hitch, ain't you? Well, you just put your trust in Ben Gunn – Ben Gunn's the man to do it. Would you think it likely, now, that your squire would prove a liberal-minded one in case of help – him being in a clove-hitch, as you remark?'

I told him the squire was the most liberal of men.

'Ay, but you see,' returned Ben Gunn, 'I didn't mean giving me a gate to keep, and a shuit of livery clothes, and such; that's not my mark, Jim. What I mean is, would he be likely to come down to the toon of, say one thousand pounds out of money that's as good as a man's own already?'

'I am sure he would,' said I. 'As it was, all hands were to share.'

'And a passage home?' he added, with a look of great shrewdness.

'Why,' I cried, 'the squire's a gentleman. And besides, if we got rid of the others, we should want you to help work the vessel home.'

'Ah,' said he, 'so you would.' And he seemed very much relieved.

'Now, I'll tell you what,' he went on. 'So much I'll tell you, and no more. I were in Flint's ship when he buried the treasure; he and six along – six strong seamen. They was ashore nigh a week, and us standing off and on in the old *Walrus*. One fine day up went the signal, and here come Flint by himself in a little boat, and his head done up in a blue scarf. The sun was getting up, and mortal white he looked about the cutwater. But, there he was, you mind, and the six all dead – dead and buried. How he done it, not a man aboard us could make out. It was battle, murder, and sudden death, leastways – him against six. Billy Bones was the mate; Long John, he was quartermaster; and they asked him where the treasure was. "Ah," says he, "you can go ashore, if you like, and stay," he says: "But as for the ship, she'll beat up for more, by thunder!" That's what he said.

'Well, I was in another ship three years back, and we sighted this island. "Boys," said I, "here's Flint's treasure; let's land and find it." The cap'n was displeased at that; but my messmates were all of a mind, and landed. Twelve days they looked for it, and every day they had the worse word for me, until one fine morning all hands went aboard. "As for you, Benjamin Gunn," says they, "here's a musket," they says, "and a spade, and a pickaxe. You can stay here, and find Flint's money for yourself," they says.

'Well, Jim, three years have I been here, and not a bite of Christian diet from that day to this. But now, you look here; look at me. Do I look like a man before the mast? No, says you. Nor I weren't neither, I says.'

With that he winked and pinched me hard.

'Just you mention them words to your squire, Jim,' he went on: 'Nor he weren't, neither – that's the words. Three years he were the man of this island, light and dark, fair and rain; and sometimes he would, maybe, think upon a prayer (says you), and sometimes he would, maybe, think of his old mother, so be as she's alive (you'll say); but the most part of Gunn's time (this is what you'll say) – the most part of his time was took up with another matter. And then you'll give him a nip, like I do.'

And he pinched me again in the most confidential manner.

'Then,' he continued – 'then you'll up, and you'll say this: Gunn is a good man (you'll say), and he puts a precious sight more confidence – a precious sight, mind that – in a gen'leman born than in these gen'lemen of fortune, having been one hisself.'

'Well,' I said, 'I don't understand one word that you've been saying. But that's neither here nor there; for how am I to get on board?'

'Ah,' said he, 'that's the hitch, for sure. Well, there's my boat, that I made with my two hands. I keep her under the white rock. If the worst come to the worst, we might try that after dark. Hi!' he broke out, 'what's that?'

For just then, although the sun had still an hour or two to run, all the echoes of the island awoke and bellowed to the thunder of a cannon.

'They have begun to fight!' I cried. 'Follow me.'

And I began to run towards the anchorage, my terrors all forgotten; while, close at my side, the marooned man in his goatskins trotted easily and lightly.

'Left, left,' says he; 'keep to your left hand, mate Jim! Under the trees with you! Theer's where I killed my first goat. They don't come down here now; they're all mastheaded on them mountings for the fear of Benjamin Gunn. Ah! and there's the cetemery' – cemetery he must have meant. 'You see the mounds? I come here and prayed, nows and thens, when I thought maybe a Sunday would be about doo. It weren't quite a chapel, but it seemed more solemn like; and then, says you, Ben Gunn was short-handed – no chapling, nor so much as a Bible and a flag, you says.'

So he kept talking as I ran, neither expecting nor receiving any answer.

The cannon-shot was followed, after a considerable interval, by a volley of small arms.

Another pause, and then, not a quarter of a mile in front of me, I beheld the Union Jack flutter in the air above a wood.

PART FOUR

CHAPTER ONE

Narrative continued by the Doctor: How the Ship was Abandoned

IT WAS ABOUT HALF-PAST ONE – three bells in the sea phrase – that the two boats went ashore from the *Hispaniola*. The captain, the squire, and I were talking matters over in the cabin. Had there been a breath of wind we should have fallen on the six mutineers who were left aboard with us, slipped our cable, and away to sea. But the wind was wanting; and, to complete our helplessness, down came Hunter with the news that Jim Hawkins had slipped into a boat and was gone ashore with the rest.

It never occurred to us to doubt Jim Hawkins; but we were alarmed for his safety. With the men in the temper they were in, it seemed an even chance if we should see the lad again. We ran on deck. The pitch was bubbling in the seams; the hasty stench of the place turned me sick; if ever a man smelt fever and dysentery, it was in that abominable anchorage. The six scoundrels were sitting grumbling under a sail in the forecastle; ashore we could see the gigs made fast, and a man sitting in each, hard by where the river runs in. One of them was whistling *Lillibullero*.

Waiting was a strain; and it was decided that Hunter and I should go ashore with the jolly-boat, in quest of information. The gigs had leaned to their right; but Hunter and I pulled straight in, in the direction of the stockade upon the chart. The two who were left guarding their boats seemed in a bustle at our appearance; *Lillibullero* stopped off, and I could see the pair discussing what they ought to do. Had they gone and told Silver, all might have turned out differently; but they had their orders, I suppose, and decided to sit quietly where they were and hark back again to *Lillibullero*.

There was a slight bend in the coast, and I steered so as to put it between us; even before we landed we had thus lost sight of the gigs. I jumped out, and came as near running as I durst, with a big silk handkerchief under my hat for coolness' sake, and a brace of pistols ready primed for safety.

I had not gone a hundred yards when I came on the stockade.

This was how it was: a spring of clear water rose almost at the top of a knoll. Well, on the knoll, and enclosing the spring, they had clapped a stout log-house, fit to hold two-score people on a pinch, and loopholed for musketry on every side. All round this they had cleared a wide space, and then the thing was completed by a paling six feet high, without door or opening, too strong to pull down without time and labour, and too open to shelter the besiegers. The people in the log-house had them in every way; they stood quiet in shelter and shot the others like partridges. All they wanted was a good watch and food; for, short of a complete surprise, they might have held the place against a regiment.

What particularly took my fancy was the spring. For, though we had a good enough place of it in the cabin of the *Hispaniola*, with plenty of arms and ammunition, and things to eat, and excellent wines, there had been one thing overlooked – we had no water. I was thinking this over, when there came ringing over the island the cry of a man at the point of death. I was not new to violent death – I have served His Royal Highness the Duke of Cumberland, and got a wound myself at Fontenoy – but I know my pulse went dot and carry one. 'Jim Hawkins is gone,' was my first thought.

It is something to have been an old soldier, but more still to have been a doctor. There is no time to dilly-dally in our work. And so now I made up my mind instantly, and with no time lost returned to the shore, and jumped on board the jolly-boat.

By good fortune Hunter pulled a good oar. We made the water fly; and the boat was soon alongside, and I aboard the schooner.

I found them all shaken, as was natural. The squire was sitting down, as white as a sheet, thinking of the harm he had led us to, the good soul! and one of the six forecastle hands was little better.

'There's a man,' says Captain Smollett, nodding towards him, 'new to this work. He came nigh-hand fainting, doctor, when he heard the cry. Another touch of the rudder and that man would join us.'

I told my plan to the captain, and between us we settled on the details of its accomplishment.

We put old Redruth in the gallery between the cabin and the forecastle, with three or four loaded muskets and a mattress for protection. Hunter brought the boat round under the stern-port, and Joyce and I set to work loading her with powder tins, muskets, bags of biscuits, kegs of pork, a cask of cognac, and my invaluable medicine chest.

In the meantime, the squire and the captain stayed on deck, and the latter hailed the coxswain, who was the principal man aboard.

'Mr Hands,' he said, 'here are two of us with a brace of pistols each. If any one of you six make a signal of any description, that man's dead.'

They were a good deal taken aback; and, after a little consultation, one and all tumbled down the fore companion, thinking, no doubt, to take us on the rear. But when they saw Redruth waiting for them in the sparred gallery, they went about-ship at once, and a head popped out again on deck.

'Down, dog!' cried the captain.

And the head popped back again; and we heard no more, for the time, of these six very faint-hearted seamen.

By this time, tumbling things in as they came, we had the jolly-boat loaded as much as we dared. Joyce and I got out through the stern-port, and we made for shore again, as fast as oars could take us.

This second trip fairly aroused the watchers along shore. *Lillibullero* was dropped again; and just before we lost sight of them behind the little point, one of them whipped ashore and disappeared. I had half a mind to change my plan and destroy their boats, but I feared that Silver and the others might be close at hand, and all might very well be lost by trying for too much.

We had soon touched land in the same place as before, and set to provision the blockhouse. All three made the first journey, heavily laden, and tossed our stores over the palisade. Then, leaving Joyce to guard them – one man, to be sure, but with half a dozen muskets – Hunter and I returned to the jolly-boat, and loaded ourselves once more. So we proceeded without pausing to take a breath, till the whole cargo was bestowed, when the two servants took up their position in the blockhouse, and I, with all my power, sculled back to the *Hispaniola*.

That we should have risked a second boat-load seems more daring than it really was. They had the advantage of numbers, of course, but we had the advantage of arms. Not one of them ashore had a musket, and before they could get within range for pistol shooting, we flattered ourselves we should be able to give a good account of a half-dozen at least.

The squire was waiting for me at the stern window, all his faintness gone from him. He caught the painter and made it fast, and we fell to loading the boat for our very lives. Pork, powder, and biscuit was the cargo, with only a musket and cutlass apiece for squire and me and Redruth and the captain. The rest of the arms and powder we dropped overboard in two fathoms and a half of water, so that we could see the bright steel shining far below us in the sun, on the clean, sandy bottom.

By this time the tide was beginning to ebb, and ship was swinging round to her anchor. Voices were heard faintly halloaing in the direction of the two gigs; and though this reassured us for Joyce and Hunter, who were well to the eastward, it warned our party to be off.

Redruth retreated from his place in the gallery, and dropped into the boat, which we then brought round to the ship's counter, to be handier for Captain Smollett.

'Now, men,' said he, 'do you hear me?'

There was no answer from the forecastle.

'It's to you, Abraham Gray – it's to you I am speaking.'

Still no reply.

'Gray,' resumed Mr Smollett, a little louder, 'I am leaving this ship, and I order you to follow your captain. I know you are a good man at bottom, and I dare say not one of the lot of you's as bad as he makes out. I have my watch here in my hand; I give you thirty seconds to join me in.'

There was a pause.

'Come, my fine fellow,' continued the captain, 'don't hang so long in stays. I'm risking my life and the lives of these good gentlemen every second.'

There was a sudden scuffle, a sound of blows, and out burst Abraham Gray with a knife-cut on the side of the cheek, and came running to the captain, like a dog to the whistle.

'I'm with you, sir,' said he.

And the next moment he and the captain had dropped aboard of us, and we had shoved off and given way.

We were clear out of the ship; but not yet ashore in our stockade.

CHAPTER TWO

Narrative continued by the Doctor: The Jolly-boat's Last Trip

THIS FIFTH TRIP WAS QUITE different from any of the others. In the first place, the little gallipot of a boat that we were in was gravely overloaded. Five grown men, and three of them – Trelawney, Redruth, and the captain – over six feet high, was already more than she was meant to carry. Add to that the powder, pork, and bread-bags. The gunwale was lipping astern. Several times we shipped a little water, and my breeches and the tails of my coat were all soaking wet before we had gone a hundred yards.

The captain made us trim the boat, and we got her to lie a little more evenly. All the same, we were afraid to breathe.

In the second place, the ebb was now making – a strong rippling current running westward, through the basin, and then south'ard and seaward down the straits by which we had entered in the morning. Even the ripples were a danger to our overloaded craft; but the worst of it was that we were swept out of our true course, and away from our proper landing-place behind the point. If we let the current have its way we should come ashore beside the gigs, where the pirates might appear at any moment.

'I cannot keep her head for the stockade, sir,' said I to the captain. I was steering, while he and Redruth, two fresh men, were at the oars. 'The tide keeps washing her down. Could you pull a little stronger?'

'Not without swamping the boat,' said he. 'You must bear up, sir, if you please – bear up until you see you're gaining.'

I tried, and found by experiment that the tide kept sweeping us westward until I had laid her head due east, or just about right angles to the way we ought to go.

'We'll never get ashore at this rate,' said I.

'If it's the only course that we can lie, sir, we must even lie it,' returned the captain. 'We must keep upstream. You see, sir,' he went on, 'if once we dropped to leeward of the landing-place, it's hard to say where we should get ashore, besides the chance of being boarded by the gigs; whereas, the way we go the current must slacken, and then we can dodge back along the shore.'

'The current's less a'ready, sir,' said the man Gray, who was sitting in the fore-sheets; 'you can ease her off a bit.'

'Thank you, my man,' said I, quite as if nothing had happened: for we had all quietly made up our minds to treat him like one of ourselves.

Suddenly the captain spoke up again, and I thought his voice was a little changed.

'The gun!' said he.

'I have thought of that,' said I, for I made sure he was thinking of a bombardment of the fort. 'They could never get the gun ashore, and if they did, they could never haul it through the woods.'

'Look astern, doctor,' replied the captain.

We had entirely forgotten the long nine; and there, to our horror, were the five rogues busy about her, getting off her jacket, as they called the stout tarpaulin cover under which she sailed. Not only that, but it flashed into my mind at the same moment that the round-shot and the powder for the gun had been left behind, and a stroke with an axe would put it all into the possession of the evil ones aboard.

'Israel was Flint's gunner,' said Gray, hoarsely.

At any risk, we put the boat's head direct for the landing-place. By this time we had got so far out of the run of the current that we kept steerage way even at our necessarily gentle rate of rowing, and I could keep her steady for the goal. But the worst of it was, that with the course I now held, we turned our broadside instead of our stern to the Hispaniola, and offered a target like a barn door.

I could hear, as well as see, that brandy-faced rascal, Israel Hands, plumping down a round-shot on the deck.

'Who's the best shot?' asked the captain.

'Mr Trelawney, out and away,' said I.

'Mr Trelawney, will you please pick me off one of these men, sir? – Hands, if possible,' said the captain.

Trelawney was as cool as steel. He looked to the priming of his gun.

'Now,' cried the captain, 'easy with that gun, sir, or you'll swamp the boat. All hands stand by to trim her when he aims.'

The squire raised his gun, the rowing ceased, and we leaned over to the other side to keep the balance, and all was so nicely contrived that we did not ship a drop.

They had the gun, by this time, slewed round upon the swivel, and Hands, who was at the muzzle with the rammer, was, in consequence, the most exposed. However, we had no luck; for just as Trelawney fired, down he stooped, the ball whistled over him, and it was one of the other four who fell.

The cry he gave was echoed, not only by his companions on board, but by a great number of voices from the shore, and looking in that direction I saw the other pirates trooping out from among the trees and tumbling into their places in the boats.

'Here come the gigs, sir,' said I.

'Give way then,' cried the captain. 'We mustn't mind if we swamp her now. If we can't get ashore, all's up.'

'Only one of the gigs is being manned, sir,' I added, 'the crew of the other most likely going round by shore to cut us off.'

'They'll have a hot run, sir,' returned the captain. 'Jack ashore, you know. It's not them I mind; it's the round-shot. Carpet bowls! My lady's maid couldn't miss. Tell us, squire, when you see the match, and we'll hold water.'

In the meanwhile we had been making headway at a good pace for a boat so overloaded, and we had shipped but little water in the process. We were now close in; thirty or forty strokes and we should beach her; for the ebb had already disclosed a narrow belt of sand below the clustering trees. The gig was no longer to be feared; the little point had already concealed it from our eyes. The ebb-tide, which had so cruelly delayed us, was now making reparation, and delaying our assailants. The one source of danger was the gun.

'If I durst,' said the captain, 'I'd stop and pick off another man.'

But it was plain that they meant nothing should delay their shot. They had never so much as looked at their fallen comrade, though he was not dead, and I could see him trying to crawl away.

'Ready!' cried the squire.

'Hold!' cried the captain, quick as an echo.

And he and Redruth backed with a great heave that sent her stern bodily under water. The report fell in at the same instant of time. This was the first that Jim heard, the sound of the squire's shot not having reached him. Where the ball passed, not one of us precisely knew; but I fancy it must have been over our heads, and that the wind of it may have contributed to our disaster.

At any rate the boat sank by the stern, quite gently, in three feet of water, leaving the captain and myself, facing each other, on our feet. The other three took complete headers, and came up again, drenched and bubbling.

So far there was no great harm. No lives were lost, and we could wade ashore in safety. But there were all our stores at the bottom, and, to make things worse, only two guns out of five remained in a state for service. Mine I had snatched from my knees and held over my head, by a sort of instinct. As for the captain, he had carried his over his shoulder by a bandoleer, and, like a wise man, lock uppermost. The other three had gone down with the boat.

To add to our concern we heard voices already drawing near us in the woods along shore; and we had not only the danger of being cut off from the stockade in our half-crippled state, but the fear before us whether, if Hunter and Joyce were attacked by half a dozen, they would have the sense and conduct to stand firm. Hunter was steady, that we knew; Joyce was a doubtful case – a pleasant, polite man for a valet, and to brush one's clothes, but not entirely fitted for a man of war.

With all this in our minds, we waded ashore as fast as we could, leaving behind us the poor jolly-boat, and a good half of all our powder and provisions.

CHAPTER THREE

Narrative continued by the Doctor: End of the First Day's Fighting

WE MADE OUR BEST SPEED across the strip of wood that now divided us from the stockade; and at every step we took the voices of the buccaneers rang nearer. Soon we could hear their footfalls as they ran, and the cracking of the branches as they breasted across a bit of thicket.

I began to see we should have a brush for it in earnest, and looked to my priming.

'Captain,' said I, 'Trelawney is the dead shot. Give him your gun; his own is useless.'

They exchanged guns, and Trelawney, silent and cool as he had been since the beginning of the bustle, hung a moment on his heel to see that all was fit for service. At the same time, observing Gray to be unarmed, I handed him my cutlass. It did all our hearts good to see him spit in his hand, knit his brows, and make the blade sing through the air. It was plain from every line of his body that our new hand was worth his salt.

Forty paces further we came to the edge of the wood and saw the stockade in front of us. We struck the enclosure about the middle of the south side, and, almost at the same time, seven mutineers – Job Anderson, the boatswain, at their head – appeared in full cry at the south-western corner.

They paused, as if taken aback; and before they recovered, not only the squire and I, but Hunter and Joyce from the blockhouse, had time to fire. The four shots came in rather a scattering volley; but they did the business; one of the enemy actually fell, and the rest, without hesitation, turned and plunged into the trees.

After reloading, we walked down the outside of the palisade to see to the fallen enemy. He was stone dead – shot through the heart.

We began to rejoice over our good success, when just at that moment a pistol cracked in the bush, a ball whistled close past my ear, and poor Tom Redruth stumbled, and fell his length on the ground. Both the squire and I returned the shot; but as we had nothing to aim at, it is probable we only wasted powder. Then we reloaded, and turned our attention to poor Tom.

The captain and Gray were already examining him; and I saw with half an eye that all was over.

I believe the readiness of our return volley had scattered the mutineers once more, for we were suffered without further molestation to get the poor old gamekeeper hoisted over the stockade, and carried, groaning and bleeding, into the log-house.

Poor old fellow, he had not uttered one word of surprise, complaint, fear, or even acquiescence, from the very beginning of our troubles till now, when we had laid him down in the log-house to die. He had lain like a Trojan behind his mattress in the gallery; he had followed every order silently, doggedly, and well; he was the oldest of our party by a score of years; and now, sullen, old, serviceable servant, it was he that was to die.

The squire dropped down beside him on his knees and kissed his hand, crying like a child.

'Be I going, doctor?' he asked.

'Tom, my man,' said I, 'you're going home.'

'I wish I had had a lick at them with the gun first,' he replied.

'Tom,' said the squire, 'say you forgive me, won't you?'

'Would that be respectful-like, from me to you, squire?' was the answer. 'Howsoever, so be it, amen!'

After a little while of silence, he said he thought somebody might read a prayer. 'It's the custom, sir,' he added, apologetically. And not long after, without another word, he passed away.

In the meantime the captain, whom I had observed to be wonderfully swollen about the chest and pockets, had turned out a great many various stores – the British colours, a Bible, a coil of stoutish rope, pen, ink, the log-book, and pounds of tobacco. He had found a longish fir-tree lying felled and cleared in the enclosure, and with the help of Hunter, he had set it up at the corner of the log-house where the trunks crossed and made an angle. Then, climbing on the roof, he had with his own hand bent and run up the colours.

This seemed mightily to relieve him. He re-entered the log-house, and set about counting up the stores, as if nothing else existed. But he had an eye on Tom's passage for all that; and as soon as all was over, came forward with another flag, and reverently spread it on the body.

'Don't you take on, sir,' he said, shaking the squire's hand. 'All's well with him; no fear for a hand that's been shot down in his duty to captain and owner. It mayn't be good divinity, but it's a fact.'

Then he pulled me aside.

'Dr Livesey,' he said, 'in how many weeks do you and squire expect the consort?'

I told him it was a question, not of weeks, but of months; that if we were not back by the end of August, Blandly was to send to find us; but neither sooner nor later. 'You can calculate for yourself,' I said.

'Why, yes,' returned the captain, scratching his head, 'and making a large allowance, sir, for all the gifts of Providence, I should say we were pretty close hauled.'

'How do you mean?' I asked.

'It's a pity, sir, we lost that second load. That's what I mean,' replied the captain. 'As for powder and shot, we'll do. But the rations are short, very short — so short, Dr Livesey, that we're, perhaps, as well without that extra mouth.'

And he pointed to the dead body under the flag.

Just then, with a roar and a whistle, a round-shot passed high above the roof of the log-house and plumped far beyond us in the wood.

'Oho!' said the captain. 'Blaze away! You've little enough powder already, my lads.'

At the second trial, the aim was better, and the ball descended inside the stockade, scattering a cloud of sand, but doing no further damage.

'Captain,' said the squire, 'the house is quite visible from the ship. It must be the flag they are aiming at. Would it not be wiser to take it in?'

'Strike my colours!' cried the captain. 'No, sir, not I'; and, as soon as he had said the words, I think we all agreed with him. For it was not only a piece of stout, seamanly, good feeling; it was good policy besides, and showed our enemies that we despised their cannonade.

All through the evening they kept thundering away. Ball after ball flew over or fell short, or kicked up the sand in the enclosure; but they had to fire so high that the shot fell dead and buried itself in the soft sand. We had no ricochet to fear; and though one popped in through the roof of the log-house and out again through the floor, we soon got used to that sort of horse-play, and minded it no more than cricket.

'There is one thing good about all this,' observed the captain: 'the wood in front of us is likely clear. The ebb has made a good while; our stores should be uncovered. Volunteers to go and bring in pork.'

Gray and Hunter were the first to come forward. Well armed, they stole out of the stockade; but it proved a useless mission. The mutineers were bolder than we fancied, or they put more trust in Israel's gunnery. For five of them were busy carrying off our stores, and wading out with them to one of the gigs that lay close by, pulling an oar or so to hold her steady against the current. Silver was in the stern-sheets in command; and every man of them was now provided with a musket from some secret magazine of their own.

The captain sat down to his log, and here is the beginning of the entry:

Alexander Smollett, master; David Livesey, ship's doctor; Abraham Gray, carpenter's mate; John Trelawney, owner; John Hunter and Richard Joyce, owner's servants, landsmen – being all that is left faithful of the ship's company – with stores for ten days at short rations, came ashore this day, and flew British colours on the log-house in Treasure Island. Thomas Redruth, owner's servant, landsman, shot by the mutineers; James Hawkins, cabin-boy——

And at the same time I was wondering over poor Jim Hawkins's fate.

A hail on the land side.

'Somebody hailing us,' said Hunter, who was on guard.

'Doctor! squire! captain! Hullo, Hunter, is that you?' came the cries.

And I ran to the door in time to see Jim Hawkins, safe and sound, come climbing over the stockade.

CHAPTER FOUR

Narrative Resumed by Jim Hawkins: The Garrison in the Stockade

AS SOON AS BEN GUNN SAW the colours he came to a halt, stopped me by the arm, and sat down.

'Now,' said he, 'there's your friends, sure enough.'

'Far more likely it's the mutineers,' I answered.

'That!' he cried. 'Why, in a place like this, where nobody puts in but gen'lemen of fortune, Silver would fly the Jolly Roger, you don't make no doubt of that. No; that's your friends. There's been blows, too, and I reckon your friends has had the best of it; and here they are ashore in the old stockade, as was made years and years ago by Flint. Ah, he was the man to have a head-piece, was Flint! Barring rum, his match were never seen. He were afraid of none, not he; on'y Silver – Silver was that genteel.'

'Well,' said I, 'that may be so, and so be it; all the more reason that I should hurry on and joint my friends.'

'Nay, mate,' returned Ben, 'not you. You're a good boy, or I'm mistook; but you're on'y a boy, all told. Now, Ben Gunn is fly. Rum wouldn't bring me there, where you're going – not rum wouldn't, till I see your born gen'leman, and gets it on his word of honour. And you won't forget my words: "A precious sight (that's what you'll say), a precious sight more confidence" – and then nips him.'

And he pinched me the third time with the same air of cleverness.

'And when Ben Gunn is wanted, you know where to find him, Jim. Just wheer you found him to-day. And him that comes is to have a white thing in his hand: and he's to come alone. Oh! and you'll say this: "Ben Gunn," says you, "has reasons of his own.'''

'Well,' said I, 'I believe I understand. You have something to propose, and you wish to see the squire or the doctor; and you're to be found where I found you. Is that all?'

'And when? says you,' he added. 'Why, from about noon observation to about six bells.'

'Good,' said I, 'and now may I go?'

'You won't forget?' he inquired, anxiously. 'Precious sight, and reasons of his own, says you. Reasons of his own; that's the mainstay; as between man and man. Well, then,' – still holding me – 'I reckon you can go, Jim. And, Jim, if you was to see Silver, you wouldn't go for to sell Ben Gunn? wild horses would't draw it from you? No, says you. And if them pirates camp ashore, Jim, what would you say but there'd be widders in the morning?'

He was interrupted by a loud report, and a cannon ball came tearing through the trees and pitched in the sand, not a hundred yards from where we two were talking. The next moment each of us had taken to his heels in a different direction.

For a good hour to come frequent reports shook the island, and balls kept crashing through the woods. I moved from hiding-place to hiding-place, always pursued, or so it seemed to me, by these terrifying missiles. But towards the end of the bombardment, though still I durst not venture in the direction of the stockade, where the balls fell oftenest, I had begun, in a manner, to pluck up my heart again; and after a long detour to the east, crept down among the shore-side trees.

The sun had just set, the sea breeze was rustling and tumbling in the woods, and ruffling the grey surface of the anchorage; the tide, too, was far out, and great tracts of sand lay uncovered; the air, after the heat of the day, chilled me through my jacket.

The *Hispaniola* still lay where she had anchored; but, sure enough, there was the Jolly Roger – the black flag of piracy – flying from her peak. Even as I looked, there came another red flash and another report, that sent the echoes clattering, and one more round-shot whistled through the air. It was the last of the cannonade.

I lay for some time, watching the bustle which succeeded the attack. Men were demolishing something with axes on the beach near the stockade; the poor jolly-boat, I afterwards discovered. Away, near the mouth of the river, a great fire was glowing among the trees, and between that point and the ship one of the gigs kept coming and going, the men, whom I had seen so gloomy, shouting at the oars like children. But there was a sound in their voices which suggested rum.

At length I thought I might return towards the stockade. I was pretty far down on the low, sandy spit that encloses the anchorage to the east, and is joined at half-water to Skeleton Island; and now, as I rose to my feet, I saw, some distance further down the spit, and rising from among low bushes, an isolated rock, pretty high, and peculiarly white in colour. It occurred to me that this might be the white rock of which Ben Gunn had spoken, and that some day or other a boat might be wanted, and I should know where to look for one.

Then I skirted among the woods until I had regained the rear, or shoreward side, of the stockade, and was soon warmly welcomed by the faithful party.

I had soon told my story, and began to look about me. The log-house was made of unsquared trunks of pine – roof, walls, and floor. The latter stood in several places as much as a foot or a foot and a half above the surface of the sand. There was a porch at the door, and under this porch the little spring welled up into an artificial basin of a rather odd kind – no other than a great ship's kettle of iron, with the bottom knocked out, and sunk 'to her bearings,' as the captain said, among the sand.

Little had been left beside the framework of the house; but in one corner there was a stone slab laid down by way of a hearth, and an old rusty iron basket to contain the fire.

The slopes of the knoll and all the inside of the stockade had been cleared of timber to build the house, and we could see by the stumps what a fine and lofty grove had been destroyed. Most of the soil had been washed away or buried in drift after the removal of the trees; only where the streamlet ran down from the kettle a thick bed of moss and some ferns and little creeping bushes were still green among the sand. Very close around the stockade – too close for defence, they said – the wood still flourished high and dense, all of fir on the land side, but towards the sea with a large admixture of live oaks.

The cold evening breeze, of which I have spoken, whistled through every chink of the rude building, and sprinkled the floor with a continual rain of fine sand. There was sand in our eyes, sand in our teeth, sand in our suppers, sand dancing in the spring at the bottom of the kettle, for all the world like porridge beginning to boil. Our chimney was a square hole in the roof: it was but a little part of the smoke that found its way out, and the rest eddied about the house, and kept us coughing and wiping the eye.

Add to this that Gray, the new man, had his face tied up in a bandage for a cut he had got in breaking away from the mutineers; and that poor old Tom Redruth, still unburied, lay along the wall, stiff and stark, under the Union Jack.

If we had been allowed to sit idle, we should all have fallen in the blues, but Captain Smollett was never the man for that. All hands were called up before him, and he divided us into watches. The doctor, and Gray, and I, for one; the squire, Hunter, and Joyce upon the other. Tired as we all were, two were sent out for firewood; two more were set to dig a grave for Redruth; the doctor was named cook; I was put sentry at the door; and the captain himself went from one to another, keeping up our spirits, and lending a hand wherever it was wanted.

From time to time the doctor came to the door for a little air and to rest his eyes, which were almost smoked out of his head; and whenever he did so, he had a word for me.

'That man Smollett,' he said once, 'is a better man than I am. And when I say that it means a deal, Jim.'

Another time he came and was silent for a while. Then he puts his head on one side, and looked at me.

'Is this Ben Gunn a man?' he asked.

'I do not know, sir,' said I. 'I am not very sure whether he's sane.'

'If there's any doubt about the matter, he is,' returned the doctor. 'A man who has been three years biting his nails on a desert island, Jim, can't expect to appear as sane as you or me. It doesn't lie in human nature. Was it cheese you said he had a fancy for?'

'Yes, sir, cheese,' I answered.

'Well, Jim,' says he, 'just see the good that comes of being dainty in your food. You've seen my snuff-box, haven't you? And you never saw me take snuff; the reason being that in my snuff-box I carry a piece of Parmesan cheese – a cheese made in Italy, very nutricious. Well, that's for Ben Gunn!'

Before supper was eaten we buried old Tom in the sand, and stood round him for a while bare-headed in the breeze. A good deal of firewood had been got in, but not enough for the captain's fancy; and he shook his head over it, and told us we 'must get back to this tomorrow rather livelier.' Then, when we had eaten our pork, and each had a good stiff glass of brandy grog, the three chiefs got together in a corner to discuss our prospects.

It appears they were at their wits' end what to do, the stores being so low that we must have been starved into surrender long before help came. But our best hope, it was decided, was to kill off the buccaneers until they either hauled down their flag or ran away with the *Hispaniola*. From nineteen they were already reduced to fifteen, two others were wounded, and one, at least – the man shot beside the gun – severely wounded, if he were not dead. Every time we had a crack at them, we were to take it, saving our own lives, with the extremest care. And, besides that, we had two able allies – rum and the climate.

As for the first, though we were about half a mile away, we could hear them roaring and singing late into the night; and as for the second, the doctor staked his wig that, camped where they were in the marsh and unprovided with remedies, the half of them would be on their backs before a week.

'So,' he added, 'if we are not all shot down first they'll be glad to be packing in the schooner. It's always a ship, and they can get to buccaneering again, I suppose.'

'First ship that ever I lost,' said Captain Smollett.

I was dead tired, as you may fancy; and when I got to sleep, which was not till after a great deal of tossing, I slept like a log of wood.

The rest had long been up, and had already breakfasted and increased the pile of firewood by about half as much again, when I was awakened by a bustle and the sound of voices.

'Flag of truce!' I heard someone say; and then, immediately after, with a cry of surprise: 'Silver himself!'

And, at that, up I jumped, and, rubbing my eyes, ran to a loophole in the wall.

CHAPTER FIVE

Silver's Embassy

SURE ENOUGH, THERE WERE two men just outside the stockade, one of them waving a white cloth; the other, no less a person than Silver himself, standing placidly by.

It was still quite early, and the coldest morning that I think I ever was abroad in; a chill that pierced into the marrow. The sky was bright and cloudless overhead, and the tops of the trees shone rosily in the sun. But where Silver stood with his lieutenant all was still in shadow, and they waded knee deep in a low, white vapour, and had crawled during the night out of the morass. The chill and the vapour taken together told a poor tale of the island. It was plainly a damp, feverish, unhealthy spot.

'Keep indoors, men,' said the captain. 'Ten to one this is a trick.'

Then he hailed the buccaneer.

'Who goes? Stand, or we fire.'

'Flag of truce,' cried Silver.

The captain was in the porch, keeping himself carefully out of the way of a treacherous shot should any be intended. He turned and spoke to us:

'Doctor's watch on the look-out. Dr Livesey, take the north side, if you please; Jim, the east; Gray, west. The watch below, all hands to load muskets. Lively, men, and careful.'

And then he turned again to the mutineers.

'And what do you want with your flag of truce?' he cried.

This time it was the other man who replied.

'Cap'n Silver, sir, to come on board and make terms.' he shouted.

'Cap'n Silver! Don't know him. Who's he?' cried the captain. And we could hear him adding to himself: 'Cap'n, is it? My heart, and here's promotion!'

Long John answered for himself.

'Me, sir. These poor lads have chosen me cap'n, after your desertion, sir' – laying a particular emphasis upon the word 'desertion.' 'We're willing to submit, if we can come to terms, and no bones about it. All I ask is your word, Cap'n Smollett, to let me safe and sound out of this here stockade, and one minute to get out o' shot before a gun is fired.

'My man,' said Captain Smollett, 'I have not the slightest desire to talk to you. If you wish to talk to me, you can come, that's all. If there's any treachery, it'll be on your side, and the Lord help you.'

'That's enough, cap'n,' shouted Long John, cheerily. 'A word from you's enough. I know a gentlemen, and you may lay to that.'

We could see the man who carried the flag of truce attempting to hold Silver back. Nor was that wonderful, seeing how cavalier had been the captain's answer. But Silver laughed at him aloud, and slapped him on the back, as if the idea of alarm had been absurd. Then he advanced to the stockade, threw over his crutch, got a leg up, and with great vigour and skill succeeded in surmounting the fence and dropping safely to the other side.

I will confess that I was far too much taken up with what was going on to be of the slightest use as sentry; indeed, I had already deserted my eastern loophole, and crept up behind the captain, who had now seated himself on the threshold, with his elbows on his knees, his head in his hands, and his eyes fixed on the water, as it bubbled out of the old iron kettle in the sand. He was whistling to himself: *Come, Lasses and Lads.*

Silver had terrible hard work getting up the knoll. What with the steepness of the incline, the thick tree stumps, and the soft sand, he and his crutch were as helpless as a ship in stays. But he stuck to it like a man in silence, and at last arrived before the captain, whom he saluted in the handsomest style. He was tricked out in his best; an immense blue coat, thick with brass buttons, hung as low as to his knees, and a fine laced hat was set on the back of his head.

'Here you are, my man,' said the captain, raising his head. 'You had better sit down.'

'You ain't a-going to let me inside, cap'n?' complained Long John. 'It's a cold morning, to be sure, sir, to sit outside upon the sand.'

'Why, Silver,' said the captain, 'if you had pleased to be an honest man, you might have been sitting in your galley. It's your own doing. You're either my ship's cook – and then you were treated handsome – or Cap'n Silver, a common mutineer and pirate, and then you can go hang!'

'Well, well, cap'n,' returned the sea cook, sitting down as he was bidden on the sand, 'you'll have to give me a hand up again, that's all. A sweet pretty place you have of it here. Ah, there's Jim! The top of the morning to you, Jim. Doctor, here's my service. Why, there you all are together like a happy family, in a manner of speaking.'

'If you have anything to say, my man, better say it,' said the captain.

'Right you were, Cap'n Smollett,' replied Silver. 'Dooty is dooty, to be sure. Well, now, you look here, that was a good lay of yours last night. I don't deny it was a good lay. Some of you pretty handy with a hand-spike-end. And I'll not deny neither but what some of my people was shook – maybe all was shook; maybe I was shook myself; maybe that's why I'm here for terms. But you mark me, cap'n, it won't do twice, by thunder! We'll have to do sentry-go, and ease off a point or so on the rum. Maybe you think we were all a sheet in the wind's eye. But I'll tell you I was sober; I was on'y dog tired; and if I'd awoke a second sooner I'd a' caught you at the act, I would. He wasn't dead when I got round to him, not he.'

'Well?' says Captain Smollett, as cool as can be.

All that Silver said was a riddle to him, but you would never have guessed it from his tone. As for me, I began to have an inkling. Ben Gunn's last words came back to my mind. I began to suppose that he had paid the buccaneers a visit while they all lay drunk together round their fire, and I reckoned up with glee that we had only fourteen enemies to deal with.

'Well, here it is,' said Silver. 'We want that treasure, and we'll have it – that's our point! You would just as soon save your lives, I reckon; and that's yours. You have a chart, haven't you?'

'That's as may be,' replied the captain.

'Oh, well, you have, I know that,' returned Long John. 'You needn't be so husky with a man; there ain't a particle of service in that, and you may lay to it. What I mean is, we want your chart. Now, I never meant you no harm, myself.'

'That won't do with me, my man,' interrupted the captain. 'We know exactly what you meant to do, and we don't care; for now, you see, you can't do it.'

And the captain looked at him calmly, and proceeded to fill a pipe.

'If Abe Gray——' Silver broke out.

'Avast there!' cried Mr Smollett. 'Gray told me nothing, and I asked him nothing; and what's more, I would see you and him and this whole island blown clear out of the water into blazes first. So there's my mind for you, my man, on that.'

This little whiff of temper seemed to cool Silver down. He had been growing nettled before, but now he pulled himself together.

'Like enough,' said he. 'I would set no limits to what gentlemen might consider shipshape, or might not, as the case were. And, seein' as how you are about to take a pipe, cap'n, I'll make so free as do likewise.'

And he filled a pipe and lighted it; and the two men sat silently smoking for a while, now looking each other in the face, now stopping their tobacco, now leaning forward to spit. It was as good as the play to see them.

'Now,' resumed Silver, 'here it is. You give us the chart to get the treasure by, and drop shooting poor seamen, and stoving of their heads in while asleep. You do that, and we'll offer you a choice. Either you come aboard along of us, once the treasure's shipped, and then I'll give you my affy-davy, upon my word of honour, to clap you somewhere safe ashore. Or, if that ain't to your fancy, some of my hands being rough, and having old scores, on account of hazing, then you can stay here, you can. We'll divide stores with you, man for man; and I'll give my affy-davy, as before, to speak the first ship I sight, and send 'em here to pick you up. Now you'll own that's talking. Handsomer you couldn't look to get, not you. And I hope' – raising his voice – 'that all hands in this here blockhouse will overhaul my words, for what is spoke to one is spoke to all.'

Captain Smollett rose from his seat, and knocked out the ashes of his pipe in the palm of his left hand.

'Is that all?' he asked.

'Every last word, by thunder!' answered John. 'Refuse that, and you've seen the last of me but musketballs.'

'Very good,' said the captain. 'Now you'll hear me. If you'll come up one by one, unarmed, I'll engage to clap you all in irons, and take you home to a fair trial in England. If you won't, my name is Alexander Smollett, I've flown my sovereign's colours, and I'll see you all to Davy Jones. You can't find the treasure. You can't sail the ship – there's not a man among you fit to sail the ship. You can't fight us – Gray, there, got away from five of you. Your ship's in irons, Master Silver; you're on a lee shore, and so you'll find. I stand here and tell you so; and they're the last good words you'll get from me, for, in the name of heaven, I'll put a bullet in your back when next I meet you. Tramp, my lad. Bundle out of this, please, hand over hand and double quick.'

Silver's face was a picture; his eyes started in his head with wrath. He shook the fire out of his pipe.

'Give me a hand up!' he cried.

'Not I,' returned the captain.

'Who'll give me a hand up?' he roared.

Not a man among us moved. Growling the foulest imprecations, he crawled along the sand till he got hold of the porch and could hoist himself again upon his crutch. Then he spat into the spring.

'There,' he cried, 'that's what I think of ye. Before an hour's out, I'll stove in your old blockhouse like a rum-puncheon. Laugh, by thunder, laugh! Before an hour's out, ye'll laugh upon the other side. Them that die'll be the lucky ones.'

And with a dreadful oath he stumbled off, ploughed down the sand, was helped across the stockade, after four or five failures, by the man with the flag of truce, and disappeared in an instant afterwards among the trees.

CHAPTER SIX

The Attack

AS SOON AS SILVER DISAPPEARED, the captain, who had been closely watching him, turned towards the interior of the house, and found not a man of us at his post but Gray. It was the first time we had ever seen him angry.

'Quarters!' he roared. And then, as we all slunk back to our places, 'Gray,' he said, 'I'll put your name in the log; you've stood by your duty like a seaman. Mr Trelawney, I'm surprised at you, sir. Doctor, I thought you had worn the king's coat! If that was how you served at Fontenoy, sir, you'd have been better in your berth.'

The doctor's watch were all back at their loopholes, the rest were busy, loading the spare muskets, and every one with a red face, you may be certain, and a flea in his ear, as the saying is.

The captain looked on for a while in silence. Then he spoke.

'My lads,' said he, 'I've given Silver a broadside. I pitched it in red-hot on purpose; and before the hour's out, as he said, we shall be boarded. We're outnumbered, I needn't tell you that, but we fight in shelter; and, a minute ago, I should have said we fought with discipline. I've no manner of doubt that we can drub them, if you choose.'

Then he went the rounds, and saw, as he said, that all was clear.

On the two short sides of the house, east and west, there were only two loopholes; on the south side where the porch was, two again; and on the north side, five. There was a round score of muskets for the seven of us; the firewood had been built into four piles – tables, you might say – one about the middle of each side, and on each of these tables some ammunition and four loaded muskets were laid ready to the hand of the defenders. In the middle, the cutlasses lay ranged.

'Toss out the fire,' said the captain; 'the chill is past, and we mustn't have smoke in our eyes.'

The iron fire basket was carried bodily out by Mr Trelawney, and the embers smothered among sand.

'Hawkins hasn't had his breakfast. Hawkins, help yourself, and back to your post to eat it,' continued Captain Smollett. 'Lively, now, my lad; you'll want it before you've done. Hunter, serve out a round of brandy to all hands.'

And while this was going on, the captain completed, in his own mind, the plan of the defence.

'Doctor, you will take the door,' he resumed. 'See, and don't expose yourself; keep within, and fire through the porch. Hunter, take the east side, there. Joyce, you stand by the west, my man. Mr Trelawney, you are the best shot – you and Gray will take this long north side, with the five loopholes; it's there the danger is. If they can get up to it, and fire in upon us through our own ports, things would begin to look dirty. Hawkins, neither you nor I are much account at the shooting; we'll stand by to load and bear a hand.'

As the captain had said, the chill was past. As soon as the sun had climbed above our girdle of trees, it fell with all its force upon the clearing, and drank up the vapours at a draught. Soon the sand was baking and the resin melting in the logs of the blockhouse. Jackets and coats were flung aside; shirts blown open at the neck, and rolled up to the shoulders; and we stood there, each at his post, in a fever of heat and anxiety.

An hour passed away.

'Hang them!' said the captain. 'This is as dull as the doldrums. Gray, whistle for a wind.'

And just at that moment came the first news of the attack.

'If you please, sir,' said Joyce, 'if I see any one am I to fire?'

'I told you so!' cried the captain.

'Thank you, sir,' returned Joyce, with the same quiet civility.

Nothing followed for a time; but the remark had set us all on the alert, straining ears and eyes – the musketeers with their pieces balanced in their hands, the captain out in the middle of the blockhouse, with his mouth very tight and a frown on his face.

So some seconds passed, till suddenly Joyce whipped up his musket and fired. The report had scarcely died away ere it was repeated and repeated from without in a scattering volley, shot behind shot, like a string of geese, from every side of the enclosure. Several bullets struck the log-house, but not one entered; and, as the smoke cleared away and vanished, the stockade and the woods around it looked as quiet and empty as before. Not a bough waved, not the gleam of a musket-barrel betrayed the presence of our foes.

'Did you hit your man?' asked the captain.

'No, sir,' replied Joyce. 'I believe not, sir.'

'Next best thing to tell the truth,' muttered Captain Smollett. 'Load his gun, Hawkins. How many should you say there were on your side, doctor?'

'I know precisely,' said Dr Livesey. 'Three shots were fired on this side. I saw the three flashes – two close together – one further to the west.'

'Three!' repeated the captain. 'And how many on yours, Mr Trelawney?'

But this was not so easily answered. There had come many from the north – seven, by the squire's computation; eight or nine, according to Gray. From the east and west only a single shot had been fired. It was plain, therefore, that the attack would be developed from the north, and that on the other three sides we were only to be annoyed by a show of hostilities. But Captain Smollett made no change in his arrangements. If the mutineers succeeded in crossing the blockade, he argued, they would take possession of any unprotected loophole, and shoot us down like rats in our own stronghold.

Nor had we much time left to us for thought. Suddenly, with a loud huzza, a little cloud of pirates leaped from the woods on the north side, and ran straight on the stockade. At the same moment, the fire was once more opened from the woods, and a rifle-ball sang through the doorway, and knocked the doctor's musket into bits.

The boarders swarmed over the fence like monkeys. Squire and Gray fired again and yet again; three men fell, one forwards into the enclosure, two back on the outside. But of these, one was evidently more frightened than hurt, for he was on his feet again in a crack, and instantly disappeared among the trees.

Two had bit the dust, one had fled, four had made good their footing inside our defences; while from the shelter of the woods seven or eight men, each evidently supplied with several muskets, kept up a hot though useless fire on the log-house.

The four who had boarded made straight before them for the building, shouting as they ran, and the men among the trees shouted back to encourage them. Several shots were fired; but, such was the hurry of the marksmen, that not one appeared to have taken effect. In a moment, the four pirates had swarmed up the mound and were upon us.

The head of Job Anderson, the boatswain, appeared at the middle loophole. 'At 'em, all hands – all hands!' he roared, in a voice of thunder.

At the same moment, another pirate grasped Hunter's musket by the muzzle, wrenched it from his hands, plucked it through the loophole, and, with one stunning blow, laid the poor fellow senseless on the floor. Meanwhile a third, running unharmed all round the house, appeared suddenly in the doorway, and fell with his cutlass on the doctor.

Our position was utterly reversed. A moment since, we were firing, under cover, at an exposed enemy; now it was we who lay uncovered, and could not return a blow.

The log-house was full of smoke, to which we owed our comparative safety. Cries and confusion, the flashes and reports of pistol shots, and one loud groan, rang in my ears.

'Out, lads, out, and fight 'em in the open! Cutlasses!' cried the captain.

I snatched a cutlass from the pile, and someone, at the same time snatching another, gave me a cut across the knuckles which I hardly felt. I dashed out of the door into the clear sunlight. Someone was close behind, I knew not whom. Right in front, the doctor was pursuing his assailant down the hill, and, just as my eyes fell upon him, beat down his guard, and sent him sprawling on his back, with a great slash across the face.

'Round the house, lads! round the house!' cried the captain; and even in the hurly-burly I perceived a change in his voice.

Mechanically I obeyed, turned eastwards, and with my cutlass raised, ran round the corner of the house. Next moment I was face to face with Anderson. He roared aloud, and his hanger went up above his head, flashing in the sunlight. I had not time to be afraid; but, as the blow still hung impending, leaped in a trice upon one side, and missing my foot in the soft sand, rolled headlong down the slope.

When I had first sallied from the door, the other mutineers had been already swarming up the palisade to make an end of us. One man, in a red night-cap, with his cutlass in his mouth, had even got upon the top and thrown a leg across. Well, so short had been the interval, that when I found my feel again all was in the same posture, the fellow with the red night-cap still half-way over, another still just showing his head above the top of the stockade. And yet, in this breath of time, the fight was over, and the victory was ours.

Gray, following close behind me, had cut down the big boatswain ere he had time to recover from his lost blow. Another had been shot at a loophole in the very act of firing into the house, and now lay in agony, the pistol still smoking in his hand. A third, as I had seen, the doctor had disposed of at a blow. Of the four who had scaled the palisade, one only remained unaccounted for, and he, having left his cutlass on the field, was now clambering out again with the fear of death upon him.

'Fire – fire from the house!' cried the doctor. 'And you, lads, back into cover.'

But his words were unheeded, no shot was fired, and the last boarder made good his escape, and disappeared with the rest into the wood. In three seconds nothing remained of the attacking party but the five who had fallen, four on the inside, and one on the outside, of the palisade.

The doctor and Gray and I ran full speed for shelter. The survivors would soon be back where they had left their muskets, and at any moment the fire might recommence.

The house was by this time somewhat cleared of smoke, and we saw at a glance the price we had paid for victory. Hunter lay beside his loophole, stunned; Joyce by his, shot through the head, never to move again; while right in the centre, the squire was supporting the captain, one as pale as the other.

'The captain's wounded,' said Mr Trelawney.

'Have they run?' asked Mr Smollett.

'All that could, you may be bound,' returned the doctor; 'but there's five of them will never run again.'

'Five!' cried the captain. 'Come, that's better. Five against three leaves us four to nine. That's better odds than we had at starting. We were seven to nineteen then, or thought we were, and that's as bad to bear.'*

*The mutineers were soon only eight in number, for the man shot by Mr Trelawney on board the schooner died that same evening of his wound. But this was, of course, not known till after by the faithful party.

PART FIVE

CHAPTER ONE

How I Began My Sea Adventure

THERE WAS NO RETURN OF the mutineers – not so much as another shot out of the woods. They had 'got their rations for that day,' as the captain put it, and we had the place to ourselves and a quiet time to overhaul the wounded and get dinner. Squire and I cooked outside in spite of the danger, and even outside we could hardly tell what we were at, for horror of the loud groans that reached us from the doctor's patients.

Out of the eight men who had fallen in the action, only three still breathed – that one of the pirates who had been shot at the loophole, Hunter, and Captain Smollett; and of these the first two were as good as dead; the mutineer, indeed, died under the doctor's knife, and Hunter, do what we could, never recovered consciousness in this world. He lingered all day, breathing loudly like the old buccaneer at home in his apoplectic fit; but the bones of his chest had been crushed by the blow and his skull fractured in falling, and some time in the following night, without a sign or sound, he went to his Maker.

As for the captain, his wounds were grievous indeed, but not dangerous. No organ was fatally injured. Anderson's ball – for it was Job that shot him first – had broken his shoulder-blade and touched the lung, not badly; the second had only torn and displaced some muscles in the calf. He was sure to recover, the doctor said, but, in the meantime and for weeks to come, he must not walk nor move his arm, nor so much as speak when he could help it.

My own accidental cut across the knuckles was a fleabite. Dr Livesey patched it up with plaster, and pulled my ears for me into the bargain.

After dinner the squire and the doctor sat by the captain's side a while in consultation; and when they had talked to their heart's content, it being then a little past noon, the doctor took up his hat and pistols, girt on a cutlass, put the chart in his pocket, and, with a musket over his shoulder, crossed the palisade on the north side, and set off briskly through the trees.

Gray and I were sitting together at the far end of the blockhouse, to be out of earshot of our officers consulting; and Gray took his pipe out of his mouth and fairly forgot to put it back again, so thunderstruck he was at this occurrence.

'Why, in the name of Davy Jones,' said he, 'is Dr Livesey mad?'

'Why, no,' says I. 'He's about the last of this crew for that, I take it!'

'Well, shipmate,' said Gray, 'mad he may not be; but if *he's* not, you mark my words, *I* am.'

'I take it,' replied I, 'the doctor has his idea; and if I am right, he's going now to see Ben Gunn.'

I was right, as appeared later; but, in the meantime, the house being stifling hot, and the little patch of sand inside the palisade ablaze with midday sun, I began to get another thought into my head, which was not by any means so right. What I began to do was to envy the doctor, walking in the cool shadow of the woods, with the birds about him, and the pleasant smell of the pines, while I sat grilling, with my clothes stuck to the hot resin, and so much blood about me, and so many poor dead bodies lying all around, that I took a disgust of the place that was almost as strong as fear.

All the time I was washing out the blockhouse, and then washing up the things from dinner, this disgust and envy kept growing stronger and stronger, till at last, being near a bread-bag, and no one then observing me, I took the first step towards my escapade, and filled both pockets of my coat with biscuit.

I was a fool, if you like, and certainly I was going to do a foolish, over-bold act; but I was determined to do it with all the precautions in my power. These biscuits, should anything befall me, would keep me, at least, from starving till far on in the next day.

The next thing I laid hold of was a brace of pistols, and as I already had a powder-horn, and bullets, I felt myself well supplied with arms.

As for the scheme I had in my head, it was not a bad one in itself. I was to go down the sandy spit that divides the anchorage on the east from the open sea, find the white rock I had observed last evening, and ascertain whether it was there or not that Ben Gunn had hidden his boat; a thing quite worth doing, as I still believe. But as I was certain I should not be allowed to leave the enclosure, my only plan was to take French leave, and slip out when nobody was watching; and that was so bad a way of doing it as made the thing itself wrong. But I was only a boy, and I had made my mind up.

Well, as things at last fell out, I found an admirable opportunity. The squire and Gray were busy helping the captain with his bandages; the coast was clear; I made a bolt for it over the stockade and into the thickest of the trees, and before my absence was observed I was out of cry of my companions.

This was my second folly, far worse than my first, as I left but two sound men to guard the house; but, like the first, it was a help towards saving all of us.

I took my way straight for the east coast of the island, for I was determined to go down the sea side of the spit to avoid all chance of observation from the anchorage. It was already late in the afternoon, although still warm and sunny. As I continued to thread the tall woods I could hear from far before me not only the continuous thunder of the surf, but a certain tossing of foliage and grinding of boughs which showed me the sea breeze had set in higher than usual. Soon cool draughts of air began to reach me; and a few steps further I came forth into the open borders of the grove, and saw the sea lying blue and sunny to the horizon, and the surf tumbling and tossing its foam along the beach.

I have never seen the sea quiet round Treasure Island. The sun might blaze overhead, the air be without a breath, the surface smooth and blue, but still these great rollers would be running along all the external coast, thundering and thundering by day and night; and I scarce believe there is one spot in the island where a man would be out of earshot of their noise.

I walked along beside the surf with great enjoyment, till, thinking I was not got far enough to the south, I took the cover of some thick bushes and crept warily up to the ridge of the spit.

Behind me was the sea, in front the anchorage. The sea breeze, as though it had the sooner blown itself out by its unusual violence, was already at an end; it had been succeeded by light, variable airs from the south and south-east, carrying great banks of fog; and the anchorage, under lee of Skeleton Island, lay still and leaden as when first we entered it. The *Hispaniola*, in that unbroken mirror, was exactly portrayed from the truck to the water-line, the Jolly Roger hanging from her peak.

Alongside lay one of the gigs, Silver in the stern-sheets – him I could always recognize – while a couple of men were leaning over the stern bulwarks, one of them with a red cap – the very rogue that I had seen some hours before stride-legs upon the palisade. Apparently they were talking and laughing, though at that distance – upwards of a mile – I could, of course, hear no word of what was said. All at once, there began the most horrid, unearthly screaming, which at first startled me badly, though I had soon remembered the voice of Captain Flint, and even thought I could make out the bird by her bright plumage as she sat perched upon her master's wrist.

Soon after the jolly-boat shoved off and pulled for shore, and the man with the red cap and his comrade went below by the cabin companion.

Just about the same time the sun had gone down behind the Spy-glass, and as the fog was collecting rapidly, it began to grow dark in earnest. I saw I must lose no time if I were to find the boat that evening.

The white rock, visible enough above the brush, was still some eighth of a mile further down the spit, and it took me a goodish while to get up with it, crawling, often on all-fours, among the scrub. Night had almost come when I laid my hand on its rough sides. Right below it there was an exceedingly small hollow of green turf, hidden by banks and a thick underwood about knee-deep, that grew there very plentifully; and in the centre of the dell, sure enough, a little tent of goat-skins, like what the gipsies carry about with them in England.

I dropped into the hollow, lifted the side of the tent, and there was Ben Gunn's boat – home-made if ever anything was home-made; a rude, lop-sided framework of tough wood, and stretched upon that a covering of goat-skin, with the hair inside. The thing was extremely small, even for me, and I can hardly imagine that it could have floated with a full-sized man. There was one thwart, set as low as possible, a kind of stretcher in the bows, and a double paddle for propulsion.

I had not then seen a coracle, such as the ancient Britons made, but I have seen one since, and I can give you no fairer idea of Ben Gunn's boat than by saying it was like the first and the worst coracle ever made by man. But the great advantage of the coracle it certainly possessed, for it was exceedingly light and portable.

Well, now that I had found the boat, you would have thought I had had enough of truantry for once; but, in the meantime, I had taken another notion, and become so obstinately fond of it, that I would have carried it out, I believe, in the teeth of Captain Smollett himself. This was to slip out under cover of the night, cut the *Hispaniola* adrift, and let her go ashore where she fancied. I had quite made up my mind that the mutineers, after their repulse of the morning, had nothing nearer their hearts than to up anchor and away to sea; this, I thought, it would be a fine thing to prevent; and now that I had seen how they left their watchmen unprovided with a boat, I thought it might be done with little risk.

Down I sat to wait for darkness, and made a hearty meal of biscuit. It was a night out of ten thousand for my purpose. The fog had now buried all heaven. As the last rays of daylight dwindled and disappeared, absolute blackness settled down on Treasure Island. And when at last I shouldered the coracle, and groped my way stumblingly out of the hollow where I had supped, there were but two points visible on the whole anchorage.

One was the great fire on shore, by which the defeated pirates lay carousing in the swamp. The other, a mere blur of light upon the darkness, indicated the position of the anchored ship. She had swung round to the ebb – her bow was now towards me – the only lights on board were in the cabin; and what I saw was merely a reflection on the fog of the strong rays that flowed from the stern window.

The ebb had already run some time, and I had to wade through a long belt of swampy sand, where I sank several times above the ankle, before I came to the edge of the retreating water, and wading a little way in, with some strength and dexterity, set my coracle, keel downwards, on the surface.

CHAPTER TWO

The Ebb-tide Runs

THE CORACLE – AS I HAD ample reason to know before I was done with her – was a very safe boat for a person of my height and weight, both buoyant and clever in a seaway; but she was the most cross-grained, lop-sided craft to manage. Do as you please, she always made more leeway than anything else, and turning round and round was the manoeuvre she was best at. Even Ben Gunn himself has admitted that she was 'queer to handle till you knew her way.'

Certainly I did not know her way. She turned in every direction but the one I was bound to go; the most part of the time we were broadside on, and I am very sure I never should have made the ship at all but for the tide. By good fortune, paddle as I pleased, the tide was still sweeping me down; and there lay the *Hispaniola* right in the fairway, hardly to be missed.

First she loomed before me like a blot of something yet blacker than darkness, then her spars and hull began to take shape, and the next moment, as it seemed (for the further I went, the brisker grew the current of the ebb), I was alongside of her hawser, and had laid hold.

The hawser was as taut as a bowstring – so strong she pulled upon her anchor. All round the hull, in the blackness, the rippling current bubbled and chattered like a little mountain stream. One cut with my sea-gully, and the *Hispaniola* would go humming down the tide.

So far so good; but it next occurred to my recollection that a taut hawser, suddenly cut, is a thing as dangerous as a kicking horse. Ten to one, if I were so foolhardy as to cut the *Hispaniola* from her anchor, I and the coracle would be knocked clean out of the water.

This brought me to a full stop, and if fortune had not again particularly favoured me, I should have had to abandon my design. But the light airs which had begun blowing from the south-east and south had hauled round after nightfall into the south-west. Just while I was meditating, a puff came, caught the *Hispaniola*, and forced her up into the current; and to my great joy, I felt the hawser slacken in my grasp, and the hand by which I held it dip for a second under water.

With that I made my mind up, took out my gully, opened it with my teeth, and cut one strand after another, till the vessel only swung by two. Then I lay quiet, waiting to sever these last when the strain should be once more lightened by a breath of wind.

All this time I had heard the sound of loud voices from the cabin; but, to say truth, my mind had been so entirely taken up with other thoughts that I had scarcely given ear. Now, however, when I had nothing else to do, I began to pay more heed.

One I recognized for the coxswain's, Israel Hands, that had been Flint's gunner in former days. The other was, of course, my friend of the red night-cap. Both men were plainly the worse of drink, and they were still drinking; for, even while I was listening, one of them, with a drunken cry, opened the stern window and threw out something, which I divined to be an empty bottle. But they were not only tipsy; it was plain that they were furiously angry. Oaths flew like hailstones, and every now and then there came forth such an explosion as I thought was sure to end in blows. But each time the quarrel passed off, and the voices grumbled lower for a while, until the next crisis came, and, in its turn, passed away without result.

On shore, I could see the glow of the great camp fire burning warmly through the shore-side trees. Someone was singing, a dull, old, droning sailors' song, with a droop and a quaver at the end of every verse, and seemingly no end to it at all but the patience of the singer. I had heard it on the voyage more than once, and remembered these words:

> But one man of her crew alive,
> What put to sea with seventy-five.

And I thought it was a ditty rather too dolefully appropriate for a company that had met such cruel losses in the morning. But, indeed, from what I saw, all these buccaneers were as callous as the sea they sailed on.

At last the breeze came; the schooner sidled and drew nearer in the dark; I felt the hawser slacken once more, and with a good, tough effort, cut the last fibres through.

The breeze had but little action on the coracle, and I was almost instantly swept against the bows of the *Hispaniola*. At the same time the schooner began to turn upon her heel, spinning slowly, end for end, across the current.

I wrought like a fiend, for I expected every moment to be swamped; and since I found I could not push the coracle directly off, I now shoved straight astern. At length I was clear of my dangerous neighbour; and just as I gave the last impulsion, my hands came across a light cord that was trailing overboard across the stern bulwarks. Instantly I grasped it.

Why I should have done so I can hardly say. It was at first mere instinct; but once I had it in my hands, and found it fast, curiosity began to get the upper hand, and I determined I should have one look through the cabin window.

I pulled in hand over hand on the cord, and, when I judged myself near enough, rose at infinite risk to about half my height, and thus commanded the roof and a slice of the interior of the cabin.

By this time the schooner and her little consort were gliding pretty swiftly through the water; indeed, we had already fetched up level with the camp fire. The ship was talking, as sailors say, loudly, treading the innumerable ripples with an incessant weltering splash; and until I got my eye above the window-sill I could not comprehend why the watchmen had taken no alarm. One glance, however, was sufficient; and it was only one glance that I durst take from that unsteady skiff. It showed me Hands and his companion locked together in deadly wrestle, each with a hand upon the other's throat.

I dropped upon the thwart again, none too soon, for I was near overboard. I could see nothing for the moment but these two furious encrimsoned faces, swaying together under the smoky lamp; and I shut my eyes to let them grow once more familiar with the darkness.

The endless ballad had come to an end at last, and the whole diminished company about the camp fire had broken into the chorus I had heard so often:

Fifteen men on the dead man's chest –
Yo-ho-ho, and a bottle of rum!
Drink and the devil had done for the rest –
Yo-ho-ho, and a bottle of rum!'

I was just thinking how busy drink and the devil were at that very moment in the cabin of the *Hispaniola*, when I was surprised by a sudden lurch of the coracle. At the same moment she yawed sharply and seemed to change her course. The speed in the meantime had strangely increased.

I opened my eyes at once. All round me were little ripples, combing over with a sharp, bristling sound and slightly phosphorescent. The *Hispaniola* herself, a few yards in whose wake I was still being whirled along, seemed to stagger in her course, and I saw her spars toss a little against the blackness of the night; nay, as I looked longer, I made sure she also was wheeling to the southward.

I glanced over my shoulder, and my heart jumped against my ribs. There, right behind me, was the glow of the camp fire. The current had turned at right angles, sweeping round along with it the tall schooner and the little dancing coracle; ever quickening, ever bubbling higher, ever muttering louder, it went spinning through the narrows for the open sea.

Suddenly the schooner in front of me gave a violent yaw, turning, perhaps, through twenty degrees; and almost at the same moment one shout followed another from on board; I could hear feet pounding on the companion ladder; and I knew that the two drunkards had at last been interrupted in their quarrel and awakened to a sense of their disaster.

I lay down flat in the bottom of that wretched skiff, and devoutly recommended my spirit to its Maker. At the end of the straits, I made sure we must fall into some bar of raging breakers, where all my troubles would be ended speedily; and though I could, perhaps, bear to die, I could not bear to look upon my fate as it approached.

So I must have lain for hours, continually beaten to and fro upon the billows, now and again wetted with flying sprays, and never ceasing to expect death at the next plunge. Gradually weariness grew upon me; a numbness, an occasional stupor, fell upon my mind even in the midst of my terrors; until sleep at last supervened, and in my sea-tossed coracle I lay and dreamed of home and the old 'Admiral Benbow'.

CHAPTER THREE

The Cruise of the Coracle

IT WAS BROAD DAY WHEN I awoke, and found myself tossing at the south-west end of Treasure Island. The sun was up, but was still hid from me behind the great bulk of the Spy-glass, which on this side descended almost to the sea in formidable cliffs.

Haulbowline Head and Mizzen-mast Hill were at my elbow; the hill bare and dark, the head bound with cliffs forty or fifty feet high, and fringed with great masses of fallen rock. I was scarce a quarter of a mile to seaward, and it was my first thought to paddle in and land.

That notion was soon given over. Among the fallen rocks the breakers spouted and bellowed; loud reverberations, heavy sprays flying and falling, succeeded one another from second to second; and I saw myself, if I ventured nearer, dashed to death upon the rough shore or spending my strength in vain to scale the beetling crags.

Nor was that all; for crawling together on flat tables of rock, or letting themselves drop into the sea with loud reports, I beheld huge slimy monsters – soft snails, as it were, of incredible bigness – two or three score of them together, making the rocks to echo with their barkings.

I have understood since that they were sea-lions, and entirely harmless. But the look of them, added to the difficulty of the shore and the high running of the surf, was more than enough to disgust me of that landing-place. I felt willing rather to starve at sea than to confront such perils.

In the meantime I had a better chance, as I supposed, before me. North of Haulbowline Head, the land runs in a long way, leaving, at low tide, a long stretch of yellow sand. To the north of that, again, there comes another cape – Cape of the Woods, as it was marked upon the chart – buried in tall green pines, which descended to the margin of the sea.

I remembered what Silver had said about the current that sets northwards along the whole west coast of Treasure Island; and seeing from my position that I was already under its influence, I preferred to leave Haulbowline Head behind me, and reserve my strength for an attempt to land upon the kindlier-looking Cape of the Woods.

There was a great, smooth swell upon the sea. The wind blowing steady and gentle from the south, there was no contrariety between that and the current, and the billows rose and fell unbroken.

Had it been otherwise, I must long ago have perished; but as it was, it is surprising how easily and securely my little and light boat could ride. Often, as I still lay at the bottom, and kept no more than an eye above the gunwale, I would see a big blue summit heaving close above me; yet the coracle would but bounce a little, dance as if on springs, and subside on the other side into the trough as lightly as a bird.

I began after a little to grow very bold, and sat up to try my skill at paddling. But even a small change in the disposition of the weight will produce violent changes in the behaviour of a coracle. And I had hardly moved before the boat, giving up at once her gentle dancing movement, ran straight down a slope of water so steep that it made me giddy, and struck her nose, with a spout of spray, deep into the side of the next wave.

I was drenched and terrified, and fell instantly back into my old position, whereupon the coracle seemed to find her head again, and led me as softly as before among the billows. It was plain she was not to be interfered with, and at that rate, since I could in no way influence her course, what hope had I left of reaching land?

I began to be horribly frightened, but I kept my head, for all that. First, moving with all care, I gradually baled out the coracle with my sea-cap; then getting my eye once more above the gunwale, I set myself to study how it was she managed to slip so quietly through the rollers.

I found each wave, instead of the big, smooth, glossy mountain it looks from shore, or from a vessel's deck, was for all the world like any range of hills on the dry land, full of peaks and smooth places and valleys. The coracle, left to herself, turning from side to side, threaded, so to speak, her way through these lower parts, and avoided the steep slopes and higher, toppling summits of the wave.

'Well, now,' thought I to myself, 'it is plain I must lie where I am, and not disturb the balance; but it is plain, also, that I can put the paddle over the side, and from time to time, in smooth places, give her a shove or two towards land.' No sooner thought than done. There I lay on my elbows, in the most trying attitude, and every now and again gave a weak stroke or two to turn her head to shore.

It was very tiring and slow work, yet I did visibly gain ground; and, as we drew near the Cape of the Woods, though I saw I must infallibly miss that point, I had still made some hundred yards of easting. I was, indeed, close in. I could see the cool, green tree-tops swaying together in the breeze, and I felt sure I should make the next promontory without fail.

It was high time, for I now began to be tortured with thirst. The glow of the sun from above, its thousandfold reflection from the waves, the sea-water that fell and dried upon me, caking my very lips with salt, combined to make my throat burn and my brain ache. The sight of the trees so near at hand had almost made me sick with longing; but the current had soon carried me past the point; and, as the next reach of sea opened out, I beheld a sight that changed the nature of my thoughts.

Right in front of me, not half a mile away, I beheld the Hispaniola under sail. I made sure, of course, that I should be taken; but I was so distressed for want of water that I scarce knew whether to be glad or sorry at the thought; and, long before I had come to a conclusion, surprise had taken entire possession of my mind, and I could do nothing but stare and wonder.

The Hispaniola was under her main-sail and two jibs, and the beautiful white canvas shone in the sun like snow or silver. When I first sighted her, all her sails were drawing; she was lying a course about north-west; and I presumed the men on board were going round the island on their way back to the anchorage. Presently she began to fetch more and more to the westward, so that I thought they had sighted me and were going about in chase. At last, however, she fell right into the wind's eye, was taken dead aback, and stood there awhile helpless, with her sails shivering.

'Clumsy fellows,' said I; 'they must still be drunk as owls.' And I thought how Captain Smollett would have set them skipping.

Meanwhile, the schooner gradually fell off, and filled again upon another tack, sailed swiftly for a minute or so, and brought up once more dead in the wind's eye. Again and again this was repeated. To and fro, up and down, north, south, east, and west, the Hispaniola sailed by swoops and dashes, and at each repetition ended as she had begun, with idly flapping canvas. It became plain to me that nobody was steering. And, if so, where were the men? Either they were dead drunk, or had deserted her, I thought, and perhaps if I could get on board, I might return the vessel to her captain.

The current was bearing coracle and schooner southward at an equal rate. As for the latter's sailing, it was so wild and intermittent, and she hung each time so long in irons, that she certainly gained nothing, if she did not even lose. If only I dared to sit up and paddle, I made sure that I could overhaul her. The scheme had an air of adventure that inspired me, and the thought of the water-breaker beside the fore companion doubled my growing courage.

Up I got, was welcomed almost instantly by another cloud of spray, but this time stuck to my purpose; and set myself, with all my strength and caution, to paddle after the unsteered Hispaniola. Once I shipped a sea so heavy that I had to stop and bale, with my heart fluttering like a bird; but gradually I got into the way of the thing, and guided my coracle among the waves, with only now and then a blow upon her bows and a dash of foam in my face.

I was now gaining rapidly on the schooner; I could see the brass glisten on the tiller as it banged about; and still no soul appeared upon her decks. I could not choose but suppose she was deserted. If not, the men were lying drunk below, where I might batten them down, perhaps, and do what I chose with the ship.

For some time she had been doing the worst thing possible for me – standing still. She headed nearly due south, yawing, of course, all the time. Each time she fell off her sails partly filled, and these brought her, in a moment, right to the wind again. I have said this was the worst thing possible for me; for, helpless as she looked in this situation, with the canvas cracking like cannon, and the blocks trundling and banging on the deck, she still continued to run away from me, not only with the speed of the current, but by the whole amount of her leeway, which was naturally great.

But now, at last, I had my chance. The breeze fell, for some seconds, very low, and the current gradually turning her, the *Hispaniola* revolved slowly round her centre, and at last presented me her stern, with the cabin window still gaping open, and the lamp over the table still burning on into the day. The main-sail hung drooped like a banner. She was stock-still, but for the current.

For the last little while I had even lost; but now redoubling my efforts, I began once more to overhaul the chase.

I was not a hundred yards from her when the wind came again in a clap; she filled on the port tack, and was off again, stooping and skimming like a swallow.

My first impulse was one of despair, but my second was towards joy. Round she came, till she was broadside on to me – round still till she had covered a half, and then two-thirds, and then three-quarters of the distance that separated us. I could see the waves boiling white under her forefoot. Immensely tall she looked to me from my low station in the coracle.

And then, of a sudden, I began to comprehend. I had scarce time to think – scarce time to act and save myself. I was on the summit of one swell when the schooner came swooping over the next. The bowsprit was over my head, I sprang to my feet, and leaped, stamping the coracle under water. With one hand I caught the jib-boom, while my foot was lodged between the stay and the brace; and as I still clung there panting, a dull blow told me that the schooner had charged down upon and struck the coracle, and that I was left without retreat on the *Hispaniola*.

CHAPTER FOUR

I Strike the Jolly Roger

I HAD SCARCE GAINED A position on the bowsprit, when the flying jib flapped and filled upon the other tack, with a report like a gun. The schooner trembled to her keel under the reverse; but next moment, the other sails still drawing, the jib flapped back again, and hung idle.

This had nearly tossed me off into the sea; and now I lost no time, crawled back along the bowsprit, and tumbled head foremost on the deck.

I was on the lee side of the forecastle, and the main-sail, which was still drawing, concealed from me a certain portion of the after-deck. Not a soul was to be seen. The planks, which had not been swabbed since the mutiny, bore the print of many feet; and an empty bottle, broken by the neck, tumbled to and fro like a live thing in the scuppers.

Suddenly the *Hispaniola* came right into the wind. The jibs behind me cracked aloud; the rudder slammed to; the whole ship gave a sickening heave and shudder, and at the same moment the main-boom swung inboard, the sheet groaning in the blocks, and showed me the lee after-deck.

There were the two watchmen, sure enough; Red-cap on his back, as stiff as a handspike, with his arms stretched out like those of a crucifix, and his teeth showing through his open lips; Israel Hands propped against the bulwarks, his chin on his chest, his hands lying open before him on the deck, his face as white, under its tan, as a tallow candle.

For a while the ship kept bucking and sidling like a vicious horse, the sails filling, now on one tack, now on another, and the boom swinging to and fro till the mast groaned aloud under the strain. Now and again, too, there would come a cloud of light sprays over the bulwark, and a heavy blow of the ship's bows against the swell; so much heavier weather was made of it by this great rigged ship than by my home-made, lop-sided coracle, now gone to the bottom of the sea.

At every jump of the schooner, Red-cap slipped to and fro; but – what was ghastly to behold – neither his attitude nor his fixed teeth-disclosing grin was anyway disturbed by this rough usage. At every jump, too, Hands appeared still more to sink into himself and settle down upon the deck, his feet sliding ever the further out, and the whole body canting towards the stern, so that his face became, little by little, hid from me; and at last I could see nothing beyond his ear and the frayed ringlet of one whisker.

At the same time, I observed, around both of them, splashes of dark blood upon the planks, and began to feel sure that they had killed each other in their drunken wrath.

While I was thus looking and wondering, in a calm moment, when the ship was still, Israel Hands turned partly round, and, with a low moan, writhed himself back to the position in which I had seen him first. The moan, which told of pain and deadly weakness, and the way in which his jaw hung open, went right to my heart. But when I remembered the talk I had overheard from the apple barrel, all pity left me.

I walked aft until I reached the main-mast.

'Come aboard, Mr Hands,' I said ironically.

He rolled his eyes round heavily; but he was too far gone to express surprise. All he could do was to utter one word: 'Brandy.'

It occurred to me there was no time to lose; and dodging the boom as it once more lurched across the deck, I slipped aft, and down the companion-stairs into the cabin.

It was such a scene of confusion as you can hardly fancy. All the lock-fast places had been broken open in quest of the chart. The floor was thick with mud, where ruffians had sat down to drink or consult after wading in the marshes round their camp. The bulkheads, all painted in clear white, and beaded round with gilt, bore a pattern of dirty hands. Dozens of empty bottles clinked together in corners to the rolling of the ship. One of the doctor's medical books lay open on the table, half of the leaves gutted out, I suppose, for pipe-lights. In the midst of all this the lamp still cast a smoky glow, obscure and brown as umber.

I went into the cellar; all the barrels were gone, and of the bottles a most surprising number had been drunk out and thrown away. Certainly, since the mutiny began, not a man of them could ever have been sober.

Foraging about, I found a bottle with some brandy left, for Hands; and for myself I routed out some biscuit, some pickled fruits, a great bunch of raisins, and a piece of cheese. With these I came on deck, put down my own stock behind the rudder-head, and well out of the coxswain's reach, went forward to the water-breaker, and had a good deep drink of water, and then, and not till then, gave Hands the brandy.

He must have drunk a gill before he took the bottle from his mouth.

'Ay,' said he, 'by thunder, but I wanted some o' that!'

I had sat down already in my own corner and begun to eat.

'Much hurt?' I asked him.

He grunted, or rather I might say, he barked.

'If that doctor was aboard,' he said, 'I'd be right enough in a couple of turns; but I don't have no manner of luck, you see, and that's what's the matter with me. As for that swab, he's good and dead, he is,' he added, indicating the man with the red cap. 'He warn't no seaman, anyhow. And where mought you have come from?'

'Well,' said I, 'I've come aboard to take possession of this ship, Mr Hands; and you'll please regard me as your captain until further notice.'

He looked at me sourly enough, but said nothing. Some of the colour had come back into his cheeks, though he still looked very sick, and still continued to slip out and settle down as the ship banged about.

'By the by,' I continued, 'I can't have these colours, Mr Hands; and, by your leave, I'll strike 'em. Better none than these,'

And, again dodging the boom, I ran to the colour lines, handed down their cursed black flag, and chucked it overboard.

'God save the king!' said I, waving my cap; 'and there's an end to Captain Silver!'

He watched me keenly and slyly, his chin all the while on his breast.

'I reckon,' he said at last – 'I reckon, Cap'n Hawkins, you'll kind of want to get ashore, now. S'pose we talks.'

'Why, yes,' says I, 'with all my heart, Mr Hands. Say on.' And I went back to my meal with a good appetite.

'This man,' he began, nodding feebly at the corpse – 'O'Brien were his name – a rank Irelander – this man and me got the canvas on her, meaning for to sail her back. Well, *he*'s dead now, he is – as dead as bilge; and who's to sail this ship, I don't see. Without I gives you a hint, you ain't that man, as far's I can tell. Now, look here, you gives me food and drink, and a old scarf or ankecher to tie my wound up, you do; and I'll tell you how to sail her; and that's about square all round, I take it.'

'I'll tell you one thing,' says I: 'I'm not going back to Captain Kidd's anchorage. I mean to get into North Inlet, and beach her quietly there.'

'To be sure you did,' he cried. 'Why, I ain't sich an infernal lubber, after all. I can see, can't I? I've tried my fling, I have, and I've lost, and it's you has the wind of me. North Inlet? Why, I haven't no ch'ice, not I! I'd help you sail her up to Execution Dock, by thunder! so I would.'

Well, as it seemed to me, there was some sense in this. We struck our bargain on the spot. In three minutes I had the *Hispaniola* sailing easily before the wind along the coast of Treasure Island, with good hopes of turning the northern point ere noon, and beating down again as far as North Inlet before high water, when we might beach her safely, and wait till the subsiding tide permitted us to land.

Then I lashed the tiller and went below to my own chest, where I got a soft silk handkerchief of my mother's. With this, and with my aid, Hands bound up the great bleeding stab he had received in the thigh, and after he had eaten a little and had a swallow or two more of the brandy, he began to pick up visibly, sat straighter up, spoke louder and clearer, and looked in every way another man.

The breeze served us admirably. We skimmed before it like a bird, the coast of the island flashing by, and the view changing every minute. Soon we were past the high lands and bowling beside low, sandy country, sparsely dotted with dwarf pines, and soon we were beyond that again, and had turned the corner of the rocky hill that ends the island on the north.

I was greatly elated with my new command, and pleased with the bright, sunshiny weather and these different prospects of the coast. I had now plenty of water and good things to eat, and my conscience, which had smitten me hard for my desertion, was quieted by the great conquest I had made. I should, I think, have had nothing left me to desire but for the eyes of the coxswain as they followed me derisively about the deck, and the odd smile that appeared continually on his face. It was a smile that had in it something both of pain and weakness – a haggard, old man's smile; but there was, besides that, a grain of derision, a shadow of treachery, in his expression as he craftily watched, and watched, and watched me at my work.

CHAPTER FIVE

Israel Hands

THE WIND, SERVING US to a desire, now hauled into the west. We could run so much the easier from the north-east corner of the island to the mouth of the North Inlet. Only, as we had no power to anchor, and dared not beach her till the tide had flowed a good deal further, time hung on our hands. The coxswain told me how to lay the ship to; after a good many trials I succeeded, and we both sat in silence over another meal.

'Cap'n,' said he, at length, with that same uncomfortable smile, 'here's my old shipmate, O'Brien; s'pose you was to heave him overboard. I ain't partic'ler as a rule, and I don't take no blame for settling his hash; but I don't reckon him ornamental, now, do you?'

'I'm not strong enough, and I don't like the job; and there he lies, for me,' said I.

'This here's an unlucky ship – this *Hispaniola*, Jim,' he went on, blinking. 'There's a power of men been killed in this *Hispaniola* – a sight o' poor seamen dead and gone since you and me took ship to Bristol. I never seen sich dirty luck, not I. There was this here O'Brien, now – he's dead, ain't he? Well, now, I'm no scholar, and you're a lad as can read and figure; and to put it straight, do you take it as a dead man is dead for good, or do he come alive again?'

'You can kill the body, Mr Hands, but not the spirit; you must know that already,'

I replied. 'O'Brien there is in another world, and maybe watching us.'

'Ah!' says he. 'Well, that's unfort'nate – appears as if killing parties was a waste of time. Howsomever, sperrits don't reckon for much, by what I've seen. I'll chance it with the sperrits, Jim. And now, you've spoke up free, and I'll take it kind if you'd step down into that there cabin and get me a – well, a – shiver my timbers! I can't hit the name on 't; well, you get me a bottle of wine, Jim – this here brandy's too strong for my head.'

Now, the coxswain's hesitation seemed to be unnatural; and as for the notion of his preferring wine to brandy, I entirely disbelieved it. The whole story was a pretext. He wanted me to leave the deck – so much was plain; but with what purpose I could in no way imagine. His eyes never met mine; they kept wandering to and fro, up and down, now with a look to the sky, now with a flitting glance upon the dead O'Brien. All the time he kept smiling, and putting his tongue out in the most guilty, embarrassed manner, so that a child could have told that he was bent on some deception. I was prompt with my answer, however, for I saw where my advantage lay; and that with a fellow so densely stupid I could easily conceal my suspicions to the end.

'Some wine?' I said. 'Far better. Will you have white or red?'

'Well, I reckon it's about the blessed same to me, shipmate,' he replied; 'so it's strong, and plenty of it, what's the odds?'

'All right,' I answered. 'I'll bring you port, Mr Hands. But I'll have to dig for it.'

With that I scuttled down the companion with all the noise I could, slipped off my shoes, ran quietly along the sparred gallery, mounted the forecastle ladder, and popped my head out of the fore companion. I knew he would not expect to see me there; yet I took every precaution possible; and certainly the worst of my suspicions proved too true.

He had risen from his position to his hands and knees; and, though his leg obviously hurt him pretty sharply when he moved – for I could hear him stifle a groan – yet it was at a good, rattling rate that he trailed himself across the deck. In half a minute he had reached the port scuppers, and picked out of a coil of rope a long knife, or rather a short dirk, discoloured to the hilt with blood. He looked upon it for a moment, thrusting forth his under-jaw, tried the point upon his hand, and then, hastily concealing it in the bosom of his jacket, trundled back again into his old place against the bulwark.

This was all that I required to know. Israel could move about; he was now armed; and if he had been at so much trouble to get rid of me, it was plain that I was meant to be the victim. What he would do afterwards – whether he would try to crawl right across the island from North Inlet to the camp among the swamps, or whether he would fire Long Tom, trusting that his own comrades might come first to help him, was, of course, more than I could say.

Yet I felt sure I could trust him in one point, since in that our interests jumped together, and that was in the disposition of the schooner. We both desired to have her stranded safe enough, in a sheltered place, and so that, when the time came, she could be got off again with as little labour and danger as might be; and until that was done I considered that my life would certainly be spared.

While I was thus turning the business over in my mind, I had not been idle with my body. I had stolen back to the cabin, slipped once more into my shoes, and laid my hand at random on a bottle of wine, and now, with this for an excuse, I made my reappearance on the deck.

Hands lay as I had left him, all fallen through in a bundle, and with his eyelids lowered, as though he were too weak to bear the light. He looked up, however, at my coming, knocked the neck off the bottle, like a man who had done the same thing often, and took a good swig with his favourite toast of 'Here's luck!' Then he lay quiet for a little, and then, pulling out a stick of tobacco, begged me to cut him a quid.

'Cut me a junk o' that,' says he, 'for I haven't no knife, and hardly strength enough, so be as I had. Ah, Jim, Jim, I reckon I've missed stays! Cut me a quid, as'll likely be the last, lad; for I'm for my long home, and no mistake.'

'Well,' said I, 'I'll cut you some tobacco; but if I was you and thought myself so badly, I would go to my prayers, like a Christian man.'

'Why?' said he. 'Now, you tell me why.'

'Why?' I cried. 'You were asking me just now about the dead. You've broken your trust; you've lived in sin and lies and blood; there's a man you killed lying at your feet this moment; and you ask me why! For God's mercy, Mr Hands, that's why.'

I spoke with a little heat, thinking of the bloody dirk he had hidden in his pocket, and designed, in his ill thoughts, to end me with. He, for his part, took a great draught of the wine, and spoke with the most unusual solemnity.

'For thirty years,' he said, 'I've sailed the seas, and seen good and bad, better and worse, fair weather and foul, provisions running out, knives going, and what not. Well, now I tell you, I never seen good come o' goodness yet. Him as strikes first is my fancy; dead men don't bite; them's my views – amen, so be it. And now, you look here,' he added, suddenly changing his tone, 'we've had about enough of this foolery. The tide's made good enough by now. You just take my orders, Cap'n Hawkins, and we'll sail slap in and be done with it.'

All told, we had scarce two miles to run; but the navigation was delicate, the entrance to this northern anchorage was not only narrow and shoal, but lay east and west, so that the schooner must be nicely handled to be got in. I think I was a good, prompt subaltern, and I am very sure that Hands was an excellent pilot; for we went about and about, and dodged in, shaving the banks, with a certainty and a neatness that were a pleasure to behold.

Scarcely had we passed the heads before the land closed around us. The shores of North Inlet were as thickly wooded as those of the southern anchorage; but the space was longer and narrower, and more like, what in truth it was, the estuary of a river. Right before us, at the southern end, we saw the wreck of a ship in the last stages of dilapidation. It had been a great vessel of three masts, but had lain so long exposed to the injuries of the weather, that it was hung about with great webs of dripping seaweed, and on the deck of it shore bushes had taken root, and now flourished thick with flowers. It was a sad sight, but it showed us that the anchorage was calm.

'Now,' said Hands, 'look there; there's a pet bit for to beach a ship in. Fine flat sand, never a catspaw, trees all around of it, and flowers a-blowing like a garding on that old ship.'

'And once beached,' I inquired, 'how shall we get her off again?'

'Why, so,' he replied; 'you take a line ashore there on the other side at low water: take a turn about one o'them big pines; bring it back, take a turn round the capstan, and lie-to for the tide. Come high water, all hands take a pull upon line, and off she comes as sweet as natur'. And now, boy, you stand by. We're near the bit now, and she's too much way on her. Starboard a little – so – steady – starboard – larboard a little – steady – steady!'

So he issued his commands, which I breathlessly obeyed; till, all of a sudden, he cried: 'Now, my hearty, luff!' And I put the helm hard up, and the *Hispaniola* swung round rapidly, and ran stem on for the low wooded shore.

The excitement of these last manœuvres had somewhat interfered with the watch I had kept hitherto, sharply enough, upon the coxswain. Even then I was still so much interested, waiting for the ship to touch, that I had quite forgot the peril that hung over my head, and stood craning over the starboard bulwarks and watching the ripples spreading wide before the bows. I might have fallen without a struggle for my life, had not a sudden disquietude seized upon me, and made me turn my head. Perhaps I had heard a creak, or seen his shadow moving with the tail of my eye; perhaps it was an instinct like a cat's; but, sure enough, when I looked round, there was Hands, already half-way towards me, with the dirk in his right hand.

We must both have cried out aloud when our eyes met; but while mine was the shrill cry of terror, his was a roar of fury like a charging bull's. At the same instant he threw himself forward, and I leapt sideways towards the bows. As I did so, I left hold of the tiller, which sprang sharp to leeward; and I think this saved my life, for it struck Hands across the chest, and stopped him, for the moment, dead.

Before he could recover, I was safe out of the corner where he had me trapped, with all the deck to dodge about. Just forward of the mainmast I stopped, drew a pistol from my pocket, took a cool aim, though he had already turned and was once more coming directly after me, and drew the trigger. The hammer fell, but there followed neither flash nor sound; the priming was useless with sea water. I cursed myself for my neglect. Why had not I, long before, reprimed and reloaded my only weapons? Then I should not have been, as now, a mere fleeing sheep before this butcher.

Wounded as he was, it was wonderful how fast he could move, his grizzled hair tumbling over his face, and his face itself as red as a red ensign with his haste and fury. I had no time to try my other pistol, nor, indeed, much inclination, for I was sure it would be useless. One thing I saw plainly: I must not simply retreat before him, or he would speedily hold me boxed into the bows, as a moment since he had so nearly boxed me in the stern. Once so caught, and nine or ten inches of the blood-stained dirk would be my last experience on this side of eternity. I placed my palms against the mainmast, which was of a goodish bigness, and waited, every nerve upon the stretch.

Seeing that I meant to dodge, he also paused; and a moment or two passed in feints on his part, and corresponding movements upon mine. It was such a game as I had often played at home about the rocks of Black Hill Cove; but never before, you may be sure, with such a wildly beating heart as now. Still, as I say, it was a boy's game, and I thought I could hold my own at it, against an elderly seaman with a wounded thigh. Indeed, my courage had begun to rise so high, that I allowed myself a few darting thoughts on what would be the end of the affair; and while I saw certainly that I could spin it out for long, I saw no hope of any ultimate escape.

Well, while things stood thus, suddenly the *Hispaniola* struck, staggered, ground for an instant in the sand, and then, swift as a blow, canted over to the port side, till the deck stood at an angle of forty-five degrees, and about a puncheon of water splashed into the scupper holes, and lay, in a pool, between the deck and bulwark.

We were both of us capsized in a second, and both of us rolled, almost together, into the scuppers; the dead Red-cap, with his arms still spread out, tumbling stiffly after us. So near were we, indeed, that my head came against the coxswain's foot with a crack that made my teeth rattle. Blow and all, I was the first afoot again; for Hands had got involved with the dead body. The sudden canting of the ship had made the deck no place for running on; I had to find some new way of escape, and that upon this instant, for my foe was almost touching me. Quick as thought I sprang into the mizzen shrouds, rattled up hand over hand, and did not draw a breath till I was seated on the cross-trees.

I had been saved by being prompt; the dirk had struck not half a foot below me, as I pursued my upward flight; and there stood Israel Hands with his mouth open and his face upturned to mine, a perfect statue of surprise and disappointment.

Now that I had a moment to myself, I lost no time in changing the priming of my pistol, and then, having one ready for service, and to make assurance doubly sure, I proceeded to draw the load of the other, and recharge it afresh from the beginning.

My new employment struck Hands all of a heap; he began to see the dice going against him; and after an obvious hesitation, he also hauled himself heavily into the shrouds, and, with the dirk in his teeth, began slowly and painfully to mount. It cost him no end of time and groans to haul his wounded leg behind him; and I had quietly finished my arrangements before he was much more than a third of the way up. Then, with a pistol in either hand, I addressed him.

'One more step, Mr Hands,' said I, 'and I'll blow your brains out! Dead men don't bite, you know,' I added, with a chuckle.

He stopped instantly. I could see by the working of his face that he was trying to think, and the process was so slow and laborious that, in my new-found security, I laughed aloud. At last, with a swallow or two, he spoke, his face still wearing the same expression of extreme perplexity. In order to speak he had to take the dagger from his mouth, but in all else he remained unmoved.

'Jim,' says he, 'I reckon we're fouled, you and me, and we'll have to sign articles. I'd have had you but for that there lurch; but I don't have no luck, not I; and I reckon I'll have to strike, which comes hard, you see, for a master mariner, to a ship's younker like you, Jim.'

I was drinking in his words and smiling away, as conceited as a cock upon a wall, when, all in a breath, back went his right hand over his shoulder. Something sang like an arrow through the air; I felt a blow and then a sharp pang, and there I was pinned by the shoulder to the mast. In the horrid pain and surprise of the moment – I scarce can say it was by my own volition, and I am sure it was without a conscious aim – both my pistols went off, and both escaped out of my hands. They did not fall alone; with a choked cry, the coxswain loosed his grasp upon the shrouds, and plunged head first into the water.

CHAPTER SIX

'Pieces of Eight'

OWING TO THE CANT OF the vessel, the masts hung far out over the water, and from my perch on the cross-trees I had nothing below me but the surface of the bay. Hands, who was not so far up, was, in consequence, nearer to the ship, and fell between me and the bulwarks. He rose once to the surface in a lather of foam and blood, and then sank again for good. As the water settled I could see him lying huddled together on the clean, bright sand in the shadow of the vessel's sides. A fish or two whipped past his body. Sometimes, by the quivering of the water, he appeared to move a little, as if he were trying to rise. But he was dead enough, for all that, being shot and drowned, and was food for fish in the very place where he had designed my slaughter.

I was no sooner certain of this than I began to feel sick, faint, and terrified. The hot blood was running over my back and chest. The dirk, where it had pinned my shoulder to the mast, seemed to burn like a hot iron; yet it was not so much these real sufferings that distressed me, for these, it seemed to me, I could bear without a murmur; it was the horror I had upon my mind of falling from the cross-trees into that still green water, beside the body of the coxswain.

I clung with both hands till my nails ached, and I shut my eyes as if to cover up the peril. Gradually my mind came back again, my pulses quieted down to a more natural time, and I was once more in possession of myself.

It was my first thought to pluck forth the dirk; but either it stuck too hard or my nerve failed me; and I desisted with a violent shudder. Oddly enough, that very shudder did the business. The knife, in fact, had come the nearest in the world to missing me altogether; it held me by a mere pinch of skin, and this the shudder tore away. The blood ran down the faster, to be sure; but I was my own master again, and only tacked to the mast by my coat and shirt.

These last I broke through with a sudden jerk, and then regained the deck by the starboard shrouds. For nothing in the world would I have again ventured, shaken as I was, upon the overhanging port shrouds, from which Israel had so lately fallen.

I went below, and did what I could for my wound; it pained me a good deal, and still bled freely; but it was neither deep nor dangerous, nor did it greatly gall me when I used my arm. Then I looked around me, and as the ship was now, in a sense, my own, I began to think of clearing it from its last passenger – the dead man, O'Brien.

He had pitched, as I have said, against the bulwarks, where he lay like some horrible, ungainly sort of puppet; life-sized, indeed, but how different from life's colour or life's comeliness! In that position, I could easily have my way with him; and as the habit of tragical adventures had worn off almost all my terror for the dead, I took him by the waist as if he had been a sack of bran, and, with one good heave, tumbled him overboard. He went in with a sounding plunge; the red cap came off, and remained floating on the surface; and as soon as the splash subsided, I could see him and Israel lying side by side, both wavering with the tremulous movement of the water. O'Brien, though still quite a young man, was very bald. There he lay, with that bald head across the knees of the man who had killed him, and the quick fishes steering to and fro over both.

I was now alone upon the ship; the tide had just turned. The sun was within so few degrees of setting that already the shadow of the pines upon the western shore began to reach right across the anchorage, and fall in patterns on the deck. The evening breeze had sprung up, and though it was well warded off by the hill with the two peaks upon the east, the cordage had begun to sing a little softly to itself and the idle sails to rattle to and fro.

I began to see a danger to the ship. The jibs I speedily doused and brought tumbling to the deck; but the mainsail was a harder matter. Of course, when the schooner canted over, the boom had swung outboard, and the cap of it and a foot or two of sail hung even under water. I thought this made it still more dangerous; yet the strain was so heavy that I half feared to meddle. At last, I got my knife and cut the halyards. The peak dropped instantly, a great belly of loose canvas floated broad upon the water; and since, pull as I liked, I could not budge the downhaul, that was the extent of what I could accomplish. For the rest, the Hispaniola must trust to luck, like myself.

By this time the whole anchorage had fallen into shadow – the last rays, I remember, falling through a glade of the wood, and shining bright as jewels, on the flowery mantle of the wreck. It began to be chill; the tide was rapidly fleeting seaward, the schooner settling more and more on her beam-ends.

I scrambled forward and looked over. It seemed shallow enough, and holding the cut hawser in both hands for a last security, I let myself drop softly overboard. The water scarcely reached my waist; the sand was firm and covered with ripple marks, and I waded ashore in great spirits, leaving the Hispaniola on her side, with her main-sail trailing wide upon the surface of the bay. About the same time the sun went fairly down, and the breeze whistled low in the dusk among the tossing pines.

At least, and at last, I was off the sea, nor had I returned thence empty-handed. There lay the schooner, clear at last from buccaneers and ready for our own men to board and get to sea again. I had nothing nearer my fancy than to get home to the stockade and boast of my achievements. Possibly I might be blamed a bit for my truantry, but the recapture of the Hispaniola was a clenching answer, and I hoped that even Captain Smollett would confess I had not lost my time.

So thinking, and in famous spirits, I began to set my face homeward for the blockhouse and my companions. I remembered that the most easterly of the rivers which drain into Captain Kidd's anchorage ran from the two-peaked hill upon my left; and I bent my course in that direction that I might pass the stream while it was small. The wood was pretty open, and keeping along the lower spurs, I had soon turned the corner of the hill, and not long after waded to the mid-calf across the water-course.

This brought me near to where I had encountered Ben Gunn, the maroon;

and I walked more circumspectly, keeping an eye on every side. The dusk had come nigh hand completely, and, as I opened out the cleft between the two peaks, I became aware of a wavering glow against the sky, where, as I judged, the man of the island was cooking his supper before a roaring fire. And yet I wondered, in my heart, that he should show himself so careless. For if I could see this radiance, might it not reach the eyes of Silver himself where he camped upon the shore among the marshes?

Gradually the night fell blacker; it was all I could do to guide myself even roughly towards my destination; the double hill behind me and the Spy-glass on my right hand loomed faint and fainter; the stars were few and pale; and in the low ground where I wandered I kept tripping among bushes and rolling into sandy pits.

Suddenly a kind of brightness fell about me. I looked up; a pale glimmer of moonbeams had alighted on the summit of the Spy-glass, and soon after I saw something broad and silvery moving low down behind the trees, and knew the moon had risen.

With this to help me, I passed rapidly over what remained to me of my journey; and, sometimes walking, sometimes running, impatiently drew near to the stockade. Yet, as I began to thread the grove that lies before it, I was not so thoughtless but that I slacked my pace and went a trifle warily. It would have been a poor end of my adventures to get shot down by my own party in mistake.

The moon was climbing higher and higher; its light began to fall here and there in masses through the more open districts of the wood; and right in front of me a glow of a different colour appeared among the trees. It was red and hot, and now and again it was a little darkened – as it were the embers of a bonfire smouldering.

For the life of me, I could not think what it might mean.

At last I came right down upon the borders of the clearing. The western end was already steeped in moonshine; the rest, and the blockhouse itself, still lay in a black shadow, chequered with long, silvery streaks of light. On the other side of the house an immense fire had burned itself into clear embers and shed a steady, red reverberation, contrasted strongly with the mellow paleness of the moon. There was not a soul stirring, nor a sound beside the noises of the breeze.

I stopped, with much wonder in my heart, and perhaps a little terror also. It had not been our way to build great fires; we were, indeed, by the captain's orders, somewhat niggardly of firewood; and I began to fear that something had gone wrong while I was absent.

I stole round by the eastern end, keeping close in shadow, and at a convenient place, where the darkness was thickest, crossed the palisade.

To make assurance surer, I got upon my hands and knees, and crawled, without a sound, towards the corner of the house. As I drew nearer, my heart was suddenly and greatly lightened. It is not a pleasant noise in itself, and I have often complained of it at other times; but just them it was like music to hear my friends snoring together so loud and peaceful in their sleep. The sea-cry of the watch, that beautiful 'All's well,' never fell more reassuringly on my ear.

In the meantime, there was no doubt of one thing; they kept an infamous bad watch. If it had been Silver and his lads that were now creeping in on them, not a soul would have seen daybreak. That was what it was, thought I, to have the captain wounded; and again I blamed myself sharply for leaving them in that danger with so few to mount guard.

By this time I had got to the door and stood up. All was dark within, so that I could distinguish nothing by the eye. As for sounds, there was the steady drone of the snorers, and a small occasional noise, a flickering or pecking that I could in no way account for.

With my arms before me I walked steadily in. I should lie down in my own place (I thought, with a silent chuckle) and enjoy their faces when they found me in the morning.

My foot struck something yielding – it was a sleeper's leg; and he turned and groaned, but without awaking.

And then, all of a sudden, a shrill voice broke forth out of the darkness:

'Pieces of eight! pieces of eight! pieces of eight! pieces of eight! pieces of eight!' and so forth, without pause or change, like the clacking of a tiny mill.

Silver's green parrot, Captain Flint! It was she whom I had heard pecking at a piece of bark; it was she, keeping better watch than any human being, who thus announced my arrival with her wearisome refrain.

I had no time left me to recover. At the sharp, clipping tone of the parrot, the sleepers awoke and sprang up; and with a mighty oath, the voice of Silver cried:

'Who goes?'

I turned to run, struck violently against one person, recoiled, and ran full into the arms of a second, who, for his part, closed upon and held me tight.

'Bring a torch, Dick,' said Silver, when my capture was thus assured.

And one of the men left the log-house and presently returned with a lighted brand.

PART SIX

CHAPTER ONE

In The Enemy's Camp

THE RED GLARE OF THE torch, lighting up the interior of the blockhouse, showed me the worst of my apprehensions realized. The pirates were in possession of the house and stores; there was the cask of cognac, there were the pork and bread, as before; and, what tenfold increased my horror, not a sign of any prisoner. I could only judge that all had perished, and my heart smote me sorely that I had not been there to perish with them.

There were six of the buccaneers, all told; not another man was left alive. Five of them were on their feet, flushed and swollen, suddenly called out of the first sleep of drunkenness. The sixth had only risen upon his elbow: he was deadly pale, and the blood-stained bandage round his head told that he had recently been wounded, and still more recently dressed. I remembered the man who had been shot and had run back among the woods in the great attack, and doubted not that this was he.

The parrot sat, preening her plumage, on Long John's shoulder. He himself, I thought, looked somewhat paler and more stern that I was used to. He still wore the fine broadcloth suit in which he had fulfilled his mission, but it was bitterly the worse for wear, daubed with clay and torn with the sharp briers of the wood.

'So,' said he, 'here's Jim Hawkins, shiver my timbers! dropped in, like, eh? Well, come, I take that friendly.'

And thereupon he sat down across the brandy cask, and began to fill a pipe.

'Give me a loan of the link, Dick,' said he; and then, when he had a good light, 'That'll do, lad,' he added; 'stick the glim in the wood heap; and you, gentlemen, bring yourselves to! – you needn't stand up for Mr Hawkins; he'll excuse you, you may lay to that. And so, Jim' – stopping the tobacco – 'here you were, and quite a pleasant surprise for poor old John. I see you were smart when I first set my eyes on you; but this here gets away from me clean, it do.'

To all this, as may be well supposed, I made no answer. They had set me with my back against the wall; and I stood there, looking Silver in the face, pluckily enough, I hope, to all outward appearance, but with black despair in my heart.

Silver took a whiff or two of his pipe, with great composure, and then ran on again.

'Now, you see, Jim, so be as you *are* here,' says he, 'I'll give you a piece of my mind. I've always liked you, I have, for a lad of spirit, and the picter of my own self when I was young and handsome. I always wanted you to jine and take your share, and die a gentleman, and now, my cock, you've got to. Cap'n Smollett's a fine seaman, as I'll own up to any day, but stiff on discipline. "Dooty is dooty," says he, and right he is. Just you keep clear of the cap'n. The doctor himself is gone dead again you – "ungrateful scamp" was what he said; and the short and long of the whole story is about here: you can't go back to your own lot, for they won't have you; and without you start a third ship's company all by yourself, which might be lonely, you'll have to jine with Cap'n Silver.'

So far so good. My friends, then, were still alive, and though I partly believed the truth of Silver's statement, that the cabin party were incensed at me for my desertion, I was more relieved than distressed by what I heard.

'I don't say nothing as to your being in our hands,' continued Silver, 'though there you are, and you may lay to it. I'm all for argyment; I never seen good come out o' threatening. If you like the service, well, you'll jine; and if you don't, Jim, why, you're free to answer no – free and welcome, shipmate; and if fairer can be said by mortal seaman, shiver my sides!'

'Am I to answer, then?' I asked, with a very tremulous voice. Through all this sneering talk, I was made to feel the threat of death that overhung me, and my cheeks burned and my heart beat painfully in my breast.

'Lad,' said Silver, 'no-one's a-pressing of you. Take your bearings. None of us won't hurry you, mate; time goes so pleasant in your company, you see.'

'Well,' says I, growing a bit bolder, 'if I'm to choose, I declare I have a right to know what's what, and why you're here, and where my friends are.'

'Wot's wot?' repeated one of the buccaneers, in a deep growl. 'Ah, he'd be a lucky one as knowed that!'

'You'll, perhaps, batten down your hatches till you're spoke, my friend,' cried Silver truculently to this speaker. And then, in his first gracious tones, he replied to me: 'Yesterday morning, Mr Hawkins,' said he, 'in the dogwatch, down came Dr Livesey with a flag of truce. Says he: "Cap'n Silver, you're sold out. Ship's gone." Well, maybe we'd been taking a glass, and a song to help it round. I won't say no. Leastways none of us had looked out. We looked out, and, by thunder! the old ship was gone. I never seen a pack of fools look fishier; and you may lay to that, if I tells you that looked the fishiest. "Well," says the doctor, "let's bargain." We bargained, him and I, and here we are: stores, brandy, blockhouse, the firewood you was thoughtful enough to cut, and in a manner of speaking, the whole blessed boat from cross-trees to kelson. As for them, they've tramped; I don't know wheres they are.'

He drew again quietly at his pipe.

'And lest you should take it into that head of yours,' he went on, 'that you was included in the treaty, here's the last word that was said: "How many are you," says I, "to leave?" "Four," says he – "four, and one of us wounded. As for that boy, I don't know where he is, confound him," says he, "nor I don't much care. We're about sick of him." These was his words.'

'Is that all?' I asked.

'Well, it's all that you're to hear, my son,' returned Silver.

'And now I am to choose?'

'And now you are to choose, and you may lay to that,' said Silver.

'Well,' said I, 'I am not such a fool but I know pretty well what I have to look for. Let the worst come to the worst, it's little I care. I've seen too many die since I fell in with you. But there's a thing or two I have to tell you,' I said, and by this time I was quite excited; 'and the first is this: here you are in a bad way: ship lost, treasure lost, men lost; your whole business gone to wreck; and if you want to know who did it – it was I! I was in the apple barrel the night we sighted land, and I heard you, John, and you, Dick Johnson, and Hands, who is now at the bottom of the sea, and told every word you said before the hour was out. And as for the schooner, it was I who cut her cable, and it was I that killed the men you had aboard of her, and it was I who brought her where you'll never see her more, not one of you. The laugh's on my side; I've had the top of this business from the first; I no more fear you than I fear a fly. Kill me, if you please, or spare me. But one thing I'll say, and no more; if you spare me, bygones are bygones, and when you fellows are in court for piracy, I'll save you all I can. It is for you to choose. Kill another and do yourselves no good, or spare me and keep a witness to save you from the gallows.'

I stopped, for, I tell you, I was out of breath, and, to my wonder, not a man of them moved, but all sat staring at me like as many sheep. And while they were still staring, I broke out again:

'And now, Mr Silver,' I said, 'I believe you're the best man here, and if things go the worst, I'll take it kind if you let the doctor know the way I took it.'

'I'll bear it in mind,' said Silver, with an accent so curious that I could not, for the life of me, decide whether he were laughing at my request, or had been favourably affected by my courage.

'I'll put one to that,' cried the old mahogany-faced seaman – Morgan by name – whom I had seen in Long John's public-house upon the quays of Bristol. 'It was him that knowed Black Dog.'

'Well, and see here,' added the sea-cook, 'I'll put another again to that, by thunder! for it was this same boy that faked the chart from Billy Bones. First and last, we've split upon Jim Hawkins!'

'Then here goes!' said Morgan, with an oath.

And he sprang up, drawing his knife as if he had been twenty.

'Avast there!' cried Silver. 'Who are you, Tom Morgan? Maybe you thought you was cap'n here, perhaps. By the powers, but I'll teach you better! Cross me, and you'll go where many a good man's gone before you, first and last, these thirty years back – some to the yard-arm, shiver my sides! and some by the board, and all to feed the fishes. There's never a man looked me between the eyes and seen a good day a'terwards, Tom Morgan, you may lay to that.'

Morgan paused; but a hoarse murmur rose from the others.

'Tom's right,' said one.

'I stood hazing long enough from one,' added another. 'I'll be hanged if I'll be hazed by you, John Silver.'

'Did any of you gentlemen want to have it out with *me?*' roared Silver, bending far forward from his position on the keg, with his pipe still glowing in his right hand. 'Put a name on what you're at; you ain't dumb, I reckon. Him that wants shall get it. Have I lived this many years, and a son of a rum puncheon cock his hat athwart my hawse at the latter end of it? You know the way; you're all gentlemen o' fortune, by your account. Well, I'm ready. Take a cutlass, him that dares, and I'll see the colour of his inside, crutch and all, before that pipe's empty.'

Not a man stirred; not a man answered.

'That's your sort, is it?' he added, returning his pipe to his mouth. 'Well, you're a gay lot to look at, anyway. Not much worth to fight, you ain't. P'r'aps you can understand King George's English. I'm cap'n here by 'lection. I'm cap'n here because I'm the best man by a long sea-mile. You won't fight as gentlemen o' fortune should; then, by thunder, you'll obey, and you may lay to it! I like that boy, now; I never seen a better boy than that. He's more a man than any pair of rats of you in this here house, and what I say is this: let me see him that'll lay a hand on him – that's what I say, and you may lay to it.'

There was a long pause after this. I stood straight up against the wall, my heart still going like a sledge-hammer, but with a ray of hope now shining in my bosom. Silver leant back against the wall, his arms crossed, his pipe in the corner of his mouth, as calm as though he had been in church; yet his eye kept wandering furtively, and he kept the tail of it on his unruly followers. They, on their part, drew gradually together towards the far end of the blockhouse, and the low hiss of their whispering sounded in my ear continuously like a stream. One after another they would look up, and the red light of the torch would fall for a second on their nervous faces; but it was not towards me, it was towards Silver that they turned their eyes.

'You seem to have a lot to say,' remarked Silver, spitting far into the air. 'Pipe up and let me hear it, or lay to.'

'Ax your pardon, sir,' returned one of the men; 'you're pretty free with some of the rules; maybe you'll kindly keep an eye upon the rest. This crew's dissatisfied; this crew don't vally bullying a marlin-spike; this crew has its rights like other crews, I'll make so free as that; and by your own rules, I take it we can talk together. I ax your pardon, sir, acknowledging you for to be capting at this present; but I claim my right, and steps outside for a council.'

And with an elaborate sea-salute, this fellow, a long, ill-looking, yellow-eyed man of five-and-thirty, stepped coolly towards the door and disappeared out of the house. One after another, the rest followed his example; each making a salute as he passed; each adding some apology. 'According to rules,' said one. 'Fo'c's'le council,' said Morgan. And so with one remark or another, all marched out, and left Silver and me alone with the torch.

The sea-cook instantly removed his pipe.

'Now, look you here, Jim Hawkins,' he said, in a steady whisper, that was no more than audible, 'you're within half a plank of death, and, what's a long sight worse, of torture. They're going to throw me off. But, you mark, I stand by you through thick and thin. I didn't mean to; no, not till you spoke up. I was about desperate to lose that much blunt, and be hanged into the bargain. But I see you was the right sort. I says to myself: You stand by Hawkins, John, and Hawkins'll stand by you. You're his last card, and, by the living thunder, John, he's yours! Back to back, says I. I save your witness, and he'll save your neck!'

I began to dimly understand.

'You mean all's lost?' I asked.

'Ay, by gum, I do!' he answered. 'Ship gone, neck gone – that's the size of it. Once I looked into that bay, Jim Hawkins, and seen no schooner – well, I'm tough, but I gave out. As for that lot and their council, mark me, they're outright fools and cowards. I'll save your life – if so be as I can – from them. But, see here, Jim – tit for tat – you save Long John from swinging.'

I was bewildered; it seemed a thing so hopeless he was asking – he, the old buccaneer, the ringleader throughout.

'What I can do, that I'll do,' I said.

'It's a bargain!' cried Long John. 'You speak up plucky, and, by thunder! I've a chance.'

He hobbled to the torch, where it stood propped among the firewood, and took a fresh light to his pipe.

'Understand me, Jim,' he said, returning. 'I've a head on my shoulders, I have. I'm on squire's side now. I know you've got that ship safe somewheres. How you done it, I don't know, but safe it is. I guess Hands and O'Brien turned soft. I never much believed in neither of *them*. Now you mark me. I ask no questions, nor I won't let others. I know when a game's up, I do; and I know a lad that's staunch. Ah, you that's young – you and me might have done a power of good together!'

He drew some cognac from the cask into a tin cannikin.

'Will you taste, messmate?' he asked; and when I had refused: 'Well, I'll take a drain myself, Jim,' said he. 'I need a caulker, for there's trouble on hand. And, talking o' trouble, why did that doctor give me the chart, Jim?'

My face expressed a wonder so unaffected that he saw the needlessness of further questions.

'Ah, well, he did, though,' said he. 'And there's something under that, no doubt – something, surely, under that, Jim – bad or good.'

And he took another swallow of the brandy, shaking his great fair head like a man who looks forward to the worst.

CHAPTER TWO

The Black Spot Again

THE COUNCIL OF THE BUCCANEERS had lasted some time when one of them re-entered the house, and with a repetition of the same salute, which had in my eyes an ironical air, begged for a moment's loan of the torch. Silver briefly agreed; and this emissary retired again, leaving us together in the dark.

'There's a breeze coming, Jim,' said Silver, who had, by this time, adopted quite a friendly and familiar tone.

I turned to the loophole nearest me and looked out. The embers of the great fire had so far burned themselves out, and now glowed so low and duskily, that I understood why these conspirators desired a torch. About half-way down the slope to the stockade, they were collected in a group; one held the light; another was on his knees in their midst, and I saw the blade of an open knife shine in his hand with varying colours, in the moon and torchlight. The rest were all somewhat stooping, as though watching the manœuvres of this last. I could just make out that he had a book as well as a knife in his hand; and was still wondering how anything so incongruous had come in their possession, when the kneeling figure rose once more to his feet, and the whole party began to move together towards the house.

'Here they come,' said I; and I returned to my former position, for it seemed beneath my dignity that they should find me watching them.

'Well, let 'em come, lad – let 'em come,' said Silver, cheerily. 'I've still a shot in my locker.'

The door opened, and the five men, standing huddled together just inside, pushed one of their number forward. In any other circumstances it would have been comical to see his slow advance, hesitating as he set down each foot, but holding his closed right hand in front of him.

'Step up, lad,' cried Silver. 'I won't eat you. Hand it over, lubber. I know the rules, I do; I won't hurt a depytation.'

Thus encouraged, the buccaneer stepped forth more briskly, and having passed something to Silver, from hand to hand, slipped yet more smartly back again to his companions.

The sea-cook looked at what had been given him.

'The black spot! I thought so,' he observed. 'Where might you have got the paper? Why, hillo! look here, now: this ain't lucky! You've gone and cut this out of a Bible. What fool's cut a Bible?'

'Ah, there!' said Morgan – 'there! Wot did I say? No good'll come o' that, I said.'

'Well, you've about fixed it now among you,' continued Silver. 'You'll all swing now, I reckon. What soft-headed lubber had a Bible?'

'It was Dick,' said one.

'Dick, was it? Then Dick can get to prayers,' said Silver. 'He's seen his slice of luck, has Dick, and you may lay to that.'

But here the long man with the yellow eyes struck in.

'Belay that talk, John Silver,' he said. 'This crew has tipped you the black spot in full council, as in dooty bound; just you turn it over, as in dooty bound, and see what's wrote there. Then you can talk.'

'Thanky, George,' replied the sea-cook. 'You always was brisk for business, and has the rules by heart, George, as I'm pleased to see. Well, what is it, anyway? Ah! "Deposed" – that's it, is it? Very pretty wrote, to be sure; like print, I swear. Your hand o' write, George? Why, you was gettin' quite a leadin' man in this here crew. You'll be cap'n next, I shouldn't wonder. Just oblige me with that torch again, will you? this pipe don't draw.'

'Come, now,' said George, 'you don't fool this crew no more. You're a funny man, by your account; but you're over now, and you'll maybe step down off that barrel and help vote.'

'I thought you said you knowed the rules.' returned Silver, contemptuously. 'Leastways, if you don't, I do; and I wait here – and I'm still your cap'n, mind – till you outs with your grievances, and I reply; in the meantime, your black spot ain't worth a biscuit. After that, we'll see.'

'Oh,' replied George, 'you don't be under no kind of apprehension; we're all square, we are. First, you've made a hash of this cruise – you'll be a bold man to say no to that. Second, you let the enemy out o' this here trap for nothing. Why did they want out? I dunno; but it's pretty plain they wanted it. Third, you wouldn't let us go at them upon the march. Oh, we see through you, John Silver; you want to play booty, that's what's wrong with you. And then, fourth, there's this here boy.'

'Is that all?' asked Silver quietly.

'Enough, too,' retorted George. 'We'll all swing and sun-dry for your bungling.'

'Well, now, look here, I'll answer these four p'ints; one after another I'll answer 'em. I made a hash o' this cruise, did I? Well, now, you all know what I wanted; and you all know, if that had been done, that we'd 'a' been aboard the *Hispaniola* this night as ever was, every man of us alive, and fit, and full of good plum-duff, and the treasure in the hold of her, by thunder! Well, who crossed me? Who forced my hand, as was the lawful cap'n? Who tipped me the black spot the day we landed, and began this dance? Ah, it's a fine dance – I'm with you there – and looks mighty like a hornpipe in a rope's end at Execution Dock by London town, it does. But who done it? Why, it was Anderson, and Hands, and you, George Merry! And you're the last above board of that same meddling crew; and you have the Davy Jones's insolence to up and stand for cap'n over me – you, that sank the lot of us! By the powers; but this tops the stiffest yarn to nothing.'

Silver paused, and I could see by the faces of George and his late comrades that these words had not been said in vain.

'That's for number one,' cried the accused, wiping the sweat from his brow, for he had been talking with a vehemence that shook the house. 'Why, I give you my word, I'm sick to speak to you. You've neither sense nor memory, and I leave it to fancy where your mothers was that let you come to sea. Sea! Gentlemen o' fortune! I reckon tailors is your trade.'

'Go on, John,' said Morgan. 'Speak up to the others.'

'Ah, the others!' returned John. 'They're a nice lot, ain't they? You say this cruise is bungled. Ah! by gum, if you could understand how bad it's bungled, you would see! We're that near the gibbet that my neck's stiff with thinking on it. You've seen 'em, maybe, hanged in chains, birds about 'em, seamen p'inting 'em out as they go down with the tide. "Who's that?" says one. "That! Why, that's John Silver. I knowed him well," says another. And you can hear the chains a-jangle as you go about and reach for the other buoy. Now that's about where we are, every mother's son of us, thanks to him, and Hands, and Anderson, and other ruination fools of you. And if you want to know about number four, and that boy, why, shiver my timbers! isn't he a hostage? Are we a-going to waste a hostage? No, not us; he might be our last chance, and I shouldn't wonder. Kill that boy? not me, mates! And number three? Ah, well, there's a deal to say to number three. Maybe you don't count it nothing to have a real college doctor come to see you every day – you, John, with your head broke – or you, George Merry, that had the ague shakes upon you not six hours agone, and has your eyes the colour of lemon-peel to this same moment on the clock? And maybe, perhaps, you didn't know there was a consort coming, either? But there is; and not so long till then; and we'll see who'll be glad to have a hostage when it comes to that. And as for number two, and why I make a bargain – well, you came crawling on your knees to me to make it – on your knees you came, you was that downhearted – and you'd have starved, too, if I hadn't – but that's a trifle! you look there – that's why!'

And he cast down upon the floor a paper that I instantly recognized – none other than the chart on yellow paper, with the three red crosses, that I had found in the oilcloth at the bottom of the captain's chest. Why the doctor had given it to him was more than I could fancy.

But if it were inexplicable to me, the appearance of the chart was incredible to the surviving mutineers. They leaped upon it like cats upon a mouse. It went from hand to hand, one tearing it from another; and by the oaths and the cries and the childish laughter with which they accompanied their examination, you would have thought, not only they were fingering the very gold, but were at sea with it, besides, in safety.

'Yes,' said one, 'that's Flint, sure enough. J. F., and a score below with a clove hitch to it; so he done ever.'

'Mighty pretty,' said George. 'But how are we to get away with it, and us no ship?'

Silver suddenly sprang up, and supporting himself with a hand against the wall: 'Now I give you warning, George,' he cried. 'One more word of your sauce, and I'll call you down and fight you. How? Why, how do I know? You had ought to tell me that – you and the rest, that lost me my schooner, with your interference, burn you! But not you, you can't; you hain't got the invention of a cockroach. But civil you can speak, and shall, George Merry, you may lay to that.'

'That's fair enow,' said the old man Morgan.

'Fair! I reckon so,' said the sea-cook. 'You lost the ship; I found the treasure. Who's the better man at that? And now I resign, by thunder! Elect whom you please to be your cap'n now; I'm done with it.'

'Silver!' they cried. 'Barbecue for ever! Barbecue for cap'n!'

'So that's the toon, is it?' cried the cook. 'George, I reckon you'll have to wait another turn, friend! and lucky for you as I'm not a revengeful man. But that was never my way. And now, shipmates, this black spot? 'Tain't much good now, is it? Dick's crossed his luck and spoiled his Bible, and that's about all.'

'It'll do to kiss the book on still, won't it?' growled Dick, who was evidently uneasy at the curse he had brought upon himself.

'A Bible with a bit cut out!' returned Silver derisively. 'Not it. It don't bind no more'n a ballad-book.'

'Don't it, though?' cried Dick, with a sort of joy. 'Well, I reckon that's worth having, too.'

'Here, Jim – here's a cur'osity for you,' said Silver; and he tossed me the paper.

It was a round about the size of a crown piece. One side was blank, for it had been the last leaf; the other contained a verse or two of Revelation – these words among the rest, which struck sharply home upon my mind: 'Without are dogs and murderers.' The printed side had been blackened with wood ash, which already began to come off and soil my fingers; on the blank side had been written with the same material the one word 'Depposed'. I have that curiosity beside me at this moment; but not a trace of writing now remains beyond a single scratch, such as a man might make with his thumb-nail.

That was the end of the night's business. Soon after, with a drink all round, we lay down to sleep, and the outside of Silver's vengeance was to put George Merry up for sentinel and threaten him with death if he should prove unfaithful.

It was long ere I could close an eye, and Heaven knows I had matter enough for thought in the man whom I had slain that afternoon, in my own most perilous position, and, above all, in the remarkable game that I saw Silver now engaged upon – keeping the mutineers together with one hand, and grasping, with the other, after every means, possible and impossible, to make his peace and save his miserable life. He himself slept peacefully, and snored aloud; yet my heart was sore for him, wicked as he was, to think on the dark perils that environed, and the shameful gibbet that awaited him.

CHAPTER THREE

On Parole

I WAS WAKENED – INDEED, we were all wakened, for I could see even the sentinel shake himself together from where he had fallen against the door-post – by a clear, hearty voice hailing us from the margin of the wood:

'Blockhouse, ahoy!' it cried. 'Here's the doctor.'

And the doctor it was. Although I was glad to hear the sound, yet my gladness was not without admixture. I remembered with confusion my insubordinate and stealthy conduct; and when I saw where it had brought me – among what companions and surrounded by what dangers – I felt ashamed to look him in the face.

He must have risen in the dark, for the day had hardly come; and when I ran to a loophole and looked out, I saw him standing, like Silver once before, up to the mid-leg in creeping vapour.

'You, doctor! Top o' the morning to you, sir!' cried Silver, broad awake and beaming with good nature in a moment. 'Bright and early, to be sure; and it's the early bird, as the saying goes, that gets the rations. George, shake up your timbers, son, and help Dr Livesey over the ship's side. All a-doin' well, your patients was – all well and merry.'

So he pattered on, standing on the hill-top, with his crutch under his elbow, and one hand upon the side of the log-house – quite the old John in voice, manner, and expression.

'We've quite a surprise for you, too, sir,' he continued. 'We've a little stranger here – he! he! A noo boarder and lodger, sir, and looking fit and taut as a fiddle; slep' like a supercargo, he did, right alongside of John – stem to stem we was, all night.'

Dr Livesey was by this time across the stockade and pretty near the cook; and I could hear the alteration in his voice as he said:

'Not Jim?'

'The very same as ever was,' says Silver.

The doctor stopped outright, although he did not speak, and it was some seconds before he seemed able to move on.

'Well, well,' he said, at last, 'duty first and pleasure afterwards, as you might have said yourself, Silver. Let us overhaul these patients of yours.'

A moment afterwards he had entered the blockhouse, and, with one grim nod to me, proceeded with his work among the sick. He seemed under no apprehension, though he must have known that his life, among these treacherous demons, depended on a hair; and he rattled on to his patients as if he were paying an ordinary professional visit in a quiet English family. His manner, I suppose, reacted on the men; for they behaved to him as if nothing had occurred – as if he were still ship's doctor, and they still faithful hands before the mast.

'You're doing well, my friend,' he said to the fellow with the bandaged head; 'and if ever any person had a close shave, it was you; your head must be as hard as iron. Well, George, how goes it? You're a pretty colour, certainly; why, your liver, man, is upside down. Did you take that medicine? Did he take that medicine, men?'

'Ay, ay, sir, he took it, sure enough,' returned Morgan.

'Because, you see, since I am mutineers' doctor, or prison doctor, as I prefer to call it,' says Dr Livesey, in his pleasantest way, 'I make it a point of honour not to lose a man for King George (God bless him!) and the gallows.'

The rogues looked at each other, but swallowed the home-thrust in silence.

'Dick don't feel well, sir,' said one.

'Don't he?' replied the doctor. 'Well, step up here, Dick, and let me see your tongue. No, I should be surprised if he did! the man's tongue is fit to frighten the French. Another fever.'

'Ah, there,' said Morgan, 'that comed of sp'iling Bibles.'

'That comed – as you call it – of being arrant asses,' retorted the doctor, 'and not having sense enough to know honest air from poison, and the dry land from a vile, pestiferous slough. I think it most probable – though, of course, it's only an opinion – that you'll all have the deuce to pay before you get that malaria out of your systems. Camp in a bog, would you? Silver, I'm surprised at you. You're less of a fool than many, take you all round; but you don't appear to me to have the rudiments of a notion of the rules of health.'

'Well,' he added, after he had dosed them round, and they had taken his prescriptions, with really laughable humility, more like charity school-children than blood-guilty mutineers and pirates – 'well, that's done for to-day. And now I should wish to have a talk with that boy, please.'

And he nodded his head in my direction carelessly.

George Merry was at the door, spitting and spluttering over some bad-tasting medicine; but at the first word of the doctor's proposal he swung round with a deep flush and cried 'No!' and swore.

Silver struck the barrel with his open hand.

'Si-lence!' he roared, and looked about him positively like a lion. 'Doctor,' he went on, in his usual tones, 'I was a-thinking of that, knowing as how you had a fancy for the boy. We're all humbly grateful for your kindness, and, as you see, puts faith in you, and takes the drugs down like that much grog. And I take it, I've found a way as'll suit all. Hawkins, will you give me your word of honour as a young gentleman – for a young gentleman you are, although poor born – your word of honour not to slip your cable?'

I readily gave the pledge required.

'Then, doctor,' said Silver, 'you just step outside o' that stockade, and once you're there, I'll bring the boy down on the inside, and I reckon you can yarn through the spars. Good day to you, sir, and all our dooties to the squire and Cap'n Smollett.'

The explosion of disapproval, which nothing but Silver's black looks had restrained, broke out immediately the doctor had left the house. Silver was roundly accused of playing double – of trying to make a separate peace for himself – of sacrificing the interests of his accomplices and victims; and, in one word, of the identical, exact thing that he was doing. It seemed to me so obvious, in this case, that I could not imagine how he was to turn their anger. But he was twice the man the rest were; and his last night's victory had given him a huge proponderance on their minds. He called them all the fools and dolts you can imagine, said it was necessary I should talk to the doctor, fluttered the chart in their faces, asked them if they could afford to break the treaty the very day they were bound a-treasure-hunting.

'No, by thunder!' he cried, 'it's us must break the treaty when the time comes; and till then I'll gammon that doctor, if I have to ile his boots with brandy.'

And then he bade them get the fire lit, and stalked out upon his crutch, with his hand on my shoulder, leaving them in a disarray, and silenced by his volubility rather than convinced.

'Slow, lad, slow,' he said. 'They might round upon us in a twinkle of an eye, if we was seen to hurry.'

Very deliberately, then, did we advance across the sand to where the doctor awaited us on the other side of the stockade, and as soon as we were within easy speaking distance, Silver stopped.

'You'll make a note of this here also, doctor,' says he, 'and the boy'll tell you how I saved his life, and were deposed for it, too, and you may lay to that. Doctor, when a man's steering as near the wind as me – playing chuck-farthing with the last breath in his body, like – you wouldn't think it too much, mayhap, to give him one good word? You'll please bear in mind it's not my life only now – it's that boy's into the bargain; and you'll speak me fair, doctor, and give me a bit o' hope to go on, for the sake of mercy.'

Silver was a changed man, once he was out there and had his back to his friends and the blockhouse; his cheeks seemed to have fallen in, his voice trembled; never was a soul more dead in earnest.

'Why, John, you're not afraid?' asked Dr Livesey.

'Doctor, I'm no coward! no, not I – not so much!' and he snapped his fingers. 'If I was I wouldn't say it. But I'll own up fairly, I've the shakes upon me for the gallows. You're a good man and a true; I never seen a better man! And you'll not forget what I done good, not any more than you'll forget the bad, I know. And I step aside – see here – and leave you and Jim alone. And you'll put that down for me, too, for it's a long stretch, is that!'

So saying, he stepped back a little way, till he was out of earshot, and there sat down upon a tree-stump and began to whistle; spinning round now and again upon his seat so as to command a sight, sometimes of me and the doctor, and sometimes of his unruly ruffians as they went to and fro in the sand, between the fire – which they were busy rekindling – and the house, from which they brought forth pork and bread to make the breakfast.

'So, Jim,' said the doctor sadly, 'here you are. As you have brewed, so shall you drink, my boy. Heaven knows, I cannot find it in my heart to blame you; but this much I will say, be it kind or unkind; when Captain Smollett was well, you dared not have gone off, and when he was ill, and couldn't help it, by George, it was downright cowardly!'

I will own that I here began to weep. 'Doctor,' I said, 'you might spare me. I have blamed myself enough; my life's forfeit anyway, and I should have been dead by now, if Silver hadn't stood for me; and, doctor, believe this, I can die – and I dare say I deserve it – but what I fear is torture. If they come to torture me——'

'Jim,' the doctor interrupted, and his voice was quite changed, 'Jim, I can't have this. Whip over, and we'll run for it.'

'Doctor,' said I, 'I passed my word.'

'I know, I know,' he cried. 'We can't help that, Jim, now. I'll take it on my shoulders, holus bolus, blame and shame, my boy; but stay here, I cannot let you. Jump! One jump and you're out, and we'll run for it like antelopes.'

'No,' I replied, 'you know right well you wouldn't do the thing yourself; neither you, nor squire, nor captain; and no more will I. Silver trusted me; I passed my word, and back I go. But, doctor, you did not let me finish. If they come to torture me, I might let slip a word of where the ship is; for I got the ship, part by luck and part by risking, and she lies in North Inlet, on the southern beach, and just below high water. At half-tide she must be high and dry.'

'The ship!' exlaimed the doctor.

Rapidly I described to him my adventures, and he heard me out in silence.

'There is a kind of fate in this,' he observed, when I had done. 'Every step, it's you that saves our lives; and do you suppose by any chance that we are going to let you lose yours? That would be a poor return, my boy. You found out the plot; you found Ben Gunn – the best deed that ever you did, or will do, though you live to ninety. Oh, by Jupiter, and talking of Ben Gunn! why, this is the mischief in person. Silver!' he cried, 'Silver! – I'll give you a piece of advice,' he continued as the cook drew near again; 'don't you be in any great hurry after that treasure.'

'Why, sir, I do my possible, which that ain't,' said Silver. 'I can only, asking your pardon, save my life and the boy's by seeking for that treasure; and you may lay to that.'

'Well, Silver,' replied the doctor, 'if that is so, I'll go one step further: look out for squalls when you find it.'

'Sir,' said Silver, 'as between man and man, that's too much and too little. What you're after, why you left the blockhouse, why you given me that there chart, I don't know, now, do I? and yet I done your bidding with my eyes shut and never a word of hope! But, no, this here's too much. If you won't tell me what you mean plain out, just say so, and I'll leave the helm.'

'No,' said the doctor, musingly, 'I've no right to say more; it's not my secret, you see, Silver, or, I give you my word, I'd tell it you. But I'll go as far with you as I dare go, and a step beyond; for I'll give you a bit of hope: Silver, if we both get alive out of this wolf-trap, I'll do my best to save you, short of perjury.'

Silver's face was radiant. 'You couldn't say more, I'm sure, sir, not if you was my mother,' he cried.

'Well, that's my first concession,' added the doctor. 'My second is a piece of

advice: keep the boy close beside you, and when you need help, halloo. I'm off
to seek it for you, and that itself will show you if I speak at random. Good-bye,
Jim.'

And Dr Livesey shook hands with me through the stockade, nodded to Silver,
and set off at a brisk pace into the wood.

CHAPTER FOUR

The Treasure Hunt – Flint's Pointer

'JIM,' SAID SILVER, WHEN we were alone, 'if I saved your life, you saved mine; and
I'll not forget it. I seen the doctor waving to you to run for it – with the tail of my
eye, I did; and I seen you say no, as plain as hearing. Jim, that's one to you. This
is the first glint of hope I had since the attack failed, and I owe it you. And now,
Jim, we're to go in for this here treasure-hunting, with sealed orders, too, and I
don't like it; and you and me must stick close, back to back like, and we'll save
our necks in spite o' fate and fortune.'

Just then a man hailed us from the fire that breakfast was ready, and we were
soon seated here and there about the sand over biscuit and fried junk. They had
lit a fire to roast an ox; and it was now grown so hot that they could only
approach it from the windward, and even there not without precaution. In the
same wasteful spirit, they had cooked, I suppose, three times more than we could
eat; and one of them, with an empty laugh, threw what was left into the fire,
which blazed and roared again over this unusual fuel. I never in my life saw men
so careless of the morrow; hand to mouth is the only word that can describe their
way of doing; and what with wasted food and sleeping sentries, though they were
bold enough for a brush and be done with it, I could see their entire unfitness for
anything like a prolonged campaign.

Even Silver, eating away, with Captain Flint upon his shoulder, had not a
word of blame for their recklessness. And this the more surprised me, for I
thought he had never shown himself so cunning as he did then.

'Ay, mates,' said he, 'it's lucky you have Barbecue to think for you with this
here head. I got what I wanted, I did. Sure enough, they have the ship. Where
they have it, I don't know yet; but once we hit the treasure, we'll have to jump
about and find out. And then, mates, us that has the boats, I reckon, has the
upper hand.'

Thus he kept running on, with his mouth full of the hot bacon; thus he
restored their hope and confidence, and, I more than suspect, repaired his own
at the same time.

'As for hostage,' he continued, 'that's his last talk, I guess, with them he loves
so dear. I've got my piece o' news, and thanky to him for that; but it's over and
done. I'll take him in a line when we go treasure-hunting, for we'll keep him like
so much gold, in case of accidents, you mark, and in the meantime. Once we got

the ship and treasure both, and off to sea like jolly companions, why, then, we'll talk Mr Hawkins over, we will, and we'll give him his share, to be sure, for all his kindness.'

It was no wonder the men were in a good humour now. For my part, I was horribly cast down. Should the scheme he had now sketched prove feasible, Silver, already doubly a traitor, would not hesitate to adopt it. He had still a foot in either camp, and there was no doubt he would prefer wealth and freedom with the pirates to a bare escape from hanging, which was the best he had to hope on our side.

Nay, and even if things so fell out that he was forced to keep his faith with Dr Livesey, even then what danger lay before us! What a moment that would be when the suspicions of his followers turned to certainty, and he and I should have to fight for dear life – he, a cripple, and I, a boy – against five strong and active seamen!

Add to this double apprehension, the mystery that still hung over the behaviour of my friends; their unexplained desertion of the stockade; their inexplicable cession of the chart; or, harder still to understand, the doctor's last warning to Silver: 'Look out for squalls when you find it'; and you will readily believe how little taste I found in my breakfast, and with how uneasy a heart I set forth behind my captors on the quest for treasure.

We made a curious figure, had any one been there to see us; all in soiled sailor clothes, and all but me armed to the teeth. Silver had two guns slung about him – one before and one behind – besides the great cutlass at his waist, and a pistol in each pocket of his square-tailed coat. To complete his strange appearance, Captain Flint sat perched upon his shoulder and gabbling odds and ends of purposeless sea-talk. I had a line about my waist, and followed obediently after the sea-cook, who held the loose end of the rope, now in his free hand, now between his powerful teeth. For all the world, I was led like a dancing bear.

The other men were variously burthened; some carrying picks and shovels – for that had been the very first necessary they brought ashore from the *Hispaniola* – others laden with pork, bread, and brandy for the midday meal. All the stores, I observed, came from our stock; and I could see the truth of Silver's words the night before. Had he not struck a bargain with the doctor, he and his mutineers, deserted by the ship, must have been driven to subsist on clear water and the proceeds of their hunting. Water would have been little to their taste; a sailor is not usually a good shot; and besides all that, when they were so short of eatables, it was not likely they would be very flush of powder.

Well, thus equipped, we all set out – even the fellow with the broken head, who should certainly have kept in shadow – and straggled, one after another, to the beach, where the two gigs awaited us. Even these bore trace of the drunken folly of the pirates, one in a broken thwart, and both in their muddied and unbaled condition. Both were to be carried along with us, for the sake of safety; and so, with our numbers divided between them, we set forth upon the bosom of the anchorage.

As we pulled over, there was some discussion on the chart. The red cross was, of course, far too large to be a guide; and the terms of the note on the back, as you will hear, admitted of some ambiguity. They ran, the reader may remember, thus:

Tall tree, Spy-glass Shoulder, bearing a point to the N. of N.N.E.
Skeleton Island E.S.E. and by E.
Ten feet.

A tall tree was thus the principal mark. Now, right before us, the anchorage
was bounded by a plateau from two to three hundred feet high, adjoining on the
north the sloping shoulder of the Spy-glass, and rising again towards the south
into the rough cliffy eminence called the Mizzen-mast Hill. The top of the
plateau was dotted thickly with pine trees of varying heights. Every here and
there, one of a different species rose forty or fifty feet clear above its neighbours,
and which of these was the particular 'tall tree' of Captain Flint could only be
decided on the spot, and by the readings of the compass.

Yet, although that was the case, every man on board the boats had picked a
favourite of his own ere we were half-way over, Long John alone shrugging his
shoulders and bidding them wait till they were there.

We pulled easily, by Silver's directions, not to weary the hands prematurely;
and, after quite a long passage, landed at the mouth of the second river – that
which runs down a woody cleft of the Spy-glass. Thence, bending to our left, we
began to ascend the slope towards the plateau.

At the first outset, heavy, miry ground and a matted, marish vegetation
greatly delayed our progress; but by little and little the hill began to steepen and
become stony under foot, and the wood to change its character and to grow in a
more open order. It was, indeed, a most pleasant portion of the island that we
were now approaching. A heavy-scented broom and many flowering shrubs had
almost taken the place of grass. Thickets of green nutmeg trees were dotted here
and there with the red columns and the broad shadow of the pines; and the first
mingled their spice with the aroma of the others. The air, besides, was fresh and
stirring, and this, under the sheer sunbeams, was a wonderful refreshment to our
senses.

The party spread itself abroad, in a fan shape, shouting and leaping to and fro.
About the centre, and a good way behind the rest, Silver and I followed – I
tethered by my rope, he ploughing, with deep pants, among the sliding gravel.
From time to time, indeed, I had to lend him a hand, or he must have missed his
footing and fallen backward down the hill.

We had thus proceeded for about half a mile, and were approaching the brow
of the plateau, when the man upon the farthest left began to cry aloud, as if in
terror. Shout after shout came from him, and the others began to run in his
direction.

'He can't 'a' found the treasure,' said old Morgan, hurrying past us from the
right, 'for that's clean a-top.'

Indeed, as we found when we also reached the spot, it was something very
different. At the foot of a pretty big pine, and involved in a green creeper,
which had even partly lifted some of the smaller bones, a human skeleton lay,
with a few shreds of clothing, on the ground. I believe a chill struck for a
moment to every heart.

'He was a seaman,' said George Merry, who, bolder than the rest, had gone up
close, and was examining the rags of clothing. 'Leastways, this is good sea-

cloth.'

'Ay, ay,' said Silver, 'like enough; you wouldn't look to find a bishop here, I reckon. But what sort of a way is that for bones to lie? 'Tain't in natur'.'

Indeed, on a second glance, it seemed impossible to fancy that the body was in a natural position. But for some disarray (the work, perhaps, of the birds that had fed upon him, or of the slow-growing creeper that had gradually enveloped his remains) the man lay perfectly straight – his feet pointing in one direction, his hands, raised above his head like a diver's, pointing directly in the opposite.

'I've taken a notion into my old numskull,' observed Silver. 'Here's the compass; there's the tip-top p'int o' Skeleton Island, stickin' out like a tooth. Just take a bearing, will you, along the line of them bones.'

It was done. The body pointed straight in the direction of the island, and the compass read duly E.S.E. and by E.

'I thought so,' cried the cook; 'this here is a p'inter. Right up there is our line for the Pole Star and the jolly dollars. But, by thunder! if it don't make me cold inside to think of Flint. This is one of *his* jokes, and no mistake. Him and these six was alone here; he killed 'em, every man; and this one he hauled here and laid down by compass, shiver my timbers! They're long bones, and the hair's been yellow. Ay, that would be Allardyce. You mind Allardyce, Tom Morgan?'

'Ay, ay,' returned Morgan, 'I mind him; he owed me money, he did, and took my knife ashore with him.'

'Speaking of knives,' said another, 'why don't we find his'n lying round? Flint warn't the man to pick a seaman's pocket; and the birds, I guess, would leave it be.'

'By the powers, and that's true!' cried Silver.

'There ain't a thing left here,' said Merry, still feeling round among the bones, 'not a copper doit nor a baccy-box. It don't look nat'ral to me.'

'No, by gum, it don't,' agreed Silver; 'not nat'ral, nor not nice, says you. Great guns! messmates, but if Flint was living, this would be a hot spot for you and me. Six they were, and six we are; and bones is what they are now.'

'I saw him dead with these here deadlights,' said Morgan. 'Billy took me in. There he laid, with penny-pieces on his eyes.'

'Dead – ay, sure enough he's dead and gone below,' said the fellow with the bandage; 'but if ever sperrit walked, it would be Flint's. Dear heart, but he died bad, did Flint!'

'Ay, that he did,' observed another; 'now he raged, and now he hollered for the rum, and now he sang. *Fifteen Men* were his only song, mates; and I tell you true, I never rightly liked to hear it since. It was main hot, and the windy was open, and I hear that old song comin' out as clear as clear – and the death-haul on the man already.'

'Come, come,' said Silver, 'stow this talk. He's dead, and he don't walk, that I know; leastways, he won't walk by day, and you may lay to that. Care killed a cat. Fetch ahead for the doubloons.'

We started, certainly; but in spite of the hot sun and the staring daylight, the pirates no longer ran separate and shouting through the wood, but kept side by side and spoke with bated breath. The terror of the dead buccaneer had fallen on their spirits.

CHAPTER FIVE

The Treasure Hunt – the Voice Among the Trees

PARTLY FROM THE DAMPING influence of this alarm, partly to rest Silver and the sick folk, the whole party sat down as soon as they had gained the brow of the ascent.

The plateau being somewhat tilted towards the west, this spot on which we had paused commanded a wide prospect on either hand. Before us, over the tree-tops, we beheld the Cape of the Woods fringed with surf; behind, we not only looked down upon the anchorage and Skeleton Island, but saw – clear across the spit and the eastern lowlands – a great field of open sea upon the east. Sheer above us rose the Spy-glass, here dotted with single pines, there black with precipices. There was no sound but that of the distant breakers, mounting from all round, and the chirp of countless insects in the brush. Not a man, not a sail upon the sea; the very largeness of the view increased the sense of solitude.

Silver, as he sat, took certain bearings with his compass.

'There are three "tall trees",' said he, 'about in the right line from Skeleton Island. "Spy-glass Shoulder," I take it, means that lower p'int there. It's child's play to find the stuff now. I've half a mind to dine first.'

'I don't feel sharp,' growled Morgan. 'Thinkin' o' Flint – I think it were – has done me.'

'Ah, well, my son, you praise your stars he's dead,' said Silver.

'He were an ugly devil,' cried a third pirate, with a shudder; 'that blue in the face, too!'

'That was how the rum took him,' added Merry. 'Blue! well, I reckon he was blue. That's a true word.'

Ever since they had found the skeleton and got upon this train of thought, they had spoken lower and lower, and they had almost got to whispering by now, so that the sound of their talk hardly interrupted the silence of the wood. All of a sudden, out of the middle of the trees in front of us, a thin, high, trembling voice struck up the well-known air and words:

> 'Fifteen men on the dead man's chest –
> Yo-ho-ho, and a bottle of rum!'

I never have seen men more dreadfully affected than the pirates. The colour went from their six faces like enchantment; some leaped to their feet, some clawed hold of others; Morgan grovelled on the ground.

'It's Flint, by ——!' cried Merry.

The song had stopped as suddenly as it began – broken off, you would have said, in the middle of a note, as though someone had laid his hand upon the singer's mouth. Coming so far through the clear, sunny atmosphere among the green tree-tops, I thought it had sounded airily and sweetly; and the effect on my companions was the stranger.

'Come,' said Silver, struggling with his ashen lips to get the word out, 'this won't do. Stand by to go about. This is a rum start, and I can't name the voice, but it's someone skylarking – someone that's flesh and blood, and you may lay to that.'

His courage had come back as he spoke, and some of the colour to his face along with it. Already the others had begun to lend an ear to this encouragement, and were coming a little to themselves, when the same voice broke out again – not this time singing, but in a faint distant hail, that echoed yet fainter among the clefts of the Spy-glass.

'Darby M'Graw,' it wailed – for that is the word that best described the sound – 'Darby M'Graw! Darby M'Graw!' again and again and again; and then rising a little higher, and with an oath that I leave out: 'Fetch aft the rum, Darby!'

The buccaneers remained rooted to the ground, their eyes starting from their heads. Long after the voice had died away, they still stared in silence, dreadfully, before them.

'That fixes it!' gasped one. 'Let's go.'

'They was his last words,' moaned Morgan, 'his last words above board.'

Dick had his Bible out, and was praying volubly. He had been well brought up, had Dick, before he came to sea and fell among bad companions.

Still, Silver was unconquered. I could hear his teeth rattle in his head, but he had not yet surrendered.

'Nobody in this here island ever heard of Darby,' he muttered, 'not one but us that's here.' And then, making a great effort, 'Shipmates,' he cried, 'I'm here to get that stuff, and I'll not be beat by man nor devil. I never was feared of Flint in his life, and, by the powers, I'll face him dead. There's seven hundred thousand pound not a quarter of a mile from here. When did ever a gentleman o' fortune show his stern to that much dollars, for a boozy old seaman with a blue mug – and him dead, too?'

But there was no sign of reawakening courage in his followers; rather, indeed, of growing terror at the irreverence of his words.

'Belay there, John!' said Merry. 'Don't you cross a sperrit.'

And the rest were all too terrified to reply. They would have run away severally had they dared; but fear kept them together, and kept them close by John, as if his daring helped them. He, on his part, had pretty well fought his weakness down.

'Sperrit? Well, maybe,' he said. 'But there's one thing not clear to me. There was an echo. Now, no man ever seen a sperrit with a shadow; well, then, what's he doing with an echo to him, I should like to know? That ain't in natur', surely?'

This argument seemed weak enough to me. But you can never tell what will affect the superstitious, and, to my wonder, George Merry was greatly relieved.

'Well, that's so,' he said. 'You've a head upon your shoulders, John, and no mistake. 'Bout ship, mates! this here crew is on a wrong tack, I do believe. And come to think on it, it was like Flint's voice, I grant you, but not just so clear-away like it, after all. It was liker somebody else's voice, now – it was liker——'

'By the powers, Ben Gunn!' roared Silver.

'Ay, and so it were,' cried Morgan, springing on his knees. 'Ben Gunn it were!'

'It don't make much odds, do it, now?' asked Dick. 'Ben Gunn's not here in the body, any more'n Flint.'

But the older hands greeted this remark with scorn.

'Why, nobody minds Ben Gunn,' cried Merry; 'dead or alive, nobody minds him.'

It was extraordinary how their spirits had returned, and how the natural colour had revived in their faces. Soon they were chatting together, with intervals of listening; and not long after, hearing no further sound, they shouldered the tools and set forth again, Merry walking first with Silver's compass to keep them on the right line with Skeleton Island. He had said the truth: dead or alive, nobody minded Ben Gunn.

Dick alone still held his Bible, and looked around him as he went, with fearful glances; but he found no sympathy, and Silver even joked him on his precautions.

'I told you,' said he— 'I told you, you had sp'iled your Bible. If it ain't no good to swear by, what do you suppose a sperrit would give for it? Not that!' and he snapped his big fingers, halting a moment on his crutch.

But Dick was not to be comforted; indeed, it was soon plain to me that the lad was falling sick; hastened by heat, exhaustion, and the shock of his alarm, the fever, predicted by Dr Livesey, was evidently growing swiftly higher.

It was fine open walking here, upon the summit; our way lay a little downhill, for, as I have said, the plateau tilted towards the west. The pines, great and small, grew wide apart: and even between the clumps of nutmeg and azalea, wide open spaces baked in the hot sunshine. Striking, as we did, pretty near north-west across the island, we drew, on the one hand, ever nearer under the shoulders of the Spy-glass, and on the other, looked ever wider over that western bay where I had once tossed and trembled in the coracle.

The first of the tall trees was reached, and, by the bearing, proved the wrong one. So with the second. The third rose nearly two hundred feet into the air above a clump of underwood; a giant of a vegetable, with a red column as big as a cottage, and a wide shadow around in which a company could have manœuvred. It was conspicuous far to sea both on the east and west, and might have been entered as a sailing mark upon the chart.

But it was not its size that now impressed my companions; it was the knowledge that seven hundred thousand pounds in gold lay somewhere buried below its spreading shadow. The thought of the money, as they drew nearer, swallowed up their previous terrors. Their eyes burned in their heads; their feet grew speedier and lighter; their whole soul was bound up in that fortune, that whole lifetime of extravagance and pleasure, that lay waiting there for each of them.

Silver hobbled, grunting, on his crutch; his nostrils stood out and quivered; he cursed like a madman when the flies settled on his hot and shiny countenance; he plucked furiously at the line that held me to him, and, from time to time, turned his eyes upon me with a deadly look. Certainly he took no pains to hide his thoughts; and certainly I read them like print. In the immediate nearness of the gold, all else had been forgotten; his promise and the doctor's warning were both things of the past; and I could not doubt that he hoped to seize upon the treasure, find and board the *Hispaniola* under cover of night, cut every honest throat about that island, and sail away as he had at first intended, laden with crimes and riches.

Shaken as I was with these alarms, it was hard for me to keep up with the rapid pace of the treasure-hunters. Now and again I stumbled; and it was then that Silver plucked so roughly at the rope and launched at me his murderous glances. Dick, who had dropped behind us, and now brought up the rear, was babbling to himself both prayers and curses, as his fever kept rising. This also added to my wretchedness, and, to crown all, I was haunted by the thought of the tragedy that had once been acted on that plateau, when that ungodly buccaneer with the blue face – he who died at Savannah, singing and shouting for drink – had there, with his own hand, cut down his six accomplices. This grove, that was now so peaceful, must then have rung with cries, I thought; and even with the thought I could believe I heard it ringing still.

We were now at the margin of the thicket.

'Huzza, mates, all together!' shouted Merry; and the foremost broke into a run.

And suddenly, not ten yards further we beheld them stop. A low cry arose. Silver doubled his pace, digging away with the foot of his crutch like one possessed; and next moment he and I had come also to a dead halt.

Before us was a great excavation, not very recent, for the sides had fallen in and grass had sprouted on the bottom. In this were the shaft of a pick broken in two and the boards of several packing-cases strewn around. On one of these boards I saw, branded with a hot iron, the name *Walrus* – the name of Flint's ship.

All was clear to probation. The cache had been found and rifled; the seven hundred thousand pounds were gone!

CHAPTER SIX

The Fall of a Chieftain

THERE NEVER WAS SUCH AN overturn in this world. Each of these six men was as though he had been struck. But with Silver the blow passed almost instantly. Every thought of his soul had been set full-stretch, like a racer, on that money; well, he was brought up in a single second, dead; and he kept his head, found his temper, and changed his plan before the others had had time to realize the disappointment.

'Jim,' he whispered, 'take that, and stand by for trouble.'

And he passed me a double-barrelled pistol.

At the same time he began quietly moving northward, and in a few steps had put the hollow between us two and the other five. Then he looked at me and nodded, as much as to say, 'Here is a narrow corner,' as, indeed, I thought it was. His looks were now quite friendly; and I was so revolted at these constant changes, that I could not forbear whispering: 'So you've changed sides again.'

There was no time left for him to answer in. The buccaneers, with oaths and cries, began to leap, one after another, into the pit, and to dig with their fingers, throwing the boards aside as they did so. Morgan found a piece of gold. He held it up with a perfect spout of oaths. It was a two-guinea piece, and it went from hand to hand among them for a quarter of a minute.

'Two guineas!' roared Merry, shaking it at Silver. 'That's your seven hundred thousand pounds, is it? You're the man for bargains, ain't you? You're him that never bungled nothing, you wooden-headed lubber!'

'Dig away, boys,' said Silver, with the coolest insolence; 'you'll find some pig-nuts and I shouldn't wonder.'

'Pig-nuts!' repeated Merry, in a scream. 'Mates, do you hear that? I tell you, now, that man there knew it all along. Look in the face of him, and you'll see it wrote there.'

'Ah, Merry,' remarked Silver, 'standing for cap'n again? You're a pushing lad, to be sure.'

But this time every one was entirely in Merry's favour. They began to scramble out of the excavation, darting furious glances behind them. One thing I observed, which looked well for us: they all got out upon the opposite side from Silver.

Well, there we stood, two on one side, five on the other, the pit between us, and nobody screwed up high enough to offer the first blow. Silver never moved; he watched them, very upright on his crutch, and looked as cool as ever I saw him. He was brave, and no mistake.

At last, Merry seemed to think a speech might help matters.

'Mates,' says he, 'there's two of them alone there; one's the old cripple that brought us all here and blundered us down to this; the other's that cub that I mean to have the heart of. Now, mates——'

He was raising his arm and his voice, and plainly meant to lead a charge. But just then – crack! crack! crack! – three musket shots flashed out of the thicket. Merry tumbled head foremost into the excavation; the man with the bandage spun round like a teetotum, and fell all his length upon his side, where he lay, dead but still twitching; and the other three turned and ran for it with all their might.

Before you could wink, Long John had fired two barrels of a pistol into the struggling Merry; and as the man rolled up his eyes at him in the last agony, 'George,' said he, 'I reckon I settled you.'

At the same moment the doctor, Gray, and Ben Gunn joined us, with smoking muskets, from among the nutmeg trees.

'Forward!' cried the doctor. 'Double quick, my lads. We must head 'em off the boats.'

And we set off, at a great pace, sometimes plunging through the bushes to the chest.

I tell you, but Silver was anxious to keep up with us. The work that man went through, leaping on his crutch till the muscles of his chest were fit to burst, was work no sound man ever equalled; and so thinks the doctor. As it was, he was already thirty yards behind us, and on the verge of strangling, when we reached the brow of the slope.

'Doctor,' he hailed, 'see there! no hurry!'

Sure enough there was no hurry. In a more open part of the plateau, we could see the three survivors still running in the same direction as they had started, right for Mizzen-mast Hill. We were already between them and the boats; and so we four sat down to breathe, while Long John, mopping his face, came slowly up with us.

'Thank ye kindly, doctor,' says he. 'You came in in about the nick, I guess, for me and Hawkins. And so it's you, Ben Gunn!' he added. 'Well, you're a nice one, to be sure.'

'I'm Ben Gunn, I am,' replied the maroon, wriggling like an eel in his embarrassment. 'And,' he added, after a long pause, 'how do, Mr Silver? Pretty well, I thank ye, says you.'

'Ben, Ben,' murmured Silver, 'to think as you've done me!'

The doctor sent back Gray for one of the pickaxes, deserted, in their flight, by the mutineers; and then as we proceeded leisurely downhill to where the boats were lying, related, in a few words, what had taken place. It was a story that profoundly interested Silver; and Ben Gunn, the half-idiot maroon, was the hero from beginning to end.

Ben, in his long, lonely wanderings about the island, had found the skeleton – it was he that had rifled it; he had found the treasure; he had dug it up (it was the shaft of his pickaxe that lay broken in the excavation); he had carried it on his back, in many weary journeys, from the foot of the tall pine to a cave he had on the two-pointed hill at the north-east angle of the island, and there it had lain stored in safety since two months before the arrival of the *Hispaniola*.

When the doctor had wormed this secret from him, on the afternoon of the attack, and when, next morning, he saw the anchorage deserted, he had gone to Silver, given him the chart, which was now useless – given him the stores, for Ben Gunn's cave was well supplied with goats' meat salted by himself – given anything and everything to get a chance of moving in safety from the stockade to the two-pointed hill, there to be clear of malaria and keep a guard upon the money.

'As for you, Jim,' he said, 'it went against my heart, but I did what I thought best for those who had stood by their duty; and if you were not one of these, whose fault was it?'

That morning, finding that I was to be involved in the horrid disappointment he had prepared for the mutineers, he had run all the way to the cave, and, leaving squire to guard the captain, had taken Gray and the maroon, and started, making the diagonal across the island, to be at hand beside the pine. Soon, however, he saw that our party had the start of him; and Ben Gunn, being fleet of foot, had been dispatched in front to do his best alone. Then it had occurred to him to work upon the superstitions of his former shipmates; and he was so far successful that Gray and the doctor had come up and were already ambushed before the arrival of the treasure-hunters.

'Ah,' said Silver, 'it were fortunate for me that I had Hawkins here. You would have let old John be cut to bits, and never given it a thought, doctor.'

'Not a thought,' replied Dr Livesey, cheerily.

And by this time we had reached the gigs. The doctor, with the pickaxe, demolished one of them, and then we all got aboard the other and set out to go round by sea for North Inlet.

This was a run of eight or nine miles. Silver, though he was almost killed already with fatigue, was set to an oar, like the rest of us, and we were soon skimming swiftly over a smooth sea. Soon we passed out of the straits and doubled the south-east corner of the island, round which, four days ago, we had towed the *Hispaniola*.

As we passed the two-pointed hill, we could see the black mouth of Ben Gunn's cave, and a figure standing by it, leaning on a musket. It was the squire; and we waved a handkerchief and gave him three cheers, in which the voice of Silver joined as heartily as any.

Three miles further, just inside the mouth of North Inlet, what should we meet but the *Hispaniola*, cruising by herself? The last flood had lifted her; and had there been much wind, or a strong tide current, as in the southern anchorage, we should never have found her more, or found her stranded beyond help. As it was, there was little amiss, beyond the wreck of the main-sail. Another anchor was got ready, and dropped in a fathom and a half of water. We all pulled round again to Rum Cove, the nearest point for Ben Gunn's treasure house; and then Gray, single-handed, returned with the gig to the *Hispaniola*, where he was to pass the night on guard.

A gentle slope ran up from the beach to the entrance of the cave. At the top, the squire met us. To me he was cordial and kind, saying nothing of my escapade, either in the way of blame or praise. At Silver's polite salute he somewhat flushed.

'John Silver,' he said, 'you're a prodigious villain and impostor – a monstrous impostor, sir. I am told I am not to prosecute you. Well, then, I will not. But the dead men, sir, hang about your neck like millstones.'

'Thank you kindly, sir,' replied Long John, again saluting.

'I dare you to thank me!' cried the squire. 'It is a gross dereliction of my duty. Stand back!'

And thereupon we all entered the cave. It was a large airy place, with a little spring and a pool of clear water, overhung with ferns. The floor was sand. Before a big fire lay Captain Smollett; and in a far corner, only duskily flickered over by the blaze, I beheld great heaps of coin and quadrilaterals built of bars of gold. That was Flint's treasure that we had come so far to seek, and that had cost already the lives of seventeen men from the *Hispaniola*. How many it had cost in the amassing, what blood and sorrow, what good ships scuttled on the deep, what brave men walking the plank blindfold, what shot of cannon, what shame and lies and cruelty, perhaps no man alive could tell. Yet there were still three upon that island – Silver, and old Morgan, and Ben Gunn – who had each taken his share in these crimes, as each had hoped in vain to share in the reward.

'Come in, Jim,' said the captain. 'You're a good boy in your line, Jim; but I don't think you and me'll go to sea again. You're too much of the born favourite for me. Is that you, John Silver? What brings you here, man?'

'Come back to my dooty, sir,' returned Silver.

'Ah!' said the captain; and that was all he said.

What a supper I had of it that night, with all my friends around me; and what a meal it was, with Ben Gunn's salted goat, and some delicacies and a bottle of old wine from the *Hispaniola*. Never, I am sure, were people gayer or happier. And there was Silver, sitting back almost out of the firelight, but eating heartily, prompt to spring forward when anything was wanted, even joining quietly in our laughter – the same bland, polite, obsequious seaman of the voyage out.

CHAPTER SEVEN

And Last

THE NEXT MORNING WE FELL early to work, for the transportation of this great mass of gold near a mile by land to the beach, and thence three miles by boat to the *Hispaniola*, was a considerable task for so small a number of workmen. The three fellows still abroad upon the island did not greatly trouble us; a single sentry on the shoulder of the hill was sufficient to ensure us against any sudden onslaught, and we thought, besides, they had had more than enough of fighting.

Therefore the work was pushed on briskly. Gray and Ben Gunn came and went with the boat, while the rest, during their absences, piled treasure on the beach. Two of the bars, slung in a rope's-end, made a good load for a grown man – one that he was glad to walk slowly with. For my part, as I was not much use at carrying, I was kept busy all day in the cave, packing the minted money into bread-bags.

It was a strange collection, like Billy Bones's hoard for the diversity of coinage, but so much larger and so much more varied that I think I never had more pleasure than in sorting them. English, French, Spanish, Portuguese, Georges and Louises, doubloons and double guineas and moidores and sequins, the pictures of all the kings of Europe for the last hundred years, strange Oriental pieces stamped with what looked like wisps of string or bits of spider's web, round pieces and square pieces, and pieces bored through the middle, as if to wear them round your neck – nearly every variety of money in the world must, I think, have found a place in that collection; and for number, I am sure they were like autumn leaves, so that my back ached with stooping and my fingers with sorting them out.

Day after day this work went on; by every evening a fortune had been stowed aboard, but there was another fortune waiting for the morrow; and all this time we heard nothing of the three surviving mutineers.

At last – I think it was on the third night – the doctor and I were strolling on the shoulder of the hill where it overlooks the lowlands of the isle, when, from out the thick darkness below, the wind brought us a noise between shrieking and singing. It was only a snatch that reached our ears, followed by the former silence. 'Heaven forgive them,' said the doctor; ''tis the mutineers!'

'All drunk, sir,' struck in the voice of Silver from behind us.

Silver, I should say, was allowed his entire liberty, and, in spite of daily rebuffs, seemed to regard himself once more as quite a privileged and friendly dependant. Indeed, it was remarkable how well he bore these slights, and with what unwearying politeness he kept on trying to ingratiate himself with all. Yet, I think, none treated him better than a dog; unless it was Ben Gunn, who was still terribly afraid of his old quartermaster, or myself, who had really something to thank him for; although for that matter, I suppose, I had reason to think even worse of him than anybody else, for I had seen him meditating a fresh treachery upon the plateau. Accordingly, it was pretty gruffly that the doctor answered him.

'Drunk or raving,' said he.

'Right you were, sir,' replied Silver; 'and precious little odds which, to you and me.'

'I suppose you would hardly ask me to call you a humane man,' returned the doctor with a sneer, 'and so my feelings may surprise you, Master Silver. But if I were sure they were raving – as I am morally certain one, at least, of them is down with fever – I should leave this camp, and, at whatever risk to my own carcass, take them the assistance of my skill.'

'Ask your pardon, sir, you would be very wrong,' quoth Silver. 'You would lose your precious life, and you may lay to that. I'm on your side now, hand and glove; and I shouldn't wish for to see the party weakened, let alone yourself, seeing as I know what I owes you. But these men down there, they couldn't keep their word – no, not supposing they wished to; and what's more, they couldn't believe as you could.'

'No,' said the doctor. 'You're the man to keep your word, we know that.'

Well, that was about the last news we had of the three pirates. Only once we heard a gunshot a great way off, and supposed them to be hunting. A council was held, and it was decided that we must desert them on the island – to the huge glee, I must say, of Ben Gunn, and with the strong approval of Gray. We left a good stock of powder and shot, the bulk of the salt goat, a few medicines, and some other necessaries, tools, clothing, a spare sail, a fathom or two of rope, and, by the particular desire of the doctor, a handsome present of tobacco.

That was about our last doing on the island. Before that, we had got the treasure stowed, and had shipped enough water and the remainder of the goat meat, in case of any distress; and at last, one fine morning, we weighed anchor, which was about all that we could manage, and stood out of North Inlet, the same colours flying that the captain had flown and fought under at the palisade.

The three fellows must have been watching us closer than we thought for, as we soon had proved. For, coming through the narrows, we had to lie very near the southern point, and there we saw all three of them kneeling together on the spit of sand, with their arms raised in supplication. It went to all our hearts, I think, to leave them in that wretched state; but we could not risk another mutiny; and to take them home for the gibbet would have been a cruel sort of kindness. The doctor hailed them and told them of the stores we had left, and where they were to find them. But they continued to call us by name, and appeal to us, for God's sake, to be merciful, and not leave them to die in such a place.

At last, seeing the ship still bore on her course, and was now swiftly drawing out of earshot, one of them – I know not which it was – leapt to his feet with a hoarse cry, whipped his musket to his shoulder, and sent a shot whistling over Silver's head and through the main-sail.

After that, we kept under cover of the bulwarks, and when next I looked out they had disappeared from the spit, and the spit itself had almost melted out of sight in the growing distance. That was, at least, the end of that; and before noon, to my inexpressible joy, the highest rock of Treasure Island had sunk into the blue round of sea.

We were so short of men that every one on board had to bear a hand – only the captain lying on a mattress in the stern and giving his orders; for, though greatly recovered, he was still in want of quiet. We laid her head for the nearest port in Spanish America, for we could not risk the voyage home without fresh hands; and as it was, what with baffling winds and a couple of fresh gales, we were all worn out before we reached it.

It was just at sundown when we cast anchor in a most beautiful land-locked gulf, and were immediately surrounded by shore boats full of Negroes, and Mexican Indians, and half-bloods, selling fruits and vegetables, and offering to dive for bits of money. The sight of so many good-humoured faces (especially the blacks), the taste of the tropical fruits, and above all, the lights that began to shine in the town, made a most charming contrast to our dark and bloody sojourn on the island; and the doctor and the squire, taking me along with them, went ashore to pass the early part of the night. Here they met the captain of an English man-of-war, fell in talk with him, went on board his ship, and, in short, had so agreeable a time, that day was breaking when we came alongside the *Hispaniola*.

Ben Gunn was on deck alone, and, as soon as we came on board, he began, with wonderful contortions, to make us a confession. Silver was gone. The maroon had connived at his escape in a shore boat some hours ago, and he now assured us he had only done so to preserve our lives, which would certainly have been forfeit if 'that man with the one leg had stayed aboard'. But this was not all. The sea-cook had not gone empty-handed. He had cut through a bulkhead unobserved, and had removed one of the sacks of coin, worth, perhaps, three or four hundred guineas, to help him on his further wanderings.

I think we were all pleased to be so cheaply quit of him.

Well, to make a long story short, we got a few hands on board, made a good cruise home, and the *Hispaniola* reached Bristol just as Mr Blandly was beginning to think of fitting out her consort. Five men only of those who had sailed returned with her. 'Drink and the devil had done for the rest,' with a vengeance; although, to be sure, we were not quite in so bad a case as that other ship they sang about:

> 'With one man of her crew alive,
> What put to sea with seventy-five.'

All of us had an ample share of the treasure, and used it wisely or foolishly, according to our natures. Captain Smollett is now retired from the sea. Gray not only saved his money, but, being suddenly smit with a desire to rise, also studied his profession; and he is now mate and part owner of a fine full-rigged ship; married besides, and the father of a family. As for Ben Gunn, he got a thousand pounds, which he spent or lost in three weeks, or, to be more exact, in nineteen days, for he was back begging on the twentieth. Then he was given a lodge to keep, exactly as he had feared upon the island; and he still lives, a great favourite, though something of a butt, with the country boys, and a notable singer in church on Sundays and saints' days.

Of Silver we have heard no more. That formidable seafaring man with one leg has at last gone clean out of my life; but I dare say he met his old Negress, and perhaps still lives in comfort with her and Captain Flint. It is to be hoped so, I suppose, for his chances of comfort in another world are very small.

The bar silver and the arms still lie, for all that I know, where Flint buried them; and certainly they shall lie there for me. Oxen and wainropes would not bring me back again to that accursed island; and the worst dreams that ever I have are when I hear the surf booming about its coasts, or start upright in bed, with the sharp voice of Captain Flint still ringing in my ears: 'Pieces of eight! pieces of eight!'

KIDNAPPED

Dedication

MY DEAR CHARLES BAXTER,

If you ever read this tale, you will likely ask yourself more questions than I should care to answer: as for instance how the Appin murder has come to fall in the year 1751, how the Torran rocks have crept so near to Earraid, or why the printed trial is silent as to all that touches David Balfour. These are nuts beyond my ability to crack. But if you tried me on the point of Alan's guilt or innocence, I think I could defend the reading of the text. To this day you will find the tradition of Appin clear in Alan's favour. If you inquire, you may even hear the descendants of 'the other man' who fired the shot are in the country to this day. But that other man's name, inquire as you please, you shall not hear; for the Highlander values a secret for itself and for the congenial exercise of keeping it. I might go on for long to justify one point and own another indefensible; it is more honest to confess at once how little I am touched by the desire of accuracy. This is no furniture for the scholar's library, but a book for the winter evening school-room when the tasks are over and the hour for bed draws near; and honest Alan, who was a grim old fire-eater in his day, has in this new avatar no more desperate purpose than to steal some young gentleman's attention from his Ovid, carry him awhile into the Highlands and the last century, and pack him to bed with some engaging images to mingle with his dreams.

As for you, my dear Charles, I do not even ask you to like the tale. But perhaps when he is older, your son will; he may then be pleased to find his father's name on the fly-leaf; and in the meanwhile it pleases me to set it there in memory of many days that were happy and some (now perhaps as pleasant to remember) that were sad. If it is strange for me to look back from a distance both in time and space on these bygone adventures of our youth, it must be stranger for you who tread the same streets – who may tomorrow open the door of the old Speculative, where we begin to rank with Scott and Robert Emmet and the beloved and inglorious Macbean – or may pass the corner of the close where that great society, the L.J.R., held its meetings and drank its beer, sitting in the seats of Burns and his companions. I think I see you, moving there by plain daylight, beholding with your natural eyes those places that have now become for your companion a part of the scenery of dreams. How, in the intervals of present business, the past must echo in your memory! Let it not echo often without some kind thoughts of your friend.

R.L.S.

SKERRYVORE,
BOURNEMOUTH

CHAPTER ONE

I Set Off Upon My Journey to the House of Shaws

I WILL BEGIN THE STORY OF my adventures with a certain morning early in the month of June, the year of grace 1751, when I took the key for the last time out of the door of my father's house. The sun began to shine upon the summit of the hills as I went down the road; and by the time I had come as far as the manse, the blackbirds were whistling in the garden lilacs, and the mist that hung around the valley in the time of the dawn was beginning to arise and die away.

Mr Campbell, the minister of Essendean, was waiting for me by the garden gate, good man! He asked me if I had breakfasted; and hearing that I lacked for nothing, he took my hand in both of his and clapped it kindly under his arm.

'Well, Davie, lad,' said he, 'I will go with you as far as the ford, to set you on the way.'

And we began to walk forward in silence.

'Are ye sorry to leave Essendean?' said he, after a while.

'Why, sir,' said I, 'If I knew where I was going, or what was likely to become of me, I would tell you candidly. Essendean is a good place indeed, and I have been very happy there; but then I have never been anywhere else. My father and mother, since they are both dead, I shall be no nearer to in Essendean than in the Kingdom of Hungary; and, to speak truth, if I thought I had a chance to better myself where I was going, I would go with a good will.'

'Ay?' said Mr Campbell. 'Very well, Davie. Then it behoves me to tell your fortune; or so far as I may. When your mother was gone, and your father (the worthy, Christian man) began to sicken for his end, he gave me in charge a certain letter, which he said was your inheritance. "So soon," says he, "as I am gone, and the house is redd up and the gear disposed of" (all which, Davie, hath been done) "give my boy this letter into his hand, and start him off to the house of Shaws, not far from Cramond. That is the place I came from," he said, "and it's where it befits that my boy should return. He is a steady lad," your father said, "and a canny goer; and I doubt not he will come safe, and be well liked where he goes."'

'The house of Shaws!' I cried. 'What had my poor father to do with the house of Shaws?'

'Nay,' said Mr Campbell, 'who can tell that for a surety? But the name of that family, Davie boy, is the name you bear – Balfours of Shaws: an ancient, honest, reputable house, peradventure in these latter days decayed. Your father, too, was a man of learning as befitted his position; no man more plausibly conducted school; nor had he the manner or the speech of a common dominie; but (as ye will yourself remember) I took aye a pleasure to have him to the manse to meet the gentry; and those of my own house, Campbell of Kilrennet, Campbell of

Dunswire, Campbell of Minch, and others, all well-kenned gentlemen, had pleasure in his society. Lastly, to put all the elements of this affair before you, here is the testamentary letter itself, superscribed by the own hand of our departed brother.'

He gave me the letter, which was addressed in these words: 'To the hands of Ebenezer Balfour, Esquire, of Shaws, in his house of Shaws, these will be delivered by my son, David Balfour.' My heart was beating hard at this great prospect now suddenly opening before a lad of sixteen years of age, the son of a poor country dominie in the Forest of Ettrick.

'Mr Campbell,' I stammered, 'and if you were in my shoes, would you go?'

'Of a surety,' said the minister, 'that would I, and without pause. A pretty lad like you should get to Cramond (which is near in by Edinburgh) in two days of walk. If the worst came to the worst, and your high relations (as I cannot but suppose them to be somewhat of your blood) should put you to the door, ye can but walk the two days back again and risp at the manse door. But I would rather hope that ye shall be well received, as your poor father forecast for you, and for anything that I ken, come to be a great man in time. And here, Davie, laddie,' he resumed, 'it lies near upon my conscience to improve this parting, and set you on the right guard against the dangers of the world.'

Here he cast about for a comfortable seat, lighted on a big boulder under a birch by the trackside, sate down upon it with a very long, serious upper lip, and, the sun now shining in upon us between two peaks, put his pocket-handkerchief over his cocked hat to shelter him. There, then, with uplifted forefinger, he first put me on my guard against a considerable number of heresies, to which I had no temptation, and urged upon me to be instant in my prayers and reading of the Bible. That done, he drew a picture of the great house that I was bound to, and how I should conduct myself with its inhabitants.

'Be soople, Davie, in things immaterial,' said he. 'Bear ye this in mind, that, though gentle born, ye have had a country rearing. Dinnae shame us, Davie, dinnae shame us! In yon great, muckle house, with all these domestics, upper and under, show youself as nice, as circumspect, as quick at the conception, and as slow of speech as any. As for the laird – remember he's the laird; I say no more: honour to whom honour. It's pleasure to obey a laird; or should be, to the young.'

'Well, sir,' said I, 'it may be; and I'll promise you I'll try to make it so.'

'Why, very well said,' replied Mr Campbell, heartily. 'And now to come to the material, or (to make a quibble) to the immaterial. I have here a little packet which contains four things.' He tugged it, as he spoke, and with some difficulty, from the skirt pocket of his coat. 'Of these four things, the first is your legal due: the little pickle money for your father's books and plenishing, which I have bought (as I have explained from the first) in the design of re-selling at a profit to the incoming dominie. The other three are gifties that Mrs Campbell and myself would be blithe of your acceptance. The first, which is round, will likely please ye best at the first off-go; but, O Davie, laddie, it's but a drop of water in the sea; it'll help you but a step, and vanish like the morning. The second, which is flat and square and written upon, will stand by you through life, like a good staff for the road, and a good pillow to your head in sickness. And as for the last, which is cubical, that'll see you, it's my prayerful wish, into a better land.'

With that he got upon his feet, took off his hat, and prayed a little while aloud, and in affecting terms, for a young man setting out into the world; then suddenly took me in his arms and embraced me very hard; then held me at arm's length, looking at me with his face all working with sorrow; and then whipped about, and crying goodbye to me, set off backward by the way that we had come at a sort of jogging run. It might have been laughable to another; but I was in no mind to laugh. I watched him as long as he was in sight; and he never stopped hurrying, nor once looked back. Then it came in upon my mind that this was all his sorrow at my departure; and my conscience smote me hard and fast, because I, for my part, was overjoyed to get away out of that quiet countryside, and go to a great, busy house, among rich and respected gentlefolk of my own name and blood.

'Davie, Davie,' I thought, 'was ever seen such black ingratitude? Can you forget old favours and old friends at the mere whistle of a name? Fie, fie; think shame!'

And I sat down on the boulder the good man had just left, and opened the parcel to see the nature of my gifts. That which he had called cubical, I had never had much doubt of; sure enough it was a little Bible, to carry in a plaid-neuk. That which he had called round, I found to be a shilling piece; and the third, which was to help me so wonderfully both in health and sickness all the days of my life, was a little piece of coarse yellow paper, written upon thus in red ink:

TO MAKE LILLY OF THE VALLEY WATER – Take the flowers of lilly of the valley and distil them in sack, and drink a spooneful or two as there is occasion. It restores speech to those that have the dumb palsey. It is good against the Gout; it comforts the heart and strengthens the memory; and the flowers, put into a Glasse, close stopt, and set into ane hill of ants for a month, then take it out, and you will find a liquor which comes from the flowers, which keep in a vial; it is good, ill or well, and whether man or woman.

And then, in the minister's own hand, was added:

Likewise for sprains, rub it in; and for the cholic, a great spoonful in the hour.

To be sure, I laughed over this; but it was rather tremulous laughter; and I was glad to get my bundle on my staff's end and set out over the ford and up the hill upon the farther side; till, just as I came on the green drove-road running wide through the heather, I took my last look of Kirk Essendean, the trees about the manse, and the big rowans in the kirkyard where my father and my mother lay.

CHAPTER TWO

I Come to My Journey's End

ON THE FORENOON OF THE second day, coming to the top of a hill, I saw the country fall away before me down to the sea; and in the midst of this descent, on a long ridge, the city of Edinburgh smoking like a kiln. There was a flag upon the castle, and ships moving or lying anchored in the firth; both of which, for as far away as they were, I could distinguish clearly; and both brought my country heart into my mouth.

Presently after, I came by a house where a shepherd lived, and got a·rough direction for the neighbourhood of Cramond; and so, from one to another, worked my way to the westward of the capital by Colinton, till I came out upon the Glasgow road. And there, to my great pleasure and wonder, I beheld a regiment marching to the fifes, every foot in time; an old red-faced general on a grey horse at the one end, and at the other the company of Grenadiers, with their Pope's-hats. The pride of life seemed to mount into my brain at the sight of the red-coats and the hearing of that merry music.

A little farther on, and I was told I was in Cramond parish, and began to substitute in my inquiries the name of the house of Shaws. It was a word that seemed to surprise those of whom I sought my way. At first I thought the plainness of my appearance, in my country habit, and that all dusty from the road, consorted ill with the greatness of the place to which I was bound. But after two, or maybe three, had given me the same look and the same answer, I began to take it in my head there was something strange about the Shaws itself.

The better to set this fear at rest, I changed the form of my inquiries; and spying an honest fellow coming along a lane on the shaft of his cart, I asked him if he had ever heard tell of a house they called the house of Shaws.

He stopped his cart and looked at me, like the others.

'Ay,' said he. 'What for?'

'It's a great house?' I asked.

'Doubtless,' says he. 'The house is a big, muckle house.'

'Ay,' said I, 'but the folk that are in it?'

'Folk?' cried he. 'Are ye daft? There's nae folk there – to call folk.'

'What?' says I; 'not Mr Ebenezer?'

'Oh, ay,' says the man, 'there's the laird, to be sure, if it's him you're wanting. What'll like be your business, mannie?'

'I was led to think that I would get a situation,' I said, looking as modest as I could.

'What?' cries the carter, in so sharp a note that his very horse started; and then, 'Well, mannie,' he added, 'it's nane of my affairs; but ye seem a decent-spoken lad; and if ye'll take a word from me, ye'll keep clear of the Shaws.'

The next person I came across was a dapper little man in a beautiful white wig, whom I saw to be a barber on his rounds; and knowing well that barbers were great gossips, I asked him plainly what sort of a man was Mr Balfour of the Shaws.

'Hoot, hoot, hoot,' said the barber, 'nae kind of a man, nae kind of a man at all'; and began to ask me very shrewdly what my business was; but I was more than a match for him at that, and he went on to his next customer no wiser than he came.

I cannot well describe the blow this dealt to my illusions. The more indistinct the accusations were, the less I liked them, for they left the wider field to fancy. What kind of a great house was this, that all the parish should start and stare to be asked the way to it? or what sort of a gentleman, that his ill-fame should be thus current on the wayside? If an hour's walking would have brought me back to Essendean, I had left my adventure then and there, and returned to Mr Campbell's. But when I had come so far a way already, mere shame would not suffer me to desist till I had put the matter to the touch of proof; I was bound, out of mere self-respect, to carry it through; and little as I liked the sound of what I heard, and slow as I began to travel, I still kept asking my way and still kept advancing.

It was drawing on to sundown when I met a stout, dark, sour-looking woman coming trudging down a hill; and she, when I had put my usual question, turned sharp about, accompanied me back to the summit she had just left, and pointed to a great bulk of building standing very bare upon a green in the bottom of the next valley. The country was pleasant round about, running in low hills, pleasantly watered and wooded, and the crops, to my eyes, wonderfully good; but the house itself appeared to be a kind of ruin; no road led up to it; no smoke arose from any of the chimneys; nor was there any semblance of a garden. My heart sank. 'That!' I cried.

The woman's face lit up with a malignant anger. 'That is the house of Shaws!' she cried. 'Blood built it; blood stopped the building of it; blood shall bring it down. See here!' she cried again – 'I spit upon the ground, and crack my thumb at it! Black be its fall! If ye see the laird, tell him what ye hear; tell him this makes the twelve hunner and nineteen time that Jennet Clouston has called down the curse on him and his house, byre, and stable, man, guest, and master, wife, miss, or bairn – black, black be their fall!'

And the woman, whose voice had risen to a kind of eldritch sing-song, turned with a skip, and was gone. I stood where she left me, with my hair on end. In those days folk still believed in witches and trembled at a curse; and this one, falling so pat, like a wayside omen, to arrest me ere I carried out my purpose, took the pith out of my legs.

I sat me down and stared at the house of Shaws. The more I looked, the pleasanter that countryside appeared; being all set with hawthorn bushes full of flowers; the fields dotted with sheep; a fine flight of rooks in the sky; and every sign of a kind soil and climate; and yet the barrack in the midst of it went sore against my fancy.

Country folk went by from the fields as I sat there on the side of the ditch, but I lacked the spirit to give them a good-e'en. At last the sun went down, and then, right up against the yellow sky, I saw a scroll of smoke go mounting, not much thicker, as it seemed to me, than the smoke of a candle; but still there it was, and meant a fire, and warmth, and cookery, and some living inhabitant that must have lit it; and this comforted my heart wonderfully – more, I feel sure, than a whole flask of the lily of the valley water that Mrs Campbell set so great a store by.

So I set forward by a little faint track in the grass that led in my direction. It was very faint indeed to be the only way to a place of habitation; yet I saw no other. Presently it brought me to stone uprights, with an unroofed lodge beside them, and coats of arms upon the top. A main entrance, it was plainly meant to be, but never finished; instead of gates of wrought iron, a pair of hurdles were tied across with a straw rope; and as there were no park walls, nor any sign of avenue, the track that I was following passed on the right hand of the pillars, and went wandering on toward the house.

The nearer I got to that, the drearier it appeared. It seemed like the one wing of a house that had never been finished. What should have been the inner end stood open on the upper floors, and showed against the sky with steps and stairs of uncompleted masonry. Many of the windows were unglazed, and bats flew in and out like doves out of a dovecote.

The night had begun to fall as I got close; and in three of the lower windows, which were very high up, and narrow, and well barred, the changing light of a little fire began to glimmer.

Was this the palace I had been coming to? Was it within these walls that I was to seek new friends and begin great fortunes? Why, in my father's house on Essen-Waterside, the fire and the bright lights would show a mile away, and the door open to a beggar's knock.

I came forward cautiously, and giving ear as I came, heard someone rattling with dishes, and a little dry, eager cough that came in fits; but there was no sound of speech, and not a dog barked.

The door, as well as I could see it in the dim light, was a great piece of wood all studded with nails; and I lifted my hand with a faint heart under my jacket, and knocked once. Then I stood and waited. The house had fallen into a dead silence; a whole minute passed away, and nothing stirred but the bats overhead. I knocked again, and hearkened again. By this time my ears had grown so accustomed to the quiet, that I could hear the ticking of the clock inside as it slowly counted out the seconds; but whoever was in that house kept deadly still, and must have held his breath.

I was in two minds whether to run away; but anger got the upper hand, and I began instead to rain kicks and buffets on the door, and to shout out aloud for Mr Balfour. I was in full career, when I heard the cough right overhead, and jumping back and looking up, beheld a man's head in a tall nightcap, and the bell mouth of a blunderbuss, at one of the first storey windows.

'It's loaded,' said a voice.

'I have come here with a letter,' I said, 'to Mr Ebenezer Balfour of Shaws. Is he here?'

'From whom is it?' asked the man with the blunderbuss.

'That is neither here nor there,' said I, for I was growing very wroth.

'Well,' was the reply, 'ye can put it down upon the doorstep, and be off with ye.'

'I will do no such thing,' I cried. 'I will deliver it into Mr Balfour's hands, as it was meant I should. It is a letter of introduction.'

'A what?' cried the voice sharply.

I repeated what I had said.

'Who are ye, yourself?' was the next question, after a considerable pause.

'I am not ashamed of my name,' said I. 'They call me David Balfour.'

At that, I made sure the man started, for I heard the blunderbuss rattle on the window-sill; and it was after quite a long pause, and with a curious change of voice, that the next question followed:

'Is your father dead?'

I was so much surprised at this, that I could find no voice to answer, but stood staring.

'Ay,' the man resumed, 'he'll be dead, no doubt; and that'll be what brings ye chapping to my door.' Another pause, and then, defiantly, 'Well, man,' he said, 'I'll let ye in'; and he disappeared from the window.

CHAPTER THREE

I Make Acquaintance of My Uncle

PRESENTLY THERE CAME A great rattling of chains and bolts, and the door was cautiously opened, and shut to again behind me as soon as I had passed.

'Go into the kitchen and touch naething,' said the voice; and while the person of the house set himself to replacing the defences of the door, I gropped my way forward and entered the kitchen.

The fire had burned up fairly bright, and showed me the barest room I think I ever put my eyes on. Half-a-dozen dishes stood upon the shelves; the table was laid for supper with a bowl of porridge, a horn spoon, and a cup of small beer. Besides what I have named, there was not another thing in that great, stone-vaulted, empty chamber but lockfast chests arranged along the wall and a corner cupboard with a padlock.

As soon as the last chain was up, the man rejoined me. He was a mean, stooping, narrow-shouldered, clay-faced creature; and his age might have been anything between fifty and seventy. His nightcap was of flannel, and so was the nightgown that he wore, instead of coat and waistcoat, over his ragged shirt. He was long unshaved; but what most distressed and even daunted me, he would neither take his eyes away from me nor look me fairly in the face. What he was, whether by trade or birth, was more than I could fathom; but he seemed most like an old, unprofitable serving-man, who should have been left in charge of that big house upon board wages.

'Are ye sharp-set?' he asked, glancing at about the level of my knee. 'Ye can eat that drop parritch.'

I said I feared it was his own supper.

'Oh,' said he, 'I can do fine wanting it. I'll take the ale, though, for it slockens* my cough.' He drank the cup about half out, still keeping an eye upon me as he drank; and then suddenly held out his hand. 'Let's see the letter,' said he.

I told him the letter was for Mr Balfour; not for him.

'And who do you think I am?' says he. 'Give me Alexander's letter!'

'You know my father's name?'

'It would be strange if I didnae,' he returned, 'for he was my born brother; and little as ye seem to like either me or my house, or my good parritch, I'm your born uncle, Davie, my man, and you my born nephew. So give us the letter, and sit down and fill your kyte.'

If I had been some years younger, what with shame, weariness, and disappointment, I believe I had burst into tears. As it was, I could find no words, neither black nor white, but handed him the letter, and sat down to the porridge with as little appetite for meat as ever a young man had.

Meanwhile, my uncle, stooping over the fire, turned the letter over and over in his hands.

'Do ye ken what's in it?' he asked, suddenly.

'You see for yourself, sir,' said I, 'that the seal has not been broken.'

'Aye,' said he, 'but what brought you here?'

'To give the letter,' said I.

'No,' says he, cunningly, 'but ye'll have had some hopes, nae doubt?'

'I confess, sir,' said I, 'when I was told that I had kinsfolk well-to-do, I did indeed indulge the hope that they might help me in my life. But I am no beggar; I look for no favours at your hands, and I want none that are not freely given. For as poor as I appear, I have friends of my own that will be blithe to help me.'

'Hoot-toot' said Uncle Ebenezer, 'dinnae fly up in the snuff at me. We'll agree fine yet. And, Davie, my man, if you're done with that bit parritch, I could just take a sup of it myself. Ay,' he continued, as soon as he had ousted me from the stool and spoon, 'they're fine, halesome food – they're grand food, parritch.' He murmured a little grace to himself and fell to. 'Your father was very fond of his meat, I mind; he was a hearty, if not a great eater; but as for me, I could never do mair than pyke at food.' He took a pull at the small beer, which probably reminded him of hospitable duties; for his next speech ran thus: 'If ye're dry, ye'll find water behind the door.'

To this I returned no answer, standing stiffly on my two feet, and looking down upon my uncle with a mighty angry heart. He, on his part, continued to eat like a man under some pressure of time, and to throw out little darting glances now at my shoes and now at my home-spun stockings. Once only, when he had ventured to look a little higher, our eyes met; and no thief taken with a hand in a man's pocket could have shown more lively signals of distress. This set me in a muse, whether his timidity arose from too long a disuse of any human company; and whether perhaps, upon a little trial, it might pass off, and my uncle change into an altogether different man. From this I was awakened by his sharp voice.

'Your father's been long dead?', he asked.

'Three weeks sir,' said I.

*Moistens

'He was a secret man, Alexander – a secret, silent man,' he continued. 'He never said muckle when he was young. He'll never have spoken muckle of me?'

'I never knew, sir, till you told it me yourself, that he had any brother.'

'Dear me, dear me!' said Ebenezer. 'Nor yet of Shaws, I dare say?'

'Not so much as the name, sir,' said I.

'To think o' that!' said he. 'A strange nature of a man!' For all that, he seemed singularly satisfied, but whether with himself, or me, or with this conduct of my father's, was more than I could read. Certainly, however, he seemed to be outgrowing that distaste, or ill-will, that he had conceived at first against my person; for presently he jumped up, came across the room behind me, and hit me a smack upon the shoulder. 'We'll agree fine yet!' he cried. 'I'm just as glad I let you in. And now come awa' to your bed.'

To my surprise, he lit no lamp or candle, but set forth into the dark passage, groped his way, breathing deeply, up a flight of steps, and paused before a door, which he unlocked. I was close upon his heels, having stumbled after him as best I might; and he bade me go in, for that was my chamber. I did as he bid, but paused after a few steps, and begged a light to go to bed with.

'Hoot-toot!' said Uncle Ebenezer, 'there's a fine room.'

'Neither moon nor star, sir, and pit-mirk*,' said I. 'I cannae see the bed.'

'Hoot-toot, hoot-toot' said he. 'Lights in a house is a thing I dinnae agree with. I'm unco feared of fires. Good night to ye, Davie, my man.' And before I had time to add a further protest, he pulled the door to, and I heard him lock me in from the outside.

I did not know whether to laugh or cry. The room was as cold as a well, and the bed, when I found had my way to it, as damp as a peat-hag; but by good fortune I had caught up my bundle and my plaid, and rolling myself in the latter, I lay down upon the floor under lee of the big bedstead, and fell speedily asleep.

With the first peep of day I opened my eyes, to find myself in a great chamber, hung with stamped leather, furnished with fine embroidered furniture, and lit by three fair windows. Ten years ago, or perhaps twenty, it must have been as pleasant a room to lie down or to awake in, as a man could wish; but damp, dirt, disuse, and the mice and spiders had done their worst since then. Many of the window-panes, besides, were broken; and indeed this was so common a feature in that house, that I believe my uncle must at some time have stood a siege from his indignant neighbours – perhaps with Jennet Clouston at their head.

Meanwhile the sun was shining outside; and being very cold in that miserable room, I knocked and shouted till my gaoler came and let me out. He carried me to the back of the house, where was a draw-well, and told me to 'wash my face there, if I wanted'; and when that was done, I made the best of my own way back to the kitchen, where he had lit the fire and was making the porridge. The table was laid with two bowls and two horn spoons, but the same single measure of small beer. Perhaps my eye rested on this particular with some surprise, and perhaps my uncle observed it; for he spoke up as if in answer to my thought, asking me if I would like to drink ale – for so he called it.

I told him such was my habit, but not to put himself about.

'Na, na,' said he; 'I'll deny you nothing in reason.'

He fetched another cup from the shelf; and then, to my great surprise, instead

*Dark as the pit

of drawing more beer, he poured an accurate half from one cup to the other. There was a kind of nobleness in this that took my breath away; if my uncle was certainly a miser, he was one of that thorough breed that goes near to make the vice respectable.

When we had made an end of our meal, my uncle Ebenezer unlocked a drawer, and drew out of it a clay pipe and a lump of tobacco, from which he cut one fill before he locked it up again. Then he sat down in the sun at one of the windows and silently smoked. From time to time his eyes came coasting round to me, and he shot out one of his questions. Once it was, 'And your mother?' And when I had told him that she, too, was dead, 'Ay, she was a bonnie lassie!' Then, after another long pause, 'Whae were these friends o' yours?'

I told him they were different gentlemen of the name of Campbell; though, indeed, there was only one, and that the minister, that had ever taken the least note of me; but I began to think my uncle made too light of my position, and finding myself all alone with him, I did not wish him to suppose me helpless.

He seemed to turn this over in his mind; and then, 'Davie, my man,' said he, 'ye've come to the right bit when ye came to your Uncle Ebenezer. I've a great notion of the family, and I mean to do the right by you; but while I'm taking a bit think to mysel' of what's the best thing to put you to – whether the law, or the meenistry, or maybe the army, whilk is what boys are fondest of – I wouldnae like the Balfours to be humbled before a wheen Hieland Campbells, and I'll ask you to keep your tongue within your teeth. Nae letters; nae messages; no kind of word to onybody; or else – there's my door.'

'Uncle Ebenezer,' said I, 'I've no manner of reason to suppose you mean anything but well by me. For all that, I would have you to know that I have a pride of my own. It was by no will of mine that I came seeking you; and if you show me your door again, I'll take you at the word.'

He seemed grievously put out. 'Hoots-toots,' said he, 'ca' cannie, man – ca' cannie! Bide a day or two. I'm nae warlock, to find a fortune for you in the bottom of a parritch bowl; but just you give me a day or two, and say naething to naebody, and as sure as sure, I'll do the right by you.'

'Very well,' said I, 'enough said. If you want to help me, there's no doubt but I'll be glad of it, and none but I'll be grateful.'

It seemed to me (too soon, I daresay) that I was getting the upper hand of my uncle; and I began next to say that I must have the bed and bedclothes aired and put to sun-dry; for nothing would make me sleep in such a pickle.

'Is this my house or yours?' said he, in his keen voice, and then all of a sudden broke off. 'Na, na,' said he, 'I dinnae mean that. What's mine is yours, Davie, my man, and what's yours is mine. Blood's thicker than water; and there's naebody but you and me that ought the name.' And then on he rambled about the family, and its ancient greatness, and his father that began to enlarge the house, and himself that stopped the building as a sinful waste; and this put it in my head to give him Jennet Clouston's message.

'The limmer!' he cried. 'Twelve hunner and fifteen – that's every day since I had the limmer rowpit*! Dod, David, I'll have her roasted on red peats before I'm by with it! A witch – a proclaimed witch! I'll aff and see the session clerk.'

And with that he opened a chest, and got out a very old and well-preserved

*Sold up

blue coat and waistcoat, and a good enough beaver hat, both without lace. These he threw on anyway, and taking a staff from the cupboard, locked all up again, and was for setting out, when a thought arrested him.

'I cannae leave you by yoursel' in the house,' said he. 'I'll have to lock you out.'

The blood came into my face. 'if you lock me out,' I said, 'it'll be the last you see of me in friendship.'

He turned very pale, and sucked his mouth in. 'This is no the way,' said he, looking wickedly at a corner of the floor – 'this is no the way to win my favour, David.'

'Sir,' says I, 'with a proper reverence for your age and our common blood, I do not value your favour at a boddle's purchase. I was brought up to have a good conceit of myself; and if you were all the uncle, and all the family, I had in the world ten times over, I wouldn't buy your liking at such prices.'

Uncle Ebenezer went and looked out of the window for a while. I could see him all trembling and twitching, like a man with palsy. But when he turned round, he had a smile upon his face.

'Well, well,' said he, 'we must bear and forbear. I'll no go; that's all that's to be said of it.'

'Uncle Ebenezer,' I said, 'I can make nothing out of this. You use me like a thief; you hate to have me in this house; you let me see it, every word and every minute; it's not possible that you can like me; and as for me, I've spoken to you as I never thought to speak to any man. Why do you seek to help me, then? Let me gang back – let me gang back to the friends I have, and that like me!'

'Na, na; na, na,' he said, very earnestly. 'I like you fine; we'll agree fine yet; and for the honour of the house I couldnae let you leave the way ye came. Bide here quiet, there's a good lad; just you bide here quiet a bittie, and ye'll find that we agree.'

'well, sir,' said I, after I had thought the matter out in silence, 'I'll stay a while. It's more just I should be helped by my own blood than strangers; and if we don't agree, I'll do my best it shall be through no fault of mine.'

CHAPTER FOUR

I Run a Great Danger in the House of Shaws

FOR A DAY THAT WAS BEGUN so ill, the day passed fairly well. We had the porridge cold again at noon, and hot porridge at night; porridge and small beer was my uncle's diet. He spoke but little, and that in the same way as before, shooting a question at me after a long silence; and when I sought to lead him in talk about my future, slipped out of it again. In a room next door to the kitchen, where he suffered me to go, I found a great number of books, both Latin and English, in which I took great pleasure all the afternoon. Indeed the time passed so lightly in this good company, that I began to be almost reconciled to my residence at Shaws; and nothing but the sight of my uncle, and his eyes playing hide and seek with mine, revived the force of my distrust.

One thing I discovered, which put me in some doubt. This was an entry on the fly-leaf of a chapbook (one of Patrick Walker's) plainly written in my father's hand and thus conceived: To my brother Ebenezer on his fifth birthday.' Now, what puzzled me was this: That as my father was of course the younger brother, he must either have made some strange error, or he must have written, before he was yet five, an excellent, clear, manly hand of writing.

I tried to get this out of my head; but though I took down many interesting authors, old and new, history, poetry, and story-book, this notion of my father's hand of writing stuck to me; and when at length I went back into the kitchen, and sat down once more to porridge and small beer, the first thing I said to Uncle Ebenezer was to ask him if my father had not been very quick at his book.

'Alexander? No him!' was the reply. 'I was far quicker mysel'; I was a clever chappie when I was young. Why, I could read as soon as he could.'

This puzzled me yet more: and a thought coming into my head, I asked if he and my father had been twins.

He jumped upon his stool, and the horn spoon fell out of his hand upon the floor. 'What gars ye ask that?' he said, and caught me by the breast of the jacket, and looked this time straight into my eyes; his own, which were little and light, and bright like a bird's blinking and winking strangely.

'What do you mean?' I asked, very calmly, for I was far stronger than he, and not easily frightened. 'Take your hand from my jacket. This is no way to behave.'

My uncle seemed to make a great effort upon himself. 'Dod, man David,' he said, 'ye shouldnae speak to me about your father. That's where the mistake is.' He sat a while and shook, blinking in his plate; 'He was all the brother that ever I had,' he added, but with no heart in his voice; and then he caught his spoon and fell to supper again, but still shaking.

Now this last passage, this laying of hands upon my person and sudden profession of love for my dead father, went so clean beyond my comprehension that it put me into both fear and hope. On the one hand, I began to think my uncle was perhaps insane and might be dangerous; on the other, there came up into my mind (quite unbidden by me and even discouraged) a story like some ballad I had heard folk singing, of a poor lad that was a rightful heir and a wicked kinsman that tried to keep him from his own. For why should my uncle play a part with a relative that came, almost a beggar, to his door, unless in his heart he had some cause to fear him?

With this notion, all unacknowledged, but nevertheless getting firmly settled in my head, I now began to imitate his covert looks; so that we sat at table like a cat and a mouse, each stealthily observing the other. Not another word had he to say to me, black or white, but was busy turning something secretly over in his mind; and the longer we sat and the more I looked at him, the more certain I became that the something was unfriendly to myself.

When he had cleared the platter, he got out a single pipeful of tobacco, just as in the morning, turned round a stool into the chimney corner, and sat a while smoking, with his back to me.

'Davie,' he said at length, 'I've been thinking'; then he paused, and said it again. 'There's a wee bit siller that I half promised ye before ye were born,' he continued; 'promised it to your father. Oh, naething legal, ye understand; just gentlemen daffing at their wine. Well I keepit that bit money separate – it was a great expense, but a promise is a promise – and it has grown by now to be a maitter of just precisely – just exactly' – and here he paused and stumbled – 'of just exactly forty pounds!' This last he rapped out with a sidelong glance over his shoulder; and the next moment added, almost with a scream, 'Scots!'

The pound Scots being the same thing as an English shilling, the difference made by this second thought was considerable; I could see, besides, that the whole story was a lie, invented with some end which it puzzled me to guess; and I made no attempt to conceal the tone of raillery in which I answered——

'Oh, think again, sir! Pounds sterling, I believe!'

'That's what I said,' returned my uncle: 'pounds sterling! And if you'll step out-by to the door a minute, just to see what kind of a night it is, I'll git it out to ye and call ye in again.'

I did his will, smiling to myself in my contempt that he should think I was so easily to be deceived. It was a dark night, with a few stars low down; and as I stood just outside the door, I heard a hollow moaning of wind far off among the hills. I said to myself there was something thundery and changeful in the weather, and little knew of what a vast importance that should prove to me before the evening passed.

When I was called in again, my uncle counted out into my hand seven and thirty golden guinea pieces; the rest was in his hand, in small gold and silver; but his heart failed him there, and he crammed the change into his pocket.

'There,' said he, 'that'll show you! I'm a queer man, and strange wi' strangers; but my word is my bond, and there's the proof of it.'

Now, my uncle seemed so miserly that I was struck dumb by this sudden generosity, and could find no words in which to thank him.

'No a word!' said he. 'Nae thanks: I want nae thanks. I do my duty; I'm no saying that everybody would have done it; but for my part (though I'm a careful body, too) it's a pleasure to me to do the right by my brother's son; and it's a pleasure to me to think that now we'll agree as such near friends should.'

I spoke him in return as handsomely as I was able; but all the while I was wondering what would come next, and why he had parted with his precious guineas; for as to the reason he had given, a baby would have refused it.

Presently, he looked towards me sideways.

'And see here,' says he, 'tit for tat.'

I told him I was ready to prove my gratitude in any reasonable degree, and then waited, looking for some monstrous demand. And yet, when at last he plucked up courage to speak, it was only to tell me (very properly, as I thought) that he was growing old and a little broken, and that he would expect me to help him with the house and the bit garden.

I answered, and expressed my readiness to serve.

'Well,' he said, 'let's begin.' He pulled out of his pocket a rusty key. 'There,' says he, 'there's the key of the stairtower at the far end of the house. Ye can only win into it from the outside, for that part of the house is no finished. Gang ye in there, and up the stairs, and bring me down the chest that's at the top. There's papers in't,' he added.

'Can I have a light, sir?' said I.

'Na,' said he, very cunningly, 'Nae lights in my house.'

'Very well, sir,' said I. 'Are the stairs good?'

'They're grand,' said he; and then as I was going, 'Keep to the wall,' he added; 'there's nae banisters. But the stairs are grand under foot.'

Out I went into the night. The wind was still moaning in the distance, though never a breath of it came near the house of Shaws. It had fallen blacker then ever; and I was glad to feel along the wall, till I came the length of the stair-tower door at the far end of the unfinished wing. I had got the key into the keyhole and had just turned it, when all upon a sudden, without sound of wind or thunder, the whole sky lighted up with wild fire and went black again. I had to put my hand over my eyes to get back to the colour of the darkness; and indeed I was already half blinded when I stepped into the tower.

It was so dark inside, it seemed a body could scarce breathe; but I pushed out with foot and hand, and presently struck the wall with the one and the lowermost round of the stair with the other. The wall, by the touch, was of fine hewn stone; the steps too, though somewhat steep and narrow, were of polished mason-work, and regular and solid under foot. Minding my uncle's word about the banisters, I kept close to the tower side, and felt my way in the pitch darkness with a beating heart.

The house of Shaws stood some five full storeys high, not counting lofts. Well, as I advanced, it seemed to me the stair grew airier and a thought more lightsome; and I was wondering what might be the cause of this change, when a second blink of the summer lightning came and went. If I did not cry out, it was because fear had me by the throat; and if I did not fall, it was more by Heaven's mercy than my own strength. It was not only that the flash shone in on every side through breaches in the wall, so that I seemed to be clambering aloft upon an open scaffold, but the same passing brightness showed me the steps were of unequal length, and that one of my feet rested that moment within two inches of the well.

This was the grand stair! I thought; and with the thought, a gust of a kind of angry courage came into my heart. My uncle had sent me here, certainly to run great risks, perhaps to die. I swore I would settle that 'perhaps', if I should break my neck for it; got me down upon my hands and knees; and as slowly as a snail, feeling before me every inch, and testing the solidity of every stone, I continued to ascend the stair. The darkness, by contrast with the flash, appeared to have redoubled; nor was that all, for my ears were now troubled and my mind confounded by a great stir of bats in the top part of the tower, and the foul beasts, flying downwards, sometimes beat about my face and body.

The tower, I should have said, was square; and in every corner the step was made of a great stone of a different shape, to join the flights. Well, I had come close to one of these turns, when, feeling forward as usual, my hand slipped upon an edge and found nothing but emptiness beyond it. The stair had been carried no higher: to set a stranger mounting it in the darkness was to send him straight to his death; and (although, thanks to the lightning and my own precautions, I was safe enough) the mere thought of the peril in which I might have stood, and the dreadful height I might have fallen brought out the sweat upon my body and relaxed my joints.

But I knew what I wanted now, and turned and groped my way down again, with a wonderful anger in my heart. About half-way down, the wind sprang up in a clap and shook the tower, and died again; the rain followed; and before I had reached the ground level it fell in buckets. I put out my head into the storm, and looked along towards the kitchen. The door, which I had shut behind me when I left, now stood open, and shed a little glimmer of light; and I thought I could see a figure standing in the rain, quite still, like a man hearkening. And then there came a blinding flash, which showed me my uncle plainly, just where I had fancied him to stand; and hard upon the heels of it, a great tow-row of thunder.

Now, whether my uncle thought the crash to be the sound of my fall, or whether he heard in it God's voice denouncing murder, I will leave you to guess. Certain it is, at least, that he was seized on by a kind of panic fear, and that he ran into the house and left the door open behind him. I followed as softly as I could, and coming unheard into the kitchen, stood and watched him.

He had found time to open the corner cupboard and bring out a great case bottle of aqua vitae, and now sat with his back towards me at the table. Ever and again he would be seized with a fit of deadly shuddering and groan aloud, and carrying the bottle to his lips, drink down the raw spirits by the mouthful.

I stepped forward, came close behind him where he sat, and suddenly clapping my two hands down upon his shoulders – 'Ah!' cried I.

My uncle gave a kind of broken cry like a sheep's bleat, flung up his arms, and tumbled to the floor like a dead man. I was somewhat shocked at this; but I had myself to look to first of all, and did not hesitate to let him lie as he had fallen. The keys were hanging in the cupboard; and it was my design to furnish myself with arms before my uncle should come again to his senses and the power of devising evil. In the cupboard were a few bottles, some apparently of medicine; a great many bills and other papers, which I should willingly enough have rummaged, had I had the time; and a few necessaries, that were nothing to my purpose. Thence I turned to the chests. The first was full of meal; the second of money-bags and papers tied into sheaves; in the third, with many other things (and these for the most part clothes), I found a rusty, ugly-looking Highland dirk without the scabbard. This, then, I concealed inside my waistcoat, and turned to my uncle.

He lay as he had fallen, all huddled, with one knee up and one arm sprawling abroad; his face had a strange colour of blue, and he seemed to have ceased breathing. Fear came on me that he was dead; then I got water and dashed it in his face; and with that he seemed to come a little to himself, working his mouth and fluttering his eyelids. At last he looked up and saw me, and there came into his eyes a terror that was not of this world.

'Come, come,' said I, 'sit up.'

'Are ye alive?' he sobbed. 'O man, are ye alive?'

'That am I,' said I. 'Small thanks to you!'

He had begun to seek for his breath with deep sighs. 'The blue phial,' said he – 'in the aumry – the blue phial.' His breath came slower still.

I ran to the cupboard, and, sure enough, found there a blue phial of medicine, with the dose written on it on a paper, and this I administered to him with what speed I might.

'It's the trouble,' said he, reviving a little; 'I have a trouble, Davie. It's my heart.'

I set him on a chair and looked at him. It is true I felt some pity for a man that looked so sick, but I was full besides of righteous anger; and I numbered over before him the points on which I wanted explanation: why he lied to me at every word; why he feared that I should leave him; why he disliked it to be hinted that he and my father were twins – 'Is that because it is true?' I asked; why he had given me money to which I was convinced I had no claim; and, last of all, why he had tried to kill me. He heard me all through in silence; and then, in a broken voice, begged me to let him go to bed.

'I'll tell ye the morn,' he said; 'as sure as death I will.'

And so weak was he that I could do nothing but consent. I locked him into his room, however, and pocketed the key; and then returning to the kitchen, made up such a blaze as had not shone there for many a long year, and wrapping myself in my plaid, lay down upon the chests and fell asleep.

CHAPTER FIVE

I Go to the Queen's Ferry

MUCH RAIN FELL IN THE night; and the next morning there blew a bitter wintry wind out of the north-west, driving scattered clouds. For all that, and before the sun began to peep or the last of the stars had vanished, I made my way to the side of the burn, and had a plunge in a deep whirling pool. All aglow from my bath, I sat down once more beside the fire, which I replenished, and began gravely to consider my position.

There was now no doubt about my uncle's enmity; there was no doubt I carried my life in my hand, and he would leave no stone unturned that he might compass my destruction. But I was young and spirited, and like most lads that have been country-bred, I had a great opinion of my shrewdness. I had come to his door no better than a beggar and little more than a child; he had met me with treachery and violence; it would be a fine consummation to take the upper hand, and drive him like a herd of sheep.

I sat there nursing my knee and smiling at the fire; and I saw myself in fancy smell out his secrets one after another, and grow to be that man's king and ruler. The warlock of Essendean, they say, had made a mirror in which men could read the future; it must have been of other stuff than burning coal; for in all the shapes and pictures that I sat and gazed at, there was never a ship, never a seaman with a hairy cap, never a big bludgeon for my silly head, or the least sign of all those tribulations that were ripe to fall on me.

Presently, all swollen with conceit, I went upstairs and gave my prisoner his liberty. He gave me good morning civilly; and I gave the same to him, smiling down upon him from the heights of my sufficiency. Soon we were set to breakfast, as it might have been the day before.

'Well, sir,' said I, with a jeering tone, 'have you nothing more to say to me?' And then, as he made no articulate reply, 'It will be time, I think, to understand each other,' I continued. 'You took me for a country Johnnie Raw, with no more mother-wit or courage than a porridge-stick. I took you for a good man, or no worse than others at the least. It seems we were both wrong. What cause you have to fear me, to cheat me, and to attempt my life——'

He murmured something about a jest, and that he liked a bit of fun; and then, seeing me smile, changed his tone, and assured me he would make all clear as soon as we had breakfasted. I saw by his face that he had no lie ready for me, though he was hard at work preparing one; and I think I was about to tell him so, when we were interrupted by a knocking at the door.

Bidding my uncle sit where he was, I went to open it, and found on the door-step a half-grown boy in sea-clothes. He had no sooner seen me that he began to dance some steps of the sea-hornpipe (which I had never before heard of, far less seen), snapping his fingers in the air and footing it right cleverly. For all that, he was blue with the cold; and there was something in his face, a look between tears and laughter, that was highly pathetic and consisted ill with this gaity of manner.

'What cheer, mate?' says he, with a cracked voice.

I asked him soberly to name his business.

'Oh, pleasure!' says he; and then began to sing:

> 'For it's my delight, of a shiny night,
> In the season of the year.'

'Well,' said I, 'If you have no business at all, I will even be so unmannerly as to shut you out.'

'Stay brother!' he cried. 'Have you no fun about you? or do you want to get me thrashed? I've brought a letter from old Heasy-oasy to Mr Belflower.' He showed me a letter as he spoke. 'And I say, mate,' he added, 'I'm mortal hungry.'

'Well,' said I, 'come into the house, and you shall have a bite if I go empty for it.'

With that I brought him in and set him down to my own place, where he fell-to greedily on the remains of breakfast, winking to me between whiles, and making many faces which I think the poor soul considered manly. Meanwhile, my unle had read the letter and sat thinking; then, suddenly, he got to his feet with a great air of liveliness, and pulled me apart into the farthest corner of the room.

'Read that,' said he, and put the letter in my hand.

Here it is, lying before me as I write:

The Hawes Inn, at the Queen's Ferry.

SIR. – I lie here with my hawser up and down, and send my cabin-boy to informe. If you have any further commands for over-seas, to-day will be the last occasion, as the wind will serve us well out of the firth. I will not seek to deny that I have had crosses with your doer*, Mr Rankeillor; of which, If not speedily redd up, you may looke to see some losses follow. I have drawn

*Agent

a bill upon you, as per margin, and am, sir, your most obedt, humble
servant,

ELIAS HOSEASON

'You see, Davie,' resumed my uncle, as soon as he saw that I had done, 'I have
a venture with this man Hoseason, the captain of a trading brig, the *Covenant*,
of Dysart. Now, if you and me was to walk over with yon lad, I could see the
captain at the Hawes, or maybe on board the *Covenant*, if there was papers to be
signed; and so far from a loss of time, we can jog on to the lawyer, Mr
Rankeillor's. After a' that's come and gone, ye would be swier* to believe me
upon my naked word; but ye'll believe Rankeillor. He's factor to half the gentry
in these parts; an auld man, forby: highly respeckit; and he kenned your father.'
    I stood awhile and thought. I was going to some place of shipping, which was
doubtless populous, and where my uncle durst attempt no violence, and, indeed,
even the society of the cabin-boy so far protected me. Once there, I believed I
could force on the visit to the lawyer, even if my uncle were now insincere in
proposing it; and perhaps, in the bottom of my heart, I wished a nearer view of
the sea and ships. You are to remember I had lived all my life in the inland hills,
and just two days before had my first sight of the firth lying like a blue floor, and
the sailed ships moving on the face of it, no bigger than toys. One thing with
another, I made up my mind.
    'Very well,' says I, 'let us go to the Ferry.'
    My uncle got into his hat and coat, and buckled an old rusty cutlass on; and
then we trod the fire out, locked the door, and set forth upon our walk.
    The wind, being in that cold quarter, the north-west, blew nearly in our faces
as we went. It was the month of June; the grass was all white with daisies and the
trees with blossom; but, to judge by our blue nails and aching wrists, the time
might have been winter and the whiteness a December frost.
    Uncle Ebenezer trudged in the ditch, jogging from side to side like an old
ploughman coming home from work. He never said a word the whole way; and I
was thrown for talk on the cabin-boy. He told me his name was Ransome, and
that he had followed the sea since he was nine, but could not say how old he
was, as he had lost his reckoning. He showed me tattoo marks, baring his breast
in the teeth of the wind and in spite of my remonstrances, for I thought it was
enough to kill him; he swore horribly whenever he remembered, but more like a
silly schoolboy than a man; and boasted of many wild and bad things that he had
done: stelthy thefts, false accusations, ay, and even murder; but all with such a
dearth of likelihood in the details, and such a weak and crazy swagger in the
delivery, as disposed me rather to pity than to believe him.
    I asked him of the brig (which he declared was the finest ship that sailed) and
of Captain Hoseason, in whose praise he was equally loud. Heasy-oasy (for so he
still named the skipper) was a man, by his account, that minded for nothing
either in heaven or earth; one that, as people said, would 'crack on all sail into
the day of judgement'; rough, fierce, unscrupulous, and brutal; and all this my
poor cabin-boy had taught himself to admire as something seamanlike and
manly. He would only admit one flaw in his idol. 'He ain't no seaman,' he
admitted. 'That's Mr Shuan that navigates the brig; he's the finest seaman in the
*Unwilling

trade, only for drink; and I tell you I believe it! Why, look 'ere'; and turning down his stocking, he showed me a great, raw, red wound that made my blood run cold. 'He done that – Mr Shuan done it,' he said, with an air of pride.

'What!' I cried, 'do you take such savage usage at his hands? Why, you are no slave, to be so handled!'

'No,' said the poor moon-calf, changing his tune at once, 'and so he'll find! See 'ere'; and he showed me a great case-knife, which he told me was stolen. 'Oh,' says he, 'let me see him try; I dare him to; I'll do for him! Oh, he ain't the first!' And he confirmed it with a poor, silly, ugly oath.

I have never felt such pity for anyone in this wide world as I felt for that half-witted creature; and it began to come over me that the brig Covenant (for all her pious name) was little better than a hell upon the seas.

'Have you no friends?' said I.

He said he had a father in some English seaport, I forgot which. 'He was a fine man, too,' he said; 'but he's dead.'

'In Heaven's name,' cried I, 'can you find no reputable life on shore?'

'Oh, no,' says he, winking and looking very sly; 'they would put me to a trade. I know a trick worth two of that, I do!'

I asked him what trade could be so dreadful as the one he followed, where he ran the continual peril of his life, not alone from wind and sea, but by the horrid cruelty of those who were his masters. He said it was very true; and then began to praise the life, and tell what a pleasure it was to get on shore with money in his pocket, and spend it like a man, and buy apples, and swagger, and surprise what he called stick-in-the-mud boys. 'And then it's not all so bad as that,' says he; 'there's worse off than me: there's the twenty-pounders. Oh, laws! you should see them taking on. Why, I've seen a man as old as you, I dessay' – (to him I seemed old) – 'ah, and he had a beard too, – well, and as soon as we cleared out of the river, and he had the drug out of his head – my how he cried and carried on! I made a fine fool of him, I tell you! And then there's little uns, too; oh, little by me! I tell you, I keep them in order. When we carry little uns, I have a rope's end of my own to wollop 'em.' And so he ran on, until it came in on me that what he meant by twenty-pounders were those unhappy criminals who were sent overseas to slavery in North America, or the still more unhappy innocents who were kidnapped or trepanned (as the word went) for private interest or vengeance.

Just then we came to the top of the hill, and looked down on the Ferry and the Hope. The Firth of Forth (as is very well known) narrows at this point to the width of a good-sized river, which makes a convenient ferry going north, and turns the upper reach into a land-locked haven for all manner of ships. Right in the midst of the narrows lies an islet with some ruins; on the south shore they have built a pier for the service of the Ferry; and at the end of the pier, on the other side of the road, and backed against a pretty garden of holly-trees and hawthorns, I could see the building which they call the Hawes Inn.

The town of Queensferry lies farther west, and the neighbourhood of the inn looked pretty lonely at that time of day, for the boat had just gone north with passengers. A skiff, however, lay beside the pier, with some seamen sleeping on the thwarts; This, as Ransome told me, was the brig's boat waiting for the captain; and about half a mile off, and all alone in the anchorage, he showed me the Covenant herself. There was a sea-going bustle on board; yards were swinging into place; and as the wind blew from that quarter, I could hear the song of the sailors as they pulled upon the ropes. After all I had listened to upon the way, I looked at that ship with an extreme abhorrence; and from the bottom of my heart I pitied all poor souls that were condemned to sail in her.

We had all three pulled up on the brow of the hill; and now I marched across the road nd addressed my uncle. 'I think it right to tell you, sir,' says I 'there's nothing that will bring me on board that Covenant.'

He seemed to waken from a dream. 'Eh?' he said. 'What's that?'

I told him over again.

'Well, well,' he said, 'we'll have to please ye, I suppose. But what are we standing here for? It's perishing cold; and if I'm no mistaken, they're busking the Covenant for sea.'

CHAPTER SIX

What Befell at the Queen's Ferry

AS SOON AS WE CAME TO THE inn, Ransome led us up the stair to a small room, with a bed in it, and heated like an oven by a great fire of coal. At a table hard by the chimney, a tall, dark, sober-looking man sat writing. In spite of the heat of the room, he wore a thick sea-jacket, buttoned to the neck, and a tall hairy cap drawn down over his ears; yet I never saw any man, not even a judge upon the bench, look cooler, or more studious and self-possessed, than this ship-captain.

He got to his feet at once, and coming forward, offered his large hand to Ebenezer. 'I am proud to see you, Mr Balfour,' said he, in a fine deep voice, 'and glad that ye are here in time. The wind's fair, and the tide upon the turn; we'll see the old coal-bucket burning on the Isle of May before tonight.'

'Captain Hoseason,' returned my uncle, 'you keep your room unco hot.'

'It's a habit I have, Mr Balfour,' said the skipper. 'I'm a cold-rife man by my nature; I have a cold blood, sir. There's neither fur, nor flannel – no, sir, nor hot rum, will warm up what they call the temperature. Sir, it's the same with most men that have been carbonadoed, as they call it, in the tropic seas.'

'Well, well, captain,' replied my uncle, 'we must all be the way we're made.'

But it chanced that this fancy of the captain's had a great share in my misfortunes. For though I had promised myself not to let my kinsman out of sight, I was both so impaitent for a nearer look at the sea, and so sickened by the closeness of the room, that when he told me to 'run downstairs and play myself awhile', I was fool enough to take him at his word.

Away I went, therefore, leaving the two men sitting down to a bottle and a great mass of papers; and crossing the road in front of the inn, walked down upon the beach. With the wind in that quarter, only little wavelets, not much bigger than I had seen upon a lake, beat upon the shore. But the weeds were new to me – some green, some brown and long, and some with little bladders that cracked between my fingers. Even so far up the firth, the smell of the sea water was exceedingly salt and stirring; the *Covenant*, besides, was beginning to shake out her sails, which hung upon the yards in clusters; and the spirit of all that I beheld put me in thoughts of far voyages and foreign places.

I looked, too, at the seamen with the skiff – big brown fellows, some in shirts, some with jackets, some with coloured handkerchiefs about their throats, one with a brace of pistols stuck into his pockets, two or three with knotty bludgeons, and all with their case-knives. I passed the time of day with one that looked less desperate than his fellows, and asked him of the sailing of the brig. He said they would get under way as soon as the ebb set, and expressed his gladness to be out of port where there were no taverns and fiddlers; but all with such horrifying oaths, that I made haste to get away from him.

This threw me back on Ransome, who seemed the least wicked of that gang, and who soon came out of the inn and ran to me, crying for a bowl of punch. I told him I would give him no such thing, for neither he nor I was of an age for such indulgences. 'But a glass of ale you may have, and welcome,' said I. He mopped and mowed at me, and called me names; but he was glad to get the ale, for all that; and presently we were set down at a table in the front room of the inn, and both eating and drinking with a good appetite.

Here it occurred to me that, as the landlord was a man of that county, I might do well to make a friend of him. I offered him a share, as was much the custom in these days; and he was far too great a man to sit with such poor customers as Ransome and myself, and he was leaving the room, when I called him back to ask if he knew Mr Rankeillor.

'Hoot, ay,' says he, 'and a very honest man. And, oh, by the by,' says he, 'was it you that came in with Ebenezer?' And when I had told him yes, 'Ye'll be no friend of his?' he asked, meaning, in the Scottish way, that I would be no relative.

I told him no, none.

'I thought not,' said he, 'and yet ye have a kind of gliff* of Mr Alexander.'

I said it seemed that Ebenezer was ill-seen in the country.

'Nae doubt,' said the landlord. 'He's a wicked auld man, and there's many would like to see him girning in a tow†: Jennet Clouston and mony mair that he has harried out of house and hame. And yet he was ance a fine young fellow, too. But that was before the sough‡ gaed abroad about Mr Alexander; that was like the death of him.'

'And what was it?' I asked.

'Ou, just that he had killed him,' said the landlord. 'Did ye never hear that?'

'And what would he kill him for?' said I.

'And what for, but just to get the place,' said he.

'The place?' said I, 'The Shaws?'

'Nae other place that I ken,' said he.

'Ay, man?' said I. 'Is that so? Was my – was Alexander the eldest son?'

''Deed was he,' said the landlord. 'What else would he have killed him for?'

*Look
†Rope
‡Report

And with that he went away, as he had been impatient to do from the beginning.

Of course, I had guessed it a long while ago; but it is one thing to guess, another to know; and I sat stunned with my good fortune, and could scarce grow to believe that the same poor lad who had trudged in the dust from Ettrick Forest not two days ago, was now one of the rich of the earth, and had a house and broad lands, and if he but knew how to ride, might mount his horse tomorrow. All these pleasant things, and a thousand others, crowded into my mind, as I sat staring before me out of the inn window, and paying no heed to what I saw; only I remember that my eye lighted on Captain Hoseason down on the pier among his seamen, and speaking with some authority. And presently he came marching back towards the house, with no mark of a sailor's clumsiness, but carrying his fine, tall figure with a manly bearing, and still with the same sober, grave expression on his face. I wondered if it was possible that Ransome's stories could be true, and half disbelieved them; they fitted so ill with the man's looks. But indeed, he was neither so good as I supposed him, nor quite so bad as Ransome did; for, in fact, he was two men, and left the better one behind as soon as he set foot on board his vessel.

The next thing, I heard my uncle calling me, and found the pair in the road together. It was the captain who addressed me, and that with an air (very flattering to a young lad) of grave equality.

'Sir,' said he, 'Mr Balfour tells me great things of you; and for my own part, I like your looks. I wish I was for longer here, that we might make the better friends; but we'll make the most of what we have. Ye shall come on board my brig for half an hour, till the ebb sets, and drink a bowl with me.'

Now, I longed to see the inside of a ship more than words can tell; but I was not going to put myself in jeopardy, and I told him my uncle and I had an appointment with a lawyer.

'Ay, ay,' said he, 'he passed me word of that. But, ye see, the boat'll set ye ashore at the town pier, and that's but a penny stonecast from Rankeillor's house.' And here he suddenly leaned down and whispered in my ear: 'Take care of the old tod*; he means mischief. Come aboard till I can get a word with ye.' And then, passing his arm through mine, he continued aloud, as he set off towards his boat: 'But come, what can I bring ye from the Carolinas? Any friend of Mr Balfour's can command. A roll of tobacco? Indian featherwork? a skin of a wild beast? a stone pipe? the mocking-bird that mews for all the world like a cat? the cardinal bird that is as red as blood? – take your pick and say your pleasure.'

By this time we were at the boat-side, and he was handing me in. I did not dream of hanging back; I thought (the poor fool!) that I had found a good friend and helper, and I was rejoiced to see the ship. As soon as we were all set in our places, the boat was thrust off from the pier and began to move over the waters; and what with my pleasure in this new movement and my surprise at our low position, and the appearance of the shores, and the growing bigness of the brig as we drew near to it, I could hardly understand what the captain said, and must have answered him at random.

As soon as we were alongside (where I sat fairly gaping at the ship's height, the strong humming of the tide against its sides, and the pleasant cries of the
*Fox

seamen at their work) Hoseason, declaring that he and I must be the first aboard, ordered a tackle to be sent down from the mainyard. In this I was whipped into the air and set down again on the deck, where the captain stood ready waiting for me, and instantly slipped back his arm under mine. There I stood some while, a little dizzy with the unsteadiness of all around me, perhaps a little afraid, nd yet vastly pleased with these strange sights; the captain meanwhile pointing out the strangest, and telling me their names and uses.

'But where is my uncle?' said I, suddenly.

'Ay,' said Hoseason, with a sudden grimness, 'that's the point.'

I felt I was lost. With all my strength, I plucked myself clear of him and ran to the bulwarks. Sure enough, there was the boat pulling for the town, with my uncle sitting in the stern. I gave a piercing cry – 'Help, help! Murder!' – so that both sides of the anchorage rang with it, and my uncle turned round where he was sitting, and showed me a face full of cruelty and terror.

It was the last I saw. Already strong hands had been plucking me back from the ship's side; and now a thunderbolt seemed to strike me; I saw a great flash of fire, and fell senseless.

CHAPTER SEVEN

I Go to Sea in the Brig Covenant *of Dysart*

I CAME TO MYSELF IN darkness, in great pain, bound hand and foot, and deafened by many unfamiliar noises. There sounded in my ears a roaring of water as of a huge milldam; the thrashing of heavy sprays, the thundering of the sails, and the shrill cries of seamen. The whole world now heaved giddily up, and now rushed giddily downward; and so sick and hurt was I in body, and my mind so much confounded, that it took me a long while, chasing my thoughts up and down, and ever stunned again by a fresh stab of pain, to realize that I must be lying somewhere bound in the belly of that unlucky ship, and that the wind must have strengthened to a gale. With the clear perception of my plight, there fell upon me a blackness of despair, a horror of remorse at my own folly, and a passion of anger at my uncle, that once more bereft me of my senses.

When I returned again to life, the same uproar, the same confused and violent movements, shook and deafened me; and presently, to my other pains and distresses, there was added the sickness of an unused landsman on the sea. In that time of my adventurous youth, I suffered many hardships; but none that was so crushing to my mind and body, or lit by so few hopes, as these first hours on board the brig.

I heard a gun fire, and supposed the storm had proved too strong for us, and we were firing signals of distress. The thought of deliverance, even by death in the deep sea, was welcome to me. Yet it was no such matter; but (as I was afterwards told) a common habit of the captain's, which I here set down to show that even the worst man have his kindlier sides. We were then passing, it appeared, within some miles of Dysart, where the brig was built, and where old Mrs Hoseason, the captain's mother, had come some years before to live; and whether outward or inward bound, the *Covenant* was never suffered to go by that place by day without a gun fired and colours shown.

I had no measure of time; day and night were alike in that ill-smelling cavern of the ship's bowels where I lay; and the misery of my situation drew out the hours to double. How lond, therefore, I lay waiting to hear the ship split upon some rock, or to feel her reel head foremost into the depths of the sea, I have not the means of computation. But sleep at length stole from me the consciousness of sorrow.

I was awakened by the light of a hand-lantern shining in my face. A small man of about thirty, with green eyes and a tangle of fair hair, stood looking down at me.

'Well,' said he, 'how goes it?'

I answered by a sob; and my visitor then felt my pulse and temples and set himself to wash and dress the wound upon my scalp.

'Ay,' said he, 'a sore dunt*. What, man? Cheer up! The world's no done; you've made a bad start of it, but you'll make a better. Have you had any meat?'

I said I could not look at it; and thereupon he gave me some brandy and water in a tin pannikin, and left me once more to myself.

The next time he came to see me, I was lying betwixt sleep and waking, my eyes wide open in the darkness, the sickness quite departed, but succeeded by a horrid giddiness and swimming that was almost worse to bear. I ached besides, in every limb, and the cords that bound me seemed to be on fire. The smell of the hole in which I lay seemed to have become a part of me; and during the long interval since his last visit I had suffered tortures of fear, now from the scurrying of the ship's rats, that sometimes pattered on my very face, and now from the dismal imaginings that haunt the bed of fever.

The glimmer of the lantern, as a trap opened, shone in like the heaven's sunlight; and though it only showed me the strong, dark beams of this ship that was my prison, I could have cried aloud for gladness. The man with the green eyes was the first to descend the ladder, and I noticed that he came somewhat unsteadily. He was followed by the captain. Neither said a word; but the first set to and examined me, and dressed my wound as before, while Hoseason looked me in my face with an odd, black look.

'Now, sir, you see for yourself,' said the first: 'a high fever, no appetite, no light, no meat, you see for yourself what that means.'

'I am no conjurer, Mr Riach,' said the captain.

'Give me leave sir,' said Riach; 'you've a good head upon your shoulders, and a good Scotch tongue to ask with; but I will leave you no manner of excuse; I want that boy taken out of this hole and put in the forecastle.'

'What ye may want, sir, is a matter of concern to nobody but yoursel',' returned the captain; 'but I can tell ye that which is to be. Here he is; here he shall bide.'

'Admitting that you have been paid in a proportion,' said the other, 'I will crave leave humbly to say that I have not. Paid I am, and none too much, to be
*Stroke

the second officer of this old tub; and you ken very well if I do my best to earn it. But I was paid for nothing more.'

'If ye could hold back your hand from the tin-pan, Mr Riach, I would have no complaint to make of ye,' returned the skipper; 'and instead of asking riddles, I make bold to say that ye would keep your breath to cool your porridge. We'll be required on deck,' he added, in a sharper note, and set one foot upon the ladder.

But Mr Riach caught him by the sleeve.

'Admitting that you have been paid to do a murder——' he began.

Hoseason turned upon him with flash.

'What's that?' he cried. 'What kind of talk is that?'

'It seems it is the talk that you can understand,' said Mr Riach, looking him steadily in the face.

'Mr Riach I have sailed with ye three cruises,' replied the captain. 'In all that time, sir, ye should have learned to know me; I'm a stiff man, and a dour man; but for what ye say now – fie, fie – it comes from a bad heart and a black conscience. If ye say the lad will die——'

'Ay, will he!' said Mr Riach.

'Well, sir, is not that enough?' said Hoseason. 'Flit him where ye please!'

Thereupon the captain ascended the ladder; and I, who had lain silent throughout this strange conversation, beheld Mr Riach turn after him and bow as low as to his knees in what was plainly a spirit of derision. Even in my then state of sickness, I perceived two things; that the mate was touched with liquor, as the captain hinted, and that (drunk or sober) he was like to prove a valuable friend.

Five minutes afterwards my bonds were cut, I was hoisted on a man's back, carried up to the forecastle, and laid in a bunk on some sea-blankets; where the first thing that I did was to lose my senses.

It was a blessed thing indeed to open my eyes again upon the daylight, and to find myself in the society of men. The forecastle was a roomy place enough, set all about with berths, in which the men of the watch below were seated smoking, or lying down asleep. The day being calm and the wind fair, the scuttle was open, and not only the good daylight, but from time to time (as the ship rolled) a dusty beam of sunlight shone in, and dazzled and delighted me. I had no sooner moved, moreover, than one of the men brought me a drink of something healing which Mr Riach had prepared, and bade me lie still and I should soon be well again. There were no bones broken, he explained: 'A clour* on the head was naething. Man,' said he, 'it was me that gave it ye!'

Here I lay for the space of many days a close prisoner, and not only got my health again, but come to know my companions. They were a rough lot indeed, as sailors mostly are; being men rooted out of all the kindly parts of life, and condemned to toss together on the rough seas, with masters no less cruel. There were some among them that had sailed with the pirates and seen things it would be a shame even to speak of; some were men that had run from the king's ships, and went with a halter round their necks, of which they made no secret; and all, as the saying goes, were 'at a word and a blow' with their best friends. Yet I had not been many days shut up with them before I began to be ashamed of my first judgement, when I had drawn away from them at the Ferry pier, as though they

*Blow

had been unclean beasts. No class of man is altogether bad; but each has its own faults and virtues; and these shipmates of mine were no exception to the rule. Rough they were, sure enough; and bad, I suppose; but they had many virtues. They were kind when it occurred to them, simple even beyond the simplicity of a country lad like me, and had some glimmerings of honesty.

There was one man of maybe forty, that would sit on my berthside for hours, and tell me of his wife and child. He was a fisher that had lost his boat, and thus been driven to the deep-sea voyaging. Well, it is years ago now: but I have never forgotten him. His wife (who was 'young by him', as he often told me) waited in vain to see her man return; he would never again make the fire for her in the morning, nor yet keep the bairn when she was sick. Indeed, many of these poor fellows (as the event proved) were upon their last cruise; the deep seas and cannibal fish received them; and it is a thankless business to speak ill of the dead.

Among other good deeds that they did, they returned my money, which had been shared among them; and though it was about a third short, I was very glad to get it, and hoped great good from it in the land I was going to. The ship was bound for the Carolinas; and you must not suppose that I was going to that place merely as an exile. The trade was even then much depressed; since that, and with the rebellion of the colonies and the formation of the United States, it has, of course, come to an end; but in these days of my youth, white men were still sold into slavery on the plantations, and that was the destiny to which my wicked uncle had condemned me.

The cabin-boy Ransome (from whom I had first heard of these atrocities) came in at times from the round-house, where he berthed and served, now nursing a bruised limb in silent agony, now raving against the cruelty of Mr Shuan. It made my heart bleed; but the men had a great respect for the chief mate, who was, as they said, 'the only seaman of the whole jing-bang, and none such a bad man when he was sober.' Indeed, I found there was a strange peculiarity about our two mates: that Mr Riach was sullen, unkind, and harsh when he was sober, and Mr Shuan would not hurt a fly except when he was drinking. I asked about the captain: but I was told drink made no difference upon that man of iron.

I did my best in the small time allowed me to make something like a man, or rather I should say something like a boy, of the poor creature, Ransome. But his mind was scarce truly human. He could remember nothing of the time before he came to sea; only that his father had made clocks, and had a starling in the parlour, which could whistle 'The North Countrie'; all else had been blotted out in these years of hardship and cruelties. He had a strange notion of the dry land, picked up from sailors' stories: that it was a place where lads were put to some kind of slavery called a trade, and where apprentices were continually lashed and clapped into foul prisons. In a town, he thought every second person a decoy, and every third house a place in which seamen would be drugged and murdered. To be sure, I could tell him how kindly I had myself been used upon that dry land he was so much afraid of, and how well fed and carefully taught both by my friends and my parents: and if he had been recently hurt, he would weep bitterly and swear to run away; but if he was in his usual crackbrain humour or (still more) if he had had a glass of spirits in the round-house, he would deride the notion.

It was Mr Riach (Heaven forgive him!) who gave the boy drink; and it was, doubtless, kindly meant; but besides that it was ruin to his health, it was the pitifullest thing in life to see this unhappy, unfriended creature staggering, and dancing, and talking he knew not what. Some of the men laughed, but not all; others would grow as black as thunder (thinking, perhaps, of their own childhood or their own children) and bid him stop that nonsense, and think what he was doing. As for me, I felt ashamed to look at him, and the poor child still comes about me in my dreams.

All this time, you should know, the *Covenant* was meeting continuous head-winds and tumbling up and down against head-seas, so that the scuttle was almost constantly shut, and the forecastle lighted only by a swinging lantern on a beam. There was constant labour for all hands; the sails had to be made and shortened every hour; the strain told on the men's temper; there was a growl of quarrelling all day long from berth to berth; and as I was never allowed to set my foot on deck, you can picture to yourselves how weary of my life I grew to be, and how impaitent for a change.

And a change I was to get, as you shall hear; but I must first tell of a conversation I had with Mr Riach, which put a little heart in me to bear my troubles. Getting him in a favourable stage of drink (for indeed he never looked near me when he was sober) I pledged him to secrecy, and told him my whole story.

He declared it was like a ballad; that he would do his best to help me; that I should have paper, pen, and ink, and write one line to Mr Campbell and another to Mr Rankeillor; and that if I told the truth, ten to one he would be able (with their help) to pull me through and set me in my rights.

'And in the meantime,' says he, 'keep your heart up. You're not the only one, I'll tell you that. There's many a man hoeing tobacco over-seas that should be mounting his horse at his own door at home; many and many! And life is all a variorum, at the best. Look at me: I'm a laird's son and more than half a doctor, and here I am, man-Jack to Hoseason!'

I thought it would be civil to ask him for his story.

He whistled loud.

'Never had one,' said he. 'I liked fun, that's all.' And he skipped out of the forecastle.

CHAPTER EIGHT

The Round-House

ONE NIGHT, ABOUT NINE o'clock, a man of Mr Riach's watch (which was on deck) came down for his jacket; and instantly there began to go a whisper about the forecastle that 'Shuan had done for him at last'. There was no need of a name; we all knew who was meant; but we had scarce time to get the idea rightly in our heads, far less to speak of it, when the scuttle was again flung open, and Captain Hoseason came down the ladder. He looked sharply round the bunks in the tossing light of the lanter; and then walking straight up to me, he addressed me, to my surprise, in tones of kindness.

'My man,' said he, 'we want ye to serve in the round-house. You and Ransome are to change berths. Run away aft with ye.'

Even as he spoke, two seamen appeared in the scuttle, carrying Ransome in their arms; and the ship at that moment giving a great sheer into the sea, and the lantern swinging, the light fell direct on the boy's face. It was as white as wax, and had a look upon it like a dreadful smile. The blood in me ran cold, and I drew in my breath as if I had been struck.

'Run away aft; run away aft with ye!' cried Hoseason.

And at that I brushed by the sailors and the boy (who neither spoke nor moved), and ran up the ladder on deck.

The brig was sheering swiftly and giddily through a long, cresting swell. She was on the starboard tack, and on the left hand, under the arched foot of the foresail, I could see the sunset still quite bright. This, at such an hour of the night, surprised me greatly; but I was too ignorant to draw the true conclusion – that we were going north-about round Scotland, and were now on the high sea between the Orkney and the Shetland Islands, having avoided the dangerous currents of the Pentland Firth. For my part, who had been so long shut in the dark and knew nothing of head-winds, I thought we might be half-way or more across the Atlantic. And indeed (beyond that I wondered a little at the lateness of the sunset light) I gave no heed to it, and pushed on across the decks, running between the seas, catching at ropes, and only saved from going overboard by one of the hands on deck, who had been always kind to me.

The round-house, for which I was bound, and where I was now to sleep and serve, stood some six feet above the decks, and considering the size of the brig, was of good dimensions. Inside were a fixed table and bench, and two berths, one for the captain and the other for the two mates, turn and turn about. It was all fitted with lockers from top to bottom, so as to stow away the officers' belongings and a part of the ship's stores; there was a second storeroom underneath, which you entered by a hatchway in the middle of the deck; indeed, all the best of the meat and drink and the whole of the powder were collected in this place; and all the firearms, except the two pieces of brass ordnance, were set in a rack in the aftermost wall of the round-house. The most of the cutlasses were in another place.

A small window with a shutter on each side, and a skylight in the roof, gave it light by day; and after dark, there was a lamp always burning. It was burning when I entered, not brightly, but enough to show Mr Shuan sitting at the table, with the brandy bottle and a tin pannikin in front of him. He was a tall man, strongly made and very black; and he stared before him on the table like one stupid.

He took no notice of my coming in; nor did he move when the captain followed and leant on the berth beside me, looking darkly at the mate. I stood in great fear of Hoseason, and had my reasons for it; but something told me I need not be afraid of him just then; and I whispered in his ear, 'How is he?' He shook his head like one that does not know and does not wish to think, and his face was very stern.

Presently Mr Riach came in. He gave the captain a glance that meant the boy was dead as plain as speaking, and took his place like the rest of us; so that we all three stood without a word, staring down at Mr Shuan, and Mr Shuan (on his side) sat without a word, looking hard upon the table.

All of a sudden he put out his hand to take the bottle; and at that Mr Riach started forward and caught it away from him, rather by surprise than violence, crying out, with an oath, that there had been too much of this work altogether, and that a judgement would fall upon the ship. And as he spoke (the weather sliding-doors standing open) he tossed the bottle into the sea.

Mr Shuan was on his feet in a trice; he still looked dazed, but he meant murder, ay, and would have done it, for the second time that night, had not the captain stepped in between him and his victim.

'Sit down!' roars the captain. 'Ye sot and swine, do ye know what ye've done? Ye've murdered the boy!'

Mr Shuan seemed to understand; for he sat down again and put up his hand to his brow.

'Well,' he said, 'he brought me a dirty pannikin!'

At that word, the captain and I and Mr Riach all looked at each other for a second with a kind of frightened look; and then Hoseason walked up to his chief officer, took him by the shoulder, led him across to his bunk, and bade him lie down and go to sleep, as you might speak to a bad child. The murderer cried a little, but he took off his sea-boots and obeyed.

'Ah!' cried Mr Riach, with a dreadful voice, 'ye should have interfered long syne. It's too late now.'

'Mr Riach,' said the captain, 'this night's work must never be kennt in Dysart. The boy went overboard, sir; that's what the story is; and I would give five pounds out of my pocket it was true!' He turned to the table. 'What made ye throw the good bottle away?' he added. 'There was nae sense in that, sir. Here, David, draw me another. They're in the bottom locker'; and he tossed me a key. 'Ye'll need a glass yourself, sir,' he added, to Riach. 'Yon was an ugly thing to see.'

So the pair sat down and hob-a-nobbed; and while they did so, the murderer, who had been lying and whimpering in his berth, raised himself upon his elbow and looked at them and at me.

That was the first night of my new duties; and in the course of the next day I had got well into the run of them. I had to serve at the meals, which the captain took at regular hours, sitting down with the officer who was off duty; all the day through I would be running with a dram to one or other of my three masters; and at night I slept on a blanket thrown on the deck boards at the aftermost end of the round-house, and right in the draught of the two doors. It was a hard and a cold bed; nor was I suffered to sleep without interruption; for some one would be always coming in from deck to get a dram, and when a fresh watch was to be set, two and sometimes all three would sit down and brew a bowl together. How they kept their health, I know not, any more than how I kept my own.

And yet in other ways it was an easy service. There was no cloth to lay; the meals were either of oatmeal porridge or salt junk, except twice a week, when there was duff; and though I was clumsy enough and (not being firm on my sea-legs) sometimes fell with what I was bringing them, both Mr Riach and the captain were singularly patient. I could not but fancy they were making up leeway with their consciences, and that they would scarce have been so good with me if they had not been worse with Ransome.

As for Mr Shuan, the drink, or his crime, or the two together, had certainly troubled his mind. I cannot say I ever saw him in his proper wits. He never grew used to my being there, stared at me continually (sometimes, I could have thought, with terror) and more than once drew back from my hand when I was serving him. I was pretty sure from the first that he had no clear mind of what he had done, and on my second day in the round-house I had proof of it. We were alone, and he had been staring at me a long time, when, all at once, up he got, as pale as death, and came close up to me, to my great terror. But I had no cause to be afraid of him.

'You were not here before?' he asked.

'No sir,' said I.

'There was another boy?' he asked again; and when I had answered him, 'Ah!' says he, 'I thought that,' and went and sat down, without another word, except to call for brandy.

You may think it strange, but for all the horror I had, I was still sorry for him. He was a married man, with a wife in Leith; but whether or no he had a family, I have now forgotten; I hope not.

Altogether it was no very hard life for the time it lasted, which (as you are to hear) was not long. I was as well fed as the best of them; even their pickles, which were the great dainty, I was allowed my share of; and had I liked, I might have been drunk from morning to night, like Mr Shuan. I had company, too, and good company of its sort. Mr Riach, who had been to the college, spoke to me like a friend when he was not sulking, and told me many curious things, and some that were informing; and even the captain, though he kept me at the stick's end the most part of the time, would sometimes unbuckle a bit, and tell me of the fine countries he had visited.

The shadow of poor Ransome, to be sure, lay on all four of us, and on me and Mr Shuan, in particular, most heavily. And then I had another trouble of my own. Here I was, doing dirty work for three men that I looked down upon, and one of whom, at least, should have hung upon a gallows; that was for the present; and as for the future, I could only see myself slaving alongside of negroes in the tobacco field. Mr Riach, perhaps from caution, would never suffer me to say another word about my story; the captain, whom I tried to approach, rebuffed me like a dog and would not hear a word; and as the days came and went, my heart sank lower and lower, till I was even glad of the work which kept me from thinking.

CHAPTER NINE

The Man with the Belt of Gold

MORE THAN A WEEK WENT BY, in which the ill-luck that had hitherto pursued the *Covenant* upon this voyage grew yet more strongly marked. Some days she made a little way; others, she was driven actually back. At last we were beaten so far to the south that we tossed and tacked to and fro the whole of the ninth day, within sight of Cape Wrath and the wild, rocky coast on either hand of it. There followed on that a council of the officers, and some decision which I did not rightly understand, seeing only the result: that we had made a fair wind of a foul one and were running south.

The tenth afternoon, there was a falling swell and a thick, wet, white fog that hid one end of the brig from the other. All afternoon, when I went on deck, I saw men and officers listening hard over the bulwarks – 'for breakers', they said; and though I did not so much as understand the word, I felt danger in the air, and was excited.

Maybe about ten at night, I was serving Mr Riach and the captain at their supper, when the ship struck something with a great sound, and we heard voices singing out. My two masters leaped to their feet.

'She's struck,' said Mr Riach.

'No, sir,' said the captain. 'We've only run a boat down.'

And they hurried out.

The captain was in the right of it. We had run down a boat in the fog, and she had parted in the midst and gone to the bottom with all her crew, but one. This man (as I heard afterwards) had been sitting in the stern as a passenger, while the rest were on the benches rowing. At the moment of the blow, the stern had been thrown into the air, and the man (having his hands free, and for all he was encumbered with a frieze overcoat that came below his knees) had leaped up and caught hold of the brig's bow-sprit. It showed he had luck and much agility and unusual strength, that he should have thus saved himself from such a pass. And yet, when the captain brought him into the round-house, and I set eyes on him for the first time, he looked as cool as I did.

He was smallish in stature, but well set and as nimble as a goat; his face was of a good open expression, but sunburnt very dark, and heavily freckled and pitted with the smallpox; his eyes were unusually light and had a kind of dancing madness in them, that was both engaging and alarming; and when he took off his great-coat, he laid a pair of fine, silver-mounted pistols on the table, and I saw that he was belted with a great sword. His manners, besides, were elegant, and he pledged the captain handsomely. Altogether I thought of him, at the first sight, that here was a man I would rather call my friend than my enemy.

The captain, too, was taking his observations, but rather of the man's clothes than his person. And to be sure, as soon as he had taken off the great-coat, he showed forth mighty fine for the round-house of a merchant brig; having a hat with feathers, a red waistcoat, breeches of black plush, and a blue coat with silver buttons and handsome silver lace; costly clothes, though somewhat spoiled with the fog and being slept in.

'I'm vexed sir, about the boat,' says the captain.

'There are some pretty men gone to the bottom,' said the stranger, 'that I would rather see on the dry land again than half a score of boats.'

'Friends of yours?' said Hoseason.

'You have none such friends in your country,' was the reply. 'They would have died for me like dogs.'

'Well, sir,' said the captain, still watching him, 'there are more men in the world than boats to put them in.'

'And that's true too,' cried the other, 'and ye seem to be a gentleman of great penetration.'

'I have been in France, sir,' says the captain, so that it was plain he meant more by the words than showed upon the face of them.

'Well, sir,' says the other, 'and so has many a pretty man, for the matter of that.'

'No doubt, sir,' says the captain, 'and fine coats.'

'Oho!' says the stranger, 'is that how the wind sets?' And he laid his hand quickly on his pistols.

'Don't be hasty,' said the captain. 'Don't do a mischief, before ye see the need for it. 'Ye've a French soldier's coat upon your back and a Scotch tongue in your head, to be sure; but so has many an honest fellow in these days, and I dare say none the worse of it.'

'So?' said the gentleman in the fine coat: 'are ye of the honest party?' (meaning, Was he a Jacobite? for each side, in these sort of civil broils, takes the name of honesty for its own).

'Why, sir,' replied the captain, 'I am a true-blue Protestant, and I thank God for it.' (It was the first word of any religion I had ever heard from him, but I learnt afterwards he was a great church-goer while on shore.) 'But, for all that,' says he, 'I can be sorry to see another man with his back to the wall.'

'Can ye so, indeed?' asked the Jacobite. 'Well, sir, to be quite plain with ye, I am one of those honest gentlemen that were in trouble about the years forty-five and six; and (to be still quite plain with ye) if I got into the hands of any of the red-coated gentry, it's like it would go hard with me. Now, sir, I was for France; and there was a French ship cruising here to pick me up; but she gave us the go-by in the fog – as I wish from the heart that ye had done yoursel'! And the best that I can say is this: If ye can set me ashore where I was going, I have that upon me will reward you highly for your trouble.'

'In France?' says the captain. 'No, sir; that I cannot do. But where ye come from – we might talk of that.'

And then, unhappily, he observed me standing in my corner, and packed me off to the galley to get supper for the gentleman. I lost no time, I promise you; and when I came back into the round-house, I found the gentleman had taken a money-belt from about his waist, and poured out a guinea or two upon the table. The captain was looking at the guineas, and then at the belt, and then at the gentleman's face; and I thought he seemed excited.

'Half of it,' he cried, 'and I'm your man!'

The other swept back the guineas into the belt, and put it on again under his waistcoat. 'I have told ye, sir,' said he, 'that not one doit of it belongs to me. It belongs to my chieftain' – and here he touched his hat – 'and while I would be but a silly messenger to grudge some of it that the rest might come safe, I should show myself a hound indeed if I bought my own carcase any too dear. Thirty guineas on the seaside, or sixty if ye set me on the Linnhe loch. Take it, if ye will; if not, ye can do your worst.'

'Ay,' said Hoseason. 'And if I give ye over to the soldiers?'

'Ye would make a fool's bargain,' said the other. 'My chief, let me tell you, sir, is forfeited, like every honest man in Scotland. His estate is in the hands of the man they call King George; and it is his officers that collect the rents, or try to collect them. But for the honour of Scotland, the poor tenant bodies take a thought upon their chief lying in exile; and this money is a part of that very rent for which King George is looking. Now, sir, ye seem to me to be a man that understands things: bring this money within the reach of Government, and how much of it'll come to you?'

'Little enough, to be sure,' said Hoseason; and then, 'If they knew,' he added, dryly. 'But I think, if I was to try, that I could hold my tongue about it.'

'Ah, but I'll begowk* ye there!' cried the gentleman. 'Play me false, and I'll play you cunning. If a hand's laid upon me, they shall ken what money it is.'

'Well,' returned the captain, 'what must be must. Sixty guineas, and done. Here's my hand upon it.'

'And here's mine,' said the other.

And thereupon the captain went out (rather hurriedly, I thought), and left me alone in the round-house with the stranger.

At that period (so soon after the forty-five) there were many exiled gentlemen coming back at the peril of their lives, either to see their friends or to collect a little money; and as for the Highland chiefs that had been forfeited, it was a common matter of talk how their tenants would stint themselves to send them money, and their clansmen outface the soldiery to get it in, and run the gauntlet of our great navy to carry it across. All this I had, of course, heard tell of; and now I had a man under my eyes whose life was forfeit on all these counts and upon one more; for he was not only a rebel and a smuggler of rents, but had taken service with King Louis of France. And as if all this were not enough, he had a belt full of golden guineas round his loins. Whatever my opinions, I could not look on such a man without a lively interest.

'And so you're a Jacobite?' said I, as I set meat before him.

'Ay,' said he, beginning to eat. 'And you, by your long face, should be a Whig?'†

*Befool.

†Whig or Whigamore was the cant name for those who were loyal to King George.

'Betwixt and between,' said I, not to annoy him; for indeed I was as good a Whig as Mr Campbell could make me.

'And that's naething,' said he. 'But I'm saying, Mr Betwixt-and-Between,' he added, 'this bottle of yours is dry; and it's hard if I'm to pay sixty guineas and be grudged a dram upon the back of it.'

'I'll go and ask for the key,' said I, and stepped on deck.

The fog was as close as ever, but the swell almost down. They had laid the brig to, not knowing precisely where they were, and the wind (what little there was of it) not serving well for their true course. Some of the hands were still hearkening for breakers; but the captain and the two officers were in the waist with their heads together. It struck me, I don't know why, that they were after no good; and the first word I heard, as I drew softly near, more than confirmed me.

It was Mr Riach, crying out as if upon a sudden thought:

'Couldn't we wile him out of the round-house?'

'He's better where he is,' returned Hoseason; 'he hasn't room to use his sword.'

'Well, that's true,' said Riach; 'but he's hard to come at.'

'Hut!' said Hoseason. 'We can get the man in talk, one upon each side, and spin him by the two arms; or if that'll not hold, sir, we can make a run by both the doors and get him under hand before he has the time to draw.'

At this hearing, I was seized with both fear and anger at these treacherous greedy, bloody men that I sailed with. My first mind was to run away; my second was bolder.

'Captain,' said I, 'the gentleman is seeking a dram, and the bottle's out. Will you give me the key?'

They all started and turned about.

'Why, here's our chance to get the firearms!' Riach cried, and then to me: 'Hark ye, David,' he said, 'do ye ken where the pistols are?'

'Ay, ay,' put in Hoseason. 'David kens; David's a good lad. Ye see, David my man, yon wild Hielandman is a danger to the ship, besides being a rank foe to King George, God bless him!'

I had never been so be-Davided since I came on board; but I said yes, as if all I heard were quite natural.

'The trouble is,' resumed the captain, 'that all our firelocks, great and little, are in the round-house under this man's nose; likewise the powder. Now if I, or one of the officers, was to go in and take them, he would fall to thinking. But a lad like you, David, might snap up a horn and a pistol or two without remark. And if ye can do it cleverly, I'll bear in mind when it'll be good for you to have friends; and that's when we come to Carolina.'

Here Mr Riach whispered him a little.

'Very right, sir,' said the captain; and then to myself: 'And see here, David, yon man has a beltful of gold, and I give you my word that you shall have your fingers in it.'

I told him I would do as he wished, though indeed I had scarce breath to speak with; and upon that he gave me the key of the spirit locker, and I began to go slowly back to the round-house. What was I to do? They were dogs and thieves; they had stolen me from my own country; they had killed poor Ransome; and was I to hold the candle to another murder? But then, upon the other hand, there was the fear of death very plain before me; for what could a boy and a man, if they were as brave as lions, against a whole ship's company?

I was still arguing it back and forth, and getting no great clearness, when I came into the round-house and saw the Jacobite eating his supper under the lamp; and at that my mind was made up all in a moment. I have no credit by it; it was by no choice of mine, but as if by compulsion, that I walked right up to the table and put my hand on his shoulder.

'Do you want to be killed?' said I.

He sprang to his feet, and looked a question at me as clear as if he had spoken.

'Oh!' cried I, 'they're all muderers here; it's a ship full of them! They've murdered a boy already. Now it's you.'

'Ay, ay,' said he; 'but they haven't got me yet,' And then looking at me curiously, 'Will ye stand with me?'

'That will I!' said I, 'I am no thief, nor yet murderer. I'll stand by you.'

'Why, then,' said he, 'what's your name?'

'David Balfour,' said I; and then thinking that a man with so fine a coat must like fine people, I added for the first time 'of Shaws'.

It never occurred to him to doubt me, for a Highlander is used to see great gentlefolk in great poverty; but as he had no estate of his own, my words nettled a very childish vanity he had.

'My name is Stewart,' he said, drawing himself up. 'Alan Breck, they call me. A king's name is good enough for me, though I bear it plain and have the name of no farm-midden to clap to the hind-end of it.'

And having administered this rebuke, as though it were something of a chief importance, he turned to examine our defences.

The round-house was built very strong, to support the breaching of the seas. Of its five apertures, only the skylight and the two doors were large enough for the passage of a man. The doors, besides, could be drawn close: they were of stout oak, and ran in grooves, and were fitted with hooks to keep them either shut or open, as the need arose. The one that was already shut, I secured in this fashion; but when I was proceeding to slide to the other, Alan stopped me.

'David,' said he – 'for I cannae bring to mind the name of your landed estate, and so will make so bold as to call you David – that door, being open, is the best part of my defences.'

'It would be yet better shut,' says I.

'Not so, David,' says he, 'Ye see, I have but one face; but so long as that door is open and my face to it, the best part of my enemies will be in front of me, where I would aye wish to find them.'

Then he gave me from the rack a cutlass (of which there were a few besides the firearms), choosing it with great care, shaking his head and saying he had never in all his life seen poorer weapons; and next he set me down to the table with a powder-horn, a bag of bullets, and all the pistols, which he bade me charge.

'And that will be better work, let me tell you,' said he, 'for a gentleman of decent birth, than scraping plates and raxing* drams to a wheen tarry sailors.'

Thereupon he stood up in the midst with his face to the door, and drawing his

*Reaching

great sword, made trial of the room he had to wield it in.

'I must stick to the point,' he said, shaking his head; 'and that's a pity, too. It doesn't set my genius, which is all for the upper guard. And now,' said he, 'do you keep on charging the pistols, and give heed to me.'

I told him I would listen closely. My chest was tight, my mouth dry, the light dark to my eyes; the thought of the numbers that were soon to leap in upon us kept my heart in a flutter; and the sea, which I heard washing round the brig, and where I thought my dead body would be cast ere morning, ran in my mind strangely.

'First of all,' said he, 'how many are against us?'

I reckoned them up; and such was the hurry of my mind, I had to cast the numbers twice, 'Fifteen,' said I.

Alan whistled. 'well,' said he, 'that can't be cured. And now follow me. It is my part to keep this door, where I look for the main battle. In that, ye have no hand. And mind and dinnae fire to this side unless they get me down; for I would rather have ten foes in front of me than one friend like you cracking pistols at my back.'

I told him, indeed I was no great shot.

'And that's very bravely said,' he cried, in a great admiration of my candour. 'There's many a pretty gentleman that wouldnae dare to say it.'

'But then, sir,' said I, 'there is the door behind you, which they may perhaps break in.'

'Ay,' said he, 'and that is a part of your work. No sooner the pistols charged, then ye must climb up into yon bed where ye're handy at the window; and if they lift hand against the door, ye're to shoot. But that's not all. Let's make a bit of a soldier of ye, David. What else have ye to guard?'

'There's the skylight,' said I. 'But indeed, Mr Stewart, I would need to have eyes upon both sides to keep the two of them; for when my face is at the one, my back is to the other.'

'And that's very true,' said Alan. 'But have ye no ears to your head?'

'To be sure!' cried I. 'I must hear the bursting of the glass!'

'Ye have some rudiments of sense,' said Alan, grimly.

CHAPTER TEN

The Siege of the Round-house

BUT NOW OUR TIME OF TRUCE was come to an end. Those on deck had waited for my coming till they grew impatient; and scarce had Alan spoken, when the captain showed face in the open door.

'Stand!' cried Alan, and pointed his sword at him.

The captain stood, indeed; but he neither winced nor drew back a foot.

'A naked sword?' says he. 'This is a strange return for hospitality.'

'Do ye see me?' said Alan. 'I am come of kings; I bear a king's name. My badge is the oak. Do ye see my sword? It has slashed the heads off mair Whigamores than you have toes upon your feet. Call up your vermin to your back, sir, and fall on! The sooner the clash begins, the sooner ye'll taste this steel throughout your vitals.'

The captain said nothing to Alan, but he looked over at me with an ugly look. 'David,' said he, 'I'll mind this'; and the sound of his voice went through me with a jar.

Next moment he was gone.

'And now,' said Alan, 'let yur hand keep your head, for the grip is coming.'

Alan drew a dirk, which he held in his left hand in case they should run in under his sword. I, on my part, clambered up into the berth with an armful of pistols and something of a heavy heart, and set open the window where I was to watch. It was a small part of the deck that I could overlook, but enough for our purpose. The sea had gone down, and the wind was steady and kept the sails quiet; so that there was a great stillness in the ship, in which I made sure I heard the sound of muttering voices. A little after, and there came a clash of steel upon the deck, by which I knew they were dealing out the cutlasses and one had been let fall: and after that, silence again.

I do not know if I was what you call afraid; but my heart beat like a bird's, both quick and little; and there was a dimness came before my eyes which I continually rubbed away, and which continually returned. As for hope, I had none; but only a darkness of despair and a sort of anger against all the world that made me long to sell my life as dear as I was able. I tried to pray, I remember, but that same hurry of my mind, like a man running, would not suffer me to think upon the words, and my chief wish was to have the thing begin and be done with it.

It came all of a sudden when it did, with a rush of feet and a roar, and then a shout from Alan, and a sound of blows and someone crying out as if hurt. I looked back over my shoulder, and saw Mr Shuan in the doorway, crossing blades with Alan.

'That's him that killed the boy!' I cried.

'Look to your window!' said Alan; and as I turned back to my place, I saw him pass his sword through the mate's body.

It was none too soon for me to look to my own part; for my head was scarce back at the window, before five men carrying a spare yard for a battering-ram, ran past me and took post to drive the door in. I had never fired with a pistol in my life, and not often with a gun; far less against a fellow-creature. But it was now or never; and just as they swung the yard, I cried out, 'Take that!' and shot into their midst.

I must have hit one of them, for he sang out and gave back a step, and the rest stopped as if a little disconcerted. Before they had time to recover, I sent another ball over their heads; and at my third shot (which went as wide as the second) the whole party threw down the yard and ran for it.

Then I looked round again into the deck-house. The whole place was full of the smoke of my own firing, just as my ears seemed to be burst with the noise of the shots. But there was Alan, standing as before; only now his sword was running blood to the hilt, and himself swelled with triumph and fallen into so

fine an attitude, that he looked to be invincible. Right before him on the floor
was Mr Shuan, on his hands and knees; the blood was pouring from his mouth,
and he was sinking slowly lower, with a terrible, white face, and just as I looked,
some of those from behind caught hold of him by the heels and dragged him
bodily out of the round-house. I believe he died as they were doing it.

'There's one of your Whigs for ye!' cried Alan; and then turning to me, he
asked if I had done much execution.

I told him I had winged one, and thought it was the captain.

'And I've settled two,' says he. 'No, there's not enough blood let; they'll be
back again. To your watch, David. This was but a dram before meat.'

I settled back to my place, re-charging the three pistols I had fired, and
keeping watch with both eye and ear.

Our enemies were disputing not far off upon the deck, and that so loudly that
I could hear a word or two above the washing of the seas.

'It was Shuan bauchled* it,' I heard one say.

And another answered him with a 'Wheesht, man! He's paid the piper.'

After that the voices fell again into the same muttering as before. Only now,
one person spoke most of the time, as though laying down a plan, and first one
and then another answered him briefly, like men taking orders. By this, I made
sure they were coming on again, and told Alan.

'It's what we have to pray for,' said he. 'Unless we can give them a good
distaste of us, and done with it, there'll be nae sleep for either you or me. But
this time, mind, they'll be in earnest.'

By this, my pistols were ready, and there was nothing to do but listen and
wait. While the brush lasted, I had not the time to think if I was frightened; but
now, when all was still again, my mind ran upon nothing else. The thought of
the sharp swords and the cold steel was strong in me; and presently, when I
began to hear stealthy steps and a brushing of men's clothes against the round-
house wall, and knew they were taking their places in the dark, I could have
found it in my mind to cry out aloud.

All this was upon Alan's side; and I had begun to think my share of the fight
was at an end, when I heard someone drop softly on the roof above me.

Then there came a single call on the sea-pipe, and that was the signal. A knot
of them made one rush of it, cutlass in hand, against the door; and at the same
moment, the glass of the skylight was dashed in a thousand pieces, and a man
leaped through and landed on the floor. Before he got his feet, I had clapped a
pistol to his back, and might have shot him, too; only at the touch of him (and
him alive) my whole flesh misgave me, and I could no more pull the trigger than
I could have flown.

He had dropped his cutlass as he jumped, and when he felt the pistol,
whipped straight round and laid hold of me, roaring out an oath; and at that
either my courage came again, or I grew so much afraid as came to the same
thing; for I gave a shriek and shot him in the midst of the body. He gave the
most horrible, ugly groan and fell to the floor. The foot of a second fellow,
whose legs were dangling through the skylight, struck me at the same time upon
the head; and at that I snatched another pistol and shot this one through the
thigh, so that he slipped through and tumbled in a lump on his companion's

*Bungled

body. There was no talk of missing, any more than there was time to aim; I clapped the muzzle to the very place and fired.

I might have stood and stared at them for long, but I heard Alan shout as if for help, and that brought me to my senses.

He had kept the dorr so long; but one of the seamen, while he was engaged with others, had run in under his guard and caught him about the body. Alan was dirking him with his left hand, but the fellow clung like a leech. Another had broken in and had his cutlass raised. The door was thronged with their faces. I thought we were lost, and catching up my cutlass, fell on them in flank.

But I had not time to be of help. The wrestler dropped at last; and Alan, leaping back to get his distance, ran upon the others like a bull, roaring as he went. They broke before him like water, turning, and running, and falling one against another in their haste. The sword in his hands flashed like quicksilver into the huddle of our fleeing enemies; and at every flash there came the scream of a man hurt. I was still thinking we were lost, when lo! they were all gone, and Alan was driving them along the deck as a sheepdog chases sheep.

Yet he was no sooner out than he was back again, being as cautious as he was brave; and meanwhile the seamen continued running and crying out as if he was still behind them; and we heard them tumble one upon another into the forecastle, and clap-to the hatch upon the top.

The round-house was like a shambles; three were dead inside, another lay in his death agony across the threshold; and there were Alan and I victorious and unhurt.

He came to me with open arms. 'Come to my arms!' he cried, and embraced and kissed me hard upon both cheeks. 'David,' said he, 'I love you like a brother. And oh, man,' he cried in a kind of ecstasy, 'am I no a bonny fighter?'

Thereupon he turned to the four enemies, passed his sword clean through each of them, and tumbled them out of doors one after the other. As he did so, he keep humming and singing and whistling to himself, like a man trying to recall an air; only what *he* was trying, was to make one. All the while, the flush was in his face, and his eyes were as bright as a five-year-old child's with a new toy. And presently he sat down upon the table, sword in hand; the air that he was making all the time began to run a little clearer, and then clearer still; and then out he burst with a great voice into a Gaelic song.

I have translated it here, not in verse (of which I have no skill) but at least in the king's English. He sang it often afterwards, and the thing became popular; so that I have heard it, and had it explained to me, many's the time.

> This is the song of the sword of Alan:
> The smith made it,
> The fire set it;
> Now it shines in the hand of Alan Breck.

> Their eyes were many and bright,
> Swift were they to behold,
> Many the hands they guided:
> The sword was alone.

The dun deer troop over the hill,
They are many, the hill is one:
The dun deer vanish,
The hill remains.

Come to me from the hills of heather,
Come from the isles of the sea.
O far-beholding eagles,
Here is your meat.

Now this song which he made (both words and music) in the hour of our victory, is something less than just to me, who stood beside him in the tussle. Mr Shuan and five more were either killed outright or thoroughly disabled; but of these, two fell by my hand, the two that came by the skylight. Four more were hurt, and of that number, one (and he not the least important) got his hurt from me. So that, altogether, I did my fair share both of the killing, and the wounding, and might have claimed a place in Alan's verses. But poets (as a very wise man once told me) have to think upon their rhymes; and in good prose talk, Alan always did me more than justice.

In the meanwhile, I was innocent of any wrong being done me. For not only I knew no word of the Gaelic; but what with the long suspense of the waiting, and the scurry and strain of our two spirts of fighting, and, more than all, the horror I had of some of my own share in it, the thing was no sooner over than I was glad to stagger to a seat. There was that tightness on my chest that I could hardly breathe; the thought of the two men I had shot sat upon me like a nightmare; and all upon a sudden, and before I had a guess of what was coming, I began to sob and cry like any child.

Alan clapped my shoulder, and said I was a brave lad and wanted nothing but a sleep.

'I'll take the first watch,' said he. 'Ye've done well by me, David, first and last; and I wouldn't lose you for all Appin – no, nor for Breadalbane.'

So he made up my bed on the floor, and took the first spell, pistol in hand and sword on knee; three hours by the captain's watch upon the wall. Then he roused me up, and I took my turn of three hours; before the end of which it was broad day, and a very quiet morning, with a smooth, rolling sea that tossed the ship and made the blood run to and fro on the round-house floor, and a heavy rain that drummed upon the roof. All my watch there was nothing stirring; and by the banging of the helm, I knew they had even no one at the tiller. Indeed (as I learned afterwards) they were so many of them hurt or dead, and the rest in so ill a temper, that Mr Riach and the captain had to take turn and turn like Alan and me, or the brig might have gone ashore and nobody the wiser. It was a mercy the night had fallen so still, for the wind had gone down as soon as the rain began. Even as it was, I judged by the wailing of a great number of gulls that went crying and fishing round the ship, that she must have drifted near pretty the coast or one of the islands of the Hebrides; and at last, looking out of the door of the round-house, I saw the great stone hills of Skye on the right hand, and, a little more astern, the strange isle of Rum.

CHAPTER ELEVEN

The Captain Knuckles Under

ALAN AND I SAT DOWN TO breakfast about six of the clock. The floor was covered with broken glass and in a horrid mess of blood, which took away my hunger. In all other ways were were in a situation not only agreeable but merry; having ousted the officers from their own cabin, and having at command all the drink in the ship – both wine and spirits and all the dainty part of what was eatable, such as the pickles and a fine sort of biscuit. This, of itself, was enough to set us in good humour; but the richest part of it was this, that the two thirstiest men that ever came out of Scotland (Mr Shuan being dead) were now shut in the forepart of the ship and condemned to what they hated most – cold water.

'And depend upon it,' Alan said, 'we shall hear more of them ere long. Ye may keep a man from the fighting but never from his bottle.'

We made good company for each other. Alan, indeed, expressed himself most lovingly; and taking a knife from the table, cut me off one of the silver buttons from his coat.

'I had them,' says he, 'from my father, Duncan Stewart; and now give ye one of them to be a keepsake for last night's work. And wherever ye go and show that button, the friends of Alan Breck will come around you.'

He said this as if he had been Charlemagne, and commanded armies; and indeed, much as I admired his courage, I was always in danger of smiling at his vanity: in danger, I say, for had I not kept my countenance, I would be afraid to think what a quarrel might have followed.

As soon as we were through with our meal, he rummaged in the captain's locker till he found a clothes-brush; and then taking off his coat, began to visit his suit and brush away the stains, with such care and labour as I supposed to have been only usual with women. To be sure, he had no other; and, besides (as he said) it belonged to a King and so behoved to be royally looked after.

For all that, when I saw what care he took to pluck out the threads where the button had been cut away, I put a higher value on his gift.

He was still so engaged, when we were hailed by Mr Riach from the deck, asking for a parley; and I, climbing through the skylight and sitting on the edge of it, pistol in hand and with a bold front, though inwardly in fear of broken glass, hailed him back again and bade him speak out. He came to the edge of the round-house, and stood on a coil of rope, so that his chin was on a level with the roof; and we looked at each other a while in silence. Mr Riach, as I do not think he had been very forward in the battle, so he had got off with nothing worse than a blow upon the cheek; but he looked out of heart and very weary, having been all night afoot, either standing watch or doctoring the wounded.

'This is a bad job,' said he at last, shaking his head.

'It was none of our choosing,' said I.

'The captain,' says he, 'would like to speak with your friend. They might speak at the window.'

'And how do we know what treachery he means?' cried I.

'He means none, David,' returned Mr Riach; 'and if he did, I'll tell ye the honest truth, we couldnae get the men to follow.'

'Is that so?' said I.

'I'll tell ye more than that,' said he. 'it's not only the men; it's me. I'm frich'ened, Davie.' And he smiled across at me. 'No,' he continued, 'what we want is to be shut of him.'

Thereupon I consulted with Alan, and the parley was agreed to and parole given upon either side; but this was not the whole of Mr Riach's business, and he now begged me for a dram with such instancy and such reminders of his former kindness, that at last I handed him a pannikin with about a gill of brandy. He drank a part, and then carried the rest down uon the deck, to share it (I suppose) with his superior.

A little after, the captain came (as was agreed) to one of the windows, and stood there in the rain, with his arm in a sling, and looking stern and pale, and so old that my heart smote me for having fired upon him.

Alan at once held a pistol in his face.

'Put that thing up!' said the captain. 'Have I not passed my word, sir? or do ye seek to affront me?'

'Captain,' says Alan, 'I doubt your word is a breakable. Last night ye haggled and argle-bargled like an apple-wife; and then passed me your word, and gave me your hand to back it; and ye ken very well what was the upshot. Be damned to your word!' says he.

'Well, well, sir,' said the captain, 'ye'll get little good by swearing.' (And truly that was a fault of which the captain was quite free.) 'But we have other things to speak,' he continued, bitterly. 'Ye've made a sore hash of my brig; I haven't hands enough left to work her; and my first officer (whom I could ill spare) has got your sword throughout his vitals, and passed without speech. There is nothing left me, sir, but to put back into the port of Glasgow after hands; and there (by your leave) ye will find them that are better able to talk to you.'

'Ay?' said Alan; 'and faith, I'll have a talk with them mysel'! Unless there's naebody speaks English in that town, I have a bonny tale for them. Fifteen tarry sailors upon the one side, and a man and a halfling boy upon the other! Oh, man, it's peetiful!'

Hoseason flushed red.

'No,' continued Alan, 'that'll no do. Ye'll just have to set me ashore as we agreed.'

'Ay,' said Hoseason, 'but my first officer is dead – ye ken best how. There's none of the rest of us acquaint with this coast, sir; and it's one very dangerous to ships.'

'I give ye your choice,' says Alan. 'Set me on dry ground in Appin, or Ardgour, or in Morven, or Arisaig, or Morar; or, in brief where ye please, within thirty miles of my own country; except in a country of the Campbells. That's a broad target. If ye miss that, ye must be as feckless at the sailoring as I have

found ye at the fighting. Why, my poor country people in their bit cobles* pass
from island to island in all weathers, ay, and by night too, for the matter of that.'

'A coble's not a ship sir.' said the captain. 'It has nae draught of water.'

'Well, then, to Glasgow if ye list' says Alan. 'We'll have the laugh of ye at the
least.'

'My mind runs little upon laughing,' said the captain. 'But all this will cost
money sir.'

'Well, sir,' says Alan, 'I am nae weathercock. Thirty guineas, if ye land me on
the sea-side; and sixty, if ye put me in the Linnhe lock.'

'But see, sir, where we lie, we are but a few hours' sail from Ardnamurchan,'
said Hoseason. 'Give me sixty, and I'll set ye there.'

'And I'm to wear my brogues and run jeopardy of the red coats to please you?' cries
Alan. 'No, sir, if ye want sixty guineas, earn them, and set me in my own country.'

'It's to risk the brig, sir,' said the captain, 'and your own lives along with her.'

'Take it or want it,' says Alan.

'Could ye pilot us at all?' asked the captain, who was frowning to himself.

'Well it's doubtful,' said Alan. 'I'm more of a fighting man (as ye have seen for
yoursel') than a sailorman. But I have been often enough picked up and set
down upon this coast, and should ken something of the lie of it.'

The captain shook his head, still frowning.

'If I had lost less money on this unchancy cruise,' says he, 'I would see you in a
rope's-end before I risked my brig, sir. But be it as ye will. As soon as I get a slant
of wind (and there's some coming, or I'm the more mistaken) I'll put it in hand.
But there's one thing more. We may meet in with a king's ship and she may lay
us aboard sir, with no blame of mine: they keep the cruisers thick upon this
coast, ye ken who for. Now, sir, if that was to befall, ye might leave the money.'

'Captain,' says Alan, 'if ye see a pennant, it shall be your part to run away.
And now, as I hear you're a little short of brandy in the forepart, I'll offer ye a
change: a bottle of brandy against two buckets of water.'

That was the last clause of the treaty, and was duly executed on both sides; so
that Alan and I could at last wash out the round-house and be quit of the
memorials of those whom we had slain, and the captain and Mr Riach could be
happy again in their own way, the name of which was drink.

CHAPTER TWELVE

I Hear of the Red Fox

BEFORE WE HAD DONE cleaning out the round-house, a breeze sprang up from a
little to the east of north. This blew off the rain and brought out the sun.

And here I must explain; and the reader would do well to look at the map. On
the day when the fog fell and we ran down Alan's boat, we had been running

*Coble: a small boat used in fishing.

through the Little Minch. At dawn after the battle, we lay becalmed to the east
of the Isle of Canna or between that and the Isle Eriska in the chain of the Long
Islands. Now to get from there to the Linnhe Loch, the straight course was
through the narrows of the Sound of Mull. But the captain had no chart; he was
afraid to trust his brig so deep among the islands; and the wind serving well, he
preferred to go by west of Tiree and come up under the southern coast of the
great Isle of Mull.

All day the breeze held in the same point, and rather freshened then died
down; and towards afternoon, a swell began to set in from round the outer
Hebrides. Our course, to go round about the inner isles, was to the west of
south, so that at first we had this swell upon our beam, and were much rolled
about. But after nightfall, when we had turned the end of Tiree and began to
head more to the east, the sea came right astern.

Meanwhile, the early part of the day, before the swell came up, was very
pleasant; sailing, as we were, in a bright sunshine and with many mountainous
islands upon different sides. Alan and I sat in the round-house with the doors
open on each side (the wind being straight astern) and smoked a pipe or two of
the captain's fine tobacco. It was at this time we heard each other's stories,
which was the more important to me, as I gained some knowledge of that wild
Highland country, on which I was so soon to land. In those days, so close on the
back of the great rebellion, it was needful a man should know what he was doing
when he went upon the heather.

It was I that showed the example, telling him all my misfortune; which he
heard with great good nature. Only, when I came to mention that good friend of
mine, Mr Campbell the minister, Alan fired up and cried out that he hated all
that were of that name.

'Why,' said I, 'he is a man you should be proud to give your hand to.'

'I know nothing I would help a Campbell to,' says he, 'unless it was a leaden
bullet. I would hunt all of that name like blackcocks. If I lay dying, I would
crawl upon my knees to my chamber window for a shot at one.'

'Why, Alan,' I cried, 'what ails ye at the Campbells?'

'Well,' says he, 'ye ken very well that I am an Appin Stewart, and the
Campbells have long harried and wasted those of my name; ay, and got lands of
us by treachery – but never with the sword,' he cried loudly, and with the word
brought down his fist upon the table. But I paid the less attention to this, for I
knew it was usually said by those who have the under hand. 'There's more than
that,' he continued, 'and all in the same story: lying words, lying papers, tricks
fit for a peddler, and the show of what's legal over all, to make a man the more
angry.'

'You that are so wasteful of your buttons,' said I, 'I can hardly think you would
be a good judge of business.'

'Ah!' says he, falling again to smiling, 'I got my wastefulness from the same
man I got the buttons from; and that was my poor father, Duncan Stewart, grace
be to him! He was the prettiest man of his kindred; and the best swordsman in
the Hielands, David, and that is the same as to say, in all the world. I should
ken, for it was him that taught me. He was in the Black Watch, when first it was
mustered; and like other gentlemen privates, had a gillie at his back to carry his
firelock for him on the march. Well, the King, it appears, was wishful to see

Hieland swordsmanship; and my father and three more were chosen out and sent to London town, to let him see it at the best. So they were had into the palace and showed the whole art of the sword for two hours at a stretch, before King George and Queen Carline, and the Butcher Cumberland, and many more of whom I have nae mind. And when they were through, the King (for all he was a rank usurper) spoke them fair and gave each man three guineas in his hand. Now, as they were going out of the palace, they had a porter's lodge to go by; and it came in on my father, as he was perhaps the first private Hieland gentleman that had ever gone by that door, it was right he should give the poor porter a proper notion of their quality. So he gives the King's three guineas into the man's hand, as if it was his common custom; the three others that came behind him did the same; and there they were on the street, never a peny the better for their pains. Some say it was one, that was the first to fee the King's porter; and some say it was another; but the truth of it is, that it was Duncan Stewart, as I am willing to prove with either sword or pistol. And that was the father that I had, God rest him!'

'I think he was not the man to leave you rich,' said I.

'And that's true,' said Alan. 'He left me my breeks to cover me, and little besides. And that was how I came to enlist, which was a black spot upon my character at the best of times, and would still be a sore job for me if I fell among the red-coats.'

'What,' cried I, 'were you in the English army?'

'That was I,' said Alan. 'But I deserted to the right side at Preston Pans – and that's some comfort.'

I could scarcely share this view: holding desertion under arms for an unpardonable fault in honour. But for all I was so young, I was wiser than say my thought. 'Dear, dear,' says I, 'the punishment is death.'

'Ay,' said he, 'if they got hands on me, it would be a short shrift and a long tow for Alan! But I have the King of France's commission in my pocket, which would aye be some protection.'

'I misdoubt it much,' said I.

'I have doubts mysel',' said Alan, drily.

'And, good heaven, man,' cried I, 'you that are a condemned rebel, and a deserter, and a man of the French King's – what tempts ye back into this country? It's a braving of Providence.'

'Tut!' says Alan, 'I have been back every year since forty-six!'

'And what brings ye, man?' cried I.

'Well, ye see, I weary for my friends and country,' said he. 'France is a braw place, nae doubt; but I weary for the heather and the deer. And then I have bit things that I attend to. Whiles I pick up a few lads to serve the King of France: recruits, ye see; and that's aye a little money. But the heart of the matter is the business of my chief, Ardshiel.'

'I thought they called your chief Appin,' said I.

'Ay, but Ardshiel is the captain of the clan,' said he, which scarcely cleared my mind. 'Ye see, David, he that was all his life so great a man, and come of the blood and bearing the name of kings, is now brought down to live in a French town like a poor and private person. He that had four hundred swords at his whistle, I have seen, with these eyes of mine, buying butter in the market-place, and taking it home in a kale-leaf. This is not only a pain but a disgrace to us of his family and clan. There are the bairns forby, the children and the hope of Appin, that must be learned their letters and how to hold a sword, in that far country. Now, the tenants of Appin have to pay a rent to King George; but their hearts are staunch, they are true to their chief; and what with love and a bit of pressure, and maybe a threat or two, the poor folk scrape up a second rent for Ardshiel. Well, David, I'm the hand that carries it.' And he struck the belt about his body, so that the guineas rang.

'Do they pay both?' cried I.

'Ay, David, both,' says he.

'What? two rents?' I repeated.

'Ay, David,' said he. 'I told a different tale to yon captain man; but this is the truth of it. And it's wonderful to me how little pressure is needed. But that's the handiwork of my good kinsman and my father's friend, James of the Glens; James Stewart, that is: Ardshiel's half-brother. He it is that gets the money in, and goes the management.'

This was the first time I heard the name of that James Stewart, who was afterwards so famous at the time of his hanging. But I took little heed at the moment, for all my mind was occupied with the generosity of these poor Highlanders.

'I call it noble,' I cried. 'I'm a Whig, or little better; but I call it noble.'

'Ay,' said he, 'ye're a Whig, but ye're a gentleman; and that's what does it. Now, if ye were one of the cursed race of Campbell, ye would gnash your teeth to hear tell of it. If ye were the Red Fox,' ... And at that name, his teeth shut together, and he ceased speaking. I have seen many a grim face, but never a grimmer than Alan's when he had named the Red Fox.

'And who is the Red Fox?' I asked, daunted, but still curious.

'Who is he?' cried Alan. 'Well, and I'll tell you that. When the men of the clans were broken at Culloden, and the good cause went down, and the horses rode over the fetlocks in the best blood of the north, Ardshiel had to flee like a poor deer upon the mountains – he and his lady and his bairns. A sair job we had of it before we got him shipped; and while he still lay in the heather, the English rogues, that couldnae come at his life, were striking at his rights. They stripped him of his powers; they stripped him of his lands; they plucked the weapons from the hands of his clansmen, that had borne arms for thirty centuries; ay, and the very clothes off their backs – so that it's now a sin to wear a tartan plaid, and a man may be cast into a gaol if he has but a kilt about his legs. One thing they couldnae kill. That was the love the clansmen bore their chief. These guineas are the proof of it. And now, in there steps a man, a Campbell, red-headed Colin of Glenure——'

'Is that him you call the Red Fox?' said I.

'Will ye bring me his brush?' cries Alan, fiercely. 'Ay, that's the man. In he steps, and gets papers from King George, to be so-called King's factor on the lands of Appin. And at first he sings small, and is hail-fellow-well-met with Sheamus – that's James of the Glens, my chieftain's agent. But by and by, that came to his ears that I have just told you; how the poor commons of Appin, the farmers and the crofters and the boumen, were wringing their very plaids to get a second rent, and send it over-seas for Ardshiel and his poor bairns. What was it ye called it, when I told ye?'

'I called it noble, Alan,' said I.

'And you little better than a common Whig' cries Alan. 'But when it came to Colin Roy, the black Campbell blood in him ran wild. He sat gnashing his teeth at the wine table. What! should a Stewart get a bite of bread, and him not be able to prevent it? Ah! Red Fox, if ever I hold you at a gun's end, the Lord have pity upon ye!' (Alan stopped to swallow down his anger.) 'Well, David, what does he do? He declares all the farms to let. And thinks he, in his black heart, I'll soon get other tenants that'll overbid these Stewarts, and Maccolls, and Macrobs (for these are all names in my clan, David), "and then," thinks he, "Ardshiel will have to hold his bonnet on a French roadside."'

'Well,' said I, 'what followed?'

Alan laid down his pipe, which he had long since suffered to go out, and set his hands upon his knees.

'Ay,' said he, 'ye'll never guess that! For these same Stewarts, and Maccolls, and Macrobs (that had two rents to pay, one to King George by stark force, and one to Ardshiel by natural kindness), offered him a better price than any Campbell in all broad Scotland; and far he sent seeking them – as far as to the sides of Clyde and the cross of Edinburgh – seeking, and fleeching, and begging them to come, where there was a Stewart to be starved and a red-headed hound of a Campbell to be pleasured!'

'Well, Alan,' said I, 'that is a strange story, and a fine one, too. And Whig as I may be, I am glad the man was beaten.'

'Him beaten?' echoed Alan. 'It's little ye ken of Campbells and less of the Red Fox. Him beaten? No: nor will be, till his blood's on the hillside! But if the day comes, David man, that I can find time and leisure for a bit of hunting, there grows not enough heather in all Scotland to hide him from my venegeance!'

'Man Alan,' said I, 'ye are neither very wise nor very Christian to blow off so many words of anger. They will do the man ye call the Fox no harm, and yourself no good. Tell me your tale plainly out. What did he next?'

'And that's a good observe, David,' said Alan. 'Troth and indeed, they will do him no harm; the more's the pity! And barring that about Christianity (of which my opinion is quite otherwise, or I would be nae Christian) I am much of your mind.'

'Opinion here or opinion there,' said I, 'it's a kennt thing that Christianity forbids revenge.'

'Ay,' said he, 'it's well seen it was a Campbell taught ye! It would be a convenient world for them and their sort, if there was no such a thing as a lad and a gun behind a heather bush! But that's nothing to the point. This is what he did.'

'Ay,' said I, 'come to that.'

'Well, David,' said he, 'since he couldnae be rid of the loyal commons by fair means, he swore he would be rid of them by foul. Ardshiel was to starve: that was the thing he aimed at. And since them that fed him in his exile wouldnae be bought out – right or wrong, he would drive them out. Therefore he sent for lawyers, and papers, and red-coats to stand at his back. And the kindly folk of that country must all pack and tramp, every father's son out of his father's house, and out of the place where he was bred and fed, and played when he was a callant. And who are to succeed them? Bare-leggit beggars! King George is to whistle for his rents; he maun dow with less; he can spread his butter thinner: what cares Red Colin? If he can hurt Ardshiel, he has his wish; if he can pluck the meat from my chieftain's table, and the bit toys out of his children's hands, he will gang hame singing to Glenure!'

'Let me have a word,' said I. 'Be sure, if they take less rents, be sure Government has a finger in the pie. It's not this Campbell's fault, man – it's his orders. And if ye killed this Colin tomorrow, what better would ye be? There would be another factor in his shoes, as fast as spur can drive.'

'Ye're a good lad in a fight,' said Alan; 'but man! ye have Whig blood in ye!'

He spoke kindly enough, but there was so much anger under his contempt that I thought it was wise to change the conversation. I expressed my wonder how, with the Highlands covered with troops and guarded like a city in a siege, a man in his situation could come and go without arrest.

'It's easier than ye would think,' said Alan. 'A bare hillside (ye see) is like all one road; if there's a sentry at one place, ye just go by another. And then heather's a great help. And everywhere there are friends' houses and friends' byres and haystacks. And besides, when folk talk of a country covered with troops, it's but a kind of a byword at the best. A soldier covers nae mair of it than his bootsoles. I have fished a water with a sentry on the other side of the brae, and killed a fine trout; and I have sat in a heather bush within six feet of another, and learned a real bonny tune from his whistling. This was it,' said he, and whistled me the air.

'And then, besides,' he continued, 'it's no sae bad now as it was in forty-six. The Hielands are what they call pacified. Small wonder, with never a gun or a sword left from Cantyre to Cape Wrath, but what tenty* folk have hidden in their thatch! But what I would like to ken, David, is just how long? Not long, ye would think, with men like Ardshiel in exile and men like the Red Fox sitting birling the wine and oppressing the poor at home. But it's a kittle thing to decide what folk'll bear, and what they will not. Or why would Red Colin be riding his horse all over my poor country of Appin, and never a pretty lad to put a bullet in him?'

And with this Alan fell into a muse, and for a long time sate very sad and silent.

I will add the rest of what I have to say about my friend, that he was skilled in all kinds of music, but principally pipe-music; was a well-considered poet in his own tongue; had read several books both in French and English; was a dead shot, a good angler, and an excellent fencer with the small sword as well as with his own particular weapon. For his faults, they were on his face, and I now knew them all. But the worst of them, his childish propensity to take offence and to pick quarrels, he greatly laid aside in my case, out of regard for the battle of the round-house. But whether it was because I had done well myself, or because I had been a witness of his own much greater prowess, is more than I can tell. For though he had a great taste for courage in other men, yet he admired it most in Alan Breck.

*Careful

CHAPTER THIRTEEN

The Loss of the Brig

IT WAS ALREADY LATE AT night, and as dark as it ever would be at that season of the year (and that is to say, it was still pretty bright), when Hoseason clapped his head into the round-house door.

'Here,' said he, 'come out and see if ye can pilot.'

'Is this one of your tricks?' asked Alan.

'Do I look like tricks?' cried the captain. 'I have other things to think of – my brig's in danger!'

By the concerned look of his face, and, above all, by the sharp tones in which he spoke of his brig, it was plain to both of us he was in deadly earnest; and so Alan and I, with no great fear of treachery, stepped on deck.

The sky was clear; it blew hard, and was bitter cold; a great deal of daylight lingered; and the moon, which was nearly full, shone brightly. The brig was close hauled, so as to round the south-west corner of the Island of Mull, the hills of which (and Ben More above them all, with a wisp of mist upon the top of it) lay full upon the larboard bow. Though it was no good point of sailing for the *Covenant*, she tore through the seas at a great rate, pitching and straining, and pursued by the westerly swell.

Altogether it was no such ill night to keep the seas in; and I had begun to wonder what it was that sat so heavily upon the captain, when the brig rising suddenly on the top of a high swell, he pointed and cried to us to look. Away on the lee bow, a thing like a fountain rose out of the moonlit sea, and immediately after we heard a low sound of roaring.

'What do ye call that?' asked the captain, gloomily.

'the sea breaking on a reef,' said Alan. 'And now ye ken where it is; and what better would ye have?'

'Ay,' said Hoseason, 'if it was the only one.'

And sure enough just as he spoke there came a second fountain further to the south.

'There!' said Hoseason. 'Ye see for yourself. If I had kent of these reefs, if I had had a chart, or if Shuan had been spared, it's not sixty guineas, no, nor six hundred, would have made me risk my brig in sic a stoneyard! But you, sir, that was to pilot us, have ye never a word?'

'I'm thinking,' said Alan, 'these'll be what they call the Torran Rocks.'

'Are there many of them?' says the captain.

'Truly, sir, I am nae pilot,' said Alan; 'but it sticks in my mind there are ten miles of them.'

Mr Riach and the captain looked at each other.

'There's a way through them, I suppose?' said the captain.

'Doubtless,' said Alan; 'but where? But it somehow runs in my mind once more, that it is clearer under the land.'

'So?' said Hoseason. 'We'll have to haul our wind then, Mr Riach; we'll have to come as near in about the end of Mull as we can take her, sir; and even then we'll have the land to kep the wind off us, and that stoneyard on our lee. Well, we're in for it now, and may as well crack on.'

With that he gave an order to the steersman, and sent Riach to the foretop. There were only five men on deck, counting the officers; these were all that were fit (or, at least, both fit and willing) for their work; and two of these were hurt. So, as I say, it fell to Mr Riach to go aloft, and he sat there looking out and hailing the deck with news of all he saw.

'The sea to the south is thick,' he cried; and then, after a while, 'It does seem clearer in by the land.'

'Well, sir,' said Horseason to Alan, 'we'll try your way of it. But I think I might as well trust to a blind fiddler. Pray God you're right.'

'Pray God I am!' says Alan to me. 'But where did I hear it? Well, well, it will be as it must.'

As we got nearer to the turn of the land the reefs began to be sown here and there on our very path; and Mr Riach sometimes cried down to us to change the course. Sometimes, indeed, none too soon; for one reef was so close on the brig's weather board that when a sea burst upon it the lighter sprays fell upon her deck and wetted us like rain.

The brightness of the night showed us these perils as clearly as by day, which was, perhaps, the more alarming. It showed me, too, the face of the captain as he stood by the steersman, now on one foot, now on the other, and sometimes blowing in his hands, but still listening and looking and as steady as steel. Neither he nor Mr Riach had shown well in the fighting; but I saw they were brave in their own trade, and admired them all the more because I found Alan very white.

'Ochone, David,' says he, 'this is no the kind of death I fancy.'

'What, Alan!' I cried, 'you're not afraid?'

'No,' said he, wetting his lips, 'but you'll allow yourself it's a cold ending.'

By this time, now and then sheering to one side or the other to avoid a reef, but still hugging the wind and the land, we had got round Iona and begun to come alongside Mull. The tide at the tail of the land ran very strong, and threw the brig about. Two hands were put to the helm, and Hoseason himself would sometimes lend a help; and it was strange to see three strong men throw their weight upon the tiller, and it (like a living thing) struggle against and drive them back. This would have been the greater danger, had not the sea been for some while free of obstacles. Mr Riach, besides, announced from the top that he saw clear water ahead.

'Ye were right,' said Hoseason to Alan. 'Ye have saved the brig, sir; I'll mind that when we come to clear accounts.' And I believe he not only meant what he said, but would have done it; so high a place did the Covenant hold in his affections.

But this is matter only for conjecture, things having gone otherwise than he forecast.

'Keep her away a point,' sings out Mr Riach. 'Reef to windward!'

And just at the same time the tide caught the brig, and threw the wind out of her sails. She came round into the wind like a top, and the next moment struck the reef with such a dunch as threw us all flat upon the deck, and came near to shake Mr Riach from his place upon the mast.

I was on my feet in a minute. The reef on which we had struck was close in under the south-west end of Mull, off a little isle they called Earraid, which lay low and black upon the larboard. Sometimes the swell broke clean over us; sometimes it only ground the poor brig upon the reef, so that we could hear her beat herself to pieces; and what with the great noise of the sails, and the singing of the wind, and the flying of the spray in the moonlight, and the sense of danger, I think my head must have been partly turned, for I could scarcely understand the things I saw.

Presently I observed Mr Riach and the seamen busy round the skiff; and still in the same blank, ran over to assist them; and as soon as I set my hand to work, my mind came clear again. It was no very easy task, for the skiff lay amidships and was full of hamper, and the breaking of the heavier seas continually forced us to give over and hold on; but we all wrought like horses while we could.

Meanwhile such of the wounded as could move came clambering out of the fore-scuttle and began to help; while the rest that lay helpless in their bunks harrowed me with screaming and begging to be saved.

The captain took no part. It seemed he was struck stupid. He stood holding by the shrouds, talking to himself and groaning out aloud whenever the ship hammered on the rock. His brig was like wife and child to him; he had looked on, day by day, at the mishandling of poor Ransome; but when it came to the brig, he seemed to suffer along with her.

All the time of our working at the boat, I remember only one other thing; that I asked Alan, looking across at the shore, what country it was; and he answered, it was the worst possible for him, for it was a land of the Campbells.

We had one of the wounded men told off to keep a watch upon the seas and cry us warning. Well, we had the boat about ready to be launched, when this man sang out pretty shrill: 'For God's sake, hold on!' We knew by his tone that it was something more than ordinary; and sure enough, there followed a sea so huge that it lifted the brig right up and canted her over on her beam. Whether the cry came too late or my hold was too weak, I know not; but at the sudden tilting of the ship I was cast clean over the bulwarks into the sea.

I went down, and drank my fill; and then came up, and got a blink of the moon; and then down again. They say a man sinks the third time for good. I cannot be made like other folk, then; for I would not like to write how often I went down or how often I came up again. All the while, I was being hurled along, and beaten upon and choked, and then swallowed whole; and the thing was so distracting to my wits, that I was neither sorry nor afraid.

Presently, I found I was holding to a spar, which helped me somewhat. And then all of a sudden I was in quiet water, and began to come to myself.

It was the spare yard I had got hold of, and I was amazed to see how far I had travelled from the brig. I hailed her, indeed; but it was plain she was already out of cry. She was still holding together; but whether or not they had yet launched the boat, I was too far off and too low down to see.

While I was hailing the brig, I spied a tract of water lying between us, where no great waves came, but which yet boiled white all over and bristled in the moon with rings and bubbles. Sometimes the whole tract swung to one side, like the tail of a live serpent; sometimes, for a glimpse, it all would disappear and then boil up again. What it was I had no guess, which for the time increased my fear of it; but I now know it must have been the roost or tide race, which had carried me away so fast and tumbled me about so cruelly, and at last, as if tired of that play, had flung out me and the spare yard upon its landward margin.

I now lay quite becalmed, and began to feel that a man can die of cold as well as of drowning. The shores of Earraid were close in; I could see in the moonlight the dots of heather and the sparkling of the mica in the rocks.

'Well,' thought I to myself, 'if I cannot get as far as that, it's strange!'

I had no skill of swimming, Essen Water being small in our neighbourhood; but when I laid hold upon the yard with both arms, and kicked out with both feet, I soon began to find that I was moving. Hard work it was, and mortally slow; but in about an hour of kicking and splashing, I had got well in between the points of a sandy bay surrounded by low hills.

The sea was here quite quiet; there was no sound of any surf; the moon shone clear; and I thought in my heart I had never seen a place so desert and desolate. But it was dry land; and when at last it grew so shallow that I could leave the yard and wade ashore upon my feet, I cannot tell if I was more tired or more grateful. Both at least, I was; tired as I never was before that night; and grateful to God as I trust I have been often, though never with more cause.

CHAPTER FOURTEEN

The Islet

WITH MY STEPPING ASHORE I began the most unhappy part of my adventures. It was half past twelve in the morning, and though the wind was broken by the land, it was a cold night. I dared not sit down (for I thought I should have frozen), but took off my shoes and walked to and fro upon the sand, barefoot, and beating my breast, with infinite weariness. There was no sound of man or cattle; not a cock crew, though it was about the hour of their first waking; only the surf broke outside in the distance, which put me in mind of my perils and those of my friend. To walk by the sea at that hour of the morning, and in a place so desert-like and lonesome, struck me with a kind of fear.

As soon as the day began to break I put on my shoes and climbed a hill – the ruggedest scramble I ever undertook – falling, the whole way, between big blocks of granite or leaping from one to another. When I got to the top the dawn was come. There was no sign of the brig, which must have lifted from the reef and sunk. The boat, too, was nowhere to be seen. There was never a sail upon the ocean; and in what I could see of the land, was neither house nor man.

I was afraid to think what had befallen my shipmates, and afraid to look longer at so empty a scene. What with my wet clothes and weariness, and my belly that now began to ache with hunger, I had enough to trouble me without that. So I set off eastward along the south coast, hoping to find a house where I might warm myself, and perhaps get news of those I had lost. And at the wrst, I considered the sun would soon rise and dry my clothes.

After a little, my way was stopped by a creek or inlet of the sea, which seemed to run pretty deep into the land; and as I had no means to get across, I must needs change my direction to go about the end of it. It was still the roughest kind of walking; indeed the whole, not only of Earraid, but of the neighbouring part of Mull (which they call the Ross) is nothing but a jumble of granite rocks with heather in among. At first the creek kept narrowing as I had looked to see; but presently to my surprise it began to widen out again. At this I scratched my head, but had still no notion of the truth; until at last I came to a rising ground, and it burst upon me all in a moment that I was cast upon a little, barren isle, and cut off on every side by the salt seas.

Instead of the sun rising to dry me, it came on to rain, with a thick mist; so that my case was lamentable.

I stood in the rain, and shivered, and wondered what to do, till it occurred to me that perhaps the creek was fordable. Back I went to the narrowest point and waded in. But not three yards from shore, I plumped in head over ears; and if ever I was heard of more it was rather by God's grace than my own prudence. I was no wetter (for that could hardly be) but I was all the colder for this mishap; and having lost another hope, was the more unhappy.

And now, all at once, the yard came in my head. What had carried me through the roost, would surely serve me to cross this little quiet creek in safety. With that I set off, undaunted, across the top of the isle, to fetch and carry it back. It was a weary tramp in all ways, and if hope had not buoyed me up, I must have cast myself down and given up. Whether with the sea salt, or because I was growing fevered, I was distressed with thirst, and had to stop, as I went, and drink the peaty water out of the hags.

I came to the bay at last, more dead than alive; and at the first glance, I thought the yard was something further out than when I left it. In I went, for the third time, into the sea. The sand was smooth and firm and shelved gradually down; so that I could wade out till the water was almost to my neck and the little waves splashed into my face. But at that depth my feet began to leave me and I durst venture in no further. As for the yard, I saw it bobbing very quietly some twenty feet in front of me.

I had borne up well until this last disappointment; but at that I came ashore, and flung myself down upon the sands and wept.

The time I spent upon the island is still so horrible a thought to me, that I must pass it lightly over. In all the books I have read of people cast away, they had either their pockets full of tools, or a chest of things would be thrown upon the beach along with them, as if on purpose. My case was very different. I had nothing in my pockets but money and Alan's silver button; and being inland bred, I was as much short of knowledge as of means.

I knew indeed that shell-fish were counted good to eat; and among the rocks of the isle I found a great plenty of limpets, which at first I could scarcely strike from their places, not knowing quickness to be needful. There were, besides, some of the little shells that we call buckies; I think periwinkle is the English name. Of these two I made my whole diet, devouring them cold and raw as I found them; and so hungry was I, that at first they seemed to me delicious.

Perhaps they were out of season, or perhaps there was something wrong in the sea about my island. But at least I had no sooner eaten my first meal than I was seized with giddiness and retching, and lay for a long time no better than dead. A second trial of the same food (indeed I had no other) did better with me and I revived my strength. But as long as I was on the island, I never knew what to expect when I had eaten; sometimes all was well, and sometimes I was thrown into a miserable sickness; nor could I ever distinguish what particular fish it was that hurt me.

All day it streamed rain; the island ran like a sop; there was no dry spot to be found; and when I lay down that night, between two boulders that made a kind of roof, my feet were in a bog.

The second day I crossed the island to all sides. There was no one part of it better than another; it was all desolate and rocky; nothing living on it but game birds which I lacked the means to kill, and the gulls which haunted the outlying rocks in a prodigious number. But the creek, or straits, that cut off the isle from the main land of the Ross, opened out on the north into a bay, and the bay again opened into the sound of Iona; and it was the neighbourhood of this place that I chose to be my home; though if I had thought upon the very name of home in such a spot, I must have burst out weeping.

I had good reasons for my choice. There was in this part of the isle a little hut of a house like a pig's hut, where fishers used to sleep when they came there upon their business; but the turf roof of it had fallen entirely in; so that the hut was of no use to me, and gave me less shelter than my rocks. What was more important, the shell-fish on which I lived grew there in great plenty; when the tide was out I could gather a peck at a time; and this was doubtless a convenience. But the other reason went deeper. I had become in no way used to the horrid solitude of the isle, but still looked round me on all sides (like a man that was hunted) between fear and hope that I might see some human creature coming. Now, from a little up the hillside over the bay, I could catch a sight of the great, ancient church and the roofs of the people's houses in Iona. And on the other hand, over the low country of the Ross, I saw smoke go up, morning and evening, as if from a homestead in a hollow of the land.

I used to watch this smoke, when I was wet and cold, and had my head half turned with loneliness; and think of the fireside and the company, till my heart burned. It was the same with the roofs of Iona. Altogether, this sight I had of men's homes and comfortable lives, although it put a point on my own sufferings, yet it kept hope alive, and helped me to eat my raw shell-fish (which had soon grown to be a disgust) and saved me from the sense of horror I had whenever I was quite alone with dead rocks, and fowls, and the rain, and the cold sea.

I say it kept hope alive; and indeed it seemed impossible that I should be left to die on the shores of my own country, and within view of a church tower and the smoke of men's houses. But the second day passed; and though as long as the light lasted I kept a bright look-out for boats on the Sound or men passing on the Ross, no help came near me. It still rained; and I turned in to sleep, as wet as

ever and with a cruel sore throat, but a little comforted, perhaps, by having said
good night to my next neighbours, the people of Iona.

Charles the Second declared a man could stay outdoors more days in the year
in the climate of England than in any other. This was very like a king with a
palace at his back and changes of dry clothes. But he must have had better luck
on his flight from Worcester than I had on that miserable isle. It was the height
of the summer; yet it rained for more than twenty-four hours, and did not clear
until the afternoon of the third day.

This was the day of incidents. In the morning I saw a red deer, a buck with a
fine spread of antlers, standing in the rain on the top of the island; but he had
scarce seen me rise from under my rock, before he trotted off upon the other
side. I supposed he must have swum the straits; though what should bring any
creature to Earraid, was more than I could fancy.

A little after, as I was jumping about after my limpets, I was startled by a
guinea-piece, which fell upon a rock in front of me and glanced off into the sea.
When the sailors gave me my money again, they kept back not only about a
third of the whole sum, but my father's leather purse; so that from that day out, I
carried my gold loose in a pocket with a button. I now saw there must be a hole,
and clapped my hand to the place in a great hurry. But this was to lock the stable
door after the steed was stolen. I had left the shore at Queensferry with near on
fifty pounds; now I found no more than two guinea pieces and a silver shilling.

It is true I picked up a third guinea a little after, where it lay shining on a piece
of turf. That made a fortune of three pounds and four shillings, English money,
for a lad, the rightful heir of an estate, and now starving on an isle at the
extreme end of the wild Highlands.

This state of my affairs dashed me still further; and indeed my plight on that
third morning was truly pitiful. My clothes were beginning to rot; my stockings
in particular were quite worn through, so that my shanks went naked; my hands
had grown quite soft with the continual soaking; my throat was very sore, my
strength had much abated, and my heart so turned against the horrid stuff I was
condemned to eat, that the very sight of it came near to sicken me.

And yet the worst was not yet come.

There is a pretty high rock on the north-west of Earraid, which (because it
had a flat top and overlooked the Sound) I was much in the habit of frequenting;
not that ever I stayed in one place, save when asleep, my misery giving me no
rest. Indeed I wore myself down with continual and aimless goings and comings
in the rain.

As soon, however, as the sun came out, I lay down on the top of that rock to
dry myself. The comfort of the sunshine is a thing I cannot tell. It set me
thinking hopefully of the deliverance, of which I had begun to despair, and I
scanned the sea and the Ross with a fresh interest. On the south of my rock, a
part of the island jutted out and his the open ocean, so that a boat could thus
come quite near me upon that side, and I be none the wiser.

Well, all of a sudden, a coble with a brown sail and a pair of fishers aboard of
it, came flying round that corner of the isle, bound for Iona. I shouted out, and
then fell on my knees on the rock and reached up my hands and prayed to them.
They were near enough to hear – I could even see the colour of their hair; and
there was no doubt but they observed me, for they cried out in the Gaelic

tongue, and laughed. But the boat never turned aside, and flew on, right before my eyes, for Iona.

I could not believe such wickedness, and ran along the shore from rock to rock, crying on them piteously; even after they were out of reach of my voice, I still cried and waved to them; and when they were quite gone, I thought my heart would have burst. All the time of my troubles I wept only twice. Once, when I could not reach the yard; and now, the second time, when these fishers turned a deaf ear to my cries. But this time I wept and roared like a wicked child, tearing u the turf with my nails and grinding my face in the earth. If a wish would kill men, those two fishers would never have seen morning, and I should likely have died upon my island.

When I was a little over my anger, I must eat again, but with such loathing of the mess as I could now scarce control. Sure enough, I should have done as well to fast, for my fishes poisoned me again. I had all my first pains; my throat was so sore I could scarce swallow; I had a fit of strong shuddering, which clucked my teeth together; and there came on me that dreadful sense of illness, which we have no name for either in Scotch or English. I thought I should have died, and made my peace with God, forgiving all men, even my uncle and the fishers; and as soon as I had thus made up my mind to the worst, clearness came upon me: I observed the night was falling dry; my clothes were dried a good deal; truly, I was in a better case than ever before, since I had landed on the isle; and so I got to sleep at last, with a thought of gratitude.

The next day (which was the fourth of this horrible life of mine) I found my bodily strength run very low. But the sun shone, the air was sweet, and what I managed to eat of the shell-fish agreed well with me and revived my courage.

I was scarce back on my rock (where I went always the first thing after I had eaten) before I observed a boat coming down the Sound, and with her head, as I thought, in my direction.

I began at once to hope and fear exceedingly; for I thought these men might have thought better of their cruelty and be coming back to my assistance. But another disappointment, such as yesterday's, was more than I could bear. I turned my back, accordingly, upon the sea, and did not look again till I had counted many hundreds. The boat was still heading for the island. The next time I counted the full thousand, as slowly as I could, my heart beating so as to hurt me. And then it was out of all question. She was coming straight to Earraid.

I could no longer hold myself back, but ran to the sea side and out, from one rock to another, as far as I could go. It is a marvel I was not drowned; for when I was brought to a stand at last, my legs shook under me, and my mouth was so dry, I must wet it with sea-water before I was able to shout.

All this time the boat was coming on; and now I was able to perceive it was the same boat and the same two men as yesterday. This I knew by their hair, which the one had of a bright yellow and the other black. But now there was a third man along with them, who looked to be of a better class.

As soon as they were come within easy speech, they let down their sail and lay quiet. In spite of my supplications, they drew no nearer in, and what frightened me most of all, the new man tee-hee'd with laughter as he talked and looked at me.

Then he stood up in the boat and addressed me a long while, speaking fast and with many wavings of his hand. I told him I had no Gaelic; and at this he became very angry, and I began to suspect he thought he was talking English. Listening very close, I caught the word 'whateffer' several times; but all the rest was Gaelic, and might have been Greek and Hebrew for me.

'Whatever,' said I, to show him I had caught a word.

'Yes, yes – yes, yes,' says he, and then he looked at the other men, as much as to say, 'I told you I spoke English', and began again as hard as ever in the Gaelic.

This time I picked out another word, 'tide'. Then I had a flash of hope. I remembered he was always waving his hand towards the mainland of the Ross.

'Do you mean when the tide is out——?' I cried, and could not finish.

'Yes, yes,' said he. 'Tide.'

At that I turned tail upon their boat (where my adviser had once more begun to tee-hee with laughter), leaped back the way I had come, from one stone to another, and set off running across the isle as I had never run before. In about half an hour I came out upon the shores of the creek; and, sure enough, it was shrunk into a little trickle of water, through which I dashed, not above my knees, and landed with a shout on the main island.

A sea-bred boy would not have stayed a day on Earraid; which is only what they call a tidal islet, and except in the bottom of the neaps, can be entered and left twice in every twenty-four hours, either dry-shod, or at the most by wading. Even I, who had the tide going out and in before me in the bay, and even watched for the ebbs, the better to get my shell-fish – even I (I say), if I had sat down to think, instead of raging at my fate, must have soon guessed the secret, and got free. It was no wonder the fishers had not understood me. The wonder was rather that they had ever guessed my pitiful illusion, and taken the trouble to come back. I had starved with cold and hunger on that island for close upon one hundred hours. But for the fishers, I might have left my bones there, in pure folly. And even as it was, I had paid for it pretty dear, not only in past sufferings, but in my present case; being clothed like a beggar-man, scarce able to walk, and in great pain of my sore throat.

I have seen wicked men and fools, a great many of both; and I believe they both get paid in the end; but the fools first.

CHAPTER FIFTEEN

The Lad with the Silver Button: Through the Isle of Mull

THE ROSS OF MULL, WHICH I had now got upon, was rugged and trackless, like the isle I had just left; being all bog, and briar, and big stone. There may be roads for them that know that country well; but for my part I had no better guide than my own nose, and no other landmark than Ben More.

I aimed as well as I could for the smoke I had seen so often from the island; and with all my great weariness and the difficulty of the way, came upon the house in the bottom of a little hollow, about five or six at night. It was low and longish, roofed with turf and built of unmortared stones; and on a mound in front of it, an old gentleman sat smoking his pipe in the sun.

With what little English he had, he gave me to understand that my shipmates had got safe ashore, and had broken bread in that very house on the day after.

'Was there one,' I asked, 'dressed like a gentleman?'

He said they all wore rough great-coats; but to be sure, the first of them, the one that came alone, wore breeches and stockings, while the rest had sailors' trousers.

'Ah,' said I, 'and he would have a feathered hat?'

He told me, no, that he was bare-headed like myself.

At first I thought Alan might have lost his hat; and then the rain came in my mind, and I judged it more likely he had it out of harm's way under his great coat. This set me smiling, partly because my friend was sage, partly to think of his vanity in dress.

And then the old gentleman clapped his hand to his brow, and cried out that I must be the lad with the silver button.

'Why, yes!' said I, in some wonder.

'Well, then,' said the old gentleman, 'I have a word for you that you are to follow your friend to his country, by Torosay.'

He then asked me how I had fared, and I told him my tale. A south-country man would certainly have laughed; but this old gentleman (I call him so because of his manners, for his clothes were dropping off his back) heard me all through with nothing but gravity and pity. When I had done, he took me by the hand, led me into his hut (it was no better) and presented me before his wife, as if she had been the Queen and I a duke.

The good woman set oat-bread before me and a cold grouse, patting my shoulder and smiling to me all the time, for she had no English; and the old gentleman (not to be behind) brewed me a strong punch out of their country spirit. All the time I was eating, and after that when I was drinking the punch, I could scarce come to believe in my good fortune; and the house, though it was thick with the peat-smoke and as full of holes as a colander, seemed like a palace.

The punch threw me in a strong sweat and a deep slumber; the good people let me lie; and it was near noon of the next day before I took the road, my throat already easier and my spirits restored by good fare and good news. The old gentleman, although I pressed him hard, would take no money, and gave me an old bonnet for my head; though I am free to own I was no sooner out of view of the house, than I very jealously washed this gift of his in a wayside fountain.

Thought I to myself: 'If these are the wild Highlanders, I could wish my own folk wilder.'

I not only started late, but I must have wandered nearly half the time. True, I met plenty of people grubbing in little miserable fields that would not keep a cat, or herding little kine about the bigness of asses. The Highland dress being forbidden by law since the rebellion, and the people condemned to the lowland habit, which they much disliked, it was strange to see the variety of their array. Some went bare, only for a hanging cloak or great-coat, and carried their trousers on their backs like a useless burthen; some had made an imitation of the tartan with little parti-coloured stripes patched together like an old wife's quilt; others, again, still wore the highland philabeg, but by putting a few stitches between the legs, transformed it into a pair of trousers like a Dutchman's. All those makeshifts were condemned and punished, for the law was harshly applied, in hopes to break up the clan spirit; but in that out-of-the-way, sea-bound isle, there were few to make remarks and fewer to tell tales.

They seemed in great poverty; which was no doubt natural, now that rapine was put down, and the chiefs kept no longer an open house; and the roads (even such a wandering, country by-track as the one I followed) were infested with beggars. And here again I marked a difference from my own part of the country. For our lowland beggars – even the gownsmen themselves, who beg by patent – had a louting, flattering way with them, and if you gave them a plack and asked change, would very civilly return you a boddle. But these Highland beggars stood on their dignity, asked alms only to buy snuff (by their account) and would give no change.

To be sure, this was no concern of mine, except in so far as it entertained me by the way. What was much more to the purpose, few had any English, and these few (unless they were of the brotherhood of beggars) not very anxious to place it at my service. I knew Torosay to be my destination, and repeated the name to them and pointed; but instead of simply pointing in reply, they would give me a screed of the Gaelic that set me foolish; so it was small wonder if I went out of my road as often as I stayed in it.

At last, about eight at night and already very weary, I came to a lone house, where I asked admittance, and was refused, until I bethought me of the power of money in so poor a country, and held up one of my guineas in my finger and thumb. Thereupon, the man of the house, who had hitherto pretended to have no English, and driven me from his door by signals, suddenly began to speak as clearly as was needful, and agreed for five shillings to give me a night's lodging and guide me the next day to Torosay.

I slept uneasily that night, fearing I should be robbed; but I might have spared myself the pain; for my host was no robber, only miserably poor and a great cheat. He was not alone in his poverty; for the next morning, we must go five miles about to the house of what he called a rich man to have one of my guineas changed. This was perhaps a rich man for Mull; he would have scarce been thought so in the south; for it took all he had, the whole house was turned upside down, and a neighbour brought under contribution, before he could scrape together twenty shillings in silver. The odd shilling he kept for himself, protesting he could ill afford to have so great a sum of money lying 'locked up'. For all that he was very courteous and well spoken, made us both sit down with his family to dinner, and brewed punch in a fine china bowl, over which my rascal guide grew so merry that he refused to start.

I was for getting angry, and appealed to the rich man (Hector Maclean was his name) who had been a witness to our bargain and to my payment of the five shillings. But Maclean had taken his share of the punch, and vowed that no gentleman should leave his table after the bowl was brewed; so there was nothing for it but to sit and hear Jacobite toasts and Gaelic songs, till all were tipsy and staggered off to bed or the barn for their night's rest.

Next day (the fourth of my travels) we were up before five upon the clock; but my rascal guide got to the bottle at once, and it was three hours before I had him clear of the house, and then (as you shall hear) only for a worse disappointment.

As long as we went down a heathery valley that lay before Mr Maclean's house, all went well; only my guide looked constantly over his shoulder, and when I asked him the cause, only grinned at me. No sooner, however, had we crossed the back of a hill, and got out of sight of the house windows, than he told me Torosay lay right in front, and that a hill-top (which he pointed out) was my best landmark.

'I care very little for that,' said I, 'since you are going with me.'

The impudent cheat answered me in the Gaelic that he had no English.

'My fine fellow,' I said, 'I know very well your English comes and goes. Tell me what will bring it back? It is more money you wish?'

'Five shillings mair,' said he, 'and hersel' will bring ye there.'

I reflected a while and then offered him two, which he accepted greedily, and insisted on having in his hands at once – 'for luck', as he said, but I think it was rather for my misfortune.

The two shillings carried him not quite as many miles; at the end of which distance, he sat down upon the wayside and took off his brogues from his feet, like a man about to rest.

I was now red-hot. 'Ha!' said I, 'have you no more English?'

He said impudently, 'no'.

At that I boiled over and lifted my hand to strike him; and he, drawing a knife from his rags, squatted back and grinned at me like a wild-cat. At that, forgetting everything but my anger, I ran in upon him, put aside his knife with my left and struck him in the mouth with the right. I was a strong lad and very angry, and he but a little man; and he went down before me heavily. By good luck, his knife flew out of hand as he fell.

I picked up both that and his brogues, wished him a good morning, set off upon my way, leaving him bare-foot and disarmed. I chuckled to myself as I went, being sure I was done with that rogue, for a variety of reasons. First, he knew he could have no more of my money; next, the brogues were worth in that country only a few pence; and lastly the knife, which was really a dagger, it was against the law for him to carry.

In about half-an-hour of walk, I overtook a great, ragged man, moving pretty fast but feeling before him with a staff. He was quite blind, and told me he was a catechist, which should have put me at my ease. But his face went against me; it seemed dark and dangerous and secret; and presently, as we began to go on alongside, I saw the steel butt of a pistol sticking from under the flap of his coat-pocket. To carry such a thing menat a fine of fifteen pounds sterling upon a first offence, and transportation to the colonies upon a second. Nor could I quite see why a religious teacher should go armed, or what a blind man could be doing with a pistol.

I told him about my guide, for I was proud of what I had done, and my vanity for once got the heels of my prudence. At the mention of the five shillings he cried out so loud that I made up my mind I should say nothing of the other two, and was glad he could not see my blushes.

'Was it too much?' I asked, a little faltering.

'Too much!' cries he. 'Why, I will guide you to Torosay myself for a dram of brandy. And give you the great pleasure of my company (me that is a man of some learning) in the bargain.'

I said I did not see how a blind man could be a guide: but at that he laughed aloud, and said his stick was eyes enough for an eagle.

'In the Isle of Mull, at least,' says he, 'where I knew every stone and heather-bush by mark of head. See, now,' he said, striking right and left, as if to make sure, 'down there a burn is running; and at the head of it there stands a bit of a small hill with a stone cocked upon the top of that; and it's hard at the foot of the hill, that the way runs by to Torosay; and the way here, being for droves, is plainly trodden, and will show grassy through the heather.'

I had to own he was right in every feature, and told my wonder.

'Ha!' says he, 'that's nothing. Would ye believe me now, that before the Act came out, and when there were weapons in this country, I could shoot? Ay, could I!' cries he, and then with a leer: 'If ye had such a thing as a pistol here to try with, I would show ye how it's done.'

I told him I had nothing of the sort, and gave him a wider berth. If he had known, his pistol stuck at that time quite plainly out of his pocket, and I could see the sun twinkle on the steel of the butt. But by the better luck for me, he knew nothing, thought all was covered, and lied on in the dark.

He then began to question me cunningly, where I came from, whether I was rich, whether I could change a five-shilling piece for him (which he declared he had that moment in his sporran) and all the time he kept edging up to me and I avoiding him. We were now upon a sort of green cattle-track which crossed the hills towards Torosay, and we kept changing sides upon that like dancers in a reel. I had so plainly the upper-hand that my spirits rose, and indeed I took a pleasure in this game of blind-man's buff; but the catechist grew angrier and angrier, and at last began to swear in Gaelic and to strike for my legs with his staff.

Then I told him that, sure enough, I had a pistol in my pocket as well as he, and if he did not strike across the hill due south I would even blow his brains out.

He became at once very polite; and after trying to soften me for some time, but quite in vain, he cursed me once more in the Gaelic and took himself off. I watched him striding along, through bog and brier, tapping with his stick, until he turned the end of a hill and disappeared in the next hollow. Then I struck on again for Torosay, much better pleased to be alone than to travel with that man of learning. This was an unlucky day; and these two, of whom I had just rid myself one after the other, were the two worst men I met with in the Highlands.

At Torosay, on the Sound of Mull, and looking over to the mainland of Morven, there was an inn with an innkeeper, who was a Maclean, it appeared, of a very high family; for to keep an inn is thought even more genteel in the Highlands than it is with us, perhaps as partaking of hospitality, or perhaps because the trade is idle and drunken. He spoke good English, and finding me to be something of a scholar, tried me first in French, where he easily beat me, and then in the Latin, in which I don't know which of us did best. This pleasant rivalry put us at once upon friendly terms; and I sat up and drank punch with him (or to be more correct, sat up and watched him drink it) until he was so tipsy that he wept upon my shoulder.

I tried him, as if by accident, with a sight of Alan's button; but it was plain he had never seen or heard of it. Indeed, he bore some grudge against the family and friends of Ardshiel, and before he was drunk he read me a lampoon, in very good Latin, but with a very ill meaning, which he had made in elegiac verses upon a person of that house.

When I told him of my catechist, he shook his head, and said I was lucky to have got clear off. 'That is a very dangerous man,' he said; 'Duncan Mackiegh is his name; he can shoot by the ear at several yards, and has been often accused of highway robberies, and once of murder.'

'The cream of it is,' says I, 'that he called himself a catechist.'

'And why should he not?' says he, 'when that is what he is? It was Maclean of Duart gave it to him because he was blind. But, perhaps, it was a peety,' says my host, 'for he is always on the road, going from one place to another to hear the yound folk say their religion; and doubtless, that is a great temptation to the poor man.'

At last, when my landlord could drink no more, he showed me to a bed, and I lay down in very good spirits; having travelled the greater part of that big and crooked Island of Mull, from Earraid to Torosay, fifty miles as the crow flies and (with my wanderings) much nearer a hundred, in four days and with little fatigue. Indeed I was by far in better heart and health of body at the end of that long tramp than I had been at the beginning.

CHAPTER SIXTEEN

The Lad with the Silver Button: Across Morven

THERE IS A REGULAR FERRY from Torosay to Kinlochaline on the mainland. Both shores of the Sound are in the country of the strong clan of the Macleans, and the people that passed the ferry with me were almost all of that clan. The skipper of the boat, on the other hand, was called Neil Roy Macrob; and since Macrob was one of the names of Alan's clansmen, and Alan himself had sent me to that ferry, I was eager to come to private speech of Neil Roy.

In the crowded boat this was of course impossible, and the passage was a very slow affair. There was no wind, and as the boat was wretchedly equipped, we could pull but two oars on one side, and one on the other. The men gave way, however, with a good will, the passengers taking spells to help them, and the whole company giving the time in Gaelic boat-songs. And what with the songs, and the sea air, and the good nature and spirit of all concerned, and the bright weather, the passage was a pretty thing to have seen.

But there was one melancholy part. In the mouth of Loch Aline we found a great sea-going ship at anchor; and this I supposed at first to be one of the King's cruisers which were kept along that coast, both summer and winter, to prevent communication with the French. As we got a little nearer, it became plain she was a ship of merchandise; and what still puzzled me, not only her decks, but the sea-beach also, were quite black with people, and skiffs were continually plying to and fro between them. Yet nearer, and there began to come to our ears a great sound of mourning, the people on board and those on the shore crying and lamenting one to another so as to pierce the heart.

Then I understood this was an emigrant ship bound for the American colonies.

We put the ferry-boat alongside, and the exiles leaned over the bulwarks, weeping and reaching out their hands to my fellow-passengers, among whom they counted some near friends. How long this might have gone on I do not know, for they seemed to have no sense of time; but at last the captain of the ship, who seemed near beside himself (and no great wonder) in the midst of this crying and confusion, came to the side and begged us to depart.

Thereupon Neil sheered off; and the chief singer in our boat struck into a melancholy air, which was presently taken up both by the emigrants and their friends upon the beach, so that it sounded from all sides like a lament for the dying. I saw the tears run down the cheeks of the men and women in the boat, even as they bent at the oars; and the circumstances and the music of the song (which is one called 'Lochaber no more') were highly affecting even to myself.

At Kinlochaline I got Neil Roy upon one side on the beach, and said I made sure he was one of Appin's men.

'And what for no?' said he.

'I am seeking somebody,' said I; 'and it comes in my mind that you will have news of him. Alan Breck Stewart is his name.' And very foolishly, instead of showing him the button, I sought to pass a shilling in his hand.

At this he drew back. 'I am very much affronted,' he said; 'and this is not the way that one shentleman should behave to another at all. The man you ask for is in France; but if he was in my sporran,' says he, 'and your belly full of shillings, I would not hurt a hair upon his body.'

I saw I had gone the wrong way to work, and without wasting time upon apologies, showed him the button lying in the hollow of my palm.

'Aweel, aweel,' said Neil; 'and I think ye might have begun with that end of the stick, whatever! But if ye are the lad with the silver button, all is well, and I have the word to see that ye come safe. But if ye will pardon me to speak plainly,' says he, 'there is a name that you should never take into your mouth, and that is the name of Alan Breck; and there is a thing that ye would never do, and that is to offer your dirty money to a Hieland shentleman.'

It was not very easy to apologize; for I could scarce tell him (what was the truth) that I had never dreamed he would set up to be a gentleman until he told me so. Neil on his part had no wish to prolong his dealings with me, only to fulfil his orders and be done with it; and he made haste to give me my route. This was to lie the night in Kinlochaline in the public inn; to cross Morven the next day to Ardgour, and lie the night in the house of one John of the Claymore, who was warned that I might come; the third day, to be set across one loch at Corran and another at Balachulish, and then ask my way to the house of James of the Glens, at Aucharn in Duror of Appin. There was a good deal of ferrying, as you hear; the sea in all this part running deep into the mountains and winding about their roots. It makes the country strong to hold and difficult to travel, but full of prodigious wild and dreadful prospects.

I had some other advice from Neil: to speak with no one by the way, to avoid Whigs, Campbells, and the 'red-soldiers'; to leave the road and lie in a bush, if I saw any of the latter coming 'for it was never chancy to meet in with them'; and in brief, to conduct myself like a robber or a Jacobite agent, as perhaps Neil thought me.

The inn at Kinlochaline was the most beggarly vile place that ever pigs were styed in, full of smoke, vermin, and silent Highlanders. I was not only discontented with my lodging, but with myself for my mismanagement of Neil, and thought I could hardly be worse off. But very wrongly, as I was soon to see; for I had not been half an hour at the inn (standing in the door most of the time, to ease my eyes from the peat smoke) when a thunderstorm came close by, the springs broke in a little hill on which the inn stood, and one end of the house became a running water. Places of public entertainment were bad enough all over Scotland in those days; yet is was a wonder to myself, when I had to go from the fireside to the bed in which I slept, wading over the shoes.

Early in my next day's journey I overtook a little, stout, solemn man, walking very slowly with his toes turned out, sometimes reading in a book and sometimes marking the place with his finger, and dressed decently and plainly in something of a clerical style.

This I found to be another catechist, but of a different order from the blind man of Mull: being indeed one of those sent out by the Edinburgh Society for Propagating Christian Knowledge, to evangelize the more savage places of the Highlands. His name was Henderland; he spoke with the broad south-country tongue, which I was beginning to weary for the sound of; and besides common countryship, we soon found we had a more particular bond of interest. For my good friend, the minister of Essendean, had translated into the Gaelic in his by-time a number of hymns and pious books, which Henderland used in his work, and held in great esteem. Indeed it was one of these he was carrying and reading when we met.

We fell in company at once, our ways lying together as far as to Kingairloch. As we went, he stopped and spoke with all the wayfarers and workers that we met or passed; and though of course I could not tell what they discoursed about, yet I judged Mr Henderland must be well liked in the countryside, for I observed many of them to bring out their mulls and share a pinch of snuff with him.

I told him as far in my affairs as I judged wise; as far, that is, as they were none of Alan's; and gave Balachulish as the place I was travelling to, to meet a friend; for I thought Aucharn, or even Duror, would be too particular and might put him on the scent.

On his part he told me much of his work and the people he worked among, the hiding priests and Jacobites, the Disarming Act, the dress, and many other curiosities of the time and place. He seemed moderate; blaming Parliament in several points, and especially because they had framed the Act more severely against those who wore the dress than against those who carried weapons.

This moderation put it in my mind to question him of the Red Fox and the Appin tenants; questions which, I thought, would seem natural enough in the mouth of one travelling to that country.

He said it was a bad business. 'It's wonderful,' said he, 'where the tenants find the money, for their life is mere starvation. (Ye don't carry such a thing as snuff, do ye, Mr Balfour? No, Well, I'm better wanting it.) But these tenants (as I was saying) are doubtless partly driven to it. James Stewart in Duror (that's him they call James of the Glens) is half-brother to Ardshiel, the captain of the clan; and he is a man much looked up to, and drives very hard. And then there's one they call Alan Breck——'

'Ah!' cried I, 'what of him?'

'What of the wind that bloweth where it listeth?' said Henderland. 'He's here and awa; here today and gone tomorrow: a fair heather-cat. He might be glowering at the two of us out of yon whin-bush, and I wouldnae wonder! Ye'll no carry such a thing as snuff, will ye?'

I told him no, and that he had asked the same thing more than once.

'It's highly possible,' said he sighing. 'But it seems strange ye shouldnae carry it. However, as I was saying, this Alan Breck is a bold, desperate customer, and well kent to be James's right hand. His life is forfeit already; he would boggle at naething; and maybe, if a tenant-body was to hang back, he would get a dirk in his wame.'

'You make a poor story of it all, Mr Henderland,' said I. 'If it is all fear upon both sides, I care to hear no more of it.'

'Na,' said Mr Henderland, 'but there's love too, and self-denial that should put the like of you and me to shame. There's something fine about it; no perhaps Christian, but humanly fine. Even Alan Breck, by all that I hear, is a child to be respected. There's many a lying sneck-draw sits close in kirk in our own part of the country, and stands well in the world's eye, and maybe is a far worse man, Mr Balfour, that yon misguided shedder of man's blood. Ay, ay, we might take a lesson by them. – Ye'll perhaps think I've been too long in the Hielands?' he added, smiling to me.

I told him not at all; that I had seen much to admire among the Highlanders; and if he came to that, Mr Campbell himself was a Highlander.

'Ay,' said he, 'that's true. It's a fine blood.'

'And what is the King's agent about?' I asked.

'Colin Campbell?' says Henderland. 'Putting his head in a bees' byke!'

'He is to turn the tenants out by force, I hear?' said I.

'Yes,' says he, 'but the business has gone back and forth, as folk say. First, James of the Glens rode to Edinburgh and got some lawyer (a Stewart, nae doubt – they all hing together like bats in a steeple) and had the proceedings stayed. And then Colin Campbell cam' in again, and had the upper-hand before the Barons of Exchequer. And now they tell me the first of the tenants are to flit tomorrow. It's to begin at Duror under James's very windows, which doesnae seem wise by my humble way of it.'

'Do you think they'll fight?' I asked.

'Well,' says Henderland, 'they're disarmed – or supposed to be – for there's still a good deal of cold iron lying by in quiet places. And then Colin Campbell has the sogers coming. But for all that, if I was his lady wife, I wouldnae be well pleased till I got him home again. They're queer customers, the Appin Stewarts.'

I asked if they were worse than their neighbours.

'No they,' said he. 'And that's the worst part of it. For if Colin Roy can get his business in Appin, he has it all to begin again in the next country, which they

call Mamore, and which is one of the countries of the Camerons. He's King's
Factor upon both, and from both he has to drive out the tenant; and indeed, Mr
Balfour (to be open with ye), it's my belief that if he escapes the one lot, he'll get
his death by the other.'

So we continued talking and walking the great part of the day; until at last,
Mr Henderland, after expressing his delight in my company, and satisfaction at
meeting with a friend of Mr Campbell's ('whom,' says he, 'I will make bold to
call that sweet singer of our convenanted Zion') proposed that I should make a
short stage, and lie the night in his house a little beyond Kingairloch. To say
truth, I was overjoyed; for I had no great desire for John of the Claymore, and
since my double misadventure, first with the guide and next with the gentleman
skipper, I stood in some fear of any Highland stranger. Accordingly we shook
hands upon the bargain, and came in the afternoon to a small house, standing
alone by the shore of the Linnhe Loch. The sun was already gone from desert
mountains of Ardgour upon the hither side, but shone on those of Appin on the
farther; the loch lay as still as a lake, only the gulls were crying round the sides of
it; and the hole place seemed solemn and uncouth.

We had no sooner come to the door of Mr Henderland's dwelling, than to my
great surprise (for I was now used to the politeness of Highlanders) he burst
rudely past me, dashed into the room, caught up a jar and a small horn spoon,
and began ladling snuff into his nose in most excessive quantities. Then he had a
hearty fit of sneezing, and looked round upon me with a rather silly smile.

'It's a vow I took,' says he. 'I took a vow upon me that I wouldnae carry it.
Doubtless it's a great privation; but when I think upon the martyrs, not only to
the Scottish Covenant but to other points of Christianity, I think shame to
mind it.'

As soon as we had eaten (and porridge and whey was the best of the good
man's diet) he took a grave face and said he had a duty to perform by Mr
Campbell, and that was to inquire into my state of mind towards God. I was
inclined to smile at him, since the business of the snuff; but he had not spoken
long before he brought the tears into my eyes. There are two things that men
should never weary of, goodness and humility; we get none too much of them in
this rough world among cold, proud people; but Mr Henderland had their very
speech upon his tongue. And though I was a good deal puffed up with my
adventures and with having come off, as the saying is, with flying colours; yet he
soon had me on my knees beside a simple, poor old man, and both proud and
glad to be there.

Before we went to bed he offered me sixpence to help me on my way, out of a
scanty store he kept in the turf wall of his house; at which excess of goodness I
knew not what to do. But at last he was so earnest with me, that I thought it the
more mannerly part to let him have his way, and so left him poorer than myself.

CHAPTER SEVENTEEN

The Death of the Red Fox

THE NEXT DAY MR HENDERLAND found for me a man who had a boat of his own and was to cross the Linnhe Loch that afternoon into Appin, fishing. Him he prevailed on to take me, for he was one of his flock; and in this way I saved a long day's travel and the price of the two public ferries I must otherwise have passed.

It was near noon before we set out; a dark sky, with clouds, and the sun shining upon little patches. The sea was here very deep and still, and had scarce a wave upon it; so that I must put the water to my lips before I could believe it to be truly salt. The mountains on either side were high, rough and barren, very black and gloomy in the shadow of the clouds, but all silver-laced with little watercourses where the sun shone upon them. It seemed a hard country, this of Appin, for people to care as much about as Alan did.

There was but one thing to mention. A little after we had started, the sun shone upon a little moving clump of scarlet close in along the waterside to the north. It was much of the same red as soldiers' coats; every now and then, too, there came little sparks and lightnings, as though the sun had struck upon bright steel.

I asked my boatman what it should be; and he answered he supposed it was some of the red soldiers coming from Fort William into Appin, against the poor tenantry of the country. Well, it was a sad sight to me; and whether it was because of my thoughts of Alan, or from something prophetic in my bosom, although this was but the second time I had seen King George's troops, I had no good will to them.

At last we came so near the point of land at the entering in of Loch Leven that I beddged to be set on shore. My boatman (who was an honest fellow and mindful of his promise to the catechist) would fain have carried me on to Balachulish; but as this was to take me farther from my secret destination, I insisted, and was set on shore at last under the wood of Lettermore (or Lettervore, for I have heard it both ways) in Alan's country of Appin.

This was a wood of birches, growing on a steep, craggy side of a mountain that overhung the loch. It had many openings aand ferny dells; and a road or bridle track ran north and south through the midst of it, by the edge of which, where was a spring, I sat down to eat some oatbread of Mr Henderland's, and think upon my situation.

Here I was not only troubled by a cloud of stinging midges, but far more by the doubts of my mind. What I ought to do, why I was going to join my self with an outlaw and a would-be murderer like Alan, whether I should not be acting more like a man of sense to tramp back to the south country direct, by my own guidance and at my own charges, and what Mr Campbell or even Mr Henderland would think of me if they should ever learn my folly and presumption; these were the doubts that now began to come in on me stronger than ever.

As I was sitting and thinking, a sound of men and horses came to me thrugh the wood; and presently after, at a turning of the road, I saw four travellers come into view. The way was in this part so rough and narrow that they came single and led their horses by the reins. The first was a great, red-headed gentleman, of an imperious and flushed face, who carried his hat in his hand and fanned himself, for he was in a breathing heat. The second, by his decent black garb and white wig, I correctly took to be a lawyer. The third was a servant, and wore some part of his clothes in tartan, which showed that his master was of a Highland family, and either an outlaw or else in singular good odour with the Government, since the wearing of tartan was against the Act. If I had been better versed in these things, I would have known the tartan to be of the Argyle (or Campbell) colours. This servant had a good-sized portmanteau strapped on his horse, and a net of lemons (to brew punch with) hanging at the saddle-bow; as was often enough the custom with luxurious travellers in that part of the country.

As for the fourth, who brought up the tail, I had seen his like before, and knew him at once to be a sheriff's officer.

I had no sooner seen these people coming than I made up my mind (for no reason that I can tell) to go through with my adventure; and when the first came alongside of me, I rose up from the bracken and asked him the way to Aucharn.

He stopped and looked at me, as I thought, a little oddly; and then, turning to the lawyer, 'Mungo,' said he, 'there's many a man would think this more of a warning than two pyats. Here am I on the road to Duror on the job ye ken; and here is a young lad starts up out of the bracken, and speers if I am on the way to Aucharn.'

'Glenure,' said the other, 'this is an ill subject for jesting.'

These two had now drawn close up and were gazing at me, while the two followers had halted about a stone-cast in the rear.

'And what seek ye in Aucharn?' said Colin Roy Campbell of Glenure; him they called the Red Fox; for he it was that I had stopped.

'The man that lives there,' said I.

'James of the Glens,' says Glenure, musingly; and then to the lawyer: 'Is he gathering his people, think ye?'

'Anyway,' says the lawyer, 'we shall do better to bide where we are, and let the soldiers rally us.'

'If you are concerned for me,' said I, 'I am neither of his people nor yours, but an honest subject of King George, owing no man and fearing no man.'

'Why, very well said,' replies the Factor. 'But if I may make so bold as ask, what does this honest man so far from his country? and why does he come seeking the brother of Ardshiel? I have power here, I must tell you. I am King's Factor upon several of these estates, and have twelve files of soldiers at my back.'

'I have heard a waif word in the country,' said I, a little nettled, 'that you were a hard man to drive.'

He still kept looking at me, as if in doubt.

'Well,' said he, at last, 'your tongue is bold; but I am no unfriend to plainness. If ye had asked me the way to the door of James Stewart on any other day but this, I would have set ye right and bidden ye God speed. But today – eh, Mungo?' And he turned again to look at the lawyer.

But just as he turned there came the shot of a firelock from higher up the hill; and with the very sound of it Glenure fell upon the road.

'Oh, I am dead!' he cried, several times over.

The lawyer had caught him up and held him in his arms, the servant standing over and clasping his hands. And now the wounded man looked from one to another with scared eyes, and there was a change in his voice that went to the heart.

'Take care of yourselves,' says he. 'I am dead.'

He tried to open his clothes as if to look for the wound, but his fingers slipped on the buttons. With that he gave a great sigh, his head rolled on his shoulder, and he passed away.

The lawyer said never a word, but his face was as sharp as a pen and as white as the dead man's; the servant broke out into a great noise of crying and weeping, like a child; and I, on my side, stood staring at them in a kind of horror. The sheriff's officer had run back at the first sound of the shot, to hasten the coming of the soldiers.

At last the lawyer laid down the dead man in his blood upon the road, and got to his own feet with a kind of stagger.

I believe it was his movement that brought me to my senses, for he had no sooner done so than I began to scramble up the hill, crying out, 'The murderer! the murderer!'

So little a time had elapsed, that when I got to the top of the first steepness, and could see some part of the open mountain, the murderer was still moving away at no great distance. He was a big man, in a black coat, with metal buttons, and carried a long fowling-piece.

'Here!' I cried, 'I see him!'

At that the murderer gave a little, quick look over his shoulder, and began to run. The next moment he was lost in a fringe of birches; then he came out again on the upper side, where I could see him climbing like a jackanapes, for that part was again very steep; and then he dipped behind a shoulder, and I saw him no more.

All this time I had been running on my side, and had got a good way up, when a voice cried upon me to stand.

I was at the edge of the upper wood, and so now, when I halted and looked back, I saw all the open part of the hill below me.

The lawyer and the sheriff's officer were standing just above the road, crying and waving on me to come back; and on their left, the red-coats, musket in hand, were beginning to struggle singly out of the lower wood.

'Why should I come back?' I cried. 'Come you on!'

'Ten pounds if ye take that lad!' cried the lawyer. 'He's an accomplice. He was posted here to hold us in talk.'

At that word (which I could hear quite plainly, though it was to the soldiers and not to me that he was crying it) my heart came into my mouth with quite a new kind of terror. Indeed, it is one thing to stand the danger of your life, and quite another to run the peril of both life and character. The thing, besides, had come so suddenly, like thunder out of a clear sky, that I was all amazed and helpless.

The soldiers began to spread, some of them to run, and others to put up their pieces and cover me; and still I stood.

'Jouk* in here among the trees,' said a voice, close by.

Indeed, I scarce knew what I was doing, but I obeyed; and as I did so, I heard the firelocks bang and the balls whistle in the birches.

Just inside the shelter of the trees I found Alan Breck standing, with a fishing-rod. He gave me no salutation; indeed it was no time for civilities; only 'Come!' says he, and set off running along the side of the mountain towards Balachulish; and I, like a sheep, to follow him.

Now we ran among the birches, now stooping behind low humps upon the mountain side; now crawling on all fours among the heather. The pace was deadly; my heart seemed bursting against my ribs; and I had neither time to think nor breath to speak with. Only I remembered seeing with wonder that Alan every now and then would straighten himself to his full height and look back; and every time he did so, there came a great far-away cheering and crying of the soldiers.

Quarter of an hour later, Alan stopped, clapped down flat in the heather, and turned to me.

'Now,' said he, 'it's earnest. Do as I do for your life.'

And at the same speed, but now with infinitely more precaution, we traced back again a cross the mountain side by the same way that we had come, only perhaps higher; till at last Alan threw himself down in the upper wood of Lettermore, where I had found him at the first, and lay, with his face in the bracken, panting like a dog.

My own sides so ached, my head so swam, my tongue so hung out of my mouth with heat and dryness, that I lay beside him like one dead.

CHAPTER EIGHTEEN

I Talk with Alan in the Wood of Lettermore

ALAN WAS THE FIRST TO COME round. He rose, went to the border of the wood, peered out a little, and then returned and sat down.

'Well,' said he, 'yon was a hot burst, David.'

I said nothing, nor so much as lifted my face. I had seen murder done, and a great, ruddy, jovial gentleman struck out of life in a moment; the pity of that sight was still sore within me, and yet that was but a part of my concern. Here was murder done upon the man Alan hated; here was Alan skulking in the trees and running from the troops; and whether his was the hand that fired or only the

*Duck.

head that ordered, signified but little. By my way of it, my only friend in that wild country was blood-guilty in the first degree; I held him in horror; I could not look upon his face; I would have rather lain alone in the rain on my cold isle, than in that warm wood beside a murderer.

'Are ye still wearied?' he asked again.

'No,' said I, still with my face in the bracken; 'no, I am not wearied now, and I can speak. You and me must twine*,' I said. 'I liked you very well, Alan; but your ways are not mine, and they're not God's; and the short and the long of it is just that we must twine.'

'I will hardly twine from ye, David, without some kind of reason for the same,' said Alan, mighty gravely. 'If ye ken anything against my reputation, it's the least thing that ye should do, for old aquaintance sake, to let me hear the name of it; and if ye have only taken a distaste to my society, it will be proper for me to judge if I'm insulted.'

'Alan,' said I, 'what is the sense of this? Ye ken very well yon Campbell-man lies in his blood upon the road.'

He was silent for a little; then says he, 'Did ever ye hear tell of the story of the Man and the Good People?' – by which he meant the fairies.

'No,' said I, 'nor do I want to hear it.'

'With your permission, Mr Balfour, I will tell it you, whatever,' says Alan. 'The man, ye should ken, was cast upon a rock in the sea, where it appears the Good People were in use to come and rest as they went through to Ireland. The name of this rock is called the Skerryvore, and it's not far from where we suffered shipwreck. Well, it seems the man cried so sore, if he could just see his little bairn before he died! that at last the king of the Good People took peety upon him, and sent one flying that brought back the bairn in a poke† and laid it down beside the man where he lay sleeping. So when the man woke, there was a poke beside him and something into the inside of it that moved. Well, it seems he was one of these gentry tht think aye the worst of things; and for greater security, he stuck his dirk throughout that poke before he opened it, and there was his bairn dead. I am thinking to myself, Mr Balfour, that you and the man are very much alike.'

'Do you mean you had no hand in it?' cried I, sitting up.

'I will tell you first of all, Mr Balfour of Shaws, as one friend to another,' said Alan, 'that if I were going to kill a gentleman, it would not be in my own country, to bring trouble on my clan; and I would not go wanting sword and gun, and with a long fishing-rod upon my back.'

'Well,' said I, 'that's true!'

'And now,' continued Alan, taking out his dirk and laying his hand upon it in a certain manner, 'I swear upon the Holy Iron I had neither art nor part, act nor thought in it.'

'I thank God for that!' cried I, and offered him my hand.

He did not appear to see it.

'And here is a great deal of work about a Campbell!' said he. 'They are not so scarce, that I ken!'

'At least,' said I, 'you cannot justly blame me, for you know very well what

*Part.
†Bag.

you told me in the brig. But the temptation and act are different, I thank God
again for that. We may all be tempted; but to take a life in cold blood, Alan!'
And I could say no more for the moment. 'And do you know who did it?' I
added. 'Do you know that man in the black coat?'

'I have nae clear mind about his coat,' said Alan, cunningly; 'but it sticks in
my head that it was blue.'

'Blue or black, did ye know him?' said I.

'I couldnae just conscientiously swear to him,' says Alan. 'He gaed very close
by me, to be sure, but it's a strange thing that I should just have been tying my
brogues.'

'Can you swear that you don't know him, Alan?' I cried, half angered, half in
a mind to laugh at his evasions.

'Not yet,' says he; 'but I've a grand memory for forgetting, David.'

'And yet there was one thing I saw clearly,' said I; 'and that was, that you
exposed yourself and me to draw the soldiers.'

'It's very likely,' said Alan; 'and so would any gentleman. You and me were
innocent of that transaction.'

'The better reason, since we were falsely suspected, that we should get clear,' I
cried. 'The innocent should surely come before the guilty.'

'Why, David,' said he, 'the innocent have aye a chance to get assoiled in
court; but for the lad that shot the bullet, I think the best place for him will be the
heather. Them that havenae dipped their hands in any little difficulty, should be
very mindful of the case of them that have. And that is the good Christianity.
For if it was the other way round about, and the lad whom I couldnae just clearly
see had been in our shoes, and we in his (as might very well have been(I think
we would be a good deal obliged to him oursel's if he would draw the soldiers.'

When it came to this, I gave Alan up. But he looked so innocent all the time,
and was in such clear good faith in what he said, and so ready to sacrifice himself
for what he deemed his duty, that my mouth was closed. Mr Henderland's words
came back to me: that we ourselves might take a lesson by these wild
Highlanders. Well, here I had taken mine. Alan's morals were all tail-first; but
he was ready to give his life for them, such as they were.

'Alan,' said I, 'I'll not say it's the good Christianity as I understand it, but it's
good enough. And here I offer ye my hand for the second time.'

Whereupon he gave me both of his, saying surely I had cast a spell upon him,
for he could forgive me anything. Then he grew very grave, and said we had not
much time to throw away, but must both flee that country; he, because he was a
deserter, and the whole Appin would now be searched like a chamber, and every
one obliged to give a good account of himself; and I, because I was certainly
involved in the murder.

'Oh!' says I, willing to give him a little lesson, 'I have no fear of the justice of
my country.'

'As if this was your country!' said he. 'Or as if ye would be tried here, in a
country of Stewarts!'

'It's all Scotland,' said I.

'Man, I whiles wonder at ye,' said Alan. 'This is a Campbell that's been
killed. Well, it'll be tried in Inverara, the Campbells' head place; with fifteen
Campbells in the jurybox, and the biggest Campbell of all (and that's the Duke)

sitting cocking on the bench. Justice, David? The same justice, by all the world, as Glenure found a while ago at the roadside.'

This frightened me a little, I confess, and would have frighted me more if I had known how nearly exact were Alan's predictions; indeed it was but in one point that he exaggerated, there being but eleven Campbells on the jury; though as the other four were equally in the Duke's dependence, it mattered less than might appear. Still, I cried out that he was unjust to the Duke of Argyle who (for all he was a Whig), was yet a wise and honest nobleman.

'Hoot!' cried Alan, 'the man's a Whig, nae doubt; but I would never deny he was a good chieftain to his clan. And what would the clan think if there a Campbell shot, and naebody hanged, and their own chief the Justice General? But I have often observed,' says Alan, 'that you Low-country bodies have no clear idea of what's right and wrong.'

At this I did at last laugh out aloud; when to my surprise, Alan joined in and laughed as merrily as myself.

'Na, na,' said he, 'we're in the Hielands, David; and when I tell ye to run, take my word and run. Nae doubt it's a hard thing to skulk and starve in the heather, but it's harder yet to lie shackled in a red-coat prison.'

I asked him whither we should flee; and as he told me 'to the Lowlands', I was a little better inclined to go with him; for indeed I was growing impatient to get back and have the upper hand of my uncle. Besides, Alan made so sure there would be no question of justice in the matter, that I began to be afraid he might be right. Of all deaths, I would truly like least to die by the gallows; and the picture of that uncanny instrument came into my head with extraordinary clearness (as I had once seen it engraved at the top of a pedlar's ballad) and took away my appetite for courts of justice.

'I'll chance it, Alan,' said I. 'I'll go with you.'

'But mind you,' said Alan, 'it's no small thing. Ye maun lie bare and hard, and brook many an empty belly. Your bed shall be the moorcock's, and your life shall be like the hunted deer's, and ye shall sleep with your hand upon your weapons. Ay, man, ye shall taigle many a weary foot, or we get clear! I tell ye this at the start, for it's a life that I ken well. But if ye ask what other chance ye have, I answer: Nane. Either take to the heather with me, or else hang.'

'And that's a choice very easily made,' said I; and we shook hands upon it.

'And now let's take another keek at the red-coats,' says Alan, and he led me to the north-eastern fringe of the wood.

Looking out between the trees, we could see a great side of mountain, running down exceeding steep into the waters of the loch. It was a rough part, all hanging stone, and heather, and bit scrags of birchwood; and away at the far end towards Balachulish, little wee red soldiers were dipping up and down over hill and howe, and growing smaller every minute. There was no cheering now, for I think they had other uses for what breath was left them; but they still stuck to the trail, and doubtless thought that we were close in front of them.

Alan watched them, smiling to himself.

'Ay,' said he, 'they'll be gey weary before they've got to the end of that employ! And so you and me, David, can sit down and eat a bite, and breathe a bit longer, and take a dram from my bottle. Then we'll strike for Aucharn, the house of my kinsman, James of the Glens, where I must get my clothes, and my

arms, and money to carry us along; and then David, we'll cry "Forth, Fortune!"
and take a cast among the heather.'

So we sat again and ate and drank, in a place whence we could see the sun
going down into a field of great, wild, and houseless mountains, such as I was
now condemned to wander in with my companion. Partly as we so sat, and
partly afterwards, on the way to Aucharn, each of us narrated his adventures;
and I shall here set down so much of Alan's as seems either curious or needful.

It appears he ran to the bulwarks as soon as the wave was passed; saw me, and
lost me, and saw me again, as I tumbled in the roost; and at last had one glimpse
of me clinging on the yard. It was this that put him in some hope I would maybe
get to land after all, and made him leave those clues and messages which had
brought me (for my sins) to that unlucky country of Appin.

In the meanwhile, those still on the brig had got the skiff launched, and one
or two were on board of her already, when there came a second wave greater
than the first, and heaved the brig out of her place, and would certainly have
sent her to the bottom, had she not struck and caught on some projection of the
reef. When she had struck first, it had been bows-on, so that the stern had
hitherto been lowest. But now her stern was thrown in the air, and the bows
plunged under the sea; and with that, the water began to pour into the fore-
scuttle like the pouring of a mill-dam.

It took the colour out of Alan's face, even to tell what followed. For there
were still two men lying impotent in their bunks; and these, seeing the water
pour in and thinking the ship had foundered, began to cry out aloud, and that
with such harrowing cries that all who were on deck tumbled one after another
into the skiff and fell to their oars. They were not two hundred yards away, when
there came a third great sea; and at that the brig lifted clean over the reef; her
canvas filled for a moment, and she seemed to sail in chase of them, but settling
all the while; and presently she drew down and down, as if a hand was drawing
her; and the sea closed over the *Covenant* of Dysart.

Never a word they spoke as they pulled ashore, being stunned with the horror
of that screaming; but they had scarce set foot upon the beach when Hoseason
woke up, as if out of a muse, and bade them lay hands upon Alan. They hung
back indeed, having little taste for the employment; but Hoseason was like a
fiend; crying that Alan was alone, that he had a great sum about him, that he
had been the means of losing the brig and drowning all their comrades, and that
here was both revenge and wealth upon a single cast. It was seven against one; in
that part of the shore there was no rock that Alan could set his back to; and the
sailors began to spread out and come behind him.

'And then,' said Alan, 'the little man with the red head – I havenae mind of
the name that he is called.'

'Riach,' said I.

'Ay,' said Alan, 'Riach! Well, it was him that took up the clubs for me, asked
the men if they werenae feared of a judgement, and says he, "Dod, I'll put my
back to the Hielandman's mysel'," That's none such an entirely bad little man,
yon little man with the red head,' said Alan. 'He had some spunks of decency.'

'Well,' said I, 'he was kind to me in his way.'

'And so he was to Alan,' said he; 'and by my troth, I found his way a very good
one! But ye see, David, the loss of the ship and the cries of these poor lads sat

very ill upon the man; and I'm thinking that would be the cause of it.'

'Well, I would think so,' says I; 'for he was as keen as any of the rest at the beginning. But how did Hoseason take it?'

'It sticks in my mind that he would take it very ill,' says Alan. 'But the little man cried to me to run, and indeed I thought it was a good observe, and ran. The last that I saw they were all in a knot upon the beach, like folk that were not agreeing very well together.'

'What do you mean by that?' said I.

'Well, the fists were going,' said Alan; 'and I saw one man go down like a pair of breeks. But I thought it would be better no to wait. Ye see there's a strip of Campbells in that end of Mull, which is no good company for a gentleman like me. If it hadnae been for that I would have waited aand looked for ye mysel', let alone giving a hand to the little man.' (It was droll how Alan dwelt on Mr Riach's stature, for, to say the truth, the one was not much smaller than the other). 'So,' says he, continuing, 'I set my best foot forward, and whenever I met in with anyone I cried out there was a wreck ashore. Man, they didnae stop to fash with me! Ye should have seen them linking for the beach! And when they got there they found they had had the pleasure of a run, which is aye good for a Campbell. I'm thinking it was a judgement on the clan that the brig went down in the lump and didnae break. But it was a very unlucky thing for you, that same; for if any wreck had come ashore they would have hunted high and low, and would soon have found ye.'

CHAPTER NINETEEN

The House of Fear

NIGHT FELL AS WE WERE walking, and the clouds, which had brocken up in the afternoon, settled in and thickened, so that it fell, for the season of the year, extremely dark. The way we went was over rough mountain sides; and though Alan pushed on with an assured manner, I could by no means see how he directed himself.

At last, about half past ten of the clock, we came to the top of a brae, and saw lights below us. It seemed a house door stood open and let out a beam of fire and candlelight; and all round the house and steading five or six persons were moving hurriedly about, each carrying a lighted brand.

'James must have tint his wits,' said Alan. 'If this was the soldiers instead of you and me, he would be in a bonny mess. But I dare say he'll have a sentry on the road, and he would ken well enough no soldiers would find the way that we came.'

Hereupon he whistled three times, in a particular manner. It was strange to see how, at the first sound of it, all the moving torches came to a stand, as if the bearers were affrighted; and how, at the third, the bustle began again as before.

Having thus set folks' minds at rest, we came down the brae, and were met at
the yard gate (for this place was like a well-doing farm) by a tall, handsome man
of more than fifty, who cried out to Alan in the Gaelic.

'James Stewart,' said Alan. 'I will ask ye to speak in Scotch, for here is a young
gentleman with me that has nane of the other. This is him,' he added, putting
his arm through mine, 'a young gentleman of the lowlands, and a laird in his
country too, but I am thinking it will be the better for his health if we give his
name the go-by.'

James of the Glens turned to me for a moment, and greeted me courteously
enough; the next he had turned to Alan.

'This has been a dreadful accident,' he cried. 'It will bring trouble on the
country.' And he wrung his hands.

'Hoots!' said Alan, 'ye must take the sour with the sweet, man. Colin Roy is
dead, and be thankful for that!'

'Ay,' said James, 'and by my troth, I wish he was alive again! It's all very fine
to blow and boast beforehand; but now it's done, Alan; and who's to bear the
wyte* of it? The accident fell out in Appin – mind ye that, Alan; it's Appin that
must pay; and I am a man that has a family.'

While this was going on I looked about me at the servants. Some were on
ladders, digging in the thatch of the house or the farm buildings, from which
they brought out guns, swords, and different weapons of war; others carried them
away; and by the sound of mattock blows from somewhere further down the
brae, I suppose they buried them. Though they were all so busy, there prevailed
no kind of order in their efforts; men struggled together for the same gun and ran
into each other with their burning torches; and James was continually turning
about from his talk with Alan, to cry out orders which were apparently never
understood. The faces in the torchlight were like those of people overborne with
hurry and panic; and though none spoke above his breath, their speech sounded
both anxious and angry.

It was about this time that a lassie came out of the house carrying a pack or
bundle; and it has often made me smile to think how Alan's instinct awoke at
the mere sight of it.

'What's that the lassie has?' he asked.

'We're just setting the house in order, Alan,' said James, in his frightened and
somewhat fawning way. 'They'll search Appin with candles, and we must have
all things straight. We're digging the bit guns and swords into the moss, ye see;
and these, I am thinking, will be your ain French clothes.'

'Bury my French clothes!' cried Alan. 'Troth, no!' And he laid hold upon the
packet and retired into the barn to shift himself, recommending me in the
meanwhile to his kinsman.

James carried me accordingly into the kitchen, and sat down with me at table,
smiling and talking at first in a very hospitable manner. But presently the gloom
returned upon him; he sat frowning, and biting his fingers; only remembered me
from time to time; and the gave me but a word or two and a poor smile, and back
into his private terrors. His wife sat by the fire and wept, with her face in her
hands; his eldest son was crouched upon the floor, running over a great mass of
papers and now and again setting one alight and burning it to the bitter end; all
*Blame.

the while a servant with a red face was rummaging about the room, in a blind hurry of fear, and whimpering as she went: and every now and again one of the men would thrust in his face from the yard, and cry for orders.

At last James could keep his seat no longer, and begged my permission to be so unmannerly as walk about. 'I am but poor company altogether, sir,' says he, 'but I can think of nothing but this dreadful accident, and the trouble it is like to bring upon quite innocent persons.'

A little after he observed his son burning a paper, which he thought should have been kept; and at that his excitement burst out so that it was painful to witness. He struck the lad repeatedly.

'Are you gone gyte*?' he cried. 'Do you wish to hang your father?' and forgetful of my presence, carried on at him a long time together in the Gaelic, the young man answering nothing; only the wife, at the name of hanging, throwing her apron over her face and sobbing out louder than before.

This was all wretched for a stranger like myself to hear and see; and I was right glad when Alan returned, looking like himself in his fine French clothes, though (to be sure) they were now grown almost too battered and withered to deserve the name of fine. I was then taken out in my turn by another of the sons, and given that change of clothing of which I had stood so long in need, and a pair of Highland brogues made of deer-leather, rather strange at first, but after a little practice very east to the feet.

By the time I came back Alan must have told his story; for it seemed understood that I was to fly with him, and they were all busy upon our equipment. They gave us each a sword and pistols, though I professed my inability to use the former; and with these, and some ammunition, a bag of oatmeal, an iron pan, and a bottle of right French brandy, we were ready for the heather. Money, indeed, was lacking. I had about two guineas left; Alan's belt having been despatched by another hand, that trusty messenger had no more than seventeen-pence to his whole fortune; and as for James, it appears he had brought himself so low with journeys to Edinburgh and legal expenses on behalf of the tenants, that he could only scrape together three-and-five-pence-halfpenny, the most of it in coppers.

'This'll no do,' said Alan.

'Ye must find a safe bit somewhere near by,' said James, 'and get word sent to me. Ye see, ye'll have to get this business prettily off, Alan. This is no time to be stayed for a guinea or two. They're sure to get wind of ye, sure to seek ye, and by my word of it, sure to lay on ye the wyte of this day's accident. If it falls on you, it falls on me that am your near kinsman and harboured ye while ye were in the country. And if it comes on me——' he paused, and bit his fingers, with a white face. 'It would be a painful thing for our friends if I was to hang,' said he.

'It would be an ill day for Appin,' says Alan.

'It's a day that sticks in my throat,' said James, 'Oh man, man, man – man Alan! you and me have spoken like two fools!' he cried, striking his hand upon the wall so that the house rang again.

'Well, and that's true, too,' said Alan; 'and my friend from the lowlands here' (nodding at me) 'gave me a good word upon that head, if I would only have listened to him.'

*Mad.

'But see here,' said James, returning to his former manner, 'if they lay me by the heels, Alan, it's then that you'll be needing the money. For with all that I have said and that you have said, it will look very black against the two of us; do ye mark that? Well, follow me out, and ye'll see that I'll have to get a paper out against ye mysel'; I'll have to offer a reward for ye; ay, will I! It's a sore thing to do between such near friends; but if I get the dirdum* of this dreadful accident, I'll have to fend for myself, man. Do ye see that?'

He spoke with a pleading earnestness, taking Alan by the breast of the coat.

'Ay,' said Alan, 'I see that.'

'And ye'll have to be clear of the country, Alan – ay, and clear of Scotland – you and your friend from the lowlands, too. For I'll have to paper your friend from the lowlands. Ye see that, Alan – say that ye see that!'

I thought Alan flushed a bit. 'This is unco hard on me that brought him here, James,' said he, throwing his head back. 'It's like making me a traitor!'

'Now, Alan, man!' cried James. 'Look things in the face! He'll be papered anyway; Mungo Campbell'll be sure to paper him; what matters if I paper him too? And then, Alan, I am a man that has a family.' And then, after a little pause on both sides: 'And, Alan, it'll be a jury of Campbells,' said he.

'There's one thing,' said Alan, musingly, 'that naebody kens his name.'

'Nor yet they shallnae, Alan! There's my hand on that,' cried James, for all the world as if he had really known my name and was forgoing some advantage. 'But just the habit he was in, and what he looked like, and his age, and the like? I couldnae well do less.'

'I wonder at your father's son,' cried Alan, sternly. 'Would ye sell the lad with a gift? would ye change his clothes and then betray him?'

'No, no, Alan,' said James, 'No, no: the habit he took off – the habit Mungo saw him in.' But I thought he seemed crestfallen; indeed, he was clutching at every straw, and all the time, I dare say, saw the faces of his hereditary foes on the bench and in the jury-box, and the gallows in the background.

'Well, sir,' says Alan, turning to me, 'what say ye to that? Ye are here under the safeguard of my honour; and it's my part to see nothing done but what shall please you.'

'I have but one word to say,' said I; 'for to all this dispute I am a perfect stranger. But the plain common sense is to set the blame where it belongs, and that is on the man that fired the shot. Paper him, as ye call it, set the hunt on him; and let honest, innocent folk show their faces in safety.'

But at this both Alan and James cried out in horror; bidding me hold my tongue, for that was not to be thought of; and asking me 'What the Camerons would think?' (which confirmed me, it must have been a Cameron from Mamore that did the act) and if I did not see that the lad might be caught? 'Ye havenae surely though of that?' said they, with such innocent earnestness, that my hands dropped at my side and I despaired of argument.

'Very well, then,' said I, 'paper me, if you please, paper Alan, paper King George! We're all three innocent, and that seems to be what's wanted! But at least, sir,' said I to James, recovering from my little fit of annoyance, 'I am Alan's friend, and if I can be helpful to friends of his, I will not stumble at the risk.'

* Blame.

I thought it best to put a fair face on my consent, for I saw Alan troubled; and besides (thinks I to myself) as soon as my back is turned, they will paper me, as they call it, whether I consent or not. But in this I saw I was wrong; for I had no sooner said the words, than Mrs Stewart leaped out of her chair, came running over to us, and wept first upon my neck and then on Alan's, blessing God for our goodness to her family.

'As for you, Alan, it was no more than your bounden duty,' she said. 'But for this lad that has come here and seen us at our worst, and seen the goodman fleeching like a suitor, him that by rights should give his commands like any king – as for you, my lad,' she says, 'my heart is wae not to have your name, but I have your face; and as long as my heart beats under my bosom, I will keep it, and think of it, and bless it.' And with that she kissed me, and burst once more into such sobbing, that I stood abashed.

'Hoot, hoot,' said Alan, looking mighty silly. 'The day comes unco soon in this month of July; and tomorrow there'll be a fine to-do in Appin, a fine riding of dragoons, and crying of "Cruachan!"* and running of red-coats; and it behoves you and me to be the sooner gone.'

Thereupon we said farewell, and set out again, bending somewhat eastward, in a fine mild dark night, and over much the same broken country as before.

CHAPTER TWENTY

The Flight in the Heather: the Rocks

SOMETIMES WE WALKED, sometimes ran; and as it drew on to morning, walked ever the less and ran the more. Though, upon its face, that country appeared to be a desert, yet there were huts and houses of the people, of which we must have passed more than twenty, hidden in quiet places of the hills. When we came to one of these, Alan would leave me in the way, and go himself and rap upon the side of the house and speak a while at the window with some sleeper awakened. This was to pass the news; which, in that country, was so much of a duty that Alan must pause to attend to it even while fleeing for his life; and so well attended to by others, that in more than half of the houses where we called they had heard already of the murder. In the others, as well as I could make out (standing back at a distance and hearing a strange tongue) the news was received with more of consternation than surprise.

For all our hurry, day began to come in while we were still far from any shelter. It found us in a prodigious valley, strewn with rocks and where ran a foaming river. Wild mountains stood around it; there grew there neither grass nor trees; and I have sometimes thought since then, that it may have been the valley called Glencoe, where the massacre was in the time of King William. But for the details of our itinerary, I am all to seek; our way lying now by short cuts,

*The rallying-word of the Campbells.

now by great detours; our pace beging so hurried; our time of journeying usually by night; and the names of such places as I asked and heard, being in the Gaelic tongue and the more easily forgotten.

The first peep of morning, then, showed us this horrible place, and I could see Alan knit his brow.

'This is no fit place for you and me,' he said. 'This is a place they're bound to watch.'

And with that he ran harder than ever down to the water side, in a part where the river was split in two among three rocks. It went through with a horrid thundering that made my belly quake; and there hung over the lynn a little mist of spray. Alan looked neither to the right nor to the left, but jumped clean upon the middle rock and fell there on his hands and knees to check himself, for that rock was small and he might have pitched over on the far side. I had scarce time to measure the distance or to understand the peril, before I had followed him, and he had caught and stopped me.

So there we stood side by side upon a small rock slippery with spray, a far broader leap in front of us, and the river dinning upon all sides. When I saw where I was, there came on me a deadly sickness of fear, and I put my hand over my eyes. Alan took me and shook me; I saw he was speaking, but the roaring of the falls and the trouble of my mind prevented me from hearing; only I saw his face was red with anger, and that he stamped upon the rock. The same looked showed me the water raging by, and the mist hanging in the air; and with that, I covered my eyes again and shuddered.

The next minute Alan had set the brandy bottle to my lips, and forced me to drink about a gill, which sent the blood into my head again. Then, putting his hands to his mouth and his mouth to my ear, he shouted, 'Hang or drown!' and turning his back upon me, leaped over the farther branch of the stream, and landed safe.

I was now alone upon the rock, which gave me the more room; the brandy was singing in my ears; I had this good example fresh before me, and just wit enough to see that if I did not leap at once, I should never leap at all. I bent low on my knees and flung myself forth, with that kind of anger of despair that has sometimes stood me in stead of courage. Sure enough, it was but my hands that reached the full length; these slipped, caught again, slipped again; and I was sliddering back into the lynn, when Alan seized me, first by the hair, then by the collar, and with a great strain dragged me into safety.

Never a word he said, but set off running again for his life, and I must stagger to my feet and run after him. I had been weary before, but now I was sick and bruised, and partly drunken, with the brandy; I kept stumbling as I ran, I had a stitch that came near to overmaster me; and when at last Alan paused under a great rock that stood there among a number of others, it was none too soon for David Balfour.

A great rock, I have said; but by rights it was two rocks leaning together at the top, both some twenty feet high, and at first sight inaccessible. Even Alan (though you may say he had as good as four hands) failed twice in an attempt to climb them; and it was only at the third trial, and then by standing on my shoulders and leaping up with such force as I thought must have broken my collar-bone, that he secured a lodgement. Once there, he let down his leathern girdle; and with the aid of that and a pair of shallow footholds in the rocks, I scrambled up beside him.

Then I saw why he had come there; for the two rocks, being both somewhat hollow on the top and sloping one to the other, made a kind of dish or saucer, where as many as three or four men might have lain hidden.

All this while Alan had not said a word, and had run and climbed with such a savage, silent frenzy of hurry, that I knew he was in mortal fear of some miscarriage. Even now we were on the rock he said nothing, nor so much as relaxed the frowning look upon his face; but clapped flat down, and keeping only one eye above the edge of our place of shelter, scouted all round the compass. The dawn had come quite clear; we could see the stony sides of the valley, and its bottom, which was bestrewed with rocks, and the river, which went from one side to another, and made white falls; but nowhere the smoke of a house, nor any living creature but some eagles screaming round a cliff.

Then at last Alan smiled.

'Ay,' said he, 'now we have a chance'; and then looking at me with some amusement, 'Ye're no very gleg* at the jumping,' said he.

At this I suppose I coloured with mortification, for he added at once, 'Hoots! small blame to ye! To be feared of a thing and yet to do it, is what makes the prettiest kind of a man. And then there was water there, and water's a thing that dauntons even me. No, no,' said Alan, 'it's no you that's to blame, it's me.'

I asked him why.

'Why,' said he, 'I have proved myself a gomeral this night. For first of all I take a wrong road, and that in my own country of Appin; so that the day has caught us where we should never have been; and thanks to that, we lie here in some danger and mair discomfort. And next (which is the worst of the two, for a man that has been so much among the heather as myself) I have come wanting a water-bottle, and here we lie for a long summer's day with naething but neat spirit. Ye may think that a small matter; but before it comes night, David, ye'll give me news of it.'

I was anxious to redeem my character, and offered, if he would pour out the brandy, to run down and fill the bottle at the river.

'I wouldnae waste the good spirit either,' says he. 'It's been a good friend to you this night; or in my poor opinion, ye would still be cocking on yon stone. And what's mair,' says he, 'ye may have observed (you that's a man of so much penetration) that Alan Breck Stewart was perhaps walking quicker than his ordinar'.'

'You!' I cried, 'you were running fit to burst.'

'Was I so?' said he. 'Well, then, ye may depend upon it, there was nae time to be lost. And now here is enough said; gang you to your sleep, lad, and I'll watch.'

Accordingly, I lay down to sleep; a little peaty earth had drifted in between the top of the two rocks, and some bracken grew there, to be a bed to me; the last thing I heard was still the crying of the eagles.

I dare say it would be nine in the morning when I was roughly awakened, and found Alan's hand pressed upon my mouth.

'Wheesht!' he whispered. 'Ye were snoring.'

*Brisk.

'Well,' said I, surprised at his anxious and dark face, 'and why not?'

He peered over the edge of the rock, and signed to me to do the like.

It was now high day, cloudless, and very hot. The valley was as clear as in a picture. About half a mile up the water was a camp of red-coats; a big fire blazed in their midst, at which some were cooking; and near by, on the top of a rock about as high as ours, there stood a sentry, with the sun sparkling on his arms. All the way down along the riverside were posted other sentries; here near together, there widelier scattered; some planted like the first, on places of command, some on the ground level and marching and counter-marching, so as to meet half way. Higher up the glen, where the ground was more open, the chain of posts was continued by horse-soldiers, whom we could see in the distance riding to and fro. Lower down, the infantry continued; but as the stream was suddenly swelled by the confluence of a considerable burn, they were more widely set, and only watched the fords and stepping-stones.

I took but one look at them, and ducked again into my place. It was strange indeed to see this valley, which had lain so solitary in the hour of dawn, bristling with arms and dotted with the red coats and breeches.

'Ye see,' said Alan, 'this was what I was afraid of, Davie: that they would watch the burn-side. They began to come in about two hours ago, and, man! but ye're a grand hand at the sleeping! We're in a narrow place. If they get up the sides of the hill, they could easy spy us with a glass; but if they'll only keep in the foot of the valley, we'll do yet. The posts are thinner down the water; and, come night, we'll try our hand at getting by them.'

'And what are we to do till night?' I asked.

'Lie here,' says he, 'and birstle.'

That one good Scotch word, 'birstle,' was indeed the most of the story of the day that we had now to pass. You are to remember that we lay on the bare top of a rock, like scones upon a girdle; the sun beat upon us cruelly; the rock grew so heated, a man could scarce endure the touch of it; and the little patch of earth and fern, which kept cooler, was only large enough for one at a time. We took turn about to lie on the naked rock, which was indeed like the position of that saint that was martyred on a gridiron; and it ran in my mind how strange it was, that in the same climate and at only a few days' distance, I should have suffered so cruelly, first from cold upon my island, and now from heat upon this rock.

All the while we had no water, only a raw brandy for a drink, which was worse than nothing; but we kept the bottle as cool as we could, burying it in the earth, and got some relief by bathing our breasts and temples.

The soldiers kept stirring all day in the bottom of the valley, now changing guard, now in patrolling parties hunting among the rocks. These lay round in so great a number, that to look for men among them was like looking for a needle in a bottle of hay; and being so hopeless a task, it was gone about with the less care. Yet we could see the soldiers pike their bayonets among the heather, which sent a cold thrill into my vitals; and they would sometimes hang about our rock, so that we scarce dared to breathe.

It was in this way that I first heard the right English speech; one fellow as he went by actually clapping his hand upon the sunny face of the rock on which we lay, and plucking it off again with an oath.

'I tell you it's 'ot,' says he; and I was amazed at the clipping tones and the odd sing-song in which he spoke, and no less at that strange trick of dropping out the letter h. To be sure, I had heard Ransome; but he had taken his ways from all sorts of people, and spoke so imperfectly at the best, that I set down the most of it to childishness. My surprise was all the greater to hear that manner of speaking in the mouth of a grown man; and indeed I have never grown used to it; nor yet altogether with the English grammar, as perhaps a very critical eye might here and there spy out even in these memoirs.

The tediousness and pain of these hours upon the rock grew only the greater as the day went on; the rock getting still the hotter and the sun fiercer. There were giddiness, and sickness, and sharp pangs like rheumatism, to be supported. I minded then, and have often minded since, on the lines in our Scotch psalm:

> The moon by night thee shall not smite,
> Nor yet the sun by day;

and indeed it was only by God's blessing that we were neither of us sun-smitten.

At last, about two, it was beyond men's bearing, and there was now temptation to resist, as well as pain to thole. For the sun being now got a little into the west, there came a patch of shade on the east side of our rock, which was the side sheltered from the soldiers.

'As well one death as another,' said Alan, and slipped over the edge and dropped on the ground on the shadowy side.

I followed him at once, and instantly fell all my length, so weak was I and so giddy with that long exposure. Here, then, we lay for an hour or two, aching from head to foot, as weak as water, and lying quite naked to the eye of any soldier who should have strolled that way. None came, however, all passing by on the other side; so that our rock continued to be our shield even in this new position.

Presently we began again to get a little strength; and as the soldiers were now lying closer along the riverside, Alan proposed that we should try a start. I was by this time afraid of but one thing in the world; and that was to be set back upon the rock; anything else was welcome to me; so we got ourselves at once in marching order, and began to slip from rock to rock one after the other, now crawling flat on our bellies in the shade, now making a run for it, heart in mouth.

The soldiers, having searched this side of the valley after a fashion, and being perhaps somewhat sleepy with the sultriness of the afternoon, had now laid by much of their vigilance, and stood dozing at their posts or only kept a lookout along the banks of the river; so that in this way, keeping down the valley and at the same time towards the mountains we drew steadily away from their neighbourhood. But the business was the most wearing I had ever taken part in. A man had need of a hundred eyes in every part of him, to keep concealed in that uneven country and within cry of so many and scattered sentries. When we must pass an open place, quickness was not all, but a swift judgement not only of the lie of the whole country, but of the solidity of every stone on which we must set foot; for the afternoon was now fallen so breathless that the rolling of a pebble sounded abroad like a pistol shot, and would start the echo calling among the hills and cliffs.

By sundown we had made some distance, even by our slow rate of progress, though to be sure the sentry on the rock was still plainly in our view. But now we came on something that put all fears out of season; and that was a deep rushing burn, that tore down, in that part, to join the glen river. At the sight of this we cast ourselves on the ground and plunged head and shoulders in the water; and I cannot tell which was the more pleasant, the great shock as the cool stream went over us, or the greed with which we drank of it.

We lay there (for the banks hid us), drank again and again, bathed our chests, let our wrists trail in the running water till they ached with the chill; and at last, being wonderfully renewed, we got out the meal-bag and made drammach in the iron pan. This, though it is but cold water mingled with oatmeal, yet makes a good enough dish for a hungry man; and where there are no means of making fire, or (as in our case) good reason for not making one, it is the chief stand-by of those who have taken to the heather.

As soon as the shadow of the night had fallen, we set forth again, at first with the same caution, but presently with more boldness, standing our full height and stepping out at a good pace of walking. The way was very intricate, lying up the steep sides of mountains and along the brows of cliffs; clouds had come in with the sunset, and the night was dark and cool; so that I walked without much fatigue, but in continual fear of falling and rolling down the mountains, and with no guess at our direction.

The moon rose at last and found us still on the road; it was in its last quarter and was long beset with clouds; but after a while shone out, and showed me many dark heads of mountains, and was reflected far underneath us on the narrow arm of a sea-loch.

At this sight we both paused: I struck with wonder to find myself so high and walking (as it seemed to me, upon clouds: Alan to make sure of his direction.

Seemingly he was well pleased, and he must certainly have judged us out of ear-shot of all our enemies; for throughout the rest of our night-march he beguiled the way with whistling of many tunes, warlike, merry, plaintive; reel tunes that made the foot go faster; tunes of my own south country that made me fain to be home from my adventures; and all these, on the great, dark, desert mountains, making company upon the way.

CHAPTER TWENTY-ONE

The Flight in the Heather: the Heugh of Corrynakiegh

EARLY AS DAY COMES IN THE beginning of July, it was still dark when we reached our destination, a cleft in the head of a great mountain, with a water running through the midst, and upon the one hand a shallow cave in a rock. Birches grew there in a thin, pretty wood, which a little farther on was changed into a wood of pines. The burn was full of trout; the wood of cushat-doves; on the open side of the mountain beyond, whaups would be always whistling, and cuckoos were plentiful. From the mouth of the cleft we looked down upon a part of Mamore, and on the sea-loch that divides that country from Appin; and this from so great a height, as made it my continual wonder and pleasure to sit and behold them.

The name of the cleft was the Heugh of Corrynakiegh; and although from its height and being so near upon the sea, it was often beset with clouds, yet it was on the whole a pleasant place, and the five days we lived in it went happily.

We slept in the cave, making our bed of heather bushes which we cut for that purpose, and covering ourselves with Alan's great-coat. There was a low concealed place, in a turning of the glen, where we were so bold as to make fire; so that we could warm ourselves when the clouds set in, and cook hot porridge, and grill the little trouts that we caught with our hands under the stones and overhanging banks of the burn. This was indeed our chief pleasure and business; and not only to save our meal against worse times, but with a rivalry that much amused us, we spent a great part of our days at the water side, stripped to the waist and groping about or (as they say) guddling for these fish. The largest we got might have been a quarter of a pound; but they were of good flesh and flavour, and when broiled upon the coals, lacked only a little salt to be delicious.

In any by-time Alan must teach me to use my sword, for my ignorance had much distressed him; and I think besides, as I had sometimes the upper hand of him in the fishing, he was not sorry to turn to an exercise where he had so much the upper hand of me. He made it somewhat more of a pain than need have been, for he stormed at me all through the lessons in a very violent manner of scolding, and would push me so close that I made sure he must run me through the body. I was often tempted to turn tail, but held my ground for all that, and got some profit of my lessons; if it was but to stand on guard with an assured countenance, which is often all that is required. So, though I could never in the least please my master, I was not altogether displeased with myself.

In the meantime, you are not to suppose that we neglected our chief business, which was to get away.

'It will be many a long day,' Alan said to me on our first morning, 'before the red-coats think upon seeking Corrynakiegh; so now we must get word sent to James, and he must find the siller for us.'

'And how shall we sent that word?' says I. 'We are here in a desert place, which yet we dare not leave; and unless ye get the fowls of the air to be your messengers, I see not what we shall be able to do.'

'Ay?' said Alan. 'Ye're a man of small contrivance, David.'

Thereupon he fell in a muse, looking in the embers of the fire; and presently, getting a piece of wood, he fashioned it in a cross, the four ends of which he blackened on the coals. Then he looked at me a little shyly.

'Could ye lend me my button?' says he. 'It seems a strange thing to ask a gift again, but I own I am laith to cut another.'

I gave him the button; whereupon he strung it on a strip of his great coat which he had used to bind the cross; and tying in a little sprig of birch and another of fir, he looked upon his work with satisfaction.

'Now,' said he, 'there is a little clachan' (what is called a hamlet in the English) 'not very far from Corrynakiegh, and it has the name of Koalisnacoan.

There, there are living many friends of mine whom I could trust with my life, and some that I am not just so sure of. Ye see, David, there will be money set upon our heads; James himsel' is to set money on them; and as for the Campbells, they would never spare siller where there was a Stewart to be hurt. If it was otherwise, I would go down to Koalisnacoan whatever, and trust my life into these people's hands as lightly as I would trust another with my glove.'

'But being so?' said I.

'Being so,' said he, 'I would as lief they didnae see me. There's bad folk everywhere, and what's far worse, weak ones. So when it comes dark again, I will steal down into that clachan, and set this that I have been making in the window of a good friend of mine, John Breck Maccoll, a bouman* of Appin's.'

'With all my heart,' says I; 'and if he finds it, what is he to think?'

'Well,' says Alan, 'I wish he was a man of more penetration, for by my troth I am afraid he will make little enough of it! But this is what I have in my mind. This cross is something in the nature of the crosstarrie, or fiery cross, which is the signal of gathering in our clans; yet he will know well enough the clan is not to rise, for there it is standing in his window, and no word with it. So he will say to himsel', *The clan is not to rise, but there is something.* Then he will see my button, and that was Duncan Stewart's. And then he will say to himsel', *The son of Duncan is in the heather, and has need of me.*'

'Well,' said I, 'it may be. But even supposing so, there is a good deal of heather between here and the Forth.'

'And that is a very true word,' says Alan. 'But then John Breck will see the sprig of birch and the sprig of pine; and he will say to himsel' (if he is a man of any penetration at all, which I misdoubt) *Alan will be lying in a wood which is both of pines and birches.* Then he will think to himsel', *That is not so very rife hereabout*; and then he will come and give us a look up in Corrynakiegh. And if he does not, David, the devil may fly away with him, for what I care; for he will no be worth the salt to his porridge.'

'Eh, man,' said I, drolling with him a little, 'you're very ingenious! But would it not be simpler for you to write him a few words in black-and-white?'

'And that is an excellent observe, Mr Balfour of Shaws,' says Alan, drolling with me; 'and it would certainly be much simpler for me to write to him, but it would be a sore job for John Breck to read it. He would have to go to the school for two–three years; and its possible we might be wearied waiting for him.'

So that night Alan carried down his fiery cross and set it in the bouman's window. He was troubled when he came back; for the dogs had barked and the folk run out from their houses; and he thought he had heard a clatter of arms and seen a red-coat come to one of the doors. On all accounts we lay the next day in the borders of the wood and kept a close look-out; so that if it was John Breck that came, we might be ready to guide him, and if it was the red-coats, we should have time to get away.

About noon a man was to be spied, straggling up the open side of the mountain in the sun, and looking round him as he came, from under his hand. No sooner had Alan seen him than he whistled; the man turned and came a little towards us; then Alan would give another 'peep!' and the man would come

*A bouman is a tenant who takes stock from the landlord and shares with him the increase.

still nearer; and so by the sound of whistling, he was guided to the spot where we lay.

He was a ragged, wild, bearded man, about forty, grossly disfigured with the smallpox, and looked both dull and savage. Although his English was very bad and broken, yet Alan (according to his very handsome use, whenever I was by) would suffer him to speak no Gaelic. Perhaps the strange language made him appear more backward than he really was; but I thought he had little good-will to serve us, and what he had was the child of terror.

Alan would have had him carry a message to James; but the bouman would hear of no message. 'She was forget it,' he said in his screaming voice; and would either have a letter or wash his hands of us.

I thought Alan would be gravelled at that, for we lacked the means of writing in that desert, But he was a man of more resources than I knew; searched the wood until he found the quill of a cushat-dove, which he shaped into a pen;made himself a kind of ink with gunpowder from his horn and water from the running stream; and tearing a corner from his French Military commission (which he carried in his pocket, like a talisman to keep him from the gallows) he sat down and wrote as follows:

DEAR KINSMAN, – Please send the money by the bearer to the place he kens of. – Your affectionate cousin,

A.S.

This he entrusted to the bouman, who promised to make what manner of speed he best could, and carried it off with him down the hill.

He was three full days gone, but about five in the evening of the third, we heard a whistling in the wood, which Alan answered; and presently the bouman came up the waterside, looking for us, right and left. He seemed less sulky than before, and indeed he was no doubt well pleased to have got to the end of such a dangerous commission.

He gave us the news of the country; that it was alive with red-coats; that arms were being found, and poor folk brought in trouble daily; and that James and some of his servants were already clapped in prison at Fort William, under strong suspicion of complicity. It seemed, it was noised on all sides that Alan Breck had fired the shot; and there was a bill issued for both him and me, with one hundred pounds reward.

This was all as bad as could be; and the little note the bouman had carried us from Mrs Stewart was of a miserable sadness. In it she besought Alan not to let himself be captured, assuring him, if he fell in the hands of the troops, both he and James were no better than dead men. The money she had sent was all that she could beg or borrow, and she prayed heaven we could be doing with it. Lastly, she said she enclosed us one of the bills in which we were described.

This we looked upon with great curiosity and not a little fear, partly as a man may look in a mirror, partly as he might look into the barrel of an enemy's gun to judge if it be truly aimed. Alan was advertised as 'a small, pock-marked, active man of thirty-five or thereby, dressed in a feathered hat, a French side-coat of blue with silver buttons and lace a great deal tarnished, a red waistcoat and breeches of black shag'; and I as 'a tall strong lad of about eighteen, wearing an old blue coat, very ragged, an old Highland bonnet, a long homespun waistcoat, blue breeches; his legs bare; low-country shoes, wanting the toes; speaks like a low-lander, and has no beard.'

Alan was well enough pleased to see his finery so fully remembered and set down; only when he came to the word tarnish, he looked upon his lace like one a little mortified. As for myself, I thought I cut a miserable figure in the bill; and yet was well enough pleased too, for since I had changed these rags, the description had ceased to be a danger and become a source of safety.

'Alan,' said I, 'you should change your clothes.'

'Na, troth!' said Alan, 'I have nae others. A fine sight I would be, if I went back to France in a bonnet!'

This put a second reflection in my mind: that if I were to separate from Alan and his tell-tale clothes I should be safe against arrest, and might go openly about my business. Nor was this all; for suppose I was arrested when I was alone, there was little against me; but suppose I was taken in company with the reputed murderer, my case would begin to be grave. For generosity's sake, I dare not speak my mind upon this head; but I thought of it none the less.

I thought of it all the more, too, when the bouman brought out a green purse with four guineas in gold, and the best part of another in small change. True, it was more than I had. But then Alan, with less than five guineas, had to get as far as France; I, with my less than two, not beyond Queensferry; so that, taking things in their proportion, Alan's society was not only a peril to my life but a burden on my purse.

But there was no thought of the sort in the honest head of my companion. He believed he was serving, helping, and protecting me. And what could I do but hold my peace, and chafe, and take my chance of it?

'It's little enough,' said Alan, putting the purse in his pocket, 'but it'll do my business. And now John Breck, if ye will hand me over my button, this gentleman and me will be for taking the road.'

But the bouman, after feeling about in a hairy purse that hung in front of him in the Highland manner (though he wore otherwise the lowland habit, with sea-trousers) began to roll his eyes strangely, and at last said, 'Her nainsel will loss it', meaning he thought he had lost it.

'What!' cried Alan, 'you will lose my button, that was my father's before me? Now, I will tell you what is in my mind, John Breck: it is in my mind this is the worst day's work that ever ye did since ye were born.'

And as Alan spoke, he set his hands on his knees and looked at the bouman with a smiling mouth, and that dancing light in his eyes that meant mischief to his enemies.

Perhaps the bouman was honest enough; perhaps he had meant to cheat and then, finding himself alone with two of us in a desert place, cast back to honesty as being safer; at least, and all at once, he seemed to find that button and handed it to Alan.

'Well, and it is a good thing for the honour of the Maccolls,' said Alan, and then to me, 'Here is my button back again, and I thank you for parting with it, which is of a piece with all your friendships to me.' Then he took the warmest parting of the bouman. 'For,' says he, 'ye have done very well by me, and set your neck at a venture, and I will always give you the name of a good man.'

Lastly, the bouman took himself off by one way; and Alan and I (getting our chattels together) struck into another to resume our flight.

CHAPTER TWENTY-TWO

The Flight in the Heather: The Moor

MORE THAN ELEVEN HOURS OF incessant, hard travelling brought us early in the morning to the end of a range of mountains. In front of us there lay a piece of low, broken, desert land, which we must now cross. The sun was not long up, and shone straight in our eyes; a little, thin mist went up from the face of the moorland like a smoke; so that (as Alan said) there might have been twenty squadron of dragoons there and we none the wiser.

We sat down, therefore, in a howe of the hillside till the mist should have risen, and made ourselves a dish of drammach, and held a council of war.

'David,' said Alan, 'this is the kettle bit. Shall we lie here till it comes night, or shall we risk it and stave on ahead?'

'Well,' said I, 'I am tired indeed, but I could walk as far again, if that was all.'

'Ay, but it isnae,' said Alan, 'nor yet the half. This is how we stand: Appin's fair death to us. To the south it's all Campbells, and no to be thought of. To the north; well, there's no muckle to be gained by going north; neither for you, that wants to get to Queensferry, nor yet for me, that wants to get to France. Well, then, we'll can strike east.'

'East be it!' says I, quite cheerily; but I was thinking, in to myself: 'Oh, man, if you would only take one point of the compass and let me take any other, it would be the best for both of us.'

'Well, then, east, ye see, we have the muirs,' said Alan. 'Once there, David, it's mere pitch-and-toss. Out on yon bald, naked, flat place, where can a body turn to? Let the red-coats come over a hill, they can spy you miles away; and the sorrow's in their horses' heels, they would soon ride you down. It's no good place, David; and I'm free to say, it's worse by daylight than by dark.'

'Alan,' said I, 'hear my way of it. Appin's death for us; we have none too much money, nor yet meal; the longer they seek, the nearer they may guess where we are; it's all a risk; and I give my word to go ahead until we drop.'

Alan was delighted. 'There are whiles,' said he, 'when ye are altogether too canny and Whiggish to be company for a gentleman like me; but there come other whiles when ye show yoursel' a mettle spark; and it's then, David, that I love ye like a brother.'

The mist rose and died away, and showed us that country lying as waste as the sea; only the moorfowl and the peewees crying upon it, and far over to the east, a herd of deer, moving like dots. Much of it was red with heather; much of the rest broken up with bogs and hags and peaty pools; some had been burnt black in a heath fire; and in another place there was quite a forest of dead firs, standing like skeletons. A wearier looking desert man never saw; but at least it was clear of troops, which was our point.

We went down accordingly into the waste, and began to make our toilsome and devious travel towards the eastern verge. There were the tops of mountains all round (you are to remember) from whence we might be spied at any moment; so it behoved us to keep in the hollow parts of the moor, and when these turned aside from our direction, to move upon its naked face with infinite care. Sometimes, for half an hour together, we must crawl from one heather bush to another, as hunters do when they are hard upon the deer. It was a clear day again, with a blazing sun; the water in the brandy bottle was soon gone; and altogether, if I had guessed what it would be to crawl half the time upon my belly and to walk much of the rest stooping nearly to the knees, I should certainly have held back from such a killing enterprise.

Toiling and resting and toiling again, we wore away the morning; and about noon lay down in a thick bush of heather to sleep. Alan took the first watch; and it seemed to me I had scarce closed my eyes before I was shaken up to take the second. We had no clock to go by; and Alan stuck a sprig of heath in the ground to serve instead; so that as soon as the shadow of the bush should fall so far to the east, I might know to rouse him. But I was by this time so weary that I could have slept twelve hours at a stretch; I had the taste of sleep in my throat; my joints slept even when my mind was waking; the hot smell of the heather, and the drone of the wild bees, were like possets to me; and every now and again I would give a jump and find I had been dozing.

The last time I woke I seemed to come back from farther away, and thought the sun had taken a great start in the heavens. I looked at the sprig of heather, and at that I could have cried aloud; for I saw I had betrayed my trust. My head was nearly turned with fear and shame; and at what I saw, when I looked out around me on the moor, my heart was like dying in my body. For sure enough a body of horse-soldiers had come down during my sleep, and were drawing near to us from the south-east, spread out in shape of a fan and riding their horses to and fro in the deep parts of the heather.

When I waked Alan, he glanced first at the soldiers, then at the mark and the position of the sun, and knitted his brows with a sudden, quick look, both ugly and anxious, which was all the reproach I had of him.

'What are we to do now?' I asked.

'We'll have to play at being hares,' said he. 'Do ye see yon mountain?' pointing to one on the north-eastern sky.

'Ay,' said I.

'Well, then,' says he, 'let us strike for that. Its name is Ben Alder; it is a wild, desert mountain full of hills and hollows, and if we can win to it before the morn, we may do yet.'

'But, Alan,' cried I, 'that will take us across the very coming of the soldiers!'

'I ken that fine,' said he; 'but if we are driven back on Appin, we are two dead men. So now, David man, be brisk!'

With that he began to run forward on his hands and knees with an incredible quickness, as though it were his natural way of going. All the time, too, he kept winding in and out in the lower parts of the moorland where we were the best concealed. Some of these had been burned or at least scathed with fire; and there rose in our faces (which were close to the ground) a blinding, choking dust as fine as smoke. The water was long out; and this posture of running on the hands and knees brings an overmastering weakness and weariness, so that the joints ache and the wrists faint under your weight.

Now and then, indeed, where was a big bush of heather we lay a while, and panted, and putting aside the leaves, looked back at the dragoons. They had not spied us, for they held straight on; a half-troop, I think, covering about two miles of ground, and beating it mighty thoroughly as they went. I had awakened just in time; a little later, and we must have fled in front of them, instead of escaping on one side. Even as it was, the least misfortune might betray us; and now and again, when a grouse rose out of the heather with a clap of wings, we lay as still as the dead and were afraid to breathe.

The aching and faintness of my body, the labouring of my heart, the soreness of my hands, and the smarting of my throat and eyes in the continual smoke of dust and ashes, had soon grown to be so unbearable that I would gladly have given up. Nothing but the fear of Alan lent me enough of a false kind of courage to continue. As for himself (and you are to bear in mind that he was cumbered with a great coat), he had first turned crimson, but as time went on, the redness began to be mingled with patches of white; his breath cried and whistled as it came; and his voice, when he whispered his observations in my ear during our halts, sounded like nothing human. Yet he seemed in no way dashed in spirits, nor did he at all abate in his activity; so that I was driven to marvel at the man's endurance.

At length, in the first gloaming of the night, we heard a trumpet sound, and looking back from among the heather, saw the troops beginning to collect. A little after, they had built a fire and camped for the night, about the middle of the waste.

At this I begged and besought that we might lie down and sleep.

'There shall be no sleep the night!' said Alan. 'From now on, these weary dragoons of yours will keep the crown of the muirland, and none will get out of Appin but winged fowls. We got through in the nick of time, and shall we jeopard what we've gained? Na, na, when the day comes, it shall find you and me in a fast place on Ben Alder.'

'Alan,' I said, 'it's not the want of will: it's the strength that I want, if I could, I would; but as sure as I'm alive I cannot.'

'Very well, then,' said Alan. 'I'll carry ye.'

I looked to see if he were jesting; but no, the little man was in dead earnest; and the sight of so much resolution shamed me.

'Lead away!' said I, 'I'll follow.'

He gave me one look, as much as to say 'Well done, David!' and off he set again at his top speed.

It grew cooler and even a little darker (but not much) with the coming of the night. The sky was cloudless; it was still early in July, and pretty far north; in the darkest part of that night, you would have needed pretty good eyes to read, but for all that, I have often seen it darker in a winter midday. Heavy dew fell and drenched the moor like rain; and this refreshed me for a while. When we stopped to breathe, and I had time to see all about me, the clearness and sweetness of the night, the shapes of the hills like things asleep, and the fire dwindling away behind us, like a bright spot in the midst of the moor, anger would come upon me in a clap that I must still drag myself in agony and eat the dust like a worm.

By what I have read in books, I think few that have held a pen were ever really wearied, or they would write of it more strongly. I had no care of my life, neither past nor future, and I scarce remembered there was such a lad as David Balfour. I did not think of myself, but just of each fresh step which I was sure would be my last, with despair – and of Alan, who was the cause of it, with hatred. Alan was in the right trade as a soldier; this is the officer's part ot make men continue to do things, they know not wherefore, and when, if the choice was offered, they would lie down where they were and be killed. And I dare say I would have made a good enough private; for in these last hours, it never occurred to me that I had any choice, but just to obey as long as I was able, and die obeying.

Day began to come in, after years, I thought; and by that time we were past the greatest danger, and could walk upon our feet like men, instead of crawling like brutes. But, dear heart have mercy! what a pair we must have made, going double like old grandfathers, stumbling like babes, and as white as dead folk. Never a word passed between us; each set his mouth and kept his eyes in front of him, and lifted up his foot and set it down again, like people lifting weights at a country play*; all the while, with the moorfowl crying 'peep!' in the heather, and the light comijg slowly clearer in the east.

I say Alan did as I did. Not that ever I looked at him, for I had enough to keep my feet; but because it is plain he must have been as stupid with weariness as myself, and looked as little where we were going, or we should not have walked into an ambush like blind men.

It fell in this way. We were going down a heathery brae, Alan leading and I following a pace or two behind, like a fiddler and his wife; when upon a sudden the heather gave a rustle, three or four ragged men leaped out, and the next moment we were lying on our backs, each with a dirk at his throat.

I don't think I cared; the pain of this rough handling was quite swallowed up by the pains of which I was already full; and I was too glad to have stopped walking to mind about a dirk. I lay looking up in the face of the man that held me; and I mind his face was black with the sun and his eyes very light, but I was not afraid of him. I heard Alan and another whispering in the Gaelic; and what they said was all one to me.

Then the dirks were put up, our weapons were taken away, and we were set face to face, sitting in the heather.

'They are Cluny's men,' said Alan. 'We couldnae have fallen better. We're just to bide here with these, which are his out-sentries, till they can get word to the chief of my arrival.'

Now Cluny Macpherson, the chief of the clan Vourich, had been one of the leaders of the great rebellion six years before; there was a price on his life; and I had supposed him long ago in France, with the rest of the heads of that desperate party. Even tired as I was, the surprise of what I heard half wakened me.

'What?' I cried, 'Is Cluny still here?'

'Ay is he so!' said Alan, 'Still in his own country and kept by his own clan. King George can do no more.'

I think I would have asked further, but Alan gave me the put-off. 'I am rather
*Village fair.

wearied,' he said, 'and I would like fine to get a sleep.' And without more words, he rolled on his face in a deep heather bush, and seemed to sleep at once.

There was no such thing possible for me. You have heard grasshoppers whirring in the grass in the summer time? Well, I had no sooner closed my eyes, than my body and above all my head, belly, and wrists, seemed to be filled with whirring grasshoppers; and I must open my eyes again at once, and tumble and toss, and sit up and lie down; and look at the sky which dazzled me, or at Cluny's wild and dirty sentries, peering out over the top of the brae and chattering to each other in the Gaelic.

That was all the rest I had, until the messenger returned; when, as it appeared that Cluny would be glad to receive us, we must get once more upon our feet and set forward. Alan was in excellent good spirits, much refreshed by his sleep, very hungry, and looking pleasantly forward to a dram and a dish of hot collops, of which, it seems, the messenger had brought him word. For my part, it made me sick to hear of eating. I had been dead-heavy before, and now I felt a kind of dreadful lightness, which would not suffer me to walk. I drifted like a gossamer; the ground seemed to me a cloud, the hills a feather-weight, the air to have a current, like a running burn, which carried me to and fro. With all that, a sort of horror of despair set on my mind, so that I could have wept at my own helplessness.

I saw Alan knitting his brows at me, and supposed it was in anger; and that gave me a pang of light-headed fear, like what a child may have. I remember, too, that I was smiling, and could not stop smiling, hard as I tried; for I thought it was out of place at such a time. But my good companion had nothing in his mind but kindness; and the next moment, two of the gillies had me by the arms, and I began to be carried forward with great swiftness (or so it appeared to me, although I dare say it was slowly enough in truth) through a labyrinth of dreary glens and hollows and into the heart of that dismal mountain of Ben Alder.

CHAPTER TWENTY-THREE

Cluny's Cage

WE CAME AT LAST TO THE FOOT of an exceeding steep wood, which scrambled up a craggy hillside, and was crowned by a naked precipice.

'It's here,' said one of the guides, and we struck up hill.

The trees clung upon the slope, like sailors on the shrouds of a ship; and their trunks were like the rounds of a ladder, by which we mounted.

Quite at the top, and just before the rocky face of the cliff sprang above the foliage, we found that strange house which was known in the country as 'Cluny's Cage'. The trunks of several trees had been wattled across, the intervals strengthened with stakes, and the ground behind this barricade levelled up with earth to make the floor. A tree, which grew out from the hillside, was the living centre beam of the roof. The walls were of wattle and covered with moss. The whole house had something of an egg shape; and it half hung, half stood in that steep, hillside thicket, like a wasps' nest in a green hawthorn.

Within, it was large enough to shelter five or six persons with some comfort. A projection of the cliff had been cunningly employed to be the fireplace; and the smoke rising against the face of the rock, and being not dissimilar in colour, readily escaped notice from below.

This was but one of Cluny's hiding places; he had caves, besides, and underground chambers in several parts of his country; and following the reports of his scouts, he moved from one to another as the soldiers drew near or moved away. By this manner of living, and thanks to the affection of his clan, he had not only stayed all this time in safety, while so many others had fled or been taken and slain; but stayed four or five years longer, and only went to France at last by the express command of his master. There he soon died; and it is strange to reflect that he may have regretted his Cage upon Ben Alder.

When we came to the door he was seated by his rock chimney, watching a gillie about some cookery. He was mighty plainly habited, with a knitted nightcap drawn over his ears, and smoked a foul cutty pipe. For all that he had the manners of a king, and it was quite a sight to see him rise out of his place to welcome us.

'Well, Mr Stewart, come awa' sir!' said he, 'and bring in your friend that as yet I dinna ken the name of.'

'And how is yourself, Cluny?' said Alan. 'I hope ye do brawly, sir. And I am proud to see ye, and to present to ye my friend the Laird of Shaws, Mr David Balfour.'

Alan never referred to my estate without a touch of a sneer, when we were alone; but with strangers, he rang the words out like a herald.

'Step in by, the both of ye, gentlemen,' said Cluny. 'I make ye welcome to my house, which is a queer, rude place for certain, but one where I have entertained a royal personage, Mr Stewart – ye doubtless ken the personage I have in my eye. We'll take a dram for luck, and as soon as this handless man of mine has the collops ready, we'll dine and take a hand at the cartes as gentlemen should. My life is a bit driegh,' says he, pouring out the brandy; 'I see little company, and sit and twirl my thumbs, and mind upon a great day that is gone by, and weary for another great day that we all hope will be upon the road. And so here's a toast to ye: The Restoration!'

Thereupon we all touched glasses and drank. I am sure I wished no ill to King George; and if he had been there himself in proper person, it's like he would have done as I did. No sooner had I taken out the dram than I felt hugely better, and could look on and listen, still a little mistily perhaps, but no longer with the same groundless horror and distress of mind.

It was certainly a strange place, and we had a strange host. In his long hiding, Cluny had grown to have all manner of precise habits, like those of an old maid. He had a particular place, where no one else must sit; the Cage was arranged in a particular way, which none must disturb; cookery was one of his chief fancies, and even while he was greeting us in, he kept an eye to the collops.

It appears, he sometimes visited or received visits from his wife and one or two of his nearest friends, under the cover of night; but for the most part lived quite alone, and communicated only with his sentinels and the gillies that waited on him in the Cage. The first thing in the morning, one of them, who was a barber, came and shaved him, and gave him the news of the country, of which he was immoderately greedy. There was no end to his questions; he put them as earnestly as a child; and at some of the answers, laughed out of all bounds of reason, and would break out again laughing at the mere memory, hours after the barber was gone.

To be sure, there might have been a purpose in his questions; for though he was thus sequestered, and like the other landed gentlemen of Scotland, stripped by the late Act of Parliament of legal powers, he still exercised a patriarchal justice in his clan. Disputes were brought to him in his hiding-hole to be decided; and the men of his country, who would have snapped their fingers at the Court of Session, laid aside revenge and paid down money at the bare word of this forfeited and hunted outlaw. When he was angered, which was often enough, he gave his commands and breathed threats of punishment like any king; and his gillies trembled and crouched away from him like children before a hasty father. With each of them, as he entered, he ceremoniously shook hands, both parties touching their bonnets at the same time in a military manner. Altogether, I had a fair chance to see some of the inner workings of a Highland clan; and this was a proscribed, fugitive chief; his country conquered; the troops riding upon all sides in quest of him, sometimes within a mile of where he lay; and when the least of the ragged fellows whom he rated and threatened, could have made a fortune by betraying him.

On that first day as soon as the collops were ready, Cluny gave them with his own hand a squeeze of a lemon (for he was well supplied with luxuries) and bade us draw in to our meal.

'They', said he, meaning the collops, 'are such as I gave His Royal Highness in this very house; bating the lemon juice, for at that time we were glad to get the meat and never fashed for kitchen*. Indeed, there were mair dragoons than lemons in my country in the year forty-six.'

I do not know if the collops were truly very good, but my heart rose against the sight of them, and I could eat but little. All the while Cluny entertained us with stories of Prince Charlie's stay in the Cage, giving us the very words of the speakers, and rising from his place to show us where they stood. By these, I gathered the Prince was a gracious, spirited boy, like the son of a race of polite kings, but not so wise as Solomon. I gathered, too, that while he was in the Cage, he was often drunk; so the fault that has since, by all accounts, made such a wreck of him, had even then begun to show itself.

We were no sooner done eating than Cluny brought out an old thumbed, greasy pack of cards, such as you may find in a mean inn; and his eys brightened in his face as he proposed that we should fall to playing.

Now this was one of the things I had been brought up to eschew like disgrace; it being held by my father neither the part of a Christian nor yet a gentleman, to set his own livelihood and fish for that of others, on the cast of painted pasteboard. To be sure, I might have pleaded my fatigue, which was excuse enough; but I thought it behoved that I should bear a testimony. I must have got very red in the face, but I spoke steadily, and told them I had no call to be a
*Condiment.

judge of others, but for my own part, it was a matter in which I had no clearness.

Cluny stopped mingling the cards. 'What in deil's name is this?' says he. 'What kind of Whiggish, canting talk is this, for the house of Cluny Macpherson?'

'I will put my hand in the fire for Mr Balfour,' says Alan. 'He is an honest and a mettle gentleman, and I would have ye bear in mind who says it. I bear a king's name,' says he, cocking his hat; 'and I and any that I call friend are company for the best. But the gentleman is tired, and should sleep; if he had no mind to the cartes, it will never hinder you and me. And I'm fit and willing, sir, to play ye any game that ye can name.'

'Sir,' says Cluny, 'in this poor house of mine I would have you ken tht any gentleman may follow his pleasure. If your friend would like to stand on his head, he is welcome. And if either he, or you, or any other man, is not preceesely satisfied, I will be proud to step outside with him.'

I had no will that these two friends should cut their throats for my sake.

'Sir,' said I, 'I am very wearied, as Alan says; and what's more, as you are a man that likely has sons of your own, I may tell you it was a promise to my father.'

'Say nae mair, say nae mair,' said Cluny, and pointed me to a bed of heather in a corner of the Cage. For all that he was displeased enough, looked at me askance, and grumbled when he looked. And indeed it must be owned that both my scruples and the words in which I declared them, smacked somewhat of the Covenanter, and were little in their place among wild Highland Jacobites.

What with the brandy and the venison, a strange heaviness had come over me; and I had scarce lain down upon the bed before I fell into a kind of trance, in which I continued almost the whole time of our stay in the Cage. Sometimes I was broad awake and understood what passed; sometimes I only heard voices or men snoring, like the voice of a silly river; and the plaids upon the wall dwindled down and swelled out again, like firelight shadows on the roof. I must sometimes have spoken or cried out, for I remember I was now and then amazed at being answered; yet I was conscious of no particular nightmare, only of a general, black, abiding horror – a horror of the place I was in, and the bed I lay in, and the plaids on the wall, and the voices, and the fire, and myself.

The barber-gillie, who was a doctor too, was called in to prescribe for me; but as he spoke in the Gaelic, I understood not a word of his opinion, and was too sick even to ask for a translation. I knew well enough I was ill, and that was all I cared about.

I paid little heed while I lay in this poor pass. But Alan and Cluny were most of the time at the cards, and I am clear that Alan must have begun by winning; for I remember sitting up, and seeing them hard at it, and a great glittering pile of as much as sixty or a hundred guineas on the table. It looked strange enough, to see all this wealth in a nest upon a cliff-side, wattled about growing trees. And even then, I thought it seemed deep water for Alan to be riding, who had no better battle-horse than a green purse and a matter of five pounds.

The luck, it seems, changed on the second day. About noon I was awakened as usual for dinner, and as usual refused to eat, and was given a dram with some bitter infusion which the barber had prescribed. The sun was shining in at the open door of the Cage, and this dazzled and offended me. Cluny sat at the table,

biting the pack of cards. Alan had stooped over the bed, and had his face close
to my eyes; to which, troubled as they were with the fever, it seemed of the most
shocking bigness.

He asked me for a loan of my money.

'What for?' said I.

'Oh, just for a loan,' said he.

'But why?' I repeated. 'I don't see.'

'Hut, David!' said Alan, 'ye wouldnae grudge me a loan?'

I would though, if I had my senses. But all I thought of then was to get his face
away, and I handed him my money.

On the morning of the third day, when we had been forty-eight hours in the
Cage, I awoke with a great relief of spirits, very weak and weary indeed, but
seeing things of the right size and with their honest, everyday appearance. I had
a mind to eat, moreover; rose from bed of my own movement; and as soon as we
had breakfasted, stepped to the entry of the Cage and sat down outside in the
top of the wood. It was a grey day with a cold, mild air: and I sat in a dream all
morning, only disturbed by the passing by of Cluny's scouts and servants coming
with provisions and reports; for as the coast was at that time clear, you might
almost say he held court openly.

When I returned, he and Alan had laid the cards aside, and were questioning
a gillie; and the chief turned about and spoke to me in the Gaelic.

'I have no Gaelic, sir,' said I.

Now since the card question, everything I said or did had the power of
annoying Cluny. 'Your name has more sense than yourself then,' said he,
angrily; 'for it's good Gaelic. But the point is this. My scout reports all clear in
the south, and the question is have ye the strength to go?'

I saw cards on the table, but no gold; only a heap of little written papers, and
these all on Cluny's side. Alan, besides, had an odd look, like man not very well
content; and I began to have a strong misgiving.

'I do not know if I am as well as I should be,' said I, looking at Alan; 'but the
little money we have has a long way to carry us.'

Alan took his under-lip into his mouth, and looked upon the ground.

'David,' says he, at last, 'I've lost it; there's the naked truth.'

'My money too?' said I.

'Your money too,' says Alan, with a groan. 'Ye shouldnae have given it me.
I'm daft when I get to the cartes.'

'Hoot-toot, hoot-toot,' said Cluny. 'It was all daffing; it's all nonsense. Of
course, ye'll have your money back again, and the double of it, if ye'll make so
free with me. It would be a singular thing for me to keep it. It's not to be
supposed that I would be any hindrance to gentlemen in your situation; that
would be a singular thing!' cries he, and began to pull gold out of his pocket,
with a mighty red face.

Alan said nothing, only looked on the ground.

'Will you step to the door with me, sir?' said I.

Cluny said he would be very glad, and followed me readily enough, but he
looked flustered and put out.

'And now sir,' says I, 'I must first acknowledge your generosity.'

'Nonsensical nonsense!' cries Cluny. 'Where's the generosity? This is just a most unfortunate affair; but what would ye have me do – boxed up in this bee-skep of a cage of mine – but just set my friends to the cartes, when I can get them? And if they lose, of course, it's not to be supposed——' And here he came to a pause.

'Yes,' said I, 'if they lose, you give them back their money; and if they win, they carry away yours in their pouches! I have said before that I grant your generosity; but to me, sir, it's a very painful thing to be placed in this position.'

There was a little silence, in which Cluny seemed always as if he was about to speak, but said nothing. All the time he grew redder and redder in the face.

'I am a young man,' said I, 'and I ask your advice. Advise me as you would your son. My friend fairly lost this money, after having fairly gained a far greater sum of yours; can I accept it back again? would that be the right part for me to play? Whatever I do, you can see for yourself it must be hard upon a man of any pride.'

'It's rather hard on me, too, Mr Balfour,' said Cluny, 'and ye give me very much the look of a man that has entrapped poor people to their hurt. I wouldnae have my friends come to any house of mine to accept affronts; no,' he cried, with a sudden heat of anger, 'nor yet to give them!'

'And so you see, sir,' said I, 'there is something to be said upon my side; and this gambling is a very poor employ for gentlefolks. But I am still waiting your opinion.'

I am sure if ever Cluny hated any man it was David Balfour. He looked me all over with a warlike eye, and I saw the challenge at his lips. But either my youth disarmed him, or perhaps his own sense of justice. Certainly it was a mortifying matter for all concerned, and not least for Cluny; the more credit that he took it as he did.

'Mr Balfour,' said he, 'I think you are too nice and covenanting, but for all that you have the spirit of a very pretty gentleman. Upon my honest word, ye may take this money – it's what I would tell my son – and here's my hand along with it!'

CHAPTER TWENTY-FOUR

The Flight in the Heather: the Quarrel

ALAN AND I WERE PUT ACROSS Loch Errocht under cloud of night, and went down its eastern shore to another hiding place near the head of Loch Rannoch, whither we were led by one of the gillies from the Cage. This fellow carried all our luggage and Alan's great-coat in the bargain, trotting along under the burden, far less than the half of which used to weigh me to the ground, like a stout hill pony with a feather; yet he was a man that, in plain contest, I could have broken on my knee.

Doubtless it was a great relief to walk disencumbered; and perhaps without that relief, and the consequent sense of liberty and lightness, I could not have walked at all. I was but new risen from a bed of sickness; and there was nothing in the state of our affairs to hearten me for much exertion; travelling, as we did, over the most dismal deserts in Scotland, under a cloudy heaven, and with divided hearts among the travellers.

For long, we said nothing, marching alongside or one behind the other, each with a set countenance; I, angry and proud, and drawing what strength I had from these two violent and sinful feelings: Alan angry and ashamed, ashamed that he had nost my money, angry that I should take it so ill.

The thought of a separation ran always the stronger in my mind; and the more I approved of it, the more ashamed I grew of my approval. It would be a fine, handsome, generous thing, indeed, for Alan to turn round and say to me: 'Go, I am in the most danger, and my company only increases yours.' But for me to turn to the friend who certainly loved me, and say to him: 'You are in great danger, I am in but little; your friendship is a burden; go take your risks and bear your hardships alone' – no, that was impossible; and even to think of it privily to myself, made my cheeks to burn.

And yet Alan had behaved like a child and (what is worse) a treacherous child. Wheedling my money from me while I lay half-conscious, was scarce better than theft; and yet here he was trudging by my side, without a penny to his name, and by what I could see, quite blithe to sponge upon the money he had driven me to beg. True, I was ready to share it with him; but it made me rage to see him count upon my readiness.

These were the two things uppermost in my mind; and I could open my mouth upon neither without black ungenerosity. So I did the next worst, and said nothing, nor so much as looked once at my companion, save with the tail of my eye.

At last, upon the other side of Loch Errocht, going over a smooth, rushy place, where the walking was easy, he could bear it no longer, and came close to me.

'David,' says he, 'this is no way for two friends to take a small accident. I have to say that I'm sorry; and so that's said. And now if you have anything, ye'd better say it.'

'Oh,' says, I, 'I have nothing.'

He seemed disconcerted; at which I was meanly pleased.

'No,' said he, with rather a trembling voice, 'but when I say I was to blame?'

'Why, of course, ye were to blame,' said I, coolly; 'and you will bear me out that I have never reproached you.'

'Never,' says he; 'but ye ken very well that ye've done worse. Are we to part? Ye said so once before. Are ye to say it again? There's hills and heather enough between here and the two seas, David; and I will own I'm no very keen to stay where I'm no wanted.'

This pierced me like a sword, and seemed to lay bare my private disloyalty.

'Alan Breck!' I cried; and then: 'Do you think I am one to turn my back on you in your chief need? You dursn't say it to my face. My whole conduct's there to give the lie to it. It's true, I fell asleep upon the muir; but that was from weariness, and you do wrong to cast it up to me——'

'Which is what I never did,' said Alan.

'But aside from that,' I continued, 'what have I done that you should even me to dogs by such a supposition? I never yet failed a friend, and it's not likely I'll begin with you. There are things between us that I can never forget, even if you can.'

'I will only say this to ye, David,' said Alan, very quietly, 'that I have long been owing ye my life, and now I owe ye money. Ye should try to make that burden light for me.'

This ought to have touched me, and in a manner it did, but the wrong manner. I felt I was behaving badly; and was now not only angry with Alan, but angry with myself in the bargain; and it made me the more cruel.

'You asked me to speak,' said I. 'Well, then, I will. You own yourself that you have done me a disservice; I have had to swallow an affront: I have never reproached you, I never named the thing till you did. And now you blame me,' cried I, 'because I cannae laugh and sing as if I was glad to be affronted. The next thing will be that I'm to go down upon my knees and thank you for it! Ye should think more of others, Alan Breck. If ye thought more of others, ye would perhaps speak less about yourself; and when a friend that likes you very well, has passed over an offence without a word, you would be blithe to let it lie, instead of making it a stick to break his back with. By your own way of it, it was you that was to blame; then it shouldnae be you to seek the quarrel.'

'Aweel,' said Alan, 'say nae mair.'

And we fell back into our former silence; and came to our journey's end, and supped, and lay down to sleep, without another word.

The gillie put us across Loch Rannoch in the dusk of the next day, and gave us his opinion as to our best route. This was to get us up at once into the tops of the mountains: to go round by a circuit, turning the heads of Glen Lyon, Glen Lochay, and Glen Dochart, and come down upon the lowlands by Kippen and the upper waters of the Forth. Alan was little pleased with a route which led us through the country of his blood-foe, the Glenorchy Campbells. He objected that by turning to the east, we should come almost at once among the Athole Stewarts, a race of his own name and lineage although following a different chief, and come besides by a far easier and swifter way to the place whither we were bound. But the gillie, who was indeed the chief man of Cluny's scouts, had good reasons to give him on all hands, naming the force of troops in every district, and alleging finally (as well as I could understand) that we should nowhere be so little troubled as in a country of the Campbells.

Alan gave way at last, but with only half a heart. 'It's one of the dowiest countries in Scotland,' said he. 'There's naething there that I ken, but heath and crows, and Campbells. But I see that ye're a man of some penetration; and be it as ye please!'

We set forth accordingly by this itinerary; and for the best part of three nights travelled on eerie mountains and among the well-heads of wild rivers; often buried in mist, almost continually blown and rained upon, and not once cheered by any glimpse of sunshine. By day, we lay and slept in the drenching heather; by night, incessantly clambered upon breakneck hills and among rude crags. We often wandered; we were often so involved in fog, that we must lie quiet till it lightened. A fire was never to be thought of. Our only food was drammach and a portion of cold meat that we had carried from the Cage; and as for drink, Heaven knows we had no want of water.

This was a dreadful time, rendered the more dreadful by the gloom of the weather and the country. I was never warm; my teeth chattered in my head; I was troubled with a very sore throat, such as I had on the isle; I had a painful stitch in my side, which never left me; and when I slept in my wet bed, with the rain beating above and the mud oozing below me, it was to live over again in fancy the worst part of my adventures – to see the tower of Shaws lit by lightning, Ransome carried below on the men's backs, Shuan dying on the round-house floor, or Colin Campbell grasping at the bosom of his coat. From such broken slumbers, I would be aroused in the gloaming, to sit up in the smae puddle where I had slept, and sup cold drammach; the rain driving sharp in my face or running down my back in icy trickles; the mist enfolding us like as in a gloomy chamber – or perhaps, if the wind blew, falling suddenly apart and showing us the gulf of some dark valley where the streams were crying aloud.

The sound of an infinite number of rivers came up from all round. In this steady rain the springs of the mountain were broken up; every glen gushed water like a cistern; every stream was in high spate, and had filled and overflowed its channel. During our night tramps, it was solemn to hear the voice of them below in the valleys, now booming like thunder, now with an angry cry. I could well understand the story of the Water Kelie, that demon of the streams, who is fabled to keep wailing and roaring at the ford until the coming of the doomed traveller. Alan I saw believed it, or half believed it; and when the cry of the river rose more than usually sharp, I was little surprised (though, of course, I would still be shocked) to see him cross himself in the manner of the Catholics.

During all these horrid wanderings we had no familiarity, scarcely even that of speech. The truth is that I was sickening for my grave, which is my best excuse. But besides that I was of an unforgiving disposition from my birth, slow to take offence, slower to forget it, and now incensed both against my companion and myself. For the best part of two days he was unweariedly kind; silent, indeed, but always ready to help, and always hoping (as I could very well see) that my displeasure would blow by. For the same length of time I stayed in myself, nursing my anger, roughly refusing his services, and passing him over with my eyes as if he had been a bush or a stone.

The second night, or rather the peep of the third day, found us upon a very open hill, so that we could not follow our usual plan and lie down immediately to eat and sleep. Before we had reached a place of shelter, the grey had come pretty clear, for though it still rained, the clouds ran higher; and Alan, looking in my face, showed some marks of concern.

'Ye had better let me take your pack,' said he, for perhaps the ninth time since we had parted from the scout beside Loch Rannoch.

'I do very well, I thank you,' said I, as cold as ice.

Alan flushed darkly. 'I'll not offer it again,' he said. 'I'm not a patient man, David.'

'I never said you were,' said I, which was exactly the rude, silly speech of a boy of ten.

Alan made no answer at the time, but his conduct answered for him. Henceforth, it is to be thought, he quite forgave himself for the affair at Cluny's; cocked his hat again, walked jauntily, whistled airs, and looked at me upon one side with a provoking smile.

The third night we were to pass through the western end of the country of
Balquidder. It came clear and cold, with a touch in the air like frost, and a
northerly wind that blew the clouds away and made the stars bright. The streams
were full, of course, and still made a great noise among the hills; but I observed
that Alan thought no more upon the Kelpie, and was in high good spirits. As for
me, the change of weather came too late; I had lain in the mire so long that (as
the Bible has it) my very clothes 'abhorred me'; I was dead weary, deadly sick,
and full of pains and shiverings; the chill of the wind went through me, and the
sound of it confused my ears. In this poor state I had to bear from my companion
something in the nature of a persecution. He spoke a good deal, and never
without a taunt. 'Whig' was the best name he had to give me. 'Here,' he would
say, 'here's a dub for ye to jump, my Whiggie! I ken you're a fine jumper!' And so
on; all the time with a gibing voice and face.

I knew it was my own doing, and no one else's; but I was too miserable to
repent. I felt I could drag myself but little farther; pretty soon, I must lie down
and die on these wet mountains like a sheep or a fox, and my bones must whiten
there like the bones of a beast. My head was light, perhaps; but I began to love
the prospect, I began to glory in the thought of such a death, alone in the desert,
with the wild eagles besieging my last moments. Alan would repent then, I
thought; he would remember, when I was dead, how much he owed me, and the
remembrance would be torture. So I went like a sick, silly, and bad-hearted
schoolboy, feeding my anger against a fellow-man, when I would have been
better on my knees, crying on God for mercy. And at each of Alan's taunts, I
hugged myself. 'Ah!' thinks I to myself, 'I have a better taunt in readiness; when
I lie down and die, you will feel it like a buffet in your face; ah, what a revenge!
ah, how you will regret your ingratitude and cruelty!'

All the while, I was growing worse and worse. Once I had fallen, my legs
simply doubling under me, and this had struck Alan for the moment; but I was
afoot so briskly, and set off again with such a natural manner, that he soon
forgot the incident. Flushes of heat went over me, and then spasms of
shuddering. The stitch in my side was hardly bearable. At last I began to feel
that I could trail myself no farther; and with that, there came on me all at once
the wish to have it out with Alan, let my anger blaze, and be done with my life
in a more sudden manner. He had just called me 'Whig'. I stopped.

'Mr Stewart,' said I, in a voice that quivered like a fiddlestring, 'you are older
than I am, and should know your manners. Do you think it either very wise or
very witty to cast my politics in my teeth? I thought, where folk differed, it was
the part of gentlemen to differ civilly; and if I did not, I may tell you I could find
a better taunt than some of yours.'

Alan had stopped opposite to me, his hat cocked, his hands in his breeches
pockets, his head a little to one side. He listened, smiling evilly, as I could see by
the starlight; and when I had done he began to whistle a Jacobite air. It was the
air made in mockery of General Cope's defeat at Preston Pans:

Hey, Johnnie Cope, are ye waukin' yet?
And are your drums a-beatin' yet?

And it came in my mind that Alan, on the day of that battle, had been engaged upon the royal side.

'Why do ye take that air, Mr Stewart?' said I. 'Is that to remind me you have been beaten on both sides?'

The air stopped on Alan's lips. 'David!' said he.

'But it's time these manners ceased,' I continued; 'and I mean you shall henceforth speak civilly of my King and my good friends the Campbells.'

'I am a Stewart——' began Alan.

'Oh,' says I, 'I ken ye bear a king's name. But you are to remember, since I have been in the Highlands, I have seen a good many of those that bear it; and the best I can say of them is this, that they would be none the worse of washing.'

'Do you know that you insult me?' said Alan, very low.

'I am sorry for that,' said I, 'for I am not done; and if you distaste the sermon, I doubt the pirliecue* will please you as little. You have been chased in the field by the grown men of my party; it seems a poor kind of pleasure to outface a boy. Both the Campbells and the Whigs have beaten you; you have run before them like a hare. It behoves you to speak of them as of your betters.'

Alan stood quite still, the tails of his great-coat clapping behind him in the wind.

'This is a pity,' he said at last. 'There are things said that cannot be passed over.'

'I never asked you to,' said I. 'I am as ready as yourself.'

'Ready?' said he.

'Ready,' I repeated. 'I am no blower and boaster like some that I could name. Come on!' And drawing my sword, I fell on guard as Alan himself had taught me.

'David!' he cried. 'Are ye daft? I cannae draw upon ye, David. It's fair murder.'

'That was your look-out when you insulted me,' said I.

'It's the truth!' cried Alan, and he stood for a moment, wringing his mouth in his hand like a man in sore perplexity. 'It's the bare truth,' he said, and drew his sword. But before I could touch his blade with mine, he had thrown it from him and fallen to the ground. 'Na, na,' he kept saying, 'na, na – I cannae, I cannae.'

At this the last of my anger oozed all out of me; and I found myself only sick, and sorry, and blank, and wondering at myself. I would have given the world to take back what I had said; but a word once spoken, who can recapture it? I minded me of all Alan's kindness and courage in the past, how he had helped and cheered and borne with me in our evil days; and then recalled my own insults, and saw that I had lost for ever that doughty friend. At the same time, the sickness that hung upon me seemed to redouble, and the pang in my side was like a sword for sharpness. I thought I must have swooned where I stood.

This it was that gave me a thought. No apology could blot out what I had said; it was needless to think of one, none could cover the offence; but where an apology was vain, a mere cry for help might bring Alan back to my side. I put my pride away from me. 'Alan!' I said; 'if you cannae help me, I must just die here.'

He started up sitting, and looked at me.

'It's true,' said I. 'I'm by with it. Oh, let me get into the bield of a house – I'll can die there easier.' I had no need to pretent; whether I chose or not, I spoke in

*A second sermon.

a weeping voice that would have melted a heart of stone.

'Can ye walk?' asked Alan.

'No,' said I, 'not without help. This last hour, my legs have been fainting under me; I've a stitch in my side like a red-hot iron; I cannae breathe right. If I die, Ye'll can forgive me, Alan? In my heart, I liked ye fine – even when I was the angriest.'

'Wheesht, wheesht!' cried Alan. 'Dinnae say that! David man, ye ken——' He shut his mouth upon a sob. 'Let me get my arm about ye,' he continued; 'that's the way! Now lean upon me hard. Gude kens where there's a house! We're in Balwhidder, too; there should be no want of houses, no, nor friends' houses here. Do ye gang easier so, Davie?'

'Ay,' said I, 'I can be doing this way'; and I pressed his arm with my hand.

Again he came near sobbing. 'Davie,' said he, 'I'm no a right man at all; I have neither sense nor kindness; I couldnae remember ye were just a bairn, I couldnae see ye were dying on your feet; Davie, ye'll have to try and forgive me.'

'Oh, man, let's say no more about it!' said I. 'We're neither one of us to mend the other – that's the truth! We must just bear and forbear, man Alan! Oh, but my stitch is sore! Is there nae house?'

'I'll find a house to ye, David,' he said, stoutly. 'We'll follow down the burn, where there's bound to be houses. My poor man, will ye no be better on my back?'

'Oh, Alan,' says I, 'and me a good twelve inches taller?'

'Ye're no such a thing,' cried Alan, with a start. 'There may be a trifling matter of an inch or two; I'm no saying I'm just exactly what ye would call a tall man, whatever; and dare say,' he added, his voice trailing off in a laughable manner, 'now when I come to think of it, I dare say ye'll be just about right. Ay, it'll be a foot, or near hand; or may be even mair!'

It was sweet and laughable to hear Alan eat his words up in the fear of some fresh quarrel. I could have laughed, had not my stitch caught me so hard; but if I had laughed, I think I must have wept too.

'Alan,' cried I, 'what makes ye so good to me? What makes ye care for such a thankless fellow?'

'Deed, and I don't know,' said Alan. 'For just precisely what I thought I liked about ye, was that ye never quarrelled; – and now I like ye better!'

CHAPTER TWENTY-FIVE

In Balquhidder

AT THE DOOR OF THE FIRST house we came to, Alan knocked, which was no very safe enterprise in such a part of the Highlands as the Braes of Balquidder. No great clan held rule there; it was filled and disputed by small septs, and broken remnants, and what they call 'chiefless folk', driven into the wild country about the springs of Forth and Teith by the advance of the Campbells. Here were Stewarts and Maclarens, which came to the same thing, for the Maclarens followed Alan's chief in war, and made but one clan with Appin. Here, too, were many of that old, proscribed, nameless, red-handed clan of the Macgregors. They had always been ill considered, and now worse than ever, having credit with no side or party in the whole country of Scotland. Their chief, Macgregor of Macgregor, was in exile; the more immediate leader of that part of them about Balquidder, James More, Rob Roy's eldest son, lay waiting his trial in Edinburgh Castle; they were in ill-blood with Highlander and Lowlander, with the Grahames, the Maclarens and the Stewarts; and Alan, who took up the quarrel of any friend however distant, was extremely wishful to avoid them.

Chance served us very well; for it was a household of Maclarens that we found, where Alan was not only welcome for his name's sake but known by reputation. Here then I was got to bed without delay, and a doctor fetched, who found me in a sorry plight. But whether because he was a very good doctor, or I a very young, strong man, I lay bed-ridden for no more than a week, and before a month I was able to make the road again with a good heart.

All this time Alan would not leave me; though I often pressed him, and indeed his foolhardiness in staying was a common subject of outcry with the two or three friends that were let into the secret. He hid by day in a hole of the braes under a little wood; and at night when the coast was clear, would come into the house to visit me. I need not say if I was pleased to see him; Mrs Maclaren, our hostess, thought nothing good enough for such a guest; and as Duncan Dhu (which was the name of our host) had a pair of pipes in his house and was much of a lover of music, the time of my recovery was quite a festival, and we commonly turned night into day.

The soldiers let us be; although once a party of two companies and some dragoons went by in the bottom of the valley, where I could see them through the windows as I lay in bed. What was much more astonishing, no magistrate came near me, and there was no question put of whence I came or whither I was going; and in that time of excitement, I was as free of all inquiry as though I had lain in a desert. Yet my presence was known before I left to all the people in Balquidder and the adjacent parts; many coming about the house on visits and these (after the custom of the country) spreading the news among their neighbours. The bills, too, had now been printed. There was one pinned near the foot of my bed, where I could read my own not very flattering portrait and, in larger characters, the amount of the blood money that had been set upon my life. Duncan Dhu and the rest that knew that I had come there in Alan's company, could have entertained no doubt of who I was; and many others must have had their guess. For though I had changed my clothes, I could not change my age or person; and lowland boys of eighteen were not so rife in these parts of the world, and above all about that time, that they could fail to put one thing with another and connect me with the bill. So it was, at least. Other folk keep a secret among two or three near friends, and somehow it leaks out; but among these clansmen, it is told to a whole countryside, and they will keep it for a century.

There was but one thing happened worth narrating; and that is the visit I had of Robin Oig, one of the sons of the notorious Rob Roy. He was sought upon all sides on a charge of carrying a young woman from Balfron and marrying her (as was alleged) by force; yet he stepped about Balquidder like a gentleman in his own walled policy. It was he who had shot James Maclaren at the plough stilts, a quarrel never satisfied; yet he walked into the house of his blood enemies as a rider* might into a public inn.

Duncan had time to pass me word of who it was; and we looked at one another in concern. You should understand, it was then close upon the time of Alan's coming; the two were little likely to agree; and yet if we sent word or sought to make a signal, it was sure to arouse suspicion in a man under so dark a cloud as the Macgregor.

He came in with a great show of civility, but like a man among inferiors; took off his bonnet to Mrs Maclaren, but clapped it on his head again to speak to Duncan; and having thus set himself (as he would have thought) in a proper light, came to my bedside and bowed.

'I am given to know, sir,' says he, 'that your name is Balfour.'

'They call me David Balfour,' said I, 'at your service.'

'I would give ye my name in return sir,' he replied, 'but it's one somewhat blown upon of late days; and it's perhaps suffice if I tell ye that I am own brother to James More Drummond or Macgregor, of whom ye will scarce have failed to hear.'

'No, sir,' said I, a little alarmed; 'nor yet of your father, Macgregor-Campbell.' And I sat up and bowed in bed; for I thought to compliment him, in case he was proud of having had an outlaw to his father.

He bowed in return. 'But what I am come to say, sir,' he went on, 'is this. In the year '45, my brother raised a part of the "Gregara", and marched six companies to strike a stroke for the good side; and the surgoen that marched with our clan and cured my brother's leg when it was broken in the brush at Preston Pans, was a gentleman of the same name precisely as yourself. He was brother to Balfour of Baith; and if you are in any reasonable degree of nearness one of the genetleman's kin, I have come to put myself and my people at your command.'

You are to remember that I knew no more of my descent than any cadger's dog; my uncle, to be sure, had prated of some of our high connexions, but nothing to the present purpose; and there was nothing left me but that bitter disgrace of owning that I could not tell.

Robin told me shortly he was sorry he had put himself about, turned his back upon me without a sign of salutation, and as he went towards the door, I could hear him telling Duncan that I was 'only some kinless loon that didn't know his own father'. Angry as I was at these words and ashamed of my own ignorance, I could scarce keep from smiling that a man who was under the lash of the law (and was indeed hanged some three years later) should be so nice as to the descent of his acquaintances.

Just in the door, he met Alan coming in; and the two drew back and looked at each other like strange dogs. They were neigher of them big men, but they seemed fairly to swell out with pride. Each wore a sword, and by a movement of his haunch, thrust clear the hilt of it, so that it might be the more readily grasped and the blade drawn.

*Commercial traveller.

'Mr Stewart, I am thinking,' says Robin.

'Troth, Mr Macgregor, it's not a name to be ashamed of,' answered Alan.

'I did not know ye were in my country, sir,' says Robin.

'It sticks in my mind that I am in the country of my friends the Maclarens,' says Alan.

'That's a kittle point,' returned the other. 'There may be two words to say to that. But I think I will have heard that you are a man of your sword?'

'Unless ye were born deaf, Mr Macgregor, ye will have heard a good deal more than that,' says Alan. 'I am not the only man that can draw steel in Appin; and when my kinsman and captain, Ardshiel, had a talk with a gentleman of your name, not so may years back, I could never hear that the Macgregor had the best of it.'

'Do ye mean my father, sir,' says Robin.

'Well, I wouldnae wonder,' said Alan. 'The gentleman I have in my mind had the ill-taste to clap Campbell to his name.'

'My father was an old man,' returned Robin. 'The match was unequal. You and me would make a better pair, sir.'

'I was thinking that,' said Alan.

I was half out of bed, and Duncan had been hanging at the elbow of these fighting cocks, ready to intervene upon the least occasion. But when the word was uttered, it was a case of now or never; and Duncan, with something of a white face to be sure, thrust himself between.

'Gentlemen,' said he, 'I will have been thinking of a very different matter, whateffer. Here are my pipes, and here are you two gentlemen who are baith acclaimed pipers. It's an auld dispute which one of ye's the best. Here will be a braw chance to settle it.'

'Why, sir,' said Alan, still addressing Robin, from whom indeed he had not so much as shifted his eyes, nor yet Robin from him, 'why, sir,' says Alan, 'I think I will have heard some sough of the sort. Have ye music, as folk say? Are ye a bit of a piper?'

'I can pipe like a Macrimmon!' cries Robin.

'And that is a very bold word,' quoth Alan.

'I have made bolder words good before now,' returned Robin, 'and that against better adversaries.'

'It is easy to try that,' says Alan.

Duncan Dhu made haste to bring out the pair of pipes that was his principal possession, and to set before his guests a mutton-ham and a bottle of that drink which the call Athole brose, and which is made of old whiskey, strained honey, and sweet cream, slowly beaten together in the right order and porportion. The two enemies were still on the very breach of a quarrel; but down they sat, one upon each side of the peat fire, with a mighty show of politeness. Maclaren pressed them to taste his mutton-ham and 'the wife's brose', reminding them the wife was out of Athole and had a name far and wide for her skill in that confection. But Robin put aside these hospitalities as bad for the breath.

'I would have ye to remark, sir,' said Alan, 'that I havenae broken bread for near upon ten hours, which will be worse for the breath than any brose in Scotland.'

'I will take no advantages, Mr Stewart,' replied Robin. 'Eat and drink; I'll follow you.'

Each ate a small portion of the ham and drank a glass of the brose to Mrs
Maclaren; and then after a great number of civilities, Robin took the pipes and
played a little spring in a very ranting manner.

'Ay, ye can blow,' said Alan; and taking the instrument from his rival, he first
played the same spring in a manner identical with Robin's; and then wandered
into variations, which, as he went on, he decorated with a perfect flight of
grace-notes, such as pipers love, and call the 'warblers'.

I had been pleased with Robin's playing, Alan's ravished me.

'That's not very bad, Mr Stewart,' said the rival, 'but ye show a poor device in
your warblers.'

'Me!' cried Alan, the blood starting to his face. 'I give ye the lie.'

'Do ye own yourself beaten at the pipes, then,' said Robin, 'that ye seek to
change them for the sword?'

'And that's very well said, Mr Macgregor,' returned Alan; 'and in the
meantime' (laying a strong accent on the word) 'I take back the lie. I appeal to
Duncan.'

'Indeed, ye need appeal to naebody,' said Robin. 'Ye're a far better judge than
any Maclaren in Balquidder: for it's a God's truth that you're a very creditable
piper for a Stewart. Hand me the pipes.'

Alan did as he asked; and Robin proceeded to imitate and correct some part of
Alan's variations, which it seemed that he remembered perfectly.

'Ay, ye have music,' said Alan, gloomily.

'And now be the judge yourself, Mr Stewart,' said Robin; and taking up the
variations from the beginning, he worked them throughout to so new a purpose,
with some ingenuity and sentiment, and with so odd a fancy and so quick a
knack in the grace-notes, that I was amazed to hear him.

As for Alan, his face grew dark and hot, and he sat and gnawed his fingers,
like a man under some deep affront. 'Enough!' he cried. 'Ye can blow the pipes –
make the most of that.' And he made as if to rise.

But Robin only held out his hand as if to ask for silence, and struck into the
slow measure of a pibroch. It was a fine piece of music in itself, and nobly played;
but it seems besides it was a piece peculiar to the Appin Stewarts and a chief
favourite with Allan. The first notes were scarce out, before there came a change
in his face; when the time quickened, he seemed to grow restless in his seat; and
long before that piece was at an end, the last signs of his anger died from him,
and he had no thought but for the music.

'Robin Oig,' he said, when it was done, 'ye are a great piper. I am not fit to
blow in the same kingdom with ye. Body of me! ye have mair music in your
sporran that I have in my head! And though it still sticks in my mind that I
could maybe show ye another of it with the cold steel, I warn ye beforehand –
it'll no be fair! It would go against my heart to haggle a man that can blow the
pipes as you can!'

Thereupon the quarrel was made up; all night long the brose was going and
the pipes changing hands; and the day had come pretty bright, and the three
men were none the better for what they had been taking, before Robin as much
as thought upon the road.

It was the last I saw of him, for I was in the Low Countries at the University of

Leyden, when he stood his trial, and was hanged in the Grassmarket. And I have told this at so great length, partly because it was the last incident of any note that befell me on the wrong side of the Highland Line, and partly because (as the man came to be hanged) it's in a manner history.

CHAPTER TWENTY-SIX

End of the Flight: we Pass the Forth

THE MONTH, AS I HAVE SAID, was not yet out, but it was already far through August, and beautiful warm weather, with every sign of an early and great harvest, when I was pronounced able for my journey. Our money was now run to so low an ebb that we must think first of all on speed; for if we came not soon to Mr Rankeillor's, or if when we came there he should fail to help me, we must surely starve. In Alan's view, besides, the hunt must have now greatly slackened; and the line of the Forth and even Stirling Bridge, which is the main pass over that river, would be watched with little interest.

'It's a chief principle in military affairs,' said he, 'to go where ye are least expected. Forth is our trouble; ye ken the saying, "Forth bridles the wild Hielandman". Well, if we seek to creep round about the head of that river and come down by Kippen or Balfron, it's just precisely there that they'll bo looking to lay hands on us. But if we stave on straight to the auld Brig of Stirling, I'll lay my sword they let us pass unchallenged.'

The first night, accordingly, we pushed to the house of a Maclaren in Strathire, a friend of Duncan's, where we slept the twenty-first of the month, and whence we set forth again about the fall of night to make another easy stage. The twenty-second we lay in a heather bush on a hillside in Uam Var, within view of a herd of deer, the happiest ten hours of sleep in a fine, breathing sunshine and on bone-dry ground, that I have ever tasted. That night we struck Allan Water, and followed it down; and coming to the edge of the hills saw the whole Carse of Stirling underfoot, as flat as a pancake, with the town and castle on a hill in the midst of it, and the moon shining on the Links of Forth.

'Now,' said Alan, 'I kenna if ye care, but ye're in your own land again. We passed the Hieland Line in the first hour; and now if we could but pass yon crooked water, we might cast our bonnets in the air.'

In Allan Water, near by where it falls into the Forth, we found a little sandy islet, overgrown with burdock, butterbur, and the like low plants, that would just cover us if we lay flat. Here it was we made our camp, within plain view of Stirling Castle, whence we could hear the drums beat as some part of the garrison paraded. Shearers worked all day in a field on one side of the river, and we could hear the stones going on the hooks and the voices and even the words of the men talking. It behoved to lie close and keep silent. But the sand of the little isle was sun-warm, the green plants gave us shelter for our heads, we had food and drink in plenty; and to crown all, we were within sight of safety.

As soon as the shearers quit their work and the dusk began to fall, we waded ashore and struck for the Bridge of Stirling, keeping to the fields and under the field fences.

The bridge is close under the castle hill, an old high, narrow bridge with pinnacles along the parapet; and you may conceive with how much interest I looked upon it, not only as a place famous in history, but as the very doors of salvation to Alan and myself. The moon was not yet up when we came there; a few lights shone along the front of the fortress, and lower down a few lighted windows in the town; but it was all mighty still, and there seemed to be no guard upon the passage.

I was for pushing straight across; but Alan was more wary.

'It looks unco' quiet,' said he; 'but for all that we'll lie down here cannily behind a dyke, and make sure.'

So we lay for about a quarter of an hour, whiles whispering, whiles lying still and hearing nothing earthly but the washing of the water on the pier. At last there came by an old, hobbling woman with a crutch stick; who first stopped a little, close to where we lay, and bemoaned herself and the long way she had travelled; and then set forth again up the steep spring of the bridge. The woman was so little, and the night still so dark, that we soon lost sight of her; only heard the sound of her steps, and her stick and a cough that she had by fits, draw slowly farther away.

'She's bound to be across now,' I whispered.

'Na,' said Alan, 'her foot still sounds boss* upon the bridge.'

And just then – 'Who goes?' cried a voice, and we heard the butt of a musket rattle on the stones. I must suppose the sentry had been sleeping, so that had we tried, we might have passed unseen; but he was awake now, and the chance forfeited.

'This'll never do,' said Alan. 'This'll never, never do for us, David.'

And without another word, he began to crawl away through the fields; and a little after, being well out of eyeshot, got to his feet again, and struck along a road that led to the eastward. I could not conceive what he was doing; and indeed I was so sharply cut by the disappointment, that I was little likely to be pleased with anything. A moment back, and I had seen myself knocking at Mr Rankeillor's door to claim my inheritance, like a hero in a ballad; and here was I back again, a wandering, hunted blackguard, on the wrong side of Forth.

'Well?' said I.

'Well,' said Alan, 'what would ye have? They're none such fools as I took them for. We have still the Forth to pass, Davie – weary fall the rains that fed the hillsides that guided it!'

'And why go east?' said I.

'Ou, just upon the chance!' said he, 'If we cannae pass the river, we'll have to see what can do for the firth.'

'There are fords upon the river, and none upon the firth,' said I.

'To be sure there are fords, and a bridge forby,' quoth Alan: 'and of what service, when they are watched?'

'Well,' said I, 'but a river can be swum.'

*Hollow

'By them that have the skill of it,' returned he; 'But I have yet to hear that either you or me is much of a hand as that exercise; and for my own part, I swim like a stone.'

'I'm not up to you in talking back, Alan,' I said; 'but I can see we're making bad worse. If it's hard to pass a river, it stands to reason it must be worse to pass a sea.'

'But there's such a thing as a boat,' says Alan, 'or I'm the more deceived.'

'Ay, and such a thing as money,' says I. 'But for us that have neither one nor other, they might just as well not have been invented.'

'Ye think so?' said Alan.

'I do that,' said I.

'David,' says he, 'ye're a man of small invention and less faith. But let me set my wits upon the hone, and if I cannae beg, borrow, nor yet steal a boat, I'll make one!'

'I think I see ye!' said I. 'And what's more than all that: if ye pass a bridge, it can tell no tales; but if we pass the firth, there's the boat on the wrong side – somebody must have brought it – the countryside will all be in a bizz——'

'Man!' cried Alan, 'if I make a boat, I'll make a body to take it back again! So deave me with no more of your nonsense, but walk (for that's what you've got to do) – and let Alan think for ye.'

All night, then, we walked through the north side of the Carse under the high line of the Ochil mountains; and by Alloa and Clackmannan and Culross, all of which we avoided; and about ten in the morning, mighty hungry and tired, came to the little clachan of Limekilns. This is a place that sits near in by the waterside, and looks across the Hope to the town of the Queensferry. Smoke went up from both of these, and from other villages and farms upon all hands. The fields were being reaped; two ships lay anchored and boats were coming and going on the Hope. It was altogether a right pleasant sight to me; and I could not take my fill of gazing at these comfortable, green, cultivated hills and the busy people both of the field and sea.

For all that, there was Mr Rankeillor's house on the south shore, where I had no doubt wealth awaited me; and here was I upon the north, clad in poor enough attire of an outlandish fashion, with three silver shillings left to me of all my fortune, a price set upon my head, and an outlawed man for my sole company.

'O, Alan!' said I, 'to think of it! Over there, there's all that heart could want waiting me; and the birds go over, and the boats go over – all that please can go, but just me only! O, man, but it's a heartbreak!'

In Limekilns we entered a small change-house, which we only knew to be a public by the wand over the door, and bought some bread and cheese from a good-looking lass that was the servant. This we carried with us in a bundle, meaning to sit and eat it in a bush of wood on the seashore, that we saw some third part of a mile in front. As we went, I kept looking across the water and sighing to myself; and though I took no heed of it, Alan had fallen into a muse. At last he stopped in the way.

'Did ye take heed of the lass we bought this of?' says he, tapping on the bread and cheese.

'To be sure,' said I, 'and a bonny lass she was.'

'Ye thought that?' cried he. 'Man David, that's good news.'

'In the name of all that's wonderful, why so?' says I, 'What good can that do?'

'Well,' said Alan, with one of his droll looks, 'I was rather in hopes it would maybe get us that boat.'

'If it were the other way about, it would be liker it,' said I.

'That's all that you ken, ye see,' said Alan. 'I don't want the lass to fall in love with ye, I want her to be sorry for ye, David; to which end, there is no manner of need that she should take you for a beauty. Let me see' (looking me curiously over). 'I wish ye were a wee thing paler; but apart from that ye'll do fine for my purpose – ye have a fine, hang-dog, rag-and-tatter, clappermaclaw kind of a look to ye, as if ye had stolen the coat from a potato-bogle. Come; right about, and back to the change-house for that boat of ours.'

I followed him laughing.

'David Balfour,' said he, 'ye're a very funny gentleman by your way of it, and this is a very funny employ for ye, no doubt. For all that, if ye have any affection for my neck (to say nothing of your own) ye will perhaps be kind enough to take this matter responsibly. I am going to do a bit of play-acting, the bottom ground of which is just exactly as serious as the gallows for the pair of us. So bear it, if ye please, in mind, and conduct yourself according.'

'Well, well,' said I, 'have it as you will.'

As we got near the clachan, he made me take his arm and hang upon it like one almost helpless with weariness; and by the time he pushed open the change-house door, he seemed to be half carrying me. The maid appeared surprised (as well she might be) at our speedy return; but Alan had no words to spare for her in explanation, helped me to a chair, called for a tass of brandy with which he fed me in little sips, and then breaking up the bread and cheese helped me to eat it like a nursery-lass; the whole with that grave, concerned, affectionate countenance, that might have imposed upon a judge. It was small wonder if the maid were taken with the picture we presented, of a poor sick, overwrought lad and his most tender comrade. She drew quite near, and stood leaning with her back on the next table.

'What's like wrong with him?' said she at last.

Alan turned upon her, to my great wonder, with a kind of fury. 'Wrong?' cries he. 'He's walked more hundreds of miles than he has hairs upon his chin, and slept oftener in wet heather than dry sheets. Wrong, quo' she! Wrong enough, I would think! Wrong indeed!' and he kept grumbling to himself, as he fed me, like a man ill-pleased.

'He's young for the like of that,' said the maid.

'Ower young,' said Alan, with his back to her.

'He would be better riding,' says she.

'And where could I get a horse to him?' cried Alan turning on her with the same appearance of fury. 'Would ye have me steal?'

I thought this roughness would have sent her off in dudgeon, as indeed it closed her mouth for the time. But my companion knew very well what he was doing; and for as simple as he was in some things of life, had a great fund of roguishness in such affairs as these.

'Ye neednae tell me,' she said at last – 'ye're gentry.'

'Well,' said Alan, softened a little (I believe against his will) by this artless comment, 'and suppose we were? Did ever you hear that gentrice put money in folk's pockets?'

She sighed at this, as if she were herself some disinherited great lady. 'No,' says she, 'that's true indeed.'

I was all this while chafing at the part I played, and sitting tongue-tied between shame and merriment; but somehow at this I could hold in no longer, and bade Alan let me be, for I was better already. My voice struck in my throat, for I ever hated to take part in lies; but my very embarrassment helped on the plot, for the lass no doubt set down my husky voice to sickness and fatigue.

'Has he nae friends?' said she, in a tearful voice.

'That has he so!' cried Alan, 'if we could but win to them! – friends and rich friends, beds to lie in, food to eat, doctors to see to him – and here he must tramp in the dubs and sleep in the heather like a beggarman.'

'And why that?' says the lass.

'My dear,' says Alan, 'I cannae very safely say; but I'll tell ye what I'll do instead,' says he, 'I'll whistle ye a bit tune.' And with that he leaned pretty far over the table, and in a mere breath of a whistle, but with a wonderful pretty sentiment, gave her a few bars of 'Charlie is my darling'.

'Wheesht,' says she, and looked over her shoulder to the door.

'That's it,' said Alan.

'And him so young!' cried the lass.

'He's old enough to——' and Alan struck his forefinger on the back part of his neck, meaning that I was old enough to lose my head.

'It would be a black shame,' she cried, flushing high.

'It's what will be, though,' said Alan, 'unless we manage the better.'

At this the lass turned and ran out of that part of the house, leaving us alone together, Alan in high good humour at the furthering of his schemes, and I in bitter dudgeon at being called a Jacobite and treated like a child.

'Alan,' I cried, 'I can stand no more of this.'

'Ye'll have to sit it then, Davie,' said he. 'For if ye upset the pot now, ye may scrape your own life out of the fire, but Alan Breck is a dead man.'

This was so true that I could only groan; and even my groan served Alan's purpose, for it was overheard by the lass as she came flying in again with a dish of white puddings and a bottle of strong ale.

'Poor lamb!' says she, and had no sooner set the meat before us, than she touched me on the shoulder with a little friendly touch, as much as to bid me cheer up. Then she told us to fall to, and there would be no more to pay; for the inn was her own, or at least her father's, and he was gone for the day to Pittencrieff. We waited for no second bidding, for bread and cheese is but cold comfort and the puddings smelt excellently well; and while we sat and ate, she took up that same place by the next table, looking on, and thinking, and frowning to herself, and drawing the string of her apron through her hand.

'I'm thinking ye have rather a long tongue,' she said at last to Alan.

'Ay,' said Alan; 'but ye see I ken the folk I speak to.'

'I would never betray ye,' said she, 'if ye mean that.'

'No,' said he, 'ye're not that kind. But I'll tell ye what ye would do, ye would help.'

'I couldnae,' said she, shaking her head. 'Na, I couldnae.'

'No,' said he, 'but if ye could?'

She answered him nothing.

'Look here my lass,' said Alan, 'there are boats in the kingdom of Fife, for I saw two (no less) upon the beach, as I came in by your town's end. Now if we could have the use of a boat to pass under cloud of night into Lothian, and some secret, decent kind of a man to bring that both back again and keep his counsel, there would be two souls saved – mine to all likelihood – his to a dead surety. If we lack that boat, we have but three shillings left in this wide world; and where to go, and how to do, and what other place there is for us except the chains of a gibbet – I give you my naked word, I kenna! Shall we go wanting, lassie? Are ye to lie in your warm bed and think upon us, when the wind gowls in the chimney and the rain tirls on the roof? Are ye to eat your meat by the cheeks of a red fire, and think upon this poor sick lad of mine, biting his finger ends on a blae muir for cauld and hunger? Sick or sound, he must aye be moving; with the death grapple at his throat he must aye be trailing in the rain on the lang roads; and when he gants his last on a rickle of cauld stanes, there will be nae friends near him but only me and God.'

At this appeal, I could see the lass was in great trouble of mind, being tempted to help us, and yet in some fear she might be helping malefactors; and so now I determined to step in myself and to allay her scruples with a portion of the truth.

'Did ever you hear,' said I, 'of Mr Rankeillor of the Ferry?'

'Rankeillor the writer?' said she. 'I daursay that!'

'Well,' said I, 'it's to his door that I am bound, so you may judge by that if I am an ill-doer; and I will tell you more, that though I am indeed, by a dreadful error, in some peril of my life, King George has no truer friend in all Scotland than myself.'

Her face cleared up mightily at this, although Alan's darkened.

'That's more than I would ask,' said she. 'Mr Rankeillor is a kennt man.' And she bade us finish our meat, get clear of the clachan as soon as might be, and lie close in the bit wood on the sea beach. 'And ye can trust me,' says she, 'I'll find some means to put you over.'

At this we waited for no more, but shook hands with her upon the bargain, made short work of the puddings, and set forth again from Limekilns as far as to the wood. It was a small piece of perhaps a score of elders and hawthorns and a few young ashes, not thick enough to veil us from passers-by upon the road or beach. Here we must lie, however, making the best of the brave warm weather and the good hopes we now had of a deliverance, and planning more particularly what remained for us to do.

We had but one trouble all day; when a strolling piper came and sat in the same wood with us; a red-nosed, blear-eyed, drunken dog, with a great bottle of whisky in his pocket, and a long story of wrongs that had been done him by all sorts of persons, from the Lord President of the Court of Session who had denied him justice, down to the Baillies of Inverkeithing who had given him more of it than he desired. It was impossible but he should conceive some suspicion of two men lying all day concealed in a thicket and having no business to allege. As long as he stayed there he kept us in hot water with prying questions; and after he was gone, as he was a man not very likely to hold his tongue, we were in the greater impatience to be gone ourselves.

The day came to an end with the same brightness; the night fell quiet and clear; lights came out in houses and hamlets and then, one after another, began to be put out; but it was past eleven, and we were long since strangely tortured with anxieties, before we heard the grinding of oars upon the rowing pins. At that, we looked out and saw the lass herself comig rowing to us in a boat. She had trusted no one with our affairs, not even her sweetheart, if she had one; but as soon as her father was asleep, had left the house by a window, stolen a neighbour's boat, and come to our assistance single-handed.

I was abashed how to find expression for my thanks; but she was no less abashed at the thought of hearing them; begged us to lose no time and to hold our peace, saying (very properly) that the heart of our matter was in haste and silence; and so, what with one thing and another, she had set us on the Lothian shore not far from Carriden, had shaken hands with us, and was out again at sea and rowing for Limekilns, before there was one word said either of her service or our gratitude.

Even after she was gone, we had nothing to say, as indeed nothing was enough for such a kindness. Only Alan stood a great while upon the shore shaking his head.

'It is a very fine lass,' he said at last. 'David, it is a very fine lass.' And a matter of an hour later, as we were lying in a den on the seashore and I had been already dozing, he broke out again in commendations of her character. For my part, I could say nothing, she was so simple a creature that my heart smote me both with remorse and fear; remorse because we had traded upon her ignorance; and fear lest we should have anyway involved her in the dangers of our situation.

CHAPTER TWENTY-SEVEN

I Come to Mr Rankeillor

THE NEXT DAY IT WAS AGREED that Alan should fend for himself till sunset; but as soon as it began to grow dark, he should lie in the fields by the roadside near to Newhalls, and stir for naught until he heard me whistling. At first I proposed I should give him for a signal the 'Bonnie House of Airlie', which was a favourite of mine; but he objected that as the piece was very commonly known, any ploughman might whistle it by accident; and taught me instead a little fragment of a Highland air, which has run in my head from that day to this, and will likely run in my head when I lie dying. Every time it comes to me, it takes me off to that last day of my uncertainty, with Alan sitting up in the bottom of the den, whistling and beating the measure with a finger, and the grey of the dawn coming on his face.

I was in the long street of Queensferry before the sun was up. It was a fairly built burgh, the houses of good stone, many slated; the town-hall not so fine, I thought, as that of Peebles, nor yet the street so noble; but take it altogether, it put me to shame for my foul tatters.

As the morning went on, and the fires began to be kindled, and the windows to open, and the people to appear out of the houses, my concern and despondency grew ever the blacker. I saw now that I had no grounds to stand upon; and no clear proof of my rights, nor so much as of my own identity. If it was all a bubble, I was indeed sorely cheated and left in a sore pass. Even if things were as I conceived, it would in all likelihood take time to establish my contentions; and what time had I to spare with less than three shillings in my pocket, and a condemned, hunted man upon my hands to ship out of the country? Truly, if my hope broke with me, it might come to the gallows yet for both of us. And as I continued to walk up and down, and saw people looking askance at me upon the street or out of windows, and nudging or speaking one to another with smiles, I began to take a fresh apprehension; that it might be no easy matter even to come to speech of the lawyer, far less to convince him of my story.

For the life of me I could not muster up the courage to address any of these reputable burghers; I thought shame even to speak with them in such a pickle of rags and dirt; and if I had asked for the house of such a man as Mr Rankeillor, I supposed they would have burst out laughing in my face. So I went up and down, and through the street, and down to the harbour-side, like a dog that has lost its master, with a strange gnawing in my inwards, and every now and then a movement of despair. It grew to be high day at last, perhaps nine in the forenoon; and I was worn with these wanderings, and chanced to have stopped in front of a very good house on the landward side, a house with beautiful, clear glass windows, flowering knots upon the sills, the walls new-harled,* and a chase-dog sitting yawning on the step like one that was at home. Well, I was even envying this dumb brute, when the door fell open and there issued forth a shrewd, ruddy, kindly, consequential man in a well-powered wig and spectacles. I was in such a plight that no one set eyes on me once, but he looked at me again; and this gentleman, as it proved, was so much struck with my poor appearance that he came straight up to me and asked me what I did.

I told him I was come to the Queensferry on business, and taking heart of grace, asked him to direct me to the house of Mr Rankeillor.

'Why,' said he, 'that is his house that I have just come out of; and for a rather singular chance, I am that very man.'

'Then, sir,' said I, 'I have to beg the favour of an interview.'

'I do not know your name,' said he, 'nor yet your face.'

'My name is David Balfour,' said I.

'David Balfour?' he repeated, in rather a high tone, like one surprised. 'And where have you come from, Mr David Balfour?' he asked, looking me pretty drily in the face.

'I have come from a great many strange places, sir,' said I; 'but I think it would be as well to tell you where and how in a more private manner.'

He seemed to muse awhile, holding his lip in his hand, and looking now at me and now upon the causeway of the street.

'Yes,' says he, 'that will be the best, no doubt,' And he led me back with him into his house, cried out to someone whom I could not see that he would be

*Newly rough-cast.

engaged all morning, and brought me into a little dusty chamber full of books and documents. Here he sat down, and bade me be seated; though I thought he looked a little ruefully from his clean chair to my muddy rags. 'And now,' says he, 'if you have any business, pray be brief and come swiftly to the point. *Nec gemino bellum Trojanum orditur ab ovo* – do you understand that?' says he, with a keen look.

'I will even do as Horace says, sir,' I answered, smiling, 'and carry you *in medias res.*' He nodded as if he was well pleased, and indeed his scrap of Latin had been set to test me. For all that, and though I was somewhat encouraged, the blood came in my face when I added I have reason to believe myself some rights on the estate of Shaws.'

He got a paper book out of a drawer and set it before him open. 'Well?' said he.

But I had shot my bolt and sat speechless.

'Come, come, Mr Balfour,' said he, 'you must continue Where were you born?'

'In Essendea, sir,' said I, 'the year 1734, the 12th of March.'

He seemed to follow this statement in his paper book; but what that meant I knew not. 'Your father and mother?' said he.

'My father was Alexander Balfour, schoolmaster of that place,' said I, 'and my mother Grace Pitarrow; I think her people were from Angus.'

'Have you any papers proving your identity?' asked Mr Rankeillor.

'No, sir,' said I, 'but they are in the hands of Mr Campbell, the minister, and could be readily produced. Mr Campbell, too, would give me his word; and for that matter, I do not think my uncle would deny me.'

'Meaning Mr Ebenezer Balfour?' says he.

'The same,' said I.

'Whom you have seen?' he asked.

'By whom I was received into his own house,' I answered.

'Did you ever meet a man of the name of Hoseason?' asked Mr Rankeillor.

'I did so, sir, for my sins,' said I; 'for it was by his means and the procurement of my uncle, that I was kidnapped within sight of this town, carried to sea, suffered shipwreck and a hundred other hardships, and stand before you today in this poor accoutrement.'

'You say you were shipwrecked,' said Rankeillor; 'where was that?'

'Off the south end of the Isle of Mull,' said I. 'The name of the isle on which I was cast up is the Island Earraid.'

'Ah!' says he, smiling, 'you are deeper than me in the geography. But so far, I may tell you, this agrees pretty exactly with other information that I hold. But you say you were kidnapped; in what sense?'

'In the plain meaning of the word, sir,' said I. 'I was on my way to your house, when I was trepanned on board the brig, cruelly struck down, thrown below, and knew no more of anything till we were far at sea. I was destined for the plantations; a fate that, in God's providence, I have escaped.'

'The brig was lost on June the 27th,' says he, looking in his book, 'and we are now at August the 24th. Here is a considerable hiatus, Mr Balfour, of near upon two months. It has already caused a vast amount of trouble to your friends; and I own I shall not be very well contented until it is set right.'

'Indeed, sir,' said I, 'these months are very easily filled up; but yet before I told my story, I would be glad to know that I was talking to a friend.'

'This is to argue in a circle,' said the lawyer. 'I cannot be convinced till I have heard you. I cannot be your friend till I am properly informed. If you were more trustful, it would better befit your time of life. And you know, Mr Balfour, we have a proverb in the country that evil-doers are aye evil-dreaders.'

'You are not to forget, sir,' said I, 'that I have already suffered by my trustfulness; and was shipped off to be a slave by the very man that (if I rightly understand) is your employer.'

All this while, I had been gaining ground with Mr Rankeillor, and in proportion as I gained ground, gaining confidence. But at this sally, which I made with something of a smile myself, he fairly laughed aloud.

'No, no,' said he, 'it is not so bad as that. *Fui, non sum.* I *was* indeed your uncle's man of business; but while you (*imberbis juvenis custode remoto*) were gallivanting in the west, a good deal of water has run under the bridge; and if your ears did not sing, it was not for lack of being talked about. On the very day of your sea disaster, Mr Campbell stalked into my office, demanding you from all the winds. I had never heard of your existence; but I had known your father; and from matters in my competence (to be touched upon hereafter) I was disposed to fear the worst. Mr Ebenezer admitted having seen you; declared (what seemed improbable) that he had given you considerable sums; and that you had started for the continent of Europe, intending to fulfil your education, which was probable and praiseworthy. Interrogated how you had come to send no word to Mr Campbell, he deponed that you had expressed a great desire to break with your past life. Further interrogated where you now were, protested ignorance, but believed you were in Leyden. That is a close sum of his replies. I am not exactly sure that anyone believed him,' continued Mr Rankeillor with a smile; 'and in particular he so much disrelished some expressions of mine that (in a word) he showed me to the door. We were then at a full stand; for whatever shrewd suspicions we might entertain, we had no shadow of probation. In the very article, comes Captain Hoseason with the story of your drowning; whereupon all fell through; with no consequence but concern to Mr Campbell, injury to my pocket, and another blot upon your uncle's character, which could very ill afford it. And now, Mr Balfour,' said he, 'you understand the whole process of these matters, and can judge for yourself to what extent I may be trusted.'

Indeed he was more pedantic than I can represent him, and placed more scraps of Latin in his speech; but it was all uttered with a fine geniality of eye and manner which went far to conquer my distrust. Moreover, I could see he now treated me as if I was myself beyond a doubt; so that first point of my identity seemed fully granted.

'Sir,' said I, 'if I tell you my story, I must commit a friend's life to your discretion. Pass me your word it shall be sacred; and for what touches myself, I will ask no better guarantee than just your face.'

He passed me his word very seriously. 'But,' said he, 'these are rather alarming prolocutions; and if there are in your story any little jostles to the law, I would beg you to bear in mind that I am a lawyer, and pass lightly.'

Thereupon I told him my story from the first, he listening with his spectacles thrust up and his eyes closed, so that I sometimes feared he was asleep. But no such matter! he heard every word (as I found afterwards) with such quickness of hearing and precision of memory as often surprised me. Even strange, outlandish Gaelic names, heard for that time only, he remembered and would remind me of, years after. Yet when I called Alan Breck in full, we had an odd scene. The name of Alan had of course rung through Scotland, with the news of the Appin murder and the offer of the reward; and it had no sooner escaped me than the lawyer moved in his seat and opened his eyes.

'I would name no unnecessary names, Mr Balfour,' said he; 'above all of Highlanders, many of whom are obnoxious to the law.'

'Well, it might have been better not,' said I; 'but since I have let it slip, I may as well continue.'

'Not at all,' said Mr Rankeillor. 'I am somewhat dull of hearing, as you may have remarked; and I am far from sure I caught the name exactly. We will call your friend, if you please, Mr Thomson – that there may be no reflections. And in future, I would take some such way with any Highlander that you may have to mention – dead or alive.'

By this, I saw he must have heard the name all too clearly and had already guessed I might be coming to the murder. If he chose to play this part of ignorance, it was no matter of mine; so I smiled, said it was no very Highland sounding name, and consented. Through all the rest of my story Alan was Mr Thomson; which amused me the more, as it was a piece of policy after his own heart. James Stewart, in like manner, was mentioned under the style of Mr Thomson's kinsman; Colin Campbell passed as a Mr Glen; and to Cluny, when I came to that part of my tale, I gave the name of 'Mr Jameson, a Highland chief'. It was truly the most open farce, and I wondered that the lawyer should care to keep it up; but after all it was quite in the taste of that age, when there were two parties in the state, and quiet persons, with no very high opinions of their own, sought out every cranny to avoid offence to either.

'Well, well,' said the lawyer, when I had quite done, 'this is a great epic, a great Odyssey of yours. You must tell it, sir, in a sound Latinity when your scholarship is riper; or in English if you please, though for my part I prefer the stronger tongue. You have rolled much; *quae regio in terris* – what parish in Scotland (to make a homely translation) has not been filled with your wanderings? You have shown, besides, a singular aptitude for getting into false positions; and, yes, upon the whole, for behaving well in them. This Mr Thomson seems to me a gentleman of some choice qualities, though perhaps a trifle bloody-minded. It would please me none the worse, if (with all his merits) he were soused in the North Sea; for the man, Mr David, is a sore embarrassment. But you are doubtless quite right to adhere to him; indubitably, he adhered to you. *It comes* – we may say – he was your true companion; nor less, *paribus curis vestigia figit*, for I dare say you would both take an orra thought upon the gallows. Well, well, these days are fortunately by; and I think (speaking humanly) that you are near the end of your troubles.'

As he thus moralized on my adventures, he looked upon me with so much humour and benignity that I could scarce contain my satisfaction. I had been so long wandering with lawless people, and making my bed upon the hills and under the bare sky, that to sit once more in a clean, covered house, and to talk amicably with a gentleman in broadcloth, seemed mighty elevations. Even as I thought so, my eye fell on my unseemly tatters, and I was once more plunged in confusion. But the lawyer saw and understood me. He rose, called over the stair to lay another plate, for Mr Balfour would stay to dinner, and led me into a bedroom in the upper part of the house. Here he set before me water and soap and a comb; and laid out some clothes that belonged to his son; and here, with another apposite tag, he left me to my toilet.

CHAPTER TWENTY-EIGHT

I Go in Quest of My Inheritance

I MADE WHAT CHANGE I COULD in my appearance; and blithe was I to look in the glass and find the beggar-man a thing of the past, and David Balfour come to life again. And yet I was ashamed of the change too, and above all, of the borrowed clothes. When I had done, Mr Rankeillor caught me on the stair, made me his compliments, and had me again into the cabinet.

'Sit ye down, Mr David,' said he, 'and now that you are looking a little more like yourself, let me see if I can find you any news. You will be wondering, no doubt, about your father and your uncle? To be sure it is a singular tale; and the explanation is one that I blush to have to offer you. For,' says he, really with embarrassment, 'the matter hinges on a love affair.'

'Truly,' said I, 'I cannot very well join that notion with my uncle.'

'But your uncle, Mr David, was not always old,' replied the lawyer, 'and what may perhaps surprise you more, not always ugly. He had a fine gallant air; people stood in their doors to look after him, as he went by upon a mettle horse. I have seen it with these eyes, and I ingenuously confess, not altogether without envy; for I was a plain lad myself and a plain man's son; and in those days, it was a case of *Odi te, qui bellus es, Sabelle.*'

'It sounds like a dream,' said I.

'Ay, ay,' said the lawyer, 'that is how it is with youth and age. Nor was that all, but he had a spirit of his own that seemed to promise great things in the future. In 1715, what must he do but run away to join the rebels? It was your father that pursued him, found him in a ditch, and brought him back *multum gementem*; to the mirth of the whole country. However, *majora canamus* – the two lads fell in love, and that with the same lady. Mr Ebenezer, who was the admired and the beloved, and the spoiled one, made, no doubt, mighty certain of the victory; and when he found he had deceived himself, screamed like a peacock. The whole county heard of it; now he lay sick at home, with his silly family standing round the bed in tears; now he rode from public house to public house, and shouted his sorrows into the lug of Tom, Dick, and Harry. Your father, Mr David, was a kind gentleman; but he was weak, dolefully weak; took all this folly with a long countenance; and one day – by your leave – resigned the lady. She was no such fool, however; its from her you must inherit your excellent good sense; and she refused to be bandied from one to another. Both got upon their knees to her; and the upshot of the matter for that while, was that she showed both of them the door. That was in August; dear me! the same year I came from college. The scene must have been highly farcical.'

I thought myself it was a silly business, but I could not forget my father had a hand in it. 'Surely, sir, it had some note of tragedy,' said I.

'Why, no, sir, not at all,' returned the lawyer. 'For tragedy implies some ponderable matter in dispute, some *dignus vindice nodus*; and this piece of work was all about the petulance of a young ass that had been spoiled, and wanted nothing so much as to be tied up and soundly belted. However, that was not your father's view; and the end of it was, that from concession to concession on your father's part, and from one height to another of squalling, sentimental selfishness upon your uncle's, they came at last to drive a sort of bargain, from whose ill-results you have recently been smarting. The one man took the lady, the other the estate. Now, Mr David, they talk a great deal of charity and generosity; but in this disputable state of life, I often think the happiest consequences seem to flow when a gentleman consults his lawyers and takes all the law allows him. Anyhow, this piece of quixotry upon your father's part, as it was unjust in itself, has brought forth a monstrous family of injustices. Your father and mother lived and died poor folk; you were poorly reared; and in the meanwhile, what a time it has been for the tenants on the estate of Shaws! And I might add (if it was a matter I cared much about) what a time for Mr Ebenezer!'

'And yet that is certainly the strangest part of all,' said I, 'that a man's nature should thus change.'

'True,' said Mr Rankeillor. 'And yet I imagine it was natural enough. He could not think that he had played a handsome part. Those who knew the story gave him the cold shoulder; those who knew it not, seeing one brother disappear, and the other succeed in the estate, raised a cry of murder; so that upon all sides, he found himself evited. Money was all he got by his bargain; well, he came to think the more of money. He was selfish when he was young, he is selfish now that he is old; and the latter end of all these pretty manners and fine feelings, you have seen for yourself.'

'Well, sir,' said I, 'and in all this, what is my position?'

'The estate is yours beyond a doubt,' replied the lawyer. 'It matters nothing what your father signed, you are the heir of entail. But your uncle is a man to fight the indefensible; and it would be likely your identity that he would call in question. A lawsuit is always expensive, and a family lawsuit always scandalous; besides which, if any of your doings with your friend Mr Thomson were to come out, we might find that we had burned our fingers. The kidnapping, to be sure, would be a court card upon our side, if we could only prove it. But it may be difficult to prove; and my advice (upon the whole) is to make a very easy bargain with your uncle, perhaps even leaving him at Shaws where he has taken root for a quarter of a century, and contenting yourself in the meanwhile with a fair provision.'

I told him I was very willing to be easy, and that to carry family concerns before the public was a step from which I was naturally much averse. In the meantime (thinking to myself) I began to see the outlines of that scheme on which we afterwards acted.

'The great affair,' I asked, 'is to bring home to him the kidnapping?'

'Surely,' said Mr Rankeillor, 'and if possible, out of court. For mark you here, Mr David; we could no doubt find some men of the Covenant who would swear to your reclusion; but once they were in the box, we could no longer check their testimony, and some word of your friend Mr Thomson must certainly crop out. Which (from what you have let fall) I cannot think to be desirable.'

'Well sir,' said I, 'here is my way of it.' And I opened my plot to him.

'But this would seem to involve my meeting the man Thomson?' says he, when I had done.

'I think so, indeed, sir,' said I.

'Dear doctor!' cries he, rubbing his brow. 'Dear doctor! No, Mr David, I am afraid your scheme is inadmissible. I say nothing against your friend Mr Thomson; I know nothing against him; and if I did – mark this, Mr David! – it would be my duty to lay hands on him. Now I put it to you: is it wise to meet? He may have matters to his charge. He may not have told you all. His name may not be even Thomson!' cries the lawyer, twinkling; 'for some of these fellows will pick up names by the roadside as another would gather haws.'

'You must be the judge, sir,' said I.

But it was clear my plan had taken hold upon his fancy, for he kept musing to himself till we were called to dinner and the company of Mrs Rankeillor; and that lady had scarce left us again to ourselves and a bottle of wine, ere he was back harping on my proposal. When and where was I to meet my friend Mr Thomson; was I sure of Mr T's discretion; supposing we could catch the old fox tripping, would I consent to such and such a term of an agreement – these and the like questions he kept asking at long intervals, while he thoughtfully rolled his wine upon his tongue. When I had answered all of them, seemingly to his contentment, he fell into a still deeper muse, even the claret being now forgotten. Then he got a sheet of paper and a pencil, and set to work writing and weighing every word; and at last touched a bell and had his clerk into the chamber.

'Torrance,' said he, 'I must have this written out fair against tonight; and when it is done, you will be so kind as to put on your hat and be ready to come along with this gentleman and me, for you will probably be wanted as a witness.'

'What, sir,' cried I, as soon as the clerk was gone, 'are you to venture it?'

'Why, so it would appear,' says he, filling his glass. 'But let us speak no more of business. The very sight of Torrance brings in my head a little, droll matter of some years ago, when I had made a tryst with the poor oaf at the cross of Edinburgh. Each had gone his proper errand; and when it came four o'clock, Torrance had been taking a glass a nd did not know his master, and I, who had forgot my spectacles, was so blind without them, that I give you my word I did not know my own clerk.' And thereupon he laughed heartily.

I said it was an odd chance, and smiled out of politeness; but what held me all the afternoon in wonder, he kept returning and dwelling on this story, and telling it again with fresh details and laughter; so that I began at last to be quite put out of countenance and feel ashamed for my friend's folly.

Towards the time I had appointed with Alan, we set out from the house, Mr Rankeillor and I arm in arm, and Torrance following behind with the deed in his pocket and a covered basket in his hand. All through the town, the lawyer was bowing right and left, and continually being button-holed by gentlemen on matters of burgh or private business; and I could see he was greatly looked up to in the county. At last we were clear of the houses, and began to go along the side of the haven and towards the Hawes Inn and the ferry pier, the scene of my misfortune. I could not look upon the place without emotion, recalling how many that had been there with me that day were now no more: Ransome taken, I could hope, from the evil to come; Shuan passed where I dared not follow him; and the poor souls that had gone down with the brig in her last plunge. All these, and the brig herself, I had out-lived; and come through these hardships and fearful perils without scathe. My only thought should have been of gratitude; and yet I could not behold the place without sorrow for others and a chill of recollected fear.

I was so thinking when, upon a sudden, Mr Rankeillor cried out, clapped his hand to his pockets, and began to laugh.

'Why,' he cries, 'if this be not a farcical adventure! After all that I said, I have forgotten my glasses!'

At that, of course, I understood the purpose of his anecdote, and knew that if he had left his spectacles at home, it had been done on purpose, so that he might have the benefit of Alan's help without the awkwardness of recognizing him. And indeed it was well thought upon; for now (suppose things to go the very worst) how could Rankeillor swear to my friend's identity, or how be made to bear damaging evidence against myself? For all that, he had been a long while of finding out his want, and had spoken to and recognized a good few persons as we came through the town; and I had little doubt myself that he saw reasonably well.

As soon as we were past the Hawes (where I recognized the landlord smoking his pipe in the door, and was amazed to see him look no older) Mr Rankeillor changed the order of march, walking behind with Torrance and sending me forward in the manner of a scout. I went up the hill, whistling from time to time my Gaelic air; and at length I had the pleasure to hear it answered and to see Alan rise from behind a bush. he was somewhat dashed in spirits, having passed a long day alone skulking in the country, and made but a poor meal in an alehouse near Dundas. But at the mere sight of my clothes, he began to brighten up; and as soon as I had told him in what a forward state our matters were, and the part I looked to him to play in what remained, he sprang into a new man.

'And that is a very good notion of yours,' says he; 'and I dare say that you could lay your hands upon no better man to put it through, than Alan Breck. It is not a thing (mark ye) that anyone could do, but takes a gentleman of penetration. But it sticks in my head your lawyer-man will be somewhat wearying to see me,' says Alan.

Accordingly I cried and waved on Mr Rankeillor, who came up alone and was presented to my friend, Mr Thomson.

'Mr Thomson, I am pleased to meet you,' said he. 'But I have forgotten my glasses; and our friend, Mr David here' (clapping me on the shoulder) 'will tell you that I am little better than blind, and that you must not be surprised if I pass you by tomorrow.'

This he said, thinking that Alan would be pleased; but the Highlandman's vanity was ready to startle at a less matter than that.

'Why, sir,' said he, stiffly, 'I would say it mattered the less as we are met here for a particular end, to see justice done to Mr Balfour; and by what I can see, not very likely to have much else in common. But I accept your apology, which was a very proper one to make.'

'And that is more than I could look for, Mr Thomson,' said Rankeillor, heartily. 'And now as you and I are the chief actors in this enterprise, I think we should come into a nice agreement; to which end, I porpose that you should lend me your arm, for (what with the dusk and the want of my glasses) I am not very clear as to the path; and as for you, Mr David, you will find Torrance a pleasant kind of body to speak with. Only let me remind you, it's quite needless he should hear more of your adventures or those of ahem – Mr Thomson.'

Accordingly these two went on ahead in very close talk, and Torrance and I brought up the rear.

Night was quite come when we came in view of the house of Shaws. Ten had been gone some time; it was dark and mild, with a pleasant, rustling wind in the south-west that covered the sound of our approach; and as we drew near we saw no glimmer of light in any portion of the building. It seemed my uncle was already in bed, which was indeed the best thing for our arrangements. We made our last whispered consultations some fifty yards away; and then the lawyer and Torrance and I crept quietly up and crouched down beside the corner of the house; and as soon as we were in our places, Alan strode to the door without concealment and began to knock.

CHAPTER TWENTY-NINE

I Come into My Kingdom

FOR SOME TIME ALAN VOLLEYED upon the door, and his knocking only roused the echoes of the house and neighbourhood. At last however, I could hear the noise of a window gently thrust up, and knew that my uncle had come to his observatory. By what light there was he would see Alan standing, like a dark shadow, on the steps; the three witnesses were hidden quite out of his view; so that there was nothing to alarm an honest man in his own house. For all that, he studied his visitor awhile in silence, and when he spoke his voice had a quaver of misgiving.

'What's this?' says he. 'This is nae kind of time of night for decent folk; and I hae nae trokings* wi' nighthawks. What brings ye here? I have a blunderbush.'

'Is that yoursel', Mr Balfour?' returned Alan, stepping back and looking up into the darkness. 'have a care of that blunderbuss; they're nasty things to burst.'

'What brings ye here? and whae are ye?' says my uncle, angrily.

'I have no manner of inclination to rowt out my name to the countryside,'
*Dealings.

said Alan; 'but what brings me here is another story, being more of your affairs than mine; and if ye're sure it's what ye would like, I'll set it to a tune and sing it to you.'

'And what is't?' asked my uncle.

'David,' says Alan.

'What was that?' cried my uncle, in a mighty changed voice.

'Shall I give ye the rest of the name, then?' said Alan.

There was a pause; and then, 'I'm thinking I'll better let ye in,' says my uncle, doubtfully.

'I dare say that,' said Alan; 'but the point is, Would I go? Now I will tell you what I am thinking. I am thinking that it is here upon this doorstep that we must confer upon this business; and it shall be here or nowhere at all whatever; for I would have you to understand that I am as stiff-necked as yoursel', and a gentleman of better family.'

This change of note disconcerted Ebenezer; he was a little while digesting it; and then says he, 'Weel, weel, what must be must,' and shut the window. But it took him a long time to get downstairs, and a still longer to undo the fastenings, repenting (I dare say) and taken with fresh claps of fear at every second step and every bolt and bar. At last, however, we heard the creak of the hinges, and it seems my uncle slipped gingerly out and (seeing that Alan had stepped back a pace or two) sate him down on the top doorstep with the blunderbuss ready in his hands.

'And now,' says he, 'mind I have my blunderbush, and if ye take a step nearer y're as good as deid.'

'And a very civil speech,' said Alan, 'to be sure.'

'Na,' says my uncle, 'but this is no a very chancy kind of a proceeding, and I'm bound to be prepared. And now that we understand each other, ye'll can name your business.

'Why,' says Alan, 'you that are a man of so much understanding, will doubtless have perceived that I am a Hieland gentleman. My name has nae business in my story; but the county of my friends is no very far from the Isle of Mull, of which ye will have heard. It seems there was a ship lost in those parts; and the next day a gentleman of my family was seeking wreckwood for his fire among the hands, when he came upon a lad that was half drowned. Well, he brought him to; and he and some other gentlemen took and clapped him in an auld, ruined castle, where from that day to this he has been a great expense to my friends. My friends are a wee wild-like, and not so particular about the law as some that I could name; and finding that the lad owned some decent folk, and was your born nephew, Mr Balfour, they asked me to give ye a bit call and to confer upon the matter. And I may tell ye at the off-go, unless we can agree upon some terms, ye are little likely to set eyes upon him. For my friends,' added Alan, simply, 'are no very well off,'

My uncle cleared his throat. 'I'm no very caring,' says he. 'He wasnae a good lad at the best of it, and I've nae call to interfere.'

'Ay, ay,' said Alan, 'I see what ye would be at: pretending ye don't care, to make the ransome smaller.'

'Na,' said my uncle, 'it's the mere truth. I take nae manner of interest in the lad, and I'll pay nae ransom, and ye can make a kirk and a mill of him for what I care.'

'Hoot, sir,' says Alan, 'Blood's thicker than water, in the deil's name! Ye cannae desert your brother's son for the fair shame of it; and if ye did, and it came to be kennt, ye wouldnae by very popular in your countryside, or I'm the more deceived.'

'I'm no just very popular the way it is,' returned Ebenezer; 'and I dinnae see how it would come to be kennt. No by me, onyway; nor by you or your friends. So that's idle talk, my buckie,' says he.

'Then it'll have to be David that tells it,' said Alan.

'How that?' says my uncle, sharply.

'Ou, just this way,' says Alan. 'My friends would doubtless keep your nephew as long as there was any likelihood of siller to be made of it, but if there was nane, I am clearly of opinion they would let him gang where he pleased, and be damned to him.'

'Ay, but I'm no very caring about that either,' said my uncle. 'I wouldnae be muckle made up with that.'

'I was thinking that,' said Alan.

'And what for why?' asked Ebenezer.

'Why, Mr Balfour,' replied Alan, 'by all that I could hear, there were two ways of it: either ye liked David and would pay to get him back; or else ye had very good reasons for not wanting him, and would pay for us to keep him. It seems it's not the first; well then, it's the second; and blythe am I to ken it, for it should be a pretty penny in my pocket and the pockets of my friends.'

'I dinnae follow ye there,' said my uncle.

'No?' said Alan. 'Well, see here; you dinnae want the lad back; well, what do ye want down with him, and how much will ye pay?'

My uncle made no answer, but shifted uneasily on his seat.

'Come, sir,' cried Alan. 'I would have ye ken that I am a gentleman; I bear a king's name; I am nae rider to kick my shanks at your hall door. Either give me an answer in civility, and that out of hand; or by the top of Glencoe, I will ram three feet of iron through your vitals.'

'Eh, man,' cried my uncle, scrambling to his feet, 'give me a meenit! What's like wrong with ye? I'm just a plain man, and nae dancing master; and I'm trying to be as ceevil as it's morally possible. As for that wild talk, it's fair disreputable. Vitals, says you! And where would I be with my blunderbush?' he snarled.

'Power and your auld hands are but as the snail to the swallow against the bright stell in the hands of Alan,' said the other. 'Before your jottering finger could find the trigger, the hilt would dirl on your breast bane.'

'Eh, man, whae's denying it?' said my uncle. 'Pit it as ye please, hae't your ain way; I'll do naething to cross ye. Just tell me what like ye'll be wanting, and ye'll see that we'll can agree fine.'

'Troth, sir,' said Alan, 'I ask for nothing but plain dealing. In two words: do ye want the lad killed or kept?'

'O, sirs!' cried Ebenezer. 'O, sirs, me! that's no kind of language!'

'Killed or kept?' repeated Alan.

'Oh, keepit, keepit!' wailed my uncle. 'We'll have nae bloodshed, if you please.'

'Well,' says Alan, 'as ye please; that'll be the dearer.'

'The dearer?' cries Ebenezer. 'Would ye fyle your hands wi' crime?'

'Hoot!' said Alan, 'they're baith crime, whatever! And the killing's easier, and quicker, and surer. Keeping the lad'll be a fashious* job, a fashious, kittle business.'

'I'll have him keepit, though,' returned my uncle. 'I never had naething to do with onything morally wrong; and I'm no gaun to begin to pleasure a wild Hielandman.'

'Ye're unco scrupulous,' sneered Alan.

'I'm a man o' principle,' said Ebenezer simply; 'and if I have to pay for it, I'll have to pay for it. And besides,' says he, 'ye forget the lad's my brother's son.'

'Well, well,' said Alan, 'and now about the price. It's no very easy for me to set a name upon it; I would first have to ken some small matters. I would have to ken, for instance, what ye gave Hoseason at the first off-go?'

'Hoseason?' cries my uncle, struck aback. 'What for?'

'For kidnapping David,' says Alan.

'It's a lee, it's a black lee!' cried my uncle. 'He was never kidnapped. He leed in his throat that tauld ye that. Kidnapped? He never was!'

'That's no fault of mine or yet of yours,' said Alan; 'nor yet of Hoseason's, if he's a man that can be trusted.'

'What do ye mean?' cried Ebenezer. 'Did Hoseason tell ye?'

'Why, ye donnered auld runt, how else would I ken?' cried Alan. 'Hoseason and I are partners; we gang shares; so ye can see for yoursel', what good ye can do leeing. And I must plainly say ye drove a fool's bargain when ye let a man like the sailor-man so far forward in your private matters. But that's past praying for; and ye must lie on your bed the way ye made it. And the point in hand is just this: what did ye pay him?'

'Has he tauld ye himsel',' asked my uncle.

'That's my concern,' said Alan.

'Weel,' said my uncle, 'I dinnae care what he said, he leed, and the solemn God's truth is this, that I gave him twenty pound. But I'll be perfec'ly honest with ye: forby that, he was to have the selling of the lad in Caroliny, whilk would be as muckle mair, but no from my pocket, ye see.'

'Thank you, Mr Thomson. That will do excellently well,' said the lawyer, stepping forward; and then mighty civilly, 'Good evening, Mr Balfour,' said he.

And, 'Good evening, uncle Ebenezer,' said I.

And, 'It's a braw nicht, Mr Balfour,' added Torrance.

Never a word said my uncle, neither black nor white; but just sat where he was on the top doorstep and stared upon us like a man turned to stone. Alan filched away his blunderbuss; and the lawyer, taking him by the arm, plucked him up from the doorstep, led him into the kitchen, whither we all followed, and set him down in a chair beside the hearth, where the fire was out and only a rush-light burning.

There we all looked upon him for a while, exulting greatly in our success, but yet with a sort of ity for the man's shame.

'Come, come, Mr Ebenezer,' said the lawyer, 'you must not be down-hearted, for I promise you we shall make easy terms. In the meanwhile give us the cellar key, and Torrance shall draw us a bottle of your father's wine in honour of the
*Troublesome.

event.' Then, turning to me and taking me by the hand, 'Mr David,' says he, 'I wish you all joy in your good fortune, which I believe to be deserved.' And then to Alan, with a spice of drollery, 'Mr Thomson, I pay you my compliment; it was most artfully conducted; but in one point you somewhat outran my comprehension. Do I understand your name to be James? or Charles? or is it George perhaps?'

'And why should it be any of the three, sir?' quoth Alan, drawing himself, up like one who smelt an offence.

'Only, sir, that you mentioned a king's name,' replied Rankeillor; 'and as there has never yet been a King Thomson, or his fame at least has never come my way, I judged you must refer to that you had in baptism.'

This was just the stab that Alan would feel keenest, and I am free to confess he took it very ill. Not a word would he answer, but stept off to the far end of the kitchen, and sat down and sulked; and it was not till I stepped after him, and gave him my hand, and thanked him by title as the chief spring of my success, that he began to smile a bit, and was at last prevailed upon to join our party.

By that time we had the fire lighted, and a bottle of wine uncorked; a good supper came out of the basket, to which Torrance and I and Alan set ourselves down; while the lawyer and my uncle passed into the next chamber to consult. They stayed there closeted about an hour; at the end of which period there had come to a good understanding, and my uncle and I set our hands to the agreement in a formal manner. By the terms of this, my uncle bound himself to satisfy Rankeillor as to his intromissions, and to pay me two thirds of the yearly income of Shaws.

So the beggar in the ballad had come home; and when I lay down that night on the kitchen chests, I was a man of means and had a name in the country. Alan and Torrance and Rankeillor slept and snored on their hard beds; but for me, who had lain out under heaven and upon dirt and stones, so many days and nights, and often with an empty belly, and in fear of death, this good change in my case unmanned me more than any of the former evil ones; and I lay till dawn, looking at the fire on the roof and planning the future.

CHAPTER THIRTY

Good-Bye

SO FAR AS I WAS CONCERNED myself, I had come to port; but I had still Alan, to whom I was so much beholden, on my hands; and I felt besides a heavy charge in the matter of the murder and James of the Glens. On both these heads I unbosomed to Rankeillor the next morning, walking to and fro about six of the clock before the house of Shaws, and with nothing in view but the fields and woods that had been my ancestors' and were now mine. Even as I spoke on these grave subjects, my eye would take a glad bit of a run over the prospect, and my heart jump with pride.

About my clear duty to my friend, the lawyer had no doubt; I must help him out of the county at whatever risk; but in the case of James, he was of a different mind.

'Mr Thomson,' says he, 'is one thing, Mr Thomson's kinsman quite another. I know little of the facts; but I gather that a great noble (whom we will call, if you like, the D. of A.*) has some concern and is even supposed to feel some animosity in the matter. The D. of A. is doubtless an excellent nobleman; but, Mr David, *timeo qui nocuere deos*. If you interfere to baulk his vengeance, you should remember there is one way to shut your testimony out; and that is to put you in the dock. There, you would be in the same pickle as Mr Thomson's kinsman. You will object that you are innocent; well, but so is he. And to be tried for your life before a Highland jury, on a Highland quarrel, and with a Highland judge upon the bench, would be a brief transition to the gallows.'

Now I had made all these reasonings before and found no very good reply to them; so I put on all the simplicity I could. 'In that case, sir,' said I, 'I would just have to be hanged – would I not?'

'My dear boy,' cries he, 'go in God's name, and do what you think is right. It is a poor thought that at my time of life I should be advising you to choose the safe and shameful; and I take it back with an apology. Go and do your duty; and be hanged, if you must, like a gentleman. There are worse things in the world than to be hanged.'

'Not many, sir,' said I, smiling.

'Why, yes, yes, sir,' he cried, 'very many. And it would be ten times better for your uncle (to go no farther afield) if he were dangling decently upon a gibbet.'

Thereupon he turned into the house (still in a great fervour of mind, so that I saw I had pleased him heartily) and there he wrote me two letters, making his comments on them as he wrote.

'This,' says he, 'is to my bankers, the British Linen Company, placing a credit to your name. Consult Mr Thomson; he will know of ways; and you, with this credit, can supply the means. I trust you will be a good husband of your money; but in the affairs of a friend like Mr Thomson, I would be even prodigal. Then, for his kinsman, there is no better way than that you should seek the Advocate, tell him your tale, and offer testimony; whether he may ask it or not, is quite another matter, and will turn on the D. of A. Now that you may reach the Lord Advocate well recommended, I give you here a letter to a namesake of your own the learned Mr Balfour of Pilrig, a man whom I esteem. It will look better that you should be presented by one of your own name; and the laird of Pilrig is much looked up to in the Faculty and stands well with the Lord Advocate Grant. I would not trouble him, if I were you, with any particulars; and (do you know?) I think it would be needless to refer to Mr Thomson. Form yourself upon the laird, he is a good model; when you deal with the Advocate, be discreet; and in all these matters, may the Lord guide you, Mr David!'

Thereupon he took his farewell, and set out with Torrance for the Ferry, while Alan and I turned our faces for the city of Edinburgh. As we went by the footpath and beside the gateposts and the unfinished lodge, we kept looking back at the house of my fathers. It stood there, bare and great and smokeless,

*The Duke of Argyle.

like a place not lived in; only in one of the top windows, there was the peak of a nightcap bobbing up and down and back and forward, like the head of a rabbit from a burrow. I had little welcome when I came, and less kindness while I stayed; but at least I was watched as I went away.

Alan and I went slowly forward upon our way, having little heart either to walk or speak. The same thought was uppermost in both, that we were near the time of our parting; and remembrance of all the bygone days sate upon us sorely. We talked indeed of what should be done; and it was resolved that Alan should keep to the country, biding now here, now there, but coming once in the day to a particular place where I might be able to communicate with him, either in my own person or by messenger. In the meanwhile, I was to seek out a lawyer, who was an Appin Stewart, and a man therefore to be wholly trusted; and it should be his part to find a ship and to arrange for Alan's safe embarkation. No sooner was this business done, than the words seemed to leave us; and though I would seek to jest with Alan under the name of Mr Thomson, and he with me on my new clothes and my estate, you could feel very well that we were nearer tears than laughter.

We came the by-way over the hill of Corstorphine; and when we got near to the place called Rest-and-be-Thankful, and looked down on Corstorphine bogs and over to the city and the castle on the hill, we both stopped, for we both knew without a word said, that we had come to where our ways parted. Here he repeated to me once again what had been agreed upon between us; the address of the lawyer, the daily hour at which Alan might be found, and the signals that were to be made by any that came seeking him. Then I gave what money I had (a guinea or two of Rankeillor's) so that he should not starve in the meanwhile; and then we stood a space, and looked over at Edinburgh in silence.

'Well, good-bye,' said Alan, and held out his left hand.

'Good-bye,' said I, and gave the hand a little grasp, and went off down hill.

Neither one of us looked the other in the face, nor so long as he was in my view did I take one back glance at the friend I was leaving. But as I went on my way to the city, I felt so lost and lonesome, that I could have found it in my heart to sit down by the dyke, and cry and weep like any baby.

It was coming near noon when I passed in by the West Kirk and the Grassmarket into the streets of the capital. The huge height of the buildings, running up to ten and fifteen storeys, the narrow arched entries that continually vomited passengers, the wares of the merchants in their windows, the hubbub and endless stir, the foul smells and the fine clothes, and a hundred other particulars too small to mention, struck me into a kind of stupor of surprise, so that I let the crowd carry me to and fro; and yet all the time what I was thinking of was Alan at Rest-and-be-Thankful; and all the time (although you would think I would not choose but be delighted with these braws and novelties) there was a cold gnawing in my inside like a remorse for something wrong.

The hand of Providence brought me in my drifting to the very doors of the British Linen Company's bank.

[Just there, with his hand upon his fortune, the present editor inclines for the time to say farewell to David. How Alan escaped, and what was done about the murder, with a variety of other delectable particulars, may be some day set forth. That is a thing however, that hinges on the public fancy. The editor has a great kindness for both Alan and David, and would gladly spend much of his life in their society; but in this he may find himself to stand alone. In the fear of which, and lest any one should complain of scurvy usage, he hastens to protest that all went well with both, in the limited and human sense of the word 'well'; that whatever befell them, it was not dishonour, and whatever failed them, they were not found wanting to themselves.]

WEIR OF
HERMISTON

TO MY WIFE

I saw rain falling and the rainbow drawn
On Lammermuir. Hearkening I heard again
In my precipitous city beaten bells
Winnow the keen sea wind. And here afar.
Intent on my own race and place, I wrote.
  Take thou the writing: thine it is. For who
Burnished the sword, blew on the drowsy coal,
Held still the target higher, chary of praise
And prodigal of counsel – who but thou?
So now, in the end, if this the least be good,
If any deed be done, if any fire
Burn in the imperfect page, the praise be thine.

INTRODUCTORY

IN THE WILD END OF A moorland parish, far out of the sight of any house, there stands a cairn among the heather, and a little by east of it, in the going down of the braeside, a monument with some verses half defaced. It was here that Claverhouse shot with his own hand the Praying Weaver of Balweary, and the chisel of Old Mortality has clinked on that lonely gravestone. Public and domestic history have thus marked with a bloody finger this hollow among the hills; and since the Cameronian gave his life there, two hundred years ago, in a glorious folly, and without comprehension or regret, the silence of the moss has been broken once again by the report of firearms and the cry of the dying.

The Deil's Hags was the old name. But the place is now called Francie's Cairn. For a while it was told that Francie walked. Aggie Hogg met him in the gloaming by the cairnside, and he spoke to her with chattering teeth, so that his words were lost. He pursued Rob Todd (if any one could have believed Robbie) for the space of half a mile with pitiful entreaties. But the age is one of incredulity; these superstitious decorations speedily fell off; and the facts of the story itself, like the bones of a giant buried there and half dug up, survived, naked and imperfect, in the memory of the scattered neighbours. To this day, of winter nights, when the sleet is on the window and the cattle are quiet in the byre, there will be told again, amid the silence of the young and the additions and corrections of the old, the tale of the Justice-Clerk and of his son, young Hermiston, that vanished from men's knowledge; of the two Kirsties and the Four Black Brothers of the Cauldstaneslap; and of Frank Innes, 'the young fool advocate,' that came into these moorland parts to find his destiny.

CHAPTER ONE

Life and Death of Mrs Weir

THE LORD JUSTICE-CLERK was a stranger in that part of the country; but his lady wife was known there from a child, as her race had been before her. The old 'riding Rutherfords of Hermiston,' of whom she was the last descendant, had been famous men of yore, ill neighbours, ill subjects, and ill husbands to their wives though not their properties. Tales of them were rife for twenty miles about; and their name was even printed in the page of our Scots histories, not always to their credit. One bit the dust at Flodden; one was hanged at his peel door by James the Fifth; another fell dead in a carouse with Tom Dalyell; while a fourth (and that was Jean's own father) died presiding at a Hell-Fire Club, of which he was the founder. There were many heads shaken in Crossmichael at that judgment; the more so as the man had a villainous reputation among high and low, and both with the godly and the worldly. At that very hour of his demise, he had ten going pleas before the Session, eight of them oppressive. And the same doom extended even to his agents; his grieve, that had been his right hand in many a left-hand business, being cast from his horse one night and drowned in a peat-hag on the Kye-skairs; and his very doer (although lawyers have long spoons) surviving him not long, and dying on a sudden in a bloody flux.

In all these generations, while a male Rutherford was in the saddle with his lads, or brawling in a change-huse, there would be always a white-faced wife immured at home in the old peel or the later mansion-house. It seemed this succession of martyrs bided long, but took their vengeance in the end, and that was in the person of the last descendant, Jean. She bore the name of the Rutherfords, but she was the daughter of their trembling wives. At the first she was not wholly without charm. Neighbours recalled in her, as a child, a strain of elfin wilfulness, gentle little mutinies, sad little gaieties, even a morning gleam of beauty that was not to be fulfilled. She withered in the growing, and (whether it was the sins of her sires or the sorrows of her mothers) came to her maturity depressed, and, as it were, defaced; no blood of life in her, no grasp or gaiety; pious, anxious, tender, tearful, and incompetent.

It was a wonder to many that she had married – seeming so wholly of the stuff that makes old maids. But chance cast her in the path of Adam Weir, then the new Lord Advocate, a recognized, risen man, the conqueror of many obstacles, and thus late in the day beginning to think upon a wife. He was one who looked rather to obedience than beauty, yet it would seem he was struck with her at the first look. 'Wha's she?' he said, turning to his host; and, when he had been told, 'Ay,' says he, 'she looks menseful. She minds me——'; and then, after a pause (which some have been daring enough to set down to sentimental recollections), 'Is she releegious?' he asked, and was shortly after, at his own request, presented. The acquaintance, which it seems profane to call a courtship, was pursued with Mr Weir's accustomed industry, and was long a legend, or rather a source of legends, in the Parliament House. He was described coming, rosy with much port, into the drawing-room, walking direct up to the lady, and assailing her with pleasantries, to which the embarrassed fair one responded, in what seemed a kind of agony, 'Eh, Mr Weir!' or 'O, Mr Weir!' or 'Keep me, Mr Weir!' On the very eve of their engagement, it was related that one had drawn near to the tender couple, and had overheard the lady cry out, with the tones of one who talked for the sake of talking, 'Keep me, Mr Weir, and what became of him?' and the profound accents of the suitor reply, 'Haangit, mem, haangit.' The motives upon either side were much debated. Mr Weir must have supposed his bride to be somehow suitable; perhaps he belonged to that class of men who think a weak head the ornament of women – an opinion invariably punished in this life. Her descent and her estate were beyond question. Her wayfaring ancestors and her litigious father had done well by Jean. There was ready money and there were broad acres, ready to fall wholly to the husband, to lend dignity to his descendants, and to himself a title, when he should be called upon the Bench. On the side of Jean, there was perhaps some fascination of curiosity as to this unknown male animal that approached her with the roughness of a ploughman and the *aplomb* of an advocate. Being so trenchantly opposed to all she knew, loved, or understood, he may well have seemed to her the extreme, if scarcely the ideal, of his sex. And besides, he was an ill man to refuse. A little over forty at the period of his marriage, he looked already older, and to the force of manhood added the senatorial dignity of years; it was, perhaps, with an unreverend awe, but he was awful. The Bench, the Bar, and the most experienced and reluctant witness, bowed to his authority – and why not Jeannie Rutherford?

The heresy about foolish women is always punished, I have said, and Lord Hermiston began to pay the penalty at once. His house in George Square was wretchedly ill-guided; nothing answerable to the expense of maintenance but the cellar, which was his own private care. When things went wrong at dinner, as they continually did, my lord would look up the table at his wife: 'I think these broth would be better to sweem in than to sup.' Or else to the butler: 'Here, M'Killop, awa' wi' this Raadical gigot – tak' it to the French, man, and bring me some puddocks! It seems rather a sore kind of a business that I should be all day in Court haanging Raadicals, and get nawthing to my denner.' Of course this was but a manner of speaking, and he had never hanged a man for being a radical in his life; the law, of which he was the faithful minister, directing otherwise. And of course these growls were in the nature of pleasantry, but it was of a recondite sort; and uttered as they were in his resounding voice, and commented on by that expression which they called in the Parliament House 'Hermiston's hanging face' – they struck mere dismay into the wife. She sat before him speechless and fluttering; at each dish, as at a fresh ordeal, her eye hovered toward my lord's countenance and fell again; if he but ate in silence, unspeakable relief was her portion; if there were complaint, the world was darkened. She would seek out the cook, who was always her *sister in the Lord*. 'O, my dear, this is the most dreidful thing that my lord can never be contented in his own house!' she would begin; and weep and pray with the cook; and then the cook would pray with Mrs Weir; and the next day's meal would never be a penny the better – and the next cook (when she came) would be worse, if anything, but just as pious. It was often wondered that Lord Hermiston bore it as he did; indeed, he was a stoical old voluptuary, contented with sound wine and plenty of it. But there were moments when he overflowed. Perhaps half a dozen times in the history of his married life – 'Here! tak' it awa', and bring me a piece bread and kebbuck!' he had exclaimed, with an appalling explosion of his voice and rare gestures. None thought to dispute or to make excuses; the service was arrested; Mrs Weir sat at the head of the table whimpering without disguise; and his lordship opposite munched his bread and cheese in ostentatious disregard. Once only Mrs Weir had ventured to appeal. He was passing her chair on his way into the study.

'O, Edom!' she wailed, in a voice tragic with tears, and reaching out to him both hands, in one of which she held a sopping pocket-handkerchief.

He paused and looked upon her with a face of wrath, into which there stole, as he looked, a twinkle of humour.

'Noansense!' he said. 'You and your noansense! What do I want with a Christian faim'ly? I want Christian broth! Get me a lass that can plain-boil a potato, if she was a whüre off the streets.' And with these words, which echoed in her tender ears like blasphemy, he had passed on to his study and shut the door behind him.

Such was the housewifery in George Square. It was better at Hermiston, where Kirstie Elliott, the sister of a neighbouring bonnet-laird, and an eighteenth cousin of the lady's, bore the charge of all, and kept a trim house and a good country table. Kirstie was a woman in a thousand, clean, capable, notable; once a moorland Helen, and still comely as a blood horse and healthy as the hill wind. High in flesh and voice and colour, she ran the house with her whole intemperate soul, in a bustle, not without buffets. Scarce more pious than decency in those days required, she was the cause of many an anxious thought and many a tearful prayer to Mrs Weir. Housekeeper and mistress renewed the parts of Martha and Mary; and though with a pricking conscience, Mary reposed on Martha's strength as on a rock. Even Lord Hermiston held Kirstie in a particular regard. There were few with whom he unbent so gladly, few whom he favoured with so many pleasantries. 'Kirstie and me maun have our joke,' he would declare, in high good humour, as he buttered Kirstie's scones, and she waited at table. A man who had no need either of love or of popularity, a keen reader of men and of events, there was perhaps only one truth for which he was quite unprepared: he would have been quite unprepared to learn that Kirstie hated him. He thought maid and master were well matched; hard, handy, healthy, broad Scots folk, without a hair of nonsense to the pair of them. And the fact was that she made a goddess and an only child of the effete and tearful lady; and even as she waited at table her hands would sometimes itch for my lord's ears.

Thus, at least, when the family were at Hermiston, not only my lord, but Mrs Weir too, enjoyed a holiday. Free from the dreadful looking-for of the miscarried dinner, she would mind her seam, read her piety books, and take her walk (which was my lord's orders), sometimes by herself, sometimes with Archie, the only child of that scarce natural union. The child was her next bond to life. Her frosted sentiment bloomed again, she breated deep of life, she let loose her heart, in that society. The miracle of her motherhood was ever new to her. The sight of the little man at her skirt intoxicated her with the sense of power, and froze her with the consciousness of her responsibility. She looked forward, and, seeing him in fancy grow up and play his diverse part on the world's theatre, caught in her breath and lifted up her courage with a lively effort. It was only with the child that she forgot herself and was at moments natural; yet it was only with the child that she had conceived and managed to pursue a scheme of conduct. Archie was to be a great man and a good; a minister if possible, a saint for certain. She tried to engage his mind upon her favourite books, Rutherford's *Letters*, Scougal's *Grace Abounding*, and the like. It was a common practice of hers (and strange to remember now) that she would carry the child to the Deil's Hags, sit with him on the Praying Weaver's stone, and talk of the Covenanters till their tears ran down. Her view of history was wholly artless, a design in snow and ink; upon the one side, tender innocents with psalms upon their lips; upon the other, the persecutors, booted, bloody-minded, flushed with wine: a suffering Christ, a raging Beelzebub. *Persecutor* was a word that knocked upon the woman's heart; it was her highest thought of wickedness, and the mark of it was on her house. Her great-great-grandfather had drawn the sword against the Lord's anointed on the field of Rullion Green, and breathed his last (tradition said) in the arms of the detestable Dalyell. Nor could she blind herself to this, that had they lived in those old days, Hermiston himself would have been numbered alongside of Bloody Mackenzie and the politic Lauderdale and Rothes, in the band of God's immediate enemies. The sense of this moved her to the more fervour; she had a voice for that name of *persecutor* that thrilled in the child's marrow; and when one day the mob hooted and hissed them all in my lord's travelling carriage, and cried, 'Down with the persecutor! down with Hanging Hermiston!' and mamma covered her eyes and wept, and papa let down the glass and looked out upon the rabble with his droll formidable face, bitter and smiling, as they said he sometimes looked when he gave sentence, Archie was for the moment too much amazed to be alarmed, but he had scarce got his mother by herself before his shrill voice was raised demanding an explanation: Why had they called papa a persecutor?

'Keep me, my precious!' she exclaimed. 'Keep me, my dear! this is poleetical. Ye must never ask me anything poleetical, Erchie. Your faither is a great man, my dear, and it's no for me or you to be judging him. It would be telling us all, if we behaved ourselves in our several stations the way your faither does in his high office; and let me hear no more of any such disrespectful and undutiful questions! No that you meant to be undutiful, my lamb; and your mother kens that – she kens it well, dearie!' And so slid off to safer topics, and left on the mind of the child an obscure but ineradicable sense of something wrong.

Mrs Weir's philosophy of life was summed in one expression – tenderness. In her view of the universe, which was all lighted up with a glow out of the doors of hell, good people must walk there in a kind of ecstasy of tenderness. The beasts and plants had no souls; they were here but for a day, and let their day pass gently! And as for the immortal men, on what black, downward path were many of them wending, and to what a horror of an immortality! 'Are not two sparrows,' 'Whosoever shall smite thee,' 'God sendeth His rain,' 'Judge not, that ye be not judged' – these texts made her body of divinity; she put them on in the morning with her clothes and lay down to sleep with them at night; they haunted her like a favourite air, they clung about her like a favourite perfume. Their minister was a marrowy expounder of the law, and my lord sat under him with relish; but Mrs Weir respected him from far off; heard him (like the cannon of a beleaguered city) usefully booming outside on the dogmatic ramparts; and meanwhile, within and out of shot, dwelt in her private garden which she watered with grateful tears. It seems strange to say of this colourless and ineffectual woman, but she was a true enthusiast, and might have made the sunshine and the glory of a cloister. Perhaps none but Archie knew she could be eloquent; perhaps none but he had seen her – her colour raised, her hands clasped or quivering – glow with gentle ardour. There is a corner of the policy of Hermiston, where you come suddenly in view of the summit of Black Fell, sometimes like the mere grass top of a hill, sometimes (and this is her own expression) like a precious jewel in the heavens. On such days, upon the sudden view of it, her hand would tighten on the child's fingers, her voice rise like a song. '*I to the hills!*' she would repeat. 'And O, Erchie, are'na these like the hills of Naphtali?' and her tears wuld flow.

Upon an impressionable child the effect of this continual and pretty accompaniment to life was deep. The woman's quietism and piety passed on to his different nture undiminished; but whereas in her it was a native sentiment, in him it was only an implanted dogma. Nature and the child's pugnacity at times revolted. A cad from the Potterrow once struck him in the mouth; he struck back, the pair fought it out in the back stable lane towards the Meadows, and Archie returned with a considerable decline in the number of his front teeth, and unregenerately boasting of the losses of the foe. It was a sore day for Mrs Weir; she wept and prayed over the infant backslider until my lord was due from Court, and she must resume that air of tremulous composure with which she always greeted him. The judge was that day in an observant mood, and remarked upon the absent teeth.

'I am afraid Erchie will have been fechting with some of they blagyard lads,' said Mrs Weir.

My lord's voice rang out as it did seldom in the privacy of his own house. 'I'll have nonn of that, sir!' he cried. 'Do you hear me? – nonn of that! No son of mine shall be speldering in the glaur with any dirty raibble.'

The anxious mother was grateful for so much support; she had even feared the contrary. And that night when she put the child to bed – 'Now, my dear, ye see!' she said, 'I told you what your faither would think of it, if he heard ye had fallen into this dreidful sin; and let you and me pray to God that ye may be keepit from the like temptation or stren'thened to resist it!'

The womanly falsity of this was thrown away. Ice and iron cannot be welded; and the points of view of the Justice-Clerk and Mrs Weir were not less unassimilable. The character and position of his father had long been a stumbling-block to Archie, and with every year of his age the difficulty grew more instant. The man was mostly silent; when he spoke at all, it was to speak of the things of the world, always in a worldly spirit, often in language that the child had been schooled to think coarse, and sometimes with words that he knew to be sins in themselves. Tenderness was the first duty, and my lord was invariably harsh. God was love; the name of my lord (to all who knew him) was fear. In the world, as schematised for Archie by his mother, the place was marked for such a creature. There were some whom it was good to pity and well (though very likely useless) to pray for; they were named reprobates, goats, God's enemies, brands for the burning; and Archie tallied every mark of identification, and drew the inevitable private inference that the Lord Justice-Clerk was the chief of sinners.

The mother's honesty was scarce complete. There was one influence she feared for the child and still secretly combated; that was my lord's; and half unconsciously, half in a wilful blindness, she continued to undermine her husband with his son. As long as Archie remained silent, she did so ruthlessly, with a single eye to heaven and the child's salvation; but the day came when Archie spoke. It was 1801, and Archie was seven, and beyond his years for curiosity and logic, when he brought the case up openly. If judging were sinful and forbidden, how came papa to be a judge? to have that sin for a trade? to bear the name of it for a distinction?

'I can't see it,' said the little Rabbi, and wagged his head.

Mrs Weir abounded in commonplace replies.

'No, I canna see it,' reiterated Archie. 'And I'll tell you what, mamma, I don't think you and me's justifeed in staying with him.'

The woman awoke to remorse; she saw herself disloyal to her man, her sovereign and bread-winner, in whom (with what she had of worldliness) she took a certain subdued pride. She expatiated in reply on my lord's honour and greatness; his useful services in this world of sorrow and wrong, and the place in which he stood, far above where babes and innocents could hope to see or criticise. But she had builded too well – Archie had his answers pat: Were not babes and innocents the type of the kingdom of heaven? Were not honour and greatness the badges of the world? And at any rate, how about the mob that had once seethed about the carriage?

'It's all very fine,' he concluded, 'but in my opinion, papa has no right to be it. And it seems that's not the worst yet of it. It seems he's called "the Hanging Judge" – it seems he's crooool. I'll tell you what it is, mamma, there's a tex' borne in upon me: It were better for that man if a milestone were bound upon his back and him flung into the deepestmost pairts of the sea.'

'O, my lamb, ye must never say the like of that!' she cried. 'Ye're to honour faither and mother, dear, that your days may be long in the land. It's Atheists that cry out against him – French Atheists, Erchie! Ye would never surely even yourself down to be saying the same thing as French Atheists? It would break my heart to think that of you. And O, Erchie, here are'na *you* setting up to *judge*? And have ye no forgot God's plain command – the First with Promise, dear? Mind you upon the beam and the mote!'

Having thus carried the war into the enemy's camp, the terrified lady breathed again. And no doubt it is easy thus to circumvent a child with catchwords, but it may be questioned how far it is effectual. An instinct in his breast detects the quibble, and a voice condemns it. He will instantly submit, privately hold the same opinion. For even in this simple and antique relation of the mother and the child, hypocrisies are multiplied.

When the Court rose that year and the family returned to Hermiston, it was a common remark in all the country that the lady was sore failed. She seemed to loose and seize again her touch with life, now sitting inert in a sort of durable bewilderment, anon waking to feverish and weak activity. She dawdled about the lasses at their work, looking stupidly on; she fell to rummaging in old cabinets and presses, and desisted when half through; she would begin remarks with an air of animation and drop them without a struggle. Her common appearance was of one who has forgotten something and is trying to remember; and when she overhauled, one after another, the worthless and touching mementoes of her youth, she might have been seeking the clue to that lost thought. During this period, she gave many gifts to the neighbours and house lasses, giving them with a manner of regret that embarrassed the recipients.

The last night of all she was busy on some female work, and toiled upon it with so manifest and painful a devotion that my lord (who was not often curious) inquired as to its nature.

She blushed to the eyes. 'O, Edom, it's for you!' she said. 'It's slippers. I – I hae never made ye any.'

'Ye daft auld wife!' returned his lordship. 'A bonny figure I would be, palmering about in bauchles!'

The next day, at the hour of her walk, Kirstie interfered. Kirstie took this decay of her mistress very hard; bore her a grudge, quarrelled with and railed upon her, the anxiety of a genuine love wearing the disguise of temper. This day of all days she insisted disrespectfully, with rustic fury, that Mrs Weir should stay at home. But, 'No, no,' she said, 'It's my lord's orders,' and set forth as usual. Archie was visible in the acre bog, engaged upon some childish enterprise, the instrument of which was mire; and she stood and looked at him a while like one about to call; then thought otherwise, sighed, and shook her head, and proceeded on her rounds alone. The house lasses were at the burnside washing, and saw here pass with her loose, weary, dowdy gait.

'She's a terrible feckless wife, the mistress!' said the one.

'Tut,' said the other, 'the wumman's seeck.'

'Weel, I canna see nae differ in her,' returned the first. 'A füshionless quean, a feckless carline.'

The poor creature thus discussed rambled a while in the grounds without a purpose. Tides in her mind ebbed and flowed, and carried her to and fro like seaweed. She tried a path, paused, returned, and tried another; questing, forgetting her quest; the spirit of choice extinct in her bosom, or devoid of sequency. On a sudden, it appeared as though she had remembered, or had formed a resolution, wheeled about, returned with hurried steps, and appeared in the dining-room, where Kirstie was at the cleaning, like one charged with an important errand.

'Kirstie!' she began, and paused; and then with conviction, 'Mr Weir isna speeritually minded, but he has been a good man to me.'

It was perhaps the first time since her husband's elevation that she had forgotten the handle to his name, of which the tender, inconsistent woman was not a little proud. And when Kirstie looked up at the speaker's face, she was aware of a change.

'Godsake, what's the maitter wi' ye, mem?' cried the housekeeper, starting from the rug.

'I do not ken,' answered her mistress, shaking her head. 'But he is not speeritually minded, my dear.'

'Here, sit down with ye! Godsake, what ails the wife?' cried Kirstie, and helped and forced her into my lord's own chair by the cheek of the hearth.

'Keep me, what's this?' she gasped. 'Kirstie, what's this? I'm frich'ened.'

They were her last words.

It was the lowering nightfall when my lord returned. He had the sunset in his back, all clouds and glory; and before him, by the wayside, spied Kirstie Elliott waiting. She was dissolved in tears, and addressed him in the high, false note of barbarous mourning, such as still lingers modified among Scots heather.

'The Lord peety ye, Hermiston! the lord prepare ye!' she keened out. 'Weary upon me, that I should have to tell it!'

He reined in his horse and looked upon her with the hanging face.

'Has the French landit?' cried he.

'Man, man,' she said, 'is that a' ye can think of? The Lord prepare ye: the Lord comfort and support ye!'

'Is onybody deid?' says his lordship. 'It's no Erchie?'

'Bethankit, no!' exclaimed the woman, startled into a more natural tone. 'Na, na, it's no sae bad as that. It's the mistress, my lord; she just fair flittit before my e'en. She just gi'ed a sab and was by wi' it. Eh, my bonny Miss Jeannie, that I mind sae weel!' and forth again upon that pouring tide of lamentation in which women of her class excel and over-abound.

Lord Hermiston sat in the saddle beholding her. Then he seemed to recover command upon himself.

'Weel, it's something of the suddenest,' said he. 'But she was a dwaibly body from the first.'

And he rode home at a precipitate amble with Kirstie at his horse's heels.

Dressed as she was for her last walk, they had laid the dead lady on her bed. She was never interesting in life; in death she was not impressive; and as her husband stood before her, with his hands crossed behind his powerful back, that which he looked upon was the very image of the insignificant.

'Her and me were never cut out for one another,' he remarked at last. 'It was a daft-like marriage.' And then, with a most unusual gentleness of tone, 'Puir bitch,' said he, 'puir bitch!' then suddenly: 'Where's Erchie?'

Kirstie had decoyed him to her room and given him 'a jeely-piece.'

'Ye have some kind of gumption, too,' observed the judge, and considered his housekeeper grimly. 'When all's said,' he added, 'I micht have done waur – I micht have been marriet upon a skirling Jezebel like you!'

'There's naebody thinking of you, Hermiston!' cried the offended woman. 'We think of her that's out of her sorrows. And could *she* have done waur? Tell me that, Hermiston – tell me that before her clay-cauld corp!'

'Weel, there's some of them gey an' ill to please,' observed his lordship.

CHAPTER TWO

Father and Son

MY LORD JUSTICE-CLERK WAS known to many; the man Adam Weir perhaps to none. He had nothing to explain or to conceal; he sufficed wholly and silently to himself; and that part of our nature which goes out (too often with false coin) to acquire glory or love, seemed in him to be omitted. He did not try to be loved, he did not care to be; it is probable the very thought of it was a stranger to his mind. He was an admired lawyer, a highly unpopular judge; and he looked down upon those who were his inferiors in either distinction, who were lawyers of less grasp or judges not so much detested. In all the rest of his days and doings, not one trace of vanity appeared; and he went on through life with a mechanical movement, as of the unconscious, that was almost august.

He saw little of his son. In the childish maladies with which the boy was troubled, he would make daily inquiries and daily pay him a visit, entering the sick-room with a facetious and appalling countenance, letting off a few perfunctory jests, and going again swiftly, to the patient's relief. Once, a court holiday falling opportunely, my lord had his carriage, and drove the child himself to Hermiston, the customary place of convalescence. It is conceivable he had been more than usually anxious, for that journey always remained in Archie's memory as a thing apart, his father having related to him from beginning to end, and with much detail, three authentic murder cases. Archie went the usual round of other Edinburgh boys, the high school and the college; and Hermiston looked on, or rather looked away, with scarce an affectation of interest in his progress. Daily, indeed, upon a signal after dinner, he was brought in, given nuts and a glass of port, regarded sardonically, sarcastically questioned. 'Well, sir, and what have you donn with your book to-day?' my lord might begin, and set him posers in law Latin. To a child just stumbling into Corderius, Papinian and Paul proved quite invincible. But papa had memory of no other. He was not harsh to the little scholar, having a vast fund of patience learned upon the bench, and was at no pains whether to conceal or to express his disappointment. 'Well, ye have a long jaunt before ye yet!' he might observe, yawning, and fall back on his own thoughts (as like as not) until the time came for separation, and my lord would take the decanter and the glass, and be off to the back chamber looking on the Meadows, where he toiled on his cases till the hours were small. There was no 'fuller man' on the bench; his memory was marvellous, though wholly legal; if he had to 'advise' extempore, none did it better; yet there was none who more earnestly prepared. As he thus watched in the night, or sat at table and forgot the presence of his son, no doubt but he tasted deeply of recondite pleasures. To be wholly devoted to some intellectual exercise is to have succeeded in life; and perhaps only in law and the higher mathematics may this devotion be maintained, suffice to itself without reaction, and find continual rewards without excitement. This atmosphere of his father's sterling industry was the best of Archie's education. Assuredly it did not attract him; assuredly it rather rebutted and depressed. Yet it was still present, unobserved like the ticking of a clock, an arid ideal, a tasteless stimulant in the boy's life.

But Hermiston was not all of one piece. He was, besides, a mighty toper; he could sit at wine until the day dawned, and pass directly from the table to the bench with a steady hand and a clear head. Beyond the third bottle, he showed the plebeian in a larger print; the low, gross accent, the low, foul mirth, grew broader and commoner; he became less formidable, and infinitely more disgusting. Now, the boy had inherited from Jean Rutherford a shivering delicacy, unequally mated with potential violence. In the playing-fields, and amongst his own companions, he repaid a coarse expression with a blow; at his father's table (when the time came for him to join these revels) he turned pale and sickened in silence. Of all the guests whom he there encountered, he had toleration for only one: David Keith Carnegie, Lord Glenalmond. Lord Glenalmond was tall and emaciated, with long features and long delicate hands. He was often compared with the statue of Forbes of Culloden in the Parliament House; and his blue eye, at more than sixty, preserved some of the fire of youth. His exquisite disparity with any of his fellow-guests, his appearance as of an artist and an aristocrat stranded in rude company, riveted the boy's attention; and as curiosity and interest are the things in the world that are the most immediately and certainly rewarded, Lord Glenalmond was attracted by the boy.

'And so this is your son, Hermiston?' he asked, laying his hand on Archie's shoulder. 'He's getting a big lad.'

'Hout!' said the gracious father, 'just his mother over again – daurna say boo to a goose!'

But the stranger retained the boy, talked to him, drew him out, found in him a taste for letters, and a fine, ardent, modest, youthful soul; and encouraged him to be a visitor on Sunday evenings in his bare, cold, lonely dining-room, where he sat and read in the isolation of a bachelor grown old in refinement. The beautiful gentleness and grace of the old judge, and the delicacy of his person, thoughts, and language, spoke to Archie's heart in its own tongue. He conceived the ambition to be such another, and, when the day came for him to choose a profession, it was in emulation of Lord Glenalmond, not of Lord Hermiston, that he chose the Bar. Hermiston looked on at this friendship with some secret pride, but openly with the intolerance of scorn. He scarce lost an opportunity to put them down with a rough jape; and, to say truth, it was not difficult, for they were neither of them quick. He had a word of contempt for the whole crowd of poets, painters, fiddlers, and their admirers, the bastard race of amateurs, which was continually on his lips. 'Signor Feedle-eerie!' he would say. 'O, for Goad's sake, no more of the Signor!'

'You and my father are great friends, are you not?' asked Archie once.

'There is no man that I more respect, Archie,' replied Lord Glenalmond. 'He is two things of price. He is a great lawyer, and he is upright as the day.'

'You and he are so different,' said the boy, his eyes dwelling on those of his old friend, like a lover's on his mistress's.

'Indeed so,' replied the judge; 'very different. And so I fear are you and he. Yet I would like it very ill if my young friend were to misjudge his father. He has all the Roman virtues: Cato and Brutus were such; I think a son's heart might well be proud of such an ancestry of one.'

'And I would sooner he were a plaided herd,' cried Archie, with sudden bitterness.

'And that is neither very wise, nor I believe entirely true,' returned Glenalmond. 'Before you are done you will find some of these expressions rise on you like a remorse. They are merely literary and decorative; they do not aptly express your thought, nor is your thought clearly apprehended, and no doubt your father (if he were here) would say, "Signor Feedle-eerie!"'

With the infinitely delicate sense of youth, Archie avoided the subject from that hour. It was perhaps a pity. Had he but talked – talked freely – let himself gush out in words (the way youth loves to do and should), there might have been no tale to write upon the Weirs of Hermiston. But the shadow of a threat of ridicule sufficed; in the slight tartness of these words he read a prohibition; and it is likely that Glenalmond meant it so.

Besides the veteran, the boy was without confidant or friend. Serious and eager, he came through school and college, and moved among a crowd of the indifferent, in the seclusion of his shyness. He grew up handsome, with an open, speaking countenance, with graceful, youthful ways; he was clever, he took prizes, he shone in the Speculative Society. It should seem he must become the centre of a crowd of friends; but something that was in part the delicacy of his mother, in part the austerity of his father, held him aloof from all. It is a fact, and a strange one, that among his contemporaries Hermiston's son was thought to be a chip of the old block. 'You're a friend of Archie Weir's?' said one to Frank Innes; and Innes replied, with his usual flippancy and more than his usual insight: 'I know Weir, but I never met Archie.' No one had met Archie, a malady most incident to only sons. He flew his private signal, and none heeded it; it seemed he was abroad in a world from which the very hope of intimacy was banished; and he looked round about him on the concourse of his fellow-students, and forward to the trivial days and acquaintances that were to come, without hope or interest.

As time went on, the tough and rough old sinner felt himself drawn to the son of his loins and sole continuator of his new family, with softnesses of sentiment that he could hardly credit and was wholly impotent to express. With a face, voice, and manner trained through forty years to terrify and repel, Rhadamanthus may be great, but he will scarce be engaging. It is a fact that he tried to propitiate Archie, but a fact that cannot be too lightly taken; the attempt was so unconspicuously made, the failure so stoically supported. Sympathy is not due to these steadfast iron natures. If he failed to gain his son's friendship, or even his son's toleration, on he went up the great, bare staircase of his duty, uncheered and undepressed. There might have been more pleasure in his relations with Archie, so much he may have recognized at moments; but pleasure was a by-product of the singular chemistry of life, which only fools expected.

An idea of Archie's attitude, since we are all grown up and have forgotten the days of our youth, it is more difficult to convey. He made no attempt whatsover to understand the man with whom he dined and breakfasted. Parsimony of pain, glut of pleasure, these are the two alternating ends of youth; and Archie was of the parsimonious. The wind blew cold out of a certain quarter – he turned his back upon it; stayed as little as was possible in his father's presence; and when there, averted his eyes as much as was decent from his father's face. The lamp shone for many hundred days upon these two at table – my lord, ruddy, gloomy, and unreverend; Archie with a potential brightness that was always dimmed and veiled in that society; and there were not, perhaps, in Christendom two men more radically strangers. The father, with a grand simplicity, either spoke of what interested himself, or maintained an unaffected silence. The son turned in his head for some topic that should be quite safe, that would spare him fresh evidences either of my lord's inherent grossness or of the innocence of his inhumanity; treading gingerly the ways of intercourse, like a lady gathering up her skirts in a by-path. If he made a mistake, and my lord began to abound in matter of offence, Archie drew himself up, his brow grew dark, his share of the talk expired; but my lord would faithfully and cheerfully continue to pour out the worst of himself before his silent and offended son.

'Well, it's a poor hert that never rejoices!' he would say, at the conclusion of such a nightmare interview. 'But I must get to my plew-stilts.' And he would seclude himself as usual in the back room, and Archie go forth into the night and the city quivering with animosity and scorn.

CHAPTER THREE

In the Matter of the Hanging of Duncan Jopp

IT CHANCED IN THE YEAR 1813 that Archie strayed one day into the Judiciary Court. The macer made room for the son of the presiding judge. In the dock, the centre of men's eyes, there stood a whey-coloured, misbegotten caitiff, Duncan Jopp, on trial for his life. His story, as it was raked out before him in that public scene, was one of disgrace and vice and cowardice, the very nakedness of crime; and the creature heard and it seemed at times as though he understood – as if at times he forgot the horror of the place he stood in, and remembered the shame of what had brought him there. He kept his head bowed and his hands clutched upon the rail; his hair dropped in his eyes and at times he flung it back; and now he glanced about the audience in a sudden fellness of terror, and now looked in the face of his judge and gulped. There was pinned about his throat a piece of dingy flannel; and this it was perhaps that turned the scale in Archie's mind between disgust and pity. The creature stood in a vanishing point; yet a little while, and he was still a man, and had eyes and apprehension; yet a little longer, and with a last sordid piece of pageantry, he would cease to be. And here, in the meantime, with a trait of human nature that caught at the beholder's breath, he was tending a sore throat.

Over against him, my Lord Hermiston occupied the bench in the red robes of criminal jurisdiction, his face framed in the white wig. Honest all through, he did not affect the virtue of impartiality; this was no case for refinement; there was a man to be hanged, he would have said, and he was hanging him. Nor was it possible to see his lordship, and acquit him of gusto in the task. It was plain he gloried in the exercise of his trained facilities, in the clear sight which pierced at once into the joint of fact, in the rude, unvarnished gibes with which he demolished every figment of defence. He took his ease and jested, unbending in that solemn place with some of the freedom of the tavern; and the rag of man with the flannel round his neck was hunted gallowsward with jeers.

Duncan had a mistress, scarce less forlorn and greatly older than himself, who came up, whimpering and curtseying, to add the weight of her betrayal. My lord gave her the oath in his most roaring voice, and added an intolerant warning.

'Mind what ye say now, Janet,' said he. 'I have an e'e upon ye, I'm ill to jest with.'

Presently, after she was tremblingly embarked on her story, 'And what made ye do this, ye auld runt?' the Court interposed. 'Do ye mean to tell me ye was the panel's mistress?'

'If you please, ma loard,' whined the female.

'Godsake! ye made a bonny couple,' observed his lordship; and there was something so formidable and ferocious in his scorn that not even the galleries thought to laugh.

The summing up contained some jewels. 'These two peetiable creatures seem to have made up thegither, it's not for us to explain why.' – 'The panel, who (whatever else he may be) appears to be equally ill set-out in mind and boady,' – 'Neither the panel nor yet the old wife appears to have had so much common sense as even to tell a lie when it was necessary.' And in the course of sentencing, my lord had this *obiter dictum*: 'I have been the means, under God, of haanging a great number, but never just such a disjaskit rascal as yourself.' The words were strong in themselves; the light and heat and detonation of their delivery, and the savage pleasure of the speaker in his task, made them tingle in the ears.

When all was over, Archie came forth again into a changed world. Had there been the least redeeming greatness in the crime, any obscurity, any dubiety, perhaps he might have understood. But the culprit stood, with his sore throat, in the sweat of his mortal agony, without defence or excuse: a thing to cover up with blushes: a being so much sunk beneath the zones of sympathy that pity might seem harmless. And the judge had pursued him with a monstrous, relishing gaiety, horrible to be conceived, a trait for nightmares. It is one thing to spear a tiger, another to crush a toad; there are aesthetics even of the slaughterhouse; and the loathsomeness of Duncan Jopp enveloped and infected the image of his judge.

Archie passed by his friends in the High Street with incoherent words and gestures. He saw Holyrood in a dream, remembrance of its romance awoke in him and faded; he had a vision of the old radiant stories, of Queen Mary and Prince Charlie, of the hooded stag, of the splendour and crime, the velvet and bright iron of the past; and dismissed them with a cry of pain. He lay and moaned in the Hunter's Bog, and the heavens were dark above him and the grass of the field an offence. 'This is my father,' he said. 'I draw my life from him; the

flesh upon my bones is his, the bread I am fed with is the wages of these horrors.'
He recalled his mother, and ground his forehead in the earth. He thought of
flight, and where was he to flee to? of other lives, but was there any life worth
living in this den of savage and jeering animals?

The interval before the execution was like a violent dream. He met his father;
he would not look at him, he could not speak to him. It seemed there was no
living creature but must have been swift to recognize that imminent animosity;
but the hide of the Justice-Clerk remained impenetrable. Had my lord been
talkative the truce could never have subsisted; but he was by fortune in one of
his humours of sour silence; and under the very guns of his broadside, Archie
nursed the enthusiasm of rebellion. It seemed to him, from the top of his
nineteen years' experience, as if he were marked at birth to be the perpetrator of
some signal action, to set back fallen Mercy, to overthrow the usurping devil
that sat, horned and hoofed, on her throne. Seductive Jacobin figments, which
he had often refuted at the Speculative, swam up in his mind and startled him as
with voices: and he seemed to himself to walk accompanied by an almost
tangible presence of new beliefs and duties.

On the named morning he was at the place of execution. He saw the fleering
rabble, the flinching wretch produced. He looked on for a while at a certain
parody of devotion, which seemed to strip the wretch of his last claim to
manhood. Then followed the brutal instant of extinction, and the paltry
dangling of the remains like a broken jumping-jack. He had been prepared for
something terrible, not for this tragic meanness. He stood a moment silent, and
then – 'I denounce this God-defying murder,' he shouted; and his father, if he
must have disclaimed the sentiment, might have owned the stentorian voice
with which it was uttered.

Frank Innes dragged him from the spot. The two handsome lads followed the
same course of study and recreation, and felt a certain mutual attraction,
founded mainly on good looks. It had never gone deep; Frank was by nature a
thin, jeering creature, not truly susceptible whether of feeling or inspiring
friendship; and the relation between the pair was altogether on the outside, a
thing of common knowledge and the pleasantries that spring from a common
acquaintance. The more credit to Frank that he was appalled by Archie's
outburst, and at least conceived the design of keeing him in sight, and, if
possible, in hand, for the day. But Archie, who had just defied – was it God or
Satan? – would not listen to the word of a college companion.

'I will not go with you,' he said. 'I do not desire your company, sir; I would be
alone.'

'Here, Weir, man, don't be absurd,' said Innes, keeping a tight hold upon his
sleeve. 'I will not let you go until I know what you mean to do with yourself; it's
no use brandishing that staff.' For indeed at that moment Archie had made a
sudden – perhaps a warlike – movement. 'This has been the most insane affair;
you know it has. You know very well that I'm playing the good Samaritan. All I
wish is to keep you quiet.'

'If quietness is what you wish, Mr Innes,' said Archie, 'and you will promise to
leave me entirely to myself, I will tell you so much, that I am going to walk in
the country and admire the beauties of nature.'

'Honour bright?' asked Frank.

'I am not in the habit of lying, Mr Innes,' retorted Archie. 'I have the honour of wishing you good-day.'

'You won't forget the Spec.?' asked Innes.

'The Spec.?' said Archie. 'O no, I won't forget the Spec.'

And the one young man carried his tortured spirit forth of the city and all the day long, by one road and another, in an endless pilgrimage of misery; while the other hastened smilingly to spread the news of Weir's access of insanity, and to drum up for that night a full attendance at the Speculative, where further eccentric developments might certainly be looked for. I doubt if Innes had the least belief in his prediction; I think it flowed rather from a wish to make the story as good and the scandal as great as possible; not from any ill-will to Archie – from the mere pleasure of beholding interested faces. But for all that his words were prophetic. Archie did not forget the Spec.; he put in an appearance there at the due time, and, before the evening was over, had dealt a memorable shock to his companions. It chanced he was the president of the night. He sat in the same room where the Society still meets – only the portraits were not there: the men who afterwards sat for them were then but beginning their career. The same lustre of many tapers shed its light over the meeting; the same chair, perhaps, supported him that so many of us have sat in since. At times he seemed to forget the business of the evening, but even in these periods he sat with a great air of energy and determination. At times he meddled bitterly, and launched with defiance those fines which are the precious and rarely used artillery of the president. He little thought, as he did so, how he resembled his father, but his friends remarked upon it, chuckling. So far, in his high place above his fellow-students, he seemed set beyond the possibility of any scandal; but his mind was made up – he was determined to fulfil the sphere of his offence. He signed to Innes (whom he had just fined, and who just impeached his ruling) to succeed him in the chair, stepped down from the platform, and took his place by the chimney-piece, the shine of many wax tapers from above illuminating his pale face, the glow of the great red fire relieving from behind his slim figure. He had to propose, as an amendment to the next subject in the case-book, 'Whether capital punishment be consistent with God's will or man's policy?'

A breath of embarrassment, of something like alarm, passed round the room, so daring did these words appear upon the lips of Hermiston's only son. But the amendment was not seconded; the previous question was promptly moved and unanimously voted, and the momentary scandal smuggled by. Innes triumphed in the fulfilment of his prophecy. He and Archie were now become the heroes of the night; but whereas every one crowded about Innes, when the meeting broke up, but one of all his companions came to speak to Archie.

'Weir, man! That was an extraordinary raid of yours!' observed this courageous member, taking him confidentially by the arm as they went out.

'I don't think if a raid,' said Archie grimly. 'More like a war. I saw that poor brute hanged this morning, and my gorge rises at it yet.'

'Hut-tut,' returned his companion, and, dropping his arm like something hot, he sought the less tense society of others.

Archie found himself alone. The last of the faithful – or was it only the boldest of the curious? – had fled. He watched the black huddle of his fellow-students draw off down and up the street, in whispering or boisterous gangs. And the isolation of the moment weighed upon him like an omen and an emblem of his destiny in life. Bred up in unbroken fear himself, among trembling servants, and in a house which (at the least ruffle in the master's voice) shuddered into silence, he saw himself on the brink of the red valley of war, and measured the danger and length of it with awe. He made a detour in the glimmer and shadow of the streets, came into the back stable lane, and watched for a long while the light burn steady in the Judge's room. The longer he gazed upon that illuminated window-blind, the more blank became the picture of the man who sat behind it, endlessly turning over sheets of process, pausing to sip a glass of port, or rising and passing heavily about his book-lined walls to verify some reference. He could not combine the brutal judge and the industrious, dispassionate student; the connecting link escaped him, from such a dual nature, it was impossible he should predict behaviour; and he asked himself if he had done well to plunge into a business of which the end could not be foreseen? and presently after, with a sickening decline of confidence, if he had done loyally to strike his father? For he had struck him – defied him twice over and before a cloud of witnesses – struck him a public buffet before crowds. Who had called him to judge his father in these precarious and high questions? The office was usurped. It might have become a stranger; in a son – there was no blinking it – in a son, it was disloyal. And now, between these two natures so antipathetic, so hateful to each other, there was depending an unpardonable affront: and the providence of God alone might foresee the manner in which it would be resented by Lord Hermiston.

These misgivings tortured him all night and arose with him in the winter's morning; they followed him from class to class, they made him shrinkingly sensitive to every shade of manner in his companions, they sounded in his ears through the current voice of the professor; and he brought them home with him at night unabated and indeed increased. The cause of this increase lay in a chance encounter with the celebrated Dr Gregory. Archie stood looking vaguely in the lighted window of a book-shop, trying to nerve himself for the approaching ordeal. My lord and he had met and parted in the morning as they had now done for long, with scarcely the ordinary civilities of life; and it was plain to the son that nothing had yet reached the father's ears. Indeed, when he recalled the awful countenance of my lord, a timid hope sprang up in him that perhaps there would be found no one bold enough to carry tales. If this were so, he asked himself, would be begin again? and he found no answer. It was at this moment that a hand was laid upon his arm, and a voice said in his ear, 'My dear Mr Archie, you had better come and see me.'

He started, turned round, and found himself face to face with Dr Gregory. 'And why should I come to see you?' he asked, with the defiance of the miserable.

'Because you are looking exceeding ill,' said the doctor, 'and you very evidently want looking after, my young friend. Good folk are scarce, you know; and it is not every one that would be quite so much missed as yourself. It is not every one that Hermiston would miss.'

And with a nod and a smile, the doctor passed on.

A moment after, Archie was in pursuit, and had in turn, but more roughly, seized him by the arm.

'What do you mean? What did you mean by saying that? What makes you think that Hermis – my father would have missed me?'

The doctor turned about and looked him all over with a clinical eye. A far more stupid man than Dr Gregory might have guessed the truth; but ninety-nine out of a hundred, even if they had been equally inclined to kindness, would have blundered by some touch of charitable exaggeration. The doctor was better inspired. He knew the father well; in that white face of intelligence and suffering he divined something of the son; and he told, without apology or adornment, the plain truth.

'When you had the measles, Mr Archibald, you had them gey and ill; and I thought you were going to slip between my fingers,' he said. 'Well, your father was anxious. How did I know it? says you. Simply because I am a trained observer. The sign that I saw him make, ten thousand would have missed; and perhaps – *perhaps*, I say, because he's a hard man to judge of – but perhaps he never made another. A strange thing to consider! It was this. One day I came to him: "Hermiston," said I, "there's a change." He never said a word, just glowered at me (if ye'll pardon the phrase) like a wild beast. 'A change for the better,' said I. And I distinctly heard him take his breath.'

The doctor left no opportunity for anticlimax; nodding his cocked hat (a piece of antiquity to which he clung) and repeating 'Distinctly' with raised eyebrows, he took his departure, and left Archie speechless in the street.

The anecdote might be called infinitely little, and yet its meaning for Archie was immense. 'I did not know the old man had so much blood in him.' He had never dreamed this sire of his, this aboriginal antique, this adamantine Adam, had even so much of a heart as to be moved in the least degree for another – and that other himself, who had insulted him! With the generosity of youth, Archie was instantly under arms upon the other side: had instantly created a new image of Lord Hermiston, that of a man who was all iron without and all sensibility within. The mind of the vile jester, the tongue that had pursued Duncan Jopp with unmanly insults, the unbeloved countenance that he had known and feared for so long, were all forgotten; and he hastened home, impatient to confess his misdeeds, impatient to throw himself on the mercy of this imaginary character.

He was not to be long without a rude awakening. It was in the gloaming when he drew near the doorstep of the lighted house, and was aware of the figure of his father approaching from the opposite side. Little daylight lingered; but on the door being opened, the strong yellow shine of the lamp gushed out upon the landing and shone full on Archie, as he stood, in the old-fashioned observance of respect, to yield precedence. The Judge came without haste, stepping stately and firm; his chin raised, his face illumined, his mouth set hard. There was never a wink of change in his expression; without looking to the right or left, he mounted the stair, passed close to Archie, and entered the house. Instinctively, the boy, upon his first coming, had made a movement to meet him; instinctively, he recoiled against the railing, as the old man swept by him in a pomp of indignation. Words were needless; he knew all – perhaps more than all – and the hour of judgment was at hand.

It is possible that, in this sudden revulsion of hope, and before these symptoms of impending danger, Archie might have fled. But not even that was left to him. My lord, after hanging up his cloak and hat, turned round in the lighted entry, and made him an imperative and silent gesture with his thumb, and with the strange instinct of obedience, Archie followed him into the house.

All dinner-time there reigned over the Judge's table a palpable silence, and as soon as the solids were despatched he rose to his feet.

'M'Killop, tak' the wine into my room,' said he; and then to his son: 'Archie, you and me has to have a talk.'

It was at this sickening moment that Archie's courage, for the first and last time, entirely deserted him. 'I have an appointment,' said he.

'It'll have to be broken, then,' said Hermiston, and led the way into his study.

The lamp was shaded, the fire trimmed to a nicety, the table covered deep with orderly documents, the backs of law books made a frame upon all sides that was only broken by the window and the doors.

For a moment Hermiston warmed his hands at the fire, presenting his back to Archie; then suddenly disclosed on him the terrors of the Hanging Face.

'What's this I hear of ye?' he asked.

There was no answer possible to Archie.

'I'll have to tell ye, then,' pursued Hermiston. 'It seems ye've been skirling against the father that begot ye, and one of His Maijesty's Judges in this land; and that in the public street, and while an order of the Court was being executit. Forbye which, it would appear that ye've been airing your opeenions in A Coallege Debatin' Society'; he paused a moment: and then, with extraordinary bitterness, added: 'Ye damned eediot.'

'I had meant to tell you,' stammered Archie. 'I see you are well informed.'

'Muckle obleeged to ye,' said his lordship, and took his usual seat. 'And so you disapprove of Caapital Punishment?' he added.

'I am sorry, sir, I do,' said Archie.

'I am sorry, too,' said his lordship. 'And now, if you please, we shall approach this business with a little more parteecularity. I hear that at the hanging of Duncan Jopp – and, man! ye had a fine client there – in the middle of all the riff-raff of the ceety, ye thought fit to cry out, "This is a damned murder, and my gorge rises at the man that haangit him."'

'No, sir, these were not my words,' cried Archie.

'What were yer words, then?' asked the Judge.

'I believe I said, "I denounce it as a murder!"' said the son. 'I beg your pardon – a God-defying murder. I have no wish to conceal the truth,' he added, and looked his father for a moment in the face.

'God, it would only need that of it next!' cried Hermiston. 'There was nothing about your gorge rising, then?'

'That was afterwards, my lord, as I was leaving the Speculative. I said I had been to see the miserable creature hanged, and my gorge rose at it.'

'Did ye, though?' said Hermiston. 'And I suppose ye knew who haangit him?'

'I was present at the trial; I ought to tell you that, I ought to explain. I ask your pardon beforehand for any expression that may seem undutiful. The position in which I stand is wretched,' said the unhappy hero, now fairly face to face with the business he had chosen. 'I have been reading some of your cases. I was present while Jopp was tried. It was a hideous business. Father, it was a hideous thing! Grant he was vile, why should you hunt him with a vileness equal to his own? It was done with glee – that is the word – you did it with glee; and I looked on, God help me! with horror.'

'You're a young gentleman that doesna approve of Caapital Punishment,' said Hermiston. 'Weel, I'm an auld man that does. I was glad to get Jopp haangit, and what for would I pretend I wasna? You're all for honesty, it seems; you couldn't even steik your mouth on the public street. What for should I steik mines upon the bench, the King's officer, bearing the sword, a dreid to evil-doers, as I was from the beginning, and as I will be to the end! Mair than enough of it! Heedious! I never gave twa thoughts to heediousness, I have no call to be bonny. I'm a man that gets through with my day's business, and let that suffice.'

The ring of sarcasm had died out of his voice as he went on; the plain words became invested with some of the dignity of the Justice-seat.

'It would be telling you if you could say as much,' the speaker resumed. 'But ye cannot. Ye've been reading some of my cases, ye say. But it was not for the law in them, it was to spy out your faither's nakedness, a fine employment in a son. You're splairging; you're running at lairge in life like a wild nowt. It's impossible you should think any longer of coming to the Bar. You're not fit for it; no splairger is. And another thing: son of mines or no son of mines, you have flung fylement in public on one of the Senators of the Coallege of Justice, and I would make it my business to see that ye were never admitted there yourself. There is a kind of a decency to be observit. Then comes the next of it – what am I to do with ye next? Ye'll have to find some kind of a trade, for I'll never support ye in idleset. What do ye fancy ye'll be fit for? The pulpit? Na, they could never get diveenity into that bloackhead. Him that the law of man whammles is no likely to do muckle better by the law of God. What would ye make of hell? Wouldna your gorge rise at that? Na, there's no room for splairgers under the fower quarters of John Calvin. What else is there? Speak up. Have ye got nothing of your own?'

'Father, let me go to the Peninsula,' said Archie. 'That's all I'm fit for – to fight.'

'All? quo' he!' returned the Judge. 'And it would be enough too, if I thought it. But I'll never trust ye so near the French, you that's so Frenchifeed.'

'You do me injustice there, sir,' said Archie. 'I am loyal; I will not boast; but any interest I may have ever felt in the French——'

'Have ye been so loyal to me?' interrupted his father.

There came no reply.

'I think not,' continued Hermiston. 'And I would send no man to be a servant to the King, God bless him! that has proved such a shauchling son to his own faither. You can splairge here on Edinburgh street, and where's the hairm? It doesna play buff on me! And if there were twenty thousand eediots like yourself, sorrow a Duncan Jopp would hang the fewer. But there's no splairging possible in a camp; and if you were to go to it, you would find out for yourself whether Lord Well'n'ton approves of caapital punishment or not. You a sodger!' he cried, with a sudden burst of scorn. 'Ye auld wife, the sodjers would bray at ye like cuddies!'

As at the drawing of a curtain, Archie was aware of some illogicality in his position, and stood abashed. He had a strong impression, besides, of the essential valour of the old gentleman before him, how conveyed it would be hard to say.

'Well, have ye no other proposeetion?' said my lord again.

'You have taken this so calmly, sir, that I cannot but stand ashamed,' began Archie.

'I'm nearer voamiting, though, than you would fancy,' said my lord.

The blood rose to Archie's brow.

'I beg your pardon, I should have said that you had accepted my affront. . . . I admit it was an affront; I did not think to apologize, but I do, I ask your pardon; it will not be so again, I pass you my word of honour. . . . I should have said that I admired your magnanimity with – this – offender,' Archie concluded with a gulp.

'I have no other son, ye see,' said Hermiston. 'A bonny one I have gotten! But I must just do the best I can wi' him, and what am I to do? If ye had been younger, I would have wheepit ye for this rideeculous exhibeetion. The way it is, I have just to grin and bear. But one thing is to be clearly understood. As a faither, I must grin and bear it; but if I had been the Lord Advocate instead of the Lord Justice-Clerk, son or no son, Mr Erchibald Weir would have been in a jyle the night.'

Archie was now dominated. Lord Hermiston was coarse and cruel; and yet the son was aware of a bloomless nobility, an ungracious abnegation of the man's self in the man's office. At every word, this sense of the greatness of Lord Hermiston's spirit struck more home; and along with it that of his own impotence, who had struck – and perhaps basely struck – at his own father, and not reached so far as to have even nettled him.

'I place myself in your hands without reserve,' he said.

'That's the first sensible word I've had of ye the night,' said Hermiston. 'I can tell ye, that would have been the end of it, the one way or the other; but it's better ye should come there yourself, than what I would have had to hirstle ye. Weel, by my way of it – and my way is the best – there's just the one thing it's possible that ye might be with decency, and that's a laird. Ye'll be out of hairm's way at the least of it. If ye have to rowt, ye can rowt amang the kye; and the maist feck of the caapital punishment ye're like to come across'll be guddling trouts. Now, I'm for no idle lairdies; every man has to work, if it's only at peddling ballants; to work, or to be wheeped, or to be haangit. If I set ye down at Hermiston, I'll have to see you work that place the way it has never been workit yet; ye must ken about the sheep like a herd; ye must be my grieve there, and I'll see that I gain by ye. Is that understood?'

'I will do my best,' said Archie.

'Well, then, I'll send Kirstie word the morn, and ye can go yourself the day after,' said Hermiston. 'And just try to be less of an eediot!' he concluded, with a freezing smile, and turned immediately to the papers on his desk.

CHAPTER FOUR

Opinions of the Bench

LATE THE SAME NIGHT, AFTER a disordered walk, Archie was admitted into Lord Glenalmond's dining-room, where he sat, with a book upon his knee, beside three frugal coals of fire. In his robes upon the bench, Glenalmond had a certain air of burliness: plucked of these, it was a maypole of a man that rose unsteadily from his chair to give his visitor welcome. Archie had suffered much in the last days, he had suffered again that evening; his face was white and drawn, his eyes wild and dark. But Lord Glenalmond greeted him without the least mark of surprise or curiosity.

'Come in, come in,' said he. 'Come in and take a seat. Carstairs' (to his servant) 'make up the fire, and then you can bring a bit of supper,' and again to Archie, with a very trivial accent; 'I was half expecting you,' he added.

'No supper,' said Archie. 'It is impossible that I should eat.'

'Not impossible,' said the tall old man, laying his hand upon his shoulder, 'and, if you will believe me, necessary.'

'You know what brings me?' said Archie, as soon as the servant had left the room.

'I have a guess, I have a guess,' replied Glenalmond. 'We will talk of it presently – when Carstairs has come and gone, and you have had a piece of my good Cheddar cheese and a pull at the porter tankard: not before.'

'It is impossible I should eat,' repeated Archie.

'Tut, tut!' said Lord Glenalmond. 'You have eaten nothing to-day, and I venture to add, nothing yesterday. There is no case that may not be made worse; this may be a very disagreeable business, but if you were to fall sick and die, it would be still more so, and for all concerned – for all concerned.'

'I see you must know all,' said Archie. 'Where did you hear it?'

'In the mart of scandal, in the Parliament House,' said Glenalmond. 'It runs riot below among the bar and the public, but it sifts up to us upon the bench, and rumour has some of her voices even in the divisions.'

Castairs returned at this moment, and rapidly laid out a little supper; during which Lord Glenalmond spoke at large and a little vaguely on indifferent subjects, so that it might be rather said of him that he made a cheerful noise, than that he contributed to human conversation; and Archie sat upon the other side, not heeding him, brooding over his wrongs and errors.

But so soon as the servant was gone, he broke forth again at once. 'Who told my father? Who dared to tell him? Could it have been you?'

'No, it was not me,' said the Judge; 'although – to be quite frank with you, and after I had seen and warned you – it might have been me. I believe it was Glenkindie.'

'That shrimp!' cried Archie.

'As you say, that shrimp,' returned my lord; 'although really it is scarce a fitting mode of expression for one of the senators of the College of Justice. We were hearing the parties in a long, crucial case, before the fifteen; Creech was moving at some length for an infeftment; when I saw Glenkindie lean forward to Hermiston with his hand over his mouth and make him a secret communication. No one could have guessed its nature from your father; from Glenkindie, yes, his malice sparked out of him a little grossly. But your father, no. A man of granite. The next moment he pounced upon Creech. 'Mr Creech,' says he, 'I'll take a look of that sasine,' and for thirty minutes after,' said Glenalmond, with a smile, 'Messrs Creech and Co. were fighting a pretty uphill battle, which resulted, I need hardly add, in their total rout. The case was dismissed. No, I doubt if ever I heard Hermiston better inspired. He was literally rejoicing *in apicibus juris.*'

Archie was able to endure no longer. He thrust his plate away and interrupted the deliberate and insignificant stream of talk. 'Here,' he said, 'I have made a fool of myself, if I have not made something worse. Do you judge between us – judge between a father and a son. I can speak to you; it is not like . . . I will tell you what I feel and what I mean to do; and you shall be the judge,' he repeated.

'I decline jurisdiction,' said Glenalmond, with extreme seriousness. 'But, my dear boy, if it will do you any good to talk, and if it will interest you at all to hear what I may choose to say when I have heard you, I am quite at your command. Let an old man say it, for once, and not need to blush: I love you like a son.'

There came a sudden sharp sound in Archie's throat. 'Ay,' he cried, 'and there it is! Love! Like a son! And how do you think I love my father?'

'Quietly, quietly,' says my lord.

'I will be very quiet,' replied Archie. 'And I will be baldly frank. I do not love my father; I wonder sometimes if I do not hate him. There's my shame; perhaps my sin; at least, and in the sight of God, not my fault. How was I to love him? He has never spoken to me, never smiled upon me; I do not think he ever touched me. You know the way he talks? You do not talk so, yet you can sit and hear him without shuddering, and I cannot. My soul is sick when he begins with it; I could smite him in the mouth. And all that's nothing. I was at the trial of this Jopp. You were not there, but you must have heard him often; the man's notorious for it, for being – look at my position! he's my father and this is how I have to speak of him – notorious for being a brute and cruel and a coward. Lord Glenalmond, I give you my word, when I came out of that Court, I longed to die – the shame of it was beyond my strength: but I – I——' he rose from his seat and began to pace the room in a disorder. 'Well, who am I? A boy, who have never been tried, have never done anything except this twopenny impotent folly with my father. But I tell you, my lord, and I know myself, I am at least that kind of a man – or that kind of a boy, if you prefer it – that I could die in torments rather than that any one should suffer as that scoundrel suffered. Well, and what have I done? I see it now. I have made a fool of myself, as I said in the beginning; and I have gone back, and asked my father's pardon, and placed myself wholly in his hands – and he has sent me to Hermiston,' with a wretched smile, 'for life, I suppose – and what can I say? he strikes me as having done quite right, and let me off better than I had deserved.'

'My poor, dear boy!' observed Glenalmond. 'My poor dear and, if you will allow me to say so, very foolish boy! You are only discovering where you are; to one of your temperament, or of mine, a painful discovery. The world was not made for us; it was made for ten hundred millions of men, all different from each other and from us; there's no royal road there, we just have to sclamber and tumble. Don't think that I am at all disposed to be surprised; don't suppose that I ever think of blaming you; indeed I rather admire! But there fall to be offered one or two observations on the case which occur to me and which (if you will listen to them dispassionately) may be the means of inducing you to view the matter more calmly. First of all, I cannot acquit you of a good deal of what is called intolerance. You seem to have been very much offended because your father talks a little sculduddery after dinner, which it is perfectly licit for him to do, and which (although I am not very fond of it myself) appears to be entirely an affair of taste. Your father, I scarcely like to remind you, since it is so trite a commonplace, is older than yourself. At least, he is *major* and *sui juris*, and may please himself in the matter of his conversation. And, do you know, I wonder if he might not have as good an answer against you and me? We say we sometimes find him *coarse*, but I suspect he might retort that he finds us always dull. Perhaps a relevant exception.'

He beamed on Archie, but no smile could be elicited.

'And now,' proceeded the Judge, 'for "Archibald on Capital Punishment." This is a very plausible academic opinion; of course I do not and I cannot hold it; but that's not to say that many able and excellent persons have not done so in the past. Possibly, in the past also, I may have a little dipped myself in the same heresy. My third client, or possibly my fourth, was the means of a return in my opinions. I never saw the man I more believed in; I would have put my hand in the fire, I would have gone to the cross for him; and when it came to trial he was gradually pictured before me, by undeniable probation, in the light of so gross, so cold-blooded, and so black-hearted a villain, that I had a mind to have cast my brief upon the table. I was then boiling against the man with even a more tropical temperature than I had been boiling for him. But I said to myself: "No, you have taken up his case; and because you have changed your mind it must not be suffered to let drop. All that rich tide of eloquence that you prepared last night with so much enthusiasm is out of place, and yet you must not desert him, you must say something." So I said something, and I got him off. It made my reputation. But an experience of that kind is formative. A man must not bring his passions to the bar – or to the bench,' he added.

The story had slightly rekindled Archie's interest. 'I could never deny,' he began – 'I mean I can conceive that some men would be better dead. But who are we to know all the springs of God's unfortunate creatures? Who are we to trust ourselves where it seems that God Himself must think twice before He treads, and to do it with delight? Yes, with delight. *Tigris ut aspera.*'

'Perhaps not a pleasant spectacle,' said Glenalmond. 'And yet, do you know, I think somehow a great one.'

'I've had a long talk with him tonight,' said Archie.

'I was supposing so,' said Glenalmond.

'And he struck me – I cannot deny that he struck me as something very big,' pursued the son. 'Yes, he is big. He never spoke about himself; only about me. I suppose I admired him. The dreadful part——'

'Suppose we did not talk about that,' interrupted Glenalmond. 'You know it very well, it cannot in any way help that you should brood upon it, and I sometimes wonder whether you and I – who are a pair of sentimentalists – are quite good judges of plain men.'

'How do you mean?' asked Archie.

'*Fair* judges, I mean,' replied Glenalmond. 'Can we be just to them? Do we not ask too much? There was a word of yours just now that impressed me a little when you asked me who we were to know all the springs of God's unfortunate creatures. You applied that, as I understood, to capital cases only. But does it – I ask myself – does it not apply all through? Is it any less difficult to judge of a good man or of a half-good man, than of the worst criminal at the bar? And may not each have relevant excuses?'

'Ah, but we do not talk of punishing the good,' cried Archie.

'No, we do not talk of it,' said Glenalmond. 'But I think we do it. Your father, for instance.'

'You think I have punished him?' cried Archie.

Lord Glenalmond bowed his head.

'I think I have,' said Archie. 'And the worst is, I think he feels it! How much, who can tell, with such a being? But I think he does.'

'And I am sure of it,' said Glenalmond.

'Has he spoken to you, then?' cried Archie.

'O no,' replied the judge.

'I tell you honestly,' said Archie, 'I want to make it up to him. I will go, I have already pledged myself to go, to Hermiston. That was to him. And, now I pledge myself to you, in the sight of God, that I will close my mouth on capital punishment and all other subjects where our views may clash, for – how long shall I say? when shall I have sense enough? – ten years. Is that well?'

'It is well,' said my lord.

'As far as it goes,' said Archie. 'It is enough as regards myself, it is to lay down enough of my conceit. But as regards him, whom I have publicly insulted? What am I to do to him? How do you pay attentions to a – an Alp like that?'

'Only in one way,' replied Glenalmond. 'Only by obedience, punctual, prompt, and scrupulous.'

'And I promise that he shall have it,' answered Archie. 'I offer you my hand in pledge of it,'

'And I take your hand as a solemnity,' replied the judge. 'God bless you, my dear, and enable you to keep your promise. God guide you in the true way, and spare your days, and preserve to you your honest heart.' At that, he kissed the young man upon the forehead in a gracious, distant, antiquated way; and instantly launched, with a marked change of voice, into another subject, 'And now, let us replenish the tankard; and I believe, if you will try my Cheddar again, you would find you had a better appetite. The Court has spoken, and the case is dismissed.'

'No, there is one thing I must say,' cried Archie. 'I must say it in justice to himself. I know – I believe faithfully, slavishly, after our talk – he will never ask me anything unjust. I am proud to feel it, that we have that much in common, I am proud to say it to you.'

The Judge, with shining eyes, raised his tankard. 'And I think perhaps that we might permit ourselves a toast,' said he. 'I should like to propose the health of a man very different from me and very much my superior – a man from whom I have often differed, who has often (in the trivial expression) rubbed me the wrong way, but whom I have never ceased to respect and, I may add, to be not a little afraid of. Shall I give you his name?'

'The Lord Justice-Clerk, Lord Hermiston,' said Archie, almost with gaiety; and the pair drank the toast deeply.

It was not precisely easy to re-establish, after these emotional passages, the natural flow of conversation. But the Judge eked out what was wanting with kind looks, produced his snuff-box (which was very rarely seen) to fill in a pause, and at last, despairing of any further social success, was upon the point of getting down a book to read a favourite passage, when there came a rather startling summons at the front door, and Carstairs ushered in my Lord Glenkindie, hot from a midnight supper. I am not aware that Glenkindie was ever a beautiful object, being short, and gross-bodied, and with an expression of sensuality comparable to a bear's. At that moment, coming in hissing from many potations, with a flushed countenance and blurred eyes, he was strikingly contrasted with the tall, pale, kingly figure of Glenalmond. A rush of confused thought came over Archie – of shame that this was one of his father's elect friends; of pride, that at the least of it Hermiston could carry his liquor; and last of all, of rage, that he should have here under his eyes the man that had betrayed him. And then that too passed away; and he sat quiet, biding his opportunity.

The tipsy senator plunged at once into an explanation with Glenalmond. There was a point reserved yesterday, he had been able to make neither head nor tail of it, and seeing lights in the house, he had just dropped in for a glass of porter – and at this point he became aware of the third person. Archie saw the cod's mouth and the blunt lips of Glenkindie gape at him for a moment, and the recognition twinkle in his eyes.

'Who's this?' said he. 'What? is this possibly you, Don Quickshot? And how are ye? And how's your father? And what's all this we hear of you? It seems you're a most extraordinary leveller, by all tales. No king, no parliaments, and your gorge rises at the macers, worthy men! Hoot, toot! Dear, dear me! Your father's son too! Most rideeculous!'

Archie was on his feet, flushing a little at the reappearance of his unhappy figure of speech, but perfectly self-possessed. 'My lord – and you, Lord Glenalmond, my dear friend,' he began, 'this is a happy chance for me, that I can make my confession and offer my apologies to two of your at once.'

'Ah, but I don't know about that. Confession? It'll be judeecial, my young friend,' cried the jocular Glenkindie. 'And I'm afraid to listen to ye. Think if ye were to make me a coanvert!'

'If you would allow me, my lord,' returned Archie, 'what I have to say is very serious to me; and be pleased to be humorous after I am gone!'

'Remember, I'll hear nothing against the macers!' put in the incorrigible Glenkindie.

But Archie continued as though he had not spoken. 'I have played, both yesterday and to-day, a part for which I can only offer the excuse of youth. I was so unwise as to go to an execution; it seems I made a scene at the gallows; not content with which, I spoke the same night in a college society against capital punishment. This is the extent of what I have done, and in case you hear more alleged against me, I protest my innocence. I have expressed my regret already to my father, who is so good as to pass my conduct over – in a degree, and upon the condition that I am to leave my law studies.'. . .

CHAPTER FIVE

Winter on the Moors

1. *At Hermiston*

THE ROAD TO HERMISTON RUNS for a great part of the way up the valley of a stream, a favourite with anglers and with midges, full of falls and pools, and shaded by willows and natural woods of birch. Here and there, but at great distances, a byway branches off, and a gaunt farmhouse may be descried above in a fold of the hill; but the more part of the time, the road would be quite empty of passage and the hills of habitation. Hermiston parish is one of the least populous in Scotland; and, by the time you came that length, you would scarce be surprised at the inimitable smallness of the kirk, a dwarfish, ancient place seated for fifty, and standing in a green by the burn-side among two-score gravestones. The manse close by, although no more than a cottage, is surrounded by the brightness of a flower-garden and the straw roofs of bees; and the whole colony, kirk and manse, garden and graveyard, finds harbourage in a grove of rowans, and is all the year round in a great silence broken only by the drone of the bees, the tinkle of the burn, and the bell on Sundays. A mile beyond the kirk the road leaves the valley by a precipitous ascent, and brings you a little after to the place of Hermiston, where it comes to an end in the back-yard before the coach-house. All beyond and about is the great field of the hills; the plover, the curlew, and the lark cry there; the wind blows as it blows in a ship's rigging, hard and cold and pure; and the hilltops huddle one behind another, like a herd of cattle, into the sunset.

The house was sixty years old, unsightly, comfortable; a farmyard and a kitchen-garden on the left, with a fruit wall where little hard green pears came to their maturity about the end of October.

The policy (as who should say the park) was of some extent, but very ill reclaimed; heather and moorfowl had crossed the boundary wall and spread and roosted within; and it would have tasked a landscape gardener to say where policy ended and unpolicied nature began. My lord had been led by the influence of Mr Sheriff Scott into a considerable design of planting; many acres were accordingly set out with fir, and the little feathery besoms gave a false scale and lent a strange air of a toy-shop to the moors. A great, rooty sweetness of bogs was in the air, and at all seasons an infinite melancholy piping of hill birds. Standing so high and with so little shelter, it was a cold, exposed house, splashed by showers, drenched by continuous rains that made the gutters to spout, beaten upon and buffeted by all the winds of heaven; and the prospect would be often black with tempest, and often white with the snows of winter. But the house was wind and weather proof, the hearths were kept bright, and the rooms pleasant with live fires of peat; and Archie might sit of an evening and hear the squalls bugle on the moorland, and watch the fire prosper in the earthy fuel, and the smoke winding up the chimney, and drink deep of the pleasures of shelter.

Solitary as the place was, Archie did not want neighbours. Every night, if he chose, he might go down to the manse and share a 'brewst' of toddy with the minister – a hare-brained ancient gentleman, long and light and still active, though his knees were loosened with age, and his voice broke continually in childish trebles – and his lady wife, a heavy, comely dame, without a word to say for herself beyond good-even and good-day. Harum-scarum, clodpole young lairds of the neighbourhood paid him the compliment of a visit. Young Hay of Romanes rode down to call, on his crop-eared pony; young Pringle of Drumanno came up on his bony grey. Hay remained on the hospitable field, and must be carried to bed; Pringle got somehow to his saddle about 3 a.m., and (as Archie stood with the lamp on the upper doorstep) lurched, uttered a senseless view-holloa, and vanished out of the small circle of illumination like a wraith. Yet a minute or two longer the clatter of his breakneck flight was audible, then it was cut off by the intervening steepness of the hill; and again, a great while after, the renewed beating of phantom horse-hoofs, far in the valley of the Hermiston, showed that the horse at least, if not his rider, was still on the homeward way.

There was a Tuesday club at the 'Crosskeys' in Crossmichael, where the young bloods of the countryside congregated and drank deep on a percentage of the expense, so that he was left gainer who should have drunk the most. Archie had no great mind to this diversion, but he took it like a duty laid upon him, went with a decent regularity, did his manfullest with the liquor, held up his head in the local jests, and got home again and was able to put up his horse, to the admiration Kirstie and the lass that helped her. He dined at Driffel, supped at Windielaws. He went to the New Year's ball at Huntsfield and was made welcome, and thereafter rode to hounds with my Lord Muirfell, upon whose name, as that of a legitimate Lord of Parliament, in a work so full of Lords of Session, my pen should pause reverently. Yet the same fate attended him here as in Edinburgh. The habit of solitude tends to perpetuate itself, and an austerity of which he was quite unconscious, and a pride which seemed arrogance, and perhaps was chiefly shyness, discouraged and offended his new companions. Hay did not return more than twice, Pringle never at all, and there came a time when Archie even desisted from the Tuesday Club, and became in all things – what he had had the name of almost from the first – the Recluse of Hermiston. High-nosed Miss Pringle of Drumanno and high-stepping Miss Marshall of the Mains were understood to have had a difference of opinion about him the day after the ball – he was none the wiser, he could not suppose himself to be remarked by these entrancing ladies. At the ball itself my Lord Muirfell's daughter, the Lady Flora, spoke to him twice, and the second time with a touch of appeal, so that her colour rose and her voice trembled a little in his ear, like a passing grace in music. He stepped back with a heart on fire, coldly and not ungracefully excused himself, and a little after watched her dancing with young

Drumanno of the empty laugh, and was harrowed at the sight, and raged to himself that this was a world in which it was given to Drumanno to please, and to himself only to stand aside and envy. He seemed excluded, as of right, from the favour of such society – seemed to extinguish mirth wherever he came, and was quick to feel the wound, and desist, and retire into solitude. If he had but understood the figure he presented, and the impression he made on these bright eyes and tender hearts; if he had but guessed that the Recluse of Hermiston, young, graceful, well spoken, but always cold, stirred the maidens of the county with the charm of Byronism when Byronism was new, it may be questioned whether his destiny might not ven yet have been modified. It may be questioned, and I think it should be doubted. It was in his horoscope to be parsimonious of pain to himself, or of the chance of pain, even to the avoidance of any opportunity of pleasure; to have a Roman sense of duty, an instinctive aristocracy of manners and taste; to be the son of Adam Weir and Jean Rutherford.

2. Kirstie

Kirstie was now over fifty, and might have sat to a sculptor. Long of limb, and still light of foot, deep-breasted, robust-loined, her golden hair not yet mingled with any trace of silver, the years had but caressed and embellished her. By the lines of a rich and vigorous maternity, she seemed destined to be the bride of heroes and the mother of their children; and behold, by the iniquity of fate, she had passed through her youth alone, and drew near to the confines of age, a childless woman. The tender ambitions that she had received at birth had been, by time and disappointment, diverted into a certain barren zeal of industry and fury of interference. She carried her thwarted ardours into housework, she washed floors with her empty heart. If she could not win the love of one with love, she must dominate all by her temper. Hasty, wordy, and wrathful, she had a drawn quarrel with most of her neighbours, and with the others not much more than armed neutrality. The grieve's wife had been 'sneisty'; the sister of the gardener who kept house for him had shown herself 'upsitten'; and she wrote to Lord Hermiston about once a year demanding the discharge of the offenders, and justifying the demand by much wealth of detail. For it must not be supposed that the quarrel rested with the wife and did not take in the husband also – or with the gardener's sister, and did not speedily include the gardener himself. As the upshot of all this petty quarrelling and intemperate speech, she was practically excluded (like a lightkeeper on his tower) from the comforts of human association; except with her own indoor drudge, who, being but a lassie and entirely at her mercy, must submit to the shifty weather of 'the mistress's' moods without complaint, and be willing to take buffets or caresses according to the temper of the hour. To Kirstie, thus situate and in the Indian summer of her heart, which was slow to submit to age, the gods sent this equivocal good thing of Archie's presence. She had known him in the cradle and paddled him when he misbehaved; and yet, as she had not so much as set eyes on him since he was eleven and had his last serious illness, the tall slender, refined, and rather melancholy young gentleman of twenty came upon her with the shock of a new acquaintance. He was 'Young Hermiston,' 'the laird himsel'': he had an air of distinctive superiority, a cold straight glance of his black eyes, that abashed the woman's tantrums in the beginning, and therefore the possibility of any quarrel was excluded. He was new, and therefore immediately aroused her curiosity; he was reticent, and kept it awake. And lastly he was dark and she fair, and he was male and she female, the everlasting fountains of interest.

Her feeling partook of the loyalty of a clanswoman, the hero-worship of a maiden aunt, and the idolatry due to a god. No matter what he had asked of her, ridiculous or tragic, she would have done it and joyed to do it. Her passion, for it was nothing less, entirely filled her. It was a rich physical pleasure to make his bed or light his lamp for him when he was absent, to pull off his wet boots or wait on him at dinner when he returned. A young man who should have so doted on the idea, moral and physical, of any woman, might be properly described as being in love, head and heels, and would have behaved himself accordingly. But Kirstie – though her heart leaped at his coming footsteps – though, when he patted her shoulder, her face brightened for the day – had not a hope or thought beyond the present moment and its perpetuation to the end of time. Till the end of time she would have had nothing altered, but still continue delightedly to serve her idol, and be repaid (say twice in the month) with a clap on the shoulder.

I have said her heart leaped – it is the accepted phrase. But rather, when she was alone in any chamber of the house, and heard his foot passing on the corridors, something in her bosom rose slowly until her breath was suspended, and as slowly fell again with a deep sigh, when the steps had passed and she was disappointed of her eyes' desire. This perpetual hunger and thirst of his presence kept her all day on the alert. When he went forth at morning, she would stand and follow him with admiring looks. As it grew late and drew to the time of his return, she would steal forth to a corner of the policy wall and be seen standing there sometimes by the hour together, gazing with shaded eyes, waiting the exquisite and barren pleasure of his view a mile off on the mountains. When at night she had trimmed and gathered the fire, turned down his bed, and laid out his night-gear – when there was no more to be done for the king's pleasure, but to remember him fervently in her usually very tepid prayers, and go to bed brooding upon his perfections, his future career, and what she should give him the next day for dinner – there still remained before her one more opportunity; she was still to take in the tray and say good-night. Sometimes Archie would glance up from his book with a preoccupied nod and a perfunctory salutation which was in truth a dismissal; sometimes – and by degrees more often – the volume would be laid aside, he would meet her coming with a look of relief; and the conversation would be engaged, last out the supper, and be prolonged till the small hours by the waning fire. It was no wonder that Archie was fond of company after his solitary days; and Kirstie, upon her side, exerted all the arts of her vigorous nature to ensnare his attention. She would keep back some piece of news during dinner to be fired off with the entrance of the supper tray, and form as it were the *lever de rideau* of the evening's entertainment. Once he had heard her tongue wag, she made sure of the result. From one subject to another she moved by insidious transitions, fearing the least silence, fearing almost to give him time for an answer lest it should slip into a hint of separation. Like so many people of her class, she was a brave narrator; her place was on the hearth-rug and she made it a rostrum, miming her stories as she told them, fitting them with

vital detail, spinning them out with endless 'quo' he's' and 'quo' she's,' her voice
sinking into a whisper over the supernatural or the horrific; until she would
suddenly spring up in affected surprise, and pointing to the clock, 'Mercy, Mr
Archie!' she would say, 'whatten a time o' night is this of it! God forgive me for a
daft wife!' So it befell, by good management, that she was not only the first to
begin these nocturnal conversations, but invariably the first to break them off; so
she managed to retire and not to be dismissed.

3. A Border Family

Such an unequal intimacy has never been uncommon in Scotland, where the
clan spirit survives; where the servant tends to spend her life in the same service,
a helpmeet at first, then a tyrant, and at last a pensioner; where, besides, she is
not necessarily destitute of the pride of birth, but is, perhaps, like Kirstie, a
connection of her master's, and at least knows the legend of her own family, and
may count kinship with some illustrious dead. For that is the mark of the Scot of
all classes: that he stands in an attitude towards the past unthinkable to
Englishmen, and remembers and cherishes the memory of his forebears, good or
bad; and there burns alive in him a sense of identity with the dead even to the
twentieth generation. No more characteristic instance could be found than in
the family of Kirstie Elliott. They were all, and Kirstie the first of all, ready and
eager to pour forth the particulars of their genealogy, embellished with every
detail that memory had handed down or fancy fabricated; and behold! from
every ramification of that tree there dangled a halter. The Elliotts themselves
have had a chequered history; but these Elliotts deduced, besides, from three of
the most unfortunate of the border clans – the Nicksons, the Ellwalds, and the
Crozers. One ancestor after another might be seen appearing a moment out of
the rain and the hill mist upon his furtive business, speeding home, perhaps,
with a paltry booty of lame horses and lean kine, or squealing and dealing death
in some moorland feud of the ferrets and the wild cats. One after another closed
his obscure adventures in mid-air, triced up to the arm of the royal gibbet or the
Baron's dule-tree. For the rusty blunderbuss of Scots criminal justice, which
usually hurt nobody but jurymen, became a weapon of precision for the
Nicksons, the Ellwalds, and the Crozers. The exhilaration of their exploits
seemed to haunt the memories of their descendants alone, and the shame to be
forgotten. Pride glowed in their bosoms to publish their relationship to 'Andrew
Ellwald of the Laverockstanes, called 'Unchancy Dand,' who was justifeed wi'
seeven mair of the same name at Jeddart in the days of King James the Sax.' In
all this tissue of crime and misfortune, the Elliots of Cauldstaneslap had one
boast which must appear legitimate: the males were gallows-birds, born outlaws,
petty thieves, and deadly brawlers; but, according to the same tradition, the
females were all chaste and faithful. The power of ancestry on the character is
not limited to the inheritance of cells. If I buy ancestors by the gross from the
benevolence of Lyon King of Arms, my grandson (if he is Scottish) will feel a
quickening emulation of their deeds. The men of the Elliotts were proud,
lawless, violent as of right, cherishing and prolonging a tradition. In like
manner with the women. And the woman, essentially passionate and reckless,
who crouched on the rug, in the shine of the peat fire, telling these tales, had
cherished through life a wild integrity of virtue.

Her father Gilbert had been deeply pious, a savage disciplinarian in the antique style, and withal a notorious smuggler. 'I mind when I was a bairn getting mony a skelp and being shoo'd to bed like pou'try,' she would say. 'That would be when the lads and their bit kegs were on the road. We've had the riffraff of two-three counties in our kitchen, mony's the time, betwix' the twelve and the three; and their lanterns would be standing in the forecourt, ay, a score o' them at once. But there was nae ungodly talk permitted at Cauldstaneslap; my faither was a consistent man in walk and conversation; just let slip an aith, and there was the door to ye! He had that zeal for the Lord, it was a fair wonder to hear him pray, but the faimily has aye had a gift that way.' This father was twice married, once to a dark woman of the old Ellwald stock, by whom he had Gilbert, presently of Cauldstaneslap; and, secondly, to the mother of Kirstie. 'He was an auld man when he married her, a fell auld man wi' a muckle voice – you could hear him rowting from the top o' the Kye-skairs,' she said; 'but for her, it appears she was a perfit wonder. It was gentle blood she had, Mr Archie, for it was your ain. The countryside gaed gyte about her and her gowden hair. Mines is no to be mentioned wi' it, and there's few weemen has mair hair than what I have, or yet a bonnier colour. Often would I tell my dear Miss Jeannie – that was your mother, dear, she was cruel ta'en up about her hair, it was unco tender, ye see – "Houts, Miss Jeannie," I would say, "just fling your washes and your French dentifrishes in the back o' the fire, for that's the place for them; and awa' down to a burn side, and wash yersel' in cauld hill water, and dry your bonny hair in the caller wind o' the muirs, the way that my mother aye washed hers, and that I have aye made it a practice to have wishen mines – just you do what I tell ye, my dear, and ye'll give me news of it! Ye'll have hair, and routh of hair, a pigtail as thick's my arm," I said, "and the bonniest colour like the clear gowden guineas, so as the lads in kirk'll no can keep their eyes off it!" Weel, it lasted out her time, puir thing! I cuttit a lock of it upon her corp that was lying there sae cauld. I'll show it ye some of thir days if ye're good. But, as I was sayin', my mither——'

On the death of the father there remained golden-haired Kirstie, who took service with her distant kinsfolk, the Rutherfords, and black-a-vised Gilbert, twenty years older, who farmed the Cauldstaneslap, married, and begot four sons between 1773 and 1784, and a daughter, like a postscript, in '97, the year of Camperdown and Cape St Vincent. It seemed it was a tradition in the family to wind up with a belated girl. In 1804, at the age of sixty, Gilbert met an end that might be called heroic. He was due home from market any time from eight at night till five in the morning, and in any condition from the quarrelsome to the speechless, for he maintained to that age the goodly customs of the Scots farmer. It was known on this occasion that he had a good bit of money to bring home; the word had gone round loosely. The laird had shown his guineas, and if anybody had but noticed it, there was an ill-looking vagabond crew, the scum of Edinburgh, that drew out of the market long ere it was dusk and took the hill-road by Hermiston, where it was not to be believed that they had lawful business. One of the countryside, one Dickieson, they took with them to be their guide, and dear he paid for it. Of a sudden, in the ford of the Broken Dykes, this vermin clan fell on the laird, six to one, and him three parts asleep, having drunk hard. But it is ill to catch an Elliott. For a while, in the night and the black water that was deep as to his saddle-girths, he wrought with his staff like a smith at his stithy, and great was the sound of oaths and blows. With that the ambuscade was burst, and he rode for home with a pistol-ball in him, three knife wounds, the loss of his front teeth, a broken rib and bridle, and a dying horse. That was a race with death that the laird rode! In the mirk night, with his broken bridle and his head swimming, he dug his spurs to the rowels in the horse's side, and the horse, that was even worse off than himself, the poor creature! screamed out loud like a person as he went, so that hills echoed with it, and the folks at Cauldstaneslap got to their feet about the table and looked at each other with white faces. The horse fell dead at the yard gate, the laird won the length of the house and fell there on the threshold. To the son that raised him he gave the bag of money. 'Hae,' said he. All the way up the thieves had seemed to him to be at his heels, but now the hallucination left him – he saw them again in the place of the ambuscade – and the thirst of vengeance seized on his dying mind. Raising himself and pointing with an imperious finger into the black night from which he had come, he uttered the single command, 'Brocken Dykes,' and fainted. He had never been loved, but he had been feared in honour. At that sight, at that word, gasped out at them from a toothless and bleeding mouth, the old Elliott spirit awoke with a shout in the four sons. 'Wanting the hat,' continues my author, Kirstie, whom I but haltingly follow, for she told this tale like one inspired, 'wanting guns, for there wasna twa grains o' pouder in the house, wi' nae mair weepons than their sticks into their hands, the fower o' them took the road. Only Hob, and that was the eldest, hunkered at the doorsill where the blood had rin, fyled his hand wi' it, and haddit it up to Heeven in the way o' the auld Border aith. "Hell shall have her ain again this nicht!" he raired, and rode forth upon that earrand.' It was three miles to Broken Dykes, down hill, and a sore road. Kirstie had seen men from Edinburgh dismounting there in plain day to lead their horses. But the four brothers road it as if Auld Hornie were behind and Heaven in front. Come to the ford, and there was Dickieson. By all tales, he was not dead, but breathed and reared upon his elbow, and cried out to them for help. It was at a graceless face that he asked mercy. As soon as Hob saw, by the glint of the lantern, the eyes shining and the whiteness of the teeth in the man's face, 'Damn you!' says he; 'ye hae your teeth, hae ye?' and rode his horse to and fro upon that human remnant. Beyond that, Dandie must dismount with the lantern to be their guide; he was the youngest son, scarce twenty at the time. 'A' nicht long they gaed in the wet heath and jennipers, and whaur they gaed they neither knew nor cared, but just followed the bluidstains and the footprints o' their faither's murderers. And a' nicht Dandie had his nose to the grund like a tyke, and the ithers followed and spak' naething, neither black nor white. There was nae noise to be heard, But just the sough of the swalled burns, and Hob, the dour yin, risping his teeth as he gaed.' With the first glint of the morning they saw they were on the drove-road, and at that the four stopped and had dram to their breakfasts, for they knew that Dand must have guided them right, and the rogues could be but little ahead, hot foot for Edinburgh by the way of the Pentland Hills. By eight o'clock they had word of them – a shepherd had seen four men 'uncoly mishandled' go by in the last hour. 'That's yin a piece,' says Clem, and swung his cudgel. 'Five o' them!' says Hob. 'God's death, but the faither was a man! And him drunk!' And then there befell them what my author termed 'a sair misbegowk,' for they were overtaken by a posse of mounted neighbours come to aid in the pursuit. Four sour faces looked on the reinforcement. 'The Deil's broughten you!' said Clem, and they rode thenceforward in the rear of the party with hanging heads. Before ten they had found and secured the rogues, and by three of the afternoon, as they rode up the Vennel with their prisoners, they were aware of a concourse of people bearing in their midst something that dripped. 'For the boady of the saxt,' pursued Kirstie, 'wi' his head smashed like a hazel-nit, had been a' that nicht in the chairge o' Hermiston Water, and it dunting it on the stanes, and grunding it on the shallows, and flinging the deid thing heels-ower hurdie at the Fa's o' Spango; and in the first o' the day, Tweed had got a hold o' him and carried him off like a wind, for it was uncoly swalled, and raced wi' him, bobbing under brae-sides, and was long playing with the creature in the drumlie lynns under the castle, and at the hinder end of all cuist him up on the starling of Crossmichael brig. Sae there they were a'thegither at last (for Dickieson had been brought in on a cart long syne), and folk could see what mainner o' man my brither had been that had held his head again sax and saved the siller, and him drunk!' Thus died of honourable injuries and in the savour of fame Gilbert Elliott of the Cauldstaneslap; but his sons had scarce less glory out of the business. Their savage haste, the skill with which Dand had found and followed the trail, the barbarity to the wounded Dickieson (which was like an open secret in the county), and the doom which it was currently supposed they had intended for the others, struck and stirred popular imagination. Some centuries earlier the last of the minstrels might have fashioned the last of the ballads out of that Homeric fight and chase; but the spirit was dead, or had been reincarnated already in Mr Sheriff Scott, and the degenerate moorsmen must be content to tell the tale in prose, and to make of the 'Four Black Brothers' a unit after the fashion of the 'Twelve Apostles' or the 'Three Musketeers.'

Robert, Gilbert, Clement, and Andrew – in the proper Border diminutives, Hob, Gib, Clem, and Dand Elliott – these ballad heroes, had much in common; in particular, their high sense of the family and the family honour; but they went diverse ways, and prospered and failed in different businesses. According to Kirstie, 'they had a' bees in their bonnets but Hob.' Hob the laird was, indeed, essentially a decent man. An elder of the Kirk, nobody had heard an oath upon his lips, save, perhaps, thrice or so at the sheep-washing, since the chase of his father's murderers. The figure he had shown on that eventful night disappeared as if swallowed by a trap. He who had ecstatically dipped his hand in the red blood, he who had ridden down Dickieson, became, from that moment on, a stiff and rather graceless model of the rustic proprieties; cannily profiting by the high war prices, and yearly stowing away a little nest-egg in the bank against calamity; approved of and sometimes consulted by the greater lairds for the massive and placid sense of what he said, when he could be induced to say anything; and particularly valued by the minister, Mr Torrance, as a right-hand man in the parish, and a model to parents. The transfiguration had been for the moment only; some Barbarossa, some old Adam of our ancestors, sleeps in all of us till the fit circumstance shall call it into action; and, for as sober as he now seemed, Hob had given once for all the measure of the devil that haunted him. He was married, and, by reason of the effulgence of that legendary night, was adored by his wife. He had a mob of little lusty, barefoot children who marched

in a caravan the long miles to school, the stage of whose pilgrimage were marked
by acts of spoliation and mischief, and who were qualified in the countryside as
'fair pests.' But in the house, if 'faither was in,' they were quiet as mice. In short,
Hob moved through life in a great peace – the reward of any one who shall have
killed his man, with any formidable and figurative circumstance, in the midst of
a country gagged and swaddled with civilization.

It was a current remark that the Elliots were 'guid and bad, like sanguishes';
and certainly there was a curious distinction, the men of business coming
alternately with the dreamers. The second brother, Gib, was a weaver by trade,
had gone out early into the world to Edinburgh, and come home again with his
wings singed. There was an exaltation in his nature which had led him to
embrace with enthusiasm the principles of the French Revolution, and had
ended by bringing him under the hawse of my Lord Hermiston in that furious
onslaught of his upon the Liberals, which sent Muir and Palmer into exile and
dashed the party into chaff. It was whispered that my lord, in his great scorn for
the movement, and prevailed upon a little by a sense of neighbourliness, had
given Gib a hint. Meeting him one day in the Potterrow, my lord had stopped in
front of him: "Gib, ye eediot,' he had said, 'what's this I hear of you? Poalitics,
poalitics, poalitics, weaver's poalitics, is the way of it, I hear. If ye are'na
a'thegither dozened with eediocy, ye'll gang your ways back to Cauldstaneslap,
and ca' your loom, and ca' your loom, man!' And Gilbert had taken him at the
word and returned, with an expedition almost to be called flight, to the house of
his father. The clearest of his inheritance was that family gift of prayer of which
Kirstie had boasted; and the baffled politician now turned his attention to
religious matters – or, as others said, to heresy and schism. Every Sunday
morning he was in Crossmichael, where he had gathered together, one by one, a
sect of about a dozen persons, who called themselves 'God's Remnant of the
True Faithful,' or, for short, 'God's Remnant.' To the profane, they were known
as 'Gib's Deils.' Bailie Sweedie, a noted humorist in the town, vowed that the
proceedings always opened to the tune of 'The Deil Fly Away with the
Exciseman,' and that the sacrament was dispensed in the form of hot whisky-
toddy; both wicked hits at the evangelist, who had been suspected of smuggling
in his youth, and had been overtaken (as the phrase went) on the streets of
Crossmichael one Fair day. It was known that every Sunday they prayed for a
blessing on the arms of Bonaparte. For this, 'God's Remnant,' as they were
'skailing' from the cottage that did duty for a temple, had been repeatedly stoned
by the bairns, and Gib himself hooted by a squadron of Border volunteers in
which his own brother, Dand, rode in a uniform and with a drawn sword. The
'Remnant' were believed, besides, to be 'antinomian in principle,' which might
otherwise have been a serious charge, but the way public opinion then blew it
was quite swallowed up and forgotten in the scandal about Bonaparte. For the
rest, Gilbert had set up his loom in an outhouse at Cauldstaneslap, where he
laboured assiduously six days of the week. His brothers, appalled by his political
opinions, and willing to avoid dissension in the household, spoke but little to
him; he less to them, remaining absorbed in the study of the Bible and almost
constant prayer. The gaunt weaver was dry-nurse at Cauldstaneslap, and the
bairns loved him dearly. Except when he was carrying an infant in his arms, he
was rarely seen to smile – as, indeed, there were few smilers in that family.

When his sister-in-law rallied him, and proposed that he should get a wife and bairns of his own, since he was so fond of them, 'I have no clearness of mind upon that point,' he would reply. If nobody called him in to dinner, he stayed out. Mrs Hob, a hard, unsympathetic woman, once tried the experiment. He went without food all day, but at dusk, as the light began to fail him, he came into the house of his own accord, looking puzzled. 'I've had a great gale of prayer upon my speerit,' said he. 'I canna mind sae muckle's what I had for denner.' The creed of God's Remnant was justified in the life of its founder. 'And yet I dinna ken,' said Kirstie. 'He's maybe no more stockfish than his neeghbours! He rode wi' the rest o' them, and had a good stamach to the work, by a' that I hear! God's Remnant! The deil's clavers! There wasna muckle Christianity in the way Hob guided Johnny Dickieson, at the least of it; but Guid kens! Is he a Christian even? He might be a Mahommedan or a Deevil or a Fireworshipper, for what I ken.'

The third brother had his name on a door-plate, no less, in the city of Glasgow, 'Mr Clement Elliott,' as long as your arm. In his case, that spirit of innovation which had shown itself timidly in the case of Hob by the admission of new manures, and which had run to waste with Gilbert in subversive politics and heretical religions, bore useful fruit in many ingenious mechanical improvements. In boyhood, from his addiction to strange devices of sticks and string, he had been counted the most eccentric of the family. But that was all by now; and he was a partner of his firm, and looked to die a bailie. He too had married, and was rearing a plentiful family in the smoke and din of Glasgow; he was wealthy, and could have bought out his brother, the cock-laird, six time over, it was whispered; and when he slipped away to Cauldstaneslap for a well-earned holiday, which he did as often as he was able, he astonished the neighbours with his broadcloth, his beaver hat, and the ample plies of his neckcloth. Though an eminently solid man at bottom, after the pattern of Hob, he had contracted a certain Glasgow briskness and *aplomb* which set him off. All the other Elliotts were as lean as a rake, but Clement was laying on fat, and he panted sorely when he must get into his boots. Dand said, chuckling: 'Ay, Clem has the elements of a corporation,' 'A provost and corporation,' returned Clem. And his readiness was much admired.

The fourth brother, Dand, was a shepherd to his trade, and by starts, when he could bring his mind to it, excelled in the business. Nobody could train a dog like Dandie; nobody, through the peril of great storms in the winter time, could do more gallantly. But if his dexterity were exquisite, his diligence was but fitful; and he served his brother for bed and board, and a trifle of pocket-money when he asked for it. He loved money well enough, knew very well how to spend it, and could make a shrewd bargain when he liked. But he preferred a vague knowledge that he was well to windward to any counted coins in the pocket; he felt himself richer so. Hob would expostulate: 'I'm an amature herd.' Dand would reply, 'I'll keep your sheep to you when I'm so minded, but I'll keep my liberty too. Thir's no man can coandescend on what I'm worth.' Clem would expound to him the miraculous results of compound interest, and recommend investments. 'Ay, man?' Dand would say; 'and do you think, if I took Hob's siller that I wouldna drink it or wear it on the lassies? And, anyway, my kingdom is no of this world. Either I'm a poet or else I'm nothing.' Clem would remind him of

old age. 'I'll die young, like Robbie Burns,' he would say stoutly. No question
but he had a certain accomplishment in minor verse. His 'Hermiston Burn,'
with its pretty refrain:

> 'I love to gang thinking whaur ye gang linking,
> Hermiston burn, in the howe;'

his 'Auld, auld Elliotts, clay-cauld Elliotts, dour, bauld Elliotts of auld,' and his
really fascinating piece about the Praying Weaver's stone, had gained him in the
neighbourhood the reputation, still possible in Scotland, of a local bard; and,
though not printed himself, he was recognized by others who were and who had
become famous. Walter Scott owed to Dandie the text of the 'Raid of Wearie' in
the *Minstrelsy*; and made him welcome at his house, and appreciated his talents,
such as they were, with all his usual generosity. The Ettrick Shepherd was his
sworn crony; they would meet, drink to excess, roar out their lyrics in each
other's faces, and quarrel and make it up again till bedtime. And besides these
recognitions, almost to be called official, Dandie was made welcome for the sake
of his gift through the farmhouses of several contiguous dales, and was thus
exposed to manifold temptations which he rather sought than fled. He had
figured on the stool of repentance, for once fulfilling to the letter the tradition of
his hero and model. His humorous verses to Mr Torrance on that occasion –
'Kenspeckle here my lane I stand' – unfortunately too indelicate for further
citation, ran through the country like a fiery cross; they were recited, quoted,
paraphrased, and laughed over as far away as Dumfries on the one hand and
Dunbar on the other.

These four brothers were united by a close bond, the bond of that mutual
admiration – or rather mutual hero-worship – which is so strong among the
members of secluded families who have much ability and little culture. Even the
extremes admired each other. Hob, who had as much poetry as the tongs,
professed to find pleasure in Dand's verses; Clem, who had no more religion than
Claverhouse, nourished a heartfelt, at least an open-mouthed, admiration of
Gib's prayers; and Dandie followed with relish the rise of Clem's fortunes.
Indulgence followed hard on the heels of admiration. The laird, Clem, and
Dand, who were Tories and patriots of the hottest quality, excused to
themselves, with a certain bashfulness, the radical and revolutionary heresies of
Gib. By another division of the family, the laird, Clem, and Gib, who were men
exactly virtuous, swallowed the dose of Dand's irregularities as a kind of clog or
drawback in the mysterious providence of God affixed to bards, and distinctly
probative of poetical genius. To appreciate the simplicity of their mutual
admiration it was necessary to hear Clem, arrived upon one of his visits, and
dealing in a spirit of continuous irony with the affairs and personalities of that
great city of Glasgow where he lived and transacted business. The various
personages, ministers of the church, municipal officers, mercantile big-wigs,
whom he had occasion to introduce, were all alike denigrated, all served but as
reflectors to cast back a flattering sidelight on the house of Cauldstaneslap. The
Provost, for whom Clem by exception entertained a measure of respect, he
would liken to Hob. 'He minds me o' the laird there,' he would say. 'He has
some of Hob's grand, whunstane sense, and the same way with him of steiking

his mouth when he's no very pleased.' And Hob, all unconscious, would draw down his upper lip and produce, as if for comparison, the formidable grimace referred to. The unsatisfactory incumbent of St Enoch's Kirk was thus briefly dismissed: 'If he had but twa fingers o' Gib's, he would waken them up.' And Gib, honest man! would look down and secretly smile. Clem was a spy whom they had sent out into the world of men. He had come back with the good news that there was nobody to compare with the Four Black Brothers, no position that they would not adorn, no official that it would not be well they should replace, no interest of mankind, secular or spiritual, which would not immediately bloom under their supervision. The excuse of their folly is in two words: scarce the breadth of a hair divided them from the peasantry. The measure of their sense is this: that these symposia of rustic vanity were kept entirely within the family, like some secret ancestral practice. To the world their serious faces were never deformed by the suspicion of any simper of self-contentment. Yet it was known. 'They hae a guid pride o' themsel's!' was the word in the countryside.

Lastly, in a Border story, there should be added their 'to-names.' Hob was The Laird. 'Roy ne puis, prince ne daigne'; he was the laird of Cauldstaneslap – say fifty acres – *ipsissimus*. Clement was Mr Elliott, as upon his door-plate, the earlier Dafty having been discarded as no longer applicable, and indeed only a reminder of misjudgment and the imbecility of the public; and the youngest, in honour of his perpetual wanderings, was known by the sobriquet of Randy Dand.

It will be understood that not all this information was communicated by the aunt, who had too much of the family failing herself to appreciate it thoroughly in others. But as time went on, Archie began to observe an omission in the family chronicle.

'Is there not a girl too?' he asked.

'Ay: Kirstie. She was named for me, or my grandmother at least – it's the same thing,' returned the aunt, and went on again about Dand, whom she secretly preferred by reason of his gallantries.

'But what is your niece like?' said Archie at the next opportunity.

'Her? As black's your hat! But I dinna suppose she would maybe be what you would ca' *ill-looked* a'thegither. Na, she's a kind of a handsome jaud – a kind o' gipsy,' said the aunt, who had two sets of scales for men and women – or perhaps it would be more fair to say that she had three, and the third and the most loaded was for girls.

'How comes it that I never see her in church?' said Archie.

''Deed, and I believe she's in Glesgie with Clem and his wife. A heap good she's like to get of it! I dinna say for men folk, but where weemen folk are born, there let them bide. Glory to God, I was never far'er from here than Crossmichael.'

In the meanwhile it began to strike Archie as strange, that while she thus sang the praises of her kinsfolk, and manifestly relished their virtues and (I may say) their vices like a thing creditable to herself, there should appear not the least sign of cordiality between the house of Hermiston and that of Cauldstaneslap. Going to church of a Sunday, as the lady housekeeper stepped with her skirts kilted, three tucks of her white petticoat showing below, and her best India shawl upon her back (if the day were fine) in a pattern of radiant dyes, she would sometimes overtake her relatives preceding her more leisurely in the same direction. Gib of course was absent: by skreigh of day he had been gone to Crossmichael and his fellow-heretics; but the rest of the family would be seen marching in open order: Hob and Dand, stiff-necked, straight-backed six-footers, with severe dark faces, and their plaids about their shoulders; the convoy of children scattering (in a state of high polish) on the wayside, and every now and again collected by the shrill summons of the mother; and the mother herself, by a suggestive circumstance which might have afforded matter of thought to a more experienced observer than Archie, wrapped in a shawl nearly identical with Kirstie's, but a thought more gaudy and conspicuously newer. At the sight, Kirstie grew more tall – Kirstie showed her classical profile, nose in air and nostril spread, the pure blood came in her cheek evenly in a delicate living pink.

'A braw day to ye, Mistress Elliott,' said she, and hostility and gentility were nicely mingled in her tones. 'A fine day, mem,' the laird's wife would reply with a miraculous curtsey, spreading the while her plumage – setting off, in other words, and with arts unknown to the mere man, the pattern of her India shawl. Behind her, the whole Cauldstaneslap contingent marched in closer order, and with an indescribable air of being in the presence of the foe; and while Dandie saluted his aunt with a certain familiarity as of one who was well in court, Hob marched on in awful immobility. There appeared upon the face of this attitude in the family the consequences of some dreadful feud. Presumably the two women had been principals in the original encounter, and the laird had probably been drawn into the quarrel by the ears, too late to be included in the present skin-deep reconciliation.

'Kirstie,' said Archie one day, 'what is this you have against your family?'

'I dinna complean,' said Kirstie, with a flush. 'I say naething.'

'I see you do not – not even good-day to your own nephew,' said he.

'I hae naething to be ashamed of,' said she. 'I can say the Lord's prayer with a good grace. If Hob was ill, or in preeson or poverty, I would see to him blithely. But for curtchying and complimenting and colloguing, thank ye kindly!'

Archie had a bit of a smile: he leaned back in his chair. 'I think you and Mrs Robert are not very good friends,' says he slyly, 'when you have your India shawls on?'

She looked upon him in silence, with a sparkling eye but an indecipherable expression; and that was all that Archie was ever destined to learn of the battle of the India shawls.

'Do none of them ever come here to see you?' he inquired.

'Mr Archie,' said she, 'I hope that I ken my place better. It would be a queer thing, I think, if I was to clamjamfry up your faither's house – that I should say it! – wi' a dirty, black-a-vised clan, no ane o' them it was worth while to mar soap upon but just mysel'! Na, they're all damnifeed wi' the black Ellwalds. I have nae patience wi' black folk.' Then, with a sudden consciousness of the case of Archie, 'No that it maitters for men sae muckle,' she made haste to add, 'but there's naebody can deny that it's unwomanly. Long hair is the ornament o' woman ony way; we've good warrandise for that – it's in the Bible – and wha can doubt that the Apostle had some gowden-haired lassie in his mind – Apostle and all, for what was he but just a man like yersel'?'

CHAPTER SIX

A Leaf from Christina's Psalm-Book

ARCHIE WAS SEDULOUS AT church. Sunday after Sunday he sat down and stood up with that small company, heard the voice of Mr Torrance leaping like an ill-played clarionet from key to key, and had an opportunity to study his moth-eaten gown and the black thread mittens that he joined together in prayer, and lifted up with a reverent solemnity in the act of benediction. Hermiston pew was a little square box, dwarfish in proportion with the kirk itself, and enclosing a table not much bigger than a footstool. There sat Archie, an apparent prince, the only undeniable gentleman and the only great heritor in the parish, taking his ease in the only pew, for no other in the kirk had doors. Thence he might command an undisturbed view of that congregation of solid plaided men, strapping wives and daughters, oppressed children, and uneasy sheep-dogs. It was strange how Archie missed the look of race; except the dogs, with their refined foxy faces and inimitably curling tails, there was no one present with the least claim to gentility. The Cauldstaneslap party was scarcely an exception; Dandie perhaps, as he amused himself making verses through the interminable burden of the service, stood out a little by the glow in his eye and a certain superior animation of face and alertness of body; but even Dandie slouched like a rustic. The rest of the congregation, like so many sheep, oppressed him with a sense of hob-nailed routine, day following day – of physical labour in the open air, oatmeal porridge, peas bannock, the somnolent fireside in the evening, and the night-long nasal slumbers in a box-bed. Yet he knew many of them to be shrewd and humorous, men of character, notable women, making a bustle in the world and radiating an influence from their low-browed doors. He knew besides they were like other men; below the crust of custom, rapture found a way; he had heard them beat the timbrel before Bacchus – had heard them shout and carouse over their whisky-toddy; and not the most Dutch-bottomed and severe faces among them all, not even the solemn elders themselves, but were capable of singular gambols at the voice of love. Men drawing near to an end of life's adventurous journey – maids thrilling with fear and curiosity on the threshold of entrance – women who had borne and perhaps buried children, who could remember the cinging of the small dead hands and the patter of the little feet now silent – he marvelled that among all those faces there should be no face of expectation, none that was mobile, none into which the rhythm and poetry of life had entered. 'O for a live face,' he thought; and at times he had a memory of Lady Flora; and at times he would study the living gallery before him with despair, and would see himself go on to waste his days in that joyless, pastoral place, and death come to him, and his grave be dug under the rowans, and the Spirit of the Earth laugh out in a thunder-peal at the huge fiasco.

On this particular Sunday, there was no doubt but that the spring had come at last. It was warm, with a latent shiver in the air that made the warmth only the more welcome. The shallows of the stream glittered and tinkled among bunches of primrose. Vagrant scents of the earth arrested Archie by the way with moments of ethereal intoxication. The grey, Quakerish dale was still only awakened in places and patches from the sobriety of its winter colouring; and he wondered at its beauty; an essential beauty of the old earth it seemed to him, not resident in particulars but breathing to him from the whole. He surprised himself by a sudden impulse to write poetry – he did so sometimes, loose, galloping octosyllabics in the vein of Scott – and when he had taken his place on a boulder, near some fairy falls and shaded by a whip of a tree that was already radiant with new leaves, it still more surprised him that he should find nothing to write. His heart perhaps beat in time to some vast indwelling rhythm of the universe. By the time he came to a corner of the valley and could see the kirk, he had so lingered by the way that the first psalm was finishing. The nasal psalmody, full of turns and trills and graceless graces, seemed the essential voice of the kirk itself upraised in thankgiving. 'Everything's alive,' he said; and again cries it aloud, 'thank God, everything's alive!' He lingered yet a while in the kirk-yard. A tuft of primroses was blooming hard by the leg of an old, black table tombstone, and he stopped to contemplate the random apologue. They stood forth on the cold earth with a trenchancy of contrast; and he was struck with a sense of incompleteness in the day, the season, and the beauty that surrounded him – the chill there was in the warmth, the gross black clods about the opening primroses, the damp earthy smell that was everywhere intermingled with the scents. The voice of the aged Torrance within rose in an ecstasy. And he wondered if Torrance also felt in his old bones the joyous influence of the spring morning; Torrance, or the shadow of what once was Torrance, that must come so soon to lie outside here in the sun and rain with all his rheumatisms, while a new minister stood in his room and thundered from his own familiar pulpit? The pity of it, and something of the chill of the grave, shook him for a moment as he made haste to enter.

He went up the aisle reverently, and took his place in the pew with lowered eyes, for he feared he had already offended the kind old gentleman in the pulpit, and was sedulous to offend no further. He could not follow the prayer, not even the heads of it. Brightnesses of azure, clouds of fragrance, a tinkle of falling water and singing birds, rose like exhalations from some deeper, aboriginal memory, that was not his, but belonged to the flesh on his bones. His body remembered; and it seemed to him that his body was in no way gross, but ethereal and perishable like a strain of music; and he felt for it an exquisite tenderness as for a child, an innocent, full of beautiful instincts and destined to an early death. And he felt for old Torrance – of the many supplications, of the few days – a pity that was near to tears. The prayer ended. Right over him was a tablet in the wall, the only ornament in the roughly masoned chapel – for it was no more; the tablet commemorated, I was about to say the virtues, but rather the existence of a former Rutherford of Hermiston; and Archie, under that trophy of his long descent and local greatness, leaned back in the pew and contemplated vacancy with the shadow of a smile between playful and sad, that became him strangely. Dandie's sister, sitting by the side of Clem in her new Glasgow finery, chose that moment to observe the young laird. Aware of the stir of his entrance, the little formalist had kept her eyes fastened and her face prettily composed during the prayer. It was not hypocrisy, there was no one further from a hypocrite. The girl had been taught to behave: to look up, to look down, to look unconscious, to look seriously impressed in church, and in every conjuncture to look her best. That was the game of female life, and she played it frankly. Archie was the one person in church who was of interest, who was somebody new, reputed eccentric, known to be young, and a laird, and still unseen by Christina. Small wonder that, as she stood there in her attitude of pretty decency, her mind should run upon him! if he spared a glance in her direction, he should know she was a well-behaved young lady who had been to Glasgow. In reason he must admire her clothes, and it was possible that he should think her pretty. At that her heart beat the least thing in the world; and she proceeded, by way of a corrective, to call up and dismiss a series of fancied pictures of the young man who should now, by rights, be looking at her. She settled on the plainest of them – a pink short young man with a dish face and no figure, at whose admiration she could afford to smile; but for all that, the consciousness of his gaze (which was really fixed on Torrance and his mittens) kept her in something of a flutter till the word Amen. Even then, she was far too well-bred to gratify her curiosity with any impatience. She resumed her seat languidly – this was a Glasgow touch – she composed her dress, rearranged her nosegay of primroses, looked first in front, then behind upon the other side, and at last allowed her eyes to move, without hurry, in the direction of the Hermiston pew. For a moment, they were riveted. Next she had plucked her gaze home again like a tame bird who should have meditated flight. Possibilities crowded on her; she hung over the future and grew dizzy; the image of this young man, slim, graceful, dark, with the inscrutable half-smile, attracted and repelled her like a chasm. 'I wonder, will I have met my fate?' she thought, and her heart swelled.

Torrance was got some way into his first exposition, positing a deep layer of texts as he went along, laying the foundations of his discourse, which was to deal with a nice point in divinity, before Archie suffered his eyes to wander. They fell first of all on Clem, looking insupportably prosperous, and patronizing Torrance with the favour of a modified attention, as of one who was used to better things in Glasgow. Though he had never before set eyes on him, Archie had no difficulty in identifying him, and no hesitation in pronouncing him vulgar, the worst of the family. Clem was leaning lazily forward when Archie first saw him. Presently he leaned nonchalantly back; and that deadly instrument, the maiden, was suddenly unmasked in profile. Though not quite in the front of the fashion (had anybody cared!), certain artful Glasgow mantua-makers, and her own inherent taste, had arrayed her to great advantage. Her accoutrement was, indeed, a cause of heart-burning, and almost of scandal, in that infinitesimal kirk company. Mrs Hob had said her say at Cauldstaneslap. 'Daft-like!' she had pronounced it. 'A jaiket that'll no meet! Whaur's the sense of a jaiket that'll no button upon you, if it should come to be weet? What do ye ca thir things? Demmy brokens, d'ye say? They'll be brokens wi' a vengeance or ye can win back! Weel, I have naething to do wi' it – it's no good taste.' Clem, whose purse had thus metamorphosed his sister, and who was not insensible to the

WEIR OF HERMISTON

advertisement, had come to the rescue with a 'Hoot, woman! What do you ken of good taste that has never been to the ceety?' And Hob, looking on the girl with pleased smiles, as she timidly displayed her finery in the midst of the dark kitchen, had thus ended the dispute: 'The cutty looks weel,' he had said, 'and it's no very like rain. Wear them the day, hizzie; but it's no a thing to make a practice o'.' In the breasts of her rivals, coming to the kirk very conscious of white underlinen, and their faces splendid with much soap, the sight of the toilet had raised a storm of varying emotion, from the mere unenvious admiration that was expressed in a long-drawn 'Eh!' to the angrier feeling that found vent in an emphatic 'Set her up!' her frock was of straw-coloured jaconet muslin, cut low at the bosom and short at the ankle, so as to display her *demi-broquins* of Regency violet, crossing with many straps upon a yellow cobweb stocking. According to the pretty fashion in which our grandmothers did not hesitate to appear, and our great-aunts went forth armed for the pursuit and capture of our great-uncles, the dress was drawn up so as to mould the ontour of both breasts, and in the nook between, a cairngorm brooch maintained it. Here, too, surely in a very enviable position, trembled the nosegay of primroses. She wore on her shoulders – or rather, on her back and not her shoulders, which it scarcely passed – a French coat of sarsenet, tied in front with Margate braces, and of the same colour with her violet shoes. About her face clustered a disorder of dark ringlets, a little garland of yellow French roses surmounted her brow, and the whole was crowned by a village hat of chipped straw. Amongst all the rosy and all the weather faces that surrounded her in church, she glowed like an open flower – girl and raiment, and the cairngorm that caught the daylight and returned it in a fiery flash, and the threads of bronze and gold that played in her hair.

Archie was attracted by the bright thing like a child. He looked at her again and yet again, and their looks crossed. The lip was lifted from her little teeth. He saw the red blood work vividly under her tawny skin. Her eye, which was great as a stag's, struck and held his gaze. He knew who she must be – Kirstie, she of the harsh diminutive, his housekeeper's niece, the sister of the rustic prophet, Gib – and he found in her the answer to his wishes.

Christina felt the shock of their encountering glances, and seemed to rise, clothed in smiles, into a region of the vague and bright. But the gratification was not more exquisite than it was brief. She looked away abruptly, and immediately began to blame herself for that abruptness. She knew what she should have done, too late – turned slowly with her nose in the air. And meantime his look was not removed, but continued to play upon her like a battery of cannon constantly aimed, and now seemed to isolate her alone with him, and now seemed to uplift her, as on a pillory, before the congregation. For Archie continued to drink her in with his eyes, even as a wayfarer comes to a well-head on a mountain, and stoops his face, and drinks with thirst unassuageable. In the cleft of her little breasts the fiery eye of the topaz and the pale florets of primrose fascinated him. He saw the breasts heave, and the flowers shake with the heaving, and marvelled what should so much discompose the girl. And Christina was conscious of his gaze – saw it, perhaps, with the dainty plaything of an ear that peeped among her ringlets; she was conscious of changing colour, conscious of her unsteady breath. Like a creature tracked, run down, surrounded, she sought in a dozen ways to give herself a countenance. She used her handkerchief – it was a really fine one – then she desisted in a panic: 'He would only think I was too warm.' She took to reading in the metrical psalms, and then remembered it was sermon-time. Last she put a 'sugar-bool' in her mouth, and the next moment repented of the step. It was such a homely-like thing! Mr Archie would never be eating sweeties in kirk; and, with a palpable effort, she swallowed it whole, and her colour flamed high. At this signal of distress Archie awoke to a sense of his ill-behaviour. What had he been doing? He had been exquisitely rude in church to the niece of his housekeeper; he had stared like a lackey and a libertine at a beautiful and modest girl. It was possible, it was even likely, he would be presented to her after service in the kirk-yard, and then how was he to look? And there was no excuse. He had marked the tokens of her shame, of her increasing indignation, and he was such a fool that he had not understood them. Shame bowed him down, and he looked resolutely at Mr Torrance; who little supposed, good, worthy man, as he continued to expound justification by faith, what was his true business: to play the part of derivative to a pair of children at the old game of falling in love.

Christina was greatly relieved at first. It seemed to her that she was clothed again. She looked back on what had passed. All would have been right if she had not blushed, a silly fool! There was nothing to blush at, if she *had* taken a sugar-bool. Mrs MacTaggart, the elder's wife in St Enoch's, took them often. And if he had looked at her, what was more natural than that a young gentleman should look at the best-dressed girl in church? And at the same time, she knew far otherwise, she knew there was nothing casual or ordinary in the look, and valued herself on its memory like a decoration. Well, it was a blessing he had found something else to look at! And presently she began to have other thoughts. It was necessary, she fancied, that she should put herself right by a repetition of the incident, better managed. If the wish was father to the thought, she did not know or she would not recognize it. It was simply as a manoeuvre of propriety, as something called for to lessen the significance of what had gone before, that she should a second time meet his eyes, and this time without blushing. And at the memory of the blush, she blushed again, and became one general blush burning from head to foot. Was ever anything so indelicate, so forward, done by a girl before? And here she was, making an exhibition of herself before the congregation about nothing! She stole a glance upon her neighbours, and behold! they were steadily indifferent, and Clem had gone to sleep. And still the one idea was becoming more and more potent with her, that in common prudence she must look again before the service ended. Something of the same sort was going forward in the mind of Archie, as he struggled with the load of penitence. So it chanced that, in the flutter of the moment when the last psalm was given out, and Torrance was reading the verse, and the leaves of every psalm-book in church were rustling under busy fingers, two stealthy glances were sent out like antennae among the pews and on the indifferent and absorbed occupants, and drew timidly nearer to the straight line between Archie and Christina. They met, they lingered together for the least fraction of time, and that was enough. A charge as of electricity passed through Christina, and behold! the leaf of her psalm-book was torn across.

Archie was outside by the gate of the graveyard, conversing with Hob and the

minister and shaking hands all round with the scattering congregation, when
Clem and Christina were brought up to be presented. The laird took off his hat
and bowed to her with grace and respect. Christina made her Glasgow curtsey to
the laird, nd went on again up the road for Hermiston and Cauldstaneslap,
walking fast, breathing hurriedly with a heightened colour, and in this strange
frame of mind, that when she was alone she seemed in high happiness, and
when any one addressed her she resented it like a contradiction. A part of the
way she had the company of some neighbour girls and a loutish young man;
never had they seemed so insipid, never had she made herself so disagreeable.
But these struck aside to their various destinations or were out-walked and left
behind; and when she had driven off with sharp words the proffered convoy of
some of her nephews and nieces, she was free to go on alone up Hermiston brae,
walking on air, dwelling intoxicated among clouds of happiness. Near to the
summit she heard steps behind her, a man's steps, light and very rapid. She
knew the foot at once and walked the faster. 'If it's me he's wanting, he can run
for it,' she thought, smiling.

Archie overtook her like a man whose mind was made up.

'Miss Kirstie,' he began.

'Miss Christina, if you please, Mr Weir,' she interrupted. 'I canna bear the
contraction.'

'You forget it has a friendly sound for me. Your aunt is an old friend of mine,
and a very good one. I hope we shall see much of you at Hermiston?'

'My aunt and my sister-in-law doesna agree very well. Not that I have much
ado with it. But still when I'm stopping in the house, if I was to be visiting my
aunt, it would not look considerate-like.'

'I am sorry,' said Archie.

'I thank you kindly, Mr Weir,' she said. 'I whiles think myself it's a great
peety.'

'Ah, I am sure your voice would always be for peace!' he cried.

'I wouldna be too sure of that,' she said. 'I have my days like other folk, I
suppose.'

'Do you know, in our old kirk, among our good old grey dames, you made an
effect like sunshine.'

'Ah, but that would be my Glasgow clothes!'

'I did not think I was so much under the influence of pretty frocks.'

She smiled with a half look at him. 'There's more than you!' she said. 'But you
see I'm only Cinderella. I'll have to put all these things by in my trunk; next
Sunday I'll be as grey as the rest. They're Glasgow clothes, you see, and it would
never do to make a practice of it. It would seem terrible conspicuous.'

By that they were come to the place where their ways severed. The old grey
moors were all about them; in the midst a few sheep wandered; and they could
see on the one hand the straggling caravan scaling the braes in front of them for
Cauldstaneslap, and on the other, the contingent from Hermiston bending off
and beginning to disappear by detachments into the policy gate. It was in these
circumstances that they turned to say farewell, and deliberately exchanged a
glance as they shook hands. All passed as it should, genteelly; and in Christina's
mind, as she mounted the first steep ascent for Cauldstaneslap, a gratifying sense
of triumph prevailed over the recollection of minor lapses and mistakes. She had

kilted her gown, as she did usually at that rugged pass; but when she spied Archie still standing and gazing after her, the skirts came down again as if by enchantment. Here was a piece of nicety for that upland parish, where the matrons marched with their coats kilted in the rain, and the lasses walked barefoot to kirk through the dust of summer, and went bravely down by the burn-side, and sat on stones to make a public toilet before entering! It was perhaps an air wafted from Glasgow; or perhaps it marked a stage of that dizziness of gratified vanity, in which the instinctive act passed unperceived. He was looking after! She unloaded her bosom of a prodigious sigh that was all pleasure, and betook herself to run. When she had overtaken the stragglers of her family, she caught up the niece whom she had so recently repulsed, and kissed and slapped her, and drove her away again, and ran after her with pretty cries and laughter. Perhaps she thought the laird might still be looking! But it chanced the little scene came under the view of eyes less favourable; for she overtook Mrs Hob marching with Clem and Dand.

'You're shürely fey, lass!' quoth Dandie.

'Think shame to yersel', miss!' said the strident Mrs Hob. 'Is this the gait to guide yersel' on the way hame frae kirk? You're shürely no sponsible the day! And anyway I would mind my guid claes.'

'Hoot!' said Christina, and went on before them head in air, treading the rough track with the tread of a wild doe.

She was in love with herself, her destiny, the air of the hills, the benediction of the sun. All the way home, she continued under the intoxication of these sky-scraping spirits. At table she could talk freely of young Hermiston; gave her opinion of him offhand and with a loud voice, that he was a handsome young gentleman, real well mannered and sensible-like, but it was a pity he looked doleful. Only – the moment after – a memory of his eyes in church embarrassed her. But for this inconsiderable check, all through meal-time she had a good appetite, and she kept them laughing at table, until Gib (who had returned before them from Crossmichael and his separative worship) reproved the whole of them for their levity.

Singing 'in to herself' as she went, her mind still in the turmoil of a glad confusion, she rose and tripped upstairs to a little loft, lighted by four panes in the gable, where she slept with one of her nieces. The niece, who followed her, presuming on 'Auntie's' high spirits, was flounced out of the apartment with small ceremony, and retired, smarting and half tearful, to bury her woes in the byre among the hay. Still humming, Christina divested herself of her finery, and put her treasures one by one in her great green trunk. The last of these was the psalm-book; it was a fine piece, the gift of Mistress Clem, in distinct old-faced type, on paper that had begun to grow foxy in the warehouse – not by service – and she was used to wrap it in a handkerchief every Sunday after its period of service was over, and bury it end-wise at the head of her trunk. As she now took it in hand the book fell open where the leaf was torn, and she stood and gazed upon that evidence of her bygone discomposure. There returned again the vision of the two brown eyes staring at her, intent and bright, out of that dark corner of the kirk. The whole appearance and attitude, the smile, the suggested gesture of young Hermiston came before her in a flash at the sight of the torn page. 'I was surely fey!' she said, echoing the words of Dandie, and at the suggested doom her high spirits deserted her. She flung herself prone upon the bed, and lay there, holding the psalm-book in her hands for hours, for the more part in a mere stupor of unconsenting pleasure and unreasoning fear. The fear was super-stitious; there came up again and again in her memory Dandie's ill-omened words, and a hundred grisly and black tales out of the immediate neighbourhood read her a commentary on their force. The pleasure was never realized. You might say the joints of her body thought and remembered, and were gladdened, but her essential self, in the immediate theatre of consciousness, talked feverishly of something else, like a nervous person at a fire. The image that she most complacently dwelt on was that of Miss Christina in her character of the Fair Lass of Cauldstaneslap, carrying all before her in the straw-coloured frock, the violet mantle, and the yellow cobweb stockings. Archie's image, on the other hand, when it presented itself was never welcomed – far less welcomed with any ardour, and it was exposed at times to merciless criticism. In the long vague dialogues she held in her mind, often with imaginary, often with unrealized interlocutors, Archie, if he were referred to at all, came in for savage handling. He was described as 'looking like a stirk,' 'staring like a caulf,' 'a face like a ghaist's.' 'Do you call that manners?' she said; or, 'I soon put him in his place.' "*Miss Christina, if you please, Mr Weir!*" says I, and just flyped up my skirt tails.' With gabble like this she would entertain herself long whiles together, and then her eye would perhaps fall on the torn leaf, and the eyes of Archie would appear again from the darkness of the wall, and the voluble words deserted her, and she would lie still and stupid, and think upon nothing with devotion, and be sometimes raised by a quiet sigh. Had a doctor of medicine come into that loft, he would have diagnosed a healthy, well-developed, eminently vivacious lass lying on her face in a fit of the sulks; not one who had just contracted, or was just contracting, a mortal sickness of the mind which should yet carry her towards death and despair. Had it been a doctor of psychology, he might have been pardoned for divining in the girl a passion of childish vanity, self-love *in excelsis*, and no more. It is to be understood that I have been painting chaos and describing the inarticulate. Every lineament that appears is too precise, almost every word used too strong. Take a finger-post in the mountains on a day of rolling mists; I have but copied the names that appear upon the pointers, the names of definite and famous cities far distant, and now perhaps basking in sunshine; but Christina remained all these hours, as it were, at the foot of the post itself, not moving, and enveloped in mutable and blinding wreaths of haze.

The day was growing late and the sunbeams long and level, when she sat suddenly up, and wrapped in its handkerchief and put by that psalm-book which had already played a part so decisive in the first chapter of her love-story. In the absence of the mesmerist's eye, we are told nowadays that the head of a bright nail may fill his place, if it be steadfastly regarded. So that torn page had riveted her attention on what might else have been but little, and perhaps soon forgotten; while the ominous words of Dandie – heard, not heeded, and still remembered – had lent to her thoughts, or rather to her mood, a cast of solemnity, and that idea of Fate – a pagan Fate, uncontrolled by any Christian deity, obscure, lawless, and august – moving indissuadably in the affairs of Christian men. Thus even that phenomenon of love at first sight, which is so rare and seems so simple and violent, like a disruption of life's tissue, may be decomposed into a sequence of accidents happily concurring.

She put on a grey frock and a pink kerchief, looked at herself a moment with approval in the small square of glass that served her for a toilet mirror, and went softly downstairs through the sleeping house that resounded with the sound of afternoon snoring. Just outside the door, Dandi was sitting with a book in his hand, not reading, only honouring the Sabbath by a sacred vacancy of mind. She came near him and stood still.

'I'm for off up the muirs, Dandie,' she said.

There was something unusually soft in her tones that made him look up. She was pale, her eyes dark and bright; no trace remained of the levity of the morning.

'Ay, lass? Ye'll have yer ups and downs like me, I'm thinkin',' he observed.

'What for do ye say that?' she asked.

'O, for naething,' says Dand. 'Only I think ye're mair like me than the lave of them. Ye've mair of the poetic temper, tho' Guid kens little enough of the poetic taalent. It's an ill gift at the best. Look at yoursel'. At denner you were all sunshine and flowers and laughter, and now you're like the star of evening on a lake.'

She drank in this hackneyed compliment like wine, and it glowed in her veins.

'But I'm saying, Dand' – she came nearer him – 'I'm for the muirs. I must have a braith of air. If Clem was to be speiring for me, try and quaiet him, will ye no?'

'What way?' said Dandie. 'I ken but the ae way, and that's leein'. I'll say ye had a sair heed, if ye like.'

'But I havena,' she objected.

'I daursay no',' he returned. 'I said I would say ye had; and if ye like to nay-say me when ye come back, it'll no mateerially maitter, for my chara'ter's clean gane a'ready past reca'.'

'O, Dand, are ye a leear?' she asked, lingering.

'Folks say sae,' replied the bard.

'Wha says sae?' she pursued.

'Them that should ken the best,' he responded. 'The lassies, for ane.'

'But, Dand, you would never lee to me?' she asked.

'I'll leave that for your pairt of it, ye girzie,' said he. 'Ye'll lee to me fast eneuch, when ye hae gotten a jo. I'm tellin' ye and it's true; when you have a jo, Miss Kirstie, it'll be for guid and ill. I ken: I was made that way mysel', but the deil was in my luck! Here, gang awa wi' ye to your muirs, and let me be; I'm in an hour of inspiraution, ye upsetting tawpie!'

But she clung to her brother's neighbourhood, she knew not why.

'Will ye no gie's a kiss, Dand?' she said. 'I aye likit ye fine.'

He kissed her and considered her a moment; he found something strange in her. But he was a libertine through and through, nourished equal contempt and suspicion of all womankind, and paid his way among them habitually with idle compliments.

'Gae wa' wi' ye!' said he. 'ye're a dentie baby, and be content wi' that!'

That was Dandie's way; a kiss and a comfit to Jenny – a bawbee and my blessing to Jill – and good-night to the whole clan of ye, my dears! When anything approached the serious, it became a matter for men, he both throught

and said. Women, when they did not absorb, were only children to be shoo'd
away. Merely in his character of connoisseur, however, Dandie glanced
carelessly after his sister as she crossed the meadow. 'The brat's no that bad!' he
thought with surprise, for though he had just been paying her compliments, he
had not really looked at her. 'Hey! what's yon?' For the grey dress was cut with
short sleeves and skirts, and displayed her trim strong legs clad in pink stockings
of the same shade as the kerchief she wore round her shoulders, and that
shimmered as she went. This was not her way in undress; he knew her ways and
the ways of the whole sex in the countryside, no one better; when they did not
go barefoot, they wore stout 'rig and furrow' woollen hose of an invisible blue
mostly, when they were not black outright; and Dandie, at sight of this
daintiness, put two and two together. It was a silk handkerchief, then they
would be silken hose; they matched – then the whole outfit was a present of
Clem's, a costly present, and not something to be worn through bog and briar,
or on a late afternoon of Sunday. He whistled. 'My denty May, either your heid's
fair turned, or there's some ongoings!' he observed, and dismissed the subject.

She went slowly at first, but ever straighter and faster for the Cauldstaneslap,
a pass among the hills to which the farm owed its name. The Slap opened like a
doorway between two rounded hillocks; and through this ran the short cut to
Hermiston. Immediately on the other side it went down through the Deil's
Hags, a considerably marshy hollow of the hill tops, full of springs, and
crouching junipers, and pools where the black peatwater slumbered. There was
no view from here. A man might have sat upon the Praying Weaver's stone a
half century, and seen none but the Cauldstaneslap children twice in the
twenty-four hours on their way to the school and back again, an occasional
shepherd, the irruption of a clan of sheep, or the birds who haunted about the
springs, drinking and shrilly piping. So, when she had once passed the Slap,
Kirstie was received into seclusion. She looked back a last ime at the farm. It
still lay deserted except for the figure of Dandie, who was now seen to be
scribbling in his lap, the hour of expected inspiration having come to him at
last. Thence she passed rapidly through the morass, and came to the farther end
of it, where a sluggish burn discharges, and the path for Hermiston accompanies
it on the beginning of its downward way. From this corner a wide view was
opened to her of the whole stretch of braes upon the other side, still sallow and
in places rusty with the winter, with the path marked boldly, here and there by
the burn-side a tuft of birches, and – two miles off as the crow flies – from its
enclosures and young plantations, the windows of Hermiston glittering in the
western sun.

Here she sat down and waited, and looked for a long time at these far-away
bright panes of glass. It amused her to have so extended a view, she thought. It
amused her to see the house of Hermiston – to see 'folk'; and there was an
indistinguishable human unit, perhaps the gardener, visibly sauntering on the
gravel paths.

By the time the sun was down and all the easterly braes lay plunged in clear
shadow, she was aware of another figure coming up the path at a most unequal
rate of approach, now half running, now pausing and seeming to hesitate. She
watched him at first with a total suspension of thought. She held her thought as
a person holds his breathing. Then she consented to recognize him. 'He'll no be

coming here, he canna be; it's no possible.' And there began to grow upon her a subdued choking suspense. He *was* coming; his hesitations had quite ceased, his step grew firm and swift; no doubt remained; and the question loomed up before her instant: what was she to do? It was all very well to say that her brother was a laird himself; it was all very well to speak of casual intermarriages and to count cousinship, like Auntie Kirstie. The difference in their social station was trenchant; propriety, prudence, all that she had ever learned, all that she knew, bade her flee. But on the other hand the cup of life now offered to her was too enchanting. For one moment, she saw the question clearly, and definitely made her choice. She stood up and showed herself an instant in the gap relieved upon the sky line; and the next, fled trembling and sat down glowing with excitement on the Weaver's stone. She shut her eyes, seeking, praying for composure. Her hand shook in her lap, and her mind was full of incongruous and futile speeches. What was there to make a work about? She could take care of herself, she supposed. There was no harm in seeing the laird. It was the best thing that could happen. She would mark a proper distance to him once and for all. Gradually the wheels of her nature ceased to go round so madly, and she sat in passive expectation, a quiet, solitary figure in the midst of the grey moss. I have said she was no hypocrite, but here I am at fault. She never admitted to herself that she had come up the hill to look for Archie. And perhaps after all she did not know, perhaps came as a stone falls. For the steps of love in the young, and especially in girls, are instinctive and unconscious.

In the meantime Archie was drawing rapidly near, and he at least was consciously seeking her neighbourhood. The afternoon had turned to ashes in his mouth; the memory of the girl had kept him from reading and drawn him as with cords; and at last, as the cool of the evening began to come on, he had taken his hat and set forth, with a smothered ejaculation, by the moor path to Cauldstaneslap. He had no hope to find her; he took the off chance without expectation of result and to relieve his uneasiness. The greater was his surprise, as he surmounted the slope and came into the hollow of the Deil's Hags, to see there, like an answer to his wishes, the little womanly figure in the grey dress and the pink kerchief sitting little, and low, and lost, and acutely solitary, in these desolate surroundings and on the weather-beaten stone of the dead weaver. Those things that still smacked of winter were all rusty about her, and those things that already relished of the spring had put forth the tender and lively colours of the season. Even in the unchanging face of the death-stone, changes were to be remarked; and in the channelled lettering, the moss began to renew itself in jewels of green. By an afterthought that was a stroke of art, she had turned up over her head the back of the kerchief; so that it now framed becomingly her vivacious and yet pensive face. Her feet were gathered under her on the one side, and she leaned on her bare arm, which showed out strong and round, tapered to a slim wrist, and shimmered in the fading light.

Young Hermiston was struck with a certain chill. He was reminded that he now dealt in serious matters of life and death. This was a grown woman he was approaching, endowed with her mysterious potencies and attractions, the treasury of the continued race, and he was neither better nor worse than the average of his sex and age. He had a certain delicacy which had preserved him hitherto unspotted, and which (had either of them guessed it) made him a more dangerous companion when his heart should be really stirred. His throat was dry as he came near; but the appealing sweetness of her smile stood between them like a guardian angel.

For she turned to him and smiled, though without rising. There was a shade in this cavalier greeting that neither of them perceived; neither he, who simply thought it gracious and charming as herself; nor yet she, who did not observe (quick as she was) the difference between rising to meet the laird, and remaining seated to receive the expected admirer.

'Are ye stepping west, Hermiston?' said she, giving him his territorial name after the fashion of the countryside.

'I was,' said he, a little hoarsely, 'but I think I will be about the end of my stroll now. Are you like me, Miss Christina? The house would not hold me. I came here seeking air.'

He took his seat at the other end of the tombstone and studied her, wondering what was she. There was infinite import in the question alike for her and him.

'Ay,' she said. 'I couldna bear the roof either. It's a habit of mine to come up here about the gloaming when it's quaiet and caller.'

'It was a habit of my mother's also,' he said gravely. The recollection half startled him as he expressed it. He looked around. 'I have scarce been here since. It's peaceful,' he said, with a long breath.

'It's no like Glasgow,' she replied. 'A weary place, yon Glasgow! But what a day have I had for my hame-coming, and what a bonny evening!'

'Indeed, it was a wonderful day,' said Archie. 'I think I will remember it years and years until I come to die. On days like that – I do not know if you feel as I do – but everything appears so brief, and fragile, and exquisite, that I am afraid to touch life. We are here for so short a time; and all the old people before us – Rutherfords of Hermiston, Elliotts of the Cauldstaneslap – that were here but a while since riding about and keeping up a great noise in this quiet corner – making love too, and marrying – why, where are they now? It's deadly commonplace, but, after all, the commonplaces are the great poetic truths.'

He was sounding her, semi-consciously, to see if she could understand him; to learn if she were only an animal the colour of flowers, or had a soul in her to keep her sweet. She, on her part, her means well in hand, watched, womanlike, for any opportunity to shine, to abound in his humour, whatever that might be. The dramatic artist, that lies dormant or only half awake in most human beings, had in her sprung to his feet in a divine fury, and chance had served her well. She looked upon him with a subdued twilight look that became the hour of the day and the train of thought; earnestness shone through her like stars in the purple west; and from the great but controlled upheaval of her whole nature there passed into her voice, and rang in her lightest words, a thrill of emotion.

'Have you mind of Dand's song?' she answered. 'I think he'll have been trying to say what you have been thinking.'

'No, I never heard it,' he said. 'Repeat it to me, can you?'

'It's nothing wanting the tune,' said Kirstie.

'Then sing it me,' said he.

'On the Lord's Day? That would never do, Mr Weir!'

'I am afraid I am not so strict a keeper of the Sabbath, and there is no one in this place to hear us, unless the poor old ancient under the stone.'

'No that I'm thinking that really,' she said. 'By my way of thinking, it's just as serious as a psalm. Will I sooth it to ye then?'

'If you please,' said he, and, drawing near to her on the tombstone, prepared to listen.

‿ She sat up as if so sing. 'I'll only can sooth it to ye,' she explained. 'I wouldna like to sing out loud on the Sabbath. I think the birds would carry news of it to Gilbert,' and she smiled. 'It's about the Elliotts,' she continued, 'and I think there's few bonnier bits in the book-poets, though Dand has never got printed yet.'

And she began, in the low, clear tones of her half voice, now sinking almost to a whisper, now rising to a particular note which was her best, and which Archie learned to wait for with growing emotion:

'O they rade in the rain, in the days that are gane,
   In the rain and the wind and the lave,
They shoutit in the ha' and they routit on the hill,
   But they're a' quaitit noo in the grave.
Auld, auld Elliotts, clay-cauld Elliotts, dour, bauld Elliotts of auld!'

All the time she sang she looked steadfastly before her, her knees straight, her hands upon her knee, her head cast back and up. The expression was admirable throughout, for had she not learned it from the lips and under the criticism of the author? When it was done, she turned upon Archie a face softly bright, and eyes gently suffused and shining in the twilight, and his heart rose and went out to her with boundless pity and sympathy. His question was answered. She was a human being tuned to a sense of the tragedy of life; there were pathos and music and a great heart in the girl.

He arose instinctively, she also; for she saw she had gained a point, and scored the impression deeper, and she had wit enough left to flee upon a victory. They were but commonplaces that remained to be exchanged, but the low, moved voices in which they passed made them sacred in the memory. In the falling greyness of the evening he watched her figure winding through the morass, saw it turn a last time and wave a hand, and then pass through the Slap; and it seemed to him as if something went along with her out of the deepest of his heart. And something surely had come, and come to dwell there. He had retained from childhood a picture, now half obliterated by the passage of time and the multitude of fresh impressions, of his mother telling him, with the fluttered earnestness of her voice, and often with dropping tears, the tale of the 'Praying Weaver,' on the very scene of his brief tragedy and long repose. And now there was a companion piece; and he beheld, and he should behold for ever, Christina perched on the same tomb, in the grey colours of the evening, gracious, dainty, perfect as a flower, and she also singing:

'Of old, unhappy far-off things,
And battles long ago,'

of their common ancestors now dead, of their rude wars composed, their weapons buried with them, and of these strange changelings, their descendants, who lingered a little in their places, and would soon be gone also, and perhaps sung of by others at the gloaming hour. By one of the unconscious arts of tenderness the two women were enshrined together in his memory. Tears, in that hour of sensibility, came into his eyes indifferently at the thought of either; and the girl, from being something merely bright and shapely, was caught up into the zone of things serious as life and death and his dead mother. So that in all ways and on either side, Fate played his game artfully with this poor pair of children. The generations were prepared, the pangs were made ready, before the curtain rose on the dark drama.

In the same moment of time that she disappeared from Archie, there opened before Kirstie's eyes the cup-like hollow in which the farm lay. She saw, some five hundred feet below her, the house making itself bright with candles, and this was a broad hint to her to hurry. For they were only kindled on a Sabbath night with a view to that family worship which rounded in the incomparable tedium of the day and brought on the relaxation of supper. Already she knew that Robert must be within-sides at the head of the table, 'waling the portions'; for it was Robert in his quality of family priest and judge, not the gifted Gilbert, who officiated. She made good time accordingly down the steep ascent, and came up to the door panting as the three younger brothers, all roused at last from slumber, stood together in the cool and the dark of the evening with a fry of nephews and nieces about them, chatting and awaiting the expected signal. She stood back; she had no mind to direct attention to her late arrival or to her labouring breath.

'Kirstie, ye have shaved it this time, my lass,' said Clem. 'Whaur were ye?'

'O, just taking a dander by mysel',' said Kirstie.

And the talk continued on the subject of the American War, without further reference to the truant who stood by them in the covert of the dusk, thrilling with happiness and the sense of guilt.

The signal was given, and the brothers began to go in one after another, amid the jostle and throng of Hob's children.

Only Dandie, waiting till the last, caught Kirstie by the arm. 'When did ye begin to dander in pink hosen, Mistress Elliott?' he whispered slyly.

She looked down; she was one blush. 'I maun have forgotten to change them,' said she; and went into prayers in her turn with a troubled mind, between anxiety as to whether Dand should have observed her yellow stockings at church, and should thus detect her in a palpable falsehood, and shame that she had already made good his prophecy. She remembered the words of it, how it was to be when she had gotten a jo, and that that would be for good and evil. 'Will I have gotten my jo now?' she thought with a secret rapture.

And all through prayers, where it was her principal business to conceal the pink stockings from the eyes of the indifferent Mrs Hob – and all through supper, as she made a feint of eating and sat at the table radiant and constrained – and again when she had left them and come into her chamber, and was alone with her sleeping niece, and could at last lay aside the armour of society – the same words sounded within her, the same profound note of happiness, of a world all changed and renewed, of a day that had been passed in Paradise, and of a night that was to be heaven opened. All night she seemed to be conveyed smoothly upon a shallow stream of sleep and waking, and through the bowers of

Beulah; all night she cherished to her heart that exquisite hope; and if, towards morning, she forgot it a while in a more profound unconsciousness, it was to catch again the rainbow thought with her first moment of awaking.

CHAPTER SEVEN

Enter Mephistopheles

TWO DAYS LATER A GIG FROM Crossmichael deposited Frank Innes at the doors of Hermiston. Once in a way, during the past winter, Archie, in some acute phase of boredom, had written him a letter. It had contained something in the nature of an invitation, or a reference to an invitation – precisely what, neither of them now remembered. When Innes had received it, there had been nothing further from his mind than to bury himself in the moors with Archie; but not even the most acute political heads are guided through the steps of life with unerring directness. That would require a gift of prophecy which has been denied to man. For instance, who could have imagined that, not a month after he had received the letter, and turned it into mockery, and put off answering it, and in the end lost it, misfortunes of a gloomy cast should begin to thicken over Frank's career? His case may be briefly stated. His father, a small Morayshire laird with a large family, became recalcitrant and cut off the supplies; he had fitted himself out with the beginnings of quite a good law library, which, upon some sudden losses on the turf, he had been obleged to sell before they were paid for; and his bookseller, hearing some rumour of the event, took out a warrant for his arrest. Innes had early word of it, and was able to take precautions. In this immediate welter of his affairs, with an unpleasant charge hanging over him, he had judged it the part of prudence to be off instantly, had written a fervid letter to his father at Inverauld, and put himself in the coach for Crossmichael. Any port in a storm! He was manfully turning his back on the Parliament House and its gay babble, on porter and oysters, the racecourse and the ring; and manfully prepared, until these clouds should have blown by, to share a living grave with Archie Weir at Hermiston.

To do him justice, he was no less surprised to be going than Archie was to see him come; and he carried off his wonder with an infinitely better grace. 'Well, here I am!' said he, as he alighted. 'Pylades has come to Orestes at last. By the way, did you get my answer? No? How very provoking! Well, here I am to answer for myself, and that's better still.'

'I am very glad to see you, of course,' said Archie. 'I make you heartily welcome, of course. But you surely have not come to stay, with the Courts still sitting; is that not most unwise?'

'Damn the Courts!' says Frank. 'What are the Courts to friendship and a little fishing?'

And so it was agreed that he was to stay, with no term to the visit but the term

which he had privily set to it himself – the day, namely, when his father should
have come down with the dust, and he should be able to pacify the bookseller.
On such vague conditions there began for these two young men (who were not
even friends) a life of great familiarity and, as the days drew on, less and less
intimacy. They were together at meal times, together o' nights when the hour
had come for whisky-toddy; but it might have been noticed (had there been any
one to pay heed) that they were rarely so much together by day. Archie had
Hermiston to attend to, multifarious activities in the hills, in which he did not
require, and had even refused, Frank's escort. He would be off sometimes in the
morning and leave only a note on the breakfast table to announce the fact; and
sometimes, with no notice at all, he would not return for dinner until the hour
was long past. Innes groaned under these desertions; it required all his
philosophy to sit down to a solitary breakfast with composure, and all his
unaffected good-nature to be able to greet Archie with friendliness on the more
rare occasions when he came home late for dinner.

'I wonder what on earth he finds to do, Mrs Elliott?' said he one morning,
after he had just read the hasty billet and sat down to table.

'I suppose it will be business, sir,' replied the housekeeper dryly, measuring his
distance off to him by an indicated curtsey.

'But I can't imagine what business!' he reiterated.

'I suppose it will be *his* business,' retorted the austere Kirstie.

He turned to her with that happy brightness that made the charm of his
disposition, and broke into a peal of healthy and natural laughter.

'Well played, Mrs Elliott!' he cried; and the housekeeper's face relaxed into
the shadow of an iron smile. 'Well played indeed!' said he. 'But you must not be
making a stranger of me like that. Why, Archie and I were at the High School
together, and we've been to college together, and we were going to the Bar
together, when – you know! Dear, dear me! what a pity that was! A life spoiled,
a fine young fellow as good as buried here in the wilderness with rustics; and all
for what? A frolic, silly, if you like, but no more. God, how good your scones
are, Mrs Elliott!'

'They're no mines, it was the lassie made them,' said Kirstie; 'and, saving your
presence, there's little sense in taking the Lord's name in vain about idle vivers
that you fill your kyte wi'.'

'I dare say you're perfectly right, ma'am,' quoth the imperturbable Frank. 'But
as I was saying, this is a pitiable business, this about poor Archie; and you and I
might do worse than put our heads together, like a couple of sensible people, and
bring it to an end. Let me tell you, ma'am, that Archie is really quite a
promising young man, and in my opinion he would do well at the Bar. As for his
father, no one can deny his ability, and I don't fancy any one would care to deny
that he has the deil's own temper——'

'If you'll excuse me, Mr Innes, I think the lass is crying on me,' said Kirstie,
and flounced from the room.

'The damned, cross-grained, old broomstick!' ejaculated Innes.

In the meantime, Kirstie had escaped into the kitchen, and before her vassal
gave vent to her feelings.

'Here, ettercap! Ye'll have to wait on yon Innes! I canna haud myself in. "Puir
Erchie!" I'd "puir Erchie" him, if I had my way! And Hermiston with the deil's

ain temper! God, let him take Hermiston's scones out of his mouth first. There's no a hair on ayther o' the Weirs that hasna mair spunk and dirdum to it than what he has in his hale dwaibly body! Settin' up his snash to me! Let him gang to the black toon where he's mebbe wantit – birling in a curricle – wi' pimatum on his heid – making a mess o' himsel' wi' nesty hizzies – a fair disgrace!' It was impossible to hear without admiration Kirstie's graduated disgust, as she brought forth, one after another, these somewhat baseless charges. Then she remembered her immediate purpose, and turned again to her fascinated auditor. 'Do ye no hear me, tawpie? Do ye no hear what I'm tellin' ye? Will I have to shoo ye in to him? If I come to attend to ye, mistress!' And the maid fled the kitchen, which had become practically dangerous, to attend on Innes's wants in the front parlour.

Tantaene irae? Has the reader perceived the reason? Since Frank's coming there were no more hours of gossip over the supper tray! All his blandishments were in vain; he had started handicapped on the race for Mrs Elliott's favour.

But it was a strange thing how misfortune dogged him in his efforts to be genial. I must guard the reader against accepting Kirstie's epithets as evidence; she was more concerned for their vigour than for their accuracy. Dwaibly, for instance; nothing could be more calumnious. Frank was the very picture of good looks, good humour, and manly youth. He had bright eyes with a sparkle and a dance to them, curly hair, a charming smile, brilliant teeth, and admirable carriage of the head, the look of a gentleman, the address of one accustomed to please at first sight and to improve the impression. And with all these advantages, he failed with every one about Hermiston; with the silent shepherd, with the obsequious grieve, with the groom who was also the ploughman, with the gardener and the gardener's sister – a pious, down-hearted woman with a shawl over her ears – he failed equally and flatly. They did not like him, and they showed it. The little maid, indeed, was an exception; she admired him devoutly, probably dreamed of him in her private hours; but she was accustomed to play the part of silent auditor to Kirstie's tirades and silent recipient of Kirstie's buffets, and she had learned not only to be a very capable girl of her years, but a very secret and prudent one besides. Frank was thus conscious that he had one ally and sympathizer in the midst of that general union of disfavour that surrounded, watched, and waited on him in the house of Hermiston; but he had little comfort or society from that alliance, and the demure little maid (twelve on her last birthday) preserved her own counsel, and tripped on his service, brisk, dumbly responsive, but inexorably unconversational. For the others, they were beyond hope and beyond endurance. Never had a young Apollo been cast among such rustic barbarians. But perhaps the cause of his ill-success lay in one trait which was habitual and unconscious with him, yet diagnostic of the man. It was his practice to approach any one person at the expense of someone else. He offered you an alliance against the someone else; he flattered you by slighting him; you were drawn into a small intrigue against him before you knew how. Wonderful are the virtues of this process generally; but Frank's mistake was in the choice of the someone else. He was not politic in that; he listened to the voice of irritation. Archie had offended him at first by what he had felt to be rather a dry reception, had offended him since by his frequent absences. He was besides the one figure continually present in Frank's

eye; and it was to his immediate dependants that Frank could offer the snare of
his sympathy. Now the truth is that the Weirs, father and son, were surrounded
by a posse of strenuous loyalists. Of my lord they were vastly proud. It was a
distinction in itself to be one of the vassals of the 'Hanging Judge,' and his gross,
formidable joviality was far from unpopular in the neighbourhood of his home.
For Archie they had, one and all, a sensitive affection and respect which
recoiled from a word of belittlement.

Nor was Frank more successful when he went farther afield. To the Four Black
Brothers, for instance, he was antipathetic in the highest degree. Hob thought
him too light, Gib too profane. Clem, who saw him but for a day or two before
he went to Glasgow, wanted to know what the fule's business was, and whether
he meant to stay here all session-time! 'Yon's a drone,' he pronounced. As for
Dand, it will be enough to describe their first meeting, when Frank had been
whipping a river and the rustic celebrity chanced to come along the path.

'I'm told you're quite a poet,' Frank had said.

'Wha tell't ye that, mannie?' had been the unconciliating answer.

'O, everybody!' says Frank.

'God! Here's fame!' said the sardonic poet, and he had passed on his way.

Come to think of it, we have here perhaps a truer explanation of Frank's
failures. Had he met Mr Sheriff Scott he could have turned a neater
compliment, because Mr Scott would have been a friend worth making. Dand,
on the other hand, he did not value sixpence, and he showed it even while he
tried to flatter. Condescension is an excellent thing, but it is strange how one-
sided the pleasure of it is! He who goes fishing among the Scots peasantry with
condescension for a bait will have an empty basket by evening.

In proof of this theory Frank made a great success of it at the Crossmichael
Club, to which Archie took him immediately on his arrival; his own last
appearance on that scene of gaiety. Frank was made welcome there at once,
continued to go regularly, and had attended a meeting (as the members ever
after loved to tell) on the evening before his death. Young Hay and young
Pringle appeared again. There was another supper at Windielaws, another
dinner at Driffel; and it resulted in Frank being taken to the bosom of the county
people as unreservedly as he had been repudiated by the country folk. He
occupied Hermiston after the manner of an invader in a conquered capital. He
was perpetually issuing from it, as from a base, to toddy parties, fishing-parties,
and dinner parties, to which Archie was not invited, or to which Archie would
not go. It was now that the name of The Recluse became general for the young
man. Some say that Innes invented it; Innes, at least, spread it abroad.

'How's all with your Recluse today?' people would ask.

'O, reclusing away!' Innes would declare, with his bright air of saying
something witty; and imediately interrupt the general laughter which he had
provoked much more by his air than his words, 'Mind you, it's all very well
laughing, but I'm not very well pleased. Poor Archie is a good fellow, an
excellent fellow, a fellow I always liked. I think it small of him to take his little
disgrace so hard and shut himself up. 'Grant that it is a ridiculous story, painfully
ridiculous,' I keep telling him. 'Be a man! Live it down, man!' But not he. Of
course it's just solitude, and shame, and all that. But I confess I'm beginning to
fear the result. It would be all the pities in the world if a really promising fellow

like Weir was to end ill. I'm seriously tempted to write to Lord Hermiston, and put it plainly to him.'

'I would if I were you,' some of his auditors would say, shaking the head, sitting bewildered and confused at this new view of the matter, so deftly indicated by a single word. 'A capital idea!' they would add, and wonder at the *aplomb* and position of this young man, who talked as a matter of course of writing to Hermiston and correcting him upon his private affairs.

And Frank would proceed, sweetly confidential: 'I'll give you an idea, now. He's actually sore about the way that I'm received and he's left out in the county – actually jealous and sore. I've rallied him and I've reasoned with him, told him that everyone was most kindly inclined towards him, told him even that *I* was received merely because I was his guest. But it's no use. He will neither accept the invitations he gets, nor stop brooding about the ones where he's left out. What I'm afraid of is that the wound's ulcerating. He had always one of those dark, secret, angry natures – a little underhand and plenty of bile – you know the sort. He must have inherited it from the Weirs, whom I suspect to have been a worthy family of weavers somewhere; what's the cant phrase? – sedentary occupation. It's precisely the kind of character to go wrong in a false position like what his father's made for him, or he's making for himself, whichever you like to call it. And for my part, I think it a disgrace,' Frank would say generously.

Presently the sorrow and anxiety of this disinterested friend took shape. He began in private, in conversations of two, to talk vaguely of bad habits and low habits. 'I must say I'm afraid he's going wrong altogether,' he would say. 'I'll tell you plainly, and between ourselves, I scarcely like to stay there any longer; only, man, I'm positively afraid to leave him alone. You'll see, I shall be blamed for it later on. I'm staying at a great sacrifice. I'm hindering my chances at the Bar, and I can't blind my eyes to it. And what I'm afraid of is that I'm going to get kicked for it all round before all's done. You see, nobody believes in friendship nowadays.'

'Well, Innes,' his interlocutor would reply, 'it's very good of you, I must say that. If there's any blame going, you'll always be sure of *my* good word, for one thing.'

'Well,' Frank would continue, 'candidly, I don't say it's pleasant. He has a very rough way with him; his father's son, you know. I don't say he's rude – of course, I couldn't be expected to stand that – but he steers very near the wind. No, it's not pleasant; but I tell ye, man, in conscience I don't think it would be fair to leave him. Mind you, I don't say there's anything actually wrong. What I say is that I don't like the looks of it, man!' and he would press the arm of his momentary confidant.

In the early stages I am persuaded there was no malice. He talked but for the pleasure of airing himself. He was essentially glib, as becomes the young advocate, and essentially careless of the truth, which is the mark of the young ass; and so he talked at random. There was no particular bias, but that one which is indigenous and universal, to flatter himself and to please and interest the present friend. And by thus milling air out of his mouth, he had presently built up a presentation of Archie which was known and talked of in all corners of the county. Wherever there was a residential house and a walled garden, wherever there was a dwarfish castle and a park, wherever a quadruple cottage by the ruins of a peel-tower showed an old family going down, and wherever a handsome villa with a carriage approach and a shrubbery marked the coming up of a new one – probably on the wheels of machinery – Archie began to be regarded in the light of a dark, perhaps a vicious mystery, and the future developments of his career to be looked for with uneasiness and confidential whispering. He had done something disgraceful, my dear. What, was not precisely known, and that good kind young man, Mr Innes, did his best to make light of it. But there it was. And Mr Innes was very anxious about him now; he was really uneasy, my dear; he was positively wrecking his own prospects because he dared not leave him alone. How wholly we all lie at the mercy of a single prater, not needfully with any malign purpose! And if a man but talks of himself in the right spirit, refers to his virtuous actions by the way, and never applies to them the name of virtue, how easily his evidence is accepted in the court of public opinion!

All this while, however, there was a more poisonous ferment at work between the two lads, which came late indeed to the surface, but had modified and magnified their dissensions from the first. To an idle, shallow, easy-going customer like Frank, the smell of a mystery was attractive. It gave his mind something to play with, like a new toy to a child; and it took him on the weak side, for like many young men coming to the Bar, and before they have been tried and found wanting, he flattered himself he was a fellow of unusual quickness and penetration. They knew nothing of Sherlock Holmes in those days, but there was a good deal said of Talleyrand. And if you could have caught Frank off his guard he would have confessed with a smirk that, if he resembled any one, it was the Marquis de Talleyrand-Périgord. It was on the occasion of Archie's first absence that this interest took root. It was vastly deepened when Kirstie resented his curiosity at breakfast, and that same afternoon there occurred another scene which clinched the business. He was fishing Swingleburn, Archie accompanying him, when the latter looked at his watch.

'Well, good-bye,' said he. 'I have something to do. See you at dinner.'

'Don't be in such a hurry,' cries Frank. 'Hold on till I get my rod up. I'll go with you; I'm sick of flogging this ditch.'

And he began to reel up his line.

Archie stood speechless. He took a long while to recover his wits under this direct attack; but by the time he was ready with his anwer, and the angle was almost packed up, he had become completely Weir, and the hanging face gloomed on his young shoulders. He spoke with a laboured composure, a laboured kindness even; but a child could see that his mind was made up.

'I beg your pardon, Innes; I don't want to be disagreeable, but let us understand one another from the beginning. When I want your company, I'll let you know.'

'O!' cries Frank, 'you don't want my company, don't you?'

'Apparently not just now,' replied Archie. 'I even indicated to you when I did, if you'll remember – and that was at dinner. If we two fellows are to live together pleasantly – and I see no reason why we should not – it can only be by respecting each other's privacy. If we begin intruding——'

'O, come! I'll take this at no man's hands. Is this the way you treat a guest and an old friend?' cried Innes.

'Just go home and think over what I said by yourself,' continued Archie, 'whether it's reasonable, or whether it's really offensive or not; and let's meet at dinner as though nothing had happened. I'll put it this way, if you like – that I know my own character, that I'm looking forward (with great pleasure, I assure you) to a long visit from you, and that I'm taking precautions at the first. I see the thing that we – that I, if you like – might fall out upon, and I step in and *obsto principiis*. I wager you five pounds you'll end by seeing that I mean friendliness, and I assure you, Francie, I do,' he added, relenting.

Bursting with anger, but incapable of speech, Innes shouldered his rod, made a gesture of farewell, and strode off down the burnside. Archie watched him go without moving. He was sorry, but quite unashamed. He hated to be inhospitable, but in one thing he was his father's son. He had a strong sense that his house was his own and no man else's; and to lie at a guest's mercy was what he refused. He hated to seem harsh. But that was Frank's lookout. If Frank had been commonly discreet, he would have been decently courteous. And there was another consideration. The secret he was protecting was not his own merely; it was hers: it belonged to that inexpressible she who was fast taking possession of his soul, and whom he would soon have defended at the cost of burning cities. By the time he had watched Frank as far as the Swingleburnfoot, appearing and disappearing in the tarnished heather, still stalking at a fierce gait but already dwindled in the distance into less than the smallness of Lilliput, he could afford to smile at the occurrence. Either Frank would go, and that would be a relief – or he would continue to stay, and his host must continue to endure him. And Archie was now free – by devious paths, behind hillocks and in the hollow of burns – to make for the trysting-place where Kirstie, cried about by the curlew and the plover, waited and burned for his coming by the Covenanter's stone.

Innes went off down-hill in a passion of resentment, easy to be understood, but which yielded progressively to the needs of his situation. He cursed Archie for a cold-hearted, unfriendly, rude, rude dog; and himself still more passionately for a fool in having come to Hermiston when he might have sought refuge in almost any other house in Scotland. But the step, once taken, was practically irretrievable. He had no more ready money to go anywhere else; he would have to borrow from Archie the next clubnight; and ill as he thought of his host's manners, he was sure of his practical generosity. Frank's resemblance to Talleyrand strikes me as imaginary; but at least not Talleyrand himself could have more obediently taken his lesson from the facts. He met Archie at dinner without resentment, almost with cordiality. You must take your friends as you find them, he would have said. Archie couldn't help being his father's son, or his grandfather's, the hypothetical weaver's grandson. The son of a hunks, he was still a hunks at heart, incapable of true generosity and consideration; but he had other qualities with which Frank could divert himself in the meanwhile, and to enjoy which it was necessary that Frank should keep his temper.

So excellently was it controlled that he awoke next morning with his head full of a different, though a cognate subject. What was Archie's little game? Why did he shun Frank's company? What was he keeping secret? Was he keeping tryst with somebody, and was it a woman? It would be a good joke and a fair revenge to discover. To that task he set himself with a great deal of patience, which might have surprised his friends, for he had been always credited not with patience so much as brilliancy; and little by little, from one point to another, he at last succeeded in piecing out the situation. First he remarked that, although Archie set out in all the directions of the compass, he always came home again from some point between the south and west. From the study of a map, and in consideration of the great expanse of untenanted moorland running in that direction towards the sources of the Clyde, he laid his finger on Cauldstaneslap and two other neighbouring farms, Kingsmuirs and Polintarf. But it was difficult to advance farther. With his rod for a pretext, he vainly visited each of them in turn; nothing was to be seen suspicious about this trinity of moorland settlements. He would have tried to follow Archie, had it been the least possible, but the nature of the land precluded the idea. He did the next best, ensconced himself in a quiet corner, and pursued his movements with a telescope. It was equally in vain, and he soon wearied of his futile vigilance, left the telescope at home, and had almost given the matter up in despair, when, on the twenty-seventh day of his visit, he was suddenly confronted with the person whom he sought. The first Sunday Kirstie had managed to stay away from kirk on some pretext of indisposition, which was more truly modesty; the pleasure of beholding Archie seeming too sacred, too vivid for that public place. On the two following, Frank had himself been absent on some of his excursions among the neighbouring families. It was not until the fourth, accordingly, that Frank had occasion to set eyes on the enchantress. With the first look, all hesitation was over. She came with the Cauldstaneslap party; then she lived at Cauldstaneslap. Here was Archie's secret, here was the woman, and more than that – though I have need here of every manageable attenuation of language – with the first look, he had already entered himself as rival. It was a good deal in pique, it was a little in revenge, it was much in genuine admiration: the devil may decide the proportions! I cannot, and it is very likely that Frank could not.

'Mighty attractive milkmaid,' he observed, on the way home.

'Who?' said Archie.

'O, the girl you're looking at – aren't you? Forward there on the road. She came attended by the rustic bard; presumably, therefore, belongs to his exalted family. The single objection! for the four black brothers are awkward customers. If anything were to go wrong, Gib would gibber, and Clem would prove inclement; and Dand fly in danders, and Hob blow up in gobbets. It would be a Helliott of a business!'

'Very humorous, I am sure,' said Archie.

'Well I am trying to be so,' said Frank. 'It's none too easy in this place, and with your solemn society, my dear fellow. But confess that the milkmaid has found favour in your eyes, or resign all claim to be a man of taste.'

'It is no matter,' returned Archie.

But the other continued to look at him, steadily and quizzically, and his colour slowly rose and deepened under the glance, until not impudence itself could have denied that he was blushing. And at this Archie lost some of his control. He changed his stick from one hand to the other, and – 'O, for God's sake, don't be an ass!' he cried.

'Ass? That's the retort delicate without doubt,' says Frank. 'Beware of the homespun brothers, dear. If they come into the dance, you'll see who's an ass.

Think now, if they only applied (say) a quarter as much talent as I have applied to the question of what Mr Archie does with his evening hours, and why he is so unaffectedly nasty when the subject's touched on——'

'You are touching on it now,' interrupted Archie, with a wince.

'Thank you. That was all I wanted, an articulate confession,' said Frank.

'I beg to remind you——' began Archie.

But he was interrupted in turn. 'My dear fellow, don't. It's quite needless. The subject's dead and buried.'

And Frank began to talk hastily on other matters, an art in which he was an adept, for it was his gift to be fluent on anything or nothing. But although Archie had the grace or the timidity to suffer him to rattle on, he was by no means done with the subject. When he came home to dinner, he was greeted with a sly demand, how things were looking 'Cauldstaneslap ways.' Frank took his first glass of port out after dinner to the toast of Kirstie, and later in the evening he returned to the charge again.

'I say, Weir, you'll excuse me for returning again to this affair. I've been thinking it over, and I wish to beg you very seriously to be more careful. It's not a safe business. Not safe, my boy,' said he.

'What?' said Archie.

'Well, it's you own fault if I must put a name on the thing; but really, as a friend, I cannot stand by and see you rushing head down into these dangers. My dear boy,' said he, holding up a warning cigar, 'consider! What is to be the end of it?'

'The end of what?' – Archie, helpless with irritation, persisted in this dangerous and ungracious guard.

'Well, the end of the milkmaid; or, to speak more by the card, the end of Miss Christina Elliott of the Cauldstaneslap.'

'I assure you,' Archie broke out, 'this is all a figment of your imagination. There is nothing to be said against that young lady; you have no right to introduce her name into the conversation.'

'I'll make a note of it,' said Frank. 'She shall henceforth be nameless, nameless, nameless, Gregarach!* I make a note besides of your valuable testimony to her character. I only want to look at this thing as a man of the world. Admitted she's an angel – but, my good fellow, is she a lady?'

This was torture to Archie. 'I beg your pardon,' he said, struggling to be composed, 'but because you have wormed yourself into my confidence——'

'O, come!' cried Frank. 'Your confidence? It was rosy but unconsenting. Your confidence, indeed? Now look! This is what I must say, Weir, for it concerns your safety and good character, and therefore my honour as your friend. You say I wormed myself into your confidence. Wormed is good. But what have I done? I have put two and two together, just as the parish will be doing to-morrow, and the whole of Tweeddale in two weeks, and the black brothers – well, I won't put a date on that; it will be a dark and stormy morning! Your secret, in other words, is poor Poll's. And I want to ask of you as a friend whether you like the prospect? There are two horns to your dilemma, and I must say for myself I should look mighty ruefully on either. Do you see yourself explaining to the four Black Brothers? or do you see yourself presenting the milkmaid to papa as the future

*When the Clan Macgregor was proscribed, even the use of the name was forbidden.

lady of Hermiston? Do you? I tell you plainly, I don't!'

Archie rose. 'I will hear no more of this,' he said, in a trembling voice.

But Frank again held up his cigar. 'Tell me one thing first. Tell me if this is not a friend's part that I am playing?'

'I believe you think it so,' replied Archie. 'I can go as far as that. I can do so much justice to your motives. But I will hear no more of it. I am going to bed.'

'That's right, Weir,' said Frank heartily. 'Go to bed and think over it; and I say, man, don't forget your prayers! I don't often do the moral – don't go in for that sort of thing – but when I do there's one thing sure, that I mean it.'

So Archie marched off to bed, and Frank sat alone by the table for another hour or so, smiling to himself richly. There was nothing vindictive in his nature; but, if revenge came in his way, it might as well be good, and the thought of Archie's pillow reflections that night was indescribably sweet to him. He felt a pleasant sense of power. He looked down on Archie as on a very little boy whose strings he pulled – as on a horse whom he had backed and bridled by sheer power of intelligence, and whom he might ride to glory or the grave at pleasure. Which was it to be? He lingered long, relishing the details of schemes that he was too idle to pursue. Poor cork upon a torrent, he tasted that night the sweets of omnipotence, and brooded like a deity over the strands of that intrigue which was to shatter him before the summer waned.

CHAPTER EIGHT

A Nocturnal Visit

KIRSTIE HAD MANY CAUSES of distress. More and more as we grow old – and yet more and more as we grow old and are women, frozen by the fear of age – we come to rely on the voice as the single outlet of the soul. Only thus, in the curtailment of our means, can we relieve the straitened cry of the passion within us; only thus, in the bitter and sensitive shyness of advancing years, can we maintain relations with those vivacious figures of the young that still show before us and tend daily to become no more than the moving wall-paper of life. Talk is the last link, the last relation. But with the end of the conversation, when the voice stops and the bright face of the listener is turned away, solitude falls again on the bruised heart. Kirstie had lost her 'cannie hour at e'en'; she could no more wander with Archie, a ghost if you will, but a happy ghost, in fields Elysian. And to her it was as if the whole world had fallen silent; to him, but an unremarkable change of amusements. And she raged to know it. The effervescency of her passionate and irritable nature rose within her at times to bursting point.

This is the price paid by age for unseasonable ardours of feeling. It must have been so for Kirstie at any time when the occasion chanced; but it so fell out that she was deprived of this delight in the hour when she had most need of it, when she had most to say, most to ask, and when she trembled to recognize her sovereignty not merely in abeyance but annulled. For, with the clairvoyance of a genuine love, she had pierced the mystery that had so long embarrassed Frank. She was conscious, even before it was carried out, even on that Sunday night when it began, of an invasion of her rights; and a voice told her the invader's name. Since then, by arts, by accident, by small things observed, and by the general drift of Archie's humour, she had passed beyond all possibility of doubt. With a sense of justice that Lord Hermiston might have envied, she had that day in church considered and admitted the attractions of the younger Kirstie; and with the profound humanity and sentimentality of her nature, she had recognized the coming of fate. Not thus would she have chosen. She had seen, in imagination, Archie wedded to some tall, powerful, and rosy heroine of the golden locks, made in her own image, for whom she would have strewed the bride-bed with delight; and now she could have wept to see the ambition falsified. But the gods had pronounced, and her doom was otherwise.

She lay tossing in bed that night, besieged with feverish thoughts. There were dangerous matters pending, a battle was toward, over the fate of which she hung in jealousy, sympathy, fear, and alternate loyalty and disloyalty to either side. Now she was reincarnated in her niece, and now in Archie. Now she saw, through the girl's eyes, the youth on his knees to her, heard his persuasive instances with a deadly weakness, and receiving his overmastering caresses. Anon, with a revulsion, her temper raged to see such utmost favours of fortune and love squandered on a brat of a girl, one of her own house, using her own name – a deadly ingredient – and that 'didna ken her ain mind an' was as black's your hat.' Now she trembled lest her deity should plead in vain, loving the idea of success for him like a triumph of nature; anon, with returning loyalty to her own family and sex, she trembled for Kirstie and the credit of the Elliotts. And again she had a vision of herself, the day over for her old-world tales and local gossip, bidding farewell to her last link with life and brightness and love; and behind and beyond, she saw but the blank butt-end where she must crawl to die. Had she then come to the lees? she, so great, so beautiful, with a heart as fresh as a girl's and strong as womanhood? It could not be, and yet it was so; and for a moment her bed was horrible to her as the sides of the grave. And she looked forward over a waste of hours, and saw herself go on to rage, and tremble, and be softened, and rage again, until the day came and the labours of the day must be renewed.

Suddenly she heard feet on the stairs – his feet, and soon after the sound of a window-sash flung open. She sat up with her heart beating. He had gone to his room alone, and he hd not gone to bed. She might again have one of her night cracks; and at the entrancing prospect a change came over her mind; with the approach of this hope of pleasure, all the baser metal became immediately obliterated from her thoughts. She rose, all woman, and all the best of woman, tender, pitiful, hating the wrong, loyal to her own sex – and all the weakest of that dear miscellany, nourishing, cherishing next her soft heart, voicelessly flattering, hopes that she would have died sooner than have acknowledged. She tore off her nightcap, and her hair fell about her shoulders in profusion. Undying coquetry awoke. By the faint light of her nocturnal rush, she stood before the looking-glass, carried her shapely arms above her head, and gathered up the treasures of her tresses. She was never backward to admire herself; that kind of modesty was a stranger to her nature; and she paused, struck with a pleased wonder at the sight. 'Ye daft auld wife!' she said, answering a thought that was not; and she blushed with the innocent consciousness of a child. Hastily she did up the massive and shining coils, hastily donned a wrapper, and with the rushlight in her hand, stole into the hall. Below stairs she heard the clock ticking the deliberate seconds, and Frank jingling with the decanters in the dining-room. Aversion rose in her, bitter and momentary. 'Nesty, tippling puggy!' she thought; and the next moment she had knocked guardedly at Archie's door and was bidden enter.

Archie had been looking out into the ancient blackness, pierced here and there with a rayless star; taking the sweet air of the moors and the night into his bosom deeply; seeking, perhaps finding, peace after the manner of the unhappy. He turned round as she came in, and showed her a pale face against the windowframe.

'Is that you Kirstie?' he asked. 'Come in!'

'It's unco late, my dear,' said Kirstie, affecting unwillingness.

'No, no,' he answered, 'not at all. Come in, if you want a crack. I am not sleepy, God knows!'

She advanced, took a chair by the toilet-table and the candle, and set the rushlight at her foot. Something – it might be in the comparative disorder of her dress, it might be the emotion that now welled in her bosom – had touched her with a wand of transformation, and she seemed young with the youth of goddesses.

'Mr Erchie,' she began, 'what's this that's come to ye?'

'I am not aware of anything that has come,' said Archie, and blushed, and repented bitterly that he had let her in.

'O, my dear, that'll no dae!' said Kirstie. 'It's ill to blend the eyes of love. O, Mr Erchie, tak' a thocht ere it's ower late. Ye shouldna be impatient o' the braws o' life, they'll a' come in their saison, like the sun and the rain. Ye're young yet; ye've mony cantie years afore ye. See and dinna wreck yersel' at the outset like sae mony ithers! Hae patience – they telled me aye that was the owercome o' life – hae patience, there's a braw day coming yet. Gude kens it never cam' to me; and here I am, wi' nayther man nor bairn to ca' my ain, wearying a' folks wi' my ill tongue, and you just the first, Mr Erchie!'

'I have a difficulty in knowing what you mean,' said Archie.

'Weel, and I'll tell ye,' she said. 'It's just this, that I'm feared. I'm feared for ye, my dear. Remember, your faither is a hard man, reaping where he hasna sowed and gaithering where he hasna strawed. It's easy speakin', but mind! Ye'll have to look in the gurly face o'm, where it's ill to look, and vain to look for mercy. Ye mind me o' a bonny ship pitten oot into the black and gowsty seas – ye're a' safe still, sittin' quait and crackin' wi' Kirstie in your lown chalmer; but whaur will ye be the morn, and in whatten horror o' the fearsome tempest, cryin' on the hills to cover ye?'

'Why, Kirstie, you're very enigmatical tonight – and very eloquent,' Archie put in.

'And, my dear Mr Erchie,' she continued, with a change of voice, 'ye maunna think that I canna sympathize wi' ye. Ye maunna think that I havena been young mysel'. Lang syne, when I was a bit lassie, no twenty yet——' She paused and sighed. 'Clean and caller, wi' a fit like the hinney bee,' she continued. 'I was aye big and buirdly, ye maun understand; a bonny figure o' a woman, though I say it that suldna – built to rear bairns – braw bairns they suld hae been, and grand I would hae likit it! But I was young, dear, wi' the bonny glint o' youth in my e'en, and little I dreamed I'd ever be tellin' ye this, an auld, lanely, rudas wife! Weel, Mr Erchie, there was a lad cam' courtin' me, as was but naetural. Mony had come before, and I would nane o' them. But this yin had a tongue to wile the birds frae the lift and the bees frae the foxglove bells. Deary me, but it's lang syne. Folk have dee'd sinsyne and been buried, and are forgotten, and bairns been born and got merrit and got bairns o' their ain. Sinsyne woods have been plantit, and have grawn up and are bonny trees, and the joes sit in their shadow; and sinsyne auld estates have changed hands, and there have been wars and rumours of wars on the face of the earth. And here I'm still – like an auld droopit craw – lookin' on and craikin'! But, Mr Erchie, do ye no think that I have mind o' it a' still? I was dwalling then in my faither's house; and it's a curious thing that we were whiles trysted in the Deil's Hags. And do ye no think that I have mind of the bonny simmer days, the lang miles o' the bluid-red heather, the cryin' o' the whaups, and the lad and the lassie that was trysted? Do ye no think that I mind how the hilly sweetness ran about my hairt? Ay, Mr Erchie, I ken the way o' it – fine do I ken the way – how the grace o' God takes them, like Paul of Tarsus, when they think it least, and drives the pair o' them into a land which is like a dream, and the world and the folks in 't are nae mair than clouds to the puir lassie, and heeven nae mair than windle-straes, if she can but pleesure him! Until Tam dee'd – that was my story,' she broke off to say, 'he dee'd, and I wasna at the buryin'. But while he was here, I could take care o' mysel'. And can yon puir lassie?'

Kirstie, her eyes shining with unshed tears, stretched out her hand towards him appealingly; the bright and the dull gold of her hair flashed and smouldered in the coils behind her comely head, like the rays of an eternal youth; the pure colour had risen in her face; and Archie was abashed alike by her beauty and her story. He came towards her slowly from the window, took up her hand in his and kissed it.

'Kirstie,' he said hoarsely, 'you have misjudged me sorely. I have always thought of her, I wouldna harm her for the universe, my woman!'

'Eh, lad, and that's easy sayin',' cried Kirstie, 'but it's nane sae easy doin'! Man, do ye no comprehend that it's God's wull we should be blendit and glamoured, and have nae command over our ain members at a time like that? My bairn,' she cried, still holding his hand, 'think o' the puir lass! have pity upon her, Erchie! and O, be wise for twa! Think o' the risk she rins! I have seen ye, and what's t prevent ithers! I saw ye once in the Hags, in my ain howf, and I was wae to see ye there – in pairt for the omen, for I think there's a weird on the place – and in pairt for pure nakit envy and bitterness o' hairt. It's strange ye should forgather there tae! God! but yon puir, thrawn, auld Covenanter's seen a heap o' human natur' since he lookit his last on the musket-barrels, if he never saw nane afore,' she added, with a kind of wonder in her eyes.

'I swear by my honour I have done her no wrong,' said Archie. 'I swear by my honour and the redemption of my soul that there shall none be done her. I have heard of this before. I have been foolish, Kirstie, but not unkind and, above all, not base.'

'There's my bairn!' said Kirstie, rising. 'I'll can trust ye noo, I'll can gang to my bed wi' an easy hairt.' And then she saw in a flash how barren had been her triumph. Archie had promised to spare the girl, and he would keep it; but who had promised to spare Archie? What was to be the end of it? Over a maze of difficulties she glanced, and saw, at the end of every passage, the flinty countenance of Hermiston. And a kind of horror fell upon her at what she had done. She wore a tragic mask. 'Erchie, the Lord peety you, dear, and peety me! I have buildit on this foundation' – laying her hand heavily on his shoulder – 'and buildit hie, and pit my hairt in the buildin' of it. If the hale hypothec were to fa', I think, laddie, I would dee! Excuse a daft wife that loves ye, and that kenned your mither. And for His name's sake keep yersel' frae inordinate desires; haud your heart in baith your hands, carry it canny and laigh; dinna send it up like a bairn's kite into the collishangie o' the wunds! Mind, Maister Erchie dear, that this life's a' disappointment, and a mouthfu' o' mools is the appointed end.'

'Ay, but Kirstie, my woman, yu're asking me ower much at last,' said Archie, profoundly moved, and lapsing into the broad Scots. 'Ye're asking what nae man can grant ye, what only the Lord of heaven can grant ye if He see fit. Ay! And can even He? I can promise ye what I shall do, and you can depend on that. But how I shall feel – my woman, that is long past thinking of!'

They were both standing by now opposite each other. The face of Archie wore the wretched semblance of a smile; hers was convulsed for a moment.

'Promise me ae thing,' she cried, in a sharp voice. 'Promise me ye'll never do naething without telling me.'

'No, Kirstie, I canna promise ye that,' he replied. 'I have promised enough, God kens!'

'May the blessing of God lift and rest upon ye, dear!' she said.

'God bless ye, my old friend,' said he.

CHAPTER NINE

At the Weaver's Stone

IT WAS LATE IN THE AFTERNOON when Archie drew near by the hill path to the Praying Weaver's stone. The Hags were in shadow. But still, through the gate of the Slap, the sun shot a last arrow, which sped far and straight across the surface of the moss, here and there touching and shining on a tussock, and lighted at length on the gravestone and the small figure awaiting him there. The emptiness and solitude of the great moors seemed to be concentrated there, and Kirstie pointed out by that figure of sunshine for the only inhabitant. His first sight of her was thus excruciatingly sad, like a glimpse of a world from which all light, comfort, and society were on the point of vanishing. And the next moment, when she had turned her face to him and the quick smile had enlightened it, the whole face of nature smiled upon him in her smile of welcome. Archie's slow pace was quickened; his legs hasted to her though his heart was hanging back. The girl, upon her side, drew herself together slowly and stood up, expectant; she was all languor, her face was gone white; her arms ached for him, her soul was on tip-toes. But he deceived her, pausing a few steps away, not less white than herself, and holding up his hand with a gesture of denial.

'No, Christina, not to-day,' he said. 'To-day I have to talk to you seriously. Sit ye down, please, there where you were. Please!' he repeated.

The revulsion of feeling in Christina's heart was violent. To have longed and waited these weary hours for him, rehearsing her endearments – to have seen him at last come – to have been ready there, breathless, wholly passive, his to do what he would with – and suddenly to have found herself confronted with a grey-faced, harsh schoolmaster – it was too rude a shock. She could have wept, but pride withheld her. She sat down on the stone, from which she had arisen, part with the instinct of obedience, part as though she had been thrust there. What was this? Why was she rejected? Had she ceased to please? She stood here offering her wares, and he would none of them! And yet they were all his! His to take and keep, not his to refuse though! In her quick petulant nature, a moment ago on fire with hope, thwarted love and wounded vanity wrought. The schoolmaster that there is in all men, to the despair of all girls and most women, was now completely in possession of Archie. He had passed a night of sermons, a day of reflection; he had come wound up to do his duty; and the set mouth, which in him only betrayed the effort of his will, to her seemed the expression of an averted heart. It was the same with his constrained voice and embarrassed utterance; and if so – if it was all over – the pang of the thought took away from her the power of thinking.

He stood before her some way off. 'Kirstie, there's been too much of this. We've seen too much of each other.' She looked up quickly and her eyes contracted. 'There's no good ever comes of these secret meetings. They're not frank, not honest truly, and I ought to have seen it. People have begun to talk; and it's not right of me. Do you see?'

'I see somebody will have been talking to ye,' she said sullenly.

'They have, more than one of them,' replied Archie.

'And whae were they?' she cried. 'And what kind o' love do ye ca' that, that's ready to gang round like a whirligig at folk talking? Do ye think they havena talked to me?'

'Have they indeed?' said Archie, with a quick breath. 'That is what I feared. Who were they? Who has dared——?'

Archie was on the point of losing his temper.

As a matter of fact, not any one had talked to Christina on the matter; and she strenuously repeated her own first question in a panic of self-defence.

'Ah, well! what does it matter?' he said. 'They were good folk that wished well to us, and the great affair is that there are people talking. My dear girl, we have to be wise. We must not wreck our lives at the outset. They may be long and happy yet, and we must see to it, Kirstie, like God's rational creatures and not like fool children. There is one thing we must see to before all. You're worth waiting for, Kirstie! worth waiting for a generation; it would be enough reward.'

– And here he remembered the schoolmaster again, and very unwisely took to following wisdom. 'The first thing that we must see to, is that there shall be no scandal about for my father's sake. That would ruin all; do ye no see that?'

Kirstie was a little pleased, there had been some show of warmth of sentiment in what Archie had said last. But the dull irritation still persisted in her bosom; with the aboriginal instinct, having suffered herself, she wished to make Archie suffer.

And besides, there had come out the word she had always feared to hear from his lips, the name of his father. It is not to be supposed that, during so many days with a love avowed between them, some reference had not been made to their conjoint future. It had in fact been often touched upon, and from the first had been the sore point. Kirstie had wilfully closed the eye of thought; she would not argue even with herself; gallant, desperate little heart, she had accepted the command of that supreme attraction like the call of fate, and marched blindfold on her doom. But Archie, with his masculine sense of responsibility, must reason; he must dwell on some future good, when the present good was all in all to Kirstie; he must talk – and talk lamely, as necessity drove him – of what was to be. Again and again he had touched on marriage; again and again been driven back into indistinctness by a memory of Lord Hermiston. And Kirstie had been swift to understand and quick to choke down and smother the understanding; swift to leap up in flame at a mention of that hope, which spoke volumes to her vanity and her love, that she might one day be Mrs Weir of Hermiston; swift, also, to recognize in his stumbling or throttled utterance the death-knell of these expectations, and constant, poor girl! in her large-minded madness, to go on and to reck nothing of the future. But these unfinished references, these blinks in which his heart spoke, and his memory and reason rose up to silence it before the words were well uttered, gave her unqualified agony. She was raised up and dashed down again bleeding. The recurrence of the subject forced her, for however short a time, to open her eyes on what she did not wish to see; and it had invariably ended in another disappointment. So now again, at the mere wind of its coming, at the mere mention of his father's name – who might seem indeed to have accompanied them in their whole moorland courtship, an awful figure in a wig with an ironical and bitter smile, present to guilty consciousness – she fled from it head down.

'Ye havena told me yet,' she said, 'who was it spoke?'

'Your aunt for one,' said Archie.

'Auntie Kirstie?' she cried. 'And what do I care for my Auntie Kirstie?'

'She cares a great deal for her niece,' replied Archie, in kind reproof.

'Troth, and it's the first I've heard of it,' retorted the girl.

'The question here is not who it is, but what they say, what they have noticed,' pursued the lucid schoolmaster. 'That is what we have to think of in self-defence.'

'Auntie Kirstie, indeed! A bitter, thrawn auld maid that's fomented trouble in the country before I was born, and will be doing it still, I daur say, when I'm deid! It's in her nature; it's as natural for her as it's for a sheep to eat.'

'Pardon me, Kirstie, she was not the only one,' interposed Archie. 'I had two warnings, two sermons, last night, both most kind and considerate. Had you been there, I promise you you would have grat, my dear! And they opened my eyes. I saw we were going a wrong way.'

'Who was the other one?' Kirstie demanded.

By this time Archie was in the condition of a hunted beast. He had come, braced and resolute; he was to trace out a line of conduct for the pair of them in a few cold, convincing sentences; he had now been there some time, and he was still staggering round the outworks and undergoing what he felt to be a savage cross-examination.

'Mr Frank!' she cried. 'What nex', I would like to ken?'

'He spoke most kindly and truly.'

'What like did he say?'

'I am not going to tell you; you have nothing to do with that,' cried Archie, startled to find he had admitted so much.

'Oh, I have naething to do with it?' she repeated, springing to her feet. 'A'body at Hermiston's free to pass their opinions upon me, but I have naething to do wi' it! Was this at prayers like? Did ye ca' the grieve into the consultation? Little wonder if a'body's talking, when ye make a'body yer confidants! But as you say, Mr Weir – most kindly, most considerately, most truly, I'm sure – I have naething to do with it. And I think I'll better be going. I'll be wishing you good evening, Mr Weir.' And she made him a stately curtsey, shaking as she did so from head to foot, with the barren ecstasy of temper.

Poor Archie stood dumbfounded. She had moved some steps away from him before he recovered the gift of articulate speech.

'Kirstie!' he cried. 'Oh, Kirstie woman!'

There was in his voice a ring of appeal, a clang of mere astonishment that showed the schoolmaster was vanquished.

She turned round on him. 'What do ye Kirstie me for?' she retorted. 'What have ye to do wi' me? Gang to your ain freends and deave them!'

He could only repeat the appealing 'Kirstie!'

'Kirstie, indeed!' cried the girl, her eyes blazing in her white face. 'My name is Miss Christina Elliott, I would have ye to ken, and I daur ye to ca' me out of it. If I canna get love, I'll have respect, Mr Weir. I'm come of decent people, and I'll have respect. What have I done that ye should lightly me? What have I done? What have I done? O, what have I done?' and her voice rose upon the third repetition. 'I thocht – I thocht – I thocht I was sae happy!' and the first sob broke from her like the paroxysm of some mortal sickness.

Archie ran to her. He took the poor child in his arms, and she nestled to his breast as to a mother's, and clasped him in hands that were strong like vices. He felt her whole body shaken by the throes of distress, and had pity upon her beyond speech. Pity, and at the same time a bewildered fear of this explosive engine in his arms, whose works he did not understand, and yet had been tampering with. There arose from before him the curtains of boyhood, and he saw for the first time the ambiguous face of woman as she is. In vain he looked back over the interview; he saw not where he had offended. It seemed unprovoked, a wilful convulsion of brute nature. . . .

THE MASTER
OF BALLANTRAE

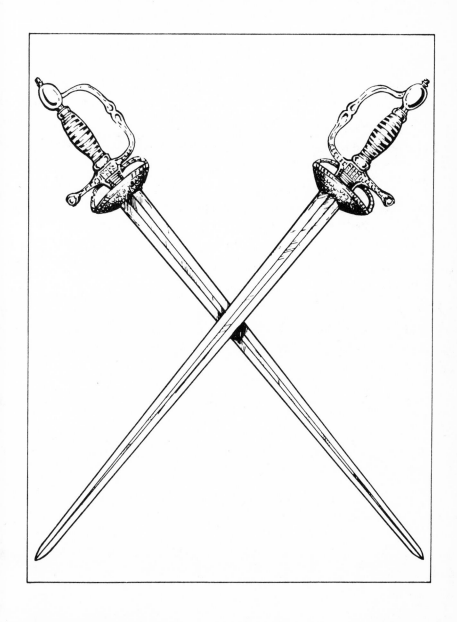

To
SIR PERCY FLORENCE AND LADY SHELLEY

HERE IS A TALE WHICH extends over many years and travels into many countries. By a peculiar fitness of circumstance the writer began, continued it, and concluded it among distant and diverse scenes. Above all, he was much upon the sea. The character and fortune of the fraternal enemies, the hall and shrubbery of Durrisdeer, the problem of Mackellar's homespun and how to shape it for superior flights; these were his company on deck in many star-reflecting harbours, ran often in his mind at sea to the tune of slatting canvas, and were dismissed (something of the suddenest) on the approach of squalls. It is my hope that these surroundings of its manufacture may to some degree find favour for my story with seafarers and sea-lovers like yourselves.

And at least here is a dedication from a great way off: written by the loud shores of a subtropical island near upon ten thousand miles from Boscombe Chine and Manor: scenes which rise before me as I write, along with the faces and voices of my friends.

Well, I am for the sea once more; no doubt Sir Percy also. Let us make the signal B.R.D.!

R.L.S.

WAIKIKI,
May 17, 1889.

Preface

ALTHOUGH AN OLD, CONSISTENT exile, the editor of the following pages revisits now and again the city of which he exults to be a native; and there are few things more strange, more painful, or more salutary, than such revisitations. Outside, in foreign spots, he comes by surprise and awakens more attention than he had expected; in his own city, the relation is reversed, and he stands amazed to be so little recollected. Elsewhere he is refreshed to see attractive faces, to remark possible friends; there he scouts the long streets, with a pang at heart, for the faces and friends that are no more. Elsewhere he is delighted with the presence of what is new, there tormented by the absence of what is old. Elsewhere he is content to be his present self; there he is smitten with an equal regret for what he once was and for what he once hoped to be.

He was feeling all this dimly, as he drove from the station, on his last visit; he was feeling it still as he alighted at the door of his friend Mr Johnstone Thomson, W.S., with whom he was to stay. A hearty welcome, a face not altogether changed, a few words that sounded of old days, a laugh provoked and shared, a glimpse in passing of the snowy cloth and bright decanters and the Piranesis on the dining-room wall, brought him to his bedroom with a somewhat lightened cheer, and when he and Mr Thomson sat down a few minutes later, cheek by jowl, and pledged the past in a preliminary bumper, he was already almost consoled, he had already almost forgiven himself his two unpardonable errors, that he should ever have left his native city, or ever returned to it.

'I have something quite in your way,' said Mr Thomson. 'I wished to do honour to your arrival; because, my dear fellow, it is my own youth that comes back along with you; in a very tattered and withered state, to be sure, but – well! – all that's left of it.'

'A great deal better than nothing,' said the editor. 'But what is this which is quite in my way?'

'I was coming to that,' said Mr Thomson: 'Fate has put it in my power to honour your arrival with something really original by way of dessert. A mystery.'

'A mystery?' I repeated.

'Yes,' said his friend, 'a mystery. It may prove to be nothing, and it may prove to be a great deal. But in the meanwhile it is truly mysterious, no eye having looked on it for near a hundred years; it is highly genteel, for it treats of a titled family; and it ought to be melodramatic, for (according to the superscription) it is concerned with death.'

'I think I rarely heard a more obscure or a more promising annunciation,' the other remarked. 'But what is It?'

'You remember my predecessor's, old Peter M'Brair's business?'

'I remember him acutely; he could not look at me without a pang of reprobation, and he could not feel the pang without betraying it. He was to me a man of a great historical interest, but the interest was not returned.'

'Ah well, we go beyond him,' said Mr Thomson. 'I dare say old Peter knew as little about this as I do. You see, I succeeded to a prodigious accumulation of old law-papers and old tin boxes, some of them of Peter's hoarding, some of his father's, John, first of the dynasty, a great man in his day. Among other collections were all the papers of the Durrisdeers.'

'The Durrisdeers!' cried I. 'My dear fellow, these may be of the greatest interest. One of them was out in the '45; one had some strange passages with the devil – you will find a note of it in Law's *Memorials*, I think; and there was an unexplained tragedy, I know not what, much later, about a hundred years ago——'

'More than a hundred years ago,' said Mr Thomson. 'In 1783.'

'How do you know that? I mean some death.'

'Yes, the lamentable deaths of my lord Durrisdeer and his brother, the Master of Ballantrae (attainted in the troubles),' said Mr Thomson with something the tone of a man quoting. 'Is that it?'

'To say truth,' said I, 'I have only seen some dim reference to the things in memoirs; and heard some traditions dimmer still, through my uncle (whom I think you knew). My uncle lived when he was a boy in the neighbourhood of St Bride's; he has often told me of the avenue closed up and grown over with grass, the great gates never opened, the last lord and his old maid sister who lived in the back parts of the house, a quiet, plain poor, humdrum couple it would seem – but pathetic too, as the last of that stirring and brave house – and, to the country folk, faintly terrible from some deformed traditions.'

'Yes,' said Mr Thomson. 'Henry Graeme Durie, the last lord, died in 1820; his sister, the Honourable Miss Katherine Durie, in '27; so much I know; and by what I have been going over the last few days, they were what you say, decent, quiet people and not rich. To say truth, it was a letter of my lord's that put me on the search for the packet we are going to open this evening. Some papers could not be found; and he wrote to Jack M'Brair suggesting they might be among those sealed up by a Mr Mackellar. M'Brair answered, that the papers in question were all in Mackellar's own hand, all (as the writer understood) of a purely narrative character; and besides, said he, 'I am bound not to open them before the year 1889.' You may fancy if these words struck me: I instituted a hunt through all the M'Brair repositories; and at last hit upon that packet which (if you have had enough wine) I propose to show you at once.'

In the smoking-room, to which my host now led me, was a packet, fastened with many seals and enclosed in a single sheet of strong paper thus endorsed:

Papers relating to the lives and lamentable deaths of the late Lord Durisdeer, and his elder brother James, commonly called Master of Ballantrae, attainted in the troubles: entrusted into the hands of John M'Brair in the Lawnmarket of Edinburgh, W.S.; this 20th day of September Anno Domini 1789; by him to be kept secret until the revolution of one hundred years complete, or until the 20th day of September 1889: the same compiled and written by me,

EPHRAIM MACKELLAR,
For near forty years Land Steward on the
estates of His Lordship.

As Mr Thomson is a married man, I will not say what hour had struck when we laid down the last of the following pages; but I will give a few words of what ensued.

'Here,' said Mr Thomson, 'is a novel ready to your hand: all you have to do is to work up the scenery, develop the characters, and improve the style.'

'My dear fellow,' said I, 'they are just the three things that I would rather die than set my hand to. It shall be published as it stands.'

'But it's so bald,' objected Mr Thomson.

'I believe there is nothing so noble as baldness,' replied I, 'and I am sure there is nothing so interesting. I would have all literature bald, and all authors (if you like) but one.'

'Well, well,' said Mr Thomson, 'we shall see.'

CHAPTER ONE

Summary of events during the Master's wanderings

THE FULL TRUTH OF THIS ODD matter is what the world has long been looking for, and public curiosity is sure to welcome. It so befell that I was intimately mingled with the last years and history of the house; and there does not live one man so able as myself to make these matters plain, or so desirous to narrate them faithfully. I knew the Master; on many secret steps of his career I have an authentic memoir in my hand; I sailed with him on his last voyage almost alone; I made one upon that winter's journey of which so many tales have gone abroad; and I was there at the man's death. As for my late Lord Durrisdeer, I served him and loved him near twenty years; and thought more of him the more I knew of him. Altogether, I think it not fit that so much evidence should perish; the truth is a debt I owe my lord's memory; and I think my old years will flow more smoothly, and my white hair lie quieter on the pillow, when the debt is paid.

The Duries of Durrisdeer and Ballantrae were a strong family in the south-west from the days of David First. A rhyme still current in the countryside

> Kittle folk are the Durrisdeers,
> They ride wi' ower mony spears

bears the mark of its antiquity; and the name appears in another, which common report attributes to Thomas of Ercildoune himself – I cannot say how truly, and which some have applied – I dare not say with how much justice – to the events of this narration:

> Twa Duries in Durrisdeer,
> Ane to tie and ane to ride,
> An ill day for the groom
> And a waur day for the bride.

Authentic history besides is filled with their exploits, which (to our modern eyes) seem not very commendable: and the family suffers its full share of those ups and downs to which the great houses of Scotland have been ever liable. But all these I pass over, to come to that memorable year 1745, when the foundations of this tragedy were laid.

At that time there dwelt a family of four persons in the house of Durrisdeer, near St Bride's, on the Solway shore; a chief hold of their race since the Reformation. My old lord, eighth of the name, was not old in years, but he suffered prematurely from the disabilities of age; his place was at the chimney-side; there he sat reading, in a lined gown, with few words for any man, and wry

words for none: the model of an old retired housekeeper; and yet his mind very
well nourished with study, and reputed in the country to be more cunning than
he seemed. The Master of Ballantrae, James in baptism, took from his father the
love of serious reading; some of his tact perhaps as well, but that which was only
policy in the father became black dissimulation in the son. The face of his
behaviour was merely popular and wild: he sat late at wine, later at the cards;
had the name in the country of 'an unco man for the lasses'; and was ever in the
front of broils. But for all he was the first to go in, yet it was observed he was
invariably the best to come off; and his partners in mischief were usually alone to
pay the piper. This luck or dexterity got him several ill-wishers, but with the rest
of the country, enhanced his reputation; so that great things were looked for in
his future, when he should have gained more gravity. One very black mark he
had to his name; but the matter was hushed up at the time, and so defaced by
legends before I came into those parts, that I scruple to set it down. If it was true,
it was a horrid fact in one so young; and if false, it was a horrid calumny. I think
it notable that he had always vaunted himself quite implacable, and was taken at
his word; so that he had the addition among his neighbours of 'an ill man to
cross.' Here was altogether a young nobleman (not yet twenty-four in the year
'45) who had made a figure in the country beyond his time of life. The less
marvel if there were little heard of the second son, Mr Henry (my late Lord
Durrisdeer), who was neither very bad nor yet very able, but an honest, solid
sort of lad like many of his neighbours. Little heard, I say; but indeed it was a
case of little spoken. He was known among the salmon fishers in the firth, for
that was a sport that he assiduously followed; he was an excellent good horse-
doctor besides; and took a chief hand, almost from a boy, in the management of
the estates. How hard a part that was, in the situation of that family, none
knows better than myself; nor yet with how little colour of justice a man may
there acquire the reputation of a tyrant and a miser. The fourth person in the
house was Miss Alison Graeme, a near kinswoman, an orphan, and the heir to a
considerable fortune which her father had acquired in trade. This money was
loudly called for by my lord's necessities; indeed the land was deeply mortgaged;
and Miss Alison was designed accordingly to be the Master's wife, gladly enough
on her side; with how much good-will on his, is another matter. She was a
comely girl, and in those days very spirited and self-willed; for the old lord
having no daughter of his own, and my lady being long dead, she had grown up
as best she might.

   To these four came the news of Prince Charlie's landing, and set them
presently by the ears. My lord, like the chimney-keeper that he was, was all for
temporizing. Miss Alison held the other side, because it appeared romantical;
and the Master (though I have heard they did not agree often) was for this once
of her opinion. The adventure tempted him, as I conceive; he was tempted by
the oppotunity to raise the fortunes of the house, and not less by the hope of
paying off his private liabilities, which were heavy beyond all opinion. As for Mr
Henry, it appears he said little enough at first; his part came later on. It took the
three a whole day's disputation before they agreed to steer a middle course, one
son going forth to strike a blow for King James, my lord and the other staying at
home to keep in favour with King George. Doubtless this was my lord's decision;
and, as is well known, it was the part played by many considerable families. But

the one dispute settled, another opened. For my lord, Miss Alison, and Mr Henry all held the one view: that it was the cadet's part to go out; and the Master, what with restlessness and vanity, would at no rate consent to stay at home. My lord pleaded, Miss Alison wept, Mr Henry was very plain spoken: all was of no avail.

'It is the direct heir of Durrisdeer that should ride by his King's bridle,' says the Master.

'If we were playing a manly part,' says Mr Henry, 'there might be sense in such talk. But what are we doing? Cheating at cards!'

'We are saving the house of Durrisdeer, Henry,' his father said.

'And see, James,' said Mr Henry, 'if I go, and the Prince has the upper hand, it will be easy to make your peace with King James. But if you go, and the expedition fails, we divide the right and the title. And what shall I be then?'

'You will be Lord Durrisdeer,' said the Master. 'I put all I have upon the table.'

'I play at no such game,' cries Mr Henry. 'I shall be left in such a situation as no man of sense and honour could endure. I shall be neither fish nor flesh!' he cried. And a little after he had another expression, plainer perhaps than he intended. 'It is your duty to be here with my father,' said he. 'You know well enough you are the favourite.'

'Ay?' said the Master. 'And there spoke Envy! Would you trip up my heels – Jacob?' said he, and dwelled upon the name maliciously.

Mr Henry went and walked at the low end of the hall without reply; for he had an excellent gift of silence. Presently he came back.

'I am the cadet and I *should* go,' said he. 'And my lord here is the master, and he says I *shall* go. What say ye to that, my brother?'

'I say this, Harry,' returned the Master, 'that when very obstinate folk are met, there are only two ways out: Blows – and I think none of us could care to go so far; or the arbitrament of chance – and here is a guinea piece. Will you stand by the toss of the coin?'

'I will stand and fall by it,' said Mr Henry. 'Heads, I go; shield, I stay.'

The coin was spun, and it fell shield. 'So there is a lesson for Jacob,' says the Master.

'We shall live to repent of this,' says Mr Henry, and flung out of the hall.

As for Miss Alison, she caught up that piece of gold which had just sent her lover to the wars, and flung it clean through the family shield in the great painted window.

'If you loved me as well as I love you, you would have stayed,' cried she.

'I could not love you, dear, so well, loved I not honour more,' sang the Master.

'Oh!' she cried, 'you have no heart – I hope you may be killed!' and she ran from the room, and in tears, to her own chamber.

It seems the Master turned to my lord with his most comical manner, and says he, 'This looks like a devil of a wife.'

'I think you are a devil of a son to me,' cried his father, 'you that have always been the favourite, to my shame be it spoken. Never a good hour have I gotten of you, since you were born; no, never one good hour,' and repeated it again the third time. Whether it was the Master's levity, or his insubordination, or Mr Henry's word about the favourite son, that had so much disturbed my lord, I do not know; but I incline to think it was the last, for I have it by all accounts that Mr Henry was more made up to from that hour.

Altogether it was in pretty ill blood with his family that the Master rode to the North; which was the more sorrowful for others to remember when it seemed too late. By fear and favour he had scraped together near upon a dozen men, principally tenants' sons; they were all pretty full when they set forth, and rode up the hill by the old abbey, roaring and singing, the white cockade in every hat. It was a desperate venture for so small a company to cross the most of Scotland unsupported; and (what made folk think so the more) even as that poor dozen was clattering up the hill, a great ship of the king's navy, that could have brought them under with a single boat, lay with her broad ensign streaming in the bay. The next afternoon, having given the Master a fair start, it was Mr Henry's turn; and he rode off, all by himself, to offer his sword and carry letters from his father to King George's Government. Miss Alison was shut in her room, and did little but weep, till both were gone; only she stitched the cockade upon the Master's hat, and (as John Paul told me) it was wetted with tears when he carried it down to him.

In all that followed, Mr Henry and my old lord were true to their bargain. That ever they accomplished anything is more than I could learn; and that they were anyway strong on the king's side, more than I believe. But they kept the letter of loyalty, corresponded with my Lord President, sat still at home, and had little or no commerce with the Master while that business lasted. Nor was he, on his side, more communicative. Miss Alison, indeed, was always sending him expresses, but I do not know if she had many answers. Macconochie rode for her once, and found the Highlanders before Carlisle, and the Master riding by the Prince's side in high favour; he took the letter (so Macconochie tells), opened it, glanced it through with a mouth like a man whistling, and stuck it in his belt, whence, on his horse passaging, it fell unregarded to the ground. It was Macconochie who picked it up; and he still kept it, and indeed I have seen it in his hands. News came to Durrisdeer of course, by the common report, as it goes travelling through a country, a thing always wonderful to me. By that means the family learned more of the Master's favour with the Prince, and the ground it was said to stand on: for by a strange condescension in a man so proud – only that he was a man still more ambitious – he was said to have crept into notability by truckling to the Irish. Sir Thomas Sullivan, Colonel Burke, and the rest, were his daily comrades, by which course he withdrew himself from his own country-folk. All the small intrigues he had a hand in fomenting; thwarted my Lord George upon a thousand points; was always for the advice that seemed palatable to the Prince, no matter if it was good or bad; and seems upon the whole (like the gambler he was all through life) to have had less regard to the chances of the campaign than to the greatness of favour he might aspire to, if, by any luck, it should succeed. For the rest, he did very well in the field; no one questioned that; for he was no coward.

The next was the news of Culloden, which was brought to Durrisdeer by one of the tenants' sons – te only survivor, he declared, of all those tht had gone singing up the hill. By an unfortunate chance John Paul and Macconochie had that very morning found the guinea piece – which was the root of all the evil – sticking in a holly bush; they had been 'up the gait,' as the servants say at

Durrisdeer, to the change-house; and if they had left of the guinea, they had less of their wits. What must John Paul do but burst into the hall where the family sat at dinner, and cry the news to them that 'Tam Macmorland was but new lichtit at the door, and – wirra, wirra – there were nane to come behind him'?

They took the word in silence like folk condemned; only Mr Henry carrying his palm to his face, and Miss Alison laying her head outright upon her hands. As for my lord, he was like ashes.

'I have still one son,' says he. 'And, Henry, I will do you this justice – it is the kinder that is left.'

It was a strange thing to say in such a moment; but my lord had never forgotten Mr Henry's speech, and he had years of injustice on his conscience. Still it was a strange thing, and more than Miss Alison could let pass. She broke out and blamed my lord for his unnatural words, and Mr Henry because he was sitting there in safety when his brother lay dead, and herself because she had given her sweetheart ill words at his departure, calling him the flower of the flock, wringing her hands, protesting her love, and crying on him by his name – so that the servants stood astonished.

Mr Henry got to his feet, and stood holding his chair. It was he that was like ashes now.

'Oh!' he burst out suddenly, 'I know you loved him.'

'The world knows that, glory be to God!' cries she; and then to Mr Henry: 'There is none but me to know one thing – that you were a traitor to him in your heart.'

'God knows,' groans he, 'it was lost love on both sides.'

Time went by in the house after that without much change; only they were now three instead of four, which was a perpetual reminder of their loss. Miss Alison's money, you are to bear in mind, was highly needful for the estates; and the one brother being dead, my lord soon set his heart upon her marrying the other. Day in, day out, he would work upon her, sitting by the chimney-side with his finger in his Latin book, and his eyes set upon her face with a kind of pleasant intentness that became the old gentleman very well. If she wept, he would condole with her like an ancient man that has seen worse times and begins to think lightly even of sorrow; if she raged, he would fall to reading again in his Latin book, but always with some civil excuse; if she offered, as she often did, to let them have her money in a gift, he would show her how little it consisted with his honour, and remind her, even if he should consent, that Mr Henry would certainly refuse. *Non vi sed saepe cadendo* was a favourite word of his; and no doubt this quiet persecution wore away much of her resolve; no doubt, besides, he had a great influence on the girl, having stood in the place of both her parents; and, for that matter, she was herself filled with the spirit of the Duries, and would have gone a great way for the glory of Durrisdeer; but not so far, I think, as to marry my poor patron, had it not been – strangely enough – for the circumstance of his extreme unpopularity.

This was the work of Tam Macmorland. There was not much harm in Tam; but he had that grievous weakness, a long tongue; and as the only man in that country who had been out – or, rather who had come in again – he was sure of listeners. Those that have the underhand in any fighting, I have observed, are ever anxious to persuade themselves they were betrayed. By Tam's account of it, the rebels had been betrayed at every turn and by every officer they had; they had been betrayed at Derby, and betrayed at Falkirk; the night march was a step of treachery of my Lord George's; and Culloden was lost by the treachery of the Macdonalds. This habit of imputing treason grew upon the fool, till at last he must have in Mr Henry also. Mr Henry (by his account) had betrayed the lads of Durrisdeer; he had promised to follow with more men, and instead of that he had ridden to King George. 'Ay, and the next day!' Tam would cry. 'The puir bonnie Master, and the puir, kind lads that rade wi' him, were hardly ower the scaur, or he was aff – the Judis! – Ay, weel – he has his way o't: he's to be my lord, nae less, and there's mony a cold corp amang the Hieland heather!' And at this, if Tam had been drinking, he would begin to weep.

Let anyone speak long enough, he will get believers. This view of Mr Henry's behaviour crept about the country by little and little; it was talked upon by folk that knew the contrary, but were short of topics; and it was heard and believed and given out for gospel by the ignorant and the ill-willing. Mr Henry began to be shunned; yet awhile, and the commons began to murmur as he went by, and the women (who are always the most bold because they are the most safe) to cry out their reproaches to his face. The Master was cried up for a saint. It was remembered how he had never any hand in pressing the tenants; as, indeed, no more he had, except to spend the money. He was a little wild perhaps, the folk said; but how much better was a natural wild lad that would soon have settled down, than a skinflint and a sneck-draw, sitting, with his nose in an account book, to persecute poor tenants! One trollop, who had had a child to the Master, and by all accounts been very badly used, yet made herself a kind of champion of his memory. She flung a stone one day at Mr Henry.

'Whaur's the bonnie lad that trustit ye?' she cried.

Mr Henry reined in his horse and looked upon her, the blood flowing from his lip. 'Ay, Jess?' says he. 'You, too? And yet ye should ken me better.' For it was he who had helped her with money.

The woman had another stone ready, which she made as if she would cast; and he, to ward himself, threw up the hand that held his riding-rod.

'What, would ye beat a lassie, ye ugly――?' cries she, and ran away screaming as though he had struck her.

Next day word went about the country like wildfire that Mr Henry had beaten Jessie Broun within an inch of her life. I give it as one instance of how this snowball grew, and one calumny brought another; until my poor patron was so perished in reputation that he began to keep the house like my lord. All this while, you may be very sure, he uttered no complaints at home; the very ground of the scandal was too sore a matter to be handled; and Mr Henry was very proud and strangely obstinate in silence. My old lord must have heard of it, by John Paul, if by no one else; and he must at least have remarked the altered habits of his son. Yet even he, it is probable, knew not how high the feeling ran; and as for Miss Alison, she was ever the last person to hear news, and the least interested when she heard them.

In the height of the ill-feeling (for it died away as it came, no man could say why) there was an election forward in the town of St Bride's, which is the next to Durrisdeer, standing on the Water of Swift; some grievance was fermenting, I forget what, if ever I heard; and it was currently said there would be broken heads ere night, and that the sheriff had sent as far as Dumfries for soldiers. My lord moved that Mr Henry should be present, assuring him it was necessary to appear, for the credit of the house. 'It will soon be reported,' said he, 'that we do not take the lead in our own country.'

'It is a strange lead that I can take,' said Mr Henry; and when they had pushed him further, 'I tell you the plain truth,' he said, 'I dare not show my face.'

'You are the first of the house that ever said so,' cried Miss Alison.

'We will go all three,' said my lord; and sure enough he got into his boots (the first time in four years – a sore business John Paul had to get them on), and Miss Alison into her riding-coat, and all three rode together to St Bride's.

The streets were full of the riff-raff of all the countryside, who had no sooner clapped eyes on Mr Henry than the hissing began, and the hooting, and the cries of 'Judas!' and 'Where was the Master?' and 'Where were the poor lads that rode with him?' Even a stone was cast; but the more part cried shame at that, for my old lord's sake, and Miss Alison's. It took not ten minutes to persuade my lord that Mr Henry had been right. He said never a word, but turned his horse about, and home again, with his chin upon his bosom. Never a word said Miss Alison; no doubt she thought the more; no doubt her pride was stung, for she was a bone-bred Durie; and no doubt her heart was touched to see her cousin so unjustly used. That night she was never in bed; I have often blamed my lady – when I call to mind that night, I readily forgive her all; and the first thing in the morning she came to the old lord in his usual seat.

'If Henry still wants me,' said she, 'he can have me now.' To himself she had a different speech: 'I bring you no love, Henry; but God knows, all the pity in the world.'

June the 1st, 1748, was the day of their marriage. It was December of the same year that first saw me alighting at the doors of the great house; and from there I take up the history of events as they befell under my own observation, like a witness in a court.

CHAPTER TWO

Summary of Events (continued)

I MADE THE LAST OF MY journey in the cold end of December, in a mighty dry day of frost, and who should be my guide but Patey Macmorland, brother of Tam! For a tow-headed, bare-legged brat of ten, he had more ill tales upon his tongue than ever I heard the match of; having drunken betimes in his brother's cup. I was still not so old myself; pride had not yet the upper hand of curiosity; and indeed it would have taken any man, that cold morning, to hear all the old clashes of the country, and be shown all the places by the way where strange things had fallen out. I had tales of Claverhouse as we came through the bogs, and tales of the devil as we came over the top of the scaur. As we came in by the abbey I heard somewhat of the old monks, and more of the freetraders, who use its ruins for a magazine, landing for that cause within a cannon-shot of Durrisdeer; and along all the road the Duries and poor Mr Henry were in the first rank of slander. My mind was thus highly prejudiced against the family I was about to serve, so that I was half surprised when I beheld Durrisdeer itself, lying in a pretty, sheltered bay, under the Abbey Hill; the house most commodiously built in the French fashion, or perhaps Italianate, for I have no skill in these arts; and the place the most beautified with gardens, lawns, shrubberies, and trees I have ever seen. The money sunk here unproductively would have quite restored the family; but as it was, it cost a revenue to keep it up.

Mr Henry came himself to the door to welcome me; a tall dark young gentleman (the Duries are all black men) of a plain and not cheerful face, very strong in body, but not so strong in health: taking me by the hand without any pride, and putting me at home with plain kind speeches. He led me into the hall, booted as I was, to present me to my lord. It was still daylight; and the first thing I observed was a lozenge of clear glass in the midst of the shield in the painted window, which I remember thinking a blemish on a room otherwise so handsome, with its family portraits, and the pargeted ceiling with pendants, and the carved chimney, in one corner of which my old lord sat reading in his Livy. He was like Mr Henry, with much the same plain countenance, only more subtle and pleasant, and his talk a thousand times more entertaining. He had many questions to ask me, I remember, of Edinburgh College, where I had just received my mastership of arts, and of the various professors, with whom and their proficiency he seemed well acquainted; and thus, talking of things that I knew, I soon got liberty of speech in my new home.

In the midst of this came Mrs Henry into the room; she was very far gone, Miss Katharine being due in about six weeks, which made me think less of her beauty at the first sight; and she used me with more of condescension than the rest; so that upon all accounts, I kept her in the third place of my esteem.

It did not take long before all Patey Macmorland's tales were blotted out of my belief, and I was become, what I have ever since remained, a loving servant of the house of Durrisdeer. Mr Henry had the chief part of my affection. It was with him I worked; and I found him an exacting master, keeping all his kindness for those hours in which we were unemployed, and in the steward's office not only loading me with work, but viewing me with a shrewd supervision. At length one day he looked up from his paper with a kind of timidness, and says he, 'Mr Mackellar, I think I ought to tell you that you do very well.' That was my first word of commendation; and from that day his jealousy of my performance was relaxed; soon it was 'Mr Mackellar' here, and 'Mr Mackellar' there, with the whole family; and for much of my service at Durrisdeer, I have transacted everything at my own time, and to my own fancy, and never a farthing challenged. Even while he was driving me, I had begun to find my heart go out to Mr Henry; no doubt, partly in pity, he was a man so palpably unhappy, He would fall into a deep muse over our accounts, staring at the page or out of the window; and at those times the look of his face, and the sigh that would break from him, awoke in me strong feelings of curiosity and commiseration. One day, I remember, we were late upon some business in the steward's room. This room is in the top of the house, and has a view upon the bay, and over a little wooded cape, on the long sands; and there, right over against the sun, which was then dipping, we saw the freetraders, with a great force of men and horses, scouring on the beach. Mr Henry had been staring straight west, so that I marvelled he was not blinded by the sun; suddenly he frowns, rubs his hand upon his brow, and turns to me with a smile.

'You would not guess what I was thinking,' says he. 'I was thinking I would be a happier man if I could ride and run the danger of my life, with these lawless companions.'

I told him I had observed he did not enjoy good spirits; and that it was a common fancy to envy others nd think we should be the better of some change; quoting Horace to the point, like a young man fresh from college.

'Why, just so,' said he. 'And with that we may get back to our accounts.'

It was not long before I began to get wind of the causes that so much depressed him. Indeed a blind man must have soon discovered there was a shadow on the house, the shadow of the Master of Ballantrae. Dead or alive (and he was then supposed to be dead) that man was his brother's rival: his rival abroad, where there was never a good word for Mr Henry, and nothing but regret and praise for the Master; and his rival at home, not only with his father and his wife, but with the very servants.

They were two old serving-men that were the leaders. John Paul, a little, bald, solemn, stomachy man, a great professor of piety and (take him for all in all) a pretty faithful servant, was the chief of the Master's faction. None durst go so far as John. He took a pleasure in disregarding Mr Henry publicly, often with a slighting comparison. My lord and Mrs Henry took him up, to be sure, but never so resolutely as they should; and he had only to pull his weeping face and begin his lamentations for the Master – 'his laddie,' as he called him – to have the whole condoned. As for Henry, he let these things pass in silence, sometimes with a sad and sometimes with a black look. There was no rivalling the dead, he knew that; and how to censure an old serving-man for a fault of loyalty, was more than he could see. His was not the tongue to do it.

Macconochie was chief upon the other side; an old, ill-spoken, swearing, ranting, drunken dog; and I have often thought it an odd circumstance in human nature that these two serving-men should each have been the champion of his contrary, and blackened their own faults and made light of their own virtues when they beheld them in a master. Macconochie had soon smelled out my secret inclination, took me much into his confidence, and would rant against the Master by the hour, so that even my work suffered. 'They're a' daft here,' he would cry, 'and be damned to them! The Master – the deil's in their thrapples that should call him sae! it's Mr Henry should be master now! They were nane sae fond o' the Master when they had him, I'll can tell ye that. Sorrow on his name! Never a guid word did I hear on his lips, nor naebody else, but just fleering and flyting and profane cursing – deil hae him! There's nane kent his wickedness: him a gentleman! Did ever ye hear tell, Mr Mackellar, o' Wully White the wabster? No? Aweel, Wully was an unco praying kind o' man; a dreigh body, nane o' my kind, I never could abide the sight o' him; onyway he was a great hand by his way of it, and he up and rebukit the Master for some of his on-goings. It was a grand thing for the Master o' Ball'ntrae to tak up a feud wi' a' wabster, was-nae't?' Macconochie would sneer; indeed, he never took the

full name upon his lips but with a sort of a whine of hatred. 'But he did! A fine
employ it was; chapping at the man's door, and crying 'boo' in his lum, and
puttin' poother in his fire, and pee-oys* in his window; till the man thocht it was
auld Hornie was come seekin' him. Weel, to make a lang story short, Wully gaed
gyte. At the hinder end, they couldnae get him frae his knees, but he just roared
and prayed and grat straucht on, till he got his release. It was fair murder, a'body
said that. Ask John Paul – he was brawly ashamed o' that game, him that's sic a
Christian man! Grand doin's for the Master o' Ball'ntrae!' I asked him what the
Master had thought of it himself. 'How would I ken?' says he. 'He never said
naething.' And on again in his usual manner of banning and swearing, with
every now and again a 'Master of Ballantrae' sneered through his nose. It was in
one of these confidences that he showed me the Carlisle letter, the print of the
horse-shoe still stamped in the paper. Indeed, that was our last confidence; for
he then expressed himself so ill-naturedly of Mrs Henry that I had to reprimand
him sharply, and must thenceforth hold him at a distance.

My old lord was uniformly kind to Mr Henry; he had even pretty ways of
gratitude, and would sometimes clap him on the shoulder and say, as if to the
world at large: 'This is a very good son to me.' And grateful he was, no doubt,
being a man of sense and justice. But I think that was all, and I am sure Mr
Henry thought so. The love was all for the dead son. Not that this was often
given breath to; indeed, with me but once. My lord had asked me one day how I
got on with Mr Henry, and I had told him the truth.

'Ay,' said he, looking sideways on the burning fire, 'Henry is a good lad, a very
good lad,' said he. 'You have heard, Mr Mackellar, that I had another son? I am
afraid he was not so virtuous a lad as Mr Henry; but dear me, he's dead, Mr
Mackellar! and while he lived we were all very proud of him, all very proud. If
he was not all he should have been in some ways, well, perhaps we loved him
better!' This last he said looking musingly in the fire; and then to me, with a
great deal of briskness, 'But I am rejoiced you do so well with Mr Henry. You will
find him a good master.' And with that he opened his book, which was the
customary signal of dismission. But it would be little that he read, and less that
he understood; Culloden field and the Master, these would be the burthen of his
thought; and the burthen of mine was an unnatural jealousy of the dead man for
Mr Henry's sake, that had even then begun to grow on me.

I am keeping Mrs Henry for the last, so that this exression of my sentiment
may seem unwarrantably strong: the reader shall judge for himself when I have
done. But I must first tell of another matter, which was the means of bringing me
more intimate. I had not yet been six months at Durrisdeer when it chanced that
John Paul fell sick and must keep his bed; drink was the root of his malady, in my
poor thought; but he was tended, and indeed carried himself, like an afflicted
saint; and the very minister, who came to visit him, professed himself edified
when he went away. The third morning of his sickness, Mr Henry comes to me
with something of a hang-dog look.

'Mackellar,' says he, 'I wish I could trouble you upon a little service. There is a
pension we pay; it is John's part to carry it, and now that he is sick I know not to
whom I should look unless it was yourself. The matter is very delicate; I could
not carry it with my own hand for a sufficient reason; I dare not send

*A kind of firework made with damp powder.

Macconochie, who is a talker, and I am – I have – I am desirous this should not come to Mrs Henry's ears,' says he, and flushed to his neck as he said it.

To say truth, when I found I was to carry money to one Jessie Broun, who was no better than she should be, I supposed it was some trip of his own that Mr Henry was dissembling. I was the more impressed when the truth came out.

It was up a wynd off a side street in St Bride's that Jessie had her lodging. The place was very ill inhabited, mostly by the freetrading sort. There was a man with a broken head at the entry; half-way up, in a tavern, fellows were roaring and singing, though it was not yet nine in the day. Altogether, I had never seen a worse neighbourhood, even in the great city of Edinburgh, and I was in two minds to go back. Jessie's room was of a piece with her surroundings, and herself no better. She would not give me the receipt (which Mr Henry told me to demand, for he was very methodical) until she had sent out for spirits, and I had pledged her in a glass; and all the time she carried on in a light-headed, reckless way – now aping the manners of a lady, now breaking into unseemly mirth, now making coquettish advances that oppressed me to the ground. Of the money she spoke more tragically.

'It's blood money!' said she; 'I take it for that; blood money for the betrayed! See what I'm brought down to! Ah, if the bonnie lad were back again, it would be changed days. But he's deid – he's lyin' deid amang the Hieland hills – the bonnie lad, the bonnie lad!'

She had a rapt manner of crying on the bonnie lad, clasping her hands and casting up her eyes, that I think she must have learned of strolling players; and I thought her sorrow very much of an affectation, and that she dwelled upon the business because her shame was now all she had to be proud of. I will not say I did not pity her, but it was a loathing pity at the best; and her last change of manner wiped it out. This was when she had had enough of me for an audience, and had set her name at last to the receipt. 'There!' says she, and taking the most unwomanly oaths upon her tongue, bade me begone and carry it to the Judas who had sent me. It was the first time I had heard the name applied to Mr Henry; I was staggered besides at her sudden vehemence of word and manner, and got forth from the room, under this shower of curses, like a beaten dog. But even then I was not quit, for the vixen threw up her window, and, leaning forth, continued to revile me as I went up the wynd; the freetraders, coming to the tavern door, joined in the mockery, and one had even the inhumanity to set upon me a very savage small dog, which bit me in the ankle. This was a strong lesson, had I required one, to avoid ill company; and I rode home in much pain from the bite and considerable indignation of mind.

Mr Henry was in the steward's room, affecting employment, but I could see he was only impatient to hear of my errand.

'Well?' says he, as soon as I come in; and when I had told him something of what passed, and that Jessie seemed an undeserving woman and far from grateful: 'She is no friend to me,' said he; 'but, indeed, Mackellar, I have few friends to boast of, and Jessie has some cause to be unjust. I need not dissemble what all the country knows: she was not very well used by one of our family.' This was the first time I had heard him refer to the Master even distantly; and I think he found his tongue rebellious even for that much, but presently he resumed: 'This is why I would have nothing said. It would give pain to Mrs

Henry . . . and to my father,' he added with another flush.

'Mr Henry,' said I, 'if you will take a freedom at my hands, I would tell you to let that woman be. What service is your money to the like of her? She has no sobriety and no economy – as for gratitude, you will as soon get milk from a whin-stone; and if you will pretermit your bounty, it will make no change at all but just to save the ankles of your messengers.'

Mr Henry smiledd. 'But I am grieved about your ankle,' said he, the next moment, with a proper gravity.

'And observe,' I continued, 'I give you this advice upon consideration; and yet my heart was touched for the woman in the beginning.'

'Why, there it is, you see!' said Mr henry. 'And you are to remember that I knew her once a very decent lass. Besides which, although I speak little of my family, I think much of its repute.'

And with that he broke up the talk, which was the first we had together in such confidence. But the same afternoon I had the proof that his father was perfectly acquainted with the business, and that it was only from his wife that Mr Henry kept it secret.

'I fear you had a painful errand today,' says my lord to me, 'for which, as it enters in no way among your duties, I wish to thank you, and to remind you at the same time (in case Mr Henry should have neglected) how very desirable it is that no word of it should reach my daughter. Reflections on the dead, Mr Mackellar, are doubly painful.'

Anger glowed in my heart; and I could have told my lord to his face how little he had to do, bolstering up the image of the dead in Mrs Henry's heart, and how much better he were employed to shatter that false idol; for by this time I saw very well how the land lay between my patron and his wife.

My pen is clear enough to tell a plain tale; but to render the effect of an infinity of small things, not one great enough in itself to be narrated; and to translate the story of looks, and the message of voices when they are saying no great matter; and to put in half a page the essence of near eighteen months – this is what I despair to accomplish. The fault, to be very blunt, lay all in Mrs Henry. She felt it a merit to have consented to the marriage, and she took it like a martyrdom; in which my old lord, whether he knew it or not, fomented her. She made a merit, besides, of her constancy to the dead, though its name, to a nicer conscience, should have seemed rather disloyalty to the living; and here also my lord gave her his countenance. I suppose he was glad to talk of his loss, and ashamed to dwell on it with Mr Henry. Certainly, at least, he made a little coterie apart in that family of three, and it was the husband who was shut out. It seems it was an old custom when the family were alone in Durrisdeer, that my lord should take his wine to the chimney-side, and Miss Alison, instead of withdrawing, should bring a stool to his knee, and chatter to him privately; and after she had become my patron's wife the same manner of doing was continued. It should have been pleasant to behold this ancient gentleman so loving with his daughter, but I was too much a partisan of Mr Henry's to be anything but wroth at his exclusion. Many's the time I have seen him make an obvious resolve, quit the table, and go and join himself to his wife and my Lord Durrisdeer; and on their part, they were never backward to make him welcome, turned to him smilingly as to an intruding child, and took him into their talk with an effort so ill-concealed that he was soon back again me at the table, whence (so great is the hall of Durrisdeer) we could but hear the murmur of voices at the chimney. There he would sit and watch, and I along with him; and sometimes by my lord's head sorrowfully shaken, or his hand laid on Mrs Henry's head, or hers upon his knee as if in consolation, or sometimes by an exchange of tearful looks, we would draw our conclusion that the talk had gone to the old subject and the shadow of the dead was in the hall.

I have hours when I blame Mr Henry for taking all too patiently; yet we are to remember he was married in pity, and accepted his wife upon that term. And, indeed, he had small encouragement to make a stand. Once, I remember, he announced he had found a man to replace the pane of the stained window, which, as it was he that managed all the business, was a thing clearly within his attributions. But to the Master's fanciers, that pane was like a relic; and on the first word of any change, the blood flew to Mrs Henry's face.

'I wonder at you!' she cried.

'I wonder at myself,' says Mr Henry, with more of bitterness than I had ever heard him to express.

Thereupon my old lord stepped in with his smooth talk, so that before the meal was at an end all seemed forgotten; only that, after dinner, when the pair had withdrawn as usual to the chimney-side, we could see her weeping with her head upon his knee. Mr Henry kept up the talk with me upon some topic of the estates – he could speak of little else but business, and was never the best of company; but he kept it up that day with more continuity, his eye straying ever and again to the chimney, and his voice changing to another key, but without check of delivery. The pane, however, was not replaced; and I believe he counted it a great defeat.

Whether he was stout enough or no, God knows he was kind enough. Mrs Henry had a manner of condescension with him, such as (in a wife) would have pricked my vanity into an ulcer; he took it like a favour. She held him at the staff's end; forgot and then remembered and unbent to him, as we do to children; burthened him with cold kindness; reproved him with a change of colour and a bitten lip, like one shamed by his disgrace; ordered him with a look of the eye, when she was off her guard; when she was on the watch, pleaded with him for the most natural attentions, as though they were unheard-of favours. And to all this he replied with the most unwearied service; loving, as folks say, the very ground she trod on, and carrying that love in his eyes as bright as a lamp. When Miss Katharine was to be born, nothing would serve but he must stay in the room behind the head of the bed. There he sat, as white (they tell me) as a sheet, and the sweat dropping from his brow; and the handkerchief he had in his hand was crushed into a little ball no bigger than a musket-bullet. Nor could he bear the sight of Miss Katharine for many a day; indeed, I doubt if he was ever what he should have been to my young lady; for the which want of natural feeling he was loudly blamed.

Such was the state of this family down to the 7th April, 1749, when there befell the first of that series of events which were to break so many hearts and lose so many lives.

On that day I was sitting in my room a little before supper when John Paul

burst open the door with no civility of knocking, and told me there was one
below that wished to speak with the steward; sneering at the name of my office.

I asked what manner of man, and what his name was; and this disclosed the
excuse of John's ill-humour, for it appeared the visitor refused to name himself
except to me, a sore affront to the major-demo's consequence.

'Well,' said I, smiling a little, 'I will see what he wants.'

I found in the entrance hall a big man, very plainly habited, and wrapped in a
sea-cloak, like one new landed, as indeed he was. Not far off Macconochie was
standing, with his tongue out of his mouth and his hand upon his chin, like a
dull fellow thinking hard; and the stranger, who had brought his cloak about his
face, appeared uneasy. He had no sooner seen me coming than he went to meet
me with an effusive manner.

'My dear man,' said he, 'a thousand apologies for disturbing you, but I'm in
the most awkward position. And there's a son of a ramrod there that I should
know the looks of, and more betoken I believe that he knows mine. Being in
this family, sir, and in a place of some responsibility (which was the cause I took
the liberty to send for you), you are doubtless of the honest party?'

'You may be sure at least,' says I, 'that all of that party are quite safe in
Durrisdeer.'

'My dear man, it is my very thought,' says he. 'You see, I have just been set on
shore here by a very honest man, whose name I cannot remember, and who is to
stand off and on for me till morning, at some danger to himself; and, to be clear
with you, I am a little concerned lest it should be at some to me. I have saved my
life so often, Mr——, I forget your name, which is a very good one – that, faith,
I would be very loath to lose it after all. And the son of a ramrod, whom I
believe I saw before Carlisle ...'

'Oh, sir,' said I, 'you can trust Macconochie until tomorrow.'

'Well, and it's a delight to hear you say so,' says the stranger. 'The truth is that
my name is not a very suitable one in this country of Scotland. With a
gentleman like you, my dear man, I would have no concealments, of course; and
by your leave I'll just breathe it in your ear. They call me Francis Burke –
Colonel Francis Burke; and I am here, at a most damnable risk to myself, to see
your masters – if you'll excuse me, my good man, for giving them the name, for
I'm sure it's a circumstance I would never have guessed from your appearance.
And if you would just be so very obliging as to take my name to them, you might
say that I come bearing letters which I am sure they will be very rejoiced to have
the reading of.'

Colonel Francis Burke was one of the Prince's Irishmen, that did his cause
such an infinity of hurt, and were so much distasted of the Scots at the time of
the rebellion; and it came at once into my mind, how the Master of Ballantrae
had astonished all men by going with that party. In the same moment a strong
foreboding of the truth possessed my soul.

'If you will step in here,' said I, opening a chamber door, 'I will let my lord
know.'

'And I am sure it's very good of you, Mr What's-your-name,' says the Colonel.

Up to the hall I went, slow-footed. There they were, all three – my old lord in
his place, Mrs Henry at work by the window, Mr Henry (as was much his
custom) pacing the low end. In the midst was the table laid for supper. I told

them briefly what I had to say. My old lord lay back in his seat. Mrs Henry sprang up standing with a mechanical motion, and she and her husband stared at each other's eyes across the room: it was the strangest challenging look these two exchanged, and as they looked, the colour faded in their faces. Then Mr Henry turned to me; not to speak, only to sign with his finger; but that was enough, and I went down again for the Colonel.

When we returned these three were in much the same position I had left them in; I believe no word had passed.

'My Lord Durrisdeer, no doubt?' says the Colonel, bowing, and my lord bowed in answer. 'And this,' continues the Colonel, 'should be the Master of Ballantrae?'

'I have never taken that name,' said Mr Henry; 'but I am Henry Durie, at your service.'

Then the Colonel turns to Mrs Henry, bowing with his hat upon his heart and the most killing airs of gallantry. 'There can be no mistake about so fine a figure of a lady,' says he. 'I address the seductive Miss Alison, of whom I have so often heard?'

Once more husband and wife exchanged a look.

'I am Mrs Henry Durie,' she said; 'but before my marriage my name was Alison Graeme.'

Then my lord spoke up. 'I am an old man, Colonel Burke,' said he, 'and a frail one. It will be mercy on your part to be expeditious. Do you bring me news of—
—' he hesitated, and then the words broke from him with a singular change of voice – 'my son?'

'My dear lord, I will be round with you like a soldier,' said the Colonel. 'I do.'

My lord held out a wavering hand; he seemed to wave a signal, but whether it was to give him time or to speak on, was more than we could guess. At length he got out the one word, 'Good?'

'Why, the very best in the creation!' cries the Colonel. 'For my good friend and admired comrade is at this hour in the fine city of Paris, and as like as not, if I know anything of his habits, he will be drawing in his chair to a piece of dinner. – Bedad, I believe the lady's fainting.'

Mrs Henry was indeed the colour of death, and drooped against the window-frame. But when Mr Henry made a movement as if to run to her, she straightened with a sort of shiver. 'I am well,' she said, with her white lips.

Mr Henry stopped, and his face had a strong twitch of anger. The next moment he had turned to the Colonel. 'You must not blame yourself,' says he, 'for this effect on Mrs Durie. It is only natural; we were all brought up like brother and sister.'

Mrs Henry looked at her husband with something like relief or even gratitude. In my way of thinking, that speech was the first step he made in her good graces.

'You must try to forgive me, Mrs Durie, for indeed and I am just an Irish savage,' said the Colonel; 'and I deserve to be shot for not breaking the matter more artistically to a lady. But here are the Master's own letters; one for each of the three of you; and to be sure (if I know anything of my friend's genius) he will tell his own story with a better grace.'

He brought the three letters forth as he spoke, arranged them by their superscriptions, presented the first to my lord, who took it greedily, and advanced towards Mrs Henry holding out the second.

But the lady waved it back. 'To my husband,' says she, with a choked voice.

The Colonel was a quick man, but at this he was somewhat nonplussed. 'To be sure!' says he; 'how very dull of me! To be sure!' But he still held the letter.

At last Mr Henry reached forth his hand, and there was nothing to be done but give it up. Mr Henry took the letters (both hers and his own), and looked upon their outside, with his brows knit hard, as if he were thinking. He had surprised me all through by his excellent behaviour; but he was to excel himself now.

'Let me give you a hand to your room,' said he to his wife. 'This has come something of the suddenest; and, at any rate, you will wish to read your letter by yourself.'

Again she looked upon him with the same thought of wonder; but he gave her no time, coming straight to where she stood. 'It will be better so, believe me,' said he; 'and Colonel Burke is too considerate not to excuse you.' And with that he took her hand by the fingers, and led her from the hall.

Mrs Henry returned no more that night; and when Mr Henry went to visit her next morning, as I heard long afterwards, she gave him the letter again, still unopened.

'Oh, read it and be done!' he had cried.

'Spare me that,' said she.

And by these two speeches, to my way of thinking, each undid a great part of what they had previously done well. But the letter, sure enough, came into my hands, and by me was burned, unopened.

To be very exact as to the adventures of the Master after Culloden, I wrote not long ago to Colonel Burke, now a Chevalier of the Order of St Louis, begging him for some notes in writing, since I could scarce depend upon my memory at so great an interval. To confess the truth, I have been somewhat embarrassed by his response; for he sent me the complete memoirs of his life, touching only in places on the Master; running to a much greater length than my whole story, and not everywhere (as it seems to me) designed for edification. He begged in his letter, dated from Ettenheim, that I would find a publisher for the whole, after I had made what use of it I required; and I think I shall best answer my own purpose and fulfil his wishes by printing certain parts of it in full. In this way my readers will have a detailed and, I believe, a very genuine account of some essential matters; and if any publisher should take a fancy to the Chevalier's manner of narration, he knows where to apply for the rest, of which there is plenty at his service. I put in my first extract here, so that it may stand in the place of what the Chevalier told us over our wine in the hall of Durrisdeer; but you are to suppose it was not the brutal fact, but a very varnished version that he offered to my lord.

CHAPTER THREE

The Master's Wanderings
From the Memoirs of the Chevalier de Burke

... I LEFT RUTHVEN (it's hardly necessary to remark) with much greater satisfaction than I had come to it; but whether I missed my way in the deserts, or whether my companions failed me, I soon found myself alone. This was a predicament very disagreeable; for I never understood this horrid country or savage people, and the last stroke of the Prince's withdrawal had made us of the Irish more unpopular than ever. I was reflecting on my poor chances, when I saw another horseman on the hill, whom I supposed at first to have been a phantom, the news of his death in the very front at Culloden being current in the army generally. This was the Master of Ballantrae, my Lord Durrisdeer's son, a young nobleman of the rarest gallantry and parts, and equally designed by nature to adorn a Court and to reap laurels in the field. Our meeting was the more welcome to both, as he was one of the few Scots who had used the Irish with consideration, and as he might now be of very high utility in aiding my escape. Yet what founded our particular friendship was a circumstance by itself as romantic as any fable of King Arthur.

This was on the second day of our flight, after we had slept one night in the rain upon the inclination of a mountain. There was an Appin man, Alan Black Stewart (or some such name,* but I have seen him since in France), who chanced to be passing the same way, and had a jealousy of my companion. Very uncivil expressions were exchanged; and Stewart calls upon the Master to alight and have it out.

'Why, Mr Stewart,' says the Master, 'I think at the present time I would prefer to run a race with you.' And with the word claps spurs to his horse.

Stewart ran after us, a childish thing to do, for more than a mile; and I could not help laughing, as I looked back at last and saw him on a hill, holding his hand to his side, and nearly burst with running.

'But, all the same,' I could not help saying to my companion, 'I would let no man run after me for any such proper purpose, and not give him his desire. It was a good jest, but it smells a trifle cowardly.'

He bent his brows at me. 'I do pretty well,' says he, 'when I saddle myself with the most unpopular man in Scotland, and let that suffice for courage.'

'O, bedad,' says I, 'I could show you a more unpopular with the naked eye. And if you like not my company, you can "saddle" yourself on someone else.'

'Colonel Burke,' says he, 'do not let us quarrel; and, to that effect, let me assure you I am the least patient man in the world.'

'I am as little patient as yourself,' said I. 'I care not who knows that.'

*Note by Mr Mackellar. Should not this be Alan *Breck* Stewart, afterwards notorious as the Appin murderer? The Chevalier is sometimes very weak on names.

'At this rate,' says he, reining in, 'we shall not go very far. And I propose we do one of two things upon the instant: either quarrel and be done; or make a sure bargain to bear everything at each other's hands.'

'Like a pair of brothers?' said I.

'I said no such foolishness,' he replied. 'I have a brother of my own, and I think no more of him than of a colewort. But if we are to have our noses rubbed together in this course of flight, let us each dare to be ourselves like savages, and each swear that he will neither resent nor deprecate the other. I am a pretty bad fellow at bottom, and I find the pretence of virtues very irksome.'

'O, I am as bad as yourself,' said I. 'There is no skim milk in Francis Burke. But which is it to be? Fight or make friends?'

'Why,' says he, 'I think it will be the best manner to spin a coin for it.'

This proposition was too highly chivalrous not to take my fancy; and, strange as it may seem of two well-born gentlemen of today, we span a half-crown (like a pair of ancient paladins) whether we were to cut each other's throats or be sworn friends. A more romantic circumstance can rarely have occurred; and it is one of those points in my memoirs, by which we may see the old tales of Homer and the poets are equally true to-day – at least, of the noble and genteel. The coin fell for peace, and we shook hands upon our bargain. And then it was that my companion explained to me his thought in running away from Mr Stewart, which was certainly worthy of his political intellect. The report of his death, he said, was a great guard to him; Mr Stewart having recognized him had become a danger: and he had taken the briefest road to that gentleman's silence. 'For,' says he, 'Alan Black is too vain a man to narrate any such story of himself.'

Towards afternoon we came down to the shores of that loch for which we were heading; and there was the ship, but newly come to anchor. She was the *Sainte-Marie-des-Anges*, out of the port of Havre-de-Grace. The Master, after we had signalled for a boat, asked me if I knew the captain. I told him he was a countryman of mine, of the most unblemished integrity, but, I was afraid, a rather timorous man.

'No matter,' says he. 'For all that, he should certainly hear the truth.'

I asked him if he meant about the battle, for if the captain once knew the standard was down, he would certainly put to sea again at once.

'And even then!' said he; 'the arms are now of no sort of utility.'

'My dar man,' said I, 'who thinks of the arms? But, to be sure, we must remember our friends. They will be close upon our heels, perhaps the Prince himself, and if the ship be gone, a great number of valuable lives may be imperilled.'

'The captain and the crew have lives also, if you come to that,' says Ballantrae.

This I declared was but a quibble, and that I would not hear of the captain being told; and then it was that Ballantrae made me a witty answer, for the sake of which (and also because I have been blamed myself in this business of the *Sainte-Marie-des-Anges*) I have related the whole conversation as it passed.

'Frank,' says he, 'remember our bargain. I must not object to your holding your tongue, which I hereby even encourage you to do; but, by the same terms, you are not to resent my telling.'

I could not help laughing at this; though I still forewarned him what would come of it.

'The devil may come of it for what I care,' says the reckless fellow. 'I have always done exactly as I felt inclined.'

As is well known, my prediction came true. The captain had no sooner heard the news than he cut his cable and to sea again; and before morning broke, we were in the Great Minch.

The ship was very old; and the skipper, although the most honest of men (and Irish too), was one of the least capable. The wind blew very boisterous, and the sea raged extremely. All that day we had little heart whether to eat or drink; went early to rest in some concern of mind; and (as if to give us a lesson) in the night the wind chopped suddenly into the north-east, and blew a hurricane. We were awaked by the dreadful thunder of the tempest and the stamping of the mariners on deck; so that I supposed our last hour was certainly come; and the terror of my mind was increased out of all measure by Ballantrae, who mocked at my devotions. It is in hours like these that a man of any piety appears in his true light, and we find (what we are taught as babes) the small trust that can be set in worldly friends: I would be unworthy of my religion if I let this pass without particular remark. For three days we lay in the dark in the cabin, and had but a biscuit to nibble. On the fourth the wind fell, leaving the ship dismasted and heaving on vast billows. The captain had got a guess of whither we were blown; he was stark ignorant of his trade, and could do naught but bless the Holy Virgin; a very good thing, too, but scarce the whole of seamanship. It seemed our one hope was to be picked up by another vessel; and if that should prove to be an English ship, it might be no great blessing to the Master and myself.

The fifth and sixth days we tossed there helpless. The seventh some sail was got on her, but she was an unwieldy vessel at the best, and we made little but leeway. All the time, indeed, we had been drifting to the south and west, and during the tempest must have driven in that direction with unheard-of voilence. The ninth dawn was cold and black, with a great sea running, and every mark of foul weather. In this situation we were overjoyed to sight a small ship on the horizon, and to perceive her go about and head for the *Sainte-Marie*. But our gratification did not very long endure; for when she had laid to and lowered a boat, it was immediately filled with disorderly fellows, who sang and shouted as they pulled across to us, and swarmed in on our deck with bare cutlasses, cursing loudly. Their leader was a horrible villain, with his face blacked and his whiskers curled in ringlets; Teach, his name; a most notorious pirate. He stamped about the deck, raving and crying out that his name was Satan, and his ship was called Hell. There was something about him like a wicked child or a half-witted person, that daunted me beyond expression. I whispered in the ear of Ballantrae that I would not be the last to volunteer, and only prayed God they might be short of hands; he approved my purpose with a nod.

'Bedad,' said I to Master Teach, 'if you are Satan, here is a devil for ye.'

The word pleased him; and (not to dwell upon these shocking incidents) Ballantrae and I and two others were taken for recruits, while the skipper and all the rest were cast into the sea by the method of walking the plank. It was the first time I had seen this done; my heart died within me at the spectacle; and Master Teach or one of his acolytes (for my head was too much lost to be precise) remarked upon my pale face in a very alarming manner. I had the strength to cut a step or two of a jig, and cry out some ribaldry, which saved me for that time; but my legs were like water when I must get down into the skiff among these miscreants; and what with my horror of my company and fear of the monstrous billows, it was all I could do to keep an Irish tongue and break a jest or two as we were pulled aboard. By the blessing of God, there was a fiddle in the pirate ship, which I had no sooner seen than I fell upon; and in my quality of crowder I had the heavenly good luck to get favour in their eyes. *Crowding Pat* was the name they dubbed me with; and it was little I cared for a name so long as my skin was whole.

What kind of a pandemonium that vessel was, I cannot describe, but she was commanded by a lunatic, and might be called a floating Bedlam. Drinking, roaring, singing, quarrelling, dancing, they were never all sober at one time; and there were days together when, if a squall had supervened, it must have sent us to the bottom; or if a king's ship had come along, it would have found us quite helpless for defence. Once or twice we sighted a sail, and, if we were sober enough, overhauled her, God forgive us! and if we were all too drunk, she got away, and I would bless the saints under my breath. Teach ruled, if you can call that rule which brought no order, by the terror he created; and I observed the man was very vain of his position. I have known marshals of France – ay, and even Highland chieftains – that were less openly puffed up; which throws a singular light on the pursuit of honour and glory. Indeed, the longer we live, the more we perceive the sagacity of Aristotle and the other old philosophers; and though I have all my life been eager for legitimate distinctions, I can lay my hand upon my heart, at the end of my career, and declare there is not one – no, nor yet life itself – which is worth acquiring or preserving at the slightest cost of dignity.

It was long before I got private speech of Ballantrae; but at length one night we crept out upon the bowsprit, when the rest were better employed, but commiserated our position.

'None can deliver us but the saints,' said I.

'My mind is very different,' said Ballantrae; 'for I am going to deliver myself. This Teach is the poorest creature possible; we make no profit of him, and lie continually open to capture; and,' says he. 'I am not going to be a tarry pirate for nothing, nor yet to hang in chains if I can help it.' And he told me what was in his mind to better the state of the ship in the way of discipline, which would give us safety for the present, and a sooner hope of deliverance when they should have gained enough and should break up their company.

I confessed to him ingenuously that my nerve was quite shook amid these horrible surroundings, and I durst scarce tell him to count upon me.

'I am not very easy frightened,' said he, 'nor very easy beat.'

A few days after, there befell an accident which had nearly hanged us all; and offers the most extraordinary picture of the folly that ruled in our concerns. We were all pretty drunk: and some bedlamite spying a sail, Teach put the ship about in chase without a glance, and we began to bustle up the arms and boast of the horrors that should follow. I observed Ballantrae stood quiet in the bows, looking under the shade of his hand; but for my part, true to my policy among these savages, I was at work with the busiest and passing Irish jests for their diversion.

'Run up the colours,' cries Teach. 'Show the ——s the Jolly Roger!'

It was the merest drunken braggadocio at such a stage, and might have lost us a valuable prize; but I thought it no part of mine to reason, and I ran up the black flag with my own hand.

Ballantrae steps presently aft with a smile upon his face.

'You may perhaps like to know, you drunken dog,' says he, 'that you are chasing a king's ship.'

Teach roared him the lie; but he ran at the same time to the bulwarks, and so did they all. I have never seen so many drunken men struck suddenly sober. The cruiser had gone about, upon our impudent display of colours; she was just then filling on the new tack; her ensign blew out quite plain to see; and even as we stared, there came a puff of smoke, and then a report, and a shot plunged in the waves a good way short of us. Some ran to the ropes, and got the *Sarah* round with an incredible swiftness. One fellow fell on the rum barrel, which stood broached upon the deck, and rolled it promptly overboard. On my part, I made for the Jolly Roger, struck it, tossed it in the sea; and could have flunged myself after, so vexed was I with our mismanagement. As for Teach, he grew as pale as death, and incontinently went down to his cabin. Only twice he came on deck that afternoon; went to the taffrail; took a long look at the king's ship, which was still on the horizon heading after us; and then, without speech, back to his cabin. You may say he deserted us; and if it had not been for one very capable sailor we had on board, and for the lightness of the airs that blew all day, we must certainly have gone to the yard-arm.

It is to be supposed Teach was humiliated, and perhaps alarmed for his position with the crew; and the way in which he set about regaining what he had lost, was highly characteristic of the man. Early next day we smelled him burning sulphur in his cabin and crying out of 'Hell, hell!' which was well understood among the crew, and filled their minds with apprehension. Presently he comes on deck, a perfect figure of fun, his face blacked, his hair and whiskers curled, his belt stuck full of pistols; chewing bits of glass so that the blood ran down his chin, and brandishing a dirk. I do not know if he had taken these manners from the Indians of America, where he was a native; but such was his way, and he would always thus announce that he was wound up to horrid deeds. The first that came near him was the fellow who had sent the rum overboard the day before; him he stabbed to the heart, damning him for a mutineer; and then capered about the body, raving and swearing and daring us to come on. It was the silliest exhibition; and yet dangerous too, for the cowardly fellow was plainly working himself up to another murder.

All of a sudden Ballantrae stepped forth. 'Have done with this play-acting,' says he. 'Do you think to frighten us with making faces? We saw nothing of you yesterday, when you were wanted; and we did well without you, let me tell you that.'

There was a murmur and a movement in the crew, of pleasure and alarm, I thought, in nearly equal parts. As for Teach, he gave a barbarous howl, and swung his dirk to fling it, an art in which (like many seamen) he was very expert.

'Knock that out of his hand!' says Ballantrae, so sudden and sharp that my arm obeyed him before my mind had understood.

Teach stood like one stupid, never thinking on his pistols.

'Go down to your cabin,' cries Ballantrae, 'and come on deck again when you are sober. Do you think we are going to hang for you, you black-faced, half-witted, drunken brute and butcher? Go down!' And he stamped his foot at him with such a sudden smartness that Teach fairly ran for it to the companion.

'And now, mates,' says Bellantrae, 'a word with you. I don't know if you are gentlemen of fortune for the fun of the thing, but I am not. I want to make money, and get ashore again, and spend it like a man. And on one thing my mind is made up: I will not hang if I can help it. Come: give me a hint; I'm only a beginner! Is there no way to get a little discipline and common sense about this business?'

One of the men spoke up: he said by rights they should have a quartermaster; and no sooner was the word out of his mouth than they were all of that opinion. The thing went by acclamation, Ballantrae was made quartermaster, the rum was put in his charge, laws were passed in imitation of those of a pirate by the name of Roberts, and the last proposal was to make an end of Teach. But Ballantrae was afraid of a more efficient captain, who might be a counterweight to himself, and he opposed this stoutly. Teach, he said, was good enough to board ships and to frighten fools with his blacked face and swearing; we could scarce get a better man than Teach for that; and besides, as the man was now disconsidered and as good as deposed, we might reduce his proportion of the plunder. This carried it; Teach's share was cut down to a mere derision, being actually less than mine; and there remained only two points: whether he would consent, and who was to announce to him this resolution.

'Do not let that stick you,' says Ballantrae, 'I will do that.'

And he stepped to the companion and down alone into the cabin to face that drunken savage.

'This is the man for us,' cries one of the hands. 'Three cheers for the quartermaster!' which were given with a will, my own voice among the loudest, and I dare say these plaudits had their effect on Master Teach in the cabin, as we have seen of late days how shouting in the streets may trouble even the minds of legislators.

What passed precisely was never known, though some of the heads of it came to the surface later on; and we were all amazed, as well as gratified, when Ballantrae came on deck with Teach upon his arm, and announced that all had been consented.

I pass swiftly over those twelve or fifteen months in which we continued to keep the sea in the North Atlantic, getting our food and water from the ships we overhauled, and doing on the whole a pretty fortunate business. Sure, no one could wish to read anything so ungenteel as the memoirs of a pirate, even an unwilling one like me! Things went extremely better with our designs, and Ballantrae kept his lead, to my admiration, from that day forth. I would be tempted to suppose that a gentleman must everywhere be first, even aboard a rover: but my birth is every whit as good as any Scottish lord's, and I am not ashamed to confess that I stayed Crowding Pat until the end, and was not much better than the crew's buffoon. Indeed, it was no scene to bring out my merits. My health suffered from a variety of reasons; I was more at home to the last on a horse's back than a ship's deck; and, to be ingenuous, the fear of the sea was constantly in my mind, battling with the fear of my companions. I need not cry myself up for courage; I have done well on many fields under the eyes of famous generals, and earned my late advancement by an act of the most distinguished valour before many witnesses. But when we must proceed on one of our

abordages, the heart of Francis Burke was in his boots; the little egg-shell skiff in
which we must set forth, the horrible heaving of the vast billows, the height of
the ship that we must scale, the thought of how many there might be there in
garrison upon their legitimate defence, the scowling heavens which (in that
climate) so often looked darkly down upon our exploits, and the mere crying of
the wind in my ears, were all considerations most unpalatable to my valour.
Besides which, as I was always a creature of the nicest sensibility, the scenes that
must follow on our success tempted me as little as the chances of defeat. Twice
we found women on board; and though I have seen towns sacked, and of late
days in France some very horrid public tumults, there was something in the
smallness of the numbers engaged, and the bleak, dangerous sea-surroundings,
that made these acts of piracy far the most revolting. I confess ingenuously I
could never proceed unless I was three parts drunk; it was the same even with
the crew; Teach himself was fit for no enterprise till he was full of rum; and it was
one of the most difficult parts of Ballantrae's performance, to serve us with liquor
in the proper quantities. Even this he did to admiration; being upon the whole
the most capable man I ever met with, and the one of the most natural genius.
He did not even scrape favour with the crew, as I did, by continual buffoonery
made upon a very anxious heart; but preserved on most occasions a great deal of
gravity and distance: so that he was like a parent among a family of young
children, or a schoolmaster with his boys. What made his part the harder to
perform, the men were most inveterate grumblers; Ballantrae's discipline, little
as it was, was yet irksome to their love of licence; and what was worse, being
kept sober they had time to think. Some of them accordingly would fall to
repenting their abominable crimes; one in particular, who was a good Catholic,
and with whom I would sometimes steal apart for prayer; above all in bad
weather, fogs, lashing rain and the like, when we would be the less observed;
and I am sure no two criminals in the cart have ever performed their devotions
with more anxious sincerity. But the rest, having no such grounds of hope, fell
to another pastime, that of computation. All day long they would be telling up
their shares or glooming over the result. I have said we were pretty fortunate.
But an observation falls to be made: that in this world, in no business that I have
tried, do the profits rise to a man's expectations. We found many ships and took
many; yet few of them contained much money, their goods were usually nothing
to our purpose – what did we want with a cargo of ploughs, or even of tobacco? –
and it is quite a painful reflection how many whole crews we have made to walk
the plank for no more than a stock of biscuit or an anker or two of spritis.

   In the meanwhile our ship was growing very foul, and it was high time we
should make for our *port de carénage*, which was in the estuary of a river among
swamps. It was openly understood that we should then break up and go and
squander our proportions of the spoil; and this made every man greedy of a little
more, so that our decision was delayed from day to day. What finally decided
matters was a trifling accident, such as an ignorant person might suppose
incidental to our way of life. But here I must explain: on only one of all the ships
we boarded, the first on which we found women, did we meet with any genuine
resistance. On that occasion we had two men killed and several injured, and if it
had not been for the gallantry of Ballantrae, we had surely been beat back at
last. Everywhere else the defence (where there was any at all) was what the

worst troops in Europe would have laughed at; so that the most dangerous part of our employment was to clamber up the side of the ship; and I have even known the poor souls on board to cast us a line, so eager were they to volunteer instead of walking the plank. This constant immunity had made our fellows very soft, so that I understood how Teach had made so deep a mark upon their minds; for indeed the company of that lunatic was the chief danger in our way of life. The accident to which I have referred was this: – We had sighted a little full-rigged ship very close under our board in a haze; she sailed near as well as we did – I should be nearer truth if I said, near as ill; and we cleared the bow-chaser to see if we could bring a spar or two about their ears. The swell was exceedingly great; the motion of the ship beyond description; it was little wonder if our gunners should fire thrice and be still quite broad of what they aimed at. But in the meanwhile the chase had cleared a stern gun, the thickness of the air concealing them; and being better marksmen, their first shot struck us in the bows, knocked our two gunners into mincemeat, so that we were all sprinkled with the blood, and plunged through the deck into the forecastle where we slept. Ballantrae would have held on; indeed, there was nothing in this *contretemps* to affect the mind of any soldier; but he had a quick perception of the men's wishes, and it was plain this lucky shot had given them a sickener of their trade. In a moment they were all of one mind: the chase was drawing away from us, it was needless to hold on, the *Sarah* was too foul to overhaul a bottle, it was mere foolery to keep the sea with her; and on these pretended grounds her head was incontinently put about and the course laid for the river. It was strange to see what merriment fell on that ship's company, and how they stamped about the deck jesting, and each computing what increase had come to his share by the death of the two gunners.

We were nine days making our port, so light were the airs we had to sail on, so foul was the ship's bottom; but early on the tenth, before dawn, and in a light lifting haze, we passed the head. A little after, the haze lifted, and fell again, showing us a cruiser very close. This was a sore blow, happening so near our refuge. There was a great debate of whether she had seen us, and if so whether it was likely they had recognized the *Sarah*. We were very careful, by destroying every member of those crews we overhauled, to leave no evidence as to our own persons; but the appearance of the *Sarah* herself we could not keep so private; and above all of late, since she had been foul, and we had pursued many ships without success, it was plain that her description had been often published. I supposed this alert would have made us separate upon the instant. But here again that original genius of Ballantrae's had a surprise in store for me. He and Teach (and it was the most remarkable step of his success) had gone hand in hand since the first day of his appointment. I often questioned him upon the fact, and never got an answer but once, when he told me he and Teach had an understanding 'which would very much surprise the crew if they should hear of it, and would surprise himself a good deal if it was carried out.' Well, here again he and Teach were of a mind; and by their joint procurement the anchor was no sooner down than the whole crew went off upon a scene of drunkenness indescribable. By afternoon we were a mere shipful of lunatical persons, throwing of things overboard, howling of different songs at the same time, quarrelling and falling together, and then forgetting our quarrels to embrace. Ballantrae had bid me drink nothing, and feign drunkenness, as I valued my life;

and I have never passed a day so wearisomely, lying the best part of the time upon the forecastle and watching the swamps and thickets by which our little basin was entirely surrounded for the eye. A little after dusk Ballantrae stumbled up to my side, feigned to fall, with a drunken laugh, and before he got his feet again, whispered me too 'reel down into the cabin and seem to fall asleep upon a locker, for there would be need of me soon.' I did as I was told, and coming into the cabin, where it was quite dark, let myself fall on the first locker. There was a man there already; by the way he stirred and threw me off, I could not think he was much in liquor; and yet when I had found another place, he seemed to continue to sleep on. My heart now beat very hard, for I saw some desperate matter was in act. Presently down came Ballantrae, lit the lamp, looked about the cabin, nodded as if pleased, and on deck again without a word. I peered out from between my fingers, and saw there were three of us slumbering, or feigning to slumber, on the lockers: myself, one Dutton, and one Gradey, both resolute men. On deck the rest were got to a pitch of revelry quite beyond the bounds of what is human; so that no reasonable name can describe the sounds they were now making. I have heard many a drunken bout in my time, many on board that very *Sarah*, but never anything the least like this, which made me early suppose the liquor had been tampered with. It was a long while before these yells and howls died out into a sort of miserable moaning, and then to silence; and it seemed a long while after that before Ballantrae came down again, this time with Teach upon his heels. The latter cursed at the sight of us three upon the lockers.

'Tut,' says Ballantrae, 'you might fire a pistol at their ears. You know what stuff they have been swallowing.'

There was a hatch in the cabin floor, and under that the richest part of the booty was stored against the day of division. It fastened with a ring and three padlocks, the keys (for greater security) being divided; one to Teach, one to Ballantrae, and one to the mate, a man called Hammond. Yet I was amazed to see they were now all in the one hand; and yet more amazed (still looking through my fingers) to observe Ballantrae and Teach bring up several packets, four of them in all, very carefully made up and with a loop for carriage.

'And now,' says Teach, 'let us be going.'

'One word,' says Ballantrae. 'I have discovered there is another man besides your-self who knows a private path across the swamp; and it seems it is shorter than yours.'

Teach cried out, in that case, they were undone.

'I do not know for that,' says Ballantrae. 'For there are several other circumstances with which I must acquaint you. First of all, there is no bullet in your pistols, which (if you remember) I was kind enough to load for both of us this morning. Secondly, as there is someone else who knows a passage, you must think it highly improbable I should saddle myself with a lunatic like you. Thirdly, these gentlemen (who need no longer pretend to be asleep) are those of my party, and will now proceed to gag and bind you to the mast; and when your men awaken (if they ever do awake after the drugs we have mingled in their liquor), I am sure they will be so obliging as to deliver you, and you will have no difficulty, I daresay, to explain the business of the keys.'

Not a word said Teach, but looked at us like a frightened baby as we gagged and bound him.

'Now you see, you moon-calf,' says Ballantrae, 'why we make four packets.

Heretofore you have been called Captain Teach, but I think you are now rather Captain Learn.'

That was our last word on board the *Sarah*. We four, with our four packets, lowered ourselves softly into a skiff, and left that ship behind us as silent as the grave, only for the moaning of some of the drunkards. There was a fog about breast-high upon the waters; so that Dutton, who knew the passage, must stand on his feet to direct our rowing; and this, as it forced us to row gently, was the means of our deliverance. We were yet but a little way from the ship, when it began to come grey, and the birds to fly abroad upon the water. All of a sudden Dutton clapped down upon his hams, and whispered us to be silent for our lives, and hearken. Sure enough, we heard a little faint creak of oars upon one hand, and then again, and further off, a creak of oars upon the other. It was clear we had been sighted yesterday in the morning; here were the cruiser's boats to cut us out; here were we defenceless in their very midst. Sure, never were poor souls more perilously placed; and as we lay there on our oars, praying God the mist might hold, the sweat poured from my brow. Presently we heard one of the boats where we might have thrown a biscuit in her. 'Softly, men,' we heard an officer whisper; and I marvelled they could not hear the drumming of my heart.

'Never mind the path,' says Ballantrae; 'we must get shelter anyhow; let us pull straight ahead for the sides of the basin.'

This we did with the most anxious precaution, rowing, as best we could, upon our hands, and steering at a venture in the fog, which was (for all that) our only safety. But Heaven guided us; we touched ground at a thicket; scrambled ashore with our treasure; and having no other way of concealment, and the mist beginning already to lighten, hove down the skiff and let her sink. We were still but new under cover when the sun rose; and at the same time, from the midst of the basin, a great shouting of seamen sprang up, and we knew the *Sarah* was being boarded. I heard afterwards the officer that took her got great honour; and it's true the approach was creditably managed, but I think he had an easy capture when he came to board. *

I was still blessing the saints for my escape, when I became aware we were in trouble of another kind. We were here landed at random in a vast and dangerous swamp; and how to come at the path was a concern of doubt, fatigue, and peril. Dutton, indeed, was of opinion we should wait until the ship was gone, and fish up the skiff; for any delay would be more wise than to go blindly ahead in that morass. One went back accordingly to the basin-side and (peering through the thicket) saw the fog already quite drunk up, and English colours flying on the *Sarah*, but no movement made to get her under way. Our situation was now very doubtful. The swamp was an unhealthful place to linger in; we had been so greedy to bring treasures that we had brought but little food; it was highly desirable, besides, that we should get clear of the neighbourhood and into the settlements before the news of the capture went abroad; and against all these considerations, there was only the peril of the passage on the other side. I think it not wonderful we decided on the active part.

*Note by Mr Mackellar. This Teach of the *Sarah* must not be confused with the celebrated *Blackbeard*. The dates and facts by no means tally. It is possible the second Teach may have at once borrowed the name and imitated the more excessive part of his manners from the first. Even the Master of Ballantrae could make admirers.

It was already blistering hot when we set forth to pass the marsh, or rather to strike the path, by compass. Dutton took the compass and one or other of us three carried his proportion of the treasure. I promise you he kept a sharp eye to his rear, for it was like the man's soul that he must trust us with. The thicket was as close as a bush; the ground very treacherous, so that we often sank in the most terrifying manner, and must go round about; the heat, besides, was stifling, the air singularly heavy, and the stinging insects abounded in such myriads that each of us walked under his own cloud. It has often been commented on, how much better gentlemen of birth endure fatigue than persons of the rabble; so that walking officers who must tramp in the dirt beside their men, shame them by their constancy. This was well to be observed in the present instance; for here were Ballantrae and I, two gentlemen of the highest breeding, on the one hand; and on the other Grady, a common mariner, and a man nearly a giant in physical strength. The case of Dutton is not in point, for I confess he did as well as any of us. * But as for Grady, he began early to lament his case, tailed in the rear, refused to carry Dutton's packet when it came his turn, clamoured continually for rum (of which we had too little), and at last even threatened us from behind with a cocked pistol, unless we should allow him rest. Ballantrae would have fought it out, I believe; but I prevailed with him the other way; and we made a stop and ate a meal. It seemed to benefit Grady little; he was in the rear again at once, growling and bemoaning his lot; and at last, by some carelessness, not having followed properly in our tracks, stumbled into a deep part of the slough where it was mostly water, gave some very dreadful screams, and before we could come to his aid had sunk along with his booty. His fate, and above all these screams of his, appalled us to the soul; yet it was, on the whole, a fortunate circumstance, and the means of our deliverance, for it moved Dutton to mount into a tree, whence he was able to perceive and to show me, who had climbed after him, a high piece of the wood, which was a landmark for the path. He went forward the more carelessly, I must suppose; for presently we saw him sink a little down, draw up his feet and sink again, and so twice. Then he turned his face to us, pretty white.

'Lend a hand,' said he, 'I am in a bad place.'

'I don't know about that,' said Ballantrae, standing still.

Dutton broke out into the most violent oaths, sinking a little lower as he did, so that the mud was nearly to his waist, and plucking a pistol from his belt, 'Help me,' he cries, 'or die and be damned to you!'

'Nay,' says Ballantrae, 'I did but jest. I am coming.' And he set down his own packet and Dutton's, which he was then carrying. 'Do not venture near till we see if you are needed,' said he to me, and went forward alone to where the man was bogged. He was quiet now, though he still held the pistol; and the marks of terror in his countenance were very moving to behold.

'For the Lord's sake,' says he, 'look sharp.'

Ballantrae was now got close up. 'Keep still,' says he, and seemed to consider; and then, 'Reach out both your hands!'

Dutton laid down his pistol, and so watery was the top surface that it went clear out of sight; with an oath he stooped to snatch it; and as he did so,

*Note by Mr Mackellar. And is not this the whole explanation? since this Dutton, exactly like the officers, enjoyed the stimulus of some responsibility.

Ballantrae leaned forth and stabbed him between the shoulders. Up went his hands over his head – I know not whether with the pain or to ward himself; and the next moment he doubled forward in the mud.

Ballantrae was already over the ankles; but he plucked himself out, and came back to me, where I stood with my knees smiting one another. 'The devil take you, Francis!' says he. 'I believe you are a half-hearted fellow, after all. I have only done justice on a pirate. And here we are quite clear of the *Sarah*! Who shall now say that we have dipped our hands in any irregularities?'

I assured him he did me injustice; but my sense of humanity was so much affected by the horridness of the fact that I could scarce find breath to answer with.

'Come,' said he, 'you must be more resolved. The need for this fellow ceased when he had shown you where the path ran; and you cannot deny I would have been daft to let slip so fair an opportunity.'

I could not deny but he was right in principle; nor yet could I refrain from shedding tears, of which I think no man of valour need have been ashamed; and it was not until I had a share of the rum that I was able to proceed. I repeat, I am far from ashamed of my generous emotion; mercy is honourable in the warrior; and yet I cannot altogether censure Ballantrae, whose step was really fortunate, as we struck the path without further misadventure, and the same night, about sundown, came to the edge of the morass.

We were too weary to seek far; on some dry sands, still warm with the day's sun, and close under a wood of pines, we lay down and were instantly plunged in sleep.

We awaked the next morning very early, and began with a sullen spirit a conversation that came near to end in blows. We were now cast on shore in the southern provinces, thousands of miles from any French settlement; a dreadful journey and a thousand perils lay in front of us; and sure, if there was ever need for amity, it was in such an hour. I must suppose that Ballantrae had suffered in his sense of what is truly polite; indeed, and there is nothing strange in the idea, after the seawolves we had consorted with so long; and as for myself, he fubbed me off unhandsomely, and any gentleman would have resented his behaviour.

I told him in what light I saw his conduct; he walked a little off, I following to upbraid him; and at last he stopped me with his hand.

'Frank,' says he, 'you know what we swore; and yet there is no oath invented would induce me to swallow such expressions, if I did not regard you with sincere affection. It is impossible you should doubt me there: I have given proofs. Dutton I had to take, because he knew the pass, and Grady because Dutton would not move without him; but what call was there to carry you along? You are a perpetual danger to me with your cursed Irish tongue. By rights you should now be in irons in the cruiser. And you quarrel with me like a baby for some trinkets!'

I considered this one of the most unhandsome speeches ever made; and indeed to this day I can scarce reconcile it to my notion of a gentleman that was my friend. I retorted upon him with his Scotch accent, of which he had not so much as some, but enough to be very barbarous and disgusting, as I told him plainly; and the affair would have gone to a great length, but for an alarming intervention.

We had got some way off upon the sand. The place where we had slept, with the packets lying undone and the money scattered openly, was now between us and the pines; and it was out of these the stranger must have come. There he was at least, a great hulking fellow of the country, with a broad axe on his shoulder, looking open-mouthed, now at the treasure, which was just at his feet, and now at our disputation, in which we had gone far enough to have weapons in our hands. We had no sooner observed him than he found his legs and made off again among the pines.

This was no scene to put our minds at rest; a couple of armed men in sea-clothes found quarrelling over a treasure, not many miles from where a pirate had been captured – here was enough to bring the whole country about our ears. The quarrel was not even made up; it was blotted from our minds; and we got our packets together in the twinkling of an eye, and made off, running with the best will in the world. But the trouble was, we did not know in what direction, and must continually return upon our steps. Ballantrae had indeed collected what he could from Dutton; but it's hard to travel upon hearsay; and the estuary, which spreads into a vast irregular harbour, turned us off upon every side with a new stretch of water.

We were near beside ourselves, and already quite spent with running, when, coming to the top of a dune, we saw we were again cut off by another ramification of the bay. This was a creek, however, very different from those that had arrested us before; being set in rocks, and so precipitously deep that a small vessel was able to lie alongside, made fast with a hawser; and her crew had laid a plank to the shore. Here they had lighted a fire, and were sitting at their meal. As for the vessel herself, she was one of those they build in the Bermudas.

The love of gold and the great hatred that everybody has to pirates were motives of the most influential, and would certainly raise the country in our pursuit. Besides, it was now plain we were on some sort of straggling peninsula, like the fingers of a hand; and the wrist, or passage to the mainland, which we should have taken at the first, was by this time not improbably secured. These considerations put us on a bolder counsel. For as long as we dared, looking every moment to hear sounds of the chase, we lay among some bushes on the top of the dune; and having by this means secured a little breath and recomposed our appearance, we strolled down at last, with a great affectation of carelessness, to the party by the fire.

It was a trader and his negroes, belonging to Albany, in the province of New York, and now on the way home from the Indies with a cargo; his name I cannot recall. We were amazed to learn he had put in here from terror of the *Sarah*; for we had no thought our exploits had been so notorious. As soon as the Albanian heard she had been taken the day before, he jumped to his feet, gave us a cup of spirits for our good news, and sent his negroes to get sail on the Bermudan. On our side, we profited by the dram to become more confidential, and at last offered ourselves as passengers. He looked askance at our tarry clothes and pistols, and replied civilly enough that he had scarce accommodation for himself; nor could either our prayers or our offers of money, in which we advanced pretty far, avail to shake him.

'I see, you think ill of us,' says Ballantrae, 'but I will show you how well we think of you by telling you the truth. We are Jacobite fugitives, and there is a price upon our heads.'

At this, the Albanian was plainly moved a little. He asked us many questions as to the Scotch war, which Ballantrae very patiently answered. And then, with a wink, in a vulgar manner, 'I guess you and your Prince Charlie got more than you cared about,' said he.

'Bedad, and that we did,' said I. 'And, my dear man, I wish you would set a new example and give us just that much.'

This I said in the Irish way, about which there is allowed to be something very engaging. It's a remarkable thing, and a testimony to the love with which our nation is regarded, that this address scarce ever fails in a handsome fellow. I cannot tell how often I have seen a private soldier escape the horse, or a beggar wheedle out a good alms by a touch of the brogue. And, indeed, as soon as the Albanian had laughed at me I was pretty much at rest. Even then, however, he made many conditions, and – for one thing – took away our arms, before he suffered us aboard; which was the signal to cast off; so that in a moment after, we were gliding down the bay with a good breeze, and blessing the name of God for our deliverance. Almost in the mouth of the estuary, we passed the cruiser, and a little after, the poor *Sarah* with her prize crew; and these were both sights to make us tremble. The Bermudan seemed a very safe place to be in, and our bold stroke to have been fortunately played, when we were thus reminded of the case of our companions. For all that, we had only exchanged traps, jumped out of the frying-pan into the fire, run from the yard-arm to the block, and escaped the open hostility of the man-of-war to lie at the mercy of the doubtful faith of our Albanian merchant.

From many circumstances, it chanced we were safer than we could have dared to hope. The town of Albany was at that time much concerned in contraband trade across the desert with the Indians and the French. This, as it was highly illegal, relaxed their loyalty, and as it brought them in relation with the politest people on the earth, divided even their sympathies. In short, they were like all the smugglers in the world, spies and agents ready-made for either party. Our Albanian, besides, was a very honest man indeed, and very greedy; and, to crown our luck, he conceived a great delight in our society. Before we had reached the town of New York we had come to a full agreement, that he should carry us as far as Albany upon his ship, and thence put us on a way to pass the boundaries and join the French. For all this we were to pay at a high rate; but beggars cannot be choosers, nor outlaws bargainers.

We sailed, then, up the Hudson River, which I protest is a very fine stream, and put at the 'King's Arms' in Albany. The town was full of the militia of the province, breathing slaughter against the French. Governor Clinton was there himself, a very busy man, and, by what I could learn, very near distracted by the factiousness of his Assembly. The Indians on both sides were on the war-path; we saw parties of them bringing in prisoners and (what was much worse) scalps, both male and female, for which they were paid at a fixed rate; and I assure you the sight was not encouraging. Altogether, we could scarce have come at a period more unsuitable for our designs; our position in the chief inn was dreadfully conspicuous; our Albanian fubbed us off with a thousand delays, and seemed upon the point of a retreat from his engagements; nothing but peril appeared to environ the poor fugitives, and for some time we drowned our concern in a very irregular course of living.

This too, proved to be fortunate; and it's one of the remarks that fall to be made upon our escape, how providentially our steps were conducted to the very end. What a humiliation to the dignity of man! My philosophy, the extraordinary genius of Ballantrae, our valour, in which I grant that we were equal – all these might have proved insufficient without the Divine blessing on our efforts. And how true it is, as the Church tells us, that the Truths of Religon are, after all, quite applicable even to daily affairs! At least, it was in the course of our revelry that we made the acquaintance of a spirited youth by the name of Chew. He was one of the most daring of the Indian traders, very well acquainted with the secret paths of the wilderness, needy, dissolute, and, by a last good fortune, in some disgrace with his family. Him we persuaded to come to our relief; he privately provided what was needful for our flight, and one day we slipped out of Albany, without a word to our former friend, and embarked, a little above, in a canoe.

To the toils and perils of this journey, it would require a pen more elegant than mine to do full justice. The reader must conceive for himself the dreadful wilderness which we had now to thread; its thickets, swamps, precipitous rocks, impetuous rivers, and amazing waterfalls. Among these barbarous scenes we must toil all day, now paddling, now carrying our canoe upon our shoulders; and at night we slept about a fire, surrounded by the howling of wolves and other savage animals. It was our design to mount the headwaters of the Hudson, to the neighbourhood of Crown Point, where the French had a strong place in the woods, upon Lake Champlain. But to have done this directly were too perilous; and it was accordingly gone upon by such a labyrinth of rivers, lakes, and portages as makes my head giddy to remember. These paths were in ordinary times entirely desert; but the country was now up, the tribes on the war-path, the woods full of Indian scouts. Again and again we came upon these parties when we least expected them; and one day, in particular, I shall never forget, how, as dawn was coming in, we were suddenly surrounded by five or six of these painted devils, uttering a very dreary sort of cry, and brandishing their hatchets. It passed off harmlessly, indeed, as did the rest of our encounters; for Chew was well known and highly valued among the different tribes. Indeed, he was a very gallant, respectable young man; but even with the advantage of his companion-ship, you must not think these meetings were without sensible peril. To prove friendship on our part, it was needful to draw upon our stock of rum – indeed, under whatever disguise, that is the true business of the Indian trader, to keep a travelling public-house in the forest; and when once the braves had got their bottle of *scaura* (as they call this beastly liquor), it behoved us to set forth and paddle for our scalps. Once they were a little drunk, good-bye to any sense or decency; they had but one thought, to get more *scaura*. They might easily take it in their heads to give us chase, and had we been overtaken, I had never written these memoirs.

We were come to the most critical portion of our course, where we might equally expect to fall into the hands of French or English, when a terrible calamity befell us. Chew was taken suddenly sick with symptoms like those of poison, and in the course of a few hours expired in the bottom of the canoe. We thus lost at once our guide, our interpreter, our boatman, and our passport, for he was all these in one; and found ourselves reduced, at a blow, to the most desperate and irremediable distress. Chew, who took a great pride in his knowledge, had indeed often lectured us on the geography; and Ballantrae, I believe, would listen. But for my part I have always found such information highly tedious; and beyond the fact that we were now in the country of the Adirondack Indians, and not so distant from our destination, could we but have found the way, I was entirely ignorant. The wisdom of my course was soon the more apparent; for with all his pains, Ballantrae was no further advanced than myself. He knew we must continue to go up one stream; then, by way of a portage, down another; and they up a third. But you are to consider in a mountain country, how many streams came rolling in from every hand. And how is a gentleman, who is a perfect stranger in that part of the world, to tell any one of them from any other? Nor was this our only trouble. We were great novices, besides, in handling a canoe; the portages were almost beyond our strength, so that I have seen us sit down in despair for half an hour at a time without one word; and the appearance of a single Indian, since we had now no means of speaking to them, would have been in all probability the means of our destruction. There is altogether some excuse if Ballantrae showed something of a glooming disposition; his habit of imputing blame to others, quite as capable as himself, was less tolerable, and his language it was not always easy to accept. Indeed, he had contracted on board the pirate ship a manner of address which was in a high degree unusual between gentlemen; and now, when you might say he was in a fever, it increased upon him hugely.

The third day of these wanderings, as we were carrying the canoe up a rocky portage, she fell, and was entirely bilged. The portage was between two lakes, both pretty extensive; the track, such as it was, opened at both ends upon the water, and on both hands was enclosed by the unbroken woods; and the sides of the lakes were quite impassable with bog: so that we beheld ourselves not only condemned to go without our boat and the greater part of our provisions, but to plunge at once into impenetrable thickets and to desert what little guidance we still had – the course of the river. Each stuck his pistols in his belt, shouldered an axe, made a pack of his treasure and as much food as he could stagger under; and deserting the rest of our possessions, even to our swords, which would have much embarrassed us among the woods, we set forth on this deplorable adventure. The labours of Hercules, so finely described by Homer, were a trifle to what we now underwent. Some parts of the forest were perfectly dense down to the ground, so that we must cut our way like mites in a cheese. In some the bottom was full of deep swamp, and the whole wood entirely rotten I have leapt on a great fallen log and sunk to the knees in touchwood; I have sought to stay myself, in falling, against what looked to be a solid trunk, and the whole thing has whiffed away at my touch like a sheet of paper. Stumbling, falling, bogging to the knees, hewing our way, our eyes almost put out with twigs and branches, our clothes plucked from our bodies, we laboured all day, and it is doubtful if we made two miles. What was worse, as we could rarely get a view of the country, and were perpetually justled from our path by obstacles, it was impossible even to have a guess in what direction we were moving.

A little before sundown, in an open place with a stream, and set about with barbarous mountains, Ballantrae threw down his pack. 'I will go no further,' said he, and bade me light the fire, damning my blood in terms not proper for a chairman.

I told him to try to forget he had ever been a pirate, and to remember he had been a gentleman.

'Are you mad?' he cried. 'Don't cross me here!' And then, shaking his fist at the hills, 'To think,' cries he, 'that I must leave my bones in this miserable wilderness! Would God I had died upon the scaffold like a gentleman!' This he said ranting like an actor; and then sat biting his fingers and staring on the ground, a most unchristian object.

I took a certain horror of the man, for I thought a soldier and a gentleman should confront his end with more philosophy. I made him no reply, therefore, in words; and presently the evening fell so chill that I was glad, for my own sake, to kindle a fire. And yet God knows, in such an open spot, and the country alive with savages, the act was little short of lunacy. Ballantrae seemed never to observe me; but at last, as I was about parching a little corn, he looked up.

'Have you ever a brother?' said he.

'By the blessing of Heaven,' said I, 'not less than five.'

'I have the one,' said he, with a strange voice; and then presently, 'He shall pay me for all this,' he added. And when I asked him what was his brother's part in our distress, 'What!' he cried, 'he sits in my place, he bears my name, he courts my wife; and I am here alone with a damned Irishman in this tooth-chattering desert! Oh, I have been a common gull!' he cried.

The explosion was in all ways so foreign to my friend's nature that I was daunted out of all my just susceptibility. Sure, an offensive expression, however vivacious, appers a wonderfully small affair in circumstances so extreme! But here there is a strange thing to be noted. He had only once before referred to the lady with whom he was contracted. That was when we came in view of the town of New York, when he had told me, if all had their rights, he was now in sight of his own property, for Miss Graeme enjoyed a large estate in the province. And this was certainly a natural occasion; but now here she was named a second time; and what is surely fit to be observed, in this very month, which was November, '47, and I believe upon that very day as we sat among these barbarous mountains, his brother and Miss Graeme were married. I am the least superstitious of men; but the hand of Providence is here displayed too openly not to be remarked.*

The next day, and the next, were passed in similar labours; Ballantrae often deciding on our course by the spinning of a coin; and once, when I expostulated on this childishness, he had an odd remark that I have never forgotten. 'I know no better way,' said he, 'to express my scorn of human reason.' I think it was the third day that we found the body of a Christian, scalped and most abominably mangled, and lying in a pudder of his blood; the birds of the desert screaming over him, as thick as flies. I cannot describe how dreadfully this sight affected us; but it robbed me of all strength and all hope for this world. The same day, and only a little after, we were scrambling over a part of the forest that had been burned, when Ballantrae, who was a little ahead, ducked suddenly behind a fallen trunk. I joined him in this shelter, whence we could look abroad without being seen ourselves; and in the bottom of the next vale, beheld a large war party of the savages going by across our line. There might be the value of a weak battalion present; all naked to the waist, blacked with grease and soot, and

*Note by Mr Mackellar. A complete blunder: there was at this date no word of the marriage: see above in my own narration.

painted with white lead and vermilion, according to their beastly habits. They went one behind another like a string of geese, and at a quickish trot; so that they took but a little while to rattle by, and disappear again among the woods. Yet I suppose we endured a greater agony of hesitation and suspense in these few minutes than goes usually to a man's whole life. Whether they were French or English Indians, whether they desired scalps or prisoners, whether we should declare ourselves upon the chance, or lie quiet and continue the heart-breaking business of our journey: sure, I think these were questions to have puzzled the brains of Aristotle himself. Ballantrae turned to me with a face all wrinkled up and his teeth showing in his mouth, like what I have read of people starving; he said no word, but his whole appearance was a kind of dreadful question.

'They may be of the English side,' I whispered; 'and think! the best we could then hope, is to begin this over again.'

'I know – I know,' he said. 'Yet it must come to a plunge at last.' And he suddenly plucked out his coin, shook it in his closed hands, looked at it, and then lay down with his face in the dust.

Addition by Mr Mackellar. – I drop the Chevalier's narration at this point because the couple quarrelled and separated the same day; and the Chevalier's account of the quarrel seems to me (I must confess) quite incompatible with the nature of either of the men. Henceforth they wandered alone, undergoing extraordinary sufferings; until first one and then the other was picked up by a party from Fort St Frederick. Only two things are to be noted. And first (as most important for my purpose) that the Master, in the course of his miseries, buried his treasure, at a point never since discovered, but of which he took a drawing in his own blood on the lining of his hat. And second, that on his coming thus penniless to the Fort, he was welcomed like a brother by the Chevalier, who thence paid his way to France. The simplicity of Mr Burke's character leads him at this point to praise the Master exceedingly; to an eye more worldly wise, it would seem it was the Chevalier alone that was to be commended. I have the more pleasure in pointing to this really very noble trait of my esteemed correspondent, as I fear I may have wounded him immediately before. I have refrained from comments on any of his extraordinary and (in my eyes) immoral opinions, for I know him to be jealous of respect. But his version of the quarrel is really more than I can reproduce; for I knew the Master myself, and a man more insusceptible of fear is not conceivable. I regret this oversight of the Chevalier's, and all the more because the tenor of his narrative (set aside a few flourishes) strikes me as highly ingenuous.

CHAPTER FOUR

Persecutions Endured by Mr Henry

YOU CAN GUESS ON WHAT PART of his adventures the Colonel principally dwelled. Indeed, if we had heard it all, it is to be thought the current of this business had been wholly altered; but the pirate ship was very gently touched upon. Nor did I heard the Colonel to an end even of that which he was willing to disclose; for Mr Henry, having for some while been plunged in a brown study, rose at last from his seat and (reminding the Colonel there were matters that he must attend to) bade me follow him immediately to the office.

Once there, he sought no longer to dissemble his concern, walking to and fro in the room with a contorted face, and passing his hand repeatedly upon his brow.

'We have some business,' he began at last; and there broke off, declared we must have wine, and sent for a magnum of the best. This was extremely foreign to his habitudes; and what was still more so, when the wine had come, he gulped down one glass upon another like a man careless of appearances. But the drink steadied him.

'You will scarce be surprised, Mackellar,' says he, 'when I tell you that my brother – whose safety we are all rejoiced to learn – stands in some need of money.'

I told him I had misdoubted as much; but the time was not very fortunate, as the stock was low.

'Not mine,' said he. 'There is the money for the mortgage.'

I reminded him it was Mrs Henry's.

'I will be answerable to my wife,' he cried violently.

'And then,' said I, 'there is the mortgage.'

'I know,' said he; 'it is on that I would consult you.'

I showed him how unfortunate a time it was to divert this money from its destination; and how, by so doing, we must lose the profit of our past economies, and plunge back the estate into the mire. I even took the liberty to plead with him; and when he still opposed me with a shake of the head and a bitter dogged smile, my zeal quite carried me beyond my place. 'This is midsummer madness,' cried I; 'and I for one will be no party to it.'

'You speak as though I did it for my pleasure,' says he. 'But I have a child now; and, besides, I love order; and to say the honest truth, Mackellar, I had begun to take a pride in the estates.' He gloomed for a moment. 'But what would you have?' he went on. 'Nothing is mine, nothing. This day's news has knocked the bottom out of my life. I have only the name and the shadow of things – only the shadow; there is no substance in my rights.'

'They will prove substantial enough before a court,' said I.

He looked at me with a burning eye, and seemed to repress the word upon his lips; and I repented what I had said, for I saw that while he spoke of the estate he had still a side-thought to his marriage. And then, of a sudden, he twitched the letter from his pocket, where it lay all crumpled, smoothed it violently on the table, and read these words to me with a trembling tongue: – '"My dear Jacob" – This is how he begins!' cried he – '"My dear Jacob, I once called you so, you may remember; and you have now done the business, and flung my heels as high as Criffel." What do you think of that, Mackellar,' says he, 'from an only brother? I declare to God I liked him very well; I was always staunch to him; and this is how he writes! But I will not sit down under the imputation' – walking to and fro – 'I am as good as he; I am a better man than he, I call on God to prove it! I cannot give him all the monstrous sum he asks; he knows the estate to be incompetent; but I will give him what I have, and it is more than he expects. I have borne all this too long. See what he writes further on; read it for yourself: "I know you are a niggardly dog." A niggardly dog! I niggardly? Is that true, Mackellar? You think it is?' I really thought he would have struck me at that. 'Oh, you all think so! Well, you shall see, and he shall see, and God shall see. If I ruin the estate and go barefoot, I shall stuff this bloodsucker. Let him ask all – all, and he shall have it! It is all his by rights. Ah!' he cried, 'and I foresaw all this, and worse, when he would not let me go.' He poured out another glass of wine, and was about to carry it to his lips, when I made so bold as to lay a finger on his arm. He stopped a moment. 'You are right,' said he, and flung glass and all in the fireplace. 'Come, let us count the money.'

I durst no longer oppose him; indeed, I was very much affected by the sight of so much disorder in a man usually so controlled; and we sat down together, counted the money, and made it up in packets for the greater ease of Colonel Burke, who was to be the bearer. This done, Mr Henry returned to the hall, where he and my old lords sat all night through with their guest.

A little before dawn I was called and set out with the Colonel. He would scarce have liked a less responsible convoy, for he was a man who valued himself; nor could we afford him one more dignified, for Mr Henry must not appear with the free-traders. It was a very bitter morning of wind, and as we went down through the long shrubbery the Colonel held himself muffled in his cloak.

'Sir,' said I, 'this is a great sum of money that your fiend requires. I must suppose his necessities to be very great.'

'We must suppose so,' says he, I thought drily, but perhaps it was the cloak about his mouth.

'I am only a servant of the family,' said I. 'You may deal openly with me. I think we are likely to get little good by him?'

'My dear man,' said the Colonel, 'Ballantrae is a gentleman of the most eminent natural abilities, and a man that I admire, and that I revere, to the very ground he treads on.' And then he seemed to me to pause like one in a difficulty.

'But for all that,' said I, 'we are likely to get little good by him?'

'Sure, and you can have it your own way, my dear man,' says the Colonel.

By this time we had come to the side of the creek, where the boat awaited him. 'Well,' said he, 'I am sure I am very much your debtor for your civility, Mr Whatever-your-name-is; and just as a last word, and since you show so much intelligent interest, I will mention a small circumstance that may be of use to the family. For I believe my friend omitted to mention that he has the largest pension on the Scots Fund of any refugee in Paris; and it's the more disgraceful, sir,' cries the Colonel, warming, 'because there's not one dirty penny for myself.'

He cocked his hat at me, as if I had been to blame for this partiality; then changed again into his usual swaggering civility, shook me by the hand, and set off down to the boat, with the money under his arms, and whistling as he went the pathetic air of *Shule Aroon*. It was the first time I had heard that tune; I was to hear it again, words and all, as you shall learn, but I remember how that little stave of it ran in my head after the freetraders had bade him 'Wheesht, in the deil's name,' and the grating of the oars had taken its place, and I stood and watched the dawn creeping on the sea, and the boat drawing away, and the lugger lying with her foresail backed awaiting it.

The gap made in our money was a sore embarrassment, and, among other consequences, it had this: that I must ride to Edinburgh, and there raise a new loan on very questionable terms to keep the old afloat; and was thus, for close upon three weeks, absent from the house of Durrisdeer.

What passed in the interval I had none to tell me, but I found Mrs Henry, upon my return, much changed in her demeanour. The old talks with my lord for the most part pretermitted; a certain deprecation visible towards her husband, to whom I thought she addressed herself more often; and, for one thing, she was now greatly wrapped up in Miss Katharine. You would think the change was agreeable to Mr Henry; no such matter! To the contrary, every circumstance of alteration was a stab to him; he read in each the avowal of her truant fancies. That constancy to the Master of which she was proud while she supposed him dead, she had a blush for now she knew he was alive, and these blushes were the hated spring of her new conduct. I am to conceal no truth; and I will here say plainly, I think this was the period in which Mr Henry showed the worst. He contained himself, indeed, in public; but there was a deep-seated irritation visible underneath. With me, from whom he had less concealment, he was often grossly unjust, and even for his wife he would sometimes have a sharp retort: perhaps when she had ruffled him with some unwonted kindness; perhaps upon no tangible occasion, the mere habitual tenor of the man's annoyance bursting spontaneously forth. When he would thus forget himself (a thing so strangely out of keeping with the terms of their relation), there went a shock through the whole company, and the pair would look upon each other in a kind of pained amazement.

All the time, too, while he was injuring himself by this defect of temper, he was hurting his position by a silence, of which I scarce know whether to say it was the child of generosity or pride. The freetraders came again and again, bringing messengers from the Master, and none departed empty-handed. I never durst reason with Mr Henry; he gave what was asked of him in a kind of noble rage. Perhaps because he knew he was by nature inclining to the parsimonious, he took a back-foremost pleasure in the recklessness with which he supplied his brother's exigence. Perhaps the falsity of the position would have spurred a humbler man into the same excess. But the estate (if I may say so) groaned under it; our daily expenses were shorn lower and lower; the stables were emptied, all but four roadsters; servants were discharged, which raised a dreadful murmuring in the country, and heated up the old disfavour upon Mr Henry; and at last the yearly visit to Edinburgh must be discontinued.

This was in 1756. You are to suppose that for seven years this bloodsucker had been drawing the life's blood from Durrisdeer, and that all this time my patron had held his peace. It was an effect of devilish malice in the Master that he addressed Mr Henry alone upon the matter of his demands, and there was never a word to my lord. The family had looked on, wondering at our economies. They had lamented, I have no doubt, that my patron had become so great a miser – a fault always despicable, but in the young abhorrent, and Mr Henry was not yet thirty years off age. Still, he had managed the business of Durrisdeer almost from a boy; and they bore with these changes in a silence as proud and bitter as his own until the coping-stone of the Edinburgh visit.

At this time I believe my patron and his wife were rarely together, save at meals. Immediately on the back of Colonel Burke's announcement Mrs Henry made palpable advances; you might say she had paid a sort of timid court to her husband, different, indeed, from her former manner of unconcern and distance. I never had the heart to blame Mr Henry because he recoiled from these advances; nor yet to censure the wife, when she was cut to the quick by their rejection. But the result was an entire estrangement, so that (as I say) they rarely spoke, except at meals. Even the matter of the Edinburgh visit was first broached at table, and it chanced that Mrs Henry was that day ailing and querulous. She had no sooner understood her husband's meaning than the red flew in her face.

'At last,' she cried, 'this is too much! Heaven knows what pleasure I have in my life, that I should be denied my only consolation. These shameful proclivities must be trod down; we are already a mark and an eyesore in the neighbourhood. I will not endure this fresh insanity.'

'I cannot afford it,' says Mr Henry.

'Afford!' she cried. 'For shame! But I have money of my own.'

'That is all mine, madam, by marriage,' he snarled, and instantly left the room.

My old lord threw up his hands to Heaven, and he and his daughter, withdrawing to the chimney, gave me a broad hint to be gone. I found Mr Henry in his usual retreat, the steward's room, perched on the end of the table, and plunging his penknife in it with a very ugly countenance.

'Mr Henry,' said I, 'you do yourself too much injustice, and it is time this should cease.'

'Oh!' cries he, 'nobody minds here. They think it only natural. I have shameful proclivities. I am a niggardly dog,' and he drove his knife up to the hilt. 'But I will show that fellow,' he cried with an oath, 'I will show him which is the more generous.'

'This is no generosity,' said I; 'this is only pride.'

'Do you think I want morality?' he asked.

I thought he wanted help, and I should give it him, willy-nilly; and no sooner was Mrs Henry gone to her room than I presented myself at her door and sought admittance.

She openly showed her wonder. 'What do you want with me, Mr Mackellar?' said she.

'The Lord knows, madam,' says I, 'I have never troubled you before with any freedoms; but this thing lies too hard upon my conscience, and it will out. Is it possible that two people can be so blind as you and my lord? and have lived all these years with a noble gentleman like Mr Henry, and understand so little of his nature?'

'What does this mean?' she cried.

'Do you not know where his money goes to? his – and yours – and the money for the very wine he does not drink at table?' I went on. 'To Paris – to that man! Eight thousand pounds has he had of us in seven years, and my patron fool enough to keep it secret!'

'Eight thousand pounds!' she repeated. 'It is impossible; the estate is not sufficient.'

'God knows how we have sweated farthings to produce it,' said I. 'But eight thousand and sixty is the sum, beside odd shillings. And if you can think my patron miserly after that, this shall be my last interference.'

'You need say no more, Mr Mackellar,' said she. 'You have done most properly in what you too modestly call your interference. I am much to blame; you must think me indeed a very unobservant wife' (looking upon me with a strange smile), 'But I shall put this right at once. The Master was always of a very thoughtless nature; but his heart is excellent; he is the soul of generosity. I shall write to him myself. You cannot think how you have pained me by this communication.'

'Indeed, madam, I had hope to have pleased you,' said I, for I raged to see her still thinking of the Master.

'And pleased,' said she, 'and pleased me, of course.'

That same day (I will not say but what I watched) I had the satisfaction to see Mr Henry come from his wife's room in a state most unlike himself; for his face was all bloated with weeping, and yet he seemed to me to walk upon the air. By this, I was sure his wife had made him full amends for once. 'Ah,' thought I to myself, 'i have done a brave stroke this day.'

On the morrow, as I was seated at my books, Mr Henry came in softly behind me, took me by the shoulders, and shook me in a manner of playfulness. 'I find you are a faithless fellow after all,' says he, which was his only reference to my part; but the tone he spoke in was more to me than any eloquence of protestation. Nor was this all I had effected; for when the next messenger came (as he did not long afterwards) from the Master, he got nothing away with him but a letter. For some while back it had been I myself who had conducted these affairs; Mr Henry not setting pen to paper, and I only in the dryest and most formal terms. But this letter I did not even see; it would scarce be pleasant reading, for Mr Henry felt he had his wife behind him for once, and I observed, on the day it was despatched, he had a very gratified expression.

Things went better now in the family, though it could scarce be pretended they went well. There was now at least no misconception; there was kindness upon all sides; and I believe my patron and his wife might again have drawn together if he could but have pocketed his pride, and she forgot (what was the ground of all) her brooding on another man. It is wonderful how a private thought leaks out; it is wonderful to me now how we should all have followed the current of her sentiments; and though she bore herself quietly, and had a very even disposition, yet we should have known whenever her fancy ran to Paris. And would not anyone have thought that my disclosure must have rooted up that idol? I think there is a devil in women: all these years passed, never a sight of the man, little enough kindness to remember (by all accounts) even while she had him, the notion of his death intervening, his heartless rapacity laid bare to her; that all should not do, and she must still keep the best place in her heart for this accursed fellow, is a thing to make a plain man rage. I had never much natural sympathy for the passion of love; but this unreason in my patron's wife disgusted me outright with the whole matter. I remember checking a maid because she sang some bairnly kickshaw while my mind was thus engaged; and my asperity brought about my ears the enmity of all the petticoats about the house; of which I recked very little, but it amused Mr Henry, who rallied me much upon our joint unpopularity. It is strange enough (for my own mother was certainly one of the salt of the earth, and my Aunt Dickson, who paid my fees at the University, a very notable woman), but I have never had much toleration for the female sex, possibly not much understanding; and being far from a bold man, I have ever shunned their company. Not only do I see no cause to regret this diffidence in myself, but have invariably remarked that most unhappy consequences follow those who were less wise. So much I thought proper to set down lest I show myself unjust to Mrs Henry. And, besides, the remark arose naturally, on a reperusal of the letter which was the next step in these affairs, and reached me, to my sincere astonishment, by a private hand, some week or so after the departure of the last messenger.

Letter from Colonel BURKE *(afterwards Chevalier) to*

MR MACKELLAR.

TROYES IN CHAMPAGNE,

July 12, 1756.

MY DEAR SIR, – You will doubtless be surprised to receive a communication from one so little known to you; but on the occasion I had the good fortune to rencounter you at Durrisdeer, I remarked you for a young man of a solid gravity of character: a qualification which I profess I admire and revere next to natural genius or the bold chivalrous spirit of the soldier. I was, besides, interested in the noble family which you have the honour to serve, or (to speak more by the book) to be the humble and respected friend of; and a conversation I had the pleasure to have with you very early in the morning has remained much upon my mind.

Being the other day in Paris, on a visit from this famous city, where I am in garrison, I took occasion to inquire your name (which I profess I had forgot) at my friend, the Master of B.; and a fair opportunity occurring, I write to inform you of what's new.

The Master of B. (when we had last some some talk of him together) was in receipt, as I think I then told you, of a highly advantageous pension on the Scots Fund. He next received a company, and was soon after advanced to a regiment of his own. My dear sir, I do not offer to explain this circumstance; any more than why I myself, who have rid at the right hand of Princes, should be fubbed off with a pair of colours and sent to rot in a hole at the bottom of the province. Accustomed as I am to Courts, I cannot but feel it is no atmosphere for a plain soldier; and I could never hope to advance by similar means, even could I stoop to the endeavour. But our friend has a particular aptitude to succeed by the means of ladies; and if all be true that I have heard, he enjoyed a remarkable protection. It is like this turned against him; for when I had the honour to shake him by the hand, he was but newly released from the Bastile, where he had been cast on a sealed letter; and, though now released, has both lost his regiment and his pension. My dear sir, the loyalty of a plain Irishman will ultimately succeed in the place of craft; as I am sure a gentleman of your probity will agree.

Now, sir, the Master is a man whose genius I admire beyond expression, and, besides, he is my friend; but I thought a little word of this revolution in his fortunes would not come amiss, for, in my opinion, the man's desperate. He spoke, when I saw him, of an adventure upon India (whither I am myself in some hope of accompanying my illustrious countryman, Mr Lally); but for this he would require (as I understood) more money than was readily at this command. You may have heard a military proverb: that it is a good thing to make a bridge of gold to a flying enemy? I trust you will take my meaning, and I subscribe myself, with proper respects to my Lord Durrisdeer, to his son, and to the beauteous Mrs Durie,

My dear Sir,
Your obedient humble servant,
FRANCIS BURKE.

This missive I carried at once to Mr Henry; and I think there was but the one thought between the two of us: that it had come a week too late. I made haste to send an answer to Colonel Burke, in which I begged him, if he should see the Master, to assure him his next messenger would be attended to. But with all my haste I was not in time to avert what was impending; the arrow had been drawn, it must now fly. I could almost doubt the power of Providence (and certainly His will) to stay the issue of events; and it is a strange thought, how many of us had been storing up the elements of this catastrophe, for how long a time, and with how blind an ignorance of what we did.

From the coming of the Colonel's letter, I had a spy-glass in my room, began to drop questions to the tenant folk, and as there was no great secrecy observed, and the freetrade (in our part) went by force as much as stealth, I had soon got together a knowledge of the signals in use, and know pretty well to an hour when any messenger might be expected. I say, I questioned the tenants; for with the traders themselves, desperate blades that went habitually armed, I could never bring myself to meddle willingly. Indeed, by what proved in the sequel an unhappy chance, I was an object of scorn to some of these braggadocios; who had not only gratified me with a nickname, but catching me one night upon a by-path, and being all (as they would have said) somewhat merry, had caused me to dance for their diversion. The method employed was that of cruelly chipping at my toes with naked cutlasses, shouting at the same time 'Square Toes'; and though they did me no bodily mischief, I was none the less deplorably affected, and was indeed for several days confined to my bed: a scandal on the state of Scotland on which no comment is required.

It happened on the afternoon on November 7th, in this same unfortunate year, that I espied, during my walk, the smoke of a beacon fire upon the Muckleross. It was drawing near time for my return; but the uneasiness upon my spirits was that day so great that I must burst through the thicket to the edge of what they call the Craig Head. The sun was already down, but there was still a broad light in the west, which showed me some of the smugglers treading out their signal fire upon the Ross, and in the bay the lugger lying with her sails brailed up. She was plainly but new come to anchor, and yet the skiff was already lowered and pulling for the landing-place at the end of the long shrubbery. And this I knew could signify but one thing, the coming of a messenger for Durrisdeer.

I laid aside the remainder of my terrors, clambered down the brae – a place I had never ventured through before – and was hid among the shore-side thickets in time to see the boat touch. Captain Crail himself was steering, a thing not usual; by his side there sat a passenger; and the men gave way with difficulty, being hampered with near upon half a dozen portmanteaus, great and small. But the business of landing was briskly carried through; and presently the baggage was all tumbled on shore, the boat on its return voyage to the lugger, and the passenger standing alone upon the point of rock, a tall slender figure of a gentleman, habited in black, with a sword by his side and a walking-cane upon his wrist. As he so stood, he waved the cane to Captain Crail by way of salutation, with something both of grace and mockery that wrote the gesture deeply on my mind.

No sooner was the boat away with my sworn enemies than I took a sort of half-courage, came forth to the margin of the thicket, and there halted again, my mind being greatly pulled about between natural diffidence and a dark foreboding of the truth. Indeed, I might have stood there swithering all night, had not the stranger turned, spied me through the mists, which were beginning to fall, and waved and cried on me to draw near. I did so with a heart like lead.

'Here, my good man,' said he, in the English accent, 'here are some things for Durrisdeer.'

I was now near enough to see him, a very handsome figure and countenance, swarthy, lean, long, with a quick, alert, black look, as of one who was a fighter, and accustomed to command; upon one cheek he had a mole, not unbecoming; a large diamond sparkled on his hand; his clothes, although of the one hue, were of a French and foppish design; his ruffles, which he wore longer than common, of exquisite lace; and I wondered the more to see him in such a guise when he was but newly landed from a dirty smuggling lugger. At the same time he had a better look at me, toised me a second time sharply, and then smiled.

'I wager, my friend,' says he, 'that I know both your name and your nickname. I divined these very clothes upon your hand of writing, Mr Mackellar.'

At these words I fell to shaking.

'Oh,' says he, 'you need not be afraid of me. I bear no malice for your tedious letters; and it is my purpose to employ you a good deal. You may call me Mr Bally: it is the name I have assumed; or rather (since I am addressing so great a precisian) it is so I have curtailed my own. Come now, pick up that and that' – indicating two of the portmanteaus. 'That will be as much as you are fit to bear, and the rest can very well wait. Come, lose no time, if you please.'

His tone was so cutting that I managed to do as he bid by a sort of instinct, my mind being all the time quite lost. No sooner had I picked up the portmanteaus than he turned his back and marched off through the long shrubbery, where it began already to be dusk, for the wood is thick and evergreen. I followed behind, loaded almost to the dust, though I profess I was not conscious of the burthen; being swallowed up in the monstrosity of this return, and my mind flying like a weaver's shuttle.

On a sudden I set the portmanteaus to the ground and halted. He turned and looked back at me.

'Well?' said he.

'You are the Master of Ballantrae?'

'You will do me the justice to observe,' says he, 'that I have made no secret with the astute Mackellar.'

'And in the name of God,' cries I, 'what brings you here? Go back, while it is yet time.'

'I thank you,' said he. 'Your master has chosen his way, and not I; but since he has made the choice, he (and you also) must abide by the result. And now pick up these things of mine, which you have set down in a very boggy place, and attend to that which I have made your business.'

But I had no thought now of obedience; I came stright up to him. 'If nothing will move you to go back,' said I; 'though sure, under all the circumstances, any Christian or even any gentleman would scruple to go forward . . .'

'These are gratifying expressions,' he threw in.

'If nothing will move you to go back,' I continued, 'there are still some decencies to be observed. Wait here with your baggage, and I will go forward and prepare your family. Your father is an old man; and . . .' I stumbled . . . 'there are decencies to be observed.'

'Truly,' said he, 'this Mackellar improves upon acquaintance. But look you here, my man, and understand it once for all – you waste your breath upon me, and I go my own way with inevitable motion.'

'Ah!' says I. 'Is that so? We shall see then!'

And I turned and took to my heels for Durrisdeer. He clutched at me and cried out angrily, and then I believed I heard him laugh, and then I am certain he pursued me for a step or two, and (I supposee) desisted. One thing at least is sure, that I came but a few minutes later to the door of the great house, nearly strangled for the lack of breath, but quite alone. Straight up the stair I ran, and burst into the hall, and stopped before the family without the power of speech; but I must have carried my story in my looks, for they rose out of their places and stared on me like changelings.

'He has come,' I panted out at last.

'He?' said Mr Henry.

'Himself,' said I.

'My son?' cried my lord. 'Imprudent, imprudent boy! Oh, could he not stay where he was safe!'

Never a word says Mrs Henry; nor did I look at her, I scarce knew why.

'Well,' said Mr Henry, with a very deep breath, 'and where is he?'

'I left him in the long shrubbery,' said I.

'Take me to him,' said he.

So we went out together, he and I, without another word from anyone; and in the midst of the gravelled plot encountered the Master strolling up, whistling as he came, and beating the air with his cane. There was still light enough overhead to recognize, though not to read, a countenance.

'Ah! Jacob,' says the Master. 'So here is Esau back.'

'James,' says Mr Henry, 'for God's sake, call me by my name. I will not pretend that I am glad to see you; but I would fain make you as welcome as I can in the house of our fathers.'

'Or in *my* house? or *yours?*' says the Master. 'Which were you about to say? But this is an old sore, and we need not rub it. If you would not share with me in Paris, I hope you will yet scarce deny your elder brother a corner of the fire at Durrisdeer?'

'That is very idle speech,' replied Mr Henry. 'And you understand the power of your position excellently well.'

'Why, I believe I do,' said the other with a little laugh. And this, though they had never touched hands, was (as we may say) the end of the brothers' meeting; for at this the Master turned to me and bade me fetch his baggage.

I, on my side, turned to Mr Henry for a confirmation; perhaps with some defiance.

'As long as the Master is here, Mr Mackellar, you will very much oblige me by regarding his wishes as you would my own,' says Mr Henry. 'We are constantly troubling you: will you be so good as send one of the servants?' – with an accent on the word.

If this speech were anything at all, it was surely a well-deserved reproof upon the stranger; and yet, so devilish was his impudence, he twisted it the other way.

'And shall we be common enough to say "Sneck up"?' inquires he softly, looking upon me sideways.

Had a kingdom depended on the act, I could not have trusted myself in words; even to call a servant was beyond me; I had rather serve the man myself than speak; and I turned away in silence and went into the long shrubbery, with a heart full of anger and despair. It was dark under the trees, and I walked before me and forgot what business I was come upon, till I near broke my shin on the portmanteaus. Then it was that I remarked a strange particular; for whereas I had before carried both and scarce observed it, it was now as much as I could do to manage one. And this, as it forced me to make two journeys, kept me the longer from the hall.

When I got there, the business of welcome was over long ago; the company was already at supper; and, by an oversight that cut me to the quick, my place had been forgotten. I had seen one side of the Master's return; now I was to see the other. It was he who first remarked my coming in and standing back (as I did) in some annoyance. He jumped from his seat.

'And if I have not got the good Mackellar's place!' cries he. 'John, lay another for Mr Bally; I protest he will disturb no one, and your table is big enough for all.'

I could scarce credit my ears, nor yet my senses, when he took me by the shoulders and thrust me, laughing, into my own place – such an affectionate playfulness was in his voice. And while John laid the fresh place for him (a thing on which he still insisted), he went and leaned on his father's chair and looked down upon him, and the old man turned about and looked upwards on his son, with such a pleasant mutual tenderness that I could have carried my hand to my head in mere amazement.

Yet all was of a piece. Never a harsh word fell from him, never a sneer showed upon his lip. He had laid aside even his cutting English accent, and spoke with the kindly Scots tongue, that set a value on affectionate words; and though his manners had a graceful elegance mighty foreign to our ways in Durrisdeer, it was still a homely courtliness, that did not shame but flattered us. All that he did throughout the meal, indeed, drinking wine with me with a notable respect, turning about for a pleasant word with John, fondling his father's hand, breaking into little merry tales of his adventures, calling up the past with happy reference – all he did was so becoming, and himself so handsome, that I could scarce wonder if my lord and Mrs Henry sat about the board with radiant faces, or if John waited behind with dropping tears.

As soon as supper was over, Mrs Henry rose to withdraw.

'This was never your way, Alison,' said he.

'It is my way now,' she replied: which was notoriously false, 'and I will give you a good-night, James, and a welcome – from the dead,' said she, and her voice dropped and trembled.

Poor Mr Henry, who had made rather a heavy figure through the meal, was more concerned than ever; pleased to see his wife withdraw, and yet half displeased, as he thought upon the cause of it; and the next moment altogether dashed by the fervour of her speech.

On my part, I thought I was now one too many; and was stealing after Mrs Henry, when the Master saw me.

'Now, Mr Mackellar,' says he, 'I take this near on an unfriendliness. I cannot have you go: this is to make a stranger of the prodigal son; and let me remind you where – in his own father's house! Come, sit ye down, and drink another glass with Mr Bally.'

'Ay, ay, Mr Mackellar,' says my lord, 'we must not make a stranger either of him or you. I have been telling my son,' he added, his voice brightening as usual on the word, 'how much we valued all your friendly service.'

So I sat there, silent, till my usual hour; and might have been almost deceived in the man's nature but for one passage, in which his perfidy appeared too plain. Here was the passage; of which, after what he knows of the brothers' meeting, the reader shall consider for himself. Mr Henry sitting somewhat dully, in spite of his best endeavours to carry things before my lord, up jumps the Master, passes about the board, and claps his brother on the shoulder.

'Come, come, _Hairry lad_,' says he, with a broad accent such as they must have used together when they were boys, 'you must not be downcast because your brother has come home. All's yours, that's sure enough, and little I grudge it you. Neither must you grudge me my place beside my father's fire.'

'And that is too true, Henry,' says my old lord with a little frown, a thing rare with him. 'You have been the elder brother of the parable in the good sense; you must be careful of the other.'

'I am easily put in the wrong,' said Mr Henry.

'Who puts you in the wrong?' cried my lord, I thought very tartly for so mild a man. 'You have earned my gratitude and your brother's many thousand times: you may count on its endurance; and let that suffice.'

'Ay. Harry, that you may,' said the Master: and I thought Mr Henry looked at him with a kind of wildness in his eye.

On all the miserable business that now followed, I have four questions that I asked myself often at the time, and ask myself still: – Was the man moved by a particular sentiment against Mr Henry? or by what he thought to be his interest? or by a mere delight in cruelty such as cats display and theologians tell us of the devil? or by what he would have called love? My common opinion halts among the three first; but perhaps there lay at the spring of his behaviour an element of all. As thus: – Animosity to Mr. Henry would explain his hateful usage of him when they were alone; the interests he came to serve would explain his very different attitude before my lord; that and some spice of a design of gallantry, his care to stand well with Mrs Henry; and the pleasure of malice for itself, the pains he was continually at to mingle and oppose these lines of conduct.

Partly because I was a very open friend to my patron, partly because in my letters to Paris I had often given myself some freedom of remonstrance, I was included in his diabolical amusement. When I was alone with him, he pursued me with sneers; before the family he used me with the extreme of friendly condescension. This was not only painful in itself; not only did it put me continually in the wrong; but there was in it an element of insult indescribable. That he should thus leave me out in his dissimulation, as though even my testimony were too despicable to be considered, galled me to the blood. But what it was to me is not worth notice. I make but memorandum of it here; and chiefly for this reason, that it had one good result, and gave me the quicker sense of Mr Henry's martydrom.

It was on him the burthen fell. How was he to respond to the public advances of one who never lost a chance of gibing him in private? How was he to smile back on the deceiver and the insulter? He was condemned to seem ungracious. He was condemned to silence. Had he been less proud, had he spoken, who would have credited the truth? The acted calumny had done its work; my lord and Mrs Henry were the daily witnesses of what went on; they could have sworn in court that the Master was a model of long-suffering good-nature, and Mr Henry a pattern of jealousy and thanklessness. And ugly enough as these must have appeared in anyone, they seemed tenfold uglier in Mr Henry; for who could forget that the Master lay in peril of his life, and that he had already lost his mistress, his title, his fortune?

'Henry, will you ride with me?' asks the Master one day.

And Mr Henry, who had been goaded by the man all morning, raps out: 'I will not.'

'I sometimes wish you would be kinder, Henry,' says the other, wistfully.

I give this for a specimen; but such scenes befell continually. Small wonder if Mr Henry was blamed; small wonder if I fretted myself into something near upon a bilous fever; nay, and at the mere recollection feel a bitterness in my blood.

Sure, never in this world was a more diabolical contrivance: so perfidious, so simple, so impossible to combat. And yet I think again, and I think always, Mrs Henry might have read between the lines; she might have had more knowledge of her husband's nature; after all these years of marriage she might have commanded or captured his confidence. And my old lord, too – that very watchful gentleman – where was all his observation? But, for one thing, the deceit was practised by a master hand, and might have gulled an angel. For another (in the case of Mrs Henry), I have observed there are no persons so far away as those who are both married and estranged, so that they seem out of earshot or to have no common tongue. For a third (in the case of both of these spectators), they were blinded by old ingrained predilection. And for a fourth, the risk the Master was supposed to stand in (supposed, I say – you will soon hear why) made it seem the more ungenerous to criticize; and keeping them in a perpetual tender solicitude about his life, blinded them the more effectually to his faults.

It was during this time that I perceived most clearly the effect of manner, and was led to lament most deeply the plainness of my own. Mr Henry had the essence of a gentleman; when he was moved, when there was any call of circumstance, he could play his part with dignity and spirit; but in the day's commerce (it is idle to deny it) he fell short of the ornamental. The Master (on the other hand) had never a movement but it commended him. So it befell that when the one appeared gracious and the other ungracious, every trick of their bodies seemed to call out confirmation. Not that alone: but the more deeply Mr Henry floundered in his brother's toils, the more clownish he grew; and the more the Master enjoyed his spiteful entertainment, the more engagingly, the more smilingly, he went! So that the plot, by its own scope and progress, furthered and confirmed itself.

It was one of the man's arts to use the peril in which (as I say) he was supposed to stand. He spoke of it to those who loved him with a gentle pleasantry, which made it the more touching. To Mr Henry he used it as a cruel weapon of offence. I remember his laying his finger on the clean lozenge of the painted window one day when we three were alone together in the hall. 'Here went your lucky guinea, Jacob,' said he. And when Mr Henry only looked upon him darkly, 'Oh!' he added, 'you need not look such impotent malice, my good fly. You can be rid of your spider when you please. How long, O Lord? When are you to be wrought to the point of a denunciation, scupulous brother? It is one of my interests in this dreary hole. I ever loved experiment.' Still Mr Henry only stared upon him with a glooming brow and a changed colour; and at last the Master broke out in a laugh and clapped him on the shoulder, calling him a sulky dog. At this my patron leaped back with a gesture I thought very dangerous; and I must suppose the Master thought so too, for he looked the least in the world discountenanced, and I do not remember him again to have laid hands on Mr' Henry.

But though he had his peril always on his lips in the one way or the other, I thought his conduct strangely incautious, and began to fancy the Government – who had set a price upon his head – was gone sound asleep. I will not deny I was tempted with the wish to denounce him; but two thoughts withheld me: one, that if he were thus to end his life upon an honourable scaffold, the man would be canonized for good in the minds of his father and my patron's wife; the other, that if I was anyway mingled in the matter, Mr Henry himself would scarce escape some glancings of suspicion. And in the meanwhile our enemy went in and out more than I could have thought possible, the fact that he was home again was buzzed about all the country-side, and yet he was never stirred. Of all these so-many and so-different persons who were acquainted with his presence, none had the least greed – as I used to say in my annoyance – or the least loyalty; and the man rode here and there – fully more welcome, considering the lees of old unpopularity, than Mr Henry – and considering the freetraders, far safer than myself.

Not but what he had a trouble of his own; and this, as it brought about the gravest consequences, I must now relate. The reader will scarce have forgotten Jessie Broun; her way of life was much among the smuggling party; Captain Crail himself was of her intimates; and she had early word of Mr Bally's presence at the house. In my opinion, she had long ceased to care two straws for the Master's person; but it was become her habit to connect herself continually with the Master's name; that was the ground of all her play-acting; and so now, when he was back, she thought she owed it to herself to grow a haunter of the neighbourhood of Durrisdeer. The Master could scarce go abroad but she was there in wait for him; a scandalous figure of a woman, not often sober; haling him wildly as 'her bonny laddie,' quoting pedlar's poetry, and, as I receive the story, even seeking to weep upon his neck. I own I rubbed my hands over this persecution; but the Master, who laid so much upon others, was himself the least patient of men. There were strange scenes enacted in the policies. Some say he took his cane to her, and Jessie fell back upon her former weapons – stones. It is certain at least that he made a motion to Captain Crail to have the woman trepanned, and that the Captain refused the proposition with uncommon vehemence. And the end of the matter was victory for Jessie. Money was got together; an interview took place, in which my proud gentleman must consent to be kissed and wept upon; and the woman was set up in a public of her own, somewhere on Solway side (but I forget where), and, by the only news I ever had of it, extremely ill-frequented.

This is to look forward. After Jessie had been but a little while upon his heels, the Master comes to me one day in the steward's office, and with more civility than usual, 'Mackellar,' says he, 'there is a damned crazy wench comes about here. I cannot well move in the matter myself, which brings me to you. Be so good as to see to it; the men must have a strict injunction to drive the wench away.'

'Sir,' said I, trembling a little, 'you can do your own dirty errands for yourself.'

He said not a word to that, and left the room.

Presently came Mr Henry. 'Here is news!' cried he. 'It seems all is not enough, and you must add to my wretchedness. It seems you have insulted Mr Bally.'

'Under your kind favour, Mr Henry,' said I, 'it was he that insulted me, and, as I think, grossly. But I may have been careless of your position when I spoke; and if you think so when you know all, my dear patron, you have but to say the word. For you I would obey in any point whatever, even to sin, God pardon me!' And thereupon I told him what had passed.

Mr Henry smiled to himself; a grimmer smile I never witnessed. 'You did exactly well,' said he. 'He shall drink his Jessie Broun to the dregs.' And then, spying the Master outside, he opened the window, and crying to him by the name of Mr Bally, asked him to step up and have a word.

'James,' said he, when our persecutor had come in and closed the door behind him, looking at me with a smile, as if he thought I was to be humbled, 'you brought me a complaint against Mr Mackellar, into which I have inquired. I need not tell you I would always take his word against yours; for we are alone, and I am going to use something of your own freedom. Mr Mackellar is a gentleman I value; and you must contrive, so long as you are under this roof, to bring yourself into no more collisions with one whom I will support at any possible cost to me or mine. As for the errand upon which you came to him, you must deliver yourself from the consequences of your own cruelty, and none of my servants shall be at all employed in such a case.'

'My father's servants, I believe,' says the Master.

'Go to him with this tale,' said Mr Henry.

The Master grew very white. He pointed at me with his finger. 'I want that man discharged,' he said.

'He shall not be,' said Mr Henry.

'You shall pay pretty dear for this,' says the Master.

'I have paid so dear already for a wicked brother,' said Mr Henry, 'that I am bankrupt even of fears. You have no place left where you can strike me.'

'I will show you about that,' says the Master, and went softly away.

'What will he do next, Mackellar?' cries Mr Henry.

'Let me go away,' said I. 'My dear patron, let me go away; I am but the beginning of fresh sorrows.'

'Would you leave me quite alone?' said he.

We were not long in suspense as to the nature of the new assault. Up to that hour the Master had played a very close game with Mrs Henry; avoiding pointedly to be alone with her, which I took at the time for an effect of decency, but now think to be a most insidious art; meeting her, you may say, at meal-time only; and behaving, when he did so, like an affectionate brother. Up to that hour, you may say he had scarce directly interfered between Mr Henry and his wife; except in so far as he had manoeuvred the one quite forth from the good graces of the other. Now all that was to be changed; but whether really in revenge, or because he was wearying of Durrisdeer and looked about for some diversion, who but the devil shall decide?

From that hour, at least, began the siege of Mrs Henry; a thing so deftly carried on that I scarce know if she was aware of it herself, and that her husband must look on in silence. The first parallel was opened (as was made to appear) by accident. The talk fell, as it did often, on the exiles in France; so it glided to the matter of their songs.

'There is one,' says the Master, 'if you are curious in these matters, that has always seemed to me very moving. The poetry is harsh; and yet, perhaps because of my situation, it has always found the way to my heart. It is supposed to be sung, I should tell you, by an exile's sweetheart; and represents perhaps, not so much the truth of what she is thinking, as the truth of what he hopes of her, poor soul! in these far lands.' And here the Master sighed. 'I protest it is a pathetic sight when a score of rough Irish, all common sentinels, get to this song; and you may see, by their falling tears, how it strikes home to them. It goes thus, father,' says he, very adroitly taking my lord for his listener, 'and if I cannot get to the end of it, you must think it is a common case with us exiles.'

And thereupon he struck up the same air as I had heard the Colonel whistle; but now to words, rustic indeed, yet most pathetically setting forth a poor girl's aspirations for an exiled lover; of which one verse indeed (or something like it) still sticks by me:

> O, I will dye my petticoat red,
> With my dear boy I'll beg my bread,
> Though all my friends should wish me dead,
> For Willie among the rushes, O!

He sang it well, even as a song; but he did better yet as a performer. I have heard famous actors, when there was not a dry eye in the Edinburgh theatre; a great wonder to behold; but no more wonderful than how the Master played upon that little ballad, and on those who heard him, like an instrument, and seemed now upon the point of failing, and now to conquer his distress, so that words and music seemed to pour out of his own heart and his own past, and to be aimed directly at Mrs Henry. And his art went further yet; for all was so delicately touched, it seemed impossible to suspect him of the least design; and so far from making a parade of emotion, you would have sworn he was striving to be calm. When it came to an end, we all sat silent for a time; he had chosen the dusk of the afternoon, so that none could see his neighbour's face; but it seemed as if we held our breathing; only my old lord cleared his throat. The first to move was the singer, who got to his feet suddenly and softly, and went and walked softly to and fro in the low end of the hall, Mr Henry's customary place. We were to suppose that he there struggled down the last of his emotion; for he presently returned and launched into a disquisition on the nature of the Irish (always so much miscalled, and whom he defended) in his natural voice; so that before the lights were brought, we were in the usual course of talk. But even then, methought Mrs Henry's face was a shade pale; and, for another thing, she withdrew almost at once.

The next sign was a friendship this insidious devil struck up with innocent Miss Katharine; so that they were always together, hand in hand, or she climbing on his knee, like a pair of children. Like all his diabolical acts, this cut in several ways. It was the last stroke to Mr Henry, to see his own babe debauched against him; it made him harsh with the poor innocent; which brought him still a peg lower in his wife's esteem; and (to conclude) it was a bond of union between the lady and the Master. Under this influence, their old reserve melted by daily stages. Presently there came walks in the long shrubbery, talks in the Belvedere, and I know not what tender familiarity. I am sure Mrs Henry was like many a good woman; she had a whole conscience, but perhaps by the means of a little winking. For even to so dull an observer as myself, it was plain her kindness was of a more moving nature than the sisterly. The tones of her voice appeared more numerous: she had a light softness in her eye; she was more gentle with all of us, even with Mr Henry, even with myself; methought she breathed of some quiet melancholy happiness.

To look on at this, what a torment it was for Mr Henry! And yet it brought our ultimate deliverance, as I am soon to tell.

The purport of the Master's stay was no more noble (gild it as they might) than to wring money out. He had some design of a fortune in the French Indies, as the Chevalier wrote me; and it was the sum required for this that he came seeking. For the rest of the family it spelled ruin; but my lord, in his incredible partiality, pushed ever for the granting. The family was now so narrowed down (indeed, there were no more of them than just the father and the two sons) that it was possible to break the entail and alienate a piece of land. And to this, at first by hints, and then by open pressure, Mr Henry was brought to consent. He never would have done so, I am very well assured, but for the weight of the distress under which he laboured. But for his passionate eagerness to see his brother gone, he would not thus have broken with his own sentiment and the traditions of his house. And even so, he sold them his consent at a dear rate, speaking for once openly, and holding the business up in its own shameful colours.

'You will observe,' he said, 'this is an injustice to my son, if ever I have one.'

'But that you are not likely to have,' said my lord.

'God knows!' said Mr Henry. 'And considering the cruel falseness of the position in which I stand to my brother, and that you, my lord, are my father, and have a right to command me, I set my hand to this paper. But one thing I will say first: I have been ungenerously pushed, and when next, my lord, you are tempted to compare your sons, I call on you to remember what I have done and what he has done. Acts are the fair test.'

My lord was the most uneasy man I ever saw; even in his old face the blood came up. 'I think this is not a very wisely chosen moment, Henry, for complaints,' said he. 'This takes away from the merit of your generosity.'

'Do not deceive yourself, my lord,' said Mr Henry. 'This injustice is not done from generosity to him, but in obedience to yourself.'

'Before strangers . . .' begins my lord, still more unhappily affected.

'There is no one but Mackellar here,' said Mr Henry; 'he is my friend. And, my lord, as you make him no stranger to your frequent blame, it were hard if I must keep him one to a thing so rare as my defence.'

Almost I believe my lord would have rescinded his decision; but the Master was on the watch.

'Ah! Henry, Henry,' says he, 'you are the best of us still. Rugged and true! Ah! man, I wish I was as good.'

And at that instance of his favourite's generosity, my lord desisted from his hesitation, and the deed was signed.

As soon as it could be brought about, the land of Ochterhall was sold for much below its value, and the money paid over to our leech and sent by some private carriage into France. And now here was all the man's business brought to a successful head, and his pockets once more bulging with our gold; and yet the point for which we had consented to this sacrifice was still denied us, and the visitor still lingered on at Durrisdeer. Whether in malice, or because the time was not yet come for his adventure to the Indies, or because he had hopes of his design on Mrs Henry, or from the orders of the Government, who shall say? but linger he did, and that for weeks.

You will observe I say: from the orders of Government; for about this time the man's disreputable secret trickled out.

The first hint I had was from a tenant, who commented on the Master's stay, and yet more on his security; for this tenant was a Jacobitish sympathizer, and had lost a son at Culloden, which gave him the more critical eye. 'There is one thing,' said he, 'that I cannot but think strange; and that is how he got to Cockermouth.'

'To Cockermouth?' said I, with a sudden memory of my first wonder on beholding the man disembark so point-de-vice after so long a voyage.

'Why, yes,' says the tenant, 'it was there he was picked up by Captain Crail. You thought he had come from France by sea? And so we all did.'

I turned this news a little in my head, and then carried it to Mr Henry. 'Here is an odd circumstance,' said I, and told him.

'What matters how he came, Mackellar, so long as he is here?' groans Mr Henry.

'No, no,' said I, 'but think again! Does not this smack a little of some Government connivance? You know how much we have wondered already at the man's security.'

'Stop,' said Mr Henry. Let me think of this.' And as he thought there came that grim smile upon his face that was a little like the Master's. 'Give me paper,' said he. And he sat without another word and wrote to a gentleman of his acquaintance – I will name no unnecessary names, but he was one in a high place. This letter I despatched by the only hand I could depend upon in such a case – Macconochie's; and the old man rode hard, for he was back with the reply before even my eagerness had ventured to expect him. Again, as he read it, Mr Henry had the same grim smile.

'This is the best you have done for me yet, Mackellar,' says he. 'With this in my hand I will give him a shog. Watch for us at dinner.'

At dinner accordingly Mr Henry proposed some very public appearance for the Master; and my lord, as he had hoped, objected to the danger of the course.

'Oh!' says Mr Henry, very easily, 'you need no longer keep this up with me. I am as much in the secret as yourself.'

'In the secret?' says my lord. 'What do you mean, Henry? I give you my word, I am in no secret from which you are exluded.'

The Master had changed ountenance, and I saw he was struck in a joint of his harness.

'How?' says Mr Henry, turning to him with a huge appearance of surprise. 'I see you serve your masters very faithfully; but I had thought you would have been humane enough to set your father's mind at rest.'

'What are you talking of? I refuse to have my business publicly discussed. I order this to cease,' cries the Master, very foolishly and passionately, and indeed more like a child than a man.

'So much discretion was not looked for at your hands, I can assure you,' continued Mr Henry. 'For see what my correspondent writes' – unfolding the paper – '"It is, of course, in the interests both of the Government and the gentleman whom we may perhaps best continue to call Mr Bally, to keep this understanding secret; but it was never meant his own family should continue to endure the suspense you paint so feelingly; and I am pleased mine should be the hand to set these fears at rest. Mr Bally is as safe in Great Britain as yourself."'

'Is this possible?' cries my lord, looking at his son, with a great deal of wonder and still more of suspicion in his face.

'My dear father,' says the Master, already much recovered, 'I am overjoyed that this may be disclosed. My own instructions, direct from London, bore a very contrary sense, and I was charged to keep the indulgence secret from everyone, yourself not excepted, and indeed yourself expressly named – as I can show in black and white unless I have destroyed the letter. They must have changed their mind very swiftly, for the whole matter is still quite fresh; or rather, Henry's correspondent must have misconceived that part, as he seems to have misconceived the rest. To tell you the truth, sir,' he continued, getting visibly more easy, 'I had supposed this unexplained favour to a rebel was the effect of some application from yourself; and the injunction to secrecy among my family the result of a desire on your part to conceal your kindness. Hence I was the more careful to obey orders. It remains now to guess by what other channel indulgence can have flowed on so notorious an offender as myself; for I do not think your son need defend himself from what seems hinted at in Henry's letter. I have never yet heard of a Durrisdeer who was a turncoat or a spy,' says he proudly.

And so it seemed he had swum out of this danger unharmed; but this was to reckon without a blunder he had made, and without the pertinacity of Mr Henry, who was now to show he had something of his brother's spirit.

'You say the matter is still fresh,' says Mr Henry.

'It is recent,' says the Master, with a fair show of stoutness and yet not without a quaver.

'Is it so recent as that?' asks Mr Henry, like a man a little puzzled, and spreading his letter forth again.

In all the letter there was no word as to the date; but how was the Master to know that?

'It seemed to come late enough for me,' says he, with a laugh. And at the sound of that laugh, which rang false, like a cracked bell, my lord looked at him again across the table, and I saw his old lips draw together close.

'No,' said Mr Henry, still glancing on his letter, 'But I remember your expression. You said it was very fresh.'

And here we had a proof of our victory, and the strongest instance yet of my lord's incredible indulgence; for what must he do but interfere to save his favourite from exposure!

'I think, Henry,' says he, with a kind of pitiful eagerness, 'I think we need dispute no more. We are all rejoiced at last to find your brother safe; we are all at one on that; and, as grateful subjects, we can do no less than drink to the king's health and bounty.'

Thus was the Master extricated; but at least he had been put to his defence, he had come lamely out, and the attraction of his personal danger was now publicly plucked away from him. My lord, in his heart of hearts, now knew his favourite to be a Government spy; and Mrs Henry (however she explained the tale) was notably cold in her behaviour to the discredited hero of romance. Thus in the best fabric of duplicity there is some weak point, if you can strike it, which will loosen all; and if, by this fortunate stroke, we had not shaken the idol, who can say how it might have gone with us at the catastrophe?

And yet at the time we seemed to have accomplished nothing. Before a day or two he had wiped off the ill-results of his discomfiture, and, to all appearance, stood as high as ever. As for my Lord Durrisdeer, he was sunk in parental partiality; it was not so much love, which should be an active quality, as an apathy and torpor of his other powers; and forgiveness (so to misapply a noble word) flowed from him in sheer weakness, like the tears of senility. Mrs Henry's was a different case; and Heaven alone knows what he found to say to her, or how he persuaded her from her contempt. It is one of the worst things of sentiment, that the voice grows to be more important than the words, and the speaker than that which is spoken. But some excuse the Master must have found, or perhaps he had even struck upon some art to wrest this exposure to his own advantage; for after a time of coldness, it seemed as if things went worse than ever between him and Mrs Henry. They were then constantly together. I would not be thought to cast one shadow of blame, beyond what is due to a half-wilful blindness, on that unfortunate lady; but I do think, in these last days, she was playing very near the fire; and whether I be wrong or not in that, one thing is sure and quite sufficient: Mr Henry thought so. The poor gentleman sat for days in my room, so great a picture of distress that I could never venture to address him; yet it is to be thought he found some comfort even in my presence and the knowledge of my sympathy. There were times, too, when we talked, and a strange manner of talk it was; there was never a person named, nor an individual circumstance referred to; yet we had the same matter in our minds, and we were each aware of it. It is a strange art that can thus be practised; to talk for hours of a thing, and never name nor yet so much as hint at it. And I remember I wondered if it was by some such natural skill that the Master made love to Mrs Henry all day long (as he manifestly did), yet never startled her into reserve.

To show how far affairs had gone with Mr Henry, I will give some words of his, uttered (as I have cause not to forget) upon the 26th of February, 1757. It was unseasonable weather, a cast back into winter: windless, bitter cold, the world all white with rime, the sky low and grey: the sea black and silent like a quarry-hole. Mr Henry sat close by the fire and debated (as was now common with him) whether 'a man' should 'do things,' whether 'interference was wise,' and the like general propositions, which each of us particularly applied. I was by the window, looking out, when there passed below me the Master, Mrs Henry, and Miss Katharine, that now constant trio. The child was running to and fro, delighted with the frost; the Master spoke close in the lady's ear with what seemed (even from so far) a devilish grace of insinuation; and she on her part looked on the ground like a person lost in listening. I broke out of my reserve.

'If I were you, Mr Henry,' said I, 'I would deal openly with my lord.'

'Mackellar, Mackellar,' said he, 'you do not see the weakness of my ground. I can carry no such base thoughts to anyone – to my father least of all; that would be to fall into the bottom of his scorn. The weakness of my ground,' he continued, 'lies in myself, that I am not one who engages love. I have their gratitude, they all tell me that; I have a rich estate of it! But I am not present in their minds; they are moved neither to think with me nor to think for me. There is my loss!' He got to his feet and trod down the fire. 'But some method must be found, Mackellar,' said he, looking at me suddenly over his shoulder; 'some way must be found. I am a man of a great deal of patience – far too much – far too much. I begin to despise myself. And yet, sure, never was a man involved in such a toil!' He fell back to his brooding.

'Cheer up,' said I. 'It will burst of itself.'

'I am far past anger now,' says he, which had so little coherency with my own observation that I let both fall.

CHAPTER FIVE

Account of all that passed on the night of FEBRUARY 27TH, *1757*

ON THE EVENING OF THE interview referred to, the Master went abroad; he was abroad a great deal of the next day also, that fatal 27th; but where he went, or what he did, we never concerned ourselves to ask until next day. If we had done so, and by any chance found out, it might have changed all. But as all we did was done in ignorance, and should be so judged, I shall so narrate these passages as they appeared to us in the moment of their birth, and reserve all that I since discovered for the time of its discovery. For I have now come to one of the dark parts of my narrative, and must engage the reader's indulgence for my patron.

All the 27th that rigorous weather endured: a stifling cold; the folk passing about like smoking chimneys; the wide hearth in the hall piled high with fuel; some of the spring birds that had already blundered north into our neighbour-hood, besieging the windows of the house or trotting on the frozen turf like things distracted. About noon there came a blink of sunshine; showing a very pretty, wintry, frosty landscape of white hills and woods, with Crail's lugger waiting for a wind under the Craig Head, and the smoke mounting straight into the air from every farm and cottage. With the coming of night, the haze closed in overhead; it fell dark and still and starless, and exceeding cold: a night the most unseasonable, fit for strange events.

Mrs Henry withdrew, as was now her custom, very early. We had set ourselves of late to pass the evening with a game of cards; another mark that our visitor was wearying mightily of the life at Durrisdeer; and we had not been long at this when my old lord slipped from his place beside the fire, and was off without a word to seek the warmth of bed. The three thus left together had neither love nor courtesy to share; not one of us would have sat up one instant to oblige another; yet from the influence of custom, and as the cards had just been dealt, we continued the form of playing out the round. I should say we were late sitters; and though my lord had departed earlier than was his custom, twelve was already gone some time upon the clock, and the servants long ago in bed. Another thing I should say, that although I never saw the Master anyway affected with liquor, he had been drinking freely, and was perhaps (although he showed it not) a trifle heated.

Anyway, he now practised one of his transitions; and so soon as the door closed behind my lord, and without the smallest change of voice, shifted from ordinary civil talk into a stream of insult.

'My dear Henry, it is yours to play,' he had been saying, and now continued: 'it is a very strange thing how, even in so small a matter as a game of cards, you display your rusticity. You play, Jacob, like a bonnet laird, or a sailor in a tavern. The same dulness, the same petty greed, *cette lenteur d'hébété qui me fait rager*; it is strange I should have such a brother. Even Square-toes has a certain vivacity when his stake is imperilled; but the dreariness of a game with you I positively lack language to depict.'

Mr Henry continued to look at his cards, as though very maturely considering some play; but his mind was elsewhere.

'Dear God, will this never be done?' cries the Master. '*Quel loudeau!* But why do I trouble you with French expressions, which are lost on such an ignoramus? A *lourdeau*, my dear brother, is as we might say a bumpkin, a clown, a clodpole: a fellow without grace, lightness, quickness; any gift of pleasing, any natural brilliancy: such a one as you shall see, when you desire, by looking in the mirror. I tell you these things for your good, I assure you; and besides, Square-toes' (looking at me and stifling a yawn), 'it is one of my diversions in this very dreary spot to toast you and your master at the fire like chestnuts. I have great pleasure in your case, for I observe the nickname (rustic as it is) has always the power to make you writhe. But sometimes I have more trouble with this dear fellow here, who seems to have gone to sleep upon his cards. Do you not see the applicability of the epithet I have just explained, dear Henry? Let me show you. For instance, with all those solid qualities which I delight to recognize in you. I never knew a woman who did not prefer me – not, I think,' he continued, with the most silken deliberation, 'I think – who did not continue to prefer me.'

Mr Henry laid down his cards. He rose to his feet very softly, and seemed all the while like a person in deep thought. 'You coward!' he said gently, as if to himself. And then, with neither hurry nor any particular violence, he struck the Master in the mouth.

The Master sprang to his feet like one transfigured; I had never seen the man so beautiful. 'A blow!' he cried. 'I would not take a blow from God Almighty!'

'Lower your voice,' said Mr Henry. 'Do you wish my father to interfere for you again?'

'Gentlemen, gentlemen,' I cried, and sought to come between them.

The Master caught me by the shoulder, held me at arm's length, and still addressing his brother: 'Do you know what this means?' said he.

'It was the most deliberate act of my life,' sayd Mr Henry.

'I must have blood, I must have blood for this,' sayd the Master.

'Please God it shall be yours,' said Mr Henry; and he went to the wall and took down a pair of swords that hung there with others, naked. These he presented to the Master by the points. 'Mackellar shall see us play fair,' said Mr Henry. 'I think it very needful.'

'You need insult me no more,' said the Master, taking one of the swords at random. 'I have hated you all my life.'

'My father is but newly gone to bed,' said Mr Henry. 'We must go somewhere forth of the house.'

'There is an excellent place in the long shrubbery,' said the Master.

'Gentlemen,' said I, 'shame upon you both! Sons of the same mother, would you turn against the life she gave you?'

'Even so, Mackellar,' said Mr Henry, with the same perfect quietude of manner he had shown throughout.

'It is what I will prevent,' said I.

And now here is a blot upon my life. At these words of mine the Master turned his blade against my bosom; I saw the light run along the steel; and I threw up my arms and fell to my knees before him on the floor. 'No, no,' I cried, like a baby.

'We shall have no trouble with him,' said the Master. 'It is a good thing to have a coward in the house.'

'We must have light,' said Mr Henry, as though there had been no interruption.

'This trembler can bring a pair of candles,' said the Master.

To my shame be it said, I was still so blinded with the flashing of that bare sword that I volunteered to bring a lantern.

'We do not need a l-l-lantern,' says the Master, mocking me. 'There is no breath of air. Come, get to your feet, take a pair of lights, and go before. I am close behind with this' – making the blade glitter as he spoke.

I took up the candlesticks and went before them, steps that I would give my hand to recall; but a coward is a slave at the best; and even as I went, my teeth smote each other in my mouth. It was as he had said: there was no breath stirring; a windless stricture of frost had bound the air; and as we went forth in the shine of the candles, the blackness was like a roof over our heads. Never a word was said; there was never a sound but the creaking of our steps along the frozen path. The cold of the night fell about me like a bucket of water; I shook as I went with more than terror; but my companions, bare-headed like myself, and fresh from the warm hall, appeared not even conscious of the change.

'Here is the place,' said the Master. 'Set down the candles.' I did as he bid me, and presently the flames went up, as steady as in a chamber, in the midst of the frosted trees, and I beheld these two brothers take their places.

'The light is something in my eyes,' said the Master.

'I will give you every advantage,' replied Mr Henry, shifting his ground, 'for I think you are about to die.' He spoke rather sadly than otherwise, yet there was a ring in his voice.

'Henry Durie,' said the Master, 'two words before I begin. You are a fencer, you can hold a foil; you little know what a change it makes to hold a sword! And by that I know you are to fall. But see how strong is my situation! If you fall, I shift out of this country to where my money is before me. If I fall where are you? My father, your wife – who is in love with me, as you very well know – your child even, who prefers me to yourself: – how will these avenge me! Had you thought of that, dear Henry?' He looked at his brother with a smile; then made a fencing-room salute.

Never a word said Mr Henry, but saluted too, and the swords rang together.

I am no judge of the play; my head, besides, was gone with cold and fear and horror; but it seems that Mr Henry took and kept the upper hand from the engagement, crowding in upon his foe with a contained and glowing fury. Nearer and nearer he crept upon the man, till of a sudden the Master leaped back with a little sobbing oath; and I believe the movement brought the light once more against his eyes. To it they went again, on the fresh ground; but now methought closer, Mr Henry pressing more outrageously, the Master beyond doubt with shaken confidence. For it is beyond doubt he now recognized himself for lost, and had some taste of the cold agony of fear; or he had never attempted the foul stroke. I cannot say I followed it, my untrained eye was never quick enough to seize details, but it appears he caught his brother's blade with his left hand, a practice not permitted. Certainly Mr Henry only saved himself by leaping on one side; as certainly the Master, lunging in the air, stumbled on his knee, and before he could move the sword was through his body.

I cried out with a stifled scream, and ran in; but the body was already fallen to the ground, where it writhed a moment like a trodden worm, and then lay motionless.

'Look at his left hand,' said Mr Henry.

'It is all bloody,' said I.

'On the inside?' said he.

'It is cut on the inside,' said I.

'I thought so,' said he, and turned his back.

I opened the man's clothes; the heart was quite still, it gave not a flutter.

'God forgive us, Mr Henry!' said I. 'He is dead.'

'Dead?' he repeated, a little stupidly; and then with a rising tone, 'Dead? dead?' says he, and suddenly cast his bloody sword upon the ground.

'What must we do?' said I. 'Be yourself, sir. It is too late now: you must be yourself.'

He turned and stared at me. 'Oh, Mackellar!' says he, and put his face in his hands.

I plucked him by the coat. 'For God's sake, for all our sakes, be more courageous!' said I. 'What must we do?'

He showed me his face with the same stupid stare. 'Do?' says he. And with that his eye fell on the body, and 'Oh!' he cries out, with his hand to his brow, as if he had never remembered; and, turning from me, made off towards the house of Durrisdeer at a strange stumbling run.

I stood a moment mused; then it seemed to me my duty lay most plain on the side of the living; and I ran after him, leaving the candles on the frosty ground and the body lying in their light under the trees. But run as I pleased, he had the start of me, and was got into the house, and up to the hall, where I found him standing before the fire with his face once more in his hands, and as he so stood he visibly shuddered.

'Mr Henry, Mr Henry,' I said, 'this will be the ruin of us all.'

'What is this that I have done?' cries he, and then looking upon me with a countenance that I shall never forget, 'Who is to tell the old man?' he said.

The word knocked at my heart; but it was no time for weakness. I went and poured him out a glass of brandy. 'Drink that,' said I, 'drink it down.' I forced him to swallow it like a child; and, being still perished with the cold of the night, I followed his example.

'It has to be told, Mackellar,' said he. 'It must be told.' And he fell suddenly in a seat – my old lord's seat by the chimney-side – and was shaken with dry sobs.

Dismay came upon my soul: it was plain there was no help in Mr Henry.

'Well,' said I, 'sit there, and leave all to me.' And taking a candle in my hand, I set forth out of the room in the dark house. There was no movement; I must suppose that all had gone unobserved; and I was now to consider how to smuggle through the rest with the like secrecy. It was no hour for scruples; and I opened my lady's door without so much as a knock, and passed boldly in.

'There is some calamity happened,' she cried, sitting up in bed.

'Madam,' said I, 'I will go forth again into the passage; and do you get as quickly as you can into your clothes. There is much to be done.'

She troubled me with no questions, nor did she keep me waiting. Ere I had time to prepare a word of that which I must say to her, she was on the threshold singing me to enter.

'Madam,' said I, 'if you cannot be very brave, I must go elsewhere; for if no one helps me tonight, there is an end of the house of Durrisdeer.'

'I am very courageous,' said she; and she looked at me with a sort of smile, very painful to see, but very brave too.

'It has come to a duel,' said I.

'A duel?' she repeated. 'A duel! Henry and——'

'And the Master,' said I. 'Things have been borne so long, things of which you know nothing, which you would not believe if I should tell. But tonight it went too far, and when he insulted you——'

'Stop,' said she. 'He? Who?'

'Oh! madam,' cried I, my bitterness breaking forth, 'do you ask me such a question? Indeed, then, I may go elsewhere for help; there is none here!'

'I do not know in what I have offended you,' said she. 'Forgive me; put me out of this suspense.'

But I dared not tell her yet; I felt not sure of her; and at the doubt, and under the sense of impotence it brought with it, I turned on the poor woman with something near to anger.

'Madam,' said I, 'we are speaking of two men; one of them insulted, you, and you ask me which. I will help you to the answer. With one of these men you have spent all your hours: has the other reproached you? To one you have been always kind; to the other, as God sees me and judges between us two, I think not always: has his love ever failed you? Tonight one of these two men told the other, in my hearing – the hearing of a hired stranger – that you were in love with him. Before I say one word, you shall answer your own question: Which was it? Nay, madam, you shall answer me another: If it has come to this dreadful end, whose fault is it?'

She stared at me like one dazzled. 'Good God!' she said once, in a kind of bursting exclamation; and then a second time in a whisper to herself: 'Great God! – In the name of mercy, Mackellar, what is wrong?' she cried. 'I am made up; I can hear all.'

'You are not fit to hear,' said I. 'Whatever it was, you shall say first it was your fault.'

'Oh!' she cried, with a gesture of wringing her hands, 'this man will drive me mad! Can you not put me out of yout thoughts?'

'I think not once of you,' I cried. 'I think of none but my dear unhappy master.'

'Ah!' she cried, with her hand to her heart, 'is Henry dead!'

'Lower your voice,' said I. 'The other.'

I saw her sway like something stricken by the wind; and I know not whether in cowardice or misery, turned aside and looked upon the floor. 'These are dreadful tidings,' said I at length, when her silence began to put me in some fear; 'and you and I behove to be the more bold if the house is to be saved.' Still she answered nothing. 'There is Miss Katharine besides,' I added; 'unless we bring this matter through, her inheritance is like to be shame.'

I do not know if it was the thought of her child or the naked word shame that gave her deliverance; at least, I had no sooner spoken than a sound passed her lips, the like of it I never heard; it was as though she had lain buried under a hill and sought to move that burthen. And the next moment she had found a sort of voice.

'It was a fight,' she whispered. 'It was not——?' and she paused upon the word.

'It was a fair fight on my dear master's part,' said I. 'As for the other, he was slain in the very act of a foul stroke.'

'Not now!' she cried.

'Madam,' said I, 'hatred of that man glows in my bosom like a burning fire; ay, even now he is dead. God knows, I would have stopped the fighting, had I dared. It is my shame I did not. But when I saw him fall, if I could have spared one thought from pitying of my master, it had been to exult in that deliverance.'

I do not know if she marked; but her next words were, 'My lord?'

'That shall be my part,' said I.

'You will not speak to him as you have to me?' she asked.

'Madam,' said I, 'have you not someone else to think of? Leave my lord to me.'

'Someone else?' she repeated.

'Your husband,' said I. She looked at me with a countenance illegible. 'Are you going to turn your back on him?' I asked.

Still she looked at me; then her hand went to her heart again. 'No,' said she.

'God bless you for that word!' I said. 'Go to him now, where he sits in the hall; speak to him – it matters not what you say; give him your hand; say, "I know all"; – if God gives you grace enough, say, "Forgive me."'

'God strengthen you, and make you merciful,' said she. 'I will go to my husband.'

'Let me light you there,' said I, taking up the candle.

'I will find my way in the dark,' she said, with a shudder, and I think the shudder was at me.

So we separated – she down the stairs to where a little light glimmered in the hall-door, I along the passage to my lord's room. It seems hard to say why, but I could not burst in on the old man as I could on the young woman; with whatever reluctance, I must knock. But his old slumbers were light, or perhaps he slept not; and at the first summons I was bidden enter.

He, too, sat up in bed; very aged and bloodless he looked; and whereas he had a certain largeness of appearance when dressed for daylight, he now seemed frail and little, and his face (the wig being laid aside) not bigger than a child's. This daunted me; nor less, the haggard surmise of misfortune in his eye. Yet his voice was even peaceful as he inquired my errand. I set my candle down upon a chair, leaned on the bed-foot, and looked at him.

'Lord Durrisdeer,' said I, 'it is very well known to you that I am a partisan in your family.'

'I hope we are none of us partisans,' said he. 'That you love my son sincerely, I have always been glad to recognize.'

'Oh! my lord, we are past the hour of these civilities,' I replied. 'If we are to save anything out of the fire, we must look the face in its bare contenance. A partisan I am; partisans we have all been; it is as a partisan I am here in the middle of the night to plead before you. Hear me; before I go, I will tell you why.'

'I would always hear you, Mr Mackellar,' said he, 'and that at any hour, whether of the day or night, for I would be always sure you had a reason. You spoke once before to very proper purpose; I have not forgotten that.'

'I am here to plead the cause of my master,' I said. 'I need not tell you how he acts. You know how he is placed. You know with what generosity he has always met your other — met your wishes,' I corrected myself, stumbling at that name of son. 'You know — you must know — what he has suffered — what he has suffered about his wife.'

'Mr Mackellar!' cried my lord, rising in bed like a bearded lion.

'You said you would hear me,' I continued. 'What you do not know, what you should know, one of the things I am here to speak of, is the persecution he must bear in private. Your back is not turned before one whom I dare not name to you falls upon him with the most unfeeling taunts; twits him — pardon me, my lord — twits him with your partiality, calls him Jacob, calls him clown, pursues him with ungenerous raillery, not to be borne by man. And let but one of you appear, instantly he changes; and my master must smile and courtesy to the man who has been feeding him with insults; I know, for I have shared in some of it, and I tell you the life is insupportable. All these months it has endured; it began with the man's landing; it was by the name of Jacob that my master was greeted the first night.'

My lord made a movement as if to throw aside the clothes and rise. 'If there be any truth in this——' said he.

'Do I look like a man lying?' I interrupted, checking him with my hand.

'You should have told me at first,' he said.

'Ah, my lord! indeed I should, and you may well hate the face of this unfaithful servant!' I cried.

'I will take order,' said he, 'at once.' And again made the movement to rise.

Again I checked him. 'I have not done,' said I. 'Would God I had! All this my dear, unfortunate patron has endured without help or countenance. Your own best word, my lord, was only gratitude. Oh, but he was your son, too! He had no other father. He was hated in the country, God knows how unjustly. He had a loveless marriage. He stood on all hands without affection or support — dear, generous, ill-fated, noble heart!'

'Your tears do you much honour and me much shame,' says my lord, with a palsied trembling. 'But you do me some injustice. Henry has been ever dear to me, very dear. James (I do not deny it, Mr Mackellar), James is perhaps dearer; you have not seen my James in quite a favourable light; he has suffered under his misfortunes; and we can only remember how great and how unmerited these were. And even now his is the more affectionate nature. But I will not speak of him. All that you say of Henry is most true; I do not wonder, I know him to be very magnanimous; you will say I trade upon the knowledge? It is possible; there are dangerous virtues: virtues that tempt the encroacher. Mr Mackellar, I will make it up to him! I will take order with all this. I have been weak; and, what is worse, I have been dull.'

'I must not hear you blame yourself, my lord, with that which I have yet to tell upon my conscience,' I replied. 'You have not been weak; you have been abused by a devilish dissembler. You saw yourself how he had deceived you in the matter of his danger; he has deceived you throughout in every step of his career. I wish to pluck him from your heart; I wish to force your eyes upon your other son; ah, you have a son there!'

'No, no,' said he, 'two sons – I have two sons.'

I made some gesture of despair that struck him; he looked at me with a changed face. 'There is much worse behind?' he asked, his voice dying as it rose upon the question.

'Much worse,' I answered. 'This night he said these words to Mr Henry: "I have never known a woman who did not prefer me to you, and I think who did not continue to prefer me."'

'I will hear nothing against my daughter,' he cried; and from his readiness to stop me in this direction, I conclude his eyes were not so dull as I had fancied, and he had looked not without anxiety upon the siege of Mrs Henry.

'I think not of blaming her,' cried I. 'It is not that. These words were said in my hearing to Mr Henry; and if you find them not yet plain enough, these others but a little after: "Your wife, who is in love with me."'

'They have quarrelled?' he said.

I nodded.

'I must fly to them,' he said, beginning once again to leave his bed.

'No, no!' I cried, holding forth my hands.

'You do not know,' said he. 'These are dangerous words.'

'Will nothing make you understand, my lord?' said I.

His eyes besought me for the truth.

I flung myself on my knees by the bedside. 'Oh, my lord,' cried I, 'think on him you have left; think of this poor sinner whom you begot, whom your wife bore to you, whom we have none of us strengthened as we could; think of him, not of yourself; he is the other sufferer – think of him! That is the door for sorrow – Christ's door, God's door: oh! it stands open. Think of him, even as he thought of you. "Who is to tell the old man?" – these were his words. It was for that I came; that is why I am here pleading at your feet.'

'Let me get up,' he cried, thrusting me aside, and was on his feet before myself. His voice shook like a sail in the wind, yet he spoke with a good loudness; his face was like the snow, but his eyes were steady and dry. 'Here is too much speech,' said he. 'Where was it?'

'In the shrubbery,' said I.

'And Mr Henry?' he asked. And when I had told him he knotted his old face in thought.

'And Mr James?' says he.

'I have left him lying,' said I, 'beside the candles.'

'Candles?' he cried. And with that he ran to the window, opened it, and looked abroad. 'It might be spied from the road.'

'Where none goes by at such an hour,' I objected.

'It makes no matter,' he said. 'One might. Hark!' cries he. 'What is that?'

It was the sound of men very guardedly rowing in the bay; and I told him so.

'The freetraders,' said my lord. 'Run at once, Mackellar; put these candles out. I will dress in the meanwhile; and when you return we can debate on what is wisest.'

I groped my way downstairs, and out of the door. From quite a far way off a sheen was visible, making points of brightness in the shrubbery; in so black a night it might have been remarked for miles; and I blamed myself bitterly for my incaution. How much more sharply when I reached the place! One of the candlesticks was overthrown, and that taper quenched. The other burned steadily by itself, and made a broad space of light upon the frosted ground. All within that circle seemed, by the force of contrast and the overhanging blackness, brighter than by day. And there was the bloodstain in the midst; and a little farther off Mr Henry's sword, the pommel of which was of silver; but of the body, not a trace. My heart thumped upon my ribs, the hair stirred upon my scalp, as I stood there staring – so strange was the sight, so dire the fears it wakened. I looked right and left; the ground was so hard it told no story. I stood and listened till my ears ached, but the night was hollow about me like an empty church; not even a ripple stirred upon the shore; it seemed you might have heard a pin drop in the county.

I put the candle out, and the blackness fell about me groping dark; it was like a crowd surrounding me; and I went back to the house of Durrisdeer, with my chin upon my shoulder, startling, as I went, with craven suppositions. In the door a figure moved to meet me, and I had near screamed with terror ere I recognized Mrs Henry.

'Have you told him?' says she.

'It was he who sent me,' said I. 'It is gone. But why are you here?'

'It is gone!' she repeated. 'What is gone?'

'The body,' said I. 'Why are you not with your husband?'

'Gone?' said she. 'You cannot have looked. Come back.'

'There is no light now,' said I. 'I dare not.'

'I can see in the dark. I have been standing here so long – so long,' said she. 'Come give me your hand.'

We returned to the shrubbery hand in hand, and to the fatal place.

'Take care of the blood,' said I.

'Blood?' she cried, and started violently back.

'I suppose it will be,' said I. 'I am like a blind man.'

'No,' said she, 'nothing! Have you not dreamed?'

'Ah, would to God we had!' cried I.

She spied the sword, picked it up, and seeing the blood, let it fall again with her hands thrown wide. 'Ah!' she cried. And then, with an instant courage, handled it the second time. 'I will take it back and clean it properly,' says she, and again looked about her on all sides. 'It cannot be that he was dead?' she added.

'There was no flutter of his heart,' said I, and then remembering: 'Why are you not with your husband?'

'It is no use,' said she; 'he will not speak to me.'

'Not speak to you?' I repeated. 'Oh! you have not tried.'

'You have a right to doubt me,' she replied, with a gentle dignity.

At this, for the first time, I was seized with sorrow for her. 'God knows, madam,' I cried, 'God knows I am not so hard as I appear; on this dreadful night who can veneer his words? But I am a friend to all who are not Henry Durie's enemies.'

'It is hard, then, you should hesitate about his wife,' said she.

I saw all at once, like the rending of a veil, how nobly she had borne this unnatural calamity, and how generously my reproaches.

'We must go back and tell this to my lord,' said I.

'Him I cannot face,' she cried.

'You will find him the least moved of all of us,' said I.

'And yet I cannot face him,' said she.

'Well,' said I, 'you can return to Mr Henry: I will see my lord.'

. .s we walked back, I bearing the candlesticks, she the sword – a strange burthen for that woman – she had another thought. 'Should we tell Henry?' she asked.

'Let my lord decide,' said I.

My lord was nearly dressed when I came to his chamber. He heard me with a frown. 'The freetraders,' said he. 'But whether dead or alive?'

'I thought him——' said I, and paused, ashamed of the word.

'I know; but you may very well have been in error. Why should they remove him if not living?' he asked. 'Oh! here is a great door of hope. It must be given out that he departed – as he came – without any note of preparation. We must save all scandal.'

I saw he had fallen, like the rest of us, to think mainly of the house. Now that all the living members of the family were plunged in irremediable sorrow, it was strange how we turned to the conjoint abstraction of the family itself, and sought to bolster up the airy nothing of its reputation: not the Duries only, but the hired steward himself.

'Are we to tell Mr Henry?' I asked him.

'I will see,' said he. 'I am going first to visit him; then I go forth with you to view the shrubbery and consider.'

We went downstairs into the hall. Mr Henry sat by the table with his head upon his hand, like a man of stone. His wife stood a little back from him, her hand at her mouth; it was plain she could not move him. My old lord walked very steadily to where his son was sitting; he had a steady countenance, too, but methought a little cold. When he was quite come up, he held out both his hands and said, 'My son!'

With a broken, strangled cry, Mr Henry leaped up and fell on his father's neck, crying and weeping, the most pitiful sight that ever a man witnessed. 'Oh! father,' he cried, 'you know I loved him; you know I loved him in the beginning; I could have died for him – you know that! I would have given my life for him and you. Oh! say you know that. Oh! say you can forgive me. O father, father, what have I done – what have I done? And we used to be bairns together!' and wept and sobbed, and fondled the old man, and clutched him about the neck, with the passion of a child in terror.

And then he caught sight of his wife (you would have thought for the first time), where she stood weeping to hear him, and in a moment had fallen at her knees. 'And O my lass,' he cried, 'you must forgive me too! Not your husband – I have only been the ruin of your life. But you knew me when I was a lad; there was no harm in Henry Durie then; he meant aye to be a friend to you. It's him – it's the old bairn that played with you – oh, can ye never, never forgive him?'

Throughout all this my lord was like a cold, kind spectator with his wits about him. At the first cry, which was indeed enough to call the house about us, he had said to me over his shoulder, 'Close the door.' And now he nodded to himself.

'We may leave him to his wife now,' says he. 'Bring a light, Mr Mackellar.'

Upon my going forth again with my lord, I was aware of a strange phenomenon; for though it was quite dark, and the night not yet old, methought I smelt the morning. At the same time there went a tossing through the branches of the evergreens, so that they sounded like a quiet sea, and the air puffed at times against our faces, and the flame of the candle shook. We made the more speed, I believe, being surrounded by this bustle; visited the scene of the duel, where my lord looked upon the blood with stoicism; and passing farther on toward the landing-place, came at last upon some evidences of the truth. For, first of all, where there was a pool across the path, the ice had been trodden in, plainly by more than one man's weight; next, and but a little farther, a young tree was broken, and down by the landing-place, where the traders' boats were usually beached, another stain of blood marked where the body must have been infallibly set down to rest the bearers.

This stain we set ourselves to wash away with the seawater, carrying it in my lord's hat; and as we were thus engaged there came a sudden moaning gust and left us instantly benighted.

'It will come to snow,' says my lord; 'and the best thing that we could hope. Let us go back now; we can do nothing in the dark.'

As we went houseward, the wind being again subsided, we were aware of a strong pattering noise about us in the night; and when we issued from the shelter of the trees, we found it raining smartly.

Throughout the whole of this my lord's clearness of mind, no less than his activity of body, had not ceased to minister to my amazement. He set the crown upon it in the council we held on our return. The freetraders had certainly secured the Master, though whether dead or alive we were still left to our conjectures; the rain would, long before day, wipe out all marks of the transaction; by this we must profit. The Master had unexpectedly come after the fall of night; it must now be given out he had as suddenly departed before the break of day; and, to make all this plausible, it now only remained for me to mount into the man's chamber, and pack and conceal his baggage. True, we still lay at the discretion of the traders; but that was the incurable weakness of our guilt.

I heard him, as I said, with wonder, and hastened to obey. Mr and Mrs Henry were gone from the hall; my lord, for warmth's sake, hurried to his bed; there was still no sign of stir among the servants, and as I went up the tower stair, and entered the dead man's room, a horror of solitude weighed upon my mind. To me extreme surprise, it was all in the disorder of departure. Of his three portmanteaus, two were already locked; the third lay open and near full. At once there flashed upon me some suspicion of the truth. The man had been going, after all; he had but waited upon Crail, as Crail waited upon the wind; early in the night the seamen had perceived the weather changing; the boat had come to give notice of the change and call the passenger aboard, and the boat's crew had stumbled on him lying in his blood. Nay, and there was more behind. This prearranged departure shed some light upon his inconceivable insult of the night before; it was a parting shot, hatred being no longer checked by policy. And, for another thing, the nature of that insult, and the conduct of Mrs Henry, pointed to one conclusion, which I have never verified, and can now never verify until the great assize – the conclusion that he had at last forgotten himself, had gone too far in his advances, and had been rebuffed. It can never be verified, as I say; but as I thought of it that morning among his baggage, the thought was sweet to me like honey.

Into the open portmanteau I dipped a little ere I closed it. The most beautiful lace and linen, many suits of those fine plain clothes in which he loved to appear; a book or two, and those of the best, Caesar's *Commentaries*, a volume of Mr Hobbes the *Henriade* of M. de Voltaire, a book upon the Indies, one on the mathematics, far beyond where I have studied: these were what I observed with very mingled feelings. But in the open portmanteau no papers of any description. This set me musing. It was possible the man was dead; but, since the traders had carried him away, not likely. It was possible that he might still die of his wound; but it was also possible he might not. And in this latter case I was determined to have the means of some defence.

One after another I carried his portmanteaus to a loft in the top of the house which we kept locked; went to my own room for my keys, and, returning to the loft, had the gratification to find two that fitted pretty well. In one of the portmanteaus there was a shagreen letter-case, which I cut open with my knife; and thenceforth (so far as any credit went) the man was at my mercy. Here was a vast deal of gallant correspondence, chiefly of his Paris days; and, what was more to the purpose, here were the copies of his own reports to the English Secretary, and the originals of the Secretary's answers: a most damning series: such as to publish would be to wreck the Master's honour and to set a price upon his life. I chuckled to myself as I ran through the documents; I rubbed my hands, I sang aloud in my glee. Day found me at the pleasing task; nor did I then remit my diligence, except in so far as I went to the window – looked out for a moment, to see the frost quite gone, the world turned black again, and the rain and the wind driving in the bay – and to assure myself that the lugger was gone from its anchorage, and the Master (whether dead or alive) now tumbling on the Irish Sea.

It is proper I should add in this place the very little I have subsequently angled out upon the doings of that night. It took me a long while to gather it: for we dared not openly ask, and the freetraders regarded me with enmity, if not with scorn. It was near six months before we even knew for certain that the man survived; and it was years before I learned from one of Crail's men, turned publican on his ill-gotten gain, some particulars which smack to me of truth. It seems the traders found the Master struggled on one elbow, and now staring round him, and now gazing at the candle or at his hand which was all bloodied, like a man stupid. Upon their coming, he would seem to have found his mind, bade them carry him aboard, and hold their tongues; and on the captain asking how he had come in such a pickle, replied with a burst of passionate swearing, and incontinently fainted. They held some debate, but they were momently looking for a wind, they were highly paid to smuggle him to France, and did not care to delay. Besides which, he was well enough liked by these abominable wretches: they supposed him under capital sentence, knew not in what mischief he might have got his wound, and judged it a piece of good nature to remove him out of the way of danger. So he was taken aboard, recovered on the passage over, and was set ashore a convalescent at the Havre de Grace. What is truly notable: he said not a word to anyone of the duel, and not a trader knows to this day in what quarrel, or by the hand of what adversary, he fell. With any other man I should have set this down to natural decency; with him, to pride. He could not bear to avow, perhaps even to himself, that he had been vanquished by one whom he had so much insulted and whom he so cruelly despised.

CHAPTER SIX

Summary of Events during the Master's second absence

OF THE HEAVY SICKNESS which declared itself next morning I can think with equanimity, as of the last unmingled trouble that befell my master; and even that was perhaps a mercy in disguise; for what pain of the body could equal the miseries of his mind? Mrs Henry and I had the watching by the bed. My old lord called from time to time to take the news, but would not usually pass the door. Once, I remember, when hope was nigh gone, he stepped to the bedside, looked awhile in his son's face, and turned away with a singular gesture of the head and hand thrown up, that remains upon my mind as something tragic; such grief and such a scorn of sublunary things were there expressed. But the most of the time Mrs Henry and I had the room to ourselves, taking turns by night, and bearing each other company by day, for it was dreary watching. Mr Henry, his shaven head bound in a napkin, tossed to and fro without remission, beating the bed with his hands. His tongue never lay; his voice ran continuously like a river, so that my heart was weary with the sound of it. It was notable, and to me inexpressibly mortifying, that he spoke all the while on matters of no import: comings and goings, horses – which he was ever calling to have saddled, thinking perhaps (the poor soul!) that he might ride away from his discomfort – matters of the garden, the salmon nets, and (what I particularly raged to hear) continually of his affairs, cyphering figures and holding disputation with the tenantry. Never a word of his father or his wife, nor of the Master, save only for a day or two, when his mind dwelled entirely in the past, and he supposed himself a boy again and upon some innocent child's play with his brother. What made this the more affecting: it appeared the Master had then run some peril of his life, for there was a cry – 'Oh! Jamie will be drowned – Oh, save Jamie!' which he came over and over with a great deal of passion.

This, I say, was affecting both to Mrs Henry and myself; but the balance of my master's wanderings did him little justice. It seemed he had set out to justify his brother's calumnies; as though he was bent to prove himself a man of a dry nature, immersed in money-getting. Had I been there alone, I would not have troubled my thumb; but all the while, as I listened, I was estimating the effect on the man's wife, and telling myself that he fell lower every day. I was the one person on the surface of the globe that comprehended him, and I was bound there should be yet another. Whether he was to die there and his virtues perish: or whether he should save his days and come back to that inheritance of sorrows, his right memory: I was bound he should be heartily lamented in the one case, and unaffectedly welcomed in the other, by the person he loved the most, his wife.

Finding no occasion of free speech, I bethought me at last of a kind of documentary disclosure; and for some nights, when I was off duty and should have been asleep, I gave my time to the preparation of that which I may call my budget. But this I found to be the easiest portion of my task, and that which remained – namely, the presentation to my lady – almost more than I had fortitude to overtake. Several days I went about with my papers under my arm, spying for some juncture of talk to serve as introduction. I will not deny but that some offered; only when they did my tongue clove to the roof of my mouth; and I think I might have been carrying about my packet till this day, had not a fortunate accident delivered me from all my hesitations. This was at night, when I was once more leaving the room, the thing not yet done, and myself in despair at my own cowardice.

'What do you carry about with you, Mr Mackellar?' she asked. 'These last days, I see you always coming in and out with the same armful.'

I returned upon my steps without a word, laid the papers before her on the table, and left her to her reading. Of what that was, I am now to give you some idea; and the best will be to reproduce a letter of my own which came first in the budget and of which (according to an excellent habitude) I have preserved the scroll. It will show, too, the moderation of my part in these affairs, a thing which some have called recklessly in question.

DURRISDEER.

1757.

HONOURED MADAM,

I trust I would not step out of my place without occasion; but I see how much evil has flowed in the past to all of your noble house from that unhappy and secretive fault of reticency, and the papers on which I venture to call your attention are family papers, and all highly worthy your acquaintance.

I append a schedule with some necessary observations,

And am,

Honoured Madam,

Your ladyship's obliged, obedient servant

EPHRAIM MACKELLAR.

Schedule of Papers

A. Scroll of ten letters from Ephraim Mackellar to the Hon James Durie, Esq., by courtesy Master of Ballantrae, during the latter's residence in Paris: under dates . . . (*follow the dates*) . . . *Nota:* to be read in connection with B. and C.

B. Seven original letters from the said M^r of Ballantrae to the said E. Mackellar, under dates . . . (*follow the dates*).

C. Three original letters from the said M^r of Ballantrae to the Hon Henry Durie, Esq., under dates . . . (*follow the dates*) . . . *Nota:* given me by Mr Henry to answer: copies of my answers A4, A5 and A9 of these productions. The purport of Mr Henry's communications, of which I can find no scroll, may be gathered from those of his unnatural brother.

D. A correspondence, original and scroll, extending over a period of three years till January of the current year, between the said M^r of Ballantrae and —— ——, Under Secretary of State; twenty-seven in all. *Nota:* found among the Master's papers.

Weary as I was with watching and distress of mind, it was impossible for me to sleep. All night long I walked in my chamber, revolving what should be the issue, and sometimes repenting the temerity of my immixture in affairs so private; and with the first peep of morning I was at the sick-room door. Mrs Henry had thrown open the shutters and even the window, for the temperature was mild. She looked steadfastly before her; where was nothing to see, or only the blue of the morning creeping among woods. Upon the stir of my entrance she did not so much as turn about her face: a circumstance from which I augured very ill.

'Madam,' I began; and then again, 'Madam'; but could make no more of it. Nor yet did Mrs Henry come to my assistance with a word. In this pass I began gathering up the papers where they lay scattered on the table; and the first thing that struck me, their bulk appeared to have diminished. Once I ran them through, and twice; but the correspondence with the Secretary of State, on which I had reckoned so much against the future, was nowhere to be found. I looked in the chimney; amid the smouldering embers, black ashes of papers fluttered in the draught; and at that my timidity vanished.

'Good God, madam,' cried I, in a voice not fitting for a sick-room. 'Good God, madam, what have you done with my papers?'

'I have burned them,' said Mrs Henry, turning about. 'It is enough, it is too much, that you and I have seen them.'

'This is a fine night's work that you have done!' cried I. 'And all to save the reputation of a man that ate bread by the shedding of his comrade's blood, as I do by the shedding of ink.'

'To save the reputation of that family in which you are a servant, Mr Mackellar,' she returned, 'and for which you have already done so much.'

'It is a family I will not serve much longer,' I cried, 'for I am driven desperate. You have stricken the sword out of my hands; you have left us all defenceless. I had always these letters I could shake over his head; and now – what is to do? We are so falsely situate we dare not show the man the door; the country would fly on fire against us; and I had this one hold upon him – and now it is gone – now he may come back tomorrow, and we must all sit down with him to dinner, go for a stroll with him on the terrace, or take a hand at cards, of all things, to divert his leisure! No, madam! God forgive you, if He can find it in His heart, for I cannot find it in mine.'

'I wonder to find you so simple, Mr Mackellar,' said Mrs Henry. 'What does this man value reputation? But he knows how high we prize it; he knows we would rather die than make these letters public; and do you suppose he would not trade upon the knowledge? What you call your sword, Mr Mackellar, and which had been one indeed against a man of any remnant of propriety, would have been but a sword of paper against him. He would smile in your face at such a threat. He stands upon his degradation, he makes that his strength: it is in vain to struggle with such characters.' She cried out this last a little desperately, and then with more quiet: 'No, Mr Mackellar; I have thought upon this matter all night, and there is no way out of it. Papers or no papers, the door of this house stands open for him; he is the rightful heir, forsooth! If we sought to exclude him, all would redound against poor Henry, and I should see him stoned again upon the streets. Ah! if Henry dies, it is a different matter! They have broke the entail for their own good purposes; the estate goes to my daughter; and I shall see who sets a foot upon it. But if Henry lives, my poor Mr Mackellar, and that man returns, we must suffer: only this time it will be together.'

On the whole I was well pleased with Mrs Henry's attitude of mind; nor could I even deny there was some cogency in that which she advanced about the papers.

'Let us say no more about it,' said I. 'I can only be sorry I trusted a lady with the originals, which was an unbusinesslike proceeding at the best. As for what I said of leaving the service of the family, it was spoken with the tongue only; and you may set your mind at rest. I belong to Durrisdeer, Mrs Henry, as if I had been born there.'

I must do her the justice to say she seemed perfectly relieved; so that we began this morning, as we were to continue for so many years, on a proper ground of mutual indulgence and respect.

The same day, which was certainly prededicate to joy, we observed the first signal of recovery in Mr Henry; and about three of the following afternoon he found his mind again, recognizing me by name with the strongest evidences of affection. Mrs Henry was also in the room, at the bed-foot; but it did not appear that he observed her. And indeed (the fever being gone) he was so weak that he made but the one effort and sank again into a lethargy. The course of his restoration was now slow, but equal; every day his appetite improved; every week we were able to remark an increase both of strength and flesh; and before the end of the month he was out of bed and had even begun to be carried in his chair upon the terrace.

It was perhaps at this time that Mrs Henry and I were the most uneasy in mind. Apprehension for his days was at an end; and a worse fear succeeded. Every day we drew consciously nearer to the day of reckoning; and the days passed on, and still there was nothing. Mr Henry bettered in strength, he held long talks with us on a great diversity of subjects, his father came and sat with him and went again; and still there was no reference to the late tragedy or to the former troubles which had brought it on. Did he remember, and conceal his dreadful knowledge? or was the whole blotted from his mind? This was the problem that kept us watching and trembling all day when we were in his company and held us awake at night when we were in our lonely beds. We knew not even which alternative to hope for, both appearing so unnatural and pointing so directly to an unsound brain. Once this fear offered, I observed his conduct with sedulous particularity. Something of the child he exhibited: a cheerfulness quite foreign to his previous character, an interest readily aroused, and then very tenacious, in small matters which he had heretofore despised. When he was stricken down, I was his only confidant, and I may say his only friend, and he was on terms of division with his wife; upon his recovery, all was changed, the past forgotten, the wife first and even single in his thoughts. He turned to her with all his emotions, like a child to its mother, and seemed secure of sympathy; called her in all his needs with something of that querulous familiarity that marks a certainty of indulgence; and I must say, in justice to the woman, he was never disappointed. To her, indeed, this changed behaviour was inexpressibly affecting; and I think she felt it secretly as a reproach; so that I have seen her, in early days, escape out of the room that she might indulge herself in weeping. But to me the change appeared not natural; and viewing it along with all the rest, I began to wonder, with many head-shakings, whether his reason was perfectly erect.

As this doubt stretched over many years, endured indeed until my master's death, and clouded all our subsequent relations, I may well consider of it more at large. When he was able to resume some charge of his affairs, I had many opportunities to try him with precision. There was no lack of understanding, nor yet of authority; but the old continuous interest had quite departed; he grew readily fatigued, and fell to yawning; and he carried into money relations, where it is certainly out of place, a facility that bordered upon slackness. True, since we had no longer the exactions of the Master to contend against, there was the less occasion to raise strictness into principle or do battle for a farthing. True, again, there was nothing excessive in these relaxations, or I would have been no party to them. But the whole thing marked a change, very slight yet very perceptible; and though no man could say my master had gone at all out of his mind, no man could deny that he had drifted from his character. It was the same to the end, with his manner and appearance. Some of the heat of the fever lingered in his veins: his movements a little hurried, his speech notably more voluble, yet neither truly amiss. His whole mind stood open to happy impressions, welcoming these and making much of them; but the smallest suggestion of trouble or sorrow he received with visible impatience and dismissed again with immediate relief. It was to this temper that he owed the felicity of his later days; and yet here it was, if anywhere, that you could call the man insane. A great part of this life consists in contemplating what we cannot cure; but Mr Henry, if he could not dismiss solicitude by an effort of the mind, must instantly and at whatever cost annihilate the cause of it; so that he played alternately the ostrich and the bull. It is to this strenuous cowardice of pain that I have to set down all the unfortunate and excessive steps of his subsequent career. Certainly this was the reason of his beating M'Manus, the groom, a thing so much out of all his former practice, and which awakened so much comment at the time. It is to this, again, that I must lay the total loss of near upon two hundred pounds, more than the half of which I could have saved if his impatience would have suffered me. But he preferred loss or any desperate extreme to a continuance of mental suffering.

All this has led me far from our immediate trouble: whether he remembered or had forgotten his late dreadful act; and if he remembered, in what light he viewed it. The truth burst upon us suddenly, and was indeed one of the chief surprises of my life. He had been several times abroad, and was now beginning to walk a little with an arm, when it chanced I should be left alone with him upon the terrace. He turned to me with a singular furtive smile, such as schoolboys use when in fault; and says he, in a private whisper and without the least preface: 'Where have you buried him?'

I could not make one sound in answer.

'Where have you buried him?' he repeated. 'I want to see his grave.'

I conceived I had best take the bull by the horns. 'Mr Henry,' said I, 'I have news to give that will rejoice you exceedingly. In all human likelihood, your hands are clear of blood. I reason from certain indices; and by these it should appear your brother was not dead, but was carried in a swound on board the lugger. But now he may be perfectly recovered.'

What there was in his countenance I could not read. 'James?' he asked.

'Your brother James,' I answered. 'I would not raise a hope that may be found deceptive, but in my heart I think it very probable he is alive.'

'Ah!' says Mr Henry; and suddenly rising from his seat with more alacrity than he had yet discovered, set one finger on my breast, and cried at me in a kind of screaming whisper, 'Mackellar' – these were his words – 'nothing can kill that man. He is not mortal. He is bound upon my back to all eternity – to all God's eternity!' says he, and, sitting down again, fell upon a stubborn silence.

A day or two after, with the same secret smile, and first looking about as if to be sure we were alone, 'Mackellar,' said he, 'when you have any intelligence, be sure and let me know. We must keep an eye upon him, or he will take us when we least expect.'

'He will not show his face here again,' said I.

'Oh yes he will,' said Mr Henry. 'Wherever I am, there will he be.' And again he looked all about him.

'You must not dwell upon this thought, Mr Henry,' said I.

'No,' said he, 'that is a very good advice. We will never think of it, except when you have news. And we do not know yet,' he added; 'he may be dead.'

The manner of his saying this convinced me thoroughly of what I had scarce ventured to suspect: that, so far from suffering any penitence for the attempt, he did but lament his failure. This was a discovery I kept to myself, fearing it might do him a prejudice with his wife. But I might have saved myself the trouble; she had divined it for herself, and found the sentiment quite natural. Indeed, I could not but say that there were three of us, all of the same mind; nor could any news have reached Durrisdeer more generally welcome than tidings of the Master's death.

This brings me to speak of the exception, my old lord. As soon as my anxiety for my own master began to be relaxed, I was aware of a change in the old gentleman, his father, that seemed to threaten mortal consequences. His face was pale and swollen; as he sat in the chimneyside with his Latin, he would drop off sleeping and the book roll in the ashes; some days he would drag his foot, others stumble in speaking. The amenity of his behaviour appeared more extreme; full of excuses for the least trouble, very thoughtful for all; to myself, of a most flattering civility. One day, that he had sent for his lawyer and remained a long while private, he met me as he was crossing the hall with painful footsteps and took me kindly by the hand, 'Mr Mackellar,' said he, 'I have had many occasions to set a proper value on your services; and today, when I recast my will, I have taken the freedom to name you for one of my executors. I believe you bear love enough to our house to render me this service.' At that very time he passed the greater portion of his days in slumber, from which it was often difficult to rouse him; seemed to have lost all count of years, and had several times (particularly on waking) called for his wife and for an old servant whose very gravestone was now green with moss. If I had been put to my oath, I must have declared he was incapable of testing; and yet there was never a will drawn more sensible in every trait, or showing a more excellent judgment both of persons and affairs.

His dissolution, though it took not very long, proceeded by infinitesimal gradations. His faculties decayed together steadily; the power of his limbs was almost gone, he was extremely deaf, his speech had sunk into mere mumblings; and yet to the end he managed to discover something of his former courtesy and kindness, pressing the hand of any that helped him, presenting me with one of his Latin books, in which he had laboriously traced my name, and in a thousand ways reminding us of the greatness of that loss which it might almost be said we had already suffered. To the end, the power of articulation returned to him in flashes; it seemed he had only forgotten the art of speech as a child forgets his lesson, and at times he would call some part of it to mind. On the last night of his life he suddenly broke silence with these words from Virgil: 'Gnatique patrisque, alma, precor, miserere,' perfectly uttered, and with a fitting accent. At the sudden clear sound of it we started from our several occupations; but it was in vain we turned to him; he sat there silent, and, to all appearance, fatuous. A little later he was had to bed with more difficulty than ever before; and some time in the night, without any mortal violence, his spirit fled.

At a far later period I chanced to speak of these particulars with a doctor of medicine, a man of so high a reputation that I scruple to adduce his name. By his view of it father and son both suffered from the same affection: the father from the strain of his unnatural sorrows – the son perhaps in the excitation of the fever; each had ruptured a vessel in the brain, and there was probably (my doctor added) some predisposition in the family to accidents of that description. The father sank, the son recovered all the externals of a healthy man; but it is like there was some destruction in those delicate tissues where the soul resides and does her earthly business; her heavenly, I would fain hope, cannot be thus obstructed by material accidents. And yet, upon a more mature opinion, it matters not one jot; for He who shall pass judgment on the records of our life is the same that formed us in frailty.

The death of my old lord was the occasion of a fresh surprise to us who watched the behaviour of his successor. To any considering mind, the two sons had between them slain their father, and he who took the sword might be even said to have slain him with his hand; but no such thought appeared to trouble my new lord. He was becomingly grave; I could scarce say sorrowful, or only with a pleasant sorrow; talking of the dead with a regretful cheerfulness, relating old examples of his character, smiling at them with a good conscience; and when the day of the funeral came round, doing the honours with exact propriety. I could perceive, besides, that he found a solid gratification in his accession to the title: the which he was punctilious in exacting.

And now there came upon the scene a new character, and one that played his part, too, in the story; I mean the present lord, Alexander, whose birth (17th July, 1757) filled the cup of my poor master's happiness. There was nothing then left him to wish for; nor yet leisure to wish for it. Indeed, there never was a parent so fond and doting as he showed himself. He was continually uneasy in his son's absence. Was the child abroad? the father would be watching the clouds in case it rained. Was it night? he would rise out of his bed to observe its slumbers. His conversation grew even wearyful to strangers, since he talked of little but his son. In matters relating to the estate, all was designed with a particular eye to Alexander; and it would be: 'Let us put it in hand at once, that the wood may be grown against Alexander's majority'; or 'This will fall in again handsomely for Alexander's marriage.' Every day this absorption of the man's nature became more observable, with many touching and some very blame-worthy particulars. Soon the child could walk abroad with him, at first on the terrace, hand in hand, and afterwards at large about the policies; and this grew to be my lord's chief occupation. The sound of their two voices (audible a great way off, for they spoke loud) became familiar in the neighbourhood; and for my part I found it more agreeable than the sound of birds. It was pretty to see the pair returning, full of briers, and the father as flushed and sometimes as bemuddied as the child, for they were equal sharers in all sorts of boyish entertainment, digging in the beach, damming of streams, and what not; and I have seen them gaze through a fence at cattle with the same childish contemplation.

The mention of these rambles brings me to a strange scene of which I was a witness. There was one walk I never followed myself without emotion, so often had I gone there upon miserable errands, so much had there befallen against the house of Durriseer. But the path lay handy from all points beyond the Muckle Ross; and I was driven, although much against my will, to take my use of it perhaps once in the two months. It befell when Mr Alexander was of the age of six or seven, I had some business on the far side in the morning, and entered the shrubbery, on my homeward way, about nine of a bright forenoon. It was that time of year when the woods are all in their spring colours, the thorns all in flower, and the birds in the high season of their singing. In contrast to this merriment, the shrubbery was only the more sad, and I the more oppressed by its associations. In this situation of spirit it struck me disagreeably to hear voices a little way in front, and to recognize the tones of my lord and Mr Alexander. I pushed ahead, and came presently into their view. They stood together in the open space where the duel was, my lord with his hand on his son's shoulder, and speaking with some gravity. At least, as he raised his head upon my coming, I thought I could perceive his countenance to lighten.

'Ah!' says he, 'here comes the good Mackellar. I have just been telling Sandie the story of this place, and how there was a man whom the devil tried to kill, and how near he came to kill the devil instead.'

I had thought it strange enough he should bring the child into that scene; that he should actually be discoursing of his act, passed measure. But the worst was yet to come; for he added, turning to his son, – 'You can ask Mackellar; he was here and saw it.'

'Did you really see the devil?' asked the child.

'I have not heard the tale,' I replied; 'and I am in a press of business.' So far I said, sourly, fencing with the embarrassment of the position; and suddenly the bitterness of the past, and the terror of that scene by candlelight, rushed in upon my mind. I bethought me that, for a difference of a second's quickness in parade, the child before me might have never seen the day; and the emotion that always fluttered round my heart in that dark shrubbery burst forth in words. 'But so much is true,' I cried, 'that I have met the devil in these woods, and seen him foiled here. Blessed be God that we escaped with life – blessed be God that one stone yet stands upon another in the walls of Durrisdeer! And, oh! Mr Alexander, if every you come by this spot, thought it was a hundred years hence, and you came with the gayest and the highest in the land, I would step aside and remember a bit prayer.'

My lord bowed his head gravely. 'Ah!' says he, 'Mackellar is always in the right. Come, Alexander, take your bonnet off.' And with that he uncovered, and held out his hand. 'O Lord,' says he, 'I thank Thee, and my son thanks Thee, for Thy manifold great mercies. Let us have peace for a little; defend us from the evil man. Smite him, O Lord, upon the lying mouth!' The last broke out of him like a cry; and at that, whether remembered anger choked his utterance, or whether he perceived this was a singular sort of prayer, at least he suddenly came to a full stop; and, after a moment, set back his hat upon his head.

'I think you have forgot a word, my lord,' said I. '"Forgive us our trespasses, as we forgive them that trespass against us. For thine is the kingdom, and the power, and the glory, for ever and ever. Amen."'

'Ah! that is easy saying,' said my lord. 'That is very easy saying, Mackellar. But for me to forgive! – I think I would cut a very silly figure if I had the affectation to pretend it.'

'The bairn, my lord!' said I, with some severity, for I thought his expressions little fitted for the ears of children.

'Why, very true,' said he. 'This is dull work for a bairn. Let's go nesting.'

I forget if it was the same day, but it was soon after, my lord, finding me alone, opened himself a little more on the same head.

'Mackellar,' he said, 'I am now a very happy man.'

'I think so indeed, my lord,' said I, 'and the sight of it gives me a light heart.'

'There is an obligation in happiness – do you not think so?' says he, musingly.

'I think so indeed,' says I, 'and one in sorrow, too. If we are not here to try to do the best, in my humble opinion the sooner we are away the better for all parties.'

'Ay, but if you were in my shoes, would you forgive him?' asks my lord.

The suddenness of the attack a little gravelled me. 'It is a duty laid upon us strictly,' said I.

'Hut!' said he. 'These are expressions! Do you forgive the man yourself?'

'Well – no!' said I. 'God forgive me, I do not.'

'Shake hands upon that!' cries my lord, with a kind of joviality.

'It is an ill sentiment to shake hands upon,' said I, 'for Christian people. I think I will give you mine on some more evangelical occasion.'

This I said, smiling a little; but as for my lord, he went from the room laughing aloud.

For my lord's slavery to the child, I can find no expression adequate. He lost himself in that continual thought: business, friends, and wife being all alike forgotten, or only remembered with a painful effort, like that of one struggling with a posset. It was most notable in the matter of his wife. Since I had known Durrisdeer, she had been the burthen of his thought and the loadstone of his eyes; and now she was quite cast out. I have seen him come to the door of a room, look round, and pass my lady over as though she were a dog before the fire. It would be Alexander he was seeking, and my lady knew it well. I have heard him speak to her so ruggedly that I nearly found it in my heart to intervene: the cause would still be the same, that she had in some way thwarted Alexander. Without doubt this was in the nature of a judgment upon my lady. Without doubt she had the tables turned upon her, as only Providence can do it; she who had been cold so many years to every mark of tenderness, it was her part now to be neglected.

An odd situation resulted: that we had once more two parties in the house, and that now I was of my lady's. Not that ever I lost the love I bore my master. But, for one thing, he had the less use for my society. For another, I could not but compare the case of Mr Alexander with that of Miss Katharine; for whom my lord had never found the least attention. And for a third, I was wounded by the change he discovered to his wife, which struck me in the nature of an infidelity. I could not but admire, besides, the constancy and kindness she displayed. Perhaps her sentiment to my lord, as it had been founded from the first in pity, was that rather of a mother than of a wife; perhaps it pleased her – if I may so say – to behold her two children so happy in each other; the more as one had suffered so unjustly in the past. But for all that, and though I could never trace in her one spark of jealousy, she must fall back for society on poor neglected Miss Katharine; and I, on my part, came to pass my spare hours more and more with the mother and daughter. It would be easy to make too much of this division, for it was a pleasant family, as families go; still the thing existed; whether my lord knew it or not, I am in doubt. I do not think he did; he was bound up so entirely in his son; but the rest of us knew it, and in a manner suffered from the knowledge.

What troubled us most, however, was the great and growing danger to the child. My lord was his father over again; it was to be feared the son would prove a second Master. Time has proved these fears to have been quite exaggerate. Certainly there is no more worthy gentleman today in Scotland than the seventh Lord Durrisdeer. Of my own exodus from his employment it does not become me to speak, above all in a memorandum written only to justify his father. . . .

[Editor's Note. Five pages of Mr Mackellar's MS are her omitted. I have gathered from their perusal an impression that Mr Mackellar, in his old age, was rather an exacting servant. Against the seventh Lord Durrisdeer (with whom, at any rate, we have no concern) nothing material is alleged. – R. L. S.]

... But our fear at the time was lest he should turn out, in the person of his son, a second edition of his brother. My lady had tried to interject some wholesome discipline; she had been glad to give that up, and now looked on with secret dismay; sometimes she even spoke of it by hints; and sometimes, when there was brought to her knowledge some monstrous instance of my lord's indulgence, she would betray herself in a gesture or perhaps an exclamation. As for myself, I was haunted by the thought both day and night: not so much for the child's sake as for the father's. The man had gone to sleep, he was dreaming a dream, and any rough wakening must infallibly prove mortal. That he should survive the child's death was inconceivable; and the fear of its dishonour made me cover my face.

It was this continual preoccupation that screwed me up at last to a remonstrance; a matter worthy to be narrated in detail. My lord and I sat one day at the same table upon some tedious business of detail; I have said that he had lost his former interest in such occupations; he was plainly itching to be gone, and he looked fretful, weary, and methought older than I had ever previously observed. I suppose it was the haggard face that put me suddenly upon my enterprise.

'My lord,' said I, with my head down, and feigning to continue my occupation – 'or, rather, let me call you again by the name of Mr Henry, for I fear your anger and want you to think upon old times——'

'My good Mackellar!' said he; and that in tones so kindly that I had near forsook my purpose. But I called to mind that I was speaking for his good, and stuck to my colours.

'Has it never come in upon your mind what you are doing?' I asked.

'What I am doing?' he repeated. 'I was never good at guessing riddles.'

'What you are doing with your son?' said I.

'Well,' said he, with some defiance in his tone, 'and what am I doing with my son?'

'Your father was a very good man,' says I, straying from the direct path. 'But do you think he was a wise father?'

There was a pause before he spoke, and then: 'I say nothing against him,' he replied. 'I had the most cause perhaps; but I say nothing.'

'Why, there it is,' said I. 'You had the cause at least. And yet your father was a good man; I never knew a better, save on the one point, nor yet a wiser. Where he stumbled, it is highly possible another man should fall. He had the two sons——'

My lord rapped suddenly and violently on the table.

'What is this?' cried he. 'Speak out!'

'I will, then,' said I, my voice almost strangled with the thumping of my heart. 'If you continue to indulge Mr Alexander, you are following in your father's footsteps. Beware, my lord, lest (when he grows up) your son should follow in the Master's.'

I had never meant to put the thing so crudely; but in the extreme of fear there comes a brutal kind of courage, the most brutal indeed of all; and I burnt my ships with that plain word. I never had the answer. When I lifted my head, my lord had risen to his feet, and the next moment he fell heavily on the floor. The fit or seizure endured not very long; he came to himself vacantly, put his hand to his head, which I was then supporting, and says he, in a broken voice: 'I have been ill,' and a little after: 'Help me.' I got him to his feet, and he stood pretty well, though he kept hold of the table. 'I have been ill, Mackellar,' he said again. 'Something broke, Mackellar – or was going to break, and then all swam away. I think I was very angry. Never mind, Mackellar; never you mind, my man. I wouldnae hurt a hair upon your head. Too much has come and gone. It's a certain thing between us two. But I think, Mackellar, I will go to Mrs Henry – I think I will go to Mrs Henry.' said he, and got pretty steadily from the room, leaving me overcome with penitence.

Presently the door flew open, and my lady swept in with flashing eyes. 'What is all this?' she cried. 'What have you done to my husband? Will nothing teach you your position in this house? Will you never cease from making and meddling?'

'My lady,' said I, 'since I have been in this house I have had plenty of hard words. For a while they were my daily diet, and I swallowed them all. As for today, you may call me what you please; you will never find the name hard enough for such a blunder. And yet I meant it for the best.'

I told her all with ingenuity, even as it is written here; and when she had heard me out she pondered, and I could see her animosity fall. 'Yes,' she said, 'you meant well indeed. I have had the same thought myself, or the same temptation rather, which makes me pardon you. But, dear God, can you not understand that he can bear no more? He can bear no more!' she cried. 'The cord is stretched to snapping. What matters the future if he have one or two good days?'

'Amen,' said I. 'I will meddle no more. I am pleased enough that you should recognize the kindness of my meaning.'

'Yes,' said my lady; 'but when it came to the point, I have to suppose your courage failed you; for what you said was said cruelly.' She paused, looking at me; then suddenly smiled a little and said a singular thing: 'Do you know what you are, Mr Mackellar? You are an old maid.'

No more incident of any note occurred in the family until the return of that ill-starred man the Master. But I have to place here a second extract from the memoirs of Chevalier Burke, interesting in itself, and highly necessary for my purpose. It is our only sight of the Master on his Indian travels; and the first word in these pages of Secundra Dass. One fact, it is to observe, appears here very clearly, which if we had known some twenty years ago, how many calamities and sorrows had been spared! – that Secundra Dass spoke English.

CHAPTER SEVEN

Adventure of Chevalier Burke in India
Extracted from his Memoirs

... HERE WAS I, THEREFORE, on the street of that city, the name of which I cannot call to mind, while even then I was so ill-acquainted with its situation that I knew not whether to go south or north. The alert being sudden, I had run forth without shoes or stockings; my hat had been struck from my head in the mellay; my kit was in the hands of the English; I had no companion but the cipaye, no weapon but my sword, and the devil a coin in my pocket. In short, I was for all the world like one of those calendars with whom Mr Galland has made us acquainted in his elegant tales. These gentlemen, you will remember, were for ever falling in with extraordinary incidents; and I was myself upon the brink of one so astonishing that I protest I cannot explain it to this day.

The cipaye was a very honest man; he had served many years with the French colours, and would have let himself be cut to pieces for any of the brave countrymen of Mr Lally. It is the same fellow (his name has quite escaped me) of whom I have narrated already a surprising instance of generosity of mind – when he found Mr de Fessac and myself upon the ramparts, entirely overcome with liquor, and covered us with straw while the commandant was passing by. I consulted him, therefore, with perfect freedom. It was a fine question what to do; but we decided at last to escalade a garden wall, where we could certainly sleep in the shadow of the trees, and might perhaps find an occasion to get hold of a pair of slippers and a turban. In that part of the city we had only the difficulty of the choice, for it was a quarter consisting entirely of walled gardens, and the lanes which divided them were at that hour of the night deserted. I gave the cipaye a back, and we had soon dropped into a large enclosure full of trees. The place was soaking with dew, which, in that country is exceedingly unwholesome, above all to whites; yet my fatigue was so extreme that I was already half asleep, when the cipaye recalled me to my senses. In the far end of the enclosure a bright light had suddenly shone out, and continued to burn steadily among the leaves. It was a circumstance highly unusual in such a place and hour; and, in our situation, it behoved us to proceed with some timidity. The cipaye was sent to reconnoitre, and pretty soon returned with the intelligence that we had fallen extremely amiss, for the house belonged to a white man, who was in all likelihood English.

'Faith,' says I, 'if there is a white man to be seen, I will have a look at him; for, the Lord be praised! there are more sorts than the one!'

The cipaye led me forward accordingly to a place from which I had a clear view upon the house. It was surrounded with a wide verandah; a lamp, very well trimmed, stood upon the floor of it, and on either side of the lamp there sat a man, crosslegged, after the Oriental manner. Both, besides, were bundled up in muslin like two natives; and yet one of them was not only a white man, but a man very well known to me and the reader, being indeed that very Master of Ballantrae of whose gallantry and genius I have had to speak so often. Word had reached me that he was come to the Indies, though we had never met at least, and I head little of his occupations. But, sure, I had no sooner recognized him, and found myself in the arms of so old a comrade, than I supposed my tribulations were quite done. I stepped plainly forth into the light of the moon, which shone exceeding strong, and hailing Ballantrae by name, made him in a few words master of my grievous situation. He turned, started the least thing in the world, looked me fair in the face while I was speaking, and when I had done addressed himself to his companion in the barbarous native dialect. The second person, who was of an extraordinary delicate appearance, with legs like walking canes and fingers like the stalk of a tobacco pipe,* now rose to his feet.

'The Sahib,' says he, 'understands no English language. I understand it myself, and I see you make some small mistake – oh! which may happen very often. But the Sahib would be glad to know how you come in a garden.'

'Ballantrae!' I cried, 'have you the damned impudence to deny me to my face.'

Ballantrae never moved a muscle, staring at me like an image in a pagoda.

'The Sahib understands no English language,' says the native, as glib as before. 'He be glad to know how you come in a garden.'

'Oh! the divil fetch him,' says I. 'He would be glad to know how I come in a garden, would he? Well, now, my dear man, just have the civility to tell the Sahib, with my kind love, that we are two soldiers here whom he never met and never heard of, but the cipaye is a broth of a boy, and I am a broth of a boy myself; and if we don't get a full meal of meat, and a turban, and slippers, and the value of a gold mohur in small change as a matter of convenience, bedad, my friend, I could lay my finger on a garden where there is going to be trouble.'

They carried their comedy so far as to converse awhile in Hindustanee; and then says the Hindu, with the same smile, but sighing as if he were tired of the repetition, 'The Sahib would be glad to know how you come in a garden.'

'Is that the way of it?' says I, and laying my hand on my sword-hilt I bade the cipaye draw.

Ballantrae's Hindu, still smiling, pulled out a pistol from his bosom, and though Ballantrae himself never moved a muscle I knew him well enough to be sure he was prepared.

'The Sahib thinks you better go away,' says the Hindu.

Well, to be plain, it was what I was thinking myself; for the report of a pistol would have, under Providence, the means of hanging the pair of us.

'Tell the Sahib I consider him no gentleman,' says I, and turned away with a gesture of contempt.

I was not gone three steps when the voice of the Hindu called me back. 'The Sahib would be glad to know if you are a dam low Irishman,' says he; and at the words Ballantrae smiled and bowed very low.

'What is that?' says I.

'The Sahib say you ask your friend Mackellar,' says the Hindu. 'The Sahib he cry quits.'

*Note by Mr Mackellar. – Plainly Secundra Dass. – E. McK.

'Tell the Sahib I will give him a cure for the Scots fiddle when next we meet,' cried I.

The pair were still smiling as I left.

There is little doubt some flaws may be picked in my own behaviour; and when a man, however gallant, appeals to posterity with an account of his exploits, he must almost certainly expect to share the fate of Caesar and Alexander, and to meet with some detractors. But there is one thing that can never be laid at the door of Francis Burke: he never turned his back on a friend. . . .

(Here follows a passage which the Chevalier Burke has been at the pains to delete before sending me his manuscript. Doubtless it was some very natural complaint of what he supposed to be an indiscretion on my part; though, indeed, I can call none to mind. Perhaps Mr Henry was less guarded; or it is just possible the Master found the means to examine my correspondence, and himself read the letter from Troyes: in revenge for which this cruel jest was perpetrated on Mr Burke in his extreme necessity. The Master, for all his wickedness, was not without some natural affection; I believe he was sincerely attached to Mr Burke in the beginning; but the thought of treachery dried up the springs of his very shallow friendship, and his detestable nature appeared naked. – E. McK.)

CHAPTER EIGHT

The Enemy in the House

IT IS A STRANGE THING THAT I should be at a stick for a date – the date, besides, of an incident that changed the very nature of my life, and sent us all into foreign lands. But the truth is, I was stricken out of all my habitudes, and find my journals very ill redd-up, * the day not indicated sometimes for a week or two together, and the whole fashion of the thing like that of a man near desperate. It was late in March at least, or early in April, 1764. I had slept heavily, and awakened with a premonition of some evil to befall. So strong was this upon my spirit that I hurried downstairs in my shirt and breeches, and my hand (I remember) shook upon the rail. It was a cold, sunny morning, with a thick white frost; the blackbirds sang exceeding sweet and loud about the house of Durrisdeer, and there was a noise of the sea in all the chambers. As I came by the doors of the hall, another sound arrested me – of voices talking. I drew nearer, and stood like a man dreaming. Here was certainly a human voice, and that in my own master's house, and yet I knew it not; certainly human speech, and that in my native land; and yet, listen as I pleased, I could not catch one syllable. An old tale started up in my mind of a fairy wife (or perhaps only a wandering stranger), that came to the place of my fathers some generations

* Ordered.

back, and stayed the matter of a week, talking often in a tongue that signified nothing to the hearers; and went again, as she had come, under cloud of night, leaving not so much as a name behind her. A little fear I had but more curiosity; and I opened the hall-door and entered.

The supper-things still lay upon the table; the shutters were still closed, although day peeped in the divisions; and the great room was lighted only with a single taper and the shining of the fire. Close in the chimney sat two men. The one that was wrapped in a cloak and wore boots, I knew at once: it was the bird of ill-omen back again. Of the other, who was set close to the red embers, and made up into a bundle like a mummy, I could but see that he was an alien, of a darker hue than any man of Europe, very frailly built, with a singular tall forehead, and a secret eye. Several bundles and a small valise were on the floor; and to judge by the smallness of this luggage, and by the condition of the Master's boots, grossly patched by some unscrupulous country cobbler, evil had not prospered.

He rose upon my entrance; our eyes crossed; and I know not why it should have been, but my courage rose like a lark on a May morning.

'Ha!' said I, 'is this you?' – and I was pleased with the unconcern of my own voice.

'It is even myself, worthy Mackellar,' says the Master.

'This time you have brought the black dog visibly upon your back,' I continued.

'Referring to Secundra Dass?' asked the Master. 'Let me present you. He is a native gentleman of India.'

'Hum!' said I. 'I am no great lover of you or your friends, Mr Bally. But I will let a little daylight in, and have a look at you.' And so saying, I undid the shutters of the eastern window.

By the light of the morning I could perceive the man was changed. Later, when we were all together, I was more struck to see how lightly time had dealt with him; but the first glance was otherwise.

'You are getting an old man,' said I.

A shade came upon his face. 'If you could see yourself,' said he, 'you would perhaps not dwell upon the topic.'

'Hut!' I returned, 'old age is nothing to me. I think I have been always old; and I am now, I thank God, better known and more respected. It is not everyone that can say that, Mr Bally! The lines in *your* brow are calamities: your life begins to close in upon you like a prison; death will soon be rapping at the door: and I see not from what source you are to draw your consolations.'

Here the Master addressed himself to Secundra Dass in Hindustanee, from which I gathered (I freely confess, with a high degree of pleasure) that my remarks annoyed him. All this while, you may be sure, my mind had been busy upon other matters, even while I rallied my enemy; and chiefly as to how I should communicate secretly and quickly with my lord. To this, in the breathing-space now given me, I turned all the forces of my mind; when, suddenly shifting my eyes, I was aware of the man himself standing in the doorway, and, to all appearance, quite composed. He had no sooner met my looks than he stepped across the threshold. The Master heard him coming, and advanced upon the other side; about four feet apart, these brothers came to a full pause, and stood exchanging steady looks, and then my lord smiled, bowed a little forward, and turned briskly away.

'Mackellar,' says he, 'we must see to breakfast for these travellers.'

It was plain the Master was a trifle disconcerted; but he assumed the more impudence of speech and manner. 'I am as hungry as a hawk,' says he. 'Let it be something good, Henry.'

My lord turned to him with the same hard smile. 'Lord Durrisdeer, says he.

'Oh! never in the family,' returned the Master.

'Everyone in this house renders me my proper title,' says my lord. 'If it please you to make an exception, I will leave you to consider what appearance it will bear to strangers, and whether it may not be translated as an effect of impotent jealousy.'

I could have clapped my hands together with delight: the more so as my lord left no time for any answer, but bidding me with a sign to follow him, went straight out of the hall.

'Come quick,' says he; 'we have to sweep vermin from the house.' And he sped through the passages, with so swift a step that I could scarce keep up with him, straight to the door of John Paul, the which he opened without summons and walked in. John was, to all appearance, sound asleep, but my lord made no pretence of waking him.

'John Paul,' said he, speaking as quietly as ever I heard him, 'you served my father long, or I would pack you from the house like a dog. If in half an hour's time I find you gone, you shall continue to receive your wages in Edinburgh. If you linger here or in St Bride's – old man, old servant, and altogether – I shall find some very astonishing way to make you smart for your disloyalty. Up and begone. The door you let them in by will serve for your departure. I do not choose my son shall see your face again.'

'I am rejoiced to find you bear the thing so quietly,' said I, when we were forth again by ourselves.

'Quietly?' cries he, and put my hand suddenly against his heart, which struck upon his bosom like a sledge.

At this revelation I was filled with wonder and fear. There was no constitution could bear so violent a strain – his least of all, that was unhinged already; and I decided in my mind that we must bring this monstrous situation to an end.

'It would be well, I think, if I took word to my lady,' said I. Indeed, he should have gone himself, but I counted – not in vain – on his indifference.

'Ay,' says he, 'do. I will hurry breakfast: we must all appear at the table, even Alexander; it must appear we are untroubled.'

I ran to my lady's room, and with no preparatory cruelty disclosed my news.

'My mind was long ago made up,' said she. 'We must make our packets secretly today, and leave secretly tonight. Thank heaven, we have another house! The first ship that sails shall bear us to New York.'

'And what of him?' I asked.

'We leave him Durrisdeer,' she cried. 'Let him work his pleasure upon that.'

'Not so, by your leave,' said I. 'There shall be a dog at his heels that can hold fast. Bed he shall have, and board, and a horse to ride upon, if he behave himself; but the keys – if you think well of it, my lady – shall be left in the hands of one Mackellar. There will be good care taken; trust him for that.'

'Mr Mackellar,' she cried, 'I thank you for that thought. All shall be left in your hands. If we must go into a savage country, I bequeath it to you to take our vengeance. Send Macconochie to St Bride's to arrange privately for horses and to call the lawyer. My lord must leave procuration.'

At that moment my lord came to the door, and we opened our plan to him.

'I will never hear of it,' he cried; 'he would think I feared him. I will stay in my own house, please God, until I die. There lives not the man can beard me out of it. Once and for all, here I am, and here I stay, in spite of all the devils in hell.' I can give no idea of the vehemency of his words and utterance; but we both stood aghast, and I in particular, who had been a witness of his former self-restraint.

My lady looked at me with an appeal that went to my heart and recalled me to my wits. I made her a private sign to go, and when my lord and I were alone, went up to him where he was racing to and fro in one end of the room like a half-lunatic, and set my hand firmly on his shoulder.

'My lord,' says I, 'I am going to be the plain-dealer once more; if for the last time, so much the better, for I am grown weary of the part.'

'Nothing will change me,' he answered. 'God forbid I should refuse to hear you; but nothing will change me.' This he said firmly, with no signal of the former violence, which already raised my hopes.

'Very well,' said I. 'I can afford to waste my breath.' I pointed to a chair, and he sat down and looked at me. 'I can remember a time when my lady very much neglected you,' said I.

'I never spoke of it while it lasted,' returned my lord, with a high flush of colour; 'and it is all changed now.'

'Do you know how much?' I said. 'Do you know how much it is all changed? The tables are turned, my lord! It is my lady that now courts you for a word, a look – ay, and courts you in vain. Do you know with whom she passes her days while you are out gallivanting in the policies? My lord, she is glad to pass them with a certain dry old grieve* of the name of Ephraim Mackellar; and I think you may be able to remember what that means, for I am the more in a mistake or you were once driven to the same company yourself.'

'Mackellar!' cried my lord, getting to his feet. 'O my God, Mackellar!'

'It is neither the name of Mackellar nor the name of God that can change the truth,' said I; 'and I am telling you the fact. Now for you, that suffered so much, to deal out the same suffering to another, is that the part of any Christian? But you are so swallowed up in your new friend that the old are all forgotten. They are all clean vanished from your memory. And yet they stood by you at the darkest; my lady not the least. And does my lady ever cross your mind? Does it ever cross your mind what she went through that night? – or what manner of a wife she has been to you thenceforward? – or in what kind of a position she finds herself today? Never. It is your pride to stay and face him out, and she must stay along with you. Oh! my lord's pride – that's the great affair! And yet she is the woman, and you are a great hulking man! She is the woman that you swore to protect; and, more betoken, the own mother of that son of yours!'

'You are speaking very bitterly, Mackellar,' said he; 'but, the Lord knows, I fear you are speaking very true. I have not proved worthy of my happiness. Bring my lady back.'

*Land steward.

My lady was waiting near at hand to learn the issue. When I brought her in, my lord took a hand of each of us, and laid them both upon his bosom. 'I have had two friends in my life,' said he. 'All the comfort ever I had, it came from one or other. When you two are in a mind, I think I would be an ungrateful dog——' He shut his mouth very hard, and looked on us with swimming eyes. 'Do what ye like with me,' says he, 'only don't think——' He stopped again. 'Do what ye please with me: God knows I love and honour you.' And dropping our two hands, he turned his back and went and gazed out of the window. But my lady ran after, calling his name, and threw herself upon his neck in a passion of weeping.

I went out and shut the door behind me, and stood and thanked God from the bottom of my heart.

At the breakfast board, according to my lord's design, we were all met. The Master had by that time plucked off his patched boots and made a toilet suitable to the hour; Secundra Dass was no longer bundled up in wrappers, but wore a decent plain black suit, which misbecame him strangely; and the pair were at the great window, looking forth, when the family entered. They turned; and the black man (as they had already named him in the house) bowed almost to his knees, but the Master was for running forward like one of the family. My lady stopped him, curtseying low from the far end of the hall, and keeping her children at her back. My lord was a little in front: so there were the three cousins of Durrisdeer face to face. The hand of time was very legible on all; I seemed to read in their changed faces a *memento mori*; and what affected me still more, it was the wicked man that bore his years the handsomest. My lady was quite transfigured into the matron, a becoming woman for the head of a great tableful of children and dependants. My lord was grown slack in his limbs; he stooped; he walked with a running motion, as though he had learned again from Mr Alexander; his face was drawn; it seemed a trifle longer than of old; and it wore at times a smile very singularly mingled, and which (in my eyes) appeared both bitter and pathetic. But the Master still bore himself erect, although perhaps with effort; his brow barred about the centre with imperious lines, his mouth set as for command. He had all the gravity and something of the splendour of Satan in the *Paradise Lost*. I could not help but see the man with admiration, and was only surprised that I saw him with so little fear.

But indeed (as long as we were at the table) it seemed as if his authority were quite vanished and his teeth all drawn. We had known him a magician that controlled the elements; and here he was, transformed into an ordinary gentleman, chatting like his neighbours at the breakfast-board. For now the father was dead, and my lord and lady reconciled, in what ear was he to pour his calumnies? It came upon me in a kind of vision how hugely I had overrated the man's subtlety. He had his malice still; he was false as ever; and, the occasion being gone that made his strength, he sat there impotent; he was still the viper, but now spent his venom on a file. Two more thoughts occurred to me while yet we sat at breakfast: the first, that he was abashed – I had almost said, distressed – to find his wickedness quite unavailing; the second, that perhaps my lord was in the right, and we did amiss to fly from our dismasted enemy. But my poor master's leaping heart came in my mind, and I remembered it was for his life we played the coward.

When the meal was over, the Master followed me to my room, and, taking a chair (which I had never offered him), asked me what was to be done with him.

'Why, Mr Bally,' said I, 'the house will still be open to you for a time.'

'For a time?' says he. 'I do not know if I quite take your meaning.'

'It is plain enough,' said I. 'We keep you for our reputation; as soon as you shall have publicly disgraced yourself by some of your misconduct, we shall pack you forth again.'

'You are become an impudent rogue,' said the Master, bending his brows at me dangerously.

'I learned in a good school,' I returned. 'And you must have perceived yourself that with my old lord's death your power is quite departed. I do not fear you now, Mr Bally; I think even – God forgive me – that I take a certain pleasure in your company.'

He broke out in a burst of laughter, which I clearly saw to be assumed.

'I have come with empty pockets,' says he, after a pause.

'I do not think there will be any money going,' I replied. 'I would advise you not to build on that.'

'I shall have something to say on the point,' he returned.

'Indeed?' said I. 'I have not a guess what it will be, then.'

'Oh! you affect confidence,' said the Master. 'I have still one strong position – that you people fear a scandal, and I enjoy it.'

'Pardon me, Mr Bally,' says I. 'We do not in the least fear a scandal against you.'

He laughed again. 'You have been studying repartee,' he said. 'But speech is very easy, and sometimes very deceptive. I warn you fairly: you will find me vitriol in the house. You would do wiser to pay money down and see my back.' And with that he waved his hand to me and left the room.

A little after, my lord came with the lawyer, Mr Carlyle; a bottle of old wine was brought, and we all had a glass before we fell to business. The necessary deeds were then prepared and executed, and the Scottish estates made over in trust to Mr Carlyle and myself.

'There is one point, Mr Carlyle,' said my lord, when these affairs had been adjusted, 'on which I wish that you would do us justice. This sudden departure coinciding with my brother's return will be certainly commented on. I wish you would discourage any conjunction of the two.'

'I will make a point of it, my lord,' said Mr Carlyle. 'The Mas – Mr Bally does not, then, accompany you?'

'It is a point I must approach,' said my lord. 'Mr Bally remains at Durrisdeer, under the care of Mr Mackellar; and I do not mean that he shall even know our destination.'

'Common report, however——' began the lawyer.

'Ah! but, Mr Carlyle, this is to be a secret quite among ourselves,' interrupted my lord. 'None but you and Mackellar are to be made acquainted with my movements.'

'And Mr Bally stays here? Quite so,' said Mr Carlyle. 'The powers you leave——' Then he broke off again. 'Mr Mackellar, we have a rather heavy weight upon us.'

'No doubt, sir,' said I.

'No doubt,' said he. 'Mr Bally will have no voice?'

'He will have no voice,' said my lord; 'and I hope no influence. Mr Bally is not a good adviser.'

'I see,' said the lawyer. 'By the way, has Mr Bally means?'

'I understand him to have nothing,' replied my lord. 'I give him table, fire, and candle in this house.'

'And in the matter of an allowance? If I am to share the responsibility, you will see how highly desirable it is that I should understand your views,' said the lawyer. 'On the question of an allowance?'

'There will be no allowance,' said my lord. 'I wish Mr Bally to live very private. We have not always been gratified with his behaviour.'

'And in the matter of money,' I added, 'he has shown himself an infamous bad husband. Glance your eye upon that docket, Mr Carlyle, where I have brought together the different sums the man has drawn from the estate in the last fifteen or twenty years. The total is petty.'

Mr Carlyle made the motion of whistling. 'I had no guess of this,' said he. 'Excuse me once more, my lord, if I appear to push you; but it is really desirable that I should penetrate your intentions. Mr Mackellar might die, when I should find myself alone upon this trust. Would it not be rather your lordship's preference that Mr Bally should – ahem – should leave the country?'

My lord looked at Mr Carlyle. 'Why do you ask that?' said he.

'I gather, my lord, that Mr Bally is not a comfort to his family,' says the lawyer with a smile.

My lord's face became suddenly knotted. 'I wish he was in hell!' cried he, and filled himself a glass of wine, but with a hand so tottering that he spilled the half into his bosom. This was the second time that, in the midst of the most regular and wise behaviour, his animosity had spurted out. It startled Mr Carlyle, who observed my lord thenceforth with covert curiosity, and to me it restored the certainty that we were acting for the best in view of my lord's health and reason.

Except for this explosion the interview was very successfully conducted. No doubt Mr Carlyle would talk, as lawyers do, little by little. We could thus feel we had laid the foundations of a better feeling in the country, and the man's own misconduct would certainly complete what we had begun. Indeed, before his departure, the lawyer showed us there had already gone abroad some glimmerings of the truth.

'I should perhaps explain to you, my lord,' said he, pausing, with his hat in his hand, 'that I have not been altogether surprised with your lordship's dispositions in the case of Mr Bally. Something of this nature oozed out when he was last in Durrisdeer. There was some talk of a woman at St Bride's, to whom you had behaved extremely handsome, and Mr Bally with no small degree of cruelty. There was the entail, again, which was much controverted. In short, there was no want of talk, back and forward; and some of our wiseacres took up a strong opinion. I remained in suspense, as became one of my cloth; but Mr Mackellar's docket here has finally opened my eyes. I do not think, Mr Mackellar, that you and I will give him that much rope.'

The rest of that important day passed prosperously through. It was our policy to keep the enemy in view, and I took my turn to be his watchman with the rest. I think his spirits rose as he perceived us to be so attentive, and I know that mine insensibly declined. What chiefly daunted me was the man's singular dexterity to worm himself into our troubles. You may have felt (after a horse accident) the hand of a bone-setter artfully divide and interrogate the muscles, and settle strongly on the injured place? It was so with the Master's tongue, that was so cunning to question; and his eyes, that were so quick to observe. I seemed to have said nothing, and yet to have let all out. Before I knew where I was the man was condoling with me on my lord's neglect of my lady and myself, and his hurtful indulgence to his son. On this last point I perceived him (with panic fear) to return repeatedly. The boy had displayed a certain shrinking from his uncle; it was strong in my mind that his father had been fool enough to indoctrinate the same, which was no wise beginning: and when I looked upon the man before me, still so handsome, so apt a speaker, with so great a variety of fortunes to relate, I saw he was the very personage to captivate a boyish fancy. John Paul had left only that morning; it was not to be supposed he had been altogether dumb upon his favourite subject: so that here would be Mr Alexander in the part of Dido, with a curiosity inflamed to hear; and there would be the Master, like a diabolical Aeneas, full of matter the most pleasing in the world to any youthful ear, such as battles, sea-disasters, flights, the forests of the West, and (since his later voyage) the ancient cities of the Indies. How cunningly these baits might be employed, and what an empire might be so founded, little by little, in the mind of any boy, stood obviously clear to me. There was no inhibition, so long as the man was in the house, that would be strong enough to hold these two apart; for if it be hard to charm serpents, it is no very difficult thing to cast a glamour on a little chip of manhood not very long in breeches. I recalled an ancient sailor-man who dwelt in a lone house beyond the Figgate Whins (I believe he called it after Portobello), and how the boys would troop out of Leith on a Saturday, and sit and listen to his swearing tales, as thick as crows about a carrion: a think I often remarked as I went by, a young student, on my own more meditative holiday diversion. Many of these boys went, no doubt, in the face of an express command; many feared and even hated the old brute of whom they made their hero; and I have seen them flee from him when he was tipsy, and stone him when he was drunk. And yet there they came each Saturday! How much more easily would a boy like Mr Alexander fall under the influence of a high-looking, high-spoken gentleman-adventurer, who should conceive the fancy to entrap him; and the influence gained, how easy to employ it for the child's perversion!

I doubt if our enemy had named Mr Alexander three times before I perceived which way his mind was aiming – all this train of thought and memory passed in one pulsation through my own – and you may say I started back as though an open hole had gaped across a pathway. Mr Alexander: there was the weak point, there was the Eve in our perishable paradise; and the serpent was already hissing on the trail.

I promise you, I went the more heartily about the preparations; my last scruple gone, the danger of delay written before me in huge characters. From that moment forth I seem not to have sat down or breathed. Now I would be at my post with the Master and his Indian; now in the garret buckling a valise; now sending forth Macconochie by the side postern and the wood-path to bear it to the trysting-place; and, again, snatching some words of counsel with my lady. This was the *verso* of our life in Durrisdeer that day; but on the *recto* all appeared quite settled, as of a family at home in its paternal seat; and what perturbation may have been observable, the Master would set down to the blow of his unlooked-for coming, and the fear he was accustomed to inspire.

Supper went creditably off, cold salutations passed, and the company trooped to their respective chambers. I attended the Master to the last. We had put him next door to his Indian, in the north wing; because that was the most distant and could be severed from the body of the house with doors. I saw he was a kind friend or good master (whichever it was) to his Secundra Dass – seeing to his comfort; mending the fire with his own hand, for the Indian complained of cold; inquiring as to the rice on which the stranger made his diet; talking with him pleasantly in the Hindustanee, while I stood by, my candle in my hand, and affected to be overcome with slumber. At length the Master observed my signals of distress. 'I perceive,' says he, 'that you have all your ancient habits: early to bed and early to rise. Yawn yourself away!'

Once in my own room, I made the customary motions of undressing, so that I might time myself; and when the cycle was complete, set my tinder-box ready, and blew out my taper. The matter of an hour afterward I made a light again, put on my shoes of list that I had worn by my lord's sick-bed, and set forth into the house to call the voyagers. All were dressed and waiting – my lord, my lady, Miss Katharine, Mr Alexander, my lady's woman Christie; and I observed the effect of secrecy even upon quite innocent persons, that one after another showed in the chink of the door a face as white as paper. We slipped out of the side postern into a night of darkness, scarce broken by a star or two; so that at first we groped and stumbled and fell among the bushes. A few hundred yards up the wood-path Macconochie was waiting us with a great lantern; so the rest of the way we went easy enough, but still in a kind of guilty silence. A little beyond the abbey the path debouched on the main road; and some quarter of a mile farther, at the place called Eagles, where the moors begin, we saw the lights of the two carriages stand shining by the wayside. Scarce a word or two was uttered at our parting, and these regarded business: a silent grasping of hands, a turning of faces aside, and the thing was over; the horses broke into a trot, the lamplight sped like Will-o'-the-Wisp upon the broken moorland, it dipped beyond Stony Brae; and there were Macconochie and I alone with our lantern on the road. There was one thing more to wait for, and that was the reappearance of the coach upon Cartmore. It seems they must have pulled up upon the summit, looked back for a last time, and seen our lantern not yet moved away from the place of separation. For a lamp was taken from a carriage, and waved three times up and down by way of a farewell. And then they were gone indeed, having looked their last on the kind roof of Durrisdeer, their faces toward a barbarous country. I never knew before the greatness of that vault of night in which we two poor serving-men – the one old, and the one elderly – stood for the first time deserted; I had never felt before my own dependency upon the countenance of others. The sense of isolation burned in my bowels like a fire. It seemed that we who remained at home were the true exiles, and that Durrisdeer and Solwayside, and all that made my country native, its air good to me, and its language welcome, had gone forth and was for over the sea with my old masters.

The remainder of that night I paced to and fro on the smooth highway, reflecting on the future and the past. My thoughts, which at first dwelled tenderly on those who were just gone, took a more manly temper as I considered what remained for me to do. Day came upon the inland mountain-tops, and the fowls began to cry, and the smoke of homesteads to arise in the brown bosom of the moors, before I turned my face homeward, and went down the path to where the roof of Durrisdeer shone in the morning by the sea.

At the customary hour I had the Master called, and awaited his coming in the hall with a quiet mind. He looked about him at the empty room and the three covers set.

'We are a small party,' said he. 'How comes that?'

'This is the party to which we must grow accustomed,' I replied.

He looked at me with a sudden sharpness. 'What is all this?' said he.

'You and I and your friend Mr Dass are now all the company,' I replied. 'My lord, my lady, and the children, are gone upon a voyage.'

'Upon my word!' said he. 'Can this be possible? I have indeed fluttered your Volscians in Corioli! But this is no reason why our breakfast should go cold. Sit down, Mr Mackellar, if you please' – taking, as he spoke, the head of the table, which I had designed to occupy myself – 'and as we eat, you can give me the details of this evasion.'

I could see he was more affected than his language carried, and I determined to equal him in coolness. 'I was about to ask you to take the head of the table,' said I; 'for though I am now thrust into the position of your host, I could never forget that you were, after all, a member of the family.'

For a while he played the part of entertainer, giving directions to Macconochie, who received them with an evil grace, and attending specially upon Secundra. 'And where has my good family withdrawn to?' he asked carelessly.

'Ah! Mr Bally, that is another point,' said I. 'I have no orders to communicate their destination.'

'To me,' he corrected.

'To anyone,' said I.

'It is the less pointed,' said the Master; 'c'est de bon ton: my brother improves as he continues. And I, my dear Mr Mackellar?'

'You will have bed and board, Mr Bally,' said I. 'I am permitted to give you the run of the cellar, which is pretty reasonably stocked. You have only to keep well with me, which is no very difficult matter, and you shall want neither for wine nor for a saddle-horse.'

He made an excuse to send Macconochie from the room.

'And for money?' he inquired. 'Have I to keep well with my good friend Mackellar for my pocket-money also? This is a pleasing return to the principles of boyhood.'

'There was no allowance made,' said I; 'but I will take it on myself to see you are supplied in moderation.'

'In moderation?' he repeated. 'And you will take it on yourself?' He drew himself up, and looked about the hall at the dark rows of portraits. 'In the name of my ancestors, I thank you,' says he; and then, with a return to irony, 'But there must certainly be an allowance for Secundra Dass?' he said. 'It is not possible they have omitted that?'

'I will make a note of it, and ask instructions when I write,' said I.

And he, with a sudden change of manner and leaning forward with an elbow on the table, 'Do you think this entirely wise?'

'I execute my orders, Mr Bally,' said I.

'Profoundly modest,' said the Master; 'perhaps not equally ingenuous. You told me yesterday my power was fallen with my father's death. How comes it, then, that a peer of the realm flees under cloud of night out of a house in which his fathers have stood several sieges? that he conceals his address, which must be a matter of concern to his Gracious Majesty and to the whole republic? and that he should leave me in possession and under the paternal charge of his invaluable Mackellar? This smacks to me of a very considerable and genuine apprehension.'

I sought to interrupt him with some not very truthful denegation; but he waved me down and pursued his speech.

'I say it smacks of it,' he said; 'but I will go beyond that, for I think the apprehension grounded. I came to this house with some reluctancy. In view of the manner of my last departure, nothing but necessity could have induced me to return. Money, however, is that which I must have. You will not give with a good grace; well, I have the power to force it from you. Inside of a week, without leaving Durrisdeer, I will find out where these fools are fled to. I will follow; and when I have run my quarry down, I will drive a wedge into that family that shall once more burst it into shivers. I shall see then whether my Lord Durrisdeer' (said with indescribable scorn and rage) 'will choose to buy my absence; and you will all see whether, by that time, I decide for profit or revenge.'

I was amazed to hear the man so open. The truth is, he was consumed with anger at my lord's successful flight, felt himself to figure as a dupe, and was in no humour to weigh language.

'Do you consider this entirely wise?' said I, copying his words.

'These twenty years I have lived by my poor wisdom,' he answered, with a smile that seemed almost foolish in its vanity.

'And come out a beggar in the end,' said I, 'if beggar be a strong enough word for it.'

'I would have you to observe, Mr Mackellar,' cried he, with a sudden imperious heat, in which I could not but admire him, 'that I am scrupulously civil: copy me in that, and we shall be the better friends.'

Throughout this dialogue I had been incommoded by the observation of Secundra Dass. Not one of us, since the first word, had made a feint of eating: our eyes were in each other's faces – you might say, in each other's bosoms; and those of the Indian troubled me with a certain changing brightness, as of comprehension. But I brushed the fancy aside, telling myself once more he understood no English; only, from the gravity of both voices, and the occasional scorn and anger in the Master's, smelled out there was something of import in the wind.

For the matter of three weeks we continued to live together in the house of Durrisdeer: the beginning of that most singular chapter of my life – what I must call my intimacy with the Master. At first he was somewhat changeable in his behaviour: now civil, now returning to his old manner of flouting me to my face; and in both I met him half-way. Thanks be to Providence, I had now no measure to keep with the man; and I was never afraid of black brows, only of naked swords. So that I found a certain entertainment in these bouts of incivility, and was not always ill-inspired in my rejoinders. At last (it was at supper) I had a droll expression that entirely vanquished him. He laughed again and again; and 'Who would have guessed,' he cried, 'that this old wife had any wit under his petticoats?'

'It is no wit, Mr Bally,' said I: 'a dry Scot's humour, and something of the driest.' And, indeed, I never had the least pretension to be thought a wit.

From that hour he was never rude with me, but all passed between us in a manner of pleasantry. One of our chief times of daffing* was when he required a horse, another bottle, or some money. He would approach me then after the manner of a schoolboy and I would carry it on by way of being his father: on both sides, with infinity of mirth. I could not but perceive that he thought more of me, which tickled that poor part of mankind, the vanity. He dropped, besides (I must suppose unconsciously), into a manner that was not only familiar, but even friendly; and this on the part of one who had so long detested me, I found the more insidious. He went little abroad; sometimes even refusing invitations. 'No,' he would say, 'what do I care for these thick-headed bonnet-lairds? I will stay at home, Mackellar; and we shall share a bottle quietly, and have one of our good talks.' And, indeed, meal-time at Durrisdeer must have been a delight to anyone, by reason of the brilliancy of the discourse. He would often express wonder at his former indifference to my society. 'But you see,' he would add, 'we were upon opposite sides. And so we are today; but let us never speak of that. I would think much less of you if you were not staunch to your employer.' You are to consider he seemed to me quite impotent for any evil; and how it is a most engaging form of flattery when (after many years) tardy justice is done to a man's character and parts. But I have no thought to excuse myself. I was to blame; I let him cajole me, and, in short, I think the watch-dog was going sound asleep, when he was suddenly aroused.

I should say the Indian was continually travelling to and fro in the house. He never spoke, save in his own dialect and with the Master; walked without sound; and was always turning up where you would least expect him, fallen into a deep abstraction, from which he would start (upon your coming) to mock you with one of his grovelling obeisances. He seemed so quiet, so frail, and so wrapped in his own fancies, that I came to pass him over without much regard, or even to pity him for a harmless exile from his country. And yet without doubt the creature was still eavesdropping; and without doubt it was through his stealth and my security that our secret reached the Master.

It was one very wild night, after supper, and when we had been making more than usually merry, that the blow fell on me.

'This is all very fine,' says the Master, 'but we should do better to be buckling our valise.'

'Why so?' I cried. 'Are you leaving?'

'We are all leaving tomorrow in the morning,' said he. 'For the port of *Fooling.

Glasgow first, thence for the province of New York.'

I suppose I must have groaned aloud.

'Yes,' he continued, 'I boasted; I said a week, and it has taken me twenty days. But never mind; I shall make it up; I will go the faster.'

'Have you the money for this voyage?' I asked.

'Dear and ingenuous personage, I have,' said he. 'Blame me, if you choose, for my duplicity; but while I have been wringing shillings from my daddy, I had a stock of my own put by against a rainy day. You will pay for your own passage, if you choose to accompany us on our flank march; I have enough for Secundra and myself, but not more – enough to be dangerous, not enough to be generous. There is, however, an outside seat upon the chaise which I will let you have upon a moderate commutation; so that the whole menagerie can go together – the housedog, the monkey, and the tiger.'

'I go with you,' said I.

'I count upon it,' said the Master. 'You have seen me foiled; I mean you shall see me victorious. To gain that I will risk wetting you like a sop in this wild weather.'

'And at least,' I added, 'you know very well you could not throw me off.'

'Not easily,' said he. 'You put your finger on the point with your usual excellent good sense. I never fight with the inevitable.

'I suppose it is useless to appeal to you?' said I.

'Believe me, perfectly,' said he.

'And yet, if you would give me time, I could write——' I began.

'And what would be my Lord Durrisdeer's answer?' asks he.

'Ay,' said I, 'That is the rub.'

'And, at any rate, how much more expeditions that I should go myself!' says he. 'But all this is quite a waste of breath. At seven tomorrow the chaise will be at the door. For I start from the door, Mackellar; I do not skulk through woods and take my chaise upon the wayside – shall we say, at Eagles?'

My mind was now thoroughly made up. 'Can you spare me a quarter of an hour at St Brides?' said I. 'I have a little necessary business with Carlyle.'

'An hour, if you prefer,' said he. 'I do not seek to deny that the money for your seat is an object to me; and you could always get the first to Glasgow with saddle-horses.'

'Well,' said I, 'I never thought to leave old Scotland.'

'It will brisken you up,' says he.

'This will be an ill journey for someone,' I said. 'I think, sir, for you. Something speaks in my bosom; and so much it says plain – that this is an ill-omened journey.'

'If you take to prophecy,' says he, 'listen to that.'

There came up a violent squall off the open Solway, and the rain was dashed on the great windows.

'Do you ken what that bodes, warlock?' said he, in a broad accent: 'that there'll be a man Mackellar unco' sick at sea.'

When I got to my chamber, I sat there under a painful excitation, hearkening to the turmoil of the gale, which struck full upon that gable of the house. What with the pressure on my spiritis, the eldritch cries of the wind among the turret-tops, and the perpetual trepidation of the masoned house, sleep fled my eyelids

utterly. I sat by my taper, looking on the black panes of the window, where the
storm appeared continually on the point of bursting in its entrance; and upon
that empty field I beheld a perspective of consequences that made the hair to rise
upon my scalp. The child corrupted, the home broken up, my master dead or
worse than dead, my mistress plunged in desolation – all these I saw before me
painted brightly on the darkness; and the outcry of the wind appeared to knock
at my inaction.

CHAPTER NINE

Mr Mackellar's Journey with the Master

THE CHAISE CAME TO THE DOOR in a strong drenching mist. We took our leave in
silence: the house of Durrisdeer standing with dropping gutters and windows
closed, like a place dedicated to melancholy. I observed the Master kept his
head out, looking back on these splashed walls and glimmering roofs, till they
were suddenly swallowed in the mist; and I must suppose some natural sadness
fell upon the man at this departure; or was it some pre-vision of the end? At
least, upon our mounting the long brae from Durrisdeer, as we walked side by
side in the wet, he began first to whistle and then to sing the saddest of our
country tunes, which sets folk weeping in a tavern, *Wandering Willie*. The set of
words he used with it I have not heard elsewhere, and could never come by any
copy; but some of them which were the most appropriate to our departure linger
in my memory. One verse began.

> Home was home then, my dear, full of kindly faces;
>   Home was home then, my dear, happy for the child.

And ended somewhat thus:

> Now, when day dawns on the brow of the moorland,
>   Lone stands the house, and the chimney-stone is cold.
> Lone let it stand, now the folks are all departed,
>   The kind hearts, the true hearts, that loved the place of old.

I could never be a judge of the merit of these verses; they were so hallowed by
the melancholy of the air, and were sung (or rather 'soothed') to me by a master-
singer at a time so fitting. He looked in my face when he had done, and saw that
my eyes watered.

'Ah! Mackellar,' said he, 'do you think I have never a regret?'

'I do not think you could be so bad a man,' said I, 'if you had not all the
machinery to be a good one.'

'No, not all,' says he: 'not all. You are there in error. The malady of not wanting, my evangelist.' But methought he sighed as he mounted again into the chaise.

All day long we journeyed in the same miserable weather: the mist besetting us closely, the heavens incessantly weeping on my head. The road lay over moorish hills, where was no sound but the crying of moor-fowl in the wet weather and the pouring of the swollen burns. Sometimes I would doze off in slumber, when I would find myself plunged at once in some foul and ominous nightmare, from the which I would awake strangling. Sometimes, if the way was steep and the wheels turning slowly, I would overhear the voices from within, talking in that tropical tongue which was to me as inarticulate as the piping of the fowls. Sometimes, at a longer ascent, the Master would set foot to ground and walk by my side, mostly without speech. And all the time, sleeping or waking, I beheld the same black perspective of approaching ruin; and the same pictures rose in my view, only they were now painted upon hillside mist. One, I remember, stood before me with the colours of a true illusion. It showed me my lord seated at a table in a small room; his head, which was at first buried in his hands, he slowly raised, and turned upon me a countenance from which hope had fled. I saw it first on the black window-panes, my last night in Durrisdeer; it haunted and returned upon me half the voyage through; and yet it was no effect of lunacy, for I have come to a ripe old age with no decay of my intelligence; nor yet (as I was then tempted to suppose) a heaven-sent warning of the future, for all manner of calamities befell, not that calamity – and I saw many pitiful sights, but never that one.

It was decided we should travel on all night; and it was singular, once the dusk had fallen, my spirits somewhat rose. The bright lamps, shining forth into the mist and on the smoking horses and the hodding post-boy, gave me perhaps an outlook intrinsically more cheerful than what day had shown; or perhaps my mind had become wearied of its melancholy. At least, I spent some waking hours, not without satisfaction in my thoughts, although wet and weary in my body; and fell at last into a natural slumber without dreams. Yet I must have been at work even in the deepest of my sleep; and at work with at least a measure of intelligence. For I started broad awake, in the very act of crying out to myself:

HOME WAS HOME THEN, MY DEAR, HAPPY FOR THE CHILD,

stricken to find in it an appropriateness, which I had not yesterday observed, to the Master's detestable purpose in the present journey.

We were then close upon the city of Glasgow, where we were soon breakfasting together at an inn, and where (as the devil would have it) we found a ship in the very article of sailing. We took our places in the cabin; and, two days after, carried our effects on board. Her name was the *Nonesuch*, a very ancient ship and very happily named. By all accounts this should be her last voyage; people shook their heads upon the quays, and I had several warnings offered me by strangers in the street to the effect that she was rotten as a cheese, too deeply loaden, and must infallibly founder if we met a gale. From this it fell out we were the only passengers; the Captain, McMurtrie, was a silent, absorbed man, with the Glasgow or Gaelic accent; the mates ignorant rough seafarers, come in through the hawsehole; and the Master and I were cast upon each other's company.

The *Nonesuch* carried a fair wind out of the Clyde, and for near upon a week we enjoyed bright weather and a sense of progress. I found myself (to my wonder) a born seaman, in so far at least as I was never sick; yet I was far from tasting the usual serenity of my health. Whether it was the motion of the ship on the billows, the confinement, the salted food, or all of these together, I suffered from a blackness of spirit and a painful strain upon my temper. The nature of my errand on that ship perhaps contributed; I think it did no more; the malady (whatever it was) sprang from my environment; and if the ship were not to blame, then it was the Master. Hatred and fear are ill bedfellows; but (to my shame be it spoken) I have tasted those in other places, lain down and got up with them, and eaten and drunk with them, and yet never before, nor after, have I been so poisoned through and through, in soul and body, as I was on board the *Nonesuch*. I freely confess my enemy set me a fair example of forbearance; in our worst days displayed the most patient geniality, holding me in conversation as long as I would suffer, and when I had rebuffed his civility, stretching himself on deck to read. The book he had on board with him was Mr Richardson's famous *Clarissa*; and among other small attentions he would read me passages aloud; nor could any elocutionist have given with greater potency the pathetic portions of that work. I would retort upon him with passages out of the Bible, which was all my library – and very fresh to me, my religious duties (I grieve to say it) being always and even to this day extremely neglected. He tasted the merits of the work like the connoisseur he was; and would sometimes take it from my hand, turn the leaves over like a man that knew his way, and give me, with his fine declamation, a Roland for my Oliver. But it was singular how little he applied his reading to himself; it passed high above his head like summer thunder: Lovelace and Clarissa, the tales of David's generosity, the psalms of his penitence, the solemn questions of the Book of Job, the touching poetry of Isaiah – they were to him a source of entertainment only, like the scraping of a fiddle in a change-house. This outer sensibility and inner toughness set me against him; it seemed of a piece with that impudent grossness which I knew to underlie the veneer of his fine manners; and sometimes my gorge rose against him as though he were deformed – and sometimes I would draw away as though from something partly spectral. I had moments when I thought of him as of a man of pasteboard – as though, if one should strike smartly through the buckram of his countenance, there would be found a mere vacuity within. This horror (not merely fanciful, I think) vastly increased my detestation of his neighbourhood; I began to feel something shiver within me on his drawing near; I had at times a longing to cry out; there were days when I thought I could have struck him. This frame of mind was doubtless helped by shame, because I had dropped during our last days at Durrisdeer into a certain toleration of the man; and if anyone had then told me I should drop into it again, I must have laughed in his face. It is possible he remained unconscious of these extreme fever of my resentment; yet I think he was too quick; and rather that he had fallen, in a long life of idleness, into a positive need of company, which obliged him to confront and tolerate my unconcealed aversion. Certain, at least, that he loved the note of his own tongue, as, indeed, he entirely loved all the parts and properties of himself; a sort of imbecility which almost necessarily attends on wickedness. I have seen him driven, when I proved recalcitrant, to long discourses with the skipper; and this, although the man plainly testified his weariness, fiddling miserably with both hand and foot, and replying only with a grunt.

After the first week out we fell in with foul winds and heavy weather. The sea was high. The *Nonesuch*, being an old-fashioned ship and badly loaden, rolled beyond belief; so that the skipper trembled for his masts, and I for my life. We made no progress on our course. An unbearable ill-humour settled on the ship: men, mates, and master girding at one another all day long. A saucy word on the one hand, and a blow on the other, made a daily incident. There were times when the whole crew refused their duty; and we of the afterguard were twice got under arms – being the first time that ever I bore weapons – in the fear of mutiny.

In the midst of our evil season sprang up a hurricane of wind; so that all supposed she must go down. I was shut in the cabin from noon of one day till sundown of the next; the Master was somewhere lashed on deck. Secundra had eaten of some drug and lay insensible; so you may say I passed these hours in an unbroken solitude. At first I was terrified beyond motion, and almost beyond thought, my mind appearing to be frozen. Presently there stole in on me a ray of comfort. If the *Nonesuch* foundered, she would carry down with her into the deeps of that unsounded sea the creature whom we all so feared and hated; there would be no more Master of Ballantrae, the fish would sport among his ribs; his schemes all brought to nothing, his harmless enemies at peace. At first, I have said, it was but a ray of comfort; but it had soon grown to be broad sunshine. The thought of the man's death, of his deletion from this world, which he embittered for so many, took possession of my mind. I hugged it, I found it sweet in my belly. I conceived the ship's last plunge, the sea bursting upon all sides into the cabin, the brief mortal conflict there, all by myself, in that closed place; I numbered the horrors, I had almost said with satisfaction; I felt I could bear all and more, if the *Nonesuch* carried down with her, overtook by the same ruin, the enemy of my poor master's house. Towards noon of the second day the screaming of the wind abated; the ship lay not so perilously over, and it began to be clear to me that we were past the height of the tempest. As I hope for mercy, I was singly disappointed. In the selfishness of that vile, absorbing passion of hatred, I forgot the case of our innocent shipmates, and thought but of myself and my enemy. For myself, I was already old; I had never been young, I was not formed for the world's pleasures, I had few affections; it mattered not the toss of a silver tester whether I was drowned there and then in the Atlantic, or dribbled out a few more years, to die, perhaps no less terribly, in a deserted sick-bed. Down I went upon my knees – holding on by the locker, or else I had been instantly dashed across the tossing cabin – and, lifting up my voice in the midst of that clamour of the abating hurricane, impiously prayed for my own death. 'O God!' I cried, 'I would be liker a man if I rose and struck this creature down; but Thou madest me a coward from my mother's womb. O Lord, Thou madest me so, Thou knowest my weakness, Thou knowest that any face of death will set me shaking in my shoes. But, lo! here is Thy servant ready, his mortal weakness laid aside. Let me give my life for this creature's; take the two of them, Lord! take the two, and have mercy on the innocent!' In some such words as these, only yet more irreverent and with more sacred adjurations, I continued to pour forth my spirit. God heard me not, I must suppose in mercy; and I was still absorbed in my agony of supplication when someone, removing the tarpaulin cover, let the light of the sunset pour into the cabin. I stumbled to my feet ashamed, and was seized with surprise to find myself totter and ache like one that had been stretched upon the rack. Secundra Dass, who had slept off the effects of his drug, stood in a corner not far off, gazing at me with wild eyes; and from the open skylight the captain thanked me for my supplications.

'It's you that's saved the ship, Mr Mackellar,' says he. 'There is no craft of seamanship that could have kept her floating: well may we say "Except the Lord the city keep, the watchmen watch in vain"!'

I was abashed by the captain's error; abashed, also, by the surprise and fear with which the Indian regarded me at first, and the obsequious civilities with which he soon began to cumber me. I know now that he must have overheard and comprehended the peculiar nature of my prayers. It is certain, of course, that he at once disclosed the matter to his patron; and looking back with greater knowledge, I can now understand what so much puzzled me at the moment, those singular and (so to speak) approving smiles with which the Master honoured me. Similarly, I can understand a word that I remember to have fallen from him in conversation that same night; when, holding up his hand and smiling, 'Ah! Mackellar,' said he, 'not every man is so great a coward as he thinks he is – nor yet so good a Christian.' He did not guess how true he spoke! For the fact is, the thoughts which had come to me in the violence of the storm retained their hold upon my spirit; and the words that rose to my lips unbidden in the instancy of prayer continued to sound in my ears: with what shameful consequences it is fitting I should honestly relate; for I could not support a part of such disloyalty as to describe the sins of others and conceal my own.

The wind fell, but the sea hove ever the higher. All night the *Nonesuch* rolled outrageously; the next day dawned, and the next, and brought no change. To cross the cabin was scarce possible; old experienced seamen were cast down upon the deck, and one cruelly mauled in the concussion; every board and block in the old ship cried out aloud; and the great bell by the anchor-bitts continually and dolefully rang. One of these days the Master and I sate alone together at the break of the poop. I should say the *Nonesuch* carried a high-raised poop. About the top of it ran considerable bulwarks, which made the ship unweatherly; and these, as they approached the front on each side, ran down in a fine, old-fashioned, carven scroll to join the bulwarks of the waist. From this disposition, which seems designed rather for ornament than use, it followed there was a discontinuance of protection: and that, besides, at the very margin of the elevated part where (in certain movements of the ship) it might be the most needful. It was here we were sitting: our feet hanging down, the Master betwixt me and the side, and I holding on with both hands to the grating of the cabin skylight; for it struck me it was a dangerous position, the more so as I had continually before my eyes a measure of our evolutions in the person of the Master, which stood out in the break of the bulwarks against the sun. Now his head would be in the zenith and his shadow fall quite beyond the *Nonesuch* on the farther side; and now he would swing down till he was underneath my feet, and the line of the sea leaped high above him like the ceiling of a room. I looked on upon this with a growing fascination, as birds are said to look on snakes. My mind, besides, was troubled with an astonishing diversity of noises; for now that we had all sails spread in the vain hope to bring her to the sea, the ship sounded like a factory with their reverberations. We spoke first of the mutiny with which we had been threatened; this led us on to the topic of assassination; and that offered a temptation to the Master more strong than he was able to resist. He must tell me a tale, and show me at the same time how clever he was and how wicked. It was a thing he did always with affectation and display; generally with a good effect. But this tale, told in a high key in the midst of so great a tumult, and by a narrator who was one moment looking down at me from the skies and the next peering up from under the soles of my feet – this particular tale, I say, took hold upon me in a degree quite singular.

'My friend the count,' it was thus that he began his story, 'had for an enemy a certain German baron, a stranger in Rome. It matters not what was the ground of the count's enmity; but as he had a firm design to be revenged, and that with safety to himself, he kept it secret even from the baron. Indeed, that is the first principle of vengeance; and hatred betrayed is hated impotent. The count was a man of a curious, searching mind; he had something of the artist; if anything fell for him to do, it must always be done with an exact perfection, not only as to the result, but in the very means and instruments, or he thought the thing miscarried. It chanced he was one day riding in the outer suburbs, when he came to a disused by-road branching off into the moor which lies about Rome. On the one hand was an ancient Roman tomb; on the other a deserted house in a garden of evergreen trees. This road brought him presently into a field of ruins, in the midst of which, in the side of a hill, he saw an open door, and, not far off, a single stunted pine no greater than a currant-bush. The place was desert and very secret; a voice spoke in the count's bosom that there was something here to his advantage. He tied his horse to the pine-tree, took his flint and steel in his hand to make a light and entered into the hill. The doorway opened on a passage of old Roman masonry, which shortly after branched in two. The count took the turning to the right, and followed it, groping forward in the dark, till he was brought up by a kind of fence, about elbow high, which extended quite across the passage. Sounding forward with his foot, he found an edge of polished stone, and then vacancy. All his curiosity was now awakened, and, getting some rotten sticks that lay about the floor, he made a fire. In front of him was a profound well; doubtless some neighbouring peasant had once used it for his water, and it was he that had set up the fence. A long while the count stood leaning on the rail and looking down into the pit. It was of Roman foundation, and, like all that nation set their hands to, built as for eternity; the sides were still straight, and the joints smooth; to a man who should fall in no escape was possible. 'Now,' the count was thinking, 'a strong impulsion brought me to this place. What for? what have I gained? why should I be sent to gaze into this well?' when the rail of the fence gave suddenly under his weight, and he came within an ace of falling headlong in. Leaping back to save himself, he trod out the last flicker of his fire, which gave him thenceforth no more light, only an incommoding smoke. 'Was I sent here to my death?' says he, and shook from head to foot. And then a thought flashed in his mind. He crept forth on hands and knees to the brink of the pit, and felt above him in the air. The rail had been fast to a pair of uprights; it had only broken from the one, and still depended from the other. The count set it back again as he had found it, so that the place meant death to the first comer, and groped out of the catacomb like a sick man. The next day, riding in the Corso with the baron, he purposely betrayed a strong preoccupation. The other (as he had designed) inquired into the cause; and he, after some fencing, admitted that his spirits had been dashed by an unusual dream. This was calculated to draw on the baron – a superstitious man, who affected the scorn of superstition. Some rallying followed, and then the count, as if suddenly carried away, called on his friend to beware, for it was of him that he had dreamed. You know enough of human nature, my excellent Mackellar, to be certain of one thing: I mean that the baron did not rest till he had heard the dream. The count, sure that he would never desist, kept him in play till his curiosity was highly inflamed, and then suffered himself, with seeming reluctance, to be overborne. 'I warn you,' says he, 'evil will come of it; something tells me so. But since there is to be no peace either for you or me except on this condition, the blame be on your own head! This was the dream: I beheld you riding, I know not where, yet I think it must have been near Rome, for on your one hand was an ancient tomb, and on the other a garden of evergreen trees. Methought I cried and cried upon you to come back in a very agony of terror; whether you heard me I know not, but you went doggedly on. The road brought you to a desert place among ruins, where was a door in a hillside, and hard by the door a misbegotten pine. Here you dismounted (I still crying on you to beware), tied your horse to the pine-tree, and entered resolutely in by the door. Within, it was dark; but in my dream I could still see you and still besought you to hold back. You felt your way along the right-hand wall, took a branching passage to the right, and came to a little chamber, where was a well with a railing. At this – I know not why – my alarm for you increased a thousandfold, so that I seemed to scream myself hoarse with warnings, crying it was still time, and bidding you begone at once from that vestibule. Such was the word I used in my dream, and it seemed then to have a clear significancy; but today, and awake, I profess I know not what it means. To all my outcry you rendered not the least attention, leaning the while upon the rail and looking down intently in the water. And then there was made to you a communication; I do not think I even gathered what it was, but the fear of it plucked me clean out of my slumber, and I awoke shaking and sobbing. And now,' continues the count, 'I thank you from my heart for your insistency. This dream lay on me like a load; and now I have told it in plain words and in the broad daylight, it seems no great matter.' – 'I do not know,' says the baron. 'It is in some points strange. A communication, did you say? Oh, it is an odd dream. It will make a story to amuse our friends.' – 'I am not so sure,' says the count. 'I am sensible of some reluctancy. Let us rather forget it.' – 'By all means,' says the baron. And (in fact) the dream was not again referred to. Some days after, the count proposed a ride in the fields, which the baron (since they were daily growing faster friends) very readily accepted. On the way back to Rome, the count led them insensibly by a particular route. Presently he reined in his horse, clapped his hand before his eyes, and cried out aloud. Then he showed his face again (which was now quite white, for he was a consummate actor), and stared upon the baron. 'What ails you?' cries the baron. 'What is wrong with you?' – 'Nothing,' cries the count. 'It is nothing. A seizure, I know not what. Let us hurry back to Rome.' But in the meanwhile the baron had looked about him; and there, on the left-hand side of the way as they went back to Rome, he saw a dusty by-road with a tomb upon the one hand and a garden of evergreen trees upon the other. – 'Yes,' says he, with a changed voice. 'Let us by all means hurry back to Rome. I fear you are not well in health.' – 'Oh, for God's sake!' cries the count, shuddering, 'back to Rome and let me get to bed.' They made their return with scarce a word; and the count, who should by rights have gone into society, took to his bed and gave out he had a touch of country fever. The next day the baron's horse was found tied to the pine, but himself was never heard of from that hour. – And, now, was that a murder?' says the Master, breaking sharply off.

'Are you sure he was a count?' I asked.

'I am not certain of the title,' said he, 'but he was a gentleman of family: and the Lord deliver you, Mackellar, from an enemy so subtle!'

These last words he spoke down at me, smiling, from high above; the next, he was under my feet. I continued to follow his evolutions with a childish fixity; they made me giddy and vacant, and I spoke as in a dream.

'He hated the baron with a great hatred?' I asked.

'His belly moved when the man came near him,' said the Master.

'I have felt that same,' said I.

'Verily!' cries the Master. 'Here is news indeed! I wonder – do I flatter myself? or am I the cause of these ventral perturbations?'

He was quite capable of choosing out a graceful posture, even with no one to behold him but myself, and all the more if there were any element of peril. He sat now with one knee flung across the other, his arms on his bosom, fitting the swing of the ship with an exquisite balance, such as a featherweight might overthrow. All at once I had the vision of my lord at the table, with his head upon his hands: only now, when he showed me his countenance, it was heavy with reproach. The words of my own prayer – *I were liker a man if I struck this creature down* – shot at the same time into my memory. I called my energies together, and (the ship then heeling downward toward my enemy) thrust at him swiftly with my foot. It was written I should have the guilt of this attempt without the profit. Whether from my own uncertainty or his incredible quickness, he escaped the thrust, leaping to his feet and catching hold at the same moment of a stay.

I do not know how long a time passed by: I lying where I was upon the deck, overcome with terror and remorse and shame: he standing with the stay in his hand, backed against the bulwarks, and regarding me with an expression singularly mingled. At last he spoke.

'Mackellar,' said he, 'I make no reproaches, but I offer you a bargain. On your side, I do not suppose you desire to have this exploit made public; on mine, I own to you freely I do not care to draw my breath in a perpetual terror of assassination by the man I sit at meat with. Promise me – but no,' says he, breaking off, 'you are not yet in the quiet possession of your mind; you might think I had extorted the promise from your weakness; and I would leave no door open for casuistry to come in – that dishonesty of the conscientious. Take time to meditate.'

With that he made off up the sliding deck like a squirrel, and plunged into the cabin. About half an hour later he returned – I still lying as he had left me.

'Now,' says he, 'will you give me your troth as a Christian, and a faithful servant of my brother's, that I shall have no more to fear from your attempts?'

'I give it you,' said I.

'I shall require your hand upon it,' says he.

'You have the right to make conditions,' I replied, and we shook hands.

He sat down at once in the same place and the old perilous attitude.

'Hold on!' cried I, covering my eyes. 'I cannot bear to see you in that posture. The least irregularity of the sea might plunge you overboard.'

'You are highly inconsistent,' he replied, smiling, but doing as I asked. 'For all that, Mackellar, I would have you to know you have risen forty feet in my esteem. You think I cannot set a price upon fidelity? But why do you suppose I carry that Secundra Dass about the world with me? Because he would die or do murder for me tomorrow; and I love him for it. Well, you may think it odd, but I like you the better for this afternoon's performance. I thought you were magnetized with the Ten Commandments; but no – God damn my soul!' – he cries, 'the old wife has blood in his body after all! Which does not change the fact,' he continued, smiling again, 'that you have done well to give your promise; for I doubt if you would ever shine in your new trade.'

'I suppose,' said I, 'I should ask your pardon and God's for my attempt. At any rate, I have passed my word, which I will keep faithfully. But when I think of those you persecute——' I paused.

'Life is a singular thing,' said he, 'and mankind a very singular people. You suppose yourself to love my brother. I assure you, it is merely custom. Interrogate your memory; and when first you came to Durrisdeer, you will find you considered him a dull, ordinary youth. He is as dull and ordinary now, though not so young. Had you instead fallen in with me, you would today be as strong upon my side.'

'I would never say you were ordinary, Mr Bally,' I returned; 'but here you prove yourself dull. You have just shown your reliance on my word. In other terms, that is my conscience – the same which starts instinctively back from you, like the eye from a strong light.'

'Ah!' says he, 'but I mean otherwise. I mean, had I met you in my youth. You are to consider I was not always as I am today; nor (had I met in with a friend of your description) should I have ever been so.'

'But, Mr Bally,' says I, 'you would have made a mock of me; you would never have spent ten civil words on such a Square-toes.'

But he was now fairly started on his new course of justification, with which he wearied me throughout the remainder of the passage. No doubt in the past he had taken pleasure to paint himself unnecessarily black, and made a vaunt of his wickedness, bearing it for a coat-of-arms. Nor was he so illogical as to abate one item of his old confessions. 'But now that I know you are a human being,' he would say, 'I can take the trouble to explain myself. For I assure you I am human, too, and have my virtues, like my neighbours.' I say, he wearied me, for I had only the one word to say in answer: twenty times I must have said it: 'Give up your present purpose and return with me to Durrisdeer; then I will believe you.'

Thereupon he would shake his head at me. 'Ah! Mackellar, you might live a thousand years and never understand my nature,' he would say. 'This battle is now committed, the hour of reflection quite past, the hour for mercy not yet come. It began between us when we span a coin in the hall of Durrisdeer, now twenty years ago; we have had our ups and downs, but never either of us dreamed of giving in; and as for me, when my glove is cast, life and honour go with it.'

'A fig for your honour!' I would say. 'And by your leave, these warlike similitudes are something too high-sounding for the matter in hand. You want some dirty money; there is the bottom of your contention; and as for your means, what are they? to stir up sorrow in a family that never harmed you, to debauch (if you can) your own nephew, and to wring the heart of your born brother! A footpad that kills an old granny in a woollen mutch with a dirty bludgeon, and that for a shilling-piece and a paper of snuff – there is all the warrior that you are.'

When I would attack him thus (or somewhat thus) he would smile, and sigh like a man misunderstood. Once, I remember, he defended himself more at large, and had some curious sophistries, worth repeating, for a light upon his character.

'You are very like a civilian to think war consists in drums and banners,' said he. 'War (as the ancients said very wisely) is *ultima ratio*. When we take our advantage unrelentingly, then we make war. Ah! Mackellar, you are a devil of a soldier in the steward's room at Durrisdeer, or the tenants do you sad injustice!'

'I think little of what war is or is not,' I replied. 'But you weary me with claiming my respect. Your brother is a good man, and you are a bad one – neither more nor less.'

'Had I been Alexander——' he began.

'It is so we all dupe ourselves,' I cried. 'Had I been St Paul, it would have been all one; I would have made the same hash of that career that you now see me making of my own.'

'I tell you,' he cried, bearing down my interruption; 'had I been the least petty chieftain in the Highlands, had I been the least king of naked negroes in the African desert, my people would have adored me. A bad man, am I? Ah! but I was born for a good tyrant! Ask Secundra Dass; he will tell you I treat him like a son. Cast in your lot with me tomorrow, become my slave, my chattel, a thing I can command as I command the powers of my own limbs and spirit – you will see no more that dark side that I turn upon the world in anger. I must have all or none. But where all is given, I give it back with usury. I have a kingly nature: there is my loss!'

'It has been hitherto rather the loss of others,' I remarked, 'which seems a little on the hither side of royalty.'

'Tilly-vally!' cried he. 'Even now, I tell you, I would spare that family in which you take so great an interest: yes, even now – tomorrow I would leave them to their petty warfare, and disappear in that forest of cut-throats and thimble-riggers that we call the world. I would do it tomorrow!' says he. 'Only – only——'

'Only what?' I asked.

'Only they must beg it on their bended knees. I think in public, too,' he added, smiling. 'Indeed, Mackellar, I doubt if there be a hall big enough to serve my purpose for that act of reparation.'

'Vanity, vanity!' I moralized. 'To think that this great force for evil should be swayed by the same sentiment that sets a lassie mincing to her glass!'

'Oh! there are double words for everything: the word that swells, the word that belittles; you cannot fight me with a word!' said he. 'You said the other day that I relied on your conscience: were I in your humour of detraction, I might say I built upon your vanity. It is your pretension to be *un homme de parole*; 'tis mine not to accept defeat. Call it vanity, call it virtue, call it greatness of soul – what signifies the expression? But recognize in each of us a common strain: that we both live for an idea.'

It will be gathered from so much familiar talk, and so much patience on both sides, that we now lived together upon excellent terms. Such was again the fact, and this time more seriously than before. Apart from disputations such as that which I have tried to reproduce, not only consideration reigned, but, I am tempted to say, even kindness. When I fell sick (as I did shortly after our great storm), he sat by my berth to entertain me with his conversation, and treated me with excellent remedies, which I accepted with security. Himself commented on the circumstance. 'You see,' says he, 'you begin to know me better. A very little while ago, upon this lonely ship, where no one but myself has any smattering of science, you would have made sure I had designs upon your life. And, observe, it is since I found you had designs upon my own, that I have shown you most respect. You will tell me if this speaks of a small mind.' I found little to reply. In so far as regarded myself, I believed him to mean well; I am, perhaps, the more a dupe of his dissimulation, but I believed (and I still believe) that he regarded me with genuine kindness. Singular and sad fact! so soon as this change began, my animosity abated, and these haunting visions of my master passed utterly away. So that, perhaps, there was truth in the man's last vaunting word to me, uttered on the twenty-second day of July, when our long voyage was at last brought almost to an end, and we lay becalmed at the sea end of the vast harbour of New York, in a gasping heat, which was presently exchanged for a surprising waterfall of rain. I stood on the poop, regarding the green shores near at hand, and now and then the light smoke of the little town, our destination. And as I was even then devising how to steal a march on a familiar enemy, I was conscious of a shade of embarrassment when he approached me with his hand extended.

'I am now to bid you farewell,' said he, 'and that for ever. For now you go among my enemies, where all your former prejudices will revive. I never yet failed to charm a person when I wanted; even you, my good friend – to call you so for once – even you have now a very different portrait of me in your memory, and one that you will never quite forget. The voyage has not lasted long enough, or I should have wrote the impression deeper. But now all is at an end, and we are again at war. Judge by this little interlude how dangerous I am; and tell those fools' – pointing with his finger to the town – 'to think twice and thrice before they set me at defiance.'

CHAPTER TEN

Passages at New York

I HAVE MENTIONED I WAS resolved to steal a march upon the Master; and this, with the complicity of Captain M'Murtrie, was mighty easily effected: a boat being partly loaded on the one side of our ship and the Master placed on board of it, the while a skiff put off from the other, carrying me alone. I had no more trouble in finding a direction to my lord's house, whither I went at top speed, and which I found to be on the outskirts of the place, a very suitable mansion, in a fine garden, with an extraordinary large barn, byre, and stable, all in one. It was here my lord was walking when I arrived; indeed, it had become his chief place of frequentation, and his mind was now filled with farming. I burst in upon him breathless, and gave him my news: which was, indeed, no news at all, several ships having outsailed the *Nonesuch* in the interval.

'We have been expecting you long,' said my lord: 'and indeed, of late days, ceased to expect you any more. I am glad to take your hand again, Mackellar. I thought you had been at the bottom of the sea.'

'Ah! my lord, would God I had!' cried I. 'Things would have been better for yourself.'

'Not in the least,' says he, grimly. 'I could not ask better. There is a long score to pay, and now – at last – I can begin to pay it.'

I cried out against his security.

'Oh!' says he, 'this is not Durrisdeer, and I have taken my precautions. His reputation awaits him; I have prepared a welcome for my brother. Indeed, fortune has served me; for I found here a merchant of Albany who knew him after the '45 and had mighty convenient suspicions of a murder: someone of the name of Chew it was, another Albanian. No one here will be surprised if I deny him my door; he will not be suffered to address my children, nor even to salute my wife: as for myself, I make so much exception for a brother that he may speak to me. I should lose my pleasure else,' says my lord, rubbing his palms.

Presently he bethought himself, and set men off running with billets, to summon the magnates of the province. I cannot recall what pretext he employed; at least, it was successful; and when our ancient enemy appeared upon the scene, he found my lord pacing in front of his house under some trees of shade, with the Governor upon one hand, and various notables upon the other. My lady, who was seated in the verandah, rose with a very pinched expression and carried her children into the house.

The Master, well dressed and with an elegant walking-sword, bowed to the company in a handsome manner and nodded to my lord with familiarity. My lord did not accept the salutation, but looked upon his brother with bended brows.

'Well, sir,' says he, at last, 'what ill wind brings you hither of all places, where (to our common disgrace) your reputation has preceded you?'

'Your lordship is pleased to be civil,' cries the Master, with a fine start.

'I am pleased to be very plain,' returned my lord; 'because it is needful you should clearly understand your situation. At home, where you were so little known, it was still possible to keep appearances; that would be quite vain in this province; and I have to tell you that I am quite resolved to wash my hands of you. You have already ruined me almost to the door, as you ruined my father before me – whose heart you also broke. Your crimes escape the law; but my friend the Governor has promised protection to my family. Have a care, sir!' cries my lord, shaking his cane at him; 'if you are observed to utter two words to any of my innocent household, the law shall be stretched to make you smart for it.'

'Ah!' says the Master, very slowly. 'And so this is the advantage of a foreign land! These gentlemen are unacquainted with our story, I perceive. They do not know that I am the true Lord Durrisdeer; they do not know you are my younger brother, sitting in my place under a sworn family compact; they do not know (or they would not be seen with you in familiar correspondence) that every acre is mine before God Almighty – and every doit of the money you withhold from me, you do it as a thief, a perjurer, and a disloyal brother!'

'General Clinton,' I cried, 'do not listen to his lies. I am the steward of the estate, and there is not one word of truth in it. The man is a forfeited rebel turned into a hired spy: there is his story in two words.'

It was thus that (in the heat of the moment) I let slip his infamy.

'Fellow,' said the Governor, turning his face sternly on the Master, 'I know more of you than you think for. We have some broken ends of your adventures in the provinces, which you will do very well not to drive me to investigate. There is the disappearance of Mr Jacob Chew with all his merchandise; there is the matter of where you came ashore from with so much money and jewels, when you were picked up by a Bermudan out of Albany. Believe me, if I let these matters lie, it is in commiseration for your family, and out of respect for my valued friend, Lord Durrisdeer.'

There was a murmur of applause from the provincials.

'I should have remembered how a title would shine out in such a hole as this,' says the Master, white as a sheet: 'no matter how unjustly come by. It remains for me, then, to die at my lord's door, where my dead body will form a very cheerful ornament.'

'Away with your affectations!' cries my lord. 'You know very well I have no such meaning; only to protect myself from calumny, and my home from your intrusion. I offer you a choice. Either I shall pay your passage home on the first ship, when you may perhaps be able to resume your occupations under Government, although God knows I would rather see you on the highway! Or, if that likes you not, stay here and welcome! I have inquired the least sum on which body and soul can be decently kept together in New York; so much you shall have, paid weekly; and if you cannot labour with your hands to better it, high time you should betake yourself to learn. The condition is – that you speak with no member of my family except myself,' he added.

I do not think I have ever seen any man so pale as was the Master; but he was erect and his mouth firm.

'I have been met here with some very unmerited insults,' said he, 'from which I have certainly no idea to take refuge by flight. Give me your pittance; I take it without shame, for it is mine already – like the shirt upon your back; and I choose to stay until these gentlemen shall understand me better. Already they must spy the cloven hoof, since with all your pretended eagerness for the family honour, you take a pleasure to degrade it in my person.'

'This is all very fine,' says my lord; 'but to us who know you of old, you must be sure it signifies nothing. You take that alternative out of which you think that you can make the most. Take it, if you can, in silence; it will serve you better in the long run, you may believe me, than this ostentation of ingratitude.'

'Oh, gratitude, my lord,' cries the Master, with a mounting intonation and his forefinger very conspicuously lifted up. 'Be at rest: it will not fail you. It now remains that I should salute these gentlemen whom we have wearied with out family affairs.'

And he bowed to each in succession, settled his walking-sword, and took himself off, leaving everyone amazed at his behaviour, and me not less so at my lord's.

We were now to enter on a changed phase of this family division. The Master was by no manner of means so helpless as my lord supposed, having at his hand, and entirely devoted to his service, an excellent artist in all sorts of goldsmith work. With my lord's allowance, which was not so scanty as he had described it, the pair could support life; and all the earning of Secundra Dass might be laid upon one side for any future purpose. That this was done, I have no doubt. It was in all likelihood the Master's design to gather a sufficiency, and then proceed in quest of that treasure which he had buried long before among the mountains; to which, if he had confined himself, he would have been more happily inspired. But unfortunately for himself and all of us, he took counsel of his anger. The public disgrace of his arrival – which I sometimes wonder he could manage to survive – rankled in his bones; he was in that humour when a man – in the words of the old adage – will cut off his nose to spite his face; and he must make himself a public spectacle in the hopes that some of the disgrace might spatter on my lord.

He chose, in a poor quarter of the town, a lonely, small house of boards, overhung with some acacias. It was furnished in front with a sort of hutch opening, like that of a dog's kennel, but about as high as a table from the ground, in which the poor man that built it had formerly displayed some wares; and it was this which took the Master's fancy and possibly suggested his proceedings. It appears, on board the pirate ship he had acquired some quickness with the needle – enough, at least, to play the part of tailor in the public eye; which was all that was required by the nature of his vengeance. A placard was hung above the hutch, bearing these words in something of the following disposition:

James Durie
formerly MASTER of BALLANTRAE
Clothes Neatly Clouted

SECUNDRA DASS,
Decayed Gentleman of India
Fine Goldsmith work

Underneath this, when he had a job, my gentleman sat withinside tailorwise and busily stitching. I say, when he had a job; but such customers as came were rather for Secundra and the Master's sewing would be more in the manner of Penelope's. He could never have designed to gain even butter to his bread by such a means of livelihood: enough for him that there was the name of Durie dragged in the dirt on the placard, and the sometime heir of that proud family set up cross-legged in public for a reproach upon his brother's meanness. And in so far his device succeeded that there was murmuring in the town and a party formed highly inimical to my lord. My lord's favour with the Governor laid him more open on the other side; my lady (who was never so well received in the colony) met with painful innuendoes; in a party of women, where it would be the topic most natural to introduce, she was almost debarred from the naming of needlework; and I have seen her return with a flushed countenance and vow that she would go abroad no more.

In the meantime my lord dwelled in his decent mansion, immersed in farming; a popular man with his intimates, and careless or unconscious of the rest. He laid on flesh; had a bright, busy face; even the heat seemed to prosper with him; and my lady – in despite of her own annoyances – daily blessed Heaven her father should have left her such a paradise. She had looked on from a window upon the Master's humiliation; and from that hour appeared to feel at ease. I was not so sure myself; as time went on there seemed to me a something not quite wholesome in my lord's condition. Happy he was, beyond a doubt, but the grounds of this felicity were secret; even in the bosom of his family he brooded with manifest delight upon some private thought; and I conceived at last the suspicion (quite unworthy of us both) that he kept a mistress somewhere in the town. Yet he went little abroad, and his day was very fully occupied; indeed, there was but a single period, and that pretty early in the morning, while Mr Alexander was at his lesson-book, of which I was not certain of the disposition. It should be borne in mind, in the defence of that which I now did, that I was always in some fear my lord was not quite justly in his reason; and with our enemy sitting so still in the same town with us, I did well to be upon my guard. Accordingly I made a pretext, had the hour changed at which I taught Mr Alexander the foundation of cyphering and the mathematic, and set myself instead to dog my master's footsteps.

Every morning, fair or foul, he took his gold-headed cane, set his hat on the back of his head – a recent habitude, which I thought to indicate a burning brow – and betook himself to make a certain circuit. At the first his way was among pleasant trees and beside a graveyard, where he would sit awhile, if the day were fine, in meditation. Presently the path turned down to the waterside, and came back along the harbour-front and past the Master's booth. As he approached this second part of his circuit, my Lord Durrisdeer began to pace more leisurely, like a man delighted with the air and scene; and before the booth, half-way between that and the water's edge, would pause a little, leaning on his staff. It was the hour when the Master sate within upon his board and plied his needle. So these two brothers would gaze upon each other with hard faces; and then my lord moved on again, smiling to himself.

It was but twice that I must stoop to that ungrateful necessity of playing spy. I was then certain of my lord's purpose in his rambles and of the secret source of his delight. Here was his mistress: it was hatred and not love that gave him healthful colours. Some moralists might have been relieved by the discovery; I confess that I was dismayed. I found this situation of two brethren not only odious in itself, but big with possibilities of further evil; and I made it my practice, in so far as many occupations would allow, to go by a shorter path and be secretly present at their meeting. Coming down one day a little late, after I had been near a week prevented, I was struck with surprise to find a new development. I should say there was a bench against the Master's house, where customers might sit to parley with the shopman; and here I found my lord seated, nursing his cane and looking pleasantly forth upon the bay. Not three feet from him sate the Master, stitching. Neither spoke; nor (in this new situation) did my lord so much as cast a glance upon his enemy. He tasted his neighbourhood, I must suppose, less indirectly in the bare proximity of person; and, without doubt, drank deep of hateful pleasures.

He had no sooner come away than I openly joined him.

'My lord, my lord,' said I, 'this is no manner of behaviour.

'I grow fat upon it,' he replied; and not merely the words, which were strange enough, but the whole character of his expression shocked me.

'I warn you, my lord, against this indulgency of evil feeling,' said I. 'I know not to which it is more perilous, the soul or the reason; but you go the way to murder both.'

'You cannot understand,' said he. 'You had never such mountains of bitterness upon your heart.'

'And if it were no more,' I added, 'you will surely goad the man to some extremity.'

'To the contrary; I am breaking his spirit,' says my lord.

Every morning for hard upon a week my lord took this same place upon the bench. It was a pleasant place, under the green acacias, with a sight upon the bay and shipping, and a sound (from some way off) of mariners singing at their employ. Here the two sate without speech or any external movement, beyond that of the needle or the Master biting off a thread, for he still clung to his pretence of industry; and here I made a point to join them wondering at myself and my companions. If any of my lord's friends went by, he would hail them cheerfully, and cry out he was there to give some good advice to his brother, who was now (to his delight) grown quite industrious. And even this the Master accepted with a steady countenance; what was in his mind, God knows, or perhaps Satan only.

All of a sudden, on a still day of what they call the Indian Summer, when the woods were changed into gold and pink and scarlet, the Master laid down his needle and burst into a fit of merriment. I think he must have been preparing it a long while in silence, for the note in itself was pretty naturally pitched; but breaking suddenly from so extreme a silence, and in circumstances so averse from mirth, it sounded ominously on my ear.

'Henry,' said he, 'I have for once made a false step, and for once you have had the wit to profit by it. The farce of the cobbler ends today; and I confess to you (with my compliments) that you have had the best of it. Blood will out; and you have certainly a choice idea of hos to make yourself unpleasant.'

Never a word said my lord; it was just as though the Master had not broken silence.

'Come,' resumed the Master, 'do not be sulky; it will spoil your attitude. You can now afford (believe me) to be a little gracious; for I have not merely a defeat to accept. I had meant to continue this performance till I had gathered enough money for a certain purpose; I confess ingenuously, I have not the courage. You naturally desire my absence from this town; I have come round by another way to the same idea. And I have a proposition to make; or, if your lordship prefers, a favour to ask.'

'Ask it,' says my lord.

'You may have heard that I had once in this country a considerable treasure,' returned the Master; 'it matters not whether or no – such is the fact; and I was obliged to bury it in a spot of which I have sufficient indications. To the recovery of this has my ambition now come down; and, as it is my own, you will not grudge it me.'

'Go and get it,' says my lord. 'I make no opposition.'

'Yes,' said the Master; 'but to do so, I must find men and carriage. The way is long and rough, and the country infested with wild Indians. Advance me only so much as shall be needful: either as a lump sum, in lieu of my allowance; or, if you prefer it, as a loan, which I shall repay on my return. And then, if you so decide, you may have seen the last of me.'

My lord stared him steadily in the eyes; there was a hard smile upon his face, but he uttered nothing.

'Henry,' said the Master, with a formidable quietness, and drawing at the same time somewhat back – 'Henry, I had the honour to address you.'

'Let us be stepping homeward,' says my lord to me, who was plucking at his sleeve; and with that he rose, stretched himself, settled his hat, and still without a syllable of response, began to walk steadily along the shore.

I hesitated awhile between the two brothers, so serious a climax did we seem to have reached. But the Master had resumed his occupation, his eyes lowered, his hand seemingly as deft as ever; and I decided to pursue my lord.

'Are you mad?' I cried, so soon as I had overtook him. 'Would you cast away so fair an opportunity?'

'Is it possible you should still believe in him?' inquired my lord, almost with a sneer.

'I wish him forth of this town!' I cried. 'I wish him anywhere and anyhow but as he is.'

'I have said my say,' returned my lord, 'and you have said yours. There let it rest.'

But I was bent on dislodging the Master. That sight of him patiently returning to his needlework was more than my imagination could digest. There was never a man made, and the Master the least of any, that could accept so long a series of insults. The air smelt blood to me. And I vowed there should be no neglect of mine if, through any chink of possibility, crime could be yet turned aside. That same day, therefore, I came to my lord in his business room, where he sat upon some trivial occupation.

'My lord,' said I, 'I have found a suitable investment for my small economies. But these are unhappily in Scotland; it will take some time to lift them, and the affair presses. Could your lordship see his way to advance me the amount against my note?'

He read me awhile with keen eyes. 'I have never inquired into the state of your affairs, Mackellar,' says he. 'Beyond the amount of your caution, you may not be worth a farthing, for what I know.'

'I have been a long while in your service, and never told a lie, nor yet asked a favour for myself,' said I, 'until today.'

'A favour for the Master,' he returned, quietly. 'Do you take me for a fool, Mackellar? Understand it once and for all, I treat this beast in my own way; fear nor favour shall not move me; and before I am hoodwinked, it will require a trickster less transparent than yourself. I ask service, loyal service; not that you should make and mar behind my back, and steal my own money to defeat me.'

'My lord,' said I, 'these are very unpardonable expressions.'

'Think once more, Mackellar,' he replied; 'and you will see they fit the fact. It is your own subterfuge that is unpardonable. Deny (if you can) that you designed this money to evade my orders with, and I will ask your pardon freely. If you cannot, you must have the resolution to hear your conduct go by its own name.'

'If you think I had any design but to save you——' I began.

'Oh! my old friend,' said he, 'you know very well what I think! Here is my hand to you with all my heart; but of money, not one rap.'

Defeated upon this side, I went straight to my room, wrote a letter, ran with it to the harbour, for I knew a ship was on the point of sailing; and came to the Master's door a little before dusk. Entering without the form of any knock, I found him sitting with his Indian at a simple meal of maize porridge with some milk. The house within was clean and poor; only a few books upon a shelf distinguished it, and (in one corner) Secundra's little bench.

'Mr Bally,' said I, 'I have near five hundred pounds laid by in Scotland, the economies of a hard life. A letter goes by yon ship to have it lifted. Have so much patience till the return ship comes in, and it is all yours, upon the same condition you offered to my lord this morning.'

He rose from the table, came forward, took me by the shoulders, and looked me in the face, smiling.

'And yet you are very fond of money!' said he. 'And yet you love money beyond all things else, except my brother!'

'I fear old age and poverty,' said I, 'which is another matter.'

'I will never quarrel for a name. Call it so,' he replied. 'Ah, Mackellar, Mackellar, if this were done from any love to me, how gladly would I close upon your offer!'

'And yet,' I eagerly answered – 'I say it to my shame, but I cannot see you in this poor place without compunction. It is not my single thought, nor my first; and yet it's there! I would gladly see you delivered. I do not offer it in love, and far from that; but, as God judges me – and I wonder at it too! – quite without enmity.'

'Ah!' says he, still holding my shoulders, and now gently shaking me, 'you think of me more than you suppose. "And I wonder at it too,"' he added, repeating my expression and, I suppose, something of my voice. 'You are an honest man, and for that cause I spare you.'

'Spare me?' I cried.

'Spare you,' he repeated, letting me go and turning away. And then fronting me once more: 'You little know what I would do with it, Mackellar! Did you think I had swallowed my defeat indeed? Listen: my life has been a series of unmerited cast-backs. That fool, Prince Charlie, mismanaged a most promising affair: there fell my first fortune. In Paris I had my foot once more high up on the ladder: that time it was an accident: a letter came to the wrong hand, and I was bare again. A third time I found my opportunity; I built up a place for myself in India with an infinite patience; and then Clive came, my rajah was swallowed up, and I escaped out of the convulsion, like another Aeneas, with Secundra Dass upon my back. Three times I have had my hand upon the highest station: and I am not yet three-and-forty. I know the world as few men know it when they come to die – Court and camp, the East and the West; I know where to go, I see a thousand openings. I am now at the height of my resources, sound of health, of inordinate ambition. Well, all this I resign; I care not if I die and the world never hear of me; I care only for one thing, and that I will have. Mind yourself; lest, when the roof falls, you, too, should be crushed under the ruins.'

As I came out of his house, all hope of intervention quite destroyed, I was aware of a stir on the harbour side, and, raising my eyes, there was a great ship newly come to anchor. It seems strange I could have looked upon her with so much indifference, for she brought death to the brothers of Durrisdeer. After all the desperate episodes of this contention, the insults, the opposing interests, the fraternal duel in the shrubbery, it was reserved for some poor devil in Grub Street, scribbling for his dinner, and not caring what he scribbled, to cast a spell across four thousand miles of the salt sea, and send forth both these brothers into savage and wintry deserts, there to die. But such a thought was distant from my mind; and while all the provincials were fluttered about me by the unusual animation of their port, I passed throughout their midst on my return homeward, quite absorbed in the recollection of my visit and the Master's speech.

The same night there was brought to us from the ship a little packet of pamphlets. The next day my lord was under engagement to go with the Governor upon some party of pleasure; the time was nearly due, and I left him for a moment alone in his room and skimming through the pamphlets. When I returned, his head had fallen upon the table, his arms lying abroad amongst the crumpled papers.

'My lord, my lord!' I cried as I ran forward, for I supposed he was in some fit.

He sprang up like a figure upon wires, his countenance deformed with fury, so that in a strange place I should scarce have known him. His hand at the same time flew above his head, as though to strike me down. 'Leave me alone!' he screeched, and I fled, as fast as my shaking legs would bear me, for my lady. She, too, lost no time; but when we returned, he had the door locked within, and only cried to us from the other side to leave him be. We looked in each other's faces, very white – each supposing the blow had come at last.

'I will write to the Governor to excuse him,' says she. 'We must keep our strong friends.' But when she took up the pen, it flew out of her fingers. 'I cannot write,' said she. 'Can you?'

'I will make a shift, my lady,' said I.

She looked over me as I wrote. 'That will do,' she said, when I had done. 'Thank God, Mackellar, I have you to lean upon! But what can it be now? What, what can it be?'

In my own mind, I believed there was no explanation possible, and none required; it was my fear that the man's madness had now simply burst forth its way, like the long-smothered flames of a volcano; but to this (in mere mercy to my lady) I durst not give expression.

'It is more to the purpose to consider our own behaviour,' said I. 'Must we leave him there alone?'

'I do not dare disturb him,' she replied. 'Nature may know best; it may be Nature that cries to be alone; and we grope in the dark. Oh yes, I would leave him as he is.'

'I will, then, despatch this letter, my lady, and return here, if you please, to sit with you,' said I.

'Pray do,' cries my lady.

All afternoon we sat together, mostly in silence, watching my lord's door. My own mind was busy with the scene that had just passed, and its singular resemblance to my vision. I must say a word upon this, for the story has gone abroad with great exaggeration, and I have even seen it printed, and my own name referred to for particulars. So much was the same: here was my lord in a room, with his head upon the table, and when he raised his face, it wore such an expression as distressed me to the soul. But the room was different, my lord's attitude at the table not at all the same, and his face, when he disclosed it, expressed a painful degree of fury instead of that haunting despair which had always (except once, already referred to) characterized it in the vision. There is the whole truth at last before the public; and if the differences be great, the coincidence was yet enough to fill me with uneasiness. All afternoon, as I say, I sat and pondered upon this quite to myself; for my lady had trouble of her own, and it was my last thought to vex her with fancies. About the midst of our time of waiting, she conceived an ingenious scheme, had Mr Alexander fetched, and bid him knock at his father's door. My lord sent the boy about his business, but without the least violence, whether of manner or expression; so that I began to entertain a hope the fit was over.

At last, as the night fell and I was lighting a lamp that stood there trimmed, the door opened and my lord stood within upon the threshold. The light was not so strong that we could read his countenance; when he spoke, methought his voice a little altered but yet perfectly, steady.

'Mackellar,' said he, 'carry this note to its destination with your own hand. It is highly private. Find the person alone when you deliver it.'

'Henry,' says my lady, 'you are not ill?'

'No, no,' says he, querulously, 'I am occupied. Not at all; I am only occupied. It is a singular thing a man must be supposed to be ill when he has any business! Send me supper to this room, and a basket of wine: I expect the visit of a friend. Otherwise I am not to be disturbed.'

And with that he once more shut himself in.

The note was addressed to one Captain Harris, at a tavern on the portside. I knew Harris (by reputation) for a dangerous adventurer, highly suspected of piracy in the past, and now following the rude business of an Indian trader. What my lord should have to say to him, or he to my lord, it passed my imagination to conceive: or yet how my lord had heard of him, unless by a disgraceful trial from which the man was recently escaped. Altogether I went upon the errand with reluctance, and from the little I saw of the Captain, returned from it with sorrow. I found him in a foul-smelling chamber, sitting by a guttering candle and an empty bottle; he had the remains of a military carriage, or rather perhaps it was an affectation, for his manners were low.

'Tell my lord, with my service, that I will wait upon his lordship in the inside of half an hour,' says he, when he had read the note; and then had the servility, pointing to his empty bottle, to propose that I should buy him liquor.

Although I returned with my best speed, the Captain followed close upon my heels, and he stayed late into the night. The cock was crowing a second time when I saw (from my chamber window) my lord lighting him to the gate, both men very much affected with their potations, and sometimes leaning one upon the other to confabulate. Yet the next morning my lord was abroad again early with a hundred pounds of money in his pocket. I never supposed that he returned with it; and yet I was quite sure it did not find its way to the Master, for I lingered all morning within view of the booth. That was the last time my Lord Durrisdeer passed his own enclosure till we left New York; he walked in his barn, or sat and talked with his family, all much as usual; but the town saw nothing of him, and his daily visits to the Master seemed forgotten. Nor yet did Harris reappear; or not until the end.

I was now much oppressed with a sense of the mysteries in which we had begun to move. It was plain, if only from his change of habitude, my lord had something on his mind of a grave nature; but what it was, whence it sprang, or why he should now keep the house and garden, I could make no guess at. It was clear, even to probation, the pamphlets had some share in this revolution; I read all I could find, and they were all extremely insignificant, and of the usual kind of party scurrility; even to a high politician, I could spy out no particular matter of offence, and my lord was a man rather indifferent on public questions. The truth is, the pamphlet which was the spring of this affair, lay all the time on my lord's bosom. There it was that I found it at last, after he was dead, in the midst of the north wilderness: in such a place, in such dismal circumstances, I was to read for the first time these idle, lying words of a Whig pamphleteer declaiming against indulgency to Jacobites:– 'Another notorious Rebel, the M——r of B——e, is to have his Title restored,' the passage ran. 'This Business has been long in hand, since he rendered some very disgraceful Services in Scotland and France. His Brother, L——d D——r, is known to be no better than himself in Inclination; and the supposed Heir, who is now to be set aside, was bred up in the most detestable Principles. In the old Phrase, it is *six of the one and half a dozen of the other*; but the Favour of such a Reposition is too extreme to be passed over.' A man in his right wits could not have cared two straws for a tale so manifestly false; that Government should ever entertain the notion, was inconceivable to any reasoning creature, unless possibly the fool that penned it; and my lord, though never brilliant, was ever remarkable for sense. That he should credit such a rodomontade, and carry the pamphlet on his bosom and the words in his heart, is the clear proof of the man's lunacy. Doubtless the mere mention of Mr Alexander, and the threat directly held out against the child's succession, precipitated that which had so long impended. Or else my master had been truly mad for a long time, and we were too dull or too much used to him, and did not perceive the extent of his infirmity.

About a week after the day of the pamphlets I was late upon the harbour-side, and took a turn towards the Master's, as I often did. The door opened, a flood of light came forth upon the road, and I beheld a man taking his departure with friendly salutations. I cannot say how singularly I was shaken to recognize the adventurer Harris. I could not but conclude it was the hand of my lord that had brought him there; and prolonged my walk in very serious and apprehensive thought. It was late when I came home, and there was my lord making up his portmanteau for a voyage.

'Why do you come so late?' he cried. 'We leave tomorrow for Albany, you and I together; and it is high time you were about your preparations.'

'For Albany, my lord?' I cried. 'And for what earthly purpose?'

'Change of scene,' said he.

And my lady, who appeared to have been weeping, gave me the signal to obey without more parley. She told me a little later (when we found occasion to exchange some words) that he had suddenly announced his intention after a visit from Captain Harris, and her best endeavours, whether to dissuade him from the journey, or to elicit some explanation of its purpose, had alike proved unavailing.

CHAPTER ELEVEN

The Journey in the Wilderness

WE MADE A PROSPEROUS VOYAGE up that fine river of the Hudson, the weather grateful, the hills singularly beautified with the colours of the autumn. At Albany we had our residence at an inn, where I was not so blind and my lord not so cunning but what I could see he had some design to hold me prisoner. The work he found for me to do was not so pressing that we should transact it apart from necessary papers in the chamber of an inn; nor was it of such importance that I should be set upon as many as four or five scrolls of the same document. I submitted in appearance; but I took private measures on my own side, and had the news of the town communicated to me daily by the politeness of our host. In this way I received at last a piece of intelligence for which, I may say, I had been waiting. Captain Harris (I was told) with 'Mr Mountain, the trader,' had gone up the river in a boat. I would have feared the landlord's eye, so strong the sense of some complicity upon my master's part oppressed me. But I made out to say I had some knowledge of the Captain, although none of Mr Mountain, and to inquire who else was of the party. My informant knew not; Mr Mountain had come ashore upon some needful purchases; had gone round the town buying, drinking, and prating; and it seemed the party went upon some likely venture, for he had spoken much of great things he would do when he returned. No more was known, for none of the rest had come ashore, and it seemed they were pressed for time to reach a certain spot before the snow should fall.

And sure enough, the next day, there fell a sprinkle even in Albany; but it passed as it came, and was but a reminder of what lay before us. I thought of it lightly then, knowing so little as I did of that inclement province: the retrospect is different; and I wonder at times if some of the horror of these events which I must now rehearse flowed not from the foul skies and savage winds to which we were exposed, and the agony of cold that we must suffer.

The boat having passed by, I thought at first we should have left the town. But no such matter. My lord continued his stay in Albany, where he had no ostensible affairs, and kept me by him, far from my due employment, and making a pretence of occupation. It is upon this passage I expect, and perhaps deserve, censure. I was not so dull but what I had my own thoughts. I could not see the Master entrust himself into the hands of Harris, and not expect some underhand contrivance. Harris bore a villainous reputation, and he had been tampered with in private by my lord; Mountain, the trader, proved, upon inquiry, to be another of the same kidney; the errand they were all gone upon being the recovery of ill-gotten treasures, offered in itself a very strong incentive to foul play; and the character of the country where they journeyed promised impunity to deeds of blood. Well: it is true I had all these thoughts and fears, and guesses of the Master's fate. But you are to consider I was the same man that sought to dash him from the bulwarks of a ship in the mid-sea; the same that, a little before, very impiously but sincerely offered God a bargain, seeking to hire God to be my bravo. It is true again that I had a good deal melted towards our enemy. But this I always thought of as a weakness of the flesh and even culpable; my mind remaining steady and quite bent against him. True, yet again, that it was one thing to assume on my own shoulders the guilt and danger of a criminal attempt, and another to stand by and see my lord imperil and besmirch himself. But this was the very ground of my inaction. For (should I anyway stir in the business) I might fail indeed to save the Master, but I could not miss to make a byword of my lord.

Thus it was that I did nothing; and upon the same reasons, I am still strong to justify my course. My lord had carried with him several introductions to chief people of the town and neighbourhood; others he had before encountered in New York: with this consequence, that he went much abroad, and I am sorry to say was altogether too convivial in his habits. I was often in bed, but never asleep, when he returned; and there was scarce a night when he did not betray the influence of liquor. By day he would still lay upon me endless tasks, which he showed considerable ingenuity to fish up and renew, in the manner of Penelope's web. I never refused, as I say, for I was hired to do his bidding; but I took no pains to keep my penetration under a bushel, and would sometimes smile in his face.

I think I must be the devil and you Michael Scott,' I said to him one day. 'I have bridged the Tweed and split the Eildons; and now you set me to the rope of sand.'

He looked at me with shining eyes, and looked away again, his jaw chewing, but without words.

'Well, well, my lord,' said I, 'your will is my pleasure. I will do this thing for the fourth time; but I would beg of you to invent another task against tomorrow, for by my troth, I am weary of this one.'

'You do not know what you are saying,' returned my lord, putting on his hat and turning back to me. 'It is a strange thing you should take a pleasure to annoy me. A friend – but that is a different affair. It is a strange thing. I am a man that has had ill-fortune all my life through. I am still surrounded by contrivances. I am always treading in plots,' he burst out. 'The whole world is banded against me.'

'I would not talk wicked nonsense if I were you,' said I: 'but I will tell you what I *would* do – I would put my head in cold water, for you had more last night than you could carry.'

'Do ye think that?' said he, with a manner of interest highly awakened. 'Would that be good for me? It's a thing I never tried.'

'I mind the days when you had no call to try, and I wish, my lord, that they were back again,' said I. 'But the plain truth is, if you continue to exceed, you will do yourself a mischief.'

'I don't appear to carry drink the way I used to,' said my lord. 'I get overtaken, Mackellar. But I will be more upon my guard.'

'That is what I would ask of you,' I replied. 'You are to bear in mind that you are Mr Alexander's father: give the bairn a chance to carry his name with some responsibility.'

'Ay, ay,' said he. 'Ye're a very sensible man, Mackellar, and have been long in my employ. But I think, if you have nothing more to say to me, I will be stepping. If you have nothing more to say?' he added, with that burning, childish eagerness that was now so common with the man.

'No, my lord, I have nothing more,' said I, dryly enough.

'Then I think I will be stepping,' says my lord, and stood and looked at me, fidgeting with his hat, which he had taken off again. 'I suppose you will have no errands. No? I am to meet Sir William Johnson, but I will be more upon my guard.' He was silent for a time, and then, smiling: 'Do you call to mind a place, Mackellar – it's a little below Eagles – where the burn runs very deep under a wood of rowans. I mind being there when I was a lad – dear, it comes over me like an old song! – I was after the fishing, and I made a bonny cast. Eh, but I was happy. I wonder, Mackellar, why I am never happy now?'

'My lord,' said I, 'if you would drink with more moderation you would have the better chance. It is an old byword that the bottle is a false consoler.'

'No doubt,' said he, 'no doubt. Well, I think I will be going.'

'Good-morning, my lord,' said I.

'Good-morning, good-morning,' said he, and so got himself at last from the apartment.

I give that for a fair specimen of my lord in the morning; and I must have described my patron very ill if the reader does not perceive a notable falling off. To behold the man thus fallen: to know him accepted among his companions for a poor, muddled toper, welcome (if he were welcome at all) for the bare consideration of his title; and to recall the virtues he had once displayed against such odds of fortune; was not this a thing at once to rage and to be humbled at?

In his cups he was more excessive. I will give but the one scene, close upon the end, which is strongly marked upon my memory to this day, and at the time affected me almost with horor.

I was in bed, lying there awake, when I heard him stumbling on the stair and singing. My lord had no gift of music, his brother had all the graces of the family, so that when I say singing, you are to understand a manner of high, carolling utterance, which was truly neither speech nor song. Something not unlike is to be heard upon the lips of children, ere they learn shame; from those of a man grown elderly, it had a strange effect. He opened the door with noisy precaution; peered in, shading his candle; conceived me to slumber; entered, set his light upon the table, and took off his hat. I saw him very plain; a high feverish exultation appeared to boil in his veins, and he stood and smiled and smirked upon the candle. Presently he lifted up his arm, snapped his fingers, and fell to undress. As he did so, having once more forgot my presence, he took back to his singing; and now I could hear the words, which were those from the old song of the *Twa Corbies* endlessly repeated:

> And over his banes when they are bare
> The wind sall blaw for evermair!

I have said there was no music in the man. His strains had no logical succession except in so far as they inclined a little to the minor mode; but they exercised a rude potency upon the feelings, and followed the words, and signified the feelings of the singer with barbaric fitness. He took it first in the time and manner of a rant; presently this ill-favoured gleefulness abated, he began to dwell upon the notes more feelingly, and sank at last into a degree of maudlin pathos that was to me scarce bearable. By equal steps, the original briskness of his acts declined; and when he was stripped to his breeches, he sat on the bedside and fell to whimpering. I know nothing less respectable than the tears of drunkenness, and turned my back impatiently on this poor sight.

But he had started himself (I am to suppose) on that slippery descent of self-pity; on the which, to a man unstrung by old sorrows and recent potations, there is no arrest except exhaustion. His tears continued to flow, and the man to sit there, three parts naked, in the cold air of the chamber. I twitted myself alternately with inhumanity and sentimental weakness, now half rising in my bed to interfere, now reading myself lessons of indifference and courting slumber, until, upon a sudden, the *quantum mutatus ab illo* shot into my mind; and calling to remembrance his old wisdom, constancy, and patience, I was overborne with a pity almost approaching the passionate, not for my master alone but for the sons of man.

At this I leaped from my place, went over to his side and laid a hand on his bare shoulder, which was cold as stone. He uncovered his face and showed it me all swollen and begrutten* like a child's; and at the sight my impatience partially revived.

'Think shame to yourself,' said I. 'This is bairnly conduct. I might have been
*Tear-marked.

snivelling myself, if I had cared to swill my belly with wine. But I went to my bed sober like a man. Come: get into yours, and have done with this pitiable exhibition.'

'Oh, Mackellar,' said he, 'my heart is wae!'

'Wae?' cried I. 'For a good cause, I think. What words were these you sang as you came in? Show pity to others, we then can talk of pity to yourself. You can be the one thing or the other, but I will be no party to halfway houses. If you're a striker, strike, and if you're a bleater, bleat!'

'Ay!' cries he, with a burst, 'that's it – strike! that's talking! Man, I've stood it all too long. But when they laid a hand upon the child, when the child's threatened' – his momentary vigour whimpering off – 'my child, my Alexander!' – and he was at his tears again.

I took him by the shoulder and shook him. 'Alexander!' said I. 'Do you ever think of him? Not you! Look yourself in the face like a brave man, and you'll find you're but a self-deceiver. The wife, the friend, the child, they're all equally forgot, and you sunk in a mere bog of selfishness.'

'Mackellar,' said he, with a wonderful return to his old manner and appearance, 'you may say what you will of me, but one thing I never was – I was never selfish.'

'I will open your eyes in your despite,' said I. 'How long have we been here? and how often have you written to your family? I think this is the first time you were ever separate: have you written at all? Do they know if you are dead or living?'

I had caught him here too openly; it braced his better nature; there was no more weeping, he thanked me very penitently, got to bed and was soon fast asleep; and the first thing he did the next morning was to sit down and begin a letter to my lady: a very tender letter it was too, though it was never finished. Indeed all communication with New York was transacted by myself; and it will be judged I had a thankless task of it. What to tell my lady and in what words, and how far to be false and how far cruel, was a thing that kept me often from my slumber.

All this while, no doubt, my lord waited with growing impatiency for news of his accomplices. Harris, it is to be thought, had promised a high degree of expedition; the time was already overpast when word was to be looked for; and suspense was a very evil counsellor to a man of an impared intelligence. My lord's mind throughout this interval dwelled almost wholly in the Wilderness, following that party with whose deeds he had so much concern. He continually conjured up their camps and progresses, the fashion of the country, the perpetration in a thousand different manners of the same horrid fact, and that consequent spectacle of the Master's bones lying scattered in the wind. These private guilty considerations I would continually observe to peep forth in the man's talk, like rabbits from a hill. And it is the less wonder if the scene of his meditations began to draw him bodily.

It is well known what pretext he book. Sir William Johnson had a diplomatic errand in these parts; and my lord and I (from curiosity, as was given out) went in his company. Sir William was well attended and liberally supplied. Hunters brought us venison, fish was taken for us daily in the streams, and brandy ran like water. We proceeded by day and encamped by night in the military style; sentinels were set and changed; every man had his named duty; and Sir William was the spring of all. There was much in this that might at times have entertained me; but, for our misfortune, the weather was extremely harsh, the days were in the beginning open, but the nights frosty from the first. A painful keen wind blew most of the time, so that we sat in the boat with flue fingers, and at night, as we scorched our faces at the fire, the clothes upon our back appeared to be of paper. A dreadful solitude surrounded our steps; the land was quite dispeopled, there was no smoke of fires, and save for a single boat of merchants on the second day, we met no travellers. The season was indeed late, but this desertion of the waterways impressed Sir William himself; and I have heard him more than once express a sense of intimidation. 'I have come too late, I fear; they must have dug up the hatchet,' he said; and the future proved how justly he had reasoned.

I could never depict the blackness of my soul upon this journey. I have none of those minds that are in love with the unusual; to see the winter coming and to lie in the field so far from any house, oppressed me like a nightmare; it seemed, indeed, a kind of awful braving of God's power; and this thought, which I daresay only writes me down a coward, was greatly exaggerated by my private knowledge of the errand we were come upon. I was besides encumbered by my duties to Sir William, whom it fell upon me to entertain; for my lord was quite sunk into a state bordering on *pervigilium*, watching the woods with a rapt eye, sleeping scarce at all, and speaking sometimes not twenty words in a whole day. That which he said was still coherent; but it turned almost invariably upon the party for whom he kept his crazy look-out. He would tell Sir William often, and always as if it were a new communication, that he had 'a brother somewhere in the woods,' and beg that the sentinels should be directed 'to inquire for him.' 'I am anxious for news of my brother,' he would say. And sometimes, when we were under way, he would fancy he spied a canoe far off upon the water or a camp on the shore, and exhibit painful agitation. It was impossible but Sir William should be struck with these singularities; and at last he led me aside, and hinted his uneasiness. I touched my head and shook it; quite rejoiced to prepare a little testimony against possible disclosures.

'But in that case,' cries Sir William, 'is it wise to let him go at large?'

'Those that know him best,' said I, 'are persuaded that he should be humoured.'

'Well, well,' replied Sir William, 'it is none of my affairs. But if I had understood, you would never have been here.'

Our advance into this savage country had thus uneventfully proceeded for about a week, when we encamped for a night at a place where the river ran among considerable mountains clothed in wood. The fires were lighted in a level space at the water's edge; and we supped and lay down to sleep in the customary fashion. It chanced the night fell murderously cold; the stringency of the frost seized and bit me through my coverings, so that pain kept me wakeful; and I was afoot again before the peep of day, crouching by the fires or trotting to and fro at the stream's edge, to combat the aching of my limbs. At last dawn began to break upon hoar woods and mountains, the sleepers rolled in their robes, and the boisterous river dashing among spears of ice. I stood looking about me, swaddled in my stiff coat of a bull's fur, and the breath smoking from my scorched nostrils, when, upon a sudden, a singular, eager cry rang from the borders of the wood. The sentries answered it, the sleepers sprang to their feet, one pointed, the rest followed his direction with their eyes, and there, upon the edge of the forest and betwixt two trees we beheld the figure of a man reaching forth his hands like one in ecstasy. The next moment he ran forward, fell on his knees at the side of the camp, and burst in tears.

This was John Mountain, the trader, escaped from the most horrid perils; and his first word, when he got speech, was to ask if we had seen Secundra Dass.

'Seen what?' cries Sir William.

'No,' said I, 'we have seen nothing of him. Why?'

'Nothing?' says Mountain. 'Then I was right after all.' With that he struck his palm upon his brow. 'But what takes him back?' he cried. 'What takes the man back among dead bodies? There is some damned mystery here.'

This was a word which highly aroused our curiosity, but I shall be more perspicacious, if I narrate these incidents in their true order. Here follows a narrative which I have compiled out of three sources, not very consistent in all points:

First, a written statement by Mountain, in which everything criminal is cleverly smuggled out of view;

Second, two conversations with Secundra Dass; and

Third, many conversations with Mountain himself, in which he was pleased to be entirely plain; for the truth is he regarded me as an accomplice.

NARRATIVE OF THE TRADER, MOUNTAIN

The crew that went up the river under the joint command of Captain Harris and the Master numbered in all nine persons, of whom (if I except Secundra Dass) there was not one that had not merited the gallows. From Harris downwards the voyagers were notorious in that colony for desperate, bloody-minded miscreants; some were reputed pirates, the most hawkers of rum; all ranters and drinkers; all fit associates, embarking together without remorse upon this treacherous and murderous design. I could not hear there was much discipline or any set captain in the gang; but Harris and four others, Mountain himself, two Scotsmen – Pinkerton and Hastie – and a man of the name of Hicks, a drunken shoemaker, put their heads together and agreed upon the course. In a material sense, they were well enough provided, and the Master in particular brought with him a tent where he might enjoy some privacy and shelter.

Even this small indulgence told against him in the minds of his companions. But indeed he was in a position so entirely false (and even ridiculous) that all his habit of command and arts of pleasing were here thrown away. In the eyes of all, except Secundra Dass, he figured as a common gull and designated victim; going unconsciously to death; yet he could not but suppose himself the contriver and the leader of the expedition; he could scarce help but so conduct himself; and at the least hint of authority or condescension, his deceivers would be laughing in their sleeves. I was so used to see and to conceive him in a high authoritative attitude, that when I had conceived his position on this journey, I was pained and could have blushed. How soon he may have entertained a first surmise, we cannot know; but it was long, and the party had advanced into the Wilderness beyond the reach of any help, ere he was fully awakened to the truth.

It fell thus. Harris and some others had drawn apart into the woods for consultation, when they were startled by a rustling in the brush. They were accustomed to the arts of Indian warfare, and Mountain had not only lived and hunted, but fought and earned some reputation, with the savages. He could move in the woods without noise, and follow a trail like a hound; and upon the emergence of this alert, he was deputed by the rest to plunge into the thicket for intelligence. He was soon convinced there was a man in his close neighbourhood, moving with precaution but without art among the leaves and branches; and coming shortly to a place of advantage, he was able observe Secundra Dass crawling briskly off with many backward glances. At this he knew not whether to laugh or cry; and his accomplices, when he had returned and reported, were in much the same dubiety. There was now no danger of an Indian onslaught; but on the other hand, since Secundra Dass was at the pains to spy upon them, it was highly probable he knew English, and if he knew English it was certain the whole of their design was in the Master's knowledge. There was one singularity in the position. If Secundra Dass knew and concealed his knowledge of English, Harris was a proficient in several of the tongues of India, and as his career in that part of the world had been a great deal worse than profligate, he had not thought proper to remark upon the circumstance. Each side had thus a spy-hole on the counsels of the other. The plotters, so soon as this advantage was explained, returned to camp; Harris, hearing the Hindustani was once more closeted with his master, crept to the side of the tent; and the rest, sitting about the fire with their tobacco, awaited his report with impatience. When he came at last, his face was very black. He had overheard enough to confirm the worst of his suspicions. Secundra Dass was a good English scholar; he had been some days creeping and listening, the Master was now fully informed of the conspiracy, and the pair proposed on the morrow to fall out of line at a carrying place and plunge at a venture in the woods: preferring the full risk of famine, savage beasts, and savage men to their position in the midst of traitors.

What, then, was to be done? Some were for killing the Master on the spot; but Harris assured them that would be a crime without profit, since the secret of the treasure must die along with him that buried it. Others were for desisting at once from the whole enterprise and making for New York; but the appetizing name of treasure, and the thought of the long way they had already travelled, dissuaded the majority. I imagine they were dull fellows for the most part. Harris, indeed, had some acquirements, Mountain was no fool, Hastie was an educated man; but even these had manifestly failed in life, and the rest were the dregs of colonial rascality. The conclusion they reached, at least, was more the offspring of greed and hope, than reason. It was to temporize, to be wary and watch the Master, to be silent and supply no further aliment to his suspicions, and to depend entirely (as well as I make out) on the chance that their victim was as greedy, hopeful, and irrational as themselves, and might, after all, betray his life and treasure.

Twice in the course of the next day Secundra and the Master must have appeared to themselves to have escaped; and twice they were circumvented. The

Master, save that the second time he grew a little pale, displayed no sign of disappointment, apologized for the stupidity with which he had fallen aside, thanked his recapturers as for a service, and rejoined the caravan with all his usual gallantry and cheerfulness of mien and bearing. But it is certain he had smelled a rat; for from thenceforth he and Secundra spoke only in each other's ear, and Harris listened and shivered by the tent in vain. The same night it was announced they were to leave the boats and proceed by foot, a circumstance which (as it put an end to the confusion of the portages) greatly lessened the chances of escape.

And now there began between the two sides a silent contest, for life on the one hand, for riches on the other. They were now near that quarter of the desert in which the Master himself must begin to play the part of the guide; and using this for a pretext of persecution, Harris and his men sat with him every night about the fire, and laboured to entrap him into some admission. If he let slip his secret, he knew well it was the warrant for his death; on the other hand, he durst not refuse their questions, and must appear to help them to the best of his capacity, or he practically published his mistrust. And yet Mountain assures me the man's brow was never ruffled. He sat in the midst of these jackals, his life depending by a thread, like some easy, witty householder at home by his own fire; an answer he had for everything – as often as not a jesting answer; avoided threats, evaded insults; talked, laughed, and listened with an open countenance; and, in short, conducted himself in such a manner as must have disarmed suspicion, and went near to stagger knowledge. Indeed, Mountain confessed to me they would soon have disbelieved the Captain's story, and supposed their designated victim still quite innocent of their designs; but for the fact that he continued (however ingeniously) to give the slip to questions, and the yet stronger confirmation of his repeated efforts to escape. The last of these, which brought things to a head, I am now to relate. And first I should say that by this time the temper of Harris's companions was utterly worn out; civility was scarce pretended; and, for one very significant circumstance, the Master and Secundra had been (on some pretext) deprived of weapons. On their side, however, the threatened pair kept up the parade of friendship handsomely; Secundra was all bows, the Master all smiles; and on the last night of the truce he had even gone so far as to sing for the diversion of the company. It was observed that he had also eaten with unusual heartiness and drank deep, doubtless from design.

At least, about three in the morning, he came out of the tent into the open air, audibly mourning and complaining, with all the manner of a sufferer from surfeit. For some while, Secundra publicly attended on his patron, who at last became more easy and fell asleep on the frosty ground behind the tent, the Indian returning within. Some time after, the sentry was changed; had the Master pointed out to him, where he lay in what is called a robe of buffalo: and thenceforth kept an eye upon him (he declared) without remission. With the first of the dawn, a draught of wind came suddenly and blew open one side the corner of the robe; and with the same puff, the Master's hat whirled in the air and fell some yards away. The sentry thinking it remarkable the sleeper should not awaken, thereupon drew near; and the next moment, with a great shout, informed the camp their prisoner was escaped. He had left behind his Indian, who (in the first vicacity of the surprise) came near to pay the forfeit of his life, and was, in fact, inhumanly mishandled; but Secundra, in the midst of threats and cruelties, stuck to it with extraordinary loyalty, that he was quite ignorant of his master's plans, which might indeed be true, and of the manner of his escape, which was demonstrably false. Nothing was therefore left to the conspirators but to rely entirely on the skill of Mountain. The night had been frosty, the ground quite hard; and the sun was no sooner up than a strong thaw set in. It was Mountain's boast that few men could have followed that trail, and still fewer (even of the native Indians) found it. The Master had thus a long start before his pursuers had the scent, and he must have travelled with surprising energy for a pedestrian so unused, since it was near noon before Mountain had a view of him. At this conjuncture the trader was alone, all his companions following, at his own request, several hundred yards in the rear; he knew the Master was unarmed; his heart was besides heated with the exercise and lust of hunting; and seeing the quarry so close, so defenceless, and seeming so fatigued, he vain-gloriously determined to effect the capture with his single hand. A step or two farther brought him to one margin of a little clearing; on the other, with his arms folded and his back to a huge stone, the Master sat. It is possible Mountain may have made a rustle, it is certain, at least, the Master raised his head and gazed directly at that quarter of the thicket where his hunter lay; 'I could not be sure he saw me,' Mountain said; 'he just looked my way like a man with his mind made up, and all the courage ran out of me like rum out of a bottle.' And presently, when the Master looked away again, and appeared to resume those meditations in which he had sat immersed before the trader's coming, Mountain slunk stealthily back and returned to seek the help of his companions.

And now began the chapter of surprises, for the scout had scarce informed the others of his discovery, and they were yet preparing their weapons for a rush upon the fugitive, when the man himself appeared in their midst, walking openly and quietly, with his hands behind his back.

'Ah, men!' says he, on his beholding them. 'Here is a fortunate encounter. Let us get back to camp.'

Mountain had not mentioned his own weakness or the Master's disconcerting gaze upon the thicket, so that (with all the rest) his return appeared spontaneous. For all that, a hubbub arose; oaths flew, fists were shaken, and guns pointed.

'Let us get back to camp,' said the Master. 'I have an explanation to make, but it must be laid before you all. And in the meanwhile I would put up these weapons, one of which might very easily go off and blow away your hopes of treasure. I would not kill,' says he, smiling, 'the goose with the golden eggs.'

The charm of his superiority once more triumphed; and the party, in no particular order, set off on their return. By the way, he found accasion to get a word or two apart with Mountain.

'You are a clever fellow and bold,' says he, 'but I am not so sure that you are doing yourself justice. I would have you to consider whether you would not do better, ay, and safer, to serve me instead of serving so commonplace a rascal as Mr Harris. Consider of it,' he concluded, dealing the man a gentle tap upon the shoulder, 'and don't be in haste. Dead or alive, you will find me an ill man to quarrel with.'

When they were come back to the camp where Harris and Pinkerton stood guard over Secundra, these two ran upon the Master like viragoes, and were amazed out of measure when they were bidden by the comrades to 'stand back and hear what the gentleman had to say.' The Master had not flinched before their onslaught; nor, at this proof of the ground he had gained, did he betray the least sufficiency.

'Do not let us be in haste,' says he. 'Meat first and public speaking after.'

With that they made a hasty meal; and as soon as it was done, the Master, leaning on one elbow, began his speech. He spoke long, addressing himself to each except Harris, finding for each (with the same exception) some particular flattery. He called them 'bold, honest blades,' declared he had never seen a more jovial company, work better done, or pains more merrily supported. 'Well, then,' says he, 'someone asks me, Why the devil I ran away? But that is scarce worth answer, for I think you all know pretty well. But you know only pretty well: that is a point I shall arrive at presently, and be you ready to remark it when it comes. There is a traitor here: a double traitor: I will give you his name before I am done; and let that suffice for now. But here comes some other gentleman and asks me, "Why, in the devil, I came back?" Well, before I answer that question, I have one to put to you. It was this cur here, this Harris, that speaks Hindustani?' cries he, rising on one knee and pointing fair at the man's face, with a gesture indescribably menacing; and when he had been answered in the affirmative, 'Ah!' says he, 'then are all my suspicions verified, and I did rightly to come back. Now, men, hear the truth for the first time.' Thereupon he launched forth in a long story, told with extraordinary skill, how he had long suspected Harris, how he had found the confirmation of his fears, and how Harris must have misrepresented what passed between Secundra and himself. At this point he made a bold stroke with excellent effect. 'I suppose,' says he, 'you think you are going shares with Harris, I suppose you think you will see to that yourselves; you would naturally not think so flat a rogue could cozen you. But have a care! These half-idiots have a sort of cunning, as the skunk has its stench; and it may be news to you that Harris has taken care of himself already. Yes, for him the treasure is all money in the bargain. You must find it or go starve. But he has been paid beforehand; my brother paid him to destroy me; look at him, if you doubt – look at him, grinning and gulping, a detected thief!' Thence, having made this happy impression, he explained how he had escaped and thought better of it, and at last concluded to come back, lay the truth before the company, and take his chance with them once more: persuaded as he was, they would instantly depose Harris and elect some other leader. 'There is the whole truth,' said he: 'and with one exception, I put myself entirely in your hands. What is the exception? There he sits,' he cried, pointing once more to Harris; 'a man that has to die! Weapons and conditions are all one to me; put me face to face with him, and if you give me nothing but a stick, in five minutes I will show you a sop of broken carrion, fit for dogs to roll in.'

It was dark night when he made an end; they had listened in almost perfect silence; but the firelight scarce permitted anyone to judge, from the look of his neighbours, with what result of persuasion or conviction. Indeed, the Master had set himself in the brightest place, and kept his face there, to be the centre of men's eyes: doubtless on a profound calculation. Silence followed for a while, and presently the whole party became involved in disputation: the Master lying on his back, with his hands knit under his head and one knee flung across the other, like a person unconcerned in the result. And here, I daresay, his bravado carried him too far and prejudiced his case. At least, after a cast or two back and forward, opinion settled finally against him. It's possible he hoped to repeat the business of the pirate ship, and be himself, perhaps, on hard enough conditions, elected leader; and things went so far that way, that Mountain actually threw out the proposition. But the rock he split upon was Hastie. This fellow was not well liked, being sour and slow, with an ugly, glowering disposition, but he had studied some time for the Church at Edinburgh College, before ill conduct had destroyed his prospects, and he now remembered and applied what he had learned. Indeed he had not proceeded very far, when the Master rolled carelessly upon one side, which was done (in Mountain's opinion) to conceal the beginnings of despair upon his countenance. Hastie dismissed the most of what they had heard as nothing to the matter: what they wanted was the treasure. All that was said of Harris might be true, and they would have to see to that in time. But what had that to do with the treasure? They had heard a vast of words; but the truth was just this, that Mr Durie was damnably frightened and had several times run off. Here he was – whether caught or come back was all one to Hastie: the point was to make an end of the business. As for the talk of deposing and electing captains, he hoped they were all free men and could attend their own affairs. That was dust flung in their eyes, and so was the proposal to fight Harris. 'He shall fight no one in this camp, I can tell him that,' said Hastie. 'We had trouble enough to get his arms away from him, and we should look pretty fools to give them back again. But it it's excitement the gentleman is after, I can supply him with more than perhaps he cares about. For I have no intention to spend the remainder of my life in these mountains; already I have been too long; and I propose that he should immediately tell us where that treasure is, or else immediately be shot. And there,' says he, producing his weapon, 'there is the pistol that I mean to use.'

'Come, I call you a man,' cries the Master, sitting up and looking at the speaker with an air of admiration.

'I didn't ask you to call me anything,' returned Hastie; 'which is it to be?'

'That's an idle question,' said the Master. 'Needs must when the devil drives. The truth is we are within easy walk of the place, and I will show it you tomorrow.'

With that, as if all were quite settled, and settled exactly to his mind, he walked off to his tent, whither Secundra had preceded him.

I cannot think of these last turns and wriggles of my old enemy except with admiration; scarce even pity is mingled with the sentiment, so strongly the man supported, so boldly resisted his misfortunes. Even at that hour, when he perceived himself quite lost, when he saw he had but effected an exchange of enemies, and overthrown Harris to set Hastie up, no sign of weakness appeared in his behaviour, and he withdrew to his tent, already determined (I must suppose) upon affronting the incredible hazard of his last expedient, with the same easy, assured, genteel expression and demeanour as he might have left a theatre withal to join a supper of the wits. But doubtless within, if we could see there, his soul trembled.

Early in the night, word went about the camp that he was sick; and the first thing the next morning he called Hastie to his side, and inquired most anxiously if he had any skill in medicine. As a matter of fact, this was a vanity of that fallen divinity student's, to which he had cunningly addressed himself. Hastie examined him; and being flattered, ignorant, and highly suspicious, knew not in the least whether the man was sick or malingering. In this state he went forth again to his companions; and (as the thing which would give himself most consequence either way) announced that the patient was in a fair way to die.

'For all that,' he added with an oath, 'and if he bursts by the wayside, he must bring us this morning to the treasure.'

But there were several in the camp (Mountain among the number) whom this brutality revolted. They would have seen the Master pistolled, or pistolled him themselves, without the smallest sentiment of pity; but they seemed to have been touched by his gallant fight and unequivocal defeat the night before; perhaps, too, they were even already beginning to oppose themselves to their new leader; at least, they now declared that (if the man was sick) he should have a day's rest in spite of Hastie's teeth.

The next morning he was manifestly worse, and Hastie himself began to display something of humane concern, so easily does even the pretence of doctoring awaken sympathy. The third the Master called Mountain and Hastie to the tent, announced himself to be dying, gave them full particulars as to the position of the cache, and begged them to set out incontinently on the quest, so that they might see if he deceived them, and (if they were at first unsuccessful) he should be able to correct their error.

But here arose a difficulty on which he doubtless counted. None of these men would trust another, none would consent to stay behind. On the other hand, although the Master seemed extremely low, spoke scarce above a whisper, and lay much of the time insensible, it was still possible it was a fraudulent sickness; and if all went treasure-hunting, it might prove they had gone upon a wild-goose chase, and return to find their prisoner flown. They concluded, therefore, to hang idling round the camp, alleging sympathy to their reason; and certainly, so mingled are our dispositions, several were sincerely (if not very deeply) affected by the natural peril of the man whom they callously designed to murder. In the afternoon Hastie was called to the bedside to pray: the which (incredible as it must appear) he did with unction; about eight at night, the wailing of Secundra announced that all was over; and before ten, the Indian, with a link stuck in the ground, was toiling at the grave. Sunrise of next day beheld the Master's burial, all hands attending with great decency of demeanour; and the body was laid in the earth, wrapped in a fur robe, with only the face uncovered; which last was of a waxy whiteness, and had the nostrils plugged according to some Oriental habit of Secundra's. No sooner was the grave filled than the lamentations of the Indian once more struck concern to every heart; and it appears this gang of murderers, so far from resenting his outcries, although both distressful and (in such a country) perilous to their own safety, roughly but kindly endeavoured to console him.

But if human nature is even in the worst of men occasionally kind, it is still, and before all things, greedy; and they soon turned from the mourner to their own concerns. The cache of the treasure being hard by, although yet unidentified, it was concluded not to break camp; and the day passed, on the part of the voyagers, in unavailing exploration of the woods, Secundra the while lying on his master's grave. That night they placed no sentinel, but lay together about the fire in the customary woodman fashion, the heads outward, like the spokes of a wheel. Morning found them in the same disposition; only Pinkerton, who lay on Mountain's right, between him and Hastie, had (in the hours of darkness) been secretly butchered, and there lay, still wrapped as to his body in his mantle, but offering above that ungodly and horrific spectacle of the scalped head. The gang were that morning as pale as a company of phantoms, for the pertinacity of Indian war (or to speak more correctly, Indian murder) was well known to all. But they laid the chief blame on their unsentinelled posture; and fired with the neighbourhood of the treasure, determined to continue where they were. Pinkerton was buried hard by the Master; the survivors again passed the day in exploration, and returned in a mingled humour of anxiety and hope, being partly certain they were now close on the discovery of what they sought, and on the other hand (with the return of darkness) infected with the fear of Indians. Mountain was the first sentry; he declares he neither slept nor yet sat down, but kept his watch with a perpetual and straining vigilance, and it was even with unconcern that (when he saw by the stars his time was up) he drew near the fire to awaken his successor. This man (it was Hicks the shoemaker) slept on the lee side of the circle, something farther off in consequence than those to windward, and in a place darkened by the blowing smoke. Mountain stooped and took him by the shoulder; his hand was at once smeared by some adhesive wetness; and (the wind at the moment veering) the firelight shone upon the sleeper, and showed him, like Pinkerton, dead and scalped.

It was clear they had fallen in the hands of one of those matchless Indian bravos, that will sometimes follow a party for days, and in spite of indefatigable travel, and unsleeping watch, continue to keep up with their advance, and steal a scalp at every resting-place. Upon this discovery, the treasure-seekers, already reduced to a poor half-dozen, fell into mere dismay, seized a few necessaries, and deserting the remainder of their goods, fled outright into the forest. Their fire they left still burning, and their dead comrade unburied. All day they ceased not to flee, eating by the way, from hand to mouth; and since they feared to sleep, continued to advance at random even in the hours of darkness. But the limit of man's endurance is soon reached; when they rested at last it was to sleep profoundly; and when they woke, it was to find that the enemy was still upon their heels, and death and mutilation had once more lessened and deformed their company.

By this they had become light-headed, they had quite missed their path in the wilderness, their stores were already running low. With the further horrors, it is superfluous that I should swell this narrative, already too prolonged. Suffice it to say that when at length a night passed by innocuous, and they might breathe again in the hope that the murderer had at last desisted from pursuit, Mountain and Secundra were alone. The trader is firmly persuaded their unseen enemy was some warrior of his own acquaintance, and that he himself was spared by favour. The mercy extended to Secundra he explains on the ground that the East Indian was thought to be insane; partly from the fact that, through all the horrors of the flight and while others were casting away their food and weapons, Secundra continued to stagger forward with a mattock on his shoulder, and partly because, in the last days and with a great degree of heat and fluency, he perpetually spoke with himself in his own language. But he was sane enough when it came to English.

'You think he will be gone quite away?' he asked, upon their blest awakening in safety.

'I pray God so, I believe so, I dare to believe so,' Mountain had replied almost with incoherence, as he described the scene to me.

And indeed he was so much distempered that until he met us, the next morning, he could scarce be certain whether he had dreamed or whether it was a fact, that Secundra had thereupon turned directly about and returned without a word upon their footprints, setting his face for these wintry and hungry solitudes, along a path whose every stage was mile-stoned with a mutilated corpse.

CHAPTER TWELVE

The Journey in the Wilderness (continued)

MOUNTAIN'S STORY, AS IT WAS laid before Sir William Johnson and my lord, was shorn, of course, of all the earlier particulars, and the expedition described to have proceeded uneventfully, until the Master sickened. But the latter part was very forcibly related, the speaker visibly thrilling to his recollections; and our then situation, on the fringe of the same desert, and the private interests of each, gave him an audience prepared to share in his emotions. For Mountain's intelligence not only changed the world for my Lord Durrisdeer, but materially affected the designs of Sir William Johnson.

These I find I must lay more at length before the reader. Word had reached Albany of dubious import; it had been rumoured some hostility was to be put in act; and the Indian diplomatist had, thereupon, sped into the wilderness, even at the approach of winter, to nip that mischief in the bud. Here, on the borders, he learned that he was come too late; and a difficult choice was thus presented to a man (upon the whole) not any more bold than prudent. His standing with the painted braves may be compared to that of my Lord President Culloden among the chiefs of our own Highlanders at the 'Forty-five; that is as much as to say, he was, to these men, reason's only speaking-trumpet, and counsels of peace and moderation, if they were to prevail at all, must prevail singly through his influence. If, then, he should return, the province must lie open to all the abominable tragedies of Indian war – the houses blaze, the wayfarer be cut off, and the men of the woods collect their usual disgusting spoil of human scalps. On the other side, to go farther north, to risk so small a party deeper in the desert, to carry words of peace among warlike savages already rejoicing to return to war; here was an extremity from which it was easy to perceive his mind revolted.

'I have come too late,' he said more than once, and would fall into a deep consideration, his head bowed in his hands, his foot patting the ground.

At length he raised his face and looked upon us, that is to say upon my lord, Mountain, and myself, sitting close round a small fire, which had been made for privacy in one corner of the camp.

'My lord, to be quite frank with you, I find myself in two minds,' said he. 'I think it very needful I should go on, but not at all proper I should any longer enjoy the pleasure of your company. We are here still upon the water side; and I think the risk to southward no great matter. Will not yourself and Mr Mackellar take a single boat's crew and return to Albany?'

My lord, I should say, had listened to Mountain's narrative, regarding him throughout with a painful intensity of gaze; and since the tale concluded, had sat as in a dream. There was something very daunting in his look; something to my eyes not rightly human; the face, lean, and dark, and aged, the mouth painful, the teeth disclosed in a perpetual rictus; the eyeball swimming clear of the lids upon a field of blood-shot white. I could not behold him myself without a jarring irritation, such as, I believe, is too frequently the uppermost feeling on the sickness of those dear to us. Others, I could not but remark, were scarce able to support his neighbourhood – Sir William eviting to be near him, Mountain dodging his eye, and, when he met it, blenching and halting in his story. At this appeal, however, my lord appeared to recover his command upon himself.

'To Albany?' said he, with a good voice.

'Not short of it, at least,' replied Sir William. 'There is no safety nearer hand.'

'I would be very sweir* to return,' says my lord. 'I am not fraid – of Indians,' he added, with a jerk.

'I wish that I could say so much,' returned Sir William, smiling; 'although, if any man durst say it, it should be myself. But you are to keep in view my responsibility, and that as the voyage has now become highly dangerous, and your business – if you ever had any,' says he – 'brought quite to a conclusion by the distressing family intelligence you have received, I should be hardly justified if I even suffered you to proceed, and run the risk of some obloquy if nything regrettable should follow.'

My lord turned to Mountain. 'What did he pretend he died of?' he asked.

'I don't think I understand your honour,' said the trader, pausing, like a man very much affected, in the dressing of some cruel frostbites.

For a moment my lord seemed at a full stop: and then, with some irritation, 'I ask you what he died of. Surely that's a plain question,' said he.

'Oh! I don't know,' said Mountain. 'Hastie even never knew. He seemed to sicken natural, and just pass away.'

'There it is, you see!' concluded my lord, turning to Sir William.

'Your lordship is too deep for me,' replied Sir William.

'Why,' says my lord, 'this is a matter of succession; my son's title may be called in doubt; and the man being supposed to be dead of nobody can tell what, a great deal of suspicion would be naturally roused.'

'But, God damn me, the man's buried!' cried Sir William.

'I will never believe that,' returned my lord, painfully trembling. 'I'll never

*Unwilling

believe it!' he cried again, and jumped to his feet. 'Did he look dead?' he asked of Mountain.

'Look dead?' repeated the trader. 'He looked white. Why, what would he be at? I tell you, I put the sods upon him.'

My lord caught Sir William by the coat with a hooked hand. 'This man has the name of my brother,' says he, 'but it's well understood that he was never canny.'

'Canny?' says Sir William. 'What is that?'

'He's not of this world,' whispered my lord, 'neither him nor the black deil that serves him. I have struck my sword throughout his vitals,' he cried; 'I have felt the hilt dirl* on his breastbone, and the hot blood spirt in my very face, time and again, time and again!' he repeated, with a gesture indescribable. 'But he was never dead for that,' said he, and sighed aloud. 'Why should I think he was dead now? No, not till I see him rotting,' says he.

Sir William looked across at me with a long face. Mountain forgot his wounds, staring and gaping.

'My lord,' said I, 'I wish you would collect your spirits.' But my throat was so dry, and my own wits so scattered, I could add no more.

'No,' says my lord, 'it's not to be supposed that he would understand me. Mackellar does, for he kens all, and has seen him buried before now. This is a very good servant to me, Sir William, this man Mackellar; he buried him with his own hands – he and my father – by the light of two siller candlesticks. The other man is a familiar spirit; he brought him from Coromandel. I would have told ye this long syne, Sir William, only it was in the family,' These last remarks he made with a kind of melancholy composure, and his time of aberration seemed to pass away. 'You can ask yourself what it all means,' he proceeded. 'My bother falls sick, and dies, and is buried, or so they say; and all seems very plain. But why did the familiar go back? I think ye must see for yourself it's a point that wants some clearing.'

'I will be at your service, my lord, in half a minute,' said Sir William, rising. 'Mr Mackellar, two words with you'; and he led me without the camp, the frost crunching in our steps, the trees standing at our elbow, hoar with frost, even as on that night in the Long Shrubbery. 'Of course, this is midsummer madness,' said Sir William, as soon as we were gotten out of hearing.

'Why, certainly,' said I. 'The man is mad. I think that manifest.'

'Shall I seize and bind him?' asked Sir William. 'I will upon your authority. If these are all ravings, that should certainly be done.'

I looked down upon the ground, back at the camp, with its bright fires and the folk watching us, and about me on the woods and mountains; there was just the one way that I could not look, and that was in Sir William's face.

'Sir William,' said I at last, 'I think my lord not sane, and have long thought him so. But there are degrees in madness; and whether he should be brought under restraint – Sir William, I am no fit judge,' I concluded.

'I will be the judge,' said he. 'I ask for facts. Was there, in all that jargon, any word of truth or sanity? Do you hesitate?' he asked. 'Am I to understand you have buried this gentleman before?'

*Ring

'Not buried,' said I; and then, taking up courage at last, 'Sir William,' said I, 'unless I were to tell you a long story, which much concerns a noble family (and myself not in the least), it would be impossible to make this matter clear to you. Say the word, and I will do it, right or wrong. And, at any rate I will say so much, that my lord is not so crazy as he seems. This is a strange matter, into the tail of which you are unhappily drifted.'

'I desire none of your secrets,' replied Sir William; 'but I will be plain at the risk of incivility, and confess that I take little pleasure in my present company.'

'I would be the last to blame you,' said I, 'for that.'

'I have not asked either for your censure or your praise, sir,' returned Sir William. 'I desire simply to be quit of you: and to that effect I put a boat and complement of men at your disposal.'

'This is fairly offered,' said I, after reflection. 'But you must suffer me to say a word upon the other side. We have a natural curiosity to learn the truth of this affair; I have some of it myself; my lord (it is very plain) has but too much. The matter of the Indian's return is enigmatical.'

'I think so myself,' Sir William interrupted, 'and I propose (since I go in that direction) to probe it to the bottom. Whether or not the man has gone like a dog to die upon his master's grave, his life, at least, is in great danger, and I propose, if I can, to save it. There is nothing against his character?'

'Nothing, Sir William,' I replied.

'And the other?' he said. 'I have heard my lord, of course; but, from the circumstances of his servant's loyalty, I must suppose he had some noble qualities.'

'You must not ask that!' I cried. 'Hell may have noble flames. I have known him a score of years, and always hated, and always admired, and always slavishly feared him.'

'I appear to intrude again upon your secrets,' and Sir William, 'believe me, inadvertently. Enough that I will see the grave, and (if possible) rescue the Indian. Upon these terms, can you persuade your master to return to Albany?'

'Sir William,' said I, 'I will tell you how it is. You do not see my lord to advantage; it will seem even strange to you that I should love him; but I do, and I am not alone. If he goes back to Albany, it must be by force, and it will be the death-warrant of his reason, and perhaps his life. That is my sincere belief; but I am in your hands, and ready to obey, if you will assume so much responsibility as to command.'

'I will have no shred or responsibility; it is my single endeavour to avoid the same,' cried Sir William. 'You insist upon following this journey up; and be it so! I wash my hands of the whole matter.'

With which word, he turned upon his heel and gave the order to break camp; and my lord, who had been hovering near by, came instantly to my side.

'Which is it to be?' said he.

'You are to have your way,' I answered. 'You shall see the grave.'

The situation of the Master's grave was, between guides, easily described; it lay, indeed, beside a chief landmark of the wilderness, a certain range of peaks, conspicuous by their design and altitude, and the source of many brawling tributaries to that inland sea, Lake Champlain. It was therefore possible to strike for it direct, instead of following back the blood-stained trail of the fugitives, and to cover, in some sixteen hours of march, a distance which their perturbed wanderings had extended over more than sixty. Our boats we left under a guard upon the river; it was, indeed, probable we should return to find them frozen fast; and the small equipment with which we set forth upon the expedition included not only an infinity of furs to protect us from the cold, but an arsenal of snow-shoes to render travel possible, when the inevitable snow should fall. Considerable alarm was manifested at our departure; the march was conducted with soldierly precaution, the camp at night sedulously chosen and patrolled; and it was a consideration of this sort that arrested us, the second day, within not many hundred yards of our destination – the night being already imminent, the spot in which we stood well qualified to be a strong camp for a party of our numbers; and Sir William, therefore, on a sudden thought, arresting our advance.

Before us was the high range of mountains toward which we had been all day deviously drawing near. From the first light of the dawn, their silver peaks had been the goal of our advance across a tumbled lowland forest, thrid with rough streams, and strewn with monstrous boulders; the peaks (as I say) silver, for already at the higher altitudes the snow fell nightly; but the woods and the low ground only breathed upon with frost. All day heaven had been charged with ugly vapours in the which the sun swam and glimmered like a shilling piece; all day the wind blew on our left cheek barbarous cold, but very pure to breathe. With the end of the afternoon, however, the wind fell; the clouds, being no longer reinforced, were scattered or drunk up; the sun set behind us with some wintry splendour, and the white brow of the mountains shared its dying glow.

It was dark ere we had supper; we ate in silence, and the meal was scarce despatched before my lord slunk from the fireside to the margin of the camp; whither I made haste to follow him. The camp was on high ground, overlooking a frozen lake, perhaps a mile in its longest measurement; all about us, the forest lay in heights and hollows; above rose the white mountains; and higher yet, the moon rode in a fair sky. There was no breath of air; nowhere a twig creaked; and the sounds of our own camp were hushed and swallowed up in the surrounding stillness. Now that the sun and the wind were both gone down, it appeared almost warm, like a night of July; a singular illusion of the sense, when earth, air, and water were strained to bursting with the extremity of frost.

My lord (or what I still continued to call by his loved name) stood with his elbow in one hand, and his chin sunk in the other, gazing before him on the surface of the wood. My eyes followed his, and rested almost pleasantly upon the frosted contexture of the pines, rising in moonlit hillocks, or sinking in the shadow of small glens. Hard by, I told myself, was the grave of our enemy, now gone where the wicked cease from troubling, the earth heaped for ever on his once so active limbs. I could not but think of him as somehow fortunate to be thus done with man's anxiety and weariness, the daily expense of spirit, and that daily river of circumstance to be swum through, at any hazard, under the penalty of shame or death. I could not but think how good was the end of that long travel; and with that, my mind swung at a tangent to my lord. For was not my lord dead also? a maimed soldier, looking vainly for discharge, lingering derided in the line of battle? A kind man, I remembered him; wise, with a decent pride, a son perhaps too dutiful, a husband only too loving, one that could suffer and be silent, one whose hand I loved to press. Of a sudden, pity caught in my windpipe with a sob; I could have wept aloud to remember and behold him; and standing thus by his elbow, under the broad moon, I prayed fervently either that he should be released, or I strengthened to persist in my affection.

'Oh God,' said I, 'this was the best man to me and to himself, and now I shrink from him. He did no wrong, or not till he was broke with sorrows; these are but his honourable wounds that we begin to shrink from. Oh, cover them up, oh, take him away, before we hate him!'

I was still so engaged in my own bosom, when a sound broke suddenly upon the night. It was neither very loud, nor very near; yet, bursting as it did from so profound and so prolonged a silence, it startled the camp like an alarm of trumpets. Ere I had taken breath, Sir William was beside me, the main part of the voyagers clustered at his back, intently giving ear. Methought, as I glanced at them across my shoulder, there was a whiteness, other than moonlight, on their cheeks; and the rays of the moon reflected with a sparkle on the eyes of some, and the shadows lying black under the brows of others (according as they raised or bowed the head to listen) gave to the group a strange air of animation and anxiety. My lord was to the front, crouching a little forth, his hand raised as for silence: a man turned to stone. And still the sounds continued, breathlessly renewed with a precipitate rhythm.

Suddenly Mountain spoke in a loud, broken whisper, as of a man relieved. 'I have it now,' he said; and, as we all turned to hear him, 'the Indian must have known the cache,' he added. 'That is he – he is digging out the treasure.'

'Why, to be sure!' exclaimed Sir William. 'We were geese not to have supposed so much.'

'The only thing is,' Mountain resumed, 'the sound is very close to our old camp. And, again, I do not see how he is there before us, unless the man had wings!'

'Greed and fear are wings,' remarked Sir William. 'But this rogue has given us an alert, and I have a notion to return the compliment. What say you, gentlemen, shall we have a moonlight hunt?'

It was so agreed; dispositions were made to surround Secundra at his task; some of Sir William's Indians hastened in advance; and a strong guard being left at our headquarters, we set forth along the uneven bottom of the forest; frost crackling, ice sometimes loudly splitting under foot; and overhead the blackness of pine-woods, and the broken brightness of the moon. Our way led down into a hollow of the land; and as we descended, the sounds diminished and had almost died away. Upon the other slope it was more open, only dotted with a few pines, and several vast and scattered rocks that made inky shadows in the moonlight. Here the sounds began to reach us more distinctly; we could now perceive the ring of iron, and more exactly estimate the furious degree of haste with which the digger plied his instrument. As we neared the top of the ascent, a bird or two winged aloft and hovered darkly in the moonlight; and the next moment we were gazing through a fringe of trees upon a singular picture.

A narrow plateau, overlooked by the white mountains, and encompassed nearer hand by woods, lay bare to the strong radiance of the moon. Rough goods, such as make the wealth of foresters, were sprinkled here and there upon the ground in meaningless disarray. About the midst, a tent stood, silvered with frost: the door open, gaping on the black interior. At the one end of this small stage lay what seemed the tattered remnants of a man. Without doubt we had arrived upon the scene of Harris's encampment; there were the goods scattered in the panic of flight; it was in yon tent the Master breathed his last; and the frozen carrion that lay before us was the body of the drunken shoemaker. It was always moving to come upon the theatre of any tragic incident; to come upon it after so many days, and to find it (in the seclusion of a desert) still unchanged, must have impressed the mind of the most careless. And yet it was not that which struck us into pillars of stone; but the sight (which yet we had been half expecting) of Secundra ankle deep in the grave of his late Master. He had cast the main part of his raiment by, yet his frail arms and shoulders glistened in the moonlight with a copious sweat; his face was contracted with anxiety and expectation; his blows resounded on the grave, as thick as sobs; and behind him, strangely deformed and ink-black upon the frosty ground, the creature's shadow repeated and parodied his swift gesticulations. Some night birds arose from the boughs upon our coming, and then settled back; but Secundra, absorbed in his toil, heard or heeded not at all.

I heard Mountain whisper to Sir William, 'Good God! it's the grave! He's digging him up!' It was what we had all guessed, and yet to hear it put in language thrilled me. Sir William violently started.

'You damned sacrilegious hound!' he cried. 'What's this?'

Secundar leaped in the air, a little breathless cry escaped him, the tool flew from his grasp, and he stood one instant staring at the speaker. The next, swift as an arrow, he sped for the woods upon the farther side; and the next again, throwing up his hands with a violent gesture of resolution, he had begun already to retrace his steps.

'Well, then, you come, you help——' he was saying. But by now my lord had stepped beside Sir William; the moon shone fair upon his face, and the words were still upon Secundra's lips, when he beheld and recognized his master's enemy. 'Him!' he screamed, clasping his hands, and shrinking on himself.

'Come, come!' said Sir William. 'There is none here to do you harm, if you be innocent; and if you be guilty, your escape is quite cut off. Speak, what do you here among the graves of the dead and the remains of the unburied?'

'You no murderer?' inquired Secundra. 'You true man? You see me safe?'

'I will see you safe, if you be innocent,' returned Sir William. 'I have said the thing, and I see not wherefore you should doubt it.'

'These all murderers,' cried Secundra, 'that is why! He kill – murderer,' pointing to Mountain; 'there two hire-murderers,' pointing to my lord and myself – 'all gallows-murderers! Ah! I see you all swing in a rope. Now I go save the sahib; he see you swing in a rope. The sahib,' he continued, pointing to the grave, 'he not dead. He bury, he not dead.'

My lord uttered a little noise, moved nearer to the grave, and stood and stared in it.

'Buried and not dead?' exclaimed Sir William. 'What kind of rant is this?'

'See, sahib,' said Secundra. 'The sahib and I alone with murderers; try all way to escape, no way good. Then try this way: good way in warm climate good way in India; here, in this dam cold place, who can tell? I tell you pretty good hurry: you help, you light a fire, help rub.'

'What is the creature talking of?' cried Sir William. 'My head goes round.'

'I tell you I bury him alive,' said Secundra. 'I teach him swallow his tongue. Now dig him up pretty good hurry, and he not much worse. You light a fire.'

Sir William turned to the nearest of his men. 'Light a fire,' said he. 'My lot seems to be cast with the insane.'

'You good man,' returned Secundra. 'Now I go dig the sahib up.'

He returned as he spoke to the grave, and resumed his former toil. My lord stood rooted, and I at my lord's side, fearing I knew not what.

The frost was not yet very deep, and presently the Indian threw aside his tool, and began to scoop the dirt by handfuls. Then he disengaged a corner of a buffalo robe; and then I saw hair catch among his fingers: yet a moment more, and the moon shone on something white. A while Secundra crouched upon his knees, scraping with delicate fingers, breathing with puffed lips; and when he moved aside I beheld the face of the Master wholly disengaged. It was deadly white, the eyes closed, the ears and nostrils plugged, the cheeks fallen, the nose sharp as if in death; but for all he had lain so many days under the sod, corruption had not approached him, and (what strangely affected all of us) his lips and chin were mantled with a swarthy beard.

'My God!' cried Mountain, 'he was as smooth as a baby when we laid him there!'

'They say hair grows upon the dead,' observed Sir William, but his voice was thick and weak.

Secundra paid no heed to our remarks, digging swift as a terrier in the loose earth. Every moment the form of the Master, swathed in his buffalo robe, grew more distinct in the bottom of that shallow trough; the moon shining strong, and the shadows of the standers-by, as they drew forward and back, falling and flitting over his emergent countenance. The sight held us with a horror not before experienced. I dared not look my lord in the face; but for as long as it lasted, I never observed him to draw breath; and a little in the background one of the men (I know not whom) burst into a kind of sobbing.

'Now,' said Secundra, 'you help me lift him out.'

Of the flight of time, I have no idea; it may have been three hours, and it may have been five, that the Indian laboured to reanimate his master's body. One thing only I know, that it was still night, and the moon was not yet set, although it had sunk low, and now barred the plateau with long shadows, when Secundra uttered a small cry of satisfaction; and, leaning swiftly forth, I thought I could myself perceive a change upon the icy countenance of the unburied. The next moment I beheld his eyelids flutter; the next they rose entirely, and the week-old corpse looked me for a moment in the face.

So much display of life I can myself swear to. I have heard from others that he visibly strove to speak, that his teach showed in his beard, and that his brow was contorted as with an agony of pain aand effort. And this may have been; I know not, I was otherwise engaged. For at that first disclosure of the dead man's eyes, my Lord Durrisdeer fell to the ground, and when I raised him up, he was a corpse.

Day came, and still Secundra could not be persuaded to desist from his unavailing efforts. Sir William, leaving a small party under my command, proceeded on his embassy with the first light; and still the Indian rubbed the limbs and breathed in the mouth of the dead body. You would think such labours might have vitalized a stone; but, except for that one moment (which was my lord's death), the black spirit of the Master held aloof from its discarded clay; and by about the hour of noon, even the faithful servant was at length convinced. He took it with unshaken quietude.

'Too cold,' said he, 'good way in India, no good here.' And, asking for some food, which he ravenously devoured as soon as it was set before him, he drew near the fire and took his place at my elbow. In the same spot, as soon as he had eaten, he stretched himself out, and fell into a childlike slumber, from which I must arouse him, some hours afterwards, to take his part as one of the mourners at the double funeral. It was the same throughout; he seemed to have outlived at once, and with the same effort, his grief for his master and his terror of myself and Mountain.

One of the men left with me was skilled in stone-cutting; and before Sir William returned to pick us up, I had chiselled on a boulder this inscription, with a copy of which I may fitly bring my narrative to a close:

J. D.,

HEIR TO A SCOTTISH TITLE,

A MASTER OF THE ARTS AND GRACES,

ADMIRED IN EUROPE, ASIA, AMERICA,

IN WAR AND PEACE,

IN THE TENTS OF SAVAGE HUNTERS AND THE

CITADELS OF KINGS, AFTER SO MUCH

ACQUIRED, ACCOMPLISHED, AND

ENDURED,

LIES HERE FOR-

GOTTEN.

———

H. D.,

HIS BROTHER,

AFTER A LIFE OF UNMERITED DISTRESS,

BRAVELY SUPPORTED,

DIED ALMOST IN THE SAME HOUR,

AND SLEEPS IN THE SAME GRAVE

WITH HIS FRATERNAL ENEMY.

———

THE PIETY OF HIS WIFE AND ONE OLD

SERVANT RAISED THIS STONE

TO BOTH.

THE END

THE BLACK
ARROW

Critic on the Hearth,

NO ONE BUT MYSELF KNOWS WHAT I have suffered, nor what my books have gained, by your unsleeping watchfulness and admirable pertinacity. And now here is a volume that goes into the world and lacks your *imprimatur*: a strange thing in our joint lives; and the reason of it stranger still! I have watched with interest, with pain, and at length with amusement, your unavailing attempts to peruse THE BLACK ARROW; and I think I should lack humour indeed, if I let the occasion slip and did not place your name in the fly-leaf of the only book of mine that you have never read – and never will read.

That others may display more constancy is still my hope. The tale was written years ago for a particular audience and (I may say) in rivalry with a particular author; I think I should do well to name him – Mr Alfred R. Phillips. It was not without its reward at the time. I could not, indeed, displace Mr Phillips from his well-worn priority; but in the eyes of readers who thought less than nothing of TREASURE ISLAND, the black arrow was supposed to mark a clear advance. Those who read volumes and those who read story papers belong to different worlds. The verdict on TREASURE ISLAND was reversed in the other court: I wonder, will it be the same with its successor?

R.L.S.

Saranac Lake,
    April 8, 1888.

THE BLACK ARROW:

A TALE OF THE TWO ROSES

PROLOGUE

John Amend-All

ON A CERTAIN AFTERNOON, in the late springtime, the bell upon Tunstall Moat House was heard ringing at an unaccustomed hour. Far and near, in the forest and in the fields along the river, people began to desert their labours and hurry towards the sound; and in Tunstall hamlet a group of poor country-folk stood wondering at the summons.

Tunstall hamlet at that period, in the reign of old King Henry VI, wore much the same appearance as it wears today. A score or so of houses, heavily framed with oak, stood scattered in a long green valley ascending from the river. At the foot, the road crossed a bridge, and mounting on the other side, disappeared into the fringes of the forest on its way to the Moat House, and further forth to Holywood Abbey. Half-way up the village, the church stood among yews. On every side the slopes were crowned and the view bounded by the green elms and greening oak-trees of the forest.

Hard by the bridge, there was a stone cross upon a knoll, and here the group had collected – half a dozen women and one tall fellow in a russet smock – discussing what the bell betided. An express had gone through the hamlet half an hour before, and drunk a pot of ale in the saddle, not daring to dismount for the hurry of his errand; but he had been ignorant himself of what was forward, and only bore sealed letters from Sir Daniel Brackley to Sir Oliver Oates, the parson, who kept the Moat House in the master's absence.

But now there was the noise of a horse; and soon, out of the edge of the wood and over the echoing bridge, there rode up young Master Richard Shelton, Sir Daniel's ward. He, at the least, would know, and they hailed him and begged him to explain. He drew bridle willingly enough – a young fellow not yet eighteen, sun-browned and grey-eyed, in a jacket of deer's leather, with a black velvet collar, a green hood upon his head, and a steel crossbow at his back. The express, it appeared, had brought great news. A battle was impending. Sir Daniel had sent for every man that could draw a bow or carry a bill to go post-haste to Kettley, under pain of his severe displeasure; but for whom they were to fight, or of where the battle was expected, Dick knew nothing. Sir Oliver would come shortly himself, and Bennet Hatch was arming at that moment, for he it was who should lead the party.

'It is the ruin of this kind land,' a woman said. 'If the barons live at war, ploughfolk must eat roots.'

'Nay,' said Dick, 'every man that follows shall have sixpence a day, and archers twelve.'

'If they live,' returned the woman, 'that may very well be; but how if they die, my master?'

'They cannot better die than for their natural lord,' said Dick.

'No natural lord of mine,' said the man in the smock. 'I followed the Walsinghams; so we all did down Brierly way, till two years ago come Candlemas. And now I must side with Brackley! It was the law that did it; call ye that natural? But now, what with Sir Daniel and what with Sir Oliver – that knows more of law than honesty – I have no natural lord but poor King Harry the Sixt, God bless him! – the poor innocent that cannot tell his right hand from his left.'

'Ye speak with an ill tongue, friend,' answered Dick, 'to miscall your good master and my lord the king in the same libel. But King Harry – praised be the saints! – has come again into his right mind, and will have all things peaceably ordained. And as for Sir Daniel, y' are very brave behind his back. But I will be no tale-bearer; and let that suffice.'

'I say no harm of you, Master Richard,' returned the peasant. 'Y' are a lad; but when ye come to a man's inches, ye will find ye have an empty pocket. I say no more: the saints help Sir Daniel's neighbours, and the Blessed Maid protect his wards!'

'Clipsby,' said Richard, 'you speak what I cannot hear with honour. Sir Daniel is my good master, and my guardian.'

'Come, now, will ye read me a riddle?' returned Clipsby. 'On whose side is Sir Daniel?'

'I know not,' said Dick, colouring a little; for his guardian had changed sides continually in the troubles of that period, and every change had brought him some increase of fortune.

'Ay,' returned Clipsby, 'you, nor no man. For, indeed, he is one that goes to bed Lancaster and gets up York.'

Just then the bridge rang under horse-shoe iron, and the party turned and saw Bennet Hatch come galloping – a brown-faced, grizzled fellow, heavy of hand and grim of mien, armed with sword and spear, a steel salet on his head, a leather jack upon his body. He was a great man in these parts; Sir Daniel's right hand in peace and war, and at that time, by his master's interest, bailiff of the hundred.

'Clipsby,' he shouted, 'off to the Moat House, and send all other laggards the same gate. Bowyer will give you jack and salet. We must ride before curfew. Look to it: he that is last at the lych-gate Sir Daniel shall reward. Look to it right well! I know you for a man of naught. Nance,' he added, to one of the women, 'is old Appleyard up town?'

'I'll warrant you,' replied the woman. 'In his field, for sure.'

So the group dispersed, and while Clipsby walked leisurely over the bridge, Bennet and young Shelton rode up the road together, through the village and past the church.

'Ye will see the old shrew,' said Bennet. 'He will waste more time grumbling and prating of Harry the Fift than would serve a man to shoe a horse. And all because has been to the French wars!'

The house to which they were bound was the last in the village, standing alone among lilacs; and beyond it, on three sides, there was open meadow rising towards the borders of the wood.

Hatch dismounted, threw his rein over the fence, and walked down the field, Dick keeping close at his elbow, to where the old soldier was digging, knee-deep in his cabbages, and now and again, in a cracked voice, singing a snatch of song. He was all dressed in leather, only his hood and tippet were of black frieze, and tied with scarlet; his face was like a walnut-shell, both for colour and wrinkles; but his old grey eye was still clear enough, and his sight unabated. Perhaps he was deaf; perhaps he thought it unworthy of an old archer of Agincourt to pay any heed to such disturbances; but neither the surly notes of the alarm-bell, nor the near approach of Bennet and the lad, appeared at all to move him; and he continued obstinately digging, and piped up, very thin and shaky:

> 'Now, dear lady, if thy will be,
> I pray you that you will rue on me.'

'Nick Appleyard,' said Hatch, 'Sir Oliver commends him to you, and bids that ye shall come within this hour to the Moat House, there to take command.'

The old fellow looked up.

'Save you, my masters!' he said, grinning. 'And where goeth Master Hatch?'

'Master Hatch is off to Kettley, with every man that we can horse,' returned Bennet. 'There is a fight toward, it seems, and my lord stays a reinforcement.'

'Ay, verily,' returned Appleyard. 'And what will ye leave me to garrison withal?'

'I leave you six good men, and Sir Oliver to boot,' answered Hatch.

'It'll not hold the place,' said Appleyard; 'the number sufficeth not. It would take two score to make it good.'

'Why, it's for that we came to you, old shrew!' replied the other. 'Who else is there but you that could do aught in such a house with such a garrison?'

'Ay! when the pinch comes, ye remember the old shoe,' returned Nick. 'There is not a man of you can back a horse or hold a bill; and as for archery – St Michael! if old Harry the Fift were back again, he would stand and let ye shoot at him for a farthing a shoot!'

'Nay, Nick, there's some can draw a good bow yet,' said Bennet.

'Draw a good bow!' cried Appleyard. 'Yes! But who'll shoot me a good shoot? It's there the eye comes in, and the head between your shoulders. Now, what might you call a long shoot, Bennet Hatch?'

'Well,' said Bennet, looking about him, 'it would be a long shoot from here into the forest.'

'Ay, it would be a longish shoot,' said the old fellow, turning to look over his shoulder; and then he put up his hand over his eyes, and stood staring.

'Why, what are you looking at?' asked Bennet, with a chuckle. 'Do you see Harry the Fift?'

The veteran continued looking up the hill in silence. The sun shone broadly over the shelving meadows; a few white sheep wandered browsing; all was still but the distant jangle of the bell.

'What is it, Appleyard?' asked Dick.

'Why, the birds,' said Appleyard.

And, sure enough, over the top of the forest, where it ran down in a tongue among the meadows, and ended in a pair of goodly green elms, about a bowshoot from the field where they were standing, a flight of birds was skimming to and fro, in evident disorder.

'What of the birds?' said Bennet.

'Ay!' returned Appleyard, 'y' are a wise man to go to war, Master Bennet. Birds are a good sentry; in forest places they be the first line of battle. Look you, now, if we lay here in camp, there might be archers skulking down to get the wind of us; and here would you be, none the wiser!'

'Why, old shrew,' said Hatch, 'there be no men nearer us than Sir Daniel's, at Kettley; y' are as safe as in London Tower; and ye raise scares upon a man for a few chaffinches and sparrows!'

'Hear him!' grinned Appleyard. 'How many a rogue would give his two crop ears to have a shoot at either of us! Saint Michael, man! they hate us like two pole-cats!"

'Well, sooth it is, they hate Sir Daniel,' answered Hatch, a little sobered.

'Ay, they hate Sir Daniel, and they hate every man that serves with him,' said Appleyard; 'and in the first order of hating, they hate Bennet Hatch and old Nicholas the bowman. See ye here: if there was a stout fellow yonder in the wood-edge, and you and I stood fair for him – as, by Saint George, we stand! – which, think ye, would he choose?'

'You, for a good wager,' answered Hatch.

'My surcoat to a leather belt, it would be you!' cried the old archer. 'Ye burned Grimstone, Bennet – they'll ne'er forgive you that, my master. And as for me,' I'll soon be in a good place, God grant, and out of bow-shoot – ay, and cannon-shoot – of all their malices. I am an old man, and draw fast to homeward, where the bed is ready. But for you, Bennet, y' are to remain behind here at your own peril, and if ye come to my years unhanged, the old true-blue English spirit will be dead.'

'Y' are the shrewishest old dolt in Tunstall Forest,' returned Hatch, visibly ruffled by these threats. 'Get ye to your arms before Sir Oliver come, and leave prating for one good while. An ye had talked so much with Harry the Fift, his ears would ha' been richer than his pocket.'

An arrow sang in the air, like a huge hornet; it struck old Appleyard between the shoulder-blades, and pierced him clean through, and he fell forward on his face among the cabbages. Hatch, with a broken cry, leapt into the air; then, stooping double, he ran for the cover of the house. And in the meanwhile Dick Shelton had dropped behind a lilac, and had his crossbow bent and shouldered, covering the point of the forest.

Not a leaf stirred. The sheep were patiently browsing; the birds had settled. But there lay the old man, with a clothyard arrow standing in his back; and there were Hatch holding to the gable, and Dick crouching and ready behind the lilac bush.

'D'ye see aught?' cried Hatch.

'Not a twig stirs,' said Dick.

'I think shame to leave him lying,' said Bennet, coming forward once more with hesitating steps and a very pale countenance. 'Keep a good eye on the wood, Master Shelton – keep a clear eye on the wood. The saints assoil us! here was a good shoot!'

Bennet raised the old archer on his knee. He was not yet dead; his face worked, and his eyes shut and opened like machinery, and he had a most horrible, ugly look of one in pain.

'Can ye hear, old Nick?' asked Hatch. 'Have ye a last wish before ye wend, old brother?'

'Pluck out the shaft, and let me pass, a' Mary's name!' gasped Appleyard. 'I be done with Old England. Pluck it out!'

'Master Dick,' said Bennet, 'come hither, and pull me a good pull upon the arrow. He would fain pass, the poor sinner.'

Dick laid down his crossbow, and pulling hard upon the arrow, drew it forth. A gush of blood followed; the old archer scrambled half upon his feet, called once upon the name of God, and then fell dead. Hatch, upon his knees among the cabbages, prayed fervently for the welfare of the passing spirit. But even as he prayed, it was plain that his mind was still divided, and he kept an eye upon the corner of the wood from which the shot had come. When he had done, he got to his feet again, drew off one of his mailed gauntlets, and wiped his pale face, which was all wet with terror.

'Ay,' he said, 'it'll be my turn next.'

'Who hath done this, Bennet?' Richard asked, still holding the arrow in his hand.

'Nay, the saints know,' said Hatch. 'Here are a good two score Christian souls that we have hunted out of house and holding, he and I. He has paid his shot, poor shrew, nor will it be long, mayhap, ere I pay mine. Sir Daniel driveth over-hard.'

'This is a strange shaft,' said the lad, looking at the arrow in his hand.

'Ay, by my faith!' cried Bennet. 'Black, and black-feathered. Here is an ill-favoured shaft, by my sooth! for black, they say, bodes burial. And here be words written. Wipe the blood away. What read ye?'

'"*Appulyaird fro Jon Amend-All,*"' read Shelton. 'What should this betoken?'

'Nay, I like it not,' returned the retainer, shaking his head. 'John Amend-All! Here is a rogue's name for those that be up in the world! But why stand we here to make a mark? Take him by the knees, good Master Shelton, while I lift him by the shoulders, and let us lay him in his house. This will be a rare shog to poor Sir Oliver; he will turn paper-colour; he will pray like a windmill.'

They took up the old archer, and carried him between them into the house, where he had dwelt alone. And there they laid him on the floor, out of regard for the mattress, and sought, as best they might, to straighten and compose his limbs.

Appleyard's house was clean and bare. There was a bed, with a blue cover, a cupboard, a great chest, a pair of joint-stools, a hinged table in the chimney-corner, and hung upon the wall the old soldier's armoury of bows and defensive armour. Hatch began to look about him curiously.

'Nick had money,' he said. 'He may have had three score pounds put by. I would I could light upon 't! When ye lose an old friend, Master Richard, the best consolation is to heir him. See, now, this chest. I would go a mighty wager there is a bushel of gold therein. He had a strong hand to get, and a hard hand to keep withal, had Appleyard the archer. Now may God rest his spirit! Near eighty year he was afoot and about, and ever getting; but now he's on the broad of his back, poor shrew, and no more lacketh; and if his chattels came to a good friend, he would be merrier, methinks, in heaven.'

'Come, Hatch,' said Dick, 'respect his stone-blind eyes. Would ye rob the man before his body? Nay, he would walk!'

Hatch made several signs of the cross; but by this time his natural complexion had returned, and he was not easily to be dashed from any purpose. It would have gone hard with the chest had not the gate sounded, and presently after the door of the house opened and admitted a tall, portly, ruddy, black-eyed man of near fifty, in a surplice and black robe.

'Appleyard,' the newcomer was saying, as he entered, but he stopped dead. 'Ave Maria!' he cried. 'Saints be our shield! What cheer is this?'

'Cold cheer with Appleyard, sir parson,' answered Hatch, with perfect cheerfulness. 'Shot at his own door, and alighteth even now at purgatory gates. Ay! there, if tales be true, he shall lack neither coal nor candle.'

Sir Oliver groped his way to a joint-stool, and sat down upon it, sick and white.

'This is a judgment! O, a great stroke!' he sobbed, and rattled off a leash of prayers.

Hatch meanwhile reverently doffed his salet and knelt down.

'Ay, Bennet,' said the priest, somewhat recovering, 'and what may this be? What enemy hath done this?'

'Here, Sir Oliver, is the arrow. See, it is written upon with words,' said Dick.

'Nay,' cried the priest, 'this is a foul hearing! John Amend-All! A right Lollardy word. And black of hue, as for an omen! Sirs, this knave arrow likes me not. But it importeth rather to take counsel. Who should this be? Bethink you, Bennet. Of so many black ill-willers, which should he be that doth so hardily outface us? Simnel? I do much question it. The Walsinghams? Nay, they are not yet so broken; they still think to have the law over us, when times change. There was Simon Malmesbury, too. How think ye, Bennet?'

'What think ye, sir,' returned Hatch, 'of Ellis Duckworth?'

'Nay, Bennet, never. Nay, not he,' said the priest. 'There cometh never any rising, Bennet, from below – so all judicious chroniclers concord in their opinion; but rebellion travelleth ever downward from above; and when Dick, Tom, and Harry take them to their bills, look ever narrowly to see what lord is profited thereby. Now, Sir Daniel, having once more joined him to the Queen's party, is in ill odour with the Yorkist lords. Thence, Bennet, comes the blow – by what procuring, I yet seek; but therein lies the nerve of this discomfiture.'

'An't please you, Sir Oliver,' said Bennet, 'the axles are so hot in this country that I have long been smelling fire. So did this poor sinner, Appleyard. And, by your leave, men's spirits are so foully inclined to all of us, that it needs neither York nor Lancaster to spur them on. Hear my plain thoughts: You, that are a clerk, and Sir Daniel, that sails on any wind, ye have taken many men's goods, and beaten and hanged not a few. Y' are called to count for this; in the end, I wot not how, ye have ever the uppermost at law, and ye think all patched. But give me leave, Sir Oliver: the man that ye have dispossessed and beaten is but the angrier, and some day, when the black devil is by, he will up with his bow and clout me a yard of arrow through your inwards.'

'Nay, Bennet, y' are in the wrong. Bennet, ye should be glad to be corrected,' said Sir Oliver. 'Y' are a prater, Bennet, a talker, a babbler; your mouth is wider than your two ears. Mend it, Bennet, mend it.'

'Nay, I say no more. Have it as ye list,' said the retainer.

The priest now rose from the stool, and from the writing-case that hung about his neck took forth wax and a taper, and a flint and steel. With these he sealed up the chest and the cupboard with Sir Daniel's arms, Hatch looking on disconsolate; and then the whole party proceeded, somewhat timorously, to sally from the house and get to horse.

''Tis time we were on the road, Sir Oliver,' said Hatch, as he held the priest's stirrup while he mounted.

'Ay; but, Bennet, things are changed,' returned the parson. 'There is now no Appleyard – rest his soul! – to keep the garrison. I shall keep you, Bennet. I must have a good man to rest me on in this day of black arrows. 'The arrow that flieth by day,' saith the evangel; I have no mind of the context; nay, I am a sluggard priest, I am too deep in men's affairs. Well, let us ride forth, Master Hatch. The jackmen should be at the church by now.'

So they rode forward down the road, with the wind after them, blowing the tails of the parson's cloak; and behind them, as they went, clouds began to arise and blot out the sinking sun. They had passed three of the scattered houses that make up Tunstall hamlet, when, coming to a turn, they saw the church before them. Ten or a dozen houses clustered immediately round it; but to the back the churchyard was next the meadows. At the lych-gate, near a score of men were gathered, some in the saddle, some standing by their horses' heads. They were variously armed and mounted; some with spears, some with bills, some with bows, and some bestriding plough-horses, still splashed with the mire of the furrow; for these were the very dregs of the country, and all the better men and the fair equipments were already with Sir Daniel in the field.

'We have not done amiss, praised be the cross of Holywood! Sir Daniel will be right well content," observed the priest, inwardly numbering the troop.

'Who goes? Stand! if ye be true!' shouted Bennet.

A man was seen slipping through the churchyard among the yews; and at the sound of this summons he discarded all concealment, and fairly took to his heels for the forest. The men at the gate, who had been hitherto unaware of the stranger's presence, woke and scattered. Those who had dismounted began scrambling into the saddle: the rest rode in pursuit; but they had to make the circuit of the consecrated ground, and it was plain their quarry would escape them. Hatch, roaring an oath, put his horse at the hedge, to head him off; but the beast refused, and sent his rider sprawling in the dust. And though he was up again in a moment, and had caught the bridle, the time had gone by, and the fugitive had gained too great a lead for any hope of capture.

The wisest of all had been Dick Shelton. Instead of starting in a vain pursuit, he had whipped his crossbow from his back, bent it, and set a quarrel to the string; and now, when the others had desisted, he turned to Bennet, and asked if he should shoot.

'Shoot! shoot!' cried the priest, with sanguinary violence.

'Cover him, Master Dick,' said Bennet. 'Bring me him down like a ripe apple.'

The fugitive was now within but a few leaps of safety; but this last part of the meadow ran very steeply uphill, and the man ran slower in proportion. What with the greyness of the falling night, and the uneven movements of the runner, it was no easy aim; and as Dick levelled his bow, he felt a kind of pity, and a half desire that he might miss. The quarrel sped.

The man stumbled and fell, and a great cheer arose from Hatch and the pursuers. But they were counting their corn before the harvest. The man fell lightly; he was lightly afoot again, turned and waved his cap in a bravado, and was out of sight next moment in the margin of the wood.

'And the plague go with him!' cried Bennet. 'He has thieves' heels: he can run, by St Banbury! But you touched him, Master Shelton; he has stolen your quarrel, may he never have good I grudge him less!'

'Nay, but what made he by the church?' asked Sir Oliver. 'I am shrewdly afeared there has been mischief here. Clipsby, good fellow, get ye down from your horse, and search thoroughly among the yews.'

Clipsby was gone but a little while ere he returned, carrying a paper.

'This writing was pinned to the church door,' he said, handing it to the parson. 'I found naught else, sir parson.'

'Now, by the power of Mother Church,' cried Sir Oliver, 'but this runs hard on sacrilege! For the king's good pleasure, or the lord of the manor – well! But that every run-the-hedge in a green jerkin should fasten papers to the chancel door – nay, it runs hard on sacrilege, hard; and men have burned for matters of less weight! But what have we here? The light falls apace. Good Master Richard, y' have young eyes. Read me, I pray, this libel.'

Dick Shelton took the paper in his hand and read it aloud. It contained some lines of a very rugged doggerel, hardly even rhyming, written in a gross character, and most uncouthly spelt. With the spelling somewhat bettered, this is how they ran: –

'I had four blak arrows under my belt,
Four for the greefs that I have felt,
Four for the nomber of ill menne
That have oppressid me now and then.

One is gone; one is wele sped;
Old Apulyaird is ded.

One is for Maister Bennet Hatch,
That burned Grimstone, walls and thatch.

One for Sir Oliver Oates,
That cut Sir Harry Shelton's throat.

Sir Daniel, ye shull have the fourt;
We shall think it fair sport.

Ye shull each have your own part,
A blak arrow in each blak heart.
Get ye to your knees for to pray:
Ye are ded theeves, by yea and nay!'

'JON AMEND-ALL
of the Green Wood,
And his jolly fellaweship.

'Item, we have mo arrowes and goode hempen cord for otheres of your following.'

'Now, well-a-day for charity and the Christian graces!' cried Sir Oliver, lamentably. 'Sirs, this is an ill world, and groweth daily worse. I will swear upon the cross of Holywood I am as innocent of that good knight's hurt, whether in act or purpose, as the babe unchristened. Neither was his throat cut; for therein they are again in error, as there still live credible witnesses to show.'

'It boots not, sir parson,' said Bennet. 'Here is unseasonable talk.'

'Nay, Master Bennet, not so. Keep ye in your due place, good Bennet,' answered the priest. 'I shall make mine innocence appear. I will upon no consideration lose my poor life in error. I take all men to witness that I am clear of this matter. I was not even in the Moat House. I was sent of an errand before nine upon the clock——'

'Sir Oliver,' said Hatch, interrupting, 'since it please you not to stop this sermon, I will take other means. Goffe, sound to horse.'

And while the tucket was sounding, Bennet moved close to the bewildered parson, and whispered violently in his ear.

Dick Shelton saw the priest's eye turned upon him for an instant in a startled glance. He had some cause for thought; for this Sir Harry Shelton was his own natural father. But he said never a word, and kept his countenance unmoved.

Hatch and Sir Oliver discussed together for awhile their altered situation; ten men, it was decided between them, should be reserved, not only to garrison the Moat House, but to escort the priest across the wood. In the meantime, as Bennet was to remain behind, the command of the reinforcement was given to Master Shelton. Indeed, there was no choice; the men were loutish fellows, dull and unskilled in war, while Dick was not only popular, but resolute and grave beyond his age. Although his youth had been spent in these rough country places, the lad had been well taught in letters by Sir Oliver, and Hatch himself had shown him the management of arms and the first principles of command. Bennet had always been kind and helpful; he was one of those who are cruel as the grave to those they call their enemies, but ruggedly faithful and well-willing to their friends; and now, while Sir Oliver entered the next house to write, in his swift, exquisite penmanship, a memorandum of the last occurences to his master, Sir Daniel Brackley, Bennet came up to his pupil to wish him God-speed upon his enterprise.

'Ye must go the long way about, Master Shelton,' he said; 'round by the bridge, for your life! Keep a sure man fifty paces afore you, to draw shots; and go softly till y' are past the wood. If the rogues fall upon you, ride for 't; ye will do naught by standing. And keep ever forward, Master Shelton; turn me not back again, an ye love your life; there is no help in Tunstall, mind ye that. And now, since ye go to the great wars about the king, and I continue to dwell here in extreme jeopardy of my life, and the saints alone can certify if we shall meet again below, I give you my last counsels now at your riding. Keep an eye on Sir Daniel; he is unsure. Put not your trust in the jack-priest; he intendeth not amiss, but doth the will of others; it is a hand-gun for Sir Daniel! Get you good lordship where ye go; make you strong friends; look to it. And think ever a pater-noster-while on Bennet Hatch. There are worse rogues afoot than Bennet.

So, God-speed!'

'And Heaven be with you, Bennet!' returned Dick. 'Ye were a good friend to me-ward, and so I shall say ever.'

'And, look ye, master,' added Hatch, with a certain embarrassment, 'if this Amend-All should get a shaft into me, ye might, mayhap, lay out a gold mark or mayhap a pound for my poor soul; for it is like to go stiff with me in purgatory.'

'Ye shall have your will of it, Bennet,' answered Dick. 'But, what cheer, man! we shall meet again, where ye shall have more need of ale than masses.'

'The saints so grant it, Master Dick!' returned the other. 'But here comes Sir Oliver. An he were as quick with the long-bow as with the pen, he would be a brave man-at-arms.'

Sir Oliver gave Dick a sealed packet, with this superscription: 'To my ryght worchypful master, Sir Daniel Brackley, knyght, be thys delyvered in haste.'

And Dick, putting it in the bosom of his jacket, gave the word and set forth westward up the village.

Book I

THE TWO LADS

CHAPTER ONE

At the Sign of the Sun in Kettley

SIR DANIEL AND HIS MEN LAY in and about Kettley that night, warmly quartered and well patrolled. But the Knight of Tunstall was one who never rested from money-getting; and even now, when he was on the brink of an adventure which should make or mar him, he was up an hour after midnight to squeeze poor neighbours. He was one who trafficked greatly in disputed inheritances; it was his way to buy out the most unlikely claimant, and then, by the favour he curried with great lords about the king, procure unjust decisions in his favour; or, if that was too roundabout, to seize the disputed manor by force of arms, and rely on his influence and Sir Oliver's cunning in the law to hold what he had snatched. Kettley was one such place; it had come very lately into his clutches; he still met with opposition from the tenants; and it was to overawe discontent that he had led his troops that way.

By two in the morning, Sir Daniel sat in the inn room, close by the fireside, for it was cold at that hour among the fens of Kettley. By his elbow stood a pottle of spiced ale. He had taken off his visored headpiece, and sat with his bald head and thin, dark visage resting on one hand, wrapped warmly in a sanguine-coloured cloak. At the lower end of the room about a dozen of his men stood sentry over the door or lay asleep on benches; and, somewhat nearer hand, a young lad, apparently of twelve or thirteen, was stretched in a mantle on the floor. The host of the Sun stood before the great man.

'Now, mark me, mine host,' Sir Daniel said, 'follow but mine orders, and I shall be your good lord ever. I must have good men for head boroughs, and I will have Adam-a-More high constable; see to it narrowly. If other men be chosen, it shall avail you nothing; rather it shall be found to your sore cost. For those that have paid rent to Walsingham I shall take good measure – you among the rest, mine host.'

'Good knight,' said the host, 'I will swear upon the cross of Holywood I did but pay to Walsingham upon compulsion. Nay, bully knight, I love not the rogue Walsinghams; they were as poor as thieves, bully knight. Give me a great lord like you. Nay; ask me among the neighbours, I am stout for Brackley.'

'It may be,' said Sir Daniel, drily. 'Ye shall then pay twice.'

The innkeeper made a horrid grimace; but this was a piece of bad luck that might readily befall a tenant in these unruly times, and he was perhaps glad to make his peace so easily.

'Bring up yon fellow, Selden!' cried the knight.

And one of his retainers led up a poor, cringing old man, as pale as a candle, and all shaking with the fen fever.

'Sirrah,' said Sir Daniel, 'your name?'

'An't please your worship,' replied the man, 'my name is Condall – Condall of Shoreby, at your good worship's pleasure.'

'I have heard you ill reported on,' returned the knight. 'Ye deal in treason, rogue; ye trudge the country leasing; y' are heavily suspicioned of the death of severals. How, fellow, are ye so bold? But I will bring you down.'

'Right honourable and my reverend lord,' the man cried, 'here is some hodge-podge, saving your good presence. I am but a poor private man, and have hurt none.'

'The under-sheriff did report of you most vilely,' said the knight. '"Seize me," saith he, "that Tyndal of Shoreby."'

'Condall, my good lord; Condall is my poor name,' said the unfortunate.

'Condall or Tyndal, it is all one,' replied Sir Daniel, coolly. 'For, by my sooth, y' are here, and I do mightily suspect your honesty. If you would save your neck, write me swiftly an obligation for twenty pound.'

'For twenty pound, my good lord!' cried Condall. 'Here is midsummer madness! My whole estate amounteth not to seventy shillings.'

'Condall or Tyndal,' returned Sir Daniel, grinning, 'I will run my peril of that loss. Write me down twenty, and when I have recovered all I may, I will be good lord to you, and pardon you the rest.'

'Alas! my good lord, it may not be; I have no skill to write,' said Condall.

'Well-a-day!' returned the knight. 'Here, then, is no remedy. Yet I would fain have spared you, Tyndal, had my conscience suffered. Selden, take me this old shrew softly to the nearest elm, and hang me him tenderly by the neck, where I may see him at my riding. Fare ye well, good Master Condall, dear Master Tyndal; y' are post-haste for Paradise; fare ye then well!'

'Nay, my right pleasant lord,' replied Condall, forcing an obsequious smile, 'an ye be so masterful, as doth right well become you, I will even, with all my poor skill, do your good bidding.'

'Friend,' quoth Sir Daniel, 'ye will now write two score. Go to! y' are too cunning for a livelihood of seventy shillings. Selden, see him write me this in good form, and have it duly witnessed.'

And Sir Daniel, who was a very merry knight, none merrier in England, took a drink of his mulled ale, and lay back, smiling.

Meanwhile, the boy upon the floor began to stir, and presently sat up and looked about him with a scare.

'Hither,' said Sir Daniel; and as the other rose at his command and came slowly towards him, he leaned back and laughed outright. 'By the rood!' he cried, 'a sturdy boy!'

The lad flashed crimson with anger, and darted a look of hate out of his dark eyes. Now that he was on his legs, it was more difficult to make certain of his age. His face looked somewhat older in expression, but it was as smooth as a young child's; and in bone and body he was unusually slender, and somewhat awkward of gait.

'Ye have called me, Sir Daniel,' he said. 'Was it to laugh at my poor plight?'

'Nay, now, let laugh,' said the knight. 'Good shrew, let laugh, I pray you. An ye could see yourself, I warrant ye would laugh the first.'

'Well,' cried the lad, flushing, 'ye shall answer this when ye answer for the other. Laugh while yet ye may!'

'Nay, now, good cousin,' replied Sir Daniel, with some earnestness, 'think not that I mock at you, except in mirth, as between kinsfolk and singular friends. I will make you a marriage of a thousand pounds, go to! and cherish you exceedingly. I took you, indeed, roughly, as the time demanded; but from henceforth I shall ungrudgingly maintain and cheerfully serve you. Ye shall be Mrs Shelton – Lady Shelton, by my troth! for the lad promiseth bravely. Tut! ye will not shy for honest laughter; it purgeth melancholy. They are no rogues who laugh, good cousin. Good mine host, lay me a meal now for my cousin, Master John. Sit ye down, sweetheart, and eat.'

'Nay,' said Master John, 'I will break no bread. Since ye force me to this sin, I will fast for my soul's interest. But, good mine host, I pray you of courtesy give me a cup of fair water; I shall be much beholden to your courtesy indeed.'

'Ye shall have a dispensation, go to!' cried the knight. 'Shalt be well shriven, by my faith! Content you, then, and eat.'

But the lad was obstinate, drank a cup of water, and, once more wrapping himself closely in his mantle, sat in a far corner, brooding.

In an hour or two, there rose a stir in the village of sentries challenging and the clatter of arms and horses; and then a troop drew up by the inn door, and Richard Shelton, splashed with mud, presented himself upon the threshold.

'Save you, Sir Daniel,' he said.

'How! Dickie Shelton!' cried the knight; and at the mention of Dick's name the other lad looked curiously across. 'What maketh Bennet Hatch?'

'Please you, sir knight, to take cognizance of this packet from Sir Oliver, wherein are all things fully stated,' answered Richard, presenting the priest's letter. 'And please you farther, ye were best make all speed to Risingham; for on the way hither we encountered one riding furiously with letters, and by his report, my Lord of Risingham was sore bested, and lacked exceedingly your presence.'

'How say you? Sore bested?' returned the knight. 'Nay, then, we will make speed sitting down, good Richard. As the world goes in this poor realm of England, he that rides softliest rides surest. Delay, they say, begetteth peril; but it is rather this itch of doing that undoes men; mark it, Dick. But let me see, first, what cattle ye have brought. Selden, a link here at the door!'

And Sir Daniel strode forth into the village street, and, by the red glow of a torch, inspected his new troops. He was an unpopular neighbour and an unpopular master; but as a leader in war he was well beloved by those who rode behind his pennant. His dash, his proved courage, his forethought for the soldiers' comfort, even his rough gibes, were all to the taste of the bold blades in jack and salet.

'Nay, by the rood!' he cried, 'what poor dogs are these? Here be some as crooked as a bow, and some as lean as a spear. Friends, ye shall ride in the front of the battle; I can spare you, friends. Mark me this old villain on the piebald! A two-year mutton riding on a hog would look more soldierly! Ha! Clipsby, are ye there, old rat? Y' are a man I could lose with a good heart; ye shall go in front of all, with a bull's-eye painted on your jack, to be the better butt for archery; sirrah, ye shall show me the way.'

'I will show you any way, Sir Daniel, but the way to change sides,' returned Clipsby, sturdily.

Sir Daniel laughed a guffaw.

'Why, well said!' he cried. 'Has a shrewd tongue in thy mouth, go to! I will forgive you for that merry word. Selden, see them fed, both man and brute.'

The knight re-entered the inn.

'Now, friend Dick,' he said, 'fall to. Here is good ale and bacon. Eat, while that I read.'

Sir Daniel opened the packet, and as he read his brow darkened. When he had done he sat a little, musing. Then he looked sharply at his ward.

'Dick,' said he, 'y' have seen this penny rhyme?'

The lad replied in the affirmative.

'It bears your father's name,' continued the knight; 'and our poor shrew of a parson is, by some mad soul, accused of slaying him.'

'He did most eagerly deny it,' answered Dick.

'He did?' cried the knight, very sharply. 'Heed him not. He has a loose tongue; he babbles like a jack-sparrow. Some day, when I may find the leisure, Dick, I will myself more fully inform you of these matters. There was one Duckworth shrewdly blamed for it; but the times were troubled, and there was no justice to be got.'

'It befell at the Moat House?' Dick ventured, with a beating at his heart.

'It befell between the Moat House and Holywood,' replied Sir Daniel, calmly; but he shot a covert glance, black with suspicion, at Dick's face. 'And now,' added the knight, 'speed you with your meal; ye shall return to Tunstall with a line from me.'

Dick's face fell sorely.

'Prithee, Sir Daniel,' he cried, 'send one of the villains! I beseech you let me to the battle. I can strike a stroke, I promise you.'

'I misdoubt it not,' replied Sir Daniel, sitting down to write. 'But here, Dick, is no honour to be won. I lie in Kettley till I have sure tidings of the war, and then ride to join me with the conqueror. Cry not on cowardice; it is but wisdom, Dick; for this poor realm so tosseth with rebellion, and the king's name and custody so changeth hands, that no man may be certain of the morrow. Toss-pot and Shuttle-wit run in, but my Lord Good-Counsel sits o' one side, waiting.'

With that, Sir Daniel, turning his back to Dick, and quite at the farther end of the long table, began to write his letter, with his mouth on one side, for this business of the Black Arrow stuck sorely in his throat.

Meanwhile, young Shelton was going on heartily enough with his breakfast, when he felt a touch upon his arm, and a very soft voice whispering in his ear.

'Make not a sign, I do beseech you,' said the voice, 'but of your charity teach me the straight way to Holywood. Beseech you, now, good boy, comfort a poor soul in peril and extreme distress, and set me so far forth upon the way to my repose.'

'Take the path by the windmill,' answered Dick, in the same tone; 'it will bring you to Till Ferry; there inquire again.'

And without turning his head, he fell again to eating. But with the tail of his eye he caught a glimpse of the young lad called Master John stealthily creeping from the room.

'Why,' thought Dick, 'he is as young as I. 'Good boy' doth he call me? An I had known, I should have seen the varlet hanged ere I had told him. Well, if he goes through the fen, I may come up with him and pull his ears.'

Half and hour later, Sir Daniel gave Dick the letter, and bade him speed to the Moat House. And again, some half an hour after Dick's departure, a messenger came, in hot haste, from my Lord of Risingham.

'Sir Daniel,' the messenger said, 'ye lose great honour, by my sooth! The fight began again this morning ere the dawn, and we have beaten their van and scattered their right wing. Only the main battle standeth fast. An we had your fresh men, we should tilt you them all into the river. What, sir knight! Will ye be the last? It stands not with your good credit.'

'Nay,' cried the knight, 'I was but now upon the march. Selden, sound me the tucket. Sir, I am with you on the instant. It is not two hours since the more part of my command came in, sir messenger. What would ye have? Spurring is good meat, but yet it killed the charger. Bustle, boys!'

By this time the tucket was sounding cheerily in the morning, and from all sides Sir Daniel's men poured into the main street and formed before the inn. They had slept upon their arms, with chargers saddled, and in ten minutes five-score men-at-arms and archers, cleanly equipped and briskly disciplined, stood ranked and ready. The chief part were in Sir Daniel's livery, murrey and blue, which gave the greater show to their array. The best armed rode first; and away out of sight, at the tail of the column, came the sorry reinforcement of the night before. Sir Daniel looked with pride along the line.

'Here be the lads to serve you in a pinch,' he said.

'They are pretty men, indeed,' replied the messenger. 'It but augments my sorrow that ye had not marched the earlier.'

'Well,' said the knight, 'what would ye? The beginning of a feast and the end of a fray, sir messenger;' and he mounted into his saddle. 'Why! how now!' he cried. 'John! Joanna! Nay, by the sacred rood! where is she? Host, where is that girl?'

'Girl, Sir Daniel?' cried the landlord. 'Nay, sir, I saw no girl.'

'Boy, then, dotard!' cried the knight. 'Could ye not see it was a wench? She in the murrey-coloured mantle – she that broke her fast with water, rogue – where is she?'

'Nay, the saints bless us! Master John, ye called him,' said the host. 'Well, I thought none evil. He is gone. I saw him – her – I saw her in the stable a good hour agone; 'a was saddling a grey horse.'

'Now, by the rood!' cried Sir Daniel, 'the wench was worth five hundred pound to me and more.'

'Sir knight,' observed the messenger, with bitterness, 'while that ye are here, roaring for five hundred pounds, the realm of England is elsewhere being lost and won.'

'It is well said,' replied Sir Daniel. 'Selden, fall me out with six cross-bowmen; hunt me her down. I care not what it cost; but, at my returning, let me find her at the Moat House. Be it upon your head. And now, sir messenger, we march.'

And the troop broke into a good trot, and Selden and his six men were left behind upon the street of Kettley, with the staring villagers.

CHAPTER TWO

In the Fen

IT WAS NEAR SIX IN THE MAY morning when Dick began to ride down into the fen upon his homeward way. The sky was all blue; the jolly wind blew loud and steady; the windmill-sails were spinning; and the willows over all the fen rippling and whitening like a field of corn. He had been all night in the saddle, but his heart was good and his body sound, and he rode right merrily.

The path went down and down into the marsh, till he lost sight of all the neighbouring landmarks but Kettley windmill on the knoll behind him, and the extreme top of Tunstall Forest far before. On either hand there were great fields of blowing reeds and willows, pools of water shaking in the wind, and treacherous bogs, as green as emerald, to tempt and betray the traveller. The path lay almost straight through the morass. It was already very ancient; its foundation had been laid by Roman soldiery; in the lapse of ages much of it had sunk, and every here and there, for a few hundred yards, it lay submerged below the stagnant waters of the fen.

About a mile from Kettley, Dick came to one such break in the plain line of causeway, where the reeds and willows grew dispersedly like little islands and confused the eye. The gap, besides, was more than usually long; it was a place where any stranger might come readily to mischief; and Dick bethought him, with something like a pang, of the lad whom he had so imperfectly directed. As for himself, one look backward to where the windmill-sails were turning back against the blue of heaven – one look forward to the high ground of Tunstall Forest, and he was sufficiently directed and held straight on, the water washing to his horse's knees, as safe as on a highway.

Half-way across, and when he had already sighted the path rising high and dry upon the farther side, he was aware of a great splashing on his right, and saw a grey horse, sunk to its belly in the mud, and still spasmodically struggling. Instantly, as though it had divined the neighbourhood of help, the poor beast began to neigh most piercingly. It rolled, meanwhile, a blood-shot eye, insane with terror; and as it sprawled wallowing in the quag, clouds of stinging insects rose and buzzed about it in the air.

'Alack!' thought Dick, 'can the poor lad have perished? There is his horse, for certain – a brave grey! Nay, comrade, if thou criest to me so piteously, I will do all man can to help thee. Shalt not lie there to drown by inches!'

And he made ready his crossbow, and put a quarrel through the creature's head.

Dick rode on after this act of rugged mercy, somewhat sobered in spirit, and looking closely about him for any sign of his less happy predecessor in the way.

'I would I had dared to tell him further,' he thought; 'for I fear he has miscarried in the slough.'

And just as he was so thinking, a voice cried upon his name from the causeway side, and, looking over his shoulder, he saw the lad's face peering from a clump of reeds.

'Are ye there?' he said, reining in. 'Ye lay so close among the reeds that I had passed you by. I saw your horse bemired, and put him from his agony; which, by my sooth! an ye had been a more merciful rider, ye had done yourself. But come forth out of your hiding. Here be none to trouble you.'

'Nay, good boy, I have no arms, nor skill to use them if I had,' replied the other, stepping forth upon the pathway.

'Why call me "boy"?' cried Dick. 'Y' are not, I trow, the elder of us twain.'

'Good Master Shelton,' said the other, 'prithee forgive me. I have none the least intention to offend. Rather I would in every way beseech your gentleness and favour, for I am now worse bested than ever, having lost my way, my cloak, and my poor horse. To have a riding-rod and spurs, and never a horse to sit upon! And before all,' he added, looking ruefully upon his clothes – 'before all, to be so sorrily besmirched!'

'Tut!' cried Dick. 'Would ye mind a ducking? Blood of wound or dust of travel – that's a man's adornment.'

'Nay, then, I like him better plain,' observed the lad. 'But, prithee, how shall I do? Prithee, good Master Richard, help me with your good counsel. If I come not safe to Holywood, I am undone.'

'Nay,' said Dick, dismounting, 'I will give more than counsel. Take my horse, and I will run awhile, and when I am weary we shall change again, that so, riding and running, both may go the speedier.'

So the change was made, and they went forward as briskly as they durst on the uneven causeway, Dick with his hand upon the other's knee.

'How call ye your name?' asked Dick.

'Call me John Matcham,' replied the lad.

'And what make ye to Holywood?' Dick continued.

'I seek sanctuary from a man that would oppress me,' was the answer. 'The good Abbot of Holywood is a strong pillar to the weak.'

'And how came ye with Sir Daniel, Master Matcham?' pursued Dick.

'Nay,' cried the other, 'by the abuse of force! He hath taken me by violence from my own place; dressed me in these weeds; ridden with me till my heart was sick; gibed me till I could 'a' wept; and when certain of my friends pursued, thinking to have me back, claps me in the rear to stand their shot! I was even grazed in the right foot, and walk but lamely. Nay, there shall come a day between us; he shall smart for all!'

'Would ye shoot at the moon with a hand-gun?' said Dick. ''Tis a valiant knight, and hath a hand of iron. An he guessed I had made or meddled with your flight, it would go sore with me.'

'Ay, poor boy,' returned the other, 'y' are his ward, I know it. By the same token, so am I, or so he saith; or else he hath bought my marriage – I wot not rightly which; but it is some handle to oppress me by.'

'Boy again!' said Dick.

'Nay, then, shall I call you girl, good Richard?' asked Matcham.

'Never a girl for me,' returned Dick. 'I do abjure the crew of them!'

'Ye speak boyishly,' said the other. 'Ye think more of them than ye pretend.'

'Not I,' said Dick, stoutly. 'They come not in my mind. A plague of them, say I! Give me to hunt and to fight and to feast, and to live with jolly foresters. I never heard of a maid yet that was for any service, save one only; and she, poor shrew, was burned for a witch and the wearing of men's clothes in spite of nature.'

Master Matcham crossed himself with fervour, and appeared to pray.

'What make ye?' Dick inquired.

'I pray for her spirit,' answered the other, with a somewhat troubled voice.

'For a witch's spirit?' Dick cried. 'But pray for her, an ye list; she was the best wench in Europe, was this Joan of Arc. Old Appleyard the archer ran from her, he said, as if she had been Mahoun. Nay, she was a brave wench.'

'Well, but, good Master Richard,' resumed Matcham, 'an ye like maids so little, y' are no true natural man; for God made them twain by intention, and brought true love into the world, to be man's hope and woman's comfort.'

'Faugh!' said Dick. 'Y' are a milk-sopping baby, so to harp on women. An ye think I be no true man, get down upon the path, and whether at fists, backsword, or bow and arrow, I will prove my manhood on your body.'

'Nay, I am no fighter,' said Matcham, eagerly. 'I mean no tittle of offence. I meant but pleasantry. And if I talk of women, it is because I heard ye were to marry.'

'I to marry!' Dick exclaimed. 'Well, it is the first I hear of it. And with whom was I to marry?'

'One Joan Sedley,' replied Matcham, colouring. 'It was Sir Daniel's doing; he hath money to gain upon both sides; and, indeed, I have heard the poor-wench bemoaning herself pitifully of the match. It seems she is of your mind, or else distasted to the bridegroom.'

'Well! marriage is like death, it comes to all,' said Dick, with resignation. 'And she bemoaned herself? I pray ye now, see there how shuttle-witted are these girls: to bemoan herself before that she had seen me! Do I bemoan myself? Not I. An I be to marry, I will marry dry-eyed! But if ye know her, prithee, of what favour is she? fair or foul? And is she shrewish or pleasant?'

'Nay, what matters it?' said Matcham. 'An y' are to marry, ye can but marry. What matters foul or fair? These be but toys. Y' are no milksop, Master Richard; ye will wed with dry eyes, anyhow.'

'It is well said,' replied Shelton. 'Little I reck.'

'Your lady wife is like to have a pleasant lord,' said Matcham.

'She shall have the lord Heaven made her for,' returned Dick. 'I trow there be worse as well as better.'

'Ah, the poor wench!' cried the other.

'And why so poor?' asked Dick.

'To wed a man of wood,' replied his companion. 'O me, for a wooden husband!'

'I think I be a man of wood, indeed,' said Dick, 'to trudge afoot the while you ride my horse; but it is good wood, I trow.'

'Good Dick, forgive me,' cried the other. 'Nay, y' are the best heart in England; I but laughed. Forgive me now, sweet Dick.'

'Nay, no fool words,' returned Dick, a little embarrassed by his companion's warmth. 'No harm is done. I am not touchy, praise the saints.'

And at that moment the wind, which was blowing straight behind them as they went, brought them the rough flourish of Sir Daniel's trumpeter.

'Hark!' said Dick, 'the tucket soundeth.'

'Ay,' said Matcham, 'they have found my flight, and now I am unhorsed!' and he became pale as death.

'Nay, what cheer!' returned Dick. 'Y' have a long start, and we are near the ferry. And it is I, methinks, that am unhorsed.'

'Alack, I shall be taken!' cried the fugitive. 'Dick, kind Dick, beseech ye help me but a little!'

'Why, now, what aileth thee?' said Dick. Methinks I help you very patently. But my heart is sorry for so spiritless a fellow! And see ye here, John Matcham – sith John Matcham is your name – I, Richard Shelton, tide what betideth, come what may, will see you safe in Holywood. The saints so do to me again if I default you. Come, pick me up a good heart, Sir White-face. The way betters here; spur me the horse. Go faster! faster! Nay, mind not for me; I can run like a deer.'

So, with the horse trotting hard, and Dick running easily alongside, they crossed the remainder of the fen, and came out upon the banks of the river by the ferryman's hut.

CHAPTER THREE

The Fen Ferry

THE RIVER TILL WAS A WIDE, sluggish, clayey water, oozing out of fens, and in this part of its course it strained among some score of willow-covered, marshy islets.

It was a dingy stream; but upon this bright, spirited morning everything was become beautiful. The wind and the martens broke it up into innumerable dimples; and the reflection of the sky was scattered over all the surface in crumbs of smiling blue.

A creek ran up to meet the path, and close under the bank the ferryman's hut lay snugly. It was of wattle and clay, and the grass grew green upon the roof.

Dick went to the door and opened it. Within, upon a foul old russet cloak, the ferryman lay stretched and shivering; a great hulk of a man, but lean and shaken by the country fever.

'Hey, Master Shelton,' he said, 'be ye for the ferry? Ill times, ill times! Look to yourself. There is a fellowship abroad. Ye were better turn round on your two heels and try the bridge.'

'Nay; time's in the saddle,' answered Dick. 'Time will ride, Hugh Ferryman. I am hot in haste.'

'A wilful man!' returned the ferryman, rising. 'An ye win safe to the Moat House, y' have done lucky; but I say no more.' And then catching sight of

Matcham, 'Who be this?' he asked, as he paused, blinking, on the threshold of his cabin.

'It is my kinsman, Master Matcham,' answered Dick.

'Give ye good day, good ferryman,' said Matcham, who had dismounted, and now came forward, leading the horse. 'Launch me your boat, I prithee; we are sore in haste.'

The gaunt ferryman continued staring.

'By the mass!' he cried at length, and laughed with open throat.

Matcham coloured to his neck and winced; and Dick, with an angry countenance, put his hand on the lout's shoulder.

'How now, churl!' he cried. 'Fall to thy business, and leave mocking thy betters.'

Hugh Ferryman grumblingly undid his boat, and shoved it a little forth into the deep water. Then Dick led in the horse, and Matcham followed.

'Ye be mortal small made, master,' said Hugh, with a wide grin; 'something o' the wrong model, belike. Nay, Master Shelton, I am for you,' he added, getting to his oars. 'A cat may look at a king. I did but take a shot of the eye at Master Matcham.'

'Sirrah, no more words,' said Dick. 'Bend me your back.'

They were by that time at the mouth of the creek, and the view opened up and down the river. Everywhere it was enclosed with islands. Clay banks were falling in, willows nodding, reeds waving, martens dipping and piping. There was no sign of man in the labyrinth of waters.

'My master,' said the ferryman, keeping the boat steady with one oar, 'I have a shrewd guess that John-a-Fenne is on the island. He bears me a black grudge to all Sir Daniel's. How if I turned me up stream and landed you an arrow-flight above the path? Ye were best not meddle with John Fenne.'

'How, then? is he of this company?' asked Dick.

'Nay, mum is the word,' said Hugh. 'But I would go up water, Dick. How if Master Matcham came by an arrow?' and he laughed again.

'Be it so, Hugh,' answered Dick.

'Look ye, then,' pursued Hugh. 'Sith it shall so be, unsling me your cross-bow – so: now make it ready – good; place me a quarrel. Ay, keep it so, and look upon me grimly.'

'What meaneth this?' asked Dick.

'Why, my master, if I steal you across, it must be under force or fear,' replied the ferryman; 'for else, if John Fenne got wind of it, he were like to prove my most distressful neighbour.'

'Do these churls ride so roughly?' Dick inquired. 'Do they command Sir Daniel's own ferry?'

'Nay,' whispered the ferryman, winking. 'Mark me! Sir Daniel shall down. His time is out. He shall down. Mum!' And he bent over his oars.

They pulled a long way up the river, turned the tail of an island, and came softly down a narrow channel next the opposite bank. Then Hugh held water in midstream.

'I must land you here among the willows,' he said.

'Here is no path but willow swamps and quagmires,' answered Dick.

'Master Shelton,' replied Hugh, 'I dare not take ye nearer down, for your own sake now. He watcheth me the ferry, lying on his bow. All that go by and owe Sir Daniel goodwill, he shooteth down like rabbits. I heard him swear it by the rood. An I had not known you of old days – ay, and from so high upward – I would 'a' let you go on; but for old days' remembrance, and because ye had this toy with you that's not fit for wounds or warfare, I did risk my two poor ears to have you over whole. Content you; I can no more, on my salvation!'

Hugh was still speaking, lying on his oars, when there came a great shout from among the willows on the island, and sounds followed as of a strong man breasting roughly through the wood.

'A murrain!' cried Hugh. 'He was on the upper island all the while!' He pulled straight for shore. 'Threat me with your bow, good Dick; threat me with it plain,' he added. 'I have tried to save your skins, save you mine!'

The boat ran into a tough thicket of willows with a crash. Matcham, pale, but steady and alert, at a sign from Dick, ran along the thwarts and leaped ashore; Dick, taking the horse by the bridle, sought to follow, but what with the animal's bulk, and what with the closeness of the thicket, both stuck fast. The horse neighed and trampled; and the boat, which was swinging in an eddy, came on and óff and pitched with violence.

'It may not be, Hugh; here is no landing,' cried Dick; but he still struggled valiantly with the obstinate thicket and the startled animal.

A tall man appeared upon the shore of the island, a long-bow in his hand. Dick saw him for an instant, with the corner of his eye, bending the bow with a great effort, his face crimson with hurry.

'Who goes?' he shouted. 'Hugh, who goes?'

''Tis Master Shelton, John,' replied the ferryman.

'Stand, Dick Shelton!' bawled the man upon the island. 'Ye shall have no hurt, upon the rood! Stand! Back out, Hugh Ferryman.'

Dick cried a taunting answer.

'Nay, then, ye shall go afoot,' returned the man; and he let drive an arrow.

The horse, struck by the shaft, lashed out in agony and terror; the boat capsized, and next moment all were struggling in the eddies of the river.

When Dick came up, he was within a yard of the bank; and before his eyes were clear, his hand had closed on something firm and strong that instantly began to drag him forward. It was the riding-rod, that Matcham, crawling forth upon an overhanging willow, had opportunely thrust into his grasp.

'By the mass!' cried Dick, as he was helped ashore, 'that makes a life I owe you. I swim like a cannon-ball.' And he turned instantly towards the island.

Midway over, Hugh Ferryman was swimming with his upturned boat, while John-a-Fenne, furious at the ill-fortune of his shot, bawled to him to hurry.

'Come, Jack,' said Shelton, 'run for it! Ere Hugh can hale his barge across, or the pair of 'em can get it righted, we may be out of cry.'

And adding example to his words, he began to run, dodging among the willows, and in marshy places leaping from tussock to tussock. He had no time to look for his direction; all he could do was to turn his back upon the river, and put all his heart to running.

Presently, however, the ground began to rise, which showed him he was still in the right way, and soon after they came forth upon a slope of solid turf, where elms began to mingle with the willows.

But here Matcham, who had been dragging far into the rear, threw himself fairly down.

'Leave me, Dick!' he cried, pantingly; 'I can no more.'

Dick turned, and came back to where his companion lay.

'Nay, Jack, leave thee!' he cried. 'That were a knave's trick, to be sure, when ye risked a shot and a ducking, ay, and a drowning too, to save my life. Drowning, in sooth; for why I did not pull you in along with me, the saints alone can tell!'

'Nay,' said Matcham, 'I would 'a' saved us both, good Dick, for I can swim.'

'Can ye so?' cried Dick, with open eyes. It was the one manly accomplishment of which he was himself incapable. In the order of the things that he admired, next to having killed a man in single fight came swimming. 'Well,' he said, 'here is a lesson to despise no man. I promised to care for you as far as Holywood, and, by the rood, Jack, y' are more capable to care for me.'

'Well, Dick, we're freiends now,' said Matcham.

'Nay, I never was unfriends,' answered Dick. 'Y' are a brave lad in your way, albeit something of a milksop, too. I never met your like before this day. But, prithee, fetch back your breath, and let us on. Here is no place for chatter.'

'My foot hurts shrewdly,' said Matcham.

'Nay, I had forgot your foot,' returned Dick. 'Well, we must go the gentlier. I would I knew rightly where we were. I have clean lost the path; yet that may be for the better, too. An they watch the ferry, they watch the path, belike, as well. I would Sir Daniel were back with two-score men; he would sweep me these rascals as the wind sweeps leaves. Come, Jack, lean ye on my shoulder, ye poor shrew. Nay, y' are not tall enough. What age are ye, for a wager? – twelve?'

'Nay, I am sixteen,' said Matcham.

'Y' are poorly grown to height, then,' answered Dick. 'But take my hand. We shall go softly, never fear. I owe you a life; I am a good repayer, Jack, of good or evil.'

They began to go forward up the slope.

'We must hit the road, early or late,' continued Dick; 'and then for a fresh start. By the mass! but y' 'ave a rickety hand, Jack. If I had a hand like that, I would think shame. I tell you,' he went on, with a sudden chuckle, 'I swear by the mass I believe Hugh Ferryman took you for a maid.'

'Nay, never!' cried the other, colouring high.

''A did, though, for a wager!' Dick exclaimed. 'Small blame to him. Ye look liker maid than man; and I tell you more – y' are a strange-looking rogue for a boy; but for a hussy, Jack, ye would be right fair – ye would. Ye would be well-favoured for a wench.'

'Well,' said Matcham, 'ye know right well that I am none.'

'Nay, I know that; I do but jest,' said Dick. 'Ye'll be a man before your mother, Jack. What cheer, my bully! Ye shall strike shrewd strokes. Now, which, I marvel, of you or me, shall be first knighted, Jack? for knighted I shall be, or die for 't. 'Sir Richard Shelton, Knight:' it soundeth bravely. But 'Sir John Matcham' soundeth not amiss.'

'Prithee, Dick, stop till I drink,' said the other, pausing where a little clear spring welled out of the slope into a gravelled basin no bigger than a pocket. 'And O, Dick, if I might come by anything to eat! – my very heart aches with hunger.'

'Why, fool, did ye not eat at Kettley?' asked Dick.

'I had made a vow – it was a sin I had been led into,' stammered Matcham; 'but now, if it were but dry bread, I would eat it greedily.'

'Sit ye, then, and eat,' said Dick, 'while that I scout a little forward for the road.' And he took a wallet from his girdle, wherein were bread and pieces of dry bacon, and, while Matcham fell heartily to, struck farther forth among the trees.

A little beyond there was a dip in the ground, where a streamlet soaked among dead leaves; and beyond that, again, the trees were better grown and stood wider, and oak and beech began to take the place of willow and elm. The continued tossing and pouring of the wind among the leaves sufficiently concealed the sounds of his footsteps on the mast; it was for the ear what a moonless night is to the eye; but for all that Dick went cautiously, slipping from one big trunk to another, and looking sharply about him as he went. Suddenly a doe passed like a shadow through the underwood in front of him, and he paused, disgusted at the chance. This part of the wood had been certainly deserted, but now that the poor deer had run, she was like a messenger he should have sent before him to announce his coming; and instead of pushing farther, he turned him to the nearest well-grown tree, and rapidly began to climb.

Luck had served him well. The oak on which he had mounted was one of the tallest in that quarter of the wood, and easily out-topped its neighbours by a fathom and a half; and when Dick had clambered into the topmost fork and clung there, swinging dizzily in the great wind, he saw behind him the whole fenny plain as far as Kettley, and the Till wandering among woody islets, and in front of him, the white line of high-road winding through the forest. The boat had been righted – it was even now midway on the ferry. Beyond that there was no sign of man, nor aught moving but the wind. He was about to descend, when, taking a last view, his eye lit upon a string of moving points about the middle of the fen. Plainly a small troop was threading the causeway, and that at a good pace; and this gave him some concern as he shinned vigorously down the trunk and returned across the wood for his companion.

CHAPTER FOUR

A Greenwood Company

MATCHAM WAS WELL RESTED and revived; and the two lads, winged by what Dick had seen, hurried through the remainder of the outwood, crossed the road in safety, and began to mount into the high ground of Tunstall Forest. The trees grew more and more in groves, with heathy places in between, sandy, gorsy, and dotted with old yews. The ground became more and more uneven, full of pits and hillocks. And with every step of the ascent the wind still blew the shriller, and the trees bent before the gusts like fishing-rods.

They had just entered one of the clearings, when Dick suddenly clapped down upon his face among the brambles, and began to crawl slowly backward towards the shelter of the grove. Matcham, in great bewilderment, for he could see no reason for this flight, still imitated his companion's course; and it was not until they had gained the harbour of a thicket that he turned and begged him to explain.

For all reply, Dick pointed with his finger.

At the far end of the clearing, a fir grew high above the neighbouring wood, and planted its black shock of foliage clear against the sky. For about fifty feet above the ground the trunk grew straight and solid like a column. At that level, it split into two massive boughs; and in the fork, like a mast-headed seaman, there stood a man in a green tabard, spying far and wide. The sun glistened upon his hair; with one hand he shaded his eyes to look abroad, and he kept slowly rolling his head from side to side, with the regularity of a machine.

The lads exchanged glances.

'Let us try to the left,' said Dick. 'We had near fallen foully, Jack.'

Ten minutes afterwards they struck into a beaten path.

'Here is a piece of forest that I know not,' Dick remarked. 'Where goeth me this track?'

'Let us even try,' said Matcham.

'A few yards further, the path came to the top of a ridge and began to go down abruptly into a cup-shaped hollow. At the foot, out of a thick wood of flowering hawthorn, two or three roofless gables, blackened as if by fire, and a single tall chimney marked the ruins of a house.

'What may this be?' whispered Matcham.

'Nay, by the mass, I know not,' answered Dick. 'I am all at sea. Let us go warily.'

With beating hearts, they descended through the hawthorns. Here and there, they passed signs of recent cultivation; fruit-trees and pot-herbs ran wild among the thicket; a sun-dial had fallen in the grass; it seemed they were treading what once had been a garden. Yet a little farther and they came forth before the ruins of the house.

It had been a pleasant mansion and a strong. A dry ditch was dug deep about it; but it was now choked with masonry, and bridged by a fallen rafter. The two farther walls still stood, the sun shining through their empty windows; but the remainder of the building had collapsed, and now lay in a great cairn of ruin, grimed with fire. Already in the interior a few plants were springing green among the chinks.

'Now I bethink me,' whispered Dick, 'this must be Grimstone. It was a hold of one Simon Malmesbury; Sir Daniel was his bane! 'Twas Bennet Hatch that burned it, now five years agone. In sooth, 'twas pity, for it was a fair house.'

Down in the hollow, where no wind blew, it was both warm and still; and Matcham, laying one hand upon Dick's arm, held up a warning finger.

'Hist!' he said.

Then came a strange sound, breaking on the quiet. It was twice repeated ere they recognized its nature. It was the sound of a big man clearing his throat; and just then a hoarse, untuneful voice broke into singing.

'Then up and spake the master, the king of the outlaws:

"What make ye here, my merry men, among the greenwood shaws?"
And Gamelyn made answer – he looked never adown:
"O, they must need to walk in wood that may not walk in town!"'

The singer paused, a faint clink of iron followed, and then silence.

The two lads stood looking at each other. Whoever he might be, their invisible neighbour was just beyond the ruin. And suddenly the colour came into Matcham's face, and next moment he had crossed the fallen rafter, and was climbing cautiously on the huge pile of lumber that filled the interior of the roofless house. Dick would have withheld him, had he been in time; as it was, he was fain to follow.

Right in the corner of the ruin, two rafters had fallen crosswise, and protected a clear space no larger than a pew in church. Into this the lads silently lowered themselves. There they were perfectly concealed, and through an arrow loophole commanded a view upon the farther side.

Peering through this, they were struck stiff with terror at their predicament. To retreat was impossible; they scarce dared to breathe. Upon the very margin of the ditch, not thirty feet from where they crouched, an iron cauldron bubbled and steamed above a glowing fire; and close by, in an attitude of listening, as though he had caught some sound of their clambering among the ruins, a tall, red-faced, battered-looking man stood poised, an iron spoon in his right hand, a horn and a formidable dagger at his belt. Plainly this was the singer; plainly he had been stirring the cauldron, when some incautious step among the lumber had fallen upon his ear. A little further off another man lay slumbering, rolled in a brown cloak, with a butterfly hovering above his face. All this was in a clearing white with daisies; and at the extreme verge a bow, a sheaf of arrows, and part of a deer's carcase, hung upon a flowering hawthorn.

Presently the fellow relaxed from his attitude of attention, raised the spoon to his mouth, tasted its contents, nodded, and then fell again to stirring and singing.

"'O, they must need to walk in wood that may not walk in town,'"

he croaked, taking up his song where he had left it.

"'O, sir, we walk not here at all an evil thing to do,
But if we meet with the good king's deer to shoot a shaft into.'"

Still as he sang, he took from time to time another spoonful of the broth, blew upon it, and tasted it, with all the airs of an experienced cook. At length, apparently, he judged the mess was ready, for taking the horn from his girdle, he blew three modulated calls.

The other fellow awoke, rolled over, brushed away the butterfly, and looked about him.

'How now, brother?' he said. 'Dinner?'

'Ay, sot,' replied the cook, 'dinner it is, and a dry dinner, too, with neither ale nor bread. But there is little pleasure in the greenwood now; time was when a good fellow could live here like a mitred abbot, set aside the rain and the white frosts; he had his heart's desire both of ale and wine. But now are men's spirits dead; and this John Amend-All, save us and guard us! but a stuffed booby to scare crows withal.'

'Nay,' returned the other, 'y' are too set on meat and drinking, Lawless. Bide ye a bit; the good time cometh.'

'Look ye,' returned the cook, 'I have even waited for this good time sith that I was so high. I have been a grey friar; I have been a king's archer; I have been a shipman, and sailed the salt seas; and I have been in greenwood before this, forsooth! and shot the king's deer. What cometh of it? Naught! I were better to have bided in the cloister. John Abbot availeth more than John Amend-All. By'r Lady! here they come.'

One after another, tall likely fellows began to stroll into the lawn. Each as he came produced a knife and a horn cup, helped himself from the cauldron, and sat down upon the grass to eat. They were very variously equipped and armed; some in rusty smocks, and with nothing but a knife and an old bow; others in the height of forest gallantry, all in Lincoln green, both hood and jerkin, with dainty peacock arrows in their belts, a horn upon a baldrick, and a sword and dagger at their sides. They came in the silence of hunger, and scarce growled a salutation, but fell instantly to meat.

There were, perhaps, a score of them already gathered, when a sound of suppressed cheering arose close by among the hawthorns, and immediately after five or six woodmen carrying a stretcher debouched upon the lawn. A tall, lusty fellow, somewhat grizzled, and as brown as a smoked ham, walked before them with an air of some authority, his bow at his back, a bright boar-spear in his hand.

'Lads!' he cried, 'good fellows all, and my right merry friends, y' have sung this while on a dry whistle and lived at little ease. But what said I ever? Abide Fortune constantly; she turneth, turneth swift. And lo! here is her little firstling – even that good creature, ale!'

There was a murmur of applause as the bearers set down the stretcher and displayed a goodly cask.

'And now haste ye, boys,' the man continued. 'There is work toward. A handful of archers are but now come to the ferry; murrey and blue is their wear; they are our butts – they shall all taste arrows – no man of them shall struggle through this wood. For, lads, we are here some fifty strong, each man of us most foully wronged; for some they have lost lands, and some friends; and some they have been outlawed – all oppressed! Who, then, hath done this evil? Sir Daniel, by the rood! Shall he then profit? shall he sit snug in our houses? shall he till our fields? shall he suck the bone he robbed us of? I trow not. He getteth him strength at law; he gaineth cases; nay, there is one case he shall not gain – I have a writ here at my belt that, please the saints, shall conquer him.'

Lawless the cook was by this time already at his second horn of ale. He raised it, as if to pledge the speaker.

'Master Ellis,' he said 'y' are for vengeance – well it becometh you! – but your poor brother o' the greenwood, that had never lands to lose nor friends to think upon, looketh rather, for his poor part, to the profit of the thing. He had liever a gold noble and a pottle of canary wine than all the vengeances in purgatory.'

'Lawless,' replied the other, 'to reach the Moat House, Sir Daniel must pass the forest. We shall make that passage dearer, pardy, than any battle. Then, when he has got to earth with such ragged handful as escapeth us – all his great friends fallen and fled away, and none to give him aid – we shall beleaguer that old fox about, and great shall be the fall of him. 'Tis a fat buck; he will make a dinner for us all.'

'Ay,' returned Lawless, 'I have eaten many of these dinners beforehand; but the cooking of them is hot work, good Master Ellis. And meanwhile what do we? We make black arrows, we write rhymes, and we drink fair cold water, that discomfortable drink.'

'Y' are untrue, Will Lawless. Ye still smell of the Grey Friars' buttery; greed is your undoing,' answered Ellis. 'we took twenty pounds from Appleyard. We took seven marks from the messenger last night. A day ago we had fifty from the merchant.'

'And today,' said one of the men, 'I stopped a fat pardoner riding apace for Holywood. Here is his purse.'

Ellis counted the contents.

'Five-score shillings!' he grumbled. 'Fool, he had more in his sandal, or stitched into his tippet. Y' are but a child, Tom Cuckow; ye have lost the fish.'

But, for all that, Ellis pocketed the purse with nonchalance. He stood leaning on his boar-spear, and looked round upon the rest. They, in various attitudes, took greedily of the venison pottage, and liberally washed it down with ale. This was a good day; they were in luck; but business pressed, and they were speedy in their eating. The first-comers had by this time even despatched their dinner. Some lay down upon the grass and fell instantly asleep, like boa-constrictors; others talked together, or overhauled their weapons; and one, whose humour was particularly gay, holding forth an ale-horn, began to sing:

> 'Here is no law in good green shaw,
> Here is no lack of meat;
> 'Tis merry and quiet, with deer for our diet,
> In summer, when all is sweet.
>
> Come winter again, with wind and rain –
> Come winter, with snow and sleet,
> Get home to your places, with hoods on your faces,
> And sit by the fire and eat.'

All this while the two lads had listened and lain close; only Richard had unslung his cross-bow, and held ready in one hand the windac, or grappling-iron that he used to bend it. Otherwise they had not dared to stir; and this scene of forest life had gone on before their eyes like a scene upon a theatre. But now there came a strange interruption. The tall chimney which overtopped the remainder of the ruins rose right above their hiding-place. There came a whistle in the air, and then a sounding smack, and the fragments of a broken arrow fell about their ears. Some one from the upper quarters of the wood, perhaps the very sentinel they saw posted in the fir, had shot an arrow at the chimney-top.

Matcham could not restrain a little cry, which he instantly stifled, and even Dick started with surprise, and dropped the windac from his fingers. But to the fellows on the lawn, this shaft was an expected signal. They were all afoot together, tightening their belts, testing their bow-strings, loosening sword and dagger in the sheath. Ellis held up his hand; his face had suddenly assumed a look of savage energy; the white of his eyes shone in his sun-brown face.

'Lads,' he said, 'ye know your places. Let not one man's soul escape you. Appleyard was a whet before a meal; but now we go to table. I have three men whom I will bitterly avenge – Harry Shelton, Simon Malmesbury, and' – striking his broad bosom – 'and Ellis Duckworth, by the mass!'

Another man came, red with hurry, through the thorns.

''Tis not Sir Daniel!' he panted. 'They are but seven. Is the arrow gone?'

'It struck but now,' replied Ellis.

'A murrain!' cried the messenger. 'Methought I heard it whistle. And I go dinnerless!'

In the space of a minute, some running, some walking sharply, according as their stations were nearer or farther away, the men of the Black Arrow had all disappeared from the neighbourhood of the ruined house; and the cauldron, and the fire, which was now burning low, and the dead deer's carcase on the hawthorn, remained alone to testify they had been there.

CHAPTER FIVE

'Bloody as the Hunter'

THE LADS LAY QUIET TILL the last footstep had melted on the wind. Then they arose, and with many an ache, for they were weary with constraint, clambered through the ruins, and recrossed the ditch upon the rafter. Matcham had picked up the windac and went first, Dick following stiffly, with his cross-bow on his arm.

'And now,' said Matcham, 'forth to Holywood.'

'To Holywood!' cried Dick, 'when good fellows stand shot? Not I! I would see you hanged first, Jack!'

'Ye would leave me, would ye?' Matcham asked.

'Ay, by my sooth!' returned Dick. 'An I be not in time to warn these lads, I will go die with them. What! would ye have me leave my own men that I have lived among? I trow not! Give me my windac.'

But there was nothing further from Matcham's mind.

'Dick,' he said, 'ye sware before the saints that ye would see me safe to Holywood. Would ye be forsworn? Would you desert me – a perjurer?'

'Nay, I sware for the best,'returned Dick. 'I meant it too; but now! But look ye, Jack, turn again with me. Let me but warn these men, and, if needs must, stand shot with them; then shall all be clear, and I will on again to Holywood and purge mine oath.'

'Ye but deride me,' answered Matcham. 'These men ye go to succour are the same that hunt me to my ruin.'

Dick scratched his head.

'I cannot help it, Jack,' he said. 'Here is no remedy. What would ye? Ye run no great peril, man; and these are in the way of death. Death!' he added. 'Think of it! What a murrain do ye keep me here for? Give me the windac. Saint George! shall they all die?'

'Richard Shelton,' said Matcham, looking him squarely in the face, 'would ye, then, join party with Sir Daniel? Have ye not ears? Heard ye not this Ellis, what he said? or have ye no heart for your own kindly blood and the father that men slew? 'Harry Shelton,' he said; and Sir Harry Shelton was your father, as the sun shines in heaven.'

'What would ye?' Dick cried again. 'Would ye have me credit thieves?'

'Nay, I have heard it before now,' returned Matcham. 'The fame goeth currently, it was Sir Daniel slew him. He slew him under oath; in his own house he shed the innocent blood. Heaven wearies for the avenging on't; and you – the man's son – ye go about to comfort and defend the murderer!'

'Jack,' cried the lad, 'I know not. It may be; what know I? But, see here: This man hath bred me up and fostered me, and his men I have hunted with and played among; and to leave them in the hour of peril – O, man, if I did that, I were stark dead to honour! Nay, Jack, ye would not ask it; ye would not wish me to be base.'

'But your father, Dick?' said Matcham, somewhat wavering. 'Your father? and your oath to me? Ye took the saints to witness.'

'My father?' cried Shelton. 'Nay, he would have me go! If Sir Daniel slew him, when the hour comes this hand shall slay Sir Daniel; but neither him nor his will I desert in peril. And for mine oath, good Jack, ye shall absolve me of it here. For the lives' sake of many men that hurt you not, and for mine honour, ye shall set me free.'

'I, Dick? Never!' returned Matcham. 'An ye leave me, y' are forsworn, and so I shall declare it.'

'My blood heats,' said Dick. 'Give me the windac! Give it me!'

'I'll not,' said Matcham. 'I'll save you in your teeth.'

'Not?' cried Dick. 'I'll make you!'

'Try it,' said the other.

They stood, looking in each other's eyes, each ready for a spring. Then Dick leaped; and though Matcham turned instantly and fled, in two bounds he was overtaken, the windac was twisted from his grasp, he was thrown roughly to the ground, and Dick stood across him, flushed and menacing, with doubled fist. Matcham lay where he had fallen, with his face in the grass, not thinking of resistance.

Dick bent his bow.

'I'll teach you!' he cried, fiercely. 'Oath or no oath, ye may go hang for me!'

And he turned and began to run. Matcham was on his feet at once, and began running after him.

'What d'ye want?' cried Dick, stopping. 'What make ye after me? Stand off!'

'I will follow an I please,' said Macham. 'This wood is free to me.'

'Stand back, by'r lady!' returned Dick, raising his bow.

'Ah, y'are a brave boy!' retorted Matcham 'Shoot!'

Dick lowered his weapon in some confusion.

'See here,' he said. 'Y' have done me ill enough. Go, then. Go your way in fair wise; or, whether I will or not, I must even drive you to it.'

'Well,' said Matcham, doggedly, 'y' are the stronger. Do your worst. I shall not leave to follow thee, Dick, unless thou makest me,' he added.

Dick was almost beside himself. It went against his heart to beat a creature so defenceless; and, for the life of him, he knew no other way to rid himself of this unwelcome and, as he began to think, perhaps untrue companion.

'Y' are mad, I think,' he cried. 'Fool-fellow, I am hasting to your foes; as fast as foot can carry me, go I thither.'

'I care not, Dick,' replied the lad. 'If y' are bound to die, Dick, I'll die too. I would liever go with you to prison than to go free without you.'

'Well,' returned the other, 'I may stand no longer prating. Follow me, if ye must; but if ye play me false, it shall but little advance you, mark ye that. Shalt have a quarrel in thine inwards, boy.'

So saying, Dick took once more to his heels, keeping in the margin of the thicket, and looking briskly about him as he went. At a good pace he rattled out of the dell, and came again into the more open quarters of the wood. To the left a little eminence appeared, spotted with golden gorse, and crowned with a black tuft of firs.

'I shall see from there,' he thought, and struck for it across a healthy clearing.

He had gone but a few yards, when Matcham touched him on the arm, and pointed. To the eastward of the summit there was a dip, and, as it were, a valley passing to the other side; the heath was not yet out; all the ground was rusty, like an unscoured buckler, and dotted sparingly with yews; and there, one following another, Dick saw half a score green jerkins mounting the ascent, and marching at their head, conspicuous by his boar-spear, Ellis Duckworth in person. One after another gained the top, showed for a moment against the sky, and then dipped upon the further side, until the last was gone.

Dick looked at Matcham with kindlier eye.

'So y' are to be true to me, Jack?' he asked. 'I thought ye were of the other party.'

Matcham began to sob.

'What cheer!' cried Dick. 'Now the saints behold us! would ye snivel for a word?'

'Ye hurt me,' sobbed Matcham. 'Ye hurt me when ye threw me down. Y' are a coward to abuse your strength.'

'Nay, that is fool's talk,' said Dick, roughly. 'Y' had not title to my windac, Master John. I would 'a' done right to have well basted you. If ye go with me, ye must obey me; and so, come.'

Matcham had half a thought to stay behind; but, seeing that Dick continued to scour full-tilt towards the eminence, and not so much as looked across his shoulder, he soon thought better of that, and began to run in turn. But the ground was very difficult and steep; Dick had already a long start, and had, at any rate, the lighter heels, and he had long since come to the summit, crawled forward through the firs, and ensconced himself in a thick tuft of gorse, before Matcham, panting like a deer, rejoined him, and lay down in silence by his side.

Below, in the bottom of a considerable valley, the short cut from Tunstall hamlet wound downwards to the ferry. It was well beaten, and the eye followed it easily from point to point. Here it was bordered by open glades; there the forest closed upon it; every hundred yards it ran beside an ambush. Far down the path, the sun shone on seven steel salets, and from time to time, as the trees opened, Selden and his men could be seen riding briskly, still bent upon Sir Daniel's mission. The wind had somewhat fallen, but still tussled merrily with the trees, and, perhaps, had Appleyard been there, he would have drawn a warning from the troubled conduct of the birds.

'Now, mark,' Dick whispered. 'They be already well advanced into the wood; their safety lieth rather in continuing forward. But see ye where this wide glade runneth down before us, and in the midst of it, these two-score trees make like an island? There were their safety. An they but come sound as far as that, I will make shift to warn them. But my heart misgiveth me; they are but seven against so many, and they but carry cross-bows. The long-bow, Jack, will have the uppermost ever.'

Meanwhile, Selden and his men still wound up the path, ignorant of their danger, and momently drew nearer hand. Once, indeed, they paused, drew into a group, and seemed to point and listen. But it was something from far away across the plain that had arrested their attention – a hollow growl of cannon that came, from time to time, upon the wind, and told of the great battle. It was worth a thought, to be sure; for if the voice of the big guns were thus become audible in Tunstall Forest, the fight must have rolled ever eastward, and the day, by consequence, gone sore against Sir Daniel and the lords of the dark rose.

But presently the little troop began again to move forward, and came next to a very open, heathy portion of the way, where but a single tongue of forest ran down to join the road. They were but just abreast of this, when an arrow shone flying. One of the men threw up his arms, his horse reared, and both fell and struggled together in a mass. Even from where the boys lay they could hear the rumour of the men's voices crying out; they could see the startled horses prancing, and, presently, as the troop began to recover from their first surprise, one fellow beginning to dismount. A second arrow from somewhat farther off glanced in a wide arch; a second rider bit the dust. The man who was dismounting lost hold upon the rein, and his horse fled galloping, and dragged him by the foot along the road, bumping from stone to stone, and battered by the fleeing hoofs. The four who still kept the saddle instantly broke and scattered; one wheeled and rode, shrieking, towards the ferry; the other three, with loose rein and flying raiment, came galloping up the road from Tunstall. From every clump they passed an arrow sped. Soon a horse fell, but the rider found his feet and continued to pursue his comrades till a second shot despatched him. Another man fell; then another horse; out of the whole troop there was but one fellow left, and he on foot; only, in different directions, the noise of the galloping of three riderless horses was dying fast into the distance.

All this time not one of the assailants had for a moment showed himself. Here and there along the path, horse or man rolled, undespatched, in his agony; but no merciful enemy broke cover to put them from their pain.

The solitary survivor stood bewildered in the road beside his fallen charger. He had come the length of that broad glade, with the island of timber, pointed out by Dick. He was not, perhaps, five hundred yards from where the boys lay hidden; and they could see him plainly, looking to and fro in deadly expectation. But nothing came; and the man began to pluck up his courage, and suddenly unslung and bent his bow. At the same time, by something in his action, Dick recognized Selden.

At this offer of resistance, from all about him in the covert of the woods there went up the sound of laughter. A score of men, at least, for this was the very thickest of the ambush, joined in this cruel and untimely mirth. Then an arrow glanced over Selden's shoulder; and he leaped and ran a little back. Another dart struck quivering at his heel. He made for the cover. A third shaft leapt out right in his face, and fell short in front of him. And then the laughter was repeated loudly, rising and re-echoing from different thickets.

It was plain that his assailants were but baiting him, as men, in those days, baited the poor bull, or as the cat still trifles with the mouse. The skirmish was well over; farther down the road, a fellow in green was already calmly gathering the arrows; and now, in the evil pleasure of their hearts, they gave themselves the spectacle of their poor fellow-sinner in his torture.

Selden began to understand; he uttered a roar of anger, shouldered his crossbow, and sent a quarrel at a venture into the wood. Chance favoured him, for a slight cry responded. Then, throwing down his weapon, Selden began to run before him up the glade, and almost in a straight line for Dick and Macham.

The companions of the Black Arrow now began to shoot in earnest. But they were properly served; their chance had passed; most of them had now to shoot against the sun; and Selden, as he ran, bounded from side to side to baffle and deceive their aim. Best of all, by turning up the glade he had defeated their preparations; there were no marksmen posted higher up than the one who he had just killed or wounded; and the confusion of the foresters' counsels soon became apparent. A whistle sounded thrice, and then again twice. It was repeated from another quarter. The woods on either side became full of the sound of people bursting through the underwood; and a bewildered deer ran out into the open, stood for a second on three feet, with nose in air, and then plunged again into the thicket.

Selden still ran, bounding; ever and again an arrow followed him, but still would miss. It began to appear as if he might escape. Dick had his bow armed, ready to support him; even Matcham, forgetful of his interest, took sides at heart for the poor fugitive; and both lads glowed and trembled in the ardour of their hearts.

He was within fifty yards of them, when an arrow struck him, and he fell. He was up again, indeed, upon the instant; but now he ran staggering, and, like a blind man, turned aside from his direction.

Dick leaped to his feet and waved to him.

'Here!' he cried. 'This way! here is help! Nay, run, fellow – run!'

But just then a second arrow struck Selden in the shoulder, between the plates of his brigandine, and, piercing through his jack, brought him, like a stone, to earth.

'Oh, the poor heart!' cried Matcham, with clasped hands.

And Dick stood petrified upon the hill, a mark for archery.

Ten to one he had speedily been shot – for the foresters were furious with themselves, and taken unawares by Dick's appearance in the rear of their position – but instantly out of a quarter of the wood surprisingly near to the two lads, a stentorian voice arose, the voice of Ellis Duckworth.

'Hold!' it roared. 'Shoot not! Take him alive! It is young Shelton – Harry's son.'

And immediately after a shrill whistle sounded several times, and was again taken up and repeated farther off. The whistle, it appeared, was John Amend-All's battle trumpet, by which he published his directions.

'Ah, foul fortune!' cried Dick. 'We are undone. Swiftly, Jack, come swiftly!'

And the pair turned and ran back through the open pine clump that covered the summit of the hill.

CHAPTER SIX

To the Day's End

IT WAS, INDEED, HIGH time for them to run. On every side the company of the Black Arrow was making for the hill. Some, being better runners, or having open ground to run upon, had far outstripped the others, and were already close upon the goal; some, following valleys, had spread out to right and left, and outflanked the lads on either side.

Dick plunged into the nearest cover. I was a tall grove of oaks, firm under foot and clear of underbrush, and as it lay down hill, they made good speed. There followed next a piece of open, which Dick avoided, holding to his left. Two minutes after, and the same obstacle arising, the lads followed the same course. Thus it followed that, while the lads, bending continually to the left, drew nearer and nearer to the high road and the river which they had crossed an hour or two before, the great bulk of their pursuers were leaning to the other hand, and running towards Tunstall.

The lads paused to breathe. There was no sound of pursuit. Dick put his ear to the ground, and still there was nothing; but the wind, to be sure, still made a turmoil in the trees, and it was hard to make certain.

'On again!' said Dick; and, tired as they were, and Matcham limping with his injured foot, they pulled themselves together, and once more pelted down the hill.

Three minutes later, they were breasting through a low thicket of evergreen. High overhead, the tall trees made a continuous roof of foliage. It was a pillared grove, as high as a cathedral, and except for the hollies among which the lads were struggling, open and smoothly swarded.

On the other side, pushing through the last fringe of evergreen, they blundered forth again into the open twilight of the grove.

'Stand!' cried a voice.

And there, between the huge stems, not fifty feet before them, they beheld a stout fellow in green, sore blown with running, who instantly drew an arrow to

the head and covered them. Matcham stopped with a cry; but Dick, without a
pause, ran straight upon the forester, drawing his dagger as he went. The other,
whether he was startled by the daring of the onslaught, or whether he was
hampered by his orders, did not shoot: he stood wavering; and before he had
time to come to himself, Dick bounded at his throat, and sent him sprawling
backward on the turf. The arrow went one way and the bow another with a
sounding twang. The disarmed forester grappled his assailant; but the dagger
shone and descended twice. Then came a couple of groans, and then Dick rose
to his feet again, and the man lay motionless, stabbed to the heart.

'On!' said Dick; and he once more pelted forward, Matcham trailing in the
rear. To say truth, they made but poor speed of it by now, labouring dismally as
they ran, and catching for their breath like fish. Matcham had a cruel stitch, and
his head swam; and as for Dick, his knees were like lead. But they kept up the
form of running with undiminished courage.

Presently they came to the end of the grove. It stopped abruptly; and there, a
few yards before them, was the high road from Risingham to Shoreby, lying, at
this point, between two even walls of forest.

At the sight Dick paused; and as soon as he stopped running, he became
aware of a confused noise, which rapidly grew louder. It was at first like the rush
of a very high gust of wind, but it soon became more definite, and resolved itself
into the galloping of horses; and then, in a flash, a whole company of men-at-
arms came driving round the corner, swept before the lads, and were gone again
upon the instant. They rode as for their lives, in complete disorder; some of
them were wounded; riderless horses galloped at their side with bloody saddles.
They were plainly fugitives from the great battle.

The noise of their passage had scarce begun to die away towards Shoreby,
before fresh hoofs came echoing in their wake, and another deserter clattered
down the road; this time a single rider, and, by his splendid armour, a man of
high degree. Close after him there followed several baggage-waggons, fleeing at
an ungainly canter, the drivers flailing at the horses as if for life. These must
have run early in the day; but their cowardice was not to save them. For just
before they came abreast of where the lads stood wondering, a man in hacked
armour, and seemingly beside himself with fury, overtook the waggons, and with
the truncheon of a sword began to cut the drivers down. Some leaped from their
places and plunged into the wood; the others he sabred as they sat, cursing them
the while for cowards in a voice that was scarce human.

All this time the noise in the distance had continued to increase; the rumble
of carts, the clatter of horses, the cries of men, a great, confused rumour, came
swelling on the wind; and it was plain that the rout of a whole army was pouring,
like an inundation, down the road.

Dick stood sombre. He had meant to follow the highway till the turn for
Holywood, and now he had to change his plan. But above all, he had recognized
the colours of Earl Risingham, and he knew that the battle had gone finally
against the rose of Lancaster. Had Sir Daniel joined, and was he now a fugitive
and ruined? or had he deserted to the side of York, and was he forfeit to honour?
It was an ugly choice.

'Come,' he said, sternly; and, turning on his heel, he began to walk forward
through the grove, with Matcham limping in his rear.

For some time they continued to thread the forest in silence. It was now growing late; the sun was setting in the plain beyond Kettley; the tree-tops overhead glowed golden; but the shadows had begun to grow darker and the chill of the night to fall.

'If there was anything to eat!' cried Dick, suddenly, pausing as he spoke.

Matcham sat down and began to weep.

'Ye can weep for your own supper, but when it was to save men's lives, your heart was hard enough,' said Dick, contemptuously. 'Y' 'ave seven deaths upon your conscience, Master John; I'll ne'er forgive you that.'

'Conscience!' cried Matcham, looking fiercely up. 'Mine! And ye have the man's red blood upon your dagger! And wherefore did ye slay him, the poor soul? He drew his arrow, but he let not fly; he held you in his hand, and spared you! 'Tis as brave to kill a kitten as a man that not defends himself.'

Dick was struck dumb.

'I slew him fair. I ran me in upon his bow,' he cried.

'It was a coward blow,' returned Matcham. 'Y' are but a lout and a bully, Master Dick; ye but abuse advantages; let there come a stronger, we will see you truckle at his boot! Ye care not for vengeance, neither – for your father's death that goes unpaid, and his poor ghost that clamoureth for justice. But if there come but a poor creature in your hands that lacketh skill and strength, and would befriend you, down she shall go!'

Dick was too furious to observe that 'she.'

'Marry!' he cried, 'and here is news! Of any two the one will still be stronger. The better man throweth the worse, and the worse is well served. Ye deserve a belting, Master Matcham, for your ill-guidance and unthankfulness to me-ward; and what ye deserve ye shall have.'

And Dick, who, even in his angriest temper, still preserved the appearance of composure, began to unbuckle his belt.

'Here shall be your supper,' he said, grimly.

Matcham had stopped his tears; he was as white as a sheet, but he looked Dick steadily in the face, and never moved. Dick took a step, swinging the belt. Then he paused, embarrassed by the large eyes and the thin, weary face of his companion. His courage began to subside.

'Say ye were in the wrong, then,' he said, lamely.

'Nay,' said Matcham, 'I was in the right. Come, cruel! I be lame; I be weary; I resist not; I ne'er did thee hurt; come, beat me – coward!'

Dick raised the belt at this last provocation; but Matcham winced and drew himself together with so cruel an apprehension, that his heart failed him yet again. The strap fell by his side, and he stood irresolute, feeling like a fool.

'A plague upon thee, shrew!' he said. 'An ye be so feeble of hand, ye should keep the closer guard upon your tongue. But I'll be hanged before I beat you!' and he put on his belt again. 'Beat you I will not,' he continued; 'but forgive you? – never. I knew ye not; ye were my master's enemy; I lent you my horse; my dinner ye have eaten; y' 'ave called me a man o' wood, a coward, and a bully. Nay, by the mass! the measure is filled, and runneth over. 'Tis a great thing to be weak, I trow: ye can do your worst, yet shall none punish you; ye may steal a man's weapons in the hour of need, yet may the man not take his own again; – y' are weak, forsooth! Nay, then, if one cometh charging at you with a lance, and crieth he is weak, ye must let him pierce your body through! Tut! fool words!'

'And yet ye beat me not,' returned Matcham.

'Let be,' said Dick – 'let be. I will instruct you. Y' 'ave been ill-nurtured, methinks, and yet ye have the makings of some good, and, beyond all question, saved me from the river. Nay, I had forgotten it; I am as thankless as thyself. But, come, let us on. An we be for Holywood this night, ay, or tomorrow early, we had best set forward speedily.'

But though Dick had talked himself back into his usual good-humour, Matcham had forgiven him nothing. His violence, the recollection of the forester whom he had slain – above all, the vision of the upraised belt, were things not easily to be forgotten.

'I will thank you, for the form's sake,' said Matcham. 'But, in sooth, good Master Shelton, I had liever find my way alone. Here is a wide wood; prithee, let each choose his path; I owe you a dinner and a lesson. Fare ye well!'

'Nay,' cried Dick, 'if that be your tune, so be it, and a plague be with you!'

Each turned aside, and they began walking off severally, with no thought of the direction, intent solely on their quarrel. But Dick had not gone ten paces ere his name was called, and Matcham came running after.

'Dick,' he said, 'it were unmannerly to part so coldly. Here is my hand, and my heart with it. For all that wherein you have so excellently served and helped me – not for the form, but from the heart, I thank you. Fare ye right well.'

'Well, lad,' returned Dick, taking the hand which was offered him, 'good speed to you, if speed you may. But I misdoubt it shrewdly. Y' are too disputatious.'

So then they separated for the second time; and presently it was Dick who was running after Matcham.

'Here,' he said, 'take my cross-bow; shalt not go unarmed.'

'A cross-bow!' said Matcham. 'Nay, boy, I have neither the strength to bend nor yet the skill to aim with it. It were no help to me, good boy. But yet I thank you.'

The night had now fallen, and under the trees they could no longer read each other's face.

'I will go some little way with you,' said Dick. 'The night is dark. I would fain leave you on a path, at least. My mind misgiveth me, y' are likely to be lost.'

Without any more words, he began to walk forward, and the other once more followed him. The blackness grew thicker and thicker; only here and there, in open places, they saw the sky, dotted with small stars. In the distance, the noise of the rout of the Lancastrian army still continued to be faintly audible; but with every step they left it farther in the rear.

At the end of half an hour of silent progress they came forth upon a broad patch of heathy open. It glimmered in the light of the stars, shaggy with fern and islanded with clumps of yew. And here they paused and looked upon each other.

'Y' are weary?' Dick said.

'Nay, I am so weary,' answered Matcham, 'that methinks I could lie down and die.'

'I hear the chiding of a river,' returned Dick. 'Let us go so far forth, for I am sore athirst.'

The ground sloped down gently; and, sure enough, in the bottom, they found a little murmuring river, running among willows. Here they threw themselves down together by the brink; and putting their mouths to the level of a starry pool, they drank their fill.

'Dick,' said Matcham, 'it may not be. I can no more.'

'I saw a pit as we came down,' said Dick. 'Let us lie down therein and sleep.'

'Nay, but with all my heart!' cried Matcham.

The pit was sandy and dry; a shock of brambles hung upon one edge, and made a partial shelter; and there the two lads lay down, keeping close together for the sake of warmth, their quarrel all forgotten. And soon sleep fell upon them like a cloud, and under the dew and stars they rested peacefully.

CHAPTER SEVEN

The Hooded Face

THEY AWOKE IN THE GREY OF the morning; the birds were not yet in full song, but twittered here and there among the woods; the sun was not yet up, but the eastern sky was barred with solemn colours. Half starved and over-weary as they were, they lay without moving, sunk in a delightful lassitude. And as they thus lay, the clang of a bell fell suddenly upon their ears.

'A bell!' said Dick, sitting up. 'Can we be, then, so near to Holywood?'

A little after, the bell clanged again, but this time somewhat nearer hand; and from that time forth, and still drawing nearer and nearer, it continued to sound brokenly abroad in the silence of the morning.

'Nay, what should this betoken?' said Dick, who was now broad awake.

'It is some one walking,' returned Matcham, 'and the bell tolleth ever as he moves.'

'I see that well,' said Dick. 'But wherefore? What maketh he in Tunstall Woods? Jack,' he added, 'laugh at me an ye will, but I like not the hollow sound of it.'

'Nay,' said Matcham, with a shiver, 'it hath a doleful note. An the day were not come—'

But just then the bell, quickening its pace, began to ring thick and hurried, and then it gave a single hammering jangle, and was silent for a space.

'It is as though the bearer had run for a pater-noster-while, and then leaped the river,' Dick observed.

'And now beginneth he again to pace soberly forward,' added Matcham.

'Nay,' returned Dick – 'nay, not so soberly, Jack. 'Tis a man that walketh you right speedily. 'Tis a man in some fear of his life, or about some hurried business. See ye not how swift the beating draweth near?'

'It is now close by,' said Matcham.

They were now on the edge of the pit; and as the pit itself was on a certain eminence, they commanded a view over the greater proportion of the clearing, up to the thick woods that closed it in.

The daylight, which was very clear and grey, showed them a riband of white footpath wandering among the gorse. It passed some hundred yards from the pit, and ran the whole length of the clearing, east and west. By the line of its course, Dick judged it should lead more or less directly to the Moat House.

Upon this path, stepping forth from the margin of the wood, a white figure now appeared. It paused a little, and seemed to look about; and then, at a slow pace, and bent almost double, it began to draw near across the heath. At every step the bell clanked. Face, it had none; a white hood, not even pierced with eyeholes, veiled the head; and as the creature moved, it seemed to feel its way with the tapping of a stick. Fear fell upon the lads, as cold as death.

'A leper!' said Dick, hoarsely.

'His touch is death,' said Matcham. 'Let us run.'

'Not so,' returned Dick. 'See ye not? – he is stone-blind. He guideth him with a staff. Let us lie still; the wind bloweth towards the path, and he will go by and hurt us not. Alas, poor soul, and we should rather pity him!'

'I will pity him when he is by,' replied Matcham.

The blind leper was now about halfway towards them, and just then the sun rose and shone full on his veiled face. He had been a tall man before he was bowed by his disgusting sickness, and even now he walked with a vigorous step. The dismal beating of his bell, the pattering of the stick, the eyeless screen before his countenance, and the knowledge that he was not only doomed to death and suffering, but shut out for ever from the touch of his fellow-men, filled the lads' bosoms with dismay; and at every step that brought him nearer, their courage and strength seemed to desert them.

As he came about level with the pit, he paused, and turned his face full upon the lads.

'Mary be my shield! He sees us!' said Matcham, faintly.

'Hush!' whispered Dick. 'He doth but hearken. He is blind, fool!'

The leper looked or listened, whichever he was really doing, for some seconds. Then he began to move on again, but presently paused once more, and again turned and seemed to gaze upon the lads. Even Dick became dead-white and closed his eyes, as if by mere sight he might become infected. But soon the bell sounded, and this time, without any farther hesitation, the leper crossed the remainder of the little heath and disappeared into the covert of the woods.

'He saw us,' said Matcham. 'I could swear it!'

'Tut!' returned Dick, recovering some sparks of courage. 'He but heard us. He was in fear, poor soul! An ye were blind, and walked in a perpetual night, ye would start yourself, if ever a twig rustled or a bird cried "Peep."'

'Dick, good Dick, he saw us,' repeated Matcham. 'When a man hearkeneth, he doth not as this man; he doth otherwise, Dick. This was seeing; it was not hearing. He means foully. Hark, else, if his bell be not stopped!'

Such was the case. The bell rang no longer.

'Nay,' said Dick, 'I like not that. Nay,' he cried again, 'I like that little. What may this betoken? Let us go, by the mass!'

'He hath gone east,' added Matcham. 'Good Dick, let us go westward straight. I shall not breathe till I have my back turned upon that leper.'

'Jack, y' are too cowardly,' replied Dick. 'We shall go fair for Holywood, or as fair, at least, as I can guide you, and that will be due north.'

They were afoot at once, passed the stream upon some stepping-stones, and began to mount on the other side, which was steeper, towards the margin of the wood. The ground became very uneven, full of knolls and hollows; trees grew scattered or in clumps; it became difficult to choose a path, and the lads somewhat wandered. They were weary, besides, with yesterday's exertions and the lack of food, and they moved but heavily and dragged their feet among the sand.

Presently, coming to the top of a knoll, they were aware of the leper, some hundred feet in front of them, crossing the line of their march by a hollow. His bell was silent, his staff no longer tapped the ground, and he went before him with the swift and assured footsteps of a man who sees. Next moment he had disappeard into a little thicket.

The lads, at the first glimpse, had crouched behind a tuft of gorse; there they lay, horror-struck.

'Certain, he pursueth us,' said Dick – 'certain. He held the clapper of his bell in one hand, saw ye? that it should not sound. Now may the saints aid and guide us, for I have no strength to combat pestilence!'

'What maketh he?' cried Matcham. 'What doth he want? Who ever heard the like, that a leper, out of mere malice, should pursue unfortunates? Hath he not his bell to that very end, that people may avoid him? Dick, there is below this something deeper.'

'Nay, I care not,' moaned Dick; 'the strength is gone out of me; my legs are like water. The saints be mine assistance!'

'Would ye lie there idle?' cried Matcham. 'Let us back into the open. We have the better chance; he cannot steal upon us unawares.'

'Not I,' said Dick. 'My time is come; and peradventure he may pass us by.'

'Bend me, then, your bow!' cried the other 'What! will ye be a man?'

Dick crossed himself. 'Would ye have me shoot upon a leper?' he cried. 'The hand would fail me. Nay, now,' he added – 'nay, now, let be! With sound men I will fight, but not with ghosts and lepers. Which this is, I wot not. One or other, Heaven be our protection!'

'Now,' said Matcham, 'if this be man's courage, what a poor thing is man! But sith ye will do naught, let us lie close.'

Then came a single, broken jangle on the bell.

'He hath missed his hold upon the clapper,' whispered Matcham. 'Saints! how near he is!'

But Dick answered never a word; his teeth were near chattering.

Soon they saw a piece of the white robe between some bushes; then the leper's head was thrust forth from behind a trunk, and he seemed narrowly to scan the neighbourhood before he once again withdrew. To their stretched senses the whole bush appeared alive with rustlings and the creak of twigs; and they heard the beatings of each other's heart.

Suddenly, with a cry, the leper sprang into the open close by, and ran straight upon the lads. They, shrieking aloud, separated and began to run different ways. But their horrible enemy fastened upon Matcham, ran him swiftly down, and had him almost instantly a prisoner. The lad gave one scream that echoed high and far over the forest, he had one spasm of struggling, and then all his limbs relaxed, and he fel limp into his captor's arms.

Dick heard the cry and turned. He saw Matcham fall; and on the instant his spirit and his strength revived. With a cry of pity and anger, he unslung and bent his arblast. But ere he had time to shoot, the leper held up his hand.

'Hold your shot, Dickon!' cried a familiar voice. 'Hold your shot, mad wag! Know ye not a friend?'

And then laying down Matcham on the turf, he undid the hood from off his face, and disclosed the features of Sir Daniel Brackley.

'Sir Daniel!' cried Dick.

'Ay, by the mass, Sir Daniel!' returned the knight. 'Would ye shoot upon your guardian, rogue? But here is this——' And there he broke off, and pointing to Matcham, asked – 'How call ye him, Dick?'

'Nay,' said Dick, 'I call him Master Matcham. Know ye him not? He said ye knew him!'

'Ay,' replied Sir Daniel, 'I know the lad;' and he chuckled. 'But he has fainted; and, by my sooth, he might have had less to faint for. Hey, Dick? Did I put the fear of death upon you?'

'Indeed, Sir Daniel, ye did that,' said Dick, and sighed again at the mere recollection. 'Nay, sir, saving your respect, I had as lief 'a' met the devil in person; and to speak truth, I am yet all a-quake. But what made ye, sir, in such a guise?'

Sir Daniel's brow grew suddenly black with anger.

'What made I?' he said. 'Ye do well to mind me of it! What? I skulked for my poor life in my own wood of Tunstall, Dick. We were ill sped at the battle; we but got there to be swept among the rout. Where be all my good men-at-arms? Dick, by the mass, I know not! We were swept down; the shot fell thick among us; I have not seen one man in my own colours since I saw three fall. For myself, I came sound to Shoreby, and being mindful of the Black Arrow, got me this gown and bell, and came softly by the path for the Moat House. There is no disguise to be compared with it; the jingle of this bell would scare me the stoutest outlaw in the forest; they would all turn pale to hear it. At length I came by you and Matcham. I could see but evilly through this same hood, and was not sure of you, being chiefly, and for many a good cause, astonished at the finding you together. Moreover, in the open, where I had to go slowly and tap with my staff, I feared to disclose myself. But see,' he added, 'this poor shrew begins a little to revive. A little good canary will comfort the heart of it.'

The knight, from under his long dress, produced a stout bottle, and began to rub the temples and wet the lips of the patient, who returned gradually to consciousness, and began to roll dim eyes from one to another.

'What cheer, Jack!' said Dick. 'It was no leper, after all; it was Sir Daniel! See!'

'Swallow me a good draught of this,' said the knight. 'This will give you manhood. Thereafter, I will give you both a meal, and we shall all three on to Tunstall. For, Dick,' he continued, laying forth bread and meat upon the grass, 'I will avow to you, in all good conscience, it irks me sorely to be safe between four walls. Not since I backed a horse have I been pressed so hard; peril of life, jeopardy of land and livelihood, and to sum up, all these losels in the wood to hunt me down. But I be not yet shent. Some of my lads will pick me their way home. Hatch hath ten fellows; Selden, he had six. Nay, we shall soon be strong again; and if I can but buy my peace with my right fortunate and undeserving Lord of York, why, Dick, we'll be a man again and go a-horseback!'

And so saying, the knight filled himself a horn of canary, and pledged his ward in dumb show.

'Selden,' Dick faltered – 'Selden——' And he paused again.

Sir Daniel put down the wine untasted.

'How!' he cried in a changed voice. 'Selden? Speak! What of Selden?'

Dick stammered forth the tale of the ambush and the massacre.

The knight heard in silence; but as he listened, his countenance became convulsed with rage and grief.

'Now here,' he cried, 'on my right hand, I swear to avenge it! If that I fail, if that I spill not ten men's souls for each, may this hand wither from my body! I broke this Duckworth like a rush; I beggared him to his door; I burned the thatch above his head; I drove him from this country; and now, cometh he back to beard me? Nay, but, Duckworth, this time it shall go bitter hard!'

He was silent for some time, his face working.

'Eat!' he cried, suddenly. 'And you here,' he added to Matcham, 'swear me an oath to follow straight to the Moat House.'

'I will pledge mine honour,' replied Matcham.

'What make I with your honour?' cried the knight. 'Swear me upon your mother's welfare!'

Matcham gave the required oath; and Sir Daniel readjusted the hood over his face, and prepared his bell and staff. To see him once more in that appalling travesty somewhat revived the horror of his two companions. But the knight was soon upon his feet.

'Eat with despatch,' he said, 'and follow me yarely to mine house.'

And with that he set forth again into the woods; and presently after the bell began to sound, numbering his steps, and the two lads sat by their untasted meal, and heard it die slowly away up-hill into the distance.

'And so ye go to Tunstall?' Dick inquired.

'Yea, verily,' said Matcham, 'when needs must! I am braver behind Sir Daniel's back than to his face.'

They ate hastily, and set forth along the path through the airy upper levels of the forest, where great beeches stood apart among green lawns, and the birds and squirrels made merry on the boughs. Two hours later, they began to descend upon the other side, and already, among the tree-tops, saw before them the red walls and roofs of Tunstall House.

'Here,' said Matcham, pausing, 'ye shall take your leave of your friend Jack, whom y' are to see no more. Come, Dick, forgive him what he did amiss, as he, for his part, cheerfully and lovingly forgiveth you.'

'And wherefore so?' asked Dick. 'An we both go to Tunstall, I shall see you yet again, I trow, and that right often.'

'Ye'll never again see poor Jack Matcham,' replied the other, 'that was so fearful and burthensome, and yet plucked you from the river; ye'll not see him more, Dick, by mine honour!' He held his arms open, and the lads embraced and kissed. 'And, Dick,' continued Matcham, 'my spirit bodeth ill. Y' are now to see a new Sir Daniel; for heretofore hath all prospered in his hands exceedingly, and fortune followed him; but now, methinks, when his fate hath come upon him, and he runs the adventure of his life, he will prove but a foul lord to both of us. He may be brave in battle, but he hath the liar's eye; there is fear in his eye, Dick, and fear is as cruel as the wolf! We go down into that house. Saint Mary guide us forth again!'

And so they continued their descent in silence, and came out at last before Sir Daniel's forest stronghold, where it stood, low and shady, flanked with round towers and stained with moss and lichen, in the lilied waters of the moat. Even as they appeared, the doors were opened, the bridge lowered, and Sir Daniel himself, with Hatch and the parson at his side, stood ready to receive them.

Book II

THE MOAT HOUSE

CHAPTER ONE

Dick Asks Questions

THE MOAT HOUSE STOOD NOT far from the rough forest road. Externally, it was a compact rectangle of red stone, flanked at each corner by a round tower, pierced for archery and battlemented at the top. Within, it enclosed a narrow court. The moat was perhaps twelve feet wide, crossed by a single drawbridge. It was supplied with water by a trench, leading to a forest pool, and commanded, through its whole length, from the battlements of the two southern towers. Except that one or two tall and thick trees had been suffered to remain within half a bowshot of the walls, the house was in a good posture for defence.

In the court, Dick found a part of the garrison, busy with preparations for defence, and gloomily discussing the chances of a siege. Some were making arrows, some sharpening swords that had long been disused; but even as they worked, they shook their heads.

Twelve of Sir Daniel's party had escaped the battle, run the gauntlet through the wood, and come alive to the Moat House. But out of this dozen, three had been gravely wounded: two at Risingham in the disorder of the rout, one by John Amend-All's marksmen as he crossed the forest. This raised the force of the garrison, counting Hatch, Sir Daniel, and young Shelton, to twenty-two effective men. And more might be continually expected to arrive. The danger lay not, therefore, in the lack of men.

It was the terror of the Black Arrow that oppressed the spirits of the garrison. For their open foes of the party of York, in these most changing times, they felt but a far-away concern. 'The world,' as people said in those days, 'might change again' before harm came. But for their neighbours in the wood they trembled. It was not Sir Daniel alone who was a mark for hatred. His men, conscious of impunity, had carried themselves cruelly through all the country. Harsh commands had been harshly executed; and of the little band that now sat talking in the court, there was not one but had been guilty of some act of oppression or barbarity. And now, by the fortune of war, Sir Daniel had become powerless to protect his instruments; now, by the issue of some hours of battle, at which many of them had not been present, they had all become punishable traitors to the State, outside the buckler of the law, a shrunken company in a poor fortress that was hardly tenable, and exposed upon all sides to the just resentment of their victims. Nor had there been lacking grisly advertisements of what they might expect.

At different periods of the evening and the night, no fewer than seven riderless horses had come neighing in terror to the gate. Two were from Selden's troop; five belonged to men who had ridden with Sir Daniel to the field. Lastly, a little before dawn, a spearman had come staggering to the moat-side, pierced by three arrows; even as they carried him in, his spirit had departed; but by the words that he uttered in his agony, he must have been the last survivor of a considerable company of men.

Hatch himself showed, under his sun-brown, the pallor of anxiety; and when he had taken Dick aside and learned the fate of Selden, he fell on a stone bench and fairly wept. The others, from where they sat on stools or doorsteps in the sunny angle of the court, looked at him with wonder and alarm, but none ventured to inquire the cause of his emotion.

'Nay, Master Shelton,' said Hatch, at last – 'nay, but what said I? We shall all go. Selden was a man of his hands; he was like a brother to me. Well, he has gone second; well, we shall all follow! For what said their knave rhyme? – 'A black arrow in each black heart.' Was it not so it went? Appleyard, Selden, Smith, old Humphrey gone; and there lieth poor John Carter, crying, poor sinner, for the priest.'

Dick gave ear. Out of a low window, hard by where they were talking, groans and murmurs came to his ear.

'Lieth he there?' he asked.

'Ay, in the second porter's chamber,' answered Hatch. 'We could not bear him further, soul and body were so bitterly at odds. At every step we lifted him, he thought to wend. But now, methinks, it is the soul that suffereth. Ever for the priest he crieth, and Sir Oliver, I wot not why, still cometh not. 'Twill be a long shrift; but poor Appleyard and poor Selden, they had none.'

Dick stooped to the window and looked in. The little cell was low and dark, but he could make out the wounded soldier lying moaning on his pallet.

'Carter, poor friend, how goeth it?' he asked.

'Mr Shelton,' returned the man, in an excited whisper, 'for the dear light of heaven, bring the priest. Alack, I am sped: I am brought very low down; my hurt is to the death. Ye may do me no more service; this shall be the last. Now, for my poor soul's interest, and as a loyal gentleman, bestir you; for I have that matter on my conscience that shall drag me deep.'

He groaned, and Dick heard the grating of his teeth, whether in pain or terror.

Just then Sir Daniel appeared upon the threshold of the hall. He had a letter in one hand.

'Lads,' he said, 'we have had a shog, we have had a tumble; wherefore, then, deny it? Rather it imputeth to get speedily again to saddle. This old Harry the Sixt has had the undermost. Wash we, then, our hands of him. I have a good friend that rideth next the duke, the Lord of Wensleydale. Well, I have writ a letter to my friend, praying his good lordship, and offering large satisfaction for the past and reasonable surety for the future. Doubt not but he will lend a favourable ear. A prayer without gifts is like a song without music: I surfeit him with promises, boys – I spare not to promise. What, then, is lacking? Nay, a great thing – wherefore should I deceive you? – a great thing and a difficult: a messenger to bear it. The woods – y' are not ignorant of that – lie thick with our ill-willers. Haste is most needful; but without sleight and caution all is naught. Which, then, of this company will take me this letter, bear it to my Lord of Wensleydale, and bring me the answer back?'

One man instantly arose.

'I will, an't like you,' said he. 'I will even risk my carcase.'

'Nay, Dicky Bowyer, not so,' returned the knight. 'It likes me not. Y' are sly indeed, but not speedy. Ye were a laggard ever.'

'An't be so, Sir Daniel, here am I,' cried another.

'The saints forfend!' said the knight. 'Y' are speedy, but not sly. Ye would blunder me head-foremost into John Amend-All's camp. I thank you both for your good courage; but, in sooth, it may not be.'

Then Hatch offered himself, and he also was refused.

'I want you here, good Bennet; y' are my right hand, indeed,' returned the knight; and then several coming forward in a group, Sir Daniel at length selected one and gave him the letter.

'Now,' he said, 'upon your good speed and better discretion we do all depend. Bring me a good answer back, and before three weeks, I will have purged my forest of these vagabonds that brave us to our faces. But mark it well, Throgmorton: the matter is not easy. Ye must steal forth under night, and go like a fox; and how ye are to cross Till I know not, neither by the bridge nor ferry.'

'I can swim,' returned Throgmorton. 'I will come soundly, fear not.'

'Well, friend, get ye to the buttery,' replied Sir Daniel. 'Ye shall swim first of all in nut-brown ale.' And with that he turned back into the hall.

'Sir Daniel hath a wise tongue,' said Hatch, aside, to Dick. 'See, now, where many a lesser man had glossed the matter over, he speaketh it out plainly to his company. Here is a danger, 'a saith, and here difficulty; and jesteth in the very saying. Nay, by Saint Barbary, he is a born captain! Not a man but he is some deal heartened up! See how they fall again to work.'

This praise of Sir Daniel put a thought in the lad's head.

'Bennet,' he said, 'how come my father by his end?'

'Ask me not that,' replied Hatch. 'I had no hand nor knowledge in it; furthermore, I will even be silent, Master Dick. For look you, in a man's own business, there he may speak; but of hearsay matters and of common talk, not so. Ask me Sir Oliver – ay, or Carter, if ye will; not me.'

And Hatch set off to make the rounds, leaving Dick in a muse.

'Wherefore would he not tell me:' thought the lad. 'And wherefore named he Carter? Carter – nay, then Carter had a hand in it, perchance.'

He entered the house, and passing some little way along a flagged and vaulted passage, came to the door of the cell where the hurt man lay groaning. At his entrance Carter started eagerly

'Have ye brought the priest?' he cried.

'Not yet awhile,' returned Dick. 'Y' 'ave a word to tell me first. How came my father, Harry Shelton, by his death?'

The man's face altered instantly.

'I know not,' he replied, doggedly.

'Nay, ye know well,' returned Dick. 'Seek not to put me by.'

'I tell you I know not,' repeated Carter.

'Then,' said Dick, 'ye shall die unshriven. Here am I, and here shall stay. There shall no priest come near you, rest assured. For of what avail is penitence, an ye have no mind to right those wrongs ye had a hand in? and without penitence, confession is but mockery.'

'Ye say what ye mean not, Master Dick,' said Carter, composedly. 'It is ill threatening the dying, and becometh you (to speak truth) little. And for as little as it commends you, it shall serve you less. Stay, an ye please. Ye will condemn my soul – ye shall learn nothing! There is my last word to you.' And the wounded man turned upon the other side.

Now, Dick, to say truth, had spoken hastily, and was ashamed of his threat. But he made one more effort.

'Carter,' he said, 'mistake me not. I know ye were but an instrument in the hands of others; a churl must obey his lord; I would not bear heavily on such an one. But I begin to learn upon many sides that this great duty lieth on my youth and ignorance, to avenge my father. Prithee, then, good Carter, set aside the memory of my threatenings, and in pure good-will and honest penitence, give me a word of help.'

The wounded man lay silent; nor, say what Dick pleased, could he extract another word from him.

'Well,' said Dick, 'I will go call the priest to you as ye desired; for howsoever ye be in fault to me or mine, I would not be willingly in fault to any, least of all to one upon the last change.'

Again the old soldier heard him without speech or motion; even his groans he had suppressed; and as Dick turned and left the room, he was filled with admiration for that rugged fortitude.

'And yet,' he thought, 'of what use is courage without wit? Had his hands been clean, he would have spoken; his silence did confess the secret louder than words. Nay, upon all sides, proof floweth on me. Sir Daniel, he or his men, hath done this thing.'

Dick paused in the stone passage with a heavy heart. At that hour, in the ebb of Sir Daniel's fortune, when he was beleaguered by the archers of the Black Arrow, and proscribed by the victorious Yorkists, was Dick, also, to turn upon the man who had nourished and taught him, who had severely punished, indeed, but yet unwearyingly protected his youth? The necessity, if it should prove to be one, was cruel.

'Pray Heaven he be innocent!' he said.

And then steps sounded on the flagging, and Sir Oliver came gravely towards the lad.

'One seeketh you earnestly,' said Dick.

'I am upon the way, good Richard,' said the priest. 'It is this poor Carter. Alack, he is beyond cure.'

'And yet his soul is sicker than his body,' answered Dick.

'Have ye seen him?' asked Sir Oliver, with a manifest start.

'I do but come from him,' replied Dick.

'What said he – what said he?' snapped the priest, with extraordinary eagerness.

'He but cried for you the more piteously, Sir Oliver. It were well done to go the faster, for his hurt is grievous,' returned the lad.

'I am straight for him,' was the reply. 'Well, we have all our sins. We must all come to our latter day, good Richard.'

'Ay, sir; and it were well if we all came fairly,' answered Dick.

The priest dropped his eyes, and with an inaudible benediction hurried on.

'He, too!' thought Dick – 'he, that taught me in piety! Nay, then, what a world is this, if all that care for me be blood-guilty of my father's death! Vengeance! Alas! what a sore fate is mine, if I must be avenged upon my friends!'

The thought put Matcham in his head. He smiled at the remembrance of his strange companion, and then wondered where he was. Ever since they had come together to the doors of the Moat House the younger lad had disappeared, and Dick began to weary for a word with him.

About an hour after, mass being somewhat hastily run through by Sir Oliver, the company gathered in the hall for dinner. It was a long, low apartment, strewn with green rushes, and the walls hung with arras in a design of savage men and questing bloodhounds; here and there hung spears and bows and bucklers; a fire blazed in the big chimney; there were arras-covered benches round the wall, and in the midst the table, fairly spread, awaited the arrival of the diners. Neither Sir Daniel nor his lady made their appearance. Sir Oliver himself was absent, and here again there was no word of Matcham. Dick began to grow alarmed, to recall his companion's melancholy forebodings, and to wonder to himself if any foul play had befallen him in that house.

After dinner he found Goody Hatch, who was hurrying to my lady Brackley.

'Goody,' he said, 'where is Master Matcham, I prithee? I saw ye go in with him when we arrived.'

The old woman laughed aloud.

'Ah, Master Dick,' she said, 'y' have a famous bright eye in your head, to be sure!' and laughed again.

'Nay, but where is he, indeed?' persisted Dick.

'Ye will never see him more,' she returned; 'never. It is sure.'

'An I do not,' returned the lad, 'I will know the reason why. He came hither of his full free will; such as I am, I am his best protector, and I will see him justly used. There be too many mysteries; I do begin to weary of the game!'

But as Dick was speaking, a heavy hand fell on his shoulder. It was Bennet Hatch that had come unperceived behind him. With a jerk of his thumb, the retainer dismissed his wife.

'Friend Dick,' he said, as soon as they were alone, 'are ye a moonstruck natural? An ye leave not certain things in peace, ye were better in the salt sea than here in Tunstall Moat House. Y' have questioned me; y' have baited Carter; y' have frighted the jack-priest with hints. Bear ye more wisely, fool; and even now, when Sir Daniel calleth you, show me a smooth face, for the love of wisdom. Y' are to be sharply questioned. Look to your answers.'

'Hatch,' returned Dick, 'in all this I smell a guilty conscience.'

'An ye go not the wiser, ye will soon smell blood,' replied Bennet. 'I do but warn you. And here cometh one to call you.'

And indeed, at that very moment, a messenger came across the court to summon Dick into the presence of Sir Daniel.

CHAPTER TWO

The Two Oaths

SIR DANIEL WAS IN THE HALL; there he paced angrily before the fire, awaiting Dick's arrival. None was by except Sir Oliver, and he sat discreetly backward, thumbing and muttering over his breviary.

'Y' have sent for me, Sir Daniel?' said young Shelton.

'I have sent for you, indeed,' replied the knight. 'For what cometh to mine ears? Have I been to you so heavy a guardian that ye make hast to credit ill of me? Or sith that ye see me, for the nonce, some worsted, do ye think to quit my party? By the mass, your father was not so! Those he was near, those he stood by, come wind or weather. But you, Dick, y' are a fair-day friend, it seemeth, and now seek to clear yourself of your allegiance.'

'An't please you, Sir Daniel, not so,' returned Dick, firmly. 'I am grateful and faithful, where gratitude and faith are due. And before more is said, I thank you, and I thank Sir Oliver; y' have great claims upon me, both – none can have more; I were a hound if I forgot them.'

'It is well,' said Sir Daniel; and then, rising into anger: 'Gratitude and faith are words, Dick Shelton,' he continued; 'but I look to deeds. In this hour of my peril, when my name is attainted, when my lands are forfeit, when this wood is full of men that hunger and thirst for my destruction, what doth gratitude? what doth faith? I have but a little company remaining; is it grateful or faithful to poison me their hearts with your insidious whisperings? Save me from such gratitude! But, come, now, what is it ye wish? Speak; we are here to answer. If he have aught against me, stand forth and say it.'

'Sir,' replied Dick, 'my father fell when I was yet a child. It hath come to mine ears that he was foully done by. It hath come to mine ears – for I will not dissemble – that ye had a hand in his undoing. And in all verity, – I shall not be at peace in mine own mind, nor very clear to help you, till I have certain resolution of these doubts.'

Sir Daniel sat down in a deep settle. He took his chin in his hand and looked at Dick fixedly.

'And ye think I would be guardian to the man's son that I had murdered?' he asked.

'Nay,' said Dick, 'pardon me if I answer churlishly; but indeed ye know right well a wardship is most profitable. All these years have ye not enjoyed my revenues, and led my men? Have ye not still my marriage? I wot not what it may be worth – it is worth something. Pardon me again; but if ye were base enough to slay a man under trust, here were, perhaps, reasons enough to move you to the lesser baseness.'

'When I was a lad of your years,' returned Sir Daniel, sternly, 'my mind had not so turned upon suspicions. And Sir Oliver here,' he added, 'why should he, a priest, be guilty of this act?'

'Nay, Sir Daniel,' said Dick, 'but where the master biddeth, there will the dog go. It is well known this priest is but your instrument. I speak very freely; the time is not for courtesies. Even as I speak, so would I be answered. And answer get I none! Ye but put more questions. I rede ye beware, Sir Daniel; for in this way ye will but nourish and not satisfy my doubts.'

'I will answer you fairly, Master Richard,' said the knight. 'Were I to pretend ye have not stirred my wrath, I were no honest man. But I will be just even in anger. Come to me with these words when y' are grown and come to man's estate, and I am no longer your guardian, and so helpless to resent them. Come to me then, and I will answer you as ye merit, with a buffet in the mouth. Till then ye have two courses: either swallow me down these insults, keep a silent tongue, and fight in the meanwhile for the man that fed and fought for your infancy; or else – the door standeth open, the woods are full of mine enemies – go.'

The spirit with which these words were uttered, the looks with which they were accompanied, staggered Dick; and yet he could not but observe that he had got no answer.

'I desire nothing more earnestly, Sir Daniel, than to believe you,' he replied. 'Assure me ye are free from this.'

'Will ye take my word of honour, Dick?' inquired the knight.

'That would I,' answered the lad.

'I give it you,' returned Sir Daniel. 'Upon my word of honour, upon the eternal welfare of my spirit, and as I shall answer for my deeds hereafter, I had no hand nor portion in your father's death.'

He extended his hand, and Dick took it eagerly. Neither of them observed the priest, who, at the pronunciation of that solemn and false oath, had half arisen from his seat in an agony of horror and remorse.

'Ah,' cried Dick, 'ye must find it in your greatheartedness to pardon me! I was a churl indeed to doubt of you. But ye have my hand upon it; I will doubt no more.'

'Nay, Dick,' replied Sir Daniel, 'y' are forgiven. Ye know not the world and its calumnious nature.'

'I was the more to blame,' added Dick, 'in that the rogues pointed, not directly at yourself, but at Sir Oliver.'

As he spoke, he turned towards the priest, and paused in the middle of the last word. This tall, ruddy, corpulent, high-stepping man had fallen, you might say, to pieces; his colour was gone, his limbs were relaxed, his lips stammered prayers; and now, when Dick's eyes were fixed upon him suddenly, he cried out aloud, like some wild animal, and buried his face in his hands.

Sir Daniel was by him in two strides, and shook him fiercely by the shoulder. At the same moment Dick's suspicions reawakened.

'Nay,' he said, 'Sir Oliver may swear also. 'Twas him they accused.'

'He shall swear,' said the knight.

Sir Oliver speechlessly waved his arms.

'Ay, by the mass! but ye shall swear,' cried Sir Daniel, beside himself with fury. 'Here, upon this book, ye shall swear,' he continued, picking up the breviary, which had fallen to the ground. 'What! Ye make me doubt you! Swear, I say; swear!'

But the priest was still incapable of speech. His terror of Sir Daniel, his terror of pejury, risen to about an equal height, strangled him.

And just then, through the high stained-glass window of the hall, a black arrow crashed, and struck, and stuck quivering in the midst of the long table.

Sir Oliver, with a loud scream, fell fainting on the rushes; while the knight, followed by Dick, dashed into the court and up the nearest corkscrew stair to the battlements. The sentries were all on the alert. The sun shone quietly on green lawns dotted with trees, and on the wooded hills of the forest which enclosed the view. There was no sign of a besieger.

'Whence came that shot?' asked the knight.

'From yonder clump, Sir Daniel,' returned a sentinel.

The knight stood a little, musing. The he turned to Dick. 'Dick,' he said, 'keep me an eye upon these men; I leave you in charge here. As for the priest, he shall clear himself, or I will know the reason why. I do almost begin to share in your suspicions. He shall swear, trust me, or we shall prove him guilty.'

Dick answered somewhat coldly, and the knight, giving him a piercing glance, hurriedly returned to the hall. His first glance was for the arrow. It was the first of these missiles he had seen, and as he turned it to and fro, the dark hue of it touched him with some fear. Again there was some writing: one word – 'Earthed.'

'Ay,' he broke out, 'they know I am home, then. Earthed! Ay, but there is not a dog among them fit to dig me out.'

Sir Oliver had come to himself, and now scrambled to his feet.

'Alack, Sir Daniel!' he moaned, 'y' ave sworn a dread oath; y' are doomed to the end of time.'

'Ay,' returned the knight, 'I have sworn an oath, indeed, thou chucklehead; but thyself shalt swear a greater. It shall be on the blessed cross of Holywood. Look to it; get the words ready. It shall be sworn tonight.'

'Now, may Heaven lighten you!' replied the priest; 'may Heaven incline your heart from this iniquity!'

'Look you, my good father,' said Sir Daniel, 'if y' are for piety, I say no more; ye begin late, that is all. But if y' are in any sense bent upon wisdom, hear me. This lad beginneth to irk me like a wasp. I have a need for him, for I would sell his marriage. But I tell you, in all plainness, if that he continue to weary me, he shall go join his father. I give orders now to change him to the chamber above the chapel. If that ye can swear your innocency with a good solid oath and an assured countenance, it is well; the lad will be at peace a little, and I will spare him. If that ye stammer or blench, or anyways boggle at the swearing, he will not believe you; and by the mass, he shall die. There is for your thinking on.'

'The chamber above the chapel!' gasped the priest.

'That same,' replied the knight. 'So if ye desire to save him, save him; and if ye desire not, prithee, go to, and let me be at peace! For an I had been a hasty man, I would already have put my sword through you, for your intolerable cowardice and folly. Have ye chosen? Say!'

'I have chosen,' said the priest. 'Heaven pardon me, I will do evil for good. I will swear for the lad's sake.'

'So is it best!' said Sir Daniel. 'Send for him then, speedily. Ye shall see him alone. Yet I shall have an eye on you. I shall be here in the panel room.'

The knight raised the arras and let it fall again behind him. There was the sound of a spring opening; then followed the creaking of trod stairs.

Sir Oliver, left alone, cast a timorous glance upward at the arras-covered wall, and crossed himself with every appearance of terror and contrition.

'Nay, if he is in the chapel room,' the priest murmured, 'were it at my soul's cost, I must save him.'

Three minutes later, Dick, who had been summoned by another messenger, found Sir Oliver standing by the hall table, resolute and pale.

'Richard Shelton,' he said, 'ye have required an oath from me. I might complain, I might deny you; but my heart is moved toward you for the past, and I will even content you as ye choose. By the true cross of Holywood, I did not slay your father.'

'Sir Oliver,' returned Dick, 'when first we read John Amend-All's paper, I was convinced of so much. But suffer me to put two questions. Ye did not slay him; granted. But had ye no hand in it?'

'None,' said Sir Oliver. And at the same time he began to contort his face, and signal with his mouth and eyebrows, like one who desired to convey a warning, yet dared not utter a sound.

Dick regarded him in wonder; then he turned and looked all about him at the empty hall.

'What make ye?' he inquired.

'Why, naught,' returned the priest, hastily smoothing his countenance. 'I make naught; I do but suffer; I am sick. 'I – I – prithee, Dick, I must begone. On the true cross of Holywood, I am clean innocent alike of violence or treachery. Content ye, good lad, Farewell!'

And he made his escape from the apartment with unusual alacrity.

Dick remained rooted to the spot, his eyes wandering about the room, his face a changing picture of various emotions, wonder, doubt, suspicion, and amusement. Gradually, as his mind grew clearer, suspicion took the upper hand, and was succeeded by certainty of the worst. He raised his head, and, as he did so, violently started. High upon the wall there was the figure of a savage hunter woven in the tapesty. With one hand he held a horn to his mouth; in the other he brandished a stout spear. His face was dark, for he was meant to represent an African.

Now, here was what had startled Richard Shelton. The sun had moved away from the hall windows, and at the same time the fire had blazed up high on the wide hearth, and shed a changeful glow upon the roof and hangings. In this light the figure of the black hunter had winked at him with a white eyelid.

He continued staring at the eye. The light shone upon it like a gem; it was liquid, it was alive. Again the white eyelid closed upon it for a fraction of a second, and the next moment it was gone.

There could be no mistake. The live eye that had been watching him through a hole in the tapestry was gone. The firelight no longer shone on a reflecting surface.

And instantly Dick awoke to the terrors of his position. Hatch's warning, the mute signals of the priest, this eye that had observed him from the wall, ran together in his mind. He saw he had been put upon his trial, that he had once more betrayed his suspicions, and that, short of some miracle, he was lost.

'If I cannot get me forth out of this house,' he thought, 'I am a dead man! And this poor Matcham, too – to what a cockatrice's nest have I not led him!'

He was still so thinking, when there came one in haste, to bid him help in changing his arms, his clothing, and his two or three books, to a new chamber.

'A new chamber?' he repeated. 'Wherefore so? What chamber?'

"Tis one above the chapel,' answered the messenger.

'It hath stood long empty,' said Dick, musing. 'What manner of room is it?'

'Nay, a brave room,' returned the man. 'But yet' – lowering his voice – 'they call it haunted.'

'Haunted?' repeated Dick, with a chill. 'I have not heard of it. Nay, then, and by whom?'

The messenger looked about him; and then, in a low whisper, 'By the sacrist of St John's,' he said. 'They had him there to sleep one night, and in the morning – whew! – he was gone. The devil had taken him, they said; the more betoken, he had drunk late the night before.'

Dick followed the man with black forebodings.

CHAPTER THREE

The Room over the Chapel

FROM THE BATTLEMENTS nothing further was observed. The sun journeyed westward, and at last went down; but to the eyes of all these eager sentinels, no living thing appeared in the neighbourhood of Tunstall House.

When the night was at length fairly come, Throgmorton was led to a room overlooking an angle of the moat. Thence he was lowered with every precaution; the ripple of his swimming was audible for a brief period; then a black figure was observed to land by the branches of a willow and crawl away among the grass. For some half-hour Sir Daniel and Hatch stood eagerly giving ear; but all remained quiet. The messenger had got away in safety.

Sir Daniel's brow grew clearer. He turned to Hatch.

'Bennet,' said he, 'this John Amend-All is no more than a man, ye see. He sleepeth. We will make a good end of him, go to!'

All the afternoon and evening Dick had been ordered hither and thither, one command following another, till he was bewildered with the number and the hurry of commissions. All that time he had seen no more of Sir Oliver, and nothing of Matcham; and yet both the priest and the young lad ran continually in his mind. It was now his chief purpose to escape from Tunstall Moat House as speedily as might be; and yet, before he went, he desired a word with both of these.

At length, with a lamp in one hand, he mounted to his new apartment. It was large, low, and somewhat dark. The window looked upon the moat, and although it was so high up, it was heavily barred. The bed was luxurious, with one pillow of down, and one of lavender, and a red coverlet worked in a pattern of roses. All about the walls were cupboards, locked and padlocked, and concealed from view by hangings of dark-coloured arras. Dick made the round, lifting the arras, sounding the panels, seeking vainly to open the cupboards. He assured himself that the door was strong, and the bolt solid; then he set down his lamp upon a bracket, and once more looked all around.

For what reason had he been given this chamber? It was larger and finer than his own. Could it conceal a snare? Was there a secret entrance? Was it indeed haunted? His blood ran a little chilly in his veins.

Immediately over him the heavy foot of a sentry trod the leads. Below him, he knew, was the arched roof of the chapel; and next to the chapel was the hall. Certainly there was a secret passage in the hall; the eye that had watched him from the arras gave him proof of that. Was it not more than probable that the passage extended to the chapel, and if so, that it had an opening in his room?

To sleep in such a place, he felt, would be foolhardy. He made his weapons ready, and took his position in a corner of the room behind the door. If ill was intended, he would sell his life dear.

The sound of many feet, the challenge, and the password sounded overhead along the battlements; the watch was being changed.

And just then there came a scratching at the door of the chamber; it grew a little louder; then a whisper:

'Dick, Dick, it is I!'

Dick ran to the door, drew the bolt, and admitted Matcham. He was very pale, and carried a lamp in one hand and a drawn dagger in the other.

'Shut me the door,' he whispered. 'Swift, Dick! This house is full of spies; I hear their feet follow me in the corridors; I hear them breathe behind the arras.'

'Well, content you,' returned Dick, 'it is closed. We are safe for this while, if there be safety anywhere within these walls. But my heart is glad to see you. By the mass, lad, I thought ye were sped. Where hid ye?'

'It matters not,' returned Matcham. 'Since we be met, it matters not. But, Dick, are your eyes open? Have they told you of tomorrow's doings?'

'Not they,' replied Dick. 'What make they tomorrow?'

'Tomorrow, or tonight, I know not,' said the other; 'but one time or other, Dick, they do intend upon your life. I had the proof of it: I have heard them whisper; nay, they as good as told me.'

'Ay,' returned Dick, 'is it so? I had thought as much.'

And he told him the day's occurrences at length.

When it was done, Matcham arose and began, in turn, to examine the apartment.

'No,' he said, 'there is no entrance visible. Yet 'tis a pure certainty there is one. Dick, I will stay by you. An y' are to die, I will die with you. And I can help – look! I have stolen a dagger – I will do my best! And meanwhile, an ye know of any issue, any sally-port we could get opened, or any window that we might descend by, I will most joyfully face any jeopardy to flee with you.'

'Jack,' said Dick, 'by the mass, Jack, y' are the best soul, and the truest, and the bravest in all England! Give me your hand, Jack.'

And he grasped the other's hand in silence.

'I will tell you,' he resumed. 'There is a window out of which the messenger descended; the rope should still be in the chamber. 'Tis a hope.'

'Hist!' said Matcham.

Both gave ear. There was a sound below the floor; then it paused, and then began again.

'Some one walketh in the room below,' whispered Matcham.

'Nay,' returned Dick, 'there is no room below; we are above the chapel. It is my murderer in the secret passage. Well, let him come: it shall go hard with him!' And he ground his teeth.

'Blow me the lights out,' said the other. 'Perchance he will betray himself.'

They blew out both the lamps and lay still as death. The footfalls underneath were very soft, but they were clearly audible. Several times they came and went; and then there was a loud jar of a key turning in a lock, followed by a considerable silence.

Presently the steps began again, and then, all of a sudden, a chink of light appeared in the planking of the room in a far corner. It widened; a trap-door was being opened, letting in a gush of light. They could see the strong hand pushing it up; and Dick raised his crossbow, waiting for the head to follow.

But now there came an interruption. From a distant corner of the Moat House shouts began to be heard, and first one voice, and then several, crying aloud upon a name. This noise had plainly disconcerted the murderer, for the trap-door was silently lowered to its place, and the steps hurriedly returned, passed once more below the lads, and died away in the distance.

Here was a moment's respite. Dick breathed deep, and then, and not till then, he gave ear to the disturbance which had interrupted the attack, and which was now rather increasing than diminishing. All about the Moat House feet were running, doors were opening and slamming, and still the voice of Sir Daniel towered above all this bustle, shouting for 'Joanna.'

'Joanna!' repeated Dick. 'Why, who the murrain should this be? Here is no Joanna, nor ever hath been. What meaneth it?'

Matcham was silent. He seemed to have drawn further away. But only a little faint starlight entered by the window, and at the far end of the apartment, where the pair were, the darkness was complete.

'Jack,' said Dick, 'I wot not where ye were all day. Saw ye this Joanna?'

'Nay,' returned Matcham, 'I saw her not.'

'Nor heard tell of her?' he pursued.

The steps drew nearer. Sir Daniel was still roaring the name of Joanna from the courtyard.

'Did ye hear of her?' repeated Dick.

'I heard of her,' said Matcham.

'How your voice twitters! What aileth you?' said Dick. ''Tis a most excellent good fortune, this Joanna; it will take their minds from us.'

'Dick,' cried Matcham, 'I am lost; we are both lost! Let us flee if there be yet time. They will not rest till they have found me. Or, see! let me go forth; when they have found me, ye may flee. Let me forth, Dick – good Dick, let me away!'

She was groping for the bolt, when Dick at last comprehended.

'By the mass!' he cried, 'y' are no Jack; y' are Joanna Sedley; y' are the maid that would not marry me!'

The girl paused, and stood silent and motionless. Dick, too, was silent for a little; then he spoke again.

'Joanna,' he said, 'y' 'ave saved my life, and I have saved yours; and we have seen blood flow, and been friends and enemies – ay, and I took my belt to thrash you; and all that time I thought ye were a boy. But now death has me, and my time's out, and before I die I must say this: Y' are the best maid and the bravest under heaven, and, if only I could live, I would marry you blithely; and, live or die, I love you.'

She answered nothing.

'Come,' he said, 'speak up, Jack. Come, be a good maid, and say ye love me!'

'Why, Dick,' she cried, 'would I be here?'

'Well, see ye here,' continued Dick, 'an we but escape whole, we'll marry; and an we're to die, we die, and there's an end on't. But now that I think, how found ye my chamber?'

'I asked it of Dame Hatch,' she answered.

'Well, the dame's staunch,' he answered; 'she'll not tell upon you. We have time before us.'

And just then, as if to contradict his words, feet came down the corridor, and a fist beat roughly on the door.

'Here!' cried a voice. 'Open, Master Dick; open!'

Dick neither moved nor answered.

'It is all over,' said the girl; and she put her arms about Dick's neck.

One after another, men came trooping to the door. Then Sir Daniel arrived himself, and there was a sudden cessation of the noise.

'Dick,' cried the knight, 'be not an ass. The Seven Sleepers had been awake ere now. We know she is within there. Open, then, the door, man.'

Dick was again silent.

'Down with it,' said Sir Daniel. And immediately his followers fell savagely upon the door with foot and fist. Solid as it was, and strongly bolted, it would soon have given way, but once more fortune interfered. Over the thunderstorm of blows the cry of a sentinel was heard; it was followed by another; shouts ran along the battlements, shouts answered out of the wood. In the first moment of alarm it sounded as if the foresters were carrying the Moat House by assault. And Sir Daniel and his men, desisting instantly from their attack upon Dick's chamber, hurried to defend the walls.

'Now,' cried Dick, 'we are saved.'

He seized the great old bedstead with both hands, and bent himself in vain to move it.

'Help me, Jack. For your life's sake, help me stoutly!' he cried.

Between them, with a huge effort, they dragged the big frame of oak across the room, and thrust it endwise to the chamber door.

'Ye do but make things worse,' said Joanna, sadly. 'He will then enter by the trap.'

'Not so,' replied Dick. 'He durst not tell his secret to so many. It is by the trap that we shall flee. Hark! The attack is over. Nay, it was none!'

It had, indeed, been no attack; it was the arrival of another party of stragglers from the defeat of Risingham that had disturbed Sir Daniel. They had run the gauntlet under cover of the darkness; they had been admitted by the great gate; and now, with a great stamping of hoofs and jingle of accoutrements and arms, they were dismounting in the court.

'He will return anon,' said Dick. 'To the trap!'

He lighted a lamp, and they went together into the corner of the room. The open chink though which some light still glittered was easily discovered, and, taking a stout sword from his small armoury, Dick thrust it deep into the seam, and weighed strenuously on the hilt. The trap moved, gaped a little, and at length came widely open. Seizing it with their hands, the two young folk threw it back. It disclosed a few steps descenging, and at the foot of them, where the would-be murderer had left it, a burning lamp.

'Now,' said Dick, 'go first and take the lamp. I will follow to close the trap.'

So they descended one after the other, and as Dick lowered the trap, the blows began once again to thunder on the panels of the door.

CHAPTER FOUR

The Passage

THE PASSAGE IN WHICH DICK and Joanna now found themselves was narrow, dirty, and short. At the other end of it, a door stood partly open; the same door, without doubt, that had heard the man unlocking. Heavy cobwebs hung from the roof, and the paved flooring echoed hollow under the lightest tread.

Beyond the door there were two branches, at right angles. Dick chose one of them at random, and the pair hurried, with echoing footsteps, along the hollow of the chapel roof. The top of the arched ceiling rose like a whale's back in the dim glimmer of the lamp. Here and there were spyholes, concealed, on the other side, by the carving of the cornice; and looking down through one of these, Dick saw the paved floor of the chapel – the altar, with its burning tapers – and stretched before it on the steps, the figure of Sir Oliver praying with uplifted hands.

At the other end, they descended a few steps. The passage grew narrower; the wall upon one hand was now of wood; the noise of people talking, and a faint flickering of lights, came through the interstices; and presently they came to a round hole about the size of a man's eye, and Dick, looking down through it, beheld the interior of the hall, and some half a dozen men sitting, in their jacks, about the table, drinking deep and demolishing a venison pie. These were certainly some of the late arrivals.

'Here is no help,' said Dick. 'Let us try back.'

'Nay,' said Joanna; 'maybe the passage goeth farther.'

And she pushed on. But a few yards farther the passage ended at the top of a short flight of steps; and it became plain that, as long as the soldiers occupied the hall, escape was impossible upon that side.

They retraced their steps with all imaginable speed, and set forward to explore the other branch. It was exceedingly narrow, scarce wide enough for a large man; and it led them continually up and down by little breakneck stairs, until even Dick had lost all notion of his whereabouts.

At length it grew both narrower and lower; the stairs continued to descend; the walls on either hand became damp and slimy to the touch; and far in front of them they heard the squeaking and scuttling of the rats.

'We must be in the dungeons,' Dick remarked.

'And still there is no outlet,' added Joanna.

'Nay, but an outlet there must be!' Dick answered.

Presently, sure enough, they came to a sharp angle, and then the passage ended in a flight of steps. On the top of that there was a solid flag of stone by way of trap, and to this they both set their backs. It was immovable.

'Some one holdeth it,' suggested Joanna.

'Not so,' said Dick; 'for were a man strong as ten, he must still yield a little. But this resisteth like dead rock. There is a weight upon the trap. Here is no issue; and, by my sooth, good Jack, we are here as fairly prisoners as though the gyves were on our ankle-bones. Sit ye then down, and let us talk. After a while we shall return, when perchance they shall be less carefully upon their guard; and who knoweth? we may break out and stand a chance. But, in my poor opinion, we are as good as shent.'

'Dick!' she cried, 'alas the day that ever ye should have seen me! For like a most unhappy and unthankful maid, it is I have led you hither.'

'What cheer!' returned Dick. 'It was all written, and that which is written, willy nilly, cometh still to pass. But tell me a little what manner of a maid ye are, and how ye came into Sir Daniel's hands; that will do better than to bemoan yourself, whether for your sake or mine.'

'I am an orphan, like yourself, of father and mother,' said Joanna; 'and for my great misfortune, Dick, and hitherto for yours, I am a rich marriage. My Lord Foxham had me to ward; yet it appears Sir Daniel bought the marriage of me from the king, and a right dear price he paid for it. So here was I, poor babe, with two great and rich men fighting which should marry me, and I still at nurse! Well, then the world changed, and there was a new chancellor, and Sir Daniel bought the warding of me over the Lord Foxham's head. And then the world changed again, and Lord Foxham bought my marriage over Sir Daniel's; and from then to now it went on ill betwixt the two of them. But still Lord Foxham kept me in his hands, and was a good lord to me. And at last I was to be married – or sold, if ye like it better. Five hundred pounds Lord Foxham was to get for me. Hamley was the groom's name, and tomorrow, Dick, of all days in the years, was I to be betrothed. Had it not come to Sir Daniel, I had been wedded sure – and never seen thee, Dick – dear Dick!'

And here she took his hand, and kissed it, with the prettiest grace; and Dick drew her hand to him and did the like.

'Well,' she went on, 'Sir Daniel took me unawares in the garden, and made me dress in these men's clothes, which is a deadly sin for a woman; and, besides, they fit me not. He rode with me to Kettley, as ye saw, telling me I was to marry you; but I, in my heart, made sure I would marry Hamley in his teeth.'

'Ay!' cried Dick, 'and so ye loved this Hamley!'

'Nay,' replied Joanna, 'not I. I did but hate Sir Daniel. And then, Dick, ye helped me, and ye were right kind, and very bold, and my heart turned towards you in mine own despite; and now, if we can in any way compass it, I would marry you with right goodwill. And if, by cruel destiny, it may not be, still ye'll be dear to me. While my heart beats, it'll be true to you.'

'And I,' said Dick, 'that never cared a straw for any manner of woman until now, I took to you when I thought ye were a boy. I had a pity to you, and knew not why. When I would have belted you, the hand failed me. But when ye owned ye were a maid, Jack – for still I will call you Jack – I made sure ye were the maid for me. Hark!' he said, breaking off – 'one cometh.'

And indeed a heavy tread was now audible in the echoing passage, and the rats again fled in armies.

Dick reconnoitred his position. The sudden turn gave him a post of vantage. He could thus shoot in safety from the cover of the wall. But it was plain the light was too near him, and, running some way forward, he set down the lamp in the middle of the passage, and then returned to watch.

Presently, at the far end of the passage, Bennet hove in sight. He seemed to be alone, and he carried in his hand a burning torch, which made him the better mark.

'Stand, Bennet!' cried Dick. 'Another step and y' are dead.'

'So here ye are,' returned Hatch, peering forward into the darkness. 'I see you not. Aha! y' 'ave done wisely, Dick; y' 'ave put your lamp before you. By my sooth, but, though it was done to shoot my own knave body, I do rejoice to see ye profit of my lessons! And now, what make ye? what seek ye here? Why would ye shoot upon an old, kind friend? And have ye the young gentlewoman there?'

'Nay, Bennet, it is I should question and you answer,' replied Dick. 'Why am I in this jeopardy of my life? Why do men come privily to slay me in my bed? Why am I now fleeing in mine own guardian's strong house, and from the friends that I have lived among and never injured?'

'Master Dick, Master Dick,' said Bennet, 'what told I you? Y' are brave, but the most uncrafty lad that I can think upon!'

'Well,' returned Dick, 'I see ye know all, and that I am doomed indeed. It is well. Here, where I am, I stay. Let Sir Daniel get me out if he be able!'

Hatch was silent for a space.

'Hark ye,' he began, 'I return to Sir Daniel, to tell him where ye are, and how posted; for, in truth, it was to that end he sent me. But you, if ye are no fool, had best be gone ere I return.'

'Begone!' repeated Dick. 'I would begone already, an' I wist how. I cannot move the trap.'

'Put me your hand into the corner, and see what ye find there,' replied Bennet. 'Throgmorton's rope is still in the brown chamber. Fare ye well.'

And Hatch, turning upon his heel, disappeared again into the windings of the passage.

Dick instantly returned for his lamp, and proceed to act upon the hint. At one corner of the trap there was a deep cavity in the wall. Pushing his arm into the aperture, Dick found an iron bar, which he thrust vigorously upwards. There followed a snapping noise, and the slab of stone instantly started in its bed.

They were free of the passage. A little exercise of strength easily raised the trap; and they came forth into a vaulted chamber, opening on one hand upon the court, where one or two fellows, with bare arms, were rubbing down the horses of the last arrivals. A torch or two, each stuck in an iron ring against the wall, changefully lit up the scene.

CHAPTER FIVE

How Dick Changed Sides

DICK, BLOWING OUT HIS LAMP lest it should attract attention, led the way upstairs and along the corridor. In the brown chamber the rope had been made fast to the frame of an exceeding heavy and ancient bed. It had not been detached, and Dick, taking the coil to the window, began to lower it slowly and cautiously into the darkness of the night. Joan stood by; but as the rope lengthened, and still Dick continued to pay it out, extreme fear began to conquer her resolution.

'Dick,' she said, 'is it so deep? I may not essay it. I should infallibly fall, good Dick.'

It was just at the delicate moment of the operations that she spoke. Dick started; the remainder of the coil slipped from his grasp, and the end fell with a splash into the moat. Instantly, from the battlement above, the voice of a sentinel cried, 'Who goes?'

'A murrain!' cried Dick. 'We are paid now! Down with you – take the rope.'

'I cannot,' she cried, recoiling.

'An ye cannot, no more can I,' said Shelton. 'How can I swim the moat without you? Do ye desert me, then?'

'Dick,' she gasped, 'I cannot. The strength is gone from me.'

'By the mass, then, we are all shent!' he shouted, stamping with his foot; and then, hearing steps, he ran to the room door and sought to close it.

Before he could shoot the bolt, strong arms were thrusting it back upon him from the other side. He struggled for a second; then, feeling himself overpowered, ran back to the window. The girl had fallen against the wall in the embrasure of the window; she was more than half insensible; and when he tried to raise her in his arms, her body was limp and unresponsive.

At the same moment the men who had forced the door against him laid hold upon him. The first he poniarded at a blow, and the others falling back for a second in some disorder, he profited by the chance, bestrode the window-sill, seized the cord in both hands, and let his body slip.

The cord was knotted, which made it the easier to descend; but so furius was Dick's hurry, and so small his experience of such gymnastics, that he span round and round in mid-air like a criminal upon a gibbet, and now beat his head, and now bruised his hands, against the rugged stonework of the wall. The air roared in his ears; he saw the stars overhead, and the reflected stars below him in the moat, whirling like dead leaves before the tempest. And then he lost hold and fell, and soused head over ears into the icy water.

When he came to the surface his hand encountered the rope, which, newly lightened of his weight, was swinging wildly to and fro. There was a red glow overhead, and looking up, he saw, by the light of several torches and a cresset full of burning coals, the battlements lined with faces. He saw the men's eyes turning hither and thither in quest of him; but he was too far below, the light reached him not, and they looked in vain.

And now he perceived that the rope was considerably too long, and he began to struggle as well as he could towards the other side of the moat, still keeping his head above water. In this way he got much more than halfway over; indeed the bank was almost within reach, before the rope began to draw him back by its own weight. Taking his courage in both hands, he left go and made a leap for the trailing sprays of willow that had already, that same evening, helped Sir Daniel's messenger to land. He went down, rose again, sank a second time, and then his hand caught a branch, and with the speed of thought he had dragged himself into the thick of the tree and clung there, dripping and panting, and still half uncertain of his escape.

But all this had not been done without a considerable splashing, which had so far indicated his position to the men along the battlements. Arrows and quarrels fell thick around him in the darkness, thick like driving hail; and suddenly a torch was thrown down – flared through the air in its swift passage – struck for a moment on the edge of the bank, where it burned high and lit up its whole surroundings like a bonfire – and then, in a good hour for Dick, slipped off, plumped into the moat, and was instantly extinguished.

It had served its purpose. The marksmen had had time to see the willow, and Dick ensconced among its boughs; and though the lad instantly sprang higher up the bank and ran for his life, he was yet not quick enough to escape a shot. An arrow struck him in the shoulder, another grazed his head.

The pain of his wounds lent him wings; and he had no sooner got upon the level than he took to his heels and ran straight before him in the dark, without a thought for the direction of his flight.

For a few steps missiles followed him, but these soon ceased; and when at length he came to a halt and looked behind, he was already a good way from the Moat House, though he could still see the torches moving to and fro along its battlements.

He leaned against a tree, streaming with blood and water, bruised, wounded, and alone. For all that, he had saved his life for that bout; and though Joanna remained behind in the power of Sir Daniel, he neither blamed himself for an accident that it had been beyond his power to prevent, nor did he augur any fatal consequences to the girl herself. Sir Daniel was cruel, but he was not likely to be cruel to a young gentlewoman who had other protectors, willing and able to bring him to account. It was more probable he would make hast to marry her to some friend of his own.

'Well,' thought Dick, 'between then and now I will find me the means to bring that traitor under; for I think, by the mass, that I be now absolved from any gratitude or obligation; and when war is open, there is a fair chance for all.'

In the meanwhile, here he was in a sore plight.

For some little way further he struggled forward through the forest; but what with the pain of his wounds, the darkness of the night, and the extreme uneasiness and confusion of his mind, he soon became equally unable to guide himself or to continue to push through the close undergrowth, and he was fain at length to sit down and lean his back against a tree.

When he awoke from something betwixt sleep and swooming, the grey of the morning had begun to take the place of night. A little chilly breeze was bustling among the trees, and as he still sat staring before him, only half awake, he became aware of something dark that swung to and fro among the branches, some hundred yards in front of him. The progressive brightening of the day and the return of his own senses at last enabled him to recognize the object. It was a man hanging from the bough of a tall oak. His head had fallen forward on his breast; but at every stronger puff of wind his body span round and round, and his legs and arms tossed, like some ridiculous plaything.

Dick clambered to his feet, and, staggering and leaning on the tree-trunks as he went, drew near to this grim object.

The bough was perhaps twenty feet above the ground, and the poor fellow had been drawn up so high by his executioners that his boots swung clear above Dick's reach; and as his hood had been drawn over his face, it was impossible to recognize the man.

Dick looked about him right and left; and at last he perceived that the other end of the cord had been made fast to the trunk of a little hawthorn which grew, thick with blossom, under the lofty arcade of the oak. With his dagger, which alone remained to him of all his arms, young Shelton severed the rope, and instantly, with a dead thump, the corpse fell in a heap upon the ground.

Dick raised the hood; it was Throgmorton, Sir Daniel's messenger. He had not gone far upon his errand. A paper, which had apparently escaped the notice of the men of the Black Arrow, stuck from the bosom of his doublet, and Dick, pulling it forth, found it was Sir Daniel's letter to Lord Wensleydale.

'Come,' thought he, 'if the world changes yet again, I may have here the wherewithal to shame Sir Daniel – nay, and perchance to bring him to the block.'

And he put the paper in his own bosom, said a prayer over the dead man, and set forth again through the woods.

The fatigue and weakness increased; his ears sang, his steps faltered, his mind at intervals failed him, so low had he been brought by loss of blood. Doubtless he made many deviations from his true path, but at last he came out upon the high-road, not very far from Tunstall hamlet.

A rough voice bid him stand.

'Stand?' repeated Dick. 'By the mass, but I am nearer falling.'

And he suited the action to the word, and fell all his length upon the road.

Two men came forth out of the thicket, each in green forest jerkin, each with long-bow and quiver and short sword.

'Why, Lawless,' said the younger of the two, 'it is young Shelton.'

'Ay, this will be as good as bread to John Amend-All,' returned the other. 'Though, faith, he hath been to the wars. Here is a tear in his scalp that must 'a' cost him many a good ounce of blood.'

'And here,' added Greensheve, 'is a hole in his shoulder that must have pricked him well. Who hath done this, think ye? If it be one of ours, he may all to prayer; Ellis will give him a short shrift and a long rope.'

'Up with the cub,' said Lawless. 'Clap him on my back.'

And then, when Dick had been hoisted to his shoulders, and he had taken the lad's arms about his neck, and got a firm hold of him, the ex-Grey Friar added—

'Keep ye the post, brother Greensheve. I will on with him by myself.'

So Greensheve returned to his ambush on the wayside, and Lawless trudged down the hill, whistling as he went, with Dick, still in a dead faint, comfortably settled on his shoulders.

The sun rose as he came out of the skirts of the wood and saw Tunstall hamlet straggling up the opposite hill. All seemed quiet, but a strong post of some half a score of archers lay close by the bridge on either side of the road, and, as soon as they perceived Lawless with his burden, began to bestir themselves and set arrow to string like vigilant sentries.

'Who goes?' cried the man in command.

'Will Lawless, by the rood – ye know me as well as your own hand,' returned the outlaw, contemptuously.

'Give the word, Lawless,' returned the other.

'Now, Heaven lighten thee, thou great fool,' replied Lawless. 'Did I not tell it thee myself? But ye are all mad for this playing at soldiers. When I am in the greenwood, give me greenwood ways; and my word for this tide is, "A fig for all mock soldiery!"'

'Lawless, ye but show an ill example; give us the word, fool jester,' said the commander of the post.

'And if I had forgotten it?' asked the other.

'An ye had forgotten it – as I know y' 'ave not – by the mass, I would clap an arrow into your big body,' returned the first.

'Nay, an y' are so ill a jester,' said Lawless, 'ye shall have your word for me. "Duckworth and Shelton" is the word; and here, to the illustration, is Shelton on my shoulders, and to Duckworth do I carry him.'

'Pass, Lawless,' said the sentry.

'And where is John?' asked the Grey Friar.

'He holdeth a court, by the mass, and taketh rents as to the manner born!' cried another of the company.

So it proved. When Lawless got as far up the village as the little inn, he found Ellis Duckworth surrounded by Sir Daniel's tenants, and, by the right of his good company of archers, coolly taking rents, and giving written receipts in return for them. By the faces of the tenants, it was plain how little this proceeding pleased them; for they argued very rightly that they would simply have to pay them twice.

As soon as he knew what had brought Lawless, Ellis dismissed the remainder of the tenants, and, with every mark of interest and apprehension, conducted Dick into an inner chamber of the inn. There the lad's hurts were looked to; and he was recalled, by simple remedies, to consciousness.

'Dear lad,' said Ellis, pressing his hand, 'y' are in a friend's hands that loved your father, and loves you for his sake. Rest ye a little quietly, for ye are somewhat out of case. Then shall ye tell me your story, and betwixt the two of us we shall find a remedy for all.'

A little later in the day, and after Dick had awakened from a comfortable slumber to find himself still very weak, but clearer in mind and easier in body, Ellis returned, and sitting down by the bedside, begged him, in the name of his father, to relate the circumstance of his escape from Tunstall Moat House. There was something in the strength of Duckworth's frame, in the honesty of his brown face, in the clearness and shrewdness of his eyes, that moved Dick to obey him; and from first to last the lad told him the story of his two days' adventures.

'Well,' said Ellis, when he had done, 'see what the kind saints have done for you, Dick Shelton, not alone to save your body in so numerous and deadly perils, but to bring you into my hands that have no dearer wish than to assist your father's son. Be but true to me – and I see y' are true – and betwixt you and me, we shall bring that false-heart traitor to the death.'

'Will ye assault the house?' asked Dick.

'I were mad, indeed, to think of it,' returned Ellis. 'He hath too much power; his men gather to him; those that gave me the slip last night, and by the mass came in so handily for you – those have made him safe. Nay, Dick, to the contrary, thou and I and my brave bowmen, we must all slip from this forest speedily, and leave Sir Daniel free.'

'My mind misgiveth me for Jack,' said the lad.

'For Jack!' repeated Duckworth. 'Oh, I see, for the wench! Nay, Dick, I promise you, if there come talk of any marriage we shall act at once; till then, or till the time is ripe, we shall all disappear, even like shadows at morning; Sir Daniel shall look east and west, and see none enemies; he shall think, by the mass, that he hath dreamed awhile, and hath now awakened in his bed. But our four eyes, Dick, shall follow him right close, and our four hands – so help us all the army of the saints! – shall bring that traitor low!'

Two days later Sir Daniel's garrison had grown to such a strength that he ventured on a sally, and at the head of some two score horsemen, pushed without opposition as far as Tunstall hamlet. Not an arrow flew, not a man stirred in the thicket; the bridge was no longer guarded, but stood open to all comers; and as Sir Daniel crossed it, he saw the villagers looking timidly from their doors.

Presently one of them, taking heart of grace, came forward, and with the lowliest salutations, presented a letter to the knight.

His face darkened as he read the contents. It ran thus:

To the most untrue and cruel gentylman, Sir Daniel Brackley, Knyght, These: I fynde ye were untrue and unkynd fro the first. Ye have my father's blood upon your hands; let be, it will not wasshe. Some day ye shall perish by my procurement, so much I let you to wytte; and I let you to wytte farther, that if ye seek to wed to any other the gentyl-woman, Mistresse Joan Sedley, whom that I am bound upon a great oath to wed myself, the blow will be very swift. The first step therinne will be thy first step to the grave.

RIC. SHELTON.

Book III

MY LORD FOXHAM

CHAPTER ONE

The House by the Shore

MONTHS HAD PASSED AWAY since Richard Shelton made his escape from the hands of his guardian. These months had been eventful for England. The party of Lancaster, which was then in the very article of death, had once more raised its head. The Yorkists defeated and dispersed, their leader butchered on the field, it seemed, for a very brief season in the winter following upon the events already recorded, as if the House of Lancaster had finally triumphed over its foes.

The small town of Shoreby-on-the-Till was full of the Lancastrian nobles of the neighbourhood. Earl Risingham was there, with three hundred men-at-arms; Lord Shoreby, with two hundred; Sir Daniel himself, high in favour and once more growing rich on confiscations, lay in a house of his own, on the main street, with three score men. The world had changed indeed.

It was a black, bitter cold evening in the first week of January, with a hard frost, a high wind, and every likelihood of snow before the morning.

In an obscure alehouse in a by-street near the harbour, three or four men sat drinking ale and eating a hasty mess of eggs. They were all likely, lusty, weatherbeaten fellows, hard of hand, bold of eye; and though they wore plain tabards, like country ploughmen, even a drunken soldier might have looked twice before he sought a quarrel in such company.

A little apart before the huge fire sat a younger man, almost a boy, dressed in much the same fashion, though it was easy to see by his looks that he was better born, and might have worn a sword, had the time suited.

'Nay,' said one of the men at the table, 'I like it not. Ill will come of it. This is no place for jolly fellows. A jolly fellow loveth open country, good cover, and scarce foes; but here we are shut in a town, girt about with enemies; and, for the bull's-eye of misfortune, see if it snow not ere the morning.'

''Tis for Master Shelton there,' said another, nodding his head towards the lad before the fire.

'I will do much for Master Shelton,' returned the first; 'but to come to the gallows for any man – nay, brothers, not that!'

The door of the inn opened, and another man entered hastily and approached the youth before the fire.

'Master Shelton,' he said, 'Sir Daniel goeth forth with a pair of links and four archers.'

Dick (for this was our young friend) rose instantly to his feet.

'Lawless,' he said, 'ye will take John Capper's watch. Greensheve, follow with me. Capper, lead forward. We will follow him this time, an he go to York.'

The next moment they were outside in the dark street, and Capper, the man who had just come, pointed to where two torches flared in the wind at a little distance.

The town was already sound asleep; no one moved upon the streets, and there was nothing easier than to follow the party without observation. The two link-bearers went first; next followed a single man, whose long cloak blew about him in the wind; and the rear was brought up by the four archers, each with his bow upon his arm. They moved at a brisk walk, threading the intricate lanes and drawing nearer to the shore.

'He hath gone each night in this direction?' asked Dick, in a whisper.

'This is the third night running, Master Shelton,' returned Capper, 'and still at the same hour and with the same small following, as though his end were secret.'

Sir Daniel and his six men were now come to the outskirts of the country. Shoreby was an open town, and though the Lancastrian lords who lay there kept a strong guard on the main roads, it was still possible to enter or depart unseen by any of the lesser streets or across the open country.

The lane which Sir Daniel had been following came to an abrupt end. Before him there was a stretch of rough down, and the noise of the sea-surf was audible upon one hand. There were no guards in the neighbourhood, nor any light in that quarter of the town.

Dick and his two outlaws drew a little closer to the object of their chase, and presently, as they came forth from between the houses and could see a little farther upon either hand, they were aware of another torch drawing near from another direction.

'Hey,' said Dick, 'I smell treason.'

Meanwhile, Sir Daniel had come to a full halt. The torches were stuck into the sand, and the men lay down, as if to await the arrival of the other party.

This drew near at a good rate. It consisted of four men only – a pair of archers, a varlet with a link, and a cloaked gentleman walking in their midst.

'Is it you, my lord?' cried Sir Daniel.

'It is I, indeed; and if ever true knight gave proof I am that man,' replied the leader of the second troop; 'for who would not rather face giants, sorcerers, or pagans, than this pinching cold?'

'My lord,' returned Sir Daniel, 'beauty will be the more beholden, misdoubt it not. But shall we forth? for the sooner ye have seen my merchandise, the sooner shall we both get home.'

'But why keep ye her here, good knight?' inquired the other. 'An she be so young, and so fair, and so wealthy, why do ye not bring her forth among her mates? Ye would soon make her a good marriage, and no need to freeze your fingers and risk arrow-shots by going abroad at such untimely seasons in the dark.'

'I have told you, my lord,' replied Sir Daniel, 'the reason thereof concerneth me only. Neither do I purpose to explain it farther. Suffice it, that if ye be weary of your old gossip, Daniel Brackley, publish it abroad that y' are to wed Joanna Sedley, and I give you my word ye will be quit of him right soon. Ye will find him with an arrow in his back.'

Meantime the two gentlemen were walking briskly forward over the down; the three torches going before them, stooping against the wind and scattering clouds of smoke and tufts of flame, and the rear brought up by the six archers.

Close upon the heels of these, Dick followed. He had, of course, heard no word of this conversation; but he had recognized in the second of the speakers old Lord Shoreby himself, a man of an infamous reputation, whom even Sir Daniel affected, in public, to condemn.

Presently they came close down upon the beach. The air smelt salt; the noise of the surf increased; and here, in a large walled garden, there stood a small house of two storeys, with stables and other offices.

The foremost torch-bearer unlocked a door in the wall, and after the whole party had passed into the garden, again closed and locked it on the other side.

Dick and his men were thus excluded from any farther following, unless they should scale the wall and thus put their necks in a trap.

They sat down in a tuft of furze and waited. The red glow of the torches moved up and down and to and fro within the enclosure, as if the link-bearers steadily patrolled the garden.

Twenty minutes passed, and then the whole party issued forth again upon the down; and Sir Daniel and the baron, after an elaborate salutation, separated and turned severally homeward, each with his own following of men and lights.

As soon as the sound of their steps had been swallowed by the wind, Dick got to his feet as briskly as he was able, for he was stiff and aching with the cold. 'Capper, ye will give me a back up,' he said.

They advanced, all three, to the wall; Capper stooped, and Dick, getting upon his shoulders, clambered on to the cope-stone.

'Now, Greensheve,' whispered Dick, 'follow me up here; lie flat upon your face, that ye may be the less seen; and be ever ready to give me a hand if I fall foully on the other side.'

And so saying, he dropped into the garden.

It was all pitch dark; there was no light in the house. The wind whistled shrill among the poor shrubs, and the surf beat upon the beach; there was no other sound. Cautiously Dick footed it forth, stumbling among bushes, and groping with his hands; and presently the crisp noise of gravel underfoot told him that he had struck upon an alley.

Here he paused, and taking his cross-bow from where he kept it concealed under his long tabard, he prepared it for instant action, and went forward once more with greater resolution and assurance. The path led him straight to the group of buildings.

All seemed to be sorely dilapidated: the windows of the house were secured by crazy shutters; the stables were open and empty; there was no hay in the hay-loft, no corn in the corn-box. Any one would have supposed the place to be deserted; but Dick had good reason to think otherwise. He continued his inspection, visiting the offices, trying all the windows. At length he came round to the sea-side of the house, and there, sure enough, there burned a pale light in one of the upper windows.

He stepped back a little way, till he thought he could see the movement of a shadow on the wall of the apartment. Then he remembered that, in the stable his groping hand had rested for a moment on a ladder, and he returned with all despatch to bring it. The ladder was very short, but yet, by standing on the topmost round, he could bring his hands as high as the iron bars of the window; and seizing these, he raised his body by main force until his eyes commanded the interior of the room.

Two persons were within: the first he readily knew to be Dame Hatch; the

second, a tall and beautiful and grave young lady, in a long, embroidered dress –
could that be Joanna Sedley? his old wood-companion, Jack, whom he had
thought to punish with a belt?

He dropped back to the top round of the ladder in a kind of amazement. He
had never thought of his sweetheart as of so superior a being, and he was
instantly taken with a feeling of diffidence. But he had little opportunity for
thought. A low 'Hist!' sounded from close by, and he hastened to descend the
ladder.

'Who goes?' he whispered.

'Greensheve,' came the reply, in tones similarly guarded.

'What want ye?' asked Dick.

'The house is watched, Master Shelton,' returned the outlaw. 'We are not
alone to watch it; for even as I lay on my belly on the wall I saw men prowling in
the dark, and heard them whistle softly one to other.'

'By my sooth,' said Dick, 'but this is passing strange! Were they not men of Sir
Daniel's?'

'Nay, sir, that they were not,' returned Greensheve, 'for if I have eyes in my
head, every man-Jack of them weareth me a white badge in his bonnet,
something chequered with dark.'

'White, chequered with dark?' repeated Dick. 'Faith, 'tis a badge I know not.
It is none of this country's badges. Well, an that be so, let us slip as quietly forth
from this garden as we may; for here we are in an evil posture for defence.
Beyond all question there are men of Sir Daniel's in that house, and to be taken
between two shots is a beggarman's position. Take me this ladder; I must leave it
where I found it.'

They returned the ladder to the stable, and groped their way to the place
where they had entered.

Capper had taken Greensheve's position on the cope, and now he leaned
down his hand, and, first one and then the other, pulled them up.

Cautiously and silently they dropped again upon the other side; nor did they
dare to speak until they had returned to their old ambush in the gorse.

'Now, John Capper,' said Dick, 'back with you to Shoreby, even as for your
life. Bring me instantly what men ye can collect. Here shall be the rendezvous;
or if the men be scattered and the day be near at hand before they muster, let the
place be something farther back, and by the entering in of the town.
Greensheve and I lie here to watch. Speed ye, John Capper, and the saints aid
you to despatch! And now, Greensheve,' he continued, as soon as Capper had
departed, 'let thou and I go round about the garden in a wide circuit. I would
fain see whether thine eyes betrayed thee.'

Keeping well outwards from the wall, and profiting by every height and
hollow, they passed about two sides, beholding nothing. On the third side the
garden wall was built close upon the beach, and to preserve the distance
necessary to their purpose, they had to go some way down upon the sands.
Although the tide was still pretty far out, the surf was so high, and the sands so
flat, that at each breaker a great sheet of froth and water came careering over the
expanse, and Dick and Greensheve made this part of their inspection wading,
now to the ankles, and now as deep as to the knees, in the salt and icy waters of
the German Ocean.

Suddenly, against the comparative whiteness of the garden wall, the figure of a man was seen, like a faint Chinese shadow, violently signalling with both arms. As he dropped again to the earth, another arose a little farther on and repeated the same performance. And so, like a silent watchword, these gesticulations made the round of the beleaguered garden.

'They keep good watch,' Dick whispered.

'Let us back to land, good master,' answered Greensheve. 'We stand here too open; for, look ye, when the seas break heavy and white out there behind us, they shall see us plainly against the foam.'

'Ye speak sooth,' returned Dick. 'Ashore with us, right speedily.'

CHAPTER TWO

A Skirmish in the Dark

THOROUGHLY DRENCHED AND chilled, the two adventurers returned to their position in the gorse.

'I pray Heaven that Capper make good speed!' said Dick. 'I vow a candle to St Mary of Shoreby if he come before the hour!'

'Y' are in a hurry, Master Dick?' asked Greensheve.

'Ay, good fellow,' answered Dick; 'for in that house lieth my lady, whom I love, and who should these be that lie about her secretly by night? Unfriends for sure!'

'Well,' returned Greensheve, 'an John come speedily, we shall give a good account of them. They are not two score at the outside – I judge so by the spacing of their sentries – and, taken where they are, lying so widely, one score would scatter them like sparrows. And yet, Master Dick, an she be in Sir Daniel's power already, it will little hurt that she should change into another's. Who should these be?'

'I do suspect the Lord of Shoreby,' Dick replied. 'When came they?'

'They began to come, Master Dick,' said Greensheve, 'about the time ye crossed the wall. I had not lain there the space of a minute ere I marked the first of the knaves crawling round the corner.'

The last light had been already extinguished in the little house when they were wading in the wash of the breakers, and it was impossible to predict at what moment the lurking men about the garden might make their onslaught. Of two evils, Dick preferred the least. He preferred that Joanna should remain under the guardianship of Sir Daniel rather than pass into the clutches of Lord Shoreby; and his mind was made up, if the house should be assaulted, to come at once to the relief of the besieged.

But the time passed, and still there was no movement. From quarter of an hour to quarter of an hour the same signal passed about the garden wall, as if the leader desired to assure himself of the vigilance of his scattered followers; but in every other particular the neighbourhood of the little house lay undisturbed.

Presently Dick's reinforcements began to arrive. The night was not yet old before nearly a score of men crouched beside him in the gorse. Separating these into two bodies, he took the command of the smaller himself, and entrusted the larger to the leadership of Greensheve.

'Now, Kit,' said he to this last, 'take me your men to the near angle of the garden wall upon the beach. Post them strongly, and wait till that ye hear me falling on upon the other side. It is those upon the sea front that I would fain make certain of, for there will be the leader. The rest will run; even let them. And now lads, let no man draw an arrow; ye will but hurt friends. Take to the steel, and keep to the steel; and if we have the uppermost, I promise every man of you a gold noble when I come to mine estate.'

Out of the odd collection of broken men, thieves, murderers, and ruined peasantry, whom Duckworth had gathered together to serve the purposes of his revenge, some of the boldest and the most experienced in war had volunteered to follow Richard Shelton. The service of watching Sir Daniel's movements in the town of Shoreby had from the first been irksome to their temper, and they had of late begun to grumble loudly and threaten to disperse. The prospect of a sharp encounter and possible spoils restored them to good humour, and they joyfully prepared for battle.

Their long tabards thrown aside, they appeared, some in plain green jerkins, and some in stout leathern jacks; under their hoods many wore bonnets strengthened by iron plates; and for offensive armour, swords, daggers, a few stout boar-spears, and a dozen of bright bills, put them in a posture to engage even regular feudal troops. The bows, quivers, and tabards were concealed among the gorse, and the two bands set resolutely forward.

Dick, when he had reached the other side of the house, posted his six men in a line, about twenty yards from the garden wall, and took position himself a few paces in front. Then they all shouted with one voice, and closed upon the enemy.

These, lying widely scattered, stiff with cold, and taken at unawares, sprang stupidly to their feet, and stood undecided. Before they had time to get their courage about them, or even to form an idea of the number and mettle of their assailants, a similar shout of onslaught sounded in their ears from the far side of the enclosure. Thereupon they gave themselves up for lost and ran.

In this way the two small troops of the men of the Black Arrow closed upon the sea front of the garden wall, and took a part of the strangers, as it were, between two fires; while the whole of the remainder ran for their lives in different directions, and were soon scattered in the darkness.

For all that, the fight was but beginning. Dick's outlaws, although they had the advantage of surprise, were still considerably outnumbered by the men they had surrounded. The tide had flowed in the meanwhile; the beach was narrowed to a strip; and on this wet field between the surf and the garden wall, there began, in the darkness, a doubtful, furious, and deadly contest.

The strangers were well armed; they fell in silence upon their assailants; and the affray became a series of single combats. Dick, who had come first into the mellay, was engaged by three; the first he cut down at the first blow, but the other two coming upon him hotly he was fain to give ground before their onset.

One of these two was a huge fellow, almost a giant for stature, and armed with a two-handed sword, which he brandished like a switch. Against this opponent, with his reach of arm and the length and weight of his weapon, Dick and his bill were quite defenceless; and had the other continued to join vigorously in the attack, the lad must have indubitably fallen. This second man, however, less in stature and slower in his movements, paused for a moment to peer about him in the darkness, and to give ear to the sounds of the battle.

The giant still pursued his advantage, and still Dick fled before him, spying for his chance. Then the huge blade flashed and descended, and the lad, leaping on one side and running in, slashed sideways and upwards with his bill. A roar of agony responded, and before the wounded man could raise his formidable weapon, Dick, twice repeating his blow, had brought him to the ground.

The next moment he was engaged upon more equal terms with his second pursuer. Here there was no great difference in size, and though the man, fighting with sword and dagger against a bill, and being wary and quick of fence, had a certain superiority of arms, Dick more than made it up by his greater agility on foot. Neither at first gained any obvious advantage; but the older man was still insensibly profiting by the ardour of the younger to lead him where he would; and presently Dick found that they had crossed the whole width of the beach, and were now fighting above the knees in the spume and bubble of the breakers. Here his own superior activity was rendered useless; he found himself more or less at the discretion of his foe; yet a little, and he had his back turned upon his own men, and saw that his adroit and skilful adversary was bent upon drawing him farther and farther away.

Dick ground his teeth. He determined to decide the combat instantly; and when the wash of the next wave had ebbed and left them dry, he rushed in, caught a blow upon his bill, and leaped right at the throat of his opponent. The man went down backwards, with Dick still upon the top of him; and the next wave, speedily succeeding the last, buried him below a rush of water.

While he was still submerged, Dick forced his dagger from his grasp, and rose to his feet victorious.

'Yield ye!' he said. 'I give you life.'

'I yield me,' said the other, getting to his knees. 'Ye fight, like a young man, ignorantly and foolhardily; but, by the array of the saints, ye fight bravely!'

Dick turned to the beach. The combat was still raging doubtfully in the night; over the hoarse roar of the breakers steel clanged upon steel, and cries of pain and the shout of battle resounded.

'Lead me to your captain, youth,' said the conquered knight. 'It is fit this butchery should cease.'

'Sir,' replied Dick, 'so far as these brave fellows have a captain, the poor gentlemen who here addresses you is he.'

'Call off your dogs, then, and I will bid my villains hold,' returned the other.

There was something noble both in the voice and manner of his late opponent, and Dick instantly dismissed all fears of treachery.

'Lay down your arms, men!' cried the stranger knight. 'I have yielded me, upon promise of life.'

The tone of the stranger was one of absolute command, and almost instantly the din and confusion of the mellay ceased.

'Lawless,' cried Dick, 'are ye safe?'

'Ay,' cried Lawless, 'safe and hearty.'

'Light me the lantern,' said Dick.

'Is not Sir Daniel here?' inquired the knight.

'Sir Daniel?' echoed Dick. 'Now, by the rood, I pray not. It would go ill with me if he were.'

'Ill with you, fair sir?' inquired the other. 'Nay, then, if ye be not of Sir Daniel's party, I profess I comprehend no longer. Wherefore, then, fell ye upon mine ambush? in what quarrel, my young and very fiery friend? to what earthly purpose? and, to make a clear end of questioning, to what good gentleman have I surrendered?'

But before Dick could answer, a voice spoke in the darkness from close by. Dick could see the speaker's black and white badge, and the respectful salute which he addressed to his superior.

'My lord,' said he, 'if these gentlemen be unfriends to Sir Daniel, it is a pity, indeed, we should have been at blows with them; but it were tenfold greater that either they or we should linger here. The watchers in the house – unless they be all dead or deaf – have heard our hammering this quarter-hour agone; instantly they will have signalled to the town; and unless we be the livelier in our departure, we are like to be taken, both of us, by a fresh foe.'

'Hawksley is in the right,' added the lord. 'How please ye, sir? Whither shall we march?'

'Nay, my lord,' said Dick, 'go where you will for me. I do begin to suspect we have some ground of friendship, and if, indeed, I began our acquaintance somewhat ruggedly, I would not churlishly continue. Let us, then, separate, my lord, your laying your right hand in mine; and at the hour and place that ye shall name, let us encounter and agree.'

'Y' are too trustful, boy,' said the other; 'but this time your trust is not misplaced. I will meet you at the point of day at St Bride's Cross. Come, lads, follow?'

The strangers disappeared from the scene with a rapidity that seemed suspicious; and, while the outlaws fell to the congenial task of rifling the dead bodies, Dick made once more the circuit of the garden wall to examine the front of the house. In a little upper loophole of the roof he beheld a light set; and as it would certainly be visible in town from the back windows of Sir Daniel's mansion, he doubted not that this was the signal feared by Hawksley, and that ere long the lances of the Knight of Tunstall would arrive upon the scene.

He put his ear to the ground, and it seemed to him as if he heard a jarring and hollow noise from townward. Back to the beach he went hurrying. But the work was already done; the last body was disarmed and stripped to the skin, and four fellows were already wading seaward to commit it to the mercies of the deep.

A few minutes later, when there debouched out of the nearest lanes of Shoreby some two score horsemen, hastily arrayed and moving at the gallop of their steeds, the neighbourhood of the house beside the sea was entirely silent and deserted.

Meanwhile, Dick and his men had returned to the ale-house of the Goat and Bagpipes to snatch some hours of sleep before the morning tryst.

CHAPTER THREE

St Bride's Cross

ST BRIDE'S CROSS STOOD A little way back from Shoreby, on the skirts of Tunstall Forest. Two roads met: one, from Holywood across the forest; one, that road from Risingham down which we saw the wrecks of a Lancastrian army fleeing in disorder. Here the two joined issue, and went on together down the hill to Shoreby; and a little back from the point of junction, the summit of a little knoll was crowned by the ancient and weather-beaten cross.

Here, then, about seven in the morning, Dick arrived. It was as cold as ever; the earth was all grey and silver with the hoar-frost, and the day began to break in the east with many colours of purple and orange.

Dick set him down upon the lowest step of the cross, wrapped himself well in his tabard, and looked vigilantly upon all sides. He had not long to wait. Down the road from Holywood a gentleman in very rich and bright armour, and wearing over that a surcoat of the rarest fur's, came pacing on a splendid charger. Twenty yards behind him followed a clump of lancers; but these halted as soon as they came in view of the trysting-place, while the gentleman in the fur surcoat continued to advance alone.

His visor was raised, and showed a countenance of great command and dignity, answerable to the richness of his attire and arms. And it was with some confusion of manner that Dick arose from the cross and stepped down the bank to meet his prisoner.

'I thank you, my lord, for your exactitude,' he said louting very low. 'Will it please your lordship to set foot to earth?'

'Are ye here alone, young man?' inquired the other.

'I was not so simple,' answered Dick; 'and, to be plain with your lordship, the woods upon either hand of this cross lie full of mine honest fellows lying on their weapons.

'Y' 'ave done wisely,' said the lord. 'It pleaseth me the rather, since last night ye fought foolhardily, and more like a salvage Saracen lunatic than any Christian warrior. But it becomes not me to complain that had the undermost.'

'Ye had the undermost indeed, my lord, since ye so fell,' returned Dick; 'but had the waves not holpen me, it was I that should have had the worst. Ye were pleased to make me yours with several dagger marks, which I still carry. And in fine, my lord, methinks I had all the danger, as well as all the profit, of that little blind-man's medley on the beach.'

'Y' are shrewd enough to make light of it, I see,' returned the stranger.

'Nay, my lord, not shrewd,' replied Dick, 'in that I shoot at no advantage to myself. But when, by the light of this new day, I see how stout a knight hath yielded, not to my arms alone, but to fortune, and the darkness, and the surf –

and how easily the battle had gone otherwise, with a soldier so untried and rustic as myself – think it not strange, my lord, if I feel confounded with my victory.'

'Ye speak well,' said the stranger. 'Your name?'

'My name, an't like you, is Shelton,' answered Dick.

'Men call me the Lord Foxham,' added the other.

'Then, my lord, and under your good favour, ye are guardian to the sweetest maid in England,' replied Dick; 'and for your ransom, and the ransom of such as were taken with you on the beach, there will be no uncertainty of terms. I pray you, my lord, of your goodwill and charity, yield me the hand of my mistress, Joan Sedley; and take ye, upon the other part, your liberty, the liberty of these your followers, and (if ye will have it) my gatitude and service till I die.'

'But are ye not ward to Sir Daniel? Methought, if y' are Harry Shelton's son, that I had heard it so reported,' said Lord Foxham.

'Will it please you, my lord, to alight? I would fain tell you fully who I am, how situate, and why so bold in my demands. Beseech you, my lord, take place upon these steps, hear me to a full end, and judge me with allowance.'

And so saying Dick lent a hand to Lord Foxham to dismount; led him up the knoll to the cross; installed him in the place where he had himself been sitting; and standing respectfully before his noble prisoner, related the story of his fortunes up to the events of the evening before.

Lord Foxham listened gravely, and when Dick had done, 'Master Shelton,' he said, 'ye are a most fortunate-unfortunate young gentleman; but what fortune y' 'ave had, that ye have amply merited; and what unfortune, ye have noways deserved. Be of a good cheer; for ye have made a friend who is devoid neither of power nor favour. For yourself, although it fits not for a person of your birth to herd with outlaws, I must own ye are both brave and honourable; very dangerous in battle, right courteous in peace; a youth of excellent disposition and brave bearing. For your estates, ye will never see them till the world shall change again; so long as Lancaster hath the strong hand, so long shall Sir Daniel enjoy them for his own. For my ward, it is another matter; I had promised her before to a gentleman, a kinsman of my house, one Hamley; the promise is old——'

'Ay, my lord, and now Sir Daniel hath promised her to my lord Shoreby,' interrupted Dick. 'And his promise, for all it is but young, is still the likelier to be made good.'

'"Tis the plain truth,' returned his lordship. 'And considering, moreover, that I am your prisoner, upon no better composition than my bare life, and over and above that, that the maiden is unhappily in other hands, I will so far consent. Aid me with your good fellows'——

'My lord,' cried Dick, 'they are these same outlaws that ye blame me for consorting with.'

'Let them be what they will, they can fight,' returned Lord Foxham. 'Help me, then; and if between us we regain the maid, upon my knightly honour, she shall marry you!'

Dick bent his knee before his prisoner; but he, leaping up lightly from the cross, caught the lad up and embraced him like a son.

'Come,' he said, 'an y' are to marry Joan, we must be early friends.'

CHAPTER FOUR

The 'Good Hope'

AN HOUR THEREAFTER, DICK was back at the Goat and Bagpipes, breaking his fast, and receiving the report of his messengers and sentries. Duckworth was still absent from Shoreby; and this was frequently the case, for he played many parts in the world, shared many different interests, and conducted many various affairs. He had founded that fellowship of the Black Arrow, as a ruined man longing for vengeance and money; and yet among those who knew him best, he was thought to be the agent and emissary of the great King-maker of England, Richard, Earl of Warwick.

In his absence, at any rate, it fell upon Richard Shelton to command affairs in Shoreby; and, as he sat at meat, his mind was full of care, and his face heavy with consideration. It had been determined, between him and the Lord Foxham, to make one bold strike that evening, and, by brute force, to set Joanna free. The obstacles, however, were many; and as one after another of his scouts arrived, each brought him more discomfortable news.

Sir Daniel was alarmed by the skirmish of the night before. He had increased the garrison of the house in the garden; but not content with that, he had stationed horsemen in all the neighbouring lanes, so that he might have instant word of any movement. Meanwhile, in the court of his mansion, steeds stood saddled, and the riders, armed at every point, awaited but the signal to ride.

The adventure of the night appeared more and more difficult of execution, till suddenly Dick's countenance lightened.

'Lawless!' he cried, 'you that were a shipman, can ye steal me a ship?'

'Master Dick,' replied Lawless, 'if ye would back me, I would agree to steal York Minster.'

Presently after, these two set forth and descended to the harbour. It was a considerable basin, lying among sand hills, and surrounded with patches of down, ancient ruinous lumber, and tumble-down slums of the town. Many decked ships and many open boats either lay there at anchor, or had been drawn up on the beach. A long duration of bad weather had driven them from the high seas into the shelter of the port; and the great trooping of black clouds, and the cold squalls that followed one another, now with a sprinkling of dry snow, now in a mere swoop of wind, promised no improvement, but rather threatened a more serious storm in the immediate future.

The seamen, in view of the cold and the wind, had for the most part slunk ashore, and were now roaring and singing in the shoreside taverns. Many of the ships already rode unguarded at their anchors; and as the day wore on, and the weather offered no appearance of improvement, the number was continually being augmented. It was to these deserted ships, and, above all, to those of them that lay far out, that Lawless directed his attention; while Dick, seated upon an anchor that was half embedded in the sand, and giving ear, now to the rude, potent, and boding voices of the gale, and now to the hoarse singing of the shipmen in a neighbouring tavern, soon forgot his immediate surroundings and concerns in the agreeable recollection of Lord Foxham's promise.

He was disturbed by a touch upon his shoulder. It was Lawless, pointing to a small ship that lay somewhat by itself, and within but a little of the harbour mouth, where it heaved regularly and smoothly on the entering swell. A pale gleam of winter sunshine fell, at that moment, on the vessel's deck, relieving her against a bank of scowling cloud; and in this momentary glitter Dick could see a couple of men hauling the skiff alongside.

'There, sir,' said Lawless, 'mark ye it well! There is the ship for tonight.'

Presently the skiff put out from the vessel's side, and the two men, keeping her head well to the wind, pulled lustily for shore. Lawless turned to a loiterer.

'How call ye her?' he asked, pointing to the little vessel.

'They call her the *Good Hope*, of Dartmouth,' replied the loiterer. 'Her captain, Arblaster by name. He pulleth the bow oar in yon skiff.'

This was all that Lawless wanted. Hurriedly thanking the man, he moved round the shore to a certain sandy creek, for which the skiff was heading. There he took up his position, and as soon as they were within earshot, opened fire on the sailors of the *Good Hope*.

'What! Gossip Arblaster!' he cried. 'Why, ye be well met; nay, gossip, ye be right well met, upon the rood! And is that the *Good Hope*? Ay, I would know her among ten thousand! – a sweet shear, a sweet boat! But marry come up, my gossip, will ye drink? I have come into mine estate which doubtless ye remember to have heard on. I am now rich; I have left to sail upon the sea; I do sail now, for the most part, upon spiced ale. Come, fellow; thy hand upon 't! Come, drink with an old shipfellow!'

Skipper Arblaster, a long-faced, elderly, weatherbeaten man, with a knife hanging about his neck by a plaited cord, and for all the world like any modern seaman in his gait and bearing, had hung back in obvious amazement and distrust. But the name of an estate, and a certain air of tipsified simplicity and good-fellowship which Lawless very well affected, combined to conquer his suspicious jealousy; his countenance relaxed, and he at once extended his open hand and squeezed that of the outlaw in a formidable grasp.

'Nay,' he said, 'I cannot mind you. But what o' that? I would drink with any man, gossip, and so would my man Tom. Man Tom,' he added, addressing his follower, 'here is my gossip, whose name I cannot mind, but no doubt a very good seaman. Let's go drink with him and his shore friend.'

Lawless led the way, and they were soon seated in an alehouse, which, as it was very new, and stood in an exposed and solitary station, was less crowded than those nearer to the centre of the port. It was but a shed of timber, much like a block-house in the backwoods of today, and was coarsely furnished with a press or two, a number of naked benches, and boards set upon barrels to play the part of tables. In the middle, and besieged by half a hundred violent draughts, a fire of wreck-wood blazed and vomited thick smoke.

'Ay, now,' said Lawless, 'here is a shipman's joy – a good fire and a good stiff cup ashore, with foul weather without and an off-sea gale a-snoring in the roof! Here's to the *Good Hope*! May she ride easy!'

'Ay,' said Skipper Arblaster, "tis good weather to be ashore in, that is sooth. Man Tom, how say ye to that? Gossip, ye speak well, though I can never think upon your name; but ye speak very well. May the *Good Hope* ride easy! Amen!'

'Friend Dickon,' resumed Lawless, addressing his commander, 'ye have certain matters on hand, unless I err? Well, prithee be about them incontinently. For here I be with the choice of all good company, two tough old shipmen; and till that ye return I will go warrant these brave fellows will bide here and drink me cup for cup. We are not like shore-men, we old, tough tarry-Johns!'

'It is well meant,' returned the skipper. 'Ye can go, boy; for I will keep your good friend and my good gossip company till curfew – ay, and by St Mary, till the sun get up again! For, look ye, when a man hath been long enough at sea, the salt getteth me into the clay upon his bones; and let him drink a draw-well, he will never be quenched.'

Thus encouraged upon all hands, Dick rose, saluted his company, and going forth again into the gusty afternoon, got him as speedily as he might to the Goat and Bagpipes. Thence he sent word to my Lord Foxham that, so soon as ever the evening closed, they would have a stout boat to keep the sea in. And then leading along with him a couple of outlaws who had some experience of the sea, he returned himself to the harbour and the little sandy creek.

The skiff of the *Good Hope* lay among many others, from which it was easily distinguished by its extreme smallness and fragility. Indeed, when Dick and his two men had taken their places, and begun to put forth out of the creek into the open harbour, the little cockle dipped into the swell and staggered under every gust of wind, like a thing upon the point of sinking.

The *Good Hope*, as we have said, was anchored far out, where the swell was heaviest. No other vessel lay nearer than several cables' length; those that were the nearest were themselves entirely deserted; and as the skiff approached, a thick flurry of snow and a sudden darkening of the weather further concealed the movements of the outlaws from all possible espial. In a trice they had leaped upon the heaving deck, and the skiff was dancing at the stern. The *Good Hope* was captured.

She was a good stout boat, decked in the bows and amidships, but open in the stern. She carried one mast, and was rigged between a felucca and a lugger. It would seem that Skipper Arblaster had made an excellent venture, for the hold was full of pieces of French wine; and in the little cabin, besides the Virgin Mary in the bulkhead which proved the captain's piety, there were many lockfast chests and cupboards, which showed him to be rich and careful.

A dog, who was the sole occupant of the vessel, furiously barked and bit the heels of the boarders; but he was soon kicked into the cabin, and the door shut under his just resentment. A lamp was lit and fixed in the shrouds to mark the vessel clearly from the shore; one of the wine pieces in the hold was broached, and a cup of excellent Gascony emptied to the adventure of the evening; and then, while one of the outlaws began to get ready his bow and arrows and prepare to hold the ship against all comers, the other hauled in the skiff and got overboard, where he held on, waiting for Dick.

'Well, Jack, keep me a good watch,' said the young commander, preparing to follow his subordinate. 'Ye will do right well.'

'Why,' returned Jack, 'I shall do excellent well indeed, so long as we lie here;

but once we put the nose of this poor ship outside the harbour—— See, there she trembles! Nay, the poor shrew heard the words, and the heart misgave her in her oak-tree ribs. But look, Master Dick! how black the weather gathers!'

The darkness ahead was, indeed, astonishing. Great billows heaved up out of the blackness, one after another; and one after another the *Good Hope* buoyantly climbed, and giddily plunged upon the further side. A thin sprinkle of snow and thin flakes of foam came flying, and powdered the deck; and the wind harped dismally among the rigging.

'In sooth, it looketh evilly,' said Dick. 'But what cheer! 'Tis but a squall, and presently it will blow over.' But, in spite of his words, he was depressingly affected by the bleak disorder of the sky and the wailing and fluting of the wind; and as he got over the side of the *Good Hope* and made once more for the landing-creek with the best speed of oars, he crossed himself devoutly, and recommended to Heaven the lives of all who should adventure on the sea.

At the landing-creek there had already gathered about a dozen of the outlaws. To these the skiff was left, and they were bidden embark without delay.

A little further up the beach Dick found Lord Foxham hurrying in quest of him, his face concealed with a dark hood, and his bright armour covered by a long russet mantle of a poor appearance.

'Young Shelton,' he said, 'are ye for sea, then, truly?'

'My lord,' replied Richard, 'they lie about the house with horsemen; it may not be reached from the land side without alarum; and Sir Daniel once advertised of our adventure, we can no more carry it to a good end than, saving your presence, we could ride upon the wind. Now, in going round by sea, we do run some peril by the elements; but, what much outweigheth all, we have a chance to make good our purpose and bear off the maid.'

'Well,' returned Lord Foxham, 'lead on. I will, in some sort, follow you for shame's sake; but I own I would I were in bed.'

'Here, then,' said Dick. 'Hither we go to fetch our pilot.'

And he led the way to the rude alehouse where he had given rendezvous to a portion of his men. Some of these he found lingering round the door outside; others had pushed more boldly in, and, choosing places as near as possible to where they saw their comrade, gathered close about Lawless and the two shipmen. These, to judge by the distempered countenance and cloudy eye, had long since gone beyond the boundaries of moderation; and as Richard entered, closely followed by Lord Foxham, they were all three tuning up an old, pitiful sea-ditty, to the chorus of the wailing of the gale.

The young leader cast a rapid glance about the shed. The fire had just been replenished, and gave forth volumes of black smoke, so that it was difficult to see clearly in the further corners. It was plain, however, that the outlaws very largely outnumbered the remainder of the guests. Satisfied upon this point, in case of any failure in the operation of his plan, Dick strode up to the table and resumed his place upon the bench.

'Hey?' cried the skipper, tipsily, 'who are ye, hey?'

'I want a word with you without Master Arblaster,' returned Dick; 'and here is what we shall talk of.' And he showed him a gold noble in the glimmer of the firelight.

The shipman's eyes burned, although he still failed to recognize our hero.

'Ay, boy,' he said, 'I am with you. Gossip, I will be back anon. Drink fair, gossip;' and, taking Dick's arm to steady his uneven steps, he walked to the door of the alehouse.

As soon as he was over the threshold, ten strong arms had seized and bound him; and in two minutes more, with his limbs trussed one to another, and a good gag in his mouth, he had been tumbled neck and crop into a neighbouring hay-barn. Presently, his man Tom, similarly secured, was tossed beside him, and the pair were left to their uncouth reflections for the night.

And now, as the time for concealment had gone by, Lord Foxham's followers were summoned by a preconcerted signal, and the party, boldly taking possession of as many boats as their numbers required, pulled in a flotilla for the light in the rigging of the ship. Long before the last man had climbed to the deck of the *Good Hope*, the sound of furious shouting from the shore showed that a part, at least, of the seamen had discovered the loss of their skiffs.

But it was now too late, whether for recovery or revenge. Out of some forty fighting men now mustered in the stolen ship, eight had been to sea, and could play the part of mariners. With the aid of these, a slice of sail was got upon her. The cable was cut. Lawless, vacillating on his feet, and still shouting the chorus of sea-ballads, took the long tiller in his hands: and the *Good Hope* began to flit forward into the darkness of the night, and to face the great waves beyond the harbour bar.

Richard took his place beside the weather rigging. Except for the ship's own lantern, and for some lights, in Shoreby town, that were already fading to leeward, the whole world of air was as black as in a pit. Only from time to time, as the *Good Hope* swooped dizzily down into the valley of the rollers, a crest would break – a great cataract of snowy foam would leap in one instant into being – and, in an instant more, would stream into the wake and vanish.

Many of the men lay holding on and praying aloud; many more were sick, and had crept into the bottom, where they sprawled among the cargo. And what with the extreme violence of the motion, and the continued drunken bravado of Lawless, still shouting and singing at the helm, the stoutest heart on board may have nourished a shrewd misgiving as to the result.

But Lawless, as if guided by an instinct, steered the ship across the breakers, struck the lee of a great sandbank, where they sailed for a while in smooth water, and presently after laid her alongside a rude, stone pier, where she was hastily made fast, and lay ducking and grinding in the dark.

CHAPTER FIVE

The 'Good Hope' (continued)

THE PIER WAS NOT FAR DISTANT from the house in which Joanna lay; it now only remained to get the men on shore, to surround the house with a strong party, burst in the door and carry off the captive. They might then regard themselves as done with the *Good Hope*; it had placed them on the rear of their enemies; and the retreat, whether they should succeed or fail in the main enterprise, would be directed with a greater measure of hope in the direction of the forest and my Lord Foxham's reserve.

To get the men on shore, however, was no easy task; many had been sick, all were pierced with cold; the promiscuity and disorder on board had shaken their discipline; the movement of the ship and the darkness of the night had cowed their spirits. They made a rush upon the pier; my lord, with his sword drawn on his own retainers, must throw himself in front; and this impulse of rabblement was not restrained without a certain clamour of voices, highly to be regretted in the case.

When some degree of order had been restored, Dick, with a few chosen men, set forth in advance. The darkness on shore, by contrast with the flashing of the surf, appeared before him like a solid body; and the howling and whistling of the gale drowned any lesser noise.

He had scarce reached the end of the pier, however, when there fell a lull of the wind; and in this he seemed to hear on shore the hollow footing of horses and the clash of arms. Checking his immediate followers, he passed forward a step or two alone, even setting foot upon the down; and here he made sure he could detect the shape of men and horses moving. A strong discouragement assailed him. If their enemies were really on the watch, if they had beleaguered the shoreward end of the pier, he and Lord Foxham were taken in a posture of very poor defence, the sea behind, the men jostled in the dark upon a narrow causeway. He gave a cautious whistle, the signal previously agreed upon.

It proved to be a signal for more than he desired. Instantly there fell, through the black night, a shower of arrows sent at a venture; and so close were the men huddled on the pier that more than one was hit, and the arrows were answered with cries of both fear and pain. In this first discharge, Lord Foxham was struck down; Hawksley had him carried on board again at once; and his men, during the brief remainder of the skirmish, fought (when they fought at all) without guidance. That was perhaps the chief cause of the disaster which made haste to follow.

At the shore end of the pier, for perhaps a minute, Dick held his own with a handful; one or two were wounded upon either side; steel crossed steel; nor had there been the least signal of advantage, when in the twinkling of an eye the tide turned against the party from the ship. Someone cried out that all was lost; the men were in the very humour to lend an ear to a discomfortable counsel; the cry was taken up. 'On board, lads, for your lives!' cried another. A third, with the true instinct of the coward, raised that inevitable report on all retreats: 'We are betrayed!' And in a moment the whole mass of men went surging and jostling backward down the pier, turning their defenceless backs on their pursuers and piercing the night with craven outcry.

One coward thrust off the ship's stern, while another still held her by the bows. The fugitives leaped, screaming, and were hauled on board, or fell back and perished in the sea. Some were cut down upon the pier by the pursuers. Many were injured on the ship's deck in the blind haste and terror of the moment, one man leaping upon another, and a third on both. At last, and whether by design or accident, the bows of the *Good Hope* were liberated; and the ever-ready Lawless, who had maintained his place at the helm through all the hurly-burly by sheer strength of body and a liberal use of the cold steel, instantly clapped her on the proper tack. The ship began to move once more forward on the stormy sea, its scuppers running blood, its deck heaped with fallen men, sprawling and struggling in the dark.

Thereupon, Lawless sheathed his dagger, and turning to his next neighbour, 'I have left my mark on them, gossip,' said he, 'the yelping, coward hounds.'

Now, while they were all leaping and struggling for their lives, the men had not appeared to observe the rough shoves and cutting stabs with which Lawless had held his post in the confusion. But perhaps they had already begun to understand somewhat more clearly, or perhaps another ear had overheard the helmsman's speech.

Panic-stricken troops recover slowly, and men who have just disgraced themselves by cowardice, as if to wipe out the memory of their fault, will sometimes run straight into the opposite extreme of insubordination. So it was now; and the same men who had thrown away their weapons and been hauled, feet foremost, into the *Good Hope*, began to cry out upon their leaders, and demand that someone should be punished.

This growing ill-feeling turned upon Lawless.

In order to get a proper offing, the old outlaw had put the head of the *Good Hope* to seaward.

'What!' bawled one of the grumblers, 'he carrieth us to seaward!'

''Tis sooth,' cried another. 'Nay, we are betrayed for sure.'

And they all began to cry out in chorus that they were betrayed, and in shrill tones and with abominable oaths bade Lawless go about-ship and bring them speedily ashore. Lawless, grinding his teeth, continued in silence to steer the true course, guiding the *Good Hope* among the formidable billows. To their empty terrors, as to their dishonourable threats, between drink and dignity he scorned to make reply. The malcontents drew together a little abaft the mast, and it was plain they were like barnyard cocks, 'crowing for courage.' Presently they would be fit for any extremity of injustice or ingratitude. Dick began to mount by the ladder, eager to interpose; but one of the outlaws, who was also something of a seaman, got beforehand.

'Lads,' he began, 'y' are right wooden heads, I think. For to get back, by the mass, we must have an offing, must we not? And this old Lawless——'

Someone struck the speaker on the mouth, and the next moment, as a fire springs among dry straw, he was felled upon the deck, trampled under the feet, and despatched by the daggers of his cowardly companions. At this the wrath of Lawless rose and broke.

'Steer yourselves,' be bellowed, with a curse; and, careless of the result, he left the helm.

The *Good Hope* was, at that moment, trembling on the summit of a swell. She subsided, with sickening velocity, upon the farther side. A wave, like a great black bulwark, hove immediately in front of her; and, with a staggering blow, she plunged headforemost through that liquid hill. The green water passed right over her from stem to stern, as high as a man's knees; the sprays ran higher than the mast; and she rose again upon the other side, with an appalling, tremulous indecision, like a beast that has been deadly wounded.

Six or seven of the malcontents had been carried bodily overboard; and as for the remainder, when they found their tongues again, it was to bellow to the saints and wail upon Lawless to come back and take the tiller.

Nor did Lawless wait to be twice bidden. The terrible result of his fling of just resentment sobered him completely. He knew, better than any one on board, how nearly the *Good Hope* had gone bodily down below their feet; and he could tell, by the laziness with which she met the sea, that the peril was by no means over.

Dick, who had been thrown down by the concussion and half drowned, rose wading to his knees in the swamped well of the stern, and crept to the old helmsman's side.

'Lawless,' he said, 'we do all depend on you; y' are a brave, steady man, indeed, and crafty in the management of ships; I shall put three sure men to watch upon your safety.'

'Bootless, my master, bootless,' said the steersman, peering forward through the dark. 'We come every moment somewhat clearer of these sandbanks; with every moment, then, the sea packeth upon us heavier, and for all these whimperers, they will presently be on their backs. For, my master, 'tis a right mystery, but true, there never yet was a bad man that was a good shipman. None but the honest and the bold can endure me this tossing of a ship.'

'Nay, Lawless,' said Dick, laughing, 'that is a right shipman's byword, and hath no more of sense than the whistle of the wind. But, prithee, how go we? Do we lie well? Are we in good case?'

'Master Shelton,' replied Lawless, 'I have been a Grey Friar – I praise fortune – an archer, a thief, and a shipman. Of all these coats, I had the best fancy to die in the Grey Friar's, as ye may readily conceive, and the least fancy to die in John Shipman's tarry jacket; and that for two excellent good reasons: first, that the death might take a man suddenly; and second, for the horror of that great salt smother and welter under my foot here' – and Lawless stamped with his foot. 'Howbeit,' he went on, 'an I die not a sailor's death, and that this night, I shall owe a tall candle to our Lady.'

'Is it so?' asked Dick.

'It is right so,' replied the outlaw. 'Do ye not feel how heavy and dull she moves upon the waves? Do ye not hear the water washing in her hold? She will scarce mind the rudder even now. Bide till she has settled a bit lower; and she will either go down below your boots like a stone image, or drive ashore here, under our lee, and come all to pieces like a twist of string.'

'Ye speak with a good courage,' returned Dick. 'Ye are not then appalled?'

'Why, master,' answered Lawless, 'if ever a man had an ill crew to come to port with, it is I – a renegade friar, a thief, and all the rest on't. Well, ye may wonder, but I keep a good hope in my wallet; and if that I be to drown, I will drown with a bright eye, Master Shelton, and a steady hand.'

Dick returned no answer; but he was surprised to find the old vagabond of so resolute a temper, and fearing some fresh violence or treachery, set forth upon his quest for three sure men. The great bulk of the men had now deserted the deck, which was continually wetted with the flying sprays, and where they lay exposed to the shrewdness of the winter wind. They had gathered, instead, into the hold of the merchandise, among the butts of wine, and lighted by two swinging lanterns.

Here a few kept up the form of revelry, and toasted each other deep in Arblaster's Gascony wine. But as the *Good Hope* continued to tear through the smoking waves, and toss her stem and stern alternately high in air and deep into white foam, the number of these jolly companions diminished with every moment and with every lurch. Many sat apart, tending their hurts, but the majority were already prostrated with sickness, and lay moaning in the bilge.

Greensheve, Cuckow, and a young fellow of Lord Foxham's whom Dick had already remarked for his intelligence and spirit, were still, however, both fit to understand and willing to obey. These Dick set as a bodyguard about the person of the steersman, and then, with a last look at the black sky and sea, he turned and went below into the cabin, whither Lord Foxham had been carried by his servants.

CHAPTER SIX

The 'Good Hope' (concluded)

THE MOANS OF THE WOUNDED baron blended with the wailing of the ship's dog. The poor animal, whether he was merely sick at heart to be separated from his friends, or whether he indeed recognized some peril in the labouring of the ship, raised his cries, like the minute-guns, above the roar of wave and weather; and the more superstitious of the men heard, in these sounds, the knell of the *Good Hope*.

Lord Foxham had been laid in a berth, upon a fur cloak. A little lamp burned dim before the Virgin in the bulkhead, and by its glimmer Dick could see the pale countenance and hollow eyes of the hurt man.

'I am sore hurt,' said he. 'Come near to my side, young Shelton; let there be one by me who, at least, is gentle born; for after having lived nobly and richly all the days of my life, this is a sad pass that I should get my hurt in a little ferreting skirmish, and die here, in a foul, cold ship upon the sea, among broken men and churls.'

'Nay, my lord,' said Dick, 'I pray rather to the saints that ye will recover you of your hurt, and come soon and sound ashore.'

'How?' demanded his lordship. 'Come sound ashore? There is, then, a question of it?'

'The ship laboureth – the sea is grievous and contrary,' replied the lad; 'and by what I can learn of my fellow that steereth us, we shall do well, indeed, if we come dryshod to land.'

'Ha!' said the baron, gloomily, 'thus shall every terror attend upon the passage of my soul! Sir, pray rather to live hard, that ye may die easy, than to be fooled and fluted all through life, as to the pipe and tabor, and, in the last hour, be plunged among misfortunes! Howbeit, I have that upon my mind that must not be delayed. We have no priest aboard?'

'None,' replied Dick.

'Here, then, to my secular interests,' resumed Lord Foxham: 'ye must be as good a friend to me dead, as I found you a gallant enemy when I was living. I fall in an evil hour for me, for England, and for them that trusted me. My men are being brought by Hamley – he that was your rival; they will rendezvous in the long room at Holywood; this ring from off my finger will accredit you to represent mine orders; and I shall write, besides, two words upon this paper, bidding Hamley yield to you the damsel. Will ye obey? I know not.'

'But, my lord, what orders?' inquired Dick.

'Ay,' quoth the baron, 'ay – the orders;' and he looked upon Dick with hesitation. 'Are ye Lancaster or York?' he asked, at length.

'I shame to say it,' answered Dick, 'I can scarce clearly answer. But so much I think is certain: since I serve with Ellis Duckworth, I serve the House of York. Well, if that be so, I declare for York.'

'It is well,' returned the other; 'it is exceeding well. For truly, had ye said Lancaster, I wot not for the world what I had done. But sith ye are for York, follow me. I came hither but to watch these lords at Shoreby, while mine excellent young lord, Richard of Gloucester,* prepareth a sufficient force to fall upon and scatter them. I have made me notes of their strength, what watch they keep, and how they lie; and these I was to deliver to my young lord on Sunday, an hour before noon, at St Bride's Cross beside the forest. This tryst I am not like to keep, but I pray you, of courtesy, to keep it in my stead; and see that not pleasure, nor pain, tempest, wound, nor prestilence withhold you from the hour and place, for the welfare of England lieth upon this cast.'

'I do soberly take this upon me,' said Dick. 'In so far as in me lieth, your purpose shall be done.'

'It is good,' said the wounded man. 'My lord duke shall order you farther, and if ye obey him with spirit and good-will, then is your fortune made. Give me the lamp a little nearer to mine eyes, till that I write these words for you.'

He wrote a note 'to his worshipful kinsman, Sir John Hamley;' and then a second, which he left without external superscription.

'This is for the duke,' he said. 'The word is "England and Edward," and the counter, "England and York."'

'And Joanna, my lord?' asked Dick.

* At the date of this story, Richard Crookback could not have been created Duke of Gloucester; but for clearness with the reader's leave, he shall so be called.

'Nay, ye must get Joanna how ye can,' replied the baron. 'I have named you for my choice in both these letters; but ye must get her for yourself, boy. I have tried, as ye see here before you, and have lost my life. More could no man do.'

By this time the wounded man began to be very weary; and Dick, putting the precious papers in his bosom, bade him be of good cheer, and left him to repose.

The day was beginning to break, cold and blue, with flying squalls of snow. Close under the lee of the *Good Hope*, the coast lay in alternate rocky headlands and sandy bays; and further inland the wooded hill-tops of Tunstall showed along the sky. Both the wind and the sea had gone down; but the vessel wallowed deep, and scarce rose upon the waves.

Lawless was still fixed at the rudder; and by this time nearly all the men had crawled on deck, and were now gazing, with blank faces, upon the inhospitable coast.

'Are we going ashore?' asked Dick.

'Ay,' said Lawless, 'unless we get first to the bottom.'

And just then the ship rose so languidly to meet a sea, and the water weltered so loudly in her hold, that Dick involuntarily seized the steersman by the arm.

'By the mass!' cried Dick, as the bows of the *Good Hope* reappeared above the foam, 'I thought we had foundered, indeed; my heart was at my throat.'

In the waist, Greensheve, Hawksley, and the better men of both companies were busy breaking up the deck to build a raft; and these Dick joined himself, working the harder to drown the memory of his predicament. But, even as he worked, every sea that struck the poor ship, and every one of her dull lurches, as she tumbled wallowing among the waves, recalled him with a horrid pang to the immediate proximity of death.

Presently, looking up from his work, he saw that they were close in below a promontory; a piece of ruinous cliff, against the base of which the sea broke white and heavy, almost overplumbed the deck; and, above that again, a house appeared, crowning a down.

Inside the bay, the seas ran gaily, raised the *Good Hope* upon their foam-flecked shoulders, carried her beyond the control of the steersman, and in a moment dropped her with a great concussion on the sand, and began to break over her, half-mast high, and roll her to and fro. Another great wave followed, raised her again, and carried her yet farther in; and then a third succeeded, and left her far inshore of the more dangerous breakers, wedged upon a bank.

'Now, boys,' cried Lawless, 'the saints have had a care of us, indeed. The tide ebbs; let us but sit down and drink a cup of wine, and before half an hour ye may all march me ashore as safe as on a bridge.'

A barrel was broached, and, sitting in what shelter they could find from the flying snow and spray, the shipwrecked company handed the cup around, and sought to warm their bodies and restore their spirits.

Dick, meanwhile, returned to Lord Foxham, who lay in great perplexity and fear, the floor of his cabin washing knee-deep in water, and the lamp, which had been his only light, broken and extinguished by the violence of the blow.

'My lord,' said young Shelton, 'fear not at all; the saints are plainly for us; the seas have cast us high upon a shoal, and as soon as the tide hath somewhat ebbed, we may walk ashore upon our feet.'

It was nearly an hour before the vessel was sufficiently deserted by the ebbing sea, and they could set forth for the land, which appeared dimly before them through a veil of driving snow.

Upon a hillock on one side of their way a party of men lay huddled together, suspiciously observing the movements of the new arrivals.

'They might draw near and offer us some comfort,' Dick remarked.

'Well, an they come not to us, let us even turn aside to them,' said Hawksley. 'The sooner we come to a good fire and a dry bed, the better for my poor lord.'

But they had not moved far in the direction of the hillock before the men, with one consent, rose suddenly to their feet, and poured a flight of well-directed arrows on the shipwrecked company.

'Back! back!' cried his lordship. 'Beware, in Heaven's name, that ye reply not!'

'Nay,' cried Greensheve, pulling an arrow from his leather Jack. 'We are in no posture to fight, it is certain, being drenching wet, dog-weary, and three-parts frozen; but, for the love of old England, what aileth them to shoot thus cruelly on their poor country people in distress?'

'They take us to be French pirates,' answered Lord Foxham. 'In these most troublesome and degenerate days we cannot keep our own shores of England; but our old enemies, whom we once chased on sea and land, do now range at pleasure, robbing and slaughtering and burning. It is the pity and reproach of this poor land.'

The men upon the hillock lay, closely observing them, while they trailed upward from the beach and wound inland among desolate sand-hills; for a mile or so they even hung upon the rear of the march, ready, at a sign, to pour another volley on the weary and dispirited fugitives; and it was only when, striking at length upon a firm high-road, Dick began to call his men to some more martial order, that these jealous guardians of the coast of England silently disappeared among the snow. They had done what they desired; they had protected their own homes and farms, their own families and cattle; and their private interest being thus secured, it mattered not the weight of a straw to any one of them, although the Frenchmen should carry blood and fire to every other parish in the realm of England.

Book IV

THE DISGUISE

CHAPTER ONE

The Den

THE PLACE WHERE DICK HAD struck the line of a high road was not far from Holywood, and within nine or ten miles of Shoreby-on-the-Till; and here, after making sure that they were pursued no longer, the two bodies separated. Lord Foxham's followers departed, carrying their wounded master towards the comfort and security of the great abbey; and Dick, as he saw them wind away and disappear in the thick curtain of the falling snow, was left alone with near upon a dozen outlaws, the last remainder of his troop of volunteers.

Some were wounded; one and all were furious at their ill-success and long exposure; and though they were now too cold and hungry to do more, they grumbled and cast sullen looks upon their leaders. Dick emptied his purse among them, leaving himself nothing; thanked them for the courage they had displayed, though he could have found it more readily in his heart to rate them for poltroonery; and having thus somewhat softened the effect of his prolonged misfortune, despatched them to find their way, either severally or in pairs, to Shoreby and the Goat and Bagpipes.

For his own part, influenced by what he had seen on board of the *Good Hope*, he chose Lawless to be his companion on the walk. The snow was falling, without pause or variation, in one even, blinding cloud; the wind had been strangled, and now blew no longer; and the whole world was blotted out and sheeted down below that silent inundation. There was great danger of wandering by the way and perishing in drifts; and Lawless, keeping half a step in front of his companion, and holding his head forward like a hunting dog upon the scent, inquired his way of every tree, and studied out their path as though he were conning a ship among dangers.

About a mile into the forest they came to a place where several ways met, under a grove of lofty and contorted oaks. Even in the narrow horizon of the falling snow, it was a spot that could not fail to be recognized; and Lawless evidently recognized it with particular delight.

'Now, Master Richard,' said he, 'an y' are not too proud to be the guest of a man who is neither a gentleman by birth nor so much as a good Christian, I can offer you a cup of wine and a good fire to melt the marrow in your frozen bones.'

'Lead on, Will,' answered Dick. 'A cup of wine and a good fire! Nay, I would go a far way round to see them.'

Lawless turned aside under the bare branches of the grove, and, walking resolutely forward for some time, came to a steepish hollow or den, that had now drifted a quarter full of snow. On the verge a great beech-tree hung, precariously rooted; and here the old outlaw, pulling aside some bushy underwood, bodily disappeared into the earth.

The beech had, in some violent gale, been half-uprooted, and had torn up a considerable stretch of turf; and it was under this that old Lawless had dug out his forest hiding-place. The roots served him for rafters, the turf was his thatch; for walls and floor he had his mother the earth. Rude as it was, the hearth in one corner, blackened by fire, and the presence in another of a large oaken chest well fortified with iron, showed it at one glance to be the den of a man, and not the burrow of a digging beast.

Though the snow had drifted at the mouth and sifted in upon the floor of this earth-cavern, yet was the air much warmer than without; and when Lawless had struck a spark, and the dry furze bushes had begun to blaze and crackle on the hearth, the place assumed, even to the eye, an air of comfort and of home.

With a sigh of great contentment Lawless spread his broad hands before the fire, and seemed to breathe the smoke.

'Here, then,' he said, 'is this old Lawless's rabbit-hole; pray Heaven there come no terrier! Far I have rolled hither and thither, and here and about, since that I was fourteen years of mine age and first ran away from mine abbey, with the sacrist's gold chain and a mass-book that I sold for four marks. I have been in England and France and Burgundy, and in Spain, too, on a pilgrimage for my poor soul; and upon the sea, which is no man's country. But here is my place, Master Shelton. This is my native land, this burrow in the earth. Come rain or wind – and whether it's April and the birds all sing, and the blossoms fall about my bed, or whether it's winter, and I sit alone with my good gossip the fire, and robin red-breast twitters in the woods – here is my church and market, my wife and child. It's here I come back to, and it's here, so please the saints, that I would like to die.'

''Tis a warm corner, to be sure,' replied Dick, 'and a pleasant, and a well hid.'

'It had need to be,' returned Lawless, 'for an they found it, Master Shelton, it would break my heart. But here,' he added, burrowing with his stout fingers in the sandy floor, 'here is my wine cellar and ye shall have a flask of excellent strong stingo.'

Sure enough, after but a little digging, he produced a big leathern bottle of about a gallon, nearly three parts full of a very heady and sweet wine; and when they had drunk to each other comradely, and the fire had been replenished and blazed up again, the pair lay at full length, thawing and steaming, and divinely warm.

'Master Shelton,' observed the outlaw, 'y' 'ave had two mischances this last while, and y' are like to lose the maid – do I take it aright?'

'Aright!' returned Dick, nodding his head.

'Well, now,' continued Lawless, 'hear an old fool that hath been nigh-hand everything, 'and seen nigh-hand all! Ye go too much on other people's errands, Master Dick. Ye go on Ellis's; but he desireth rather the death of Sir Daniel. Ye go on Lord Foxham's; well – the saints preserve him! – doubtless he meaneth well. But go ye upon your own, good Dick. Come right to the maid's side. Court her, lest that she forget you. Be ready; and when the chance shall come, off with her at the saddlebow.'

'Ay, but, Lawless, beyond doubt she is now in Sir Daniel's own mansion,' answered Dick.

'Thither, then, go we,' replied the outlaw.

Dick stared at him.

'Nay, I mean it,' nodded Lawless. 'And if y' are of so little faith, and stumble at a word, see here!'

And the outlaw, taking a key from about his neck, opened the oak chest, and dipping and groping deep among its contents, produced first a friar's robe, and next a girdle of rope; and then a huge rosary of wood, heavy enough to be counted as a weapon.

'Here,' he said, 'is for you. On with them!'

And then, when Dick had clothed himself in this clerical disguise, Lawless produced some colours and a pencil, and proceeded, with the greatest cunning, to disguise his face. The eyebrows he thickened and produced; to the moustache, which was yet hardly visible, he rendered a like service; while, by a few lines around his eye, he changed the expression and increased the apparent age of this young monk.

'Now,' he resumed, 'when I have done the like, we shall make as bonny a pair of friars as the eye could wish. Boldly to Sir Daniel's we shall go, and there be hospitably welcome for the love of Mother Church.'

'And how, dear Lawless,' cried the lad, 'shall I repay you?'

'Tut, brother,' replied the outlaw, 'I do naught but for my pleasure. Mind not for me. I am one, by the mass, that mindeth for himself. When that I lack, I have a long tongue and a voice like the monastery bell – I do ask, my son; and where asking faileth, I do most usually take.'

The old rogue made a humorous grimace; and although Dick was displeased to lie under so great favours to so equivocal a personage, he was yet unable to restrain his mirth.

With that, Lawless returned to the big chest, and was soon similarly disguised; but below his gown, Dick wondered to observe him conceal a sheaf of black arrows.

'Wherefore do ye that?' asked the lad. 'Wherefore arrows, when ye take no bow?'

'Nay,' replied Lawless, lightly, "tis like there will be heads broke – not to says backs – ere you and I win sound from where we're going to; and if any fall, I would our fellowship should come by the credit on't. A black arrow is the seal of our abbey; it showeth you who writ the bill.'

'An ye prepare so carefully,' said Dick, 'I have here some papers that, for mine own sake, and the interest of those that trusted me, were better left behind than found upon my body. Where shall I conceal them, Will?'

'Nay,' replied Lawless, 'I will go forth into the wood and whistle me three verses of a song; meanwhile, do you bury them where ye please, and smooth the sand upon the place.'

'Never!' cried Richard. 'I trust you, man. I were base indeed if I not trusted you.'

'Brother, y' are but a child,' replied the old outlaw, pausing and turning his face upon Dick from the threshold of the den. 'I am a kind old Christian, and no traitor to men's blood, and no sparer of mine own in a friend's jeopardy. But, fool, child, I am a thief by trade and birth and habit. If my bottle were empty and my mouth dry, I would rob you, dear child, as sure as I love, honour, and admire your parts and person! Can it be clearer spoken? No.'

And he stumped forth through the bushes with a snap of his big fingers.

Dick, thus left alone, after a wondering thought upon the inconsistencies of his companion's character, hastily produced reviewed, and buried his papers. One only he reserved to carry along with him, since it in nowise compromised his friends, and yet might serve him, in a pinch, against Sir Daniel. That was the knight's own letter to Lord Wensleydale, sent by Throgmorton, on the morrow of the defeat at Risingham, and found next day by Dick upon the body of the messenger.

Then, treading down the embers of the fire, Dick left the den, and rejoined the old outlaw, who stood awaiting him under the leafless oaks, and was already beginning to be powdered by the falling snow. Each looked upon the other, and each laughed, so thorough and so droll was the disguise.

'Yet I would it were but summer and a clear day,' grumbled the outlaw, 'that I might see myself in the mirror of a pool. There be many of Sir Daniel's men that know me; and if we fell to be recognized, there might be two words for you, my brother, but as for me, in a paternoster while, I should be kicking in a rope's-end.'

Thus they set forth together along the road to Shoreby, which, in this part of its course, kept near along the margin of the forest, coming forth, from time to time, in the open country, and passing beside poor folks' houses and small farms.

Presently at sight of one of these, Lawless pulled up.

'Brother Martin,' he said, in a voice capitally disguised, and suited to his monkish robe, 'let us enter and seek alms from these poor sinners. *Pax vobiscum!* Ay,' he added, in his voice, "tis as I feared; I have somewhat lost the whine of it; and by your leave good Master Shelton, ye must suffer me to practise in these country places, before that I risk my fat neck by entering Sir Daniel's. But look ye a little, what an excellent thing it is to be a Jack-of-all-trades! An I had not been a shipman, ye had infallibly gone down in the *Good Hope*; an I had not been a thief, I could not have painted me your face; and but that I had been a Grey Friar, and sung loud in the choir, and ate hearty at the board, I could not have carried this disguise, but the very dogs would have spied us out and barked at us for shams.'

He was by this time close to the window of the farm, and he rose on his tip-toes and peeped in.

'Nay,' he cried, 'better and better. We shall here try our false faces with a vengeance, and have a merry just on Brother Capper to boot.'

And so saying he opened the door and led the way into the house.

Three of their own company sat at the table, greedily eating. Their daggers, stuck beside them in the board, and the black and menacing looks which they continued to shower upon the people of the house, proved that they owed their entertainment rather to force than favour. On the two monks, who now, with a sort of humble dignity, entered the kitchen of the farm, they seemed to turn with a particular resentment; and one – it was John Capper in person – who seemed to play the leading part, instantly and rudely ordered them away.

'We want no beggars here!' he cried.

But another – although he was as far from recognizing Dick and Lawless – inclined to more moderate counsels.

'Not so,' he cried. 'We be strong men, and take: these be weak, and crave; but in the latter end these shall be uppermost and we below. Mind him not, my father; but come, drink of my cup, and give me a benediction.'

'Y' are men of a light mind, carnal and accursed,' said the monk. 'Now, may

the saints forbid that ever I should drink with such companions! But here, for
the pity I bear to sinners, here I do leave you a blessed relic, the which, for your
soul's interest, I bid you kiss and cherish.'

So far Lawless thundered upon them like a preaching friar; but with these
words he drew from under his robe a black arrow, tossed it on the board in front
of the three startled outlaws, turned in the same instant, and, taking Dick along
with him, was out of the room and out of sight among the falling snow before
they had time to utter a word or move a finger.

'So,' he said, 'we have proved our false faces, Master Shelton. I will now
adventure my poor carcase where ye please.'

'Good!' returned Richard. 'It irks me to be doing. Set we on for Shoreby!'

CHAPTER TWO

'In mine enemies' house'

SIR DANIEL'S RESIDENCE in Shoreby was a tall, commodious, plastered mansion,
framed in carven oak, and covered by a low-pitched roof of thatch. To the back
there stretched a garden, full of fruit-trees, alleys, and thick arbours, and
overlooked from the far end by the tower of the abbey church.

The house might contain, upon a pinch, the retinue of a greater person than
Sir Daniel; but even now it was filled with hubbub. The court rang with arms
and horse-shoe-iron; the kitchen roared with cookery like a bees'-hive;
minstrels, and the players of instruments, and the cries of tumblers, sounded
from the hall. Sir Daniel, in his profusion, in the gaiety and gallantry of his
establishment, rivalled with Lord Shoreby, and eclipsed Lord Risingham.

All guests were made welcome. Minstrels, tumblers, players of chess, the
sellers of relics, medicines, perfumes and enchantments, and along with these
every sort of priest, friar, or pilgrim, were made welcome to the lower table, and
slept together in the ample lofts, or on the bare boards of the long dining-hall.

On the afternoon following the wreck of the *Good Hope*, the buttery, the
kitchens, the stables, the covered cartshed that surrounded two sides of the
court, were all crowded by idle people, partly belonging to Sir Daniel's
establishment, and attired in his livery of murrey and blue, partly nondescript
strangers attracted to the town by greed, and received by the knight through
policy, and because it was the fashion of the time.

The snow, which still fell without interruption, the extreme chill of the air,
and the approach of night, combined to keep them under shelter. Wine, ale,
and money were all plentiful; many sprawled gambling in the straw of the barn,
many were still drunken from the noontide meal. To the eye of a modern it
would have looked like the sack of a city; to the eye of a contemporary it was like
any other rich and noble household at a festive season.

Two monks – a young and an old – had arrived late, and were now warming themselves at a bonfire in a corner of the shed. A mixed crowd surrounded them – jugglers, mountebanks, and soldiers: and with these the elder of the two had soon engaged so brisk a conversation, and exchanged so many loud guffaws and country witticisms, that the group momentarily increased in number.

The younger companion, in whom the reader has already recognized Dick Shelton, sat from the first somewhat backward, and gradually drew himself away. He listened, indeed, closely, but he opened not his mouth; and by the grave expression of his countenance, he made but little account of his companion's pleasantries.

At last his eye, which travelled continually to and fro, and kept a guard upon all the entrances of the house, lit upon a little procession entering by the main gate and crossing the court in an oblique direction. Two ladies, muffled in thick furs, led the way, and were followed by a pair of waiting-women and four stout men-at-arms. The next moment they had disappeared within the house; and Dick, slipping through the crowd of loiterers in the shed, was already giving hot pursuit.

'The taller of these twain was Lady Brackley,' he thought; 'and where Lady Brackley is, Joan will not be far.'

At the door of the house the four men-at-arms had ceased to follow, and the ladies were now mounting the stairway of polished oak, under no better escort than that of the two waiting-women. Dick followed close behind. It was already the dusk of the day; and in the house the darkness of the night had almost come. On the stair-landings torches flared in iron holders; down the long tapestried corridors a lamp burned by every door. And where the door stood open, Dick could look in upon arras-covered walls, and rush-bescattered floors, glowing in the light of the wood-fires.

Two floors were passed and at every landing the younger and shorter of the two ladies had looked back keenly at the monk. He, keeping his eyes lowered, and affecting the demure manners that suited his disguise, had but seen her once, and was unaware that he had attracted her attention. And now, on the third floor, the party separated, the younger lady continuing to ascend alone, the other, followed by the waiting-maids, descending the corridor to the right.

Dick mounted with a swift foot, and holding to the corner, thrust forth his head and followed the three women with his eyes. Without turning or looking behind them, they continued to descend the corridor.

'It is right well,' thought Dick. 'Let me but know my Lady Brackley's chamber, and it will go hard an I find not Dame Hatch upon an errand.'

And just then a hand was laid upon his shoulder, and, with a bound and a choked cry, he turned to grapple his assailant.

He was somewhat abashed to find, in the person whom he had so roughly seized, the short young lady in the furs. She, on her part, was shocked and terrified beyond expression, and hung trembling in his grasp. 'Madam,' said Dick, releasing her, 'I cry you a thousand pardons; but I have no eyes behind, and, by the mass, I could not tell ye were a maid.'

The girl continued to look at him, but, by this time, terror began to be succeeded by surprise, and surprise by suspicion. Dick, who could read these changes on her face, became alarmed for his own safety in that hostile house.

'Fair maid,' he said, affecting easiness, 'suffer me to kiss your hand, in token ye forgive my roughness, and I will even go.

'Y' are a strange monk, young sir,' returned the young lady, looking him both boldly and shrewdly in the face; 'and now that my first astonishment hath somewhat passed away, I can spy the layman in each word you utter. What do ye here? Why are ye thus sacrilegiously tricked out? Come ye in peace or war? And why spy ye after Lady Brackley like a thief?'

'Madam,' quoth Dick, 'of one thing I pray you to be very sure: I am no thief. And even if I come here in war, as in some degree I do, I make no war upon fair maids, and I hereby entreat them to copy me so far, and to leave me be. For, indeed, fair mistress, cry out – if such be your pleasure – cry but once, and say what ye have seen, and the poor gentleman before you is merely a dead man. I cannot think ye would be cruel,' added Dick; and taking the girl's hand gently in both of his, he looked at her with courteous admiration.

'Are ye then a spy – a Yorkist?' asked the maid.

'Madam,' he replied, 'I am indeed a Yorkist, and in some sort, a spy. But that which bringeth me into this house, the same which will win for me the pity and interest of your kind heart, is neither of York nor Lancaster. I will wholly put my life in your discretion. I am a lover, and my name——'

But here the young lady clapped her hand suddenly upon Dick's mouth, looked hastly up and down and east and west, and, seeing the coast clear, began to drag the young man, with great strength and vehemence, upstairs.

'Hush!' she said, 'and come. 'Shalt talk hereafter.'

Somewhat bewildered, Dick suffered himself to be pulled upstairs, bustled along a corridor, and thrust suddenly into a chamber, lit, like so many of the others, by a blazing log upon the hearth.

'Now,' said the young lady, forcing him down upon a stool, 'sit ye there and attend my sovereign good pleasure. I have life and death over you, and I will not scruple to abuse my power. Look to yourself; y' 'ave cruelly mauled my arm. He knew not I was a maid, quoth he! Had he known I was a maid, he had ta'ken his belt to me, forsooth!'

And with these words she whipped out of the room, and left Dick gaping with wonder, and not very sure if he were dreaming or awake.

'Ta'en my belt to her! he repeated. 'Ta'en my belt to her!' And the recollection of that evening in the forest flowed back upon his mind, and he once more saw Matcham's wincing body and beseeching eyes.

And then he was recalled to the dangers of the present. In the next room he heard a stir, as of a person moving; then followed a sigh, which sounded strangely near; and then the rustle of skirts and tap of feet once more began. As he stood hearkening, he saw the arras wave along the wall; there was the sound of a door being opened, the hangings divided, and, lamp in hand, Joanna Sedley entered the apartment.

She was attired in costly stuffs of deep and warm colours, such as befit the winter and the snow. Upon her head, her hair had been gathered together and became her as a crown. And she, who had seemed so little and so awkward in the attire of Matcham, was now tall like a young willow, and swam across the floor as though she scorned the drudgery of walking.

Without a start, without a tremor, she raised her lamp and looked at the young monk.

'What make ye here, good brother?' she inquired 'Ye are doubtless ill-directed. Whom do ye require?' And she set her lamp upon the bracket.

'Joanna,' said Dick; and then his voice failed him. 'Joanna,' he began again, 'ye said ye loved me; and the more fool I, but I believed it!'

'Dick!' she cried. 'Dick!'

And then, to the wonder of the lad, this beautiful and tall young lady made but one step of it, and threw her arms about his neck and gave him a hundred kisses all in one.

'Oh, the fool fellow!' she cried. 'Oh, dear Dick! Oh, if ye could see yourself! Alack!' she added, pausing, 'I have spoilt you, Dick! I have knocked some of the paint off. But that can be mended. What cannot be mended, Dick – or I much fear it cannot! – is my marriage with Lord Shoreby.'

'Is it decided, then?' asked the lad.

'Tomorrow, before noon, Dick, in the abbey church,' she answered, 'John Matcham and Joanna Sedley both shall come to a right miserable end. There is no help in tears, or I could weep mine eyes out. I have not spared myself to pray, but Heaven frowns on my petition. And, dear Dick – good Dick – but that ye can get me forth of this house before the morning, we must even kiss and say good-bye.'

'Nay,' said Dick, 'not I; I will never say that word. 'Tis like despair; but while there's life, Joanna, there is hope. Yet will I hope. Ay, by the mass, and triumph! Look ye, now, when ye were but a name to me, did I not follow – did I not rouse good men – did I not stake my life upon the quarrel? And now that I have seen you for what ye are – the fairest maid and stateliest of England – think ye I would turn? – if the deep sea were there, I would straight through it; if the way were full of lions, I would scatter them like mice.'

'Ay,' she said, dryly, 'ye make a great ado about a sky-blue robe!'

'Nay, Joan,' protested Dick, ''tis not alone the robe. But, lass, ye were disguised. Here am I disguised; and, to the proof, do I not cut a figure of fun – a right fool's figure.'

'Ay, Dick, an' that ye do!' she answered, smiling.

'Well, then!' he returned, triumphant. 'So was it with you, poor Matcham, in the forest. In sooth, ye were a wench to laugh at. But now!'

So they ran on, holding each other by both hands, exchanging smiles and lovely looks, and melting minutes into seconds; and so they might have continued all night long. But presently there was a noise behind them; and they were aware of the short young lady, with her finger on her lips.

'Saints!' she cried, 'but what a noise ye keep! Can ye not speak in compass? And now, Joanna, my fair maid of the woods, what will ye give your gossip for bringing you your sweetheart?'

Joanna ran to her, by way of answer, and embraced her fierily.

'And you, sir,' added the young lady, 'what do ye give me?'

'Madam,' said Dick, 'I would fain offer to pay you in the same money.'

'Come, then,' said the lady, 'it is permitted you.'

But Dick, blushing like a peony, only kissed her hand.

'What ails ye at my face, fair sir?' she inquired, curtseying to the very ground; and, then, when Dick had at length and most tepidly embraced her, 'Joanna,' she added, 'your sweetheart is very backward under your eyes; but I warrant you, when first we met, he was more ready. I am all black and blue, wench; trust me never, if I be not black and blue! And now,' she continued, 'have ye said your sayings? for I must speedily dismiss the paladin.'

But at this they both cried out that they had said nothing, that the night was still very young, and that they would not be separated so early.

'And supper?' asked the young lady. 'Must we not go down to supper?'

'Nay, to be sure!' cried Joan. 'I had forgotten.'

'Hide me, then,' said Dick, 'put me behind the arras, shut me in a chest, or what ye will, so that I may be here on your return. Indeed, fair lady,' he added, 'bear this in mind, that we are sore bested, and may never look upon each other's face from this night forward till we die.'

At this the young lady melted; and when, a little after, the bell summoned Sir Daniel's household to the board, Dick was planted very stiffly against the wall, at a place where a division in the tapestry permitted him to breathe the more freely, and even to see into the room.

He had not been long in this position when he was somewhat strangly disturbed. The silence in that upper storey of the house was only broken by the flickering of the flames and the hissing of a green log in the chimney; but presently, to Dick's strained hearing, there came the sound of some one walking with extreme precaution; and soon after the door opened, and a little black-faced, dwarfish fellow, in Lord Shoreby's colours, pushed first his head and then his crooked body into the chamber. His mouth was open, as though to hear the better; and his eyes, which were very bright, flitted restlessly and swiftly to and fro. He went round and round the room, striking here and there upon the hangings: but Dick, by a miracle escaped his notice. Then he looked below the furniture, and examined the lamp; and at last, with an air of cruel disappoint-ment, was preparing to go away as silently as he had come, when down he dropped upon his knees, picked up something from among the rushes on the floor, examined it, and, with every signal of delight, concealed it in the wallet at his belt.

Dick's heart sank, for the object in question was a tassel from his own girdle; and it was plain to him that this dwarfish spy, who took a malign delight in his employment, would lose no time in bearing it to his master, the baron. He was half-tempted to throw aside the arras, fall upon the scoundrel, and, at the risk of his life, remove the tell-tale token. And while he was still hesitating, a new cause of concern was added. A voice, hoarse and broken by drink, began to be audible from the stair; and presently after, uneven, wandering, and heavy footsteps sounded without along the passage.

'What make ye here, my merry men, among the greenwood shaws?' sand the voice. 'What make ye here? Hey! sots, what may ye here?' it added, with a rattle of drunken laughter; and then once more breaking into song:

'If ye should drink the clary wine,
Fat Friar John, ye friend o'mine—
If I should eat, and ye should drink,
Who shall sing the mass, d'ye think?'

Lawless, alas! rolling drunk, was wandering the house, seeking for a corner wherein to slumber off the effect of his potations. Dick inwardly raged. The spy, at first terrified, had grown reassured as he found he had to deal with an intoxicated man, and now, with a movement of cat-like rapidity, slipped from the chamber, and was gone from Richard's eyes.

What was to be done? If he lost touch of Lawless for the night he was left impotent, whether to plan or carry forth Joanna's rescue. If, on the other hand, he dared to address the drunken outlaw, the spy might still be lingering within sight, and the most fatal consequences ensue.

It was, nevertheless, upon this last hazard that Dick decided. Slipping from behind the tapestry, he stood ready in the doorway of the chamber, with a warning hand upraised. Lawless, flushed crimson, with his eyes injected, vacillating on his feet, drew still unsteadily nearer. At last he hazily caught sight of his commander, and, in despite of Dick's imperious signals, hailed him instantly and loudly by his name.

Dick leaped upon and shook the drunkard furiously.

'Beast!' he hissed – 'beast, and no man! It is worse than treachery to be so witless. We may all be shent for thy sotting.'

But Lawless only laughed and staggered, and tried to clap young Shelton on the back.

And just then Dick's quick ear caught a rapid brushing in the arras. He leaped towards the sound, and the next moment a piece of the wall-hanging had been torn down, and Dick and the spy were sprawling together in its folds. Over and over they rolled, grappling for each other's throat, and still baffled by the arras, and still silent in their deadly fury. But Dick was by much the stronger, and soon the spy lay prostrate under his knee, and, with a single stroke of the long poniard, ceased to breathe.

CHAPTER THREE

The Dead Spy

THROUGHOUT THIS FURIOUS and rapid passage, Lawless had looked on helplessly, and even when all was over, and Dick, already re-arisen to his feet, was listening with the most passionate attention to the distant bustle in the lower storeys of the house, the old outlaw was still wavering on his legs like a shrub in a breeze of wind, and still stupidly staring on the face of the dead man.

'It is well,' said Dick, at length; 'they have not heard us, praise the saints! But, now, what shall I do with this poor spy? At least, I will take my tassel from his wallet.'

So saying, Dick opened the wallet; within he found a few pieces of money, the tassel, and a letter addressed to Lord Wensleydale, and sealed with my Lord Shoreby's seal. The name awoke Dick's recollection; and he instantly broke the wax and read the contents of the letter. It was short, but, to Dick's delight, it gave evident proof that Lord Shoreby was treacherously corresponding with the House of York.

The young fellow usually carried his ink-horn and implements about him, and so now, bending a knee beside the body of the dead spy, he was able to write these words upon a corner of the paper:

My Lord of Shoreby, ye that writt the letter, wot ye why your man is ded? But let me rede you, marry not.

JON AMEND-ALL

He laid this paper on the breast of the corpse; and then Lawless, who had been looking on upon these last manoeuvres with some flickering returns of intelligence, suddenly drew a black arrow from below his robe, and therewith pinned the paper in its place. The sight of this disrespect, or, as it almost seemed, cruelty to the dead, drew a cry of horror from young Shelton; but the old outlaw only laughed.

'Nay, I will have the credit for mine order,' he hiccupped. 'My jolly boys must have the credit on't – the credit, brother;' and then, shutting his eyes tight and opening his mouth like a precentor, he began to thunder, in a formidable voice:

'If ye should drink the clary wine——'

'Peace, sot!' cried Dick, and thrust him hard against the wall. 'In two words – if so be that such a man can understand me who hath more wine that wit in him – in two words, and, a-Mary's name, begone out of this house, where, if ye continue to abide, ye will not only hang yourself, but me also! Faith, then, up foot! be yare, or, by the mass, I may forget that I am in some sort your captain, and in some your debtor! Go!'

The sham monk was now, in some degree, recovering the use of his intelligence; and the ring in Dick's voice, and the glitter in Dick's eye, stamped home the meaning of his words.

'By the mass,' cried Lawless, 'an I be not wanted, I can go;' and he turned tipsily along the corridor and proceeded to flounder downstairs, lurching against the wall.

So soon he was out of sight, Dick returned to his hiding-place, resolutely fixed to see the matter out. Wisdom, indeed, moved him to be gone; but love and curiosity were stronger.

Time passed slowly for the young man, bolt upright behind the arras. The fire in the room began to die down, and the lamp to burn low and to smoke. And still there was no word of the return of anyone to these upper quarters of the house; still the faint hum and clatter of the supper party sounded from far below; and still, under the thick fall of the snow, Shoreby town lay silent upon every side.

At length, however, feet and voices began to draw near upon the stair; and presently after several of Sir Daniel's guests arrived upon the landing, and, turning down the corridor, beheld the torn arras and the body of the spy.

Some ran forward and some back, and all together began to cry aloud.

At the sound of their cries, guests, men-at-arms, ladies, servants, and, in a word, all the inhabitants of that great house, came flying from every direction, and began to join their voices to the tumult.

Soon a way was cleared, and Sir Daniel came forth in person, followed by the bridegroom of the morrow, my Lord Shoreby.

'My lord,' said Sir Daniel, 'have I not told you of this knave Black Arrow? To the proof, behold it! There it stands, and, by the rood, my gossip, in a man of yours, or one that stole your colours!'

'In good sooth, it was a man of mine,' replied Lord Shoreby, hanging back. 'I would I had more such. He was keen as a beagle and secret as a mole.'

'Ay, gossip, truly?' asked Sir Daniel, keenly. 'And what came he smelling up so many stairs in my poor mansion? But he will smell no more.'

'An't please you, Sir Daniel,' said one, 'here is a paper written upon with some matter, pinned upon his breast.'

'Give it me, arrow and all,' said the knight. And when he had taken into his hand the shaft, he continued for some time to gaze upon it in a sullen musing. 'Ay,' he said addressing Lord Shoreby, 'here is a hate that followeth hard and close upon my heels. This black stick, or its just likeness, shall yet bring me down. And, gossip, suffer a plain knight to counsel you; and if these hounds begin to wind you, flee! 'Tis like a sickness – it still hangeth, hangeth upon the limbs. But let us see what they have written. It is as I though, my lord; y' are marked, like an old oak, by the woodman; tomorrow or next day, by will come the axe. But what wrote ye in a letter?'

Lord Shoreby snatched the paper from the arrow, read it, crumpled it between his hands, and, overcoming the reluctance which had hitherto withheld him from approaching, threw himself on his knees beside the body and eagerly groped in the wallet.

He rose to his feet with a somewhat unsettled countenance.

'Gossip,' he said, 'I have indeed lost a letter here that much imported; and could I lay my hand upon the knave that took it, he should incontinently grace a halter. But let us, first of all, secure the issues of the house. Here is enough harm already, by St George!'

Sentinels were posted close around the house and garden; a sentinel on every landing of the stair, a whole troop in the main entrance hall; and yet another about the bonfire in the shed. Sir Daniel's followers were supplemented by Lord Shoreby's; there was thus no lack of men or weapons to make the house secure, or to entrap a lurking enemy, should one be there.

Meanwhile, the body of the spy was carried out through the falling snow and deposited in the abbey church.

It was not until these dispositions had been taken, and all had returned to a decorous silence, that the two girls drew Richard Shelton from his place of concealment, and made a full report to him of what had passed. He, upon his side, recounted the visit of the spy, his dangerous discovery, and speedy end.

Joanna leaned back very faint against the curtained wall.

'It will avail but little,' she said. 'I shall be wed tomorrow, in the morning, after all!'

'What!' cried her friend. 'And here is our paladin that driveth lions like mice! Ye have little faith, of a surety. But come, friend lion-driver, give us some comfort; speak, and let us hear bold counsels.'

Dick was confounded to be thus outfaced with his own exaggerated words; but though he coloured, he still spoke stoutly.

'Truly,' said he, 'we are in straits. Yet, could I but win out of this house for half an hour, I do honestly tell myself that all might still go well; and for the marriage, it should be prevented.'

'And for the lions,' mimicked the girl, 'they shall be driven.'

'I crave your excuse,' said Dick. 'I speak not now in any boasting humour, but rather as one inquiring after help or counsel; for if I get not forth of this house through these sentinels, I can do less than naught. Take me, I pray you, rightly.'

'Why said ye he was rustic, Joan?' the girl inquired. 'I warrant he hath a tongue in his head; ready, soft, and bold is his speach at pleasure. What would ye more?'

'Nay,' sighed Joanna, with a smile, 'they have changed me my friend Dick, 'tis sure enough. When I beheld him, he was rough indeed. But it matters little; there is no help for my hard case, and I must still be Lady Shoreby!'

'Nay, then,' said Dick, 'I will even make the adventure. A friar is not much regarded; and if I found a good fairy to lead me up, I may find another belike to carry me down. How call they the name of this spy?'

'Rutter,' said the young lady; 'and an excellent good name to call him by. But how mean ye, lion-driver? What is in your mind to do?'

'To offer boldly to go forth,' returned Dick; 'and if any stop me to keep an unchanged countenance, and say I go to pray for Rutter. They will be praying over his poor clay even now.'

'The device is somewhat simple,' replied the girl, 'yet it may hold.'

'Nay,' said young Shelton, 'it is no device, but mere boldness, which serveth often better in great straits.'

'Ye say true,' she said. 'Well, go, a-Mary's name, and may heaven speed you! Ye leave here a poor maid that loves you entirely, and another that is most heartily your friend. Be wary, for their sakes, and make not shipwreck of your safety.'

'Ay,' added Joanna, 'go, Dick. Ye run no more peril, whether ye go or stay. Go; ye take my heart with you; the saints defend you!'

Dick passed the first sentry with so assured a countenance that the fellow merely fidgeted and stared; but at the second landing the man carried his spear across and bade him name his business.

'Pax vobiscum,' answered Dick. 'I go to pray over the body of this poor Rutter.'

'Like enough,' returned the sentry; 'but to go alone is not permitted you.' He leaned over the oaken balusters and whistled shrill. 'One cometh!' he cried; and then motioned Dick to pass.

At the foot of the stair he found the guard afoot and awaiting his arrival; and when he had once more repeated his story, the commander of the post ordered four men out to accompany him to the church.

'Let him not slip, my lads,' he said. 'Bring him to Sir Oliver, on your lives!'

The door was then opened; one of the men took Dick by either arm, another marched ahead with a link, and the fourth, with bent bow and the arrow on the string, brought up the rear. In this order they proceeded through the garden, under the thick darkness of the night and the scattering snow, and drew near to the dimly-illuminated windows of the abbey church.

At the western portal a picket of archers stood, taking what shelter they could find in the hollow of the arched doorways, and all powdered with the snow; and it was not until Dick's conductors had exchanged a word with these, that they were suffered to pass forth and enter the nave of the sacred edifice.

The church was doubtfully lighted by the tapers upon the great altar, and by a lamp or two that swung from the arched roof before the private chapels of illustrious families. In the midst of the choir the dead spy lay, his limbs piously composed, upon a bier.

A hurried mutter of prayer sounded along the arches; cowled figures knelt in the stalls of the choir, and on the steps of the high altar a priest in pontifical vestments celebrated mass.

Upon this fresh entrance, one of the cowled figures arose, and coming down the steps which elevated the level of the choir above that of the nave, demanded from the leader of the four men what business brought him to the church. Out of respect for the service and the dead, they spoke in guarded tones; but the echoes of that huge, empty building caught up their words, and hollowly repeated and repeated them along the aisles.

'A monk!' he returned Sir Oliver (for he it was), when he had heard the report of the archer. 'My brother, I looked not for your coming,' he added, turning to young Shelton. 'In all civility, who are ye? and at whose instance do ye join your supplications to ours?'

Dick, keeping his cowl about his face, signed to Sir Oliver to move a pace or two aside from the archers; and, so soon as the priest had done so, 'I cannot hope to deceive you, sir,' he said. 'My life is in your hands.'

Sir Oliver violently started; his stout cheeks grew pale, and for a space he was silent.

'Richard,' he said, 'what brings you here, I know not; but I much misdoubt it to be evil. Nevertheless, for the kindness that was, I would not willingly deliver you to harm. Ye shall sit all night beside me in the stalls: ye shall sit there till my Lord of Shoreby be married, and the party gone safe home; and if all goeth well, and ye have planned no evil, in the end ye shall go whither ye will. But if your purpose be bloody, it shall return upon your head. Amen!'

And the priest devoutly crossed himself, and turned and louted to the altar.

With that, he spoke a few words more to the soldiers, and taking Dick by the hand, led him up to the choir, and placed him in the stall beside his own, where, for mere decency, the lad had instantly to kneel and appear to be busy with his devotions.

His mind and his eyes, however, were continually wandering. Three of the soldiers, he observed, instead of returning to the house, had got them quietly into a point of vantage in the aisle; and he could not doubt that they had done so by Sir Oliver's command. Here, then, he was trapped. Here he must spend the night in the ghostly glimmer and shadow of the church, and looking on the pale face of him he slew; and here, in the morning he must see his sweetheart married to another man before his eyes.

But, for all that, he obtained a command upon his mind, and built himself up in patience to await the issue.

CHAPTER FOUR

In the Abbey Church

IN SHOREBY ABBEY CHURCH the prayers were kept up all night without cessation, now with the singing of psalms, now with a note or two upon the bell.

Rutter, the spy, was nobly waked. There he lay, meanwhile, as they had arranged him, his dead hands crossed upon his bosom, his dead eyes staring on the roof; and hard by, in the stall, the lad who had slain him waited, in sore disquietude, the coming of the morning.

Once only, in the course of the hours, Sir Oliver leaned across to his captive.

'Richard,' he whispered, 'my son, if ye mean me evil, I will certify, on my soul's welfare, ye design upon an innocent man. Sinful in the eye of Heaven I do declare myself! but sinful as against you I am not neither have been ever.'

'My father,' returned Dick, in the same tone of voice, 'trust me, I design nothing; but as for your innocence, I may not forget that ye cleared yourself but lamely.'

'A man may be innocently guilty,' replied the priest. 'He may be set blindfolded upon a mission, ignorant of its true scope. So it was with me. I did decoy your father to his death; but as Heaven sees us in this sacred place, I knew not what I did.'

'It may be,' returned Dick. 'But see what a strange web ye have woven, that I should be, at this hour, at once your prisoner and your judge; that ye should both threaten my days and deprecate your anger. Methinks, if ye had been all your life a true man and good priest, ye would neither thus fear nor thus detest me. And now to your prayers. I do obey you, since needs must; but I will not be burthened with your company.'

The priest uttered a sigh so heavy that it had almost touched the lad into some sentiment of pity, and he bowed his head upon his hands like a man borne down below a weight of care. He joined no longer in the psalms; but Dick could hear the beads rattle through his fingers and the prayers a-pattering between his teeth.

Yet a little, and the grey of the morning began to struggle through the painted casements of the church, and to put to shame the glimmer of the tapers. The light slowly broadened and brightened, and presently through the south-eastern clerestories a flush of rosy sunlight flickered on the walls. The storm was over; the great clouds had disburdened their snow and fled farther on and the new day was breaking on a merry winter landscape sheathed in white.

A bustle of church officers followed; the bier was carried forth to the deadhouse, and the stains of blood were cleansed from off the tiles, that no such ill-omened spectacle should disgrace the marriage of Lord Shoreby. At the same time, the very ecclesiastics who had been so dismally engaged all night began to put on morning faces, to do honour to the merrier ceremony which was about to follow. And further to announce the coming of the day, the pious of the town began to assemble and fall to prayer before their favourite shrines, or wait their turn at the confessionals.

Favoured by this stir, it was of course easily possible for any man to avoid the vigilance of Sir Daniel's sentries at the door; and presently Dick, looking about him wearily, caught the eye of no less a person than Will Lawless, still in his monk's habit.

The outlaw, at the same moment, recognized his leader, and privily signed to him with hand and eye.

Now, Dick was far from having forgiven the old rogue his most untimely drunkenness, but he had no desire to involve him in his own predicament; and he signalled back to him, as plain as he was able, to begone.

Lawless, as though he had understood, disappeared at once behind a pillar, and Dick breathed again.

What, then, was his dismay to feel himself plucked by the sleeve and to find the old robber installed beside him, upon the next seat, and, to all appearance, plunged in his devotions!

Instantly Sir Oliver arose from his place, and, gliding behind the stalls, made for the soldiers in the aisle. If the priest's suspicions had been so lightly wakened, the harm was already done, and Lawless a prisoner in the church.

'Move not,' whispered Dick. 'We are in the plaguiest pass, thanks, before all things, to thy swinishness of yestereven. When ye saw me here, so strangely seated, where I have neither right nor interest, what a murrain! could ye not smell harm and get ye gone from evil?'

'Nay,' returned Lawless, 'I thought ye had heard from Ellis, and were here on duty.'

'Ellis!' echoed Dick. 'Is Ellis then returned?'

'For sure,' replied the outlaw. 'He came last night, and belted me sore for being in wine – so there ye are avenged, my master. A furious man is Ellis Duckworth! He hath ridden me hot-spur from Craven to prevent this marriage; and, Master Dick, ye know the way of him – do so he will!'

'Nay, then,' returned Dick, with composure, 'you and I, my poor brother, are dead men; for I sit here a prisoner under suspicion, and my neck was to answer for this very marriage that he purposeth to mar. I had a fair choice, by the rood! to lose my sweetheart or else lose my life! Well, the cast is thrown – it is to be my life.'

'By the mass,' cried Lawless, half arising, 'I am gone!'

But Dick had his hand at once upon his shoulder.

'Friend Lawless, sit ye still,' he said. 'An ye have eyes, look yonder at the corner by the chancel arch; see ye not that, even upon the motion of your rising, yon armed men are up and ready to intercept you? Yield ye, friend. Ye were bold aboard ship, when ye thought to die a sea-death; be bold again, now that y' are to die presently upon the gallows.'

'Master Dick,' gasped Lawless, 'the thing hath come upon me somewhat of the suddenest. But give me a moment till I fetch my breath again; and, by the mass, I will be as stout-hearted as yourself.'

'Here is my bold fellow!' returned Dick. 'And yet, Lawless, it goes hard

against the grain with me to die; but where whining mendeth nothing,
wherefore whine?'

'Nay, that indeed!' chimed Lawless. 'And a fig for death, at worst! It has to be
done, my master, soon or late. And hanging in a good quarrel is an easy death,
they say, though I could never hear of any that came back to say so.'

And so saying the stout old rascal leaned back in his stall, folded his arms, and
began to look about him with the greatest air of insolence and unconcern.

'And for the matter of that,' Dick added, 'it is yet our best chance to keep
quiet. We wot not yet what Duckworth purposes; and when all is said, and if the
worst befall, we may yet clear our feet of it.'

Now that they ceased talking, they were aware of a very distant and thin
strain of mirthful music which steadily drew nearer, louder and merrier. The
bells in the tower began to break forth into a doubling peal, and a greater and
greater concourse of people to crowd into the church, shuffling the snow from off
their feet, and clapping and blowing in their hands. The western door was flung
wide open, showing a glimpse of sunlit, snowy street, and admitting in a great
gust the shrewd air of the morning; and in short, it became plain by every sign,
that Lord Shoreby desired to be married very early in the day, and that the
wedding-train was drawing near.

Some of Lord Shoreby's men now cleared a passage down the middle aisle,
forcing the people back with lance-stocks; and just then, outside the portal, the
secular musicians could be descried drawing near over the frozen snow, the fifers
and trumpeters scarlet in the face with lusty blowing, the drummers and the
cymbalists beating as for a wager.

These, as they drew near the door of the sacred building, filed off on either
side, and marking time to their own vigorous music, stood stamping in the snow.
As they thus opened their ranks, the leaders of this noble bridal train appeared
behind and between them; and such was the variety and gaiety of their attire,
such the display of silks and velvet, fur and satin, embroidery and lace, that the
procession showed forth upon the snow like a flower-bed in a path or a painted
window in a wall.

First came the bride, a sorry sight, as pale as winter, clinging to Sir Daniel's
arm, and attended, as bridesmaid, by the short young lady who had befriended
Dick the night before. Close behind, in the most radiant toilet, followed the
bridegroom, halting on a gouty foot, and as he passed the threshold of the sacred
building, and doffed his hat, his bald head was seen to be rosy with emotion.

And now came the hour of Ellis Duckworth.

Dick, who sat stunned among contrary emotions, grasping the desk in front of
him, beheld a movement in the crowd, people jostling backward, and eyes and
arms uplifted. Following these signs, he beheld three or four men with bent
bows, leaning from the clerestory gallery. At the same instant they delivered
their discharge, and before the clamour and cries of the astounded populace had
time to swell fully upon the ear, they had flitted from their perch and
disappeared.

The nave was full of swaying heads and voices screaming; the ecclesiastics
thronged in terror from their places; the music ceased, and though the bells
overhead continued for some seconds to clang upon the air, some wind of the
disaster seemed to find its way at last even to the chamber where the ringers were

leaping on their ropes, and they also desisted from their merry labours.

Right in the midst of the nave the bridegroom lay stone-dead, pierced by two black arrows. The bride had fainted. Sir Daniel stood, towering above the crowd in his surprise and anger, a clothyard shaft quivering in his left forearm, and his face streaming blood from another which had grazed his brow.

Long before any search could be made for them, the authors of this tragic interruption had clattered down a turnpike stair and decamped by a postern door.

But Dick and Lawless still remained in pawn; they had indeed arisen on the first alarm, and pushed manfully to gain the door; but what with the narrowness of the stalls, and the crowding of terrified priests and choristers, the attempt had been in vain, and they had stoically resumed their places.

And now, pale with horror, Sir Oliver rose to his feet and called upon Sir Daniel, pointing with one hand to Dick.

'Here,' he cried, 'is Richard Shelton – alas the hour! – blood guilty! Seize him! – bid him be seized! For all our lives' sakes, take him and bind him surely! He hath sworn our fall.'

Sir Daniel was blinded by anger – blinded by the hot blood that still streamed across his face.

'Where?' he bellowed. 'Hale him forth! By the cross of Holywood but he shall rue this hour.'

The crowd fell back, and a party of archers invaded the choir, laid rough hands on Dick, dragged him head foremost from the stall, and thrust him by the shoulders down the chancel steps. Lawless, on his part, sat as still as a mouse.

Sir Daniel, brushing the blood out of his eyes, stared blinkingly upon his captive.

'Ay,' he said, 'treacherous and insolent, I have thee fast; and by all potent oaths, for every drop of blood that now trickles in mine eyes, I will wring a groan out of thy carcase. Away with him!' he added. 'Here is no place! Off with him to my house. I will number every joint of thy body with a torture.'

But Dick, putting off his captors, uplifted his voice.

'Sanctuary!' he shouted. 'Sanctuary! Ho, there, my fathers! They would drag me from the church!'

'From the church thou has defiled with murder, boy,' added a tall man, magnificently dressed.

'On what probation?' cried Dick. 'They do accuse me, indeed, of some complicity, but have not proved one tittle. I was, in truth, a suitor for this damsel's hand; and she, I will be bold to say it, repaid my suit with favour. But what then? To love a maid is no offence, I trow – nay, nor to gain her love. In all else, I stand here free frou guiltiness.'

There was a murmur of approval among the bystanders, so boldly Dick declared his innocence; but at the same time a throng of accusers arose upon the other side, crying how he had been found last night in Sir Daniel's house, how he wore a sacrilegious disguise; and in the midst of the babel, Sir Oliver indicated Lawless, both by voice and gesture, as accomplice to the fact. He, in his turn, was dragged from his seat and set beside his leader. The feelings of the crowd rose high on either side, and while some dragged the prisoners to and fro to favour their escape, other cursed and struck them with their fists. Dick's ears rang and his brain swam dizzily, like a man struggling in the eddies of a furious river.

But the tall man who had already answered Dick, by a prodigious exercise of voice restored silence and order in the mob.

'Search them,' he said, 'for arms. We may so judge of their intentions.'

Upon Dick they found no weapon but his poniard, and this told in his favour, until one man officiously drew it from its sheath, and found it still uncleansed of the blood of Rutter. At this there was a great shout among Sir Daniel's followers, which the tall man suppressed by a gesture and an imperious glance. But when it came to the turn of Lawless, there was found under his gown a sheaf of arrows identical with those that had been shot.

'How say ye now?' asked the tall man, frowningly at Dick.

'Sir,' replied Dick, 'I am here in sanctuary, is it not so? Well, sir, I see by your bearing that ye are high in station, and I read in your countenance the marks of piety and justice. To you, then, I will yield me prisoner, and that blithely, foregoing the advantage of this holy place. But rather than to be yielded into the discretion of that man – whom I do here accuse with a loud voice to be the murderer of my natural father and the unjust detainer of my lands and revenues – rather than that, I would beseech you, under favour, with your own gentle hand, to despatch me on the spot. Your own ears have heard him, how before that I was proven guilty he did threaten me with torments. It standeth not with your own honour to deliver me to my sworn enemy and old oppressor, but to try me fairly by the way of law, and, if that I be guilty indeed, to slay me mercifully.'

'My lord,' cried Sir Daniel, 'ye will not hearken to this wolf? His bloody dagger reeks him the lie into his face.'

'Nay, but suffer me, good knight,' returned the tall stranger; 'your own vehemence doth somewhat tell against yourself.'

And here the bride, who had come to herself some minutes past and looked wildly on upon this scene, broke loose from those that held her, and fell upon her knees before the last speaker.

'My Lord of Risingham,' she cried, 'hear me, in justice. I am here in this man's custody by mere force, reft from mine own people. Since that day I had never pity, countenance, nor comfort from the face of man – but from him only – Richard Shelton – whom they now accuse and labour to undo. My lord, if he was yesternight in Sir Daniel's mansion, it was I that brought him there; he came but at my prayer, and thought to do no hurt. While yet Sir Daniel was a good lord to him, he fought with them of the Black Arrow loyally; but when his foul guardian sought his life by practices, and he fled by night, for his soul's sake, out of that bloody house, whither was he to turn – he, helpless and penniless? Or if he be fallen among ill company, whom should ye blame – the lad that was unjustly handled, or the guardian that did abuse his trust?'

And then the short young lady fell on her knees by Joanna's side.

'And I, my good lord and natural uncle,' she added, 'I can bear testimony, on my conscience and before the face of all, that what this maiden saith is true. It was I, unworthy, that did lead the young man in.'

Earl Risingham had heard in silence, and when the voices ceased, he still stood silent for a space. Then he gave Joanna his hand to arise, though it was to be observed that he did not offer like courtesy to her who had called herself his niece.

'Sir Daniel,' he said, 'here is a right intricate affair, the which, with your good leave, it shall be mine to examine and adjust. Content ye, then; your business is in careful hands; justice shall be done you; and in the meanwhile, get ye incontinently home, and have your hurts attended. The air is shrewd, and I would not ye took cold upon these scratches.'

He made a sign with his hand; it was passed down the nave by obsequious servants, who waited there upon his smallest gesture. Instantly, without the church, a tucket sounded shrill, and through the open portal archers and men-at-arms, uniformly arrayed in the colours and wearing the badge of Lord Risingham, began to file into the church, took Dick and Lawless from those who still detained them, and, closing their files about the prisoners, marched forth again and disappeared.

As they were passing, Joanna held both her hands to Dick and cried him her farewell; and the bridesmaid, nothing downcast by her uncle's evident displeasure, blew him a kiss, with a 'Keep your heart up, lion-driver!' that for the first time since the accident called up a smile to the faces of the crowd.

CHAPTER FIVE

Earl Risingham

EARL RISINGHAM, ALTHOUGH by far the most important person then in Shoreby, was poorly lodged in the house of a private gentleman upon the extreme outskirts of the town. Nothing but the armed men at the doors, and the mounted messengers that kept arriving and departing, announced the temporary resident of a great lord.

Thus it was that, from lack of space, Dick and Lawless were clapped into the same apartment.

'Well spoken, Master Richard,' said the outlaw! 'it was excellently well spoken, and, for my part, I thank you cordially. Here we are in good hands; we shall be justly tried, and some time this evening, decently hanged on the same tree.'

'Indeed, my poor friend, I do believe it,' answered Dick.

'Yet have we a string to our bow,' returned Lawless. 'Ellis Duckworth is a man out of ten thousand; he holdeth you right near his heart, both for your own and for your father's sake; and knowing you guiltless of this fact, he will stir earth and heaven to bear you clear.'

'It may not be,' said Dick. 'What can he do? He hath but a handful. Alack, if it were but tomorrow – could I but keep a certain tryst an hour before noon tomorrow – all were, I think, otherwise. But now there is no help.'

'Well,' concluded Lawless, 'an ye will stand to it for my innocence, I will stand to it for yours, and that stoutly. It shall naught avail us; but an I be to hang, it shall not be for lack of swearing.'

And then, while Dick gave himself over to his reflections, the old rogue curled himself down into a corner, pulled his monkish hood about his face, and composed himself to sleep. Soon he was loudly snoring, so utterly had his long life of hardship and adventure blunted the sense of apprehension.

It was long after noon, and the day was already failing, before the door was opened and Dick taken forth and led upstairs to where, in a warm cabinet, Earl Risingham sat musing over the fire.

On his captive's entrance he looked up.

'Sir,' he said, 'I knew your father, who was a man of honour, and this inclineth me to be the more lenient; but I may not hide from you that heavy charges lie against your character. Ye do consort with murderers and robbers; upon a clear probation ye have carried war against the king's peace; ye are suspected to have piratically seized upon a ship; ye are found skulking with a counterfeit presentment in your enemy's house; a man is slain that very evening——'

'An it like you, my lord,' Dick interposed, 'I will at once avow my guilt, such as it is. I slew this fellow Rutter; and to the proof' – searching in his bosom – 'here is a letter from his wallet.'

Lord Risingham took the letter, and opened and read it twice.

'Ye have read this?' he inquired.

'I have read it,' answered Dick.

'Are ye for York or Lancaster?' the earl demanded.

'My lord, it was but a little while back that I was asked that question, and knew not how to answer it,' said Dick; 'but having answered once, I will not vary. My lord, I am for York.'

The earl nodded approvingly.

'Honestly replied,' he said. 'But wherefore, then, deliver me this letter?'

'Nay, but against traitors, my lord, are not all sides arrayed?' cried Dick.

'I would they were, young gentleman,' returned the earl; 'and I do at least approve your saying. There is more youth than guile in you, I do perceive; and were not Sir Daniel a mighty man upon our side, I were half tempted to espouse your quarrel. For I have inquired, and it appears that you have been hardly dealt with, and have much excuse. But look ye, sir, I am, before all else, a leader in the queen's interest; and though by nature a just man, as I believe, and leaning even to the excess of mercy, yet must I order my goings for my party's interest, and, to keep Sir Daniel, I would go far about.'

'My lord,' returned Dick, 'ye will think me very bold to counsel you: but do ye count upon Sir Daniel's faith? Methought he had changed sides intolerably often.'

'Nay, it is the way of England. What would ye have?' the earl demanded. 'But ye are unjust to the knight of Tunstall; and as faith goes, in this unfaithful generation, he hath of late been honourably true to us of Lancaster. Even in our last reverses he stood firm.'

'An it please you, then,' said Dick, 'to cast your eye upon this letter, ye might somewhat change your thought of him,' and he handed to the earl Sir Daniel's letter to Lord Wensleydale.

The effect upon the earl's countenance was instant; he lowered like an angry lion, and his hand, with a sudden movement, clutched at his dagger.

'Ye have read this also?' he asked.

'Even so,' said Dick. 'It is your lordship's own estate he offers to Lord Wensleydale.'

'It is my own estate, even as ye say!' returned the earl. 'I am your bedesman for this letter. It hath shown me a fox's hole. Command me, Master Shelton; I will not be backward in gratitude, and to begin with, York or Lancaster, true man or thief, I do now set you at freedom. Go, a Mary's name! But judge it right that I retain and hang your fellow, Lawless. The crime hath been most open, and it were fitting that some open punishment should follow.'

'My lord, I make it my first suit to you to spare him also,' pleaded Dick.

'It is an old condemned rogue, thief, and vagabond, Master Shelton,' said the earl. 'He hath been gallows-ripe this score of years. And, whether for one thing or another, whether tomorrow or the day after, where is the great choice?'

'Yet, my lord, it was through love to me that he came hither,' answered Dick, 'and I were churlish and thankless to desert him.'

'Master Shelton, ye are troublesome,' replied the earl, severely. 'It is an evil way to prosper in this world. Howbeit, and to be quit of your importunity, I will once more humour you. Go then, together; but go warily, and get swiftly out of Shoreby town. For this Sir Daniel (whom may the saints confound!) thirsteth most greedily to have your blood.'

'My lord, I do now offer you in words my gratitude, trusting at some brief date to pay you some of it in service,' replied Dick, as he turned from the apartment.

CHAPTER SIX

Arblaster Again

WHEN DICK AND LAWLESS were suffered to steal, by a back way, out of the house where Lord Risingham held his garrison, the evening had already come.

They paused in shelter of the garden wall to consult on their best course. The danger was extreme. If one of Sir Daniel's men caught sight of them and raised the view-hallo, they would be run down and butchered instantly. And not only was the town of Shoreby a mere net of peril for their lives, but to make for the open country was to run the risk of the patrols.

A little way off, upon some open ground, they spied a windmill standing; and hard by that, a very large granary with open doors.

'How if we lay there until the night fall?' Dick proposed.

And Lawless having no better suggestion to offer, they made a straight push for the granary at a run, and concealed themselves behind the door among some straw. The daylight rapidly departed; and presently the moon was silvering the frozen snow. Now or never was their opportunity to gain the Goat and Bagpipes unobserved and change their tell-tale garments. Yet even then it was advisable to go round by the outskirts, and not run the gauntlet of the market-place, where, in the concourse of people, they stood the more imminent peril to be recognized and slain.

This course was a long one. It took them not far from the house by the beach, now lying dark and silent, and brought them forth at last by the margin of the harbour. Many of the ships, as they could see by the clear moonshine, had weighed anchor, and, profiting by the calm sky, proceeded for more distant parts; answerably to this, the rude alehouses along the beach (although in defiance of the curfew law, they still shone with fire and candle) were no longer thronged with customers, and no longer echoed to the chorus of sea-songs.

Hastily, half-running, with their monkish raiment kilted to the knee, they plunged through the deep snow and threaded the labyrinth of marine lumber; and they were already more than half way round the harbour when, as they were passing close before an alehouse, the door suddenly opened and let out a gush of light upon their fleeting figures.

Instantly they stopped, and made believe to be engaged in earnest conversation.

Three men, one after another, came out of the alehouse, and the last closed the door behind him. All three were unsteady upon their feet, as if they had passed the day in deep potations, and they now stood wavering in the moonlight, like men who knew not what they would be after. The tallest of the three was talking in a loud, lamentable voice.

'Seven pieces of as good Gascony as ever a tapster broached,' he was saying, 'the best ship out o' the port o' Dartmouth, a Virgin Mary parcel-gilt, thirteen pounds of good gold money——'

'I have bad losses, too,' interrupted one of the others. 'I have had losses of mine own, gossip Arblaster. I was robbed at Martinmas of five shillings and a leather wallet well worth ninepence farthing.'

Dick's heart smote him at what he heard. Until that moment he had not perhaps thought twice of the poor skipper who had been ruined by the loss of the *Good Hope*; so careless, in those days, were men who wore arms of the goods and interests in their inferiors. But this sudden encounter reminded him sharply of the high-handed manner and ill-ending of his enterprise; and both he and Lawless turned their heads the other way, to avoid the chance of recognition.

The ship's dog had, however, made his escape from the wreck and found his way back again to Shoreby. He was not at Arblaster's heels, and suddenly sniffing and pricking his ears, he darted forward and began to bark furiously at the two sham friars.

His master unsteadily followed him.

'Hey shipmates!' he cried. 'Have ye ever a penny piece for a poor old shipman, clean destroyed by pirates? I am a man that would have paid for you both o' Thursday morning; and now here I be o' Saturday night, begging for a flagon of ale! Ask my man Tom, if ye misdoubt me. Seven pieces of Good Gascon wine, a ship that was mine own, and was my father's before me, a Blessed Mary of plane-tree wood and parcel-gilt, and thirteen pounds in gold and silver. Hey! what say ye? A man that fought the French, too; for I have fought the French; I have cut more French throats upon the high seas than ever a man that sails out of Dartmouth. Come, a penny piece.'

Neither Dick nor Lawless durst answer him a word, lest he should recognize their voices; and they stood there as helpless as a ship ashore, not knowing where to turn nor what to hope.

'Are ye dumb, boy?' inquired the skipper. 'Mates,' he added, with a hiccup, 'they be dumb. I like not this manner of discourtesy; for an a man be dumb, so be as he's courteous, he will still speak when he was spoken to, methinks.'

By this time the sailor, Tom, who was a man of great personal strength, seemed to have conceived some suspicion of these two speechless figures; and being soberer than his captain, stepped suddenly before him, took Lawless roughly by the shoulder, and asked him, with an oath, what ailed him that he held his tongue. To this the outlaw, thinking all was over, made answer by a wrestling feint that stretched the sailor on the sand, and, calling upon Dick to follow him, took to his heels among the lumber.

The affair passed in a second. Before Dick could run at all, Arblaster had him in his arms; Tom, crawling on his face, had caught him by one foot, and the third man had a drawn cutlass brandishing above his head.

It was not so much the danger, it was not so much the annoyance, that now bowed down the spirits of young Shelton; it was the profound humiliation to have escaped Sir Daniel, convinced Lord Risingham, and now fall helpless in the hands of this drunken sailor; and not merely helpless, but, as his conscience loudly told him when it was too late, actually guilty – actually the bankrupt debtor of the man whose ship he had stolen and lost.

'Bring me him back into the alehouse, till I see his face,' said Arblaster.

'Nay, nay,' returned Tom; 'but let us first unload his wallet, lest the other lads cry share.'

But though he was searched from head to foot not a penny was found upon him; nothing but Lord Foxham's signet, which they plucked savagely from his finger.

'Turn me him to the moon,' said the skipper; and taking Dick by the chin, he cruelly jerked his head into the air. 'Blessed Virgin!' he cried, 'it is the pirate.'

'Hey!' cried Tom.

'By the Virgin of Bordeaux, it is the man himself!' repeated Arblaster. 'What, sea-thief, do I hold you?' he cried. 'Where is my ship? Where is my wine? Hey! have I you in my hands? Tom, give me one end of a cord here; I will so truss me this sea-thief, hand and foot together, like a basting turkey – marry, I will so bind him up – and thereafter I will so beat – so beat him!'

And so he ran on, winding the cord meanwhile about Dick's limbs with the dexterity peculiar to seamen, and at every turn and cross securing it with a knot, and tightening the whole fabric with a savage pull.

When he had done, the lad was a mere package in his hands – as helpless as the dead. The skipper held him at arm's length, and laughed aloud. Then he fetched him a stunning buffet on the ear; and then turned him about, and furiously kicked and kicked him. Anger rose up in Dick's bosom like a storm; anger strangled him, and he thought to have died; but when the sailor, tired of this cruel play, dropped him all his length upon the sand and turned to consult with his companions, he instantly regained command of his temper. Here was a momentary respite; ere they began again to torture him, he might have found some method to escape from this degrading and fatal misadventure.

Presently, sure enough, and while his captors were still discussing what to do with him, he took heart of grace, and, with a pretty steady voice, addressed them.

'My masters,' he began, 'are ye gone clean foolish? Here hath Heaven put into your hands as pretty an occasion to grow rich as ever shipman had – such as ye might make thirty over-sea adventures and not find again – and, by the mass! what do ye? Beat me? – nay; so would an angry child! But for long-headed tarry-Johns, that fear not fire nor water, and that love gold as they love beef, methinks ye are not wise.'

'Ay,' said Tom, 'now y' are trussed ye would cozen us.'

'Cozen you!' repeated Dick. 'Nay, if ye be fools, it would be easy. But if ye be shrewd fellows, as I trow ye are, ye can see plainly where your interest lies. When I took your ship from you, we were many, we were well clad and armed; but now, bethink you a little, who mustered that array? One incontestably that hath made much gold. And if he, being already rich, continueth to hunt after more even in the face of storms – bethink you once more – shall there not be a treasure somewhere hidden?'

'What meaneth he?' asked one of the men.

'Why, if ye have lost an old skiff and a few jugs of vinegary wine,' continued Dick, 'forget them, for the trash they are; and do ye rather buckle to an adventure worth the name, that shall, in twelve hours, make or mar you for ever. But take me up from where I lie, and let us go somewhere near at hand and talk across a flagon, for I am sore and frozen, and my mouth is half among the snow.'

'He seeks but to cozen us,' said Tom, contemptuously.

'Cozen! cozen!' cried the third man. 'I would I could see the man that could cozen me! He were a cozener indeed! Nay, I was not born yesterday. I can see a church when it hath a steeple on it; and for my part, gossip Arblaster, methinks there is some sense in this young man. Shall we go hear him, indeed? Say, shall we go hear him?'

'I would look gladly on a pottle of strong ale, good Master Pirret,' returned Arblaster. 'How say ye, Tom? But then the wallet is empty.'

'I will pay,' said the other – 'I will pay. I would fain see this matter out; I do believe, upon my conscience, there is gold in it.'

'Nay, if ye get again to drinking, all is lost!' cried Tom.

'Gossip Arblaster, ye suffer your fellow to have too much liberty,' returned Master Pirret. 'Would ye be led by a hired man? Fy, fy!'

'Peace, fellow!' said Arblaster, addressing Tom. 'Will ye put your oar in? Truly a fine pass, when the crew is to correct the skipper?'

'Well, then, go your way,' said Tom; 'I wash my hands of you.'

'Set him, then, upon his feet,' said Master Pirret. 'I know a privy place where we may drink and discourse.'

'If I am to walk, my friends, ye must set my feet at liberty,' said Dick, when he had been once more planted upright like a post.

'He saith true,' laughed Pirret. 'Truly, he could not walk accoutred as he is. Give it a slit – out with your knife and slit, it gossip.'

Even Arblaster paused at this proposal; but as his companion continued to insist, and Dick had the sense to keep the merest wooden indifference of expression, and only shrugged his shoulders over the delay, the skipper consented at last, and cut the cords which tied his prisoner's feet and legs. Not only did this enable Dick to walk; but the whole network of his bonds being proportionately loosened, he felt the arm behind his back begin to move more freely, and could hope, with time and trouble, to entirely disengage it. So much he owed already to the owlish silliness and greed of Master Pirret.

That worthy now assumed the lead, and conducted them to the very same rude alehouse where Lawless had taken Arblaster on the day of the gale. It was now quite deserted; the fire was a pile of red embers, radiating the most ardent heat; and when they had chosen their places, and the landlord had set before them a measure of mulled ale, both Pirret and Arblaster stretched forth their legs and squared their elbows like men bent upon a pleasant hour.

The table at which they sat, like all the others in the alehouse, consisted of a heavy, square board, set on a pair of barrels; and each of the four curiously-assorted cronies sat at one side of the square, Pirret facing Arblaster, and Dick opposite to the common sailor.

'And now, young man,' said Pirret, 'to your tale. It doth appear, indeed, that ye have somewhat abused our gossip Arblaster; but what then? Make it up to him – show him but this chance to become wealthy – and I will go pledge he will forgive you.'

So far Dick had spoken pretty much at random; but it was now necessary, under the supervision of six eyes, to invent and tell some marvellous story, and, if it were possible, get back into his hands the all-important signet. To squander time was the first necessity. The longer his stay lasted, the more would his captors drink, and the surer should he be when he attempted his escape.

Well, Dick was not much of an inventor, and what he told was pretty much the tale of Ali Baba, with Shoreby and Tunstall Forest substituted for the East, and the treasures of the cavern rather exaggerated than diminished. As the reader is aware, it is an excellent story, and has but one drawback – that it is not true; and so, as these three simple shipmen now heard it for the first time, their eyes stood out of their faces, and their mouths gaped like codfish at a fishmonger's.

Pretty soon a second measure of mulled ale was called for; and while Dick was still artfully spinning out the incidents a third followed the second.

Here was the position of the parties towards the end:

Arblaster, three-parts drunk and one-half asleep, hung helpless on his stool. Even Tom had been much delighted with the tale, and his vigilance had abated in proportion. Meanwhile, Dick had gradually wormed his right arm clear of its bonds, and was ready to risk all.

'And so,' said Pirret, 'y' are one of these?'

'I was made so,' replied Dick, 'against my will; but an I could but get a sack or two of gold coin to my share, I should be a fool indeed to continue dwelling in a filthy cave, and standing shot and buffet like a soldier. Here be we four; good! Let us, then, go forth into the forest tomorrow ere the sun be up. Could we come honestly by a donkey, it were better; but an we cannot, we have our four strong backs, and I warrant me we shall come home staggering.'

Pirret licked his lips.

'And this magic,' he said – 'this password, whereby the cave is opened – how call ye it, friend?'

'Nay, none know the word but the three chiefs,' returned Dick; 'but here is your great good fortune, that, on this very evening, I should be the bearer of a spell to open it. It is a thing not trusted twice a year beyond the captain's wallet.'

'A spell!' said Arblaster, half awakening, and squinting upon Dick with one eye. 'Aroint thee! no spells! I be a good Christian. Ask my man Tom, else.'

'Nay, but this is white magic,' said Dick. 'It doth naught with the devil; only the powers of numbers, herbs, and planets.'

'Ay, ay,' said Pirret; "tis but white magic, gossip. There is no sin therein, I do assure you. But proceed, good youth. This spell – in what should it consist?'

'Nay, that I will incontinently show you,' answered Dick. 'Have ye there the ring ye took from my finger? Good! Now hold it forth before you by the extreme finger-ends, at the arm's length, and over against the shining of these embers. 'Tis so exactly. Thus, then, is the spell.'

With a haggard glance, Dick saw the coast was clear between him and the door. He put up an internal prayer. Then whipping forth his arm, he made but one snatch of the ring, and at the same instant, levering up the table, he sent it bodily over upon the seaman Tom. He, poor soul, went down bawling under the ruins; and before Arblaster understood that anything was wrong, or Pirret could collect his dazzled wits, Dick had run to the door and escaped into the moonlit night.

The moon, which now rode in the mid-heavens, and the extreme whiteness of the snow, made the open ground about the harbour bright as day; and young Shelton leaping, with kilted robe, among the lumber, was a conspicuous figure from afar.

Tom and Pirret followed him with shouts; from every drinking-shop they were joined by others whom their cries aroused; and presently a whole fleet of sailors was in full pursuit. But Jack ashore was a bad runner, even in the fifteenth century, and Dick, besides, had a start, which he rapidly improved, until, as he drew near the entrance of a narrow lane, he even paused and looked laughingly behind him.

Upon the white floor of snow, all the shipmen of Shoreby came clustering in an inky mass, and tailing out rearward in isolated clumps. Every man was shouting or screaming; every man was gesticulating with both arms in air; some one was continually falling; and to complete the picture, when one fell, a dozen would fall upon the top of him.

The confused mass of sound which they rolled up as high as to the moon was partly comical and partly terrifying to the fugitive whom they were hunting. In itself, it was impotent, for he made sure no seaman in the port could run him down. But the mere volume of noise, in so far as it must awake all the sleepers in Shoreby, and bring all the skulking sentries to the street, did really threaten him with danger in the front. So, spying a dark doorway at a corner, he whipped briskly into it, and let the uncouth hunt go by him, still shouting and gesticulating, and all red with hurry, and white with tumbles in the snow.

It was a long while, indeed, before this great invasion of the town by the harbour came to an end, and it was long before silence was restored. For long, lost sailors were still to be heard pounding and shouting through the streets in all directions and in every quarter of the town. Quarrels followed, sometimes among themselves, sometimes with the men of the patrols; knives were drawn, blows given and received, and more than one dead body remained behind upon the snow.

When, a full hour later, the last seaman returned grumblingly to the harbour side and his particular tavern, it may fairly be questioned if he had ever known what manner of man he was pursuing, but it was absolutely sure that he had now forgotten. By next morning there were many strange stories flying; and a little while after, the legend of the devil's nocturnal visit was an article of faith with all the lads of Shoreby.

But the return of the last seaman did not, even yet, set free young Shelton from his cold imprisonment in the doorway.

For some time after, there was a great activity of patrols; and special parties came forth to make the round of the place and report to one or other of the great lords, whose slumbers had been thus unusually broken.

The night was already well spent before Dick ventured from his hiding-place and came, safe and sound, but aching with cold and bruises, to the door of the Goat and Bagpipes. As the law required, there was neither fire nor candle in the house; but he groped his way into a corner of the icy guest-room, found an end of a blanket, which he hitched around his shoulders, and creeping close to the nearest sleeper, was soon lost in slumber.

Book V

CROOKBACK

CHAPTER ONE

The Shrill Trumpet

VERY EARLY THE NEXT MORNING, before the first peep of the day, Dick arose, changed his garments, armed himself once more like a gentleman, and set forth for Lawless's den in the forest. There, it will be remembered, he had left Lord Foxham's papers; and to get these and be back in time for the tryst with the young Duke of Gloucester could only be managed by an early start, and the most vigorous walking.

The frost was more rigorous than ever; the air was windless and dry, and stinging to the nostril. The moon had gone down, but the stars were still bright and numerous, and the reflection from the snow was clear and cheerful. There was no need for a lamp to walk by; nor, in that still but ringing air, the least temptation to delay.

Dick had crossed the greater part of the open ground between Shoreby and the forest, and had reached the bottom of the little hill, some hundred yards below the Cross of St Bride, when, through the stillness of the black morn, there rang forth the note of a trumpet, so shrill, clear, and piercing, that he thought he had never heard the match of it for audibility. It was blown once, and then hurriedly a second time; and then the clash of steel succeeded.

At this young Shelton pricked his ears, and drawing his sword, ran forward up the hill.

Presently he came in sight of the cross, and was aware of a most fierce encounter raging on the road before it. There were seven or eight assailants, and but one to keep head against them; but so active and dexterous was this one, so desperately did he charge and scatter his opponents, so deftly keep his footing on the ice, that already, before Dick could intervene, he had slain one, wounded another, and kept the whole in check.

Still, it was by a miracle that he continued his defence, and at any moment, any accident, the least slip of foot or error of hand, his life would be a forfeit.

'Hold ye well, sir! Here is help!' cried Richard; and forgetting that he was alone, and that the cry was somewhat irregular, 'To the Arrow! to the Arrow!' he shouted, as he fell upon the rear of the assailants.

These were stout fellows also, for they gave not an inch at this surprise, but faced about, and fell with astonishing fury upon Dick. Four against one, the steel flashed about him in the starlight; the sparks flew fiercely; one of the men opposed to him fell – in the stir of the fight he hardly knew why; then he himself was struck across the head, and though the steel cap below his hood protected him, the blow beat him down upon one knee, with a brain whirling like a windmill sail.

Meanwhile the man whom he had come to rescue, instead of joining in the conflict, had, on the first sign of intervention, leaped aback and blown again, and yet more urgently and loudly, on that same shrill-voiced trumpet that began the alarm. Next moment, indeed, his foes were on him, and he was once more charging and fleeing, leaping, stabbing, dropping to his knee, and using indifferently sword and dagger, foot and hand, with the same unshaken courage and feverish energy and speed.

But that ear-piercing summons had been heard at last. There was a muffled rushing in the snow; and in a good hour for Dick, who saw the sword-points glitter already at his throat, there poured forth out of the wood upon both sides a disorderly torrent of mounted men-at-arms, each cased in iron, and with visor lowered, each bearing his lance in rest, or his swored bared and raised, and each carrying, so to speak, a passenger, in the shape of an archer or page, who leaped one after another from their perches, and had presently doubled the array.

The original assailants, seeing themselves outnumbered and surrounded, threw down their arms without a word.

'Seize me these fellows!' said the hero of the trumpet; and when his order had been obeyed, he drew near to Dick and looked him in the face.

Dick, returning this scrutiny, was surprised to find in one who had displayed such strength, skill and energy, a lad no older than himself – slightly deformed, with one shoulder higher than the other, and of a pale, painful, and distorted countenance.* The eyes, however, were very clear and bold.

'Sir,' said this lad, 'ye came in good time for me, and none to early.'

'My lord,' returned Dick, with a faint sense that he was in the presence of a great personage, 'ye are yourself so marvellous a good swordsman that I believe ye had managed them single-handed. Howbeit, it was certainly well for me that your men delayed no longer than they did.'

'How knew ye who I was?' demanded the stranger.

'Even now, my lord,' Dick answered, 'I am ignorant of whom I speak with.'

'Is it so?' asked the other. 'And yet ye threw yourself head first into this unequal battle.'

'I saw one man valiantly contending against many,' replied Dick, 'and I had thought myself dishonoured not to bear him aid.'

A singular sneer played about the young nobleman's mouth as he made answer:

'These are very brave words. But to the more essential – are ye Lancaster or York?'

'My lord, I make no secret; I am clear for York,' Dick answered.

'By the mass!' replied the other, 'it is well for you.'

And so saying, he turned towards one of his followers.

'Let me see,' he continued, in the same sneering and cruel tones – 'let me see a clean end of these brave gentlemen. Truss me them up.'

There were but five survivors of the attacking party. Archers seized them by the arms; they were hurried to the borders of the wood, and each placed below a tree of suitable dimensions; the rope was adjusted: an archer, carrying the end of it, hastily clambered overhead, and before a minute was over, and without a word passing upon either hand, the five men were swinging by the neck.

'And now,' cried the deformed leader, 'back to your posts, and when I summon you next, be readier to attend.'

* Richard Crookback would have been really far younger at this date.

'My lord duke,' said one man, 'beseech you, tarry not here alone. Keep but a handful of lances at your hand.'

'Fellow,' said the duke, 'I have forborne to chide you for your slowness. Cross me not, therefore. I trust my hand and arm, for all that I be crooked. Ye were backward when the trumpet sounded: and ye are now too forward with your counsels. But it is ever so; last with the lance and first with tongue. Let it be reversed.'

And with a gesture that was not without a sort of dangerous nobility, he waved them off.

The footmen climbed again to their seats behind the men-at-arms, and the whole party moved slowly away and disappeared in twenty different directions, under the cover of the forest.

The day was by this time beginning to break, and the stars to fade. The first grey glimmer of dawn shone upon the countenances of the two young men, who now turned once more to face each other.

'Here,' said the duke, 'ye have seen my vengeance, which is, like my blade, both sharp and ready. But I would not have you, for all Christendom, suppose me thankless. You that came to my aid with a good sword and a better courage – unless that ye recoil from my mis-shapeness – come to my heart.'

And so saying the young leader held out his arms for an embrace.

In the bottom of his heart Dick already entertained a great terror and some hatred for the man whom he had rescued; but the invitation was so worded that it would not have been merely discourteous, but cruel, to refuse or hesitate, and he hastened to comply.

'And now, my lord duke,' he said, when he had regained his freedom, 'do I suppose aright? Are ye my Lord Duke of Gloucester?'

'I am Richard of Gloucester,' returned the other. 'And you – how call they you?'

Dick told him his name, and presented Lord Foxham's signet, which the duke immediately recognized.

'Ye come too soon,' he said; 'but why should I complain? Ye are like me, that was here at watch two hours before the day. But this is the first sally of mine arms; upon this adventure, Master Shelton, shall I make or mar the quality of my renown. There lie mine enemies, under two old, skilled captains, Risingham and Brackley, well posted for strength, I do believe, but yet upon two sides without retreat, enclosed betwixt the sea, the harbour, and the river. Methinks, Shelton, here were a great blow to be stricken, an we could strike it silently and suddenly.'

'I do think so, indeed,' cried Dick, warming.

'Have ye my Lord Foxham's notes?' inquired the duke.

And then Dick, having explained how he was without them for the moment, made himself bold to offer information every jot as good, of his own knowledge.

'And for mine own part, my lord duke,' he added, 'an ye had men enough, I would fall on even at this present. For, look ye, at the peep of day the watches of the night are over; but by day they keep neither watch nor ward – only scour the outskirts with horsemen. Now, then, when the night-watch is already unarmed, and the rest are at their morning cup – now were the time to break them.'

'How many do ye count?' asked Gloucester.

'They number not two thousand,' Dick replied.

'I have seven hundred in the woods behind us,' said the duke; 'seven hundred follow from Kettley, and will be here anon; behind these, and farther, are four hundred more; and my Lord Foxham hath five hundred half-a-day from here, at Holywood. Shall we attend their coming, or fall on?'

'My lord,' said Dick, 'when ye hanged these five poor rogues ye did decide the question. Churls although they were, in these uneasy times they will be lacked and looked for, and the alarm be given. Therefore, my lord, if ye do count upon the advantage of a surprise, ye have not, in my poor opinion, one whole hour in front of you.'

'I do think so indeed,' returned Crookback. 'Well, before an hour, ye shall be in the thick on't, winning spurs. A swift man to Holywood, carrying Lord Foxham's signet; another along the road to speed my laggards! Nay, Shelton, by the roof, it may be done!'

Therewith he once more set his trumpet to his lips and blew.

This time he was not long kept waiting. In a moment the open space about the cross was filled with horse and foot. Richard of Gloucester took his place upon the steps, and despatched messenger after messenger to hasten the concentration of the seven hundred men that lay hidden in the immediate neighbourhood among the woods; and before a quarter of an hour had passed, all his dispositions being taken, he put himself at their head, and began to move down the hill towards Shoreby.

His plan was simple. He was to seize a quarter of the town of Shoreby lying on the right hand of the high road, and make his position good there in the narrow lanes until his reinforcements followed.

If Lord Risingham chose to retreat, Richard would follow upon his rear, and take him between two fires; or, if he preferred to hold the town, he would be shut in a trap, there to be gradually overwhelmed by force of numbers.

There was but one danger, but that was imminent and great – Gloucester's seven hundred might be rolled up and cut to pieces in the first encounter, and, to avoid this, it was needful to make the surprise of their arrival as complete as possible.

The footmen, therefore, were all once more taken up behind the riders, and Dick had the signal honour meted out to him of mounting behind Gloucester himself. For as far as there was any cover the troops moved slowly, and when they came near the end of the trees that lined the highway, stopped to breathe and reconnoitre.

The sun was now well up, shining with a frosty brightness out of a yellow halo, and right over against the luminary, Shoreby, a field of snowy roofs and ruddy gables, was rolling up its columns of morning smoke.

Gloucester turned round to Dick.

'In that poor place,' he said, 'where people are cooking breakfast, either you shall gain your spurs and I begin a life of mighty honour and glory in the world's eye, or both of us, as I conceive it, shall fall dead and be unheard of. Two Richards are we. Well then, Richard Shelton, they shall be heard about, these two! Their swords shall not ring more loudly on men's helmets than their names shall ring in people's ears.'

Dick was astonished at so great a hunger after fame, expressed with so great vehemence of voice and language; and he answered very sensibly and quietly, that, for his part, he promised he would do his duty, and doubted not of victory if everyone did the like.

By this time the horses were well breathed, and the leader holding up his sword and giving rein, the whole troop of chargers broke into the gallop and thundered, with their double load of fighting men, down the remainder of the hill and across the snow-covered plain that still divided them from Shoreby.

CHAPTER TWO

The Battle of Shoreby

THE WHOLE DISTANCE TO BE crossed was not above a quarter of a mile. But they had no sooner debouched beyond the cover of the trees than they were aware of people fleeing and screaming in the snowy meadows upon either hand. Almost at the same moment a great rumour began to rise, and spread and grow continually louder in the town; and they were not yet halfway to the nearest house before the bells began to ring backward from the steeple.

The young duke ground his teeth together. By these so early signals of alarm he feared to find his enemies prepared; and if he failed to gain a footing in the town, he knew that his small party would soon be broken and exterminated in the open.

In the town, however, the Lancastrians were far from being in so good a posture. It was as Dick had said. The night-guard had already doffed their harness; the rest were still hanging – unlatched, unbraced, all unprepared for battle – about their quarters; and in the whole of Shoreby there were not, perhaps, fifty men full armed, or fifty chargers ready to be mounted.

The beating of the bells, the terrifying summons of men who ran about the streets crying and beating upon the doors, aroused in an incredibly short space at least two score out of that half hundred. These got speedily to horse, and, the alarm still flying wild and contrary, galloped in different directions.

Thus it befell that, when Richard of Gloucester reached the first house of Shoreby, he was met in the mouth of the street by a mere handful of lances, whom he swept before his onset as the storm chases the bark.

A hundred paces into the town, Dick Shelton touched the duke's arm; the duke, in answer, gathered his reins, put the shrill trumpet to his mouth, and blowing a concerted point, turned to the right hand out of the direct advance. Swerving like a single rider, his whole command turned after him, and, still at the full gallop of the chargers, swept up the narrow bye-street. Only the last score of riders drew rein and faced about in the entrance; the footmen, whom they carried behind them, leapt at the same instant to the earth, and began, some to bend their bows, and other to break into and secure the houses upon either hand.

Surprised at this sudden change of direction, and daunted by the firm front of the rear-guard, the few Lancastrians, after a momentary consultation, turned and rode farther into town to seek for reinforcements.

The quarter of the town upon which, by the advice of Dick, Richard of Gloucester had now seized, consisted of five small streets of poor and ill-inhabited houses, occupying a very gentle eminence, and lying open towards the back.

The five streets being each secured by a good guard, the reserve would thus occupy the centre, out of shot, and yet ready to carry aid wherever it was needed.

Such was the poorness of the neighbourhood that none of the Lancastrian lords, and but few of their retainers, had been lodged therein; and the inhabitants, with one accord, deserted their houses and fled, squalling, along the streets or over garden walls.

In the centre, where the five ways all met, a somewhat ill-favoured alehouse displayed the sign of the Chequers; and here the Duke of Gloucester chose his headquarters for the day.

To Dick he assigned the guard of one of the five streets.

'Go,' he said, 'win your spurs. Win glory for me; one Richard for another. I tell you, if I rise, ye shall rise by the same ladder. Go,' he added, shaking him by the hand.

But, as soon as Dick was gone, he turned to a little shabby archer at his elbow.

'Go, Dutton, and that right speedily,' he added. 'Follow that lad. If ye find him faithful, ye answer for his safety, a head for a head. Woe unto you, if ye return without him! But if he be faithless – or, for one instant, ye misdoubt him – stab him from behind.'

In the meanwhile Dick hastened to secure his post. The street he had to guard was very narrow, and closely lined with houses, which projected and overhung the roadway; but narrow and dark as it was, since it opened upon the market-place of the town, the main issue of the battle would probably fall to be decided on that spot.

The market-place was full of townspeople fleeing in disorder; but there was as yet no sign of any foeman ready to attack, and Dick judged he had some time before him to make ready his defence.

The two houses at the end stood deserted, with open doors, as the inhabitants had left them in their flight, and from these he had the furniture hastily tossed forth and piled into a barrier in the entry of the lane. A hundred men were placed at his disposal, and of these he threw the more part into the houses, where they might lie in shelter and deliver their arrows from the windows. With the rest, under his own immediate eye, he lined the barricade.

Meanwhile the utmost uproar and confusion had continued to prevail throughout the town; and what with the hurried clashing of bells, the sounding of trumpets, the swift movement of bodies of horse, the cries of the commanders, and the shrieks of women, the noise was almost deafening to the ear. Presently, little by little, the tumult began to subside; and soon after, files of men in armour and bodies of archers began to assemble and form in line of battle in the market-place.

A large portion of this body were in murrey and blue, and in the mounted knight who ordered their array Dick recognized Sir Daniel Brackley.

Then there befell a long pause, which was followed by the almost simultaneous sounding of four trumpets from four different quarters of the town. A fifth rang in answer from the market-place, and at the same moment the files began to move, and a shower of arrows rattled about the barricade, and sounded like blows upon the walls of the two flanking houses.

The attack had begun, by a common signal, on all the five issues of the quarter. Gloucester was beleaguered upon every side; and Dick judged, if he would make good his post, he must rely entirely on the hundred men of his command.

Seven volleys of arrows followed one upon the other, and in the very thick of the discharges Dick was touched from behind upon the arm, and found a page holding out to him a leathern jack, strengthened with bright plates of mail.

'It is from my Lord of Gloucester,' said the page. 'He hath observed, Sir Richard, that ye went unarmed.'

Dick, with a glow at his heart at being so addressed, got to his feet and, with the assistance of the page, donned the defensive coat. Even as he did so, two arrows rattled harmlessly upon the plates, and a third struck down the page, mortally wounded, at his feet.

Meantime the whole body of the enemy had been steadily drawing nearer across the market-place; and by this time were so close at hand that Dick gave the order to return their shot. Immediately, from behind the barrier and from the windows of the houses, a counterblast of arrows sped, carrying death. But the Lancastrians, as if they had but waited for a signal, shouted loudly in answer; and began to close at a run upon the barrier, the horsemen still hanging back, with visors lowered.

Then followed an obstinate and deadly struggle, hand to hand. The assailants, wielding their falchions with one hand, strove with the other to drag down the structure of the barricade. On the other side, the parts were reversed; and the defenders exposed themselves like madmen to protect their rampart. So for some minutes the contest raged almost in silence, friend and foe falling one upon another. But it is always easier to destroy; and when a single note upon the tucket recalled the attacking party from this desperate service, much of the barricade had been removed piecemeal, and the whole fabric had sunk to half its height, and tottered to a general fall.

And now the footmen in the market-place fell back, at a run, on every side. The horsemen, who had been standing in a line two deep, wheeled suddenly, and made their flank into their front; and as swift as a striking adder, the long, steel-clad column was launched upon the ruinous barricade.

Of the first two horsemen, one fell, rider and steed, and was ridden down by his companions. The second leaped clean upon the summit of the rampart, transpiercing an archer with his lance. Almost in the same instant he was dragged from the saddle and his horse despatched.

And then the full weight and impetus of the charge burst upon and scattered the defenders. The men-at-arms, surmounting their fallen comrades, and carried onward by the fury of their onslaught, dashed through Dick's broken line and poured thundering up the lane beyond, as a stream bestrides and pours across a broken dam.

Yet was the fight not over. Still, in the narrow jaws of the entrance, Dick and a few survivors plied their bills like woodmen; and already, across the width of the passage, there had been formed a second, a higher, and a more effectual rampart of fallen men and disembowelled horses, lashing in the agonies of death.

Baffled by this fresh obstacle, the remainder of the cavalry fell back; and as, at the sight of this movement, the flight of arrows redoubled from the casements of the houses, their retreat had, for a moment, almost degenerated into flight.

Almost at the same time, those who had crossed the barricade and charged farther up the street, being met before the door of the Chequers by the formidable hunchback and the whole reserve of the Yorkists, began to come scattering backward, in the excess of disarray and terror.

Dick and his fellows faced about, fresh men poured out of the houses; a cruel blast of arrows met the fugitives full in the face, while Gloucester was already riding down their rear; in the inside of a minute and a half there was no living Lancastrian in the street.

Then, and not till then, did Dick hold up his reeking blade and give the word to cheer.

Meanwhile Gloucester dismounted from his horse and came forward to inspect the post. His face was as pale as linen; but his eyes shone in his head like some strange jewel, and his voice, when he spoke, was hoarse and broken with the exultation of battle and success. He looked at the rampart, which neither friend nor foe could now approach without precaution, so fiercely did the horses struggle in the throes of death, and at the sight of that great carnage he smiled upon one side.

'Despatch these horses,' he said; 'they keep you from your vantage. Richard Shelton,' he added, 'ye have pleased me. Kneel.'

The Lancastrians had already resumed their archery, and the shafts fell thick in the mouth of the street; but the duke, minding them not at all, deliberately drew his sword and dubbed Richard a knight upon the spot.

'And now, Sir Richard,' he continued, 'if that ye see Lord Risingham, send me an express upon the instant. Were it your last man, let me hear of it incontinently. I had rather venture the post than lose my stroke at him. For mark me, all of ye,' he added, raising his voice, 'if Earl Risingham fall by another hand than mine, I shall count this victory a defeat.'

'My lord duke,' said one of his attendants, 'is your grace not weary of exposing his dear life unneedfully? Why tarry we here?'

'Catesby,' returned the duke, 'here is the battle, not elsewhere. The rest are but feigned onslaughts. Here must we vanquish. And for the exposure – if ye were an ugly hunchback, and the children gecked at you upon the street, ye would count your body cheaper, and an hour of glory worth a life. Howbeit, if ye will, let us ride on and visit the other posts. Sir Richard here, my namesake, he shall still hold this entry, where he wadeth to the ankles in hot blood. Him can we trust. But mark it, Sir Richard, ye are not yet done. The worst is yet to ward. Sleep not.'

He came right up to young Shelton, looking him hard in the eyes, and taking his hand in both of his, gave it so extreme a squeeze that the blood had nearly spurted. Dick quailed before his eyes. The insane excitement, the courage, and the cruelty that he read therein, filled him with dismay about the future. This young duke's was indeed a gallant spirit, to ride foremost in the ranks of war; but after the battle, in the days of peace and in the circle of his trusted friends, that mind, it was to be dreaded, would continue to bring forth the fruits of death.

CHAPTER THREE

The Battle of Shoreby (concluded)

DICK, ONCE MORE LEFT TO his own counsels, began to look about him. The arrow-shot had somewhat slackened. On all sides the enemy were falling back; and the greater part of the market-place was now left empty, the snow here trampled into orange mud, there splashed with gore, scattered all over with dead men and horses, and bristling thick with feathered arrows.

On his own side the loss had been cruel. The jaws of the little street and the ruins of the barricade were heaped with the dead and dying; and out of the hundred men with whom he had begun the battle, there were not seventy left who could still stand to arms.

At the same time the day was passing. The first reinforcements might be looked for to arrive at any moment; and the Lancastrians, already shaken by the result of their desperate but unsuccessful onslaught, were in an ill-temper to support a fresh invader.

There was a dial in the wall of one of the two flanking houses; and this, in the frosty, winter sunshine, indicated ten of the forenoon.

Dick turned to the man who was at his elbow, a little insignificant archer, binding a cut in his arm.

'It was well fought,' he said, 'and, by my sooth, they will not charge us twice.'

'Sir,' said the little archer, 'ye have fought right well for York, and better for yourself. Never hath man in so brief space prevailed so greatly on the duke's affections. That he should have entrusted such a post to one he knew not is a marvel. But look to your head, Sir Richard! If ye be vanquished – ay, if ye give way one foot's breadth – axe or cord shall punish it; and I am set if ye do aught doubtful, I will tell you honestly, here to stab you from behind.'

Dick looked at the little man in amaze.

'You!' he cried. 'And from behind!'

'It is right so,' returned the archer; 'and because I like not the affair I tell it you. Ye must make the post good, Sir Richard, at your peril. O, our Crookback is a bold blade and a good warrior; but whether in cold blood or in hot, he will have all things done exact to his commandment. If any fail or hinder, they shall die the death.'

'Now, by the saints!' cried Richard, 'is this so? And will men follow such a leader?'

'Nay, they follow him gleefully,' replied the other; 'for if he be exact to punish, he is most open-handed to reward. And if he spare not the blood and sweat of others, he is ever liberal of his own, still in the first front of battle, still the last to sleep. He will go far, will Crookback Dick o' Gloucester!'

The young knight, if he had before been brave and vigilant, was now all the more inclined to watchfulness and courage. His sudden favour, he began to perceive, had brought perils in its train. And he turned from the archer, and once more scanned anxiously the market-place. It lay empty as before.

'I like not this quietude,' he said. 'Doubtless they prepare us some surprise.'

And, as if in answer to his remark, the archers began once more to advance against the barricade, and the arrows to fall thick. But there was something hesitating in the attack. They came not on roundly, but seemed rather to await a further signal.

Dick looked uneasily about him, spying for a hidden danger. And sure enough, about half way up the little street, a door was suddenly opened from within, and the house continued, for some seconds, and both by door and window, to disgorge a torrent of Lancastrian archers. These, as they leaped down, hurriedly stood to their ranks, bent their bows, and proceeded to pour upon Dick's rear a flight of arrows.

At the same time, the assailants in the market-place redoubled their shot, and began to close in stoutly upon the barricade.

Dick called down his whole command out of the houses, and facing them both ways, and encouraging their valour both by word and gesture, returned as best he could the double shower of shafts that fell about his post.

Meanwhile house after house was opened in the street, and the Lancastrians continued to pour out of the doors and leap down from the windows, shouting victory, until the number of enemies upon Dick's rear was almost equal to the number in his face. It was plain that he could hold the post no longer; what was worse, even if he could have held it, it had now become useless; and the whole Yorkist army lay in a posture of helplessness upon the brink of a complete disaster.

The men behind him formed the vital flaw in the general defence; and it was upon these that Dick turned, charging at the head of his men. So vigorous was the attack, that the Lancastrian archers gave ground and staggered, and, at last, breaking their ranks, began to crowd back into the houses from which they had so recently and so vaingloriously sallied.

Meanwhile the men from the market-place had swarmed across the undefended barricade, and fell on hotly upon the other side; and Dick must once again face about, and proceed to drive them back. Once again the spirit of his men prevailed; they cleared the street in a triumphant style, but even as they did so the others issued again out of the houses, and took them, a third time, upon the rear.

The Yorkists began to be scattered; several times Dick found himself alone among his foes and plying his bright sword for life; several times he was conscious of a hurt. And meanwhile the fight swayed to and fro in the street without determinate result.

Suddenly Dick was aware of a great trumpeting about the outskirts of the town. The war-cry of York began to be rolled up to heaven, as by many and triumphant voices. And at the same time the men in front of him began to give ground rapidly, streaming out of the street and back upon the market-place.

Some one gave the word to fly. Trumpets were blown distractedly, some for a rally, some to charge. It was plain that a great blow had been struck, and the Lancastrians were thrown, at least for the moment, into full disorder, and some degree of panic.

And then, like a theatre trick, there followed the last act of Shoreby Battle. The men in front of Richard turned tail, like a dog that has been whistled home, and fled like the wind. At the same moment there came through the market-place a storm of horsemen, fleeing and pursuing, the Lancastrians turning back to strike with the sword, the Yorkists riding them down at the point of the lance.

Conspicuous in the mellay, Dick beheld the Crookback. He was already giving a foretaste of that furious valour and skill to cut his way across the ranks of war, which, years afterwards upon the field of Bosworth, and when he was stained with crimes, almost sufficed to change the fortunes of the day and the destiny of the English throne. Evading, striking, riding down, he so forced and so manoeuvred his strong horse, so aptly defended himself, and so liberally scattered death to his opponents, that he was now far ahead of the foremost of his knights, hewing his way, with the truncheon of a bloody sword, to where Lord Risingham was rallying the bravest. A moment more and they had met; the tall, splendid, and famous warrior against the deformed and sickly boy.

Yet Shelton had never a doubt of the result; and when the fight next opened for a moment, the figure of the earl had disappeared; but still, in the first of the danger, Crookback Dick was launching his big horse and plying the truncheon of his sword.

Thus, by Shelton's courage in holding the mouth of the street against the first attack, and by the opportune arrival of his seven hundred reinforcements, the lad, who was afterwards to be handed down to the execration of posterity under the name of Richard III, had won his first considerable fight.

CHAPTER FOUR

The Sack of Shoreby

THERE WAS NOT A FOE LEFT within striking distance; and Dick, as he looked rue-fully about him on the remainder of his gallant force, began to count the cost of victory. He was himself, now that the danger was ended, so stiff and sore, so bruised and cut and broken, and, above all, so utterly exhausted by his desperate and unremitting labours in the fight, that he seemed incapable of any fresh exertion.

But this was not yet the hour for repose. Shoreby had been taken by assault; and though an open town, and not in any manner to be charged with the resistance, it was plain that these rough fighters would be not less rough now that the fight was over, and that the more horrid part of war would fall to be enacted. Richard of Gloucester was not the captain to protect the citizens from his infuriated soldiery; and even if he had the will, it might be questioned if he had the power.

It was, therefore, Dick's business to find and to protect Joanna; and with that end he looked about him at the faces of his men. The three or four who seemed likeliest to be obedient and to keep sober he drew aside; and promising them a rich reward and a special recommendation to the duke, led them across the market-place, now empty of horsemen, and into the streets upon the farther side.

Every here and there small combats of from two to a dozen still raged upon the open street; here and there a house was being besieged, the defenders throwing out stools and tables on the heads of the assailants. The snow was strewn with arms and corpses; but except for these partial combats the streets were deserted, and the houses, some standing open, and some shuttered and barricaded, had for the most part ceased to give out smoke.

Dick, threading the skirts of these skirmishers, led his followers briskly in the direction of the abbey church; but when he came the length of the main street, a cry of horror broke from his lips. Sir Daniel's great house had been carried by assault. The gates hung in splinters from the hinges, and a double throng kept pouring in and out through the entrance, seeking and carrying booty. Meanwhile, in the upper storeys, some resistance was still being offered to the pillagers; for just as Dick came within eyeshot of the building, a casement was burst open from within, and a poor wretch in murrey and blue, screaming and resisting, was forced through the embrasure and tossed into the street below.

The most sickening apprehension fell upon Dick. He ran forward like one possessed, forced his way into the house among the foremost, and mounted without pause to the chamber on the third floor where he had last parted from Joanna. It was a mere wreck; the furniture had been overthrown, the cupboards broken open, and in one place a trailing corner of the arras lay smouldering on the embers of the fire.

Dick, almost without thinking, trod out the incipient conflagration, and then stood bewildered. Sir Daniel, Sir Oliver, Joanna, all were gone; but whether butchered in the rout or safe escaped from Shoreby, who should say?

He caught a passing archer by the tabard.

'Fellow,' he asked, 'were ye here when this house was taken?'

'Let be,' said the archer. 'A murrain! let be, or I strike.'

'Hark ye,' returned Richard, 'two can play at that. Stand and be plain.'

But the man, flushed with drink and battle, struck Dick upon the shoulder with one hand, while with the other he twitched away his garment. Thereupon the full wrath of the young leader burst from his control. He seized the fellow in his strong embrace, and crushed him on the plates of his mailed bosom like a child; then, holding him at arm's length, he bid him speak as he valued life.

'I pray you mercy!' gasped the archer. 'An I had thought ye were so angry I would 'a' been charier of crossing you. I was here indeed.'

'Know ye Sir Daniel?' pursued Dick.

'Well do I know him,' returned the man.

'Was he in the mansion?'

'Ay, sir, he was,' answered the archer; 'but even as we entered by the yard gate he rode forth by the garden.'

'Alone?' cried Dick.

'He may 'a' had a score of lances with him,' said the man.

'Lances! No women, then?' asked Shelton.

'Troth, I saw not,' said the archer. 'But there were none in the house, if that be your quest.'

'I thank you,' said Dick. 'Here is a piece for your pains.' But groping in his wallet, Dick found nothing. 'Inquire for me tomorrow,' he added – 'Richard Shel—— Sir Richard Shelton,' he corrected, 'and I will see you handsomely rewarded.

And then an idea struck Dick. He hastily descended to the courtyard, ran with all his might across the garden, and came to the great door of the church. It stood wide open; within, every corner of the pavement was crowded with fugitive burghers, surrounded by their families and laden with the most precious of their possessions, while, at the high altar, priests in full canonicals were imploring the mercy of God. Even as Dick entered, the loud chorus began to thunder in the vaulted roofs.

He hurried through the groups of refugees, and came to the door of the stair that led into the steeple. And here a tall churchman stepped before him and arrested his advance.

'Whither, my son?' he asked, severely.

'My father,' answered Dick, 'I am here upon an errand of expedition. Stay me not. I command here for my Lord of Gloucester.'

'For my Lord of Gloucester?' repeated the priest. 'Hath, then, the battle gone so sore?'

'The battle, father, is at an end, Lancaster clean sped, my Lord of Risingham – Heaven rest him! left upon the field. And now, with your good leave, I follow mine affairs.' And thrusting on one side the priest, who seemed stupefied at the news, Dick pushed open the door and rattled up the stairs four at a bound, and without pause or stumble, till he stepped upon the open platform at the top.

Shoreby Church tower not only commanded the town, as in a map, but looked far, on both sides, over sea and land. It was now near upon noon; the day exceeding bright, the snow dazzling. And as Dick looked around him, he could measure the consequences of the battle.

A confused, growling uproar reached him from the streets, and now and then, but very rarely, the clash of steel. Not a ship, not so much as a skiff remained in harbour; but the sea was dotted with sails and rowboats laden with fugitives. On shore, too, the surface of the snowy meadows was broken up with bands of horsemen, some cutting their way towards the borders of the forest, others, who were doubtless of the Yorkist side, stoutly interposing and beating them back upon the town. Over all the open ground there lay a prodigious quantity of fallen men and horses, clearly defined upon the snow.

To complete the picture, those of the foot soldiers as had not found place upon a ship still kept up an archery combat on the borders of the port, and from the cover of the shoreside taverns. In that quarter, also, one or two houses had been fired, and the smoke towered high in the frosty sunlight, and blew off to sea in voluminous folds.

Already close upon the margin of the woods, and somewhat in the line of Holywood, one particular clump of fleeing horsemen riveted the attention of the young watcher on the tower. It was fairly numerous; in no other quarter of the field did so many Lancastrians still hold together; thus they had left a wide, discoloured wake upon the snow, and Dick was able to trace them step by step from where they had left the town.

While Dick stood watching them, they had gained, unopposed, the first fringe of the leafless forest, and turning a little from their direction, the sun fell for a moment full on their array, as it was relieved against the dusky wood.

'Murrey and blue!' cried Dick. 'I swear it – murrey and blue!'

The next moment he was descending the stairway.

It was now his business to seek out the Duke of Gloucester, who alone, in the disorder of the forces, might be able to supply him with a sufficiency of men. The fighting in the main town was now practically at an end; and as Dick ran hither and thither, seeking the commander, the streets were thick with wandering soldiers, some laden with more booty than they could well stagger under, others shouting drunk. None of them, when questioned, had the least notion of the duke's whereabouts; and, at last, it was by sheer good fortune that Dick found him, where he sat in the saddle, directing operations to dislodge the archers from the harbour side.

'Sir Richard Shelton, ye are well found,' he said. 'I owe you one thing that I value little, my life; and one that I can never pay you for, this victory. Catesby, if I had ten such captains as Sir Richard, I would march forthright on London. But now, sir, claim your reward.'

'Freely, my lord,' said Dick, 'freely and loudly. One hath escaped to whom I owe some grudges, and taken with him one whom I owe love and service. Give me, then, fifty lances, that I may pursue; and for any obligation that your graciousness is pleased to allow, it shall be clean discharged.'

'How call ye him?' inquired the duke.

'Sir Daniel Brackley,' answered Richard.

'Out upon him, double-face!' cried Gloucester. 'Here is no reward, Sir Richard; here is fresh service offered, and, if that ye bring his head to me, a fresh debt upon my conscience. Catesby, get him these lances; and you, sir, bethink ye, in the meanwhile, what pleasure, honour, or profit it shall be mine to give you.'

Just then the Yorkist skirmishers carried one of the shoreside taverns, swarming in upon it on three sides, and driving out or taking its defenders. Crookback Dick was pleased to cheer the exploit, and pushing his horse a little nearer, called to see the prisoners.

There were four or five of them – two men of my Lord Shoreby's and one of Lord Risingham's among the number, and last, but in Dick's eyes not least, a tall, shambling grizzled old shipman, between drunk and sober, and with a dog whimpering and jumping at his heels.

The young duke passed them for a moment under a severe review.

'Good,' he said. 'Hang them.'

And he turned the other way to watch the progress of the fight.

'My lord,' said Dick, 'so please you, I have found my reward. Grant me the life and liberty of yon old shipman.'

Gloucester turned and looked the speaker in the face.

'Sir Richard,' he said, 'I make not war with peacock's feathers, but steel shafts. Those that are mine enemies I slay, and that without excuse or favour. For, bethink ye, in this realm of England, that is so torn in pieces, there is not a man of mine but hath a brother or a friend upon the other party. If, then, I did begin to grant these pardons, I might sheathe my sword.'

'It may be so, my lord; and yet I will be overbold, and, at the risk of your disfavour, recall your lordship's promise,' replied Dick.

Richard of Gloucester flushed.

'Mark it right well,' he said, harshly. 'I love not mercy, nor yet mercymongers. Ye have this day laid the foundations of high fortune. If ye oppose to me my word, which I have plighted, I will yield. But, by the glory of heaven, there your favour dies!'

'Mine is the loss,' said Dick.

'Give him his sailor,' said the duke; and wheeling his horse, he turned his back upon young Shelton.

Dick was nor glad nor sorry. He had seen too much of the young duke to set great store on his affection; and the origin and growth of his own favour had been too flimsy and too rapid to inspire much confidence. One thing alone he feared – that the vindictive leader might revmoke the offer of the lances. But here he did justice neither to Gloucester's honour (such as it was) nor, above all, to his decision. If he had once judged Dick to be the right man to pursue Sir Daniel, he was not one to change; and he soon proved it by shouting after Catesby to be speedy, for the paladin was waiting.

In the meantime, Dick turned to the old shipman, who had seemed equally indifferent to his condemnation and to his subsequent release.

'Arblaster,' said Dick, 'I have done you ill; but now, by the rood, I think I have cleared the score.'

But the old skipper only looked upon him dully and held his peace.

'Come,' continued Dick, 'a life is a life, old shrew, and it is more than ships or liquor. Say ye forgive me; for if your life is worth nothing to you, it hath cost me the beginnings of my fortune. come, I have paid for it dearly; be not so churlish.'

'An I had had my ship, said Arblaster, 'I would 'a' been forth and safe on the high seas – I and my man Tom. But ye took my ship, gossip, and I'm a beggar; and for my man Tom, a knave fellow in russet shot him down. "Murrain!" quoth he, and spake never again. "Murrain" was the last of his words, and the poor spirit of him passed. 'A will never sail no more, will my Tom.'

Dick was seized with unavailing penitence and pity; he sought to take the skipper's hand, but Arblaster avoided his touch.

'Nay,' said he, 'let be. Y' have played the devil with me, and let that content you.'

The words died in Richard's throat. He saw, through tears, the poor old man, bemused with liquor and sorrow, go shambling away, with bowed head, across the snow, and the unnoticed dog whimpering at his heels; and for the first time began to understand the desperate game that we play in life, and how a think once done is not to be changed or remedied by any penitence.

But there was no time left to him for vain regret. Catesby had now collected the horsemen, and riding up to Dick he dismounted, and offered him his own horse.

'This morning,' he said, 'I was somewhat jealous of your favour; it hath not been of a long growth; and now, Sir Richard, it is with a very good heart that I offer you this horse – to ride away with.'

'Suffer me yet a moment,' replied Dick. 'This favour of mine – whereupon was it founded?'

'Upon your name,' answered Catesby. 'It is my lord's chief superstition. Were my name Richard, I should be an earl tomorrow.'

'Well, sir, I thank you,' returned Dick; 'and since I am little likely to follow these great fortunes, I will even say farewell. I will not pretend I was displeased to think myself upon the road to fortune; but I will not pretend, neither, that I am over-sorry to be done with it. Command and riches, they are brave things, to be sure; but a word in your ear – yon duke of yours, he is a fearsome lad.'

Catesby laughed.

'Nay,' said he, 'of a verity he that rides with Crooked Dick will ride deep. Well, God keep us all from evil! Speed ye well.'

Thereupon Dick put himself at the head of his men, and giving the word of command, rode off.

He made straight across the town, following what he supposed to be the route of Sir Daniel, and spying around for any signs that might decide if he were right.

The streets were strewn with the dead and the wounded, whose fate, in the bitter frost, was far the more pitiable. Gangs of the victors went from house to house, pillaging and stabbing, and sometimes singing together as they went.

From different quarters, as he rode on, the sounds of violence and outrage came to young Shelton's ears; now the blows of the sledge-hammer on some barricaded door, and now the miserable shrieks of women.

Dick's heart had just been awakened. He had just seen the cruel consequences of his own behaviour; and the thought of the sum of misery that was now acting in the whole of Shoreby filled him with despair.

At length he reached the outskirts, and there, sure enough, he saw straight before him the same broad beaten track across the snow that he had marked from the summit of the church. Here, then, he went the faster on; but still, as he rode, he kept a bright eye upon the fallen men and horses that lay beside the track. Many of these, he was relieved to see, wore Sir Daniel's colours, and the faces of some, who lay upon their back, he even recognized.

About halfway between the town and the forest, those whom he was following had plainly been assailed by archers; for the corpses lay pretty closely scattered, each pierced by an arrow. And here Dick spied among the rest the body of a very young lad, whose face was somehow hauntingly familiar to him.

He halted his troop, dismounted, and raised the lad's head. As he did so, the hood fell back, and a profusion of long brown hair unrolled itself. At the same time the eyes opened.

'Ah! lion driver!' said a feeble voice. 'She is farther on. Ride – ride fast!'

And then the poor young lady fainted once again.

One of Dick's men carried a flask of some strong cordial, and with this Dick succeeded in reviving consciousness. Then he took Joanna's friend upon his saddle-bow, and once more pushed toward the forest.

'Why do ye take me?' said the girl. 'Ye but delay your speed.'

'Nay, Mistress Risingham,' replied Dick. 'Shoreby is full of blood and drunkenness and riot. Here ye are safe; content ye.'

'I will not be beholden to any of your faction,' she cried; 'set me down.'

'Madam, ye know not what ye say,' returned Dick. 'Y' are hurt'——

'I am not,' she said. 'It was my horse was slain.'

'It matters not one jot,' replied Richard. 'Ye are here in the midst of open snow, and compassed about with enemies. Whether ye will or not, I carry you with me. Glad am I to have the occasion; for thus shall I repay some portion of our debt.'

For a little while she was silent. Then, very suddenly, she asked:

'My uncle?'

'My Lord Risingham?' returned Dick. 'I would I had good news to give you, madam; but I have none. I saw him once in the battle, and once only. Let us hope the best.'

CHAPTER FIVE

Night in the Woods: Alicia Risingham

IT WAS ALMOST CERTAIN THAT Sir Daniel had made for the Moat House; but, considering the heavy snow, the lateness of the hour, and the necessity under which he would lie of avoiding the few roads and striking across the wood, it was equally certain that he could not hope to reach it ere the morrow.

There were two courses open to Dick; either to continue to follow in the knight's trail, and, if he were able, to fall upon him that very night in camp, or to strike out a path of his own, and seek to place himself between Sir Daniel and his destination.

Either scheme was open to serious objection, and Dick, who feared to expose Joanna to the hazards of a fight, had not yet decided between them when he reached the borders of the wood.

At this point Sir Daniel had turned a little to his left, and then plunged straight under a grove of very lofty timber. His party had then formed to a narrower front, in order to pass between the trees, and the track was trod proportionately deeper in the snow. The eye followed it, under the leafless tracery of the oaks, running direct and narrow; the trees stood over it, with knotty joints and the great, uplifted forest of their boughs; there was no sound, whether of man or beast – not so much as the stirring of a robin; and over the field of snow the winter sun lay golden among netted shadows.

'How say ye,' asked Dick of one of the men, 'to follow straight on, or strike across for Tunstall?'

'Sir Richard,' replied the man-at-arms, 'I would follow the line until they scatter.'

'Ye are, doubtless, right,' returned Dick; 'but we came right hastily upon the errand, even as the time commanded. Here are no houses, neither for food nor shelter, and by the morrow's dawn we shall know both cold fingers and an empty belly. How say ye, lads? Will ye stand a pinch for expedition's sake, or shall we turn by Holywood and sup with Mother Church? The case being somewhat doubtful, I will drive no man; yet if ye would suffer me to lead you, ye would choose the first.'

The men answered, almost with one voice, that they would follow Sir Richard where he would.

And Dick, setting spur to his horse, began once more to go forward.

The snow in the trail had been trodden very hard, and the pursuers had thus a great advantage over the pursued. They pushed on, indeed, at a round trot, two hundred hoofs beating alternately on the dull pavement of the snow, and the jingle of weapons and the snorting of horses raising a warlike noise along the arches of the silent wood.

Presently, the wide slot of the pursued came out upon the high road, from Holywood; it was there, for a moment, indistinguishable; and, where it once more plunged into the unbeaten snow upon the farther side, Dick was surprised to see it narrower and lighter trod. Plainly, profiting by the road, Sir Daniel had begun already to scatter his command.

At all hazards, one chance being equal to another, Dick continued to pursue the straight trail; and that, after an hour's riding, in which it led into the very depths of the forest, suddenly split, like a bursting shell, into two dozen others, leading to every point of the compass.

Dick drew bridle in despair. The short winter's day was near an end; the sun, a dull red orange, shorn of rays, swam low among the leafless thickets; the shadows were a mile long upon the snow; the frost bit cruelly at the finger-nails; and the breath and steam of the horses mounted in a cloud.

'Well, we are outwitted,' Dick confessed. 'Strike we for Holywood, after all. It is still nearer us than Tunstall – or should be by the station of the sun.'

So they wheeled to their left, turning their backs on the red shield of sun, and made across country for the abbey. But now times were changed with them; they could no longer sprank forth briskly on a path beaten firm by the passage of their foes, and for a goal to which that path itself conducted them. Now they must plough at a dull pace through the encumbering snow, continually pausing to decide their course, continually floundering in drifts. The sun soon left them; the glow of the west decayed; and presently they were wandering in a shadow of blackness, under frosty stars.

Presently, indeed, the moon would clear the hilltops, and they might resume their march. But till then, every random step might carry them wider of their march. There was nothing for it but to camp and wait.

Sentries were posted; a spot of ground was cleared of snow, and after some failures, a good fire blazed in the midst. The men-at-arms sat close about this forest hearth, sharing such provisions as they had, and passing about the flask; and Dick, having collected the most delicate of the rough and scanty fare, brought it to Lord Risingham's niece, where she sat apart from the soldiery against a tree.

She sat upon one horse-cloth, wrapped in another, and stared straight before her at the firelit scene. At the offer of food she started, like one wakened from a dream, and then silently refused.

'Madam,' said Dick, 'let me beseech you, punish me not so cruelly. Wherein I have offended you, I know not; I have, indeed, carried you away, but with a friendly violence; I have, indeed, exposed you to the inclemency of night, but the hurry that lies upon me hath for its end the preservation of another, who is no less frail and no less unfriended than yourself. At least, madam, punish not yourself; and eat, if not for hunger, then for strength.'

'I will eat nothing at the hands that slew my kinsman,' she replied.

'Dear madam,' Dick cried, 'I swear to you upon the rood I touched him not.'

'Swear to me that he still lives,' she returned.

'I will not palter with you,' answered Dick. 'Pity bids me to wound you. In my heart I do believe him dead.'

'And ye ask me to eat!' she cried. 'Ay, and they call you "sir"! Y' have won your spurs by my good kinsman's murder. And had I not been fool and traitor both, and saved you in your enemy's house, ye should have died the death, and he – he that was worth twelve of you – were living.'

'I did but my man's best, even as your kinsman did upon the other party,' answered Dick. 'Were he still living – as I vow to Heaven I wish it! – he would praise, not blame me.'

'Sir Daniel hath told me,' she replied. 'He marked you at the barricade. Upon you, he saith, their party foundered; it was you that won the battle. Well, then, it was you that killed my good Lord Risingham, as sure as though ye had strangled him. And ye would have me eat with you – and your hands not washed from killing? But Sir Daniel hath sworn your downfall. He 'tis that will avenge me!'

The unfortunate Dick was plunged in gloom. Old Arblaster returned upon his mind, and he groaned aloud.

'Do ye hold me so guilty?' he said; 'you that defended me – you that are Joanna's friend?'

'What made ye in the battle?' she retorted. 'Y' are of no party; y' are but a lad – but legs and body, without government of wit or counsel! Wherefore did ye fight? For the love of hurt, pardy!'

'Nay,' cried Dick, 'I know not. But as the realm of England goes, if that a poor gentleman fight not upon the one side, perforce he must fight upon the other. He may not stand alone; 'tis not in nature.'

'They that have no judgment should not draw the sword,' replied the young lady. 'Ye that fight but for a hazard, what are ye but a butcher? War is but noble by the cause, and y' have disgraced it.'

'Madam,' said the miserable Dick, 'I do partly see mine error. I have made too much haste; I have been busy before my time. Already I stole a ship – thinking, I do swear it, to do well – and thereby brought about the death of many innocent, and the grief and ruin of a poor old man whose face this very day hath stabbed me like a dagger. And for this morning, I did but design to do myself credit, and get fame to marry with, and, behold! I have brought about the death of your dear kinsman that was good to me. And what besides, I know not. For, alas! I may have set York upon the throne, and that may be the worser cause, and may do hurt to England. O, madam, I do see my sin. I am unfit for life. I will, for penance sake and to avoid worse evil, once I have finished this adventure, get me to a cloister. I will forswear Joanna and the trade of arms. I will be a friar, and pray for your good kinsman's spirit all my days.'

It appeared to Dick, in this extremity of his humiliation and repentance, that the young lady had laughed.

Raising his countenance, he found her looking down upon him, in the fire-light, with a somewhat peculiar but not unkind expression.

'Madam,' he cried, thinking the laughter to have been an illusion of his hearing, but still, from her changed looks, hoping to have touched her heart – 'madam, will not this content you? I give up all to undo what I have done amiss; I make heaven certain for Lord Risingham. And all this upon the very day that I have won my spurs, and thought myself the happiest young gentleman on ground.'

'Oh, boy,' she said – 'good boy!'

And then, to the extreme surprise of Dick, she first very tenderly wiped the tears away from his cheeks, and then, as if yielding to a sudden impulse, threw both her arms about his neck, drew up his face, and kissed him. A pitiful bewilderment came over simple-minded Dick.

'But come,' she said, with great cheerfulness, 'you that are a captain, ye must eat. Why sup ye not?'

'Dear Mistress Risingham,' replied Dick, 'I did but wait first upon my prisoner; but, to say truth, penitence will no longer suffer me to endure the sight of food. I were better to fast, dear lady, and to pray.'

'Call me Alicia,' she said; 'are we not old friends? And now, come, I will eat with you, bit for bit and sup for sup; so if ye eat not, neither will I; but if ye eat hearty, I will dine like a ploughman.'

So there and then she fell to; and Dick, who had an excellent stomach, proceeded to bear her company, at first with great reluctance, but gradually, as he entered into the spirit, with more and more vigour and devotion; until, at last, he forgot even to watch his model, and most heartily repaired the expenses of his day of labour and excitement.

'Lion-driver,' she said, at length, 'ye do not admire a maid in a man's jerkin?'

The moon was now up; and they were only waiting to repose the wearied horses. By the moon's light, the still penitent but now well-fed Richard beheld her looking somewhat coquettishly down upon him.

'Madam'—— he stammered, surprised at this new turn in her manners.

'Nay,' she interrupted, 'it skills not to deny; Joanna hath told me, but come, Sir Lion-driver, look at me – am I so homely – come!'

And she made bright eyes at him.

'Ye are something smallish, indeed'—— began Dick.

And here again she interrupted him, this time with a ringing peal of laughter that completed his confusion and surprise.

'Smallish!' she cried. 'Nay, now, be honest as ye are bold; I am a dwarf, or little better; but for all that – come, tell me! – for all that, passably fair to look upon; is't not so?'

'Nay, madam, exceedingly fair,' said the distressed knight, pitifully trying to seem easy.

'And a man would be right glad to wed me?' she pursued.

'O, madam, right glad!' agreed Dick.

'Call me Alicia,' said she.

'Alicia,' quoth Sir Richard.

'Well, then, lion-driver,' she continued, 'sith that ye slew my kinsmen, and left me without stay, ye owe me, in honour, every reparation; do ye not?'

'I do, madam,' said Dick. 'Although, upon my heart, I do hold me, but partially guilty of that brave knight's blood.'

'Would ye evade me?' she cried.

'Madam, not so. I have told you; at your bidding, I will even turn me a monk,' said Richard.

'Then, in honour, ye belong to me?' she concluded.

'In honour, madam, I suppose'—— began the young man.

'Go to!' she interrupted; 'ye are too full of catches. In honour do ye belong to me, till ye have paid the evil?'

'In honour I do,' said Dick.

'Hear, then,' she continued. 'You would make but a sad friar, methinks; and since I am to dispose of you at pleasure, I will even take you for my husband. Nay, now, no words!' cried she. 'They will avail you nothing. For see how just it is, that you who deprived me of one home, should supply me with another. And as for Joanna, she will be the first, believe me, to commend the change; for, after all, as we be dear friends, what matters it with which of us ye wed? Not one whit!'

'Madam,' said Dick, 'I will go into a cloister, an ye please to bid me; but to wed with anyone in this big world besides Joanna Sedley is what I will consent to neither for man's force nor yet for lady's pleasure. Pardon me if I speak my plain thoughts plainly; but where a maid is very bold, a poor man must even be the bolder.'

'Dick,' she said, 'ye sweet boy, ye must come and kiss me for that word. Nay, fear not, ye shall kiss me for Joanna, and when we meet, I shall give it back to her, and say I stole it. And as for what ye owe me, why, dear simpleton, methinks ye were not alone in that great battle; and even if York be on the throne, it was not you that set him there. But for a good, sweet, honest heart, Dick, y' are all that; and if I could find it in my soul to envy your Joanna anything, I would even envy her your love.'

CHAPTER SIX

Night in the Woods (concluded) Dick and Joan

THE HORSES HAD BY THIS TIME finished the small store of provender, and fully breathed from their fatigues. At Dick's command, the fire was smothered in snow; and while his men got once more wearily to saddle, he himself, remembering, somewhat late, true woodland caution, chose a tall oak, and nimbly clambered to the topmost fork. Hence he could look far abroad on the moonlit and snow-paven forest. On the south-west, dark against the horizon, stood those upland heathy quarters where he and Joanna had met with the terrifying misadventure of the leper. And there his eye was caught by a spot of ruddy brightness no bigger than a needle's eye.

He blamed himself sharply for his previous neglect. Were that, as it appeared to be, the shining of Sir Daniel's camp-fire, he should long ago have seen and marched for it; above all, he should, for no consideration, have announced his neighbourhood by lighting a fire of his own. But now he must no longer squander valuable hours. The direct way to the uplands was about two miles in length; but it was crossed by a very deep, precipitous dingle, impassable to mounted men; and for the sake of speed, it seemed to Dick advisable to desert the horses and attempt the adventure on foot.

Ten men were left to guard the horses; signals were agreed upon by which they could communicate in case of need; and Dick set forth at the head of the remainder, Alicia Risingham walking stoutly by his side.

The men had freed themselves of heavy armour, and left behind their lances; and they now marched with a very good spirit in the frozen snow, and under the exhilarating lustre of the moon. The descent into the dingle, where a stream strained sobbing through the snow and ice, was effected with silence and order; and on the further side, being then within a short half mile of where Dick had seen the glimmer of the fire, the party halted to breathe before the attack.

In the vast silence of the wood, the lightest sounds were audible from far; and Alicia, who was keen of hearing, held up her finger warningly, and stooped to listen. All followed her example; but besides the groans of the choked brook in the dingle close behind, and the barking of a fox at a distance of many miles among the forest, to Dick's acutest hearkening not a breath was audible.

'But yet, for sure, I heard the clash of harness,' whispered Alicia.

'Madam,' returned Dick, who was more afraid of that young lady than of ten stout warriors, 'I would not hint ye were mistaken; but it might well have come from either of the camps.'

'It came not thence. It came from westward,' she declared.

'It may be what it will,' returned Dick; 'and it must be as Heaven please. Reck we not a jot, but push on the livelier, and put it to the touch. Up, friends – enough breathed.'

As they advanced, the snow became more and more trampled with hoof-marks, and it was plain that they were drawing near to the encampment of a considerable force of mounted men. Presently they could see the smoke pouring from among the trees, ruddily coloured on its lower edge and scattering bright sparks.

And here, pursuant to Dick's orders, his men began to open out, creeping stealthily in the covert, to surround on every side the camp of their opponents. He himself, placing Alicia in the shelter of a bulky oak, stole straight forth in the direction of the fire.

At last, through an opening of the wood, his eye embraced the scene of the encampment. The fire had been built upon a heathy hummock of the ground, surrounded on three sides by thicket, and it now burned very strong, roaring aloud and brandishing flames. Around it there sat not quite a dozen people, warmly cloaked; but though the neighbouring snow was trampled down as by a regiment, Dick looked in vain for any horse. He began to have a terrible misgiving that he was out-manoeuvred. At the same time, in a tall man with a steel salet, who was spreading his hands before the blaze, he recognized his old friend and still kindly enemy, Bennet Hatch; and in two others, sitting a little back, he made out, even in their male disguise, Joanna Sedley and Sir Daniel's wife.

'Well,' thought he to himself, 'even if I lose my horses, let me get my Joanna, and why should I complain?'

And then, from the further side of the encampment, there came a little whistle, announcing that his men had joined and the investment was complete.

Bennet, at the sound, started to his feet; but ere he had time to spring upon his arms, Dick hailed him.

'Bennet,' he said – 'Bennet, old friend, yield ye. Ye will but spill men's lives in vain if ye resist.'

''Tis Master Shelton, by St Barbary!' cried Hatch. 'Yield me? Ye ask much. What force have ye?'

'I tell you, Bennet, ye are both outnumbered and begirt,' said Dick. 'Caesar and Charlemagne would cry for quarter. I have two score men at my whistle, and with one shoot of arrows I could answer for you all.'

'Master Dick,' said Bennet, 'It goes against my heart; but I must do my duty. The saints help you!' and therewith he raised a little tucket to his mouth and wound a rousing call.

Then followed a moment of confusion; for while Dick, fearing for the ladies, still hesitated to give the word to shoot, Hatch's little band sprang to their weapons and formed back to back as for a fierce resistance. In the hurry of their change of place, Joanna sprang from her seat and ran like an arrow to her lover's side.

'Here, Dick!' she cried, as she clasped his hand in hers.

But Dick still stood irresolute; he was yet young to the more deplorable necessities of war, and the thought of old Lady Brackley checked the command upon his tongue. His own men became restive. Some of them cried on him by name; others, of their own accord, began to shoot; and at the first discharge poor Bennet bit the dust. Then Dick awoke.

'On!' he cried. 'Shoot, boys, and keep to cover. England and York!'

But just then the dull beat of many horses on the snow suddenly arose in the hollow ear of the night, and, with incredible swiftness, drew nearer and swelled louder. At the same time, answering tuckets repeated and repeated Hatch's call.

'Rally, rally!' cried Dick. 'Rally upon me! Rally for your lives!'

But his men – afoot, scattered, taken in the hour when they had counted on an easy triumph – began instead to give ground severally, and either stood wavering or dispersed into the thickets. And when the first of the horsemen came charging through the open avenues and fiercely riding their steeds into the underwood, a few stragglers were overthrown or speared among the brush, but the bulk of Dick's command had simply melted at the rumour of their coming.

Dick stood for a moment, bitterly recognizing the fruits of his precipitate and unwise valour. Sir Danile had seen the fire; he had moved out with his main force, whether to attack his pursuers or to take them in the rear if they should venture the assault. His had been throughout the part of a sagacious captain; Dick's the conduct of an eager boy. And here was the young knight, his sweetheart, indeed, holding him tightly by the hand, but otherwise alone, his whole command of men and horses dispersed in the night and the wide forest, like a paper of pins in a hay barn.

'The saints enlighten me!' he thought. 'It is well I was knighted for this morning's matter; this doth me little honour.'

And thereupon, still holding Joanna, he began to run.

The silence of the night was now shattered by the shouts of the men of Tunstall, as they galloped hither and thither, hunting fugitives; and Dick broke boldly through the underwood and ran straight before him like a deer. The silver clearness of the moon upon the open snow increased, by contrast, the obscurity of the thickets; and the extreme dispersion of the vanquished led the pursuers into widely divergent paths. Hence, in but a little while, Dick and Joanna paused, in a close covert, and heard the sounds of the pursuit, scattering abroad, indeed, in all directions, but yet fainting already in the distance.

'An I had but kept a reserve of them together,' Dick cried, bitterly, 'I could have turned the tables yet! Well, we live and learn; next time, it shall go better, by the rood.'

'Nay, Dick,' said Joanna, 'what matters it? Here we are together once again.'

He looked at her, and there she was – John Matcham, as of yore, in hose and doublet. But now he knew her; now, even in that ungainly dress, she smiled upon him, bright with love; and his heart was transported with joy.

'Sweetheart,' he said, 'if ye forgive this blunderer, what care I? Make we direct for Holywood; there lieth your good guardian and my better friend, Lord Foxham. There shall we be wed; and whether poor or wealthy, famous or unknown, what matters it? This day, dear love, I won my spurs; I was commended by great men for my valour; I thought myself the goodliest man of war in all broad England. Then, first, I fell out of my favour with the great; and now have I been well thrashed, and clean lost my soldiers. There was a downfall for conceit! But, dear, I care not – dear, if ye still love me and will wed, I would have my knighthood done away, and mind it not a jot.'

'My Dick!' she cried. 'And did they knight you?'

'Ay, dear, ye are my lady now,' he answered, fondly; 'or ye shall, ere noon tomorrow – will ye not?'

'That will I, Dick, with a glad heart,' she answered.

'Ay, sir? Methought ye were to be a monk said a voice in their ears.

'Alicia!' cried Joanna.

'Even so,' replied the young lady, coming forward. 'Alicia, whom ye left for dead, and whom your lion-driver found, and brought to life again, and, by my sooth, made love to, if ye want to know.'

'I'll not believe it,' cried Joanna. 'Dick!'

'Dick!' mimicked Alicia. 'Dick, indeed! Ay, fair sir, and ye desert poor damsels in distress,' she continued, turning to the young knight. 'Ye leave them planted behind oaks. But they say true – the age of chivalry is dead.'

'Madam,' cried Dick, in despair, 'upon my soul I had forgotten you outright. Madam, ye must try to pardon me. Ye see, I had new found Joanna!'

'I did not suppose that ye had done it o' purpose,' she retorted. 'But I will be cruelly avenged. I will tell a secret to my Lady Shelton – she that is to be,' she added, curtseying. 'Joanna,' she continued, 'I believe, upon my soul, your sweetheart is a bold fellow in a fight, but he is, let me tell you plainly, the softest-hearted simpleton in England. Go to – ye may do your pleasure with him!

And now, fool children, first kiss me, either one of you, for luck and kindness; and then kiss each other just one minute by the glass, and not one second longer; and then let us all three set forth for Holywood as fast as we can stir; for these woods, methinks, are full of peril and exceeding cold.'

'But did my Dick make love to you?' asked Joanna, clinging to her sweetheart's side.

'Nay, fool girl,' returned Alicia; 'it was I made love to him. I offered to marry him, indeed; but he bade me go marry with my likes. These were his words. Nay, that I will say: he is more plain than pleasant. But now, children, for the sake of sense, set forward. Shall we go once more over the dingle, or push straight for Holywood?'

'Why,' said Dick, 'I would like dearly to get upon a horse; for I have been sore mauled and beaten, one way and another, these last days, and my poor body is one bruise. But how think ye? If the men, upon the alarm of the fighting, had fled away, we should have gone about for nothing. 'Tis but some three short miles to Holywood direct; the bell hath not beat nine; the snow is pretty firm to walk upon, the moon clear; how if we went even as we are?'

'Agreed,' cried Alicia; but Joanna only pressed upon Dick's arm.

Forth, then, they went, through open leafless groves and down snow-clad alleys, under the white face of the winter moon; Dick and Joanna walking hand in hand and in a heaven of pleasure; and their light-minded companion, her own bereavements heartily forgotten, followed a pace or two behind, now rallying them upon their silence, and now drawing happy pictures of their future and united lives.

Still, indeed, in the distance of the wood, the riders of Tunstall might be heard urging their pursuit; and from time to time cries or the clash of steel announced the shock of enemies. But in these young folk, bred among the alarms of war, and fresh from such a multiplicity of dangers, neither fear nor pity could be lightly wakened. Content to find the sounds still drawing farther and farther away, they gave up their hearts to the enjoyment of the hour, walking already as Alicia put it, in a wedding procession; and neither the rude solitude of the forest, nor the cold of the freezing night, had any force to shadow or distract their happiness.

At length, from a rising hill, they looked below them on the dell of Holywood. The great windows of the forest abbey shone with torch and candle; its high pinnacles and spires arose very clear and silent, and the gold rood upon the topmost summit glittered brightly in the moon. All about it, in the open glade, camp-fires were burning, and the ground was thick with huts; and across the midst of the picture the frozen river curved.

'By the mass,' said Richard, 'there are Lord Foxham's fellows still encamped. The messenger hath certainly miscarried. Well, then, so better. We have power at hand to face Sir Daniel.'

But if Lord Foxham's men still lay encamped in the long holm at Holywood, it was from a different reason from the one supposed by Dick. They had marched, indeed, for Shoreby; but ere they were half way thither, a second messenger met them, and bade them return to their morning's camp, to bar the road against Lancastrian fugitives, and to be so much nearer to the main army of York. For Richard of Gloucester, having finished the battle and stamped out his foes in that district, was already on the march to rejoin his brother; and not long after the return of my Lord Foxham's retainers, Crookback himself drew rein before the abbey door. It was in honour of this august visitor that the windows shone with lights; and at the hour of Dick's arrival with his sweetheart and her friend, the whole ducal party was being entertained in the refectory with the splendour of that powerful and luxurious monastery.

Dick, not quite with his good will, was brought before them. Gloucester, sick with fatigue, sat leaning upon one hand his white and terrifying countenance; Lord Foxham, half recovered from his wound, was in a place of honour on his left.

'How, sir?' asked Richard. 'Have ye brought me Sir Daniel's head?'

'My lord duke,' replied Dick, stoutly enough, but with a qualm at heart, 'I have not even the good fortune to return with my command. I have been, so please your grace, well beaten.'

Gloucester looked upon him with a formidable frown.

'I gave you fifty lances,* sir,' he said.

'My lord duke, I had but fifty men-at-arms,' replied the young knight.

'How is this?' said Gloucester. 'He did ask me fifty lances.'

'May it please your grace,' replied Catesby, smoothly, 'for a pursuit we gave him but the horsemen.'

'It is well,' replied Richard, adding, 'Shelton, ye may go.'

'Stay!' said Lord Foxham. 'This young man likewise had a charge from me. It may be he hath better sped. Say, Master Shelton, have he found the maid?'

'I praise the saints, my lord,' said Dick, 'she is in this house.'

'Is it even so? Well, then, my lord the duke,' resumed Lord Foxham, 'with your good will, tomorrow, before the army march, I do propose a marriage. This young squire——'

'Young knight,' interrupted Catesby.

'Say ye so, Sir William?' cried Lord Foxham.

'I did myself, and for good service, dub him knight,' said Gloucester. 'He hath twice manfully served me. It is not valour of hands, it is a man's mind of iron, that he lacks. He will not rise, Lord Foxham. 'Tis a fellow that will fight indeed bravely in a mellay but hath a capon's heart. Howbeit, if he is to marry, marry him in the name of Mary, and be done!'

'Nay, he is a brave lad – I know it,' said Lord Foxham. 'Content ye, then, Sir Richard. I have compounded this affair with Master Hamley, and tomorrow ye shall wed.'

Whereupon Dick judged it prudent to withdraw; but he was not yet clear of the refectory, when a man, but newly alighted at the gate, came running four stairs at a bound, and brushing through the abbey servants, threw himself on one knee before the duke.

'Victory, my lord,' he cried.

And before Dick had got to the chamber set apart for him as Lord Foxham's guest, the troops in the holm were cheering around their fires; for upon that same day, not twenty miles away, a second crushing blow had been dealt to the power of Lancaster.

* Technically, the term 'lance' included a not quite certain number of foot soldiers attached to a man-at-arms.

CHAPTER SEVEN

Dick's Revenge

THE NEXT MORNING DICK WAS afoot before the sun, and having dressed himself to the best advantage with the aid of the Lord Foxham's baggage, and got good reports of Joan, he set forth on foot to walk away his impatience.

For some while he made rounds among the soldiery, who were getting to arms in the wintry twilight of the dawn and by the red glow of torches; but gradually he strolled further afield, and at length passed clean beyond the outpost, and walked alone in the frozen forest, waiting for the sun.

His thoughts were both quiet and happy. His brief favour with the duke he could not find it in his heart to mourn; with Joan to wife, and my Lord Foxham for a faithful patron, he looked most happily upon the future; and in the past he found but little to regret.

As he thus strolled and pondered, the solemn light of the morning grew more clear, the east was already coloured by the sun, and a little scathing wind blew up the frozen snow. He turned to go home; but even as he turned, his eye lit upon a figure behind a tree.

'Stand!' he cried. 'Who goes?'

The figure stepped forth and waved its hand like a dumb person. It was arrayed like a pilgrim, the hood lowered over the face, but Dick, in an instant recognized Sir Daniel.

He strode up to him, drawing his sword; and the knight, putting his hand in his bosom, as if to seize a hidden weapon, steadfastly awaited his approach.

'Well, Dickon,' said Sir Daniel, 'how is it to be? Do ye make war upon the fallen?'

'I made no war upon your life,' replied the lad; 'I was your true friend until ye sought for mine; but ye have sought for it greedily.'

'Nay – self-defence,' replied the knight. And now, boy, the news of this battle, and the presence of yon crooked devil here in mine own wood, have broken me beyond all help. I go to Holywood for sanctuary; thence overseas, with what I can carry, and to begin life again in Burgundy or France.'

'Ye may not go to Holywood,' said Dick.

'How! May not?' asked the knight.

'Look ye, Sir Daniel, this is my marriage morn,' said Dick; 'and yon sun that is to rise will make the brightest day that ever shone for me. Your life is forfeit – doubly forfeit, for my father's death and your own practices to me-ward. But I myself have done amiss; I have brought about men's deaths; and upon this glad day I will be neither judge nor hangman. An ye were the devil, I would not lay a hand on you. An ye were the devil, ye might go where ye will for me. Seek God's forgiveness; mine ye have freely. But to go on to Holywood is different. I carry arms for York, and I will suffer no spy within their lines. Hold it, then, for certain, if ye set one foot before another, I will uplift my voice and call the nearest post to seize you.'

'Ye mock me,' said Sir Daniel. 'I have no safety out of Holywood.'

'I care no more,' returned Richard. 'I let you go east, west or south; north I will not. Holywood is shut against you. Go, and seek not to return. For, once ye are gone, I will warn every post about this army, and there will be so shrewd a watch upon all pilgrims that, once again, were ye the very devil, ye would find it ruin to make the essay.'

'Ye doom me,' said Sir Daniel, gloomily.

'I doom you not,' returned Richard. 'If it so please you to set your valour against mine, come on; and though I fear it be disloyal to my party, I will take the challenge openly and fully, fight you with mine own single strength, and call for none to help me. So shall I avenge my father, with a perfect conscience.'

'Ay,' said Sir Daniel, 'y' have a long sword against my dagger.'

'I rely upon Heaven only,' answered Dick, casting his sword some way behind him on the snow. 'Now, if your ill-fate bids you, come; and, under the pleasure of the Almighty, I make myself bold to feed your bones to foxes.'

'I did but try you, Dickon,' returned the knight, with an uneasy semblance of a laugh. 'I would not spill your blood.'

'Go, then, ere it be too late,' replied Shelton. 'In five minutes I will call the post. I do perceive that I am too long-suffering. Had but our places been reversed, I should have been bound hand and foot some minutes past.'

'Well, Dickon, I will go,' replied Sir Daniel. 'When we next meet, it shall repent you that ye were so harsh.'

And with these words, the knight turned and began to move off under the trees. Dick watched him with strangely-mingled feelings, as he went, swiftly and warily, and ever and again turning a wicked eye upon the lad who had spared him, and whom he still suspected.

There was upon one side of where he went a thicket, strongly matted with green ivy, and, even in its winter state, impervious to the eye. Herein, all of a sudden, a bow sounded like a note of music. An arrow flew, and with a great, choked cry of agony, the Knight of Tunstall threw up his hands and fell forward in the snow.

Dick bounded to his side and raised him. His face desperately worked; his whole body was shaken by contorting spasms.

'Is the arrow black?' he gasped.

'It is black,' replied Dick, gravely.

And then, before he could add one word, a desperate seizure of pain shook the wounded man from head to foot, so that his body leaped in Dick's supporting arms, and with the extremity of that pang his spirit fled in silence.

The young man laid him back gently on the snow and prayed for that unprepared and guilty spirit, and as he prayed the sun came up at a bound, and the robins began chirping in the ivy.

When he rose to his feet, he found another man upon his knees but a few steps behind him, and, still with uncovered head, he waited until that prayer also should be over. It took long; the man, with his head bowed and his face covered with his hands, prayed like one in a great disorder or distress of mind;

and by the bow that lay beside him, Dick judged that he was no other than the archer who had laid Sir Daniel low.

At length he also rose, and showed the countenance of Ellis Duckworth.

'Richard,' he said, very gravely, 'I heard you. Ye took the better part and pardoned; I took the worse, and there lays the clay of mine enemy. Pray for me.'

And he wrung him by the hand.

'Sir,' said Richard, 'I will pray for you, indeed; though how I may prevail I wot not. But if ye have so long pursued revenge, and find it now of such a sorry flavour, bethink ye, were it not well to pardon others? Hatch – he is dead, poor shrew! I would have spared a better; and for Sir Daniel, here lies his body. But for the priest, if I might anywise prevail, I would have you let him go.'

A flash came into the eyes of Ellis Duckworth.

'Nay,' he said, 'the devil is still strong within me. But be at rest; the Black Arrow flieth nevermore – the fellowship is broken. They that still live shall come to their quiet and ripe end, in Heaven's good time, for me; and for yourself, go where your better fortune calls you, and think no more of Ellis.'

CHAPTER EIGHT

Conclusion

ABOUT NINE IN THE MORNING, Lord Foxham was leading his ward, once more dressed as befitted her sex, and followed by Alicia Risingham, to the church of Holywood, when Richard Crookback, how brow already heavy with cares, crossed their path and paused.

'Is this the maid?' he asked; and when Lord Foxham had replied in the affirmative, 'Minion,' he added, 'hold up your face until I see its favour.'

He looked upon her sourly for a little.

'Ye are fair,' he said at last, 'and, as they tell me, dowered. How if I offered you a brave marriage, as became your face and parentage?'

'My lord duke,' replied Joanna, 'may it please your grace, I had rather wed with Sir Richard.'

'How so?' he asked, harshly. 'Marry but the man I name to you, and he shall be my lord, and you my lady, before night. For Sir Richard, let me tell you plainly, he will die Sir Richard.'

'I ask no more of Heaven, my lord, than but to die Sir Richard's wife,' returned Joanna.

'Look ye at that, my lord,' said Gloucester, turning to Lord Foxham. 'Here be a pair for you. The lad, when for good services I gave him his choice of my favour, chose but the grace of an old, drunken shipman. I did warn him freely, but he was stout in his besottedness. "Here dieth your favour," said I; and he, my lord, with the most assured impertinence, "Mine be the loss," quoth he. It shall be so, by the rood!'

'Said he so?' cried Alicia. 'Then well said, Lion-driver!'

'Who is this?' asked the duke.

'A prisoner of Sir Richard's,' answered Lord Foxham; 'Mistress Alicia Risingham.'

'See that she be married to a sure man,' said the duke.

'I had thought of my kinsman, Hamley, an it like your grace,' returned Lord Foxham. 'He hath well served the cause.'

'It likes me well, said Richard. 'Let them be wedded speedily. Say, fair maid, will you wed?'

'My lord duke,' said Alicia, 'so as the man is straight——' And there, in a perfect consternation, the voice died on her tongue.

'He is straight, my mistress,' replied Richard, calmly. 'I am the only crookback of my party; we are else passably well shapen. Ladies, and you, my lord,' he added, with a sudden change to grave courtesy, 'judge me not too churlish if I leave you. A captain, in the time of war, hath not the ordering of his hours.'

And with a very handsome salutation he passed on, followed by his officers.

'Alack,' cried Alicia, 'I am shent!'

'Ye know him not,' replied Lord Foxham. 'It is but a trifle; he hath already clean forgot your words.'

'He is, then, the very flower of knighthood,' said Alicia.

'Nay, he but mindeth other things,' returned Lord Foxham. 'Tarry we no more.'

In the chancel they found Dick waiting, attended by a few young men; and there were he and Joan united. When they came forth again, happy and yet serious, into the frosty air and sunlight, the long files of the army were already winding forward up the road; already the Duke of Gloucester's banner was unfolded and began to move from before the abbey in a clump of spears; and behind it, girt by steel-clad knights, the bold, black-hearted, and ambitious hunchback moved on towards his brief kingdom and his lasting infamy. But the wedding party turned upon the other side, and sat down, with sober merriment, to breakfast. The father cellarer attended on their wants, and sat with them at table. Hamley, all jealousy forgotten, began to ply the nowise loth Alicia with courtship. And there, amid the sounding of tuckets and the clash of armoured soldiery and horses continually moving forth, Dick and Joan sat side by side, tenderly held hands, and looked, with ever growing affection, in each other's eyes.

Thenceforth the dust and blood of that unruly epoch passed them by. They dwelt apart from alarms in the green forest where their love began.

Two old men in the meanwhile enjoyed pensions in great prosperity and peace, and with perhaps a superfluity of ale and wine, in Tunstall hamlet. One had been all his life a shipman, and continued to the last to lament his man Tom. The other, who had been a bit of everything, turned in the end towards piety, and made a most religious death under the name of Brother Honestus in the neighbouring abbey. So Lawless had his will, and died a friar.

THE STRANGE CASE OF
DR JEKYLL
AND MR HYDE

To
KATHARINE DE MATTOS

It's ill to loose the bands that God decreed to bind;
Still will we be the children of the heather and the wind;
Far away from home, O it's still for you and me
That the broom is blowing bonnie in the north countrie.

CHAPTER ONE

Story of the Door

MR UTTERSON THE LAWYER was a man of a rugged countenance, that was never lighted by a smile; cold, scanty and embarrassed in discourse; backward in sentiment; lean, long, dusty, dreary, and yet somehow lovable. At friendly meetings, and when the wine was to his taste, something eminently human beaconed from his eye; something indeed which never found its way into his talk, but which spoke not only in these silent symbols of the after-dinner face, but more often and loudly in the acts of his life. He was austere with himself; drank gin when he was alone, to mortify a taste for vintages; and though he enjoyed the theatre, had not crossed the doors of one for twenty years. But he had an approved tolerance for others; sometimes wondering, almost with envy, at the high pressure of spirits involved in their misdeeds; and in any extremity inclined to help rather than to reprove. 'I incline to Cain's heresy,' he used to say quaintly: 'I let my brother go to the devil in his own way.' In this character it was frequently his fortune to be the last reputable acquaintance and the last good influence in the lives of down-going men. And to such as these, so long as they came about his chambers, he never marked a shade of change in his demeanour.

No doubt the feat was easy to Mr Utterson; for he was undemonstrative at the best, and even his friendships seemed to be founded in a similar catholicity of good-nature. It is the mark of a modest man to accept his friendly circle ready made from the hands of opportunity; and that was the lawyer's way. His friends were those of his own blood, or those whom he had known the longest; his affections, like ivy, were the growth of time, they implied no aptness in the object. Hence, no doubt, the bond that united him to Mr Richard Enfield, his distant kinsman, the well-known man about town. It was a nut to crack for many, what these two could see in each other, or what subject they could find in common. It was reported by those who encountered them in their Sunday walks, that they said nothing, looking singularly dull, and would hail with obvious relief the appearance of a friend. For all that, the two men put the greatest store by these excursions, counted them the chief jewel of each week, and not only set aside occasions of pleasure, but even resisted the calls of business, that they might enjoy them uninterrupted.

It chanced on one of these rambles that their way led them down a by-street in a busy quarter of London. The street was small and what is called quiet, but it drove a thriving trade on the week-days. The inhabitants were all doing well, it seemed, and all emulously hoping to do better still, and laying out the surplus of their gains in coquetry; so that the shop fronts stood along that thoroughfare with an air of invitation, like rows of smiling saleswomen. Even on Sunday, when it veiled its more florid charms and lay comparatively empty of passage, the street shone out in contrast to its dingy neighbourhood, like a fire in a forest; and with its freshly painted shutters, well-polished brasses, and general cleanliness and gaiety of note, instantly caught and pleased the eye of the passenger.

Two doors from one corner, on the left hand going east, the line was broken by the entry of a court; and just at that point, a certain sinister block of building thrust forward its gable on the street. It was two storeys high; showed no window, nothing but a door on the lower storey and a blind forehead of discoloured wall on the upper; and bore in every feature the marks of prolonged and sordid negligence. The door, which was equipped with neither bell nor knocker, was blistered and distained. Tramps slouched into the recess and struck matches on the panels; children kept shop upon the steps; the schoolboy had tried his knife on the mouldings; and for close on a generation no one had appeared to drive away these random visitors or to repair their ravages.

Mr Enfield and the lawyer were on the other side of the by-street; but when they came abreast of the entry, the former lifted up his cane and pointed.

'Did you ever remark that door?' he asked; and when his companion had replied in the affirmative, 'It is connected in my mind,' added he, 'with a very odd story.'

'Indeed!' said Mr Utterson, with a slight change of voice, 'and what was that?'

'Well, it was this way,' returned Mr Enfield: 'I was coming home from some place at the end of the world, about three o'clock of a black winter morning, and my way lay through a part of town where there was literally nothing to be seen but lamps. Street after street, and all the folks asleep – street after street, all lighted up as if for a procession, and all as empty as a church – till at last I got into that state of mind when a man listens and listens and begins to long for the sight of a policeman. All at once, I saw two figures: one a little man who was stumping along eastward at a good walk, and the other a girl of maybe eight or ten who was running as hard as she was able down a cross-street. Well, sir, the two ran into one another naturally enough at the corner; and then came the horrible part of the thing; for the man trampled calmly over the child's body and left her screaming on the ground. It sounds nothing to hear, but it was hellish to see. It wasn't like a man; it was like some damned Juggernaut. I gave a view halloa, took to my heels, collared my gentleman, and brought him back to where there was already quite a group about the screaming child. He was perfectly cool and made no resistance, but gave me one look, so ugly that it brought the sweat on me like running. The people who had turned out were the girl's own family; and pretty soon the doctor, for whom she had been sent, put in his appearance. Well, the child was not much the worse, more frightened, according to the Sawbones; and there you might have supposed would be an end to it. But there was one curious circumstance. I had taken a loathing to my gentleman at first sight. So had the child's family, which was only natural. But the doctor's case was what struck me. He was the usual cut-and-dry apothecary, of no particular age and colour, with a strong Edinburgh accent, and about as emotional as a bagpipe. Well, sir, he was like the rest of us: every time he looked at my prisoner, I saw that Sawbones turned sick and white with the desire to kill him. I knew what was in his mind, just as he knew what was in mine; and killing being out of the question, we did the next best. We told the man we could and would make such a scandal out of this, as should make his name stink from one end of London to the other. If he had any friends or any credit, we undertook that he should lose them. And all the time, as we were pitching it in red hot, we were keeping the women off him as best we could, for they were as wild as harpies. I never saw a circle of such hateful faces; and there was the man in the middle, with a kind of black sneering coolness – frightened, too, I could see that – but carrying it off, sir, really like Satan. "If you choose to make capital out of this accident," said he, "I am naturally helpless. No gentleman but wishes to avoid a scene," says he. "Name your figure." Well, we screwed him up to a hundred pounds for the child's family; he would have clearly liked to stick out; but there was something about the lot of us that means mischief, and at last he struck. The next thing was to get the money; and where do you think he carried us but to that place with the door? – whipped out a key, went in, and presently came back with the matter of ten pounds in gold and a cheque for the balance on Coutts's, drawn payable to bearer, and signed with a name that I can't mention, though it's one of the points of my story, but it was a name at least very well known and often printed. The figure was stiff; but the signature was good for more than that, if it was only genuine. I took the liberty of pointing out to my gentleman that the whole business looked apocryphal; and that a man does not, in real life, walk into a cellar door at four in the morning and come out of it with another man's cheque for close upon a hundred pounds. But he was quite easy and sneering. "Set your mind at rest," says he; "I will stay with you till the banks open, and cash the cheque myself." So we all set off, the doctor, and the child's father, and our friend and myself, and passed the rest of the night in my chambers; and next day, when we had breakfasted, went in a body to the bank. I gave in the cheque myself, and said I had every reason to believe it was a forgery. Not a bit of it. The cheque was genuine.'

'Tut-tut!' said Mr Utterston.

'I see you feel as I do,' said Mr Enfield. 'Yes, it's a bad story. For my man was a fellow that nobody could have to do with, a really damnable man; and the person that drew the cheque is the very pink of the properties, celebrated too, and (what makes it worse) one of your fellows who do what they call good. Blackmail, I suppose; an honest man paying through the nose for some of the capers of his youth. Blackmail House is what I call that place with the door, in consequence. Though even that, you know, is far from explaining all,' he added; and with the words fell into a vein of musing.

From this he was recalled by Mr Utterson asking rather suddenly: 'And you don't know if the drawer of the cheque lives there?'

'A likely place, isn't it?' returned Mr Enfield. 'But I happened to have noticed his address; he lives in some square or other.'

'And you never asked about – the place with the door?' said Mr Utterson.

'No, sir: I had a delicacy,' was the reply. 'I feel very strongly about putting questions; it partakes too much of the style of the day of judgment. You start a question, and it's like starting a stone. You sit quietly on the top of a hill; and away the stone goes, starting others; and presently some bland old bird (the last you would have thought of) is knocked on the head in his own back garden, and the family have to change their name. No, sir, I make it a rule of mine: the more it looks like Queer Street, the less I ask.'

'A very good rule, too,' said the lawyer.

'But I have studied the place for myself,' continued Mr Enfield. 'It seems scarcely a house. There is no other door, and nobody goes in or out of that one, but, once in a great while, the gentleman of my adventure. There are three windows looking on the court on the first floor; none below; the windows are always shut, but they're clean. And then there is a chimney, which is generally smoking; so somebody must live there. And yet it's not so sure; for the buildings are so packed together about that court, that it's hard to say where one ends and another begins.'

The pair walked on again for a while in silence; and then – 'Enfield,' said Mr Utterson, 'that's a good rule of yours.'

'Yes, I think it is,' returned Enfield.

'But for all that,' continued the lawyer, 'there's one point I want to ask: I want to ask the name of that man who walked over the child.'

'Well,' said Mr Enfield, 'I can't see what harm it would do. It was a man of the name of Hyde.'

'Hm,' said Mr Utterson. 'What sort of a man is he to see?'

'He is not easy to describe. There is something wrong with his appearance; something displeasing, something downright detestable. I never saw a man I so disliked, and yet I scarce know why. He must be deformed somewhere; he gives a strong feeling of deformity, although I couldn't specify the point. He's an extraordinary-looking man, and yet I really can name nothing out of the way. No, sir; I can make no hand of it; I can't describe him. And it's not want of memory; for I declare I can see him this moment.'

Mr Utterson again walked some way in silence, and obviously under a weight of consideration. 'You are sure he used a key?' he inquired at last.

'My dear sir . . .' began Enfield, surprised out of himself.

'Yes, I know,' said Utterson; 'I know it must seem strange. The fact is, if I do not ask you the name of the other party, it is because I know it already. You see, Richard, your tale has gone home. If you have been inexact in any point, you had better correct it.'

'I think you might have warned me,' returned the other, with a touch of sullenness. 'But I have been pedantically exact, as you call it. The fellow had a key; and, what's more, he has it still. I saw him use it, not a week ago.'

Mr Utterson sighed deeply, but said never a word; and the young man presently resumed. 'Here is another lesson to say nothing,' said he. 'I am ashamed of my long tongue. Let us make a bargain never to refer to this again.'

'With all my heart,' said the lawyer. 'I shake hands on that, Richard.'

CHAPTER TWO

Search for Mr Hyde

THAT EVENING MR UTTERSON came home to his bachelor house in sombre spirits, and sat down to dinner without relish. It was his custom on a Sunday, when this meal was over, to sit close by the fire, a volume of some dry divinity on his reading-desk, until the clock of the neighbouring church rang out the hour of twelve, when he would go soberly and gratefully to bed. On this night, however, as soon as the cloth was taken away, he took up a candle and went into his business room. There he opened his safe, took from the most private part of it a document endorsed on the envelope as Dr Jekyll's Will, and sat down with a clouded brow to study its contents. The will was holograph; for Mr Utterson, though he took charge of it now that it was made, had refused to lend the least assistance in the making of it; it provided not only that, in case of the decease of Henry Jeckyll, M.D., D.C.L., LL.D., F.R.S., &c., all his possessions were to pass into the hands of his 'friend and benefactor Edward Hyde'; but that in case of Dr Jeckyll's 'disappearance or unexplained absence for any period exceeding three calendar months,' the said Edward Hyde should step into the said Henry Jeckyll's shoes without further delay, and free from any burden or obligation, beyond the payment of a few small sums to the member's of the doctor's household. This document had long been the lawyer's eyesore. It offended him both as a lawyer and as a lover of the sane and customary sides of life, to whom the fanciful was the immodest. And hitherto it was his ignorance of Mr Hyde that had swelled his indignation; now, by a sudden turn, it was his knowledge. It was already bad enough when the name was but a name of which he could learn no more. It was worse when it began to be clothed upon with detestable attributes; and out of the shifting, insubstantial mists that had so long baffled his eye, there leaped up the sudden, definite presentment of a fiend.

'I thought it was madness,' he said, as he replaced the obnoxious paper in the safe; 'and now I begin to fear it is disgrace.'

With that he blew out his candle, put on a great-coat, and set forth in the direction of Cavendish Square, that citadel of medicine, where his friend the great Dr Lanyon, had his house and received his crowding patients. 'If any one knows, it will be Lanyon,' he had thought.

The solemn butler knew and welcomed him; he was subjected to no stage of delay, but ushered direct from the door to the dining-room, where Dr Lanyon sat alone over his wine. This was a hearty, healthy, dapper, red-faced gentleman, with a shock of hair prematurely white, and a boisterous and decided manner. At sight of Mr Utterson, he sprang up from his chair and welcomed him with both hands. The geniality, as was the way of the man, was somewhat theatrical to the eye; but it reposed on genuine feeling. For these two were old friends, old mates both at school and college, both thorough respecters of themselves and of each other, and, what does not always follow, men who thoroughly enjoyed each other's company.

After a little rambling talk, the lawyer led up to the subject which so disagreeably preoccupied his mind.

'I suppose, Lanyon,' he said, 'you and I must be the two oldest friends that Henry Jekyll has?'

'I wish the friends were younger,' chuckled Dr Lanyon. 'But I suppose we are. And what of that? I see little of him now.'

'Indeed!' said Utterson. 'I thought you had a bond of common interest.'

'We had,' was his reply. 'But it is more than ten years since Henry Jekyll became too fanciful for me. He began to go wrong, wrong in mind; and though, of course, I continue to take an interest in him for old sake's sake as they say, I see and I have seen devilish little of the man. Such unscientific balderdash,' added the doctor, flushing suddenly purple, 'would have estranged Damon and Pythias.'

This little spirit of temper was somewhat of a relief to Mr Utterson. 'They have only differed on some point of science,' he thought; and being a man of no scientific passions (except in the matter of conveyancing), he even added: 'It is nothing worse than that!' He gave his friend a few seconds to recover his composure, and then approached the question he had come to put.

'Did you ever come across a *protégé* of his – one Hyde?' he asked.

'Hyde?' repeated Lanyon. 'No. Never heard of him. Since my time.'

That was the amount of information that the lawyer carried back with him to the great, dark bed on which he tossed to and fro until the small hours of the morning began to grow large. It was a night of little ease to his toiling mind, toiling in mere darkness and besieged by questions.

Six o'clock struck on the bells of the church that was so conveniently near to Mr Utterson's dwelling, and still he was digging at the problem. Hitherto it had touched him on the intellectual side alone; but now his imagination also was engaged, or rather enslaved; and as he lay and tossed in the gross darkness of the night and the curtained room, Mr Enfield's tale went by before his mind in a scroll of lighted pictures. He would be aware of the great field of lamps of a nocturnal city; then of the figure of a man walking swiftly; then of a child running from the doctor's; and then these met, and that human Juggernaut trod the child down and passed on regardless of her screams. Or else he would see a room in a rich house, where his friend lay asleep, dreaming and smiling at his dreams; and then the door of that room would be opened, the curtains of the bed plucked apart, the sleeper recalled, and, lo! there would stand by his side a figure to whom power was given, and even at that dead hour he must rise and do its bidding. The figure in these two phases haunted the lawyer all night; and if at any time he dozed over, it was but to see it glide more stealthily through sleeping houses, or move the more swiftly, and still the more swiftly, even to dizziness, through wider labyrinths of lamp-lighted city, and at every street corner crush a child and leave her screaming. And still the figure had no face by which he might know it; even in his dreams it had no face, or one that baffled him and melted before his eyes; and thus it was that there sprang up and grew apace in the lawyer's mind a singularly strong, almost an inordinate, curiosity to behold the features of the real Mr Hyde. If he could but once set eyes on him, he thought the mystery would lighten and perhaps roll altogether away, as was the habit of mysterious things when well examined. He might see a reason for his friend's strange preference or bondage (call it which you please), and even for the startling clauses of the will. And at least it would be a face worth seeing: the face of a man who was without bowels of mercy: a face which had but to show itself to raise up, in the mind of the unimpressionable Enfield, a spirit of enduring hatred.

From that time forward, Mr Utterson began to haunt the door in the by-street of shops. In the morning before office hours, at noon when business was plenty and time scarce, at night under the face of the fogged city moon, by all lights and at all hours of solitude or concourse, the lawyer was to be found on his chosen post.

'If he be Mr Hyde,' he had thought, 'I shall be Mr Seek.'

And at last his patience was rewarded. It was a fine dry night; frost in the air; the streets as clean as a ballroom floor; the lamps, unshaken by any wind, drawing a regular pattern of light and shadow. By ten o'clock, when the shops were closed, the by-street was very solitary, and, in spite of the low growl of London from all round, very silent. Small sounds carried far; domestic sounds out of the houses were clearly audible on either side of the roadway; and the rumour of the approach of any passenger preceded him by a long time. Mr Utterson had been some minutes at his post when he was aware of an odd light footstep drawing near. In the course of his nightly patrols he had long grown accustomed to the quaint effect with which the footfalls of a single person, while he is still a great way off, suddenly spring out distinct from the vast hum and clatter of the city. Yet his attention had never before been so sharply and decisively arrested; and it was with a strong, superstitious prevision of success that he withdrew into the entry of the court.

The steps drew swiftly nearer, and swelled out suddenly louder as they turned the end of the street. The lawyer, looking forth from the entry of the court, could soon see what manner of man he had to deal with. He was small, and very plainly dressed; and the look of him, even at that distance, went somehow strongly against the watcher's inclination. But he made straight for the door, crossing the roadway to save time; and as he came, he drew a key from his pocket, like one approaching home.

Mr Utterson stepped out and touched him on the shoulder as he passed. 'Mr Hyde, I think?'

Mr Hyde shrank back with a hissing intake of the breath. But his fear was only momentary; and though he did not look the lawyer in the face, he answered coolly enough: 'That is my name. What do you want?'

'I see you are going in,' returned the lawyer. 'I am an old friend of Dr Jekyll's – Mr Utterson, of Gaunt Street – you must have heard my name; and meeting you so conveniently, I thought you might admit me.'

'You will not find Dr Jekyll; he is from home,' replied Mr Hyde, blowing in the key. And then suddenly, but still without looking up, 'How did you know me?' he asked.

'On your side,' said Mr Utterson, 'will you do me a favour?'

'With pleasure,' replied the other. 'What shall it be?'

'Will you let me see your face?' asked the lawyer.

Mr Hyde appeared to hesitate; and then, as if upon some sudden reflection, fronted about with an air of defiance; and the pair stared at each other pretty fixedly for a few seconds. 'Now I shall know you again,' said Mr Utterson. 'It may be useful.'

'Yes,' returned Mr Hyde, 'it is as well we have met; and *à propos*, you should have my address.' And he gave a number of a street in Soho.

'Good God!' thought Mr Utterson, 'can he too have been thinking of the will?' But he kept his feelings to himself, and only grunted in acknowledgment of the address.

'And now,' said the other, 'how did you know me?'

'By description,' was the reply.

'Whose description?'

'We have common friends,' said Mr Utterson.

'Common friends!' echoed Mr Hyde, a little hoarsely. 'Who are they?'

'Jekyll, for instance,' said the lawyer.

'He never told you,' cried Mr Hyde, with a flush of anger. 'I did not think you would have lied.'

'Come,' said Mr Utterson, 'that is not fitting language.'

The other snarled aloud into a savage laugh; and the next moment, with extraordinary quickness, he had unlocked the door and disappeared into the house.

The lawyer stood awhile when Mr Hyde had left him, the picture of disquietude. Then he began slowly to mount the street, pausing every step or two, and putting his hand to his brow like a man in mental perplexity. The problem he was thus debating as he walked was one of a class that is rarely solved. Mr Hyde was pale and dwarfish; he gave an impression of deformity without any namable malformation, he had a displeasing smile, he had borne himself to the lawyer with a sort of murderous mixture of timidity and boldness, and he spoke with a husky, whispering and somewhat broken voice, – all these were points against him; but not all of these together could explain the hitherto unknown disgust, loathing and fear with which Mr Utterson regarded him. 'There must be something else,' said the perplexed gentleman. 'There *is* something more, if I could find a name for it. God bless me, the man seems hardly human! Something troglodytic, shall we say? or can it be the old story of Dr Fell? or is it the mere radiance of a foul soul that thus transpires through, and transfigures, its clay continent? The last, I think; for, O my poor old Harry Jekyll, if ever I read Satan's signature upon a face, it is on that of your new friend!'

Round the corner from the by-street there was a square of ancient, handsome houses, now for the most part decayed from their high estate, and let in flats and chambers to all sorts and conditions of men: map-engravers, architects, shady lawyers, and the agents of obscure enterprises. One house, however, second from the corner, was still occupied entire; and at the door of this, which wore a great air of wealth and comfort, though it was now plunged in darkness except for the fan-light, Mr Utterson stopped and knocked. A well-dressed, elderly servant opened the door.

'Is Dr Jekyll at home, Poole?' asked the lawyer.

'I will see, Mr Utterson,' said Poole, admitting the visitor, as he spoke, into a large, low-roofed, comfortable hall, paved with flags, warmed (after the fashion of a country house) by a bright, open fire, and rnished with costly cabinets of oak. 'Will you wait here by the fire, sir? or shall I give you a light in the dining-room?'

'Here, thank you,' said the lawyer; and he drew near and leaned on the tall fender. This hall, in which he was now left alone, was a pet fancy of his friend the doctor's; and Utterson himself was wont to speak of it as the pleasantest room in London. But tonight there was a shudder in his blood; the face of Hyde sat heavy on his memory; he felt (what was rare with him) a nausea and distate of life; and in the gloom of his spirits, he seemed to read a menace in the flickering of the firelight on the polished cabinets and the uneasy starting of the shadow on the roof. He was ashamed of his relief when Poole presently returned to announce that Dr Jekyll was gone out.

'I saw Mr Hyde go in by the old dissecting-room door, Poole,' he said. 'Is that right, when Dr Jekyll is from home?'

'Quite right, Mr Utterson, sir,' replied the servant. 'Mr Hyde has a key.'

'Your master seems to repose a great deal of trust in that young man, Poole,' resumed the other, musingly.

'Yes, sir, he do indeed,' said Poole. 'We have all orders to obey him.'

'I do not think I ever met Mr Hyde?' asked Utterson.

'O dear no, sir. He never *dines* here,' replied the butler. 'Indeed, we see very little of him on this side of the house; he mostly comes and goes by the laboratory.'

'Well, good-night, Poole.'

'Good-night, Mr Utterson.'

And the lawyer set out homeward with a very heavy heart. 'Poor Harry Jekyll,' he thought, 'my mind misgives me he is in deep waters! He was wild when he was young; a long while ago, to be sure; but in the law of God there is no statute of limitations. Ah, it must be that; the ghost of some old sin, the cancer of some concealed disgrace; punishment coming, *pede claudo*, years after memory has forgotten and self-love condoned the fault.' And the lawyer, scared by the thought, brooded awhile on his own past, groping in all the corners of memory, lest by chance some Jack-in-the-Box of an old iniquity should leap to light there. His past was fairly blameless; few men could read the rolls of their life with less apprehension; yet he was humbled to the dust by the many ill things he had done, and raised up again into a sober and fearful gratitude by the many that he had come so near to doing, yet avoided. And then by a return on his former subject, he conceived a spark of hope. 'This Master Hyde, if he were studied,' thought he, 'must have secrets of his own: black secrets, by the look of him; secrets compared to which poor Jekyll's worst would be like sunshine. Things cannot continue as they are. It turns me cold to think of this creature stealing like a thief to Harry's bedside; poor Harry, what a wakening! And the danger of it! for if this Hyde suspects the existence of the will, he may grow impatient to inherit. Ay, I must put my shoulder to the wheel – if Jekyll will but let me,' he added, 'if Jekyll will only let me.' For once more he saw before his mind's eye, as clear as a transparency, the strange clauses of the will.

CHAPTER THREE

Dr Jekyll Was Quite at Ease

A FORTNIGHT LATER, BY excellent good fortune, the doctor gave one of his pleasant dinners to some five or six old cronies, all intelligent reputable men, and all judges of good wine; and Mr Utterson so contrived that he remained behind after the others had departed. This was no new arrangement, but a thing that had befallen many scores of times. Where Utterson was liked, he was liked well. Hosts loved to detain the dry lawyer, when the light-hearted and the loose-tongued had already their foot on the threshold; they liked to sit awhile in his unobtrusive company, practising for solitude, sobering their minds in the man's rich silence, after the expense and strain of gaiety. To this rule Dr Jekyll was no exception; and as he now sat on the opposite side of the fire – a large, well-made, smooth-faced man of fifty, with something of a slyish cast perhaps, but every mark of capacity and kindness – you could see by his looks that he cherished for Mr Utterson a sincere and warm affection.

'I have been wanting to speak to you, Jekyll,' began the latter. 'You know that will of yours?'

A close observer might have gathered that the topic was distasteful; but the doctor carried it off gaily. 'My poor Utterson,' said he, 'you are unfortunate in such a client. I never saw a man so distressed as you were by my will; unless it were that hide-bound pedant, Lanyon, at what he called my scientific heresies. O, I know he's a good fellow – you needn't frown – an excellent fellow, and I always mean to see more of him; but a hide-bound pedant for all that; an ignorant, blatant pedant. I was never more disappointed in any man than Lanyon.'

'You know I never approved of it,' pursued Utterson, ruthlessly disregarding the fresh topic.

'My will? Yes, certainly, I know that,' said the doctor, a trifle sharply. 'You have told me so.'

'Well, I tell you so again,' continued the lawyer. 'I have been learning something of young Hyde.'

The large handsome face of Dr Jekyll grew pale to the very lips, and there came a blackness about his eyes. 'I do not care to hear more,' said he. 'This is a matter I thought we had agreed to drop.'

'What I heard was abominable,' said Utterson.

'It can make no change. You do not understand my position,' returned the doctor, with a certain incoherency of manner. 'I am painfully situated, Utterson; my position is a very strange – a very strange one. It is one of those affairs that cannot be mended by talking.'

'Jekyll,' said Utterson, 'You know me: I am a man to be trusted. Make a clean breast of this in confidence; and I make no doubt I can get you out of it.'

'My good Utterson,' said the doctor, 'this is very good of you, this is downright good of you, and I cannot find words to thank you in. I believe you fully; I would trust you before any man alive, ay, before myself, if I could make the choice; but indeed it isn't what you fancy; it is not so bad as that; and just to put your good heart at rest, I will tell you one thing: the moment I choose, I can be rid of Mr Hyde. I give you my hand upon that; and I thank you again and again; and I will just add one little word, Utterson, that I'm sure you'll take in good part: this is a private matter, and I beg of you to let it sleep.'

Utterson reflected a little, looking in the fire.

'I have no doubt you are perfectly right,' he said at last, getting to his feet.

'Well, but since we have touched upon this business, and for the last time, I hope,' continued the doctor, 'there is one point I should like you to understand. I have really a very great interest in poor Hyde. I know you have seen him; he told me so; and I fear he was rude. But I do sincerely take a great, a very great interest in that young man; and if I am taken away, Utterson, I wish you to promise me that you will bear with him and get his rights for him. I think you would, if you knew all; and it would be a weight off my mind if you would promise.'

'I can't pretend that I shall ever like him,' said the lawyer.

'I don't ask that,' pleaded Jekyll, laying his hand upon the other's arm; 'I only ask for justice; I only ask you to help him for my sake, when I am no longer here.'

Utterson heaved an irrepressible sigh. 'Well,' said he, 'I promise.'

CHAPTER FOUR

The Carew Murder Case

NEARLY A YEAR LATER, IN the month of October, 18—, London was startled by a crime of singular ferocity, and rendered all the more notable by the high position of the victim. The details were few and startling. A maid-servant living alone in a house not far from the river had gone upstairs to bed about eleven. Although a fog rolled over the city in the small hours, the early part of the night was cloudless, and the lane, which the maid's window overlooked, was brilliantly lit by the full moon. It seems she was romantically given; for she sat down upon her box, which stood immediately under the window, and fell into a dream of musing. Never (she used to say, with streaming tears, when she narrated that experience), never had she felt more at peace with all men or thought mord kindly of the world. And as she so sat she became aware of an aged and beautiful gentleman with white hair drawing near along the lane; and advancing to meet him, another and very small gentleman, to whom at first she paid less attention. When they had come within speech (which was just under the maid's eyes) the older man bowed and accosted the other with a very pretty manner of politeness.

It did not seem as if the subject of his address were of great importance; indeed, from his pointing, it sometimes appeared as if he were only inquiring his way; but the moon shone on his face as he spoke, and the girl was pleased to watch it, it seemed to breathe such an innocent and old-world kindness of disposition, yet with something high too, as of a well-founded self-content. Presently her eye wandered to the other, and she was surprised to recognize in him a certain Mr Hyde, who had once visited her master, and from whom she had conveived a dislike. He had in his hand a heavy cane, with which he was trifling; but he answered never a word, and seemed to listen with an ill-contained impatience. And then all of a sudden he broke out in a great flame of anger, stamping with his foot, brandishing the cane, and carrying on (as the maid described it) like a madman. The gentleman took a step back, with the air of one very much surprised and a trifle hurt; and at that Mr Hyde broke out of all bounds, and clubbed him to the earth. And next moment, with ape-like fury, he was trampling his victim under foot, and hailing down a storm of blows, under which the bones were audibly shattered and the body jumped upon the roadway. At the horror of these sights and sounds the maid fainted.

It was two o'clock when she came to herself and called for the police. The murderer was gone long ago; but there lay his victim in the middle of the lane, incredibly mangled. The stick with which the deed had been done, although it was of some rare and very tough and heavy wood, had broken in the middle under the stress of this insensate cruelty; and one splindered half had rolled in the neighbouring gutter – the other, without doubt, had been carried away by the murderer. A purse and a gold watch were found upon the victim; but no cards or papers, except a sealed and stamped envelope. Which he had been probably carrying to the post, and which bore the name and address of Mr Utterson.

This was brought to the lawyer the next morning, before he was out of bed; and he had no sooner seen it, and been told the circumstances, than he shot out a solemn lip. 'I shall say nothing till I have seen the body,' said he; 'this may be very serious. Have the kindness to wait while I dress.' And with the same grave countenance he hurried through his breakfast and drove to the police station, whither the body had been carried. As soon as he came into the cell, he nodded.

'Yes,' said he, 'I recognize him. I am sorry to say that this is Sir Danvers Carew.'

'Good God,sir!' exclaimed the officer, 'is it possible?' And the next moment his eye lighted up with professional ambition. 'This will make a deal of noise,' he said. 'And perhaps you can help us to the man.' And he briefly narrated what the maid had seen and showed the broken stick.

Mr Utterson had already quailed at the name of Hyde; but when the stick was laid before him, he could doubt no longer: broken and battered as it was, he recognized it for one that he had himself presented many years before to Henry Jekyll.

'Is this Mr Hyde a person of small stature?' he inquired.

'Particularly small and particularly wicked-looking, is what the maid calls him,' said the officer.

Mr Utterson reflected; and then, raising his head, 'If you will come with me in my cab,' he said, 'I think I can take you to his house.'

It was by this time about nine in the morning, and the first fog of the season. A great chocolate-coloured pall lowered over heaven, but the wind was continually charging and routing these embattled vapours; so that as the cab crawled from street to street, Mr Utterson beheld a marvellous number of degrees and hues of twilight; for here it would be dark like the back-end of evening; and there would be a glow of a rich, lurid brown, like the light of some strange conflagration; and here, for a moment, the fog would be quite broken up, and a haggard shaft of daylight would glance in between the swirling wreaths. The dismal quarter of Soho seen under these changing glimpses, with its muddy ways, and slatternly passengers, and its lamps, which had never been extinguished or had been kindled afresh to combat this mournful reinvasion of darkness, seemed, in the lawyer's eyes, like a district of some city in a nightmare. The thoughts of his mind, besides, were of the gloomiest dye; and when he glanced at the companion of his drive, he was conscious of some touch of that terror of the law and the law's officers which may at times assail the most honest.

As the cab drew up before the address indicated, the fog lifted a little and showed him a dingy street, a gin palace, a low French eating-house, a shop for the retail of penny numbers and twopenny salads, many ragged children huddled in the doorways, and many women of many different nationalities passing out, key in hand, to have a morning glass; and the next moment the fog settled down again upon that part, as brown as umber, and cut him off from his blackguardly surroundings. This was the home of Henry Jekyll's favourite; of a man who was heir to a quarter of a million sterling.

An ivory-faced and silvery-haired old woman opened the door. She had an evil face, smoothed by hypocrisy; but her manners were excellent. Yes, she said, this was Mr Hyde's, but he was not at home; he had been in that night very late, but had gone away again in less than an hour: there was nothing strange in that; his habits were very irregular, and he was often absent; for instance, it was nearly two months since she had seen him till yesterday.

'Very well then, we wish to see his rooms,' said the lawyer; and when the woman began to declare it was impossible, 'I had better tell you who this person is,' he added. 'This is Inspector Newcomen, of Scotland Yard.'

A flash of odious joy appeared upon the woman's face. 'Ah!' said she, 'he is in trouble! What has he done?'

Mr Utterson and the inspector exchanged glances. 'He don't seem a very popular character,' observed the latter. 'And now, my good woman, just let me and this gentleman have a look about us.'

In the whole extent of the house, which but for the old woman remained otherwise empty, Mr Hyde had only used a couple of rooms; but these were furnished with luxury and good taste. A closet was filled with wine; the plate was of silver, the napery elegant; a good picture hung upon the walls, a gift (as Utterson supposed) from Henry Jekyll, who was much of a connoisseur; and the carpets were of many plies and agreeable in colour. At this moment, however, the rooms bore every mark of having been recently and hurriedly ransacked; clothes lay about the floor, with their pockets inside out; lockfast drawers stood open; and on the hearth there lay a pile of gray ashes, as though many papers had been burned. From these embers the inspector disinterred the butt end of a green cheque book which had resisted the action of the fire; the other half of the stick was found behind the door; and as this clinched his suspicions, the officer declared himself delighted. A visit to the bank, where several thousand pounds were found to be lying to the murderer's credit, completed his gratification.

'Yoy may depend upon it, sir,' he told Mr Utterson: 'I have him in my hand. He must have lost his head, or he never would have left the stick, or, above all, burned the cheque book. Why, money's life to the man. We have nothing to do but wait for him at the bank, and get out the handbills.'

This last, however, was not so easy of accomplishment; for Mr Hyde had numbered few familiars – even the master of the servant-maid had only seen him twice; his family could nowhere be traced; he had never been photographed; and the few who could describe him differed widely, as common observers will. Only on one point were they agreed; and that was the haunting sense of unexpressed deformity with which the fugitive impressed his beholders.

CHAPTER FIVE

Incident of the Letter

IT WAS LATE IN THE AFTERNOON when Mr Utterson found his way to Dr Jekyll's door, where he was at once admitted by Poole, and carried down by the kitchen offices and across a yard which had once been a garden, to the building which was indifferently known as the laboratory or the dissecting-rooms. The doctor had bought the house from the heirs of a celebrated surgeon; and his own tastes being rather chemical than anatomical, had changed the destination of the block at the bottom of the garden. It was the first time that the lawyer had been received in that part of his friend's quarters; and he eyed the dingy windowless structure with curiosity, and gazed round with a distateful sense of strangeness as he crossed the theatre, once crowded with eager students and now lying gaunt and silent, the tables laden with chemical apparatus, the floor strewn with crates and littered with packing straw, and the light falling dimly through the foggy cupola. At the further end, a flight of stairs mounted to a door covered with red baize; and through this Mr Utterson was at last received into the doctor's cabinet. It was a large room, fitted round with glass presses, furnished, among other things, with a cheval-glass and a business table, and looking out upon the court by three dusty windows barred with iron. The fire burned in the grate; a lamp was set lighted on the chimney-shelf, for even in the houses the fog began to lie thickly; and there, close up to the warmth, sat Dr Jekyll, looking deadly sick. He did not rise to meet his visitor, but held out a cold hand, and bade him welcome in a changed voice.

'And now,' said Mr Utterson, as soon as Poole had left them, 'you have heard the news?'

The doctor shuddered. 'They were crying it in the square,' he said. 'I heard them in my dining-room.'

'One word,' said the lawyer. 'Carew was my client, but so are you; and I want to know what I am doing. You have not been mad enough to hide this fellow?'

'Utterson, I swear to God,' cried the doctor, 'I swear to God I will never set eyes on him again. I bind my honour to you that I am done with him in this world. It is all at an end. And indeed he does not want my help; you do not know him as I do; he is safe, he is quite safe; mark my words, he will never more be heard of.'

The lawyer listened gloomily; he did not like his friend's feverish manner. 'You seem pretty sure of him,' said he; 'and for your sake, I hope you may be right. If it came to a trial, your name might appear.'

'I am quite sure of him,' replied Jekyll; 'I have grounds for certainty that I cannot share with any one. But there is one thing on which you may advise me. I have – I have received a letter; and I am at a loss whether I should show it to the police. I should like to leave it in your hands, Utterson; you would judge wisely, I am sure; I have so great a trust in you.'

'You fear, I suppose, that it might lead to his detection?' asked the lawyer.

'No,' said the other. 'I cannot say that I care what becomes of Hyde; I am quite done with him. I was thinking of my own character, which this hateful business has rather exposed.'

Utterson ruminated awhile; he was surprised at his friend's selfishness, and yet relieved by it 'Well,' said he, at last, 'let me see the letter.'

The letter was written in an odd, upright hand, and signed 'Edward Hyde'; and it signified, briefly enough, that the writer's benefactor, Dr Jekyll, whom he had long so unworthily repaid for a thousand generosities, need labour under no alarm for his safety, as he had means of escape on which he placed a sure dependence. The lawyer liked this letter well enough: it put a better colour on the intimacy than he had looked for; and he blamed himself for some of his past suspicions.

'Have you the envelope?' he asked.

'I burned it,' replied Jekyll, 'before I thought what I was about. But it bore no postmark. The note was handed in.'

'Shall I keep this and sleep upon it?' asked Utterson.

'I wish you to judge for me entirely,' was the reply. 'I have lost confidence in myself.'

'Well, I shall consider,' returned the lawyer. 'And now one word more: it was Hyde who dictated the terms in your will about that disappearance?'

The doctor seemed seized with a qualm of faintness; he shut his mouth tight and nodded.

'I knew it,' said Utterson. 'He meant to murder you. You have had a fine escape.'

'I have had what is far more to the purpose,' returned the doctor solemnly: 'I have had a lesson – O God, Utterson, what a lesson I have had!' And he covered his face for a moment with his hands.

On his way out, the lawyer stopped and had a word or two with Poole. 'By the by,' said he, 'there was a letter handed in today: what was the messenger like?' But Poole was positive nothing had come except by post; 'and only circulars by that,' he added.

This news sent off the visitor with his fears renewed. Plainly the letter had come by the laboratory door; possibly, indeed, it had been written in the cabinet; and, if that were so, it must be differently judged, and handled with the more caution. The news-boys, as he went, were crying themselves hoarse along the footways. 'Special edition. Shocking murder of an M.P.' That was the funeral oration of one friend and client; and he could not help a certain apprehension lest the good name of another should be sucked down in the eddy of the scandal. It was, at least, a ticklish decision that he had to make; and, self-reliant as he was by habit, he began to cherish a longing for advice. It was not to be had directly; but perhaps, he thought, it might be fished for.

Presently after, he sat on one side of his own hearth, with Mr Guest, his head clerk, upon the other, and midway between, at a nicely calculated distance from the fire, a bottle of a particular old wine that had long dwelt unsunned in the foundations of his house. The fog still slept on the wing above the drowned city, where the lamps glimmered like carbuncles; and through the muffle and smother of these fallen clouds, the procession of the town's life was still rolling in through the great arteries with a sound as of a mighty wind. But the room was gay with firelight. In the bottle the acids were long ago resolved; the imperial dye had softened with time, as the colour grows richer in stained windows; and the glow of hot autumn afternoons on hillside vineyards was ready to be set free and to disperse the fogs of London. Insensibly the lawyer melted. There was no man from whom he kept fewer secrets than Mr Guest; and he was not always sure that he kept as many as he meant. Guest had often been on business to the doctor's: he knew Poole; he could scarce have failed to hear of Mr Hyde's familiarity about the house; he might draw conclusions: was it not as well, then, that he should see a letter which put that mystery to rights? and, above all, since Guest, being a great student and critic of handwriting, would consider the step natural and obliging? The clerk, besides, was a man of counsel; he would scarce read so strange a document without dropping a remark; and by that remark Mr Utterson might shape his future course.

'This is a sad business about Sir Danvers,' he said.

'Yes, sir, indeed. It has elicited a great deal of public feeling,' returned Guest. 'The man, of course, was mad.'

'I should like to hear your views on that,' replied Utterson. 'I have a document here in his handwriting; it is between ourselves, for I scarce know what to do about it; it is an ugly business at the best. But there it is; quite in your way: a murderer's autograph.'

Guest's eyes brightened, and he sat down at once and studied it with passion. 'No, sir,' he said; 'not mad; but it is an odd hand.'

'And by all accounts a very odd writer,' added the lawyer.

Just then the servant entered with a note.

'Is that from Dr Jekyll, sir?' inquired the clerk. 'I thought I knew the writing. Anything private, Mr Utterson?'

'Only an invitation to dinner. Why? do you want to see it?'

'One moment. I thank you, sir'; and the clerk laid the two sheets of paper alongside and sedulously compared their contents. 'Thank you, sir,' he said at last, returning both; 'it's a very interesting autograph.'

There was a pause, during which Mr Utterson struggled with himself. 'Why did you compare them, Guest?' he inquired suddenly.

'Well, sir,' returned the clerk, 'there's a rather singular resemblance; the two hands are in many points identical; only differently sloped.'

'Rather quaint,' said Utterson.

'It is, as you say, rather quaint,' returned Guest.

'I wouldn't speak of this note, you know,' said the master.

'No, sir,' said the clerk. 'I understand.'

But no sooner was Mr Utterson alone that night than he locked the note into his safe, where it reposed from that time forward. 'What!' he thought. 'Henry Jekyll forge for a murderer!' And his blood ran cold in his veins.

CHAPTER SIX

Remarkable Incident of Dr Lanyon

TIME RAN ON; THOUSANDS of pounds were offered in reward, for the death of Sir Danvers was resented as a public injury; but Mr Hyde had disappeared out of the ken of the police as though he had never existed. Much of his past was unearthed, indeed, and all disreputable: tales came out of the man's cruelty, at once so callous and violent, of his vile life, of his strange associates, of the hatred that seemed to have surrounded his career; but of his present whereabouts, not a whisper. From the time he had left the house in Soho on the morning of the murder, he was simply blotted out; and gradually, as time drew on, Mr Utterson began to recover from the hotness of his alarm, and to grow more at quiet with himself. The death of Sir Danvers was, to his way of thinking, more than paid for by the disappearance of Mr Hyde. Now that evil influence had been withdrawn, a new life began for Dr Jekyll. He came out of his seclusion, renewed relations with his friends, became once more their familiar guest and entertainer; and whilst he had always been known for charities, he was now no less distinguished for religion. He was busy, he was much in the open air, he did good; his face seemed to open and brighten, as if with an inward consciousness of service; and for more than two months the doctor was at peace.

On the 8th of January Utterson had dined at the doctor's with a small party; Lanyon had been there; and the face of the host had looked from one to the other as in the old days when the trio were inseparable friends. On the 12th, and again on the 14th, the door was shut against the lawyer. 'the doctor was confined to the house,' Poole said, 'and saw no one.' On the 15th he tried again, and was again refused; and having now been used for the last two months to see his friend almost daily, he found this return of solitude to weigh upon his spirits. The fifth night he had in Guest to dine with him; and the sixth he betook himself to Dr Lanyon's.

There at least he was not denied admittance; but when he came in, he was shocked at the change which had taken place in the doctor's appearance. He had his death-warrant written legibly upon his face. The rosy man had grown pale; his flesh had fallen away; he was visibly balder and older; and yet it was not so much these tokens of a swift physical decay that arrested the lawyer's notice, as a look in the eye and quality of manner that seemed to testify to some deep-seated terror of the mind. It was unlikely that the doctor should fear death; and yet that was what Utterson was tempted to suspect. 'Yes,' he thought; 'he is a doctor, he must know his own state and that his days are counted; and the knowledge is more than he can bear.' And yet when Utterson remarked on his ill looks, it was with an air of great firmness that Lanyon declared himself a doomed man.

'I have had a shock,' he said, 'and I shall never recover. It is a question of weeks. Well, life has been pleasant; I liked it; yes, sir, I used to like it. I sometimes think if we knew all, we should be more glad to get away.'

'Jekyll is ill, too,' observed Utterson. 'Have you seen him?'

But Lanyon's face changed, and he held up a trembling hand. 'I wish to see or hear no more of Dr Jekyll,' he said, in a loud, unsteady voice. 'I am quite done with that person; and I beg that you will spare me any allusion to one whom I regard as dead.'

'Tut, tut!' said Mr Utterson; and then, after a considerable pause, 'Can't I do anything?' he inquired. 'We are three very old friends, Lanyon; we shall not live to make others.'

'Nothing can be done,' returned Lanyon; 'ask himself.'

'He will not see me,' said the lawyer.

'I am not surprised at that,' was the reply. 'Some day, Utterson, after I am dead, you may perhaps come to learn the right and wrong of this. I cannot tell you. And in the meantime, if you can sit and talk with me of other things, for God's sake, stay and do so; but if you cannot keep clear of this accursed topic, the, in God's name, go, for I cannot bear it.'

As soon as he got home, Utterson sat down and wrote to Jekyll, complaining of his exclusion from his house, and asking the cause of this unhappy break with Lanyon; and the next day brought him a long answer, often very pathetically worded, and sometimes darkly mysterious in drift. The quarrel with Lanyon was incurable. 'I do not blame our old friend,' Jekyll wrote, 'but I share his view that we must never meet. I mean from henceforth to lead a life of extreme seclusion; you must not be surprised, nor must you doubt my friendship, if my door is often shut even to you. You must suffer me to go my own dark way. I have brought on myself a punishment and a danger that I cannot name. If I am the chief of sinners, I am the chief of sufferers also. I could not think that this earth contained a place for sufferings and terrors so unmanning; and you can do but one thing, Utterson, to lighten this destiny, and that is to respect my silence.'

Utterson was amazed; the dark influence of Hyde had been withdrawn, the doctor had returned to his old tasks and amities; a week ago, the prospect had smiled with every promise of a cheerful and an honoured age; and now in a moment, friendship and peace of mind and the whole tenor of his life were wrecked. So great and unprepared a change pointed to madness; but in view of Lanyon's manner and words, there must lie for it some deeper ground.

A week afterwards Dr Lanyon took to his bed, and in something less than a fortnight he was dead. The night after the funeral, at which he had been sadly affected, Utterson locked the door of his business room, and sitting there by the

light of a melancholy candle, drew out and set before him an envelope addressed
by the hand and sealed with the seal of his dead friend. 'PRIVATE: for the hands of
J.G. Utterson ALONE, and in case of his predecease *to be destroyed unread*,' so it
was emphatically superscribed; and the lawyer dreaded to behold the contents. 'I
have buried one friend today,' he thought: 'what if this should cost me another?'
And then he condemned the fear as a disloyalty, and broke the seal. Within
there was another enclosure, likewise sealed, and marked upon the cover as 'not
to be opened till the death or disappearance of Dr Henry Jekyll.' Utterson could
not trust his eyes. Yes, it was disappearance; here again, as in the mad will,
which he had long ago restored to its author, here again were the idea of a
disappearance and the name of Henry Jekyll bracketed. But in the will, that idea
had sprung from the sinister suggestion the man Hyde; it was set there with a
purpose all too plain and horrible. Written by the hand of Lanyon, what should
it mean? A great curiosity came to the trustee, to disregard the prohibition and
dive at once to the bottom of these mysteries; but professional honour and faith
to his dead friend were stringent obligations; and the packet slept in the inmost
corner of his private safe.

It is one thing to mortify curiosity, another to conquer it; and it may be
doubted if, from that day forth, Utterson desired the society of his surviving
friend with the same eagerness. He thought of him kindly; but his thoughts were
disquieted and fearful. He went to call indeed; but he was perhaps relieved to be
denied admittance; perhaps, in his heart, he preferred to speak with Poole upon
the doorstep, and surrounded by the air and sounds of the open city, rather than
to be admitted into that house of voluntary bondage, and to sit and speak with
its inscrutable recluse. Poole had, indeed, no very pleasant news to communicate. The doctor, it appeared, now more than ever confined himself to the
cabinet over the laboratory, where he would sometimes even sleep: he was out of
spirits, he had grown very silent, he did not read; it seemed as if he had
something on his mind. Utterson became so used to the unvarying character of
these reports, that he fell off little by little in the frequency of his visits.

CHAPTER SEVEN

Incident at the Window

IT CHANCED ON SUNDAY, WHEN Mr Utterson was on his usual walk with Mr
Enfield, that their way lay once again through the by-street; and that when they
came in front of the door, both stopped to gaze on it.

'Well,' said Enfield, 'that story's at an end, at least. We shall never see more
of Mr Hyde.'

'I hope not,' said Utterson. 'Did I ever tell you that I once saw him, and
shared your feeling of repulsion?'

'It was impossible to do the one without the other,' returned Enfield. 'And, by the way, what an ass you must have thought me, not to know that this was a back way to Dr Jekyll's! It was partly your own fault that I found it out even when I did.'

'So you found it out, did you?' said Utterson. 'But if that be so, we may step into the court and take a look at the windows. To tell you the truth, I am uneasy about poor Jekyll; and even outside, I feel as if the presence of a friend might do him good.'

The court was very cool and a little damp, and full of premature twilight, although the sky, high up overhead, was still bright with sunset. The middle one of the three windows was half-way open; and sitting close beside it, taking the air with an infinite sadness of mien, like some disconsolate prisoner, Utterson saw Dr Jekyll.

'What! Jekyll!' he cried. 'I trust you are better.'

'I am very low, Utterson,' replied the doctor drearily; 'very low. It will not last long, thank God.'

'You stay too much indoors,' said the lawyer. 'You should be out, whipping up the circulation, like Mr Enfield and me. (This is my cousin – Mr Enfield – Dr Jekyll.) Come, now; get your hat, and take a quick turn with us.'

'You are very good,' sighed the other. 'I should like to very much; but no, no, no; it is quite impossible; I dare not. But indeed, Utterson, I am very glad to see you; this is really a great pleasure. I would ask you and Mr Enfield up, but the place is really not fit.'

'Why then, said the lawyer, good-naturedly, 'the best thing we can do is to stay down here, and speak with you from where we are?'

'That is just what I was about to venture to propose,' returned the doctor, with a smile. But the words were hardly uttered, before the smile was struck out of his face and succeeded by an expression of such abject terror and despair, as froze the very blood of the two gentlemen below. They saw it but for a glimpse, for the window was instantly thrust down; but that glimpse had been sufficient, and they turned and left the court without a word. In silence, too, they traversed the by-street; and it was not until they had come into a neighbouring thoroughfare, where even upon a Sunday there were still some stirrings of life, that Mr Utterson at last turned and looked at his companion. They were both pale; and there was an answering horror in their eyes.

'God forgive us! God forgive us!' said Mr Utterson.

But Mr Enfield only nodded his head very seriously, and walked on once more in silence.

CHAPTER EIGHT

The Last Night

MR UTTERSON WAS SITTING by his fireside one evening after dinner, when he was surprised to receive a visit from Poole.

'Bless me, Poole, what brings you here?' he cried; and then, taking a second look at him, 'What ails you?' he added; 'is the doctor ill?'

'Mr Utterson,' said the man, 'there is something wrong.'

'Take a seat, and here is a glass of wine for you,' said the lawyer. 'Now, take your time, and tell me plainly what you want.'

'You know the doctor's ways, sir,' replied Poole, 'and how he shuts himself up. Well, he's shut up again in the cabinet; and I don't like it, sir – I wish I may die if I like it. Mr Utterson, sir, I'm afraid.'

'Now, my good man,' said the lawyer, 'be explicit. What are you afraid of?'

'I've been afraid for about a week,' returned Poole, doggedly disregarding the question; 'and I can bear it no more.'

The man's appearance amply bore out his words; his manner was altered for the worse; and except for the moment when he had first announced his terror, he had not once looked the lawyer in the face. Even now, he sat with the glass of wine untasted on his knee, and his eyes directed to a corner of the floor. 'I can bear it no more,' he repeated.

'Come,' said the lawyer, 'I see you have some good reason, Poole; I see there is something seriously amiss. Try to tell me what it is.'

'I think there's been foul play,' said Poole, hoarsely.

'Foul play!' cried the lawyer, a good deal frightened, and rather inclined to be irritated in consequence. 'What foul play? What does the man mean?'

'I daren't say, sir,' was the answer; 'but will you come along with me and see for yourself?'

Mr Utterson's only answer was to rise and get his hat and great-coat; but he observed with wonder the greatness of the relief that appeared upon the butler's face, and perhaps with no less, that the wine was still untasted when he set it down to follow.

It was a wild, cold, seasonable night of March, with a pale moon, lying on her back as though the wind had tilted her, and a flying wrack of the most diaphanous and lawny texture. The wind made talking difficult, and flecked the blood into the face. It seemed to have swept the street unusually bare of passengers, besides; for Mr Utterson thought he had never seen that part of London so deserted. He could have wished it otherwise; never in his life had he been conscious of so sharp a wish to see and touch his fellow-creatures; for, struggle as he might, there was borne in upon his mind a crushing anticipation of calamity. The square, when they got there, was all full of wind and dust, and the thin trees in the garden were lashing themselves along the railing. Poole, who had kept all the way a pace or two ahead, now pulled up in the middle of the pavement, and in spite of the biting weather, took off his hat and mopped his brow with a red pocket-handkerchief. But for all the hurry of his coming, these were not the dews of exertion that he wiped away, but the moisture of some strangling anguish; for his face was white, and his voice, when he spoke, harsh and broken.

'Well, sir,' he said, 'here we are, and God grant there be nothing wrong.'

'Amen, Poole,' said the lawyer.

Thereupon the servant knocked in a very guarded manner; the door was opened on the chain; and a voice asked from within, 'Is that you, Poole?'

'It's all right,' said Poole. 'Open the door.'

The hall, when they entered it, was brightly lighted up; the fire was built high; adn about the hearth the whole of the servants, men and women, stood huddled together like a flock of sheep. At the sight of Mr Utterson, the housemaid broke into hysterical whimpering; and the cook, crying out, 'Bless God! it's Mr Utterson,' ran forward as if to take him in her arms.

'What, what? Are you all here?' said the lawyer, peevishly. 'Very irregular, very unseemly: your master would be far from pleased.'

'They're all afraid,' said Poole.

Blank silence followed, no one protesting; only the maid lifted up her voice, and now wept loudly.

'Hold your tongue!' Poole said to her, with a ferocity of accent that testified to his own jangled nerves; and indeed when the girl had so suddenly raised the note of her lamentation, they had all started and turned towards the inner door with faces of dreadful expectation. 'And now,' continued the butler, addressing the knife-boy, 'reach me a candle, and we'll get this through hands at once.' And then he begged Mr Utterson to follow him, and led the way to the back garden.

'Now, sir,' said he, 'you come as gently as you can. I want you to hear, and I don't want you to be heard. And see here, sir, if by any chance he was to ask you in, don't go.'

Mr Utterson's nerves, at this unlooked-for termination, gave a jerk that nearly threw him from his balance; but he re-collected his courage, and followed the butler into the laboratory building and through the surgical theatre, with its lumber of crates and bottles, to the foot of the stair. Here Poole, motioned him to stand on one side and listen; while he himself, setting down the candle and making a great and obvious call on his resolution, mounted the steps, and knocked with a somewhat uncertain hand on the red baize of the cabinet door.

'Mr Utterson, sir, asking to see you,' he called; and even as he did so, once more violently signed to the lawyer to give ear.

A voice answered from within: 'Tell him I cannot see any one,' it said, complainingly.

'Thank you, sir,' said Poole, with a note of something like triumph in his voice; and taking up his candle, he led Mr Utterson back across the yard and into the great kitchen, where the fire was out and the beetles were leaping on the floor.

'Sir,' he said, looking Mr Utterson in the eyes, 'was that my master's voice?'

'It seems much changed,' replied the lawyer, very pale, but giving look for look.

'Changed? Well, yes, I think so,' said the butler. 'Have I been twenty years in this man's house, to be deceived about his voice? No, sir; master's made away with; he was made away with eight days ago, when we heard him cry out upon the name of God; and who's in there instead of him, and why it stays there, is a thing that cries to Heaven, Mr Utterson!'

'This is a very strange tale, Poole; this is rather a wild tale, my man,' said Mr Utterson, biting his finger. 'Suppose it were as you suppose, supposing Dr Jekyll to have been – well, murdered, what could induce the murderer to stay? That won't hold water; it doesn't commend itself to reason.'

'Well, Mr Utterson, you are a hard man to satisfy, but I'll do it yet,' said Poole. 'All this last week (you must know), him, or it, or whatever it is that lives in that cabinet, has been crying night and day for some sort of medicine and cannot get it to his mind. It was sometimes his way – the master's, that is – to write his orders on a sheet of paper and throw it on the stair. We've had nothing else this week back; nothing but papers, and a closed door, and the very meals left there to be smuggled in when nobody was looking. Well, sir, every day, ay, and twice and thrice in the same day, there have been orders and complaints, and I have been sent flying to all the wholesale chemists in town. Every time I brought the stuff back, there would be another paper telling me to return it, because it was not pure and another order to a different firm. This drug is wanted bitter bad, sir, whatever for.'

'Have you any of these papers?' asked Mr Utterson.

Poole felt in his pocket and handed out a crumpled note, which the lawyer, bending nearer to the candle, carefully examined. Its contents ran thus: 'Dr Jekyll presents his compliments to Messrs Maw. He assures them that their last sample is impure and quite useless for his present purpose. In the year 18—, Dr J. purchased a somewhat large quantity from Messrs M. He now begs them to search with the most sedulous care, and should any of the same quality be left, to forward it to him at once. Expense is no consideration. The importance of this to Dr J. can hardly be exaggerated.' So far the letter had run composedly enough; but here, with a sudden splutter of the pen, the writer's emotion had broken loose. 'For God's sake,' he had added, 'find me some of the old.'

'This is a strange note,' said Mr Utterson; and then sharply, 'How do you come to have it open?'

'The man at Maw's was main angry, sir, and he threw it back to me like so much dirt,' returned Poole.

'This is unquestionably the doctor's hand, do you know?' resumed the lawyer.

'I thought it looked like it,' said the servant, rather sulkily; and then, with another voice, 'But what matters hand of write?' he said. 'I've seen him!'

'Seen him?' repeated Mr Utterson. 'Well?'

'That's it!' said Poole. 'It was this way. I came suddenly into the theatre from the garden. It seems he had slipped out to look for this drug, or whatever it is; for the cabinet door was open, and there he was at the far end of the room, digging among the crates. He looked up when I came in, gave a kind of cry, and whipped upstairs into the cabinet. It was but for one minute that I saw him, but the hair stood upon my head like quills. Sir, if that was my master, why had he a mask upon his face? If it was my master, why did he cry like a rat and run from me? I have served him long enough. And then . . .' the man paused, and passed his hand over his face.

'These are all very strange circumstances,' said Mr Utterson, 'but I think I begin to see daylight. Your master, Poole, is plainly seized with one of those maladies that both torture and deform the sufferer; hence, for aught I know, the alteration of his voice; hence the mask and his avoidance of his friends; hence his eagerness to find this drug, by means of which the poor soul retains some hope of ultimate recovery – God grant that he be not deceived! There is my explanation; it is sad enough, Poole, ay, and appalling to consider; but it is plain and natural, hangs well together, and delivers us from all exorbitant alarms.'

'Sir,' said the butler, turning to a sort of mottled pallor, 'that thing was not my master, and there's the truth. My master' – here he looked round him, and began to whisper – 'is a tall fine build of a man, and this was more of a dwarf.' Utterson attempted to protest. 'O, sir,' cried Poole, 'do you think I do not know my master after twenty years? do you think I do not know where his head comes to in the cabinet door, where I saw him every morning of my life? No, sir, that thing in the mask was never Dr Jekyll – God knows what it was, but it was never Dr Jekyll; and it is the belief of my heart that there was murder done.'

'Poole,' replied the lawyer, 'if you say that, it will become my duty to make certain. Much as I desire to spare your master's feelings, much as I am puzzled about this note, which seems to prove him to be still alive, I shall consider it my duty to break in that door.'

'Ah, Mr Utterson, that's talking!' cried the butler.

'And now comes the second question,' resumed Utterson: 'Who is going to do it?'

'Why, you and me, sir,' was the undaunted reply.

'That is very well said,' returned the lawyer; 'and whatever comes of it, I shall make it my business to see you are no loser.'

'There is an axe in the theatre,' continued Poole; 'and you might take the kitchen poker for yourself.'

The lawyer took that rude but weighty instrument into his hand, and balanced it. 'Do you know, Poole,' he said, looking up, 'that you and I are about to place ourselves in a position of some peril?'

'You may say so, sir, indeed,' returned the butler.

'It is well, then, that we should be frank,' said the other. 'We both think more than we have said; let us make a clean breast. This masked figure that you saw, did you recognize it?'

'Well, sir, it went so quick, and the creature was so doubled up, that I could hardly swear to that,' was the answer. 'But if you mean, was it Mr Hyde? – why, yes, I think it was! You see, it was much of the same bigness; and it had the same quick light way with it; and then who else could have got in by the laboratory door? You have not forgot, sir, that at the time of the murder he had still the key with him? But that's not all. I don't know, Mr Utterson, if ever you met this Mr Hyde?'

'Yes,' said the lawyer, 'I once spoke with him.'

'Then you must know, as well as the rest of us, that there was something queer about that gentleman – something that gave a man a turn – I don't know rightly how to say it, sir, beyond this: that you felt it in your marrow – kind of cold and thin.'

'I own I felt something of what you describe,' said Mr Utterson.

'Quite so, sir,' returned Poole. 'Well, when that masked thing like a monkey jumped from among the chemicals and whipped into the cabinet, it went down my spine like ice. O, I know it's not evidence, Mr Utterson; I'm book-learned enough for that; but a man has his feelings; and I give you my bible-word it was Mr Hyde!'

'Ay, ay,' said the lawyer. 'My fears incline to the same point. Evil, I fear, founded – evil was sure to come – of that connection. Ay, truly, I believe you; I believe poor Harry is killed; and I believe his murderer (for what purpose, God alone can tell) is still lurking in his victim's room. Well, let our name be vengeance. Call Bradshaw.'

The footman came at the summons, very white and nervous.

'Pull yourself together, Bradshaw,' said the lawyer. 'This suspense, I know, is telling upon all of you; but it is now our intention to make an end of it. Poole, here, and I are going to force our way into the cabinet. If all is well, my shoulders are broad enough to bear the blame. Meanwhile, lest anything should really be amiss, or any malefactor seek to escape by the back, you and the boy must go round the corner with a pair of good sticks, and take your post at the laboratory door. We give you ten minutes to get to your stations.'

As Bradshaw left, the lawyer looked at his watch. 'And now, Poole, let us get to ours,' he said; and taking the poker under his arm, he led the way into the yard. The scud had banked over the moon, and it was now quite dark. The wind, which only broke in puffs and draughts into that deep well of building, tossed the light of the candle to and fro about their steps, until they came into the shelter of the theatre, where they sat down silently to wait. London hummed solemnly all around; but nearer at hand, the stillness was only broken by the sound of a footfall moving to and fro along the cabinet floor.

'So it will walk all day, sir,' whispered Poole; 'ay, and the better part of the night. Only when a new sample comes from the chemist, there's a bit of a break! Ah, it's an ill conscience that's such an enemy to rest! Ah, sir, there's blood foully shed in every step of it! But hark again, a little closer – put your heart in your ears, Mr Utterson, and tell me, is that the doctor's foot?'

The steps fell lightly and oddly, with a certain swing, for all they went so slowly; it was different indeed from the heavy creaking tread of Henry Jekyll. Utterson sighed. 'Is there never anything else?' he asked.

Poole nodded. 'Once,' he said. 'Once I heard it weeping!'

'Weeping? how that?' said the lawyer, conscious of a sudden chill of horror.

'Weeping like a woman or a lost soul,' said the butler. 'I came away with that upon my heart, that I could have wept too.'

But now the ten minutes drew to an end. Poole disinterred the axe from under a stack of packing straw; the candle was set upon the nearest table to light them to the attack; and they drew near with bated breath to where that patient foot was still going up and down, up and down in the quiet of the night.

'Jekyll,' cried Utterson, with a loud voice, 'I demand to see you.' He paused a moment, but there came no reply. 'I give you fair warning, our suspicions are aroused, and I must and shall see you,' he resumed; 'if not by fair means, then by foul – if not of your consent, they by brute force!'

'Utterson,' said the voice, 'for God's sake, have mercy!'

'Ah, that's not Jekyll's voice – it's Hyde's!' cried Utterson. 'Down with the door, Poole!'

Poole swung the axe over his shoulder; the blow shook the building, and the red baize door leaped against the lock and hinges. A dismal screech, as of mere animal terror, rang from the cabinet. Up went the axe again, and again the panels crashed and the frame bounded; four times the blow fell; but the wood was tough and the fittings were of excellent workmanship; and it was not until the fifth that the lock suddenly burst in sunder, and the wreck of the door fell inwards on the carpet.

The beseigers, appalled by their own riot and the stillness that had succeeded, stood back a little and peered in. There lay the cabinet before their eyes in the quiet lamplight, a good fire glowing and chattering on the hearth, the kettle singing its thin strain, a drawer or two open, papers neatly set forth on the business table, and nearer the fire, the things laid out for tea; the quietest room, you would have said, and, but for the glazed presses full of chemicals, the most commonplace that night in London.

Right in the midst there lay the body of a man sorely contorted and still twitching. They drew near on tiptoe, turned it on its back, and beheld the face of Edward Hyde. He was dressed in clothes far too large for him, clothes of the doctor's bigness; the cords of his face still moved with a semblance of life, but life was quite gone; and by the crushed phial in the hand and the strong smell of kernels that hung upon the air, Utterson knew that he was looking on the body of a self-destroyer.

'We have come too late,' he said sternly, 'whether to save or punish. Hyde is gone to his account; and it only remains for us to find the body of your master.'

The far greater proportion of the building was occupied by the theatre, which filled almost the whole ground storey, and was lighted from above, and by the cabinet, which formed an upper storey at one end and looked upon the court. A corridor joined the theatre to the door on the by-street; and with this, the cabinet communicated separately by a second flight of stairs. There were besides a few dark closets and a spacious cellar. All these they now thoroughly examined. Each closet needed but a glance, for all were empty, and all, by the dust that fell from their doors, had stood long unopened. The cellar, indeed, was filled with crazy lumber, mostly dating from the times of the surgeon who was Jekyll's predecessor; but even as they opened the door, they were advertised of the uselessness of further search by the fall of a perfect mat of cobweb which had for years sealed up the entrance. Nowhere was there any trace of Henry Jekyll, dead or alive.

Poole stamped on the flags of the corridor. 'He must be buried here,' he said, hearkening to the sound.

'Or he may have fled,' said Utterson, and he turned to examine the door in the by-street. It was locked; and lying near by on the flags, they found the key, already stained with rust.

'This does not look like use,' observed the lawyer.

'Use!' echoed Poole. 'Do you not see, sir, it is broken? much as if a man had stamped on it.'

'Ah,' continued Utterson, 'and the fractures, too, are rusty.' The two men looked at each other with a scare. 'This is beyond me, Poole,' said the lawyer. 'Let us go back to the cabinet.'

They mounted the stair in silence, and still, with an occasional awestruck glance at the dead body, proceeded more thoroughly to examine the contents of the cabinet. At one table there were traces of chemical work, various measured heaps of some white salt being laid on glass saucers, as though for an experiment in which the unhappy man had been prevented.

'That is the same drug that I was always bringing him,' said Poole; and even as he spoke, the kettle with a startling noise boiled over.

This brought them to the fireside, where the easy chair was drawn cosily up, and the tea things stood ready to the sitter's elbow, the very sugar in the cup. There were several books on a shelf; one lay beside the tea things open, and Utterson was amazed to find it a copy of a pious work for which Jekyll had several times expressed a great esteem, annotated, in his own hand, with startling blasphemies.

Next, in the course of the review of the chamber, the searchers came to the cheval-glass, into whose depth they looked with an involuntary horror. But it was so turned as to show them nothing but the rosy glow playing on the roof, the fire sparkling in a hundred repetitions along the glazed front of the presses, and their own pale and fearful countenances stooping to look in.

'This glass has seen some strange things, sir,' whispered Poole.

'And surely none stranger than itself,' echoed the lawyer, in the same tone. 'For what did Jekyll' – he caught himself up at the word with a start, and then conquering the weakness – 'what could Jekyll want with it?' he said.

'You may say that!' said Poole.

Next they turned to the business table. On the desk, among the neat array of papers, a large envelope was uppermost, and bore, in the doctor's hand, the name of Mr Utterson. The lawyer unsealed it, and several enclosures fell to the floor. The first was a will, drawn in the same eccentric terms as the one which he had returned six months before, to serve as a testament in case of death and as a deed of gift in case of disappearance; but in place of the name of Edward Hyde, the lawyer, with indescribable amazement, read the name of Gabriel John Utterson. He looked at Poole, and then back at the papers, and last of all at the dead malefactor stretched upon the carpet.

'My head goes round,' he said. 'He has been all these days in possession; he had no cause to like me; he must have raged to see himself displaced; and he has not destroyed this document.'

He caught the next paper; it was a brief note in the doctor's hand, and dated at the top. 'O Poole!' the lawyer cried, 'he was alive and here this day. He cannot have been disposed of in so short a space; he must be still alive, he must have fled! And then, why fled? and how? and in that case can we venture to declare this suicide? O, we must be careful. I foresee that we may yet involve your master in some dire catastrophe.'

'Why don't you read it, sir?' asked Poole.

'Because I fear,' replied the lawyer, solemnly. 'God grant I have no cause for it!' And with that he brought the paper to his eye, and read as follows:

MY DEAR UTTERSON, – When this shall fall into your hands, I shall have disappeared, under what circumstances I have not the penetration to foresee; but my instincts and all the circumstances of my nameless situation tell me that the end is sure and must be early. Go then, and first read the narrative which Lanyon warned me he was to place in your hands; and if you care to hear more, turn to the confession of

Your unworthy and unhappy friend,

HENRY JEKYLL.

'There was a third enclosure?' asked Utterson.

'Here, sir,' said Poole, and gave into his hands a considerable packet sealed in several places.

The lawyer put it in his pocket. 'I would say nothing of this paper. If your master has fled or is dead, we may at least save his credit. It is now ten; I must go home and read these documents in quiet; but I shall be back before midnight, when we shall send for the police.'

They went out, locking the door of the theatre behind them; and Utterson, once more leaving the servants gathered about the fire in the hall, trudged back to his office to read the two narratives in which this mystery was now to be explained.

CHAPTER NINE

Dr Lanyon's Narrative

ON THE NINTH OF JANUARY, now four days ago, I received by the evening delivery a registered envelope, addressed in the hand of my colleague and old school-companion, Henry Jekyll. I was a good deal surprised by this; for we were by no means in the habit of correspondence; I had seen the man, dined with him, indeed, the night before; and I could imagine nothing in our intercourse that should justify the formality of registration. The contents increased my wonder; for this is how the letter ran:

10th December 18–.

DEAR LANYON, – You are one of my oldest friends; and although we may have differed at times on scientific questions, I cannot remember, at least on my side, any break in our affection. There was never a day when, if you had said to me, 'Jekyll, my life, my honour, my reason, depend upon you.' I would not have sacrificed my fortune or my left hand to help you. Lanyon, my life, my honour, my reason, are all at your mercy; if you fail me tonight, I am lost. You might suppose, after this preface, that I am going to ask you for something dishonourable to grant. Judge for yourself.

I want you to postpone all other engagements for tonight – ay, even if you were summoned to the bedside of an emperor; to take a cab, unless your carriage should be actually at the door; and, with this letter in your hand for consultation, to drive straight to my house. Poole, my butler, has his orders; you will find him waiting your arrival with a locksmith. The door of my cabinet is then to be forced; and you are to go in alone; to open the glazed press (letter E) on the left hand, breaking the lock if it be shut; and to draw out, *with all its contents as they stand*, the fourth drawer from the top or (which is the same thing) the third from the bottom. In my extreme distress of mind, I have a morbid fear of misdirecting you; but even if I am in error you may know the right drawer by its contents: some powders a phial, and a paper book. This drawer I beg of you to carry back with you to Cavendish Square exactly as it stands.

That is the first part of the service: now for the second. You should be back, if you set out at once on the receipt of this, long before midnight; but I will leave you that amount of margin, not only in the fear of one of those obstacles that can neither be prevented nor foreseen, but because an hour when your servants are in bed is to be preferred for what will then remain to do. At midnight, then, I have to ask you to be alone in your consulting-room, to admit with your own hand into the house a man who will present himself in my name, and to place in his hands the drawer that you will have brought with you from my cabinet. Then you will have played your part, and earned my gratitude completely. Five minutes afterwards, if you insist upon an explanation, you will have understood that these arrangements are of capital importance; and that by the neglect of one of them, fantastic as they must appear, you might have charged your conscience with my death or the shipwreck of my reason.

Confident as I am that you will not trifle with this appeal, my heart sinks and my hand trembles at the bare thought of such a possibility. Think of me at this hour, in a strange place, labouring under a blackness of distress that no fancy can exaggerate, and yet well aware that, if you will but punctually serve me, my troubles will roll away like a story that is told. Serve me, my dear Lanyon, and save

Your friend,
H. J.

P.S. – I had already sealed this up when a fresh terror struck upon my soul. It is possible that the post office may fail me, and this letter not come into your hands until tomorrow morning. In that case, dear Lanyon, do my errand when it shall be most convenient for you in the course of the day; and once more expect my messenger at midnight. It may then already be too late; and if that night passes without event, you will know that you have seen the last of Henry Jekyll.

Upon the reading of this letter, I made sure my colleague was insane; but till that was proved beyond the possibility of doubt, I felt bound to do as he requested. The less I understood of this farrago, the less I was in a position to judge of its importance; and an appeal so worded could not be set aside without a grave responsibility. I rose accordingly from table, got into a hansom, and drove straight to Jekyll's house. The butler was awaiting my arrival; he had received by the same post as mine a registered letter of instruction, and had sent at once for a locksmith and a carpenter. The tradesmen came while we were yet speaking; and we moved in a body to old Dr Denman's surgical theatre, from which (as you are doubtless aware) Jekyll's private cabinet is most conveniently entered. The door was very strong, the lock excellent; the carpenter avowed he would have great trouble, and have to do much damage, if force were to be used; and the locksmith was near despair. But this last was a handy fellow, and after two hours' work, the door stood open. The press marked E was unlocked; and I took out the drawer, had it filled up with straw and tied in a sheet and returned with it to Cavendish Square.

Here I proceeded to examine its contents. The powders were neatly enough made up, but not with the nicety of the dispensing chemist; so that it was plain they were of Jekyll's private manufacture; and when I opened one of the wrappers, I found what seemed to me a simple crystalline salt of a white colour. The phial, to which I next turned my attention, might have been about half full of a blood-red liquor, which was highly pungent to the sense of smell, and seemed to me to contain phosphorus and some volatile ether. At the other ingredients I could make no guess. The book was an ordinary version book, and contained little but a series of dates. These covered a period of many years; but I observed that the entries ceased nearly a year ago, and quite abruptly. Here and there a brief remark was appended to a date, usually no more than a single word: 'double' occurring perhaps six times in a total of several hundred entries; and once very early in the list, and followed by several marks of exclamation, 'total failure!!!' All this, though it whetted my curiosity, told me little that was definite. Here were a phial of some tincture, a paper of some salt, and the record of a series of experiments that had led (like too many of Jekyll's investigations) to no end of practical usefulness. How could the presence of these articles in my house affect either the honour, the sanity, or the life of my flighty colleague? If his messenger could go to one place, why could he not go to another? And even granting some impediment, why was this gentleman to be received by me in secret? The more I reflected, the more convinced I grew that I was dealing with a case of cerebral disease; and though I dismissed my servants to bed, I loaded an old revolver, that I might be found in some posture of self-defence.

Twelve o'clock had scarce rung out over London, ere the knocker sounded very gently on the door. I went myself at the summons, and found a small man crouching against the pillars of the portico.

'Are you come from Dr Jekyll?' I asked.

He told me 'yes' by a constrained gesture; and when I had bidden him enter, he did not obey me without a searching backward glance into the darkness of the square. There was a policeman not far off, advancing with his bull's-eye open; and at the sight, I thought my visitor started and made greater haste.

These particulars struck me, I confess, disagreeably; and as I followed him into the bright light of the consulting-room, I kept my hand ready on my weapon. Here, at last, I had my chance of clearly seeing him. I had never set eyes on him before, so much was certain. He was small, as I have said; I was struck besides with the shocking expression of his face, with his remarkable

combination of great muscular activity and great apparent debility of constitution, and – last but not least – with the odd, subjective disturbance
caused by his neighbourhood. This bore some resemblance to incipient rigor,
and was accompanied by a marked sinking of the pulse. At the time, I set it
down to some idiosyncratic, personal distaste, and merely wondered at the
acuteness of the symptoms; but I have since had reason to believe the cause
to lie much deeper in the nature of man, and to turn on some nobler hinge
than the principle of hatred.

This person (who had thus, from the first moment of his entrance, struck in
me what I can only describe as a disgustful curiosity) was dressed in a fashion
that would have made an ordinary person laughable; his clothes, that is to say,
although they were of rich and sober fabric, were enormously too large for him in
every measurement – the trousers hanging on his legs and rolled up to keep them
from the ground, the waist of the coat below his haunches, and the collar
sprawling wide upon his shoulders. Strange to relate, this ludicrous accoutrement was far from moving me to laughter. Rather, as there was something
abnormal and misbegotten in the very essence of the creature that now faced me
– something seizing, surprising and revolting – this fresh disparity seemed but to
fit in with and to reinforce it; so that to my interest in the man's nature and
character there was added a curiosity as to his origin, his life, his fortune and
status in the world.

These observations, though they have taken so great a space to be set down
in, were yet the work of a few seconds. My visitor was indeed, on fire with
sombre excitement.

'Have you got it?' he cried. 'Have you got it?' And so lively was his impatience
that he even laid his hand upon my arm and sought to shake me.

I put him back, conscious at his touch of a certain icy pang along my blood.
'Come, sir,' said I. 'You forget that I have not yet the pleasure of your
acquaintance. Be seated, if you please.' And I showed him an example, and sat
down myself in my customary seat and with as fair an imitation of my ordinary
manner to a patient as the lateness of the hour, the nature of my preoccupations,
and the horror I had of my visitor would suffer me to muster.

'I beg your pardon. Dr Lanyon,' he replied, civilly enough. 'What you say
is very well founded; and my impatience has shown its heels to my
politeness. I come here at the instance of your colleague, Dr Henry Jekyll, on
a piece of business of some moment; and I understood . . .' he paused and put
his hand to his throat, and I could see, in spite of his collected manner, that
he was wrestling against the approaches of hysteria – 'I understood, a
drawer . . .'

But here I took pity on my visitor's suspense, and some perhaps on my own
growing curiosity.

'There it is, sir,' said I, pointing to the drawer, where it lay on the floor
behind a table, and still covered with the sheet.

He sprang to it, and then paused, and laid his hand upon his heart; I could
hear his teeth grate with the convulsive action of his jaws; and his face was so
ghastly to see that I grew alarmed both for his life and reason.

'Compose yourself,' said I.

He turned a dreadful smile to me, and, as if with the decision of despair, plucked away the sheet. At sight of the contents, he uttered one loud sob of such immense relief that I sat petrified. And the next moment, in a voice that was already fairly well under control, 'Have you a graduated glass?' he asked.

I rose from my place with something of an effort, and gave him what he asked.

He thanked me with a smiling nod, measured out a few minims of the red tincture and added one of the powders. The mixture, which was at first of a reddish hue, began, in proportion as the crystals melted, to brighten in colour, to effervesce audibly, and to throw off small fumes of vapour. Suddenly, and at the same moment, the ebullition ceased, and the com-pound changed to a dark purple, which faded again more slowly to a watery green. My visitor, who had watched these metamorphoses with a keen eye, smiled, set down the glass upon the table, and then turned and looked upon me with an air of scrutiny.

'And now,' said he, 'to settle what remains. Will you be wise? will you be guided? will you suffer me to take this glass in my hand, and to go forth from your house without further parley? or has the greed of curiosity too much command of you? Think before you answer, for it shall be done as you decide. As you decide, you shall be left as you were before, and neither richer nor wiser, unless the sense of service rendered to a man in mortal distress may be counted as a kind of riches of the soul. Or, if you shall so prefer to choose, a new province of knowledge and new avenues to fame and power shall be laid open to you, here, in this room, upon the instant; and your sight shall be blasted by a prodigy to stagger the unbelief of Satan.'

'Sir,' said I, affecting a coolness that I was far from truly possessing, 'you speak enigmas, and you will perhaps not wonder that I hear you with no very strong impression of belief. But I have gone too far in the way of inexplicable services to pause before I see the end.'

'It is well,' replied my visitor. 'Lanyon, you remember your vows: what follows is under the seal of our profession. And now, you who have so long been bound to the most narrow and material views, you who have denied the virtue of transcendental medicine, you who have derided your superiors – behold!'

He put the glass to his lips, and drank at one gulp. A cry followed; he reeled, staggered, clutched at the table and held on, staring with injected eyes, gasping with open mouth; and as I looked, there came, I thought, a change – he seemed to swell – his face became suddenly black, and the features seemed to melt and alter – and the next moment I had sprung to my feet and leaped back against the wall, my arm raised to shield me from that prodigy, my mind submerged in terror.

'O God!' I screamed, and 'O God!' again and again; for there before my eyes – pale and shaken, and half fainting, and groping before him with his hands, like a man restored from death – there stood Henry Jekyll!

What he told me in the next hour I cannot bring my mind to set on paper. I saw what I saw, I heard what I heard, and my soul sickened at it; and yet, now when that sight has faded from my eyes I ask myself if I believe it, and I cannot answer. My life is shaken to its roots; sleep has left me; the deadliest terror sits by me at all hours of the day and night; I feel that my days are numbered, and that I must die; and yet I shall die incredulous. As for the moral turpitude that man unveiled to me, even with tears of penitence, I cannot, even in memory, dwell on it without a start of horror. I will say but one thing, Utterson, and that (if you can bring your mind to credit it) will be more than enough. The creature who crept into my house that night was, on Jekyll's own confession, known by the name of Hyde and hunted for in every corner of the land as the murderer of Carew.

HASTIE LANYON

CHAPTER TEN

Henry Jekyll's Full Statement of the Case

I WAS BORN IN THE YEAR 18— to a large fortune, endowed besides with excellent parts, inclined by nature to industry, fond of the respect of the wise and good among my fellow-men, and thus, as might have been supposed, with every guarantee of an honourable and distinguished future. And indeed, the worst of my faults was a certain impatient gaiety of disposition, such as has made the happiness of many, but such as I found it hard to reconcile with my imperious desire to carry my head high, and wear a more than commonly grave countenance before the public. Hence it came about that I concealed my pleasures; and that when I reached years of reflection, and began to look round me, and take stock of my progress and position in the world, I stood already committed to a profound duplicity of life. Many a man would have even blazoned such irregularities as I was guilty of; but from the high views that I had set before me, I regarded and hid them with an almost morbid sense of shame. It was thus rather the exacting nature of my aspirations, than any particular degradation in my faults, that made me what I was, and, with even a deeper trench than in the majority of men, severed in me those provinces of good and ill which divide and compound man's dual nature. In this case, I was driven to reflect deeply and inveterately on that hard law of life which lies at the root of religion, and is one of the most plentiful springs of distress. Though so profound a double-dealer, I was in no sense a hypocrite; both sides of me were in dead earnest; I was no more myself when I laid aside restraint and plunged in shame, than when I laboured, in the eye of day, at the furtherance of knowledge or the relief of my scientific studies, which led wholly towards the mystic and the transcen-dental, reacted and shed a strong light on this consiousness of the perennial war among my members. With every day, and from both sides of my intelligence, the moral and the intellectual, I thus drew steadily nearer to that truth by whose partial discovery I have been doomed to such a dreadful shipwreck: that man is not truly one, but two. I say two, because the state of my own knowledge does not pass beyond that point. Others will follow, others will outstrip me on the same lines; and I hazard the guess that man will be ultimately known for a mere polity of multifarious, incongruous and independent denizens. I, for my part, from the nature of my life, advanced infallibly in one direction, and in one direction only. It was on the moral side, and in my own person, that I learned to recognize the thorough and primitive duality of man; I saw that, of the two natures that contended in the field of my consciousness, even if I could rightly be said to be either, it was only because I was radically both; and from an early date, even before the course of my scientific discoveries had begun to suggest the most naked possibility of such a miracle, I had learned to dwell with pleasure, as a beloved daydream, on the thought of the separation of these elements. If each, I told myself, could but be housed in separate identities, life would be relieved of all that was unbearable; the unjust might go his way, delivered from the aspirations and remorse of his more upright twin; and the just could walk steadfastly and securely on his upward path, doing the good things in which he found his pleasure, and no longer exposed to disgrace and penitence by the hands of this extraneous evil. It was the curse of mankind that these incongruous faggots were thus bound together – that in the agonized womb of consciousness these polar twins should be continuously struggling. How, then, were they dissociated?

I was so far in my reflections, when, as I have said, a side light began to shine upon the subject from the laboratory table. I began to perceive more deeply than it has ever yet been stated, the trembling immateriality, the mist-like transience, of this seemingly so solid body in which we walk attired. Certain agents I found to have the power to shake and to pluck back that fleshly vestment, even as a wind might toss the curtains of a pavilion. For two good reasons, I will not enter deeply into this scientific branch of my confession. First, because I have been made to learn that the doom and burthen of our life is bound for ever on man's shoulders; and when the attempt is made to cast it off, it but returns upon us with more unfamiliar and more awful pressure. Second, because, as my narrative will make, alas! too evident, my discoveries were incomplete. Enough, then, that I not only recognized my natural body for the mere aura and effulgence of certain of the powers that made up my spirit, but managed to compound a drug by which these powers should be dethroned from their supremacy, and a second form and countenance substituted, none the less natural to me because they were the expression, and bore the stamp, of lower elements in my soul.

I hesitated long before I put this theory to the test of pracice. I knew well that I risked death; for any drug that so potently controlled and shook the very fortress of identity, might by the least scruple of an overdose or at the least inopportunity in the moment of exhibition, utterly blot out that immaterial tabernacle which I looked to it to change. But the temptation of a discovery so singular and profound at last overcame the suggestions of alarm. I had long since prepared my tincture; I purchased at once, from a firm of wholesale chemists, a large quantity of a particular salt, which I knew, from my experiments, to be the last ingredient required; and, late one accursed night, I compounded the elements, watched them boil and smoke together in the glass, and when the ebullition had subsided, with a strong glow of courage, drank off the potion.

The most racking pangs succeeded: a grinding in the bones, deadly nausea, and a horror of the spirit that cannot be exceeded at the hour of birth or death. Then these agonies began swiftly to subside, and I came to myself as if out of a great sickness. There was something strange in my sensations, something indescribably new, and, from its very novelty, incredibly sweet. I felt younger, lighter, happier in body; within I was conscious of a heady recklessness, a current of disordered sensual images running like a mill race in my fancy, a solution of the bonds of obligation, an unknown but not an innocent freedom of the soul. I knew myself, at the first breath of this new life, to be more wicked, tenfold more wicked, sold a slave to my original evil; and the thought, in that moment, braced and delighted me like wine. I stretched out my hands, exulting in the freshness of these sensations; and in the act, I was suddenly aware that I had lost in stature.

There was no mirror, at that date, in my room; that which stands beside me as I write was brought there later on, and for the very purpose of those transformations. The night, however, was far gone into the morning – the morning, black as it was, was nearly ripe for the conception of the day – the inmates of my house were locked in the most rigorous hours of slumber; and I determined, flushed as I was with hope and triumph, to venture in my new shape as far as to my bedroom. I crossed the yard, wherein the constellations looked down upon me, I could have thought, with wonder, the first creature of that sort that their unsleeping vigilance had yet disclosed to them; I stole through the corridors, a stranger in my own house; and coming to my room, I saw for the first time the appearance of Edward Hyde.

I must here speak by theory alone, saying not that which I know, but that which I suppose to be most probable. The evil side of my nature, to which I had now transferred the stamping efficacy, was less robust and less developed than the good which I had just deposed. Again, in the course of my life, which had been, after all, nine-tenths a life of effort, virtue and control, it had been much less exercised and much less exhausted. And hence, as I think, it came about that Edward Hyde was so much smaller, slighter, and younger than Henry Jekyll. Even as good shone upon the countenance of the one, evil was written broadly and plainly on the face of the other. Evil besides (which I must still believe to be the lethal side of man) had left on that body an imprint of deformity and decay. And yet when I looked upon that ugly idol in the glass, I was conscious of no repugnance, rather of a leap of welcome. This, too, was myself. It seemed natural and human. In my eyes it bore a livelier image of the spirit, it seemed more express and single, than the imperfect and divided countenance I had been hitherto accustomed to call mine. And in so far I was doubtless right. I have observed that when I wore the semblance of Edward Hyde, none could come near to me at first without a visible misgiving of the flesh. This, as I take it, was because all human beings, as we meet them, are commingled out of good and evil: and Edward Hyde, alone, in the ranks of mankind, was pure evil.

I lingered but a moment at the mirror: the second and conclusive experiment had yet to be attempted; it yet remained to be seen if I had lost my identity beyond redemption and must flee before daylight from a house that was no longer mine: and hurrying back to my cabinet, I once more prepared and drank the cup, once more suffered the pangs of dissolution, and came to myself once more with the character, the stature, and the face of Henry Jekyll.

That night I had come to the fatal cross-roads. Had I approached my discovery in a more noble spirit, had I risked the experiment while under the empire of generous or pious aspirations, all must have been otherwise, and from these agonies of death and birth I had come forth an angel instead of a fiend. The drug had no discriminating action; it was neither diabolical nor divine; it but shook the doors of the prison-house of my disposition; and, like the captives of Philippi, that which stood within ran forth. At that time my virtue slumbered; my evil, kept awake by ambition, was alert and swift to seize the occasion; and the thing that was projected was Edward Hyde. Hence, although I had now two characters as well as two appearances, one was wholly evil, and the other was still the old Henry Jekyll, that incongruous compound of whose reformation and improvement I had already learned to despair. The movement was thus wholly toward the worse.

Even at that time, I had not yet conquered my aversion to the dryness of a life of study. I would still be merrily disposed at times; and as my pleasures were (to say the least) undignified, and I was not only well known and highly considered, but growing towards the elderly man, this incoherency of my life was daily growing more unwelcome. It was on this side that my new power tempted me until I fell in slavery. I had but to drink the cup, to doff at once the body of the noted professor and to assume, like a thick cloak, that of Edward Hyde. I smiled at the notion; it seemed to me at the time to be humorous; and I made my preparations with the most studious care. I took and furnished that house in Soho to which Hyde was tracked by the police; and engaged as a housekeeper a creature whom I well knew to be silent and unscrupulous. On the other side, I announced to my servants that a Mr Hyde (whom I described) was to have full liberty and power about my house in the square; and, to parry mishaps, I even called and made myself a familiar object in my second character. I next drew up that will to which you so much objected; so that if anything befell me in the person of Dr Jekyll, I could enter on that of Edward Hyde without pecuniary loss. And thus fortified, as I supposed, on every side, I began to profit by the strange immunities of my position.

Men have before hired bravos to transact their crimes, while their own person and reputation sat under shelter. I was the first that ever did so for his pleasures. I was the first that could thus plod in the public eye with a load of genial respectability, and in a moment, like a schoolboy, strip off these lendings and spring headlong into the sea of liberty. But for me, in my impenetrable mantle, the safety was complete. Think of it – I did not even exist! Let me but escape into my laboratory door, give me but a second or two to mix and swallow the draught that I had always standing ready, and, whatever he had done, Edward Hyde would pass away like the stain of breath upon a mirror; and there in his stead, quietly at home, trimming midnight lamp in his study, a man who could afford to laugh at suspicion, would be Henry Jekyll.

The pleasures which I made haste to seek in my disguise were, as I have said, undignified; I would scarce use a harder term. But in the hands of Edward Hyde they soon began to turn towards the monstrous. When I would come back from these excursions, I was often plunged into a kind of wonder at my vicarious depravity. This familiar that I called out of my own soul, and sent forth alone to do his good pleasure, was a being inherently malign and villainous; his every act and thought centred on self; drinking pleasure with bestial avidity from any degree of torture to another; relentless like a man of stone. Henry Jekyll stood at times aghast before the acts of Edward Hyde; but the situation was apart from ordinary laws, and insidiously relaxed the grasp of conscience. It was Hyde, after all, and Hyde alone, that was guilty. Jekyll was no worse; he woke again to his good qualities seemingly unimpaired; he would even make haste, where it was possible to undo the evil done by Hyde. And thus his conscience slumbered.

Into the details of the infamy at which I thus connived (for even now I can scarce grant that I committed it) I have no design of entering. I mean but to point out the warnings and the successive steps with which my chastisement approached. I met with one accident which, as it brought on no consequence, I shall no more than mention. An act of cruelty to a child aroused against me the anger of a passer-by, whom I recognized the other day in the person of your kinsman; the doctor and the child's family joined him; there were moments when I feared for my life; and at last, in order to pacify their too just resentment, Edward Hyde had to bring them to the door, and pay them in a cheque drawn in the name of Henry Jekyll. But this danger was easily eliminated from the future by opening an account at another bank in the name of Edward Hyde himself; and when, by sloping my own hand backwards, I had supplied my double with a signature, I thought I sat beyond the reach of fate.

Some two months before the murder of Sir Danvers, I had been out for one of my adventures, had returned at a late hour, and woke the next day in bed with somewhat odd sensations. It was in vain I looked about me; in vain I saw the decent furniture and tall proportions of my room in the square; in vain that I recognized the pattern of the bed curtains and the design of the mahogany frame; something still kept insisting that I was not where I was, that I had not wakened where I seemed to be, but in the little room in Soho where I was accustomed to sleep in the body of Edward Hyde. I smiled to myself, and, in my psychological way, began lazily to inquire into the elements of this illusion, occasionally, even as I did so, dropping back into a comfortable morning doze. I was still so engaged when, in one of my more wakeful moments, my eye fell upon my hand. Now, the hand of Henry Jekyll (as you have often remarked) was professional in shape and size; it was large, firm, white and comely. But the hand which I now saw, clearly enough in the yellow light of a mid-London morning, lying half shut on the bed-clothes, was lean, corded, knuckly, of a dusky pallor, and thickly shaded with a swart growth of hair. It was the hand of Edward Hyde.

I must have stared upon it for near half a minute, sunk as I was in the mere stupidity of wonder, before terror woke up in my breast as sudden and startling as the crash of cymbals; and bounding from my bed, I rushed to the mirror. At the sight that met my eyes, my blood was changed into something exquisitely thin and icy. Yes, I had gone to bed Henry Jekyll, I had awakened Edward Hyde. How was this to be explained? I asked myself; and then, with another bound of terror – how was it to be remedied? It was well on in the morning; the servants were up; all my drugs were in the cabinet – a long journey, down two pairs of stairs, through the back passage, across the open court and through the anatomical theatre, from where I was then standing horror-struck. It might indeed be possible to cover my face; but of what use was that, when I was unable to conceal the alteration in my stature? And then, with an overpowering sweetness of relief, it came back upon my mind that the servants were already used to the coming and going of my second self. I had soon dressed, as well as I was able in clothes of my own size; had soon passed through the house, where Bradshaw stared and drew back at seeing Mr Hyde at such an hour and in such a strange array; and ten minutes later, Dr Jekyll had returned to his own shape, and was sitting down, with a darkened brow, to make a feint of breakfasting.

Small indeed was my appetite. This inexplicable incident, this reversal of my previous experience, seemed, like the Babylonian finger on the wall, to be spelling out the letters of my judgment; and I began to reflect more seriously than ever before on the issues and possibilities of my double existence. That part of me which I had the power of projecting had lately been much exercised and nourished; it had seemed to me of late as though the body of Edward Hyde had grown in stature, as though (when I wore that form) I were conscious of a more generous tide of blood; and I began to spy a danger that, if this were much prolonged, the balance of my nature might be permanently overthrown, the power of voluntary change be forfeited, and the character of Edward Hyde become irrevocably mine. The power of the drug had not been always equally displayed. Once, very early in my career, it had totally failed me; since then I had been obliged on more than one occasion to double, and once, with infinite risk of death, the treble the amount; and these rare uncertainties had cast hitherto the sole shadow on my contentment. Now, however, and in the light of that morning's accident, I was led to remark that whereas, in the beginning, the difficulty had been to throw off the body of Jekyll, it had of late gradually but decidedly transferred itself to the other side. All things therefore seemed to point to this: that I was slowly losing hold of my original and better self, and becoming slowly incorporated with my second and worse.

Between these two I now felt I had to choose. My two natures had memory in common, but all other faculties were most unequally shared between them. Jekyll (who was composite), now with the most sensitive apprehensions, now with a greedy gusto, projected and shared in the pleasures and adventures of Hyde; but Hyde was indifferent to Jekyll, or but remembered him as the mountain bandit remembers the cavern in which he conceals himself from pursuit. Jekyll had more than a father's interest; Hyde had more than a son's indifference. To cast in my lot with Jekyll was to die to those appetites which I had long secretly indulged and had of late begun to pamper. To cast it in with Hyde was to die to a thousand interests and aspirations, and to become, at a blow and for ever, despised and friendless.

The bargain might appear unequal; but there was still another consideration in the scales; for while Jekyll would suffer smartingly in the fires of abstinence, Hyde would be not even conscious of all that he had lost. Strange as my circumstances were, the terms of this debate are as old and commonplace as man; much the same inducements and alarms cast the die for any tempted and trembling sinner; and it fell out with me, as it falls with so vast a majority of my fellows, that I chose the better part, and was found wanting in the strength to keep to it.

Yes, I preferred the elderly and discontented doctor, surrounded by friends, and cherishing honest hopes; and bade a resolute farewell to the liberty, the comparative youth, the light step, leaping pulses and secret pleasures, that I had enjoyed in the disguise of Hyde. I made this choice perhaps with some unconscious reservation, for I neither gave up the house in Soho, nor destroyed the clothes of Edward Hyde, which still lay ready in my cabinet. For two months, however, I was true to my determination; for two months I led a life of such severity as I had never before attained to, and enjoyed the compensations of an approving conscience. But time began at last to obliterate the freshness of my alarm; the praises of conscience began to grow into a thing of course; I began to be tortured with throes and longings, as of Hyde struggling after freedom; and at last, in an hour of moral weakness, I once again compounded and swallowed the transforming draught.

I do not suppose that when a drunkard reasons with himself upon his vice, he is once out of five hundred times affected by the dangers he runs through his brutish physical insensibility; neither had I, long as I had considered my position, made enough allowance for the complete moral insensibility and insensate readiness to evil which were the leading characters of Edward Hyde. Yet it was by these that I was punished. My devil had been long caged, he came out roaring. I was conscious, even when I took the draught, of a more unbridled, a more furious propensity to ill. It must have been this, I suppose, that stirred in my soul that tempest of impatience with which I listened to the civilities of my unhappy victim; I declare at least before God, no man morally sane could have been guilty of that crime upon so pitiful a provocation; and that I struck in no more reasonable spirit than that in which a sick child may break a plaything. But I had voluntarily stripped myself of all those balancing instincts by which even the worst of us continues to walk with some degree of steadiness among temptations; and in my case, to be tempted, however slightly, was to fall.

Instantly the spirit of hell awoke in me and raged. With a transport of glee, I mauled the unresisting body, tasting delight from every blow; and it was not till weariness had begun to succeed that I was suddenly, in the top fit of my delirium, struck through the heart by a cold thrill of terror. A mist dispersed; I saw my life to be forfeit; and fled from the scene of these excesses, at once glorying and trembling, my lust of evil gratified and stimulated, my love of life screwed to the topmost peg. I ran to the house in Soho, and (to make assurance doubly sure) destroyed my papers; thence I set out through the lamplit streets, in the same divided ecstasy of mind, gloating on my crime, light-headedly devising others in the future, and yet still hastening and still harkening in my wake for the steps of the avenger. Hyde had a song upon his lips as he compounded the draught, and as he drank it pledged the dead man. The pangs of transformation had not done tearing him, before Henry Jekyll, with streaming tears of gratitude and remorse, had fallen upon his knees and lifted his clasped hands to God. The veil of self-indulgence was rent from head to foot, I saw my life as a whole: I followed it up from the days of childhood, when I had walked with my father's hand, and through the self-denying toils of my professional life, to arrive again and again, with the same sense of unreality, at the damned horrors of the evening. I could have screamed aloud; I sought with tears and prayers to smother down the crowd of hideous images and sounds with which my memory swarmed against me; and still, between the petitions, the ugly face of my iniquity stared into my soul. As the acuteness of this remorse began to die away, it was succeeded by a sense of joy. The problem of my conduct was solved. Hyde was thenceforth impossible; whether I would or not, I was now confined to the better part of my existence; and, oh, how I rejoiced to think it! with what willing humility I embraced anew the restrictions of natural life! with what sincere renunciation I locked the door by which I had so often gone and come, and ground the key under my heel!

The next day came the news that the murder had been overlooked, that the guilt of Hyde was patent to the world, and that the victim was a man high in public estimation. It was not only a crime, it had been a tragic folly. I think I was glad to know it; I think I was glad to have my better impulses thus buttressed and guarded by the terrors of the scaffold. Jekyll was now my city of refuge; let but Hyde peep out an instant, and the hands of all men would be raised to take and slay him.

I resolved in my future conduct to redeem the past; and I can say with honesty that my resolve was fruitful of some good. You know yourself how earnestly in the last months of last year I laboured to relieve suffering; you know that much was done for others, and that the days passed quietly, almost happily for myself. Nor can I truly say that I wearied of this beneficent and innocent life; I think instead that I daily enjoyed it more completely; but I was still cursed with my duality of purpose; and as the first edge of my penitence wore off, the lower side of me, so long indulged, so recently chained down, began to growl for licence. Not that I dreamed of resuscitating Hyde; the bare idea of that would startle me to frenzy: no, it was in my own person that I was once more tempted to trifle with my conscience; and it was as an ordinary secret sinner that I at last fell before the assaults of temptation.

There comes an end to all things; the most capacious measure is filled at last; and this brief condescension to my evil finally destroyed the balance of my soul. And yet I was not alarmed; the fall seemed natural, like a return to the old days before I had made my discovery. It was a fine, clear January day, wet under foot where the frost had melted, but cloudless overhead; and the Regent's Park was full of winter chirrupings and sweet with spring odours. I sat in the sun on a bench; the animal within me licking the chops of memory; the spiritual side a little drowsed, promising subsequent penitence, but not yet moved to begin. After all, I reflected, I was like my neighbours; and then I smiled, comparing myself with other men, comparing my active goodwill with the lazy cruelty of their neglect. And at the very moment of that vainglorious thought, a qualm came over me, a horrid nausea and the most deadly shuddering. These passed away, and left me faint; and then as in its turn the faintness subsided, I began to be aware of a change in the temper of my thoughts, a greater boldness, a contempt of danger, a solution of the bonds of obligation. I looked down; my clothes hung formlessly on my shrunken limbs; the hand that lay on my knee was corded and hairy. I was once more Edward Hyde. A moment before I had been safe of all men's respect, wealthy, beloved – the cloth laying for me in the dining-room at home; and now I was the common quarry of mankind, hunted, houseless, a known murderer, thrall to the gallows.

My reason wavered, but it did not fail me utterly. I have more than once observed that, in my second character, my faculties seemed sharpened to a point and my spirits more tensely elastic; thus it came about that, where Jekyll perhaps might have succumbed, Hyde rose to the importance of the moment. My drugs were in one of the presses of my cabinet: how was I to reach them? That was the problem that (crushing my temples in my hands) I set myself to solve. The laboratory door I had closed. If I sought to enter by the house, my own servants would consign me to the gallows. I saw I must employ another hand, and thought of Lanyon. How was he to be reached? how persuaded? Supposing that I escape capture in the streets, how was I to make my way into his presence? and how should I, an unknown and displeasing visitor, prevail on the famous physician to rifle the study of his colleague, Dr Jekyll? Then I remembered that of my original character, one part remained of me: I could write my own hand; and once I had conceived that kindling spark, the way that I must follow became lighted up from end to end.

Thereupon, I arranged my clothes as best I could, and summoning a passing hansom, drove to an hotel in Portland Street, the name of which I chanced to remember. At my appearance (which was indeed comical enough, however tragic a fate these garments covered) the driver could not conceal his mirth. I gnashed my teeth upon him with a gust of devilish fury; and the smile withered from his face – happily for him – yet more happily for myself, for in another instant I had certainly dragged him from his perch. At the inn, as I entered, I looked about me with so black a countenance as made the attendants tremble; not a look did they exchange in my presence; but obsequiously took my orders, led me to a private room, and brought me wherewithal to write. Hyde in danger of his life was a creature new to me: shaken with inordinate anger, strung to the pitch of murder, lusting to inflict pain. Yet the creature was astute; mastered his fury with a great effort of the will; composed his two important letters, one to Lanyon and one to Poole, and, that he might receive actual evidence of their being posted, sent them out with directions that they should be registered.

Thenceforward, he sat all day over the fire in the private room, gnawing his nails; there he dined, sitting alone with his fears, the waiter visibly quailing before his eye; and thence, when the night was fully come, he set forth in the corner of a closed cab, and was driven to and fro about the streets of the city. He, I say – I cannot say, I. That child of Hell had nothing human; nothing lived in him but fear and hatred. And when at last, thinking the driver had begun to grow suspicious, he discharged the cab and ventured on foot, attired in his misfitting clothes, an object marked out for observation, into the midst of the nocturnal passengers, these two base passions raged within him like a tempest.

He walked fast, hunted by his fears, chattering to himself, skulking through the less frequented thoroughfares, counting the minutes that still divided him from midnight. Once a woman spoke to him, offering, I think, a box of lights. He smote her in the face, and she fled.

When I came to myself at Lanyon's, the horror of my old friend perhaps affected me somewhat: I do not know; it was at least but a drop in the sea to the abhorrence with which I looked back upon these hours. A change had come over me. It was no longer the fear of the gallows, it was the horror of being Hyde that racked me. I received Lanyon's condemnation partly in a dream; it was partly in a dream that I came home to my own house and got into bed. I slept after the prostration of the day, with a stringent and profound slumber which not even the nightmares that wrung me could avail to break. I awoke in the morning shaken, weakened, but refreshed. I still hated and feared the thought of the brute that slept within me, and I had not of course forgotten the appalling dangers of the day before; but I was once more at home, in my own house and close to my drugs; and gratitude for my escape shone so strong in my soul that it almost rivalled the brightness of hope.

I was stepping leisurely across the court after breakfast drinking the chill of the air with pleasure, when I was seized again with those indescribable sensations that heralded the change; and I had but the time to gain the shelter of my cabinet, before I was once again raging and freezing with the passions of Hyde. It took on this occasion a double dose to recall me to myself; and, alas! six hours after, as I sat looking sadly in the fire, the pangs returned, and the drug had to be re-administered. In short, from that day forth it seemed only by a great effort as of gymnastics, and only under the immediate stimulation of the drug, that I was able to wear the countenance of Jekyll. At all hours of the day and night I would be taken with the premonitory shudder; above all, if I slept, or even dozed for a moment in my chair, it was always as Hyde that I awakened. Under the strain of this continually impending doom and by the sleeplessness to which I now condemned myself, ay, even beyond what I had thought possible to man, I became, in my own person, a creature eaten up and emptied by fever, languidly weak both in body and mind, and solely occupied by one thought: the horror of my other self. But when I slept, or when the virtue of the medicine wore off, I would leap almost without transition (for the pangs of tranformation grew daily less marked) into the possession of a fancy brimming with images of terror, a soul boiling with causeless hatreds, and a body that seemed not strong enough to contain the raging energies of life. The powers of Hyde seemed to have grown with the sickliness of Jekyll. And certainly the hate that now divided them was equal on each side. With Jekyll, it was a thing of vital instinct. He had now seen the full deformity of that creature that shared with him some of the phenomena of consciousness, and was co-heir with him to death: and beyond these links of community, which in themselves made the most poignant part of his distress, he thought of Hyde, for all his energy of life, as of something not only hellish but inorganic. This was the shocking thing; that the slime of the pit seemed to utter cries and voices; that the amorphous dust gesticulated and sinned; that what was dead, and had no shape, should usurp the offices of life. And this again, that that insurgent horror was knit to him closer than a wife, closer than an eye; lay caged in his flesh, where he heard it mutter and felt it struggle to be born; and at every hour of weakness, and in the confidence of slumber, prevailed against him, and deposed him out of life. The hatred of Hyde for Jekyll was of a different order. His terror of the gallows drove him continually to commit temporary suicide, and return to his subordinate station of a part instead of a person; but he loathed the necessity, he loathed the despondency into which Jekyll was now fallen, and he resented the dislike with which he was himself regarded. Hence the apelike tricks he would play me, scrawling in my own hand blasphemies on the pages of my books, burning the letters and destroying the portrait of my father; and indeed, had it not been for his fear of death, he would long ago have ruined himself in order to involve me in the ruin. But his love of life is wonderful; I go further: I, who sicken and freeze at the mere thought of him, when I recall the abjection and passion of this attachment, and when I know how he fears my power to cut him off by suicide, I find it in my heart to pity him.

It is useless, and the time awfully fails me, to prolong this description; no one has ever suffered such torments, let that suffice; and yet even to these, habit brought – no, not alleviation – but a certain callousness of soul, a certain acquiescence of despair; and my punishment might have gone on for years, but for the last calamity which has now fallen, and which has finally severed me from my own face and nature. My provision of the salt, which had never been renewed since the date of the first experiment, began to run low. I sent out for a fresh supply, and mixed the draught; the ebullition followed, and the first change of colour, not the second; I drank it, and it was without efficiency. You will learn from Poole how I have had London ransacked; it was in vain; and I am now persuaded that my first supply was impure, and that it was that unknown impurity which lent efficacy to the draught.

About a week has passed, and I am now finishing this statement under the influence of the last of the old powders. This, then, is the last time, short of a miracle, that Henry Jekyll can think his own thoughts or see his own face (now how sadly altered!) in the glass. Nor must I delay too long to bring my writing to an end; for if my narrative has hitherto escaped destruction, it has been by a combination of great prudence and great good luck. Should the throes of change take me in the act of writing it, Hyde will tear it in pieces; but if some time shall have elapsed after I have laid it by, his wonderful selfishness and circumscription to the moment will probably save it once again from the action of his apelike spite. And indeed the doom that is closing on us both has already changed and crushed him. Half an hour from now, when I shall again and for ever reindue that hated personality, I know how I shall sit shuddering and weeping in my chair, or continue, with the most strained and fear-struck ecstasy of listening, to pace up and down this room (my last earthly refuge) and give ear to every sound of menace. Will Hyde die upon the scaffold? or will he find the courage to release himself at the last moment? God knows; I am careless; this is my true hour of death, and what is to follow concerns another than myself. Here, then, as I lay down the pen, and proceed to seal up my confession, I bring the life of that unhappy Henry Jekyll to an end.

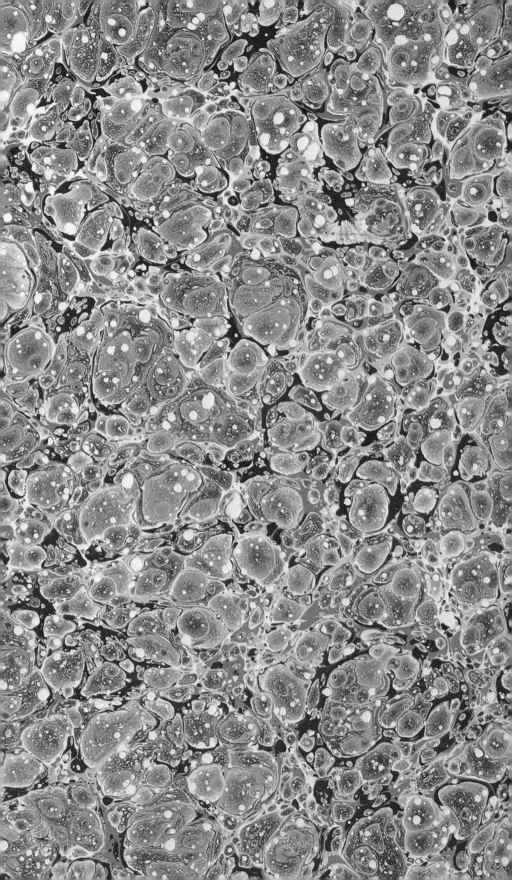